H. G. WELLS

DESPERATELY MORTAL

H. G. Wells at his desk, Hanover Terrace, 1940.

DAVID C. SMITH

H. G. WELLS
Desperately Mortal
A Biography

YALE UNIVERSITY PRESS
NEW HAVEN AND LONDON

Copyright © 1986 by David C. Smith

The author acknowledges the permission of A. P. Watts acting on behalf of the Executors of the Estate of H. G. Wells to include extracts from the writings of H. G. Wells.

Designed by Robert Baldock

Set in 11/12 pt Ehrhardt by Alan Sutton Publishing, Gloucester and printed and bound in the United States of America by The Maple—Vail Book Manufacturing Group.

Library of Congress Cataloging-in-Publication Data

Smith, David C. (David Clayton), 1929–
  H. G. Wells : desperately mortal.

  Bibliography: p.
  Includes index.
  1. Wells, H. G. (Herbert George), 1866–1946—
Biography. 2. Authors, English—20th century—Biography.
3. Authors, English—19th century—Biography.
4. Historians—Great Britain—Biography. I. Title.
PR5776.S54 1986   823′.912 [B]   86–7771
ISBN 0–300–03672–8

My thanks and acknowledgement
to the friends and
colleagues who aided
me in this work are
laid out in another place.

But, I wish to dedicate this book to
JOSHUA
in the heartfelt hope and
desire
that his world might turn
out to be a Wellsian one

CONTENTS

PART FOUR: Prophet C

ILLUSTRATIONS

SOURCES FOR ILLUSTRATIONS

H. G. Wells Papers, University of Illinois, Campaign-Urbana: 1, 2, 5, 6, 7, 8, 9, 10, 12, 17, 22, 24, 29, 31, 32, 33; BBC Hulton Picture Library: frontis., 3, 11, 14, 15, 16, 18, 23, 35, 36; Margaret Sanger Papers, Sophia Smith Collection, Smith College, Northampton, Mass.: 19, 34; The British Architectural Library, RIBA, London: 13; University of Illinois Press: 27; William Heinemann Ltd.: 28; H. G. Wells Society: 37; collection of the author: 4; United Press International (UK) Ltd.: 25. Reproduced from H. G. Wells's books: *Floor Games* (1911): 20; *Little Wars* (1913): 21; *World Brain* (1938): 26; Mrs Alison Macleod: 30. Prints of 3 and 32 were supplied by the Weidenfeld and Nicolson picture archive, and a copy of 13 by Thames Television, London.

INTRODUCTION

While talking to H. G. Wells on one occasion at the Reform Club nearly sixty years ago, Beverley Nichols put an interesting query to him. 'Let us say that an immense written examination has been set on general knowledge, would you come out "top boy"?' Wells, rather amused by the idea, told Nichols that he thought both Arnold Bennett and Gilbert Murray would have scored just ahead of him. Nichols went on to remark that Wells, sitting in a chair as he made his response, reminded him 'of a spring at tight pressure which may at any moment uncoil itself and leap out in the most surprising of directions'. And Wells himself, discussing his own time, told Nichols later that day, 'Our lives swim in expectation.'[1]

The anecdote gives us a powerful insight into the life and the meaning of H. G. Wells. Contemporaries routinely thought him one of the most brilliant minds of their time. He radiated energy: intellectual, emotional, physical, sexual energies poised for the events to come.

Few people today realize how much Wells meant to young people growing to maturity from 1890 to 1950. The use of his name to describe a scene, a style of writing or a topic for discussion came as a matter of course to their lips and pens. To take only one example, Vera Brittain, on a speaking tour in the United States in 1925 on behalf of the League of Nations Union, wrote back home to her close friend, Winifred Holtby, describing how she felt: 'It is a queer feeling to be alone in the largest hotel in the largest city in the world — a city like no other *city*, filled with terrestrial monstrosities, which at night appears like the grim ghoulish worlds imagined in some of the novels of H. G. Wells.[2]

And if it were not just the casual use of the Wellsian adjective by those of his own time, it was and has been his direct influence on western thinking and action that remains as his legacy. In 1984, Emmanuel Shinwell, 'Manny' as he was affectionately known, celebrated his hundreth birthday. On that occasion, he submitted to a longish interview in his London flat by a writer from the *Sunday Times*. The obligatory question as to the influences on his life brought forth a remark that could have been made by thousands. After he said that his parents had had little impact upon him, he

---

[1] Superior figures in the text refer to the Notes at p. 497.

went on: 'But I used to go to the public library and read everything. Darwin, H. G. Wells. Wells meant a lot to me. I've got signed copies of his books over there. I didn't care much for Plato. I liked Socrates. I used to go to the Kelvin Grove Art Gallery and look at the dinosaurs. I was always interested in evolution.'[3]

Even with this evidence, however, the Wellsian influence is not as well known today as forty years ago. Some of his books — *The Time Machine*, *The War of the Worlds*, *The Outline of History* — have remained in print almost steadily since their first publication. But the great mass of his work is relatively unknown. University literature and history courses touch his work only lightly, if at all. In fact, Wells, along with Arnold Bennett, Gilbert Murray, George Gissing, and dozens of their contemporaries are not well known. Their lives remain mysteries, their contributions over-generalized and mythic.

Modern biographies of Wells are fairly numerous. Most of them are by authors who recognize some of Wells's importance, but who are also basically repelled by him or by some aspects of his life. Others treat only a short section of his life or work, and do not put it into context. Literary analyses are quite plentiful. They vary in their resolution of Wellsian problems and most frequently ignore the man who wrote the books they study. The present book is an effort to make good these omissions, to provide a life in context, and the whole life. It is written in the belief that the attention paid to Wells while he was alive was not misdirected. He was important and that importance needs re-statement and analysis.

Let me, then, state clearly what I consider to be Wells's most important contributions. The first of these comes directly from his training and his scientific career. He took the doctrine of evolution, as taught to him by T. H. Huxley, and translated that doctrine, along with much other burgeoning science of the period, into textbooks and articles. In addition this science strongly influenced his teaching, his fiction, and his concept of writing, all directed towards young scientists and others eager to learn about the laws of nature. He used his knowledge not only to describe his own world, but also to offer a glimpse into worlds that might be.

Later, when military convulsions beset this century, Wells led the way in trying to determine the causes of these immense dislocations. Eventually he brought many of his readers (but not the governments of the time) to understand the reality of those terribly disabling years. In response to that reality, almost single-handed he created the document which he called 'a Universal Declaration of Human Rights', the foundation document for the declaration later adopted by the United Nations Organization. He believed that this document might protect ordinary people from the ravages of the bankrupt systems under which they lived.

As he surveyed the world he lived in, Wells became convinced of the need for world education, open to all, to achieve the socialist future he sought, and which he saw as a cure for the world madness. The organization of those ideas, and the propaganda efforts he undertook to establish them, led to a series of statements about human life, its purposes and capabilities which were later given form by William Beveridge and others in a postwar Britain far different from the class-ridden world of Wells's childhood. On the way to that educational goal he wrote three magnificent textbooks designed to enable any person to educate himself. One of these, *The Outline of History*, helped provide a guide road towards a universal human history, and helped change that discipline drastically for the better.

In his fiction, and in some of his other writings, Wells gave a bright glow to middle- and lower-class hopes. His description of life as it appears in *Kipps*, *Mr Polly* and *Love and Mr Lewisham* puts him in a class with Dickens. Other characters, such as Matilda Good, Uncle Ponderevo, and the students in the laboratory of 'A Slip Under the Microscope', are as vivid as any created in our language. His depiction of a possible future has led us to attempt to create that future, and to a considerable degree to succeed, even though he made it clear that his future was and is just a glimpse of what it could be — not the only road possible.

While doing this he fought, and to my mind won, a battle over the purpose and direction of fiction. The didactic novel was not much prized in his time. He, however, saw its possibilities, and pushed it forward, against the claims of academics and others interested in truth and beauty solely from their own limited perspective. By doing this, and through his support for new methods of writing, Wells opened up the modern novel in a way still not completely recognized. For those who read his novels, and those who follow his path, an incandescent trail of delight has been blazed. Although the conventional wisdom is that he lost the battle of purpose to Henry James, that is a very superficial judgement, and one, incidentally, that needs new thought from many sources.

Finally, Wells played a marvellous role in the opening out of modern feminism, a movement still spreading over all our lives. He was a supporter and advocate of birth-control at a time when few were willing to discuss the subject. He thought women could achieve anything they wished, and women who knew him well understood that he meant what he said. By his believing, he freed many to work out their own destinies. He maintained as a goal, in his fiction and in his personal life, the creation of norms of thought which would allow others to realize their own wishes and capabilities. *Ann Veronica*, *Love and Mr Lewisham*, *Marriage*, *The Secret Places of the Heart*, and *Apropos of Dolores* have widened our view of people in love far beyond the fiction of Wells's time and earlier. And when one adds to this his willingness to sponsor experimental fiction, especially that of James Joyce, Dorothy Richardson, Lewis Grassic Gibbbon, George Gissing, 'Mark Benney', 'W. N. P. Barbellion', and others, we find his influence far beyond what is normally taught. Truly he is and was a man for all times.

It may be considered a truism to say that Wells was the last polymath, but that is too slick. Instead we should note that he was a believer in a possible world, one in which this species could live up to its potential. Failure was always possible, and there were moments when that possibility seemed to crush hope itself. But H. G. Wells, the ultimate exemplar of humanity in his hopes, his fears, his failures, his occasional narrow outlook, but mostly in his soaring imagination, was for the last fifty-five years of his life a leader in thought and action. He was, in the words of the Provost in *Measure for Measure* (IV. ii), 'careless, reckless, and fearless of what's past, present, or to come; insensible of mortality, and *desperately mortal*'. It is from this line that I take my title. However, another which is as good occurs in *Henry IV, Part II*, when Warwick speaks (III. i):

> There is a history in all men's lives,
> Figuring the nature of the times deceas'd,
> The which observ'd, a man may prophesy,
> With a near aim, of the main chance of things
> As yet not come to life, which in their seeds
> And weak beginnings lie entreasured.
> Such things become *the hatch and brood of time.* . . .

When Wells reached his seventieth birthday, one of his favourite organizations, PEN, tendered him an extraordinary birthday party. When he rose to speak, to thank his friends for coming, he opened his remarks by saying that he felt as though he were a child again, and his mother was saying, 'Master Bertie. It is time to put away your toys.' Wells told his audience that he was not yet ready to go. He clung to life and to his mission to make us and our world better. As I finish this book this day, I can only say that Wells was right — it is not yet time to put away our toys and go. We have a great deal to learn, and the playtime can be marvellous fun. And, by staying on, not giving up, playing with these toys (our minds and our determination), perhaps we can still save this species and our habitat. It will be a near-run chance, no doubt, but as H. G. Wells himself would have remarked, 'If the ends don't justify the means, what the Hell does?'

1 July 1985
Bangor, Orono, Topsfield, Maine
London, Cambridge, Bridport, Reading, England

H. G. WELLS 1866–1946: *A Chronology*

1866	Born 21 September, Bromley, Kent, third son of Joseph and Sarah Wells.
1874–9	Broken leg; at Morley's Academy, Bromley. Joseph Wells injured, unable to work.
1879–82	Various apprenticeships. Sarah Wells employed from 1880 at Up Park, Sussex.
1883–4	At Midhurst (Sussex) Grammar School as pupil, and pupil teacher.
1884–7	At Normal School (later Royal College) of Science, South Kensington; edits *Science Schools Journal*.
1887–8	Teaches at Holt Academy, North Wales. Injury and illness; recuperates at Up Park, and Stoke-on-Trent. 'The Chronic Argonauts' published in *Science Schools Journal*.
1888–91	Teaches at Henley House School, Kilburn. B.Sci. degree, 1890. Tutor for University Correspondence College. Marries his cousin, Isabel Wells. 'Rediscovery of the Unique' in *Fortnightly Magazine*.
1892–3	Meets Amy Catherine Robbins. *Textbook of Biology; Honours Physiography* (with Richard A. Gregory). As health deteriorates begins to publish journalism in *Pall Mall Gazette* and elsewhere; henceforth lives by writing.
1894–5	Divorces Isabel and marries A. C. Robbins ('Jane') with whom he has been living; move to Woking. *Select Conversations with an Uncle; The Time Machine; The Wonderful Visit; The Stolen Bacillus and Other Incidents* (all 1895).
1896	Living at Worcester Park; meets George Gissing. J. B. Pinker becomes his literary agent. *The Island of Dr Moreau; The Wheels of Chance*.
1897	First correspondence with Arnold Bennett. *The Plattner Story and Others; The Invisible Man; Certain Personal Matters*.
1898	Ill again; recuperates at various Channel sites. Friendships with Conrad, Henry James, Ford Madox Hueffer (Ford). First journey abroad, to Italy with Gissing. *The War of the Worlds*.

1899   *When the Sleeper Wakes; Tales of Space and Time.*

1900   Builds Spade House, Sandgate, Kent. *Love and Mr Lewisham*
        (completed 1899).

1901   First child, G. P. ('Gip') Wells, born. *The First Men in the Moon.*
        Anticipations, first major sociological work. Begins flirtation with
        Fabian Society.

1902   *The Discovery of the Future.* Major address at the Royal Institution. *The*
        Sea Lady.

1903–4 Second son, Frank Wells, born. Death of Gissing. *Mankind in the*
        Making; Twelve Stories and a Dream. Under influence of Graham
        Wallas. Joins Fabians, much sociological commentary in press. In
        discussion group, the Co-Efficients. Friends such as G. B. Shaw,
        Sidney and Beatrice Webb, E. Ray Lankester, Violet Paget
        ('Vernon Lee') important to life and work. *The Food of the Gods.*

1905   *A Modern Utopia; Kipps.* Widening friendships, political as well as
        literary.

1906–7 *In the Days of the Comet.* Visits USA; *The Future in America.* Affairs
        with Rosamund Bland and Amber Reeves, *Socialism and the*
        Family, bring fame from left, notoriety from right. *This Misery of*
        Boots. Break with Fabians.

1908   *New Worlds for Old; First and Last Things*, a major philosophical
        statement; *The War in the Air.*

1909–10 Birth of Amber Reeves's daughter Anna Jane (December 1909), after
        her marriage to G. R. Blanco-White. Wellses move to Church
        Row, Hampstead. *Tono-Bungay; Ann Veronica* (1909); *The History*
        of Mr Polly (1910).

1911–13 *Floor Games, The New Machiavelli* (1911). Friendship with Frank
        Swinnerton. Move to Easton Glebe, on the Essex estate of Lady
        Warwick. Episode with 'Elizabeth' von Arnim. *Marriage* (1912);
        begins campaign for feminine equality; meets Rebecca West. *Little*
        Wars, The Passionate Friends (1913).

1914   First visit to Russia (January). *The Wife of Sir Isaac Harman; The World*
        Set Free. Outbreak of war; Rebecca West's son Anthony born
        (August). *The War That Will End War.*

1915   *Boon*; final breach with Henry James. *Bealby. The Research Magnificent*,
        commemorating love affair with Rebecca West.

1916–17 *Mr Britling Sees It Through; The Elements of Reconstruction*, turning
        point in journalism, from focus on England to world affairs. Tour
        of battle fronts, France and northern Italy (August 1916); *War and*

the Future. God the Invisible King, The Soul of a Bishop, second
edition of *First and Last Things* (all 1917), results of religious
phase.

1918   Work with Ministry of Information on war propaganda. *Joan and
            Peter*, first educational novel. League of Nations committee.

1919   *The Undying Fire*, reflection of friendship with F. W. Sanderson,
            Wells boys' headmaster at Oundle School.

1920   *The Outline of History* (begun in 1919). Second visit to Russia;
            interviews Lenin; encounters with Gorky, Moura Budberg; *Russia
            in the Shadows*.

1921–2   Covers World Disarmament Conference, Washington; *Washington
            and the Hope of Peace*. Relationship with Margaret Sanger. *The
            Secret Places of the Heart*, personal novel of period with Rebecca
            West and Sanger. Stands for Parliament; renews connection with
            Webbs, Labour Party. *A Short History of the World*, and major
            revision of the *Outline*.

1923–4   *Men Like Gods*. End of relationship with Rebecca West. *The Dream;
            The Story of a Great Schoolmaster* (Sanderson) (both 1924). Meets
            Odette Keun, begins habit of wintering in Mediterranean.

1925–6   *Christina Alberta's Father*. With Odette Keun at Lou Pidou, villa they
            built at Grasse, winters 1925–32. *The World of William Clissold*
            (1926), 3-vol. novel of philosophy, personal relations. Controversy
            with Hilaire Belloc over Catholic objections to the *Outline*.

1927   *Meanwhile*, novel of the 1920s; *Collected Short Stories*; Atlantic Edition
            (1924–7), with new prefaces, complete. Jane Wells dies (October).

1928   *The Book of Catherine Wells*, published as tribute to Jane. Marjorie
            Craig Wells (wife of G.P.) takes over as secretary. *Mr Blettsworthy
            on Rampole Island*. Proclaims 'Open Conspiracy'; first talks in
            world-wide campaign for peace. Becomes active in PEN.

1929–30   First BBC talk. *The Autocracy of Mr Parham*. Speech in Reichstag,
            Berlin (April 1929), published as *The Common Sense of World Peace*.
            Moves to flat in Chiltern Court, London. Second textbook, *The
            Science of Life*, with Julian Huxley and G. P. Wells (1930); trouble
            with collaborator over a third. Second version of *The Open
            Conspiracy*.

1931–2   Death of Arnold Bennett; break-up with Odette Keun. *After Democ-
            racy*; third textbook, *The Work, Wealth and Happiness of Mankind;
            The Bulpington of Blup* (all 1932). Writing now in many different
            fora.

1933   Begins liaison with Moura Budberg; new friends, Julian Huxley,
            J. B. S. Haldane, Eileen Power. *The Shape of Things to Come*, novel
            of the future. International president of PEN.

1934–5   Visit to USSR, interviews Stalin; visit to USA, interviews FDR.
            Move to 13 Hanover Terrace. *Experiment in Autobiography*, 2 vols.
            (1934). Much journalism, many talks. Collaboration with
            Alexander Korda over film version of *Shape of Things to Come*
            (released as *Things to Come*, 1936).

1936   *The Anatomy of Frustration*, a major statement of faith; *The Croquet
            Player*. PEN dinner in honour of his seventieth birthday.

1937   *Star Begotten; Brynhild; The Camford Visitation*. Chairs 'Section L' of
            British Association for the Advancement of Science.

1938–9   *The Brothers; World Brain; Apropos of Dolores* (all 1938). Visit to
            Australia, December 1938–February 1939, culminates in 'Poison
            of History' speech at ANZAAS. *Travels of a Republican Radical in
            Search of Hot Water; The Holy Terror* (both 1939). In Stockholm for
            PEN conference, September 1939, when Second World War
            breaks out.

1940   Remains in Hanover Terrace through the bombings. Active in
            proclaiming need for war aims, and in support of Declaration of
            the Rights of Man. Major speaking tour of US, autumn 1940; BA
            conference on 'Science and the World Mind'. *Babes in the Darkling
            Wood* (important for opening statement); *All Aboard for Ararat*.

1941–2   *You Can't Be Too Careful*, last novel; *Guide to the New World* (both
            1941). *The Outlook for Homo Sapiens; Phoenix; The Conquest of Time*
            (last version of *First and Last Things*) (all 1942).

1943–4   *Crux Ansata*, last attack on Catholicism (1943). Awarded the D. Sci.
            but FRS withheld. *'42 to '44* (essays and the D.Sci. thesis). At
            Hanover Terrace through the V-bomb attacks.

1945   *The Happy Turning; Mind at the End of Its Tether;* the 'Betterave
            Papers'. Growing old and ill. Out to vote; last battles with
            aristocracy. Last time out.

1946   Steadily more ill; dies in August. Memorial service, October.

PART ONE

STUDENT

1

THE FIRST YEARS, 1866–1893

> We live in an eddy: are, as it were, the creatures of that eddy. But the great stream of the universe flows past and onward. Here and there is a backwater or a whirling pool, a little fretful midge of life spinning upon its axis, or a gyrating solar system. But the main course is forward, from the things that are past and done with for ever to things that are altogether new.
>
> HGW, 'The "Cyclic" Delusion', *Saturday Review*,
> 10 November 1894

Few people in England in the year 1866 marked the eight-hundredth anniversary of the arrival on their shores of William the Bastard, any more than they noted, in the same year, that near an obscure Czechoslovakian village the armies of Austria and Prussia were fighting out the destinies of middle Europe. With Prussia's victory at Sadowa, on 3 July 1866, events were set in motion which would transform life in the twentieth century. For Prussia, triumphant in the battle for control of greater Germany, provided a matrix out of which Germany would grow masterful and energetic, eventually bringing on war after war, a period historians now are beginning to call 'the century of the German wars'. But the battle and its outcome received very little attention as it occurred, in the press or elsewhere. Russians, Americans, English, if they noted the occasion at all, dismissed it as the brawling of unruly children. In Paris, where a bit more notice was taken, what had happened was seen as untidy decadence, only momentarily disturbing the brilliant conversation in French salons.

Few in the west thought the next century would be a long-term reaction to and echo of these middle-European squabbles. Certainly a couple in England not far from Hastings, descendants of those persons who defended their land against William the Conqueror, did not regard the far-away events as important. They were taken up with the early sounds of a baby just then demanding his place in their already crowded household. For in Bromley, Kent, on 21 September 1866, a boy, their third male child, was born to Sarah and Joseph Wells. Certainly no one at Sadowa, and no one in Bromley, would have perceived any connection between the two events. However, the child, healthy, squalling, protesting his intrusion into the world's affairs, would spend a fair amount of his life analysing the place of Germany in his world, and from that study, the place of our species in the world of which that new Germany was a part. The baby, Herbert George Wells, one of the remarkable minds of the twentieth century, would also seek solutions to other problems of his time posed by nationalism, industrial growth, longer life for our species, and the gigantism from which the Prussian victory had inexorably emerged.

Wells, from practically the first moment of his life, was called Bertie by his mother and father. His two older brothers were worldly types. The elder, Fred, was to spend a good deal of time in South Africa as a clerk in a draper's shop. From their somewhat limited correspondence, it is clear that 'H.G.', as the world would call him, enjoyed and liked both his brothers. The other brother, more shadowy, died in 1931, and H.G. would name his second son, Frank, after him. His brothers always called H.G. the 'Buzzwhacker' or 'Busswhacker', although where that name came from is now lost in time. He signed his letters to them with this intimate name.

The Wells family belonged to the lowest level of the middle class. Although this may seem a narrow definition, it meant that Wells was not of the working class, with its limiting horizons, and that his family and friends could have and did hold somewhat higher expectations for him. His mother was hard-working and religious. Her religion was very important in Sarah Wells's life, and that meant that Sunday was a day of worship. The others in the family, none of them pious, allowed her to dominate that day. In fact, she dominated all days, as Joseph Wells was away from the house for much of the time. He was the nominal proprietor of a shop which sold sporting equipment, cricket bats, balls, and boots, along with a stock of glass and china. The shop was not very successful, although it remained a fixture in Bromley directories through 1887. In time the sporting equipment formed a lesser part of the stock and eventually Wells's father was listed in the directory simply as a dealer in china and glass. Joseph Wells played county cricket as a professional on the Kent side. He was a bowler, as were most professional cricketers at the time, whose duty it was to instruct others, and to bowl to the amateurs who did most of the batting. Once, while bowling for Kent against Sussex at the Oval, he took four wickets on consecutive balls, although not in the same over — a record which still stands in first-class cricket. He founded the Bromley Cricket Club and the cricket ground was where he spent his time. He played until he was fifty-three, although his career was essentially over some time before.[1]

The Wells home was centred in a below-ground kitchen and a small back garden. This was Sarah's domain and here she patched, darned, talked, and cooked. Joseph was not a willing nor a very active gardener. Soon after H.G.'s birth, while working on a grape trellis, he fell and broke his leg, and his support of the family became very limited from that time on. It was in the kitchen that Sarah taught H.G. to read and write, between his third and fourth birthdays. His first written word was 'butter'. Wells wrote intimately about his mother on several occasions and he always emphasized the hard work she invested in the home.[2] She comes across to us today as a strong representative of the Victorian lower middle class without much capability for intense thought.

In the summer of 1874, between H.G.'s seventh and eighth birthdays, the first overtly significant event in his life occurred. A friend of his father's, from a local pub, The Bell, was at the cricket ground with Joseph and H.G. The friend, Sutton, picked the boy up, threw him in the air and caught him, but when he repeated the manœuvre, Bertie slipped and twisted, fell through Sutton's arms, landed across a tent peg, and broke his tibia. The child was forced to spend some weeks in bed, in the kitchen, while the bone knitted. Joseph Wells went to the Bromley Institute library and obtained books for his son to read to pass the time. He located a book on astronomy, and Wood's *Natural History* for him. The latter book had wonderful illustrations of aspects of biology and botany, and Wells said later that the world simply opened up for him as he lay on his couch letting his mind rove over these worlds he had never seen, or, in fact, heard of. He was also to say later that this experience was important in several other ways — his need to suppress pain, the fact that religion was of little use in this activity, and the need to suppress fear of death as well, all dated from this physical trial. The experience, in another of Wells's retrospective remarks, became his 'Lucky Moment'.[3]

With the injury to the father, though, the relationships within the Wells household had changed drastically. There was not enough money now, and Sarah was forced to supplement and eventually to supply much of the family income. She had been trained as a ladies' maid, and had met Joseph when they were both in service, as his family were gardeners on large estates, and had been for several generations. The woman, Elizabeth Bullock, whom Sarah had served prior to her marriage, had married into the Fetherstonhaugh family, and now lived at Up Park in Sussex. This woman's husband had recently died and Sarah was called to fill the maid's role again. She spent much of the remainder of her life at Up Park, nominally as head housekeeper and partly as companion to her mistress. H.G. remained in Bromley, living with his father, and seeing his mother only seldom. By this time it was taken as a matter of course in the family that as soon as he was old enough, H.G. would be apprenticed to a draper, as his brothers had been.

In the two or three years prior to this apprenticeship we lose some contact with Wells. We know, from some of his writings, that he and his father walked a good deal, possibly in an effort to restore their broken legs to a normal state. We also know that Wells became fascinated by words. Later he said, 'We learned to write by reading. We ransacked the dictionary for vocabulary. . . .I was still writing Babu English at seventeen.' His brother Frank later described him as 'a masterful child'. He gave recitations, produced many drawings, and was, again in Frank's words, 'unorthodox and critical'. By the time he was twelve, Wells had begun to write in a very small way. He produced two or three primitive strip cartoons with a story-line, and at least one longer story, filled with adventure, and with his distinctive drawings, which he always called 'picshuas'.[4]

Formal education for the class of persons from which Wells came was now available, but frequently problematical. However, the Education Act of 1870 did extend the possibility of education for the middle class by providing more money for teacher training, and by the time Wells was in his teens, he was given the impetus to propel himself out of the draper's shops he seemed destined to inhabit. Prior to that time, his education was patchy. He attended a dame school for a few months, run by a Mrs Knott and her daughter, Miss Salmon. We know little of this school, other than that the Wells boys all apparently went there. Most of the pupils were girls. From 1874 to 1879 Wells did attend Thomas Morley's Bromley Academy, a fixture in the town, at 74 High Street. It was still possible to see remnants of the building until the mid-'70s of this century. Wells was apparently poor at games, but he did have some local fame as a talker. In his days at the school he was taught to be polite and responsive to adults, as were most of Mr Morley's students. Later Wells was adamant in denial when some thought he had caricatured Thomas Morley in his writing. He said at this time that Morley had a 'commanding urbanity, florid, portly, with the pretentious portliness of an encyclopaedia'.

One senses the education he received had little impact on Wells. Bromley was, however, clearly a place in which he was relatively happy, although he returned there seldom once he left. He wrote about it movingly in *The New Machiavelli*, and in an early unsigned article in the *Pall Mall Gazette*, in which he recalled the Bromley of his youth in what were to be the last of the best years for the area. The railway had recently opened that part of Kent to commuters to London, and the river running through the town was increasingly used as an outfall for the sewage. Now the fish were dead, algae covered the water, the river seemed smaller, there were more houses and roads, and Wells was happy that he had not been born later to grow up in the new urban and much less pleasant Bromley.[5]

Wells did not talk or write much about his early life. He regretted the events that meant his mother and father were separated, and felt oppressed by his family's poverty, at least in retrospect. However, he did not react negatively towards it, and when he read a book, years later, by 'Mark Benney', whom he had befriended, he told Benney not to be so negative about his own early poverty:

Gissing had that [hatred of his early poverty]. Dickens hadn't. I haven't, now. I slept in greasy torn sheets. I lived mostly on bread and butter and cheese. I am two inches shorter than I ought to be and I was too under-vitalized to play games well but somehow there was never any sense of guilt or glory about it, due I think largely to the mixture of derision and impatient contempt with which my father regarded all our inconveniences. He shot well and he bowled well but he never wanted to get on in the world.[6]

Wells, however, was very angry at the circumstances that denied him a first-class education and commented on this many times. In his view denial of opportunity to first-class minds was the greatest crime of the modern state.

Sarah Wells was convinced that becoming a draper would be a significant step up in the world for her son. To that end she apprenticed Bertie to that life, at first, in 1879, to Rodgers and Denyer in Windsor. He was later to serve briefly as a chemist's apprentice at Midhurst. These positions did not work out well at all. Wells at thirteen was a poor worker and was only useful for such tasks as washing windows. By mutual consent the agreements were soon terminated and he was then sent to Hyde the Draper, in the Kings Road, Southsea. Here he spent what he later termed 'the most miserable years of my life'. The work ritual was horrible. His supervisors were autocratic shop-walkers, alert to every false move by their charges. Wells was a failure at the work and was constantly reminded of the failures, both by his superiors and by the other workers with whom he was lodged. He was the lowest man in a rigidly fixed hierarchy. Work began at 7.30 a.m. and lasted until 8 p.m., or even later, in the dark, forbidding building where the shop was located. It is significant that no person from this period of Wells's life emerges at a later time.

Wells seemed destined, in these first fifteen years of his life, to spend much of his time underground, in dark and dismal surroundings. Raised in an underground kitchen, from which, through the grating, he could see only the feet of passers-by, he lodged in cellars or garrets, dim, closed in, filled with shadows, away from the sun, in all of the apprentice homes where he was forced to stay. Even at Up Park, access to the kitchens and the area 'below stairs' (and in this case, 'below ground') was through dark, winding, unlit tunnels. Wells used these experiences overtly in his famous pamphlet *This Misery of Boots* (1907), but when one considers the number of times his work contrasts suppressed life underground with periods of sunlight and escape, it is clear that these early childhood experiences were of considerable psychic significance as well.

While describing his work as a draper's apprentice some years later, but to a sympathetic group, he remarked, 'I knew the pinch of it all; the intolerable hours, the brutal competition, the many petty tyrannies of retail trade, and I only wish I could see my way to suggest drastic reforms that would at one blow remove these evils.' Wells went on to encourage kindliness towards others, hard work, and urged each person to create a vision by which one could escape the life. In another place he revealed in a moving passage that 'the life then offered me was a hideous insult to my possibilities; and had I not been able to believe that there was a way out of the systematized drudgery that forced itself upon me, I would deliberately have "got out" of a world that could misuse me so.'[7]

The only escape from the monotonous horror of the draper's shop was the occasional holiday. On Sundays one could choose between 'pub, piety, or the pavement'. Cycling was an escape for Wells and many others. With this extension of his horizon he could go along the sea front and participate in stereotyped romances. Here he was blessedly away from the retail trade. 'The daily life of a shop assistant may not be exactly available, but, depend upon it, the margin is a thing worth having, and almost, indeed, worth being a shop assistant for. Fancy a holiday, ye men of the Long Vacation, without a solitary trouble except the sense that it must end.'[8]

Life at Southsea was unpleasant and Wells longed and schemed to be out of it. He beseeched his mother and father to allow him to break his articles of apprenticeship. He threatened suicide at least once, if not more. At least once he walked the miles to Up Park to see his mother and plead personally with her. By the summer of 1883, he was at the end of his tether. He had wangled a place at Midhurst Grammar School, to study but also to assist as a pupil teacher, as his quick mind had attracted some attention. Teaching salaries were in part dependent on pupil results at this time; and although no money was available to Wells directly, assistance was promised by Horace Byatt, headmaster of the school, if he did well in his work.

H.G. wrote to his mother nearly every day while the decision as to his future was being discussed. At first his theme was 'Do as you wish and I shall be happy in the execution of your wishes but if you wish me to go to the Midhurst I shall be happy in a superlative degree'. Later he became more importunate: 'Time here is wasted. I can not study here . . . and you do not imagine that I shall be able to pass examinations without study. I shall not leave Midhurst and be an expense to you until I have matriculated. . . .' When his father was recalcitrant about signing the papers cancelling his indenture to Hyde, Bertie was blunt: '. . . remind him of all that he has received from you in the last few years. Ask him to sign the agreement or expect no more. He is now blocking my path in life and he will be a continued threat for the next two years unless he signs. . . .' Finally Joseph Wells gave in and Wells reported that the boys at Midhurst School were happy he was coming, 'and I hope to find my new circle very much more pleasant than the one in which I now move.' At about the same time he apologized for his early intemperate letter, and thanked his mother, as he was 'not well fitted to be a business man . . . '. Surely this last comment was one of the great understatements of all time!

Wells was free at last, though, with these papers signed, and on his way to intellectual life. The draper's existence was behind him, but not entirely, as it had scarred him in quite extraordinary ways. He could not imagine doing that sort of work again. But it did mean that he was always remarkably tolerant of waiters, servants, and others caught up in a life of drudgery and no hope — a life that few could escape. He was happy at his own prospects, but he knew how lucky he had been.[9]

Midhurst Grammar School had reopened for teaching in April 1880. The new headmaster, Horace Byatt, had high hopes of his ability to train people to take advantage of the considerable possibilities under the Education Act. Wells remained at the school for just under two years, cramming knowledge in every spare minute to obtain high enough marks so that he could attend the Normal School of Science (later the Royal College of Science), his new goal. During much of this time he was assistant master, taking care of the details of work, living in Byatt's home, with other boys, always on call. The school kept classes from 9.30 a.m. to 12.30, and from 2 to 4 in the afternoons, except Saturday, which was a half-holiday. Wells was very serious in his approach to this opportunity. Occasionally in later life, his pupils wrote to thank him for his interest in their lives and work. He also worked very hard on his preparation. On one letter in which he had complained to his mother of no news, she wrote at the bottom, '*Six* I *have* sent him. No reply until. . . .' But he was extremely busy. Later, commenting to her on the examinations he was taking, he said that he needed books badly. He asked her to send on what books he had, as well as others: French, Latin, books on geography and grammar. 'It will require hard work and time but I can give that if I can obtain books', was his judgement. The Up Park library provided some of the books necessary for the young grind.

Wells literally crammed himself full of facts. Byatt encouraged him, not only for the prizes which Wells earned towards his education, but also because it gave publicity and brought additional funds to Midhurst School. Wells took and passed an extraordinary number of examinations, each producing its guinea or occasionally two guineas for finishing at the top. He hated the cramming and spoke in scathing tones on the subject as soon as he was free of it. He termed it 'mental engorgement, learning without digestion', describing it as like making sausages, a simile he also used in a poem, although he did recognize the good side of the learning for some.

Others in England were pursuing similar paths, most especially, in Devon, Richard Arman Gregory; and, in Northumberland, from an even poorer background, Ernest Barker. Their lives would intertwine with Wells's and the bond of common experience drew them together in an ideological way as well. The Education Act, faulty as it was in many ways, did enable very bright boys to achieve a certain status. For these three, however, it remained a tragedy that many with similar gifts did not have that opportunity because of their circumstances; and, of course, the Act only applied in its limited form to one sex. Wells spoke of these problems on many occasions, but never more clearly than in 1893 when, free of the life, he looked back with admiration on those who continued the struggle to better themselves against the odds:

> There is something splendid and titanic about these ambitious and self-taught men. They work in the dark and under a tremendous disadvantage; they have often to content themselves with few and insufficient books, second-hand books, haphazard, at the most difficult points, and yet withal they will often emerge at last with ideas cleverer, sounder, and stronger than many a student who has had all the advantages — and relaxation — of a University. There is, I believe, a great future before these pilgrims from the proletariat to wisdom.[10]

Wells entered the Normal School of Science at South Kensington in the autumn of 1884, just eighteen years old. Education in South Kensington was geared towards producing teachers of science, mostly destined for the new schools which had sprung up after the Education Act. It was not yet part of the University of London, although T. H. Huxley, Wells's teacher, hoped that it soon would be. That controlling and supervisory organization would eventually provide certain standards for the congeries of institutes and schools of Wells's time. A dream of democratic education was beginning, and Huxley had a strong vision of what it might be. He spoke often on the subject, and his and later Wells's friend, E. Ray Lankester, responded to one of these speeches with a letter which might have been illuminating to a scholar like Wells. 'It always seemed to me to be a thing greatly to be desired — that the common man or ruck of students should be taught by the best possible professors so as to give them a chance. Amongst the men who go through bad cram classes and listen to futile lecturers there must be a proportion who would blossom out under the stimulus of really able and original professors,' said Lankester.[11] Huxley, of course, fitted this ideal exactly.

Wells did very well in his studies. He got either a first or a second in every course for which he registered except astronomical physics; this last he failed in 1886, but he finished with a second-class on repeating the course in 1887. He also failed geology in 1887, but this was due to his interest in the student magazine, and he already knew that he did not need the course for success in the other matters of life.[12] Clearly he mastered the material, as his later writing in that field attests.

He did particularly well in zoology, taught by Huxley, who was scheduled to give thirty-eight lectures between January and June of that first year. It is not easy to know exactly of what Huxley's courses consisted. The laboratory exercises for his elementary botany and the work in his biology laboratories are still on record, however. There was a good deal of histology in the botany class, focusing on the cornflower, various yeasts, and the sunflower. Young hellebore plants and the embryos of gymnosperm were studied in detail. In the biology laboratory, the demonstrations were mostly by G. B. Hawes who was Huxley's assistant from 1884 to 1896. Wells spent nineteen days on the general anatomy of the mammal, supplemented by detailed work on a sheep's brain, an ox eye, and a dog's larynx. This was followed by work on the hydra, the amoeba, some time on the general histology of the mammal (four days), four days on the earthworm, nine days on the arthropods, especially the astares, three days on the echinoderms (starfish), three days on the molluscs (oysters) (in all of these last demonstrations some time was spent on the larval stage of the animal), and one day on the infusoria. Some of the lectures were given by the demonstrator, as Huxley was ill during part of the term.[13]

Wells has left us several statements of his attitude towards Huxley. The best of these pieces appeared soon after his master's death. In it Wells described the opening of the class, with the formal placement of a rabbit to be dissected; and 'then Huxley appeared'. Wells said he looked like his photographs, more than most people do, and he recounted the difficulty he had in continuing his work when the great man was near by. He described the 'studied nonchalance of the first cut' on the specimen, and closed his encomium with, 'And I do not know if the students of today will quite understand just how one felt for our dean — we read his speeches, we borrowed the books he wrote. . . .' Wells spoke once to him, he remembered, and lifted his hat. Huxley was the only professor worth that gesture, thought the young radical, who remarked: 'I believed then he was the greatest man I was ever likely to meet, and I believe that all the more firmly today.' Wells went on to boast that if he were asked if he had been at the Royal College in Huxley's time, he always remarked in an offhand manner, and with dishonest intent, 'Oh yes, *I was one of his men.*'[14] This may seem like the recollection of anyone who has had a strong personality as his mentor, but in Wells's case, the feeling was honest, real, and accurate. Huxley was the greatest man he ever met, and Wells devoted his life to translating Huxleyan principles into the life of our species.

Wells entered the Royal College with great hopes, as he told his brother, of obtaining his first degree by October 1888, and with luck, of completing a doctorate by 1900. By 1886, however, after two years, his desires were less lofty, and as he had decided by that time to get married, one more year was all that he now planned. This year was not a good one, as his activities on the College magazine, as well as his proposed marriage, to his cousin Isabel Wells, interfered with his work. For those reasons, he then planned to teach for a bit before actually taking his examinations.[15] R. A. Gregory, A. T. Simmons, and others of his friends at the Royal College were sympathetic to the delay, as they felt, apparently, that the possible horizons of the young scholar were as yet unknown.

Wells described his days at the school after his graduation, in an article published under a pseudonym. He described himself as 'awestruck', as he appeared with a 'cheap shiny handbag and a quarto notebook, coloured pencils, and a book of appliances'. He went on to say that 'no human being is so absolutely free as the South Kensington student, male or female, save that it is expected that lecture notes be copied, somewhere in the interval.' He went on in the article to describe the types of students with whom he associated. One of these (though he met her much later) was clearly Amy Catherine Robbins, who became his second wife. After describing her solitary life in a flat, he went on to remark, 'Subsequently, in another course, one of the demonstrators, so it is said, saw her notes of his demonstrations so beautifully, so methodically, and so fully written out, that the scientific severity of his life was suddenly irradiated by a glow of novel sentiment. The two are now married.' Wells described Amy as 'a meek-looking, soft-voiced, little soul in a plain black dress'. Another of the student types he described may also have been a well-known personage. This person was 'an illiterate wretch of fifteen from the hinterland of Sussex who had conducted his own education. He had no manners, but was within three marks of top of his class and was [at the time of writing] a provincial professor, now gentlemanly, but still uneducated.'

Wells went on in the same article to discuss the various museums in the South Kensington area which the students used. He, in particular, was familiar with their contents. There was, unfortunately, little other outside intellectual life, only the debating society, called 'the Talking Club'; but the frequency of examinations meant that 'the students had to choose more or less wittingly between high and conspicuous proficiency in science and mental culture'. If one were prepared to modify the first, a very good education was possible, as Wells apparently rationalized his own experience. 'I am sometimes inclined to think that the authorities who rein in the students so tightly, so far as their hours of study are concerned, scarcely realize all that their college, with its adjacent museums and libraries, might become.'[16]

To change the situation in which he found himself, Wells, along with a few other students, began a magazine to record student life. He was elected editor, and soon became the primary contributor to the journal, as many of those anxious at the beginning to work found that they could not keep up with all that needed to be done. Wells addressed his first leading article 'To the Average Man', and said he would edit the journal for that person. 'I conceal from every eye beneath this calm, hopeful, even proud exterior, the devastation of the furies, the fierce, ceaseless assault of fear, remorse, and despair. Like the Roman sentinel at Pompeii, or better, like a responsible public official before an election', was his description of himself. Wells used the *Science Schools Journal* to try out his growing desire to write, and primitive versions of most aspects of his writing appear in one form or another in the journal.[17]

He was well known at the College, not only from the *Journal*, and made some of his closest and life-long friends there. One of them, Elizabeth Healey, was slightly older than Wells. She was the daughter of one of his professors, and Wells thought of her as an older sister, or so it seems. He wrote confessional letters to her until the First World War period, and the correspondence, which continued until he died, remains an excellent source for his life, especially in the earliest days of the letters. Years later this friend remembered standing in a corridor, waiting for a class to begin, when someone near by said, 'There comes Wells.' Not only for Elizabeth Healey and his other fellow students: that salutation must always have marked his entrance, as for the rest of his life people everywhere noticed him and hoped that he would illuminate their dull, drab lives.[18] Richard Gregory, A. T. 'Tommy' Simmons, and A. Morley Davies were the other closest companions of these days. All remained close to him as long as they lived.

By the end of his time at South Kensington, Wells had explored much of London, riding on the horse-drawn omnibuses which connected various areas of the city. Many of these scenes would illuminate his early essays, and they will be noticed in passing at a later time, but for now it is enough to see the quick active man, with sandy hair and thin moustache, wearing his red tie to proclaim his socialism, going to the places appropriate for a socialist to go to. For instance, Wells made the obligatory pilgrimage to Kelmscott House at Hammersmith to hear William Morris speak. Originally, he said, he had hoped to see those persons who would direct the new world, but was shown instead 'a comedy of picturesque personalities'. The two who stood out were Shaw, 'always careful to make himself misunderstood', and 'the grand head, rough voice, the sturdy figure, sedulously plain speech and lovable bearing of William Morris'.[19]

Wells himself was slight of build, and early photographs convey the sense of a forlorn demeanour, as he gazes into the slow lens of the period. He appears in cheap sack suits, with longish hair, and eventually the moustache, which in one form or another remained throughout his life. He was short, had tiny feet, and a high, almost atonal, voice, but the words uttered in that voice soon eliminated any impression of inferiority or pathos he might have given. Wells himself always attributed his non-athletic build and lack of stamina to dietary deficiencies in the dark days of his Bromley childhood and his apprentice meals of bread, dripping, and old cheese. The moustache may have been grown originally to give an appearance of maturity, and to counter the high-pitched and occasionally unpleasant voice. He spoke on several occasions of words 'cascading down' through his moustache to his shirtfront. The photographs show a person who could have passed for a somewhat weedy shop assistant ('counter-jumper' in the argot), or a slightly pathetic beginning teacher who worried about keeping discipline among his pupils. As money began to come in, Wells ate better, exercised more, and lived a more regular life. He began to develop a portly appearance, his clothes were better made, and the moustache was managed. His size, his small feet, and the intonation of his voice, though a source of ridicule by a few enemies, were of no consequence measured against the power of his intellect and his general *bonhomie* with guests and acquaintances.

Wells described his writing at this time as 'toy dog yaps to an unyielding world'. His failure in geology, coupled with his strong desire to get married and his very small literary success, forced him to take a position at a poor and marginal public school, Holt Academy, at Wrexham. It was 'an uncongenial environment', according to a letter of the period. He did discover a 'damosel', although we know little of her. She was the only thing that made life worth living, or so he told A. M. Davies, his chief correspondent at this time. The young woman, Annie, took up much of his spare time. The teaching was not difficult, but the students were dull and loutish. He told Elizabeth Healey, after he had left the school, that he 'had to grind Euclid, among other things, into some wretched apologies for immortal souls ... '. Another of his duties was to officiate at football matches. One of the clods he taught, in an apparently deliberate act, fouled him with a kick to the kidneys. Wells began to spit blood and when the doctors examined him they also found evidence of tuberculosis — consumption, as it was called then. His situation was desperate: no money, badly ill, and now coughing blood whenever he took any strenuous exercise.[20]

His surviving letters from the period alternate despair at the prospect that his life would be ended before he could make a contribution, with a grim desire to survive, what he would later call his 'sustaining vanity'. He apparently attempted to return to the classroom too soon after the injury, had a relapse, and found himself an invalid at Up Park where his mother's employer took him in. One consolation now was the opportunity to use again the great library, as he began his recuperation. As well as the library, he explored the attic of the house. Here he located the parts of a telescope, relic of some earlier era. He put it together and spent a substantial time studying the stars and the moon, while thinking about the immense distances the lens was opening to him. Among the books he read again, and which had a major impact upon him, were Plato's *Republic*, Winwood Reade's *The Martyrdom of Man*, and Burton's *Anatomy of Melancholy*. Later in life Wells was to use the Platonic dialogue form several times, most notably in *Babes in the Darkling Wood*. Burton's work was emulated in his own work *The Anatomy of Frustration*, and it is not too much to see themes in *The Outline of History* originating in Reade's book. The latter, published first in 1872, is a free-thinker's history of mankind and remained in print in its 24th edition until at least 1936. Reading it today one is struck by the force of this early attempt at analysing the impact of Darwinian thought, along with the inherent promise of the species. Wells was strongly affected

by the book (as was Winston Churchill, among others) and continued to
mention it as a formative work whenever he discussed such matters. Reade,
an explorer, died at a young age but his book remains a monument to
clarity of thought long after he has been forgotten.

The illness, though, was a difficult experience for the young scholar, and
Wells knew instinctively that 'the only chance [for me] now for a living is
literature. . . . I think the groove I shall drop into will be cheap nov-
eletteering, not with my entire approval though. I hanker after essays and
criticism — vainly,' he told one of his friends. He did continue his interest
in the College, and when one student election did not go to his satisfaction,
he asked his friend A. M. Davies, 'Why in God's name didn't you cook the
meeting? *I* always did.' Gradually Wells began to improve somewhat. He
read Heine and sent a copy of the poems on to Davies, and at a Christmas
party held below-stairs at Up Park, he danced three contras and a waltz, as
well as singing a duet with his brother Frank. He also apparently had a
brief romantic liaison with a young woman named Mary, working at Up
Park, although he later maintained that it was confined to a series of kisses,
in a closet. To most eyes, though, he must have been a pathetic specimen
— doomed with no future.[21]

It soon became necessary for the invalid to have a better convalescent
home than this busy country house, and he moved to Stoke-on-Trent,
where he found lodgings with a young curate, his fellow student William
Burton. His doctors advised him to walk and read, both of which he did,
although he indulged himself with a visit to the College in April 1888.
These same doctors apparently also told him several times that he might
not live, but they did provide him with a list of persons who had succeeded
even though invalids. Wells rejected that concept. He continued to spit
blood, however, and as late as May 1888, he said he was growing steadily
weaker. But this apparently marked the low point in his trials, and his
letters after this improve steadily in tone.

One of the results of his brush with death was his complete rejection of
religion, although he had been on the verge of that decision since at least
1885, when he had written a satirical anti-religious poem. For his mother's
sake, he did not make a parade of his views, but was quick to tell Elizabeth
Healey, as when he remarked to her, 'I know now that the whole Universe
is a sham, a tin simulacrum of ideals, veneered deal pretending to
mahogany. If I had not been an ass I should have understood that, when
the cardboard religious structure I constructed in my kid-calfhood caved in
when I came to lean on it.'[22]

As Wells began to recover he knew that he had to pass his examinations in
order to get anywhere in life, and he again began to cram himself with
material. 'My mind runs on kinetic energy, equations to chords of contact,
binomial theorem, Mendeleff's theory, macrospezungia(?) [megasporangia
is the modern term], and fields of inadequate force', was the way he

described the process to a correspondent. His first set of examinations was finished by August 1889, and he, his cousin Isabel, and his Aunt Mary went off to Whitstable for a brief holiday, prior to his taking on the Honours examinations at the end of the year.[23] During this time he was employed in London, teaching and invigilating examinations at Henley House School in Kilburn, where he met among others a former student, Alfred C. Harmsworth, later Lord Northcliffe, who had founded and edited the school journal. Harmsworth apparently provided Wells with a bit of pocket money writing paragraphs for *Tit-Bits* and *Answers to Correspondents*, the earliest of the successful Harmsworth newspapers.

A student of Wells's in those days was A.A. Milne, son of the headmaster of Henley House School, who also remembered him afterward with some fondness. Wells seems to have made something of a mark at the school. The school magazine noticed his success in his B. Sci. examination, and remarked the event with the words, 'May his shadow get a good deal broader', which may have had two meanings. When Wells had come to the school it was announced that he would take science and drawing throughout the school, but in order to impress both the boys and their parents, the magazine listed his various advanced teaching certificates: Wells was qualified, it was said, to instruct in zoology, botany, geology (mineralogy and palaeontology), physics, chemistry, mathematics, practical geometry, and drawing, which was defined as free-hand, model, geometrical, and perspective. The writer of the piece, probably J. V. Milne, the headmaster, said at the end of the introduction, 'he has already awakened a thirst for science and a spirit of enquiry.'

Wells himself also gives a glimpse of the school, and his teaching, with a short piece for the magazine which describes the summer experiments in science he had set for the boys. Sending them into the fields to observe, he adjured them, 'It is everywhere for those that have eyes to see; and it is difficult indeed to account for the eyes that cannot. *Science is the understanding of things*, not the collecting of them merely, and certainly not the naming of them.'[24]

After his examinations were passed, Wells was elected a Fellow of the Zoological Society in early 1890, and soon William Briggs, proprietor of the University Correspondence College at Cambridge, offered him employment as a reader of correspondence lessons for those persons wishing an external degree. Briggs had begun his school to take advantage of the possibilities inherent in the Education Act, and it was quite successful. In the teaching part of the enterprise Briggs paid 2s. 4d. per hour for a third-class degree person's work, 2s. 6d. for a second-class degree, and 2s. 8d. for a first-class degree. For the correcting of lessons, employees such as Wells were paid by the item. Wells journeyed to Cambridge to be interviewed by Briggs, and it was here that he first met Walter Low, also in Briggs's stable of teachers and writers. Low had been employed there for some time, and had written several in Briggs's series of textbooks. He and Wells became fast friends.

At first Wells did no teaching. And, as he was paid by the paper, the more he read the more he earned. As a result, feeling the pinch, he worked very hard. By October 1891, he had saved enough so that he and his cousin Isabel could be married. They set up housekeeping at 28 Haldon Road in East Putney in an eight-room house, rented at £30 a year. Isabel was able to contribute some funds through her work at a photograph-retouching studio where she remained as an employee. Wells's work habits continued to be good enough so that by January 1893, they had accumulated a bank account of £52. 10s. 5d.[25]

Wells had also begun to write a number of short pieces for journals in the areas of science and education, encouraged no doubt by the extra money earned from the Harmsworth papers. He published in the *Educational Times* at this period, as did Walter Low. He also co-edited the *University Correspondent*, another of Briggs's enterprises, with Walter Low. Wells remembered that it had an annual budget of £50 for the editor and another £50 for contributors. Much of the matter in the journal was advertising, or listings of every result in every conceivable examination. There was a good deal of editorial matter, however, and apparently during this time Wells and Low produced nearly all of it. Low fell ill — he died quite soon — so Wells quickly became involved in the day-to-day work of editing. Wells was very fond of Low, and his death had a profound impact on the young writer. This death, and that of Gissing in a few years, caused Wells to develop a harsh attitude towards death which has offended many since, but the uncertainty of his own future, as well as these early losses, was important in producing the hard-boiled way in which he treated the matter.

During this period Wells's writing for these journals did not wander far from the mundane business of teaching, and invigilating examinations. But his own experience in examinations and the work he saw of the people at the correspondence school led him to write fairly extensively on these matters, and eventually to try to fill some of the gaps he saw with textbooks designed for that particular audience. Also as a result of this work he began his life-long call for more science in schools, and especially the life sciences. He urged teaching and learning in the Huxley style, that is, by using types, drawing inferences, and making comparisons as the best way of learning. He designed courses for prospective students, describing appropriate dissection kits and microscopes. Even here, though, he felt that the tyro student, 'without qualified advice, . . . will certainly meet with very considerable difficulty in his endeavours. . . . To overcome these difficulties unaided, he will need either exceptional quickness or else very exceptional perseverance.' Although Wells thought most schools of the time were terrible, he felt they could be improved through the creation by the state of scientific and technical laboratories, with lectureships available to attending students on the basis of competitive examinations outside the current framework of teachers and inspectors. The new proposals would be aimed primarily at graduate education for those teachers with some experience and who qualified.[26]

In addition to commenting on the proposed University of London, then under parliamentary consideration (Wells called for the establishment of high standards, as well as 'analytical research' especially in graduate studies), he also analysed the impact of the education bills and such efforts as that of the College of Preceptors to control teaching certification on the many levels of private education in England at the time. He thought the best schools would survive, but be made better, and he argued for state subsidies to help the weaker schools. 'The organization of secondary education in England will do more harm than good if it fails to recognize, assist, and encourage efficient private enterprises, equally with those having a public or quasi-public character.' One suggestion for how to make the money go further was to create central laboratories in the larger towns and cities.[27]

Besides publishing in tame professional journals, Wells also ventured forth with other comments on improving the education system. He claimed that science needed popularizing, and that since Darwin's time, one effect of the increase in knowledge had been to cut down broad-gauged support for research. He thought that part of the problem lay with the scientists who needed to simplify their technical language, while using greater precision when writing. In addition the scientific writer should avoid jests, and lecturing down to his audience. Wells gave examples from some recent lectures he had attended, and called for significant reforms. This paper was well received and he followed it with others on how to teach science in school (based on his Henley House School work and his extension lectures). Later, in a review, he described what he conceived to be the proper sequence of a study in science.[28] These papers brought his views to many in the educational community who found them exactly what was needed.

Simply proposing curriculum changes and urging state funding was not enough, of course, so Wells, needing money, and feeling the demands of his education as well, wrote two textbooks. The first of these, co-authored with his Royal College friend, Richard A. Gregory, was *Honours Physiography* (1893), a textbook specifically designed to fill a gap in a series which Briggs used in his correspondence programme. Wells was concerned about writing another 'cram' book, but he said in this case that 'the cheap accusation' was not true. 'Cram is the acquisition of knowledge without assimilation', and of course, his book was above that. Written to a specific syllabus, available through the correspondence school, it was designed to propel the student to 'heights quite beyond his unaided ability'. Nevertheless, it was a cram book; and it sold well to the audience needing such help. To us, today, the most important sections, as we think of the life and work of H. G. Wells, are the pages on Mars and prospective life on that planet, a section on animals based on a primitive idea of continental drift, and the chapter which covers 'The General Facts of the Distribution of Life in Time and Space'. These three sections, of course, did put the book above the average run of such books, which did not usually treat speculative matters.[29]

More important perhaps was the two-volume work, *Textbook of Biology*, which appeared the same year, 1893, although the copyright was a year earlier. This work was also part of the Tutorial Series of the correspondence school, but the volumes, one on the vertebrates and the other on the invertebrates, were of a generally higher order of analysis. The book soon came out in a second edition, with the plates, originally drawn by Wells, now substantially modified. (Those in Volume II of the new edition were drawn by Amy Catherine Robbins.) The book was completely rewritten in 1898, except for chapter 14, and reissued under the title *Textbook of Zoology*. Wells's name continued to appear on the spine of the book, which reached its sixth edition in 1913. It survived as a work until 1934 at least, when the last edition I have seen was published. All of the later editions give H.G. Wells credit for the general plan of the work, but absolve him from any further responsibility. One of the areas that changed most, edition after edition, was the chapter on the theory of evolution, as this aspect of biology underwent the greatest transformation after Wells's day. He was from time to time unhappy that his name remained on the book, but apparently could do nothing about it; he had sold the rights to Briggs and his successors.[30]

Although the text was written for examination purposes, Wells again discouraged 'the system of pure cram, which is alien to the discipline of biological science'. He called instead for the student to study in the presence of a teacher who would supervise, answer queries, and observe methods of dissection and analysis. 'In the ideal world there is a plentiful supply of such teachers, and easy access to their teaching, but in this real world only a favoured few enjoy these advantages.' He called for actual dissection by the students and recommended a 'well-boiled rabbit' for skeletonic study. He dealt with dissection and pain in another section as well, thus trying to appeal to any and all potential users of his work, and to counteract the attacks of anti-vivisectionists which were current at the time. His views on reproduction bear repeating: 'The preservation of the species is paramount. Hence in an animal's physiology and psychology we meet with a vast amount of *unselfish* provision, and its structure and happiness are more essentially dependent on the good of its kind than on narrow personal advantage.'

He had learned his lessons from Huxley very well. On evolution he remarked that there were two basic laws — the first, the law of inheritance, and the second, the law of variation. The variation could be for better or worse, of course.

It is in the demonstration of this wonderful unity in life, only the more confirmed the more exhaustive our analysis becomes, that the educational value and human interest of biology chiefly lies. . . . And the world is not made and dead like a cardboard model or a child's toy, but a living equilibrium; and every day and every hour, every living thing is being weighed in the balance and found sufficient or wanting. . . . Zoology is, indeed, a philosophy and a literature to those who can read its symbols. . . .

were his considered comments.[31]

This remarkable book, written at the age of twenty-six, very well summarized in its pages where Wells stood: just on the verge of making his mark in literature. He had had a good training, supplemented with wide reading during his periods of convalescence. He had already taken the theory of evolution to its logical extension, and shown careful readers that the idea of continual progress was chimerical. The book also had the virtue of being well written, in a clear form; and although the illustrations were not professionally drawn, they usefully enhanced the text, as they were taken from life. One reviewer, in the *Educational Times* and therefore possibly Low, Gregory, or even Wells himself, liked the book very much. The reviewer concluded his favourable comments with: 'Its value lies in the judicious condensation of a large amount of material, the scientific treatment of subjects, and the discrimination between the essential and the unimportant.' Other reviewers also liked the book: several, however, thought the illustrations were crude.[32]

By the time the *Textbook* was published, Wells was feeling confident of his powers, at least most of the time, even though this confidence came with difficulty as he overcame the psychological damage of his illness. At first he told Elizabeth Healey that his life's work 'will be to give as little trouble as possible in an uncongenial universe', but a week later he was more positive as he said, 'Two things [his illnesses] were given me to pitch stones at. Sometimes I fancy that this is the thing that gives me my profoundest pleasure — to chuck things at things and break them.'[33] His readers since would agree with his fancy.

During his recuperative periods Wells read very widely, and he began to compare his writing, and his prospects, with those of authors he read who had been successful. As examples from his judgements at that time, he liked Whitman, but felt that both Tennyson and Scott gave more to the reader. He was also quite critical of Shelley, Petrarch, and parts of Dickens (he didn't like *Bleak House*, for instance, or at least the women in the book). This was also the period in which he read extensively in but finally rejected Christianity and theology. His final conversion (or deconversion) came from reading St. Paul, whose epistles he found unpleasant and shrill. He and Isabel purchased a tricycle and as they rode about the London streets and parks they occasionally discussed his reading, but he found her responses, especially on religion, not very useful, and increasingly their conversation became limited, or so he recalled. He sent Elizabeth Healey a sort of atheist's prayer, which said, 'Leave me alone, O Lord, is my prayer. I will do the same by you. You have things in a mess, but I am not a God, I cannot help you. I can give you advice if you like. But God, you are not much of a man. Leave me alone at any rate. Else I will canvass against you. I will make your position unbearable. I will jeer and make a mock of you.' So Wells, mortal as it was possible to be, railed at immortality.

More and more also the man found it difficult to deal not only with his wife but with some of his early friends. He began to quarrel with many of them, as his imagination was simply too great for their minds, and this caused him pain. Later he ignored such people or became more tolerant of their limitations. In later life Wells's friends could do little wrong. Now, however, faced with his personal dilemmas, he threatened to write a book, 'a big book. . . . The topic is unknown, but it would be something vivid and terrible.'[34]

When Wells wrote this last comment to Davies, at the end of 1891, he was already hard at work on this big book. It would eventually become *The Time Machine*. However that was still some time away; in 1891 the manuscript was perhaps still in its third draft and would be completely reworked once or twice more before it finally appeared in the form we know it today. An earlier version, in three parts, and without much of an ending, had actually been published in the *Science Schools Journal* while Wells was the editor. He, of course, as editor, would have given it a cursory reading, but he, or another, also found it necessary to provide an editorial dig at himself about the unfinished nature of the work. To Elizabeth Healey, Wells responded to the editorial remark at that time by saying, 'There is a sequel [i.e., an ending]. It is the latest Delphic voice but the Tripod is not yet broken.'[35]

Wells was not yet a writer of fiction. He was, in fact, very much a scientist and a pedagogue. That phase of his writing, honed in the two textbooks, is clear, analytical, and deceptively simple. His task, over the next half-dozen years, with the aid of W. E. Henley and the editors of the *Pall Mall Gazette*, *Saturday Review*, and other journals, would be to bring the positive aspects of his scientific writing to bear on his imaginative work. For the moment, though, he was still a scientist engaged in producing scientific work.

A look at that work today does reveal some things about Wells and presages the later marriage of science and fiction, along with some origins of the educational theories of his later life. For instance, he wrote a number of articles and reviews on the great teachers of the past, Socrates, Charlotte Brontë's fictional tutor 'Louis Moore', Pestalozzi, and others.[36] He also gave a good deal of thought to scholasticism, or rather the intellectual frame of mind in which scholasticism could flourish. 'The temper is to the

teacher what the voice is to the singer,' he remarked in one place. He felt
that diffidence was a bad thing, as it led to indolence of thought.
Humiliation was equally bad, however, and the good teacher would be
'consistent'. Wells thought women would make the best teachers as they
'have more faith, more steadiness of confidence in themselves, and others,
and an infinitely greater patience than men'. In a second part of this
philosophical discussion of education, he said that most schools erred in
their choice of staff, because they always looked for diffidence. 'We repeat,
the proper scholastic frame of mind is adamantine, and the severest
condemnation we can write of an assistant, next to the charge of modesty,
is that of being sympathetic', for that meant instability of mood, quickly
followed by favouritism. He urged his prospective teacher and scholar
readers to follow Marcus Aurelius, Epictetus, or Herbert Spencer; to be
severely scientific, in other words, no matter where that took the thinker.
He forgot his own experiences, though, as he also urged similar behaviour
at home to one's wife. 'The perfect teacher cannot be a lover or in any way
a fervent man', was his judgement. 'Born teachers have no peace on their
frontier. . . . This passion [of pedagogy] it is that sends good men and true,
even in these milder days, out of their homes and into their neighbours'
business, with the most enlivening consequences.' He closed this rather
remarkable soliloquy with his statement that: 'A good teacher must be
self-complacent, neither reformer, artist, lover, scientific investigator, nor
philosopher, but teacher, having but one passion, the pedagogic passion,
the passion of Now-listen-to-me ruling over his scholastic life.'[37]

These remarks are from the didactic Wells, the Wells of science and
education. Much of his writing in this period was in this vein. For instance,
he took the occasion of a book on Herbert Spencer, reviewed by another,
to urge the reviewer, and his readers, to modify science teaching, especially
for the young. 'It is, however, certain that science can be made extremely
interesting and comprehensible to the young while the results of direct
school teaching in religion and art are at least, extremely dubious.'[38] This
of course was a period in which many researchers, raised in Christianity,
were attempting to reconcile their Christianity, and their science, with the
teachings or implications of Darwin, Spencer, and Huxley. Wells had no
difficulty with this. He rejected Christianity as inane, and felt a compulsion
to instruct others unwilling to take a similar stand. He wrote several pieces
dealing with extinction, and especially where it reiterated the Darwinian
threat — that although that time and ours was and is the heyday of man's
existence, it need not continue. Wells was able to point out various ways in
which existence could continue, through co-operation and symbiosis, but
still the chances were none too good, at least without serious thought.
Socialism might possibly offer the answer, he supposed, but as yet pure
intellectual effort was really the only route to ultimate success, and our
species, Wells was sure, should simply knuckle under and follow his
reasoning out to its logical conclusion.[39]

As Wells set down these prophetic judgements, he was about to make a major leap into fiction. Teaching was satisfactory, but it did not give much time for retrospective thought, and, as he said, good teachers ought not to do much of that anyway. The dreary work of correcting correspondence lessons, or even of writing textbooks, brought in money enough to survive, but not much more. His health remained precarious and the demands on his funds were fairly great, especially if he wanted to surround himself with books, the amenities of life, and the sort of home to which he aspired. His work at the College of Preceptors coupled with the correspondence-course reading was a bit more remunerative, but it still did not provide sufficient income for him and for Isabel too. For by this time, as we have seen, Wells had acquired feminine baggage; and by the end of the period under discussion, he had moved well beyond his first wife, to begin his life of love as well. To a considerable extent, it was these demands which drove him into casual journalism, and the rather frantic and almost desperate attempts to make himself a novelist.

Wells thought seriously about love and the behaviour of persons in love. He lectured Elizabeth Healey on her relations with his friend and fellow student William Burton. Wells told her that Burton had been good to him, and this was worth a lot of forgiveness. Burton may not have wanted Elizabeth to continue her correspondence with Wells — the context is unclear; but Wells took the opportunity to say to her, 'Should a man who is engaged deny himself all intercourse with the most amiable part of humanity, saving one unit, and should the free man — what ought he to do?' Wells was already engaged to his cousin Isabel when he wrote this letter. In fact, they had an understanding from about 1883 or 1884, apparently. While a student at South Kensington, after one or two unsuccessful efforts to board himself, he had found inexpensive lodgings with his father's brother's wife, whom the Wells family had known casually for some time. Her daughter, Isabel, was the first woman Wells had known with whom he felt truly free. Both were sexually precocious, apparently, and the match-makers, Wells's Aunt Mary and perhaps Isabel's Aunt Sarah, did not hesitate to throw them together. Wells's first view of Isabel was remembered later: 'She had a grave and lovely face, very firmly modelled, broad brows, and a particularly lovely mouth and chin and neck.' They experienced a profound physical attraction for each other, and even though they were first cousins, plans for the marriage followed readily.[40]

Wells's sexual desires were caught up in Victorian morality. He did not want to get married: he did want to go to bed. Wells wrote of his ambivalence, couched in the terms of that Victorian morality, of course, to Elizabeth Healey. In these letters of confession he opposed marriage for those who could not take care of themselves financially. Otherwise, one was doomed to a world of 'ha'penny economics, small pretences, humiliations, that fret all the admirable qualities of the husband and weigh the wife double with the burden of time. I know all about these marriages because I am the victim of one.' In a letter a month or so later, Wells asked Elizabeth to look after Isabel, if he should die (this was when he was recuperating from his illness and at his lowest point). Later he continued his complaint about the restraints of an engagement, and even marriage: '. . . ninety-nine per cent of marriages end in revolt or passive endurance and when two people will be loyal all through, the tie becomes simply a concession to conserve adjacent fashion.' He told his brother Fred later, after Isabel and he were married, that they were 'bringing the art of living on very little very happily to a high state of preparation', but straining beneath the jollity were the pressures of sexual life.[41]

In later years, and after Isabel had died, Wells was fairly open in his discussion of the reasons for their marriage. They were thrown together, and she became the recipient of his 'suppressed love and sexual drive', or so he said. He felt that they should rather have been brother and sister, although his sexual attraction to her remained strong even after the divorce. She was not an intellectual, and soon all they shared, having so little money, were their walks and rides about London on Sundays. Isabel, according to Wells, was unable to deal with his moods, and 'topic after topic became neutral ground'. He became, as a consequence, vulnerable to someone who would fulfil these other needs.

Amy Catherine Robbins, the student he met in his demonstration classes for the Correspondence College, fell into this niche. He had in these classes two 'lovely students', Miss Robbins and Adeline Roberts. He placed his stool between them in the laboratory in order to respond to their bright queries. Soon they were meeting for tea, and soon again it was he and Amy Catherine alone at tea, and then in her flat. He said that he still loved his cousin, and there is enough evidence to credit this, but his affinity with Amy Catherine was simply too great. He faced a terrible dilemma and after he and Isabel made a visit to Miss Robbins and her mother just before Christmas 1892, the issue became acute. Then, when Wells became ill in the spring, Amy Catherine came to visit him. It became clear to Isabel what was afoot, and she apparently, according to Fred Wells, gave H.G. his choice. Wells himself professed not to remember the circumstances, but he did give the story some credence. It was a year before the situation righted itself; when Isabel's divorce petition was accepted, Wells and Amy Catherine married.[42]

Wells continued to be disturbed by the morality of his time, and felt a strong necessity to apologize for his action. He told Davies at the time that he had been in great trouble for a year, and while it was his own error, so was the marriage:

I love my wife very tenderly but not as a husband should love his wife, and – as quickly as possible – we are going to separate this new year. . . . We are parting not in anger, but in sorrow, because our tempers,

1 Bertie Wells, aged ten

2 Sarah Wells in the 1890s

3 Wells as a student at the Royal College of Science
(a parody of a famous photograph of T. H. Huxley)

4 Wells about 1895

Nov 10th 1895,

Got to write his old stunes for 'm now.

5 (*above left*): Isabel Mary Wells, Wells's
cousin and first wife

6 (*above right*): Amy Catherine Robbins,
called 'Jane', Wells's second wife

7 (*left*): Jane Wells at her desk: a 'picshua'
by Wells

interests, desires are altogether different. Isabel has been noble, loving, and faithful to me as very few wives can be. . . . I love another woman with all my being, and it seems a hideous thing to me to continue this comfortable life of legal adultery simply because I cannot have the woman I love.

He asked Davies and his sister, as he had Elizabeth Healey, to help Isabel at this difficult time. For himself, 'in sexual matters my good name will be smirched. The popular mind makes no distinction between sentiment and sensual aberration.'[43] Here Wells was certainly putting the best face on what, in 1893, was a breakdown in the moral code of his class. On the other hand, he was in love with someone who not only loved him in return, but was prepared to see her moral code breached for that love.

In the same spring of this moral dilemma, when Wells was ill once more with consumption, it became clear that he could never teach again. From his sickbed, tortured with his moral problems, he wrote once again to Elizabeth Healey, always available for a confessional role: 'However I am not dead yet and I think I may promise with safety to write further when I am better.' A year and more later, with 'The Chronic Argonauts' rewritten and accepted for publication, he knew that he had turned the corner, and even so, he was still unsure: '. . . it's my trump card and if it does not come off very much I shall know my place for the rest of my career. Still we live in hope.'[44]

He had good reason to hope. Just twenty-eight, he had overcome a great deal: a poorish childhood, the traumas of parental marriage failure, illness, and his personal anxieties. On the other side, though, he had received a good education, had met and dealt with the moral dilemmas he would face for the rest of his life, and could now turn his attention to literary work. As he said, 'Still we live in hope', and it was hope well founded.

WALKING UP NEW GRUB STREET

> . . . though in the lower types of life, heredity and material accident may make up destiny, in the higher there is a progressive development of a new factor — the acquired factor of individual habit — impressed on instinct, modifying instinct, sometimes flatly opposing instinct, and even in some cases altogether overcoming and defeating it. . . . For if, that is, the course of mankind is — saving some mighty convulsion of nature — to be determined mainly by the development of a mental environment, by educational processes, then science and literature, the storehouse and factory of ideas and the ultimate sources of all innovations, are the central and controlling facts of civilization. And it becomes conceivable that man shall cease to be driven, a dry leaf before the winds, to fulfil his destiny.
>
> HGW, 'The Acquired Factor', *The Academy*,
> 9 January 1897

The Bertie Wells, hoping for success, who wrote the letter of hope quoted at the end of chapter 1 was pre-eminently an Englishman, a Londoner, with a touch of the cockney. Later in life he would frequently refer to himself as a descendant of the men of Kent, and think of himself as a follower of and heir to John Ball, but in his early life he never quibbled when one described him as a Londoner, or even a cockney. The London in which he lived and worked in the decade of the '90s was a lively and wonderful place for Bertie Wells, and others who had their world in front of them, and he was happy to claim membership in the city's population.

He delighted in exploring the metropolis. Much of the exploration was on foot, although he and Isabel experimented with tricycles, and he and his second wife used a custom-built tandem bicycle for their wanderings, especially after they moved first to Woking and later to Worcester Park. When no wife was available, Wells went by himself — inspecting, looking, soaking up the atmosphere much as he had crammed the scientific facts necessary to pass his examinations. And, just as he had used that experience to produce his early didactic pieces on teaching, learning, and life in the classroom, so did these new experiences form the background and source for his new work. Not that he gave up writing on educational subjects; it would be the new century before he thought of himself as writer first, not teacher, and even then teaching would lie near the surface of his thought. In fact, it is not too much to say that one of the reasons his scientific and socialist writing struck home so readily then and now was because it was delivered in a clear, concise, analytical, and even professorial tone — much as Huxley had demonstrated the dissection of the rabbit so many years before.

London in the 1890s was the great metropolis of the world, and at the height of its glory. Although there may have been a sense of *fin-de-siècle* about publications like the *Yellow Book* or the illustrations of Aubrey Beardsley, and underneath the surface those who sought it could find the cruel, brutal world of *My Secret Life*, for the majority of Englishmen and Londoners, these aspects were at the margin of life and could safely be ignored. Paris was decadent; Vienna frothy and dressed in silk and crinoline; Berlin, precise and demanding; while the New World cities, New York, Chicago, San Francisco, were thought of as wild frontiers. London was the focus of the British Empire, the centre of world power. The old Queen still sat on the throne and would for more than a decade. All things came to London, and orders issued there went out to all parts of the world for execution.

London was also a noisy, dirty, smoky, foggy town. The primary method of transport for the lower classes was still walking, while for the middle classes the horse-drawn trams, and for the upper classes, their carriages, or hansom cabs, served as means of locomotion. The streets were filled with excrement, as they had been since the Middle Ages, and the Thames was polluted so badly that from time to time Parliament was forced to take a brief recess to escape the stench. The crush of traffic was so great that some tram routes had begun to be built below ground. These routes, which would eventually become the Metropolitan Railway and would link certain stops on the Underground, are still partially open to the air — built this way originally so the passengers and horses would not be frightened, and would not suffocate in the closed atmosphere. The digging begun now would eventually, by the First World War, put much of the traffic and the communication lines below the surface. Water and sewer lines were already out of sight, the sewers using the ancient creeks, such as the Fleet, which drained into the Thames for their outfalls.

The extensive building of railways in the previous twenty years had opened up the suburbs, and the middle- and upper-class population had begun to scatter. The great railway stations — Waterloo, Charing Cross, Euston, Victoria, Paddington, and the others — had altered the city remarkably in their building. Whole areas of slums had been torn down, and others created, while the tracks and termini were being located. The restructuring in fact served only to accentuate the village character of London, which remained a city of small districts.

The great parks of the metropolis were all in place by the '90s, and Londoners in numbers had begun to use Kensington Gardens, St. James's, Hyde, and Regent's Parks for a glimpse of green and the spring flowers, while Hampstead Heath to the north, and Blackheath to the south and east, continued to be places for walks and meditation. The bicycle opened up Epping Forest and the South Downs to more adventuresome travellers. Within the city, still with a population of only about 4½ million persons, the great museums in the South Kensington area, the Tower, and the other sites of note were easily accessible, and much less crowded than today. The great gardens at Kew were still expanding, and had increasingly become a place of pilgrimage, especially in the spring. Cricket remained a sport for the upper classes, as the grounds at Lord's and the Oval drew large crowds to watch W. G. Grace, Herbert Sutcliffe, and soon the remarkable Ranji. Soccer, or Association football, had begun to claim many adherents, and the famous London clubs, West Ham, Arsenal, Tottenham Hotspur, and Chelsea, were developing their pitches and their reputations.

London was also a city of enclaves — the Irish lived in Kilburn, the Scots in Kentish and Camden Towns, while Jews and East Europeans tended to live in Shoreditch and in the East End — also home of the true cockney. Within a short time the Jewish population would begin its migration to the periphery at Golders Green and Brent Cross. The fashionable areas were the West End, Kensington High Street, Chelsea, and St. John's Wood. South of the Thames dwelt middle-class Londoners — Clapham, Balham, Tooting, an area stretching downriver towards Greenwich and Woolwich, where the great docks welcomed vessels from round the world. The young traveller could take a boat to Greenwich, visit the royal habitations, and cross the Thames underwater to the Isle of Dogs through the marvellous tunnel begun by Isambard Kingdom Brunel.

The London of the 1890s had many more bookshops, especially second-hand shops with penny benches outside, as reading was very important in leisure time. W. H. Smith had begun to experiment with inexpensive books, and the three-decker novels of W. H. Mudie's circulating libraries disappeared in the Mauve Decade. The decade also saw the beginnings of the inexpensive 'ABC' restaurants of the Aerated Bread Company, while J. Lyons & Co. opened the first of their famous tea-shops in this period. A researcher working in the Reading Room of the British Museum could obtain tea and a biscuit on the Museum premises, to relieve his hunger while seeking a way upward from the class of his birth. The city of London existed as if it were made for H. G. Wells and his colleagues and rivals. The world was theirs to open, and perhaps to change.

The London of that time is very familiar to the well-read person today. It is the London of Sherlock Holmes — with the gaslight, shadow, fog, and dark evenings which we associate with Conan Doyle's stories. However, that is the world of one class pre-eminently, and the London of the 1890s was also the London of Arthur Morrisons's Jago. The stews and slums which Morrison described so brilliantly still existed, and one of Wells's earliest residences, in Mornington Place, was on the edge of such an area. At the other end of the spectrum, George Grossmith, already famous for his creation of starring roles in the quintessentially Victorian theatre of Gilbert and Sullivan, is even better known in our time for his skewering of the upwardly bound new suburban dwellers — the Pooters. And ultimately, of course, this was the London of Mr Polly, Artie Kipps, Mr Lewisham, and of the laboratory of the Time Traveller.

In a sense reading and writing reached an apogee in England at the end of the Victorian period. No radio or television offered competition for leisure time. That leisure, coupled with machinery for more rapid typesetting, cheap paper, and a desire for education — each fuelling the other — led to an explosion of reading matter after the mid-1890s. The Education Acts only accelerated the process by providing a wider audience. Newspapers — *The Times*, the *Daily News*, *Manchester Guardian*, *Post*, *Telegraph*, and dozens of others more ephemeral — bid for the pennies of the public, while weekly and monthly magazines proliferated at an enormous rate. *Punch*, the *Pall Mall Gazette*, *Westminster Gazette*, and *Spectator* were joined by the *Saturday Review*, *Nineteenth Century*, *Black and White*, *Globe*, *Nature*, *Queen*, *Women's Weekly*, *Family Herald*, and literally dozens of others less well known. For entrepreneurs like Alfred Harmsworth, editors like Frank Harris, and authors like Grant Allen, Arthur Conan Doyle, or Baroness Orczy, London was a prospective gold mine. This was the world in which H.G. Wells hoped to succeed. He began early to throw his material into the literary lion's den.

Fortunately he had some possibilities. Editors like Harris were easily approached, and in 1891 Wells placed an early essay with him for the *Fortnightly Review*, although a second was rejected as 'incomprehensible'. Wells was also able to use sources from his correspondence-school days. By 1893 his friend Gregory had gone to work for Macmillan, who published *Nature*. In 1894 Gregory became editor of that journal and was to remain in the post until 1939, one of the great forces in modern science. Harry Cust, editor of the *Pall Mall Gazette*, a somewhat sophisticated weekly, was an almost insatiable outlet for the brief paragraph, especially if it had a sting in its tail. The *Pall Mall Gazette* also published a weekly largely devoted to more formal literature, the *Pall Mall Budget*, and it paid 5 guineas each for scientific articles and stories not much different from those Wells had earlier written for *Tit-Bits* and *Answers to Correspondents*. The staffs of the two *Pall Mall* magazines were close to the *National Observer* and its editor, W. E. Henley. The latter journal was owned by William Heinemann, who also began to publish the *New Review* at about the same time. In 1894 Frank Harris purchased the *Saturday Review*, and this circle of writers, reviewers, editors, and others round which he was orbiting seemed to Wells a marvellous source of income. It was, and in addition, it provided a way for Bertie Wells to polish his techniques and his ideas. Between 1893 and 1896 he produced an immense number of small pieces — reviews, paragraphs on science and teaching, play notices, vignettes, essays of humour or pathos, short-short stories with a twist or moral, and eventually slightly longer stories also often with a moral. By 1896 he was earning £1,000 a year from this ephemeral journalism. He had arrived, at least as a sort of scribbler, in New Grub Street.

During the period in question Wells and Jane, as he soon began to call Amy Catherine, moved four times, in each case to provide him with better writing quarters and a quieter location. They were ejected from one house in Mornington Place, as the landlady objected to their then lack of a marriage certificate. Near by they found another place, but located as it was on the edge of a slum, it was not very pleasant, even for the now newlyweds, and so they moved quickly.[1] They lived for a time in Sevenoaks, in a house called Tusculum Villa, but only long enough for Wells to write bits of novels (and to finish *The Time Machine*), for the distance from London and the location were not satisfactory. Later they moved to Woking, in the country, near the railway, to a semi-detached villa called Lynton. This locale provided the background for *The War of the Worlds*; much of its scenery remains today relatively unchanged, although Wells did move the house in the story into a slightly better neighbourhood. From Woking they moved to Heatherlea, a larger villa of their own at Worcester Park. Each of these geographical moves was a step upward socially and psychologically, but all of them also had as a goal the need to make Wells's life easier as he advanced in his profession.

By this time he had settled into a routine that would not vary much until World War II. He wrote every day, as often as he could at the same hour — in the '90s it was in the morning — and always with a pencil or pen on foolscap. His calligraphy was always distinctive; the only significant changes in it were that it lost the flourishes of youth to some degree as he grew older, and that, eventually, it grew much smaller. However, it was always recognizable as his writing to the end of his life. Whoever worked as his secretary — at first Jane, then a series of others, each for a fairly long period of time: Horace Horsnell, Lucienne Southgate, and eventually his daughter-in-law, Marjorie Craig Wells — would then make a fair copy of the material. By the mid-'90s this copy was being made on a typewriter. Wells then, usually in the afternoon, treated this copy as though it were proof sheets. He reworked it completely, often with balloons circling new clauses to be added, with words crossed out (he always had a problem with repetitive verbs), and other alterations. The most frequent changes were the addition of new explanatory matter, as Wells's mind usually raced ahead of his pen on first writing. Once the revised copy was typed, a few changes might still be made, but basically this draft was ready for the press. Wells's surviving proofs, at a time when proofreading often meant major recasting, are relatively clean. It is the first typed copy that takes the major rewriting. The first handwritten draft or outline copy was usually destroyed — at least, few of them are now known.

For most of his correspondence Wells drafted a reply on the letter received; occasionally, for longer letters, he treated the reply as though it was an article. When there was a shortage of paper, or no carbon was available, the draft became his letter. A substantial number of citations in the present work are of Wells's drafts on letters received, as the replies actually sent were lost by their recipients. When he wished to comment to the press on some matter which irritated him, he frequently drafted a letter and instructed his secretary to sign it; this was a method he used with other unwanted correspondence as well. Very little writing left his house, however, which he did not draft and authorize himself.[2] His study was well lighted, with reference books, including his own works, near by. A work of art usually hung on the wall before him — for many years this was a drawing by Alan Odle, Dorothy Richardson's husband. A cat often dozed near by.

In later life Wells wrote in the late afternoon, before and after tea, while the mornings were reserved for his correspondence. Very late in his life he used to work for a half-hour or so, with tea again, in the evening and especially when he had trouble sleeping. When his children grew older, and more and more visitors came — the Wells weekends, from Friday till Monday morning, were famous — he shifted his time for writing to mid-afternoon. He could then begin a game with his guests and children, and as soon as they were heavily involved, he would sneak off and write undisturbed. Jane always protected him from interference; his writing space and time were sacred. Few bothered him, as the writing was what produced the funds for the houses and the weekends, and both Jane and H.G. made it clear that his work was a restricted area. Her role in keeping his time and space clear for writing cannot be overestimated.

At first Wells did not use an agent, and never liked the idea. Unlike other writers of the period he was cool towards personal contact with his agents, and even J. B. Pinker was eventually turned away by the Wells coolness. He used both Pinker and A. P. Watt in the early period and eventually, after an argument with Pinker, tended to stick with Watt, although even there he fell away from time to time. In addition he was not above negotiating with prospective publishers himself, and his agents were frequently convinced that they could have done a better job than he had. As he grew more famous, he made all the arrangements on the biggest items, such as *The Outline of History*, dealing personally with William Heinemann, Nelson Doubleday, and others. Few agents could have obtained terms as generous as Wells got for himself on these works. He also had many ideas on how to sell his books, how to promote them and make the public want to purchase them. His agents tended to discourage the more bizarre of such publicity schemes, but Wells never allowed his material to be handled by others without intense and constant interest on his part. Watt was better about keeping him informed of progress, and perhaps that accounts for his eventual triumph over Pinker, who jollied his clients along; although both men worked very hard at their trade.[3]

Wells had been writing fairly steadily from the time the *Science Schools Journal* began. His stories in that magazine were rather jejune, although even there early versions of later significant work appear.[4] He referred to this sort of work as 'sputters at authorship and much wrathful burning of important efforts', but he did not have much success. 'Someday I shall succeed but it is a weary game.' He summarized his results in the late spring of 1888 as:

Item — 1 short story — sold £1
Item — 1 novel = 35,000 words Burnt 0.0
Item — 1 novel — unfinished — 25,000 Burnt 0.0
Item — much comic poetry — lost 0.0.0
— — some comic prose. sent away, never returned.
Item — Humorous story. *Globe*, did not return.
Item — Sundry stories — Burnt
Item — 1 story — Wandering.
Item — A poem — Burnt

etc. etc.

Total Income (Untaxed)   1 – 0 – 0[5]

By the summer of 1893, however, as he recovered from another onset of his kidney and tubercular troubles, he could write to his brother Fred, 'I am still taking it easy — doing a few articles and science notes. I am barely paying expenses but that itself does not matter until I get a bit better. I am not fretting about it.' And, he continued, he had 'been asked to write articles — which is very much better than making them on spec. for *Knowledge, The Ed. Times, Science and Art* & *The Correspondent*, and indeed I might be doing a lot more than I am. I am doing the science notes in *The Journal of Education* and *Knowledge*, if you see these papers.'[6]

Demand for his work increased as he was able to provide all sorts of filler material. As he told A. M. Davies, nearly a year later, 'P.M.G. keeps loyal.' He also told Davies that the *Budget* of the previous week had carried five things of his. In this letter Wells also revealed that the *National Observer* was 'publishing articles from that old corpse of the Chronic Argos much recast'. By this time his short stories were also 'going after all. One in *Truth*, and another in *St. James's*.'[7]

Later in the summer Wells reported to Davies that he could not take it as easy as Davies had hoped. He had been quite ill again, but 'This decadent style seems to have caught the fancy of Mariott-Watson, Henley and one or two others . . . '. By July he told Elizabeth Healey that 'there is talk of a book and where it will end, I don't know.' He had caught on with a vengeance, and by the spring of 1896 he was describing his life to Elizabeth as 'when I'm not racking my brains for stories or abusing my contemporaries in anonymous reviews in the *Saturday*, I am usually cycling or mooning about the canal or walking.' In fact the work-load was so great, or the demand for his material so great, that he began to be much more restrictive, by asking for more money, cutting down his production, and eventually by substantially sharpening up his criticism of pot-boiling work. Wells had arrived, and now he could be much more analytical of himself and his contemporaries.[8]

He had become very conscious of his style by this time, and the work of the latter part of this period is more clearly crafted, as when he wrote 'The Argonauts of the Air', for Grant Richards who was the editor of *Phil May's Christmas Annual*. Wells had promised the story by mid-July, and when he was a day late because of his typist, he cautioned Richards 'not to be dispirited when you read it if the story does not seem to jump in the earlier two thousand words of it. I have made that go quietly in order to enhance the wobbling flight and smash of the flying apparatus at the end of it.'[9]

He and Pinker discussed Wells's hopes and ideas about writing several times, and Wells finally submitted to an interview with Pinker in which he outlined his views quite completely. Pinker called it 'enlightened nonconformity', or at least the 'moral' tendencies of the work were described in this way. Wells, in the interview (which appeared over the name of George Lynch), told Pinker that his purpose was 'greater than the public knows', and ended with this comment, which goes far beyond the scrabbling for guineas with which he had begun the decade:

> If we must summarize the matter, I would say that the danger arising to humanity out of invention, the danger of the extreme complication of life, is only to be met by education, that is to say, the inculcation of habits of constant thought — thought at home, thought at school, spacious thought about everything in which a human being is concerned.[10]

From this interview, it was clear that Wells thought his writing was a contribution to higher education.

Relatively few of the so-called great authors have left us much to indicate how they arrived at plots, or developed their characters. To some degree this may be because many writers do not have a didactic purpose in their writing, at least not as overt a one as Wells had already defined his to be. Most writers, in fact, tell vaguely of how characters take over the books in which they occur, and the author finds himself simply following a character as it develops in its creation, from deep in the subconscious of the writer. Wells was probably no different from this; however, there is evidence that

he could at least partially will the opening of his subconscious as he wrote.
He referred throughout his life to his 'dreams', and although many of these
were actual sleeping dreams, it is apparent that he could induce a sort of
waking somnolence in which his subconscious rose to the surface and
provided him with a plot structure, if not with character traits. Wells used
the dream as a plot vehicle many times, most notably in his books *When the
Sleeper Wakes* (1899), *The Dream* (1924), *The Autocracy of Mr Parham*
(1930), and *The Happy Turning* (1945), although the idea of sleeping and
dreaming occurs in many other novels, as well as in his short stories.

Wellsian dreams are almost always of 'what may be' rather than of the
past. He projected himself into the life he wanted, and although the colours
were usually pastel shades, and the outlines of his musings are indistinct at
the centre of the dream life, the concrete descriptions are easily retrieved.
When the reader encounters these paragraphs, the sense of removal from
one's own time is immediate. This ability to transport the reader
immediately to unknown worlds is one of the reasons children have sought
out Wells's books, as their own land of make-believe lies just as close to the
surface. Almost every child of my acquaintance with any sketching ability
has presented me with a drawing of his own favourite Wells story, once he
has learned of my interest and work.

Recent critics have suggested that Wells was greatly affected by the
underground setting of his early life, his failure to achieve physical health,
and by erotic fantasies which he developed in a female-dominated world,
and these ideas may have some germ of truth to them. I believe, however,
that if one thinks of dreams, both day-dreaming and in deeper night-time
encounters, we find that H. G. Wells so harnessed his great ability to
forecast events that he could actually dream his way into his new books
and his new ideas. As early as 1893, for example, he wrote a piece for the
Pall Mall Gazette which discussed dreams, and how they provided an
alternative to disappointments in life, and in the piece he foresaw a world in
which one's best dreams could be recalled or re-dreamed as solace and for
the alleviation of bad times. Later, in a private letter in response to
someone who asked how he used his memories in his writing, Wells
responded: 'I don't hurt my own memory because I believe much more in
hallucination of memory than in hallucination of sense, but my mind is
perhaps abnormally analytical and the educated person's may be as you
say.'[11]

Wells's dreams apparently changed character somewhat as he grew older,
and he discussed the phenomenon of dreaming many times with his
colleagues, most particularly with J. W. Dunne, who was much interested in
parapsychology and whose book, *An Experiment with Time*, Wells read with
delight. Eventually Wells's dreams became fantasies in which the world of
his childhood merged with his desires of what the world might be, and the
result was the fragment, *The Happy Turning*. Before he wrote that book,
however, he summarized his life of dreams by saying, after describing the

recurrent dreams of his life, 'Dreamland is radiant with hope fulfilled.' Wells was a dreamer — that is a truism — but what is less clearly understood is how he used his dreams, fostered them, and created a world from those dreams in his novels.[12]

Whether by using his dreams or his travels, Wells found in the myriad of magazines in London an opportunity to sharpen and focus his ability to see things. Between 1893 and the early spring of 1896, he conducted a review column in the *Saturday Review*, reviewed plays for a time as the magazine's official drama critic, meanwhile writing almost continuously for the *Pall Mall Gazette*, and for other journals which were looking for what are today called 'middles'. Middles are short essays, or short stories, often with a twist, which can be read in half a dozen minutes, but which will pique the reader's attention and ultimately allow him to think, 'How true. I have done that myself', or to make some similar remark.

Most of Wells's ephemeral pieces have not been collected, and many have not even been identified as his. Wells did not automatically receive the byline his reputation demanded until after 1896 or so. Some journals had a policy of giving only one byline an issue, no matter how many pieces an author contributed to it. Wells also occasionally used pseudonyms, although these are ordinarily very easy to spot. His style became increasingly recognizable, and eventually he collected a number of these magazine pieces in two early volumes, one of which he reprinted in part in his Atlantic Edition of the 1920s. As a result, many of his early pieces are known. Some knowledge also comes from a list compiled by Jane Wells in the First World War period. But it is obvious that many early Wells items have been lost, and the *Complete Short Stories*, first published in 1927, probably misses out as many as fifteen or twenty which could have qualified for that volume. Of course, Wells himself may have been unwilling to have some of his early published work reprinted, although the correspondence does not suggest that he was ashamed of much that he wrote. After all, he had been paid for it, and by people whose judgement was not trivial.

Wells developed two or three stock characters to carry many ideas of his early essays, one probably based on his father (and perhaps partly on his older brothers), another based on his mother apparently (although the character is always referred to as an 'aunt', which may be somewhat symbolic), and a third character, 'Euphemia'. The last is usually thought to be a portrait of Jane Wells, though the figure may have some traits of Isabel as well, as is frequently true in the fiction which uses his wife as a character. Some of the pieces which were not collected later are still good reading, although many are ephemeral indeed. Wells wrote in a humorous, or sardonic, vein from time to time, but the humour frequently was fairly heavy-handed, as with his visit to a mythical island of opera, and to an overly hygienic country. Others used such ideas as the nose, and how it was evolved; there were articles about learning to skate, visiting a gallery (with careful use of adjectives designed to indicate knowledge — quite a good piece), and there was his story, 'The Jilting of Jane', which has been reprinted from time to time, and is a good example of his earliest style.[13]

Wells used his travels and his experience of science to produce some clear pictures of persons; items under the microscope are well depicted in a piece in which he predicts the microdot and the microfilm as ways of preserving material when space is at a premium. Several short stories were written about his neighbours and their houses; and he even tried his hand at the short detective story. None of these last were collected by Wells in his two short-story collections of the period, however, so perhaps he felt they were not up to his standard.[14]

His 'Uncle' character was very well received, and nearly all of the pieces featuring this bombastic old fraud with his opinions on many things were reprinted in an early book, *Select Conversations with an Uncle (Now Extinct)*. The book, published by John Lane in 1895, was published in New York by the Merriam Company the same year, and was dedicated to 'my dearest and best friend, R.A.G.'. Wells took his putative uncle through London, and eventually through a love affair. The best of the pieces involve fashionable conversation, how to listen to social music, the problems of the newly married, riding a tricycle (as opposed to a bicycle which was much less dignified); one piece not collected describes the ugliest thing in London, which turns out to be Tower Bridge, although the competition was strong from other structures such as the Albert Hall.[15]

Wells's other substantial character from this period, Euphemia, is a long-suffering wife, somewhat dim and demanding of the author's time, whose comments and life come under scrutiny. Euphemia and Aunt Charlotte together provide us with an early Wells look at women. He is a bit skittish in his writing at this point, and there is no hint of erotic or sexual involvement — perhaps as much a tribute to the time as to Wells. He is bemused by these women who occasionally trouble him with their desire to regulate his life and his habits, as well as with their pretensions to authorship, or to art. A few of the articles must have struck home, however, as when Wells wrote 'A Handy Guide to Husbands: A Discreditable Exposure', which purports to be Euphemia's answer to one of his statements on wives. His conclusion was to be careful in future, as he probably had disturbed Amy Catherine with one of his comments.

Euphemia was nearly done with as a character by the time the pieces were published, however; and although some wished her to be revived, Wells stuck to more solid ground in his essays for the remainder of the 1895–6 period. When he came to collect these early papers, he included some of the Euphemia articles, but much of that volume was taken up with more serious matters. The book includes a lovely essay explaining evolution; another which discussed astronomical observation; and his masterpieces from that period, 'Bleak March in Epping Forest' and a fine humorous piece, 'Concerning a Certain Lady', who always manages to take his seat, his place in the queue, and so on. Wells had certainly arrived as a

writer with this book, *Certain Personal Matters* (1897), and reviewers liked
it generally. It was described as 'a very pleasant moneysworth, full of wit
and humour'. The book was reprinted in 1901 in a cheaper edition, bound
in both paper and cloth, and continued to sell well; it was apparently never
remaindered.[16]

Nearly all of Wells's writings from this early period betray his desire to get
ahead, and in a way, his attempt to achieve a standard working *métier*. Upon
rereading them today, especially the humorous pieces, we get fleeting
glimpses into his interior world, but on the whole they are not very
memorable. Occasionally there is a piece which remains in the
consciousness of the reader — his work on Bromley, or on the drapery
business, both written from a deep well of emotion, are examples. Another
might be his piece of redaction on evolution, but if someone other than
Wells had written it, one doubts if it would be noticed. In fact, it is not until
we look at the Wells who is attempting to be a serious reviewer that we are
caught up with his words, for here we see the young author and teacher
beginning to establish his own theoretical position, to develop his ideas of
why and how fiction should be written, and the relationship of fiction to
other more didactic prose. It is clear from our reading today that Wells was
always concerned with his art, but never at the expense of his message.
That stance, carried to its extreme, and under great provocation, led to the
controversy with Henry James, and with James's adherents ever since; but
by the time Wells wrote *Boon* (1915), he was simply working out (exorcising
even) what had been present in his writing from the earliest period. For
that reason, his reviewing of both drama and fiction, as well as his serious
pieces dealing with science and teaching during this time of learning to
write, are very important.[17]

Harry Cust, Frank Harris, and W. E. Henley all recognized the young
writer's genius, and his high productivity. To a degree they took advantage
of his desire to advance by overworking him, and eventually helping to
cause a serious relapse into tuberculosis, after the lesser attack in 1893–4.
Wells accepted the work with full knowledge of the possible consequences,
and so the blame must be apportioned to both sides. It is true that he was in
desperate need to make a home and to make money. And equally important
was the desire to establish himself as an important writer and spokesman.
For that reason, when Cust asked him to take on the job of official drama
critic for the *Pall Mall Gazette*, Wells, who had seen only two plays in his
life, simply asked if he needed a dress suit. Cust said yes, so Wells went out
and found a custom tailor who produced the necessary apparel within
forty-eight hours. Wells then presented himself in the stalls to view the play
from the vantage-point of the professional critic. In the next sixteen weeks
he reviewed some thirty plays (the exact number is still uncertain), most of
which have disappeared into the dustbin of time. He was, however, able to
see and comment on Henry Irving, Ellen Terry, Mrs Pat Campbell, and

Yvette Guilbert, who were significant performers in their time. He also met
George Bernard Shaw for the first time (although Wells had seen Shaw at
William Morris's in those days of student visits), and he wrote two or three
reviews which brought him other friends and associates because of the
quality of his comments on these plays.

Wells and Shaw probably never really liked each other. Shaw remained,
for all his genius, a narrow, opinionated, generally acerbic and occasionally
unpleasant person. Wells did not like being patronized, which Shaw could
not help doing. Shaw, however, lived in the same London neighbourhood as
Wells, and they took to walking home together from the theatre. Neither was
faced with a rigid deadline. Wells, thinking later about Shaw and these
walks, remarked that Shaw had 'no sustained and constructive mental
training' and his thinking was weak and flimsy as a result. Wells described
Shaw as a 'philanderer with facts', while Wells, who thought in wider terms
than the theatre, also had the advantage of a scientifically trained mind, so
that facts simply meant more to him.[18] Shaw was also engaged in serious
music criticism at this time, however. He did not pay much attention to
Wells's views on the theatre or on writing, in their talks.

Wells did see one or two very important plays in this period. His first
assignment as a critic was to see Oscar Wilde's *An Ideal Husband*, which
intrigued him. And very soon, he attended the notorious first night of
Henry James's play, *Guy Domville*. James was booed and hissed off the
stage, as he had mistakenly thought the audience liked the play, which in
fact it found abhorrent. Wells was not that harsh in his comments,
describing the play's failure clearly enough, but attributing it in part to the
players, as well as to the delicate writing of the work itself. James was
apparently grateful for the young writer's soft analysis and in one sense
their relationship dates from this review. Wells also wrote good criticism of
The Importance of Being Earnest, which he described as a 'rare holiday'. His
review of *Delia Harding*, in which he savaged the leading man, and his
comments, written in cockney dialect, on *Vanity Fair*, were also good; but
Wells was clearly somewhat out of his element in this theatrical venture.
What the experience provided was a window on the minds and thoughts of
others, a trip into another world, and, of course, a further sharpening of the
pen and the wit into which it was dipped.[19]

This was serious work for Wells, even if it was short-lived. Even more
serious work was the book-reviewing he began to do for the *Saturday Review*.
Frank Harris had noticed the young man when he accepted Wells's first
serious piece in 1891, and although he had rejected a second piece when
Wells brought it to the *Fortnightly*, Harris called him into the editor's
sanctum sanctorum and commented on it and on Wells's style and ideas.
When Harris moved to the *Saturday Review*, it was natural for him to ask
Wells to begin a more or less regular column reviewing books. It was a wonderful opportunity for Wells, and over the next 29 months (from November
1894) he wrote well over 100 pieces for the *Saturday Review*, many,

if not most, of them about fiction, and in which he noticed 285 books. This is not the place to analyse that work in detail; however it is useful to note that Wells did comment on nearly all the significant novelists of his time — among them Crane, Gissing, and Henry James, as well as many others. Occasionally he was merciless, as with Grant Allen's effort at feminist comment, *The Woman Who Did*. Most of Wells's subjects took his judgements in good part; even Allen apparently could not deny the force of the Wells strictures.[20]

Wells had strong ideas about fiction. In a sardonic piece written shortly before he began his reviewing, he had closed his remarks with the following comment, which set out his reviewing ideas: 'A scholar may be a gentleman, a novelist may be a decent citizen, history may be honourable, criticism even respectable, but the true creative author has a gambling spirit, a taverning temperament, and brawling in his blood.'[20]

Wells did see the importance of many of the works he was given for review. He liked Arthur Morrison's *Child of the Jago*, although the ending was not strong enough. For Wells there was not enough didacticism, or analysis, in Morrison's brilliant account of his London slum childhood. Wells also liked Turgenev, praising his characters, who provided a look at Russian types without sacrificing their individuality. Wells thought no one in England, since Meredith, had written this 'novel of types' so well, and he commended Turgenev to his readers, as he did Meredith's later novel, *The Amazing Marriage*. This was the sort of fiction Wells liked most, at least during this period — novels in which the characters stood for something, and the reader was enlightened by what he read. For him, *Jude the Obscure* was one of the greatest works of the time, and he could not understand why the public, a public which had liked the tawdry *A Woman Who Did*, did not embrace *Jude*. Wells understood very well what the public did not, that Jude's desire for an education was overcome by his sexual desires — the natural animal instincts were, and probably always would be, triumphant. With this understanding, Wells could also perceive that Hardy was offering a 'tremendous indictment of English universities', and their continuing damage to the intellectual life of the country. Wells characterized Jude as 'the voice of the educated proletarian' and he welcomed the book. This is hardly surprising, except perhaps in the force of the comment, as much about *Jude* had its echo in the Bromley childhood and the early sexual hungers of H.G. himself.

There are very few of Wells's comments in this short period that do not bear rereading, but they should always be seen in the context of what his own writing life would come to be. For instance, to offer one more quotation, he ended a review of Richard Le Gallienne's *The Quest for the Golden Girl* with an apt remark that might have been made by a critic about certain books which had not yet been written:

Mr Le Gallienne has spoilt a pretty piece of work. But his Teaching leaves a good half of the book and many subsequent passages very pleasant reading. It is certainly his most sustained and most finished performance so far. But it is a pity that he will not abandon the attempt to combine deleterious instruction with his entertainment.[22]

Wells was to review a great many more books in his lifetime, but after this rather fewer of them were fiction. In fact, his comments on style, technique, plot, and the purposes of fiction generally occcur in other places — in introductions to his own and others' work, or in correspondence, and finally in his quarrel with Henry James, and the opening essay in *Babes in the Darkling Wood* (1940). For that reason these early journalistic efforts are more important than they might otherwise be: both the reviews and the comments he was constrained to give as a result of the reviews. Much about the later life of H. G. Wells can be discerned here.

For instance, in a signed piece in late spring 1895, he said that the reviewer really needed a form, like a wedding form supplied by the newspapers, and in addition the reviewer had a responsibility not to 'smash' early works, especially ones by those who were just learning their trade. If one did true justice to several varieties of work, they would not be read, so the reviewer had a duty to prospective readers as well as analysts in his comments. Later, in a speech to other authors, he expanded on this theme by saying that authors were seedlings, needing to be nurtured, but all critics did not know that. He classed reviewers as three kinds — slug-reviewers who prey on the tender leaves, bird-reviewers who peck here and there and possibly do damage, and heavy-reviewers who thrash about crushing whole beds of shoots at once. Wells said some also act like irrigationists who drench the plants with the water of flattery and drown them, while still others withhold the water until the plants dry up. There are a few far-seeing horticulturists, according to Wells, but they are uncommon. The authors in his audience must have received these remarks, not only with laughter, but with a wry pain of recollection at their own earlier treatment. However, even here Wells was not entirely sure of his public, as he remarked in almost the same week, in a review, that 'The public does not want ideas, it does not want memories, it does not want an elaborated, meditated, and sedulously pruned story; it wants a good long read.'[23]

Wells certainly did have an eye for what was good, and whether the public would read works of social comment with the warts left on or not, he thought such works needed support, and he, for one, was prepared to give it. In a symposium conducted by the *Academy* at the end of 1896, Wells cited as good books of the year, Conrad's *Outcast of the Islands*, Crane's *Maggie* and *George's Mother*, Barrie's *Margaret Ogilvie*, Silliman's *The Flame Thrower*, Stevenson's *Weir of Hermiston*, and Steevens's *Monologues of the Dead*. However, as he said — and today we would agree with most of his choices — none of these books made 'such a distinctive effect as *Jude the Obscure* in '95'.[24] A good comment, that. And an indication that the aspiring author now knew what had to be done; it only remained to do it, according to his own standards.

Wells was clearly transforming himself into a novelist, as well as a critic and analyst of fiction. However, as he went into his new life, creative writing, the earlier profession for which he had trained, as scientist and teacher, clung to him. He continued to think and function primarily as a teacher, as well as as a scientist, during this period. His comments on education have a good deal of significance for the understanding of his later life because at this time of almost ferocious mental activity those comments are of extremely high quality. After this fertile period he does not comment much on education for some time to come, except indirectly. Later in his life, however, this visionary marriage of education, science, and fiction produced the Wells whose view of the future was so clear, and yet so disliked by the very persons he had hoped would lead the new world — the teachers. For now, though, it is sufficient to look at these early writings on education, most of which have lain relatively unremarked in their publications since the '90s.

At first Wells used his *Pall Mall Gazette* and *Saturday Review* outlets for his comments on the sins of education and educationists. As an example, he posited a land where examiners were examined and always failed. Here they were asked to respond to queries such as 'What is difficult?', which Wells thought was similar to those in the examinations then being used — 'Who was Becket?' or 'What is a fraction?'. He and his former classmate, A. T. 'Tommy' Simmons, who was a close collaborator of R. A. Gregory's and for a long time editor of the *School World*, as well as author of many textbooks, collaborated on another satirical piece, 'The Miscellaneous as an Educational Curriculum'. Modern veterans of discussions of 'what' should be in the standard curricula will appreciate this savage attack. As Wells and Simmons remarked, 'The Miscellaneous is the natural expression of "liberal opinions", that want of consciousness, that intellectual silliness that has a pride in believing in everything a little, and nothing much.'[25]

Wells and Simmons took a mythical student through the English curriculum from infant school to research degree at Cambridge, and then into his profession, that of master over those to come along after him. They gave him a report card on his learned abilities, once through this educational maze. A sample will suffice:

English — Loose and inelegant; tendency to employ terms in a technical sense in ordinary conversation; difficulty with the subjunctive.

Geology — An extensive knowledge; names, mixed; faults, faulted.

Wells wrote several such satirical comments, but his enemies remained unscathed by his wit, so he also began to try to improve them through sweet reason. (Anyone who has ever tried to lead an academic group into a new route, or to change and modify the methods of procedure, will quickly recognize that Wells had simply come up against the turgid body of educational theory, and his attacks on it follow the predictable patterns of others.)[26]

Although Wells had hoped for a more positive response to his sardonic work, his formal presentations of his position were almost always well received, and frequently stirred up substantial comment. For instance, he wrote a three-part article entitled 'The Sins of the Secondary Schoolmaster' for the *Pall Mall Gazette* at the end of 1894. Here Wells drew heavily on his own life experiences as he pilloried his former teachers under headings such as 'His Technical Incapacity', 'His Remarkable Examination Results', 'His Technical Training'. Not much of the current experience was worth keeping, thought Wells, upon mature reflection. These teachers were causing incalculable damage to the state. 'Our middle class is still shamefully equipped for the business of life. . . . They are condemned to live narrowly, work feebly, think darkly, and die with the best things in life unknown', was his passionate cry. He called for a complete revision of the curriculum, with the addition of much science, and better courses in pedagogy — with 'Carefully graded experiments and carefully elucidated reasoning . . . its essence'.[27]

The week the third part of this article appeared Wells delivered a formal address to the College of Preceptors, responsible for the training of schoolmasters, of which he was a Fellow. This address, noticed in a half-dozen contemporary journals, was entitled 'Science Teaching — An Ideal and Some Realities'. Wells was now clearly in command of what was needed in this area, as he began his address:

> There are two chief aspects from which we may survey almost any question of human interest — or, at least, almost any question outside the domain of theology. We may regard things as they are, or we may regard things as they might be; we may grope among thorny tangles of facts in search of truth, or we may wander free and unconfined in the wide and beautiful domains of the ideal.[28]

This pretty opening is simply the first clear statement of what would be the Wellsian philosophy of intellectual life, and one which he would state most clearly at the Royal Institution in 1902, and finally in his doctoral thesis in 1943.

In the well-thought-out 1894 piece Wells offers a model curriculum for all students, beginning in primary and infant school and gradually developing into a systematic course of experimental demonstrations of the various laws of life. His course was designed to train eye and hand and to bring the educational processes into an integrated whole, as the expression of thought and the drawing of inferences were integral to the learning process. Even writing played an important role, as 'We can have no exact writing, without exact thinking, and we can have no exact thinking without an ample background of inductive study.' Wells said that staffs needed to be realigned to meet the new curriculum, as now there was too much 'mutual admiration in pedagogic discussion'. He called for the development and use of charts, introduction of good historical fiction, and a systematic theme in the teaching of these disciplines. He took on his *bêtes noires*, the classical languages, and their inordinate prominence in the curriculum of his time, and dealt forcefully with the problem of who would teach the teachers. He ended his comments by anticipating the row he would stir up. 'We hear very much of the conflict of studies, but it is a protracted, a guerrilla warfare. I should be glad to find that I had done something to bring about a decisive engagement.' This early, strong paper marks a major turning-point in Wells's thinking. Here we find more than the germs: now it is the backbone of what would be the educational ideas which occupied so much of his time after World War I. That later H. G. Wells was one based firmly and clearly on this Wells, the beginning writer of the 1890s.[29]

These articles and comments, coupled with Wells's articles in the popular journals, and his riveting books, which were now beginning to appear, made him a well-known figure. In addition, of course, they increased his income substantially, from £380. 13s. 7d. in 1893, to £583. 17s. 7d. in 1894, and to £1056. 7s. 9d. in 1895. These were substantial sums, but Wells had begun to need such sums by this time. His mother had been discharged at Up Park, because of her deafness and her inability to meet the demands of her position, and she was now at a loose end. Joseph Wells, after his bankruptcy, had never worked again, and the two of them were living in a cottage at Liss, at first rented and later purchased by Wells. His older brother, Frank, never very good at the drapery trade, lived at Liss with his parents, and began a precarious itinerant peddling of watches and other jewellery. The evidence is that this was remarkably unsuccessful, and we have a mental picture of Frank as a sort of high-class tramp. In any case these three cost money, Wells's own ménage cost money, and his desires were always greater than his finances at this time. But he could market nearly anything as long as it was controversial, and when Alfred Harmsworth from his Henley House days, now owner of the *Daily Mail*, offered him his columns for a series on public education, Wells was happy to oblige.[30]

The series lasted through six articles. The first discussed schoolmasters again, and here, for the first time, Wells raised the possibility that the Germans, with their new methods, were far ahead of and continuing to gain on the English. The English version, he said, was 'the dull, pretentious, classical examinee, head-master of the upper-class school, boring away with his sham learning of Greek and Latin, his pure, scrupulously pure, mathematics, his unspeakable French, and his isolated books of British science'. A vigorous reorganization was needed in the unequal struggle with other countries.[31]

The remainder of the articles dealt with the mechanics of Wells's new curriculum, much as he had suggested in outline in the previous year's work. He sought to do away with the teaching of dead languages, which he thought ought to be buried, and said the method and use of them today was 'intellectually demoralizing'. This paper stirred up so many responses that Wells was constrained to answer them before he went on with the series. Many of his correspondents apparently thought he was calling for book-keeping and secretarial training to replace the languages, and Wells simply put them straight in a parenthetical article. After that he was able to return to his ideal curriculum, although the debate dribbled on somewhat as Sylvanus Thayer, his chief opponent on the London University reorganization, also responded, and Wells felt obliged to refute him in print.

When the series did resume, Wells discussed the teaching of mathematics, which he also found wanting:

> Even now as I write comes back the sense of stupefaction, of wandering in a great desert of unreason, the mental stress and perplexity with which under the guidance of a middle-class schoolmaster, I confronted 'sums', in 'cube root' — a matter which taught as an incident of algebraic study, presents not an atom of difficulty.

Four days later he took on the sciences as they were then performed. Here he was caustic about the lack of proper instruments of measure. He advocated a complete overhaul and held forth great promise of intellectual honesty and mental acuity as a result. He closed, in this era of jingo politics, with a remark that many must have accepted readily: 'It is in the teaching of Science in our middle-class schools that our ultimate victory or defeat by the United States or Germany in the great commercial war mainly depends.'[32]

Wells, of course, always thought of himself as a scientist. He continued throughout his life to describe himself in this way, and attempted to keep up with the general trends and changes in research findings. This, in fact, was made much easier because his old friend Gregory was editor of *Nature*. Wells read the journal regularly and contributed reviews and comments to it. And Gregory provided another service. He was always available, having the information himself or suggesting another source if he did not, to answer the scientific questions raised in increasing number by Wells's fiction. Gregory monitored Wells's writings, and kept him from making gross errors. This sort of aid has made the Wells science-fiction work of the period still extremely readable, while much of that from his competitors simply was not very good science, and is now not very good reading.[33] In fact, most of Wells's early work in the genre is still in print.

In other work in this period Wells begins to demonstrate his remarkable ability to forecast the future, although as yet there is little evidence of his using that ability in his fiction. For instance, an article on the potential of flight appeared as early as 1893. After a brief discussion of the research of Langley and Lilienthal, Wells said manned flight was coming. From this beginning, he went on to describe London in the year 2000 with a vision of hordes of winged persons flying out to the suburbs. More appropriate to his scientific training, he tended to return again and again to the teachings of evolution. Man is supreme now, said Wells, but there is nothing in the historical or fossil record to indicate that this must remain so. He said that giant air-breathing crustaceans might overcome man, or air-breathing octopi, or other cephalopods, or even giant ants. If such an animal appeared, how could we fight it, was his question. And, if this did not occur, there was always the possibility of disease. He dealt with the cycles of nature, which he believed to be only delusions fostered by persons with short temporal and visual horizons. According to Wells, ' . . . the great stream of the universe flows past us and onward. . . . But the main course is forward, from the things that are past and done with for ever to things that are altogether new.' In fact, said Wells, the by-products of evolution are much more interesting to the serious student. 'You cannot make a haycart that will refuse to carry roses,' remarked Wells, and he urged closer study of human potentials. In 1896 he dealt with the possibility of life on the moon and on Mars, both speculations that would lead inevitably to major pieces of science-fiction writing. Wells only warned against an excessive anthropomorphism in the speculative mind.[34]

By the summer of 1896, he was getting a byline whenever he commented, and especially for his statements on science. He had a few last prescriptions to make here as well, much as he had on teaching, before illness forced his retirement from journalism. For these articles he chose journals with the widest and strongest circulations he could locate. The first, in the *Saturday Review*, picked up on his theme of national competition, as when after his failure to effect a change in science teaching, he remarked that until England was willing to ask for rigorous standards in scientific tools, and to make them readily available, she would always be in second place or further back. The best example of this was the failure to provide inexpensive microscopes for students. The cheapest English version sold for 5 guineas and wasn't very good. The Germans, on the other hand, had long since solved the problem. 'It is not only a question of lost trade,' Wells said, 'but one of intellectual hindrance', and if the stupidity of protectionism was not done away with, the Germans would not only reign supreme over the world of science, the English with their expensive, badly made, protected products would be forced to attempt to compete. This article created a storm of response, to which Wells answered equally strongly, egged on by Gregory (and probably by other scientists) who accepted that Wells was undertaking the work of the scientific establishment.[35]

Wells also addressed himself to the current discussion of the significance of the evolutionary theory, and whether or not it was possible to modify the direction of events through education. In other words, were all man's characteristics hereditary? Wells thought that they probably were; however, our species could modify the direction enough to be of major significance, if we only wished. He thought, for instance, that all civilizations pass from being militaristic to a phase much more static — and that this was the time to intervene, and intervene with a state-produced education with a better life as its objective. He called for 'a rational code of morality', and asked his readers to think about these questions:

> Are we not at the present time on a level of intellectual and moral attainment sufficiently high to permit of the formulation of a moral code, without irrelevant reference, upon which educational people can agree? . . . And yet one may dream of an informal, unselfish, unauthorized body of workers, a real and conscious apparatus of education and moral suggestion, held together by a common faith and a common sentiment, and shaping the minds and arts and destinies of mankind.[36]

Here, more than thirty years before it was announced, is a clear statement of what Wells would eventually call the Open Conspiracy. With this article and others, at the end of a decade of intense work, he began to sound the clarion call to what would be the primary object of the remainder of his life. Of course, if he had not had a major success, such calls would not have been printed. It was the author, not just of these articles and reviews, but above all of *The Time Machine*, that remarkable effort at putting into fictional form the ideas he set out in a straightforward way in these pieces, whose views counted so much. So it is to Wells, and to the Time Traveller, we must look for the force behind the theory he espoused.

Of all the books Wells wrote, *The Time Machine* is perhaps the most famous. It certainly has not been out of print since its first edition, produced in 1895, and once it was published it modified and changed English and American fiction for ever. As we read the work today, after ninety years of other reading and analyses, and with, for most readers, the guilty memory of the first reading, under the covers with a torch, hoping one's parents would not stop the illicit experience just as it became almost unbearable, we realize that it is a very short book, almost a novella in fact. In addition we realize that the plot — the transference of a time traveller to other places and deep into the future — although well done, remains a beautiful piece of imaginative writing but one in which, no matter how much we want to, we cannot now believe.

The book had its beginning in the first of Wells's writings; a draft was perhaps under way as early as 1884. Extracts were published under the title, 'The Chronic Argonauts', during Wells's editorship of the *Science Schools Journal*. This was a period in which a fourth dimension, time, was beginning to exercise the minds of many scientists, and Wells's efforts to create a world with a fourth dimension led him to the abortive article, 'The Universe Rigid', which Frank Harris rejected so forcefully in 1891.

Wells continued to work on the Argonauts, and from time to time offered a new version, or occasionally parts of the original, to other journals. Some parts of it, or parts of the idea, appeared in his *Pall Mall Gazette* pieces. Henley read the Argonauts in its second (or third) form, and decided that it would make a series of unconnected articles for the *National Observer*. Seven portions of the manuscript did appear in that journal. It, however, changed hands; and the Traveller lay dormant for a time. Henley then became editor of a different journal, the *New Review*; and he called on Wells to give him more of his work. In fact he now offered Wells £100 for the work as a rewritten serial.

This time Henley also offered some good criticism of the work as Wells redid it. This editorial comment was all-important in making it into the book we know today. Henley coddled Wells along by describing the work as 'wonderful' in a letter of September 1894, gingered him when the pieces did not arrive quickly, made him rewrite the introductory chapters, and finally forced him to write a completely new beginning. With these aids to composition, though, the work became strong and Henley began its serial publication.[37]

Wells remembered the trials of the book with some diffidence in 1931 when a new illustrated edition appeared in the United States. Asked to write a new introduction, he responded with four pages of comment. He remembered discussing the ideas of the book at Knole Park 'with that dear companion who sustained me so stoutly through these adventurous years of short commons and hopeful uncertainty'. Wells also said the book was very juvenile, the work of a very inexperienced author, and one in which the second half in particular was not realized. He said that he had been influenced fairly heavily by Jonathan Swift, especially in his discussions of the Eloi and the Morlocks, as he had been in his other book of that precise period, *The Island of Dr Moreau* (1896). Wells said that all geologists and biologists of his time believed that the world would freeze up eventually, and this was the basis for the Time Traveller's last visit into the future. By 1931 Wells viewed the near future much more positively, saying that 'the only trace of pessimism left in the human prospect today is the faint regret that one was born too soon. And even from that distress, modern psychological and biological philosophy offers ways of escape.'[38] Thus Wells remembered the book thirty-five years later.

A. P. Watt began in 1895 to offer the serial round for book publication, and after a brief delay, Heinemann agreed to publish it. Wells gave the printers the *New Review* version of *The Time Machine*, but still further revised. Heinemanns did not produce the book as rapidly as Wells had hoped, and he attempted to generate greater speed in their production. However, he assured his new publisher that he was 'quite prepared to place myself in your hands with regard to price, get up, etc., only if the price is to be 1/6 or lower, I think I ought to have 20% after the first 5,000. But I don't want to haggle about details of that sort — the important thing is to get the book published.' Wells also asked about a special Christmas edition, and American publication, and offered advice on review copies.[39]

The book was reviewed widely and well. Grant Richards (or Henley —
they argued over who had done it) called the book to the attention of W.T.
Stead, who noticed it very strongly in the *Review of Reviews*, calling Wells 'A
Man of Genius'. Sidney Low apparently also reviewed it favourably
somewhere, although the review has not as yet been located. Wells however
did not get a comment from the source he must have most wanted one
from. For ultimately, the book was written for T. H. Huxley. In the last
dozen years a great many theories have been put forward on the origins of
The Time Machine, ranging from Wellsian obsession with underground
places to crude and vulgar Marxism. But what Wells was doing in this
book was putting evolutionary theory into fictional practice. That was all.
As he told Huxley when he sent him a copy:

> Lynton
> Maybury Road
> Woking
>
> May 1895
>
> Dear Sir:
> I am sending you a little book that I fancy may be of interest to you.
> The central idea — of degeneration following security — was the
> outcome of a certain amount of biological study. I daresay your position
> subjects you to a good many such displays of the range of authors but I
> have this much excuse — I was one of your pupils at the Royal College
> of Science and finally [?]: The book is a very little one.
>
> I am, Dr Sir
> Very Faithfully yours
>
> H. G. WELLS
>
> Professor Huxley[40]

With this letter Wells paid his first formal tribute to the influence of Huxley
in his life. It is clear in this context that *The Time Machine* should be read as
Wells himself indicated — as a statement of the possibilities of evolution,
even the probabilities — no more, no less.

The book ended a life totally committed to journalism. Wells would
never have to look back financially. As he told Grant Richards near the end
of 1895, 'I am dropping all journalism now and barring a story to keep the
wolf from the door am concentrating upon two long stories — one of these
is a cycling romance (I am a cyclist), the other a big scientific story remotely
resembling *The Time Machine*.'[41]

The great spurt of writing from 1893 to 1895 had taken a fearful toll on
Wells, however. He had suffered one relapse into his tubercular state
(although the evidence today is that his illness may have been related to an
ulcer, or to his kidney injury) in 1893, and in 1898 had another bad relapse.
His friends and his physician (Henry Hick, who came recommended by

George Gissing) were very disturbed at the possibility that Wells might not survive this attack. Henley said, 'For Heavens' sake, take care of yourself. You have a unique talent and you've produced three books within a year and are up to the elbows in a fourth. It is magnificent, of course, but it can't be literature.' Watt, too, was concerned, as were Wells's old friends Bowkett, Gregory, and Simmons. Gregory investigated the possibility of Roentgen ray analysis, but had to report that it would be of no use in diagnosis. Wells himself knew that he had much to do, and was equally disturbed by the breakdown.

In response to a query, he told an interviewer, and eventually his readers, that his purpose was greater than the public had yet realized. For instance, *The Time Machine* was about 'the responsibility of men to mankind. Unless humanity hangs together, unless all strive for the species as a whole, we shall end in disaster'; although he went on to say that he was always an optimist.[42] All of his friends and his readers welcomed every new item, but many also worried as to how long he could keep producing such brilliant attacks on and analyses of modern life. In any case, with the new flare-up, his doctors told him he must leave London, seek the sea air, and take it easy. Too much work was threatening his life. Jane and Bertie now began to use their tandem wheel to search for a home on the Channel coast. He had arrived, but now, it appeared, at tremendous cost to himself.

FICTION ABOUT THE FUTURE

Very thin indeed is the curtain between us and the unknown. There is a fear of the night that is begotten of ignorance and superstition, a nightmare fear, the fear of the night — of the starlit night — that comes with knowledge, when we see in its true proportion this little life of ours with all its phantasmal environment of cities and stores and arsenals, and the habits, prejudices and promises of men.

HGW (unsigned), 'From an Observatory', *Saturday Review*, 1 December 1894

After *The Time Machine* appeared, H.G. Wells's life was never the same. But literature and the art of fiction were also substantially changed by the appearance of the slight and much rewritten book. For Wells had produced a significant and seminal work. After four tries with the same material he provided readers with a masterpiece — not a masterpiece of plot, construction, or even of character, but a masterful marriage of the fictive art and theoretical science; a marriage which could not have come before his time, as neither partner was ready for the embrace. But in 1895, it was as if the nuptials had only been waiting for the cathedral organ, as Benjamin Franklin waited for the sky to prove him right, or Newton waited for the apple to drop.

There had been tremendous growth in scientific understanding in the previous forty or fifty years. This change was fostered by the work of Charles Darwin, who, after the voyages and discoveries in the Galapagos and elsewhere, finally published in 1859 his truly pivotal work, *The Origin of Species*. After this book, science, the theoretical explanation of what had previously been the domain of philosophy and metaphysics, began to dominate rational thought. That domination attracted many of the greatest minds of the period, and the advances in knowledge created out of this matrix had been remarkable. It is not too much to say that Darwin's work brought together a body of thought which produced a world explosion of knowledge. H. G. Wells had grown to manhood in the middle of the first burst of creative energy, and his thinking was to a substantial degree forged in the heat of it. In *The Time Machine* he took the process into another realm.

Darwin's chief interpreter in England had been and still was at this time T. H. Huxley, Wells's mentor. Huxley readily grasped the meaning of the evolutionary doctrine; he asked, and began in his own work to respond to, the questions of ethics raised by the theory and put, to some degree, by Darwin himself in *The Descent of Man*. Wells, aided by others also trained and influenced by Huxley — especially by Richard A. Gregory, but also by E. Ray Lankester, initially, and in the second generation by J. B. S. Haldane, Julian Huxley, and eventually C. P. Snow — would carry these questions to their ultimate end. The questions, What more can be learned? and, Can man replace the biblical God as creator? have not yet been answered, of course, although they had begun to be put in their strongest form by the time *The Time Machine* was published. Indeed it could be said that the book contributed to the search for the meaning of those questions, and even perhaps, in a timid and jejune way, began to provide some early and tentative answers. What is certain is that much of Wells's later life would be devoted to an effort to refine these first tentative responses.

Elsewhere other scientists began to respond to the Darwinian impetus, and in their own fields to provide further data to frame theoretical responses to the same questions. Louis Agassiz, while visiting the glaciers of his native Switzerland, began to doubt the age of the earth as then posited. He quickly found substantial evidence for extending the earth's age. In his studies of glaciers, and his related work on palaeolithic fish, Agassiz also began to ask questions which were difficult for contemporary theology to answer. Once he had been to North America and made new discoveries it appeared that his glacier theories were completely vindicated, and by the time of Darwin's book other geologists had begun with great strides to push the age of the earth back into deep time.

The two related sciences, biology and geology, began to provide a glimpse of the extraordinarily long existence of the solar system. Scientists in those fields also came generally to the understanding that *Homo sapiens*, now the dominant species, had been present for only a very short period in that history, and dominant for much less than that. The great animals of the past — many no longer present in the fauna — the trilobites, the megatherium, the animals of the Jurassic, and even many of the diatoms of the sea, had all preceded man and had disappeared. It was but a short step from this understanding to the view that man's tenure might be as short. With a certain amount of anthropomorphism it might be said that man's tenure was part of a logical progression, and one that had perhaps reached its natural apex, but it was much more likely that the only thing that set man apart was that he was able to see, very dimly, some of the past, and even more dimly, to look into the future. Extension of these peeps into time might enable this one species to extend and continue its domination, but there was nothing in the physical record that made that inevitable, or even likely. Wells, in writing *The Time Machine*, provided a more distinct look into the future, but just as his Time Traveller had returned to reality, so others to come might also look at the future, and attempt to modify it to their own advantage when they came back to their mental base. There was a sort of vague promise in the book, but one which would be worked out much more strongly in other Wellsian productions.

The two disciplines, geology and biology, had been Wells's major studies at the Royal College. There he had learnt of the most recent efforts to find a true answer to the questions of life. His third discipline, astronomy, and astronomical physics, were just on the verge of their knowledge explosion when Wells began his studies. Men had peered into the heavens since time immemorial, and much, if not all, of the religious explanation for the behaviour of the natural world had come as a way of providing a sort of answer to the immensity of the heavens, and their changing but apparently returning and cyclical patterns. Only those persons who had built the great megalithic monuments, both in England and on the Continent, and perhaps their counterparts in the valley of the Nile, had studied the heavens long enough to realize that the cyclical nature that had been posited was only another delusion, for time, the fourth dimension, went on into great unforeseen depths. These civilizations had left no record of their musings, nothing but their observatories, or temples (and the two uses were probably closely related). In the fifty years before Wells came to the Royal College, mechanical genius had designed better tools for use in viewing the heavens — the camera, with larger, more smoothly ground lenses, and even better, observatory platforms. But a standard time was not fixed at Greenwich until 1884; so the science of astronomy was still in an infant state as Wells began his studies.

Now, however, an explosion of information seemed possible in this realm as well. Percival Lowell, using the new tools and a powerful imagination, posited life on other plants and especially on Mars. Study of the solar system reached fever pitch. The application of mathematics and physics to that study would enhance exceptionally the knowledge of man, through the discovery of new elements, as well as new aspects of the solar system. The intellectual world which produced H. G. Wells was also, very soon, to produce Clyde Tombaugh from the plains of Kansas, who would eventually discover Planet X (Pluto) and substantially increase our knowledge of the solar system. Wells would aid indirectly in this work by his speculation as to how and why these other worlds might have existed, and for whom. The questions remained the same no matter what science was involved.

The fourth great science of this period was chemistry. Wells was not a chemist, but he could appreciate the beauty of the laboratory, and the effort it took to isolate the relationships of individual groups of molecules. The tiny worlds of the atom were equally attractive to look at, with all the potential they might offer. The periodic table was restructured and Wells wrote about that, while in the opening chapters of *The World Set Free* he provided a glimpse of the fantastic joy of making discoveries in experimental science — a glimpse unmatched in our literature, even in the memoirs of the discoverers themselves. The book, published in 1914, shone a light into the future, for it seemed by that time that the purpose of science was to provide answers to the questions of how and why the universe was as it was.

In a sense Wells could not have written *The Time Machine* and his other creations before he did; there simply was not enough factual knowledge available. By the time he began to invent explanations of what might occur, science was in a position to test these hypotheses in a routine way, no matter how peculiar they might seem to those outside the temples of science. What Wells could do, which science usually resisted, was to posit ethical questions to be associated with the working-out of the scientific method. Others could have posed these questions, but most of the philosophers of the time (with the exception, perhaps, of William James) had asked the questions in the context of Christianity, and they did not realize, or even opposed the possibility, that the answers could be sought outside the metaphysics of the mind. In the early days of the scientific excitement after Darwin's monumental book, Andrew Dickson White, president of a newly founded university in Ithaca, New York (created with the express purpose of providing a place where any student could find an answer to any question), asked these same tough questions, and provided his own answers in a highly significant book, *The Warfare of Science With Theology*, published in 1879. Wells and his compatriots took the warfare as given, knew the results, and carried on with their work. The literature produced by these workers, both in science and art, would be their response. Again, *The Time Machine* was but an early, though very powerful, gun in the battle.

It is true that the spurt of scientific activity could have taken place almost without the knowledge of the ordinary inhabitants of the US, England, or most European countries, but what was different about this explosion was that some of the citizens of those countries did watch, and comment, as it took place. Part of the reason for their interest, of course, was the implications for religion of the questions posed by the new discoveries. Some religious observances were state-sponsored, or even state-mandated. This meant that when scientific research as well was sponsored, promoted, or funded by the state, the two might and did come into conflict.

The new science challenged the old theology. Even this would have interested only a few persons, except that an explosion of literacy had also occurred. In the last twenty-five years of the nineteenth century the curve indicating increased leisure time and that showing diminished hours of work coincided, to bring about what the democratic revolutions of the previous century had promised implicitly. The mechanical changes created by the Industrial Revolution combined with the physical and social changes of the democratic revolution to prefigure a truly democratic state — that is, one in which all citizens could take part. Inevitably, but very slowly, these ideas also combined with the scientific ideas of the significance of species, not nationalities, to hold out the promise (for some) of a world state. In 1895, of course, few people were ready to accept or even discuss that idea.

They were, however, ready to discuss almost everything else. The invention of cheap paper (in the United States, paper from wood pulp brought the price of newsprint from 20 plus cents a pound in 1865 down to less than 1/4 cent a pound by 1890) made reading matter of every kind available to everyone at very little cost. Every major newspaper in the United States shifted to the cheaper paper in the decade after it was first successfully produced commercially in 1867. The cheaper paper also came along just when leisure time was increasing, as machines lightened the work load and electricity lengthened the work day. Continuous-flow manufacture (whether in assembly lines or not) in this new condition of artificial sunlight soon provided (after some labour travail) the eight-hour and the three-shift day. The amount of work asked for from each worker diminished substantially in many areas, and although the slack was taken up by more service jobs of one kind or another, it was also taken up with more and more leisure time. Socialists assumed that workers would use the leisure time gained to seek further education, and this certainly occurred; they also used it for travel, making wider and different use of holiday time, and for other activities suited to the rising expectations of the newly benefited group — mainly middle class.

Much of the new leisure time was spent in literary pursuits of one kind or another. Many new and widely differing newspapers became available at very small cost. Numerous magazines and journals were founded as well. The success of Alfred Harmsworth's *Tit-Bits, Answers to Correspondents*, and *Comic Cuts* in England, and of their American counterparts, the Beadle Dime Novels, Edward Bok's various magazines for the millions, and the Hearst and Pulitzer yellow press, indicates how great a void was there to be filled by the new journalism. It was this world which provided an opportunity for the young H. G. Wells to make his way initially. Others, many others, wrote for this market: A. Conan Doyle, H. Rider Haggard, Rudyard Kipling, Grant Allen, A. E. W. Mason, John Buchan, Ned Buntline (of the dime novel). Regional novelists of the United States wrote for magazines, as did Anthony Hope, Victor Whitechurch, and dozens of others whose work lies buried in the bound files of the *Strand, Pearson's Magazine*, or the *Cosmopolitan*. The names of the first and third of these journals indicate to a degree the aspirations of the new reading public. Closely associated with the expansion in magazine and newspaper publishing was the publication of fiction in translation (Wells's work was translated, almost immediately, into French, German, Swedish, Spanish, Russian, and Italian, for instance). Inexpensive paperbound English versions of novels were sold in railway kiosks on the Continent. More than 2,000 titles were eventually issued in these Tauchnitz editions for the anglophone traveller, and were part of this same explosion in knowledge. A number of Wells's novels of the future were published by Tauchnitz, offering the traveller a look at the new science and the new questions.

The questions increased in number towards the end of the century. To some degree the *fin de siècle* attitude might have provided a mathematical edge to many of the queries anyway, but in this period of great scientific change the edge was sharper and more persistent. Added to this in Britain was the fact of the old Queen's age, and the prospect that the Victorian era would soon be over. Men like Wells and Conan Doyle were, in their books, proclaiming a sort of Edwardian successor long before the Diamond Jubilee. As time went on Victoria's Empire seemed under constant attack, and the series of little wars to preserve its boundaries brought unpleasant comparisons with the reign of Hadrian. Germany, on the one hand, offered a major threat, and the literature of the period from 1895 to 1914 is filled with the notion of potential German aggression. From *The Battle of Dorking* (1871), through *The Riddle of the Sands* (1903), to *When William Came* (1911), reading Englishmen were apprised of the German problem. Wells's work *The War of the Worlds*, and later *The War in the Air*, simply fitted in with this general feeling. The Boer War was viewed almost as a proxy war with the Germans, or 'Dutch'; but even if seen as simply putting down peasant barbarians, it served to heighten the feeling. The frantic joy of Mafeking Night could be treated only as a hysterical indication that ordinary people thought these menaces were closed off for a while. There were those in Britain who knew that joy was merely a temporary respite, persons able to look at the reality of tragedies like Rorke's Drift, but they were in a very silent minority. On the other side of the Atlantic, the United States also offered a major threat, and Americans like Theodore Roosevelt, Brooks Adams, or Mayor William Thompson of Chicago were mainly interested in speeding the process of transition. Wells spoke to them as well with his prophecies of new worlds to come.

The fiction which Wells (along with others) wrote so well had deep roots in standard Anglo-American literature. Some aspects of this fiction were part of an ordinary education. Wells had read *Vathek*, a great ur-novel of fantasy, and he knew Edgar Allan Poe as well. Poe used a sort of science, or scientific query, to heighten the tension in his work. 'The Masque of the Red Death', 'The Fall of the House of Usher', and above all, *The Narrative of Arthur Gordon Pym*, are all written with a ghost of scientific enquiry as part of their strength. Wells in his writing was following a pattern established long before he was born.

There was, of course, another tradition of fiction which also used science as a motif, usually misapplied or unethical science, as in the case of Mary Shelley's Frankenstein and his creation, the monster. She did not ask the ethical questions posed by later writers of science fiction, but all of the elements for it were present in her book. More to the point were books which used travel to unusual or invented places to ask questions about man's future. Wells was extremely impressed by the Platonic dialogues, the *Republic* and the *Laws*. One of his earliest pieces dealt with the death of Socrates, and eventually he would himself use the dialogue form in one of his late, strong novels, asking questions about why and how we might meet great world crises. He was also taken with the writing of Sir Thomas More, and wrote a famous introduction to *Utopia*. Wells did not mention the *Persian Letters* in which Montesquieu posed somewhat similar questions, but he did mention, and in fact acknowledged his debt to, Swift and Gulliver.[1]

Science had not progressed far enough for earlier efforts in the genre to use scientific discovery, or the scientific mind, to elaborate their purposes; Wells's contribution was to add this element. Jules Verne had played about with it, but his command of science and the scientific method was weak — his books function best as adventure stories, even when scientifically plausible, as in the development of the submarine in *Twenty Thousand Leagues Under the Sea*. To my mind the best Verne novel is *The Mysterious Island*, which is much more in the vein of *Swiss Family Robinson*. Wells disagreed with this view in his introduction to the Knopf edition of his major science fiction in 1934, but the piece reads like Wells in a tongue-in-cheek mood.[2]

If the dream of the future is a precursor of time travel, it had not been used till now outside the context of the dream. Earlier writers had been constrained, in their use of dreams, either to show a possible future which could be achieved or prevented by some action, as when Dickens shows Scrooge the Fezziwigs' ball, or, more usually, as a plot device to transpose the action to a different place, as when Alice goes down the rabbit hole, or through the looking-glass. In neither case does the reader think that Alice, or he, the reader, has any opportunity other than to observe what is occurring. Wells's brilliant variation on this, in *The Time Machine*, was to show the visitor the future via science, and let the reader make up his own mind about the meaning of the viewed result. Later, in *The Sleeper Awakes* (1910), it is much more clear what the reader can do to modify, create, or change the future. It was not until very much later that Wells dealt with the obverse of the question, discussing modifications which might be bad, whether for Brownlow in a short story, or for the world in which the characters of his novels of the late 1930s, *The Brothers*, *The Camford Visitation*, or *The Croquet Player*, functioned. In all these cases Wells took a fictional method and a style of thought and married it to the science which he had learned so well. In so doing he took his fiction and the fiction of his time ahead in great jumps of technique and meaning.

Ultimately Wells's contribution to fiction writing was to apply real science, and the questions and techniques of science, rather than the

8 How hard work in literature leads to success: an 1895 'picshua' by Wells

The Authors' Syndicate.

Envelopes.

Bankers:
THE UNION BANK,
Chancery Lane.

Solicitors:
Messrs. FIELD, ROSCOE & CO.,
Lincoln's Inn Fields.

Auditors:
Messrs. OSCAR BERRY & CARR.

Telegraphic Address:
Another, London.

4, Portugal Street, Lincoln's Inn Fields, W.C.

14th March 1896

Dear Mr. Wells,

Mr. Pearson is anxious to see the remainder of your story "The War of the Worlds" as soon as possible. As far as he has read he likes it very much, but says that a great deal depends on the finish of the story. I shall be glad if you will let me know when you think you can send me the remainder.

Faithfully yours,

9 Encouraging news on *The War of the Worlds*, 1896

10 R. A. Gregory

pseudo-science of his competitors. Here his relationship with Richard Gregory and the other 'men of science', as they called themselves, was crucial, for they monitored his science before it went to the printer and publisher. They, and Wells, had a sense of the purity of science, which they received from Huxley. In this context Wells's novel, *The Island of Dr Moreau*, and his beautiful story, 'A Slip Under the Microscope', take on added significance: they can best be read, finally, as vicious attacks from the centre of the scientific community on bad science, unethical science, science which is not only not pure, but ultimately evil.

Exactly how much H. G. Wells saw of these questions at the time of the writing of *The Time Machine* is difficult to say; but the sending of a copy to Huxley is significant, and the writing of *Dr Moreau* at almost the same time is not coincidental. And an even more interesting question for his fiction can be raised: at what point did Wells realize that that fiction was important, not only because it incorporated the new science, but because by incorporating it one could ask other things of it — ask, in fact, exactly how and what the new and better world would be? Increasingly, his fiction would be written to provide explicit answers to those questions, and it is that shift in purpose which is worth documenting. For the present, one can simply notice that Wells at first called his work 'scientific romance'; but when, later in his life, he came to discuss it in theoretical terms he described it, in a formal address, as 'fiction about the future'. What he did in his work was to marry science and art — to follow, in an anticipatory way, C. P. Snow's prescription for how our species could best survive, using ideas of bridging the abyss, the chasm, between the two sides of modern educational thought. Wells's major contribution to that task was to provide an educational plan which not only allowed but promoted the building of that bridge. In that sense, *World Brain*, the original *When the Sleeper Wakes*, *A Modern Utopia*, and *The Time Machine* are strongly connected, in the ongoing work, just as — to anticipate — *Mind at the End of Its Tether* is part of, and follows on directly from, not only *The Time Machine* but also 'The Rediscovery of the Unique' and *The Discovery of the Future*.

With the publication of *The Time Machine* and his related work, H. G. Wells began his significant impact on the twentieth century and its problems. Enjoyable as these works may be to read, they also help us to understand his time and our own, from the point of view not only of those who accepted his contribution, but also of those who resisted and fought everything that he stood for.

From 1895 on through the twenty years before World War I blotted out most efforts to use science to make over the world, at least for a time, Wells was at his most prolific. As he aged from twenty-nine to forty-eight, he wrote nine novels and fifty-odd short stories that can legitimately be regarded as 'science fiction'. His 'fiction about the future', to give it its later name, using his remarkable dream-life production, fused his science from

South Kensington with his compulsive writing of short pieces for the *Saturday Review* and the *Pall Mall Gazette*. This writing slowly turned into didactic prescriptions about the future, or macabre warnings of what it might become without serious attention. Books in the latter form, *When the Sleeper Wakes*, *The Food of the Gods*, and *The World Set Free*, which are the strongest of this type, come from the most intense period of this fusion of thought.

Inevitably Wells's personal life at this time, focused on literary friendships in his new home near the Channel, influenced the other forms taken by his writing of the period — those evolving from his false step into Fabianism, as well as his efforts to create his own share of the literature his friends were so sure they were purveying. *Mr Polly*, *Kipps*, and *Tono-Bungay* can all be read in this context (and especially so if one analyses the criticism of Wells's friends and compatriots), and to some degree, the false starts of 'Esau Common' and 'Mr Waddy'. However, Wells's personal life also intruded strongly on his work, much more than the mere remembrance of youth, and under that influence he produced his masterpieces of love and human relationships from this period, *Love and Mr Lewisham*, *Ann Veronica*, and even *In the Days of the Comet*.

When one considers the books of travel, comment, socialist prediction, utopias, and the lesser novels written during these nineteen years, Wells's production is amazing. From 1895 to 1914, he wrote thirty-two books, enough stories to fill eight volumes, dozens of other pieces of uncollected journalism, and maintained a house (occasionally two), while becoming a world-renowned scholar and pundit. Although critics since, and Wells himself from time to time, have been concerned 'about a certain streak of slovenliness which seems to be an almost unavoidable defect in me', as he phrased it in his introduction to the *Sleeper*, even with this streak of vulgar, or sloppy, work, his output was enormous. The top level of his work during the period, even with the 'streak', is still read, and will likely be read as long as this language is written.[3]

Wells was a veritable writing machine during this period. He had a compulsive need to rid himself of material generated in his youth and by his education, and this need was fanned by near-breakdowns suffered in 1898, 1900, and the profound melancholia set off by the death of George Gissing. Amy Catherine — 'Jane' to Wells, by the time of the move to Sandgate — was significant in the effort leading to this production. She acted as his secretary (both personal and literary), organized Spade House weekends, to a considerable degree raised the children herself, provided a retreat for Wells — from London, from love affairs, from the demands and from the vulgarity of the outside world — a haven in which his writing could take place, his dreams be dreamed, and the proofs corrected. His periodic illnesses fuelled the creative pump, while she provided the lubricant which kept it silently going.

One wishes one knew more about the psychological nature of Wells's illnesses; modern science suggests that he probably did not have tuberculosis, and that although his kidney was weak after the injury at football, he had conquered that problem by 1895. The illnesses were almost certainly brought on by overwork, but one asks whether they were an effort by the body, or mind, to lie fallow for a time, or whether they occurred when the creative springs were running dry, from shock at that possibility. The religious experience during the stress of World War I may also be seen as a sort of illness, culminating as it did in the great textbooks and the drive towards the world state. Wells was an intense bundle of force and desire. But whether he would have had as great an achievement, on as wide a front, without Amy Catherine Robbins (and one or two other women) seems unlikely.

The Time Machine was the first of Wells's remarkable productions. It took him a long time to write, and only appeared after many false starts. He remained dissatisfied with the novel, continued to work on it, and in free periods in 1898 and 1899 again rewrote part of the book, cutting and changing once more to provide some 'improvements in expression', as well as rearranging it slightly. It was this later version that appeared in the Atlantic Edition and is usually the one reprinted today.[4]

The book opens with a group discussion among persons representing well-known types, who are led by their host at dinner in a conversation about ideas of time, the fourth dimension. The host has constructed a machine which speeds time fantastically so that years go by in a second, and he shows the creation to his guests. The Time Traveller then describes a trip taken 'with a kind of madness growing upon me, . . . I flung myself into futurity.' On arrival, he first sees a statue (a sort of Ozymandias motif) and then discovers people whose evolution arises from *Homo sapiens*. They are vegetarians, as no animals exist in this world, and their architecture appears dilapidated and worn. In addition, these persons, of the year 802,701 A.D., have extremely short attention spans and somewhat limited intelligence. Wells's better world has come with the passage of time, but with it all evidence of struggle, toil, and violence has disappeared, even the natural biological struggle. As the Traveller muses on his own time, 'We are kept keen on the grindstone of pain and necessity, and, it seemed to me, that here was that hateful grindstone broken at last!' However, this theory was wrong, as he later learns that two species of humans have evolved — the Eloi, whom he had first met, and the Morlocks, who dwell below ground. Capital and labour have thus produced their logical results. The Morlocks are carnivorous and feed on the Eloi, whom they 'farm' in a way for their use. The Traveller — Wells himself, or so it seems to the reader — now discovers the true reality of the future:

'. . . . how brief the dream of the human intellect had been. It had committed suicide. It had set itself steadfastly towards comfort and ease, a balanced society with security and permanency as its watchword, it had attained its hopes — to come to this at last. . . . It is a law of nature we overlook, that intellectual versatility is the compensation for change, danger, and trouble.'

(Chapter 10)

What is worse is that the Time Traveller now discovers still another iron law of reality, that progress does not continue for ever in an unending line; sooner or later it slows down, and as the Traveller goes on in time he finds the earth at rest, one side turned permanently towards a dying red sun. Here on the shore of the sea he sees monster crabs, lichens, and pale white butterflies of a huge size, the results of evolution; and then, stopping thirty million years later, nothing appears on the earth but cold skies now, eternal sunset, and an essentially lifeless green slime, blobs of protoplasm and chlorophyll as the world comes to its inevitable end.

The Time Traveller thus offers to readers two versions of the future — one sure, that of geology and astronomic physics — one which cannot be denied, but prior to that time, another, in which we could go the way of the Eloi and the Morlocks. But, as the narrator remarks after the Traveller has returned to the future, if we do not wish this world, ' . . . it remains for us to live as though it were not so.'

The Time Machine is a powerful book, and it is not difficult to appreciate why readers purchased it in such numbers. Combining as it does science, in the form of evolutionary theory, and hope, in the view that if we will only try to anticipate the future, we can create a world in which the Eloi and Morlocks live in a symbiosis without the cruel death the Traveller sees, and in which life can be filled out for all, Wells's book appealed to an audience just beginning to realize the promise of both education and science. Nearly a century after its publication the Time Traveller's challenge remains, however, and the book lingers as a powerful potential guide to only one future.

As Wells was offering this possibly positive and good view of science, he also produced his most sardonic attack and assault on science without thought and purpose, *Dr Moreau*, about a scientist without ethics. In this early work, as in his story, 'A Slip Under the Microscope', Wells demonstrated clearly what science could be — both positively and negatively. He offered some choice in these works but without indicating his views on what would come in the wake of the choice.

In the second novel the hero, Edward Prendick, is shipwrecked, and saved by a strange vessel, manned by odd-looking bestial sailors who take him to an island, a biological research station owned by a Dr Moreau. Moreau is vaguely familiar to Prendick as the famous, even notorious, subject of a vivisection scandal in previous years. Soon Prendick realizes that Moreau is continuing his terrible experiments, using grafting techniques to fuse animals into parodies of human beings. Prendick escapes the central buildings of the station and finds himself surrounded by the animals, led by even more grotesque creatures who chant parodic versions of Kipling's 'Law of the Jungle'. These new or pseudo-animals cannot go on all fours, suck up their drink, eat flesh or fish, claw the bark of trees, or chase other men. '*That* is the Law. Are we not Men?' they ask in their terrible song.

The animals revere Moreau, out of a dread fear of the pain he inflicts, but in a sort of diabolic worship of the changes he creates as well. Moreau, who meets Prendick again, explains that he is able to accomplish anything with his grafts, except the grafting of humanity into the brains and emotions of his patients. (This section of the book, chapter 14, appeared in a substantially different form in the *Saturday Review*. Here it is an effort to provide a guide for knowledgeable laymen as to the reasons for research.) As a result, the animals inevitably revert to their true nature. Soon one of them kills another, and with this violation of the Law, others now experience a need for blood and meat. Although an effort is made to locate those guilty of the law-breaking at a conclave of the Moreau creations, it does not work out. Prendick is forced to kill other animals in self-defence, and a great wild chase follows across and around the island.

The struggle of the animals against Moreau, their master, who has given them this law which they cannot comprehend, occupies the last part of the book. Moreau dies; the animals then ask Prendick for an alternative law, but all he is able to provide is a codicil — 'Fear the Law as he is not dead but watches.' With this the laboratory is destroyed, and fire consumes the horror of Moreau's work. Prendick is unable to rule, as he finds himself just another among the beast people, as they take on their more realistic ways, although remaining different and strange in many traits. Prendick kills those (the hyena) who change the least, and who have murdered his companion (the dog creation), and finally escapes alone, in a boat cast up by another storm. He leaves the island, still filled with terror, and once at home he finds he is able to view people only in their beastlike characteristics, as animals reverting to their more bestial real nature.

In the short story, 'A Slip Under the Microscope', set in a laboratory very like Huxley's, and apparently based on a scandalous event of the time, a scholarship student of the lower classes makes an error, and is punished for it, while losing a female student with whom he is in love. His upper-class opponent is able to win out, both in love and science, as *class* is more important than scientific *truth*. The moral one can draw from the story is that science will not achieve its true role until ethics governs decisions, just as it must govern 'research' like that of Dr Moreau.

Wells in these works is attacking science run amok, science which he saw as being used by the state for evil purposes, and science conducted without a view as to its purpose. The prospect of Moreau's island becoming a reality has haunted thinking scientists ever since, and for many has remained the observed norm outside the scientific community. The book is too close to the bone — Wells understood that a Moreau, or a Montgomery, the doctor's drunken assistant, lurks inside each of us, and he makes that point directly when Prendick is unable to save the animals or provide them with a good law, and in fact, can only mouth the horror that the pain-giver is still watching. All Prendick can do is observe and react, even after his escape.

Dr Moreau, for all its difficult and anxious message, was sought after by publishers, and William Heinemann, who eventually published the work, gave Wells an advance of £60 (Wells wanted £100), and also what were good terms for a relatively unknown author — 15 per cent on the first 5,000 copies sold, and 20 per cent thereafter. The book, which sold for 6*s.*, earned an additional 2½*d.* per copy on colonial sales. In addition the serial rights were sold, both in the US and in England, although Wells did not do as well out of these as he had hoped. Henley had suggested writing the book version first, and then making the serial version from it, but Wells tried to do it the other way round, and although the text hung together reasonably well, it did not serialize effectively. Wells became convinced that Heinemann had not given him a true accounting of the sales, and in 1899, through the Society of Authors, threatened litigation. He eventually offered to buy back the rights, the plates, and stock of unsold copies, but Heinemann knew a good thing when he had it, and kept the book in his list. Both Wells and the publisher eventually made a good deal of money from the work.[5]

The message of *Dr Moreau* met with strong reactions. The prominent scientist P. Chalmers Mitchell, whose books Wells had reviewed, reacted vigorously in the *Saturday Review*. Mitchell said he had read the book with dismay, after the promise of *The Time Machine* and *The Wonderful Visit*. He disliked the revolting details with which Wells filled the book, and urged the young author to return to the sane transmutations of which he was so capable. He skirted the problem of genetics, as to whether living tissue from one species could be affixed to another, but raised the issue implicitly. Wells was stung into a response, in which he dealt with the grafting question, citing articles in the *British Medical Journal* and elsewhere, as well as with the details to which Mitchell objected. Mitchell replied to this, giving Wells his scientific due, but remarking that Wells 'ought to be more grateful for the huge advertisement my criticism seems to have given his book'.[6]

Others liked the book, even with its horrible potential, as they realized that the world was real, and that science could be horrific. As Wells remarked to his friend, R. Cyprian, who had written to him praising the work, 'The book was unlucky at the outset, but I think it has the vitality to live through its troubles.'[7] He was right, and in a world which has produced the scientific horror of Buchenwald and Belsen, Dr Moreau remains as a terrible reminder of what science without ethics, without goals, and science for science's sake (to parody the Latin tag) can bring about in evil hands. Wells, in this work, took Mary Shelley's Frankenstein to his ultimate end, and although some might not like the prospect, it loomed ahead, nevertheless, for those who would not work against it.

With these two books Wells achieved considerable fame. His views on the future began to be sought by magazines and newspapers. His readers and contemporaries began to think in terms of time travel, of the future, and occasionally, although it was painful, about bad science and its consequences. Wells had more to teach his audience, of course, but before he did so two lighter works came from his pen. The first, *The Wonderful Visit* (1895), originated in a remark attributed to John Ruskin, that if an angel came to earth most Englishmen would simply want to bag it as a new species of bird. Wells's plot was no more substantial than that premise, although the angelic visit does allow him some worthwhile observations, especially from a tramp character, on the state of England, English education, and other matters in which H.G. was interested.

More significant was his novel, *The Invisible Man* (1897). As Wells said later, the title was a misnomer, as his man is, in fact, transparent. The transparency is achieved by modifying the refraction in the eyes of his viewers, and through the fact that the man, Griffin, has very light, near-albino, pigmentation. The story revolves around the search for the reasons for Griffin's transparency and the efforts of the invisible visitor to dominate others, to use his power — generally in a violent, and often criminal, way. The novel is tightly written, using Wells's Midhurst experience, and in its treatment of complacent rural folk anticipates *The War of the Worlds*. The book probably provided the novelist Ralph Ellison, an important black observer of America, with the title for his work *Invisible Man* (1952), and perhaps with its theme, that blacks in America remain invisible while going about their daily lives, although promising that their emergence will be significant. Wells's novel again attacks science without ethics, undertaken for no purpose, with disagreeable results.

The book is an interesting phenomenon in another way. It sold well for a month, after which the sales collapsed entirely, yet it was a steady producer of revenue throughout Wells's life, especially in the US. Every six months a royalty cheque arrived. As late as January 1935 (at the height of the Depression) the cheque was for £42. 17s. 5d., for example. In the 1920s the film rights to the book became valuable, and gave Wells an opportunity to increase his income substantially. Famous Players offered to buy the work outright, but Wells, wise in the ways of the world, said he did not believe in such sales; he preferred to grant options on a short-term basis, with each successive option bringing in more funds. Wells asked £4,000 for an option for a reasonable number of years, while the Hollywood magnates offered $25,000 with $2,000 deductible if they took up the option to film within sixty days; this last Wells accepted. The film, when made in 1933, starred

Claude Rains, and was a modest hit. The Invisible Man certainly brought
in visible funds.[8]

Interesting as these two short novels were, neither was in a class with H.G.
Wells's next production in this genre, *The War of the Worlds* (1898). To
some extent the book has been overshadowed by the extraordinary impact
of the Orson Welles Hallowe'en radio show of 1938, using the same
theme, which panicked much of eastern America. By now, from films and
television, we all have images for a Martian invasion; but Wells's novel was
and is a significant book in its own right. It was written at a time when the
British Empire was under attack. Opponents, notably Germany, lurked just
across the Channel, and the invasion of the London area was a logical
eventuality in the minds of many people. In addition, the possibility of there
being inhabitants on the planet Mars, or on other nearby worlds, had
become a part of the standard wisdom of the time, and the question of what
such creatures might look like, how they might behave, and whether the
citizens of Earth could conquer them, as they had much of the rest of the
known world in the century preceding the book, were not unusual. In other
words, the audience for the book was highly sympathetic: it appealed to
their more obvious thoughts, but struck a chord in their subconscious as
well. The book is as popular now as when it first appeared, because it still
touches those chords, albeit with less direct force today.

Wells had a great interest in the subject, and had discussed it several
times with his brother Frank, who suggested to Bertie the germ of the idea.
According to H.G., Frank Wells doubted even more strongly than his
brother that our civilization had the ability to meet crises either bravely or
intelligently, and the book was written to deal with that problem. Wells was
also thinking at the time of the destruction of the Tasmanian aborigines, a
subject which had created substantial debate, although unfortunately after
the fact. Moreover, Wells wrote widely in this period on the idea that
substances which could provide a basis for life, particularly silicon, might
be found on other planets, and this notion crept into his description of the
Martian invaders, although we see much more of their fighting machines
than of the invaders themselves. As early as 1893, in the narrow confines of
their cram book, *Honours Physiography*, Wells (and Gregory) had discussed
Martian dwellers. In fact they discussed the supposed sighting of Martian
canals, and in his days of writing for the *Saturday Review*, the young
scientist gave the subject a strong treatment in his piece 'Intelligence on
Mars'.[9]

In this piece Wells had said that, as far as was known at that time, Mars
was very similar to Earth, and he saw no reason why protoplasm could not
have evolved into beings designed to inhabit their area. However, he
warned that they would not be like humans, as conditions were bound to be
different further from the sun, and he described several possible types
within the bounds of known hereditary theory. In fact Wells said that to

assume that these beings would be like us was the worst sort of naïve anthropomorphism, and was only an aspect of the 'cosmogonies and religions invented by the childish conceit of primitive man'. Wells was very careful in his own novel not to go beyond what was possible, even asking his doctor, Henry Hick, for advice on a disease which might prevent the Martian takeover, as their world was different from ours.[10]

The War of the Worlds is a *tour de force*, and one of its joys for the modern analyst is that with early versions of the Ordnance Survey maps it is still possible to follow exactly where the Martians went, even which houses they destroyed. Wells wrote the book while living in Woking, and the area behind his house on Horsell Common is the scene of the first confrontation.

The book opens with a discussion of the idea that Mars seems, to observers, to be growing colder and dying. The Martians simply need a new home, and Wells uses the Tasmanian aborigines as an example.

The Martians land near London on their quest, and their need causes them to repel, with a Heat-Ray projected from a parabolic mirror, the initial deputation of Earth men. The insect-like beings, buried in the top layers of the earth, now begin to construct machines in which they can travel in their desire for conquest. As humans discuss generally their methods of repelling the invaders, while doing nothing about it, Wells reminds us of our anthropomorphism by likening us to the dodo, lording it in his nest, discussing the arrival of the sailors 'in want of animal food'. 'We will peck them to death tomorrow, my dear.'

Ten missiles of invaders have been launched, each creating its own Fighting Machine which strides on its tripod legs, first over Maybury Hill, the Oriental College and other sites in Woking, but then outward. Battle ensues, and although one fighting machine is destroyed with a lucky hit, the invaders are inexorable. The narrator meets various types of human response in his and their flight before the Martians, especially that of a curate who passes on the visits as simply an indication that what was foretold in the Book of Revelation is occurring. We are able in the book to see the machines move over the countryside, down the valley of the Thames, from the reports of the narrator's brother. We find that the Martians communicate with their compatriots with a sort of mechanical ululation, and when harassed are able to release a gaseous death-ray as well as their heat weapon.

The descriptions of the flight of the English before the monsters is extremely well done, as Wells uses to great advantage detail from his many bicycle trips all over the south-east of England. We are, so to speak, always on home ground, and the details of the crowds give tremendous credibility to the descriptions. Wells describes these events, in chapter 17, as 'It was the beginning of the rout of civilization, of the massacre of mankind', and the reader does not think that this is excessive, as he reads of the breakdown of morals, ethics, and the brutalization of the frightened hosts.

In this section we are enlightened by the last valiant efforts of a naval vessel, the *Thunder Child*, but even the exertions of the senior service, extraordinary and brave as they may be, are not enough. The Martians win everywhere.

In Book II we meet the Martians close up, observed from a hide under a destroyed building. They are beings which consist mostly of head, with no visible nostrils, a beak and two large eyes. There are sixteen tentacles near the mouth, used as hands, but these beings are mostly brain and lungs, evolved in the thinner Martian atmosphere. They live by injecting food (blood from other animals in the earth's environment) directly into their veins. On Mars, Wells deduces from his observations, their food is human-like beef cattle with a silicon base to their skeletonic structure. Another fact about the Martians is that they work twenty-four hours a day, and are never tired or fatigued. In this context Wells cites, indirectly, his own article on 'The Man of the Year Million' as proof of the scientific base of his observations.

However, the Martians have not prepared for everything, as earth bacteria first attack the red weed which succeeds the death-ray, and then the Martians in the Fighting Machines themselves. This does not occur until the Martians have begun the construction of a flying machine to conquer other areas. The narrator and an artilleryman, also an escapee from the first fight at Horsell Common, join forces and observe these activities. The artilleryman offers some comments on survival which are significant, about the need to preserve the species until we can learn enough about the invader, and the need to sacrifice the drones of the area, if necessary, in order to survive, while relying on controlled breeding and education to reach the heights necessary for survival. Alas, the artilleryman is like most others, all talk and no action, but fortunately for the narrator and the reader, the bacteria intervene to do the job instead. The last Martian dies, attempting to communicate with his fellows: 'Ulla, ulla, ulla' echoes from Primrose Hill, and is heard by the narrator as he reconnoitres 'dead London', close to his South Kensington site, highly symbolic — as, of course, is much of the work.

Wells, the scientist, does offer a moral for the reader. On earth the natural selection process has left humans resistant to the bacteria, but not the Martians. Implicit in this is the view that although we may be resistant today, we will not be so for all time — the end is inexorable, evolution and natural selection will combine with astronomy to end the world, perhaps not as the Martians did, but inevitably just the same.

In the story Londoners and others now begin to pick up the pieces, and restore the world, allowing the narrator to preach his moral unhindered. As he says, 'We have learned now that we cannot regard this planet as being fenced in and a secure abiding-place for Man; we can never anticipate the unseen good or evil that may come upon us suddenly out of space. . . .' Wells went on to remark that it was necessary to support scientific research and 'the conception of the commonweal of mankind'.

His book is a rattling good yarn, and has formed the basis for literally dozens of books since which deal with the threat of invasions from outer space, as well as the basis for our own journeys as the earth begins to cool down. Wells had another point to make, however, and that is that although we should be alert to these problems, half of the success needed can come from anticipation, education, and above all the concerted efforts of the species, not the frantic response of London to the Fighting Machines.

The War of the Worlds moved rapidly to tremendous success. Pinker was avid in his desire to promote the work, through illustrations, and posters throughout England. He worked very hard, in what was perhaps his first great success as an agent, to get excellent terms for Wells, not only for the book but also for the serial rights, sold eventually to *Pearson's* in Britain and *Cosmopolitan* in the US. The reviews were almost uniformly favourable, and such persons as J. M. Barrie wrote ecstatically of the book and its impact on them. Barrie toyed in fact with a dramatic version, but Wells had a greater sense of reality, and after a desultory six months of discussion, the two friends agreed not to do any further work and celebrated by going to a cricket match. Even without the play, however, it was clear, and soon after publication, that Wells had a hit on his hands. The book has never been out of print; it clearly set patterns for much science fiction since that time, and has been a money-spinner for the Wells Estate, with its film versions as well as the novel itself. One can be forgiven the query as to whether the success of the book has overshadowed its message of the need for co-operation. Certainly most of those who have written on the subject since have not used that as a theme, assuming, as Wells did when he spoke in the person of the artilleryman, that talk was easy, but the work was probably more than human beings were willing to undertake.[11]

If one of the great desires of humans is to be invisible to others, and this apparently is a childhood fantasy for many persons, an even greater fantasy and desire is (or at least was, before it was actually achieved) to go to the moon. Popular songs, and popular fantasy, have provided the moon with many odd versions of our own species. As a place for lovers to spend a honeymoon, or other time away from reality, the moon has long had a leading place in the minds and myths of humans. Jules Verne had written one such fantasy in the 1880s in his *Voyage to the Moon*, but Wells was not satisfied with the science in that book. His own next work in this vein, eventually published as a book in 1901, was entitled *The First Men in the Moon*. When he came to reprint the book in the Atlantic Edition he described it as an 'imaginative spree', and said, 'it is probably the writer's best "scientific romance".'[12]

One of the reasons it is the best of Wells's work based on science is that all the scientific aspects — gravity on the moon, the impact of the sun on the moon's surface, and even what that surface might be like — were vetted by Richard Gregory, who called on leading experts in astronomy, astronomical physics, and other disciplines to ensure that the book was accurate, within the bounds of knowledge and theory of that time.[13]

The novel was written as a serial; in fact, it originally began life as a series of three interconnected short stories, but the *Strand*'s editor, Greenhalgh Smith, liked the work well enough to ask Wells to extend it to ten, and later even more, instalments. For that reason, the second part of the book seems appended, tacked on, and is of less interest to modern readers. It is amusing to find that the novel begins with the narrator, Bedford, off by himself attempting to write a play, but not succeeding. Wells was thinking of the stage at this time and he was writing with a wry view of his efforts. This part of the book, and the meeting with the inventor of the moon vehicle, Cavor (the original stories), are quite humorous, and it was not until the piece was extended that it became more serious. In the next section Wells deals with the concepts of gravity and the earth's resistance, weightlessness in space (a good description of what travellers later experienced), the concept of the solar wind, and other matters of concern to moon visitors. On the moon his travellers are caught, escape, and one, the narrator, is able to return to earth. The remainder of the work consists mainly of fragments of messages from Cavor, who is stranded on the moon. In these Wells again describes differing education for differing castes, with the sum of knowledge maintained in brains in a central storehouse by the Selenites. Each denizen of the moon is educated for the one thing in his life, and that is all. There is no general knowledge or education for the sake of learning in this society. Wells carries this part of the story a bit further than in earlier work, when the leading Selenite, the Grand Lunar, subjects Cavor to a major inquisition on earth and its characteristics. The Grand Lunar cannot understand the folly of separate languages, of warfare rather than co-operation, but does not do very much more with these contrasts than marvel on them. Wells himself sees a world of caste, limited possibility, and suppression; the Grand Lunar sees conflict, violence, and warfare. Neither world seems very good, in fact, and the messages from Cavor die away 'for evermore into the Unknown — into the dark, into that silence that has no end', as the book itself dies away.

Again we have the phenomenon of a book that was very well received. As has been said, it grew by demand of the magazine editor, and when it was published in book form considerable care was taken over the illustrations. Even though unrest over the Boer War cut back book sales in Britain generally, Wells's work continued to move very well, although not as well as Pinker and Wells hoped. Pinker surveyed Mudie's, and the other lending libraries, and reassured the author that it was not just his books that were down, but reading generally. He told him that people would read again once the tide had turned in the war, and the present tragedy was over. However, even with the unrest, Wells's books did sell in the US, and both in the colonies and at home. He was now able to obtain advances that were substantial for that time: £500, for example, for the 'Amazing Adventures of Mr Cavor', as the book was originally called, and this for the US rights alone.[14].

Wells fumbled a bit in his purpose with *The First Men in the Moon*, good as the science was. His message was blurred, the book ended weakly, and although it kept his name before the public because in general it was well written, and was well received, his interest in his other work (especially *Love and Mr Lewisham* and *Anticipations*) meant that he had skimped his possibilities somewhat. When he returned to scientific romance it would be with a volume not only filled with meaning, but with some of his tightest and most evocative writing as well. That book, *The Food of the Gods*, published in 1904, was a major contribution to his work in this genre.

Wells himself later termed the book 'the completest statement of the conception that human beings are now in violent reaction to a profound change in conditions demanding the most complex and extensive readjustments in the scope and scale of their ideas'. Wells remarked in his preface to the novel in the Atlantic Edition that that conception was the general premise underlying nearly all of his work, both fiction and non-fiction, and he urged that *Food of the Gods* be read in conjunction with *Anticipations*.[15] There is little doubt in the reader's mind about the book's purpose, and although the theme permeates the story, the writing is of such a quality that even readers who did not accept the idea liked the story very much. It was Wells's greatest success since *The Time Machine* and *The War of the Worlds*. The message was so strong, in fact, that *Pearson's Magazine*, publishers of the serial, asked Wells to alter the book to provide some fighting and, by implication, less message: eventually Wells did tone it down somewhat in its serial form (as Pinker told him both Joseph Conrad and Henry James had found it expedient to do). He reinserted the suppressed passages when it came out in book form. Wells even gave readers of the serial one whole chapter on giant kangaroos which did not appear in the book. In fact, the two forms of the work differ fairly substantially.[16]

The opening section of Book I defines science and scientific thought and is a considered attack on the direction of much science. The scientists portrayed are weak, bumbling caricatures. Wells's view of science as practised in most laboratories is that it stultifies real work and diminishes accomplishment, as scientists are frightened to take ideas to the natural limits of experimental work. The researcher is seen as content with limited results and, in fact, wishes only to maximize technological usage, with the possibility of great wealth for the inventor. From this beginning the reader is introduced to the invention (creation) of a miracle food which will induce great growth, to be called Herakleophorbia — in translation, the nutrition of Hercules. The inventors purchase an experimental farm in Kent where they plan to administer their new substances, but, true to type, do not have sufficient control of their experiment; and this control is diminished when their research assistants, the Skinners, prove to be veritable paragons of sloth, sloppiness, and stupidity. As a result other giants, rather than just the chickens of the experiment, emerge — wasps, earwigs, vines, and eventually giant rats. The chapter about the rats, with the hair's-breadth escape of a doctor from their attack, may well be the most frightening and most realistic writing Wells ever accomplished.

The experiment goes on, and the rats are killed by a safari. The other giant growths are also either eliminated or isolated, but the Food is now being administered to children — scientifically to the offspring of the inventors but in more casual ways to other children, such as Mrs Skinner's grandchildren, as she steals some of the Food. The inventors, after considerable discussion, agree to give the Food to the children to see what will happen. In this portion of the book Wells provides a good discussion of whether science should go on without analysis, or whether an ethical position needs to be arrived at which will study research and potential results, especially with regard to human subjects. The experiment with Herakleophorbia is justified in part, by some analysts, because others will simply attempt to create and administer the Food, and they need to be forestalled. The arguments mirror those since on a number of matters.

In Book II of the work, Wells discusses bigness, gigantism, and the growth of slackness, power for the sake of power, in terms of this Food and its results. Well-wishers wring their hands, but the Food continues to be distributed, and its results seen. As Wells says, 'It was bigness insurgent.' The latter portion of Book II discusses the dissemination of the Food and the political divisions that occur over it. Here Wells dissects a village, Cheasing Eyebright, and its reactions, to make his point, using one of his better puns to lead into the description of the local vicar who had gone 'to an ivy-clad public school in its anecdotage'. Mrs Skinner's terrible grandchild is revealed, the discovery of Lady Wondershoot, who rules the village; and Albert Edward Caddles, the child, is finally sent off to work in the Wondershoot chalk quarry, in order to confine him. The child cannot understand this, and he asks his mother, '"If it's good to work, why doesn't everyone work?"'

With this statement the meaning of the book is revealed completely: it is more than just an attack on slovenly science. Wells has the brilliant idea of using a criminal released from prison who travels through the countryside, to comment on the new Food and its impact. This discussion is devastating. The children, forty feet high, are opposed by a Tory politician, Caterham, who portrays himself as Jack the Giant-killer. The slogan of the giant-suppression group, 'Grasp your nettle before it is too late', is a delicious way of showing the limits of possible human reaction, or, in Wells's view, the limits at that time. Ordinary people emerge to join Caterham, especially as it appears that private property and private rights are under attack, and the war of the two forces is anticipated by the reader.

Wells uses a love affair among the giants to provide an opportunity for them to join together, all except Albert Edward, who takes a violent trip to London, where he is eventually killed. In the ensuing war of the two groups, the giant children, who now envisage a world under their control, one which is reformed, better and fairer, and one without violence, win the first round, or at least a stalemate is created between the two forces. Caterham, now elevated to Prime Minister, calls the inventor of the Food to him, and he agrees to act as ambassador to the children, to offer them a haven in North America, Africa, or on some other reservation.

The giants discuss the offer, and after agreeing that giants and pygmies cannot co-exist in the form they then find themselves, a spokesperson for the giants, and a son of one of the inventors, simply remarks,

> 'But that is what Caterham says! He would have us live out our lives, die one by one, till only one remains, and that one at last would die also, and they would cut down all the giant plants and weeds, kill all the giant under-life, burn out the traces of the Food — make an end to us and to the Food forever. Then the little pygmy world would be safe. They would go on — safe forever, living their little pygmy lives, doing pygmy kindnesses and pygmy cruelties each to the other; they might even perhaps attain a sort of pygmy millennium, make an end to war, make an end to over-population, sit down in a world-wide city to practise pygmy arts, worshipping one another till the world begins to freeze. . . .'
>
> (Book II, ch. 5)

The giants agree after this statement that the Food must be manufactured and made available to the world. The laws of science demand it, and the battle is on, whether one wants it or not, to make the world better. The results are inevitable, and the earth will simply be a footstool for the ultimate growth of sanity.

The reader, taken up in the glow of the Wellsian forecast, closes the book with a wide view of the prospects. Wells's attacks on science and on the routine scientific establishment mind, with the drudgery science means for most, are enhanced by the discussion of the symbolic Food, which we can take to be socialism, and which will triumph, even though under attack from the Caterhams of the time; eventually it will transform the world of pygmies into a world of giants, the home of the blessed.

Wells's friends thought this book wonderful, and were nearly ecstatic with it and its powerful view of the future. Some, G. K. Chesterton in particular, realized the threat the Wells vision posed for Edwardian life. Wells was the object of a sophisticated attack from Chesterton, in an important chapter of his book published the next year, *Heretics*. Chesterton understood clearly that the story of Jack the Giant-killer lay at the foundation of human mythology — that if the small and insignificant could not have the hope of occasional triumph, then they could not be suppressed. Their anger would lash out, and the inevitable class war would come. As Chesterton said at the end of his essay, 'If we are not tall enough to touch the giant's knees, that is no reason why we should become shorter by falling on our own. But that is at bottom the meaning of all modern hero-worship and celebration of the Strong Man, the Caesar, the Superman. That he may be something more than man, *we* must be something less.'[17]

Chesterton's celebration of individuality missed the point that the giants of Wells's book could be Everyman and that their individuality worked only if some were more equal than others — if one will, that Jack could only succceed by slaying the giant whenever he became too much to handle. Wells simply thought that this concept put too much trust in the vagaries of human nature.

Wells's other friends were less analytical, perhaps, but they certainly praised the book. Gregory wrote immediately to congratulate him, welcoming 'the divination of things of natural science and sociology that have hitherto been unheeded but are revealed by the magic rod with which you write'. Beatrice Webb found the book filled with 'wit and wisdom', although she objected to the idea of food as a device for transmitting world betterment. She said that she herself had a difficulty with food intake (she often went on rather faddish diets in the hope of controlling some mental and physical problems she thought were a legacy from her childhood romance with Joseph Chamberlain and her friendship with Herbert Spencer). The Webbs invited the adult Wellses for a weekend, and gave Wells a formal evening party the following December to honour this remarkable book and his other writings.[18]

Perhaps the strongest and most analytical comment Wells received came from Violet Paget ('Vernon Lee'), who wrote him a long detailed letter on *The Food of the Gods*. She welcomed the optimism of the book, and said in her letter (written early in their friendship), 'I am extremely interested in the development of your optimism together with your maturity as a thinker and romancer. There is infinitely more grasp, more understanding, and more in the truthfulness with which you let down the curtain on your decidedly intrusive and troublesome giants, than in the [*word illegible*] book.' (This latter book mentioned is probably not by Wells.) Paget, partially as a result of this correspondence as well as several reviews and articles she and Wells wrote about each other's work, became close friends with the Wellses, and later spent several weekends with them at Sandgate. After one such visit, she returned to London with her discussions with H.G. and Jane high in her thoughts. She was revolted by the filth and callousness of the city, but more importantly by its unwillingness to accept responsibility. 'The horrible overdressed people hurrying about in carriages — horrible greasy drum . . .' seemed to her to be what Wells was writing and thinking about.

She then asked Jane to try and limit Wells's involvement with the Fabians. The point for her was for Wells 'to write more books like *The Food of the Gods*, making people recognize immediately who is at the back of this smug reserve'. Paget, who disavowed socialism as a way to utopia, thought the Wellsian books would help create an atmosphere in which a series of accidents, or clever methods, such as cheaper foods, could get to their jointly hoped-for goals.[19] Most readers welcomed this particular well-written book of his, whether or not they accepted the road to a better life offered by H. G. Wells.

The Food of the Gods marks the transition from Wells's scientific romances to his 'fiction about the future'. The earlier novels certainly carry a message to the reader, but they can be and have been read by many who simply turn the pages in sheer enjoyment. These novels are nearly all still available, many of them as paperbacks, and a new audience springs up every decade to read and enjoy them.

Interestingly enough, a search through bookshop display cases is much less likely to turn up paperbound editions of the last three scientific fictions of this period, although large portions of these books are as well written, as clearly realized, and hold the interest of the casual reader as strongly as do the earlier works. It is simply that the message has moved to the forefront, and publishers in Wells's own time, as well as in ours, were less happy about printing large editions of these works. Wells knew that publishers are conservative by nature, in both their choice of works to sponsor and which authors to take into their stable. He always stood outside the common run, both in his own view and in theirs.

By the time of World War I, Wells had nearly ceased to write short stories. A number would be written later, and some of them are extraordinary in their impact. One thinks immediately of 'An Answer to Prayer' and 'The Pearl of Love' as works of great intellectual power; and his ventures into the novella form, *The Croquet Player*, *The Brothers*, *The Camford Visitation*, and *The Happy Turning*, all belong to this strain in his writing. Although the short story as a vehicle for art and thought no longer played a major part in his work after World War I, during the period under discussion, he wrote about fifty short stories. These were published widely in a dozen journals and collected in six books. In these books, *The Stolen Bacillus and other Incidents* (1895), *The Plattner Story and Others* (1897), *Tales of Space and Time* (1898), *Twelve Stories and a Dream* (1903), *Thirty Strange Stories* (1897), and *The Country of the Blind and Other Stories* (1911), Wells occasionally reprinted stories from others of his collections, and also occasionally included a story or two that had not previously appeared. From time to time one finds other stories uncollected.

The student of Wells needs to read these works carefully. There has been as yet no detailed analysis of their literary content and their relation to his longer works; for the present, a simple analysis of their types must suffice. The stories fall into half a dozen major categories. The first, which features large or unusual animals, came directly from the science speculation of Wells's student days. Many of these involve new species, or larger versions of known species. The best examples, at least as I read them, are 'The Moth', 'The Sea-Raiders', and 'The Valley of Spiders'. From these stories it was only a short step for Wells to fiction which dealt simply with the changed circumstances of the subjects of the work. Some of these are among his most poignant and searching work in this genre. The observer of his early life senses the immediate and detailed use of his childhood desires, the rage at the world which seemed to deny them, and the dreams and reveries of change which ensued. His heroes are often faced with the choice of whether to go on and take the change offered, or remain as they are. Occasionally the acceptance of change brings about a denouement, through the circumstances being altered beyond recognition, or through the realization that the change is illusory. 'The Door in the Wall', 'The Beautiful Suit', 'The Star', 'The Magic Shop', 'The Crystal Egg', and Wells's triumph in this genre, 'The Country of the Blind', can still be read as illuminating the desires of youth, and they provide the reader with an opportunity to observe reality through the sharp eyes of H. G. Wells.

His scientific background and speculation provided the matrix for 'The Stolen Bacillus' (with its marvellous twist from the macabre to the ludicrous), as well as the analytical strength of 'In the Abyss', and 'A Slip Under the Microscope'. Wells thought often of the world of the future, and wrote widely about it after the turn of the century – providing us with 'The Lord of the Dynamos', 'The Argonauts of the Air', and the several versions of what would be the transmuted *Sleeper*, 'The New Accelerator', 'A Dream of Armageddon', and 'A Story of the Days to Come'. As 'Armageddon' ends, '"Nightmares," he cried; "Nightmares indeed! My God! Great birds that fought and tore!"'

He used his own past much less directly in this sort of work, although 'The Cone' is a powerful story of the Potteries (but not a scientific romance). This story led to his long friendship with Arnold Bennett, who simply had to know anyone who could write as powerfully of the Five Towns as in this work. That story and 'The Sad Story of a Dramatic Critic' both come out of Wells's earlier life. Perhaps less well known today, but also worth recalling, are his efforts to discuss the past, the deep past, when it was still a very real question as to what had actually happened to Neanderthal man in the conflict which led to the adaptation that is our human form today. In recent years Jean Auel, Jorgen Kirsten, and others have ventilated this question again in fiction. Wells preceded them with 'The Grisly Folk' and the five-part 'Story of the Stone Age'.

It is remarkable how well many of the stories stand up today and from time to time are rediscovered. A few years ago a reprint was issued of *The Door in the Wall*, Wells's collaboration with Alvin Langdon Coburn, the great photographer. This collection of short stories illustrated by Coburn's romantic photographs, unavailable since 1911, was read by a reviewer for the *New Yorker* for whom it was clearly a new experience. The reviewer fell over himself to praise the compact and forceful writing. Most readers, especially those new to the books, would feel the same way.[20]

Over the years the so-called subsidiary rights in Wells's work increased in value. His books were translated into many languages. The Italian rights to the early books, translated by a Dr Vallardi, went for £12 each in 1901. The Spanish rights to *War in the Air* brought £15. The French and the Germans devoted the most care to the translation, however. Up till 1912 Henry Davray, working with B. Kosakiewicz of the Libraire of the *Mercure de France*, did most of the translation into French. Proust, enchanted with Wells, attempted some translations, although his command of English simply was not good enough to finish the task. In German the translations were carried out by Felix Paul Greve, who after his move to Canada was to produce, as F. P. Grove, some outstanding novels of the prairies, work still standard in Canadian fiction. Greve translated *Dr Moreau*, *The First Men in the Moon*, and *Sleeper*; his translation of *The Time Machine* is still the standard German version. All of these works were published by J.G.C. Bruns of Minden. Nearly every one of Wells's works was available, soon after English publication, in German, French, Italian, and Spanish. Greek and Dutch translations, and occasionally Turkish, Swedish, Norwegian, and Russian followed. Every major work of Wells's also became available in the Tauchnitz editions. It took a considerable amount of Pinker's time to supervise the translations, see that no pirated editions appeared, and to ensure that each work contributed its bit to the Wells and Pinker coffers. With Wells publishing in as many different periodicals as he did, the copyright problems were also a significant part of Pinker's work.[21]

There was a considerable clamour for new Wells stories, as their publication usually increased the sales of the journals in which they appeared. Wells was able to raise his prices for the work as the demand grew. The *Illustrated London News* paid £60, as an example, for 'The Man Who Could Work Miracles', and while *Twelve Stories and a Dream* was germinating Pinker was able to raise nearly £1,200 on the initial promise of the collection, although the publisher wanted all the stories to be up to the standard of 'Mr Ledbetter's Vacation'. In 1900 five stories for the *Pall Mall Gazette* brought in £400 more; and when *Twelve Stories* appeared, the amount of the advance had risen to £1,500. By 1903 Wells was even sought after for a humorous column, and although he took the first bite, the offer was eventually declined.[22]

Rights in the stories were valuable enough in this period to cause Wells and Pinker to expend substantial effort in recovering rights in the earlier work which Wells had placed so widely. The effort led, in 1908, to the small quarrel with Pinker after which Wells began to look to other agents. Pinker continued to handle the shorter fiction, however, selling some stories to the *Strand* in 1909, for instance. He was unable to get back the other rights, though, and he had to report his lack of success to Jane Wells in 1910. Harpers did allow Wells to reacquire rights in *Tales of Space and Time*. He was then thinking about a collected edition, which had been urged on him by his friend Arnold Bennett, and others. But the failure to obtain enough of the rights put this project into abeyance until the 1920s.[23]

When the Atlantic Edition finally appeared there was a revival of interest in the shorter work, which eventually led to *The Short Stories of H. G. Wells*, published by Benn in 1927 and still in print, with all its problems of incompleteness. Magazines also began to be interested again in Wells's stories, and there was a flurry of republication in 1927 and 1928. Increasingly, too, there was a call for the collection of single items in a volume of short stories. The standard price for reprinting a story at that period was set by Wells and his agents at 20 guineas, and few refused to pay it, as Wells's name continued to sell magazines and books. When Hugo Gernsback began to publish the pulp magazine *Amazing Stories* in 1928, he featured a Wells item in most of the early issues, at $50 a time for the author. Gernsback was notoriously slow in remitting, and the publication eventually folded. However, the Wells stories and the early support of his work by the science fiction editor and enthusiast John W. Campbell, meant that a market for Wells's work continued. The pulp market revived interest in Wellsian short fiction, especially in the United States. It has never declined since.[24]

Shorter pieces of Wells's work went into gift books, as when Newnes gave 10 guineas for 'A Slip Under the Microscope' for use in a gift volume. Wells even received a payment from the New Deal: $25 for the use of 'The Country of the Blind' in a Federal Theater production broadcast nationally in the US by WJZ in New York over the Blue Network on 20 October 1938. Ten days later Orson Welles, less scrupulous about paying in advance, was to air his version of *The War of the Worlds* which set off a great panic among those listeners who did not hear the early and slight disclaimer from the studio. Wells was very unhappy at this violation of his rights, as he felt that he had been traduced, but an exchange of letters with his New York agents led to some payment as well as an apology. The use of his book's title (and the transposed plot) was probably simply a misunderstanding. Wells was concerned that the radio show would hurt his message of the period (he had just been lecturing in America, and was on his way to Australia within a month), but in the event his stock was raised by the show, which traded on beginning fears in the US of the German and Japanese menace.[25]

Even in the last days of Wells's life subsidiary rights in his work continued to bring in money. In 1930 Random House had paid him $1,000 for a special introduction to a limited edition of *The Time Machine*, and at the end of World War II Wells was paid another $750 for a version of this piece when the book was used as a dividend for Book-of-the-Month Club members in Canada. He received $150 for the first 4,000 words of *The First Men in the Moon*, and later $1,000 for reprint rights to the novel as a whole in a volume of four early science-fiction novels. *Famous Fantastic Mysteries* serialized *Dr Moreau* and *The War of the Worlds*; Australian rights were sold to *The Time Machine, Sleeper,* and *First Men,* and the months just before his death provided another little flurry of interest with reprints in *Argosy* and the New York *Post.*[26]

Radio interest in Wells's work was very great. After he agreed to speak occasionally on the BBC, and especially on the Empire – later the World – Service in the late '20s, officials at the BBC found that there was world-wide interest in his work. They sought permission to make radio plays out of his works; and many of these plays were rebroadcast several times to their listeners. One of the fascinating things about this is the remarkable attention paid to Wells in what was then the Near East (now the Middle East); in the BBC archives are a substantial number of scripts of his works in Arabic. Wells's agreement with the BBC gave him the right to vet each of these scripts, and even on the pages in Arabic one can still see his initials signifying his approval of the form in which they would be produced. A table in the Notes (p.510) shows the dates of radio productions of Wells's work, compiled from correspondence in the BBC archives.[27]

A detailed analysis might be attempted of which novels were adapted for radio by the BBC, or even which short stories. It is instructive to note that *In the Days of the Comet* was not broadcast in the period 1927–46; the *Sleeper* was aired only once, in 1937, and Wells's work on atomic energy was not broadcast until after Hiroshima and Nagasaki. The selection of works has very little to do with their literary quality, much more with what the works might mean for listeners. Without pushing the issue very far, one might conclude that a sort of crude censorship was operating with reference to certain ideas. Certainly the BBC was always very anxious about what Wells himself would say over the air; and he, in turn, refused to have his work modified by BBC officials. They frequently reached a stalemate.

'Vernon Lee' spoke rightly in her comment on *Food of the Gods* when she urged Wells to write more specifically of the worlds he was satirizing, while hoping to change them. To this end, by 1910, he was to revise *When the Sleeper Wakes* of 1899, and retitle it *The Sleeper Awakes.* By eliminating a weak love story and a great deal of unnecessary continuity in the original plot, Wells now made it a didactic work. *In the Days of the Comet* (1906) will be discussed here only briefly and will be treated later because of its greater relevance to Wells's political and social relations with the wider English community: it too offers, in the guise of scientific analysis, a moral response to the dilemmas of modern society. The last of his novels in this vein, *The World Set Free,* published in the first month of 1914, a fateful year for Wells and others, simply takes the discoveries of modern science and creates a world in which they can be pushed to the limit in their transformation of that world – the title tells everything about Wells's purpose in the book.

Wells would have gone this route anyway. His social life, his political relationships with the Fabian leadership and the Co-Efficients, as well as with the rank-and-file Fabians, especially the younger members, would have provided a matrix for his predictions. He also pursued, for a time, the way of art for art's sake, as a result of his discussions with and his efforts to impress his literary associates in the salon he and Jane maintained on the Channel at Sandgate; so that by then he was free of the need to satisfy artistic criteria in these later novels of science. They were a normal progression in his work.

The last three novels Wells wrote before 1914 in his vein of scientific romance are different from but related to a type of British novel with which Wells was very familiar. Beginning with Richard Jefferies's *After London* (1885), a number of books had suggested that the capitalist world would eventually come to an end (although only M. P. Sheil's novel, *The Purple Cloud*, published in 1901, actually discusses the destruction). Other novels with which Wells's work might be compared are W. H. Hudson's *The Crystal Age* (1887), and William Morris's *News From Nowhere* (1891). All of these works mention some sort of warlike ending and predict a new clean England, but one which is somehow pre-industrial in nature. They are anti-capitalist, approaching Luddism. London often becomes symbolic of all that is destroyed in these accounts, and especially so in Jefferies's brilliant evocation. All of these books, along with many others less well written or realized, appeared at a time of widely discussed natural events (Krakatoa, 1883; Mount Pelee, 1902; and the coming of Halley's comet, 1910), and they are part of a growing literature of apocalypse and predictions of the end of time.[28]

The fact that Wells rewrote the *Sleeper* eleven years after its first publication may have been due in part to the problem of limited early sales, which bothered him considerably. But it was also due to the onset of a second major period of illness, which occurred while the *Sleeper* and *Mr Lewisham* were in gestation and during their birth pangs. The difficulty with the work may also reflect Wells's view of his personal life by 1910.

Wells wrote three different prefaces and introductions to the book on its various appearances. All are variations on the theme of the need to rewrite, but the first two (of 1911 and 1921) are more useful for the analyst, as they discuss Wells's feelings about the book, and his reasons for restructuring it with a tighter plot line and the elimination of the extraneous baggage of the love affair. When he came to discuss the book in the Atlantic Edition he repeated, but softened, his words on his illness, and described the *Sleeper* as 'one of the most ambitious and least satisfactory of my earlier books'. So he continued to have a strong affection for the work.[29]

And well he might have, because the *Sleeper* is an ur-book for two other novels which have been highly significant for our time. The first of these, Evgeny Zamyatin's *We*, translated in 1924, became the foundation book for Russian science-fiction writing; and for some it provided a Marxist analysis of capitalism which is useful. In fact the book was also read as an attack on the early years of Soviet society. In the west, Wells's book is the basis (with Zamyatin's work also used for part of the background) of George Orwell's *Nineteen Eighty-Four*. Both the later books end unpleasantly and provide an extremely graphic idea of what capitalism, carried to its end, will become. Wells's work, on the other hand, is somewhat more optimistic, but the end of capitalism is, as in most of his work, left to the protagonists to work out — in this case the sleeper and his story represent western civilization. Orwell referred specifically to the work as important, in an as-yet-unreprinted obituary of Wells, and Zamyatin, before his untimely death, wrote one of the good early critical essays on Wells, which was revised and became the introduction, in 1924, to the second collection of Wells's writing in Russian. (The first such collection appeared in 1912, and Wells himself wrote the introduction.) So it is that an unrealized work, rewritten to a large extent for its second edition, and one which the author, fond of it as he might have been, still felt was a failure, provided the leading ideas for books still read and discussed today, and often — perhaps usually — by people who have not read the work that inspired them.[30]

The *Sleeper* is a version of the Rip Van Winkle story, the chief difference being that the sleeper has slept for somewhat over two hundred years, rather than twenty. When he does wake up, and emerges from the catafalque on which he has been placed, he finds that compound interest, and two or three bequests, have made him owner of the world. This ownership, managed by a Council, supposedly in trust but for their own interests largely, has created a monster state, with one class of persons living a hedonistic life of pleasure, while others work on deep underground assembly lines with their only hope a vulgar version, in so-called pleasure cities, of the life of the upper class. Wells uses dream sequences and his dream motif at perhaps its most overt, at least in his pre-World War I work, in the telling of the early part of this book. In the world of the woken viewer, many of the aspects of our modern urban life appear — moving sidewalks, aerial transport, a kinetoscope (modern cinema), and 'Babble Machines' to provide a sanitized and heavily edited version of the 'news'. A phonetic spelling (like Esperanto) allows everyone in the talking world to communicate. Graham, the sleeper, is in fact viewing a world quite similar to that shown in futuristic films since that day, including *The Shape of Things to Come*, Wells's and Korda's own masterpiece of film-making.

However, the sleeper's emergence creates a controversy. For who shall lead the Council now? They attempt to seduce Graham (literally) to join them, and he is also wooed by the opposition leader, Ostrog. A great struggle for the person of the sleeper leads to a chase through the futuristic city, but Graham escapes. Ostrog, however, defeats the Council in the ensuing 'battle of the darkness'; and Graham goes to meet him, where he views on television the last stand of the Council.

Unfortunately, 'the beautiful people' also wish to possess Graham; and he is equally revolted by their ideas. In a powerful chapter entitled 'Prominent People' he discusses the sorts of persons who are now in charge in the sleeper's world. One of the most telling of his vignettes is of the Minister of Education, who tells Graham that they have conquered 'cram' in this new world. But Graham then learns that in this world, without examination, the educated learn only obedience and industry. No analysis is needed, and thus only rote learning is used to prepare for the job to be done.

In the original work the love interest is supplied by Ostrog's niece, Helen Wotton, but in the final version she appears only to offer Graham a choice between the worlds he has seen, or one in which his dreams can be put into effect. He, as owner, has every opportunity to do as he wills. In a sense capitalism is able to reform itself, according to this view, and create a utopian existence; but that depends on the will of the sleeper — the desire, in fact, of the reader.

Graham learns to fly an aircraft, enjoying an aerial view of his world. Helen Wotton then introduces him to the people and to his 'responsibility'. Graham is most repelled in his visits to the underworld by the fact that the poor must die hard, vicious deaths, while the rich have an opportunity for 'euthanasy' in their pleasure palaces when life is at an end. The contrast is unbearable, and Graham asks Ostrog how he can participate in this brutal farce. Ostrog says that the people need to be put down so that a revolution can be managed to meet his ideals, not theirs. Ostrog is, in fact, as big a manipulator as the Council. A complete reversal of liberty, equality, fraternity, and a subversion of ethics has taken place.

Ostrog now threatens imported black police to control the revolution; and this, a rare case in which Wells uses a racial stereotype, revolts Graham. War to the death follows, in the air and on the ground. Graham flies off to battle against the black intruders, and then against Ostrog himself. He is apparently triumphant; but the story ends with him falling to oblivion, 'back to earth, in a vision, in a dream'. This powerful work with its ambivalent ending suggests that if Graham really wishes, he could modify the world. Once he is back on earth, the question left to the reader's imagination is, will he succumb to Ostrog's temptation or will he let the scene play out — or will he, less likely perhaps, interfere to redress the observed wrongs? The end of the revolution is unknown.

Sleeper was a difficult book to write, and remains difficult to analyse, not least because the echoes of it in Orwell's later book colour the work for the modern reader. It did not sell very well, and this disturbed Wells, coming as it did just when his need of money was quite large because of his illness and medical bills, to say nothing of the need to move from London to obtain sea air. Pinker wrote several letters urging Wells not to be disheartened, and eventually he was able to place both it and the other book of this period, *Tales of Space and Time*, with fairly substantial advances.

Pinker told Wells that it was not his fault, 'and it is important you should be at peace *with yourself*.'[31]

Readers liked the *Sleeper*, in general. J. M. Barrie, to whom Wells had sent a copy, told him it was not up to *The War of the Worlds*; but Wells knew that already. Barrie did describe it as 'a wonderful piece of imagination', even if he was frightened that Wells might find less and less of good to write about in his futuristic work. A reviewer in the *Academy* was also disturbed at the vision. As the writer said, 'Possibly Mr Wells's pessimistic speculations concerning the trend of civilization are right, possibly they are mistaken. We hope with all our heart that they are wrong....' The reviewer said that he personally was reconciled to life now and death in due course, which meant that substitute Grahams appeared everywhere in actual fact.[32]

The novel remained in Wells's mind, and several of his shorter pieces at the end of the next decade bore a resemblance to it. In 1908, in fact, he told his New York agent that he was turning over in his mind a novel on the idea of progress, with a dream of a world five hundred years ahead. In the pieces the narrator falls into suspended animation and wakes to find a brigand population in control. He is forced to act as a Highland chief might have in similar circumstances, in order to revive civilization. In the projected work the chief, according to the letter, would later fall in love and throw the project to the winds. The agent was to ask prospective publishers for a large advance before Wells began this work, but he abandoned the idea almost immediately. Instead he revised the *Sleeper* with its similar plot, while some of the germs of the novel remained fallow in his brain waiting for *The Shape of Things to Come*, a work with strong affiliations with the *Sleeper* as well as the short stories written when these ideas occupied his thoughts.[33]

Two later novels by Wells in this period did provide a response to Graham's dilemma. The first, *In the Days of the Comet*, became much more important for its supposed depiction of Wellsian views on marriage and sex. Discussion of the work therefore belongs, as I have said, in a different place in this work. For our purposes here the story is simple. The narrator is seen as the worst that capitalism can do — he is, in addition, a prototype of the young Wells. A companion, while exclaiming, '"Science! What we want now is socialism, not science!"', is specifically refuting the world in which Wells had lived and worked. The hero falls in love, has his girlfriend stolen from him by an upper-class rival, and falls into insensate rage against the circumstances. He procures a revolver, goes to hunt down the couple, but is overcome, as is everyone else, including the warring navies of Britain and Germany, by a soft, lovely green cloud from a comet's tail, which has brushed the earth. The upshot is peace and harmony. The war ends. It is an evocation of what might have occurred if the Germans had interfered in the Boer War, or of other events to come.

Leadford, the narrator, then comes awake to a world of peace. Capitalism is overturned in the wake of the comet's impact, and a conference is called to institute the world state. Broad principles are accepted immediately — private ownership is eliminated; there is a common education for the young; and new cities (somewhat like those evoked by William Morris) spring up in the clean-up and reconstruction which follow. The new world allows the lovers, in groups of three or four, to live lives of harmony. This is a simplified view of the book, but it shows that Wells was now using his novels of science to feed directly into his desire for a better world. The comet was evoked in response to Sheil's *Purple Cloud* and perhaps partly in response to the press comments on the return of Halley's comet (always a significant part of British mythology, as it often appeared at times of great social change in Britain). The book plays also on the forthcoming struggle for supremacy between Germany and Britain; while on the personal side it has echoes of Wells's life with Jane, Amber Reeves, and others. It is a highly personal novel and came under great attack, ostensibly because of its moral content, but as often, in fact, for its prediction of socialism and its attack on the vulgarity of capital.

Wells's friends, especially Gregory, received the novel with joy and affection. 'Yours is a trumpet voice and the walls of Jericho must fall down before it in the course of time. For what you say is merciless logic. . . .' was the latter's view. Gregory understood that the comet symbolized the long-term change that was necessary as human nature stood inexorably in the way. He ended his letter, which Wells must have received with great pleasure, 'This divine afflatus must come before Socialism or Communism or any other scheme can regenerate the world.' Reviews by others were less friendly, although some appreciated the book; as the reviewer in the *Outlook* remarked, 'Yet art which clothes a book of purposely disjected earnestness like this is of great service to humanity.' Others actually thought that the work was a satire on socialism itself. But the attacks focused chiefly on Wells's views of love and family life; socialism was only a vehicle for attacking the author in these analyses,[34] and they are better treated in that later context.

Wells, who thought the title weak once he saw the book in its serial form, urged Macmillan to use an alternative. Of those he suggested he preferred *The Comet of the Sweeter Air*, but he was prepared to accept *The Lovers' Comet*, *The Comet of the Opened Hearts*, or *The Comet of the New Birth*. None of these alternatives was acceptable; and, in retrospect, they all sound artificial or forced. They do, however, give us further insight into the fact that Wells had now turned quite completely to didactic fiction, at least in this genre, by the time of the *Comet*'s genesis. His fellow futurist of the time, Robert Blatchford, writing about the book for the *Clarion*, produced what amounted to a panegyric: it was the didacticism that made the book most worthwhile for *Clarion* readers, according to Blatchford. The editor did say that comets would not produce the change of which Wells had provided such a telling description. Instead, hard work, love, the hearts of good people, all would tell the tale in time. All Wells had done was to say, '*Allons!* my children! Let us to the grindstone.' But, Blatchford remarked, '. . . if any socialist can read the whole passage aloud with dry eyes and an unbroken voice there must be something sadly amiss with his economic basis, and he ought to be hounded out of the movement.'[35]

The socialism may have been the reason that, although Joseph Conrad had liked the book very much (he read it through the night, according to his letter), he was having second thoughts on it at the time he wrote. As he informed Wells, he had observed the comet, 'but after observation comes computation. . . . In approaching a book of that sort one must do exact thinking. . . .' But Conrad had some rough conclusions. They included great praise for the intensity and lucidity with which Wells presented his youthful hero, while Nettie was 'without a shadow of a doubt the most feminine of all your women'.

Conrad, by this time more ambivalent towards Wells than in earlier days, when he had given fulsome praise and little criticism, went on to complete this very good analytical letter with a paragraph which dealt once more with Wells's shift towards a more didactic purpose:

> I am as yet under the sheer power of your art — the compulsion of it. The day of liberation may come or may never come. Very likely I shall be dead first. But if it does come that will be the day on which I shall marshall my futile objections as to the matters treated in the book.

Conrad had another point of criticism which he felt he could not entrust to a letter; he came and spent a day with Wells, but whether he offered that other criticism on that day, we may doubt. Wells disturbed him, especially in this phase of his writing; and Conrad felt that perhaps he was wasting his talent. But, more importantly, he simply could not accept the ultimate premise of the work. Conrad did not stop reading Wells, and he and Ford Madox Hueffer (later Ford) continued to be moved by the Wells vision; but nevertheless, the old problems of purpose remained for these more 'artistic' friends of Wells.[36]

The *Comet* marks a dividing line in Wellsian fiction about the future. He did not write in that vein for some time thereafter. *The War in the Air* (1908), although superficially part of this group of novels, is even more part of his warnings about the Germans and belongs much more strongly in that discussion. In fact, with the *Comet*, Wells now moved into some new areas of writing; but he returned once more to this sort of fiction in 1913, as he sat in Switzerland at the home of his current friend, 'Elizabeth'. Elizabeth von Arnim was a popular romantic writer of the day; Wells wrote his novel, *The World Set Free*, at her château, Soleil, in Randogne, Switzerland.

As he told Tommy Simmons, 'I've suddenly broken out into one of the good old scientific romances again. And I suddenly need to know quite the latest about the atomic theory and sources of energy.' He had read and mastered Frederic Soddy's book on the subject (Soddy was known to Wells and had explained his work to him, along with that of the Curies, on radium, for which they received the Nobel Prize). Wells's idea for his own book was that men would learn to set up atomic degeneration in the heavy metals, much as they had learned to control fires in coal fields. The result would be limitless energy. Simmons and Gregory were only too happy to help with this project. Wells was effusive in his thanks to them, saying that they had 'put my feet into the way they ought to have gone four or five years ago'. He said that his story idea had matured now to discuss 'artificially induced radioactivity'. And he told Simmons, 'I shall telephone you when I get to London, and we must meet to celebrate my return to science.'[37] He contemplated calling the book 'The Atom Liberates the World'.

Wells dedicated his book to Soddy; and reading it today, one is struck with the prescience of the discussion. The only thing different from our reality is that Wells thought that persons of good will — in the book, Marcus Karenin — would take the atomic power and create a world set free. Revolution was necessary in the context; and the book has a graphic description of these events. But 'highly educated and highly favoured leading and ruling men voluntarily setting themselves to the task of reshaping the world . . . ' (1921 preface) had created the new world of the novel. The book is well written and strong in a number of ways. There is, for instance, good material on the evolution of thought. Early in the book the feeling of the lecture hall, as the material is transmitted to the young, is as powerful an evocation of that setting as I have ever seen.

Wells did not think that his revolution would be easy. He said a choice was present, even after the gift of limitless energy, between agricultural subservience and the acceptance of achieved science as the basis of a new social order. He predicted the devastation of radiation but insisted that 'Civilizations do not end in this manner. Mankind will insist.' Instead, in his book a new world is rebuilt in a formal way, proceeding from rural life, to urban life, to a central language, and then to the adoption of metrics, a standard year, and standard money with token coins based on energy. A new education is analysed and presented so that the young may simply build on the new world from their experiences in the classroom.

However, at the end of the book Karenin, while discussing his life with the writer, does say that science can be a delusion as well. The book, as with so many Wellsian pieces in this genre, thus ends in an ambivalent way. The world has been set free, but at great cost, and through the determination of remarkable people; but the alternative, a bad society which will use science and the promise of atomic energy for evil purposes, is not far away. Since Hiroshima and Nagasaki (and I write this on the anniversary of those acts), and most particularly since the H-bomb explosions on Pacific atolls, readers of this work realize that Wells's second alternative has occurred and his dream remains just that.

The book was swallowed up in World War I, and although it continued to be read by some throughout the interwar period, it was not until newspapers such as the Sydney *Morning Herald* remembered the work in the autumn of 1945 that it received much later attention. Even for the post-Second World War world the message and the dream, with its failure, are too difficult for many readers to accept. Gregory, of course, welcomed the book. 'Science to me stands for truth and righteousness; but the worst of it is that very few people understand anything about its aims, methods, or results. . . . One of the noblest things you are doing is to show the greatness of scientific work and its possible consequences.' This 1914 letter is one of the longest Wells received from his old comrade, but the message for both men was soon overtaken by the horror of the Somme and other French battlefields.[38]

With this book Wells left the genre he had made so completely his own. From *The Time Machine* to *The World Set Free* took only twenty years. In that period he provided a number of 'good reads', shot full of science that made them believable, but also with a message; and a message which increased in intensity as time went on. Each of these books, however, made the subsidiary and, in the long run, more important point that the changes proposed and predicted through the intervention of science could be as evil as they could be good; and the choice of the future lay in the hands of those who saw it clearly and who were willing to take the chance when it was offered.

None of this was much different from the message Wells had been providing on these matters from very early on in his writing career. In a piece for the *Pall Mall Gazette* in 1893 entitled 'The Literature of the Future', he foundered when he predicted some matters, but hit the bullseye directly enough in this comment:

> The old literature was aristocratic, and this age is only the dawn of democracy. The old literature is full of subtle meanings, hinting quotations, faint allusions; it has a classical flavour, like a scent of lavender. The democracy will have none of your classics, it hates allusions and quotations; it likes a writer to be 'clear and sensible'. It is suspicious of being laughed at. . . . The old literature had a soft voice and a gentle insinuating manner; the new literature will be a thing of loud bawling books, shrieking headlines, and slovenly grammar.[39]

A bit later in the decade he thought that this change, in both literature and knowledge, was one that had to be taught and that intrinsic nature is not very plastic; he cited *Dr Moreau* as evidence. However, he did say that he was optimistic and his writing was designed, 'in fact, [to] reconcile a scientific faith in evolution with optimism'.[40]

Wells commented once or twice more on his scientific romances and his purpose in writing them. In 1899, for instance, he confessed to one reviewer that his purpose was greater than the public knew. He said, in fact, that the greatest threat to the hopes of the future was that 'moral intelligence' would not 'overcome the acquisitive egoism of the individual', either through political indifference or a belief that righteousness was simply part of human nature.

> If we must summarize the matter, I would say that the danger arising to humanity out of invention, the danger of the extreme complication of life, is only to be met by education, that is to say, the inculcation of habits of constant thought — thought at home, thought at school, spacious thought about everything with which a human being is concerned.[41]

He continued to be queried by the press and others on this purpose, and he continued patiently to make the sort of statements we have quoted already. Although he would later write and provide a sort of primer of writing 'Fiction About the Future', he allowed himself the luxury of strong analytical comment only once more. That was in the overall introduction to his Atlantic Edition in 1924. Here he not only told of why he wrote what he did, but he was almost brutally forthcoming about why it had been only partially successful. He thought that he provided in his work 'a profound scepticism about man's knowledge of final reality'. But, as time and space were only dimensions which differed in the mental perceptions of *Homo sapiens*, ' . . . both Newtonian space and syllogistic reasoning are simplifications imposed upon us by the limitations and imperfections of our minds.'

Wells went on to remark that this meant inevitably that ideas of Right and of God would become relative and provisional as they were only 'attempts to simplify and so bring into the compass of human reactions what is otherwise humanly inexpressible'. From this view of life Wells said he had drawn the idea of a synthetic Collective Mind, 'arising out of and using and passing on beyond our individual minds'. For Wells, his work, and especially his work in this genre, was 'the theme of . . . the reaction of the passionate ego-centred individual to the growing consciousness and the gathering imperatives of such a collective mind'.[42]

This remains a clear statement of Wellsian thought. It also helps to explain why it is still possible to read his classic pieces of scientific romance without being disturbed by the message in them, or conversely, to be so disturbed by the message that it becomes difficult simply to read them as books. Wells was ambivalent about the future, and nowhere does this appear more clearly than in these works. Conrad was disturbed by the *Comet*, and others by other works of his, but it was equally true that Gregory and Blatchford simply accepted them as wholes, at times almost uncritically. For us, on rereading these marvellous books, it is essential to try to avoid either course, and to read them as guides to the future, but with the Wellsian caveat — only if one has the will.

PART TWO

AUTHOR

FALLING AMONG THE FABIANS

Socialism is to me no clear-cut system of theories and dogmas; it is one of those solid and extensive and synthetic ideas that are better indicated by a number of different formulae than by one, just as one only realizes a statue by walking round it and seeing it from a number of points of view. . . . Socialism for me is a common step we are all taking in the great synthesis of human purpose. . . . We look towards the day, the day of the organized civilized world state. . . . Socialism is to me no more and no less than the awakening of a collective consciousness in humanity, a collective will and a collective mind out of which finer individualities may arise forever in a perpetual series of fresh endeavours and fresh achievements for the race.

HGW, *First and Last Things* (1908)

On 1 January 1901, many people in advanced industrial countries assumed that the new century would mark the triumph of some version of socialism throughout the world. A widespread feeling that capitalism had run its course permeated discussions of the future, and for many the only argument worth pursuing was which road the new state might take, or perhaps, under some circumstances, how it would be formed. Since the French Revolution spokesmen had proclaimed 'Liberty, Equality, and Fraternity'; those ideas loomed for the lower classes and their champions. But as one looks back over the nineteenth century, after that proclamation, it is studded with revolutions fought to gain those ideals, most of which failed; only a very few were moderately successful. What does appear increasingly is a growing nationalism among suppressed peoples as a result of revolutionary ardour, along with what seems to be the reaction to the revolutionary ferment — imperialism, led by the beleaguered ruling classes. This is a superficial history, perhaps, but one accepted in general by most people at the end of the last century. A specific reaction to the history, socialism (but not Marxism), was now on the rise. In Germany,

Bismarck, in England, Joseph Chamberlain, in the United States, E.V. Debs (or even Theodore Roosevelt) all conducted themselves as though socialism were not far away. H. G. Wells was no different.

This socialism implied some sort of world state, especially in the areas of police power, armament, and security for all citizens. However, very little attention was paid to the implications of the rising forces of nationalism and imperialism in the world. For the early analysts of change, free trade, better education, and municipal amenities would elevate humankind, and in that elevation perhaps the problems of war and aggression might lessen and disappear. It would take the horrors of the First World War to sharpen thinking and create a focus on these problems within a framework of analysis. Where Wells was different was that in the twenty years before the war he began to lay out a credo for himself, and for others. And, although the First War would put the finishing touches to that philosophy, it was formed and refined in several books during this period, tempered by a brief flirtation with the Fabian moderates, and finally set down rather clearly in *First and Last Things* (1908), and *The New Machiavelli* (1911).

Wells was prepared for this search both by the events of his life and by his writing in the 1890s. He had found his reason for existence in his writing. His scientific romances had been quite successful, as had his first forays into more personal fiction. His first books in the new century were volumes which dealt with the socialism he felt to be so imminent. As the century began, then, Wells was active in all three strains of his literary effort — science fiction, fiction of life, and social commentary. He was physically located and settled in his new home at Sandgate. His marriage was successful and about to be crowned with a first child. Apparently the move to the sea air had alleviated his medical problems, if not clearing them away completely. Wells used his new location, and the freedom which it, and money, gave him, to devote his life generally to working out his world view in the first decade of the new century.

His name rose rapidly in significance. Soon, many persons and groups began to try and interest him, and even to enlist him in the service of their particular views. Chief among them were the leaders of the Fabian Society, a political and economic study and pressure group founded in the late 1880s, but one now in genteel but heavy competition on the left with the newly elected MPs of the Labour Party and others also concerned with questions of social justice. Wells was intrigued by the group, as it gave him access to a new (and, on the surface, important) agency for reform; but the over-willingness of the Fabians to compromise with the opposition, and their unwillingness to listen to the views of their friends, eventually drove him away. The net result of the Fabian escapade, or diversion, was to give Wells some significant time to reflect on life, resulting in important published work.

Wells's meeting with the Fabians has been overplayed in recent writing. In truth, it did not deflect him much, and although the Fabian Society was changed somewhat, the way to power in England never lay in that direction. However, because the episode involved some remarkable characters, and incidentally spilled over into sexual activity, much has been written about those days.

Wells was a socialist long before the Fabian Society attracted him. He had worn his red tie, attended meetings of socialist groups, and vaguely felt himself part of the coming new order of things ever since his student days. In 1886 he read a paper before the Talkers Club at the Royal College on the subject of socialism, a paper which he later described as theological in method, deducing the need for socialism from self-proclaimed dogmas. It was the work of a young person. During the next three years he read widely, especially in the works of Plato, Burton's *Anatomy of Melancholy*, and Thomas More. He studied Utopias. When he returned to the Royal College to finish his formal education, he spoke on socialism again, this time in a debate with Tommy Simmons, one of his best friends. Wells again took the affirmative view, but this time he presented a positivistic statement of facts, as to why socialism was necessary and inevitable.[1]

Although Wells did not speak or write again specifically on the subject of socialism for some time, it is clear that his mind was busy with the implications of the questions he had raised in his two speeches before his fellow students. In 1894, in one article, he discussed the place of ideals in living the good life, and later that spring, in a long book review, he dealt with the question of the relationship of evolution to the coming socialism. He began reading a good deal of psychology, especially the work of C. Lloyd Morgan, at this time, and soon felt that the new science might offer a way of achieving the socialism he wanted through its ability to classify the various types of minds, so that it would then be possible to create an educational curriculum to fit individual needs. For although Wells believed that man was a creature of instinctual behaviour, nevertheless he thought it might be possible to use acquired factors to modify that instinctive behaviour somewhat. He would return to this idea a great many times over the next half-dozen years, but never more clearly than in the preface to a book by a French follower, Gabriel Tarde, in 1905. In that preface he remarked, 'Very many of us, I believe, are dreaming of the possibility of human groupings of interest and a common creative impulse rather than of injustice and a trade in help and services.'[2]

By the time Wells had written these words, he had begun to think very seriously about socialism in its broadest contexts. In some measure this was because a book of his, written partly because of suggestions from his agent J. B. Pinker and partly because of a request for a serial from Alfred Harmsworth, had taken England by storm. In a series of essays Wells had described in as complete detail as he could muster, the prospective world of the new twentieth century. Appearing serially in 1901 in the *Fortnightly Review* in England and the *North American Review* in the United States, the articles, entitled *Anticipations* (reprinted in book form with a subtitle, 'The Reaction of Mechanical and Scientific Progress Upon Human Life and Thought'), catapulted Wellsian thought into the drawing-rooms, railway cars, and clubrooms of the middle and upper classes.

Pinker had kept after Wells, telling him that it was the responsibility of 'the thinking literary men' to come forward with their views, and after the essays had begun to appear from Wells's pen, Pinker continued to monitor their style, as well as their saleability.[3] It was his push that helped create the popularity as well as the content, although he was as tireless as Wells himself in producing ideas and letters.

Wells became very popular, almost famous in fact, from *Anticipations* and the follow-up discussions. For instance, he found himself being impersonated in the US, by a person who also maintained he was his brother. Pinker told Wells that he should make an American tour, as he was so popular, and this was the genesis of the significant tour of 1906. When the essays appeared in book form, some of the reviews were concerned about the materialism in the work, although in the lee of mostly positive comments these carpers were not really significant. By the time the serial ended in the periodical press, the book was already in its third impression, and went through five more in the next twelve months. It was Wells's first non-fiction bestseller. Pinker was beside himself with pleasure, first urging Wells to write an educational book, to take advantage of the discussion of the text, and later reporting that both Smiths and Mudie's, the two major circulating libraries and booksellers, after first being sceptical, had begun to sell the book in great numbers.

As the new editions of *Anticipations* came off the press, Wells took the occasion to add footnotes commenting on his correspondence. Because of his popularity, he was asked by *Cosmopolitan* to do a series on the French Republic; they hoped as well that he would allow one of their writers, either E. V. Lucas or Arthur Waugh, to interview him. Neither idea came to anything. As discussion of the book continued, Pinker had a leaflet filled with comments on it from scientists and clergymen inserted in all of the leading weeklies, and then left for the US to push the book more vigorously. In the month before Christmas 1901, the book sold 2,430 copies (1,000 in the colonies), and in the next five months nearly 2,000 more were purchased. Eventually a cheap edition was produced, and when sold in conjunction with *Mankind in the Making* (1903), its sequel, and *New Worlds for Old* (1908), a later venture, its popularity remained high. Finally, in 1914, all three books were reissued with new introductions by Wells, who, clearly bemused at his success, took the opportunity to point out that he had not been totally right in his predictions, although the degree of accuracy was certainly phenomenal.[4]

As Wells remarked on the opening page, *Anticipations* allowed him to predict the future, based on current trends, in a way that his and other fiction about the future did not. There was no worry about plot, or verisimilitude of speech or dress. He was able to focus on such matters as the impact of transportation changes, especially the railway during the previous century. This discussion led directly to his analysis of the rush to the suburbs as transportation became easier. Because of more leisure time, the move gradually but perceptibly created a larger middle class, wrote Wells. He suggested that both the aristocracy and the working class would be diminished in size and importance by the trends and thrust of modern life. Wells thought that this change might well lead to conflict, and a chapter on war followed. There he predicted the use of 'land ironclads', long before his short story of that title, as well as offering substantial discussion of troop mobility (through the use of bicycles and motorized vehicles), and some discussion of air power.

Later in the book he also discussed language difficulties in the modern world and predicted that English would win out over French and German, its great competitors. Other languages, such as Chinese, would remain important, but he foresaw a world in which English was the first language, and native languages would be used as local dialects. The last chapters were the most controversial, as in these pages he came out strongly as an advocate of women, calling for methods of birth-control to be put into effect by the state in order to control population, along with a number of other measures which could modify life substantially, especially for women of the lower classes. In these ideas, carried to their extreme, Wells was, of course, calling for socialism; but the book was not a handbook for revolution, nor was it just a work of narrow prediction. These ideas were what Wells saw as possible in the world of the new twentieth century, no more. What made the book so successful was the willingness of the author to look at alternative futures, to discuss his ideas with readers, and to invite them to participate in his work of future-making. There is nothing shrill about the book, and it has a good deal of bemused hope for what the new century would bring.

Looking back at *Anticipations* on the eve of the war, when the publishers released it again in 1914, Wells remarked that on rereading he found it a better book than he had remembered. He regretted that 'an occasional trick of harshness and moments of leaping ignorance are in the blood of H.G. Wells; everybody who reads him has to stand that — he has to stand it himself more than any one. . . . It is like a lisp or an ugly voice.' He said he had been right on Russia, wrong on specialized roads (he had anticipated a sort of moving sidewalk for goods transport), and quite wrong on flying, which had come about much more rapidly than he thought in 1901. His views on the New Republic, discussed in the book, and the Open Conspiracy (in which he had called for joint work with others), were still present in his mind, and he was working on a novel of which they formed the substance.[5]

Wells was right. Although there may have been a few ugly places in it (mostly the long discursive footnotes added as new impressions were printed), *Anticipations* was intact, well written. Readers of every kind hailed the book; appearing just at the peak of predictions, as the century turned, it provided a clear view into the future, and one which promised to be even clearer and cleaner for his readers.

The book brought Wells many new friends and supporters. As an example, E. Ray Lankester, director of the Museum of Natural History, sent him a book, invited him to dinner at the Omar Khayyám Club, as well as giving him a tour of the museum. Lankester was much less hopeful of change in England than Wells, but welcomed the opportunity to talk. Gregory at first called the book 'wonderful', and later said that it was 'a gospel and denunciation at the same time'. He reported that he had asked Lankester to review it for *Nature*.[6]

In the event *Nature* spent a lot of time on the book. Lankester reviewed it first, acclaiming the work, and going on to discuss Wells's other work, especially his novella *The Star*. He said that he was 'haunted by . . . the thing'. Lankester chose to discuss *Anticipations* through a series of long blocks of quotation, urging his readers to read the entire work and not just these samples. He commended the section on birth-control very strongly and ended his long review with these remarks:

> It seems to me that this book should have — even for those whom it cannot fail to offend — more than the interest which attaches to clever fault-finding. It is, truly enough, an unsparing indictment of existing government, society, education, religion, and morality, but it contains also a confession of faith and is full of a spirit of hope and belief in future development.[7]

Distinguished individuals found the book fascinating. Sidney Webb said that it was his favourite book of the year, while Beatrice, writing in her diary, also described it as 'the most remarkable book of the year; a powerful imagination furnished with the data and methods of physical science working on social problems'. She didn't think Wells knew enough about social organization, but the work was filled with 'luminous hypotheses'. The Webbs went to Sandgate to visit the Wellses, and introduced him to Graham Wallas. The four planners began to exchange books and visits.[8]

Either at the Webbs' suggestion, or through some quirk of his own, Wells sent a copy of the book to G. B. Shaw. Apparently they had not met since Wells's period as a dramatic critic. Shaw responded with thanks, and with memories of their walks home to North London in 1895. As for *Anticipations*, Shaw discussed mostly Wells's ideas on bi-metallism and tidal power, offered a sort of attack on natural selection in his typical tongue-in-cheek style, and commended Wells on his choice of books for 1901, especially Reid's *Alcoholism*. It was a letter of less than fulsome praise. In it Shaw had said, 'Your business is the preaching of the synthesis, not the execution of its constituents.' To another correspondent he was more direct, declaring, 'Our ideas are no longer our exclusive property; and, as we shall never see forty again, our revolutionary bolts are shot personally. The young men are reading Wells's "Anticipations" instead of attending to us. . . .' Shaw called for reform of practice, or 'we shall go on the shelf like the Cobden Club.' William James also thought that Wells was having an impact on the youth of Britain, remarking that he would be a factor in the future social evolution of the country. 'He makes a sudden daylight break through innumerable old blankets of prejudices.' James thought Wells did not allow enough for human nature, but had not said so because 'I have relished him so amazingly and think his way of hitting the nail on the head and his impatience with conservative stupidity perfectly *Köstlich*.'[9]

From these letters and diary comments it is possible to see the extent of the Wellsian impact on British minds with this book. Every significant thinker apparently read and thought about the book. Some were threatened by the prospect of the future, or in Shaw's case, by the prospect of losing power; others thought they could use Wells to their own ends, as did the Webbs; while some simply relished his attack on obscurantism and stupidity.

Wells was very conscious of the impact the book was having — in fact, how could he not have been? So he and Pinker decided to have another shot at pushing his ideas. They arranged for Wells to give a major lecture at the Royal Institution. Wells invited all of his old friends, and a great many new ones. As he remarked to Gregory, enclosing an invitation, 'We'll have a Republic in twelve years — or at any rate we may have if the [?] Empire will pick up. The amount of latent treason that I am discovering is amazing. I shall talk treason at the R.I. I am going to write, talk and preach revolution for the next five years. If I had enough money, believe me, to keep me off the need of earning a living I would do the job myself.'[10]

Wells appeared on 24 January 1902 at the Royal Institution before an audience of invited friends and comrades, and also a large group of persons who simply wished to see this remarkable thinker in action. Wells was a very poor public speaker, and on this occasion his words, filtered through his fairly large moustache, must have been partially inaudible to some of his audience. Later Graham Wallas told him that he spoke about 25 per cent too fast as well. Still, the audience was enthralled by the message, and Pinker persuaded the publisher, Fisher Unwin, to rush a book containing the speech into print. The little book sold 6,000 copies in the first month, continued to sell, and was reprinted several times, the last printing appearing in 1925. In addition, the text of the lecture appeared in *Nature*, as well as in the *Smithsonian Institution Record* in the US. It was a *tour de force*, and remains one of the key items to an understanding of Wells's thought.[11]

In his lecture Wells identified two types of minds, distinguished by their attitude towards time, as well as the relative attention given to preparing for the future. He separated these types as differing on the importance of causes and effects, and described them as oriental and occidental, passive and active, as well as legal and legislative. After offering some brilliant passages on the impact of the dead weight of the past on such matters as urban planning and warfare, he remarked that the past was the line of least resistance, but that men of science and forethought must be able to believe in knowing the future, because those events are 'fixed, settled, and unchangeable'. He told his listeners,

> I believe that the deliberate direction of historical study, and of economic and social study towards the future, and an increasing reference, a deliberate and courageous reference to the future in moral and religious discussion, would be enormously stimulating and enormously profitable to our intellectual life.

He offered to those in the hall, and to all his readers since, a remarkable prospect. In summary, that message is: if our species will only apply its collective mind, we could be the first species to transform our future, to beat the odds; as it were, to control evolution.

> We are creatures of the twilight. But it is out of our race and lineage that minds will spring that will reach back to us in our littleness to know us better than we know ourselves, and that will reach forward fearlessly to comprehend this future that defeats our eyes. All this world is heavy with the promise of greater things, and a day will come — one day in the unending succession of days — when beings, beings who are now latent in our thoughts and hidden in our loins, will stand upon this earth as one stands upon a footstool, and laugh, and reach out their hands amidst the stars.[12]

This lecture is H. G. Wells at his finest. He used his scientific background and his command of the language to offer an opening into the future filled with light and promise. The challenge, just as it had been offered in his earlier science fiction, was to band together, reach for the future, and claim it. He did not indicate that a different future was probable, if *Homo sapiens* did not respond to the challenge. There would be plenty of time later to use that reality as a goad to his readers; for the present, riding the crest of popularity, with a wide and receptive audience, he was absolutely positive. And this positivism was accepted by nearly everyone.

Joseph Conrad called the lecture 'splendid', and 'stirring'. In fact, according to Conrad, its eloquence transcended Wells's usual audience and with this work he had begun to address a much wider group. Conrad felt, and told Wells, that most of the criticism that had been offered was grossly unfair, although he also felt that Wells could have emphasized even more the human possibilities. This difference in approach only mirrored the difference between science and art, and Conrad knew that. He simply accepted 'that anything that would help our intelligences towards the clearer view of the consequences of our social actions is of the very greatest value', and he saluted Wells for this grand piece of work.[13]

The Conrad comment, coupled with the equally expansive remarks of his friends in science, and in the areas of social analysis, meant that Wells had bridged one of the main chasms of thought. He was, with *Anticipations* and *Discovery of the Future*, a mind and a force to be reckoned with. Everyone wanted to meet him, to talk with him, have him read their manuscripts and listen to their ideas. He had become a great man. Bertie Wells had been transformed into H.G. — and he would from this time forward always be known by those initials. Just as the students at the Royal remarked, 'There comes Wells', now, everyone could say, 'Have you heard what H.G. has said?'

With the publication of these books, H. G. Wells's life changed drastically. His home at Sandgate became a mecca for visitors interested in him as a literary figure, as well as those who regarded him as a new socialist leader. He and Jane became famous for their weekend entertaining, and that aspect of his life, along with his family relationships, is important enough to warrant a chapter of its own. Many significant books and articles came from those Channel weekends. However, some of them also had their genesis in the London weeks which began now to be important to him as well. For, only a few years after the turn of the century, Wells began to maintain an apartment in town. Of course, this was necessary after he had begun his liaison with Amber Reeves, and later, with Rebecca West.

As his fame and influence grew, however, he also found it necessary to remain in town on business. He acted as his own agent, at least in part, and the handling of serialization, foreign rights, and contractual matters to do with his writing for the press as well as his future books always took time, even when Pinker or Watt was available to do the preliminary drudgery. As his books sold Wells found himself in increasing demand, and although he did not accept every invitation to dine, speak, or write, many of them were useful. He became a member of the National Liberal Club, proposed by Henry James. In addition, he dined from time to time at The Other Club, founded by Winston Churchill in an effort to free himself, and his friends, from fashionable society at Pratt's or White's. The Webbs gave Wells several dinner parties, as they were wooing him for the Fabians, and many others also sought his company. London society hostesses were hopeful that he would grace their dinner tables, and as these demands grew, and might be increasingly useful to him, he began to accept some of the invitations. Lady Elcho, wife of Lord Wemyss and mother of Cynthia Asquith, was of considerable aid to him at this time, advising him on clothes, etiquette at fashionable dinner parties, and even helping him to decide which party to attend, which weekend could be skipped, or what to say to ladies whom he was asked to take in to dinner.[14]

The Webbs gave one very significant dinner for H.G. and Jane. Present were A.J. Balfour, the Bishop of Stepney (Cosmo Lang), G.B. and Charlotte Shaw, Mrs Pember Reeves, and Frederic Thesiger, later Viscount Chelmsford, of the London County Council, a colleague of Sidney Webb's (he also served as Viceroy of India, and was president of the MCC, among many other offices). Balfour 'let himself go' at this dinner, and the party was a 'mixture of chaff and dialectic' from Shaw to Wells, to Sidney to the Bishop to Beatrice, who, describing the evening, said there was 'always method in our social adventures'. After the ladies left, the men (led by Shaw, Wells, and Lang) worked on Balfour, proposing needed reforms dealing with the unemployed. Balfour and Wells exchanged some letters on this and other matters in the next few years. Wells included him in his list of recipients for his books.[15]

In addition to attending fashionable dinner parties, Wells was in demand to speak, to meet important personages such as the Labour premier of South Australia, another dignitary from Queensland, and Herbert Samuel, as well as to be present at a meeting of the Socialist Club of Oxford — to name several invitations he accepted. He was often asked to speak on behalf of causes such as women's suffrage, but usually declined, primarily because of his inadequate voice, and a relative shyness on the stage at this time.[16]

Wells was much in demand for his writing, after the success of his book, and his prices rose accordingly. In 1902 the *Times Literary Supplement* asked him to do an occasional 'scientific' piece for them, and even offered to allow him to sign his contributions, which was unusual. He didn't write for the *TLS*, but did accept offers from the *Daily Mail* (and his Henley House friend Alfred Harmsworth), and although Wells asked 25 guineas per article and the *Daily Mail* offered only 10, eventually they did pay him 14 for each piece and gave him £25 for the publishing rights outside the United Kingdom.[17]

Books and articles practically fell from Wells's pen in this period. In addition to the serious fiction, a few short stories, book reviews, and so on, he also wrote a half-dozen serious works. Although these appear today as mostly redactions of or addenda to his *Anticipations*, and, in truth, they belong in that category, they are also glosses and refinements to the theory of socialism which he was to produce, after the Fabian period, in *First and Last Things*.

As soon as he had finished *Anticipations*, magazines began imploring him and Pinker for a sequel to run serially, as they knew how much his name enhanced circulation figures. Wells responded, after some discussion, with the pieces for *Cosmopolitan* which later became *Mankind in the Making*. This is probably the weakest of the four books on modern socialism and his predictions on the social and economic world, as he recognized when it was reprinted in 1914. However, the chapters on birth-control, and the place of the home in modern socialism, brought comment from many, and are important in the development of his thought. The first few chapters of the book were extensively criticized by Graham Wallas, and many of his suggestions (especially in the areas of better food and nutrition, as well as the various stages of child development) found their way into the book which ensued. Wells utilized many observations of his own children in this book, along with others of the offspring of his friends.[18]

Most readers of the book were less critical than Wells himself. Leopold Amery liked it, as did Tommy Simmons, who remarked that 'though you may be ignorant of it, there are lots of us being kept up to a higher standard of effort', by 'the messages of mankind which proceed from Spade House'. Others, Ford Madox Hueffer, Ray Lankester, Morley Roberts, Violet Paget (Vernon Lee), and C. F. G. Masterman, liked the book, but all of them in one way or another questioned Wells's optimism, saying that his ideas were correct, but needed refining in the light of reality.[19]

Some of the reviewers also indicated that they thought Wells was too optimistic, and not in tune with the reality of the situation, even though all of them liked the book. Wells was not yet above being miffed at such remarks in the press, and responded to several of these reviews. He was much more able to take comments from his friends, although even here he was touchy, and hurt by criticism that did not deal with his style but which disagreed with the end results. Over the years some of his strongest friends found themselves estranged for periods of time after such criticism.[20]

Even though he may have been unhappy with what seemed to be niggling comments, Wells's next books in his effort to provide a basis for a socialistic future were much more tightly written. Two others appeared within about two and a half years — *A Modern Utopia* (1905) and *New Worlds for Old* in 1908. In these works he revived his comments on the need for a New Republic, and in *A Modern Utopia* urged that it be brought about through the creation and support of a group of philosopher-kings, whom he called Samurai. He took the name from the upper-class Japanese military caste whose role he thought was to maintain ethical standards and reprove those who failed in their obligations. Wells said, in a note to the reader, that *Utopia* came about because he was not satisfied with some of his writing which seemed crude and unformed. In this book he returned, at least in part, to a more open and fictional form through a sort of dialogue, which he felt was better tuned to his desires with this book. He made several attempts at outlining this form, before writing the book. When it appeared it was very heavily influenced by Plato, in both the *Republic* and the *Laws*. When he came to reprint the book in the Atlantic Edition in 1926, his preface used most of the same words, in discussing the work, as in his earlier Note to the Reader: 'I am aiming throughout at a sort of shot-silk texture between philosophical discussion on the one hand and imaginative narrative on the other', was his comment on the style then.[21]

The book made a stronger impact than *Mankind in the Making*, although with each succeeding volume in this venture, Wells found he was receiving more penetrating criticism, as his own words began to be very caustic, especially on the subject of British (and American) upper-class perceptions of themselves. Morley Roberts, for instance, sent him a twelve-page letter urging a clearer statement of purpose, as persons training in modern psychology and philosophy would not be able to go so far without more guidance. Gregory said that the book was marvellous, 'but its greatness will not be adequately understood by this flag-waving, Empire-booming, fiscal-fencing generation as a whole.' He went on to remark that the book was exactly what Huxley would have wanted, and ended by saying, 'Oh, that I could be alive in the world when the human race is one as you describe it. . . .' Winston Churchill also liked the book, but said that it needed more jam with the suet. Wells sent him a copy of *Anticipations*, in response to that remark, and Churchill again responded with much praise, but told Wells that he believed experts could not run modern governments, as the need for unified knowledge was too great.

Joseph Conrad wrote several long letters to Wells during the publication period of these books, and his comments refer to all of them in general, but he too, while wondering at the incredible ability which he found in the books, still felt that he could not follow Wells down every road. Conrad, for instance, felt that exclusivity would not always lead to efficiency, but instead to 'cliquism, to the formation of a select group of disciples, to a fatal limiting of influence. Generally the fault I find with you is that you do not take sufficient account of human imbecility which is cunning and perfidious.' The two men met and discussed each of these books, as well as Conrad's thoughtful criticism.[22] One guesses that Wells continued to refine his style, as Conrad's English was a good litmus paper with which to test whether he was succeeding with his message or not.

Reviewers were more respectful of *A Modern Utopia* than of *Mankind in the Making*. 'F.C.S.S.', writing in *Nature*, remarked that it was instructive 'to watch the growth, both in power and hopefulness, of Mr Wells's criticism of life'. He then went on to summarize all the books that fit into this progression, and closed the review with, 'He aims rather at laying down the principles of an order which shall be capable of progressively growing towards perfection; and so it may well be that in his ideal society men will be less reluctant than now to learn from experience.'

Violet Paget, completely caught up in Wells's thought patterns, came to Sandgate for a long weekend in June 1906, when she and H.G., along with Jane, spent most of the time discussing whether the society outlined in the master's books was possible in their lifetimes. Later that year as 'Vernon Lee' she addressed a long 'Open Letter' in the *Fortnightly Review* to Wells, which he apparently saw before it appeared. She said that Wells had created a twin of our planet, where things are done much better than here. She also protested that Wells confused her, causing her to accept his words, without adding in the piece of reality which would ultimately prevent his model from becoming true. This sort of comment Wells welcomed, as it put his message before even larger audiences, and caused much discussion of the possibilities inherent in the future.[23]

All in all, the amount of intellectual discussion about these books was substantial. In fact, several Samurai societies were formed to discuss the implications of Wells's work. Maurice Browne, who apparently founded the first such group, told Wells that *Modern Utopia* 'expressed for hundreds of others, as well as for us their more or less incoherent ideas on discipline and aspiration'. Wells approved a prospectus for the group, and he and Browne laid plans for a major meeting in May 1907. Wells said that he did this with a certain diffidence, as 'the higher one climbs the steeper the cliff. . . .' and said that Chesterton, who had found Wells's view chasing him through his dreams, was correct, as his own dreams were troubled. Wells suggested that Browne contact Vernon Lee and Chesterton, as possible persons to discuss their views before the society. Later he told Browne that he was not a good leader in these ventures, as he was too impatient, and certainly could not lay down a rule to follow precisely; but he did agree to discuss his views with Browne's group.

They met at the New Reform Club, under Fabian auspices, late in April 1907. Wells told the group that all present probably believed in the inevitability of socialism, so the only thing to work out was a 'personal culture which would transform this dream to the possibility of reality'. He called for a new model of citizen, who would work out what was needed for the socialist citizen of the future. Afterwards, continual propagation of these views would bring their goal forward inexorably. A beginning might be made with rules for personal efficiency, discipline, and moral and intellectual leadership. 'Clear and definite study, understanding, reading and constant discussion, becomes a duty for the socialist, for the really earnest and organized propagandist of socialism', were his suggestions. Beatrice Webb, Haden Guest, Aylmer Maude, and other prominent persons participated, and most of them called for evolution, rather than dictates from above. The only dissentient at the meeting was Shaw, who thought his own disciples were ten times more ready than Wells's for the new world.[24]

Wells continued to be bombarded with requests for pieces on socialism, and as he wrote them he continued to refine his views still more. Some of those pieces, heavily rewritten, along with other work resulting from these articles, led to the publication, in 1908, of *New Worlds for Old*, the last of this quartet of books on the socialist future.

Wells was not satisfied with Pinker's work on the previous books, so he began to discuss his plans with other agents, and with magazine publishers themselves. Wells told S.S. McClure, as an example, that he hated the idea of class warfare, which he had found so prevalent in America on his 1906 tour. 'I want to save socialism from degeneration under the stress of political conflict into that [class warfare].' He also told McClure that in England there was a group of persons who understood his ideas as a comprehensive new scheme of life, and what he wanted to do now was to provide a text for intelligent seventeen- and eighteen-year-olds. Wells resisted writing this book for a time, but as McClure, publisher of *Everybody's Magazine*, offered a substantial advance, he finally decided to write his textbook for youth, directing it mostly towards the United States, or so he told McClure. Wells was concerned that it would 'fritter away the socialism book' he really wanted to write, but demand and returns were high enough to risk it. He later told another agent (in England) that his idea was 'a plain, clear statement of the full socialist idea' on the lines indicated in his paper (in the *Grand Magazine*), with a consideration of the stock objections as well.

New Worlds for Old was quickly produced, and was very successful. It was, in the event, a clear primer of socialism, re-stating most of Wells's ideas from the earlier three books, and especially dealing with the most common objections he had heard and read in the previous decade. Its publication marked the end of the road, however, for Pinker and Wells, as Wells simply could not help but tamper with what his agents thought was their business.[25]

As always, his friends welcomed the book. William Archer, Gregory, John Galsworthy, Ray Lankester, and Robert Blatchford all commended the book, and especially its free and easy style, the handbook concept, and the fact that it could be used by anyone as a guide to life. Conrad liked this book better than the last, and told Wells that all of his visitors were discussing the book and its significance. The letters of this time contain some of the strongest of Conrad's praise for Wells, but they also reflect Conrad's own recent successes and his more optimistic view. And here too he was commenting on the entire group of books, as well as on Wells's fiction of the period. The comments blur.[26]

Of all the comments, Wells was happiest with those from a former student at Midhurst School, who wrote to him in a different vein, recalling those days, and asking for a bibliography of socialism. Wells responded with a set of the proof sheets of *New Worlds for Old*, and they then exchanged letters about Horace Byatt, his recent death, and his reburial at the school. Professional reviewers were also happy with the book. Arnold Bennett, writing under his own name in the *New Age* (he usually appeared under the name 'Jacob Tonson'), called it a masterly work; and an anonymous reviewer in the *Labour Leader* not only liked the book very much, but compared Wells very favourably with Shaw, who was dismissed as a cynic, and with Sidney Webb, who was not idealist enough to achieve the goals of socialism. Wells saw the hopes clear, but not through revolution, according to the reviewer, who urged others to read the work for their own betterment.[27]

These books on socialism were not written in a vacuum, of course. Wells was writing other pieces during this time, and listening to a great deal of commentary from his friends who visited him on weekends. In addition, prior to his final statements on the matter, he was also tremendously busy with his efforts at reform of the Fabian Society, and finally with the major tour he made of the United States. All of these matters left a considerable impress on his thinking.

Before looking at the Fabian episode, it seems appropriate to glance at his visit across the Atlantic, although in terms of strict chronology, the visit occurred in the midst of the Fabian events, as well as the writing of the four books just described. *New Worlds for Old* was written with an American audience in mind, of course, as would be many of his publications after the trip. It was the socialism that he found, and did not find, in America, as well as the expansiveness with which he was greeted and the breezy manner of his new American friends, which helped him break away from the socialism he found in the Fabian Society and which he thought to be inbred, aristocratic, and slightly shopworn.

What marked Wells's visit to America was that, more than most visitors of his time and earlier, he went with an open mind, and he was prepared to enjoy his hosts. As Americans were very used to attacks, or if not attacks, pieces written with an eye askance at their institutions, way of life, and even their hospitality, Wells's good-humoured account was well received.[28] This was the first of what would be another half-dozen visits, in the next thirty-five years, but the success of the visit, and the generosity of his comments, meant that other visits would proceed generally without much acrimony. Wells and his subject 'knew' each other, or, at least, thought they did, which was sufficient.

Wells went aboard ship expecting that the United States *was* the new world, ready to replace the decadent aristocratic England he found so strait-laced and difficult to change. He asked a New York agent, W. Perrin, to act as his American representative, and to help him meet appropriate persons in Chicago, Philadelphia, New York, and Washington. In addition, Graham Wallas and the Webbs, all of whom had friends there from their own visits, wrote letters of introduction for him. F.B. Miles, a friend of Wallas, found Wells 'a delightful young swell of apparently 35 to 37', and after giving him dinner, spent a considerable amount of time planning out what and where for him to visit. Wells, in turn, found Miles 'a dear', and said that he had had 'a gorgeous time'. Others who befriended Wells included Ray Stannard Baker, Lincoln Steffens, who engineered a visit to the White House for him to meet Theodore Roosevelt, and Jane Addams in Chicago, who not only showed him Hull House, but also made it possible for him to see the seamier side of Chicago life, 'Hinky Dink's' saloon, and the slum environs controlled by 'Bathhouse John' Coughlin.[29]

When Wells returned to Britain he went into complete retirement for a few weeks, in order to write his book while the impressions were still fresh. However, he had a leg up on the book already, having written the first chapter before he left England, and worked on it aboard ship during the return crossing. *The Future in America* (1906) was a great success, especially as Wells was so frank about problems in the United States. Too wide a gap between the classes, and the overriding problem of racialism, as well as a sort of vulgarity seemed to inhibit progress, according to Wells. After weighing up both positive and negative influences in America, and in Britain, as he was writing the book (he was reading Henry James on America, and talked to Ford Madox Hueffer just before the latter went across the Atlantic on a similar trip; he also mentioned attacks being written on slavery and the mistreatment of blacks in Africa and India), he went on to end the book on a very positive note:

> After all is said and done, I do find the balance of my mind tilts steadily to a belief in a continuing and accelerated progress now in human affairs. And in spite of my patriotic inclinations, in spite, too, of the present high intelligence and efficiency of Germany, it seems to me that in America, by sheer virtue of its size, its free traditions, and the habit of initiative in its people, the leadership of progress [towards the New Republic] must ultimately rest.[30]

Wells's friends were much taken with the book, not only those who knew America, but also those who had never been there, and who used Wells as a guide to the unknown land. Elizabeth Healey had good comments to make on the education system, while Morley Roberts, Churchill, R.S. Baker, and others simply approved. Beatrice Webb was fulsome, saying she could not compete with the press in praise, but she did not need to do so as it was such an excellent piece of work. H.G. and Jane went to the Webbs' to visit and to dinner, mostly to discuss the trip and the book. Others at the dinner were Beatrice's sister and her husband, the Courtneys, as well as Philip Snowden. The press was also very happy with the book, the most negative review being that of the *Manchester Guardian*, which found the book had 'too much "purpose" perhaps', but otherwise thought it a significant contribution to transatlantic understanding.

Wells was unhappy, however, with the way the book was handled in Britain by Chapman & Hall, as he did not think they advertised it strongly enough. Eventually he had them send sixty-eight copies either to the press or to his friends in order to get even more notice of what the book said. Finally he told the publishers that he would have to withdraw his work from their hands. He even threatened to take over publishing his own books, but this was an idle gesture. In the event, other publishers, both British and American, were ready and available to print his work: Harpers, Macmillan, and eventually Doubleday. Of course, this meant for Wells some release from work, as the larger houses did a better job of promotion, although never up to his expectations. However, he would soon find them less able to publish some of his views, so his period of ease with publishers was relatively short-lived.[31]

The response to these books was very intense in the Fabian Society, where everything H. G. Wells said or did was important because his activities bore upon a controversy within the group in which he was the central figure. Though it now appears that Wells's flirtation with Fabianism was of relatively little importance in the general history of England, of socialism, and perhaps even in the biographies of the participants, it had undoubtedly a most profound impact on Wells himself. After this time he was careful to avoid political entanglements, at least those in which he had to be responsible to others. Though often initially the leader, he frequently left most of the day-to-day work to others. This meant that those who wished to lead or to change him often gave up their friendship with him, as Wells was unable to accept such fetters no matter how slight or silken they might be.

One of the reasons why the Fabian imbroglio has received such extended treatment is the individuals involved — not only H.G. Wells and the Webbs, but also G.B. Shaw, the Blands, and above all the young women in the Fabian Society. So, comment on these events tends to take on a prurient character, at least among many; and even today a whiff of such feelings permeates the discussion. Wells certainly 'paid his dues' in these matters, to use a current phrase, but to some degree he also paid his respects with the publication of *The New Machiavelli*.

It seems quite clear that at this stage of his life, Wells was still seeking a political and social philosophy. When one reads his foursome of books on socialism, this seems to be their major thrust. As he proceeded with these books, a workable social and political philosophy became increasingly clear to him. He was able to work out his social feelings through his fiction and his personal involvement, not only with women (Rosamund Bland, Amber Reeves, Amy Catherine Wells, Dorothy Richardson all figure directly, and Beatrice Webb, E. Nesbit, and Lady Elcho indirectly, during this time) but also with other men, and in their relations with each other. The end result was a series of remarkable novels, as well as books of social commentary.

Wells wrote in a generally limpid style, which invited adherence to his views as well as commentary on them. As has been indicated, most of his friends were only too willing to discuss and debate his views, and he found this process helpful in reaching the goals he sought. The Fabian period is simply more of that working out of ideas.

The story is fairly simple. Once Wells had written *Anticipations*, many people sought him out. Among them were Beatrice and Sidney Webb, who cycled to Sandgate to meet him and express their admiration for the book. The Webbs, although coming on their own, brought with them the ideas of the Fabian Society, now grown to include more than a thousand members; the tracts it published on socialism and public affairs had received wide notice. Many early members of the founding groups — Edward Pease, Hubert Bland, George Bernard Shaw — had continued to be active; however, with the exception of Shaw, most of them were not well known.

Graham Wallas, at first a member of the 'Old Gang', as they styled themselves (he had stood as witness at the Webbs' marriage), had become increasingly estranged from them politically, although their social intercourse had not lessened except for a diminution caused by distance, marriage, and in the case of the Wallases, a child. The Society had had a substantial impact on the views of many persons in the upper middle class in England. However, a small success on the London County Council (both Webb and Wallas were elected members), and a tiny growth in Parliament (though Fabian adherents and fellow travellers, Keir Hardie and Ramsay MacDonald had been elected as Labour Party members), had created some strain as local battles and horizons tended to obscure larger ideas. The Fabian tracts continued to be published, but membership in the Society was diminishing or stagnant. More importantly, the intake was of the same age as those already involved. Few young persons appeared to be interested in the words or deeds of the Old Gang.

This was the situation when *Anticipations* appeared, and offered what seemed to be a great possibility. If only H.G. Wells could be persuaded to join the Society, lend his name and ideas, the problems of recruitment might be solved. New blood would rejuvenate the old. One doubts that the Webbs were quite as crass as this in their thinking when they set out on their bicycles for Sandgate, although Beatrice certainly had no problem about pursuing hidden or Machiavellian tactics when the occasion arose. If the visit resulted in a recruit, it was a plus for a visit of congratulations.

Meetings after the first encounter were cordial. Discussions, although heated, were undertaken in good humour. Wells, for his part, found the attention enjoyable. It was not long before the four were on a first-name basis, were exchanging visits, dinners, and a fair amount of correspondence. As the Webbs had a number of friends who fitted this category of thinking persons, it was soon logical for Sidney to approach Wells with the idea of setting up a dining club, to meet once a month to discuss some major question of the day, debate the meaning of these questions, and enlighten each other. Such groups, whether the 'Souls', or Churchill's Other Club, were a part of this upper-class English world, and were so prevalent that several novels based on them were written at about this time. Wells joined the group with pleasure, as did others. Over the next three years or so, the group, calling themselves The Co-Efficients (the name indicates their style in solving problems), met and discussed their questions. Exactly how many of their meetings Wells attended is not now known, but he did speak several times, and afterwards the other members of the group, Leopold Amery, H. W. Massingham, Bertrand Russell, Pember Reeves, R.B. Haldane, Henry Newbolt, Sir Edward Grey, Halford Mackinder, Leo Maxse, James L. Garvin, and Lord Milner, all looked upon those meetings from 1902 to 1907 as being significant in their own development, as well as for the friendships which were created.

The names alone suggest that Wells was not only playing a game for high stakes, but that his views were getting a good airing.[32]

In addition to meeting formally in this group, the two couples, and most particularly H. G. Wells and Beatrice Webb, began to exchange much correspondence. Beatrice commented on Wells's books, especially on *New Worlds for Old* and *A Modern Utopia*. They exchanged copies of their books when they appeared. As Beatrice said, 'What I felt most on meeting you was the amount of economic, intellectual and moral sympathy between Webb and Wells.' Wells participated in a debate at the London School of Economics which Beatrice chaired, on the occasion of the opening of the Students' Union. Wells read papers at meetings of the Fabians. When he gave a copy of *A Modern Utopia* to the Webbs, he told Beatrice that the chapter on the Samurai would 'appeal to your worst instincts'. The couples were very close, at least on the evidence of Beatrice's diary, in which she records conversations as to how the world perceived her relationship with Sidney. In addition Wells wrote to her at least once about a dream in which she had figured. Although it would be far too much to suggest a physical relationship, nevertheless, as one reads the extant correspondence and diary entries, there is an air of attraction between Beatrice and H.G., a sort of sexual mist which overlays the paper today. To some degree this is true of most of the correspondence Wells addressed to women, but the mist is slightly more fragrant here.[33]

The friendships well in place, it seemed logical to invite Wells to stand for the Fabian executive. He took the offer as a challenge and from that position began to formulate a change in Fabian policy and tactics. The original charter of the group, called the Basis, provided for very limited offensive activity by the Society. Instead, the group reacted to events, trusted to education eventually to achieve their goals, and to some degree, attempted to infiltrate the group in power in the government. Over time this had boiled down to acceptance of some very small gains, and many who were sympathetic felt that the Fabians had become too conservative, that they were only interested in preserving what little power they had, and therefore generally failed to take advantage of openings in the opposition. Wells also felt this way, and the new recruits into the Society, many of them young university students or graduates, as well as other readers of his work, urged him to take an active role from the vantage point of the executive. He did so, writing a series of drafts of a new Basis (as well as a brilliant Fabian tract, *This Misery of Boots*). When the group put his new draft up for public debate, Wells found that the Old Gang did not want to be reformed — or, at least, George Bernard Shaw did not.

Shaw was a mercurial person, used to having his own way, even if that way was peculiar at times. He apparently felt that he could provide Wells with the sophisticated education which he was sure the other man lacked. His rather heavy-handed efforts to take over Wells's life were, at first, met with humour, then with sarcasm, and finally with outright opposition.

Shaw, for his part, never really took Wells very seriously, except as a threat to his power on the Fabian executive. He mobilized the Old Gang around him, taking full advantage of the sexual enmity and jealousy now present, as Wells had seduced (or had been seduced by) Rosamund Bland and Amber Reeves, among younger Fabian women. Sexual life in this group, at least on its fringe, never followed conventional morality (the Bland household certainly showed that), but sexual matters now began to impinge on political and social relations. Shaw, to give him credit, did not himself make an issue of this, and was much more open-minded about events than were, say, the Webbs, to say nothing of Hubert Bland or the Reeveses.

In any case, after postponing discussion of Wells's Basis until after his American trip, a formal debate was arranged. At the time Shaw packed the house with his supporters (Wells could have done so, but didn't bother), and then used his debating and dramatic skills to rout Wells completely. Wells attempted to recover his losses with letters, meetings, and further publications over the next few months, but found the cause a difficult and ultimately useless one. He then resigned from the executive, taking some of his young friends with him. The Society had lasted out the Wells attack, but found itself in essentially the same position thereafter as it had been before, that is, to a considerable degree moribund and out of touch. It was not until the Report of the Poor Law Commission (1909) — or rather the Minority Report on the findings of that Commission, written by Beatrice Webb — and later after World War I when the Labour Party began to revive strongly, leading eventually to the formation of a Government, that the Society was of much consequence.

Even then, it was the Parliamentary Labour Party which had the lead, along with such outsiders as Jimmy Maxton, and others who represented the Left or the ILP. Membership in the Fabian Society was a useful thing. The tracts continued to exert some influence on the thinking of the Left. But, in the final analysis, Wells and the Society left each other relatively untouched. One can wonder what might have occurred if Wells had been able to overcome the Old Gang; but a group of very gentle socialists, with mostly a reformist point of view, were not to be dominated by this sexually active, loud-voiced, vulgar representative of the lower middle class. Nothing in the English society of the time suggests that he could have won. Upon reflection he knew this, and so left the Society with few regrets, and those he was able to salve with *The New Machiavelli*.[34]

What may be less well known about the affair is that, although each side attempted to win over the other, and there was some effort at secrecy, each side had a spy (if one can use that word) in the councils of the other. Charlotte Shaw served on Wells's committee to rewrite the Basis, and every meeting of the executive at which Wells was not present was reported to him by an ally, G.R.S. Taylor. Wells, in addition, tried to recruit a number of well-known persons to join the Society, but met with almost complete refusal.[35] Many of those who refused did so for reasons similar to those that drove Wells away finally. Would the Society achieve anything, especially with the Old Gang in charge? What should be its relationship with the Labour Party? From these queries, Wells knew he was beaten early in the fight, and remained in the Society longer than anyone would have predicted — relying perhaps too much on the votes of the youth he had attracted, or, perhaps, attempting to drive the Society further along the road to the socialism which had brought the two sides together originally. Whatever the motivation, the conflict did provide a good deal of entertainment for many as well as refining the views of the participants, and especially the views of H.G. Wells.[36]

After Wells had lost, the Fabians did mount some fairly extended discussions about working more closely with a parliamentary party, although the proposal was for a Fabian parliamentary group, separate from both the Labour Party and the ILP. This proposal did not get anywhere, and the two sides agreed to part as friendly enemies. Shaw continued to harrass Wells, about the Society as well as about his writing, his views on life, and just on general principles as to the way he behaved. He called Wells such things as a 'leary, rash egotist', and told him that 'if you were a thousand H.G. Wells, there is one sacrosanct person who is greater than you all, and that is the chairman of a public meeting'. He went on to comment on Wells's speech patterns and urged him to take lessons from Shaw's superior abilities at oratory. 'It is up to you to cancel your natural disadvantages by a strenuous effort of genius and by years of perseverance.'

Wells responded to these comments with a vitriolic letter of his own, saying to Shaw,

> The more I think you over the more it comes home to me what an unmitigated imbecilic Victorian ass you are. You play about with issues like a daring [?] garrulous maiden aunt, but when it comes to an affair like the Bland affair you show the instincts of conscious gentility and the judgement of a hen. You write of Bland in a stream of sentimental exaltation. You explain the beautiful and romantic character to me — as though I don't know the man to his bone. You might be Mrs Bland herself in a paroxysm of romantic instruction. . . . You don't know, as I do, in blood and substance, lust, failure, shame, hate, love and creative passion. You don't understand and you can't understand . . . any more than you can understand the sins in the Fabian Society that your vanity has wrecked.[37]

Most of Wells's friends were happy that he had left the Society. Edward Garnett, who urged his resignation while the debate over the Basis was still active, told him he would not 'make headway as long as the restricted Fabian ideals block your way' Ramsay MacDonald, writing from the House of Commons when he learnt that a newspaper report that Wells had been struck by an automobile was in error, reminisced over his own days on the Fabian executive and remarked, 'I got more and more disgusted with the attitude of Webb, Shaw and one or two others, so that their actions in the South African war came to me as a great relief, because it enabled me to clear out.' He confessed that he didn't like them personally, and that he held them in neither honour nor respect. H. W. Massingham simply remarked, 'I'm sorry for progress and glad for literature you're out.' When the *New Age* changed editors, from Joseph Clayton to A. R. Orage and Holbrook Jackson, Wells himself was able to discuss the change in his life in terms of a move away from Fabianism to one of a broader-based socialism. He wrote to the paper, 'Socialism in England has long stood in need of what you propose to give it, a Review which, without being official, shall be representative, and which shall direct itself primarily not to propaganda nor to politics, but to the development of socialist thought.' In fact, Wells thought that the new editorial policies might help considerably to rejuvenate 'the Fabian Society by providing a freedom and vigour of irresponsibility and supply co-ordination and educational links for the new members coming in.'[38]

It is just possible that the break in relationships after the Wells resignation might have gone no further, except that Shaw, and to some degree, Sidney Webb, felt that they could continue to tap Wells's mind, and at the same time keep him under control. The two men therefore rewrote the Fabian Basis early in 1908, and sent it to Wells for comment. He refused at first, as he was too busy on the articles that would become *New Worlds for Old*, but then, eleven months later, he returned the charter completely rewritten. This occasioned the blunt letter from Shaw referred to before. In the letter Shaw also brought up the draper's assistant period in Wells's life, and referred to his father's career as a professional cricketer in derogatory terms. He even intimated that Jane Wells really preferred Shaw to Wells. This letter was written in a completely tongue-in-cheek way, but to one of Wells's sensibilities, especially as to class, it struck home with a bitter blow. Wells was acrid in his response. He told Webb that 'I happen to be something of a teacher and I want to get rid of that piece of apparatus very much. Why can't you and Shaw let me throw it out now. . . . You won't even let me enlist and train forces for you to handle. You two men are the most intolerable egotists, narrow, suspicious, obstructive, I have ever met.' To Shaw, Wells placed the blame completely on the Blands. 'Damn the Blands!! All through have been that infernal hundreds of lies that have tainted this affair and put me off my game. You don't for one minute begin to understand. You've judged me in that matter and there you are!'[39]

With these outbursts, Wells apparently thought he was finished with the Society and his onetime friends of the Society as well. The press did not allow the matter to die, however, and he soon found himself defending the Society against the attacks of others who did not know the true situation. In great part this was because H. G. Wells believed that socialism was more important than personality, and transcended these little squabbles. He told the *Daily News*, for instance, that Shaw was not the Society, and the Left in the Liberal Party was very close to Fabian socialism, regardless of what Shaw did or said. The *Nation* agreed with Wells, and remarked that Shaw was the evil genius of the Society, while calling him an 'anarch of the Nietzschian type' in an editorial article commending Wells for his gallant effort 'to pump oxygen into the body of Fabianism'. Wells responded to this by saying that too much effort had been spent on personalities, and not enough on the ends in view. According to H.G., neither Webb nor Shaw was 'sinister', and 'to regard Webb, for example, as a Machiavellian statesman is ridiculous'. Shaw, on the other hand, was 'a much more inconvenient personality in the development of socialism', as he was possessed of 'a nimble and vagrant mind', but he was not an 'intellectual vertebrate'.[40]

Clearly the Fabian episode had left scars. Both sides had been bruised, and although a cordiality remained (on the surface), the wounds were very deep. Wells's comments on Shaw must have stung the Irish playwright deeply too, and he soon broke out in print. In an article in the *Christian Commonwealth*, he called Wells 'a spoiled child. His life has been one long promotion. . . . He did what he liked; and when he did not like what he had done, he threw it aside and did something else, unhindered, unchecked, unpunished apparently, even undisliked. . . .' Shaw then said that Wells had left Fabianism worse than he found it, and although Wells did not bite on this particular piece, few could have felt that he would allow Shaw the last word.[41]

Wells was, in fact, beginning his revenge. Not only Shaw, but the Webbs, as well as many other aspects of modern life, came under his scrutiny in a novel published early in 1911 called *The New Machiavelli*. The novel caused trouble. When it was received by the publishers, Macmillans first postponed the book from their summer to their winter list, and then asked Wells to cut out the sexual episodes, which it was felt were too strong for their prospective readers. Wells made some changes, but although he told Macmillan that he was ill with worry about the book, and that his writing schedule was severely altered, it was not enough. Macmillan still did not like the book, nor its contents. H.G. had begun to find that his themes caused a good deal of trouble in the world still under the censorship spell of Victorian thought. *In the Days of the Comet* had met with adverse response in some quarters, and *Ann Veronica* (as we shall see) with even more. Wells told Sir Frederick Macmillan that *The New Machiavelli* was 'an *Ann Veronica*ish book, but only in that it gives as failure and a very tragic and destructive failure what that unfortunate book gives as success.' Wells also told his publisher that he was thinking of looking elsewhere to place his books, as the delay in *The New Machiavelli* had led to 'the development of the most perilous situation for my literary reputation and I must by any means feel secure against some inexplicable objection on the next story on my part.'[42]

The problem with the book was not so much the sexual interest as that two of its leading characters were clearly portraits of Beatrice and Sidney Webb. Wells wrote Macmillan a somewhat disingenuous letter saying, 'it now occurs to me that I wasn't free to use them as characters in the subsequent style in that account.' He then offered to give another couple room to do the dirty work previously assigned to the Webb characters, and ended by remarking, 'of course all the rest of the Bailey stuff is extending flattery to the Webbs, and there you are.' Macmillan could not accept this as sufficient, while Wells, on his part, could not accept the restrictions. He moved his books to Heinemann, and then to John Lane, who was prepared to take a libel possibility in his stride.[43]

Wells felt that the attempted censorship of his novels and their content hurt his sales, his reputation, and his ability to write. He told Macmillan, when they parted company, 'Our poor neglected *Ann Veronica* is selling very fast both here and in New York. Well, *The New Machiavelli* is a book of altogether bigger calibre than *A.V.*, it's the political companion piece to *Tono-Bungay* and I want to have a guaranteed royalty on more than 10,000.' He then went on, again rather disingenuously, to remark, 'I don't altogether agree at this prospect of giddy elevation but I'm out to see myself going up — and being properly aided up — the scale to 20,000 to 30,000 in the country. *Kipps*, *Tono-Bungay*, and *The New Machiavelli* are stages in my growth.'[44]

Wells was right even though somewhat self-serving in this letter. He was a rising literary star, and Macmillan was unhappy to lose his work, even for a brief time, just as John Lane was happy to get him. The problem was his subjects, thinly disguised treatments of his personal, political, and sexual life. *The New Machiavelli* is Wells's most autobiographical novel. It treats, in fairly blunt, open, and personal detail, his life in Bromley (Bromstead); his father, his mother (less so), Morley and his first schools (to some degree), the Webbs (Altiora and Oscar Bailey), Graham Wallas (Willersley), the Co-Efficients, Amber Reeves (Isabel), and Jane (Margaret, although it is always difficult to be sure that she is the basis for any character in Wells's work). The Webbs, in particular, were pilloried (Book II, part ii); but in this novel Wells wrote without discrimination about many of his acquaintances. As a result those who were not treated were still able to see personal references where none existed, and the rumours, excited discussion, and titillation caused by the story were high, both when it appeared in serial form and when it emerged as a book.

Wells used the book to discuss English politicians, and the political scene, developing a delicious metaphor (Book III, part ii, chapter 5) of the British Empire being like 'some of those early vertebrated monsters, the Brontosaurus and the Atlantosaurus and suchlike; it sacrifices intellect to character; its backbone, that is to say, — especially in the visceral region — is bigger than its cranium.' In Book III he also worked his way to an end of politics, submerged, says the author, in sexual desire (another reason that the Fabians both hated and were moved by the book). After accepting this ending, Wells turns it into his political philosophy: 'I have sought to show my growing realization that the essential quality of all political and social effort is the development of a great race mind behind the interplay of individual lives. That is the collective human reality, the basis of morality, the purpose of devotism. . . . I have called it the hinterland of reality. . . .'

Wells then returned to the Baileys (Webbs) in the latter part of the book, making it clear that he felt their interference and gossip had caused the great furore over his affair with Amber Reeves (Book IV, part ii, chapter 2). He even indicates that he had met the two, as a result, to discuss their views, although there is no indication that he really did. In any case they appear very badly in the work, pictured as gossipy, selfish, wilful, small-minded, and vindictive persons. Wells later (Book IV, part iii, chapter 2) indirectly blames the Baileys and other narrow-minded persons for the prospective failure of socialism, by dooming it to many years of further wandering in the wilderness. He even, at the very end of the book, puts a speech into the mouth of Margaret (Jane) which indicates that she could let Wells and Amber (in their fictional form) go, knowing that she has played her part properly. Everyone is pure, and has honest motives except the Baileys.

'You talk of beauty, both of you, as something terrible, mysterious, imperative. *Your* beauty is something altogether different from anything I know or feel. It has pain in it. . . . *My* beauty is a quiet thing. . . . My beauty is *still* beauty, and yours, is excitement. I know nothing of the fascination of the fire, or why one should go deliberately out of all the decent fine things of life to run dangers and be singed and tormented and destroyed. I don't understand. . . .'

(Book IV, part iii, chapter 5)

The novel, with its frank treatment of sexual attraction and the debility of intimate political life, quickly became the literary scandal of its day, even more than *Ann Veronica* which had been personal, not political and social, in its impact. Beatrice Webb read *The New Machiavelli* with 'much interest and amusement', calling it 'very clever in a malicious way'. She did say that it 'compels agreement on the descriptive side'. She also remarked that as 'there is a statute of limitations', she felt that he could come back into distinguished society some day, even implying that she could and would forgive him eventually.[45]

Shaw wrote to Wells, while the book was being serialized, quoting William Blake on experience, 'bought with the price of all a man hath — his house, his wife, his children'. He told Wells that this would make a good motto for *The New Machiavelli*, which he dubbed a 'frightfully unfinished masterpiece, for the truth appears to be that the parties will live happily ever after.'[46]

Others, such as C. F. G. Masterman, not pictured in the book, wrote detailed criticisms of it to Wells, but accepted its general premise; later Masterman brought Wells along for breakfast with Lloyd George so they could discuss the book, and other political statements. Lord Northcliffe (the former Alfred Harmsworth) told Wells that if he heard of any boycotting of the book, his columns were open, and he, Northcliffe himself, would interfere on Wells's behalf. Reviewers were more tentative about this book; nearly all of them accepted Wells's remarks on political philosophy, but found themselves in a very different mood as to the sexual matters intimated in the novel.[47]

Morley Roberts told Wells that the ending of the novel was weak, and that his hero, Remington, should have stayed in England and kept both Margaret and Isabel and told them all to go to hell. 'They *could* have accepted this', thought Roberts, but, of course, that would have been much too close to home even for Wells. Roberts went on, 'As you are almost the only man with real courage to write what he thinks and feels in this England of ours, I wish you'd done this. . . . In any case you've helped me in many places to more clarity — in the vile welter of our world.' Violet Paget, writing to Jane, agreed with Roberts in general, although she felt that H.G. should be more magnanimous in his treatment of those whose feelings were bruised by his writing.[48]

When Wells came to write about the book again in the preface to volume XIV of his collected edition, he was still a bit taken aback by the reception originally accorded to the book. He remarked that if he wished to write about events of his time, he was duty bound to create characters similar to those who were alive and active at that time. 'There is of course a certain element of truth in these fancies. It is only by giving from his own life and feeling that a writer gives life to a character. Writers are like God in this at least, that they make men in their own image and their own breath gives them such life as they have.'[49]

Shaw was the only character in the Fabian group who did not play a strongly recognizable part in this novel. But Wells was not done with him by this omission. In fact, in some ways he held a lower view of Shaw than he held of the Webbs, and his treatment of the playwright at other times was much more vindictive. Later, Wells used a weekend with Blatchford and Shaw at Sandgate as a focus for some articles in which he wanted to 'smack' Shaw, and they also had trouble over the Allied treatment of Russia during World War I. In Wells's preface to the second edition of *Anticipations* he describes Shaw's role in the Fabian imbroglio as 'contrived to take a leading and entirely incomprehensible part'; and then when the Fabians finally produced a new magazine of the Left, the *New Statesman*, but did not invite Wells to contribute, he was vitriolic in a review of the journal although he later came to like the weekly. He remarked that it was like coming on a ten-year-old ball programme, and gave a little rhyme:

> The world's great age begins anew;
> The Fabians return;
> The Webb doth like a snake renew
> His social creed outworn.

He went on to say that Shaw wasn't present in the journal, which was 'a pity. I know him better than anyone not a sworn admirer', and called him 'an emasculated Rebecca West (if she will forgive me)'. He remarked that 'Mrs Webb, who is about as mystical as a railway whistle, writes mystically about the soul of Japan, as once she lectured to us mystically about her own.' He called the magazine 'a stagnant marsh of dull print without any current in it at all. . . . Duller than Indigestion. Duller than a privet hedge in Leeds.' He said we love and hate, we look back, 'But I bury the hatchet.' His friends must have thought he was burying the hatchet in their skull with these remarks; however, they were forbearing, and did not respond.

Eventually Wells did become more magnanimous, as when he reviewed the Webbs' book, *The Decay of Capitalist Civilization*, favourably, accepted their help when he stood for Parliament, and even became very friendly again with Beatrice; he was more distant with Sidney, but even in that case, Wells finally was able to forgive.[50] The Webbs, for their part, played a better role. They did not score off Wells in the public prints and they accepted that he had a right to score off them. The important issue was the advancement of socialism. Wells was part of that effort. In the event, he was probably more important than Shaw. They could forgive. In the real sense of the matter, if Shaw had not been present, the Webbs might have won over Wells, or he them, as the goal of socialism was foremost. However, Wells and Shaw had antagonistic natures. As Wells said, 'Shaw had an element of cruelty in his nature, and an impulse to provocation and opposition was fundamentally part of his nature.' When one added to these features Shaw's fantastically vain personality, it is no wonder that they clashed.

Shaw made a scene at Jane's funeral, insisting that she had not had cancer, but had died of some other cause, and then insisted that Wells take his children to view the actual cremation, an insistence for which Wells was later grateful. In the World War II period the two were to come together again and exchange many letters. After Charlotte died, Wells saw Shaw only once more; but he did have the ultimate revenge, one supposes, by writing an obituary of Shaw, which appeared long after Wells's own death. In it he remarked: 'Most of us older people who have known love know that irreparable sorrow for endless wasted opportunities, for kindness, and for stupid moments of petty irritation. It might have been so much better.'[51]

What the entire series of events taught Wells was that socialism, the true goal, had to come through other means. First of all, one had to articulate a social and political philosophy, have it discussed clearly and openly, modify it if necessary, and then work through propaganda and persuasion to achieve it. At first Wells tried to work through the Liberal Party, then through Labour and the Independent Labour Party. After failing in all these cases, he began to advocate the formation of a group, outside Parliament and outside the organized political parties, to bore within the structure of the state, to convert it. Wells felt, as he said in a memorable phrase, that capitalism was dead, and what was needed was a 'Competent Receiver' to aid in the reconstruction of the world. This new grouping, called the Open Conspiracy in most of his writing about it, was a Fabian Society open to all, led by many true thinkers, not dilettantes concerned only with their power and prestige. For to H. G. Wells,

> It is not by canvassing and committees, by tricks and violence, but by the sheer power of naked reasonableness, by propaganda and open intention, by feats and devotions of the intelligence, that the great state of the future, the world state, will [would] come into being.[52]

THE FAITH OF A SOCIALIST

Socialism without a tradition of personal freedom, without free
literature whose freedom is jealously preserved, without artists,
thinkers, speakers and writing, free from official domination may
easily, because of the very completeness of its organization, become
the ugliest and most stagnant tyranny the world has ever seen. . . .
There is an ungainly, self-righteous, almost conscientiously
dishonest side to modern socialism of which I am afraid.

HGW, 'Socialism and Freedom', *Christian Commonwealth*,
8 December 1909 (Christmas number)

All the while that Wells was fencing with the Fabians, he was refining his
philosophical outlook on life. The Fabian episode sharpened the subtlety
in that process, and the end result was *First and Last Things* (1908), a
personal statement of belief. In addition, just before World War I, he
produced, along with several others, a serious statement of ideas,
suggesting what could come about if only their views were put into effect.
This book was called *The Great State* (1912). Together these make up
Wells's personal ideas. Of course no one really sits down to say, 'I am going
to write a philosophy or credo', unless much discussion occurs before, and
H. G. Wells was no exception. The difference, in his case, is that he had a
public forum, as well as many private conversations to hone his beliefs.

Alfred Harmsworth, later to be Lord Northcliffe, had offered Wells the
use of his columns whenever he liked. As early as 1897, he had said that his
'press or purse' was available for the cause of Wellsian views, and he was as
good as his word. For Wells's part, he was grateful for the offer, noting that
writing a column was 'just at present, the most efficient position in the
press. . . . I believe that I have set myself at the things. But I only rejoice . . .
to see you adding your immense influence to my ideas. In effect,
reorganization of the highest education.'[1]

In the period from 1900 to 1915, Wells on several occasions accepted Northcliffe's offer of space. It is in these pieces that his philosophy is first hammered out. For instance, in early 1904, he wrote a series of articles with the general title, 'From a Study Fireside: Some Comments'. In these pieces Wells turned his attention to religion, and the need to foster a spirit of altruism if the world was to be changed; the role of 'the people', which he felt was not yet clearly understood in the process of change; and the place of specialization in the modern era, which Wells said had been heralded but which had not yet come. He also proposed a reading list for his followers, with, if necessary, the publication of the world's classics in an easily accessible and inexpensive format. He called for construction of a simple building in every town of any size to house these books and make them available to readers. In addition, in this series he addressed such subjects as the drop in the birth rate, the place of women in society, garden cities, nurseries for mothers of young children, and other matters. These last deserve some notice in a later chapter dealing with his personal life.[2]

Wells wrote on the general theory of socialism in several other venues as well, always concerned with focusing his attack on problems he perceived, while making the result more readable, accessible, and easier to understand. Some of these articles appeared in different form in *New Worlds for Old*, while others were simply part of the learning process. Their effect was to cause considerable discussion, some dissension, and occasionally acceptance. This response was very much more useful than the Fabian debates which had changed nothing, so Wells kept up the process.[3]

At this stage of his life Wells was seeking a way out from capitalism and its extremes. Many others in the same period were engaged in similar pursuits. As a result his work was widely read, and commented upon as part of the ongoing search. 'F.W.H.' (probably Francis W. Hirst), writing in *Nature* at the end of 1904 and commenting upon *Anticipations*, *Mankind in the Making*, and *The Food of the Gods*, remarked that Wells was playing with 'great ideas in a time of flux'; and he urged scientists to read these three books as part of Wells's 'hard hitting'. Hirst suggested that Wells was simply applying the lessons of evolution to sociological study, and he said that Wells saw 'the individual as trustee for the race of the principle of life' and urged him to go further and provide 'a great synthesis'. Ray Lankester, reviewing *Anticipations* earlier for the same journal, made much the same points: 'It is the truthful statement of the outlook of a man who has grasped thoroughly the teachings of modern science and who still keeps hope alive in his heart.'[4]

Wells had considerable success with his scientific colleagues. If they did not accept his beliefs completely, at least they read his statements of them, reviewed them, thought about them, and assumed that something like his ideas was necessary to stave off catastrophe. No matter what scientific material is read from this time, whether it mentions Wells directly or not, the modern reader is continually amazed by the relative uniformity of conviction — that the future is bleak without applied reason, that our species can and must make a conscious effort to modify and 'tame' the future, and that some form of general plan (and probably some form of socialism) must be provided. H. G. Wells did provide that plan for many of his time — in England, in the United States, in France, Russia, and elsewhere.

Wells had less success with literary and social thinkers, most of whom lacked the scientific training which he brought to his studies. There was as much, or more, discussion of his ideas by these groups — what was different was the tone of the discussion. Wells said that the 'lion of politics' stood in the way of his world state and later, to another correspondent, remarked that there was 'no orthodox socialism, one and indivisible', so he was trying to get it clear for the three-quarters of the movement outside the organized parties. 'We want an open door towards progressives and liberals because we do not want to shut them out of our syntheses.' This expansive view meant a good deal of cut-and-thrust in the press, however, and there must have been times when Wells wondered about his analysts and their good will. Economists gibed at him, as did sociologists, and the sociologists were the most unreasonable and unwilling to talk, or so he thought. One person in particular, John Beattie Crozier, accused Wells of stealing most of his ideas from others and dismissed his work as that of a Hindu fakir, while claiming that it was not until a second reading that he had even determined that one work, *A Modern Utopia*, was serious in intent.

Crozier was commenting on the bulk of Wells's work in this general area, but also focused his attention on some recent articles in the *Independent Review*, as well as on the books from Wells's pen. Wells responded to the criticism by saying that he was aware that much of his work to date had been scavenging, but that his criticism of Spencer, Comte, and others was warranted, because they were guilty of sloppy thinking. For Wells there was no science of sociology, no science of economics, just as there was no scientific socialism in the Fabian Society. Just 'because writings on any subject are recognizably not literature, it does not follow they are scientific', was his response to Crozier. And although this apparently silenced that critic, others continued to yap at his heels.[5]

The *New Age*, the recently founded journal of liberal and socialist thought, provided a better forum for Wells and his critics than the capitalist journals in which previous discussion had appeared. Wells told readers of Orage's journal that persons should follow the socialist movement for life, but to beware of organized parties. Although self-advertised socialist parties might provide some recruits for the movement, their tendency was always to temporize and act in an expedient manner, and this simply diminished the intellectual pursuit of socialist truth. Socialists must continue to strive for 'the triumphant imposition of their ideas', was his view. This pronouncement brought forth a splenetic letter of response from Cecil Chesterton; and he and Wells along with others debated the issue of a socialist party for over two months in the journal.[6]

Some of the controversy in these journals occurred because this was a period in English history when the state of British arms was under substantial discussion, and especially the role of the Royal Navy. The Empire was under threat, or so thought many persons, as capitalism began to find new areas for investment and needed new vessels and larger armies to protect that investment once it was under attack. This meant that conflict inevitably arose among France, Germany, the United States, and Britain, especially with reference to their African colonies and dependencies. Wells himself was ambivalent on these matters, wanting the world state, but concerned that Germany in particular posed a threat to that state as well as to Britain itself. Although he was somewhat subdued on this issue before 1910–12, it remained at the back of his mind.

In the meantime, however, Wells's followers and friends took his views even further than he was prepared to go himself by calling for a world state, or a United States of Europe. Several peace groups were formed at Oxford whose meetings Wells apparently attended, although he would not speak in debate. He did think that many of the mainly geographical problems of a world state could be solved if the issue of racial prejudice was dealt with. On that subject, he said that if one could slay just one dragon and then perish, that dragon would have to be racial prejudice.

Widespread attacks on Wells's views continued, however, and some of his associates found it necessary to resign from editorial positions in protest against his treatment. Wells was simply too progressive a thinker for many to handle at a time when their whole world was coming under attack. 'Vernon Lee', realizing this, attempted to reassure readers of Wells of his good nature and his obvious desire to aid mankind. She told her own readers that mankind needed the broadmindedness of which Wells was the best example, and urged people to rethink his work. 'He does not dogmatize and he does not prophesy; he just thinks his own thoughts and asks us to listen to what he thinks', was her contribution to the debate.[7]

Wells began to write more frequently for socialist journals, although he often published the same material in the establishment press, usually with the expressed thanks of the socialist papers which could then have his work without paying him from their slender budgets. Such pieces as 'Will Socialism Destroy the Home?' and 'Would Modern Socialism Abolish All Property?' appeared in the *Grand Magazine* and later in the *Socialist Review*, and even in pamphlets and leaflets issued by the left-wing paper. Ramsay MacDonald in particular was in favour of this method of discussion, pushing Wells's view forward.

MacDonald drew the line somewhat, however, when Wells urged voting for Winston Churchill in a by-election in 1908. Wells thought that a vote for Churchill not only supported a personal friend (although he did not say this in the press), but, more importantly, that the alternative, 'an exceptionally undesirable person, Mr Joynson-Hicks [Jix]', who would otherwise be elected as the Socialist in the race, was a 'narrow theoretician' who appealed to almost no one. Churchill was standing as an Independent Liberal candidate; Wells characterized that party as 'standing today for all that is noblest and most hopeful in the awakening consciousness of our democracy, and on the other hand is an extreme and relatively small left wing, harsh, impracticable, insubordinate, a mere disloyal minority. . . .' Needless to say, this outburst, written vigorously, as was often the case when Wells went out of his general path, and by using such extreme language, brought down a great outpouring of wrath on Wells. In the long run, however, it contributed to the general discussion, as it meant greater debate, wider (and wiser) analysis, and Wells accepted the resulting comments as beneficial for the general movement towards socialism and the world state.[8]

All of these arguments, debates, and analyses were part of a great Wellsian effort to organize his thoughts generally. His private life was to a considerable degree in turmoil. His literary efforts, widely praised for their style and characterization, had come under attack for some of their subject matter. His efforts at remodelling the Left movements in England had led to the Fabian imbroglio in which he had lost friends, made enemies, and converted very few persons except some young followers to his banner. It was, then, time to take stock. A reading and discussion group, based originally on the Young Fabians and probably closely affiliated with the Oxford socialist movement (Ben Keeling may have been important here, as well as some young leftish poets such as Rupert Brooke — the record is very unclear), began to discuss philosophies of life. Amber Reeves, then reading widely in metaphysics and philosophy (especially Kant, Hegel, and Schopenhauer), and others working in the areas of economics and governmental structure, also played a strong role in these discussions. Wells, along with the other participants, presented his views in a series of papers for group discussion. Eventually this discussion led to his writing down a credo, a set of beliefs for himself and for others, which would lead, when put together in group fashion, to the world state.

Wells is fairly coy as to how many persons actually participated in these discussions, although he indicates that one of the revisions was read by more than ten others. If at this time he circulated his material beyond the young Fabians, it probably went also to Graham Wallas, Arnold Bennett, Richard Gregory, perhaps to Ray Lankester, also to Violet Paget, and possibly (although no evidence exists for this) to Conrad and Henry James.

Though it is difficult to determine with accuracy who might have had an impact on this philosophical creation,[9] what is clear is that Wells made a long analytical effort to clear his mind, establish his position, and to offer a guide as well as an apology during his period of turmoil and trouble. One of the significant discussions followed his reading of 'Scepticism of the Instrument', in September 1905 at an Oxford meeting.

The book that resulted, *First and Last Things*, was to remain, along with *The Great State* and two or three of the series of articles on politics, as Wells's standard of behaviour and thinking through much of the rest of his life. Remarkably, the book has received little attention from Wells scholars and biographers. It was revised fairly extensively in 1917, to take account of Wells's flirtation with theology, and later the 1917 version was again revised, returning much of the book to its earlier form, while also editing out some material on war in the modern world as no longer germane. When he reprinted the work in 1926, in the Atlantic Edition, he grouped it with *The Undying Fire* and *God the Invisible King* in a volume of 'Philosophical and Theological Speculations'. For the general public he was more restrained, reprinting *First and Last Things* in 1929, with no prefatory remarks nor with any other indication of the genesis of the book, as part of the Thinker's Library. That version remained in print until World War II, when, rather than reprint it again, Wells replaced it in the Thinker's Library with a slighter volume on similar ideas, *The Conquest of Time*. The work remained for Wells an effort at explicating his life's work as he saw it and, as he said in his original subtitle, as 'A Confession of Faith and Rule of Life'. It is to this work that we now turn, in an effort to be clear about his thinking before we investigate his social life and his literary production during this same period of seeking solutions.

The theme of the book is rooted in Wellsian science and his educational background. In Darwinian thought, especially as expounded by Huxley and the German thinkers whom Wells had read (Weismann mostly), the individual in a species might be different in some ways from all other individuals, but that individuality was quirky, of very little consequence, and the individual was ultimately submerged in the totality of the species. In fact, in all other species except man, the facts of life — birth, death, and perhaps even pain or exultation — were minimized, if they were noted at all. Each representative of a species had as its greatest drive the need to sacrifice itself for the good of the whole, and the continuation of the species. The selfish desire to carry on the group, without regard to personal problems or injury, was central to life itself in this understanding of evolutionary thought.

In man these instincts are more muted, for reasons which are not yet clear. There is a willingness to do damage to others (in some members of our species), and a fear of pain and death sometimes overrides the desire to perpetuate the species. For Wells, as for most scientists, and all socialists who have thought the matter through, what is needed is a world in which the good of the group overcomes and eliminates the baser drives to personal gratification. Education should bring out the higher motivation; but often it cannot do so because it must be at the expense of the false and intermediate groups which have emerged — church, state, region, and perhaps even family. Wells's book is a statement of these truths, although arrived at haltingly, and with many a side glance at other matters which threaten to intervene.

He was well aware that the world is not what it seems to be, at least for a good part of the time; and he was equally aware that the mind twisted reality with regard to the way that reality was received and perceived by the viewer/participant. As he said, in the sentence quoted earlier, '*The forceps of our minds are clumsy forceps, and crush the truth a little in taking hold of it. . . .*' (emphasis in the original). Wells, then, perceived that even science can be wrong. What is necessary is that every observer, whether a scientist or not, strives for the truth, the reality of life, even in the face of this discontinuity:

> We are all biassed to ignore our mental imperfections and to talk and act as though our minds were exact instruments, — something wherewith to scale the heavens with assurance, — and also we are biassed to believe that, except for perversity, all our minds work exactly alike.
>
> (Book I, sect. 12)

This, of course, is precisely the point at which most Christians develop a theological explanation, and invoke a Creator to help them through their dilemmas. Wells discussed the idea of God and eventually dismissed the concept, although he continued to use theological terms to describe his faith, which was more scientific and came from his understanding of the imperatives of life, the continuation and the good of the group.

In this same vein, he discussed perceptions of beauty, curiosity, the mandates of sexual trauma, pride, self-gratification, and physical as well as spiritual love. For Wells,

> The essential fact in man's history to my sense is the slow unfolding of a sense of community with his kind, of the possibilities of co-operations leading to scarce dreamt-of collective powers, of a synthesis of the species, of the development of a common general idea, a common general purpose out of a present confusion. In that awakening of the species, one's own personal being lives and moves — a part of it and contributing to it. *One's individual existence is not so entirely cut off as it seems at first; one's entirely separate individuality is another, a profounder, among the subtle inherent delusions of the human mind.*
>
> (Book II, sect. 8, emphasis in the original)

He goes on to say, in the next section, 'The race flows through us, the race is the drama and we are the incidents. . . . We are episodes in an experience greater than ourselves.' This is the clearest statement Wells was to make of the biological imperatives which he had learned from Huxley and in which he believed profoundly. In fact, it is so clearly his view that when he came to write his doctoral dissertation in 1942–3, he simply stated and re-stated, with evidence, the same premise exactly. But, as he remarked here, early in his life and with the disasters of the twentieth century still unknown, 'It is because we are episodical in the great synthesis of life that we have to make the utmost of our individual lives and traits and possibilities.' In other words, man is perfectible within the great instinctual drives of life, and it is to that goal that we should strive, incidentally improving the race, and cutting down on the distortions and the prismatic views which most humans accept so easily. He anticipated criticism of these statements, and so he dealt with them (as, of course, he must have done in the discussions with his peers) by criticizing the ways in which Christianity and other religions failed to subordinate the individual — in fact, usually offered rewards for individuality and punished only those instances of it that were vile (and even there usually provided absolution for the offender).

Book III of this profound discussion of traits and instincts is taken up with individual reactions to these truths. Wells discusses hate, love, family ties, the role of mothers and wives (in that benighted time, and in the time to come), sex, war, justice, and the social structure of the state. His treatment of these matters follows always from his view that we see the world dimly, need to strive intensely to improve our view, and must inevitably pursue a goal which subordinates the self to the group. The group then has a responsibility to provide a matrix in which this search is possible, is ever rewarded, and in which transgressions (especially in matters of justice and sexual love) do not bring destruction, but rather understanding.

Of course the world in which this becomes most possible is one in which socialism has triumphed, because it is socialism, for Wells, which allows the fulfilment of the individual in the greater structure of the state and the race. Socialism is a word which has taken on some hard and leathery meanings since Wells's time, and to use it forces the reader into some attitudes which may prevent him from seeing exactly what Wells meant. Above all he did not mean Marxist socialism, nor did he mean a sort of distributive Lady Bountiful socialism such as might have been practised by the Fabian Society if it had, by some miracle, been given power in 1908. His view of socialism was rooted in his view of science and metaphysics, and although in his day he did not need to spell it out clearly, we have to look at the words he uses, reflecting the scepticism in which his mind was trained, and analyse those words without the freight that three-quarters of a century has loaded upon them.

Wells divided his subject into general and particular concerns (Book II, sect. 3). There are general interests and problems which affect us all collectively, says Wells, 'from which no one may legitimately seek exemption'; and there are other problems in which individuality and the interplay of individual difference are paramount. Wells calls the great synthesis of human purpose in which these are worked out his Socialism. He defined it as:

to me no clear-cut system of theories and dogmas; . . . Its common quality from nearly every point of view is the subordination of the will of the self-seeking individual to the idea of a racial well-being embodied in an organized state, organized for every end that can be obtained collectively. . . . Socialism for me is a common step we are all taking in the great synthesis of human purpose. It is the organization, in regard to a great mass of common and fundamental interests that have hitherto been dispersedly served, of a collective purpose. . . . We look towards the day, the day of the organized civilized world state. . . . Socialism is to me no more and no less than the awakening of a collective consciousness in humanity, a collective will and a collective mind out of which finer individualities may arise forever in a perpetual series of fresh endeavours and fresh achievements for the race.

(Book III, sect. 3)

He goes on to disavow class warfare as leading to or contributing to this ideal, and says that the enemy of the good is the hatred which is engendered by such ideas. It is the duty of the citizens of the world state to provide the matrix in which that state can come to pass, to eliminate the rewards of the bad life, whether it is in the prostitution of the lady of the night, or the equally abhorrent prostitution of those who are frightened of consequences and thus are less than they might be. It is necessary to create a world in which the good, the ideal, even, is the goal for all. Those who settle for and accept lesser goals need to be educated to their potential.

This is especially true of women, who in their roles as wives and mothers (at least in Wells's time) found themselves often in conflict within the structure of their own goals. If Wells is right, though, the continuation of the species, and the acceptance of the duties that go with it, must rank as the highest of all goals; and if they are not so ranked, it is the fault of others in the state who downgrade them for their own purposes. As he said on this general subject — and it is an important statement, in the light of his own personal life, then and later:

We live in the world as it is and not in the world as it should be. . . . The normal modern married woman has to make the best of a bad position, to do her best under the old conditions, to live as though she was under the new conditions, to make good citizens, to give her spare energies as far as she can to bringing about a better state of affairs. Like the private property owner and the official in a privately conducted business, her best method of conduct is to consider herself an unrecognized public official, irregularly commanded and improperly paid. There is no good in flagrant rebellion. She has to study her particular circumstances and make what good she can out of them, keeping her face towards the coming time. I cannot better the image I have already used for the thinking and believing modern-minded people of today as an advance guard cut off from proper supplies, ill furnished so that makeshift prevails, and rather demoralized. We have to be wise as well as loyal; discretion itself is loyalty to the coming State.

(Book III, sect. 9)

Perhaps in the light of 1985, this seems a bit like special pleading for the world of men. However, that is reading into the past today's imperatives. In Wells's time women did not have the vote, except in a few states and territories of America, had very little economic power (although the Married Women's Property Act in Britain had freed them somewhat), and above all had almost no freedom in sexual and marital matters, except at very great personal risk. To Wells's credit, he understood this clearly, and although some might say that he was as guilty as anyone else in setting up ideals which he did not always reach in these matters, his ideals were greater than nearly anyone else in his own time — male or female. We will be discussing this matter in greater detail in later chapters; for the time being it is enough to note that he was a supporter of birth-control (and remained a public advocate of that cause throughout his life), supported fair and open divorce laws, accepted human love on androgynous terms, including instances of group love. As he said in the section of the book just quoted, 'We live in the world as it is and not in the world as it should be.'

Much of the remainder of *First and Last Things* (or at least that part of it which was retained in all the editions) has to do with Wells's own personal reaction to the setting down of these beliefs and ideals. There are moving passages on love, and even more so on death. He invokes the last memories of dear friends, of R. A. M. Stevenson, and especially of W.E. Henley, recalling them vividly to make his point that their deaths, no matter how bereft they may leave the living, still mark, for those who make the effort, a continual statement of their contribution to the good of the group, through their relationship with the individual involved.

When Wells wrote his words on this subject in 1908, he had not had much loss from death — Gissing, Stephen Crane, Walter Low, his mother and his father — and he had not been struck (except in the case of Low and Gissing) with the sudden bereavements which came later when Jane died, or when other dear friends were to leave him in the autumn of his own life. Nevertheless, he did not alter these words in the later editions:

Faith which feeds on personal love must at last prevail over it. If Faith has any virtue it must have it here when we find ourselves bereft and isolated, facing a world from which the light has fled leaving it bleak and strange. We live for experience and the race; these individual interludes are just helps to that; the warm inn in which we lovers met and refreshed was but a halt on a journey. When we have loved to the intensest point we have done our best with each other. To keep to that image of the inn, we must not sit overlong at our wine beside the fire.

We must go on to new experiences and new adventures. Death comes to part us and turn us out and set us on the road again.

(Book IV, sec. 4)

In fact, says Wells, much harder to accept than death is the realization of failure, misdirected effort, and wrongdoing. It is for those who survive, for all of us, to make the greatest effort not to experience that last and worst of all bereavements.

H.G. Wells was a profoundly personal writer. In his fiction, as well as in his prescriptions for the future, he is always at ease in using the personal pronoun, the autobiographical experience, the individual idiom. At times, as he himself was willing to say, this becomes cloying, or harsh, and the message is damaged by its carrying case. This book of personal belief could have fallen into that same trap, and perhaps even more easily. It did not do so, and for that reason alone *First and Last Things* remains a clear statement of his beliefs, while offering a guide for readers after his own day. That it remained in print so long, and needed so little revision, is indicative of the intellectual power which went into the initial writing and discussion. It is one of H. G. Wells's most important books, and provides a clear statement of the role of the individual, of the self and its relationship to the group, to the species, to the rushing future.

As is always the case with his work, there is an ambiguity, an ambivalence to that future, however. The duty to the race is paramount — but without the strong personal effort that a socialist must make, that duty to the race can be perverted, turned aside, and may eventually lead to suicide for the race. The choice is for those who participate. In 1908 the future seemed clearer than today, perhaps. Even when the work was revised in 1917, and then in 1926 and 1929, the future remained bright. Reading the work in 1985, one may be forgiven a slightly less sanguine view of the road ahead — but even Wells modified his views towards the end as the vista darkened and became more desolate.[10]

Few reviews of the book were published. It was, perhaps, too personal and too unusual a book. Those that were printed were very sparse in their comment, as only a limited number of persons were able to provide much of value. Leo Amery, among Wells's friends of the period, stirred himself the most, writing a sixteen-page letter, much of which was gentle criticism, especially of Wells's discussion of loyalties, to region and to country. However, Amery did remark that 'It is a long way the best thing you have done', and he said that reading it had given him 'the most intense pleasure'. John Galsworthy also commented positively, but suggested that Wells needed to join together with other writers 'to set down the truth', and not be attached to political parties except by accident.[11]

Wells's statement of faith in socialism led to a substantial debate in English political circles, as his friends, both in and out of Parliament, discussed whether England's situation did, in fact, warrant these measures, and if it did, how they were to be put into place. Should one work through the regular established political parties, or through outside interest groups, or some combination of the two? Wells contributed to this debate, as he felt, at least at this time, that the older parties could be reformed or modified enough to achieve his socialism, which seemed such a logical progression. As he said, though, socialists had an obligation to present their case in a logical manner, and not just trust to blind luck. Anti-socialists persistently misstated the socialist case, and the intellectual climate of the country was such that the misstatements won out. As he put it, everyone wanted the state to do something, but the most important thing at present was to wrest control of lives from the 'narrow-minded, cramping, tyrannous, ... and probably dishonest bureaucracy. ... Our children are growing up, and it is almost as bad for them to grow up into an atmosphere of bad argument as into an atmosphere of vitiated air.' What was needed was something that would breathe life into the cause, and end 'dull work' which produced only resentment.[12]

By 1912 the situation was so bad in England, with domestic unrest, a stalemate in the Commons, German competition looming just over the Channel, and the failure of socialism to make the inroads that had been expected, that Wells and others on the Left began to take measures which would stir the pot, create more discussion, and hasten the day in which the new world would at least appear on the horizon. This effort took two forms — a book, edited and organized by Wells, and a famous series of articles in the *Daily Mail*.

The book, eventually entitled *The Great State*, was put together by Wells with the strong assistance of G.R.S. Taylor, his old friend and confidant from within the Fabian executive. Taylor, after resigning from the *New Age* in protest at their treatment of Wells, needed something to do, and Wells hit upon this book, which would present a plan for action. Wells lined up most of the contributors, while Taylor acted, as he said, as 'midwife', as some of the contributors — such as the Countess of Warwick — had written little, if anything, before. Wells acted as editor, and the Countess (by this time Wells's landlady in Essex) was happy that he did, but was also very concerned that he, as a professional, would be too harsh on them. Wells did provide stern leadership, and weaker articles were returned forthwith for revision. Some of his work on the book was done in the South of France, in the comfortable company of Cicely Hamilton, who contributed an essay. Others whose essays appeared in the finished work were L.G. Chiozza Money, E. Ray Lankester, C. J. Bond, E. S. P. Haynes, Cecil Chesterton, Roger Fry, Conrad Noel, Herbert Trench, and Hugh P. Vowles.

Wells, in his introduction, remarked that the old and fallacious antagonism of socialists and individualists was disappearing, and he called for the formation of a 'new group to achieve the Great State by working together'. That new state, said Wells, would feature 'the ideal of a social system no longer localized, no longer immediately tied to and conditioned by the cultivation of the land, world-wide in its interests and outlook and catholic in its tolerance and sympathy, a system of great individual freedom with a universal understanding among its citizens of a collective thought and purpose'. The other chapters in the book applied these ideas to education, culture, science, art, literature, finance, parliamentary government, and country life.[13] It was a clear blueprint for the future.

A few readers were not happy with Wells's efforts, as they were convinced that he was leaving socialism, and had, by publishing the book, played into the hands of the opposition. Wells told the *Nation*, when they raised that issue in a review, that they reminded him of the Fabian Society, filled 'with that awful priggishness and that vanity of disingenuousness which have done so much to make socially constructive proposals seem dangerous and ridiculous in this country'. Later he told Fenner Brockway, concerned also for his possible apostasy, that he had not abandoned socialism, just the Social Democratic Federation and the Fabians, who were delaying socialism, and especially so with their attention to Wells's private life. Brockway returned a soft answer to Wells, and the struggle went on.[14]

The book was just one gun in the great battle of philosophies that was under way, however. In fact, most of the discussion occurred in the daily press rather than in books. The main forum for Wells was the *Daily Mail*, hospitable to articles of controversial content, and to his general work of philosophical analysis at this time. In May of 1912, the paper began a long series from Wells's pen, entitled 'The Labour Unrest'. In a leader published on the first day of the series, the newspaper (and this meant Northcliffe, of course) remarked that the controversy among the classes was the 'gravest problem' in the country; as England drifted from Parliament to Parliament, the *Mail* called for 'a sort of Grand Inquest of the Nation into the causes and significance of the ferment which is hissing and seething through all sections of the industrial world'. Wells was just the person to lead the inquest, it was thought, and readers of the paper settled down not only to serious discussion but also to some good fun, as Wells's pen often ran with vitriol when engaged in these matters.[15]

The resulting controversy has not excited as much interest as some others of the time, but the quality of the debate demands some discussion, as it did cut to matters which were of great importance in England. Some of these issues were shelved during World War I, but ultimately they led, as George Dangerfield has said, to 'The Strange Death of Liberal England'. Wells stated in his first piece that the present government was clearly not serious, for 'the real task before a governing class that means to go on governing is not just at present to get the better of an argument or the best of a bargain, but to lay hold of the imaginations of this drifting, sullen, and suspicious multitude, which is the working body of the country'. He called for the establishment of something in the nature of a 'social contract', and 'a decline in the number and influence of lawyers'. Further, he thought that the gross spectacle of pleasure and opulent luxury needed to be cut back substantially, as it diminished self-respect in those unable to participate in the society in any way, not only in this hedonistic spectacle now being put forward. 'We have in fact to "pull ourselves together" as the phrase goes and make an end to all this slack, extravagant living, this spectacle of pleasure, that has been spreading and intensifying in every civilized community for the last three or four decades', was his view.

Wells remarked that the Boer War could be, and was, papered over, but a changed spirit had to come, for reality was at hand. He asked how the work of the Great State was to be handled, and called for permanent guaranteed employment, work security, a department of business and technical instruction to provide answers to knotty problems, moving from that to guild-managed businesses, and finally pensions for those no longer able to work. He said that the bulk of Britain's population needed to be rehoused, and at least half of the money then going to support the activities of the rich on the Riviera and in Switzerland ought to be confiscated as a fund to refurbish workers' cottages, not as patronage but 'out of solicitude for the country and its citizens'.

'It is as plain now as the way from Calais to Paris that if the owning class does not attend to these amenities, the mass of the people doing its best to assuage the thing through the politicians, presently will', was his challenge to the owners. As he said, after remarking on how the Industrial Revolution had come to England in piecemeal fashion, 'I believe that in making labour a part of everyone's life, and the whole of nobody's life, lies the ultimate solution of these industrial difficulties.' He called for creation of 'a national plan, to lead', as no community had yet 'had the will and the imagination to recast and radically alter its social methods as a whole', but 'Humanity is rebelling against the continuing existence of a labour class as such . . . and only the collective intelligence, a census of brains and capabilities', would respond. As he ended the next-to-last article in the series, 'We have come to a phase in our affairs when the only alternative to a great, deliberative, renascence of will and understanding is natural order and decay.' Entitling his last article in the initial group, 'What Must Be Done Now?', he called for a complete restoration of representative government, with proportional representation to be used in the elective process, a rebirth of public thought and debate (especially in schools, and from the pulpits) to fill young people

with new realization that history is not over, that nothing is settled, and that the supreme dramatic phase in the story of England has yet to come. . . . Our schools and colleges exist for no other purpose than to give our youth a vision of the world and of its duties and possibilities in the world. . . . these schools are no longer the last preserves of an elderly orthodoxy and the last repository of a decaying gift of superseded tongues. They are needed too urgently to make our leaders leader-like and to sustain the active understandings of the race.

The series marks one of Wells's finer hours. He brought his intelligence and pen to bear on a problem that was widely discerned. He applied his faith in socialism, his trust and belief in scientific progress, and his sense that evolutionary thought and practice were at a crossroads to the possible solution of a serious national disaster. It was time to seize the issue, and turn it to the advantage of those who had most to win, or most to lose: that was his reason for interfering.

Letters, speeches, articles, and sermons flowed in response to his work. H.M. Hyndman, of the old Social Democratic Federation, remarked that revolutionary times were here, and the distrust was too great for reform — only deep revolutionary change was possible. Sidney Low agreed with Wells, while several academics called for more studies to prove or disprove Wells's comments. Some readers invoked the German success under Bismarck, while others, such as the Dean of St. Paul's, said the real problem was overpopulation and the inferior stock now being produced in Britain. The Master of Rugby thought armaments were the real difficulty behind the problems, while others suggested that extended foreign trade would provide some solutions. Several called for worker ownership, in a scheme of co-partnership, but speaker and reader alike tended to agree with Seebohm Rowntree, author of one famous work, *Poverty* (1901), who remarked that England was on the edge of the abyss, and that Wells was right when he said that the ruling class should put national welfare to the front and that unselfishness ought to be the policy of the ruling classes.

As the responses to Wells poured in to the *Mail*, and the debate intensified, the sides seemed to mirror society itself. Socialists like Hamilton Fyfe and Philip Snowden agreed with Wells as to the diagnosis, although they differed in response: Fyfe thought the answer lay ultimately in the dominions, while Snowden thought industrial organization and the seizure of political power through the ballot the only way out. Churchmen, such as Bishop Welldon of Manchester, urged the convening of workers' conferences and a return to a spirit of Christianity, while John Galsworthy asked for a major reform of the public schools, at present 'only caste factories', in his phrase. Others urged emigration, while several representatives of the schools attacked Galsworthy as being out of touch with reality; and, of course, a few individuals on the right thought the problem was one created by outside agitators.

Wells then returned to the fray himself, chiding his readers for their willingness to accept 'one single cheap remedy'. He remarked that he had observed the debate with great interest, not only in the *Mail*, but also in his clubs, and in other organs of the press, but so far all he had seen was patent medicines, while the disease continued to run wild. He again urged restatement of the national purpose, pointing out, 'It is Everyman who must be the Saviour of the State in a modern community; we cannot shift our share of the burden.' He informed his readers that an educational purge was no good, as there were no 'new men' waiting to take over. What was needed was not revolution, he thought, but 'a steadfast, continuous urgency towards effort and well-planned reconstruction and efficiency. . . . We have to think clearly, and study, and consider and reconsider our ideas about public things to the very utmost of our possibilities. . . . We are the State, and there is no better way to make it better than to give it the service of our lives.'

The next day he returned one more time, with an article which rejected Syndicalism and summarized his ideas. That summary included such matters as the abolition of the labour class as a class, the reduction of the amount of irksome work, and a regular conscription for social purposes. Workers ought to do their work with passion, and forget temporary restrictions on the amount and time of production (the coal industry was functioning on short hours and short weeks). Finally, the state would not be the only employer, as many large and specialized areas could be left free but with a co-partnership with the state, in the world which he proposed. But, Wells warned, failure to rearrange matters would bring about social war. 'Not a Labour State do we want, nor a Servile State' (referring to a work by Hilaire Belloc), 'but a powerful leisure state of free men, and to that all things are tending.'

This series of articles was a remarkable performance. It stirred up a great national debate, and to some degree set in motion some reforms in Parliament, as well as giving many persons ideas for the future. As C.F.G. Masterman said to Wells, 'D—d good in criticism, quite the best stuff you have been doing', although he thought the remedies jejune, especially proportional representation. According to Masterman the only 'high-souled, iron-willed patriots' who were kept out of power by the present party caucuses were Sidney Webb '(ha, ha, got you there)'. In fact he told Wells that the persons at the top of the industries were really the problem, for most of them were *'no good*. That's the real fact of the matter. Directly they are confronted with anything outside the grooves of their business or commerce they bluster like fools or weep like children. I can't see ten men in the country who would be any particular use in Parliament who are kept out of Parliament by the caucus.'[16]

To a considerable degree Masterman was probably right, but he also misread the Wellsian message. What Wells wanted was a major reform of education, along with the creation of a universal spirit, which would take up the challenge to the species posed by evolutionary reality. However, it would take time for that to mature, and time was simply not available. By the date of the controversy, the Balkan wars had begun, and it was less than two years before the world was caught up in and nearly swallowed by the horrors of warfare in Europe.

Wells did offer a few more efforts to redirect the drift of affairs, but these tended to become more and more pessimistic in nature. In fact he, along with others, began to shift his attention across the Channel, as it seemed increasingly to him and to many that a belligerent Germany, and the demand for rearmament in England, were sapping what vital force for reform there was. As he remarked in one place on the eve of the war,

> Our art is trivial where it is not feeble, our science is taught without spirit, and falls more and more into the hands of spiritless and inferior men, our literature sputters without protest or declines toward preciousness, because our political machinery is indifferent to and contemptuous of all these fine things in life. They become unreal because they are ineffective things.[17]

A few weeks later, after the Marconi scandals had laid bare exactly how bereft of morals and ideals Members of Parliament really were, Wells remarked, almost in despair, that although Liberalism was the 'grand old creed of England', it had been traduced. Now all he could recommend, when asked what Liberals could do, was that they go out of office and into the 'bracing wilderness of opposition': only then would 'a chastening reconstruction' become possible. And he closed with sad and disconsolate words: 'I see no other hope for us but that.' Later, responding to another attack, his bitterness continued as he said, 'But I would as soon play croquet with Alice in Wonderland as go on with those ridiculous attempts to reason with Liberals about Liberalism.'[18]

Wells had offered a creed, and an analytical response to the problems posed by his time, a prescription for others to follow — but for now all these were swallowed up in the war. When the world emerged from that conflict, new methods would emerge as well, but for H.G. Wells they were to be applied with the same creed and set of beliefs recorded in First and Last Things.

It seems appropriate to take a brief look here at The Conquest of Time (1942), which in the latter years of his life, during World War II, Wells offered as a replacement for First and Last Things. One of the reasons for writing the new work, he said, was that he had not in the original taken into account the roles of relativity in scientific and rational thought, nor had he paid enough attention to psychology, which had provided new insights, especially into the matters of pain, death, and individuality. By the time the book appeared, it seemed to Wells that, with the USSR and the USA now in the war, Nazism might be defeated, and the race between education and catastrophe might be won after all, although even here the result would be close.

He had then, of course, just gone through the exultant days of the British Association meetings which had led to Science and the World Mind (1942), and the activities leading to the Declaration of the Rights of Man were in full sway. Unfortunately for H. G. Wells, Hiroshima and Nagasaki were the true legacy of the working out of relativity. The iron truth of World War II is that co-operation never came, and *The Conquest of Time* (which would have allowed evolution to be speeded up, for the betterment of all) did not come in the way he hoped. At the end of his life, he realized that he had been deluded by events at the end of 1941, and by the time of his death, the race seemed to be going to the stronger force, catastrophic nationalist greed.

However, at the point of writing *The Conquest of Time*, his words continued to echo the promise of *First and Last Things*, and perhaps it is appropriate to place some of those words here, at the end of our discussion of 'The Faith of a Socialist'.

> The wild uproar and the stabbing demands and dangers of the present time should not blind us to the fundamental insignificance of these events. These are the birth-pangs of the human release. . . . The stars in their courses fight for the new humanity. The reality of human history flows on beneath the troubled surface of these accidents. These conflicts may seize upon our individual selves and oblige us to risk or lose our personal time, our personal work, and our personal lives; but that must not blind us to the incidentalness of these occasions that have entangled us. . . . But we must not mistake even a vast plenitude of such individual distractions for a world disaster. . . . we still have to live for a time among these guttering ruins; too often we have to judge and take sides with a lesser evil against a greater; but so long as we do not treat these warring 'Powers' and 'Faiths' as primary and permanent realities, so long as we despise them utterly in our hearts. . . . we can still keep our contact with the new way of loving and know the world is ours. These discolourations of the human mind will fade as the light grows stronger, and ultimately they will fade out of human consciousness altogether. And as our species conquers time it will reach back to realize more and more exactly, and to live again more and more fully, the contribution it has incorporated from our lives. . . . And, at the last throb, a soft dark restful curtain falls for ever upon that personal life and our contribution has been made.[19]

A LITERARY SALON ON THE CHANNEL

No, man's complacent assumption of the future is too confident. We think, because things have been easy for mankind as a whole for a generation or so, we are going on to perfect comfort and serenity in the future. . . . Even now for all we can tell, the coming terror may be crouching for its spring and the fall of humanity may be at hand. In the case of every other dominant animal the world has ever seen, we repeat, the hour of its complete ascendancy has been the beginning of its decline.

> HGW, unsigned, 'The Extinction of Man: Some Speculative
> Suggestions', *Pall Mall Gazette*, 25 September 1894

Is there any future for dreamers? or is dreaming dying out? . . . And as time and death come to take the hope and glory out of the real world, we would go to the Dream Bureau more and more, when the trusted friend had failed us, when the dear delight had turned to ashes at our touch, we would hurry to our refuge to dream back our youth, dream back the high speculation that had the taste of realization in it, dream back the lost loves and the chances gone forever. And we would dream and dream again our sweetest dreams.

> HGW, unsigned, 'The Dream Bureau: A New Entertainment',
> *Pall Mall Gazette*, 25 October 1893

After H. G. Wells finished both *When the Sleeper Wakes* and *Love and Mr Lewisham*, in the early summer of 1898, he suffered through a time of great physical and mental stress. Ever since his first period of spitting blood and kidney weakness, his health had been precarious. He had had a number of relapses, but his drive to succeed had allowed him to ignore these events. Jane attempted to take good care of him, and was quite successful, but when the urge to write was at its most intense, Wells could not be deterred. In addition he found it necessary to travel widely by bicycle, often with Jane, on their tandem special, in order to make sure the descriptions in his books and articles were accurate. He was not a good patient in this way. When, therefore, with the two books finished, his health broke down again, this time it was not a simple relapse. His physician, Henry Hick, a classmate at school of Gissing, who had recommended him to Wells, told H.G. and Jane that if Wells did not obey his orders, he could not predict the consequences. He put Wells to bed for six weeks, modified his diet very considerably, and refused to allow him to do anything other than read.

Only after that did the doctor allow Wells to carry out the second part of his recuperative regimen — to locate a house to which he could retire on the Channel coast. Both Wells and Hick feared there might be substantial periods in which Wells would be bedridden; in fact, there was some indication that he might be forced to spend much time in a wheelchair. For these reasons, the prospective house had to be easy of access for the patient, and to have extensive grounds where the invalid could spend warm and sunny days. Wells and Jane cycled along the south coast, and eventually found several places on the Kent coast, in the area between Hythe and Hastings, where they thought they might live. At last they settled on a piece of property at Sandgate, within easy access of London by rail, and began to cast about for a builder who would construct a house to their specifications.[1]

It was natural for Wells and Jane to travel by bicycle, rather than train, to view possible properties. Much of south-eastern England was seen by the two in this decade of the '90s, and the cycling gave H.G. a good deal of material for the many descriptive sections in his early writing. Everyone bicycled in those days, and the Wellses were in good company. When the autumn rains fell and the roads became rutted and muddy, letters flew back and forth complaining at their inability to cycle. Wells kept Hick apprised of his cycling progress, both when he and Jane went on holiday and as they looked for their new house site.[2]

As soon as Wells was able, he and Jane began to plan their new house. In addition to the features his health required, they hoped to have a stout, strong house in which there would be amenities for the many visitors they expected. Their neighbour in Worcester Park, and now Wells's agent, James B. Pinker, offered much good advice, as did R.A. Gregory. Pinker advanced extra funds to pay a surveyor's fee (their land crossed a former town boundary, which was an early worry), saw to it that a new tenant was found for their Worcester Park villa, Heatherlea (the lease still had three years to run), and even saw to storing their furniture. After considering various possible architects, the Wellses chose C.F.A. Voysey, since famous for his late-Victorian houses, of which theirs, called Spade House, is a good example.

It took Voysey just over a year to finish the construction, a year in which Wells recuperated, living at first in a Sandgate boarding house and later in a

11 Wells about 1900

12 (*below*): Wells with his mother at Spade House

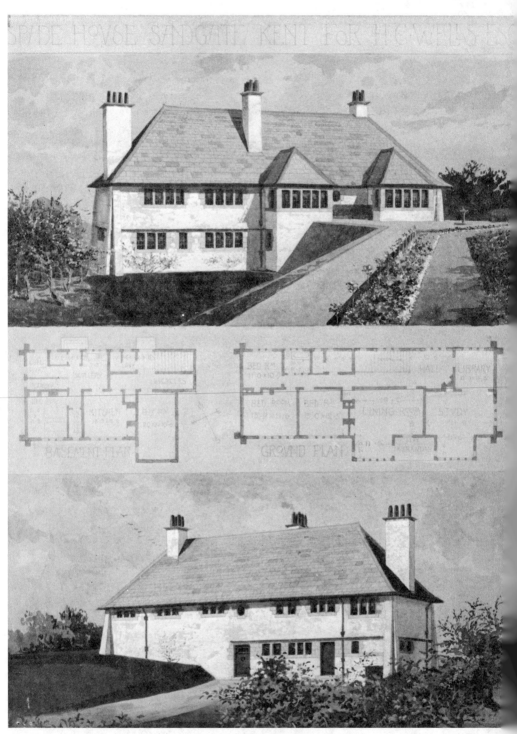

13 Spade House, Sandgate, Kent

rented house, Beach Cottage. He worried about a rumour that Voysey wasn't very good on chimneys. Word that there had been a recent landslip in the area was also vexing, until Gregory was able to reassure them on that score. Voysey was also to build a house for Pinker, so the two were able to compare progress, costs, ideas, and generally to ensure that the builder met their specifications. Voysey wanted to put the insigne of a heart on the door of the Wells house, but they were able to convince him to change it to the spade now affixed there, from which the house derived its name. The latches on the doors were also lowered to be within reach of children, much to Voysey's annoyance. However, eventually the house was finished and the Wellses moved in.[3]

Spade House still stands on the site at Sandgate. One approaches it from the rear, as the house is built to open on a vista of the sea, over the high point of land on which it sits, with a garden, croquet lawn, and spacious areas dotted with seats for reading, studying, and writing. When Wells lived there a tennis court was also prominent. The walls of the house are thick, and give a sense of almost Mediterranean solidity and permanence. Access is easy from room to room, and each of the bedrooms above is fitted with a lavatory so that guests could live as though they were in their own home. It has been said that this house was the first in England (perhaps of its size) to be constructed with these amenities. Although not the most famous of the Voysey country houses, Spade House has certainly retained its dignity, as well as its utility, over the eighty-odd years since its construction. The combination of Voysey's ideas with the needs of the Wells family created a building both useful and beautiful.[4]

The Wellses lived in Spade House for about a decade. However, as the two boys grew older, and as the pace of Wells's professional and personal life intensified, Sandgate came to seem too far from London, and the house and its grounds too small. In 1909 the family sold the house and moved to 18 Church Row, Hampstead, to a house near the Heath from which they could walk to Jack Straw's Castle or across to Highgate. After two or three years here, they moved again (although they kept the lease on the Hampstead house for some time) to a fairly large cottage on the grounds of the Easton estate in Essex, owned by a Left-leaning friend of Wells's, the Countess of Warwick. Jane and H.G. rebuilt much of that house, restored a large barn near by, constructed a garden, and then named the house Easton Glebe, to commemorate its original identity as part of the pastoral surroundings of a great estate. The Wells family lived in this fine house until Jane died in 1927. During this time Wells also maintained a flat in London, most notably in Whitehall Mansions, which he used during the week, but which was also used to some extent by Jane and the children as they grew older. In the mid-1930s Wells moved to 13 Hanover Terrace, near Regent's Park, and lived there until his death.

Wherever the family lived, there were two, and occasionally three, centres of activity. One was associated with Jane. She maintained a large garden, worked in it as soon as the early plants emerged in spring and tended it until very late autumn. Here she could be heard singing, humming, and enjoying herself as she worked in this area which might be considered her hideaway. The Easton house also had a summer-house at the end of the garden, where H.G. occasionally worked. After World War I Jane began to write a bit herself, and she kept a *pied à terre* in town which H.G. apparently never entered until her death. There, in the Bloomsbury area, near the British Museum, she had a true hiding place.

The second centre of activity was the children's quarters. They were attended by a nurse, until the older boy was about six, when this woman became the family cook, remaining with them until the move to Easton Glebe. The nurse was replaced by a governess, Fräulein M. M. Meyer, of Swiss-German origin, who was the chief teacher of the children, as well as a companion to Jane, until the boys went off to Oundle School — G.P. in 1912, and Frank two years later. Fräulein Meyer had been engaged originally to teach the boys German and French, and by the time they left school both were fluent in these languages, although G.P. had the better command of both. She also taught them other subjects, although special tutors were hired from time to time; and Wells never feared to ask particular guidance for the boys. As a result they were taught dissection by Ray Lankester, and received special training in the sciences from both him and Julian Huxley, grandson of Wells's former instructor.

The boys had large quarters for play, and Wells devised special games and toys for them. Eventually these games, for play both indoors and outdoors, were described in books which set out the benefits of playing them. In the year before the war, the boys were given intensive tutoring in language and history by a young German, Kurt Butow, of whom we will hear more later.[5]

Of course the third centre of the house and its surroundings was H.G. Wells himself, when he was there: it was his practice to spend the weekdays in London, from about 1906–7. The move to the sea air improved his health considerably; he had also, of course, a substantially better diet. He remained subject to colds, especially in late winter, and experienced periods of what was close to melancholia, although only for very short stretches and especially when under intense pressure of work. When he arrived at his home, usually on the mid-afternoon train on Friday (he returned to London on the mid-morning train on Monday), he was ready for hard physical activity. He and Jane, and later the boys, walked a good deal, thinking nothing of a fifteen-mile tramp on Saturday morning, to view the sea, a museum, or to visit Joseph Conrad or some other near-by friend. When the boys were young Wells put them to bed, told them bedtime stories, and illustrated the stories with 'picshuas'. Many of these line drawings, with appropriate captions, are in the Wells archive, or appear as illustrations in Wells family memoirs. Later H.G. and his guests would involve themselves in games with the boys, especially the outdoor war games, in which J. K. Jerome and C .F. G. Masterman, among others, were happy to take part.

After the move to Easton the weekends were even more strenuous. Evenings were filled with charades and amateur theatricals. Original plays, as well as classic dramas such as *Hamlet*, were performed by whoever was in the house. Jane had a large closet filled with potential properties for such theatrical ventures. They also played loud boisterous games of demon patience in which Jane was especially skilled. H.G. played a pianola, often classical music, while Jane frequently performed on a spinet, and later a baby grand piano; she was quite adept, especially in the music of Chopin. The boys were constantly being exposed to a high form of culture, and by the time of the move to Hampstead they usually attended the theatre with their parents, although not always on first nights, at which H.G. and Jane were often seen.

In the '20s, the family played tennis, badminton, and croquet on nearby lawns, but the most famous weekend activity was simply known as the 'ball game'. This was played with a large rubber ball, over a net (often several of them), and with all parts of the grounds in play; the object was to keep the ball moving over the net till one reached a score of fifteen. The game ranged far and wide, and was occasionally played upstairs and down in the rebuilt barn, as well as out of doors, before returning to the actual court. Everyone played, and H.G. took intense pride in matching the guests against one another so that the sides were as nearly equal as possible. Although some did not like the strenuous activity, it was mandatory at the Wells ménage, and many autobiographies and memoirs have something to say about the 'ball game'.

Wells worked every day, whether in London or not, and oftentimes the ball game was, as I have noted, simply an excuse to give him an hour with his proof sheets or for rewriting. He slept very lightly, especially when at work on a novel, and his study always had a Primus stove and supplies of tea and biscuits, so that when he rose in the night, to work for an hour or so, he could refresh himself before returning to his bed.

As one reads about this family, it is clear that each person had his own space and there was very little violation of that space by others. Of course, H.G. was in charge, but he also provided the large income which made these amenities possible, so his control lay light upon the other family members. The weekends were jolly times, and very few weekends went by without visitors, from the time of the move to Spade House until after Jane's death. A wide circle of friends came to the Wellses', to be alone with H.G. and Jane, to read each o.;er's work, to discuss political and social concerns, to relax — but, above all, to listen to what H.G. Wells had to say. His remarks were important to an increasingly large and diverse group of people, and whether at his table at the head of the stairs in the Reform

Club (his corner for thirty years or more) or at the family table in Sandgate or Easton, people gathered to listen, to comment, and in the country to be part of one of the famous weekend establishments in England in its day.[6]

Wells was a perfectionist about his work place and his work habits, never varying in time or place if he could help it. For that reason, an agent like James B. Pinker, who harried his clients, involved himself in their lives, and offered unsolicited comments on their work, tended to get on Wells's nerves. Pinker was a remarkable agent, and English literature of the early twentieth century is in great debt to his work, but he was too active for H. G. Wells, and as soon as the Wells family was well located on the Channel coast, H.G. began to cast about for another agent. As we have seen, he was eventually to use two American representatives, Perrin and Cazenove, while retaining A. P. Watt for many of his English needs. Ultimately, however, Wells preferred to act as his own agent, and did so as long as he was able.

Wells did not believe in any sort of personal promotion; he felt it was up to the publisher to carry out this activity and assume its cost. He believed in exacting 'a big cheque on account of royalties', and letting the publisher make back the royalties by promoting the book. Wells also asked for a virtually unlimited number of presentation copies (his personal list was close to a hundred copies for many of his novels). He reserved the cheap-edition rights to his books. Usually he allowed his agents to negotiate the serial publication, and the rights to his shorter pieces, but the novels were his own responsibility. Pinker had failed to sell an early novel, *The Wealth of Mr Waddy*, a book which when rewritten became *Kipps*, and it was that failure which had tended to drive Wells away from agents. The matter of agents was one of the few issues on which Arnold Bennett and Wells disagreed, but Wells's position was based, as he once said, on the fact that 'I learnt to write before I thought of a book', and his reputation allowed him to move away from the more conventional methods of placing his manuscripts.[7]

Wells was too demanding of his agents; Pinker, in particular, worked very hard to place Wellsian material. The trouble was that he also, because of his interest in Wells's work, became a part of their lives, and H.G. did not like to mix his pleasure with his business. Wells did participate in a special dinner in honour of Pinker and his work in early 1902, and gave the response to the major toast of the evening; but basically he felt that an agent was a necessary evil who took away from lawfully earned funds, did not have the need to press publishers as the author himself did (10 per cent was different from 90 per cent, after all), and he always resented the agent's role in his life. In fact, from time to time he attempted to get an agent to take a lower percentage for his work, and was occasionally successful, especially when he was earning very large amounts.[8]

Wells's income rose fairly steadily. In 1901 his sales with Pinker amounted to over £2,000; in 1903, £2,300; in 1904, over £3,100; after this time, his accounts with Pinker dropped off drastically, as he began to place his work through other agencies.[9]

As their relationship broke down, Pinker did take a reduction of his commission on the novels to 5 per cent, although he refused to take less on the short stories and articles. Wells was convinced that Pinker did not do as good a job in America as he might have, and their correspondence is filled with recriminations, apologies, and statements of trust and mistrust. Pinker told Wells that the amount of speculative funds in the US was limited. As he said to Wells, 'I would not be ashamed for anybody to see the record of your business and judge me by it, and I am sure you must know that the increases of my clients in number or importance is not going to alter your position in my regard.' This was not enough for Wells, however, and he began to negotiate directly with Macmillans in London. Wells developed 'diplomatic' illnesses when it was time to meet with Pinker, or so Pinker thought, and by the end of 1904, Jane was conducting the necessary business correspondence with the agent. Wells had used Pinker in a period when he was necessary, but did not give him any more business than he thought was absolutely essential.[10]

Of course many authors dislike their agents and feel that they are doing a shoddy job. Wells not only thought so, he let Pinker know about it, and eventually dropped him in order to conduct his business himself. Who did the better job cannot now be answered. Wells always needed more money than his work generated during this period. He lived well, often maintaining two or more homes, had an expansive social life, and also incurred expenses outside the normal ones through his extensive sexual activities. It would not be until the publication of *The Outline of History* (1920) that H.G. Wells would be free from monetary worries. By that time his need of an agent was simply nominal, of course, as someone had to do the drudgery of keeping the accounts. Jane helped by monitoring the books, but an agent could do it clearly and more smoothly. Agents remained, for Wells, a sometime necessary evil.

Wells was a very good friend to a great many people, and in no place do we see this better than in the books which he promoted for his friends; although he claimed never to write introductions, he did, in fact, write over forty, most of them for books by friends, sons of friends, or others who needed a boost. Several times Wells took a manuscript, re-worked portions of it, made extensive suggestions, and in general improved the book. Afterwards he often took the manuscript to his own publisher with the recommendation that it be read and eventually published. Of course, Wells's name was worth a lot, and if he had agreed to provide an introduction, the publisher was usually happy to accommodate him and his friend. The best-known such book was *George Meek, Bathchairman* (1910), the autobiography of a socialist friend and comrade. Wells apparently even contemplated publishing this book himself, rather than let it go unread.

Sir Harry Johnston, a famous African anthropologist and colonial governor, was another whom Wells befriended in a literary way. Johnson's novel, *The Gay-Dombeys* (1919), also introduced by Wells, was the story of the survivors of the Dickens novel, relocated in Australia. Wells apparently rewrote some portions of this work, which was the first of a half-dozen novels Johnston published in a second career. Wells met him when he was contemplating the early chapters of the *Outline of History*. Another one might mention is Brian Boru Dunne, who wrote *Cured: The 70 Adventures of A Dyspeptic* (1914). Dunne was a friend of Gissing, and the two had travelled to Italy in 1898 with Jane and H.G. A dozen other books were also placed, introduced, and aided by H.G. at various times in his life.[11]

His name was worth increasingly large amounts of money, not only on his own writings, but in helping others. His signature on appeals of various kinds was also valuable. Jane tended to keep control of just how many such appeals were responded to, but the requests were numerous. Some causes, especially in the area of literature, could not be ignored, of course. In 1906 *The Times* formed what it called a book club, which resold novels by famous writers of the day: the authors did not receive a full royalty on sales, as *The Times* maintained that it was retailing second-hand books. Shaw took the lead in opposing this project, but Wells joined in, and eventually *The Times* backed down, at least on the issue of royalties.[12]

This imbroglio, along with a problem involving copyright, especially in unauthorized overseas translations, caused Wells to become active in the Society of Authors, and eventually to be friendly to the formation of PEN. Wells, Shaw, and Barrie, along with others, were also very concerned over the censorship of plays, and wrote several letters to the press on this subject, although the censorship continued. Wells was less interested in a British academy of letters, but this had to do with his feeling that many of the original nominees did not deserve the honour. Eventually he refused membership in an important British literary body, which created further problems with Henry James; but Wells was primarily interested in helping in the case of indigent authors, not advancing the cause of 'literature' in general.[13]

Wells's home, whether at Sandgate, in Church Row, or at Easton Glebe, was a place where many of the current novelists and journalists in England met. Some of these persons became very close friends of the Wells family — Joseph Conrad, Violet Paget, Stephen Crane are examples. Perhaps closest to Wells and to Jane, however, were George Gissing, Arnold Bennett, and Frank Swinnerton. Another writer with whom Wells had an uneasy and yet intellectually profitable relationship was Henry James. Although Gissing, Paget, and Swinnerton did not live in or near the eastern part of Kent, all of the others mentioned did, and it was an easy matter to cycle or walk from one house to another. The Wells home was a centre, both geographically and intellectually. Jane Wells and H.G. liked to think of their house as a literary salon, much like those of Parisian society of an earlier time; this was what they had set out to create, with considerable success.[14]

As John Galsworthy said to H.G. after a 1907 weekend at Sandgate, 'I heartily agree with the last sentence in your letter about the time we live in — it is the best we could have had so far, though it will seem a very early Victorian period to ourselves, if we succeed in keeping ourselves afloat over these thirty years.'[15] Most people thought it could not last, just as Galsworthy indicated, and this was increasingly true as the century grew older, but in the meantime the youngish literary lions of this circle were in a great mood, improving the world, enjoying each other's comments and puns, playing together, watching their children grow, and, above all, spending delicious weekends in the Edwardian twilight — at Sandgate, in Kent or in Essex, together, remaking the world.

Fabian disagreements and discussions did not diminish the weekends for the disputants. In September 1907, Beatrice and Sidney Webb, on a five-day cycling tour round the Cinque Ports, stopped for a night with Jane while H.G. was in Switzerland with Graham Wallas. They were in a dither about the plans for Granville-Barker's play *Waste*, in which the Fabians were playing in the copyright performance, and needed to discuss these matters.[16]

All the Fabians were involved in plays and playwriting, or so it seemed. Shaw, William Archer, Lillah MacCarthy, all were present at many wonderful weekends at Sandgate. As Shaw told one correspondent, 'I am at Sandgate (Folkestone) for the sake of H.G. Wells's company.' Another reason Shaw was present was the abortive effort of Wells to make a play of *The Wheels of Chance*, and another from *The Wonderful Visit*; this was also the abandoned one-act play, *The Tail of the Comet*, which finally became the germ of the novel, *In the Days of the Comet*. Shaw read all these attempts, but cautioned Wells that his reputation was in the world of scientific fiction, and until he could

> once demonstrate that your stuff can get over the footlights, and not invoke giants, and Martians and suchlike games, you will not give much trouble to the old stagers. One thing that is almost beyond conception is the ignorance of the theatrical people of every world besides their own, however contiguous. . . . I scribble all this [he went on] to knock the thing straight in your head, as the career of a great dramatist is not to be entered on without careful consideration, and the great game in it cannot be won without an apparently reckless preliminary expenditure of genius on all sorts of side shows.[17]

This was good advice, of course, and Wells eventually abandoned his dramatic hopes.

The Fabians did act the parts in the copyright performance of *Waste*, Granville-Barker's avant-garde play which could not pass the censors. The Shaws, the Wellses, Galsworthy, St. John Heneken, and William Archer all appeared. Gilbert Murray was originally scheduled to act as well, but was ill on the day. The play made its brief appearance at the Savoy with all the censored material in place, but it could not be presented to the public in 1907, with the cuts or not.[18]

Shaw and Charlotte were at Sandgate for a weekend in 1905 and another in 1907. Shaw and Lillah MacCarthy spent Christmas week there in 1908, and when Lillah became very ill in 1910, she spent a period of recuperation at Sandgate. Afterwards, in her memoirs, she recalled the visits of Shaw, Bennett, E.V. Lucas, Barrie, and Galsworthy during the month she was there, and remembered rereading Wells, and submitting to a catechism on his work each night. At the time she visited, croquet was the rage, and there were so many guests that the evening meal had to be a buffet in order to accommodate them all.[19]

These friendships continued to be strong even with the political interference. In September 1913, at the première of *Androcles and the Lion*, Wells, John Masefield, Galsworthy, and Ellen Terry were all in attendance as supporters and special guests of Shaw. In response to a press query, Wells was reported to have remarked that the play was 'the only decent representation of Christianity he had ever seen on the stage, and the only play in London fit for children'. Still later Beatrice Webb appealed to Jane to help her with an overflow of guests (the Wellses to house the Shaws and other members of the Fabian executive) at a famous weekend party at Easton given by the Countess of Warwick. The Wellses were only too happy to renew their old acquaintances and to have at their home once more a disputatious Fabian weekend.[20]

All of the Wellses' friends looked forward to their weekends. C.F.G. Masterman, the *enfant terrible* of the Liberal Party, came several weekends to plan strategy with H.G., both political and literary. Ray Lankester was a frequent visitor, as their friendship matured, and he spent a month with the Wellses at their villa in France in the summer of 1911, after they had sold the Sandgate home. When they rented that villa for the summer, the friends who came were more carefully selected, but Violet Paget, Ella Hepworth Dixon, and Lankester were among the most prominent.[21] All remembered the travelling toy theatre which went abroad with the Wellses that summer, and this may have been the occasion of the famous enactment by Wells and Chesterton of the Minority Report on the Poor Law Commission. Later the author Philip Guedalla had so much fun at the Wells weekends that he purchased a house near by, and he and H.G. were very close well into the 1930s, again reading each other's proofs.[21]

Chief among the Wellses' friends in this period were Graham Wallas and the writer known as Vernon Lee. From their correspondence we can catch a glimpse into how these highly intellectual weekends were used to hone political and social thought, as well as restore the body. Wallas and Wells were very close friends. Wells thought of the former Fabian leader as a political mentor, and soon the two men began exchanging drafts and proofs of their more significant work. They remained friends until Wallas's death in 1931, and just before this Wallas came to Wells's aid again with a review and comment on his *Work, Wealth and Happiness of Mankind* (1932). Wells counted him as one of his dearest associates.[22]

The two men met in 1901, when Wallas sought Wells out after the chapters from *Anticipations* began to appear in the *Fortnightly*. They hit it off very well. Audrey Wallas (Ada) also began to correspond with Jane, then pregnant with G.P. Wells. Once the baby was born, the two couples spent much time together, inspecting layettes, eventually picking governesses, discussing baby food, and inevitably socialism, writing, and politics in general. As Wells wrote he sent first the chapters and later the proofs and drafts to Wallas for comment. Wallas, a slower and more methodical writer, responded in kind. The criticisms were blunt, straightforward, and immensely helpful to both men. Wallas was in the audience when Wells gave his talk at the Royal Institution in 1902, and his comments on style of presentation, as well as content, were also very useful to Wells. In fact, it is a measure of their friendship that H.G. Wells accepted such continuous direct analysis of his thought and work, for normally he was unable to carry on such relationships, as, for instance, a similar one at much the same time with Henry James.[23]

Wallas was at his best in the analytical work he did on the material which became *Mankind in the Making*. Eventually, when the book was nearly finished, Wells wrote him one of the longest letters in all of his correspondence, seven closely packed pages. After describing Wallas as 'a better man then myself' he said that '(although much wounded), contrition is my all'. They had discussed the role of the wastrel in society, especially the children begotten by such men, but now Wells went on to say, 'Temperance is the optimum amount of physical pleasure — not either abstinence or indulgence. Year by year my Christian training scales off me and I get more and more purely physiological with regard to sexual intercourse.' This letter, to be discussed in another connection later, is one of the frankest statements by Wells anywhere about his sexual needs, and it is indicative of how close he and Wallas had become. With the exception of Ray Lankester, Wells never unburdened himself to his male friends, but these two were exceptions, and important ones.[24]

Later in the letter, Wallas is told by Wells that, 'From first blast the public is going to swallow a lot from me and my affair as a good monarch is to make it go over easy.' This was in reference to Wellsian ideas of the New Republic, which would shortly see the light of day in *A Modern Utopia*. Soon the two men began to exchange frequent letters on this new book. In one such letter Wallas encouraged Wells to write even more strongly of the future. 'One is bound', he said, 'nowadays in calculating the effect of one's actions on sentient human beings to include the enormously large majority who are not yet born.'[25] As the book neared its end, the two men began gradually to plan a long hiking trip, primarily to discuss politics.

Perhaps the highlight of the Wells-Wallas friendship was this long hiking trip in Switzerland in the early autumn of 1903. They travelled together for two weeks, stopping briefly in Saas-in-Greund, Airolo, Illanz, and Ragazia — or at least these were the places to which their post was sent, and from which they sent cards to their families. Wells, who had gone hiking before, sent detailed advice on Wallas's wardrobe, and promised to provide maps, quinine, cascara, insect powder, sticking plasters, and back packs. Wallas only had to bring a change of stockings, a raincoat, and the obligatory stick. Jane, worrying that Wells had not given enough information, told Wallas that H.G. always went in a tweed knickerbocker suit, with a flannel shirt, sturdy brown hobnailed boots, and a tweed cap. He also took a panama hat, for a change. The journey was a wonderful occasion, and Wells used it to good advantage in *The New Machiavelli* where Wallas appears as Willersley. Their discussions on the trip, and thereafter, led Wells to work on *First and Last Things*, after *A Modern Utopia*, and were the germ ideas for Wallas's classic work of 1908, *Human Nature in Politics*.[26]

By 1907, after more friendly meetings and weekends, the two men were again exchanging proofs of the books they were writing. Wallas thought Wells's *New Worlds for Old* the 'best presentation of Socialism that exists', and 'of very great political importance'. He was especially careful to advise Wells to control his remarks about the Fabians, and he had, of course, offered him considerable advice during his contretemps with them, although never appearing in public to support Wells. Naturally Wells's book did not do everything, and as Wallas said, 'You still leave the rest of us some work to do on the constructive side of Socialist politics.' That remaining work was to be Wallas's, at least in part. Throughout 1907 and well into 1908, the two men exchanged many letters on the minutiae of writing, as well as on larger questions of content.[27]

When the Wallas book appeared Wells told him that he had stolen time from his novel to reread it, and, after calling it 'richly suggestive', told the older man that it was 'likely to become cardinal in the campaign of discussing democracy that lies before us. It is full of admirably chosen instances and a sort of irony that is characteristic of you. I am hoping myself to plan out a novel that shall give shape for the discussion of many of the points you raise.'

Wells went on to tell Wallas that Amber Reeves would be studying at the LSE with him some of the time during the next term, as she worked on her thesis on incentives, and hoped that this would eventually be useful to both of them as they continued the good work Wallas had under way.[28]

Wells and Wallas did not correspond quite as frequently after this time. One reason was that they saw each other often at the Reform and the

National Liberal Club; perhaps another was that Ada Wallas was less interested in seeing the Wellses, or at least H.G., once the Amber Reeves affair was known. Whatever the reason, the two men continued to be good friends, though without the closeness of the first period of their acquaintance. When Wallas published *The Great Society* in 1914 (a title, of course, similar to Wells's *The Great State*), Wells wrote a supportive and pleasant review in the *Nation*. Wells later helped Wallas in his choice of an American publisher; Wallas, in turn, introduced Wells to his protégé, Walter Lippman. Wells soon began publishing some of his material in the *New Republic*, then being edited in part by Lippman. Throughout the 1920s Wells and Wallas had casual contact, usually at their clubs, and each man always remained ready to support the other's causes. Finally, Wallas worked on Wells's great sociology textbook, and the old relationship over the proofs was renewed. Wells paid high praise to Wallas and the disinterestedness of his criticism, recalled their walk in Switzerland, as well as their general friendship in his autobiography, and also wrote a moving obituary of his companion. 'Death, when it touches me will not trouble me, for I shall not know of it; but I hate this plucking away of my friends', was his comment on the friendship. It was a significant one, which survived for over three decades, and was important in the lives of both.[29]

Another friendship very significant for Wells and Jane, which developed out of weekend visits for social purposes, was with the remarkable author and critic, Violet Paget, who wrote under the name 'Vernon Lee'. They first came to know each other when Paget wrote Wells what amounted to a fan letter about *A Modern Utopia*. Some of the material from that correspondence ended in the famous 'Open Letters', in the *Fortnightly*. Wells was moved to learn that someone as well known as she could find his work significant, and told her that he was also moved that she could 'stand my crude and floundering efforts to reason out my difficulties'. Wells urged her to read several books on Italy including Gissing's *By the Ionian Sea* and *Veranilda* (Paget lived in Florence), and ended by inviting her to visit them at Sandgate. Wells then, as he usually did with new friends, sent her copies of his own work: *The Sea Lady*, *The Time Machine*, and others. As to *The Time Machine*, he counselled her not to be too critical, for it had been hurried, as he had no 'leisure to think and I still can't afford time to read'. The idea of any sort of travel, he went on, 'except to recuperate for fresh work' were 'beyond dreaming. Consequently you will always miss in me certain qualities that you particularly admire.'[30]

Paget's letter to Wells, after a brief visit to Sandgate, is a model of dealing with an individual of Wells's personality. She was reading the books he offered and told him that she liked *Anticipations* best, describing Gissing's *Ryecroft* as his masterpiece, but closed by saying,

Dear Mr Wells, would you allow a rather obscure person of a previous literary generation to say that she has the feeling that you still have your best work to do? That you have not yet come to complete maturity (in your novels), that you have to write up to the example of *Anticipations*, but ... by yourself, for yourself, and details, atmosphere, style also answering to the original quality of your imagination.[31]

Even a letter as open as this did nothing except to cement their friendship even more, and over the next few years the two exchanged many letters, visits, and comments on life in general. Paget was one of those friends who was able to discuss the Amber Reeves affair with Wells, and those letters will be noticed later; but they felt free to comment to each other on many other things, and did. It was a literary friendship, with no other overtones (Paget was a decade older than Wells), and a powerful one for both individuals.

They exchanged books, with many compliments. Paget sent her *Gospels of Anarchy* (1908) and Wells sent her a draft of *First and Last Things* for comment. Wells commented very favourably on her Open Letters, and especially her defence of his thought in the *Albany Review* in 1907, but reproached her for 'fighting Pragmatists'. As he said, after defending the idea of pragmatism (Vernon Lee was having a public literary argument with William James), 'I do not know about you but I have been enjoying mingling intoxicating praise with results as Americans put liquors into innocent grapefruits ... I am really almost proud — no I mean properly proud — of having *got* you.'[32]

Wells was influential in getting Vernon Lee as a contributor to the *English Review*, the high-water mark for English literature before the war, and she was extremely happy to be published in this journal.[33]

Paget planned one long visit to the Wells home in 1908, but was deterred by illness while in the eastern Mediterranean; she did finally come and had 'a wonderful visit' with them in August of 1909. After this visit, Wells addressed her as 'Dear Sister in Utopia', and they exchanged intimate letters discussing Wells's romance with Amber. Paget continued to be a good friend, and whenever she was in England spent time with the Wellses and remained an influential supporter of H.G. and his work. Wells's letters to her about Amber Reeves are among the few on that subject which survive, but one suspects that very few others were written. Paget liked both Jane and H.G., was willing to put up with much that went beyond the bounds of conventional morality at that time, and for this, both of the Wellses were very grateful. In 1911, when Wells and his ménage went to Normandy for the summer, she was one of their honoured guests, and the relationship, with all its frankness, continued to thrive. Wells sent her proofs of *The New Machiavelli* for comment, and although she did not agree with his statement of the case, she did tell him his desires for the future were unexceptionable. She called for more deliberate planning, for 'inventing the future', to use her phrase, 'especially so in the way women must participate in the new world'.

She told H.G. that he was very 'useful as a loosener of prejudices, a developer of sympathies and fancies'. Wells told her that he did not expect her to like the book, but felt that he did not have to apologize for it, and she had not asked him to; 'my objectives run on different lines, I think, than yours,' he continued, 'but it makes no difference to my warm regard for you. . . . I think the day will come when you will forgive me *The New Machiavelli*, and anyhow, dear Vernon Lee, I am yours very warmly and admiringly, and affectionately.' The two authors continued to be friends, although perhaps not quite as close as before, for a break between them did not come until Wells began his strong anti-German support for the First World War. Paget was unable to accept this from her pacifist point of view, and wrote Wells a longish letter, but Wells did not take the difference amiss. He and she had had a useful and enlightening literary and personal friendship. That was important and enough for both.[34]

Wells never wrote about their weekends, even though the relationships which resulted were often very important to him both professionally and personally. However, it does not stretch the imagination much to read some of that enjoyment into a cleverly humorous novel, published in 1915 during the dark early days of the Somme, perhaps as a deliberate attempt to provide a look backward, to cheer England up, as it were. This book, *Bealby*, has essentially been neglected. It is a lesser work, no doubt, and it appeared at a difficult time, but is nevertheless worth a brief look as a Wellsian comment on country life as he saw it, though not necessarily at Sandgate or Easton Glebe.

It is the study of a young man, son of a gardener, visiting a country estate on holiday. A very funny book, it recounts the young man's first visit to a play, a flight in a gypsy caravan after he is disturbed by what he sees, and a drunken visitor, all of which are treated humorously. A love affair intervenes, after a caravan smash-up, and is introduced with the excellent paragraph:

> Then presently Miss Philips arose to her feet, gathered her skirts in her hand, and with her delicious chin raised and an expression of countenance that was almost business-like, descended towards the gathering audience below. She wore wide-flowing skirts and came down the hill in Artemisian strides.
>
> It was high time that somebody looked at her.

(Chapter 4)

The love affair is the remaining theme, along with sidelong looks by the young visitor into country life, tramp life, and social consciousness, ending with a marvellously funny battle in Crayminster, as Bealby and the tramp each attempt to pick up a reward for certain problems of the past few days (stealing vegetables, breaking up parties, and Bealby's disappearance) in which the two had joined. An effort to capture the young man, firmly ensconced on a roof, with plenty of tiles for ammunition, leads his foes to forget their dignity, all except a defender of public ways and footpaths, a figure always present in English country novels of humour, it seems. All ends relatively well, however, with Bealby home again and sanity restored, at least till the next weekend party in the country.[35]

Perhaps this does not truly represent H. G. Wells's view of country estates and country living. However, in its return to the humorous side of his writing, it does indicate how much his literary salon on the Channel meant to him, and to Jane, and, of course, to their guests. They both worked hard to make these occasions go well — probably Jane more than H.G.; and, as usual, the guests came to see him, but often remained to admire her.

'OF ART, OF LITERATURE, OF MR HENRY JAMES'

The main indictment is sound, that I sketch out scenes and individuals, often quite crudely, and resort even to conventional types and symbols, in order to get on to a discussion of relationships. The important point which I tried to argue with Henry James was that the novel of completely consistent characterization arranged beautifully in a story and painted deep and round and solid, no more exhausts the possibilities of the novel, than the art of Velasquez exhausts the possibilities of the painted picture.

> HGW, *Experiment in Autobiography*:
> 'Digression About Novels'

You may take it that my sparring and punching at you is very much due to the feeling that you were 'coming over' me, and that if I was not very careful I should find myself giving way altogether to respect. There is of course a real and very fundamental difference in our innate and developed attitudes towards life and literature. To you literature like painting is an end, to me literature like architecture is a means, it has a use.

> HGW to Henry James, 8 July 1915

These epigraphs give Wells's view of a famous literary discussion, at first between him and Henry James, but reopened since then by nearly everyone who has written on literary subjects in this century. Perhaps a bit more may still be said about these matters, especially if the discussion is placed in the context of Wells's close friendships in the literary world of his time.

Of all these friends, one of the earliest and most steadfast was George Gissing. Wells had reviewed *Eve's Ransom* and *The Paying Guest* in the old days of the *Saturday Review*, but he and Gissing did not meet until Wells was a guest in the autumn of 1896 at a dinner meeting of the Omar Khayyám Club, a literary dining group. Wells rushed up to Gissing at the dinner, told him how much he liked his work, and mentioned the curious coincidence that in *New Grub Street* Gissing's hero had lived in Mornington Road with a wife named Amy, as Wells had also done at the time the book appeared. Gissing remarked to his diary that he 'rather liked Wells's wild face and naïve manner'.[1]

The two men hit it off amazingly well and corresponded throughout the remainder of Gissing's life. Many of the letters to Gissing are missing, but with the use of his diary it is possible to trace the relationship very well. Early in 1898, Jane and H.G. went to Rome to visit Gissing, then living in the Holy City. They remained more than a month, taking in the sights, dining out, meeting other English visitors, and generally enjoying each other's company. In fact Gissing moved to the Wellses' hotel to be near them while they were there. Others who were part of the group, at least for periods of time, included E. W. Hornung, A. Conan Doyle, and Mrs Rosalind Williams (later Dobbs), Beatrice Webb's sister. Later that summer Gissing spent ten days with the Wells family learning to ride a bicycle. He wrote from their home to his publishers, and he read *The War of the Worlds* there in proof. Generally the two men, and Jane, became very fast friends.

Gissing's own life was in turmoil — he had married a prostitute early in his life and after a divorce had married another person of somewhat similar social class, but this one, unfortunately, was of unsound mind. By this time, however, he had met Gabrielle Fleury, with whom he lived in France as his third, common-law wife. Wells became caught up in these matters as Gissing confided in him and Jane. When Wells fell ill in the summer of 1898, Gissing remained close, and they visited at least once. Of course, Gissing's boyhood friend, Henry Hick, was Wells's physician. In 1900 also Gissing visited Sandgate; and in 1901, H.G. and Jane visited the Gissing establishment in Paris.

Later, just before his death, Gissing returned to England, where he remained as a guest of the Wellses and the Pinkers as well as spending time in a sanitorium. The visit was to promote Gissing's books. Although Jane Wells was able to put seven pounds on his emaciated body during the trip, Gissing's health was poor and he continued to fail. As he lay dying, Gabrielle telegraphed Wells and he went to Gissing's bedside, but left, through a misunderstanding, the day before he died. In fact, it was this death, happening so early and to such a close and sympathetic friend, that caused Wells afterwards to shun death and the manifestations of death. Many critics have felt that he treated Gissing poorly after his death; but, in truth, this was only a mark of Wells's inability to deal with such matters. Gissing's death came as a great shock to Wells, although all who saw Gissing in the last year of his life knew that he was very ill.[2]

Gissing did not leave much of an estate (less than £600) — two wives, children, small literary sales, and grave illness had eaten up what little there was. Wells and Morley Roberts, perhaps Gissing's closest other friend in

England, did what they could to obtain a pension fund for the children and to administer the estate. Eventually Clara Collet, another friend, became so domineering over the administration of the estate that Wells dropped out. He contracted, instead, to write an introduction to Gissing's unfinished novel, *Veranilda*. This was to cause even more difficulty for the bereaved friends.[3]

Gissing's associates thought that a preface by Wells to the unfinished novel might enhance its sale and increase the amount of the estate at a time when it was much needed. In the piece Wells discussed, in a very general manner, Gissing's early life, which had included a term in prison, relationships with prostitutes, and a stay in rather low conditions in Chicago. Gabrielle Fleury reacted strongly to this account and harsh letters flew back and forth. Wells and Roberts also exchanged a number of letters on the subject, and Roberts read the proposed preface and offered comments, at Wells's request. The literary world, and especially others of Gissing's friends, were very unhappy at the interference of Fleury and Collet, but Victorian sensibilities prevailed and the novel appeared with an innocuous preface by another literary figure of the time, the English positivist Frederic Harrison, who had enjoyed having Gissing as a tutor for his children. The new preface contained some errors, and did not contribute much to the Gissing estate. In fact, the publisher cut down the amount of the proposed advance when Wells was forced to withdraw. Wells told Henry Newbolt that the estate lost £150 through these silly actions.

The *Monthly Review* printed Wells's proposed introduction, so he was able to get his views into print. He rather overpraised the novel, but as he apparently told Morley Roberts, that was to increase the sales of his friend's book. Wells understood clearly enough that Gissing's reputation would ultimately stand or fall on *The Nether World*, *The Odd Women*, *Born in Exile*, and *By the Ionian Sea*, to name four books which Wells liked very much, and not on this last tired production of his great but very ill friend. Partially as a result of the contretemps Roberts also began a biography of Gissing, and Wells loaned him his Gissing correspondence. However, Roberts felt unable to publish the book immediately; and when it did come out, it appeared as a putative novel, although one in which the characters were immediately identifiable to the entire London literary world. Wells apparently read and commented on an early version of the Roberts book after the correspondence was returned; so Gissing's two old friends did what they were able to do to make the lives of Gissing's heirs more pleasant.[4]

Roberts kept his promise to Wells and eventually, in 1912, published his version of Gissing's life under the title *The Private Life of Henry Maitland*. By a literary coincidence, a second book on Gissing appeared the same month: Frank Swinnerton's *George Gissing: A Critical Study*. Swinnerton had not been able to use the Gissing correspondence with Wells, as it had been in Robert's possession at the time he was writing; but he did supplement his book through long conversations with Jane Wells. (H.G. had been unable to see him when he appeared at Easton Glebe.)

Roberts had lost all of Gissing's letters to him from the period 1880 to 1895, so his work had to depend on a flawed memory, but the novel was a good one, even so. As Roberts said to Wells, as the book neared publication, 'You did at times much for him and he knew it. I suppose if I *do* put out this volume I shall have to retire to Fiji or Namschaften. . . .' Wells reviewed the two books in *Rhythm* late in 1912. There he remarked that, after reading the books, 'I see again this scholarly, intellectual, unhappy, weakly dignified and intensely pathetic being as I knew him in my life. . . .' Wells felt Roberts should not have, or at least had had no need to, disguise his subject, and that Gissing might have benefited from a more straightforward view. He liked the Swinnerton version very much and urged the public to read both books in order to learn about his early and great friend.[5]

Frank Swinnerton became one of Wells's good friends and most vocal supporters. Wells told him once that the only figures in London literary life with whom he had not quarrelled were himself, Arnold Bennett, and G.K. Chesterton. Swinnerton lived longer than any of his contemporaries, surviving into his mid-nineties; and because of that, as well as his position first as reader, then editor, and later as important literary critic, his views on the scene in London before the war have remained significant.[6]

Swinnerton was nineteen years younger than Wells, but as he had grown up in straitened circumstances (as had most of Wells's close friends — Gissing, Bennett, and others), he appealed to Wells with his drive to excel. By the turn of the twentieth century he was employed by J. M. Dent, acting as scout and initial reader for what would become the Everyman series. From there he went to Chatto & Windus as an editor. He visited Jane at the time his book on Gissing appeared, and after Wells reviewed it. He was also present in 1911 at Wells's important lecture given under the auspices of the Times Book Club. This talk, in a hot, noisy (the room had one major window, opening on traffic, and directly behind Wells), crowded room, was also attended by Shaw and Bennett. Bennett remarked that most of the other persons in the room seemed to be women who were interested in Wells but who distinguished themselves by their crudity in dress and manner. Whether this was the case or not, the lecture, on the contemporary novel, was a statement by Wells of his own purpose in writing, as well as a discussion of the work of his contemporaries. Swinnerton thought it an important occasion, as did Bennett.[7]

As a result of this talk, Bennett invited Wells and Swinnerton to lunch. Bennett stammered badly, so he did not talk much at lunch, but Swinnerton and Wells became fast friends as a result of the meeting. Swinnerton was soon invited to dinner in Church Row. Others at the occasion included William Rothenstein, the artist, who lived near by, as well as Henry Arthur Jones, the playwright and critic, with whom Wells was to have a famous argumentative correspondence years later. Swinnerton became very ill in 1914, and Bennett and Wells took turns nursing him back to health at their country homes. Swinnerton soon began spending weekends with Wells and other times with Bennett, especially on the latter's yacht, *Velsa*, as well as accompanying Bennett on trips to Portugal, the South of France, and to Paris.

Swinnerton in 1917 wrote a remarkable novel entitled *Nocturne*, representative of the new-realism school. It did not sell well in Britain, and it was thought that the publisher had been indolent about sending out review copies, so Wells and Bennett took it upon themselves to push it. Wells, for example, wrote a strong letter to the *Daily News* urging people to read the book, wrote a preface for the American edition (without Swinnerton's knowledge), and he and Bennett also wrote articles on Swinnerton for the press. These two articles, with a third, were then published as a small book in 1920. Altogether they did what they set out to do. The book became a bestseller, remains in print, and Swinnerton became the force in English literature he deserved to be.[3]

Swinnerton returned the favour many times over, writing in his *Swinnerton: An Autobiography* and elsewhere in defence of Wells and Bennett and their novels of lower-class realism, against attacks from Henry James, and from Virginia Woolf and others of the Bloomsbury group. He was one of the ablest commentators of his time on literature generally and acted as a buffer in this controversy when Wells could not (except once or twice) and Bennett would not (primarily because of his position as critic for the *Evening Standard*) respond.[9]

The correspondence between Swinnerton and Wells is filled with accounts of occasions when they were together for weekends at Wells's home, as well as of evenings at the Reform Club, where Swinnerton used to come on Thursdays, after delivering his copy to the London *Evening News*. After a spring weekend at Easton in 1916 and exposure to the 'ball game', Swinnerton remarked that he had returned 'with stiffness in every joint'. Jane read and corrected Swinnerton's proofs on several occasions and apparently tipped off H.G. as to the strength of *Nocturne* when it appeared at Easton in proof before publication. After the First War, Swinnerton spent a fortnight with the Wellses, where he commented on *Joan and Peter* as it emerged in proof.

Wells was ill during the influenza epidemic, and Swinnerton (as well as others) was concerned about him. As he said to H.G., 'Be quick and get absolutely better. These are treacherous days.' Swinnerton also became friends with 'Elizabeth', Countess von Arnim, a Wells associate, at about this time, as their literary circle continued to expand. When PEN was being formed, Swinnerton acted as a courier for Galsworthy and Wells. In 1920 he agreed to act as Wells's executor, if Wells predeceased Jane. Swinnerton also acted as administrator of several small literary funds organized by Bennett, Wells, Galsworthy, and Edward Marsh, as the four of them felt it important to sponsor young authors as they had themselves been sponsored.[10]

When Wells went to Washington to cover the Disarmament Conference of 1920–1, Bennett and Swinnerton gave Jane a remarkable dinner to which she was invited with the following piece of inspired doggerel:

> Me and AB
> Both Agree
> That you ought to ask AB and me
> As a spree
> to dinner (merely us three)
> at your F-L-A-T
> Verbum sat. sapiente.
> We think the articles of H.G.
> From Washington Citee
> Are deserving of the highest degree
> (or Whatever it be)
> of celebritee. . . .
> And if you ask A.B. and me
> to dinner dont ask Marguere
> too as this is unreasonablee
> if you have heard nothing of she
> do not mention or speak to her when we
> come, as I think you will see
> that life has its ups and downs for A.B.
> as well as for you and me.
> Again verbum sat. sapiente or se
> As the case may be.[11]

('Marguere' was Bennett's first wife, Marguerite, with whom he was having difficulty at this period.)

Swinnerton soon fell in love, and Jane and H.G. were happy to involve themselves in the young couple's affairs and eventually to help them find a home (and perhaps even with finances, although the record is unclear). The house, Tokefield, remained as Swinnerton's home in Sussex until his death nearly sixty years later. Swinnerton later said that Wells was 'more agreeable, impulsive, inventive, and irritable' than he appeared in *Experiment in Autobiography*. He remained one of H.G.'s closest friends; and their friendship, although mostly conducted in letters and at their weekly meetings at the Reform Club after Jane's death, was a powerful force in both their lives. In 1939, just after the war broke out, 'Swinny' published a novel, called at one time *The Devil Breaks Through* (apparently an early title for *The Two Wives*). Wells was quick off the mark with high praise. Swinnerton responded to the praise with a heartfelt letter, which indicates something of their true relationship: 'But first of all believe how much your letter means to me, and how much you have always meant to me. Real affection and unalterable gratitude.' Swinnerton went on to compliment Wells on the war aims campaign, pledged his support, and urged him on: 'The one justification of this war will (or should) be a wiser world.'[12]

The other close and important friend of H. G. Wells from this earlier period was Arnold Bennett. In fact, Bennett was probably Wells's closest male friend, at least among his literary circle, with R. A. Gregory being the closest on the scientific side of his life. As Swinnerton remembered, Wells and Bennett never quarrelled; and when Bennett died, early in 1931 from typhoid, Swinnerton found Wells in his flat reading Bennett's obituary notice, and crying over the loss of his dear friend. Their correspondence was fairly extensive — more than 200 letters survive, although there are more from Bennett than Wells, probably because Wells did not write as many discursive letters as did Bennett, but also because Wells did a better job (or Jane did) of retaining his correspondence.

Bennett's novels of the lower middle classes, centring at first and most strongly on the Five Towns area of the Potteries, where he himself had grown up and where he published his first work in the *Staffordshire Signal*, have declined in popularity. Although some of his fiction, notably *The Old Wives' Tale* and the *Clayhanger* trilogy, continues to be read, his work has not had the critical revival accorded recently to Gissing, nor the steady sale certain of Wells's books have always maintained. However, Bennett's correspondence and his critical work remain significant in our understanding of the literary scene of the first half of this and the latter part of the nineteenth century. His articles in the *New Age* from 1908 to 1911 were important in the making of several literary reputations, and his weekly column in the *Evening Standard* from 1926 to his death in 1931 comes close to required reading for the period between the wars. His role in H.G. Wells's life was significant as well.[13]

Wells and Bennett were very close in age, and both came from lower-middle-class backgrounds. Each was trained for a different life from the one he chose, and each used his background to make his fiction stronger and more realistic. By coincidence each published an early and important novel (Bennett, *A Man from the North*, and Wells, *Love and Mr Lewisham*) which had as its theme the impact of profound sexual love on the career of a young man caught up in conflicting desires. It was Wells's story, 'The Cone', however, which brought the two men together, as Bennett wanted to make the acquaintance of anyone who could write about the Potteries with such skill. They became immediate friends; and throughout the decade before 1910, their correspondence is unusually clear and forceful as well as frequent. Each criticized the other's work freely, with Bennett usually offering good sound comments on Wells's sloppy habit of repeating words, and his occasional bad syntax, especially after plural and compound nouns. Wells, on the other hand, constantly urged Bennett to concentrate his powers on depicting the life of his own class and the impact of modern life upon that class. Bennett, more interested in making money and in rising socially, wrote a great many pot-boilers, which seemed frothy to Wells, as they did not advance the breakdown of the class system. The two never really fell out, however, over these matters; and the correspondence remained friendly, witty, and filled with affection.

Bennett read Wells's proofs, at least of his larger works, from 1905 to after 1921, contributing large amounts of time to dealing with Wellsian sentence construction, although he was scrupulous never to modify any of the language except to deal with infelicities. Wells, in turn, read some of Bennett's proofs, but fewer, as Bennett's style was less in need of correction. Wells introduced Bennett to Pinker and the two formed a strong alliance for the sale of Bennett's work. Bennett also became friendly with Jane Wells and was a supportive force in her life, and especially so when H.G. was in his more irascible moods, or when he was heavily involved with other women. Jane never put any obstacles in Wells's way at such times, but she did need the solace of knowing that she was needed, of which both Bennett and Swinnerton assured her at these times of stress.

Bennett, always known to his friends as 'AB', became a member of the Reform Club; and it was here that he and Wells held forth those nights (usually Monday through Thursday) when Wells was in town. Bennett wrote and had produced a large number of plays; and Wells and Jane were usually at the first night to support the work of their friend. In fact, Wells and Bennett worked together off and on for several years on a play which never reached the boards. The then manager of the Haymarket Theatre eventually refused the last version of the play, as there was to be a corpse on stage when the curtain went up. But both Bennett and Wells felt the play should not have been produced in any case, on the grounds of quality, as well as for this superstitious reason.[14]

Bennett wrote several of the better critical comments on Wells, and his views will be discussed later; however, it is significant that Wells did not, by choice, contribute to these articles, as he felt that it was for Bennett to make such judgements himself.[15]

More important for Wells, however, was the support Bennett gave him when the forces which opposed him arose. When, for instance, *Tono-Bungay* came under attack, Bennett commented strongly on it as a 'great attempt to encompass one nation's social existence', calling it a 'most distinguished and powerful book' in response to the review by 'Claudius Clear' (Robertson Nicoll) in the *British Weekly*.[16]

Later, when Wells was attacked by some for *The New Machiavelli*, attacks which focused on the serial version which did not come across with the force of the published book, Bennett was also very quick off the mark with his defence of Wells, his work, and his purpose in writing such a book. Bennett said that the book had silenced its earlier critics with 'its priceless and total sincerity'. He also said that Wells's candour, his warmth of generosity, and his inspiring faith in humanity were greater than those of any living writer, and ended his remarks with, 'H.G. Wells is a piece of sheer luck for England.'[17]

These examples, relating to H.G. Wells because he is the subject of this book, could be repeated many times over with respect to other authors whom Bennett thought victimized by philistine readers or by those who wanted sugar-coating on their literary fare. Bennett himself cut through such froth in his more significant fiction (*Sacred and Profane Love*; *The Pretty Lady*; *Lord Raingo*, to name three novels not much read today); and he admired those who followed this course even more boldly than he did himself. Bennett and Pinker, along with Wells, Barrie, and Galsworthy, were always ready to support the work of new writers whom they thought were being victimized. This support took the form of favourable reviews, letters to the press, as in the case of *Nocturne*, lobbying to obtain pensions for the families of those who, as in the case of Gissing, left little money, but also involved setting up funds for the writers themselves. The most important of the authors thus helped was James Joyce: Wells and Bennett joined Ezra Pound at first, and Sylvia Beach later, in providing funds and then vocal support for this controversial writer. Another who was helped was D. H. Lawrence, although, in a kind of comic turn-about, he eventually rejected the money as not sufficient for his needs.[18]

In an odd way, when one recalls these stories of support and help, it makes the attacks on Wells and Bennett even more remarkable. Actually, Bennett and Galsworthy bore more of the brunt than did Wells — one supposes because Wells was actually closer to contemporary writing than were the others. Whatever the case, the attacks by Henry James, Virginia Woolf, and their supporters on the Bennett–Wells–Galsworthy group as being too down-to-earth, too detailed, too full of characterization, and being unwilling to spend the time to hone their prose, to utilize the art of construction, to make the medium the message (to use terms which are familiar today) — these attacks have been well known for years. Bennett and Galsworthy accepted some of the criticism as worthwhile, and Wells spent a fair amount of time in this period of his life attempting to adjust to these critical comments. Eventually, for the two old lions, Bennett and Galsworthy, the game did not offer results worth the playing, and so they tended to ignore the attacks. For Wells, however, the criticisms struck too close to the bone: so many people had welcomed him as a new literary voice, for using powerful and relatively little-known techniques and for applying his ideas to hitherto forbidden or hidden subjects. As he went on in his life, the scientific side, with its promise (or threat), became increasingly important to him. As a result, the ends began to matter more than the means. When this time came he found it necessary to part with old friends who could not accept his views, except in general, and who continued to offer criticism. That is why he and Conrad drifted apart, on the one hand, and why, on the other, he forced the separation with Henry James through his remarkable book, *Boon*, for which some Jamesites have never quite forgiven him. The need to rid himself of what appeared to be an incubus, almost as a schoolboy needs to flee his dominating parent, was too urgent for Wells to play the game with James in any more genteel fashion. Bennett did not take the Wellsian route: he was more self-assured, perhaps, by that time; but he certainly did not neglect Wells after the James episode.

For this Wells was forever grateful. Bennett remained for him his best and closest friend. Their correspondence dwindled somewhat after the onset of the war, but this was due to circumstances. Wells began to write more and more social commentary, although Bennett continued to read and correct his proofs until after *The Outline of History* appeared; and they continued to read, comment on, and enjoy each other's work. They differed slightly on the conduct of the war, drifted apart under the pressures of the war experience, but continued to meet at the Reform to discuss and debate issues of the day. For a time at the end of the 1920s they lived in the same set of buildings, Chiltern Court, over and next to Marylebone Station off Baker Street. Wells spent winters in the South of France, after his bout with influenza, while Bennett lived abroad, in Paris and elsewhere in France, and spent a good deal of time on his yacht.

Bennett's domestic life became increasingly complicated as he separated from his first wife, Marguerite Soulié; and he began a life with Dorothy Cheston, although he was never able to marry her. (After she bore him a child, she changed her name by deed poll to Dorothy Cheston Bennett.) Wells did not get on well with Dorothy, whose demands on and views of Bennett were very cloying. This made the last days of Bennett's life somewhat difficult, as he felt separated from many of his older friends. Wells was, however, able to write to Bennett twice in the last year re-avowing his love and friendship. When, for example, Wells received *Imperial Palace*, he wrote thanking Bennett for the book, saying, 'Arnold you are a dear. You are the best friend I've ever had. . . . I've read it [the novel] with much the same surprise and delight that I felt about *The Old Wives' Tale*. . . . It's your complete conquest of a world you've raided time after time — not always to my satisfaction.'[19]

Within six months Bennett was dead. Wells was now more alone than at any other time of his life. Jane was gone, as were most of those who had frequented the noisy weekends at Sandgate and Easton. Wells, nearly ready to break off his relationship with Odette Keun, was on his own in London. It was time to begin thinking about writing an autobiographical record of his loves and his friendships. He had remained friends and comrades with a few from those early days, but now, with the exception of Gregory and Swinnerton, they were gone. Both Conrad and James were gone as well — and although their deaths had moved him, they had not done so in a personal way, as did the loss of Bennett. For Wells had closed off his relationships with those other two friends, and closed them off over the issues for which he and Bennett had stood when they emerged as writers at the end of the previous century. For both of them, and for Wells especially, the message was more important. The ends did justify (or even dictate) the means of delivery. Bennett knew that, even as Conrad and James had rejected the point.[20]

Wells's relationships with his contemporaries were often very prickly. This was especially true when he felt that they might be laughing at him, or worse still, instructing him as to how to behave, either in person or in his fiction. He, Bennett, Gissing, Swinnerton, and perhaps 'Vernon Lee' and G. K. Chesterton were more or less free of the emotions — part jealousy, part class-consciousness, part fear — that prompted such onslaughts. However, with both Joseph Conrad and Henry James the emotions underlying Wells's thinking about fiction and about his art or work boiled over at the end of the relationship. Prior to that time he was uneasy with both the others — and the correspondence that remains (most of Wells's letters to the other two have disappeared) shows the uneasiness, the tenderness, the offhand way in which overtures were made and received.

Conrad was much less of a threat to Wells, of course. He was born to and raised among the Polish aristocracy, went to sea for a long period of time as a young man, and used these experiences to write, in his later life, some very extraordinary fiction. Eventually his muse seemed somewhat to dry up; and although at one time he worked in close collaboration with his (and Wells's) friend, Ford Madox Hueffer (later Ford), Conrad is remembered today for a half-dozen novels he wrote on his own, which use the sea and the dark recesses of male minds as a way of probing our perceptions of reality and the carapace we put between ourselves and that ultimate reality, at least for most of the time.

Conrad lived near where Wells eventually settled, in the eastern part of Kent. His European background, stilted command of the language, and adherence to a code of formal behaviour which had never been English, made him potentially a subject of ridicule. Wells, however, had welcomed Conrad's work when he was reviewing books for the *Saturday Review* and the émigré writer was thankful for that notice. Wells's review, though, had a sting in its tail: 'Only greatness could make books of which the detailed workmanship was so copiously bad, so well worth reading, so convincing, and so stimulating.'[21]

Conrad responded in the flowery, quasi-subservient, faintly comic language in which his letters to Wells were often couched. Thanking him for the review, 'for the guidance of your reproof, and for the encouragement of your commendation', he said: 'You have repeated aloud and distinctly the muttered warnings of my own conscience.' Conrad went on to indicate to Wells that he had not written in this way out of insincerity or affectation, but in the process of learning (the letter is incomplete and the end is cut away).[22]

In his second letter to Wells, Conrad offered some comment on *The Wonderful Visit*, and told him that he would go on to read *The Time Machine* as well as his other work. Conrad's style to Wells is well represented in the later paragraphs of this letter:

> Your book[s] lay hold of me with a grasp that can be felt. I am held by the charm of their expression and of their meaning. I surrender to their suggestion, I am delighted by the cleanness of atmosphere by the sharp definition — even of things implied — and I am convinced by the logic of your imagination so unbounded and so brilliant. I see all this — but the best I am probably unable to see.
>
> Pardon this uncouth outburst of naïve enthusiasms. I am, alas, forty and enthusiasms are precious to me and to be proud of. . . .[23]

The correspondence apparently languished for a time, although in 1897 Wells nominated *The Nigger of the 'Narcissus'* (along with James's *What Maisie Knew* and Henley's biography of Burns) as most deserving of the prize given by the *Academy* for literature published that year. In his letter of nomination Wells described *The Nigger* as the 'most striking piece of imaginative work, in prose, this year has produced'.[24] The two authors' acquaintanceship was renewed at that time.

Conrad took the opportunity to write to Wells when he heard of the younger man's illness in the summer of 1898. In his renewal-of-friendship letter he remarked that Wells's criticisms had continued to live with him since 1896; and several letters to Wells had been written but destroyed. This very long letter of Conrad's discussed his work of the moment and clearly sought to strengthen what before had been only a passing encounter. Their acquaintance increased when Wells moved near Conrad, already living in Kent.[25]

Wells and Conrad exchanged visits and books at the end of the year; and the two wives, Jane and Jessie, also became acquainted. Conrad's stilted style of response disguises the fact that the two men had a good deal to discuss, and especially about the writing of fiction. Wells's *Invisible Man* brought forth some Conradian adjectives, as he described Wells as 'O Realist of the Fantastic! whether you like it or not'; and later referred to his 'felicity of incident'. The talk between the two was conducted through a mesh, a screen of verbiage, which diminished the impact of the words, slowed them down, slurred their contact.[26]

Increasingly we find a shutter coming down over Conrad's comments (again, it is difficult to say much about the entire relationship, as the Wells half of the correspondence is missing and there are no journals covering their meetings). The comments are more and more critical of the meaning of Wells's work — but this criticism nearly always appears at the end of the letter. They are long letters with the last comments written in a warped hand, occasionally in the margin of the letter, as if Conrad wished that Wells would pay only casual attention to them. In addition, the letters nearly always end with an invitation to talk, as writing is difficult and does not convey what Conrad wishes to say. The talks were often held, although not always, but whether they solved the communication difficulty is not known. Wells did not send Conrad all his books — for instance, it is hard to tell whether Conrad received a copy of *Kipps* or read only the serial version. From early on in the relationship the two men were really working to convert each other — Conrad to make Wells into a more traditional and less political writer, Wells to make Conrad into a Fabian, a socialist, or at least into a republican who could use his knowledge of the depths of men to help illuminate possible future worlds.[27]

The Wells–Conrad relationship continued for another ten or so years, each man always maintaining a surface delight in the other; but underneath there was an ever-growing uneasiness, as the two authors drew further and further apart on the issue of the purpose of their work. Conrad read *The Time Machine* in translation while travelling in Turkey and 'neglecting my work'. But he said that he would hold off on *The Wheels of Chance* (1896) until he got along on his own work, 'now growing like a genie from the bottle in the Arabian Nights', with seventy pencilled pages since the New Year. After Conrad finished that work he visited Wells, but he complained that there 'was no sense of relief, of course. The strain has been too long.' Conrad met others of Wells's friends — Pinker, the Bowketts, Gissing — and all of them carried news back and forth from one writer to the other. Later, when thanking Wells for a copy of a book (*The Plattner Story*, probably), Conrad referred to the 'inconclusive talks' which the two men had from time to time — but 'such should be the tenor of our intercourse', he said.

Apparently feeling this was too ambiguous, however, Conrad went on in what became a longish letter to tell Wells how much he thought of his imaginative gifts: 'the lucidity of expression . . . the wonderful easiness of your work . . . your fidelity to that ideal *intention* which stands before the artist's eyes like a veiled figure at the end of a long gallery; distant, and perhaps, forever, mysterious'.[28] Taken by itself, although praise, the statement retains a considerable ambiguity as to Conrad's feelings about Wells's work.

As the Wells family grew, G.P. became an excuse for letters; and the Conrads' child, Borys, could also be used as material for discussion, thus avoiding literary traps. Conrad was always very interested in Wells's work, but he was forever bemoaning his own inability to get much on paper. 'Things are bad with me — there's no disguising the fact. Not only is the scribbling awfully in arrears, but there's no "spring" in me to grapple with it effectually. Formerly in my sea life, a difficulty nerved me to the effort; now I perceive it is not so. However don't imagine I've given up, but there is an uncomfortable sense of losing my footing in deep waters.' This remark came just after his and Hueffer's joint effort, *Romance*, had gone into a second edition — which, of course, made Conrad happy in one way, but ultimately disturbed him that his own work did not sell as readily as did his collaborations. The Wellses, both H.G. and Jane, apparently buoyed him up, chivvied him out of his black moods and encouraged him to work, for they valued his writing as others would eventually, of that they had no doubt.[29]

Conrad was never truly satisfied with his own work, much less that of others. In the letter just mentioned, he went on to say,

> After all, my dear boy, for all our faith in our good intentions and even in our achievements, a paper success (as I call it) is not a strong enough tonic. I say so because for me, writing — *the only possible writing* — is just simply the conversion of nervous force into phrases. With you too, I am sure, tho' in your case it is the disciplined intelligence which gives the signal — the impulse. For me it is a matter of chance — stupid chance.

This letter went on to thank Wells for an interview with William Archer which he had set up, and that 'in your quiet, almost stealthy way you are doing a lot for me; if it were not for you a lot of people would not know of my existence. . . .'

When Wells sent Conrad a copy of *Twelve Stories and a Dream* also in that year, the recipient was still effusive about Wells's power. But 'There is a cold jocular ferocity about the handling of that mankind in which you believe that gives me the shudders sometimes.' Moreover, even with all the praise, another voice of doubt crept in, as all the high qualities of *When the Sleeper Wakes* were not present in the new book — 'something subtly wanting'. Of course, as for Conrad himself, 'I, my dear Wells, am absolutely out of my mind with the worry and apprehension of my work.'[30]

In 1905 Conrad went off to Capri for a holiday and to help Jessie recover from an operation. *Kipps* had begun to appear and Conrad read the first two serial instalments before he left and (apparently) the book as well, once it appeared. He told Wells that he thought he was lucky to bring off the beginning, as such efforts often tended to kill the interest in the book, but still, all in all, it was an admirable effort. When he returned from Capri, he apologized for not seeing Wells, but said that he was 'fighting with disease and creeping imbecility — like a cornered rat, facing fate with a big stick that is sure to descend and crack my skull before many days are over. . . .' He and Hueffer were back working, but for Conrad, 'The damned stuff comes out only by a kind of mental convulsion. . .', leaving him not happy, but exhausted with emotion, and 'secretly irritable to the point of savagery'. That was the reason he did not come to see Wells, even though he wanted very badly to talk with him. Conrad did pass on in translation some allusions to Wells in a book he was reading by Anatole France, all of them complimentary. With the comments Conrad said, 'These things read in their proper place demonstrate that you have produced a strong impression upon a man who anyway is far above the common in his intelligence and his sympathies.' But after all this, Conrad ended the letter by saying that he feared *Kipps* would not be well received, as the critics simply would not understand what Wells was about in this great work.[31]

One reads these letters today with the utmost regret that we do not have Wells's responses. The Conrad letters are filled with troubles, domestic discontent, failure to produce, and even greater failure to impress the critics. Wells on the other hand is given the highest praise by Conrad, Hueffer, and others; but under this reception lies the niggling fear that Wells will not be understood — that only persons of a certain standing and intelligence will perceive his greatness, and this is all because of tiny instances of his not working to capacity. If, or so seems to run the underlying thread, Wells would only pay a bit more attention to construction, to the artistic qualities, to refinement of language, then his gifts of plot, characterization, and even situation would be understood to be ironic, subtly critical, and become available to an even more appreciative audience.

In further comment on *Kipps*, Conrad remarked, 'Upon a mental review of your career, my dear Wells, I am forced to the conclusion that both kinds of your work are strangely and inexplicably underestimated.' Even the attacks on Wells, for Conrad, 'only nibble away at the hem of the mantle'. 'The cause of this (setting aside the superiority of your intelligence) it would be curious to investigate and on those lines a fundamental sort of study upon H. G. Wells could be written.' Conrad wished he could say what he really meant, but 'if it ever came out' it 'would be as disappointing to you as it would be to myself.' In a later letter Conrad remarked, on another book, 'It gives a sense of the shallowness of life which yet may be made a deep hole for any of us. . . .Upon the whole, Hurrah!! There are things I want to talk over when we meet.' On the bottom of this letter was the scrawled apology, 'This is silly but is meant to express intelligent appreciation. I am stupid today.'[32]

In 1906 Conrad felt that he owed H. G. Wells a great deal, for Wells had continued to talk widely about Conrad's work, to urge others to read it, and in many ways had advanced his career. However, they were even further apart over the purpose of fiction; so the surviving correspondence becomes even more stilted. Conrad had just finished *The Secret Agent*, and he wished to dedicate it to Wells. However, on reflection he felt that the book was too superficial and perhaps Wells would be willing to wait for another volume (*Chance*) of which he 'felt more sure'.

In fact, when Wells sent Conrad a copy of *The Future in America*, Conrad acknowledged its receipt with these words: 'You know that I had rather talk than write. Words do so chill the warmth of thought, whether it is set down in a book or letter, at least so it is in my case.' However, Conrad felt that this book came from a more 'accessible Wells, a Wells mellowed as it were. . . There is a quality of light in the landscape which at certain times appeals to us — invigorates our thoughts in the way of emotion (I suppose) more than at other times.' When *The Secret Agent* was finally ready for the press, it was the book Conrad chose after all to dedicate to Wells, as a way of repayment for all Wells had done for him. It is a fulsome dedication, but even in it one feels a sense of distance between the two men, although there is no question about the emotion with which it was penned:

To

H.G. Wells

The Chronicler of Mr Lewisham's Love

The Biographer of Kipps, and

The Historian of the Ages to Come

This simple Tale of the XIXth Century

Is Affectionately Inscribed.[33]

In the letter in which he offered these words to Wells, Conrad went on to say that in the dedication he had stated 'what the perfect novel should be, — chronicles, biographies, and histories'. This meant for Wells, of course, that some of his work, and perhaps his most important work, was outside the pale — or at least the dedication could be read that way. It is appealing but still ambiguous.

Wells and Conrad were to exchange only a few more letters after this date, and to meet again on only a few occasions. In 1908 and 1909 Wells was instrumental in obtaining a pension for Conrad from the Royal Literary Fund, which eased his financial troubles, and the unhappy author was duly thankful. Conrad knew how much Wells had done for him and the impact Wellsian thought was having on other young authors. 'You get hold of them by your fertileness, your persuasiveness, by your extraordinary accessibility, and that utter absence of superior pose joined to the warmth of conviction can be felt.' But even with this compliment, Conrad was constrained to offer some words which might be taken as other than high praise. There is 'that side of your writer's genius which contains an infinite possibility. . . . Your art, whatever you do, will contain your convictions where they would be seen perhaps in a more perfect light. Your work like all work that counts must have its connections with the laborious past and its bearing in the future — the future on which you have willed (and perhaps succeeded) to put the impress of your personality which you will not see but in which your voice will be heard — till in the ever-increasing distance even that trace of our first day shall be lost.' Yet 'when all the questions [are] settled, reopened and settled again, the story of Mr Lewisham's career with love will have an unchanged significance both as an artistic version and as a life's record.' For Conrad, Wells's art was simply more important than anything else in his work.

Later, when Conrad received his copy of *The New Machiavelli*, he continued his ambivalent remarks to Wells. After calling the book 'great, great in every direction', he said, however, that he knew how to read Wells, and he would not find the words just now but would reread the book before he responded more fully. He claimed to be in 'an exclamatory but inarticulate mood', but all Wells needed to know was that he was 'most deeply touched, intellectually and emotionally'.[34]

If the two men exchanged further correspondence, it has been lost. Apparently they did meet at least once more and again discussed the meaning of literature. At this meeting they agreed to disagree and not to meet again, it seems. Wells never alluded to the meeting, except to make some faintly disagreeable remarks about Conrad in his autobiography, mostly to intimate that Conrad had been overrated and that Hueffer was as important a writer. Conrad, on the other hand, did discuss that meeting fairly widely; and in 1918, when Hugh Walpole returned from Russia, Conrad told Walpole over lunch that he had remarked to Wells at their last meeting that 'The difference between us, Wells, is fundamental. You don't care for humanity, but think they are to be improved. I love humanity but know they are not.'

Whether this is what Conrad actually said to Wells is immaterial. The words have the ineffable ring of a post-discussion *bon mot*, but it is true that the two men disagreed fundamentally over the meaning of literature, of fiction, and of their life's work.[35]

These two men had an interesting and significant relationship. Conrad liked Wells immensely, and Wells returned the feeling although probably not with as much fervour. Conrad with his European mannerisms, decorum, and even his ménage, was always something of an object of humour for Wells. The older man used Wells as a crying post, but was very thankful for the services Wells performed for him. Their fiction, however, was the dividing line. Conrad wrote of the deep recesses of men's minds and believed in the final analysis that that deep dark nature could not be improved very much and certainly given no more than a veneer of civilization. At this time and for most of his life, Wells, on the other hand, wrote out of the conviction that men could be improved, that it was the duty of the trained intellectual to show the way to that improvement, and that even in fiction it was possible to have a strong didactic purpose and one which would not interfere with the pleasure of the reading. Conrad simply disagreed.[36]

I have given detailed attention to this correspondence, even though one side is missing, because it helps us understand the fundamental break which occurred between Henry James and H. G. Wells, again over the purpose of their work. Conrad's spare prose may not entirely have met Henry James's approval, but its artistic quality would have been more welcome to him than Wells's sermons, one is sure. Ultimately, for both Conrad and James, Wells was a danger to their work.

At first glance, for one to think that Henry James and Herbert Wells would be literary enemies seems absurd; to know that they were close friends for nearly fifteen years seems bizarre. Few literary relationships of any consequence could have paired more unlikely companions. And yet, the strong relationship between these two men, nearly thirty years apart in age, coming from totally different personal environments, and writing completely different sorts of books, is one of the more important in the literary and academic history of the twentieth century. Reverberations of their meetings and discussions are still significant, seventy years after James's death, and forty years after Wells's.

Wells had been one of the few reviewers to find any merit in *Guy Domville*, when that unfortunate play made its début. Even his review is tinged with pity, however, for the reception of the author, as well as for the literary quality of the play itself. The two men did not meet that night, nor for some time to come, but when Wells sent a copy of a book or two of his, and then James came calling (actually to see if Wells needed aid from the Royal Literary Fund during his illness), they found each other interesting companions. When Wells moved to Sandgate, he found James close by at Rye, and the two could see each other with very little effort. They often found themselves in each other's homes, reading each other's work, and, above all, holding long literary conversations as to which books of which author they liked and disliked, what styles of writing carried extra meaning, and, ultimately, as to the purpose of fiction itself.

Unfortunately we have no more than a glimpse into this unusual friendship. James retained relatively few letters from Wells, and their conversations were ordinarily quite private. However, we do know that Wells delighted in being able to bring Gissing to visit James, was pleased to meet W. D. Howells and Edith Wharton at his home, and was only too happy to meet William James, the author's philosopher brother and an admirer of H.G. — even to act as go-between when William James wished to meet G. K. Chesterton, Henry James's near neighbour. One supposes that Henry James, for his part, was equally happy to meet H.G.'s young friends, and to act as mentor — *cher maître*, as he wished to be called — both to them and to Wells. It is clear, however, that although he played this role for many others, James performed it for Wells because he felt that the younger man had an extraordinary talent. Wells could be the wave of the future in fiction — his success proved that, but only if he would pay attention in form and construction to Henry James, and mend his sloppy habits.[37]

For this is exactly where the friendship came to its abrupt and uneasy ending. James believed in art for art's sake — that the construction of a piece was the important part of the work, and if that were done well, it would carry the message of artistic worth to the reader and viewer. James frequently lectured his young disciples in his orotund style of writing and speaking, and many of them must have writhed as their work was skewered and dissected. Apparently James carried his methods even further with H. G. Wells than with most others, not only because Wells did not follow the master's dictates, but also, very probably, because the promise of Wells was so great that it heightened the stakes for James. This is not to say that

Wells was not affected by the Jamesian comment. Certainly *Tono-Bungay*, not least in its ending, reflects a Jamesian point of view, and there are other pieces of 'pure' writing by Wells that owe something to the school of Henry James. However, Wells was content simply to write his accounts of lower-class life and hopes, using the abominated autobiographical method and first-person style, to bring out the sweat and stress of life, and — to use James's pet phrase — to squeeze the orange of all its juice, even that of the bitter rind.

Their correspondence and discussion continued throughout the first decade of the twentieth century, and increasingly it began to wear away at Wells's nerves. He eventually found it necessary to lash back, to defend his own position. That opportunity finally came in his 1911 discourse on 'The Contemporary Novel' at the Times Book Club.[38]

In his address Wells was quite explicit about what he believed the new novel would become, and provided a clear rationale for his and Bennett's work. 'So far as I can see', said Wells, 'it is the only medium through which we can discuss the great majority of the problems which are being raised in such bristling multitude by our contemporary social development.' Wells thought these problems all found their beginnings in the psychological problems caused by human and individual needs in modern society with its essentially group demands. Although he did not mention Henry James in the piece, it was clear whom he was talking about, especially in his peroration, where he prophesied:

> You see now the scope of the claim I am making for the novel; it is to be the social mediator, the vehicle of understanding. . . . not a new sort of pulpit. . . the novelist is going to be the most potent of artists, because he is going to present conduct, devise beautiful conduct, discuss conduct, analyse conduct, suggest conduct, illuminate it through and through. . . . And this being my view you will be prepared for the demand I am now about to make. . . We are going to write, subject only to our limitations, about the whole of human life. . . . We mean to deal with all these things, and it will need very much more than the disapproval of provincial librarians, the hostility of a few influential people in London, the scurrility of one paper [the *Spectator*], and the deep and obstinate silences of another [the *Westminster Gazette*], to stop the incoming tide of aggressive novel-writing. . . . We are going to appeal to the young and the hopeful and the curious, against the established, the dignified, and defensive. Before we have done, we will have all life within the scope of the novel.[39]

James took this bait, if that is what it was, or at least agreed to write a piece eventually entitled 'The Younger Generation', to be the featured article in the first two issues of the *Times Literary Supplement* to be made available as a separate publication. Here James was not as restrained as Wells. He responded with sharp criticism of the new realism, using his squeezed-orange metaphor three times while discussing Arnold Bennett, and implying throughout the long (and rather turgid) piece that art was all that mattered and that Wells, Bennett, and others who followed down the paths of politics and realism were prostituting their art — selling it to the highest bidder by appealing to the prurient side of man's nature.

In the piece James even held up Conrad as a model for the others in the younger group; describing *Chance*, he said the author had succeeded: 'the indispensable fusion we spoke of has taken place, . . . only it has been transformed in wondrous fashion to an unexpected, and on the whole more limited plane of operation; it has been effected not on the ground but in the air, not between our writer's idea and his machinery, but between the different parts of his genius. . . . a noble sociability of vision.'[40]

In a sense, with this article, Henry James broke the unspoken truce that had been present between him and Wells. Wells felt that too many oranges had been squeezed, that James had written off his younger colleagues for their failure to follow him. So, in retribution, he returned to a novel on which he had worked off and on since at least 1905 — a novel in which a departed author's literary remains are the focus of a discussion of the meaning of literature and the art of fiction. And, although Wells made a few crude attempts to avoid the consequences of a direct attack, by first publishing the book, *Boon*, under a fictitious name, 'Reginald Bliss', the story was soon out. To begin with there was an introduction by Wells, in which he proclaimed, after denouncing the bad taste of the work, that, 'I should be glad if I could escape the public identification I am now repudiating. Bliss is Bliss and Wells is Wells. And Bliss can write all sorts of things that Wells could not do.'[41]

Even worse than this, though, Wells left a presentation copy, with its newly written and very cruel chapter, 'Of Art, of Literature, of Mr Henry James', at the Reform Club for James. The book is a great parody of high-toned literary discussion, and includes several paragraphs which are very like a Henry James run wild. Other writers are pilloried in the book as well, although Bliss/Wells does have some fairly good things to say for Hugh Walpole, Arnold Bennett, and for James Joyce. *Boon* depicts Edward Clodd, a literary and scientific writer of the time, under the name Dodd; Robertson Nicoll, appearing as Dr Tomlinson Keyhole; George Moore, Henry James and others, as they pontificate on literature in a series of meetings, some of which are clearly set in James's garden, where many readers of *Boon* would recall similar discussions. It is a naughty, but at the same time, quite funny book.

Of course, Henry James did not think it funny, nor did his colleagues and supporters. Wells did offer some half-hearted apologies, both by letter and even in the book itself when he remarked:

I am, I learned long ago, an uncreative, unimportant man. And yet, I suppose, I do something; I count; it is better that I should help than not in the great task of literature, the great task of becoming the thought and the expressed intention of the race, the task of taming violence, organizing the aimless, destroying error, the tasks of waylaying the Wild Asses of the Devil and sending them back to Hell. It does not matter how individually feeble we writers and disseminators are; we have to hunt the Wild Asses. As the feeblest puppy has to bark at cats and burglars. And we have to do it because we know, in spite of the darkness, the wickedness, the haste and hate, we know in our hearts, though no momentary trumpeting has shown it to us, that judgement is all about us and God stands close at hand.[42]

James's response to Wells, defending art and construction, continues to be widely quoted, of course, and every literature major in America and many reading English in Britain know that James won the battle. James lives and Wells is dead, or so the received wisdom proclaims. And yet one wonders, after all. Has the Wells case, when put in less crude forms, been destroyed? Has the didactic purpose of literature been put away? Or did, to pick only one case, Orwell have another motive besides the art of construction for writing *Nineteen Eighty-Four*, or *Animal Farm*; or even, to pick a lesser book, did Ray Bradbury learn from Wells when he provided us with *Fahrenheit 451*?

Wells's book became a *cause célèbre*, although some of the controversy remained private until after the publication of a first collection of Henry James's letters in 1920. Then, for the first time, his responses to Wells became widely known. Wells himself, of course, received substantial comment on the book at the time of publication. Maurice Baring, for instance, wrote to him as soon as he had finished reading *Boon*, congratulating him on the work, and went on to say, 'I think it contains some of the finest criticism on modern things (Henry James and Chamberlain) I have ever seen. When I finished it I bewailed [that] you had not written a whole New Republic of the Pre-War World.' Later in the year, Baring, this time discussing *The Research Magnificent*, renewed his praise for *Boon* and said that he continued to think about and like the book; but he now thought that there was 'much danger of crystallizing the "artless" novel into a rigid convention', and as for him, he preferred the novel of ideas above all others.[43]

More interesting, perhaps, is the reaction of a person mentioned in the book, who was close to both James and Wells, Hugh Walpole. In fact, a comparison of the two men's relationship with James is moderately instructive. Walpole was happy to use the term *cher maître*, thought the sun rose and fell when James commanded, but also liked Wells very much. He knew Wells very well as he had served for a time as 'Elizabeth' von Arnim's secretary, and the two often attended Wells's parties throughout the period. Walpole, less known today than one would have predicted, tended to be slightly sycophantic with his elders, which James liked; nevertheless,

Walpole had an acute mind, and was a novelist of considerable distinction. James was graceful about him and especially his masterwork of the period, *The Duchess of Wrexe*, but Wells was not unkind in his treatment of Walpole in *Boon*.

Walpole was in Russia at this period, but news of *Boon* reached him and he awaited the book with much interest. When he was able to obtain a copy he described it in his journal as a 'mad incoherent thing with much cleverness'. He thought that it was 'really clever about H.J. and says just half the truth'. Walpole wondered why the book was so fierce on Conrad (now we think of the comment as being slight, of course), and he wondered who was James Joyce, and whether Stephen Crane was as good a novelist, or F. M. Hueffer as good a poet, as Wells indicated. All in all, thought Walpole, Wells had done a good job, but would have done an even better job as satirist if he had shown less personal irritability. Later, when Walpole returned to London, one of the first things he did (James was dead by this time) was to have luncheon with Bennett and Wells. Walpole mentioned this event in his journal with, 'Wells most fascinating, so that I lost all my old hatred and succumbed as I always do to him.'[44]

A few months earlier, Robert Lynd, while writing about Henry James soon after his death, had spent a fair amount of time in the *Daily News and Leader* quoting from *Boon*, as indicating the opposite to what James was really like. Wells responded in a letter to the editor, urging critics to be more careful of their language; he noted that Lynd had said that he, Wells, both adored and abused Henry James. If, Wells said, he were responsible for *Boon* (he had not yet claimed responsibility for the work), it was of 'blended origin. . . .It is a posed discussion, a devil's advocate statement, or why should it be thus detached and pseudonymized?' Wells went on to say that James was the master, and reminded critics to read *The American Scene* where his quality was best. He was gracious in his closing by saying, 'At a hundred points, the work of every young man is different because of him.'[45]

This was not quite the last word from Wells on the subject of *Boon*, and on Henry James, however. In 1925, he reprinted the book in the Atlantic Edition, along with, in the same volume, *Ann Veronica*. Although he suppressed two earlier and lesser chapters from the original edition of *Boon* as being 'dead', he still thought some of it worthwhile a decade later. 'It is the writer's weakness to be his own *enfant terrible*', his apology ran. Describing the book as an 'outbreak of naughtiness', he linked it with the *Ann Veronica* period of his life, and proclaimed that it was a response to 'various contemporary literary artists and critics', who had 'patronized and reproved' him 'to the limit of endurance'. He had written 'The Mind of the Race' to relieve his mind. But even in 1911, there had been something more to it than literary badinage, and as the Germans drove towards Paris in 1914, he had recast the book, inserted the death of Boon, and released it. As he remarked, 'In many respects it is the most frank and intimate book that he is ever likely to write. And yet — esoteric.'[46]

14 Arnold Bennett   15 Joseph Conrad

16 George Gissing

'The great author, so famous for his lofty & serene toleration of faults that ~~do~~ differ from his own, churning up something particularly ~~Hotly~~ pleasant to say about some of his less gifted contemporaries, — under the misperception of The Mind of The Race.

H.G.W,

The mind of the Race

~~Deleted by Censor.~~

Progress of G.B.S. through life, as Alice in Wonderland.
"I feel curiouser and curiouser"

G.K.C. The last phase.

New Budget
Beer f---------- per bottle

Trouser Button.

17 Wells's unused 'picshuas' for *Boon* (1915), with caricatures of Shaw, G. K. Chesterton, and 'the great author' himself

Later Wells discussed the book and the controversy in his *Experiment in Autobiography*, repeating most of what had already been said. Still the controversy remained with him, and not least the probability that he had been rude to James, and thus diminished his own authority. In 1940, writing again as the Germans drove towards Paris, but with the danger to modern life even greater, Wells published yet another book which dealt with some of the same themes. That work, *Babes in the Darkling Wood*, he described as a dialogue novel. As preface to the work he inserted a statement of his opinions on writing, entitled 'The Novel of Ideas'. In this short piece he remarked how much his early writing had been influenced by discussions of the novel and the short story by James, Conrad, Edward Garnett, Hueffer, and George Moore. He felt that novelists were ranked on their merits according to how they met these artificial standards. Wells rebelled and took up new forms. One of them was the novel of dialogue, based, to some degree, on the dialogue method of Plato, in which ideas were discussed for their own sake. Wells put his own work in context, setting at rest once and for all, or so he thought, the notion that his work was less worthy than that of his contemporaries purely on grounds of construction and style. He asked only that his work be read with regard to the ideas he presented. In fact, of course, what he was saying here was that the ends of the artist's work — its purpose — were more important than the methods he used to produce it — the means. He had not changed his position even though a quarter of a century had passed since his early work.[47]

Afterwards Herbert Read, the writer and critic, questioned Wells about James, apparently prompted by something which had appeared in the press about the controversy. Wells was patient but clear, as he remembered those days with his old opponent. He told Read that James's 'imagination lived in a sublimated world', and that what James had written on Bennett in the *TLS* had offended him, Wells, very much. *Boon* was simply his response. Wells said that 'there was a great lamentation in the genteel literary world. . . .but, believe me, Henry James asked for it.'[48]

Herbert George Wells was no philistine. Although there are several generations of students who, if they think about it at all, probably believe that he represented the *derrière-garde* of his time, nothing could be further from the truth. He championed high cultural activities throughout his life. He was a close friend of William Rothenstein, and wrote a foreword to a catalogue of Rothenstein's Indian sketches. He was a sponsor, investor, and contributor to the *English Review*, the epitome of artistic literary comment of its time. He supported the work of Ford Madox Hueffer, Violet Hunt, Middleton Murry, and Katherine Mansfield, contributing an important statement on literary merit to their publication, *Rhythm*, and he later contributed money and the use of his name to the *Transatlantic Review*. Indeed Jane Wells was to publish a number of pieces in this journal, Hueffer's later, and highly artistic, review. Furthermore Wells was one of the earliest persons to recognize the merits of James Joyce: he wrote one of the earliest and most distinguished reviews of *A Portrait of the Artist*, which was widely used to sell the book at the time, and is still quoted on the back of the Penguin edition. He enjoyed classical music (his taste was probably more for the Romantic composers than ours would be — but many in his time shared his preference). Moreover, he sponsored Diaghilev's visit to London in 1926, when *Les Noces* was given its première performance, and wrote a letter of appreciation to *Dancing Times* on the occasion. Wells was an early subscriber to the limited edition of *Ulysses*, smuggled a copy into Britain soon after it was printed, and with Galsworthy and Bennett, as well as J. M. Barrie, contributed to a fund which allowed Joyce to live in the style he wished in Zurich.[49]

Wells was often unassuming when dealing with casual correspondents, as when he remarked to a Mr Evans, 'Will you run down here [Sandgate] to lunch one day? Then I can explain to you what an entirely futile person I am to put anyone in the way of anything. I spin theories about conduct. I try to write novels and I have never done any practical social work in my life.' He was a good deal more forthcoming with friends such as Henry Newbolt, whom he told that he 'never shall be a gentleman', when apologizing for a *faux pas*. Earlier he and Newbolt exchanged a number of fascinating letters about poetry (which Newbolt apparently sent him for criticism). Wells told Newbolt, 'I am a poet whose medium is a lean prose, but so far as my poor power goes I mean some men here and there shall glimpse a worthier mistress to dream about than the "old school" of Victoria R. . . .' Wells went on to say, 'I do think many of the things upon which men waste loyalty and love, our kingdom for example [are] diablish tawdry street-walking ideals. . . .' Other letters on style passed back and forth just at the time when many thought Wells was only interested in socialism or his own finances.[50]

No one in his own time would have thought Wells a philistine. Persons who were the epitome of the opposite of that term, such as Ford Hueffer, would have laughed at the idea. When he first conceived the idea of the *English Review* Hueffer sought Wells's help. Wells offered *Tono-Bungay*, arguably his most artistic book, and agreed as well to approach several potential contributors with whom Hueffer did not get on. In fact when the journal was delayed Wells was forced to ask his publisher to delay the appearance of the book, as 'it is really a vital matter to me'. Hueffer blamed Wells for the delay, and a long and acrimonious exchange ensued; actually, Wells, and through him Violet Paget, had been willing to help publish the journal as a co-operative venture, but they were the only authors who would. The review was a marvellous success, but lost immense amounts of money — the ultimate artistic triumph, one supposes.[51]

Even though the *English Review* went bankrupt and cost Wells and others money, he continued to support Hueffer's efforts, writing to Chesterton in

1915 to complain of an attack on Hueffer in the *New Witness*, and later apologizing, as he knew full well that G. K. Chesterton was not responsible for his brother Cecil's comments. Later Ford (as Hueffer by then was) and Wells exchanged some views on writing, in a later incarnation of the *English Review*; and Wells supported Ford at other times, most especially on the *Transatlantic Review*, even contributing funds when Ford was destitute in 1930, as well as supporting his approach to the Royal Literary Fund. Ford was, of course, not an easy person to deal with, but Wells, recognizing his merit, was very forbearing in the relationship.[52]

Wells had a great many friends and supporters in these matters, even though not all of them would have gone as far as he did in his statement of the place of art. But he was a close friend of Alvin Langdon Coburn, the great art photographer of this period, and wrote an introduction to one of his books, as well as collaborating with Coburn on another. Ella Hepworth Dixon, the original of Zuleika Dobson in Beerbohm's famous novel of that title, was a frequent visitor to the Wellses' home, and such individuals as Augustine Birrell, Osbert Sitwell, Edmund Gosse, and Gerald Du Maurier frequently joined Wells and Bennett at lunch.[53]

One can belabour the obvious, but perhaps it is best to end this defence of Wells, if that is what it is, with a brief account of his relationship with Stephen Crane. Wells had noticed Crane's work while writing for the *Saturday Review*; calling his review, 'Another View of *Maggie*', he described that work as 'art', and said that Crane had clearly written the book 'to please himself'. Later, when noticing another Crane book, Wells compared him favourably with Gissing, and in 1900, after Crane's death, he wrote a long, laudatory, and analytical article on Crane and his fiction. This piece was important enough to cause other literary magazines to quote from it at length and to urge their readers to seek it out.[54]

Crane was very ill by the time of their acquaintance, but they exchanged several visits and went to a number of parties together. Even Wells could not see him in the last days, however, as the American was haemorrhaging so badly. After Crane died, Wells gave Cora Crane some money and she went from him to Conrad and James, but Pinker, who knew her (she had been the proprietress of a whorehouse and is said to have returned to that, work in the US later), was able to head them off from giving her full support. Wells had done his part, however, though it was too late.[55]

This incident gives, in fact, a much clearer and closer view of H.G. Wells. He supported young artists of all varieties, and did it willingly. He put no bounds on their methods and modes of expression, and encouraged them, much as his friend, the French writer Paul Valéry, had done for him at the end of the '90s and would do for others.[56] That the critical response to Wells was so strong in France is indicative of his place in these matters. However, he did have a tremendous argument with Henry James. Some of the roots of the argument undoubtedly lay in their respective backgrounds. Wells simply could not be subservient, and James called for submission, almost as a matter of course. He pressed his ideas on Wells, too much so probably, but it was because he believed Wells had much to give. Wells accepted more of them than is usually understood, but ultimately the attacks came to be too difficult to accept.

It is instructive to note that when Wells retaliated, it was primarily because of the slights to his great friend, Bennett. His riposte, however rude it may have been, came from that deep wellspring of friendship, but also a well which was closely related to his difficult experiences with *Ann Veronica*. That book, and others like it, were volumes which came from Wells's own clear and deep personal life — they involved his sexual longings, and ultimately those feelings, along with the fiction, needed expression. In a way, this was what the Jamesians were unhappy about; but they had no experience of those profound longings, and so probably, in the final analysis, never understood what Wells was really all about.

WOMEN AND FICTION: I

I feel tonight, *so* tired of playing wiv' making the place comfy, and as if there was only one dear rest place in the world, and that were in the arms of you.

There is the only place I shall ever find in this world where one has sometimes peace from the silly wasteful muddle of one's life. Think! I am thinking continually of the disappointing news of it. The high bright ambitions one begins with, the dismal concessions, the growth, like a clogging hard crust over one of home and furniture and a lot of clothes and books and gardens, a load dragging me down. If I set out to make a comfortable home for you [to live in] and do work in, I merely succeed in continuing a place where you are bored to death. I make love to you and have you for my friend to the exclusion of plenty of people who would be infinitely more satisfying to you. Well, dear, I don't think I ought to send such a letter. It's only a mood you know... I have been letting myself go in a foolish fashion. It's alright you know really only I've had so much of my own society now, I am naturally getting sick of such a person as I am. How you can *ever* stand it.

Jane Wells to HGW, 26 February 1906

Whether the letter quoted above was ever posted is problematical. It now lies in pencil, unrevised, among Wells's papers at Illinois. It was written to H.G. while he was in America and probably represents the height of Jane's frustration, not only at his ability to travel thither and yon, but also at the fact that he had carved out a sexual existence different from hers. Although she apparently shared him willingly in order to preserve what she could for herself, she, in the world in which she lived, did not feel as free as he was; nor did she ever attempt to achieve the sexual equality she might have had along with the physical and social equality she had or was granted as the occasion arose. The fact that the letter does lie there, though, makes it important to an understanding of H.G. Wells and his relationships with women, with his friends, with his family. (Jane served as his secretary until well into the mid-1920s. As a result, there are some gaps in his correspondence as she weeded it. In fact, much of the personal material, some of which is the foundation for parts of this chapter, was returned to Wells after her death, to be part of the documentation of *Experiment in Autobiography*. Other letters lie in other depositories, unregarded generally. Marjorie Craig Wells returned such personal correspondence to Wells's friends early in 1947 before the estate holdings were sold.)

When one views H. G. Wells and his life, it is often difficult to remember that he came from a different time with generally different mores. Due in part to the fact that he broke down or helped in the destruction of many of those mores, but also due to the timelessness of many of his words, we tend to think of him as a sort of elderly inhabitant of our own world. He was, however, born at the height of the old Queen's reign, reared in a very Victorian (with all the freight that word carries) household, received a conventional education until he went into science, and had lived a third of his life before he gave any indication that he would be a much different product from dozens, if not hundreds, of others from that same world.

What made him different? What made him rebel, wish to modify, even be revolutionary in his approach to the relations between men and women? Patricia Stubbs, in her remarkable book, *Women and Fiction* (1979), from which I borrow the title to this chapter, implies that all men writing about women must be anti-feminist. If that is the case, Wells falls out of her paradigm. For he was a feminist, in the sense that he crusaded for equality for women and believed in an androgynous life. He also understood his own world far better than most of us today and realized that for women to achieve their rights, massive revolutionary changes would have to occur in the social fabric.

In addition Wells understood something else — which perhaps we also forget. Our species, both male and female, lives in a world of biological necessity which demands sexual expression to foster the species. It also demands, because of the circumstances and nature of human propagation, some separation of female functions, at least during part of pregnancy and while nursing takes place. It is true that modern society has tended to go further and further with this division of work, to modify it, and even to change or refer certain phases of it to helpers. However, the fact remains that a man cannot give birth to or nurse a child, and during these times he becomes of necessity the provider. This separation of function has been lengthened and strengthened by custom and events, although it is a moot and difficult question as to how long a separation is endemic to our species. One suspects that Wells would have believed in the separation of function for some length of time. He would have been taught that in any case. To change the world in that respect, as in other ways, meant education; and Wells was prepared to help. In the meantime he moved through life more free than most, because of his understanding, but also propelled apparently by a stronger sexual urge than most. He did not think his own urge much stronger than that of most men and many women, but few have been as free to exercise their desires as he was willing to be.

Significant relationships in fiction tend to fall into three categories, or so it seems to me. The first of these, of more concern today in the United States and Australia, but in the nineteenth century a major province of English writing, is the relationship of human beings to the land; what role does the environment, the place, occupy in modifying human relationships? Scott, Trollope (to some degree), Zola, and Cooper all wrote well in this genre. Wells only occasionally penetrates this world in his science fiction. Even in novels in which place is fairly important — *The Camford Visitation* or *The Wheels of Chance* are examples — other matters take precedence.

The second of the relationships is that of humans to time. In a vulgar way this is seen in historical novels, with *Forever Amber* or *Under Two Flags* the epitome of the bad example. On a somewhat higher plane one can think of the work of Alfred Duggan, Bryher, or, in another context, Scott and Dickens. In the case of the last-named I am thinking of *Bleak House* and *David Copperfield*. In our own time the theme has found a place in serious and important work. Hugh MacLennan, C. P. Snow, and Anthony Powell (all males) write on such subjects with great subtlety. Doris Lessing, and perhaps Virginia Woolf (*The Waves, To the Lighthouse*), would be feminine examples. Their message is that our species is forever under a debt to the past, and all actions must come, directly or not, from that matrix and accept its modifications. One has no choice. Wells writes most freely in this vein. Much of his science fiction, most importantly perhaps *In the Days of the Comet* but also *The Time Machine* and straight novels like *William Clissold*, are books in which time, the dead or heavy hand of the past, and the desire to escape, are paramount.

The relationship most difficult for the writer to deal with is that of human to human — the significance of raw power and sex as a driving force. Women write better about this world, mostly because they write from a perception of themselves as victims of the power or of the relentless pursuit of that power, no matter the effect upon those who are pursued. True, many men also write well about such matters. Trollope in the Palliser novels mingles the drive for both physical and political power with the demands of sex, in works which remain as guidebooks for the understanding. Dickens also wrote well in this vein — *Nicholas Nickleby, Great Expectations, Dombey and Son* leap off the page in this regard. Still, one tends to turn to the fiction of women — Mrs Gaskell, Joyce Carol Oates, or Marguerite Yourcenar might be examples. Of all the men who have written or attempted to write in this area, however, H. G. Wells ranks very near the top.

In his novels of love and power — *Love and Mr Lewisham, Ann Veronica, Marriage, The New Machiavelli* from this period of his life, and later

Apropos of Dolores — Wells treats this subject with dignity and with a perception of the roles of both the power seeker and the recipient, even when, as in *Mr Lewisham* or *Dolores*, the reader laughs at the antics the power relationships bring about. As Wells himself said, though, he wrote better about love affairs when they were declining or at their height, than when they were commencing or growing. In fact, courtship is never treated well in Wells's novels and the writing is often quite bad in those portions. That aspect was simply too personal, too difficult to transfer to the printed page, one suspects. Wells, more than most people, wrote highly personal accounts in his fiction. One would not, of course, assume, with Wells or anyone, that what we are reading is simply a courtroom transcript from the point of view of the defendant; for, given any author's general desire to heighten and intensify events and tension, the books are fiction.

However, even with this in mind, in Wellsian novels we are close to the action. It is, of course, this aspect that made him notorious in his own time. For the vulgar or less perceptive reader a Wells novel was a transcript. Wells of course denied any connection and said that the works were entirely fiction; but when one comes to the pages today, it is always with the realization that he was discussing some version of reality, though one frequently heightened by his desire to write well. This is why *Kipps, Mr Polly*, and even *Ann Veronica* remain as close pictures of a way of life, even a way of Wellsian life, but transcend that to become novels which are now near-classics, part of our own personal intellectual freight; and why they, in turn, influence what we think about the period and above all, about H.G. Wells.

We need to provide two or three more things to think about, however, before we turn to Wells and his novels in this period. The first is the point that, try as we might, we cannot forget that Wells wrote 'shocking' books in his time (*In the Days of the Comet* and *Ann Veronica* are the best examples). People did not read them in polite company. They were to be smuggled away to read alone. Mothers and aunts often forbade these books. Like the steamier work of Frank Harris, the novels carry a sexual redolence, an odour, a mist of the boudoir (or even the bordello), and reading them brings titillation. It makes no difference that this view of them is untrue. What matters is the perception. When people read H. G. Wells, they know that they are going to find fiction about the future in some books and novels of passion in others. It is up to us to read his books for something beneath that layer. We must see what Wells was really saying to his time and to ours. We need, in other words, to view him historically and aesthetically and to do this by shelving the baggage of the past as much as is possible.

Recently we have been provided with the hidden volume III of Wells's *Experiment in Autobiography*. The book, entitled *H. G. Wells in Love*, purports to give us all that was missing in the earlier two-volume work, for much had to be left out as people were still alive. To a degree those omissions are made good in the suppressed portion, and modern readers and reviewers have read the new volume with the same sort of attention once given to *In the Days of the Comet* and *Ann Veronica*. However, they have again fallen into the old trap and have taken the book at face value and treated it as legal tender for all debts. But Wells is still writing as a gifted novelist. He heightens some matters, depresses others, tells only part of the story, continues, as it were, to give us the defendant's brief. Moreover, the volume does not tell all. Many women with whom he was intimate over long periods of time do not appear in the book, even in minor roles. In addition, and this is important, Wells never, here or in his other work, indicates how these relationships turned out, how the women concerned lingered on in his life, nor does he tell us much about the other side of the relationships involved.

The most significant thing he does provide, however, is the term 'lover-shadow'; used to describe his search for a physical relationship. This concept is closely related to, if not identical with, Jung's concept of 'shadow' governing our lives in most matters. In Wells's case, he is describing an anima, his feminine counterpart; or to put it directly, if he had actually located his 'lover-shadow', their relationship on all levels would have been perfect or, in a more telling phrase, completely 'androgynous'. Together, the soul-mates would have transcended the biological imperative, the drag of time and custom, and even the pursuit of power for power's sake, to live in complete harmony. Wells did not find such a person (one is tempted to add, 'of course'), but he came close with Isabel (for a brief time), with Amy Catherine (for nearly all their lives), with Rebecca West (for some time), and with Amber Reeves (perhaps closest of all of those with whom he did not live for any length of time). He thought he was very close with Moura Budberg (although it was her refusal to accept him in this way that may have made her even more elusively attractive). In any case Wells sought through much of his life for such relationships, came much closer than most to finding them, and wrote of them in his fiction about the real and the ideal in the world of human love and passion.[1]

Wells had close family ties. Some of his family papers have been lost, but those fragments that remain show him to be a kind and loving brother and son, as well as a loving, affectionate, but more distant and demanding father. As long as his brother Fred was in England, they saw each other fairly often; and after that older brother left for South Africa in 1893, there ensued a fond correspondence usually illustrated with Wells's drawings of his life and activities. He saw his mother and father frequently, and they were regular visitors to Spade House. Although he had rented and then purchased a cottage for them at Liss, for Sarah Wells at least this was not close enough; and she hoped to live in Hastings or even nearer to Sandgate. Interestingly enough, in these later letters she was asking Wells's permission even to think about such matters, showing how the family roles had changed. Joseph Wells was a bit more distant; but even he wrote almost weekly, letters filled with mundane gossip, as those to H.G. in the summer of 1899. His cousin, Ruth Neal, spent Christmas with H.G. and Jane in 1897; and afterwards he (and later Jane) made small loans to keep her family afloat. Wells continued to send her copies of his books, and as late as 1934 provided funds to insure her automobile. Wells told Marjorie Craig Wells that she could supply 'up to fifty pounds'.

After the Wells children were in school, Jane also wrote to Fred of their progress on a number of occasions. Of course the children were special to grandparents and to uncles, so there are a number of photographs of these scenes; perhaps the most moving, however, is one of R. A. Gregory, a sort of honorary uncle, with G. P. Wells at Sandgate, along with a teddy bear. On the other side, though, there is a plaintive letter from G. P. Wells to Jane asking, 'When is Daddy coming to have a look at me?'. He told his mother that if he sold Wells's signatures at sixpence each he would be nearly a millionaire. Wells responded with some money and later went to visit the boy at his school.[2]

Wells also remained close to many of his friends, some of them dating back to his Royal College days. Few were closer than A. T. 'Tommy' Simmons. Simmons spent the Christmas holidays of 1896 with H.G. and Jane. Wells observed his progress in life closely. So closely, in fact, that a year later Simmons wrote to thank him for the interest, but closed the letter with, 'but, old chap, if after a gallant try it doesn't come off, you won't drop me, will you?'. There was no danger of that. We know that Wells and Simmons remained very close until Simmons died. Wells got back his correspondence with Simmons in 1904, to destroy some of the more personal pieces, but this made no difference to their affection. Simmons provided books for the children when they first began mathematics. Wells went to an old boys' dinner (in fact, the founding dinner of the Royal College of Science Association) with Simmons, much against his will, in 1909, and they renewed their relationship even more strongly at the time of *The World Set Free*. Simmons died suddenly in 1921, and Wells and Gregory felt an obligation to help the surviving children. Wells lent £600 to Winifred Simmons until Tommy's will could be probated and afterwards paid some of the Simmons children's fees at Oundle School. He continued to follow their careers and provide them with funds if he felt they were in need. Winifred Simmons was at the Wells cremation service. Wells remained very close to his early friends and companions because he thought they had helped him at a time when he needed it, but also because he had a strong sense of affection for those who could withstand his sharp tongue.[3]

In order to get even closer to the point of understanding Wells and his friendships, one can turn to Elizabeth Healey and their relationship. Healey too remained close to Wells all his life. When he died, she was one of the first persons to be notified. In the '30s, when her husband fell ill and was unable to work full-time, Wells provided her with a smallish annual income; and after the husband died Wells continued to send her his books (including a second complete set, autographed, for her to sell) as well as gifts such as a case of wine at Christmas. Wells relied on her judgement; she was slightly older than he, and she remained a link with Isabel as long as his first wife was still alive. They were, of course, closer in the '90s when she was still living in London and could offer pieces of advice direct, as when she reported on a party given for William Briggs which Wells could not attend as he had a severe cold. She remarked that he had been discussed there, as he was clearly on the verge of success, but they 'make the mistake of taking all your epigrammatic remarks and conversational fireworks as absolutely literally expressing your fixed creed, and so being the fixed star of your existence'. Later, when she fell in love herself, she brought the man around for Wells to meet and approve. Bruce was an instructor in mathematics at the University College of South Wales and Monmouthshire, where she was then teaching. The two made the long trip to London in April 1910 to see Wells. His relationship with her, strong over time, apparently never developed into anything more than sincere and open friendship. Wells always relied on such female friends (others were Lady Elcho and, in a slightly different sense, Eileen Power, Christabel Aberconway, and Cynthia Asquith).[4]

With Healey, Wells was very open. In 1888, after he and Isabel had fallen in love but before they were married, he asked her views on love, and his response tells us today much of how he viewed the Victorian restraints which he was to break so utterly in a few years. He asked Elizabeth, in the fragment of the letter we still have.

> Don't you think there is a frightful lot of sentimental distortion of this important factor of human life called Love? The code of rules whereby two young people have to meet each other, go through all sorts of ceremonials and finally pass under the yoke, which exists in this effete state of humanity, is one of the most ghastly difficulties that the ambitious writer of stories has to encounter — for myself, who is a doubter and contemner of almost all the amenities of social intercourse, there is a simply frightful temptation to be glaringly improper in what I write — I am one of those human beings who with the simplest and purest of lives, have the most shocking scale of morals believable. . . .[5]

Wells would have been happy in a world without the marital restraints which many persons felt necessary. He continued to love Isabel (or at least he says so, and there is indication enough to accept his word), but it was a physical love and need. He remarked in *Experiment in Autobiography* of his sexual desire for her being aroused again when he met her years after their divorce. He kept track of her movements and tried to make her life easier. In 1894, after Elizabeth Healey had told him something of Isabel's life since the divorce, he asked Elizabeth,

Is there anything I can do to help Isabel? I don't know how she is situated
even. . . . I hope you go to see her if you properly can and I'd be very glad
to know about her. She writes to me but it is scarcely to be expected she
would tell me very much. It's a dismal tragedy and it's *entirely my fault*.
Don't blame anyone else. I can't stop the hum until death. So far as I can
see all that is possible for me is to go on with my own work and keep her
at least from urgent material necessity and give her the possibility of new
interests.

Wells went on in the letter to suggest possible friends, 'but beyond that the
less I come into her life the better'.[6]

One doubts if Isabel ever entirely recovered from the divorce, even
though she did remarry and had a child. By 1898 she was helping her
husband, Fowler-Smith, run an egg farm. For a time, after the marriage,
Wells continued to pay her alimony. Sarah Wells also apparently wrote to
her. Isabel in turn kept in touch with H.G., worried about his health, even
commented on the changes in *The War of the Worlds* from the serial version,
when H.G. sent her the book. As her marriage now seemed secure and she
no longer needed support, there is a gap of a decade in the correspondence, although Wells kept sending alimony cheques until 1902 or 1903.
When he stopped finally, he reported to Elizabeth, 'So, this remarkably
false start of my youth comes to a decent end.' Wells asked Healey to burn
their correspondence on the grounds that 'it might save my widow some
day something highly disagreeable'. Later he retracted the request
(although it was at that time that he asked for his letters back from
Simmons, and perhaps from others of this period, and destroyed them).
When he did so, he discussed the alimony payments, remarking afterwards
that 'she[Jane]'s really my biggest fluke and I conceal with difficulty a pretty
abject gratitude to her for being what she is to me'. He told Elizabeth that
he had 'a sort of sturdy loyalty "to women", a most gorgeous and
thank-heaven-for aspect of a Universe'.[7]

Isabel soon turned up again, however. In 1908 she became short of
money, as a debt owed her was not repaid. She sought funds from Wells
with 'time heals many scars and we are first cousins'. He took over her
interests for a time, collected the debts and reorganized her finances.
Fowler-Smith was not very successful, and after he died Wells bought
Isabel a partnership in a laundry. For a time, in the years just before the
War, she also typed manuscripts for Wells at Easton Glebe, and several
persons remarked on seeing her and Jane working together to make H.G.'s
life more tolerable when he was creating a new novel. During the First War
Wells found her a position at Somerset House where she continued to
work. She was finally able to repay the money Wells had advanced, but he
invested it in war bonds for her daughter, Joy.

Isabel and Wells continued to correspond, and until she died he received
an annual birthday letter. He in turn sent copies of his books and an

occasional cheque, usually on her birthday. Eventually Joy went to an advanced secretarial school; she came to visit Wells, who discussed her future with her and apparently also paid for part of her education. When the *Experiment in Autobiography* was serialized, many were struck with the good will that Wells showed in it towards Isabel. Elizabeth Healey, for instance, writing from the vantage point of the many confidences she had shared with both parties, remarked to him, 'I can't tell you how much I admire your tender appreciation of Isabel. You know I was always very fond of her sweet dignity — and she never ceased to love you — that I know from many talks with her — till quite near the time of her death we never met without her telling me about you and your unfailing generosity to her.'[8]

From this story one can begin to see a rather different H. G. Wells from the caricatures often presented. He had a strong and passionate love for women, a deep biological urge, which in the case of Isabel manifested itself quickly. The marriage was an error, although the physical attraction remained. Wells knew that he had done wrong by the standards of the day, but was prepared to accept the responsibility for the act. Isabel knew that she could rely upon him. The other women whom he loved also knew this. Part of their willingness to go against moral standards may have been that knowledge. He understood his own nature, but also accepted theirs, as well as their emotional and physical needs.

We need to look at Wellsian thought on these matters in two ways: first, to survey his comments in the public press where he often wrote explicitly on these ideas; and second, to review his correspondence on his feelings about women and their relationship to him. Wells, of course, was asked to write on a great many matters, and he occasionally refused to comment, either because he was busy or because he did not know enough about the question to respond. Once, however, when asked to write on American women, he refused for a different reason. Aware that his remarks could be and would be seized on and reported out of context, he refused a commission from *Woman*, saying that he could not do what was wanted. 'The American woman is a very coarse [?common] sort of female — I can't say that and I won't say anything else.'[9] It seems clear that he would only say things he meant; and if that damaged so fragile a cause as feminism, he would remain silent.

When he did comment it was well thought out and presented a viewpoint often controversial, but one which could nevertheless be debated; and the debate might further his goals of equality. Again it was the *Daily Mail* and Northcliffe who gave the space for these statements. In May of 1904, for instance, Wells responded to the Bishop of Ripon who had preached on a drop in the birth rate as an alarming indication of England's decline. Wells was sarcastic in his article, asking the Bishop if he had carried his views to their ultimate extreme, for then he would have to favour more child brides and more children in tenements. Wells said the question itself was not important; what was important was making the lives of women and children safer and better; and if limiting the number of children helped, so much the better. Wells asked the Bishop if he thought that rabbits should inherit the earth, as they were the most fecund species presently available. This piece was the first by Wells in what would be a life-long support of birth-control measures.[10]

The Bishop did not respond to Wells; and the matter was allowed to rest until the next year when, in his occasional column in the same newspaper, Wells began a series on Utopian cities and his ideas of a better life for English people. This series began with a scarcely veiled attack on Ebenezer Howard, who had invented the 'garden city' concept to deal with urban sprawl, large populations, and modern transport. Wells thought Howard's plans too small — the railways were too close, the factories too oppressive. With modern transport there was no need for people to live so close to their work. As Wells said,

> About all modern industrial operations are obnoxious to the homes; they rattle and clatter, they bang and roar, they disgorge smoke and steam and foul the air. They make mud and refuse and muddle, they absorb and emit sudden rushes and crowds of people. They smell, they hoot, they fill the air with dust and black, they beget a teeming tumult of vans, lorries, trucks that crush and damage children.

In Wells's Utopian city, no one would live near his work, as was now necessary in the Potteries district, an example he used (as had Howard). He also called for moving populations out of the East End of London; but when he contemplated the erection of gas works in the garden cities, as had already occurred, 'My first bright vision of beautiful homes among glowing gardens comes to me no more.'[11]

Two weeks later he returned to discuss his view of what the housing for workers in his proposed garden cities might be like. He rejected the myth of the cottage in a garden, as these were in fact often without water or sanitary facilities. Women's work was harder, if anything, in such 'idyllic' spots. He told his readers that he would provide a solution to the problem, however, in his next article. That article was delayed, in the event, while Wells was answered, first by Keble Howard who defended the country cottage and claimed that Wells would do away with 'love, passion, and, in fact, emotion of all sorts. . .', in his world. A second response, more dignified and to Wells's point, came from Ebenezer Howard himself, who told Wells that he was mistaken, that his earlier plan had no fixed timetable, and that such things as the circular plan of the garden cities could be modified without difficulty. For Howard, the significant factor was a limitation of size. He thought workers should be able to go home to lunch, grow gardens, and use the money saved from their lowered travel costs to finance holidays. For Wells, of course, this simply was not enough. Howard's cities would still prevent anyone from rising out of the class of people imprisoned in this new town.[12]

When Wells returned to the debate his answer was not in terms of circularity of towns nor the size or height of buildings. Instead, he dealt with the possibility that in his Utopia women could be relieved of many of the problems of child-bearing and -raising. He told his readers he was interested in improving the lives not only of the men in these new cities, but of all the inhabitants. He believed that the world could be changed: 'Wifehood (which commonly implies motherhood) is the predominant profession of women all about the Globe. The future of the world, the future of any state, rests finally upon the quality of its children, and the profession of mother, therefore, is the most important of all.'

Wells thought that if women had a choice, which they didn't, they would wish to have smaller families. He thought that the state should play a part in family planning, in the sense that it provided nurseries and all the things necessary to make the lives of children and mothers better, and in this way make possible smaller, better, cleaner families. And if a disaster should occur in a home, he urged the state to act immediately to take the children away so as not to let them be sacrificed. As he said, 'If the state wants sound and healthy children, the state must be prepared to put people who can produce them in a better position than those that can't.' The state must be prepared to pay in one way or another, and he called for increases in taxes and rates.[13]

His next article went even further. He called for the founding of associations through which the care of babies, laundry, and other chores would be done in common. Although he knew that some would say this would impinge on the natural habits of mankind, he dismissed that argument, calling instead for a sort of extended family, saying that there should be a return to a social and more co-operative life. Common dinner tables, reading rooms, social rooms, nurses, doctors, and hospitals would all make life better. Individuals could subscribe to a joint fund which would ensure the quality of service; and if a large outlay was required, co-operative efforts could bring it about. He went on to say that this life could be very like that of a college; he suggested that the initial and rudimentary steps towards it had already been taken by the poor, and cited Gissing's novels as evidence.

Later still Wells took his ideas a step further, repeating that a public crèche, playrooms, recreation rooms, gymnasia and swimming pools were all useful and possible ideas. If hot water were available in compact and centralized laundry rooms, women's lives would be made much easier. They could focus on their children's education, have plenty of time and space for social activities, along with self-improvement. He called for an end to duplication in building and described something very like a modern shopping centre with colonnades and shops, lined with pictures, flowers, and other delights. 'That is how they do in Utopia. That is how we shall do before many years.'[14]

At about this same time, Wells, although not specifically calling for a change, went still further by supporting some research into eugenics. As this was the period when the Mendelian laws were being rediscovered and research on such matters made public all over the world, it is not surprising that Wells should have commented. Although the claim that he went very far indeed towards the championing of eugenics was to surface off and on throughout his life, he did not, in truth, go far at all. In fact, what he did say, in commenting on a paper by Francis Galton, was fairly tame. He remarked that the idea was very premature, because in 1905 no one really had enough knowledge. But, if such knowledge came, he predicted that the change would be in 'the sterilization of failures, and not in the selection of successes for breeding', in all areas and not just with humans. He said that this change would allow the survival of the fitter, not the fittest. Later Wells was bedevilled, in both America and Britain, by the misrepresentation of his views on these matters, and this spilled over into public criticism of his views after the publication of *In the Days of the Comet*.[15]

Of course, all these matters were in the context of Wells's discussion of socialism. He was aware that some readers might be hostile to him, so he put his case in terms of the growing needs of the state, useful in a time when nationalism ran high. However, he always thought of what social change would mean for all human beings, not just English people. He described his ideas as 'the rustling hem of the garment of advancing socialism', saying that private property was passé and the middle-class social structure along with it. His view was that middle-class families stood to benefit from his ideas as much as the lower classes, not only in education but also from the assurance of a planned future for children and with it only slightly weakened individual control. He regarded the entire matter as inevitable. As intelligence grew, the emancipation of women from work and drudgery would come. He urged 'A Strike Against Parentage' as it was presently constituted, saying that 'the discontent of women is a huge available force for Socialism'. Socialism, as he outlined it, could only ameliorate these discontents; and parents and children would then go forward into a bright future.[16]

A decade later Wells commented again on the matter, citing how much the solidarity of women (especially around the issue of suffrage) had in the meantime hastened the possibility of major change. A decline in the marriage and birth rates, coupled with an economic revolution, a rise in the standards of education, and the solidarity of women in the battle for suffrage, had helped to increase the prospects immeasurably. 'She [the 'old' woman] makes her stilted passage across the arena upon which the new womanhood of western Europe shows its worth. It is an exit.'[17]

Wells did not compaign actively for women's suffrage, while supporting it throughout, for he felt that to focus on that issue took away from the broader and more necessary goals of changing life. He called himself an 'adult suffragist', saying that the vote was a useful symbol; but for him, the real problem was the 'extravagant sex-mania of our social system'. 'Humanity is obsessed with sex', was his comment. However, he went on to say, 'I have always been able to take sex rather lightly, and to think we make a quite unnecessary fuss about it; I write for an imaginary reader whom I never think of as specifically male or female, and consequently I have never cared to write for such deliberately and self-consciously female publications as this [the *Freewoman*].'

He urged his readers in that journal not to focus on Mr Asquith as their enemy, as he would presently die anyway. For Wells, 'I am capable of my own dream of a woman, level-eyed with a man, brave, absolutely loyal, free and his fellow. . . . The cause of women is immortal.'[18]

At the time of writing this Wells had not yet met Rebecca West, who was soon to be an important contributor to the *Freewoman*, and his mistress as well as mother of his child. By the time he next appeared in the journal, however, debating with the editors over the proper amount of endowment for mothers, he and Rebecca were well known to each other. The *Freewoman* was for the endowment of mothers, but Wells said that they were too narrow in their approach — what was needed was the endowment of motherhood. In his better world, a prospective mother would begin to receive an endowment in the third month of her pregnancy, a sum large enough to provide for the child's health and care at the outset, and a smaller amount thereafter. Wells thought that this would not be an extra drain on the state, as it ended by supporting most children and dependent females anyway. He urged women to take up as a cause his idea that mothers should have full control and guardianship of their children. The state's only role would be to equalize opportunity. He did not exclude fathers from the family, but he did think that their legal role should be diminished. 'The role of the father should be, I think, one of friendly advice, and not of legally sustained intervention.' Signing himself, 'Your Constant Reader', he ended by asking whether the editors thought marriage was necessary.[19]

The *Freewoman*, although a radical publication for its time, was read fairly widely by middle- and upper-class women. They found Wells's rough-and-ready responses a bit too strong, and several reacted to them. So he returned to the fray, pointing out to the magazine's readers that if they wanted socialism they had to take the issue to its conclusion and not stop part way. They called for economic equality; and if they wanted that, they would need to finance it no matter who was affected. For Wells, again, 'Sex is a graver handicap to a woman than a man — economically. Womanhood is not something super-added to the normal citizen; it is something taking up time, nervous energy, room in the body and room in the mind.' For sex resulted not only in child-bearing but, for many, a period of disablement as well. A collective endowment was needed to correct this economic disability. In fact, he carried his analysis further than was usual, even for this paper: 'Sex in a man is a handicap only through women, not in itself. It does not incapacitate him; it may rule his being, but it does not invade it; for him it is not a physical let and incumbrance, but only desire and a possible obsession. It is for men quite as much as for women that the endowment of motherhood is needed.'

With this piece Wells put the issue of androgny directly to the chief publication of radical feminism. It was a tough and difficult pill for them to swallow, of course; and the *Freewoman*'s correspondence columns were busy for weeks, with few readers completely accepting Wells's ideas. But he, in the public prints, had presented his views cogently and honestly. Given a biological imperative, men and women needed to be equal. Where that equality did not obtain, and childhood and motherhood were the two most obvious places, the state had an obligation to interfere, to set the world right. This was the purpose of the state, and it applied to sexual relations as well as any other.[20] This was Wells's public opinion; his private opinions, although less readily expressed, did not differ all that much.

Wells was concerned with functional and traditional morality, which he found cloying, but at the same time, at least until after his marriage to Jane or even later (when access to money made him freer of other people's opinions), he still found himself paying some attention to the views of others. Early in his life he described morality as 'the artificial factor in man', 'a moral padding for instinct', and said that as far as he could see, sexual morality only repressed or modified the natural instinct to replenish the species. In fact, he thought that our species had probably advanced far enough to write out a moral code which would overcome these matters. Later he told one friend that although love affairs gave him 'indigestion [!]', he did believe that it was possible to have what he termed 'non-jealous marriages'. However, he refused an opportunity to write on the delicate issue of whether men had a different moral standard from women and whether it would even be reasonable for both sexes to have the same standard. Later in his life he said that chastity was 'a purely technical virtue'. He went on to explain, 'It means in effect repression of sexual instinct unless a duly ordained priest has given a limited sanction to desire. Then what was forbidden becomes in its lowly way virtuous.' Wells found that offensive, if not contrary to nature, and proclaimed again to his interviewer that there was in reality no chastity.[21]

One of the first persons with whom Wells discussed these and similar matters was the author Grant Allen. They were cycling companions and fairly good friends at the end of the '90s. Wells begged off a trip with Allen in 1896, saying that the builders and others working on his house at Worcester Park would not take Jane's views as to what should be done. Wells found this utterly offensive and complained that the setting of fashions was one of the most insulting things done to humans. Later on the two men had a vigorous discussion of childbirth and marriage which went even closer to Wells's feelings. He told Allen that 'getting people born and educating them are after all the *real* human concerns' — all other things were secondary. This was after Wells's reviews and discussions of Allen's book, *The New Woman*, which Wells disliked, and after his own publication of *The Time Machine, Dr Moreau*, and some other realistic work. He did ask Allen to ponder whether illegitimate children were more active than others and whether this was due to the types of parents who had illegitimate children (that is, children outside wedlock). It seems clear that some of these matters were of interest to Wells, but not of abiding interest just yet.[22]

Still, this was a rather limited correspondence on a subject increasingly important. More such letters were probably written, but only a very few survive. One to Graham Wallas in 1902 is extremely forthcoming. Written before Wells had had much extramarital experience (possibly a brief encounter with Ivy Low's mother; possibly a first flirtation with Dorothy Richardson, but as yet he had not had his major experiences with Richardson, Rosamund Bland, Amber Reeves, or West), it still sets his views out quite well.

Wells was writing his *Mankind in the Making* chapters and was attempting to establish how the species should function in the better world of tomorrow. He apologized to Wallas for not giving him better copy (Wallas had cut the previous chapter severely), but went on to remark that it was a difficult subject to discuss properly.

> I think I'm clear enough that the wastrel (bless his heart) may have his simple or complicated pleasures as far as I'm concerned so long as he doesn't have children. But really it isn't my affair whether he practices — not temperance because temperance is the *optimum* amount of physical pleasure — but either abstinence or indulgence.
>
> Year by year my Christian training scales off me and I get more and more purely physiological with regard to sexual intercourse. A man or a woman ought to have sexual intercourse. Few people are mentally, or morally, or physically in health without it. For everyone there is a minimum and maximum below which lies complete efficiency. Find out your equation, say I, and then keep efficient.
>
> Since it became clear to me that reproduction and sexual activity can be disconnected, the whole human [*indecipherable word or words*] not. The ungovernable complication venereal disease. Over and above sensations there are of course emotions in these affairs, but the emotions can be [?] overcome by suggestion and interruptions in a thousand different ways. Our system stresses all the emotions into jealousy. A Maori is proud to marry a girl who has had many lovers.
>
> We've got to rationalize the sentiment in these affairs. But that's a matter for morals, I submit. Anyhow I don't intend to raise the flames of public sexuality by specifically recommending preventions now. One thing at a time. From first blast the public is going to swallow a lot from me and my affair as a good monarch is to make it go over easy.[23]

This is a letter written with regard to a proposed book; but it is, nevertheless, a very straightforward letter; and as it shows Wells's views clearly, it deserves the rather long quotation. Wells never veered from his view that sexual procreation was instinctively ordered to fulfil the demands of the species, but with the development of readily available and inexpensive protective devices, he thought it likely that sexual activity would become much more widespread; and much of it would be outside conventional marriage and morality. In fact, he saw nothing wrong with this — he called such events 'passades' and pursued his instincts as he liked. We shall look presently at the reaction of his partners to these beliefs.

Occasionally some of Wells's correspondents tried to get him to think more clearly. 'Vernon Lee' (Violet Paget) told him that if he were a woman she might ask him if his hat were on perfectly straight. In other words he needed to be more careful about his choice of words. 'I cannot bear your not acting up to the perfect kindliness and sincerity which always distinguishes you from other writers on these subjects.' Later she would be even more forthright in her comments on Wells's relationship with Amber Reeves, on their child, and the novel which dealt with some of this affair, *Ann Veronica*. She always watched him, however, even though she generally accepted his point of view.[24]

Where Wells received much more than he bargained for, at least so it seems, was after the Reeves affair and others, and after *The New Machiavelli* had been published. Wells did not, as he had agreed, stop seeing Amber Reeves; and he was about to set up a formal liaison with Rebecca West, as well as his shorter but equally passionate affair with Elizabeth von Arnim. During the summer of 1911, with Spade House sold and the family not yet living at Easton Glebe, the Wellses rented a château in France for the summer. It was a good choice of location, near enough for their friends; and while it was a summer in which England was especially wet, the Continent remained pleasant and summery. Wells invited Violet Paget and Ray Lankester, among others, to Normandy to stay for part of the summer with the family. While there, he took both Paget and Lankester to an offshore island for a picnic and an extensive talk. His talk with Paget turned on their discussions of *The New Machiavelli* and Wells's treatment of the Fabians, but his discussions with Lankester were apparently about sexual desire, and especially sexual desire outside marriage. Lankester thought long and hard over the subject, and two weeks after he had left the Wells household, he sent H.G. a letter with his considered views. The fact that the letter was saved is important, but equally important for an understanding of Wells is that it did not deter or limit his friendship with Lankester in the slightest amount.[25]

The talk on the island had apparently been very frank, and the letter, written by an older Victorian bachelor, although one formally trained and excelling in biological science, is a masterpiece of treading on thin ice, trying to lecture Wells without losing a dear friend. Lankester told Wells that he had spent a great deal of time reflecting on 'the interesting subject' which they had talked about in the wood. Lankester now thought the differences between them probably a matter of their past histories, but even then they might disagree. Lankester distinguished sharply between the views of the individual and the community, even in sex which he admitted 'had an irresistible and at first disconcerting attraction for me'. But he believed that there were two kinds of women — one group 'naughty but fascinating', admirably professional, but hardly suited for permanent relationships; and a second group which he termed 'angelic creatures' and later 'angeloids', only to be approached, 'however desirable', on the basis of marriage and family assent. Whilst deeply involved with the first group, he remarked, 'I always placed the second on a pedestal and should as soon [have] thought of temporary amusement or a passionate outburst with one of them as robbing a bank.' He went on to say that he would go to a strip show or an exhibition of professional nudity, as he termed it, of the first group, but would avoid even a look at a leg or the breast of a representative of the second type. If a person who appeared to be of the second group acted in a way foreign to that group, he would shun her immediately.

He went on to lecture Wells in detail about his angelic class, and told him that those women who were out of their class or group needed education or, if necessary, to be placed in a nunnery or even be spayed (his word). The ladies of the night knew their place and performed accordingly, and the state perhaps should recognize their work with pensions because the two classes of women were both needed and both played an important role.

Lankester told Wells that Wells's experience was untypical and that his point of view

> appears to be determined by the fact that you had not appreciated the merits of professional ladies before you were led off by a quasi-angelic female into conduct which should be reserved for the alcoves of a professional and you have maintained your taste for what I may call the aberrant angelic female who the professionals would say takes the bread out of honest women's mouths.

Lankester told Wells that he wasn't playing the game properly. He should let such 'sports', in the biological sense, alone, and if need be, resolve his problems by having recourse to professionals. Lankester thought that Wells's ideas were even worse because Wells was blessed, in Jane Wells, with an admirable example of the 'angeloid group'. (One wonders what he would have said if he had known of their days in Mornington Place.)

> I have never reached that phase of happiness — now at my age I know how great is the good fortune of those who have a devoted wife ready to bear and do everything for the sake of the man and his children. If I were in such a case and in natural need of the relief and nerved rest given by 'naughtiness' — I would seek it from the best type of professional lady at my leisure and keep it a dead secret. That is I imagine what hundreds of men do.

Lankester asked Wells if he believed that his ideas could be translated into general practice or whether he truly thought that Lankester was wrong.

Wells's response is apparently not available, although it is clear from the context of Lankester's letter that Wells had been somewhat hurt by the plain talk of the older man. Still they exchanged views once more, and this time Lankester was a bit less strict and strait-laced in his views. Now he began to ask some practical questions to be applied to Wells's ideas of group or mutual marriage:

> The difficulty about adopting practical polygamy and unlimited selection in the male [said Lankester], is, I think, that we have not for some centuries been playing that game but another — and that consequently the women are not trained to meet the difficulties of the new game nor are other men duly advised of it and ready for it. Even as it is, — I have constantly observed that girls of fine qualities and great beauty — are snatched up and as it were infatuated by this or that young man of no merit but reckless audacity — simply because the chance was that the reckless youth appeared on the scene and proposed marriage — not because there was selection based upon adequate experience either in the man's or the girl's part.[26]

This correspondence too is given in some detail because it represents a high point in the conversations which Wells held with several friends; but also it provides a glimpse into affairs about which many were exercised at this time of rapidly changing morality. H.G. Wells was responsible for much of that change and it is necessary to look at his fiction, as well as at his treatment of his wife and his mistresses, all of whom modified his views to some extent. These women figure in one sense or another in his realistic novels, which rapidly began to replace the science fiction which had made his name. In addition, it will be logical eventually to look at how those women, or some of them at least, dealt with him in their own fashion. For each side changed the other dramatically. The theories laid out in conversations with Ray Lankester and Violet Paget, the statements of belief published in the *Daily Mail*, dissolved rapidly in bed where desire became paramount.

For when Wells met a young girl to whom he was attracted, he did not hide his desire. As an example, in 1917 or so he met the very young and very beautiful Enid Bagnold, later famous for her novel, *National Velvet*. Wells fell head over heels into a state of infatuation and penned her a very indiscreet letter. Other such letters were mostly destroyed, but Bagnold, by retaining this along with others more sedate, allows us to observe Wells when his instincts overcame his ideals, his morality, or even his sensibilities.

He wrote to the young girl inviting her to lunch, at which he also hoped to have Rebecca West present. Then, apparently realizing what this might mean, he went on to say hurriedly, 'then I will watch you two clever humans surveying each other. You ought to love each other but you never know. . . .' But he soon went more directly to the point of his writing:

> Every man and particularly me is a rather horrid boy of 14 and something else. If somebody did a surgical operation to my brain and removed certain small bits of it, I should become a lascivious urchin and extremely happy. If you were a man I shouldn't have the urgent desire to get friends with you that I do now. It's quite irrational. . . .

He went on to say that his attitude towards her could be described as 'honourable and respectful but I don't think that it is *strictly* honourable'. However, he did promise to show restraint when they next met. He closed by remarking that when he died he hoped to be translated to a Moslem paradise, 'and Rebecca (whom I adore) won't want me to keep. . . .' The letter ends in the ellipse.[27]

Bagnold did not go to the next meeting, but Wells kept up his pursuit although with a bit more dignity. They soon met again and became good friends. He was, after all, simply a normal man, but one whose life allowed him an opportunity to break out, to play by different rules; and his relationships with women were such that most accepted them for what they were, took what he was willing to give them, and enjoyed their moments together. Interestingly enough, Bagnold, when discussing their second meeting, makes it clear that she was apparently willing, but Wells's attachment to Rebecca was in the way.[28]

Wells is quite frank in *Experiment in Autobiography* about his relations with both Isabel and Jane. However, one gets the feeling while reading his words that perhaps our view might be clearer if we could read their words as well. He certainly was jealous of Isabel, although eventually his sexual longings for her passed, and with them his jealousy. Afterward he regretted his earlier action, especially as he had torn up her photographs. He was forced to rely on Elizabeth Healey to provide him with the ones he reproduced in the autobiography. However, he was a man with better control than that anecdote indicates; and so one may doubt whether he actually went through all the storms of jealousy and hate he described. Some of the same attitudes must have been present in his relationship with Jane.

Initially they had an equally strong sexual attraction for each other, attested by a series of childish nicknames for each other. She was 'Bits', 'Miss Bits', 'Bins', 'Snitch-It', while he was 'Mr Bins', 'Bins', and so on. Of course, his family used such names — like the 'Busswacker', 'Busswuss', 'Buzzie', and other similar-sounding names his brothers used for him. He and Jane became adults together. They (and she was a beautiful girl already in revolt) quickly made an alliance which fostered their desires for escape from the morality and strictures both found so binding. (Although *Ann Veronica* is said to be the story of Amber Reeves, I have always felt that that book should also be read as at least a partial portrait of Amy Catherine Robbins.)

What seems apparent is that for the first half-dozen years of their marriage H.G. and Jane were truly partners. Partners in writing (she produced a few pieces of journalism in this time), partners in ideas, sexual partners, and even equal partners in discovering new worlds. At the end of that time he had become a famous man, and a famous man who had had two close encounters with death. In a sense then he came to be more daring than he might otherwise have been.

This daring took him first into a complete advocacy of socialism, then to the transfer of his abilities to more didactic writing, both fiction and non-fiction, and finally to a willingness to be free of all the trammels of society. This drive was enhanced by his brush with the Fabians in which he learned the lesson that he did better alone. He was a planner, not an executor. So much was obvious. In sexual matters he also freed himself from normal restraints. As a highly sexed individual, he had always had a roving eye, apparently. With the availability of birth-control devices (and he makes a good deal of this in his autobiography), he began to experiment outside his marriage. Apparently the sexual side of his and Jane's marriage diminished fairly quickly. However, it is equally clear that other relationships grew rapidly.

He greatly depended on her just the same. She, in turn, depended even more greatly on doing for him. His rise to fame and fortune became a goal for her, and she was apparently content to make his house comfortable, his life easy, and to allow that fertile mind to create even more fantasies for his readers. She became his typist and his amanuensis — correcting, retyping, giving advice, and eventually shielding him from his agents, other unwanted interruptions, and probably even from the intrusions of his children except at fixed times. He makes it plain in his account of his life with her that she controlled the purse, the home, their external life — all with reference, of course, to what would smooth his path.

He, in turn, communicated his views to her indirectly. The use of drawings, baby talk, poems, and other less open means to give an indirect view of his needs suited her perfectly, or so it seems. At some time early in the marriage, he even modified her name to 'Jane', with all the implications of 'plain Jane'. He may even have used the name 'Euphemia' for her, while writing those pieces. Pinker certainly called her that. As well as playing a portion of the heroine's role in *Ann Veronica*, she is also probably present as Aunt Susan in *Tono-Bungay*, although this is in her later place in his life. Jane Wells, for her part, increasingly adopted a second persona as 'Catherine Wells', a writer of the Mansfield/Woolf school. In this persona she had relatively little contact with H.G., at least until after her death when he put together a collection of her work. He probably learned a good deal he had not known before from that exercise, and his introduction to the book supports that view.

In any case, they drifted into different channels, although continuing to love and respect each other greatly. For Wells, with his strong biological urge, this meant a search for other partners — a search that was readily rewarded by a series of women, usually much younger that he, most of them also 'rebels' of a sort, and usually with literary ambitions as well. Occasionally, as we learn from the suppressed volume of his autobiography, he did resort to professionals, but these incidents were very limited in number. There were always younger women about. His mind, his ideas, his willingness to flout custom, and, in fact, his utter willingness to treat them as human beings meant that he was very attractive to these potentially available partners. Apparently he continued to make physical love to Jane, but not as frequently. There is one letter, an unusual letter, in which he tells a correspondent that these times tended to be sudden, unplanned, and often took place in the garden. They maintained a summer house in the garden for him to work in, and one supposes that it was convenient.

Wells was such an open person that his life is subject to misinterpretation. At first glance he appears as simply an ageing roué and libertine, but this description falls away quickly when one realizes that no one who knew him at all believed this. Jane Wells, on the other hand, may appear as a compliant, weak sort of individual, but this description also fails. Wells said that their love operated best in a '*modus vivendi*' state, and so it did, but one is still left with the feeling that perhaps, just perhaps, he is making the situation slightly better than it actually was between them. He remained an author of fiction at all times.[29]

As I have said, relatively few of their letters survive, other than those from the earliest days. There are one or two from his American trip in 1906, several from Switzerland (mostly dealing with the collapse of Wallas, as Wells set him too rough a walking pace), and a few from his 1920 Russian trip. Those from her are filled with expressions of deep love along with the baby talk and the always-present nicknames. Only occasionally did Jane allow herself the sort of comment quoted at the head of this chapter, and one may doubt that that was actually sent.

Perhaps a quotation or two may indicate the depth of feeling, however. In 1901 or thereabouts (G.P. is either just born or about to be born), she wrote to him with:

> Dearest, dearest, dearest, dearest — do not forget me — do not fail me. My dear love do not doubt. Do believe in me a little — till I make you quite believe — till I can show you. Oh, but I love you and I am just longing, longing for the time to come. My very very dear.
>
>   Your (shameless) wife in love.

A year later, after he had left her on some unknown occasion, she followed him with this letter:

> Dear one, I am very sorry, I was all silly and crying when you went. I didn't feel a bit dismal, only somehow I think you reduce me to a sort of dewpoint — and the foolish thing is always being tearful and doesn't want to be.

Again, a few months later, she is still unsure of herself, or at least the letter seems to indicate insecurity about their relationship:

> It's very queer that I always regard myself as fixed in this world up to ripe old age, quite solidly, and you seem to hang beside me by the slenderest thread of chance that any instant may snap. (Silly old Bitz.)

H.G. apparently felt that these letters and their private talk indicated too limited a position. He wrote her a long letter (and it is indicative of their relationship that he wrote to her) in which he counselled some moderation in her approach to him and to their home.

Addressed to 'Dst Person', it is signed 'Bins'. It is a very long letter, filled with advice and often given as though a father or an elder brother were writing:

> My dearest love to you, P.C.B., and don't think me an outrageous squasher of hopes. But what we want before all things is a household we can leave with a tranquil mind at any time without any chance of explosive or dissident elements. . . .
> You put a sort of artistic anxiety into your home management, a constructive and reconstructive solicitude that keeps the home far too sharply focused. . . . My home is not made with hands, my success, our success is not to be a measure of material things, our reality is dreamland and the unseen. . . .
> The [*word left out in original*] don't deserve to break you of nights. There's a waste and tax of heart and brain that are made for better things. Things signify a little more than patience or chess. . . .[30]

Wells needed a home which was not disrupted either by moody family members or tyrannical workmen. This put a good deal of pressure on Jane, one supposes; after the boys were in school, she dealt with this pressure by taking long holidays skiing in the Alps, especially when Wells was in the South of France. She took photographs and kept diaries of her trips; and when they met again, they discussed them in detail. She also maintained a flat in town to which he did not come, and eventually, she wrote. Her stories appeared in the *Strand*, the *New English Review*, and other journals in the decade before she died. Frank Swinnerton, Arnold Bennett, and others of Wells's friends, as well as his voluminous business correspondence, all took the place he had occupied for her in their earlier life. Whether she was entirely acquiescent or not, we do not know; but we do know that she tolerated it, defended him, and accepted the love he was willing to give her.[31] He could not have been an easy person to live with, as one more letter of his will indicate:

> My instability at home is due to the unsettled feeling due to plumbing [?] I do not think you understand what a *torment* it is to an impatient man to feel the phantom future here failing to realize itself. I hate things

unfinished and out of place. I want things settled. I want a home to live in and have people in it. People one can talk with. At present home is a noisy, unsympathetic, uninteresting mudhole. I want to get at it. I want to feel it changing. I feel like *Research*. When we get it all cleared up perhaps it will be possible to get human beings interested in things that matter about us again. Anyway we must try. . . . cannot bring a visitor down or get to feel that my work is anything but an income-getting toil. It must be changed in that respect.

But he goes on in the letter to complain even more of other matters:

And when I have been at the Rectory for a few days, I get into a state of instability — because of sexual exasperation. Later on I shall be able to get pacified in London. — For that [?means ?news] I still fail to see any perfect solution I confess. But the present situation is particularly calculated to make a peaceful sojourn at L. Easton impossible. . . .Later in every respect I think it will be better. The brute fact is that I am not and never have been — if there is such a thing — a passionate lover. I am affectionate and need only interesting things and brief [?interludes] and I want a healthy woman to stay my needs and leave me most free for real things. I love you very warmly, you are in so many things, love young love and flesh young flesh, and [?mine]. I must keep you. I like your company and I doubt about never spending that holiday together and so on. But the thing is a physical necessity. That's the [*indecipherable*] hitch.

He finishes the letter, again signed 'Bins', with a promise of better days ahead for both of them. Of course, this letter was written under the press of war, and it is a product of the move to Little Easton; but it is also a product of the time in which Rebecca West is giving birth to his son. The cry for sexual relief and the bluntness with which it is put tells us a good deal about H.G. Wells, but also about Amy Catherine Wells.[32] In the long run one doubts whether any of the other women with whom Wells was linked could have provided him with the home and understanding she did, but even for her, it must have been extremely difficult at times.

Whether his sexual needs were greater than hers, or whether she simply decided that she did not wish to be as active, we do not know. What we do know is that by 1906 or so, H. G. Wells was beginning to seek some sexual gratification outside his marriage and this was apparently with Jane Wells's consent or at least acquiescence. These escapades, if that is an appropriate word, involved him with Rosamund Bland, Amber Reeves, Dorothy Richardson, Rebecca West, and Elizabeth von Arnim, at the very least. All of these left some evidence of the involvement and three of these women were made pregnant by Wells. We will soon look at these events, along with the novels the encounters produced, but before that perhaps it is appropriate also to look at three novels of this period — *Kipps, Mr Polly*, and *Tono-Bungay*. These three works are of central importance to our study of H. G. Wells. For with these works, brilliantly conceived, remarkably well written, their author is able to claim a permanent place in English fiction, close to Dickens because of the extraordinary humanity of some of his characters, but also because of his ability to invoke a *place*, a *class*, a *social scene*. These novels are very personal as well, treating aspects of Wells's own life, matters which would come under attack later, but only after he added his sexual and extramarital views to the personal side of his work. What is remarkable is that these works appeared in the same decade as his provocative excursions into socialism, and some of his best science fiction, as well as significant journalism.

Although there had been attempts at the personal, or even the more or less overtly autobiographical novel prior to Wells's efforts, such attempts had not been well received, nor had they, in fact, probed very deeply into the personal and power relationships found in marriage, sexual love, and desire for class and social advancement, or even into private unfulfilled longings. The democratic revolution, with the opening of some peepholes into a better life, along with the changes brought about by the machine revolution, altered all that. With the open frontier in Canada, Australia, and America offering an easily perceived possibility for escape now joining the leisure-time revolution, ordinary people could aspire to a life far beyond that of their parents and grandparents. Wells's personal novels provide a glimpse of the impact these external changes made on lower-middle-class minds and thought, both in the new horizons that were offered, and in the psychological trauma caused in those who beheld this new, possible and very threatening world.[33]

As these matters became more important to Wells, he began to plan a great novel in which the process of changing class, here through the impact of a bequest, would be illuminated. That novel, *The Wealth of Mr Waddy*, grew immensely, and was never fully realized. Eventually it was abandoned, which seems unfortunate, as some of Wells's more remarkable characters appear in the draft version. In the book he finally produced they play very little part, however. In the draft there are good accounts of Wells's schools, both the ones in which he taught and those he attended. Kipps, a draper's apprentice in both books, is a more slapstick version in the unpublished work. Scenes of the death of Waddy, and the resulting destruction of the various Waddy Wills, all scenes barely mentioned in *Kipps*, remain vivid in the mind of the reader of the abandoned sketch.

However, *Kipps* itself is a very good book. Wells uses his draper's apprenticeship to remarkable effect, and the scene in which Chitterlow introduces Kipps to whisky is marvellously funny. Other good things in the published version are the precise descriptions of places such as Coote's parlour, Chitterlow's flat, and also of Kipps's first visits to London, with the secret fear that he will not behave properly in the hotel, on the street, and elsewhere. After the legacy comes, Kipps builds a home, and there is a delightful scene with the architect, based somewhat, one assumes, on Wells's encounters with Voysey. Although Kipps loses his money, which is a relief, as living out of his class has been traumatic for him and his wife, by a trick of the novelist's desire he obtains enough of it back to live a comfortable life. At the last he appears chastened by the experience, not wanting more than is really useful, able to come to terms with expectations, both his own and others'; and the book ends with Artie Kipps, in a rowboat with Ann, attempting to understand the aesthetic possibilities of life, but eventually accepting himself, Ann, and their world:

> Out of the darkness beneath the shallow, weedy stream of his being rose a question, a question that looked up dimly and never reached the surface. It was the question of the wonder of the beauty, the purposeless, inconsecutive beauty, that falls so strangely among the happenings and memories of life. It never reached the surface of his mind, it never took to itself substance or form; it looked up merely as the phantom of a face might look, out of deep waters, and sank again into nothingness.
>
> (Book III, chapter 3)[34]

Mr Waddy was in gestation at the end of 1897. Pinker took the early effort and tried to place it as a serial, and eventually, when serialization failed, as a novel. The agent tried to get Wells to work harder on *Waddy*, as the bits and pieces were simply not enough to sell the idea, but it was too large a task, and Wells abandoned the work for a time, before reviving his Kipps character who had been introduced about halfway into the manuscript. Even when *Kipps* was finally finished, in the late spring of 1904, Pinker had difficulty in moving the manuscript, and described the book, after six months of negotiations, as a 'very present anxiety. . . I am not hopeless yet but the possibilities are narrowing.' The serial rights were eventually sold, and then Macmillan decided to publish the novel. Wells assured Frederick Macmillan of the purpose of the book, its 'subdued humour and the enforced pathos of feebleness and inadequacy. . . *Kipps* is designed to present a typical member of the English lower middle class in all of its pitiful limitations and feebleness, and by means of a treatment deliberately kind and genial links a sustained and fairly exhaustive criticism of the ideals and ways of life of the great mass of middle-class English people.'

Macmillan did not spend the amount of money on advertising Wells wanted, and the two exchanged a number of letters on methods of publicity (Wells wanted sandwich-men at theatre entrances), but Macmillan felt the book would only appeal to a highly literate public. Wells brought forward Henry James's praise of *Kipps*, and urged Macmillan to push it even more. The book did not move well at first, although it has remained in print ever since, and eventually became one of Wells's greatest sellers. It was the different, and to a slight degree unrealized, nature of the novel which has made it endure, but at the same time those features inhibited its early sale and the responses to it.[35]

C. F. G. Masterman, writing in the *Daily Mail*, described the book as 'the best story he has yet given us', and in a letter told Wells that *Kipps*, along with *Love and Mr Lewisham*, was the most likely of his work to endure. Morley Roberts echoed the sentiment in his correspondence, and told Wells that the book had provoked a nightmare which lingered in his mind for forty-eight hours. James felt the same pleasure with the book, describing his efforts at discussing his reaction as 'drivel' and using words such as 'gem', 'the first intelligently and consistently ironic or satiric novel', 'extraordinary life', while he worried that the criticism had not been up to the standard of the book. In fact, all the fears of Wells, Pinker, and Macmillan were for nothing. The book was on its way to being received as a masterpiece. Wells had reached the first of his peaks outside of his scientifically focused writing.[36]

If *Kipps* is a masterpiece, *Tono-Bungay* and *Mr Polly* must also rank in that category. *Tono-Bungay* (1909) is on the surface an account of a get-rich-quick scheme of Uncle Ponderevo (a man somewhat similar to Wells's father), who creates a patent nostrum which sweeps England, bringing a huge income and an almost magical change of life's structures for the Uncle, Aunt Susan (partially, as we have noted, a portrait of Jane), and the narrator; but in all the book is a massive, humorous, and dissecting attack on capitalism, on how money is made, and with what little humane purpose.

The book swept England much as had the potion of its title. It was readily accepted by those who hated the structure of society and could revel in the attack on it, as well as by those who cherished the Wellsian ability to pick out character types and illuminate their habitat, describing them with a fidelity and humour which is infectious. Both groups could accept the book on its merits, and put it in their intellectual baggage. *Tono-Bungay* used the beginning craze over flying, and Wells's own experience of flying, which began very early. There are bits and pieces from the drapery background; his mother's experiences at Up Park are well recounted in his view of life on a country estate; there is even a brief, passionate, and unfulfilled love affair with Beatrice — all events which appealed to his readers, both because of their naturalness, and because of the humour and pathos implicit in them.

The book ends with a truly remarkable account of coming down the Thames, past the bridges of London, and on out into the open sea. As Wells wrote, 'The river passes — London passes, England passes', and then one of the finer endings in all English fiction:

It is a note of crumbling and confusion, of change and seemingly aimless swelling, of a bubbling up and medley of futile loves and sorrows. But through the confusion sounds another note. Through the confusion something drives, something that is at once human achievement and the most inhuman of all existing things. Something comes out of it. . . .

Sometimes I call this reality Science, sometimes I call it Truth. But it is something we draw by pain and effort out of the heart of life, that we disentangle and make clear. Other men serve it, I know, in art, in literature, in social invention, and see it in a thousand different figures, under a hundred names. I see it always as austerity, as beauty. This thing we make clear is the heart of life. . . .

I have come to see myself from the outside, my country from the outside — without illusions. We make and pass.

We are all things that pass, striving upon a hidden mission, out to the open sea.

(Book IV, chapter 3)

Wells knew how significant his book was. He planned it carefully, and constructed it with love and attention to detail. In fact, he dropped the book to finish *The War in the Air*, on which he was working concurrently, as he felt that *Tono-Bungay* was so superior that he wanted the other out of the way, as it would interfere in the creative process.

Later when he came to look at *Tono-Bungay* again, he said that he was 'disposed to regard it as the finest and most finished novel upon the accepted lines' that he had written or was ever likely to write'. And, even earlier, when talking to his agent about the *Comet* and *Tono-Bungay*, the first being printed and the second under construction, he said:

What damned fools these people are. Here am I offering my religion and guts and everything to them and I suppose they'd rather have — they don't know what they'd rather have but anything that isn't offered. . . . They can't feel safe. The books all *do* come off but always there is this silly fencing, simply because the things aren't an evident repetition of the previous pattern. No literature is.[37]

The Fabians did not like the book very much — but by that time they were unhappy with Wells for a variety of reasons. Hubert Bland savaged the book, in the *Daily Chronicle*, and Beatrice Webb, who liked the book, did compare it unfavourably with *The War in the Air* both in her diary and in a letter to Wells. Robertson Nicoll, writing as 'Claudius Clear' in the *British Weekly*, criticized the book as an attack on chastity and for discussing unmentionable indecencies. These comments were of little moment, however. The reviewer in the *Daily Telegraph* referred to *Tono-Bungay* as 'full-fledged, four-square', and said that it appeared 'with all the intense conviction of a masterpiece'.

Wells's friends were equally pleased in their private comments. Masterman, again early off the mark, thought the novel was better than *Kipps* and told Wells that he still had more to say about women, and urged him forward still:

> Give us life, my dear, and life as seen without spectacles or opium. You are going nearer to doing it than any other literary man. You have gone further, especially in sex — in this latest book than ever before.
>
> But sex, and religion, and ambition, and love of power will [*word illegible*] sense of futility before the *iron* dominance of the *melancholy* present — beating butterfly wings against a rusty iron gate — with such pathetic side tricks and failures in realization as the suffragette movement, or the bypaths of religious emotion. By God, Mr H.G. Wells, writer of novels, here's a subject made for your head.[38]

Others were as strong in their praise. Gilbert Murray wrote three letters to Wells on the book, and in the last compared Wells to Tolstoy in his power of description. *T.P.'s Weekly* said Wells was producing a series of *tours de force*, praising the interior art of the book, although they thought that Wells had fallen into the old trap of scamping his conclusions. *T.P.'s* returned to the discussion two weeks later, as the book lingered in their writer's mind, telling readers that Susan Ponderevo was one of the great characters in English fiction, quoting items about her in detail in a long article. The *Christian Commonwealth* also felt moved to defend Wells against religious attacks; they ran a photograph of him (along with other Socialists) on the cover, and provided a brief biography as well as a review of *Tono-Bungay*. The *Commonwealth* welcomed the book, and said, '*Tono-Bungay* is designed to flame that discontent, which must stir in the hearts of the mass of Englishmen, before the conditions of waste described by Mr Wells can begin to give place to others saner and more beautiful.'[39]

The third of a remarkable trio of personal novels with males as the central focus, all of which treat changes in status, and the reaction to them, is *The History of Mr Polly*, published in 1910. Polly is a complete comic miracle, with his habit of twisting words into caricatures of themselves which at the same time catch the satirical side of Wells's view of life. Traditions are smashed in the book, with some of the funnier writing in English literature skewering the rites of marriage, courtship, funerals, and shopkeeping. Everywhere Mr Polly bumbles through, commenting and reacting, while staying essentially untouched. The draper's shop is revisited, as is young love, with an *Amaryllis at the Fair* interlude; but finally Polly is captured and put in his place, only to break out with a farcical attempt at suicide, a great fire, and his final escape to another part of England.

Eventually he returns and finds his first wife, but they are both happier now and Polly goes back, to expatiate on his views in the comfortable confines of his new life. Wells is offering no moral here, simply creating one of the great comic characters in English fiction — one which he claimed to be based not on himself so much as on his dear older brother, Frank. Whatever the source, all, or nearly all, liked the book immensely, and H.G.

Wells ended this personal period with his reputation high and his spirits relatively intact.[40]

If this had been all he had written in this period, H. G. Wells would still be a force to be mentioned in modern textbooks. The depiction of the class of his origin, the comic characters of Kipps and Polly, and the structure of *Tono-Bungay* with its savage analysis of Edwardian England, ready to go under the surgeon's knife, would all have ensured that critics of taste would have discussed his contributions. But this was not all his effort, and it was the books of personal sexual hunger, the novels of unrequited and requited love, and his championing of causes such as birth-control, feminine equality, group marriages, the gratification of sexual hungers outside the marital bonds if that was necessary, as well as his acceptance that women had the same needs and hungers as men, that created the storm round his head. For here Wells took his magic descriptive pen and opened areas not normally viewed in select drawing rooms. And for his enemies what made it seem even worse was that he apparently used his own personal extramarital experiences as material for the didactic passages in his fiction.

They might have known it would come, if they had thought about it. Even before *Love and Mr Lewisham*, the first of these personal accounts, he had written *The Wonderful Visit*, which describes the descent to earth of an angel, with whom a curate falls somewhat in love. Nothing really happens (in fact the angel 'loves' another), but these slightly unusual love affairs were rather risky even for Wells. Critics were gentle with this book, calling it 'a striking fantasia wrought with tact, charm and wit', but not a novel. However, even here his iconoclasm, although welcomed, featured in reviewers' comments. The authors said that they could not prophesy his fate, but they thought, even in this early book, that he would make his mark.[41]

Even more to the possible point of illicit love was *The Sea Lady*, which appeared in 1902. Here the unlikely visitor is a mermaid, Doris Thalassia Waters, who wins the heart of the hero, Chatteris. A high point in the novel is the conversation between Chatteris's cousin and his former fiancée, who asks, what did the mermaid have that she did not? How could he be untrue to all his upbringing? In response, the cousin, Melville, just before prophesying that the Sea Lady would woo Chatteris into the deeps — untold deeps — remarks that the difference surely is that the sweetheart has

defined things — very closely. You have made it clear to him what you expect him to be, and what you expect him to do. It is like having built a house in which he is to live. For him to go to her is like going out of a house, a very fine and dignified house, I admit, into something larger, something adventurous and incalculable. She is — she has an air of being — *natural*. . . . She has the quality of the open sky, of deep tangled places, of the flight of birds. . . .

(Chapter 7, sect. ii)

In the end Chatteris chooses the new and the different — leaving the staid and set behind, again looking into the unknown, into the sea, or into the open spaces. Love, of an unusual sort, has triumphed over ordinary matters. Wells certainly was giving his reader cues — he would not be content with staid morality, and if they wished it they would be surprised and hurt, just as this sweetheart is hurt by the defection, while knowing and understanding at the same time that the defection is inevitable. It may not be too much to say that the Sea Lady, 'a hussy', as Pinker termed her, was simply the first strong reflection of the demands being made in Wells's life with Jane, demands that would take him far away from conventional morality, into the open sea that beckoned.[42]

Although these novels gave an indication of the direction Wells's mind might take in these personal matters, none of them went as far as did *Love and Mr Lewisham*, *In the Days of the Comet*, and *Ann Veronica*, to name those published in this period of his life. For it was in those books that H.G. Wells clearly laid out his views on love, marriage, and relationships among and between the sexes. *Mr Lewisham* was the first breakthrough, although it was much less controversial than the later books. It is the story of a young man attempting to make his way, via education. Wells limns clearly the desires of the undergraduate and the hopes of the teacher early in his career, and with emotion. The discussion and analysis of the hero's schema on the basis of which modern education must function in order to achieve its promise, still wakes echoes of the days when one first began to teach. However, as is often the case in Wellsian novels, and in life, love and desire enter, block or deflect the dreams, and change the character of the novel quite completely. The book is a pretty clear representation of what H.G. Wells was like in his days at the Normal School of Science, reeling from the impact of falling in love with Isabel. Lewisham is a somewhat comic hero, but at the same time he obtains the reader's sympathy, both because he is so true to life, and because we know that he is an honest effort to depict H. G. Wells at a stage in his life when he was undergoing severe physical and mental distress.

Wells said later that this novel was his first attempt at constructing a work of art. He read it aloud to Jane to purge it of slovenly phrases, and consciously made it 'clear' and 'simple'. Wells was at work on this book by the late summer of 1896, in his first great spurt of creative energy. *Dr Moreau* was out, *The Wheels of Chance* in the press, and he was already focusing on this new work, which he had promised to Dent by Christmas. In fact, Pinker read the first good draft of the book at the end of November. Dent did not do a very good job of dealing with the manuscript, or so thought the young author and his agent; actually the book was unfinished and had to be recast substantially before it was in shape to publish.[43]

In the event Wells fell ill at about this time, and he put the book aside to work on *When the Sleeper Wakes*. Although he was not happy with that book, and rewrote it a dozen years later, he felt, at least at the time of his collapse, that it and *Mr Lewisham* might be his only major contributions. He then put more work into *Mr Lewisham*, feeling that the story of young aspirants thwarted in part by love was more important than his views on the future and the social scheme in which he found himself. Wells and Jane were building Spade House by the time *Mr Lewisham* was finally finished and in circulation to prospective publishers. Pinker's letters with regard to the book contained much more detail and advice on the house than on the book, although he and Wells knew that a good sale would provide the money needed for Voysey and his builders. Pinker was concerned that Wells's illness prevented the sort of supervision of the building that was needed, and as a result the house was going to run substantially over the estimates. The agent fussed over Wells, and his house, not just because they were friends, or because he thought the house should reflect good workmanship, but primarily because, if Wells were to keep on producing work like the last novels, he would need security, a place to work, and the elimination of worries which seemed to come with an unstable environment.[44]

Wells was distraught, but finally at the end of October 1898 he was satisfied with the revisions in *Mr Lewisham* and let it go forward. When reporting his physical condition to Elizabeth Healey, he also told her that he had finished a 'moral novel' about South Kensington, 'up to your neck in sentiment'. He and Pinker were not out of the woods just yet, however, as the book was not accepted until the end of January 1899. Finally, Wells received for each of the two books, *Mr Lewisham* and *When the Sleeper Wakes*, £200 for the US serial rights, another £500 on account of US royalties at 15 per cent; his UK royalties on each were to be 17½ per cent on the first 2,000 copies sold, 20 per cent on the next 3,000, and 25 per cent thereafter, with £500 on account. There remained some bargaining over parts of the contract, which were changed slightly, but eventually serial rights in the UK were sold to *The Weekly Times* and the book appeared in the autumn.

Even now though, both Wells and Pinker were concerned about the reviews, as the first indications were that the moral issues hinted at in the book would bring down a storm on the author. The news that Gissing had liked the manuscript was cheering, and Pinker called on the proprietors of several of the semi-religious weeklies, especially the *British Weekly* and the *Examiner*, in order to try and influence the reviews. When the reviews finally did come, the earliest were very favourable, in both the *Daily Chronicle* and the *Morning Post*, and Pinker could hardly contain himself. In fact he wished to send the reviews to those who had turned the book down, but forbore after calming down somewhat.[45]

Perhaps as important for Wells were the reactions of his old friends from College days who could recall many of the events of the novel as they had occurred. Tommy Simmons thought it was simply a precursor of what

Wells could do, while Gregory compared the work to *Jude the Obscure* with its theme of hopes thwarted by sexual demands and jealousy. Gregory, married to a woman who was very sickly, broke out at the end of his letter with, 'Why the dickens are women made to interfere with the work and aspirations of men who are created to make the world better and wiser. . . ?' Elizabeth Healey also liked the book, but said that she was resisting the temptation to assign real names to the characters, as it was 'a dangerous habit to fall into'. Wells said at first that there were no portraits from life in the book, but later confessed that the heroine was 'a very composite person. But, so far as labour and thought count on these things, the writing was an altogether more serious undertaking than anything I have ever done before. . . .' He remarked that there was more work in it than in many first-class FRS theses.[46]

By the time Wells turned again to fiction depicting personal lives and antagonisms, he had become more famous. His views on eugenics, model households, the lives of women, and even on birth control were fairly well known, or at least surmised. In addition his reputation as a ladies' man had grown somewhat. Precisely how much dalliance (to use a word of that time) actually took place prior to 1906 is difficult to say. After the fact it has been fashionable to assume that his sexual drive had manifested itself even in the 1890s. A recent book on Ivy Litvinov (née Low) suggests that Wells made a pass at her mother (Walter Low's wife, and Wells's good friend), and perhaps at her aunt. It also suggests that Wells made at least suggestions to Ivy Low herself, as well as her daughter, which, if true, gives him a substantial three-generation record. However, none of these acts is authenticated. No evidence is adduced, except perhaps H. G. Wells's reputation. In the 1930s a biography of E. Nesbit (Hubert Bland's wife) appeared, in which the context was left very vague. The book was reprinted in 1966, with a long retrospective introduction on what the author had left out (and indicating incidentally that she had been, and perhaps still was, rather naïve about the relationships involved).[47]

In the Nesbit biography appears an interesting vignette of Wells going through his correspondence and withholding some letters, while letting the biographer read others, all of them dealing with the Bland household. Most of these letters no longer survive, or at least if they do, they are not in the usual archives. What have survived are a few letters, written long after the fact, from Rosamund Bland, daughter of Hubert Bland and his mistress, the housekeeper in the Bland household. These indicate that Wells and Rosamund had a few nights of sexual happiness at Dymchurch in 1906. Mrs Langley Moore's biography gives the impression that Wells may also have dallied with E. Nesbit, only a few years older than he, and a person of reasonably wide sexual experience in a household whose occupants changed beds, and partners, with some frequency. Wells was a regular visitor to the house while Rosamund was but a young girl. For example, in 1902 he simply appeared at Well House, the Bland household, declaring that he was 'there to stay'. He himself remarked that that household was one where the visitor needed to secure his bed early, if he were to retain any rights to it. Another link between him and E. Nesbit was the fact that after Horace Horsnell left Nesbit, who had employed him as a secretary, he performed the same function for some time for H. G. Wells.[48]

What is clear is that by the time that *In the Days of the Comet* appeared, Wells had a reputation as a philanderer. He was being chased, and very steadily, by the young women in the Fabian kindergarten — Amber Reeves and Rosamund Bland. Older women were aware of his sexual attraction as well, and such letters as survive indicate that flirtations were the order of the day. Several memoirs since that time suggest that Wells seduced, or was seduced by, several Fabian wives (among them Ivy Low's aunt, Mrs Haden Guest), although no names are offered. He did have a reputation as a free-thinker on matters of sex, and as a libertine. It is into this atmosphere that the *Comet* came with its message of free and group love.

Almost immediately the *Comet* came under attack for this part of its message. Wells had been very much concerned that such comments might obscure the value of the book itself, and while it was being serialized he was at his agents, urging them to see that larger and larger instalments of the work were printed; otherwise, 'it won't be read at the best value without something of a long preparatory exposition. . . . I don't see that it helps a work of literature very greatly to jam the author's face into the eye of the startled reader. . . .' So, he urged leaving out his picture, and printing 'just what I have to say'.[49]

Although the reviews of the serial were not as harsh as Wells had feared, the book version awaited further comment, especially the part where, after the comet has passed, the lovers, now a trio, go off to build the new world. Wells is frank enough about sexual desire in the work, and describes it very completely in the feast of Beltane, while eventually ending the book with a discussion of love in a group of four. This, taken together with *Socialism and the Family* (1906), led the wolves to howl after Wells's scalp. He did not like some of the things said about him, and a few editors offered Wells space to respond. What was hardest for him was that some on the other side implied that socialism achieved would mean, in the jargon of the day, free love. Wells told the *Express* that 'to say it is my dictum that the ultimate goal of socialism is free love is an outrageous lie. . . .' Wells felt that the furore caused Macmillan to dampen their efforts to push the book, so he became doubly angry at what were, to him, false and misleading comments.[50]

In October 1907, the growing tempest burst its bounds. William Joynson-Hicks, another native of Bromley, was standing for Parliament in a Midlands seat. 'Jix', as he was always called, was an extreme Conservative, and his agent felt that he was in some danger of losing the seat. The agent therefore at least commissioned, and perhaps wrote, a pamphlet saying that if the other side were elected, it was just another step on the road to free love, as evidenced by Wells's book and his ideas. This pamphlet was widely distributed over Jix's name, although there is no evidence that he himself had anything to do with it. The *Spectator* took up the cry and published an article entitled 'Socialism and Sex Relations' which was a full-blown attack on Wells and the *Comet*.

Wells responded immediately, first sending a broadside letter asking 'comrades' who spotted the offending material to send it to him so he could take appropriate action. He also wrote to Jix, although the first letter was signed by Jane Wells. In these epistles he protested against the slur on his name, and when Jix did not respond as he wished, Wells threatened libel suits against the offenders. As he said to Jix, 'One or two of your people have got it into their heads that the law of libel does not apply to Socialists and that a Socialist will not bring an action for damages. I'm out to dispel this silly delusion.' When Jix responded with a claim of innocence, Wells told him he was responsible for the acts of his agents, and that only a full-blown public apology would suffice to clear the air. Wells also urged Jix to read his work, as 'quite respectable people on your side do', and suggested he start with *Anticipations* and *The Future in America*. He informed his opponent that if he did so, he would then stop running about the country representing Wells as a nasty-minded advocate of promiscuous copulation. Wells also wrote a full statement of the case, and his views, publishing it in the *New Age*. In his remarks he was a bit dissembling, saying that some of the problem was due to sloppy writing, and he disclaimed the *Comet* as in any way a socialist tract.

He also wrote to the *Spectator*, which did apologize to him. J.C. Bottomley, the agent, also apologized, publishing in the *Manchester Courier* a rather handsome retraction. Other papers in the Midlands which had reprinted the remarks also took the occasion to apologize. Altogether about ten newspapers printed retractions to the story. Wells was fairly happy with the results. The story never did die, of course; for one thing, his own life was too similar to what had been charged to bear close scrutiny, and for another, once such stories begin to circulate they are never eliminated. However, for Wells the incident provided a lot of publicity, not only for the *Comet* but for other novels as well. The prurient could hardly wait to see what he would do next.[51]

Where there was smoke, there was also warmth, if not an actual conflagration. In the period from 1906 to 1914, Wells was at his most active as a writer and thinker, producing several books of considerable significance, and two or three novels likely to be read as long as this lauguage is spoken. During this same period he was also at his most active sexually, fathering three out-of-wedlock children (although one was stillborn), each by a different woman, and in addition being involved in at least two significant romantic episodes with still other women. Most of these affairs lingered on, either as romantic diversions or simply because the women were part of his long train of feminine followers and associates; further discussion awaits a general analysis of Wells and women in a subsequent chapter. However, for this period it is necessary to discuss one of the women, Amber Reeves, and the novel which is associated with her and Wells, *Ann Veronica*.

Amber was the daughter of Pember Reeves, a New Zealander who had first come to Britain as High Commissioner; he and his wife Maude remained on, rather as emigrants in reverse. They were wealthy, dilettantish socialists, who found in Fabianism a way to display their views without much damage to a fairly active social life. This may sound a grudging description, but one is hard-pressed to say much else about them, except that they were Amber Reeves's parents, and good examples of what Victorian colonial parents must have been like.

Amber herself was brilliant. She took a first in the Moral Philosophy Tripos at Cambridge, and went on to study with Graham Wallas at the London School of Economics. In later life she published several worthwhile books on economics and political science, and was for a time a member of the Gollancz and Left Book Club stable of writers. She was unusually pretty, appearing today, even in monochrome photographs, as a subject for a Pre-Raphaelite painting. Her black hair was thick and somewhat unruly, earning her the nickname of 'Medusa', shortened in Wells's time to Duse or Dusa. After Rosamund Bland's rather brief conquest of Wells, Reeves, who was still not twenty, began a rather public pursuit of him. Beatrice Webb, Bernard Shaw, and others remarked on the pursuit (although the Reeves family apparently noticed nothing). After nearly a year (and Shaw thought Wells had done well to last out that long), Reeves captured Wells. They were to maintain an active physical liaison for some months. It had all the elements of young love — Wells tells a story of fornicating in the woods on an issue of *The Times* which featured Mrs Humphry Ward on the subject of declining morality. Other couplings apparently took place in London flats. As her capture of Wells became known — and the evidence is that Amber boasted widely of her catch — the elder Reeveses, instructed apparently by the Webbs and perhaps by Hubert Bland (although one would have thought his ideas on the subject rather problematical), became disturbed.

Though apparently fearing the consequences, Amber and Wells (again what evidence there is suggests she was the aggressor) went on meeting, and she became pregnant. This raised the discussion to the level of scandal. Fabian letters flew back and forth, and when it became known that a follower of Pember Reeves (who had paid unsuccessful court to Amber) was willing to make things right by marrying her, many thought that would be the end of the matter — solved in a Victorian way, although perhaps with more publicity than was usual in such an escapade. The wedding duly took place, but Wells did not go away. He maintained Amber in a cottage in Sussex, and visited her frequently. The putative husband did not appear, and to make matters worse, Jane Wells oversaw the purchase of a layette, and also visited Amber at her place of confinement. The baby, when born, was named Anna Jane Blanco-White, her legal father being Rivers Blanco-White.

There has been a good deal of talk since then that Wells had agreed not to see Amber after the marriage; but there is no real evidence of that, and she appears often enough later in his life, occasionally with the child, more usually at tea or in afternoon encounters; she also received credit as partial author of one of Wells's later books. Just before World War II, Rivers Blanco-White agreed to have dinner with Wells, in the company of others, by way of accepting completely the reality that Wells and Amber had had a relationship: it was less physical after the first tumultuous days of the chase, but they had remained close. Wells asked Eileen Power to attend the dinner as well, as he felt that there might be some incident, but in the event, nothing occurred. Wells liked to surround himself with young women in times of stress, and Power, Moura Budberg, Marjorie Craig Wells, and Amber would have made quite a flanking quartet for either Blanco-White or Wells to broach.

Although this was a private matter to the individuals involved, it occurred at a time in H. G. Wells's life in which he was attempting to sort out his feelings on a wide variety of matters. *First and Last Things*, and the furore over *In the Days of the Comet*, are as much a part of these matters as is *Ann Veronica*, or even the birth of Amber's baby. Wells did have intellectual and moral support from many. 'Vernon Lee', for instance, writing at the end of December 1906, congratulated him on the *Comet* and its depiction of human follies, but went on in the letter (in a portion written nearly a week later) to ask him, 'There are some things which have provoked discussion in my and I suppose many other circles. Are you throwing dirt in our eyes for fear of the pubescent young person's parents, or are you at a loss how the question of sexual love etc. will endure after the green vapours?'[52]

Others in the literary world, sympathizing with Wells's desire to bring matters of reality and sexual progress into the open, also supported him, as when Galsworthy called his enemies a 'pack of curs'. 'But comfort yourself it is just one more instance of the impossibility of expecting that a man of generous ideas and broad views should be understood. . . .' Wells himself responded to his critics in a fairly generous way, saying that truth was 'needed', not only about what he had actually said, but about life in general. He thought the attacks on him were symptomatic of a wider attack on socialism, and that people should not be diverted by the true interests of the opposition.[53]

If H.G. and Jane had been more compatible sexually (that is, if she had been willing to accept his needs more completely), perhaps these events might not have taken place. However, they were not, and Jane accepted the consequences as simply part of the game of life. Amber chased Wells, caught him, and she too regarded it as part of the game of life; although one suspects that she was somewhat star-struck when the great man thought she had something to say. Not a small matter at this time was the fact that young women were beginning to break down old barriers, and those men, whether older or younger, who were willing to aid in the insurrection, became welcome allies, if nothing more.

Wells introduced Amber to George F. McCleary, a publisher of books, in a letter describing her work as 'epoch-making' on 'motive' in social science. He tried to get Cazenove to place a story she had written. But she became pregnant. Wells tried to play the game properly, and was aided in this venture by Bernard Shaw among others; Shaw, for example, tried very hard to keep Beatrice Webb away, even to the point of mentioning Herbert Spencer, who as an older man had encouraged the attentions of a young and impressionable Beatrice Potter. The Webbs did not actually interfere much, and met the principals involved socially within a short time.[54]

Even here the matter might have rested; but Wells then produced a novel in which some of the affair appeared in thinly disguised form. Rereading the novel today, one is caught up not with the similarities to the real-life affair so much as with the work's effort to deal with the hopes and aspirations of young women who find themselves under male tyranny. In addition to Amber Reeves, other young women (Amy Catherine Robbins, Dorothy Richardson, Rosamund Bland, and perhaps others) provided material for this theme. Frederick Macmillan did not like the book, calling it 'exceedingly distasteful', 'not amusing', and 'certainly unedifying'. The firm refused the book, and it was brought out by T. Fisher Unwin. Dedicated to A[nna] J[ane], *Ann Veronica* was a great success, and is still in print; its most recent emergence is on the Virago list, as an example of one of the frontier books in women's emancipation from male rule. Part of the reasons for this are such statements as Ann's after Ramage has propositioned her, when back in her room, thinking over the matter, she realizes, 'For the first time, it seemed to her, she faced the facts of a woman's position in the world — the meagre realities of such freedom as it permitted her, the almost unavoidable obligation to some individual man under which she must labour for even a foothold in the world.'[55]

Most reviewers, public and private, liked the book, or at least recognized it as a significant work. William Archer was supportive, as was Maurice Baring who said the book diverted him from his work, distracted him from relaxation and nailed him to a chair. Baring, writing from Russia, compared Wells to Dostoevsky, called for another book at once, and said that Wells had 'an infinite capacity for loving and understanding all human beings, not in theory but in practice'. Gregory announced himself as a 'polygamist' at least in spirit, after reading and enjoying the book immensely. The *New Age* was tentative, unable to follow Wells quite that far. (It is significant that Bennett did not review the book, as his views would have been very favourable.) *T.P.'s Weekly* gave it a lead review which was quite sympathetic, but the writer hoped that the book would not be taken as a literal guide for young women to follow, and asked whether Wells should have left his heroine to face the world unwed. In fact, by the end of the review, the writer had even begun to reverse his field. The *Spectator*, as might be imagined, thought the book 'poisonous', but Wells, responding to the review, was dignified in his remarks: '. . . I believe that the development of civilization demands a revision of the constitution of the family, and of conventions of the relations of men and women, which will give the natural instincts of women freer play.' He went on to say that the family was not working as an institution, and our species needed to know why. The book was part of the effort.[56]

Wells had not behaved badly in the affair, either of the baby, of Amber, or of his novel. He and Violet Paget exchanged several letters during this period which illustrate his position exactly. He wrote to her at first as he was worried that she had listened to gossip and that their friendship might be damaged. Wells said that they would discuss the matter in detail when she came to visit in the New Year. What remained now was to straighten out this affair, and determine how to carry on, not only here, but in life generally. As he said, in the fourth of his letters of explanation to her,

> I was and am in love with a girl half my age, we have a quite peculiar and intense mental intimacy, which is the finest and best thing we have had or can have in our lives again — and we have loved one another physically and she is going to bear me a child. . . . We are fighting to keep in touch with each other, which is a matter of quite vital importance to both of us, and we mean to keep in touch. . . . The present clamour for our divorce and that we should marry or have an absolute separation. . . . You won't for a moment tolerate it I know. . . . I won't leave my wife, whose life is built up on mine or my sons who have a need of me, I won't give up my thinking and working out my loves, I mean somehow to see my friend and my child and I mean to protect her to the best of my power from the urgent people who want her to make her marriage a real one. And that's all.[57]

Paget was sympathetic to the problem generally, saying that laws needed to be broken deliberately in order to make progress. At all events, she went on, 'what grieves me is not that those who have eaten the cake or drunk the wine should pay the price of it, but that part of the price should be paid by others who have not their share.' She is commenting on the book, here, but indirectly on the Wells marriage, of course.

And with this we get to the nub not only of her criticism, but that of many since that time. 'My experience as a woman and a friend of women persuades me', she went on, that a girl, however much she may have read and thought and talked, however willing she may think herself to assume certain responsibilities, cannot know what she is about as a married or older woman would, and that the unwritten code is right when it considers, that an experienced man owes her protection from himself — from herself. . . . But one thing you and I do, I feel sure, agree upon, namely that although those who are not tempted cannot judge of the difficulty of resisting, those on the other hand, who *are* tempted, cannot judge of the need which the community has of demanding that temptation should be resisted.

Paget said she was concerned about the possible damage to Jane, and to Utopians of the future, when comradeship between men and girls might be badly misinterpreted by those who thought this was the norm of behaviour. Paget signed herself as 'Your *Sister in Utopia*' and 'affectionate friend', although it is clear that she was worried that Wells might bring their correspondence to an end after her homilies.

However, he responded with a letter announcing the birth of his daughter, and said, 'I clutch very eagerly at the friendship you say is still mine.' He went on then to offer his own version once more.[58]

This aspect of their correspondence lingered on for another month, with Paget backing down somewhat from her more 'pedantic' position, to use her word. Finally, on 19 January, she told him, 'But I think and feel also that you are one of the greatest and dearest of living persons and that your books, even your worst books are far above the best thought of those who fall foul of you.' She urged Wells to hold back his next book on love, for a time. However, as he told her in response, while thanking her for her comments, support, and affection, it had to be published, and although she might not like the book she would read it with interest. It was *The New Machiavelli*, '*Lewisham* on a bigger scale', to use his phrase. She then, with his other friends, awaited whatever he would bring them. Most of the barriers had come down for H.G. and his supporters. He had bridged the moat of male conservatism, and done it in a very unorthodox fashion. Those who crossed the moat with him were welcomed on the other side, for the castle was much less daunting than had been perceived.[59]

Wells was concerned how others felt no matter what he said to the contrary. That concern, however, manifested itself more in what they might say or think of Jane, or the other women involved. At the time of the Bottomley affair and Jix pamphlet, Wells began work on a personal Credo which was circulated to some of his friends and which forms a clear basis for the longer statements in *First and Last Things*. The work was not published, although copies in the Wells archive show that it was worked on at several different times. The Credo was such an integral part of H.G. Wells's life, and his impact on others in his own time, that it seems worth reproducing it here in full. His values, his actions, his thoughts, are all amplified by so doing.

CREDO

1 I believe that I possess a mind of limited capacity and an essential if sometimes only slight inaccuracy and that I am thereby debarred from any final knowledge, any knowledge of permanent and ultimate things.

2 I see the Universe as a state of flux, all Being as I conceive it is becoming.

3 In order to steady and determine my life, which otherwise remains aimless and unsatisfactory, I declare that this ultimately incomprehensible Universe about me is systematic and not chaotic and that I and my will and the determinations I make, and likewise all other things are important in that scheme. I cannot prove this. I make this declaration as an Act of Faith.

4 I do not call the systematic quality of the Universe God, but I do not dispute it being called God. And I am often disposed to talk of it as God's Will or God's Purpose. I believe that this 'God's Purpose' as many people would call it, works in and through me, and the more earnestly I think and seek out what is right in my mind and heart, the nearer am I at one with it, the better everything is. But I am unable to say or prove that this should be so.

5 I am disposed to believe that I do believe that my Ego is as it were derived from my species and detached from it to the end that I may gather experience and add to the increasing thought and acquisitions of the species. I believe that the species moves forward unconsciously to a consciousness of itself and to a collective being, and that love is an emotional realization of this collective being (however partial) and that right action is what forwards it. I am a Socialist because to me Socialism is a practical material aspect of this awakening through will of the conscious collective being of humanity.

6 My ideal of living is to live as fully as possible, to know and express as much as possible, to leave permanent results of my individual self behind me when my life ends. For my master gift and passion is for imaginative construction and especially in relation to the making for humanity of an ideal world-state. To that I seek to subordinate all my other gifts, powers and passions. But what other people should plan and seek for themselves I cannot say.[60]

This summarizes well how H. G. Wells dealt with his drives and his emotions. He set new standards and goals, and one is left with admiration for the pioneer, and affection for his companions.

THE WAR TO END WAR

This monstrous conflict in Europe, the slaughtering, the famine, the confusion, the panic and hatred and lying pride, it is all of it real only in the darkness of the mind. At the coming ·of understanding it will vanish until understanding has come. It goes on only because we, who are voices, who suggest, who might elucidate and inspire, are ourselves such little scattered creatures that though we strain to the breaking point, we still have no strength to turn on the light that would save us. There have been moments in the last three weeks when life has been a waking nightmare, one of those frozen nightmares when, with salvation within one's reach, one cannot move, and the voice dies in one's throat.

HGW, 'The War of the Mind', *The Nation* (London), 29 August 1914 (also *New York World* that same week)

The war with Germany and the Central Powers that began early in August 1914 did not come as a great surprise to H. G. Wells, or to most other observers of the European power scene of the previous fifteen years. What did come as a surprise was first the ferocity of the war, soon its great length, and then the monstrous death toll and the failure to achieve victory, which finally led to a full-scale effort to determine why the war had happened, why it had taken the course it did, and above all, what could be done to prevent war from recurring. As Wells and his compatriots passed through these various intellectual stages they were very close observers of the struggle and very nearly front-line participants. London was bombed; the German navy shelled cities on the North Sea, and in Kent one could hear the noise of the great barrages quite distinctly.

In the course of the years of the war, thought patterns solidified, for some, into racial hatred of the Germans; for others a revival of religious belief swept the country after the battles of the Somme; and eventually many (though, as it happened, nearly all of them people without much political power) melded these two drives into a thrusting demand for some control of the peace once it finally came. H.G. Wells was not immune to these various changes of mood and personality. In fact, to a considerable degree, he not only contributed to them, he fuelled their flames with his writing.

Wells was unusually prolific during the wartime period. Although his fame was such that his name sold copies of newspapers and pamphlets, and there was therefore a demand for his work, it is also true that in times of great national or personal stress he always became more active in his literary endeavours. The period from 1914 to 1918 is a case in point. During this period he wrote a half-dozen novels, several of them bearing on his wartime thoughts, and published four or five collections of his newspaper pieces, which appeared in great numbers. He held a government position for a time, as well as taking a leading part both in the efforts of the British Science Guild to revise the school curriculum, and in the various attempts he hoped would bring about a form of the League of Nations he had begun to advocate very early in the war effort.

He divided his life during the period — spending about half his time at Easton with Jane and the boys, although both of them went away to school during the war period, and about half of it in London with Rebecca West and their child, Anthony, born the weekend the war began. He passed his fiftieth birthday in the early autumn of 1916. The events of the war coupled with the passage of time created an intellectual matrix out of which his kaleidoscopic ideas of God, religion, higher intellectual powers, and the horrors of war matured in book form. After passing rapidly through a religious state, however, by the end of the war he was completely committed to world government, to centralized control of all armament and methods of warfare, and to a broad liberal education available to all at state expense. These convictions, which reach a pitch of expression in several articles written in the last months of the war, and in his important novel of the period, *Joan and Peter*, mark the emergence of a new H. G. Wells. Till then, his socialism had been grounded in the English past, but had never moved far from the islands in which he spent most of his early life; the new Wells, while remaining remarkably English, looked to a world organization of mind, intellect, trade, and transport which far transcended that English background. For, by the time the war ended, H. G. Wells had undergone a significant change of mind — the second phase of his life was under way, one based in part on the first, but nevertheless radically different. No longer would small disagreements with the Fabians, Henry James, or the direction taken by British politics excite him much. The war proved to him, and to many others, that such matters were trivial. What did matter was the future of the world, of the species; to use a later phrase of his, who would win the race between education and catastrophe?

8 A literary weekend at Easton in 1913. *Back row:* R. D. Blumenfeld; Jane Wells. *Front row:* Mrs Marian Bensusan; Mrs Hugh Cranmer-Byng; H. G. Wells; Frank Wells; Lady Warwick; Lady Mercy Greville (her daughter); G. P. 'Gip' Wells; Hugh Cranmer-Byng; S. L. Bensusan

19 Otis Skinner, Margaret Sanger and Wells at Easton Glebe, *c.* 1918–19

20 Frank and 'Gip' Wells, from *Floor Games* (1911)

21 Wells at 'Little Wars', 1912

Wells had shown some curiosity about warfare, and especially modern warfare, before the war began. His childhood experiences, and his evening romps with his boys in the nursery, had led him to write two significant books on children's games, the second called *Little Wars*. This book, published in 1913, laid out a scheme for a mock battle to be waged both indoors and out. In the book he discussed the evolution of the rules of his games, ending with a plea for mankind to play his 'Little Wars', rather than big wars, in which participants died for no useful purpose. Most people to whom he sent the book, as well as its reviewers, thought his an excellent idea, and the game had a strong vogue in late-Edwardian England.[1]

Wells was also interested in the impact of the Industrial Revolution on warfare, and he wrote on several occasions on variations of that subject. He began and abandoned a novel about a cyclist soldier, 'Esau Common'; wrote his famous piece on 'The Land Ironclads'; and toyed with a full-scale novel on modern warfare. This novel, eventually called *The War in the Air*, first began in his mind as a possible sea story, with a submarine attack on Thames shipping, and a naval battle in the fog, but with aircraft as part of the battle. Wells clearly recognized the impact of Blériot's flight across the Channel in 1909, and by 1912 had flown several times himself. The implications of such developments in modern warfare did not escape him either, as he wrote several serious articles on the possible impact of these weapons on world diplomacy; although when queried about his ideas, he claimed he was being too imaginative. *The War in the Air* was a successful novel, although he thought it a pot-boiler. It is a strong depiction of Wellsian views of the military future, with relatively little of his message about world government, socialism, or education, although he did end the book with a prophetic remark from Old Tom, 'You can say what you like, it didn't ought ever to 'ave begun.' When this book was published H. G. Wells thought war was preventable. All one had to do was put one's mind to it. The horror of industrial war was, of course, present, but there was no inevitability about the war, or its consequences.[2]

Wells was very conscious of what was often called 'the German menace' in this period of war scares. He mentioned German efficiency in manufacture in his early discussion of cheap microscopes, and twice wrote his view on the Germans for French publications. In these pieces he mentioned the grandeur of medieval Germany, but he felt that it had recently been misplaced, and that the imperialism which he saw was potentially dangerous. Eventually when the war came he expatiated on this idea of two cultures, saying, 'We fight not to destroy a nation, but a nest of evil ideas.' In the article in which he coined the phrase, 'the War to End All Wars', he was actually commenting on the evil tendencies he saw in German thought, in which a weak Christian tradition had produced a faith without intellect. It was now time for everyone to educate themselves as to the difference, and after the war had been under way for some months, while reviewing a book by Ford M. Hueffer, Wells still made a sharp distinction between the German people and the modern German state when he remarked, 'Not Germany for Germans would we destroy, but that double-headed crow, Kaiserism *cum* Kruppism, which is the blackest omen mankind has ever seen.'[3]

He warned at the outset against what 'Kruppism' would mean if a war came, in a three-part series early in 1913 for the *Daily Mail*. These pieces were reprinted by the paper as a pamphlet, and during the war were credited as one of a series of important articles which had alerted England to what was coming. In the pieces Wells told his readers not to put their trust in dreadnoughts, as submarines would destroy this shield, and also not to assume that, without conscription of capital, a conscription of the poorer population would win the war simply by providing cannon fodder. Instead of these outmoded ideas, he urged that money be spent on laboratories, on agricultural experiment stations, on research and better engineering education. If it was not, England was bound to fight first the Germans, then the Slavs, and perhaps eventually even the Asians. He urged Parliament to 'Make men; that is the only sane, permanent preparation for war. So we should develop a strength and create a tradition that would not rust nor grow old-fashioned in all the years to come.'[4]

Although the war did not come as a complete surprise to persons like Wells, who had watched the drift of affairs, still, coming as the aftermath of an obscure assassination in the Balkans, the immediate onset of the conflict was both disturbing and exhilarating. Wells, in Easton for the weekend, spent those days producing an article for the press called 'The Sword of Peace — Every Sword that is Drawn Against Germany Now is a Sword Drawn for Peace'. In this piece, he distinguished sharply between the German people and Prussian militarism. He believed, as did most others at the time, that the war would be short. It was necessary, in this short war, to punish militarism for its effrontery, then perhaps it would 'open the way to disarmament and peace throughout the earth'. In the next seven weeks Wells produced ten more major pieces, which set the tone for the response in England to the war. He called for an end to hoarding of food, saying that 'The greatest danger to England at the present time is neither the German army nor the German fleet, but this morally rotten section of our community' (the aristocracy). He called for a conference at the end of the conflict, remarking that the Empire would undergo a marked change. He also called for an end to the private manufacture of armaments, an end to what he called 'Kruppism', and said that the peace conference should provide 'a new map of Europe'. His feeling was that 'No doubt the mass of mankind will still pour along the channels of chance, but the desire for a new world of a definite character will be a force, and if it is multitudinously unanimous enough, it may even be a guiding force, in shaping the new time.' He issued an appeal to the United States to join, at the very least, in the peace-making: 'What are you going to do throughout the struggle, and what will you do at the end?' He tried to inform people about the reality of

Russia, discussed a possible postwar Balkan state, and ended this remarkable series of papers by pointing out again that the war was a war of separate cultures, 'a war of ideas'. His peroration laid out the future clearly enough for those who followed his lead:

> We have to spread this idea, repeat this idea, and *impose upon this war* the idea that this war must end war. We have to create a wide common conception of a re-mapped and pacified Europe, released from the abominable dangers of a private trade in armaments, largely disarmed and pledged to mutual protection.

But, as he said at the end of this last piece, 'How are we to gather together the wills and understanding of men for the tremendous necessities and opportunities of this time?' He knew that there was work enough for every person who wrote or talked. The prospective goals would override anything else.[5]

Wells's first great flurry of writing spent itself as the war settled down to the slaughter in the trenches, in France and in the East. By Christmas of 1914, it was clear to everyone that the war would not end soon, but it was also clear that England would probably not be invaded (although there were a few hit-and-run raids, and some shelling of seaport towns in the Hartlepool area which created apprehension). Early in the New Year Wells returned to his journalistic forum while beginning to shift his ideas to a longer horizon, calling for an organized effort at foretelling the future, and the utilization of science to make the war end quicker. He began to offer a few strategic ideas, calling for smashing the Kiel Canal, bringing up long-range siege guns to shell Metz, and bombing Germany from the air. Most of all though he called for a moral and intellectual revolution, and an end to the usual English blundering and sliding through.[6]

Wells thought, after a year of war, that England was 'sweeter spirited and harder working' than when the war began, and remarked how the 'democratic army' had improved discipline, but warned that the men would be 'less submissive after the war'. He described England as 'mobile, plastic and fused', and suggested that although the future was hazy it was still time to begin to prepare for it. Responses to these remarks brought forth a series of strong articles from Wells in which he began to try out his views of that future, focusing primarily on what it would mean for England. It would not be until 1917 that his horizons shifted dramatically to cover the world and its future. In a pithy piece about his home area, he pointed out how regional and local rivalries had damaged the area's potential for growth, and called for the elimination of such barriers. This led to another piece, later also reprinted in a pamphlet, *The Peace of the World* (1915). That peace had to be arrived at slowly and thoughtfully, Wells thought, beginning with an end to stupid rivalries, private armaments and their gain to individuals, the creation of treaties of arbitration and an end to blind stupid patriotism. 'Given an immense body of opinion initiatives might break out effectively anywhere; failing it they will be fruitless everywhere', was his considered judgement of the future.[7]

By this time Wells had written his masterpiece of the wartime experience in England, *Mr Britling Sees It Through*. The novel, set in a house very like Wells's in Essex, features a character who is clearly H.G. Wells. It mirrors in its text the way in which English people had first felt about the war, but also how those ideas had changed and become more fluid as the war went on. The book was remarkably well received. The death of a character in combat, the use of a German counterpart facing the same doubts, and his ultimate death, the concept of a world forsaken by conventional Christianity, and above all, the natural way in which that world was described, combined to make the novel a great seller. Cassells, at first tentative towards the book, published it in September 1916, and by the end of November, it had been reprinted eight times. Soon it was translated into French, German, and Russian. The German edition was distributed widely behind the German lines, and the other editions were issued in inexpensive form for the troops, and for those who remained at home. The book ends with a description of Mr Britling (Wells, of course, but the name is also evocative of an eponymous Englishman: 'little Briton' might be one meaning) writing through the night as he attempts to deal with the meaning of the war, and the possible meaning of peace when it finally comes. 'Amidst the gloom of world bankruptcy he stuck to the prospectus of a braver enterprise — reckless of his chances of subscribers. . .' But '. . . Doubt had crept into this last fastness.' For,

> Man has come, floundering and wounding and suffering, out of the breeding darknesses of Time, that will presently crush and consume him again. Why not flounder with the rest, why not eat, drink, fight, scream, weep and pray, . . . and turn to the brighter aspects, the funny and adventurous aspects of the war, the Chestertonian jolliness, the *Punch* side of things?
>
> (Book III, chapter 2)

But as news of the death of the German counterpart to his son also reaches him, Britling begins to write again, this time to the boy's father, in order to send on his effects left till the war was over. Now, as he writes, he widens his audience to include all mankind, calling, as the dawn comes to Essex, for an end to war:

> Let us pledge ourselves to service. Let us set ourselves with all our minds and all our hearts to the perfecting and working out of the methods of democracy and the ending forever of the kings and emperors and priestcrafts and the bands of adventurers, the traders and owners and forestallers who have betrayed mankind into this morass of hate and blood — in which our sons are lost — in which we flounder still.
>
> (Book III, chapter 2)

The novel ends with Britling looking out of his window in the morning at the meadow, listening to a scythe being ground, but with the promise of the new day.

The book clearly mirrored how Wells felt, but it was also as great a mirror-image of how much of England felt, and by extension, one supposes, much of the world at the end of the second year of war. It is one of Wells's clearest and most accurate novels. He was able to use the letters to the Wells family from Kurt Butow, who had been tutor to his boys, and this deepened the reality of the German picture, as well as that of England.[8] Wells did not lose any children in the war (his were too young), but he did suffer heavily through the loss of his young friends, none more grievous than that of Ben Keeling, an Oxford Fabian and close friend, who fell in 1916.

The deaths of these bright flowers of intellect disturbed Wells very much. He was asked to write a preface to an edition of Keeling's letters, and there he elaborated on the waste:

> And whether they dribble away ingloriously in some sort of mean peace or are snapped off and crushed suddenly in a planless war, the lives of young men must needs go on being wasted in futile quests and vain experiments, more of them and more, until a saner world learns to speak clearly to them, to prepare tolerable social and political institutions for them, to help them with its accumulated wisdom, and to ask them plainly for all that they are so eager to give and do.[9]

Most people in England went through these extremes of hope and fear — wishing the war would end, and eventually putting great pressure on the war leadership to do something about it. This meant later for Wells, and for many writers, a guided (and controlled) trip to the front, but until these propaganda methods emerged to control thought patterns, English people, and others, simply read what Wells, Kipling, and others had to say. Kipling lost a son in France, and so a reversion to attacks on militarism by the poet of Empire was received with more intensity, perhaps, than even Wells's books. After Jutland, for example, Kipling wrote a poem about the men who had fought that battle, closing with the remarkable lines,

> Have you news of my boy, Jack?
> *Not this tide. . . .*[10]

An excellent example of Wells's inner feelings at the time of *Britling* appears in a long letter to Victor Fisher, who hoped he could attend a Socialist meeting:

> War is frightful and an evil state of affairs worse almost than the Peace of Herbert Spencer; it is the dreadful punishment of competition instead of cooperation among nations as poverty and social decay are the dreadful consequences of competition instead of co-operating among individuals.

Until nations and men learn to forget themselves in the common good of mankind poverty and war will be the substance of men's lives. We have to organize the peace and social justice of the world, we have to educate mankind to these ends, as thoroughly as the Germans have organized the State and trained their children for this war of pride and aggression upon mankind. The programme of Socialism is not complete unless it includes the peace of the world and what is to be secured not by indolence and cowardice posing as a mystical pacifism, but by the strenuous resolve of all free peoples to beat down the armed threat in their midst. The triumph of the German Emperor in this war means the end of democracy for centuries. *The democratic socialist who is not doing his utmost today to overthrow German imperialism is either a deliberate traitor or a hopeless tool.*[11]

When *Britling* was translated, Wells found that he had to soften parts of it for the German version, as it passed through Swiss and Turkish censors, who objected to certain things. The French version was a fairly straightforward translation, although the translator missed the title with his version, *Mr Britling commence a voir clair*, which means 'Mr Britling Sees Through It'; but that is a good title for the inner meaning of the book, of course. Maxim Gorky, writing to Wells from Russia, called the book, 'Without doubt[?] the finest, most courageous, truthful, and humane book written in Europe in the course of this accursed war ... at a time of universal barbarism and cruelty, your book is an important and truly humane work' — although Gorky (at this stage in his life) disagreed with the ending, and urged Wells to add more of God and religion to the work. *Britling* was used as a text at the school of instruction for chaplains, and was very useful to officers and religious leaders engaged in war activity.[12]

Just as Mr Britling looked out into the dawn, and began to work on a real peace, so did H. G. Wells. The large correspondence to Mr Britling, forwarded to him, led to a series in the *Daily Mail* which attempted to set out how people actually thought about the war. What was the war doing to ideas? was his query. Wells was disturbed that people were concerned about the spectacular (the Zeppelins, Big Bertha, the life of the trenches), and he called for deeper thinking about causation. He dealt, in the series, with conscientious objectors, the fact that many employees were resentful of war profits, and the anti-American views held by many of the upper classes. He thought the English did not think straight because their sloppy education did not train their minds to be vigorous, and held the French up as a better ideal. Wells said however that the war was causing the nation to shed its tough dead skin of the past. In the long run, though, 'this war has been an amazing display of human inadaptability', not just on the side of technology, but politically and diplomatically as well. He called for an ideal of 'internationalism', and an end to secret commercial treaties. By not speaking out he believed the British leaders were 'underlining and endorsing the claims of the German imperialists that this is a war for bare existence. They unify the German people. They prolong the war', and he wanted an end to it.[13]

One of the reasons these essays had been commissioned by the *Daily Mail* was the impact of a series by H. G. Wells in *The Times* earlier that summer. Northcliffe and Wells continued to be close and they met from time to time for lunch. Northcliffe was on the periphery of the Government, and he used Wells as a sounding-board, to learn what intellectuals who were not part of the establishment thought, especially after the feelings of many turned negative towards the war effort and the Government itself. Northcliffe and Wells discussed such matters as manpower, the French contribution, and the way the Cabinet functioned. After these talks, in which Wells was very adamant about the need for change, Northcliffe asked him to write a series of articles for *The Times*, under a pseudonym, to see if these would have any impact on the conduct of the war. Wells received 25 guineas an article (or £157. 10s. 0d. for the series) once they were published. And, although Northcliffe had promised secrecy, the articles stirred up so much discussion that Wells was forced (or felt himself forced) to claim authorship.[14]

In the articles, Wells called for a new synthesis of thought, as well as the use of proportional representation in the election of members to a new Parliament which might include the Dominions as well. A reform of education, especially science teaching, was drastically needed. Changes could come easily, as 'We can formulate and realize, big, thorough, efficient, economical, and racially beneficient schemes of education, training, selection, direction, and research.' A better scientific education was called for by Wells, with the necessary nationalization of that effort. He also urged a nationalization of industry, which would, he felt, lead eventually to a class restructuring and a change in the life of labouring persons. He said that the primary opposition to these matters would be the hidebound Parliament, filled with lawyers, prone to argument, all wanting to preserve the past, persons whose central interests were broadly inimical to those of the English people in general. Here proportional representation could alleviate much of the problem, with a system of voting which would allow the will of the people to be truly realized, according to Wells.

He called for an Imperial constitution, and toyed with the idea that the US might be part of it, at least that there should be a peace League to which the Americans would adhere. In his Imperial Parliament he felt racial groups should be represented, the Welsh, Irish, Scots, and so on; and this larger body would have responsibility for the military, the post, food, transport, trade, and would act as a Supreme Court of foreign affairs. In his lower house he thought occupational constituencies might be represented, and in the upper house the directorships of the various large (and mostly nationalized) concerns. It would follow logically, said Wells, that the Empire would also control education, both the technical and liberal varieties, and he presaged his later views by laying out a curriculum which would feature philosophy, history (and a history grounded in the physical world, with knowledge of ethnology and archaeology), along with a biological science tripos as the culmination of studies. As he said, 'Without a general liberal education we can have no massive national intelligence, no sense of a common purpose and adventure, no general willingness.' He recognized difficulties imposed by his ideas, but said that in the long view all must agree with him that

> This is an infinitely more delicate and subtle task than economic reorganization, but it is as necessary a part of the effort that lies before us if our Empire is to remain united and make its full contribution to the rising destinies of man. Happy go lucky and wait and see are at an end in mental as in material things.[15]

This series of articles remains as Wells's strongest statement of what he hoped England might look like after the war. He tinkered with his ideas from time to time, as when he hoped to influence the Americans to join the effort. As Walter Lippman told him, in response, their entrance would not come until after the autumn election of 1916 — it did not occur, of course, until April 1917, and even then only after a good deal of controversy. Lippman, thanking Wells for *Britling*, told him how much his work meant to Lippman and others who wanted the US to join England in the great fight against imperialism; but, he said, not all Americans agreed, and although Wilson was not neutral, he was stiff about the blockade imposed by England. Apparently the British Government thought about sending Wells to Washington as unofficial ambassador, to assist Cecil Spring-Rice, but this, if it was a serious idea, fell through. Wells did act as an interpreter of England to the French, both through his writings, widely translated and circulated in France, and also because he was willing to write introductions to French accounts of the war, and supported a leading French effort at explaining the English to French readers.[16]

Wells wrote frequently and widely urging a form of republicanism in Britain after the war, pieces which stirred up much antagonism. He had constantly to defend himself, saying that republics worked well in a number of areas, and that the British could benefit from others' experience, especially as they were fighting a German dynasty which held the throne. 'They lay themselves open to the sinister retort that there is then a trade union of monarchs and that all of them must stand or fall together', was his remark. Trade unions he thought equally unnecessary, as they usually served only to perpetuate poor methods of manufacture, and increased private profits. He, Shaw, and Bennett had a series of exchanges on democracy in trade unions but also elsewhere in the British scheme of life. Some of his friends, such as Bennett and Lankester, agreed with him, but most stayed away from these matters as they were very controversial.[17]

If Wells's views were controversial, and not accepted by many, even among his socialist comrades, they followed logically from his point of view on the war itself. For him, the war was throughout a war against a set of evil ideas, which for convenience could be labelled as Prussianism, or, as he called them on several occasions, 'Kruppism and Kaiserism'. However, as had not been true in the past, this war involved all the citizens of the state. It was necessary for everyone to participate, to submit to conscription, not only of bodies but of money and materials. If this meant the end of the aristocracy, or even the monarchy, all the war had done was to speed up an inevitable result. What England should do was to monitor the necessary sacrifices, and make the best of them by ensuring that better roads, better railways, better health, and better educations for everyone emerged after the war. Let the nation gain from its sacrifices, not only by eliminating the German menace, but also by cleaning up its own bad organization at home. When Wells said that he hoped that this would be 'the war to end all wars', he was looking forward to a brighter future for mankind, and especially in Britain.[18]

Late in 1915 he expressed his general ideas in their most complete fashion in a twelve-page pamphlet entitled *The War and Socialism*. Here he used his gift of language to discuss why Britain was at war, but also what reasonable men could expect once the effort had been expended. He opened the widely circulated pamphlet with this paragraph:

All the realities of this war are things of the mind. This is a conflict of cultures, and nothing else in the world. All the worldwide pain and weariness, fear and anxieties, the bloodshed and destruction, the innumerable torn bodies of men and horses, the stench of putrefaction, the misery of hundreds of millions of human beings, the waste of mankind, are but the material consequences of a false philosophy and foolish thinking. We fight not to destroy a nation, but a nest of evil ideas.

He went on later to say elsewhere, 'Intellect without faith is the devil, but faith without intellect is a negligent angel with rusty weapons. . .We need not only to call for peace, but to seek and show and organize the way to peace. . . .The desire for a new world of a definite character will be a force. . . .This is a time of incalculable plasticity. . . .It is the supreme opportunity.'[19]

In order to achieve that opportunity, of course, the war had to be won. Wells could not give his body, but he was able to use his mind. It comes as no surprise, then, to note the number of good strategic and tactical suggestions he made for the men charged with fighting the actual war. Since that time we have learned how stupid most of the Allied generals were, how unwilling to use new ideas, and of their failure to attempt to shorten the war by new methods. In 1914–18, however, although some surmised the reality of the trenches and the closed minds of the leadership, most did not. Wells worked hard at getting his ideas across to the leadership, in the hope that the war would end soon, and men and women of good will could get on to the business of total reconstruction.

He had some ideas on reorganization of the war effort and thought the use of judiciously chosen propaganda would be effective. He called for better organization of war work in England, including manufacture of items to shorten the war, even if they were not 'profitable'. To this end he hoped that the government would mobilize scientists and technicians, for if England did not, 'This war, because of our unscientific methods, our wastefulness, our administrative pettiness, and our contempt and distrust of novelty, is going to be a vastly longer, slower, bloodier, and more distressing business [than] I expected it to be.' For him the answer was, 'We must keep pace with Essen now.' England was fighting not just a war of men, but one of material, and in such a war, '. . . it is at the centre of manufacture, and not at the centre of government, that a hostile army must strike'.[20]

He called for democratization of the officer class in order to use the best people, regardless of their origin. But in addition to these general remarks, he offered specific suggestions — one, which would have speeded up the transfer of goods to the front through a system of collapsible telephone poles strung with aerial ropes, and probably saved lives, was widely discussed. A model worked very well, and although Douglas Haig felt it was too radical a method, Northcliffe and others were impressed by the invention.[21] Wells termed the idea 'telpherage'.

Wells had a greater hand in the invention of the tank. His short story, 'The Land Ironclads', stuck in the mind of Winston Churchill and others, and when war came, work began on armoured vehicles using the Wellsian idea. In late 1916 the results were tried at the battle of Cambrai, and found very successful. Later Wells found himself showered with congratulations, giving him almost complete credit for the idea, although at a somewhat farcical trial after the war others attempted to take the credit. At the trial Churchill testified under oath that the idea had originated with Wells. When he visited the front Wells wrote about the new invention, although the original dispatch was censored heavily, and not finally published until the war was over. It remains, however, a case in which fiction acted as a stimulant to the work of invention and it probably shortened the war and saved lives.[22]

Just as he had seen the great possibilities in armoured motorized vehicles, Wells also saw the tremendous potential in the air. He had remarked, after Blériot landed at Dover Castle, that the Channel no longer stood as a barrier, and once the war began he urged his country to utilize aerial possibilities to end the war, by striking at Germany through bombing raids, as well as employing aeroplanes against opposing troops. He realized how brave the pilots were (most flew without parachutes until very late in the war, as those restricted both their movement and vision while flying), and thought of them as a new breed of aristocrat, urging the training and organization of their special skills regardless of where they belonged in the social scale. Later his views on these matters led him to invent several fantasies in which airmen, through their technical and intellectual skills, would act as leaders in his world of tomorrow.[23] Eventually his interest in aircraft involved him in a major exhibition of art featuring the history of flying and aircraft, and the government asked him to serve on a committee to investigate civil air power after the war. Wells served, but only to write a minority report when the group espoused private profit, while urging the government not to be involved in civil air transport. Wells was very alert to every new change: bombing, the use of submarines, tanks, motorized and armoured vehicles, radio, and other methods of speeding both information and explosives to those who needed them.[24]

One reason he was so well versed in these subjects was that he made one of the first, and, as it happened, one of the longest and most detailed visits to the front lines; he covered not only the fairly well-known areas of France which correspondents were urged to visit, but also went to Italy, behind the front lines, and to see the mountain fighting. The articles based on these visits were widely read, and made their way into a book which sold well in both the United States and Great Britain. Wells was a good and observant war correspondent, and from his visits he came away with many new ideas to speed victory for the Allies.[25]

Wells's ideas were so provocative and his pen so prolific that within a week or two of the beginning of the war, he was being deluged with offers of publication. This led him to return to using an agent, for a time even J.B. Pinker, although he and Pinker fell out again. Pinker could not resist attacking Cazenove, Wells's New York agent, in his letters to Wells, and he went on to suggest that the amount of commission Cazenove received was out of proportion to the amount of work he did; although Pinker declared himself ready to undertake the work, even at a loss, Wells did not really appreciate being lectured to. Although some of these homilies were sugar-coated, as when Pinker remarked, 'As a matter of fact, my dear H.G., there is only one point on which we are at variance. I would probably give you a much higher place than you would claim intellectually, but I should deny that you have the temper for business, for business ultimately is the problem of dealing with men.' Pinker apparently read one piece by Jane, but did not place it, and by midsummer, after a six months' flirtation, he and H.G. had split up again.[26]

Wells did quite well financially in this period, whether Pinker handled his affairs or not. By the time the war began he was commanding a fee of £100 for three serial articles, and during the war was paid a more or less standard fee of 25 guineas for each article, although occasional special pieces received fees of up to £100. He usually ceded the US rights free of charge, prior to America's entrance into the war, but later reprints were sold at £15 each. Several new journals began publication during the war which paid substantial fees for thoughtful articles from Wells on the future. He found himself making money out of the intellectual effort he put into changing the world, and when translations into French, and later into Italian, occurred, the proceeds increased. As the editor of the *Daily News* remarked, however, thanking him for an article, '. . .and if you can remember it [their telephone number] a little oftener so much the better.' Only the pieces used to raise funds to rehabilitate the war wounded, did he allow to be published gratis; then, he was only too happy to make a donation.[27]

The war had a tremendous impact on Wellsian thought. Eventually that thought led him to explore the possibility of an end to individual governments, and the possible emergence of a world state, and although he talked somewhat of these matters early in the war, it was not until he had experienced a religious conversion, during the war, that he moved outside his emphasis on England. That conversion did not last long, and mirrored somewhat similar experiences widely recorded in France and England. It appeared to come about as the frightful toll of the war became known; as many people began enquiring into the cause of these losses, they coupled their findings with the fear that German ideals might triumph, and so sought a deeper meaning in the war. For some of them (although not Wells) the trial by fire and steel in the war was simply an indication of the nearness of Armageddon, and the end of life on earth.

Wells did not hold those beliefs, but in his own search for a meaning in the war's causes and cost, he spent a brief time refurbishing the Christianity he had been taught at home. And, although he later specifically repudiated these books (one of philosophy, and a novel which fell into the same grouping), they are worth a brief mention as an indication of the depth of his search. One source of his change of view was apparently an exchange of letters and talks with David Lubin about elements in Jewish thought similar to Wells's notion of religion as revealed faith; the main emphasis was on a sort of deistic God who set things in motion and then watched them work themselves out. This God (Wells referred to his deity as 'the Veiled Being' and 'the Invisible King') provided the intellectual possibility of survival for mankind, but did not guarantee it, and certainly not through any kind of personal redemption or salvation from the interference of others. When Wells finished his work, he and Israel Zangwill exchanged several visits and letters about his ideas and Zangwill sent copies to the Chief Rabbi in England for discussion.[28]

In *God the Invisible King* (1917), Wells's philosophical tract (much of this material also appears in the 1917 revision of *First and Last Things*, but was excised in later printings), he mentioned discussions he had had with William James. He found that the problem in modern Christianity stemmed from the ill-directed Council of Nicaea which had adopted the idea of the Trinity. He felt that God, in this version, was a sort of Deist being, a view somewhat related to T. H. Huxley's efforts to understand religion in certain of his books. Wells dealt clearly and closely with a number of prominent atheists of his time, Joseph McCabe, Elie Metchnikov, P. Chalmers Mitchell, Sir Henry Johnston, and Gilbert Murray. In fact, one way in which the book is still useful is in the attention it pays to ideas widely discussed in English intellectual circles at the time. In his book Wells defined the moral law as consisting of the biological imperatives, and discussed the role of belief in getting humans through dark places where knowledge was not yet available. In this last connection he discussed prayer, while using as examples his correspondence with persons in insane asylums who were the chief beneficiaries of the psychological benefit of prayer. Wells's definition of religious activity, even though he rejected it later, still tells us much of what was going through his mind at this time in his life:

> For us life is a matter of our personalities in space and time. Human analysis probing with philosophy and science towards the Veiled Being reveals nothing of God, reveals space and time only as necessary forms of consciousness, glimpses a dance of atoms, of whirls in the ether. Some day in the endless future there may be a knowledge, an understanding of relationship, a power and courage that will pierce into those black wrappings. To that it may be our God, the Captain of Mankind, will take us.
>
> (Chapter 1, sect. 3)

This book stirred up a stew of protest and congratulations. It was so different from what Wells normally wrote that most people did not know how to handle it. His old friend Sydney Olivier said that the book had caused him to ponder his own views, but after realizing that the war had intensified emotions, including those of himself and Wells, he told Wells his ideas had not much changed. Others wished to discuss the book with him, and Wells had lunch with the Archbishop of Canterbury, who was interested, but 'kinder to orthodoxy'. Wells and Sir Harry Johnston had a number of talks (and eventually, from these beginnings, Wells helped Johnston publish a novel, and Johnston vetted large parts of *The Outline of History*). Max Beerbohm, Maurice Hewlett, Ray Lankester, and Northcliffe were others with whom he discussed the book. In addition, *God the Invisible King* elicited a number of essays and books of commentary, most in opposition to Wells's idea of one god as opposed to the Trinity: nearly all these were also unable to accept the implicit idea that divinity was within man, not something achieved by acts of faith or prayer. Nevertheless, Wells's ideas were discussed, and insofar as they provided a basis for philosophical discussion about the war effort and its possible consequences, they probably were worthwhile, not only for Wells but for his readers.[29]

Some evidence of this traumatic intellectual experience had surfaced in the later pages of *Britling*, and Wells alluded to other aspects in some of his journalism; but the most important fictional treatment of it was in the novel,

The Soul of a Bishop (1917). It is not much of a novel, except that it does offer a good glimpse of a suffragette daughter and a marvellous Wellsian character, Lady Sunderbund, who is so taken with the Bishop's ideas of new religion (or with the Bishop himself, more likely) that she entices him from his established position. The Bishop takes drugs, has a series of visions, but eventually returns to reality, thus thwarting the delicious lady's ideas, of both church construction and whatever else came to mind. The Bishop is not quite sure if he is happy with the life he has kept, as opposed to the vision he sought briefly, and the book ends rather ambiguously, as he sits talking to himself:

> For a while he remained frowning at the fire. Then he bent forward, turned out the gas, and rose with the air of a man who relinquishes a difficult task. 'One is limited,' he said. 'All one's ideas must fall within one's limitations. Faith is a sort of *tour de force*. A feat of the imagination. For such things as we are. Naturally — naturally. . . .That alters nothing. . . .'
>
> (Chapter 9, sect. 19)

And so one bids goodbye to the Bishop, just as Wells bade goodbye to what might be called his religious escapade. It did mark a sort of personal epiphany, however, and is indicative of just how much thought he was putting into the meaning of the war. Vestiges of these ideas remained in his novel *The Undying Fire* (1919), a modern re-telling of the Job fable, as well as in later books like *The Happy Turning* (1945). Essentially, though, Wells had tried Christianity again, albeit in a version much altered from that normally taught, and had found it wanting. Other matters were more important now. Russia had left the war. Who knew whether the Allies could win? What sort of peace might emerge? Could he and his supporters return to the days and ideals of 'the war to end war', to create a peace in which the thought of further war was simply not possible? For him, it came down to the question of how we can achieve those goals — and how H. G. Wells could help in the effort. The last two years of the Great War were for Wells, as for many others, an opportunity to change the world once and for all.

As the war progressed, the international situation changed as well, and this gave even greater urgency to the demands for a peace which would withstand such diplomatic and strategic changes. The wholesale bleeding of French and British (and, of course, German) manhood was one issue. The entrance of the US into the war was another, but the issue which created the greatest urgency for Wells, and for other observers, both official and unofficial, was the Revolution in Russia, its growth and change, and finally, the decision of the Bolshevik government to leave the war entirely. Wells knew Russia well. He was one of the few observers who had actually been there, and who had contacts with Russian spokesmen. His views were sought, but, he was appalled to find, were of little consequence. Still, to achieve the peace, an effort had to be made.[30]

Relatively few Englishmen knew Russia well when the war broke out. At first it was felt in England that the Russian effort on the eastern front would drastically shorten the war. As time went on the true state of the Russian army became known. By 1916 a major effort had been made to keep Russia in the war, simply to tie down as many German troops as possible. When the Russian Revolution was in its first stages, it was with a great sigh of collective relief that the Allies accepted Kerensky's promise to remain active against the Germans. Even when the Bolsheviks replaced the Provisional Government, they continued to fight the Germans, but once it became clear that a separate peace could be negotiated, Lenin and Trotsky accepted the German terms (the treaty of Brest-Litovsk) in order to concentrate their efforts on clearing out dissident elements in Russia itself.

The Allies had failed in their attempt to keep the Russians active, and the threat of a stepped-up German campaign in the west made them angry at the Bolsheviks. Invasion of Russian territory, recriminations against the new government, and its eventual exclusion from the peace settlement at Versailles resulted. As Woodrow Wilson said, in the sixth of his Fourteen Points, how the world treated Russia after the war would determine much of the future status of European and world diplomatic affairs. The Russians took this at face value, but Wilson was thinking of pre-war Russia, not of the Bolsheviks. In a world filled with as much misinformation and recrimination as these events brought out, the knowledge of a person like Wells was in demand. His views were not those held by most observers, especially by the British Foreign Office, so considerable controversy surrounded him and what he thought of Russia.

Wells had visited Russia at the end of 1913 and the beginning of 1914. He told Jane that it 'was exactly like the stage Russia. . . . Everything is shabby. . . . Nobody speaks French or German. . . .' He elaborated on these ideas in an article in the press, in which he said that much of what he thought had been confirmed in a sort of 'kaleidoscopic intensity'. He later introduced a person he had met in Russia to Frederick Macmillan, telling him that 'Russia is a big developing thing'. He urged Macmillan to look into translations from the Russian, and especially to try to provide books about Russia in English, as well as textbooks for English readers, who would, Wells felt, have a great need to know about Russia soon.[31]

When war broke out Wells responded with a series of articles designed to interpret Russia to England. He told his readers that the 'liberal fear of Russia' was misplaced. A month later he and C. Hagberg Wright wrote a letter to the press (which was refused by Labour papers) pointing out the misconceptions about Russia commonly held in England. Later Wells and Gilbert Murray collaborated on a letter to Russian intellectuals supporting their efforts to improve life, but also the fight against German militarism. Eventually several other leading writers signed the letter as well, Galsworthy and Anthony Hope among them. As the war in the west settled down to trench warfare, Russian efforts remained important, and as the year came to an end Wells produced another small group of articles on Russia and northern Europe. He urged readers to find out as much as they could about Russia, as its participation in the war was so significant.[32]

This letter brought a response from Bernard Shaw, who told Wells that he was not democratic enough and that in his zeal for Russia he had forgotten the human misery involved. The editor of the *Chronicle* backed Wells, but a controversy ensued. Ford Madox Hueffer told Shaw, in a public letter, that he was more concerned with attacking Wells than finding truth, and as a result had supported Prussianism. Hueffer informed Shaw that Wells was one of the few persons in England who understood the reality of the war, and he urged Shaw to keep silent. Wells also responded with an article marked clearly, 'No Rights Reserved'. In it he agreed with Hueffer, but said the reason Shaw spoke out on these subjects was that he was basically 'muddle-headed'. Shaw had 'a jackdaw's idea of knowledge', shiny bits and pieces from all over. Wells prescribed a reading list on Russia for Shaw (and in a private letter added even more ideas for Shaw's perusal). The argument kept up, both in private and public. Shaw shifted his remarks to the *New Statesman* as being a more congenial forum for attacking Wells on Russia, but Wells was quick to answer here as well. The editor of the *Chronicle* told Wells how much he liked the destruction, 'the pulverization of the Shaw fetish', when the reply appeared. A greater issue was at stake, however, than just their views of Russia. Shaw had written a pamphlet, *Common Sense About the War*, which was essentially an attack on Wells and his anti-German views. This lay at the bottom of the entire affair. Shaw and Wells met at the Reform Club in the midst of the controversy and had lunch together without recrimination, although Shaw told Graham Wallas that he had feared a public scene. But both were truly concerned about the future of the war and the eventual peace, and their animosity towards each other was of no significance.[33]

In fact this marked a renewal of Shaw's and Wells's friendship and they exchanged a number of happily insulting letters over the next few years, with Wells eventually providing advice for Shaw on going to the western front, including what sort of shoes to wear and how much to tip the chauffeur.[34]

Wells continued to be a self-appointed spokesman for Russia, urging editors to send better correspondents to report on the country, as much misinformation was being issued, supporting the teaching of Russian in schools (his own boys were learning Russian at Oundle, but it had been a hard fight to get it included in the curriculum), and calling for more and better translations of Russian books.[35] (The translations of Russian fiction by Constance Garnett were extremely useful and remained standard for many years.)

When the Russian Revolution blew up in the spring of 1917, the British press began to scrabble about for information. Wells's pre-war article was reprinted as a recent source and he was asked to lead a special mission to Russia to observe the events. He did not go (in part because he was immersed in his work on war aims), but he did issue several statements welcoming the new Free Russia. These pieces were circulated widely in the United States, and published in England only two or three days later. Others — Shaw, T. P. O'Connor, Marie Corelli, Bennett, and Hall Caine, for example — issued similar statements. As Wells said, 'We had not dared to hope it. . .' but now that it (the Revolution) had come, 'it is the precursor of the world confederation of republics that will ensure the enduring peace of the world.' Although Wells knew that the diplomatic corps would not be happy, 'in the hearts of the four British nations the Russian Revolution burns like a fire.' As time went on his feelings and support intensified and his statements on the Revolution and its promise remained strong. They were widely printed and commented upon through the summer of 1917.[36]

After the Russians left the war and signed the treaty of Brest-Litovsk, a great storm of rancour arose in England. Wells did not swerve from his position, however, and outlined his views again in a long article for the Daily Mail, urging others to rethink their opposition to the Bolsheviks. He told his readers that Kerensky had proved to be a weak person. He had been overthrown because of that weakness and the growing strength of a counter-revolutionary force in Russia. Wells felt that the aims of most liberals in the world continued to coincide with Russian aims; that is, an end to German militarism, for, as he told his readers, 'Peace without a German revolution can't be a peace.' A League of Nations was needed and persons who wished this should guard against a revival of the old diplomacy, with its aristocratic ways. Opposition to the Russian Revolution had shown up the diplomats for what they really were. In fact, said Wells, on the issue of war and peace aims, '. . . it seems to me the Bolsheviks are altogether wiser and plainer than our own rulers.'[37]

These were the issues for Wells. What sort of a peace would occur? By the time he wrote this article defending the Russian Revolution, the war was well on the way to ending. The Americans were in and their armies had begun to make their presence felt in France. The old diplomacy and the pre-war diplomats had allowed the war to occur through their stupidity, thought Wells. He felt that what was now needed for the prospective victors was a clear statement of peace aims, coupled with a method of ensuring that those aims would be fulfilled. Only then could another war be prevented. He was engaged fulltime in this effort, writing out sets of aims, proposing a world government, and propagandizing for his ideas. By the spring of 1918, Wells knew that if the war was to be the war to end war, it would take strong action, planning and idealism. That was why he welcomed the Russian Revolution and continued to endorse it no matter what form it took. The issues were simply too large for the old ways to continue. A world revolution, at least in ideas, had become imperative.

Among the major reasons why World War I erupted when it did and continued with the unparalleled ferocity it soon developed was that the map of Europe and, through colonization, other areas of the world, had become very unstable. The great growth in nationalistic feeling, fuelled by rising literacy and cheaper paper, had created a community of interest in areas with a common language, folk history, and oral tradition. This change had been accentuated in much of Europe by the decline in power of the Austro-Hungarian Empire, successor to the Catholic coalition, the Holy Roman Empire. Napoleon I had upset the balance initially with his new mass armies. After the defeat at Sadowa of the Austrian bid to control Pan-Germania, the balance had been destroyed completely. The other nation with claims on the middle European area, Turkey, was weak and undergoing a revolution of its own. Efforts at creating a pan-Slavic central force, to counter the rising Pan-Germania, foundered on nationalism, ignorance, and poor logistics. The war came as swiftly as it did because countries were bound by earlier treaties to mobilize and fight, often for geographical entities barely still in existence when the war began.

Wells had travelled widely in Europe before the war. In addition to his visit to Russia, he had spent time in Italy, France, Switzerland, Belgium, Germany, Austria, and Spain. He knew the Low Countries fairly well, and had a working knowledge of Scandinavia. He was as aware as anyone else of the strains of nationalism, and when the war broke out, some of his initial newspaper articles offered his views on what was needed to stabilize Europe.

After ten days of fighting, he said, 'We begin a new period in history. . . . That means that we have to redraw the map so that there shall be, for just as far as we can see ahead, as little cause for warfare among us Western nations as possible. That means that we have to redraw it justly. And very extensively.' Among the areas he targeted for change were Alsace-Lorraine, Denmark (at least Schleswig-Holstein), Trieste, Poland (especially the parts more remote from Warsaw), a greater Romania, and a Yugoslavia (but without that name as yet). He proposed a Swiss-type confederation as perhaps the best way to deal with the Balkans. He ended his prescriptions with, 'I intend to go on redrawing the map of Europe with every intelligent person I meet.'[38]

A few days later he urged the United States to enter the war, at least symbolically, so that she could be part of the peace-making effort, and within the same week offered a more detailed account of what the Balkans might look like after the war. By 1916 Wells's experiences with the Russian language and his sons led him to urge the adoption of some sort of *lingua franca* to overcome misunderstandings 'in this vitally important effort to promote international understanding'. He also called for restoration of Palestine to the Jews, creating a real Judaea. He welcomed a new set of maps sent to him by Holbrook Jackson which illustrated his views. As he said to Jackson, 'If you will . . . [look at] an etymological map of

Europe . . .[you will] see that I merely followed the lines laid over language and race. It is my idea of a Frictionless Europe.'[39]

As the war went on he did not move very far from his earlier ideas, based as they were on the Europe he knew so well. He did refine them somewhat with ideas of free trade zones, in order to overcome some of the incipient nationalism, and he began to speak more specifically as the end of the war seemed nearer, late in 1916. He drew upon the English wartime experience, in a series of commissioned articles, to talk about the growth in significant machinery investment, large-scale production, and freer trade, and to suggest the need to think in equally large terms about the organization and administration of resources once the war was over. He thought that nationalism was still the biggest problem, as evidenced in Ireland and Poland, but if one believed in 'Home Rule for all the world', that ideal would simply have to exist side by side with alliances and in mutual toleration — though certainly not under sovereignty from above. He described nationalism as 'a good guide, but a bad master', and felt that one possibility, again using the wartime experience, was eventual large-scale international combinations to buy, produce, sell and distribute such items as food, drink, coal, shipping, and to control agriculture in general. As he said, the lessons of the war were that socialists, who had always looked towards nationalization, now realized how small states really were and that there was a great need for international economic action, once the war was finally over.[40]

It was clear to many in England that Wells was one of the more cogent thinkers on these subjects, and it was but a short step for them (and most especially C. F. G. Masterman, then in the Government as Chancellor of the Duchy of Lancaster, as well as Lord Northcliffe) to urge him to bring his ideas to bear on the propaganda efforts then being mounted against the Germans, and especially to entice the Americans into the war. Wells went to work in the Cabinet propaganda office (as part of the Advisory Committee to the Director of Propaganda, Lord Northcliffe), then located in Crewe House, where he very quickly found himself working on the general issue of what should comprise Britain's as well as the Allies' war aims. How should they be worded, and how, eventually, could they be carried out once the war was over? Both Masterman and Northcliffe had been badgered by Wells since early in 1915 to speed up their efforts, and to set out the record clearly in the press. To some extent Wells was co-opted because he did have so many ideas. Northcliffe even recommended, apparently, that he be made a member of the War Cabinet(!).[41]

Prior to his important work on war aims, Wells was also active on other pieces of anti-German propaganda. These included urging enlistment in the Artists' Rifles, a special regiment. (Others were formed of footballers, dock workers, and such.) He wrote out a parody award of a medal to the Kaiser, but it turned out that the Kaiser in question was a Sergeant L. Kaiser, an Australian volunteer artilleryman, who had performed very bravely. Wells went on to say that Kaiser was a popular German name. 'He is a good German who like many Germans in the American and [*illegible*] armies is fighting for the freedom of Germany and the League of all the Nations which will bring peace to mankind.'[42]

At this distance in time, even with the minutes of the German Section Propaganda committee (Wells's specific charge) before us, it is difficult to determine his role exactly, beyond the memorandum he quoted in his later works. But what is known is that he continued to maintain strong ties with Walter Lippman and with Bainbridge Colby (who served during the war in the American Embassy in London). When Colonel House came to Britain as President Wilson's emissary, he was entertained at Easton by the Countess of Warwick, with Wells at the table. The similarity between some of Wells's ideas and the Fourteen Points address, along with some remarks in Lady Warwick's memoirs, and several letters from Lippman, suggest that Wells may have had a hand in the material on which the address was based. In his autobiography he claimed to know very little about the matter. However, he did reprint a very long letter to Colby, which Philip Guedalla had carried to him after a discussion with them both at the Reform Club in November 1917. Wilson saw the letter, according to Colby, and so even though Wells discounted his own efforts, one should point out that that he did so after he had repudiated the League, and the Fourteen Points, as not being sufficient to bring about world peace.[43]

Wells worked assiduously on these problems before his resignation from the committee. He produced a statement of war aims and a letter for discussion at a national conference on war aims.[44] He published several letters and articles in the press on both sides of the Atlantic, and began to edit a series of pamphlets on the League of Nations for Masterman. This activity led to the formation of a second group to work for the proposed body. Wells's resignation from the one committee simply led to a greater work load for the other. He believed, and with good reason, that his views were being heard, perhaps for the first time in the highest circles of government, and that the effort he gave to these causes was paying great dividends. For that reason, of course, when his views did not prevail and were ignored at the peace table, his disillusionment was even greater. To a considerable degree this marked the end of H.G. Wells's efforts to work within the existing framework of power, and his move to tactics of propaganda, writing, speaking, and working outside normal government channels.[45]

The intense violence of the war created a demand in many parts of the world for a massive effort to prevent further outbreaks. This led eventually to an insistence that a world-wide conference be held to set up a peaceful world, to be monitored jointly by all the nations. This arrangement, usually called a League of Nations or a League of Free Nations (the names the British proponents used), began to be discussed early in the war. By 1918, there were few observers who did not use some variant of these terms, and to call for an implementation of the idea. A few questions were raised: whether the League would have a military force of its own, whether or not some bits of national sovereignty would have to be discarded, and whether the League would have punitive power over those who violated its rules.

Some of this discussion centred on Africa (rising nationalism, and substantial discoveries of useful resources, made that area potentially very valuable). Germany had established bases there in the decade before the World War, and this meant the new League might have to focus on African and other German colonial holdings. Wells addressed these issues within the context of the proposed League, calling for a voluntary sharing of sovereignty. He also said that rather than being run by the diplomats, who had helped bring on the war through their failure to perceive reality, the League should have a council comprised of elected representatives. 'The Peace Congress is too big a job for party politicians and society and county families.' He stated these views in articles appearing early in 1918; their publication created a demand for further Wellsian comment, and he wrote a series of articles. At first destined for *Lloyds News*, the articles were held up when the Ludendorff offensive began, and finally appeared in article form only in America; eventually a book that contained them was published in England in May 1918. Wells's view, presented in both the book and the articles, was that the League should be representative, should include all countries, and ought to be organized to work towards a form of world government.[46]

The book, *In the Fourth Year*, was widely read, in lieu of the articles, and many newspapers urged their readers to read and think about the views presented by Wells. Walter Lippman, who edited the pieces for the *New Republic*, thought they were excellent, and when he came to England in August, one of his first acts was to seek out Wells for 'a crucial meeting on this work similar to yours'. It was now widely believed that Wilson's Fourteen Points address would be the basis for the peace conference once the war was over. Lippman had several meetings with Wells and others, and the result was a State Department document, interpreting the Fourteen Points address, released in mid-September. At about the same time Wells published three significant articles on the League and its future. He chose as his medium for these articles the *Morning Post*, a Tory newspaper, but one which was widely read by the people likely to go to the peace conference.[47]

In the *Post* articles Wells traced the idea of a League, and the fact that the war had extended itself to civilians, thus making everyone a potential victim; he discussed the different ideas already presented, and himself proposed a central body with power to take control of armaments, shipping, distribution of staples, to provide what he described as 'a pooling of Empires'. He spoke to the readers of the *Morning Post* on the specific issues of sovereignty and nationality, predicting that without some dilution and release of these powers, a new and much worse war would come (he predicted it in 1935). J. R. Galvin, a Tory author, responded to him, saying that the strength of nationalism was a basic problem which Wells did not face. Wells said that he was facing it, and offered a proposal to diminish it, using the Scots, Welsh, and other groups in Britain as examples of nationalities that remained intact without jeopardizing the peace.

In this third article he returned again to the issue of nationalism raised by Galvin, and the attacks levied on his views. He specifically refuted the claim that the British Empire could go it alone, as it was already a world-wide organization. He told the *Post* readership that a much greater threat than nationalism was revolution, especially as no central agency had yet been able to control arms and demagoguery. Here Wells produced some facts, which he felt needed discussion:

> First, then, the range of injury in war has increased enormously since 1914, and is still increasing. . . . There seems to be no mastery of the air that can completely suppress air raids, just as there seems to be no mastery of the sea that can completely suppress submarines. . . . The actual battle zone is also steadily broadening. . . . More and more of the population of the belligerent countries are drawn into the modern war process. . . . Will be much more destructive. . . . For the purposes of air war and for purposes of civil air transit alike these islands are completely 'bottled up', and cut off from our 'ownings' overseas. . . .[48]

By the time Wells was writing these pieces, however, the war had taken a rapid turn in favour of the Allies. Time was running out. Lippman, Wells, Bainbridge Colby, and dozens of others preparing for the peace conference found themselves only partially ready. In the last week of the war, in the midst of the false armistice and the stage-posturing of the generals, Wells found time to issue a few more comments on the possible peace, but how widely they were read is another matter. On 5 November (a significant day for Britons, of course) he discussed British nationalism, then on the 6th he analysed the Foreign Office and the League of Nations. 'We are up against an idea which saturates our histories, saturates the minds of statesmen, saturates the press, saturates European thought and the thought of many spirited states outside Europe; and that is what I call the Great Power idea in human affairs. This Great Power idea and the organ and methods that embody it is the real enemy.' He continued his assault the next day, calling for an end to secret treaties and secret diplomacy; and finally on the 8th, Friday, at the beginning of the last weekend of the war, he ended his comments: 'It is up to the people to see that mankind does not, in a mood of weariness and reaction and resentment, slip into the old grooves of thought and action, and lose the harvests of peace.'[49]

He must have felt much like his old friend, Arnold Bennett, who, once the Armistice was signed, said he viewed it with relief, but not elation, as 'I should like to be assured that the guiding minds of this great and triumphant nation were more exercised about righteous principles than about political manoeuvres for position.' In the event both Wells and Bennett were right in their hopes, but they were also right in their fears.[50]

Wells and his friends still had one or two more strings to their bow. In early 1918, a League of Free Nations Society had been founded, and it began to undertake education and propaganda for its ideals. Wells criticized the board of the original League of Nations committee (founded in 1915) for its narrow outlook, and in response a subcommittee was founded to lay out a new statement of policy. Wells worked very hard for the committee. By the end of June 1918, they had hammered out a programme, calling for major publication of historical and economic facts so that the English people would know what the real issues were. Some of the meetings were stormy, but the stakes were too great for anyone to take much offence.[51]

The new provisional executive met on 24 June 1918, with Gilbert Murray, J. A. Spender, Wells, C. McCurdy, and Major David Davies present. At a second meeting, on the 26th (Wells was not present), they agreed to add Ernest Barker and William Archer to the group. Wells served as secretary of the research committee. Another who was added was G. Lowes Dickinson, and he and Wells began work on two pamphlets. Wells attended meetings of the group, although he did have a bad cold and the beginnings of the flu that summer. (This is another reason he resigned from the war aims group, as he was simply very tired. He was also writing *Joan and Peter*, as well as his newspaper journalism during this period.[52])

The two groups of supporters of the League had not been able to agree on ends, but the success of the Wellsian group led for a time to a *rapprochement* in late July. Apparently Wells had a good deal to do with a brief agreement, having urged his friends in both groups to bury the hatchet and work together. Eventually the Wells group was the sole survivor. The drafts from Dickinson and Wells went out to the research committee for comment through September, although the old split (over who could be members of the League: only democracies, or any nation) continued to plague the discussion. Wells apparently kept the organization alive with a large donation of funds, probably to pay the printer. Time ran out here as well, and the proofs of the first pamphlet did not get to Wells until mid-December. The peace conference was already under way.[53]

The work had simply been too slow, and it did not accomplish much. Too many people had to read the drafts, make comments, and generally flatter their own egos. Wells went to a major strategy meeting held in mid-January at a drinks party, along with Lord Milne, Galsworthy, Belloc, Walter Raleigh, Gerald Du Maurier, E. V. Lucas, and A. E. W. Mason. J.M. Barrie was the host. Wells went to obtain funds and signatures for the project. This was his last real effort, however, for as he confided to Philip Guedalla, he was bored, especially by Lord Bryce, who 'is the damndest old fool alive, except Asquith'. Wells soon resigned, to work alone.[54]

The end of the war was a period of great hopes. Wells and his friends did publish two useful pamphlets as their contribution. One of these, entitled *The Idea of the League of Nations*, summarized Wells's ideas, especially on history teaching as distorting the past. Basing its statements on biological imperatives, it called — using William James's phrase, the 'Moral Equivalent of War' — for 'a proposal to change the life and mentality of everyone on earth'. A second pamphlet, *The Way to the League of Nations*, was briefer, discussing the existing treaties and the possibility of transferring power to a central agency, starting with the international post, an agricultural research bureau, a medical organization, and proposing the organization of international congresses to deal with specific problems.[55]

By the time Wells resigned from the Society, most of his associates in the effort were also disillusioned. The meetings at Versailles did not deal with the realities behind the war, and although they created a League of Nations, it was a toothless and insignificant body, perhaps even more so (although that is debatable) once the US decided that it would remain outside the League. Walter Lippman left the conference in Paris, and sailed for New York. After stopping briefly to see Wells, he wrote to him from the S.S. *Calia*.

Lippman described the peace conference as 'not unhopeful', but said the last two months had been lost. He told Wells that he thought the British delegation had been more in earnest than others, and that the Empire might still play a crucial role, by bringing together the white and coloured nations of the world. 'There's no way out for the world if you don't', was his judgement. He proposed to Wells that an international organization or conference of unattached liberals of the world might be formed, which could lay out a body of doctrine for the nations to follow, 'to act', as it were, 'as the intellectual foundation of the League of Nations'. By mid-May, at home in New York, Lippman was much less sanguine. He asked Wells, 'Do you see any hope of stability in the present treaty and covenant? I confess I don't.'[56]

For Wells the disillusionment was as bad or worse. However, although he, like Lippman, looked to history for answers, he knew by this time that if changes were to be made, a new history had to be written, one which would focus on the emergence of ideas, and one which would deal with the hopes and aspirations of all people, not just the ruling classes. He hoped to get his friends from the League of Nations committee to work on such a book. They were unable to give it the time and effort needed. So, he was faced with a large decision. Should he give his time and his effort to undertake this great history? The answer was yes. The stakes remained too high to step out of the arena as yet.

PART THREE

TEACHER

TEXTBOOKS FOR THE WORLD

The need for a common knowledge of the general facts of human history throughout the world has become very evident during the tragic happenings of the last few years. Swifter means of communication have brought all men closer to one another for good or for evil. War becomes a universal disaster, blind and monstrously destructive; it bombs the baby in its cradle and sinks the food-ships that cater for the non-combatant and the neutral. There can be no peace now, we realise, but a common peace in all the world; no prosperity but a general prosperity. But *there can be no common peace and prosperity without common historical ideas*. . . . A sense of history as the common adventure of all mankind is as necessary for peace within as it is for peace between the nations.

HGW, Introduction, The Outline of History
(1919) (emphasis in original)

H. G. Wells never stopped thinking of himself as a teacher. His earliest work and his formal training continued to manifest itself in all of his writing. *Mankind in the Making* offered a curriculum for the world he foresaw, and schoolmasters and schoolmistresses appear in nearly every novel. He no longer gave as much thought to the technical art of instruction as he had in the '90s, but once his own children started on their educational path, he again became intensely interested in the content of education. The boys received private tutoring of a high quality until it was time for formal education. At that time, H.G. and Jane spent a good deal of time in seeking out the school they wanted, before they hit upon Oundle School, near Peterborough. Oundle was an experimental school, offering an individual and personal education in many fields, and one which had diminished the classics side afforded by the more traditional public schools of England. Its headmaster, F. W. Sanderson, well known for his broad views on what constituted education, was amenable to suggestions from the

Wells parents. Russian, as an example, was begun for the Wells boys, as well as for others, after H.G. visited Russia in 1914. The Wells children were also very fortunate in the sciences, not only because of Wells's own interests, but because of the attention they received from Richard Gregory, Ray Lankester, Harry Johnston, Tommy Simmons, and others of the Wells circle.

After war came in 1914 many others in England joined Wells and Sanderson in their rather vague campaign for a wider-based education, not only in public schools but in state-supported institutions as well. Ray Lankester became chairman of a group, previously headed by Lord Milner, that had been more or less active since about 1905, called the Committee on the Neglect of Science. At about the same time, Richard Gregory became the leading figure in the British Science Guild. By 1915 these two organizations had begun a joint propaganda campaign to increase the time spent in schools on science, along with a greater emphasis on experimental science in the laboratory. Wells was a significant force in both these campaigns.

The Committee on the Neglect of Science organized a meeting of over two hundred scientific workers on 3 May 1916 in the clubrooms of the Linnaean Society of London. The Vice-Chancellor of Cambridge University, the poet laureate Robert Bridges, and others spoke briefly, with main addresses coming from Wells, Sanderson, and Lankester. (In 1917 the two organizations again joined in a meeting at the Mansion House, where Wells, H. A. L. Fisher, and Lord Sydenham spoke.) At the first meeting Wells spoke against the traditional classical education, calling for more science, and more experimental science. Lankester discussed the general aims of education (to make better people and better governments), while Sanderson outlined his ideas on how the school day could be better arranged. Sanderson also called for the establishment of 'a museum of history', where the long-term development of art and science could be illustrated. The Oundle School *Guide to Experiments and Exhibits* for the 1917 school year was circulated to the audience. At their meeting the Committee adopted a motion urging that natural science be made a compulsory part of the university entrance examination, as well as the examinations for Civil Service posts. Without its being required in these two examinations, the teaching of science would not be increased in the schools because it would have no utilitarian purpose in schools designed to obtain places for their students.[1]

As the last paragraph of the report of the Committee on the Neglect of Science stated, on behalf of the speakers and those who attended these meetings: 'Soon, for very many, as now for only a few, the pursuit of Science will become a part of the Moral Law. It will be felt as an imperative that, in order to do that which is right, man must know that which is true.' But Wells and his colleagues did not end their efforts with these pious comments. More and more publications ensued. Speeches on these same points by Faraday and others of his time were reprinted. The proceedings of the various public meetings were reprinted in several forms. Lord Bryce, the distinguished historian and authority on American affairs, even lent his name to the campaign. Wells wrote a long article for the *Fortnightly Review*, the second part of which was a slightly altered version of his address to the British Science Guild. Speaking more bluntly in the published version of his views, however, as it was addressed to a slightly different audience, he remarked at the end of the article: 'These Greek monopolists have to get their trade and prejudices and privileges out of the way of our sons and our people and our public services. It is their share in the sacrifices of these creative days.'[2]

Some minor changes were made in the Civil Service requirements and the amount of science grudgingly increased in the schools, but no wholesale changes were made until after a Labour government took power in 1924. In fact, Wells did not bother much with the two organizations after this first campaign, except to endorse their efforts, leaving the work in the capable hands of Lankester and Gregory. Instead he turned his attention to his own strengths, first to fiction and later the writing of textbooks to be used in his new education. His novels of the time, *Joan and Peter* and *The Undying Fire*, especially the first, were good weapons in the battle to modernize education.

Joan and Peter (1918) is a history of the educational experiences of two young people slightly older than Wells's children. There are good descriptions of the South Kensington laboratories, and of London gene-rally at the turn of the twentieth century, but the bulk of the book is simply a discussion, through the views of Joan and Peter, of their experiences: in infant school, later on in public school education (with a good description of education for women), and with this an excellent picture of Europe on the eve of the war, including Russia, based strongly on Wells's pre-war visits. Wells uses the novel form to discuss his views on suffragism, Ireland, India, Ulster, and the coming of the war. But the war is to mark for Joan and Peter the end of rather vapid speculation on what might be done:

> All these young people who had grown up without any clear aims or any definite sense of obligations, found themselves confronted, without notice, without any preparation, by a world crisis that was also a crisis of life or death, of honour or dishonour for each one of them.
>
> (Chapter 13)

Peter fights in the war, in the air, and some of Wells's finest writing went into the discussion of what this exhilarating experience means to the young man psychologically. The impact of the war on England, taking up where *Mr Britling* left off, is clearly laid out, along with the sense of destruction, and the sacrifice of youth for the dreams of the old. By the end of the book, the two leading characters have decided to reform education, to prevent war from recurring. The forces of reaction (in Aunt Charlotte, an interesting use of the same name as in the 1890s to indicate Tory stability) are described, and the book ends with Joan and Peter discovering each other as their mentor, Oswald, who has been responsible for their educational experimentation, muses over the results, even as he begins to work on an even larger project, the extension of education to everyone for these ends of peace.

The Undying Fire (1919), much shorter and slighter, belongs to the same mode of thinking. Dedicated to 'All schoolmasters and schoolmistresses and every teacher in the world', the novel takes the form of a debate: a progressive schoolmaster, Job Huss (based loosely on F. W. Sanderson), is tested, as was the biblical Job, by many personal trials, and defends his case against individuals who wish to close his school, return to the old ways, and who attack everything the new education stands for. The book is remarkable today — as indeed is nearly every Wells book, each with at least one powerful scene, character, or a piece of fine writing. In this book it is the depiction of life in a U-boat under attack, symbolic of attacks levied at everything new, and of how such attacks are perceived by the pioneers.

Both novels spend a good deal of time discussing the role of history in education, and in the training of minds for government and state service, along with the role of research and science in mapping out the new worlds to come. Both novels are mileposts on the way to the great textbooks, and rose out of Wells's deep consciousness of the war and its impact on England and on the world.

The two books were well received by his friends, but less so by outside reviewers. Virginia Woolf, while calling attention to Wells's ability with words, thought *Joan and Peter* too didactic for successful fiction. However, Thomas Hardy, sitting in Dorset, liked it immensely, reading it aloud to his wife in the evening. He told Wells, 'You have a preternatural knowledge of what people do. I believe you could walk down a street a mile long and see through the house-fronts and describe the movements of every inhabitant.'[3]

Lankester told Wells not to concern himself with the petty notices in the press, as the writers

> are jealous of you, and are making their puny efforts to crab the book declaring it to be all schoolmaster and no story — but they can't touch you, my dear friend. You don't write to the problems they absurdly try and insist on as a sort of law of art. Never have you given more psychological insight — never handled the thoughts which make up the salad you seek to stir (as you once put it) with [more] perfect oil than this.

Wells described *Joan and Peter* as 'one of the most ambitious' of his novels. He confessed to falling in love with Joan as the story grew, but as it was issued at a time of paper shortage, and at an unusual price (9s.), it did not win many new readers for H. G. Wells. While musing on its failure, in

1926, he said that he wished he knew a better way of presenting the two sorts of novels he wrote, the novel of ideas and the novel of incidents or personality, a problem he never really solved. He reprinted the biography he was to write of Sanderson with *Joan and Peter*, as part of a two-volume set on education, as he said they represented the height of his ideas on the matter.[4]

The novels were useful, at least for Wells as a means of working out his ideas, but they did not reach a wide enough audience. Moreover, by the time they appeared Wells had become disillusioned with the League, although he thought it was still more than he had expected. He and his friends on the League of Nations committee had discussed textbooks and methods of education, as a way of preventing further wars, but time did not permit them to produce their own. Wells apparently asked members of the committee, especially Alfred Zimmern, Gilbert Murray, and Ernest Barker, to work on a new world history to replace the older nationalistic and narrow treatments. They refused, on the grounds of lack of time, lack of formal preparation, and unwillingness to give the effort. Wells decided that he must do it himself.

He and Jane agreed to take a year to research, formulate, and write a book designed to replace the histories then available. It was a remarkable gamble. The income from Wells's past writing would inevitably dry up during such a year. The boys were still at school and in university, with additional expenses. Wells was responsible for the care and education of his child by Rebecca West, and there were the expenses of his and Jane's various homes. Still, the two felt the need for such a book outshone their own personal needs. So, late in 1918, about Christmas, H.G. and Jane sat down to begin work on what would be one of the more significant and widely read books of our century, *The Outline of History*. The second phase of Wells's writing career, already begun in a partial and desultory fashion, now, with this decision, became the dominant force in his teaching, his writing, in his life. He would devote the years left to him to a campaign to educate the world — through textbooks, through speaking, through writing, through travel and through propaganda — in fact, through the very life he lived.[5]

Wells had had some experience in writing textbooks, of course, with his *Textbook of Biology* and the *Honours Physiography* of nearly a quarter-century before. It was clear from those books that his new textbook, even in this completely different field, would be filled with generalizations, both sweeping and analytical, and would not consist merely of lists of dates and names to be memorized. That sort of history could only be 'the acquisition of knowledge without assimilation'.[6]

It soon became known in England that he was working on a new history textbook, and the *Strand Magazine* asked him to agree to an interview about his plans. Wells told his interviewer, Arthur Lynch, that the idea of an epic which would describe the races of mankind had been in his mind for years. He mentioned Winwood Reade's *Martyrdom of Man* as his prototype, along with the work of the League of Nations committee, and the realization that nationalist teaching of history was dangerous and poisonous to the future of the species. Wells said he and his collaborators were attempting 'a new synthesis' to replace the older nationalism. It would include the wide use of maps and sketches, or what Wells termed 'a world-cinematograph'. He had begun the writing of the textbook before *The Undying Fire*, and had been at work on it, either on research or on a draft form of it, for nearly eighteen months. He assumed that other outlines would follow, and he welcomed them. To Marie Beets, at about this time, he described his work as 'a real workers' history, I hope. I feel more and more that we can't get much further until people's historical ideas are cleared up. . . . I want my outline to be the outline of an international history teaching the common story of mankind.' And to a clergyman who wrote to him while the parts were appearing, Wells confided, 'I'd rather be read and discussed in the public schools than anywhere else in the world.'[7]

Once the book had reached its more or less final form, Wells spoke more of his ideas while writing the work. At a debate at the London School of Economics early in 1923, while refuting L. B. Osborn of the *Morning Post*, Wells said that 'the only way to teach history is through a history of mankind', and ultimately by doing away with narrow nationalist history. His opponent was reduced to describing Wells's later books as 'alluring sociological cocktails, a mixture of Socialism and Sexualism'. A few months later, Wells spoke to an audience of assistant masters in secondary schools about their work. Calling them the most important people in the world, he told them to 'preach boldness, shamelessness, arrogance and aggression' about their work, 'to stand up and take hold of' their world. He urged generalizations, and said that he was a failed schoolmaster who had run away 'where the work was easier and the conditions of employment better'. Wells called for 'schoolmaster-statesmen' to lead the world of the future.[8]

Wells did much of the early research and reading in preparation for this book during the latter half of 1918. Jane did as much more after the first few months, taking notes, placing slips in books, organizing material. As he worked through a section he would draft a fairly complete outline, and send it off to one of the people working as collaborators. They were named on the title-page of the first several editions. Eventually H. G. Wells supervised a team of six: Jane; J. F. Horrabin (the gifted artist and illustrator, always known to his friends as 'Horrid Ben'); Gilbert Murray, an extraordinary classical scholar, who had begun to be seriously involved in diplomatic history, the role of the League of Nations, and other similar subjects; Sir E. Ray Lankester, director of the Museum of Natural History, and a noted spokesman for science; Sir Henry H. Johnston, colonial governor, African and Asian explorer, and a widely read writer in his time on cultural anthropology; and Ernest Barker, a political scientist cum historian, then at Oxford, later at King's College, London, and who was to hold a chair at Cambridge from 1928. It would have been difficult to put together a stronger intellectual team than this, and Wells played them together beautifully. Another who worked on smaller sections of the book was Henry Seidel Canby (professor of history at Yale). R. A. Gregory, Arnold Bennett, and Philip Guedalla read the proofs of the book. A dozen others were acknowledged in the first preface, and as the book went into new editions still others were added as Wells constantly revised the book in the first ten years, to incorporate new knowledge, criticism, and new insights.

Wells wrote a draft and sent it to his colleagues; they commented, and returned the material, which Wells then rewrote in more or less final form; Jane corrected the work. It was then returned to his colleagues, further comments came in (and in the first two editions, where the material was controversial, or where little was known about an issue, a footnote signed with the initials of the collaborator was printed). The book first appeared in twenty-four parts (each a signature in length), at intervals of a fortnight; the first of these signatures came out in late November 1919. The parts were then bound up (without the advertising material on the backs of the covers) in a two-volume work, essentially unchanged from its first appearance. In fact, subscribers to the part-work could have the signatures bound up by the publisher, by paying a small fee. The book was reprinted later in 1920 (US 1921), also in two volumes, but in a different format. Changes included new material, correction of errors that had crept in, new maps and new illustrations. A third edition appeared in 1920 (US 1921), in one volume, and additional changes were made. A 'Definitive' edition was published in 1923 (US 1924), again with the parts appearing at fortnightly intervals in advance of book publication. (By this time most of the footnotes had been incorporated into the text, which was fairly well rewritten in response to the wealth of comments Wells had received.) A fifth revision came out in 1930 (US 1931), and a sixth on the eve of the Second World War. A new edition (with very little changed except for the addition of material since Wells's death) by G. P. Wells and Raymond Postgate is still in print in the US.

The later revisions are often seen in multi-volume editions, with many more prints, illustrations, maps, and a generally richer format. A German edition of 1928, the text in three volumes, is the glossiest of them all, perhaps. It has all of the original illustrations, as well as many found only in this edition, in a separate fourth volume. One might add, as stemming from this work, *The Short History of the World*, written separately in 1923 for sixth-form use, and also still in print from Penguin. There were, as well, two abridged editions for younger readers. The first, adapted for school use by E. H. Carter, a Cambridge scholar, appeared in 1925, and remained in print for a dozen years; it is an adaptation of the *Short History*. In 1929 an even shorter outline version, designed for use by teachers, with experiments, exercises, and some suggested examination topics, appeared. All of these forms of the work were read and passed by H. G. Wells. And, in some cases, his collaborators also passed on portions of the work.[9]

Newnes published the parts, and the two-volume first edition. After that Macmillan, with American rights subcontracted to several publishers in the United States, published the earlier reprints. Eventually Cassells took over publication in England, and Doubleday in the US, as they published the other textbooks. Hodder & Stoughton had wanted the book badly, but did not come up with enough of an advance, and Macmillan got the rights. The various editions, especially those in the United States after 1930, were all inexpensively bound, as both Doubleday and Wells wanted the widest possible circulation for the book; although even here Wells was concerned that Doubleday would not get it down far enough in price.[10]

H. G. and Jane Wells concerned themselves with every aspect of the book, type face, illustrations, and the index. Their chief indexer, Harold Wheeler, a history master and editor, later served as indexer for the other *Outlines*, although he was paid by Cassells. He and his wife were guests of the Wellses at Easton to celebrate publication of what they felt was the book's final form, the fourth English revision.[11]

Of Wells's collaborators, Ray Lankester was especially useful in discussion of ancient peoples; he warned Wells against using anything about Piltdown Man (in 1918!), as the scientific community was concerned that it was a fraud. Lankester also supervised Horrabin's illustrations in this portion of the book, and later entertained him for a weekend while they went over all the book illustrations in detail. Lankester, as did others, continued to pass on ideas, bibliography, and to act as a postbox for still others who had something of importance to say. Wells paid each of his main contributors (Johnston, Lankester, Barker, and Murray) a fee of 100 guineas, which came as a great surprise to them, according to their letters; two of the men reported that it was the largest fee each had ever received for professional activity.[12]

Gilbert Murray vetted all the material on the ancient world, sending Wells translations in progress (especially material on Aristophanes, later used by Murray in an important work), and he also acted as a major postbox, sending on detailed comments from his colleagues at Oxford, from Arabic and French scholar friends, and others. Murray was overwhelmed with his payment.[13]

Sir Henry Johnston was at Easton Glebe (recuperating from an operation) when much of the writing of the *Outline* was done, and he worked over the proofs, as well as offering much good comment on evolution, from the point of view of an anthropologist. Ernest Barker was the closest critic of Wells's work, especially on the more recondite material on Asoka and the siege of Amritsar. He disagreed with Wells and eventually asked for his name to be removed from the title-page over this

23 Indians in London protesting against *A Short History of the World*, 1923. Wells's treatment of modern India ('An Autocracy without an Autocrat') probably inspired this attack on a great friend

24 Wells at a BBC microphone, 1929

issue. He, Murray, and Wells met several times over lunch in London to discuss exact wording of tricky passages. This sort of criticism was exactly what Wells wanted and the book was substantially stronger after it had gone through this crucible. Wells and Barker, as well as Gilbert Murray, continued to see each other well into the Second World War period, and both the dons acted as bibliographical scouts for Wells, especially on material relating to the Catholic Church. Johnston and Lankester were to die in the '20s, but as long as they were alive, they retained a strong interest in the Wells work. Other advisers emerged, once the book began to appear in parts, and they also read proofs, and provided plates and suggestions. Wells welcomed comment from every quarter.[14] Eileen Power, for instance, added much to the medieval sections in later editions.

As we look back on the *Outline* today, it is clear that the work made a number of significant contributions to our understanding of the past. Some of these were revolutionary enough still to strike chords of admiration, and, one supposes, discords of fear and hatred. Their impact on Wells himself was immense, and much of his later writing, and especially his philosophical contributions, are imbued with his historical findings.

At the end of chapter 23 of his book, he summarized his view of history as being shot through with three great themes. These were to be the significant forces in his later thought. The first is the concept of a universal knowledge, and of 'a universally understandable and communicable history and philosophy'. Herodotus and Aristotle were his exemplars. The second concept was the generalization of religion, to 'the open service of *one* universal *God of Righteousness*'. This contribution he noticed came from the Semitic peoples of the area we call the Fertile Crescent. These two matters come together in the concept of '*a world polity*' and he summarized his views with this statement:

> The rest of the history of mankind is very largely the history of those three ideas of science, of a universal righteousness, and of a human commonweal, spreading out from the minds of the rare and exceptional persons and peoples in which they first originated, into the general consciousness of the race, and giving first a new colour, then a new spirit, and then a new direction to human affairs.
>
> (Chapter 23, sect. 8)[15]

As he said later in the work, 'History is the beginning and core of all sound philosophy and all great literature . . . ' (chapter 31, section 8). History, then, to H. G. Wells, was and is a didactic discipline, and furthermore, right-thinking people needed to seek out its cold clear reality and use the results to the best ends of our species.

Wells made other contributions in the work, and they deserve summary because it was these matters that later often caused controversy over his work. First, he provided a scientific background and integrated the findings of Darwin and biological science (Book I, first 6 chapters). Then he utilized the findings of anthropology to cement these biological ideas in place (Book II, chapters 7–12). He introduced his readers to the teachings of Buddha, and to the impact of Asian thought (chapter 25, sections 3 and 5 especially). He made the central observation that the Roman Empire had declined and died because of its failure to understand the need of all inhabitants to participate in its community life (chapter 27, section 7). He called for the discussion of Jesus to be historical, not theological, and then proceeded to follow that advice, using the words of the Bible to make and buttress his points (chapter 29, especially sections 2 and 5). In other places he analysed the contribution of the Chinese (chapter 30, section 7).

In chapter 32, section 4, he committed one of his heresies by stating that early English history was of no great significance to the history of the species. In the next chapter he introduced one of his largest generalizations, although it would be a decade before he elaborated fully on this thought. In his discussion of the nomadic invasions, he clearly anticipated his idea of youth without purpose and the fact that when this group becomes powerful, wars and devastation occur as leaders need to deflect its great energies (chapter 33, especially section 1). It is but a short step to the concept of the need to channel the energies of the young and finally to the concept of a 'competent receiver' to provide the truly better world he sought. Here is the first clear statement of the Open Conspiracy.

This great book still sounds a significant call to arms more than sixty years after its appearance. When writing about the Buddha, Wells sounded a view of history one finds extremely attractive today:

> There is . . . no social order, no security, no peace or happiness, no righteous leadership or kingship, unless men *lose themselves in something greater than themselves* [my emphasis]. The study of biological progress again reveals exactly the same process — the merger of the narrow globe of the individual experience in a wider being. . . . To forget oneself in greater interests is to escape from a prison.
>
> (Chapter 25, sect. 3)

Then, a bit later, writing about Christianity, he drives this point home as the central piece of his writing:

> Sooner or later mankind must come to one universal peace, unless our race is to be destroyed by the increasing power of its own destructive inventions; and that universal peace must needs take the form of a government, that is to say a law-sustaining organization in the best sense of the word religious; a government ruling men through the educated co-ordination of their minds in a common conception of human history and human destiny.
>
> (Chapter 32, sect. 13)

The response to the book was remarkable. Wells's friends and acquaintances were moved beyond anything he had previously written. The reviews were filled with admiration, although some were splenetic. The initial criticisms, along with the Catholic repercussions, which were long-lasting, will be treated presently, as will the long-term impact of the *Outline*, especially on professional historians. For the time being, however, a brief glance at the immediate and personal reception will be rewarding.

J. H. Breasted, author of a previous attempt at a world history, and one cited by Wells, could not contain himself, and eventually came and spent a weekend with Wells to discuss the work just as it was being published. Later, when the second revision appeared, Breasted told Wells he was convinced that 'all societies must find some footing in the common human inheritance'. He was fully converted to Wellsian thought. Floyd Dell, the American radical author, told Wells he had been 'waiting for more than twenty years for such a book', and sent Wells a cheque to make sure he received it. Dell told Wells that his entire generation had benefited from Wellsian thought, and that the Darwinian controversy had lost its bite for Americans because of Wells (although this was four years before the Tennessee evolution case). Dell said Wells had taught Dell's generation to 'dream their dream'. Walter Lippman, also writing from America, said that he was 'unreservedly grateful for the book'. He told Wells, as he must have done earlier, that he had been a Harvard undergraduate when *Tono-Bungay* and *The New Machiavelli* had appeared.

> No other books have ever meant more to me than these, but in reading the *Outline of History* there comes back all the old sense of discovery and illumination of those great books. What a wonderful thing to have conceived, how much more wonderful to have paid the price and done it. Do you mind my saying to you that you are still contemporary with the younger generation? That generation grows up with Wells; it doesn't have to look back to him.

Lippman signed the letter, 'Gratefully yours'.[16]

Robert Blatchford was equally stunned by the book, and especially by a gracious comment from Wells that Blatchford might have done it better. He told Wells, 'I wonder if you realize how much you have accomplished. In my opinion such a work will have a revolutionary impact on education and will change and expand man's views of life and the universe.' Ray Lankester told H.G. it was 'a gigantic task and wonderfully carried through'. He described it as a complete '*tour de force*', especially the next to last and last chapters. Sanderson, who adopted it immediately at Oundle, was equally moved. And finally, Beatrice Webb, writing in her diary, said, 'We are reconciled to H. G. Wells.' She had received a copy of the *Outline* from Wells, and wrote to him,

> I was really very much gratified to get the great work direct from you — not merely on account of its value, but also as a token of 'mutuality' in

regard for each other's work — a regard that has been constant on my part. The book is a great achievement. . . . You take so many things in your stride, that, unless one watches you marching on and on and on towards your chosen end, one loses half the meaning of your message.

She invited Wells to come and meet Leo Kamenev and Leonid Krassin, visiting them from Russia. With this letter, the old rifts were sealed over. Both the antagonists knew that they shared the same goals, although, of course, there would remain some discussion of means, and more particularly of the speed of the transitions.[17]

Not everyone was as happy with Wells's contribution as were his close political friends. A. W. Gomme, professor of history at Glasgow, had some very strong things to say, as did Richard Downey, an Irish priest. Wells responded to both of them, revised some judgements in light of their comments, and thanked both of them in the next edition.[18] But his old friend, Hilaire Belloc, was not so easy to deal with.

Belloc was writing in opposition to the work in a world in which it was widely reviewed and widely liked. Even when criticism emerged, at least in the United States, many were willing to come forward and support the Wellsian point of view.[19] But the Belloc comments were long, involved, and they continued. Belloc began to attack the *Outline* while it was still appearing in parts. He continued his attacks, in a wide variety of Catholic periodicals, usually offering a diatribe without producing much evidence of Wells's errors. Wells responded when the attacks were too wide of the mark, and when Belloc issued *A Companion to Mr. Wells's 'Outline of History'* (1926), which mostly attacked Wells for accepting Darwin's view of natural selection, and offered non-scientific opinion as evidence, Wells was sufficiently stung to reply directly to Belloc. Belloc was an old friend, and had spent much time in Wells's house, playing Little Wars with H.G. and his children, so the vitriolic attack came as a shock to Wells. Belloc had served as an MP, and had been responsible for bringing attention to the Marconi scandal. Wells had supported him strongly at that time, in articles which he offered gratis to Belloc's newspapers (usually edited with and by Cecil Chesterton), the *New Witness* and the *Eye Witness*.

Wells's reply to Belloc was still rather soft, although it did take the form of a small book, *Mr Belloc Objects to 'The Outline of History'* (1926). In that work Wells pointed out the sparseness of Belloc's evidence, as well as his *ad hominem* mode of attack. Belloc responded with yet another book and reissued the *Companion*. Although Wells was concerned about the force of the attack, most observers read Belloc for style, not content, and so the *Outline* continued to sell. What the attack did do was to reinforce Wells's feeling that Catholic apologists, such as Belloc, did not care whether or not they used truth in their work. The infallibility of the Church was enough to cover them. Wells remained opposed to Catholic thought of this variety, and eventually delivered himself of an attack on the Church throughout history in a bilious volume of his own, *Crux Ansata*, published in 1943 (and reprinted several times since). Hilaire Belloc and H. G. Wells gave many people a humorous year or two as they issued their various attacks on each other, but in the long run Belloc made little impact on Wells, except to solidify his belief about Catholic philosophy.[20]

The best defence of Wells against the Belloc attacks came from others. As the attacks continued, Gregory told Wells that he was 'arranging a proper article' in *Nature*. Although Gregory thought Wells could take care of himself, he still felt the scientific community needed to rally round. (Gregory had also begun a campaign to have Wells made an FRS when the book appeared.) Arthur Keith demolished Belloc in a long article, 'Is Darwinism Dead?' Accusing Belloc of putting up a smokescreen to cover his Catholicism, he suggested that Belloc had not yet read *The Origin of Species*, and after quoting some 1871 attacks on Darwin by St. George Grant (*The Genesis of Species*), Keith intimated that Belloc was only a plagiarist, not a thinker.[21]

Belloc's attacks were disheartening, however, for no matter what new evidence Wells produced, Belloc bounced back. Wells was vulnerable in one or two other ways as well, for sharp-eyed readers found that he had left Shakespeare, and other notable figures, out of the book. Wells said, in defence of his omissions, that space had been at a premium, and inclusion had depended on the contribution an individual had made to the growing centralization of power, or to the increased concern for the future of the species. Shakespeare was a brilliant writer, and perhaps the most significant Englishman, but he had little to offer in this regard, and therefore had been left out. The attacks on Wells for this omission, as well as for his deprecation of Julius Caesar and his elevation of Asoka and the Buddha, only served to heighten interest in the book and, of course, to sell copies. Wells made good some of his previous omissions in later editions, although he seldom responded openly to this sort of criticism. Alan Odle, Dorothy Richardson's husband, made a delightful pen and ink sketch of a tea party, at which Wells is welcoming only persons excluded from the history.[22]

The general sense of the history, and its ideas of one collective humanity, led others to provide other outlines, much as Wells had predicted. It also meant that Wells was offered a number of chances to comment on history, and history within the context of his beliefs. In response he provided in a short book, *The New Teaching of History* . . . (1921), a recounting of his effort, along with a response to the general comments that had been made; after discussing Downey and Belloc, he called for a Catholic *Outline*, so persons could compare their ideas. He described his own views:

My vision of history is essentially one of mental synthesis and material co-operation, from the completely isolated individual life and death of the primordial animal to the continuing mental life and social organization now growing to planetary dimensions, of the human species. . . . Combined with the study of physiography, as Professor Huxley defined it, [this idea of universal history] gives something that may be made the basis of a common understanding and sympathy for all mankind. . . . On minds prepared in this fashion it would be possible to build the new conceptions of an organized world peace that struggle so helplessly at present against the dark prejudices of today.

(Sect. 4)[23]

The *Outline* and similar books created a small revolution in the teaching of history. Most notable at Oundle, or A. S. Neill's Summerhill, both of which were immediate supporters, it also had an impact elsewhere as schoolmasters and -mistresses read the work, and adopted it for their own schools. A number of such schools depended on Wells for aid and comfort and he did not disappoint them.[24]

The teaching of history at university and in higher education was also greatly modified by the *Outline*. The movement was led by such prominent figures as Carl L. Becker, who reviewed the book in high style while developing a type of historical thinking close to Wells's own, and by other well-known academics such as Albert Guerard. Many American professors adopted the book. In addition, of course, dozens who read the *Outline* chose their careers in response to the chords it struck.[25]

A more bizarre response to the *Outline* was a suit for libel and plagiarism brought against Wells by a Toronto author, Florence Deeks. She claimed that Wells had pirated her work, 'The Web of History', and passed it off as the *Outline*. She attempted to contact his collaborators, and when Ernest Barker was in Canada in 1924 he met her and discussed her views, and even looked at her manuscript. He came away sure that she was simply misguided in her opinion. When she actually filed suit in 1928, several other historians came forward to warn Wells, saying that they too had seen her manuscript, which bore no resemblance to his work; but she persisted nevertheless in the suit. A Canadian court found that she had no case, but her solicitors appealed eventually to the Privy Council. Gilbert Murray testified on Wells's behalf, and told Wells that he presumed the woman was 'mad'. Wells did not reply to the charges, and although it cost him and his publishers nearly £3,000, the suit was finally dismissed as simply a nuisance.

Wells did write a strong memorandum to his solicitors which can be read as a short history of the League of Nations committee, giving dates of their discussions, especially with H. S. Canby and W. S. Culbertson. The Ministry of Information had given the two, with other Americans, a dinner at the Reform Club at which Wells spoke, and this was apparently the first germ of the *Outline of History*. The solicitors used this in their defence brief. When the judgement in the suit was handed down, it completely exonerated Wells and the Society of Authors, who had supported him in the matter as a friend of the court. Later when Wells was in North America the Canadian Authors' Association tendered him an invitation to visit Canada, but he refused to enter the country as long as Deeks's supporters were active there. He urged them to issue a public apology. Wells never received his apology, and never set foot on Canadian soil, so far as I am able to find out. He did recapitulate the episode in an article for the *Author*, and the editors agreed with him that the practice of bringing such suits was shameful, but that little could be done as long as the courts were willing to try such frivolous actions. Lloyds offered to insure Wells against charges of libel and plagiarism, and he took up some of the options as a result of this contretemps. When one last charge was passed on to Wells in the spring of 1933, he, when settling the account, remarked to his publishers that 'She [Deeks] is just a misfortune that has come upon me, a sort of Act of God without the slightest negligence or fault of any kind on my part. . . .'[26]

Although the suit was costly, the amounts of money brought in by the book must have been immense. Over half a million copies were sold of the individual parts and the first two cloth editions. The book continued to sell in great numbers, and is still selling today. It made H. G. Wells wealthy. He never had to worry again about finances. He could continue to speak out, write as he pleased and not worry over whether or not his material would be published. Fortunately for us, he had no problem in publishing whatever he wished. Later, after the success of the book, and a related work on F. W. Sanderson and Oundle School, Wells's publishers asked him to provide two more *Outlines*, one on biology and a second on sociology, economics, and education. Although both would be difficult to do, especially with the problems of collaborators, he agreed to take on these chores, as much as anything else because he knew the need for textbooks was as great in those areas as it had been in history.

Writing the *Outline* took a great deal out of Wells, both physically and mentally. His friends commented on how grey he looked in the late autumn and winter of 1919–20. His tiredness made him susceptible to illness, and he contracted Spanish influenza, although he recovered from the illness fairly well. From this time on, however, he suffered recurrent problems with his chest and lungs in the London winter, somewhat similar to the bouts he had experienced when he was much younger. Fortunately, the sales of the *Outline* were so great that he could afford to spend the cold and raw days in the south. He began going to the Mediterranean, at first to Portugal and Spain, and later to the Riviera, for some months of the year. When he toured the United States in later years, he always tried to have a holiday in the warm, pleasant sun of Southern California.

The *Outline* not only sold very well in English; it was soon translated into Japanese, as well as French, German, Swedish, Italian, and other languages. In 1930 (US 1931), the first truly inexpensive edition appeared in English. The book was substantially rewritten for that edition, and by then, in all its editions, it had sold over a million copies. After its publication it was the greatest seller of its time, except for the Bible or the Koran, and by now has probably sold close to two million copies in all editions. But, although the success of the book enabled Wells to deal easily with his bills, his growing physical needs, and those of his various entourages, it still brought him more and more work. Though immediately under siege to provide other *Outlines* — of Science, Literature, Economics — Wells resisted these blandishments until the mid-'20s, spending the time between making two significant visits abroad (one to Russia, and one to the Disarmament Conference in Washington); he also wrote two important novels, *The Dream* and *Men Like Gods*. In addition he stood for Parliament, wrote a useful weekly newspaper column, and was active in other ways. However, throughout this period of his life, education, and a vastly remodelled education for England and for the world, occupied much of his time.

While his own children were at Oundle School, and at university, in the years of the writing of the *Outline*, he had also to watch Anthony, Rebecca's child, through his preparatory school. Publicly, he was besieged by persons wanting his advice, who wished to remodel their schools and their curriculums, and who hoped to bring the world revolution he heralded. One of these persons was F. W. Sanderson, a recent friend, and the head of Oundle School. Wells and Sanderson shared an interest in G.P.'s and Frank's education, but also had a strong interest in wider educational changes in Britain. They were both active, as we have seen, in the Committee on the Neglect of Science, and as a result of this Sanderson, somewhat against the wishes of his staff, remodelled the classics teaching at Oundle, adding a substantial programme of science, and what we would call practical engineering and economics. New buildings were built, and the avant-garde began to seek places at the school for its children. Shaw sent his nephew, as did Arnold Bennett. Sanderson and his programme became very well known throughout British educational circles.[27]

In the spring of 1919 the school put on a performance of *Arms and the Man*, and Shaw, Wells, and Bennett were in the audience. G. P. Wells had the part of Captain Bluntschli. Increasingly the talk of Wells and Sanderson at their various meetings began to be centred on a building, to be used as a study room and library, the walls of which would be covered with maps, charts, murals, panorama showing historical progress in a variety of fields. Originally Sanderson, deflected by *First and Last Things*, had thought that the building would be a chapel. Eventually he described his idea as a 'Temple of Vision'. Sanderson and Wells began to remodel the Oundle curriculum quite widely.[28]

In June 1922, Sanderson came to London to give an address on his educational views to the National Union of Scientific Workers, with H.G. in the chair. After the address, Sanderson collapsed just as the questions began, and immediately died. Wells met with Sanderson's widow at the memorial service, and undertook to prepare a memorial volume on her husband, which would incorporate Sanderson's speeches and talks on various educational topics. Wells began the task, but when the book was partially finished he quarrelled with Mrs Sanderson (or rather, she objected to Wells's view of her husband). He resigned from the committee responsible for the memorial volume, although the published book is certainly in great part his work. He did, however, himself write a life of the man, in which the educational views of Sanderson, Oundle School, and Wells himself were given a good airing.[29]

Wells's book was well received, and was serialized both in the United States and in England, although many of the reviewers thought that Oundle School worked well because of Sanderson, just as Wells's world would work well as long as he ran it. However other reviewers remarked how much Wells and Sanderson had done to rejuvenate education and provide a series of goals for young teachers. Wells's friends also liked the book, and Bertrand Russell told Wells that he wanted the *Outline* as a required set book. (Russell had by this time left the school, Telegraph House, which he and his wife Dora had founded, as his marriage had broken down. However, Dora Russell adopted the *Short History* at the school.) Wells was grateful for the good reception, especially when the comments came from friends. He told G. Lowes Dickinson that his review (very favourable) had come at the precise moment of his being attacked by the Minister of Education, Lord Gorrell, for his views on Sanderson. As Wells went on, to Dickinson, discussing the reviews,

> One realizes what a merely comic low class character one is in the eyes of journalists, school teachers and one's countrymen generally. How utterly futile it is to write anything about education to such a crowd. Then comes real friendship and approval from so respectable an academic swell as yourself. With immense reassurance, so Thank you,
> H. G. WELLS[30]

The success of the *Outline of History*, coupled with the generally good reception of the Sanderson biography, created an even greater demand for another textbook. Wells's natural interest in science and biology, and his deep belief that human history could not be understood without reference to biology, led him to propose an Outline of Biology, which from the outset was called *The Science of Life*. He offered the idea of a possible collaboration on the work to Julian Huxley, the grandson of his former teacher, and to his son, G. P. Wells. Both were fairly young men, with G.P. just at the beginning of his career, while Huxley was better known, especially for his popular treatments of scientific subjects. Huxley, when approached, had just received a chair at King's College, London, and asked for some time, as he wanted to do several technical books in order to get his 'scientific future well fortified', and not to run the risk of being called 'a paperhanger'.[31]

By 1928, however, his fears on that score were allayed, and work began on the new project. Jane Wells had died the year before. But by the end of 1928, with Huxley and his wife coming to Easton for a month's work at the New Year, Wells could report to his agent that the book would be finished by 1 February 1929. Four of the nine proposed parts were already set up in type. Huxley and the Wells duo hired researchers, secretaries, and parcelled out portions of the book. G.P. and Huxley took certain sections, researched and wrote their own parts. H.G. then refined their work, smoothing out difficult stretches, and in general created a book which could be read by the layman. He was a difficult taskmaster, forcing his collaborators to sit at a table and work, calling them in from recreation, and generally ensuring that the book went along on a tight schedule. Both young men found his leadership good discipline, but irksome at times, as neither had been used to H.G.'s sort of dedication.[32] It was the more irksome for Huxley.

The royalty arrangements for the work were eventually settled at 40 per cent for H.G., and 30 per cent for each of his two collaborators. When the book was finally finished, or at least in corrected galley proof form, Julian Huxley departed for Africa, leaving with H.G. a letter in which he claimed that the book had changed his life. 'But for that I would still be a rather overworked and rather disgruntled professor, forever hovering between articles on comparabilities [?]. Now I am a free man, with a valuable experience behind me', and he went on to apologize for not seeing the real need for the hard work at the beginning. As a result of the book, Huxley was able to give up teaching, which he did not enjoy, and went on to have a distinguished career in administrative and experimental science.

As an example of Wells's single-mindedness about the book and its deadline, one can simply quote a letter to Enid Bagnold (by this time Lady Jones): 'I hate to think', said Wells, 'I can't scrap everything and come to see you, but I must get Julian and Gip through with *The Science of Life* and the only way to do that is to sit over them and work ... the whole time.'[33]

Watt handled the arrangements on the book for the collaborators. Eventually Cassells published the work in England, and Nelson Doubleday in the United States. The correspondence over the work, and the meetings, were nearly continuous for Wells and Watt throughout this period, and that is the reason H.G. received the greater share of the royalties. He took on all this work, although he was scrupulous about getting comments from his collaborators, both of whom were only too happy to have him act for them. Watt extracted proposals from other publishers (notably Gollancz), and used these to get an increased advance for the authors.

George Doran, who was in the process of merging with Doubleday in New York, apparently attempted to obtain the rights to the book, even though the merger was already final. He came to Nice and spent several days with H. G. Wells to try to keep a hold on the book. Wells understood clearly what was going on, and kept Watt well informed. Doran proposed starting a new company, with a quarter of the stock to go to Watt and Wells, to publish at least a mail-order version of the book, and perhaps other editions later. Eventually a limited company was formed, which published the book in various forms. The trio of authors received £15,000 in advance from the English publishers, and $75,000 from the American publishers. Doran told Watt, and asked him to pass it on to Wells, that 'I should like both Mr Wells and you to realize that I consider this the most important project of the last quarter of a century.'[34]

The stock market crash and the Depression interfered with sales, after the first rush, and the publishers ended by dropping the mail-order subscriptions and concentrating on the trade edition. Fortunately that sold well, in both countries. Eventually Doubleday wound up the subscription company, and paid the authors a lump sum for their share in its holdings. One problem was that the book clubs, which had shown great interest in this book, and others, were losing members because of the slump. There was a second edition, however, for which Wells wrote a new preface. But the money, although good, was perhaps not quite as much as had been expected. Nevertheless, the three authors did very well out of the book, and did even better when a nine-volume edition was issued later in the decade. When the slump pressed even harder on Doubleday he tried to renege on some of his commitments, or at least postpone them. But Wells told him, 'My idea is that publishers *exist* to make advances. What is the world coming to?'[35]

The book was also eventually published in French. The nine-volume edition continued in print for some time. A one-volume edition (selected by the Literary Guild in the US in 1934), a two-volume edition, and a four-volume edition were also published for various markets. During World War II a one-volume edition designed to be used in military education classes was issued. The book was widely used in beginning college classes in the US as long as it remained available; some colleges in the United States were apparently using it as late as 1960. It had become a significant bestseller, perhaps not in the class of the *Outline of History*, but it was nevertheless a very successful book, both for its authors, and for the students and others who used it over the years.[36]

The book was remarkable for what it covered. It is not too much to say that it was the first modern textbook of biology; its concept of the body as a machine, the study of the patterns of life, and its extraordinary section on evolution set it apart from any of its competitors. The sections on biology through time, as well as the introduction of modern ecological concepts, also set it apart. It included a strong section on what was then known of psychology, and even had a section on thought transference, and 'borderland' science as it was called. The book bore H. G. Wells's touch throughout and ended with a positive statement on man's future, especially if science were put to good use, and not to the evil purposes which many shortsighted individuals might expect:

For the stoicism of the scientific worker at any rate, there can be no complete defeat. And these mightier experiences and joys of the race to come will be in a sense ours, they will be consequence and fulfilment of our own joys and experiences, and a part, as we are a part, of the conscious growth of life, for which no man can certainly foretell either a limit or an end.

(Book IX, chapter 2)[37]

As Wells concluded the work on *The Science of Life*, he also began to promote a third in his series of textbooks for everyman. This one, designed to discuss economics, sociology, business, labour, leisure time, and political science, was more inchoate than the previous efforts, and nothing is more revealing of this than the fact that the book had a dozen or more working titles, before it finally appeared as *The Work, Wealth and Happiness of Mankind*. When first offered to prospective publishers late in 1928 it was described as 'The Business of Mankind, the how and why of work: A Plain Account of Man's Progressive Conquest of Power, Leisure and Abundance', and although this is not a bad description of what the book actually became, even H. G. Wells had no idea of the difficulty ahead before it reached its final form.[38]

Wells went at this work with collaborators, much as for the earlier outline of science. Hugh P. Vowles (who had known Wells since the Fabian days, and who had contributed a chapter to *The Great State*) and Edmund Cressey agreed to work with him. Wells did not give them each a third of the income from the book, as he had Huxley and G.P., however, and to some extent his troubles with the book stemmed from this decision. There was nothing wrong with the decision, of course. Vowles and Cressey were hired researchers, and Wells was to do all the collating and writing, and to take all the risks; but this meant that he did not have the psychological control he had maintained over the previous work.[39]

Vowles did not do the work Wells expected. As the *New Age* said when reviewing the controversy later, 'We imagine that Mr Vowles was to select and assemble the material, and Mr Wells was to turn it into a poem; and then when Mr Wells saw the material his vision perished.' This was partly true, but it was complicated by the fact that Wells had loaned Vowles about £800 before anything appeared. (The amounts were even in dispute.) Wells rejected his work, but Vowles maintained that he had met the terms of the contract. He and Herbert Thring, Secretary to the Society of Authors, proposed to sue Wells for the total amount agreed, £6,000. Letters flew back and forth between the two. Many of Wells's friends felt that he had not behaved too well, as he had used his power of invective to slander Vowles and Thring. The upshot of it all was that Wells paid a substantial fee to Vowles, in order to get free of him, and the controversy echoed in the press and literary circles for some time, leaving a very bad taste in nearly everyone's mouth.[40]

Wells was completely dispirited by the affair, and gave up on the idea of the book for a long period of time. It was not until he had spent a month or more on the Riviera, in his comforting home with Odette Keun, and had been visited by Galsworthy, as well as his grandchildren, that he began to look on the world in a slightly better light. As he told Watt,

> Down here one can get things clearer in one's mind. I can't give up the *Science of Work and Wealth*, it is too essential a part of my career. But the original scheme won't work. . . . After the last six weeks of toil upon *The Science of Life* I felt I could never work so hard again. But the job has to be done . . . tell George that vat is fermenting. . . . I will browse about here for a time before I make my decisions. Keep your market open and all will yet be well.[41]

Wells wished to put the book off in part because he wished to be free of Vowles, and this is where the difficulty in the spring of 1929 came from. As Wells said, early in the year, 'It may be necessary to carry the war into the enemy's camp', and he urged Watt to find a team of solicitors who were interested in this sort of practice. However, by the end of the year Wells was hard at work at the new version (Vowles was paid off, and Thring had been dismissed by the Society of Authors, so Wells was free of them, even if at some cost to his pocketbook). As he said in a tone of exultation, 'The confused scratchy bale of stuff you saw before is now somewhat shaped, architectural and coherent. I am altogether satisfied with it. I'm bringing it off.' Later, he told Watt, 'Now is the time for you to get very circumspect and active about the [book].' Wells wanted Watt to seek out Heinemann as publisher, feeling that this firm was more stable in the rickety London publishing world than Cassells. The economic slump cost him dearly, and when the book was eventually published, it appeared at a lower price, and his royalties were substantially less. Wells had wanted an advance of $30,000, but when Doubleday brought home to him the reality of the slump he took $20,000, under a contract negotiated with Doubleday when Wells visited America in 1933.[42]

Wells worked much harder on the book than he had expected when it began. However, his labour must have been more pleasant, as Amber (Reeves) Blanco-White took over the sections on money and economics, and Odette Keun acted as general editor of the work. Cressey continued his work, and A. M. Carr-Saunders, the great population demographer, supplied data and read the proof of the work. For Wells, however, it must have been equally pleasant to have his old friend Graham Wallas spend a good deal of time on the book. Wallas made many suggestions, rewrote parts of the book, read most of the galley proofs, and in many ways improved the work. Wells was very grateful to his friends, and the old days of *Mankind in the Making* seemed very close indeed. Wallas died soon after the book was published, and Wells wrote a warm obituary notice for his friend. The book restored to Wells many persons from his earlier life, and this was a boon, now that Jane had gone, and Arnold Bennett too, during the period of this great writing fever. The work, incidentally, also marked the beginning of the end of his relationship with Odette Keun, although it had been crumbling long since over Wells's unwillingness to marry her after Jane died.[43]

The book sold well, even though the Depression damaged sales substantially. Sales were reported from all over the world (Tokyo took 500 copies the first week) and the book sold 17,000 copies in its first month after publication in England. Wells did not think Doubleday had done enough for him (a not uncommon complaint, with Wells, about his publishers); and when he heard that his old friend William Baxter had had trouble in a collaborative effort, Wells told him magnanimously, 'but such is collaboration'.[44]

The book is an astounding work, especially when one considers that nothing like it had ever before been published. It features strong material on banking, economics, the increase of leisure time, and a history of educational ideas. Perhaps its most outstanding feature (for 1932) were histories of leisure time, games, the theatre, and entertainment. Short discrete sections on manufacturing discussed plastics, paper, resin, iron and steel, the transmission and generation of power, production of food, the development of architectural ideas, labour unions, legal education and ideas, banking, the gold standard and its recent abandonment; there is a good discussion of various powerful and wealthy persons. Chapter 11 was devoted to 'The Role of Women in the World's Work', and it discussed such matters as competitiveness and co-operation with men, the place of motherhood (much as Wells had done in the first decade of the century), as well as suggesting a special education and training for women to ensure equality. As was usual with Wellsian works of this period, it ended on a note of optimism. Our species could and, Wells thought, would organize life and time so that peace, brotherhood, and equality could be realized by all.

> What is the culminating effect of a survey of history, of the science of life, and of existing conditions? It is an effect of steadily accelerated growth in power, range, and understanding. . . . Progress continues in spite of every human fear and folly. . . . So far and beyond, this adventure may continue and our race survive. The impenetrable clouds that bound our life at last in every direction may hide innumerable trials and dangers, but there are no conclusive limitations even in their deepest shadows, and there are times and seasons, there are modes of exaltation — moments, as it were of revelation — when the whole universe about us seems bright with the presence of as yet unimaginable things.
>
> (Chapter 16)[45]

Wells had written the book for 'the young man in spectacles, the people who want to know, the journalist, the young professional man, the teacher, the hordes of people on the verge of politics, debating and literary society people, the young labour leaders'. This description of his audience occurs in a plea to Heinemann to make his books available at even lower prices, but it does describe Wells's audience. He had created three marvellous textbooks from which people could teach themselves, and once taught, could band together to change and modify the world. Those were his goals, and they were the goals of many of his followers. As the book began to take hold of mankind, along with its two predecessors, Wells the teacher, the instructor, the educational leader could look back and realize that the decade of hard slogging work had been remarkably profitable, in all ways.[46]

But he would have known that anyway. The friends he trusted most found this book the greatest *tour de force* of all, and the three together almost more than they could comprehend. Gregory said to him, 'You are the greatest moving force of our time, and your influence upon the minds of this generation and the next must be greater than you can ever imagine.' Olaf Stapledon, already under Wells's spell, called *The Science of Life* 'an unfailing source of delight', and he and Wells agreed to meet and discuss their writing over lunch. As Stapledon ended his letter, 'The fertility of Wellsian minds is astounding to slow persons like me.' But most of all Wells must have been pleased with the encomium of his old comrade, Wallas. Wallas sent on some possible corrections for the second edition, and gave Wells even more bibliographical items to look into, but it was his comment on Wells and his book which pleased most: 'If I were now a sixth-form boy of fifteen, as I was nearly sixty years ago, it would change the whole world for me, and though I have a lifetime of social thought behind me, it [the book] has given a new importance and proportion to my knowledge and feelings and ideas.'[47]

Simply writing and producing the textbooks, good as they might be, was not enough, of course. Wells felt he had an obligation to carry the message of these works to potential readers, just as he had remarked in his letter to Heinemann. Writing, talking, travelling — all were part of his continuously active life. There was much to do. There were many people to see. But, as long as life allowed, he would carry on his pilgrimage. The three textbooks were only the visible tip of what had become a way of life for H. G. Wells.

EDUCATING THE WORLD: WRITING AND ORGANIZING, 1921–1930

> My moods have fluctuated between hope and despair. But I know that I believe so firmly in this great World at Peace that lies so close to our own, ready to come into being as our wills turn towards it, that I must needs go about this present world of disorder and darkness like an exile doing such feeble things as I can towards the world of my desire, now hopefully, now bitterly, as the moods may happen, until I die.
>
> HGW, *Washington and the Hope of Peace* (1922)

Here, in this paragraph, written as the Washington Conference came to its end early in the winter of 1921, H.G. Wells indicated clearly the course he would follow for the rest of his life. The conference, the first significant gathering of world leaders to be held in the capital of the United States, marked the ascendance of the United States to world power, a recognition of the passing of leadership from the Old World to the New. In addition, along with the conference of some European powers at Rapallo, it marked the end of the settlements after the Great War. Of course, H.G. Wells, along with other close observers of these settlements, knew that the only thing that had really happened was the purchase of a bit of time, a respite: as the world universally termed it, an Armistice.

For, if the causes of the First World War had been the necessity to work out the position of Germany (and eventually, Russia) in the European heartland, along with the logical consequences of international capitalism in a world in which time, space, and distance had been destroyed, the peace did not deal with those causes. True, the immense loss of life and the vast expenditure of wealth had weakened both Britain and France terribly, although that weakness was not yet apparent. True, the Central Powers had lost, but the perceived Draconic peace of Versailles festered in the

Germanic soul. True, Russia and the United States had emerged as world powers of tremendous potential. However, both Russia and the United States, for different reasons, would now turn their backs on Europe and look inward. So, even with all these factors, the peace would prove to be just a respite. The causes of the war were surely not yet assuaged. More killing and greater expenditure still would be necessary before those matters would be resolved. Therefore, quick and alert observers could not help alternating between optimism and pessimism. Peace could be, might be, possible, but the path to peace was clogged with many obstacles.

Whether the population of the world could overcome these obstacles was questionable. Optimism increasingly became a surface emotion, for hidden beneath the hope was the understanding by many, and they certainly included H. G. Wells, that the foreshortening of time caused by the Industrial Revolution meant that the chances of success were rapidly becoming less and less. Perhaps, as Wells had prophesied so long ago, the second law of thermodynamics, the eventual victory of entropy, would come into play before peace prevailed. However, as long as life and breath remained, H.G. and his colleagues would work for peace — even in the face of rapid and extreme vacillations of mood. One simply had no choice except to dedicate one's life to the preservation of the species, to the final achievement of world peace.

In the first decade after the War, Wells wrote constantly on these questions. He undertook two year-long series of weekly articles for the press, both reprinted throughout the world. He made early visits to, and wrote strong accounts of, the two new superpowers — Russia and America. He stood for Parliament. He wrote fiction steadily with the goals of peace in mind — novels like *Men Like Gods* and *The Dream* which set out his view of what the world could become, as well as ones like *The World of William Clissold*, a self-conscious effort to return to a novel of artistic appeal, but with a message no different from the fantasies. Increasingly, as the decade went on, he turned also to prescriptive studies of what needed to be done and by whom.

As the tragedy of the Second World War began to loom just below the horizon, he increased his activity. It then became time to take his message to the world. In the last decade before the Second War, Wells began to travel, to speak, to proselytize and propagandize, to urge his followers to join what he called an 'Open Conspiracy' to wrench power from those who had over and over proved themselves to be untrustworthy. World history, as he had said, was a race between education and catastrophe. As time went on, the race became more desperate.

Although Wells clearly perceived the difficulties raised by the weak peace of Versailles, many casual observers in the world did not. The period between the wars for them became a sort of lull, a long weekend, to use Robert Graves's apposite phrase. Even so, Wells's popularity did not diminish. After the success of the *Outline of History*, his caustic pen and keen eye for detail were in constant demand with the semi-popular press. And although he did not agree to all the offers — refusing, for instance, commissions for pieces on religion, Scotland, spiritualism, and even a weekly book column similar to Arnold Bennett's — he did take on several important projects. The first of these was a trip to Russia, where he was one of the earliest observers after the Bolshevik Revolution had more or less stabilized matters.[1]

Wells had a very strong interest in Russia. He had visited St. Petersburg and Moscow in January of 1914. Among his friends in London was Ivy Low, daughter of his former comrade, Walter Low, who had recently married Maxim Litvinov, who was to be the first ambassador to England of the Bolshevik state. Wells stayed with them in Petrograd (once St. Petersburg, it had not yet been renamed Leningrad) on his 1920 tour. Ivy Low's sister was married to Haden Guest, a Wells acquaintance from the Fabian days. (In fact, as we have seen, she may well have been the elusive Fabian wife supposedly seduced by Wells.) Haden Guest had recently travelled in Russia, as had Bertrand Russell. Both had written articles critical of the Bolsheviks on their return to England. Wells had met Maxim Gorky as early as 1906, and although they had not yet become close friends, Wells had stayed with Gorky in Moscow in 1914. It was logical for the Bolsheviks, unhappy about the British comments, and still smarting from the Allied invasion after the Revolution, along with the not-so-subtle efforts to keep them in the war during the Brest-Litovsk negotiations, to invite Wells to visit his acquaintances, in order to redress the balance.

Lev Kamenev and Leonid Krassin, trade ministers to Britain, approached Wells and asked him to come to Russia. Gorky sent him a letter as well, commenting on the British response to the Revolution with, '. . . it seems to me that the capitalist sections of Europe have become absolutely brutal in their greed and vengeance.' Gorky also told Wells how much he had liked the *Outline of History*, and discussed its translation into Russian. It seemed logical to Wells, too, to accept the invitation, to have G. P. Wells accompany him (his Russian learnt at Oundle would come in handy), and for Wells then to give his views to the press in England.[2]

Wells received £1,000 from the *Sunday Express* for articles on his Russian trip. He promised at least three (and produced five). The fee covered British, United States, and Canadian rights, and Wells also agreed not to give any long interviews or write other articles until after his *Express* pieces appeared. He stayed just over a week in Petrograd, just under a week in Moscow, and spent a weekend with Gorky. Altogether he and Gip spent fifteen days in Russia. Gip took photographs on the trip, many of which were used to illustrate a book, *Russia in the Shadows*, published early in 1921. While in Russia they met Chaliapin, Zinoviev, and Chicherin, to name three who gave Wells interviews. The visitors went to the ballet and to the opera, and were also allowed to spend a fair amount of time on their own. This was true especially after they were shown a 'Potemkin village' version of a school. Wells protested the fraud and the regime acquiesced in a greater amount of freedom.

While in Russia Wells also viewed a long film on the various nationalities of the Soviet state, made at a congress in Baku. This film returned to England with him, and was later shown in English cinemas. He had hoped to visit Lunacharsky (Commissar for Education), but was unable to do so, in the hectic aftermath of the civil war. Wells did visit the Petrograd Soviet, which he compared, in his article, to the Third Duma, which he had visited with Maurice Baring in 1914. At the Soviet, he gave a short speech in English, arranged by his Russian friends, in which he described himself as not a Marxist or a communist, but rather a collectivist. The speech had been translated into Russian, and the translation was also read out to the Soviet. It was published in great part the next day in *Pravda*. Gip's facility in Russian allowed them to monitor the translation and its publication.

The great coup of the trip for Wells was a long interview with Lenin. It was conducted in English (in which Lenin was fluent, as he was in German). The two men talked past each other, however, with Wells asking Lenin what the goals of the Revolution were and Lenin asking Wells when the English revolution was to come. Lenin also spent much of the time talking of how electrification would solve many of Russia's problems, and urged Wells to return in a decade to see what had been accomplished. Lenin was also quite indiscreet with Wells, telling him why an American financier, Frank Vanderlip, had arrived in Moscow at this same time. Vanderlip was apparently attempting to work out a deal by which the Russians would give the US a naval base on the Siberian coast, along with a treaty of friendship and alliance directed against Japan, in exchange for long-term and large amounts of American foreign aid to help in the restoration of the country. The treaty idea fell through, and mention of it today suggests how unstable and fragile the Russian state was soon after the war. For his part Lenin later described Wells (according to Trotsky) as 'an unreconstructed bourgeois'. But the interview was still a memorable and significant occasion, and allows us today yet another look at the early Bolshevik world.[3]

We have still another view of the trip, as Claire Sheridan, a famous left-wing beauty of the day, was visiting Moscow at the same time, in order to sculpt busts of Lenin and others. She and Wells knew each other, as Wells had advised her on her children's education. Wells, Gip, and Sheridan, as well as Vanderlip, were housed in the same hotel, where they found themselves being entertained by Michael Borodin, high in the government of the day. Wells told Sheridan about Lenin's indiscretion over Kamchatka, and they both assumed that the revelation, although seemingly naïve, had in fact been made on purpose. Lenin gave her the same information while she was sculpting his bust. Lenin also mentioned to her that he had just finished *Joan and Peter*, after Wells's visit; he told

Sheridan that he was impressed with Wells's powers of description. He also said that he was going to read *The War in the Air* and *The World Set Free*, for which he had not had time before. (It seems Lenin had in his office copies of the *Daily Herald* for late September 1920, which he allowed Sheridan to borrow for the Kremlin guest house.) Taken together with Wells's own account, Sheridan's diary notes extend the view we have of Wells, a middle-class Englishman, faced with the Russia of revolution, intrigued by it, and by its leaders, but also concerned that without the help, especially of America but of the west generally, Bolshevik Russia would not succeed, and with failure might bring down western civilization in the aftermath.[4]

Wells's articles in the *Express* created a furore, as they were among the first clearly sympathetic reports from Russia since the Revolution. Claire Sheridan's cousin, Winston Churchill, responded almost immediately, asking Wells if 'cancer could repent'? Wells produced an immediate rejoinder to Churchill; originally he had not wanted to comment, but, under pressure from his friends, he agreed reluctantly to respond. In the event he was vitriolic about Churchill. 'Although I am an older man than Mr Churchill', was his opening,

> and have spent most of my life watching and thinking about a world in which he has been rushing about vehemently from one excitement to another, he has the impudence to twit me with superficiality. . . . He believes quite naïvely that he belongs to a peculiarly gifted and privileged class of beings to whom the lives and affairs of common men are given over, the raw material for brilliant careers. . . . He is the running sore of waste in our Government. . . . He has smeared his vision with human blood, and we are implicated in the things he abets. He does not stand alone. This vision of his, grotesque and distorted though it may be, is no more and no less contemptible than some misshapen idol esteemed by the tribe, to which we may presently see our children sacrificed.

Wells's diatribe in the *Express*, carried over into a second week, ended by suggesting that Churchill retire from public life in order to become the brilliant painter he could with some effort be.[5] Churchill did not reply.

Another who levied a strong attack on Wells because of his views on Russia was his old friend and companion, the playwright Henry Arthur Jones. Jones addressed a series of letters to Wells in the world press, misquoting him, attributing to Wells comments he had never made, and all in the cause of preventing Wellsian views on Bolshevism from gathering much support. Wells was quite forbearing with Jones, as compared with his behaviour with Churchill, only responding to Jones to correct obvious errors and lies. Jones's method of attack was very similar to that of Belloc; he provided his own gloss on Wells's remarks, and eventually Wells described the playwright's efforts as 'senile obstinacy' with which, he said, 'he repeats lies'. But, by and large, he thought Jones 'too silly and incoherent' to respond to. The exchange of letters gave readers some moments of amusement, both in the original and in an extraordinary book, *My Dear Wells* (1921), edited by Jones, which reprinted much of the correspondence. Wells had eventually to threaten a lawsuit with regard to the book, however, before Jones would retract some of his remarks. What the incident shows is the great rift which had grown up in Britain (and in the United States) over the postwar treatment of Russia.[6]

More important than these teapot hurricanes was the fact that Wells had become a significant figure in interpreting Russia to the west. Gorky and he maintained a vigorous correspondence for some time thereafter, and Wells was instrumental in getting the British Association to send scientific books to its colleagues in Russia. Frederick Soddy's articles and work on the atom (on which *The World Set Free* was based) were among the first items translated by the Russians. Later, after the Kronstadt rebellion, Gorky asked Wells for even more help, for under martial law, which had been imposed, the scientific interchange which had begun with the earlier books was diminished. Gorky left Russia for Berlin and the west for a time, to oversee publications, but continued to report to Wells on his translation work, and Wells continued to aid him and even provided funds for the publication of certain translations, which were done in Berlin. Gorky was almost pathetically glad of Wells's help with the translation and the transmission of books, as well as over his expressions of hope, especially for the literary and scientific community. The Russians (or at least the Russian intelligentsia) knew they had in Wells, if not a friend, at least a well-disposed onlooker.[7]

After Lenin died early in 1924, the Russians continued to think of Wells as a friend, although the organization of the Russian state was such that friendship was always viewed with suspicion. Wells, when commenting on Lenin's death, said that he had not changed his mind much about Russia. He was still concerned that Russian recovery, although more rapid than he had predicted, still lagged behind because of the overt hostility of the west.[8]

Later, after more normal relations were established between Russia and Britain (that is, once the furore over the fraudulent Zinoviev Letter had died down), the new ambassador to the Court of St. James's, Ivan Maisky, renewed Russian ties with Wells. He wrote several times to Wells and the two men came to be fairly good friends, sending each other books, as well as dining and lunching together on occasion. Wells and Maisky supplemented the formal ties between the nations, and were, one supposes, useful to their respective governments. At their meetings, the two men debated the philosophical issues of the Russian Revolution, and Maisky did his best to convert Wells into a believer, but Wells resisted with very little effort. Maisky later, at Wells's request, provided some data for *The Work, Wealth and Happiness of Mankind*. Wells and Maisky were to become much more friendly when Maisky returned to London after a posting to the Far East, but for the time being, each remained a source of information to the other.[9]

The other significant trip Wells took at the beginning of the decade was to cover the Disarmament Conference in Washington in November 1921. The *New York World* asked him to cover the conference for them, and he agreed. In the event the dispatches he filed were also printed by the *Daily Mail* in London, at least until they protested at his comments on Aristide Briand. Briand had spoken at the conference in what Wells thought was a minatory and provincial way after the considerable efforts of American Secretary of State Charles Evans Hughes to get the conference off to a strong and even radical effort at true disarmament. The *Chicago Tribune*, and some other newspapers, printed most of Wells's pieces, but the *Daily Mail* took only the first fourteen. Eventually, in 1922, the entire series (twenty-nine articles) was reprinted in a book which in England bore the title *Washington and the Hope of Peace*, and in America *Washington and the Riddle of Peace*.[10]

Wells's dispatches are a very good account of the conference, thought at the time to herald a new direction in world affairs. This view was enhanced by the solemn ceremony, which Wells attended, dedicating the tomb of the American Unknown Soldier, an event analogous to one he had attended in London. However, as he noted, 'peace' as a goal soon gave way to 'security', and although some efforts were made at disarmament, the peace of the Pacific rim was not achieved, only delayed. Wells's articles in the series on Japan and China, as well as on aerial warfare, were remarkably prescient; rereading them today, one is struck by the accuracy of his predictions. He, however, was disturbed by the return of 'business (or diplomacy) as usual', and he left the conference very dispirited at its failure to achieve the great promise prefigured in the first Hughes speech. As Wells said in his article of 30 November,

> The plain fact of the Pacific situation is that there are only three courses before the world — either unchallenged Japanese domination in Eastern Asia from now on, or a war to prevent it soon, or an alliance of America, Britain, and Japan, with whatever government China may develop, and with the other powers concerned, though perhaps less urgently concerned — an alliance of all these, for mutual restraint and mutual protection.

This conference was the first such large occasion of which radio, as well as newspapers, provided coverage, a development that intrigued Wells. For that reason, coupled with the site, many newspapers covered the event. André Géraud (Pertinax) covered the meetings for the *Echo de Paris*, along with Wickham Steed (*The Times*), Maurice Low (*Morning Post*), H.W. Nevinson (*Manchester Guardian*), J.A. Spender (*Westminster Gazette*), P.W.

25 Wells arriving to cover the World Disarmament Conference in Washington, October 1921

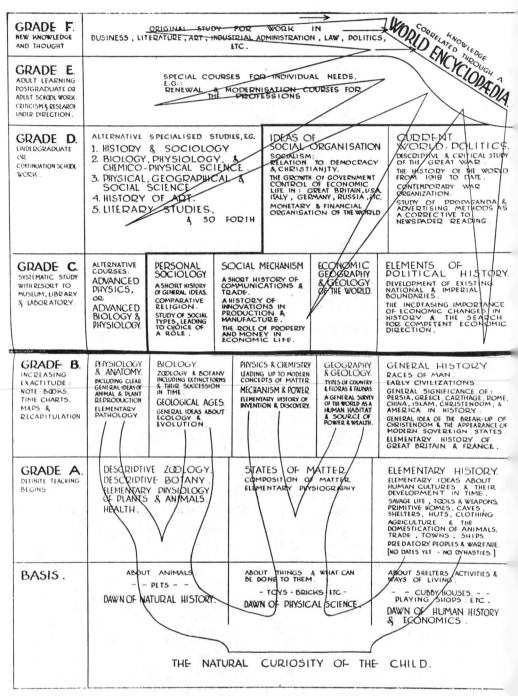

26 Chart illustrating 'The Informative Content of Education'

Wilson (*Daily News*), as well as Wells himself for the *Mail* and Charles À Court Remington for the *Telegraph*. Wells's correspondence for the period has apparently not survived, but Remington kept a diary later published. He and Wells crossed together on the S.S. *Adrianople*, along with Chaliapin, on his way to a Metropolitan Opera engagement. The three of them, with others, spent a good deal of time analysing their hopes for the conference before it began.

Wells and Remington remained in contact after the conference got under way, and to some degree Wells's understanding of the Asian situation was enhanced by the views of Remington, who had had a long service in the Far East as a military and diplomatic correspondent. Wells was bemused by the changes in America since his only previous visit, in 1906, and watched much more than he talked, according to Remington, simply viewing what was going on. He was remarkably subdued in Washington, refusing to speak at a reception for the British press at the Embassy, although he gave his views, *sotto voce*, to Remington, especially on Sir Auckland Geddes, the British ambassador, who represented much of what Wells abhorred in government. According to Remington the French attempt at censorship was the work of a malicious member of the French delegation, in a deliberate effort to shut Wells up. Remington and Wells, along with their chief companion, H. W. Nevinson, thought the conference both interesting and significant, but all three also thought that a greater opportunity had probably been missed.[11]

Whether it was the general success of these investigatory trips, or perhaps the public attention he received because of the *Outline*, Wells was persuaded to offer himself as a candidate for the seat in Parliament allotted to the University of London. Sidney Webb had contested the seat in 1918, and had lost heavily, receiving only some 1,000 votes and barely retaining his deposit. By 1922, it was clear that a general election was in the offing and Wells was now selected as the Labour candidate. R. H. Tawney made a small fuss in protest at Labour Party headquarters, saying he preferred Bertrand Russell, as Wells was 'a cad'. Beatrice and Sidney Webb both refuted this charge, however, and she remarked to her diary that it was 'hardly relevant if it is sexual morality which is to be the test' for the electorate. Once Wells was adopted as candidate, Beatrice arranged an occasion at which Jane and H.G. were to meet most of the Labour leaders. Unfortunately the participants in the meeting did not carry on the detailed discussion she wished.

Another faction also denounced Wells's candidacy because he was vice-president of the Neo-Malthusian League, and an ardent spokesman for birth control. This attack was readily answered in the press by the Reverend Cosmo Lang and G. A. Gaskell, a leader in the birth-control movement. They pointed out that his vice-presidency had nothing to do with socialism, except, as Wells had said and Lang accepted, that 'open and avowed Socialists like myself and Mr Lang ... believe ... that Birth Control, like Socialism, is inevitable'. After some further letters on the subject the correspondence was closed, although it was clear from the exchange that a new ethical standard was at least being discussed in Labour Party circles. Wells passed the only tests that were significant, however; it was his socialism that was at issue, not his sexual preferences or other notions.[12]

The election occurred fairly soon after Wells's adoption as candidate. He issued two statements (the second after the Post Office refused the first as carrying information on a book of his, which was termed advertising), and he made one significant speech for the party, at Manchester. In his formal election address, later withdrawn, he discussed the reasons he was a Labour Party representative at this time, as he believed that the party and its policy were the only 'steady, watchful, generous, comprehensive, scientific re-organization [force] amid the strained, shattered, wasteful, and life-destroying confusion in which we live today'. The other parties were simply 'adventuristic'. He said that for him the issues were better education and better medicine. He called for improvement in the League of Nations as well.

> Let us get on with scientific research and teaching, get on with education, get on with production, get on with the development of international controls and world disarmament, and at any cost to the less vital and productive elements of our community, save the homes and children, the health, the standards of life and the self-respect of our common people in the years of hardship and difficulty that are certainly before us.[13]

Although this leaflet was withdrawn, enough copies circulated for it to be read in many parts of Wells's constituency. It was replaced by the account of a talk he gave to a meeting of supporters at Millbank School in London. The talk was given on 3 November, in the week prior to the general election, and it immediately appeared as a pamphlet. Josiah Wedgwood presided at the meeting, and Wells was introduced by H. N. Brailsford. Wells gave his listeners a short history of socialism, and commented especially on the impact of the Great War. He said, as might be expected, that education was the key to the future, and accused the older parties of ducking the issue. He said that Lloyd George avoided the issue like a sparrow, and Bonar Law like an earthworm, while he proposed to meet it head-on. For Asquith the issue apparently did not exist. The Labour Party was 'the only party existing now with a real sense of obligation to the common weal'. Others on the platform were Mrs Philip Snowden and Hamilton Fyfe, editor of the *Daily Herald*. The Webbs, Eileen Power, H.J. Laski, G. D. H. Cole, Hugh Dalton, Haden Guest, Israel Zangwill, and R. A. Gregory were all apparently in the audience. Wells did poll higher than Webb had in 1918, but still came third in the postal ballot. The Tory candidate, Sydney Russell Wells, received 4,037 votes, with Professor Frederick Pollard, campaigning as a Liberal, receiving 2,593. Wells received 1,420 votes.[14]

Wells agreed to stand once more; and he did not have a long time to wait, as a new general election, which brought the Labour Party to power, was called within a year. The Countess of Warwick also stood in this election, in which the Labour Party made its strongest bid up to that time, contesting nearly every seat. Of course, both Lady Warwick and Wells were fighting seats never held by Labour representatives. (Her Tory opponent at Warwick and Leamington was Anthony Eden.) Wells worked for her, as well as for his own candidacy. This time he also worked much harder on behalf of the party. He spoke, as early as March 1923, to the University of London Club at a dinner given in his honour by his supporters. Gregory chaired the meeting. In this speech, later printed under the title *Socialism and the Scientific Method*, Wells referred to the Snowden–Mond debate recently held in the House of Commons. Snowden's speech had galvanized the country, and was the clearest statement of socialism's goals up to that time. Wells told his University supporters that it was necessary to limit wealth, and urged a capital levy to pay for needed work in the country on schools, hospitals, and health-care facilities.

> We of the Labour Party, as a party, believe in science and in the scientific motive as a motive altogether superior to profit-seeking. We believe in the salaried man, who chooses his work for the sake of his work. We believe in teachers; we believe in the spirit of creative science in the minds and hearts of men. We do not believe in the profiteer and his distinctive outlook. . . .

He made much the same points in his election address, which was posted before the election was called, and reissued once the call was official. Wells again urged increased expenditure for education and public health, and he also urged adoption of proportional representation.[15]

Wells gave other speeches as well. At a joint meeting of teachers, sponsored by the Teachers Union, held in Essex Hall, Wells spoke, as did Soddy. Others who spoke briefly were Mrs Harrison Bell, president of the National Union of Teachers, and Alderman Connors, vice-president and president-elect of the Union. Two weeks later Wells appeared in the same building, this time to address a general meeting of supporters. The crowded hall heard him say, 'We are now living in a collapsing civilization. That makes the choice [of an MP] an urgent matter.' He said that the Labour Party wanted a real League of Nations, and to abolish armament. He called for an anti-waste programme, essentially a nationalization of transport and mines, and the installation of a capital levy. Wells was also active for other candidates, as he threw himself into the campaign in a way unusual for university candidates.[16]

Pollard, the Liberal candidate, accused Wells of dividing the University of London vote, but his agent said in response that Wells had offered to withdraw, if Pollard would give some assurances to Labour. Pollard was the dog in the manger, not Wells. During the campaign, Wells also used his regular weekly column in the *Westminster Gazette* to call for proportional representation. The paper endorsed the idea, but came out for the Liberals the following week.[17]

Wells garnered a longer list of supporters this time out. About 175 persons signed the list, including D. N. Pritt, R. H. Tawney, and T.L. Humberstone, who had not been on the previous list. It did little good. Wells ran about the same; the turn-out was lower, but he still came third in the ballot:

Sydney Russell Wells (C.)	3,833
Frederick Pollard (Lib.)	2,180
H. G. Wells (Lab.)	1,427

Wells announced that he would not stand again. He said that it was 'embarrassing to mental freedom to discuss such questions as the League of Nations, vivisection, and denominational schools in the absurdly general way necessary when the immediate reaction in votes' had to be considered. Most of his friends, especially ones like Gregory, gave a sigh of relief. Wells had made his point, but it was clear to all that his place was outside Parliamentary debates.[18]

The election foray had not been wasted. It gave Wells some leverage, especially on university issues, in the newly formed Labour Government. It also gave him something more of an inside view, and his columns in the press reflected this, with a barrage of well-thought-out articles on governance, especially in the divided House which had resulted. More and more he campaigned for proportional representation. He also chastised the Labour leaders for wearing court dress and for their support of more ships for the Royal Navy. He called for a downward extension of the franchise and removal of all restrictions (this did not occur until 1945, when the university seats were also abolished). He was terribly disappointed by the Labour Party's acquiescence in business as usual, and especially by Ramsay MacDonald, although this disappointment was shared by many others.[19]

These attacks by Wells on the Labour Party itched and festered, especially as they all appeared in the Liberal paper, the *Westminster Gazette*. Because Wells was writing a weekly column at the time for the *Gazette*, many in the Labour Party felt he was a traitor. The *Daily Herald* called for a discussion of Wells's acts, but those persons who were not completely blinkered supported his right to speak, and especially so after H.W. Massingham, editor of the *Herald*, also defended his right to comment. Massingham said that many in the Cabinet actually agreed with Wells's views, especially on matters like PR and the vote for youth. Some of the attacks on Wells were levied by persons who had been conscientious objectors in the war, and they vilified him for his support of the conflict. Massingham and others simply did not allow this sort of slander and the debate wound down fairly quickly.[20]

One more piece of fall-out came through Wells's election bids. That was a brief and not very successful effort to reform scientific education in the University of London. It was led by T. L. Humberstone, a former colleague, and as indicated, a strong supporter of Wells in the election campaign; Wells returned the favour with a donation of funds and a preface to a pamphlet calling for reform. He also became involved in an equally vain attempt to create a more radical Labour paper, but, when other pledges of funds did not materialize, he withdrew the £2,000 he had originally agreed to contribute. This venture marked the virtual end of Wells's formal participation in electoral politics, although he would dabble on the fringes again a bit later.[21]

Just as Wells had been in demand for his political contributions, he was in great demand for articles of every sort for the press. He wrote his regular columns, first for the *Westminster Gazette*, and later for the *New York Times* and the *Daily Express*. He also was responsible for a great many less serious articles, mostly in monthly magazines, published on both sides of the Atlantic. It would make little sense to discuss all these pieces, many of which were topical in the extreme; on the other hand, a few are worth a brief mention, as an indication of how his words were sought in the wake of the fame created by the *Outline of History*. It gave H. G. Wells a great opportunity which he was happy to seize — both to propagandize for his views, and to increase his income, which grew rapidly throughout the decade.

As examples of the frothier type of material for which he was solicited, one could cite articles on 'The Six Greatest Men in History' (Jesus, Buddha, Aristotle, Asoka, Roger Bacon, and Abraham Lincoln). He wrote on Christianity and Christ, listed his ten most important books (Isaiah, Mark, Confucius' *The Great Learning*, Plato's *Republic*, Aristotle's *History of Animals*, *Travels of Marco Polo*, Copernicus' *Revolution of the Heavens*, Bacon's *New Atlantis*, Newton's *Principia*, and *The Origin of Species*). He urged people to read history, newspapers, *Nature* or *Scientific American*, biography, and great literature in general.

He discussed his school of the future (in response to letters about his choice of books), and called for a much greater expenditure of funds, offering Oundle School as a model. 'There is', he said, 'an enormous opposition, active and passive, on the part of the prosperous and influential undereducated. They fear education — for others and for themselves.' He went on to lay out a syllabus, not much different from that he would propose to the teachers in 1937. Later he was agreeable to making prophecies, saying he believed that a period of consolidation was due before another great spurt of invention.

He said psychoanalysis offered much for the future, as we began to understand human nature better. He thought that the future might provide an answer to the causes of crime. He discussed success, in a long article based on his close knowledge of Lord Northcliffe from his youth through his later life; and he addressed schoolmasters as to their role, in a paper already cited. Later he was asked to list the ten most important discoveries (morality, social restraint, speech, fire, the domestication of animals, cultivation of the soil, control of water, writing, the invention of money, the abolition of distance, the impact of the scientific method, and education for all — twelve, all told). Perhaps the ultimate in this type of exercise was a listing of the most important dates in history, of which he found seventeen.[22]

Although this sort of writing may seem simply pot-boiling, it is interesting that Wells took even it seriously as to construction and content. In addition, he wrote a great many other articles which were truly serious, and which as the decade went on came to dominate his thinking. At the suggestion of Winston Churchill and Brendan Bracken he wrote a long and detailed article in which he discussed the future of the British Empire, especially in a world in which communication and transportation were changing so rapidly. He discussed the possibility of an Anglo-Saxon union, and told his readers that the British Empire could be a loving trustee for an unborn heir, the world federation, led by English-speaking peoples. He summarized many of these same views, especially with regard to potential changes in transport and communication, in a long and thoughtful piece for the *Encyclopaedia Britannica* which published a two-volume work on the impact of World War I. His prescriptions will not surprise those who have read of his life to this point:

> What is necessary is a substitution for the present teaching of patriotic prejudice in schools, colleges, newspapers, pulpits, homes and every channel of diffusion and suggestion, of a teaching at least as effective and comprehensive of the idea and means of realizing the idea of a common world organization to keep the peace and exploit the resources of the race and of the earth collectively and in the common interest.[23]

He wrote on many subjects and he canvassed his friends for the latest ideas and information so that his remarks remained pithy, accurate, and with a bite to them. Sydney Olivier commented on India and imperialism, Marie Beets on railway strikes, Léon Blum offered comments on France, and Wells and Ray Lankester continued to meet and discuss matters as long as Lankester was able. Gregory also remained as close a friend as ever, of course. Others who provided Wells with information and suggestions included Bertrand Russell, Fenner Brockway, J. D. Beresford, and, of course, Arnold Bennett. As Wells said to Gregory when that old friend had provided yet another piece of information, and had ended his letter with high praise for Wells and his work, 'I do not deserve a tithe of your praise, and if I have done anything in the world it is largely because you and Simmons did so much for me in the crucial years to make me believe in myself. I have had some stout friends and you have been chief among them.'[24] Wells always attracted strong intellectual friends, and his sharp mind and analytical pen were always available to instruct those who now besieged book shops and newsagents for the results of his thinking.

Among the areas in which Wells was most interested was the potential of flying and aircraft, and this became an important part of his prescriptions for the future, along with his old *bêtes noire* of bad schools and bad teaching, and the failures of the League really to act as a Parliament of the world.[25]

His comments on other countries and other areas remain significant even after sixty years. Many of the matters he remarked upon continue as trouble spots, and it is significant that he was one of the first to analyse Fascism and Nazism; his comments on the impact of racism are also very prescient. He wrote articles on Latin America and called for a regional League to act as a forerunner for his world federation. He found Fascism abhorrent and compared its motives (after the Matteotti affair) to those of the Klan in America. His remark on the membership of such movements needs remembering:

> The underlying fact in all these matters is that the common uneducated man is a violent fool in social and public affairs. He can work in no way better than his quality. He has not sufficient understanding to work in any other way. If there were no Fascism there would be something else of the same sort. The hope of the world lies in a broader and altogether more powerful organization of education. Only as that develops will the vehement self-righteous and malignant ass abate his mischief in the world.[26]

He wrote on India, China, America, the need to save the whales (in 1924!), the drift towards dictatorship in the wake of the war, and offered ideas on how to prevent race and colour conflict from occurring. These articles and others from his year with the *Westminster Gazette* received high praise and comment, both at the time of their newspaper publication and when they appeared in book form, in *A Year of Prophesying*. Wells described the year-long effort: 'The total effect of these articles and these books of mine on my mind, is of a creature trying to find its way out of a prison into which it has fallen.' The deadlines had become simply too difficult to maintain.

Frank Swinnerton called the collection of pieces the best Christmas present he had, and even Leo Amery reached back to the old Co-efficients days to tell Wells that he disagreed with much in the book, but urged him to keep up his 'flights of fancy'; Amery described him as a 'free and irresponsible artist'. In a later paragraph, he continued his praise of Wells and his work by remarking, 'So, My dear Mr Pegasus, go on caracoling between the flowery meadows and the blue empyrean and I shall continue to enjoy watching your flights and gambols, as I pull my cart along.'[27]

Wells wrote steadily throughout the decade of the 1920s. In addition to his travel accounts, textbooks, articles, and volumes of newspaper prose, he also produced a number of novels which relate to his goals of the time. The first of these was *Men Like Gods*, a return to his fiction about the future, which appeared in 1923. In this story Mr Barnstaple is transported through a time warp (with others) into a world of the future. Those transported are English 'types' and are thinly disguised contemporary figures, Winston Churchill, Lord Beaverbrook, Edward Marsh, and others. These travellers, leaving the 'Age of Confusion', find themselves in a world filled with pastel shades, peace, a controlled environment, and generally the good life. The travellers, or at least most of them, attempt to subvert this world to one they know better. The conflict is especially well observed in the case of religious ideas. An ecological stance, through a sort of controlled eugenics, is hinted at in the new world. A moving description of the reaction of Richard Gregory and Wells to the death of Tommy Simmons (chapter 7, section 3) forms part of the dialogue between the old world and the new, as each explains to the other their differences. The earth people, however, create medical problems for the new world, and are quarantined. While they are quarrelling among themselves as to what they should do, Barnstaple is able to perceive the Utopian world clearly and to set down the five principles governing life there:

1. Principle of Privacy
2. Principle of Free Movement
3. Principle of Unlimited Knowledge
4. Principle that Lying is the Blackest Crime
5. Principle of Free Discussion and Criticism

(Book III, chapter 2)

Wells's question to the readers of the book is whether the dystopia (the earth in 1921) can become the Utopia of the five principles, and Barnstaple volunteers his services to show the way. In Utopia, entropy is finally conquered, as the old Utopian, Sungold, remarks to Barnstaple:

'Some day here and everywhere, Life of which you and I are but anticipatory atoms and eddies, life will awaken indeed, one and whole and marvellous, like a child awaking to conscious life. It will open its drowsy eyes and stretch itself and smile, looking the mystery of God in the face as one meets the morning sun. We shall be there then, all that matters of us, you and I. . . .

'And it will be no more than a beginning, no more than a beginning. . . .'

(Book III, chapter 3)

This theme of possible worlds was a strong one for Wells, and his next novel, *The Dream* (1924), essentially reverses the idea of *Men Like Gods*, to offer a lively discussion. A visitor from the future, Sarnac, returns, via a dream sequence, from his Utopian future to the Age of Confusion at about the time of World War I. The world he sees mirrors some of H. G. Wells's early life, especially his education, and there is much on the mistreatment of women in the old world. The question of drinking, the problems of single women, and the role of funeral rites in that world are all discussed. Wells creates one of his greatest characters in this book, the lodging-house keeper, Matilda Good. Her boarding house in Pimlico is a wonderful comic re-creation of that relic of Victorian life (Wells was to return to the setting in *Christina Alberta's Father* with its boarding house in Tunbridge Wells). An unfortunate marriage takes place in the old world during the trauma of the war, followed by divorce and all the terrible problems of a failed marriage. Sarnac is killed by the problem husband, after he falls totally in love with the divorced wife, and is returned to the new world. He is moved to emotional fantasy as he finishes his dream, and the book ends with the promise of the dream — a promise for the Age of Confusion more than the age of the future, where it has already been realized.

> 'It was a life,' [he says] . . . 'and it was a dream, a dream within this life; and this life too is a dream. Dreams within dreams, dreams containing dreams, until we come at last, maybe, to the Dreamer of all dreams, the Being who is all beings. Nothing is too wonderful for life and nothing is too beautiful. . . . All night we have been talking and living in the dark Ages of Confusion and now the sunrise is close at hand.'

These two novels have not had as much discussion as Wells's earlier Utopias nor his volumes on the promise of the world of the twentieth century. They are interesting books, none the less, for they mark a shift away from his occasional pessimism immediately after World War I. His public found them rather daunting, however, at a time when no one wished to think much except about himself and his immediate life. *Men Like Gods*, in particular, was hard to handle. The *Daily Herald* could not get a review copy, and enlisted Wells's help. When the review appeared it was harsh and unforgiving, and Wells responded. The paper's editor, Hamilton Fyfe, agreed with Wells, and set up a competition for reviews of the book, which resulted in much correspondence, discussion, increased newspaper and book sales, and eventually a favourable review of the novel. The winning reviewer remarked that 'the optimist is the true revolutionary', and said that that was the strength of Wells's book, calling him the 'man with the greatest vision in England'.[28]

The more established critics liked the book quite well. The *New Generation*, organ of the Neo-Malthusian group, welcomed it for its honest discussion of birth-control. 'Science has conquered all obstacles to a peaceful and happy existence,' they said, and went on to quote portions of

the book on matters of reproduction. The first issue of the *Adelphi*, a new
magazine of literary opinion founded by J. Middleton Murry, also
considered *Men Like Gods* marvellous; H. W. Tomlinson called Wells the
'most remarkable phenomenon in English literature since Dickens'.
Tomlinson said he knew instinctively that Churchill, Balfour, and
Beaverbrook were comic figures, and the book simply proved the case. The
Adelphi review was quoted at length by the *Herald*, as they attempted to
make amends to Wells. Wells himself remarked later that Churchill had
threatened to run away with the book, giving lovely speeches and starting
wars, and that he 'had to stun him' to get the novel under control. The
Churchill figure was stronger in the serial, and Walter Lippman was sorry
that that section, 'Ideas Like Wine', had been cut out in the book itself. He
told Wells that the public needed both ideas and wine and was ignorant of
them. Eventually Richard Aldington, stranded in Geneva for a weekend,
claimed that *Men Like Gods* had saved his life; so the book made a strong
impact, even with the problem of the early mediocre reviews.[29]

Most reviewers of *The Dream* did not like that novel as much, although
nearly everyone thought Matilda Good a Dickensian character and one of
Wells's best of that type. Philip Tomlinson, also writing in the *Adelphi*, after
summarizing other reviews and praising the book, said: 'In *The Dream*,
there is no mirthful ferocity; he forces us to hate the sin and love the
sinner.... this is art, surely' — perhaps the best contemporary
comment.[30]

Wells's next novel, *The World of William Clissold* (1926), is quite different
from its predecessors, but close analysis of it today shows that it is a
transitional volume, leading to *Meanwhile* and *The Open Conspiracy*, as well
as the more didactic novels at the end of the decade. *William Clissold* was a
return in some ways to the Victorian three-decker novels. It is lengthy,
discursive, filled with passages of scientific and philosophical disquisition;
at the same time, it is interesting for its depiction of the life of decaying
capitalism in the middle of the 1920s. It is also important for its treatment
of Odette Keun, who by this time had replaced Rebecca West as Wells's
mistress. It was important enough in its time to elicit a parody, *The World of
Billiam Wissold*.[31]

William Clissold opens with a seven-page 'Note Before the Title Page' in
which Wells explicitly refutes the idea that the book is a *roman à clef*. The
novel is then dedicated to Odette Keun, 'self-forgetful friend and helper'.
A long soliloquy follows in which Ray Lankester and Jung are invoked as
experts in their respective areas. Lankester appears under another name
(Sir Rupert York), but later told Wells he did not at all mind the thin
disguise. Much of this part of the book, and other pages of philosophical
speculation, are related to *First and Last Things* and *God the Invisible King*.
Wells had been rereading his earlier books, putting them together in the
Atlantic Edition, and one suspects that this exercise gave rise to the ideas

behind *William Clissold*. If there is an avatar on which the character of Clissold is based, it is perhaps Sir Alfred Mond, the self-made millionaire who was chosen by the Tories to speak for them in the famous Capitalism v. Socialism debate in the Commons soon after the Labour Party came to power in 1924. In Wells's book Clissold and his brother, who are orphaned after the father's embezzlement is discovered, find themselves 'in the collective consciousness of the race'. Clissold used *God the Invisible King* in his thinking aloud, remarking that his cousin had written the work.

Clisssold (now speaking as Wells) discovers and discards Marx, and with this revelation much of formal socialism. Many parts of the book which deal with Clissold's life, especially in Books III and IV, are actually treatments of Wells's life with Odette and others. Clementina (Odette) assumes a significant role in the book, although her harsh and demanding nature is revealed even here in the somewhat exasperated air with which Clissold treats her from time to time. In Book V, the most important of the book's speculative portions, Wells reveals the 'Open Conspiracy', based on the ideas of David Lubin and F. W. Sanderson, both of whom are mentioned by name. In the conspiracy, as Wells was beginning to outline it, self-educated persons everywhere will simply, in good time, take over the world and remake it to suit the needs of the many.

However, it is worth noting that in this book, at the end, in a section entitled 'Venus as Evening Star' and featuring the possessiveness of Clementina, it is clear that the 'Open Conspiracy' is just a dream. An automobile accident kills both Clissold and Clementina, and the house in Provence is lost. The book, a very long one, comes to us today as autobiographical in part, a statement of philosophy, the first treatment of the Open Conspiracy, as a study of international capitalism, and a predecessor to Wells's own *Experiment in Autobiography*, all of these elements having some part in the work.

Wells's friends and colleagues, although somewhat puzzled by the book, treated it with respect and good humour. Shaw, writing from Stresa, remarked that both he and Charlotte had devoured it. Shaw said that it was only a novel intermittently, but that did not bother him, as it was such a nice piece of landscape painting. He went on to write three pages of detailed commentary, most of which was positive, as the book had stimulated his thinking.[32] Graham Wallas also liked it very much; while saying, as he had done on several occasions, that he always tried to read Wells as though he, Wallas, were still in his teens, he remarked how much the book must mean to persons who were young and just beginning their intellectual life or a life of teaching. Bertrand Russell said that Dora had carried it off to read, to the detriment of her work on birth-control, and said, 'God knows how many extra babies owe their lives to its existence.' Hardy, writing from his Dorset retirement, said that his only regret was that there was no Volume IV to follow the first three. Lankester was moved by the description of himself and set up a lunch so that Wells could discuss

Marx and Engels with him. Lankester had known both men personally, and told Wells that Engels was a 'rather rotten specimen'.[33]

The reviewers, most of whom praised the book, treated it not so much as fiction as Wellsian philosophy. Many of them considered the chapters on sex, and the treatment of women, as 'must' reading, and several remarked on the catholicity and encyclopaedic nature of Wells's knowledge. The sheer size of the book put some people off, but all in all *William Clissold* was read, and widely read, whether as autobiography, fiction, or philosophy: the reader could take it as he wished.[34]

Watt handled the book for Wells and was responsible for the multi-volume format, similar to Romain Rolland's great work, *Jean-Christophe*, which had just appeared. Victor Gollancz, who was Ernest Benn's chief reader and editor at this time, and George Doran both read the book at the same time, and were very enthusiastic about its prospects. Benn gave a series of interviews in the trade press, and speculation about the book prior to its appearance in print was very great. Wells received a high royalty (27½ per cent on the sales of the first printing, 12½ per cent on colonial sales, and even 17½ per cent on the cheap edition). He asked for and received a five-year reversion clause. Wells received £3,000 in advance, in lieu of a serialization, and Benn spent £1,500 on advertising, which was an immense amount for the time. Wells and Gollancz carried on a detailed correspondence over the book and later over its progress in the market-place: H.G. objected to some of the announcements in the press, and insisted on certain illustrative material on the dust jacket.

The book received more than a hundred notices in the press, and Gollancz and Wells toyed with the idea of publishing these as a pamphlet, even of printing on facing pages those that disagreed. Most of the negative reviews, both of this book and of its immediate successor, *Meanwhile*, focused on the problem Wells posed by his attitude towards the suppression of the General Strike, about which he was vicious — on the strike itself but also on Churchill and others who led the counterattack. *William Clissold* was a success monetarily, bringing in large sums even for excerpts. Eventually, after several offers were refused because Wells and Benn were not given the right to choose the portion to be reprinted, *Cosmopolitan* took 5,000 words of the book, and paid Wells £1,000 for the excerpt. Magazines which used bits of Wells's other books, through 'misapprehension of acquired rights', were let off fairly easily, but those who wished to use parts of this book paid for it. *William Clissold* was scheduled to appear eventually as the last volume in the Essex Edition, in 1929; Wells's income-tax problems were great enough, because of its sales, for him to accept a slightly lower royalty than he usually received on the last reprinting.[35]

William Clissold, little known or read today, is a watershed book in H.G. Wells's fiction. After this book, nearly all of Wells's novels (with perhaps *Star Begotten* as an exception) are books of the changing contemporary scene. Many of them have anti-fascism as their main point (*Meanwhile*, for instance), or they discuss the coming of the war (*All Aboard for Ararat*), or they deal with women (*Brynhild*, *Apropos of Dolores*); but they all deal with contemporary affairs. Even *The Brothers*, *The Camford Visitation*, and *The Croquet Player* are novels which deal with the 1930s. The pressures of modern life and the ever-intensifying threat of fascism led H. G. Wells to treat fiction hereafter as just another means of getting his message across, but often within a somewhat bloated context; and although the characters are often very interesting, the message sometimes overwhelms them and both aspects of the novel suffer.

In fact, it looked for a time as though *William Clissold* might be the last novel, although it was successful in terms of income. As the reviews came in Wells began another weekly series in the press — the *Sunday Express* in Britain and the *New York Times* in America. The series was to be called 'The Way the World is Going' (also used as the title for the collection when the pieces appeared in book form), and a press release announced that the articles would be 'provocative', 'charming', and 'highly interesting'. Wells began the series with an article which met all of these criteria. He told his readers that, contrary to what they thought, man as a species was undergoing constant alteration. He said, moreover, that these changes were most pronounced in the way we are discarding the prime object of life: continuation and sexual purpose. By breeding later, and limiting the number of our offspring, we are the first of our species to have abundant leisure time for other matters. Wells drew from this the conclusion of the need to alter opinions on human biology, and along with that the need to utilize the time made available to ensure survival, but survival for all the species in a better world.[36]

He soon showed his readers what he meant. In rapid succession he dealt with China and the Kuomintang government, provided an analysis of Italian Fascism, and called for world control of aeroplanes and their ability to penetrate other nations' space. These articles produced an uproar. The *Express* disagreed on aircraft, the Italian government banned Wells from entering Italy, and his friends in England began to write back and forth discussing his words.[37]

Wells went on in the series to discuss the cost of modern warfare, and the fact that Parliament was very much out of touch with voters' ideas and policies. He analysed the role of wireless radio (he thought the BBC talks were sophomoric, the result of their policy of censorship), and reviewed various movies as to their artistic and social merit.[38]

He proclaimed himself an optimist about the future of ordinary people; however, he felt that such a future would be possible only with a better educational system, and he remarked that in America the situation was much worse, citing Sinclair Lewis's *Babbit* and *Elmer Gantry* as examples of how America was failing its promise. He excoriated the state of Massachusetts over the Sacco-Vanzetti case, remarking that blood was 'a

poor cement for the foundation of a civilization'. The *New York Times* did
not print this piece, as the case had stirred up such a furore in the US;
readers in America had to wait to read it in Wells's book, though a very
small minority may have found it summarized in a radical journal devoted
to the case, the *Sacco-Vanzetti Dawn*.[39]

In later articles Wells continued to antagonize proponents of the status
quo, and supporters of a Panglossian view of the times, with pieces
attacking patriotism, with 'Either you are for Cosmopolis or you are for
war'. He upheld trial marriages, discussed dreams and their relation to the
future, argued in favour of vivisection (which led to a debate with Shaw,
and a pamphlet reproducing both their views). His discussion of time
(based on J.W. Dunne's experiments with precognition) led him to discuss
immortality and to reject life beyond the grave: 'And we too live and pass,
reflecting for our moment, and in the measure of our capacity, the light and
wonder of the Eternal. And is not that enough?' A. Conan Doyle, now
completely converted to spiritualism, responded to this article, and it led
Wells to visit Lankester again, when the two old friends exchanged books
and ideas, and rehearsed the history of certain para-phenomena. This was
the summer of Jane's fatal illness, and Wells was prepared to think about
the matter of survival after death. He rejected it as a false promise,
however, and went on to discuss in *The Science of Life* the results of his
thought and findings.[40]

Wells attacked the British Empire on several scores in the series and
described the Russian version of communism as an attempt to deal with the
backward reality of that great land, rather than a coven of witches as was
generally believed. This led him to speculate on the future of labour and
the potential class war, but he described it as a small conflict compared to
the real forces in the world. He reprinted his preface to J. M. Kenworthy's
Will Civilization Crash? (1927) and went on to analyse American thought
fairly succinctly, mostly in response to the correspondence his articles had
stirred up on the other side of the Atlantic. He also wrote another
coruscating article about Shaw whom he called 'an iridescent film on the
pool of life', and his ideas 'a jackdaw's hoard'; each then accused the other
of a conditioned-reflex response. Wells urged a Lib-Lab coalition government, to be headed by Philip Snowden as the only person who could
restore 'sanity, security and peace'. This article came in the wake of the
Zinoviev Letter, and he followed it in a fortnight with a strong attack on
F. E. Smith, Lord Birkenhead, in the guise of a review of a new biography.
Wells referred to *The New Machiavelli* and urged supporters of Birkenhead
to be more realistic. (He died suddenly soon after and has become a sort of
Tory legend.) Birkenhead's son responded, as did the author of the
biography, defending the book and Birkenhead, and with this the column
came to an end.[41]

The articles did not appear in book form until late in 1928, even though
the text was with the publishers by Christmas of 1927. Part of the reason

was that Fisher Unwin, who had brought out Wells's previous collection of journalism, had lost money on the venture, and other publishers were understandably shy of the new collection. The timing of publication was also affected by Gollancz's resignation from Benns, and the book simply lay in limbo for a time. Benns said that they would increase the royalty if Wells would waive an advance, and they haggled over terms, with Wells eventually receiving £300 in Britain. Doran gave him an advance of $1,000 on the US rights, Wells getting 20 per cent in the UK and 15 per cent in the USA with a rising royalty if the book sold well. It did not sell well, and eventually Wells took a lower royalty to move the work once the Depression came down.[42]

The years 1927 and 1928 seem almost as remote from us today as the time of Louis XIV. Calvin Coolidge was President of the United States; the Tories were back in power in England, after suppressing the General Strike of 1926 with surprising ease and gleeful violence on the part of the young. Italy had succumbed to Fascism, but Germany was still in the hands of a government without much direction, while in its capital city, degradation and disillusion appeared to rule the life of the inhabitants. Hitler seemed only a minor figure. In Russia Stalin was in the process of consolidating his power after Lenin's death, the Five Year Plans providing short-term goals to drag the ancient land into modern life. In China warlords struggled for much of the country, while the Soong family attempted to establish full rule. In the meantime the peasants lived out lives not much different from fifty generations before. Lindbergh flew the Atlantic in 1927, to link the two continents by air; but for most persons, travel was by rail, if at all.

Henry Ford was about to replace the Model T Ford, standard since the mid-teens, with first the Model B, and then later the Model A. Roads still often had dirt surfaces, with mud the rule in winter, autumn, and spring. Travel was the province of the wealthy, while the long work-day, still only partially curtailed by the machine revolution, remained the lot of most people in the world. Literacy was still not widespread except in the more advanced countries; starvation remained at the back of most persons' minds; neither television nor radio had yet offered the potential for escape which has made our own world so vulnerable. Surveying all this, H.G. Wells could only marvel at the slothfulness and stolidity of his fellow humans. All the necessary inventions were in place. The failure of the old systems seemed to be so obvious. Mankind was either on the threshold of the greatest time of all, or it was on the verge of extinction. Wells's role was to focus on the choices, and to make them real to his readers. It is no wonder that these years of the locust, for most, became years of tremendous, almost frantic activity for H. G. Wells, as he moved into and through his seventh decade.

Wells, in addition to his routine articles in the press, also provided some longer and more sober versions of his ideas during this period. The

National Council for the Prevention of War republished, in somewhat longer form, one of his *Sunday Express* articles under the title *Playing at Peace*. Here Wells reiterated that although many wanted peace, few were willing to work for it. He said only a federal authority could prevent a recurrence, in worse form, of the slaughter of World War I, and challenged his readers to exercise their powers towards peace. According to him,

> a real world peace movement must be a revolutionary movement in politics, finance, industrialism, and the daily life alike. It is not a proposed change in certain formal aspects of life; it is a proposal to change the whole of life. . . . Great revolutions in human affairs need time to incubate, and the price of the peace of the world means an effort whose duration will have to be measured by lifetimes. I believe that such an effort will be made, but I believe it is a delusion to say that it has even begun.[43]

Important as this work was, he also offered longer discussions of his views, first in his novel of the impact of fascism, *Meanwhile*, and immediately thereafter with his prescription for peace, and his call to world effort, *The Open Conspiracy*. These two books are really part of the same thrust, and seem to be joined, as the fiction in this work gives way to the sermons. He had learned a lesson from *William Clissold* and its somewhat chequered reception, or so it seemed.

Meanwhile (1927) is a badly neglected novel. It is set in Italy (and in part in England) at the time of the General Strike, many of whose leading participants appear in the novel without disguise. The principal female character seems to be closely modelled on Jane Wells, and the setting in the garden at Ventimiglia is remarkably evocative for anyone who has spent time on the Italian Riviera with its aspects of green hills and bright flowers. In a villa is a company of guests, representatives of most of the significant views of the time, offering scintillating conversation similar to that of the Souls in the days of Mr Balfour, as one character remarks. Flirtations abound, and even the leading characters fell prey. And, in letters irresistibly reminiscent of those between Jane and H.G., as well as others that may have been sent, the heroine is reminded of her duty to her philandering husband, much as Jane may have been reminded at other times:

> 'You are Philip Ryland's wife. In the fullest sense and to the last possible shade of meaning, you are his wife; you are a wife by nature, and the role of a wife is not to compete and be jealous, but to understand and serve and by understanding and serving rule. Wives are rare things in life, but you are surely one. . . . Through him you may do great things in the world and in no other way will you personally ever do great things. Because you are reflective; because your initiatives are too delicate for the weight and strains of life.'

In addition to this personal and open description of married life by H.G. Wells, the novel also contains excellent descriptions of the rich on the

Riviera just before the deluge, as well as a poignant and sharp analysis of the fascist system under stress. After the preservation of a fugitive from fascism, the book moves on to discuss how fascism and its fellows can be defeated. It ends with a strong statement of the Open Conspiracy, the necessity for all persons of good will to band together against the forces of evil, to create a rebellion and revolution against events, to take control of their destiny, to wrest control from the evil forces of the past. As the Open Conspiracy is announced and described, Mrs Rylands also delivers herself of a child, a symbolic parturition marking the state of the future for the species, as well as for those in the novel. Of course, Wells knew, as he had always known, that his suggestion might not be taken, that the species might not listen, and the future could be horrible. The novel is titled *Meanwhile*, almost as though those reading the work and thinking about it were in an interlude — wondering which way to move.

The publishers liked the book and its follow-up, *The Open Conspiracy*. Gollancz bought the novel for Benn, who provided good, if not extravagant royalties. It went into a cheap edition within fifteen months, and the rights reverted to H.G. after four years. In America the Book-of-the-Month Club, recently founded, chose the book as an alternate selection, and it was translated into Danish and Norwegian, Polish and Czech, as well as other languages. By 15 September (only two months after publication) 30,000 copies had been sold in England. With a new jacket the last remaining copies (3,000) of a press run of about 50,000 were gone by the end of the summer of 1929.[44]

The Open Conspiracy (1928) also sold well. Wells granted rights for only eighteen months, reserving further rights in the book to himself, and he eventually reissued it three times, once under its original title, somewhat revised, and eventually under the title *What Are We To Do With Our Lives?* (1931), also in two editions. The theme is the same, but Wells kept revising and sharpening the prose to win even more adherents to his banner. There was some interest in serializing the book in the *New York Times*, but Wells resisted that, as he did efforts to go round him to get the book published elsewhere. Victor Gollancz, moving from Benns, published the book in his own first list. Eventually some excerpts (three articles) appeared in *The Times* and in *T.P.'s Weekly*, but only after the book had appeared, and even then only after extreme pressure (and increased payments) from Meade Minnegerode, who was acting for both papers. The book earned more than its advance within a few months, and Wells reissued it at much lower prices. Money was no great object to him at this stage of his life, and especially with a book whose message was as important as this one.[45]

The book was well received by Wells's friends. Bertrand Russell read it 'with the most complete sympathy', and said he agreed with it entirely. He went on to discuss who would join the Conspiracy, saying Einstein was a prime candidate; but that in France and England, the men of science were more interested in being elected to the Royal Society or to the Institute.

Even J. B. S. Haldane and Julian Huxley were doubtful joiners at this stage, said Russell. Beatrice Webb called the book an 'inspiring essay'; however, she reminded Wells that 'Of course you leave off where we are wont to begin: but then you and we each have our own sphere and it is very difficult to combine the two.' She then went on to say that his work was 'a magnificent introduction to the works of the Webbs'. Fabian socialism seemed still to be the way to the future. Wells responded with 'insidious you were, insidious you are. I shall drink my tea with affectionate suspicion.'[46]

A few organizations dedicated to the Open Conspiracy were formed round the world, and eventually enough were in existence for a newsletter to be published, and the organization developed some momentum. Renamed 'Cosmopolis', it will reappear in the next chapter. A few handbills survive from its earliest phase:

THE OPEN CONSPIRACY
Be a Citizen of the World
JOIN
The Open Conspiracy

Its immediate object is the introduction of hope and order into a world of frustration and chaos. . . . Its ultimate object is the establishment of a scientifically-planned World Government.[47]

For those who questioned him closely, Wells described the Open Conspiracy as following directly from and a part of the three Outlines of Knowledge. As he told one questioner, 'I feel very strongly the need of a steady patient building up of a body of ideas before we can consolidate any effective world wide constructive movements. Until we have that our efforts must necessarily be fragmentary — we shall all suffer from a sense of isolation and the lack of sympathetic co-operation. At present the world-wide propaganda of ideas is crippled by the fact that the ideas have still to be made clear and available.'

In America he thought that people had not read his message clearly enough, so the movement had languished; but in England things were more promising. A Lloyd George visit to his villa in France, Lou Pidou, led to the idea of a luncheon meeting of intellectuals, as in the old days of the Co-Efficients. Philip Guedalla, Lloyd George, C. P. Scott, Bennett, Galsworthy, Barrie, Keynes, Stampp, Russell, G.M. Trevelyan, and the Woolfs were proposed. They met once, just before Easter 1929, with Scott as the host, but apparently never again in this organized fashion. From this beginning, however, Wells did begin to have other luncheon discussions with a wide variety of people, including Harold Macmillan and Harold Nicolson, then young and energetic Members of Parliament. But Lloyd George wanted a revival of British Liberalism, which Wells and most others at the luncheon rejected, and the meetings foundered on this point.[48]

When the *Daily Herald* went to a wider-circulation format in early 1930, Wells took the opportunity to offer his advanced views on the Open

Conspiracy to its receptive audience. He called for mental and moral disarmament, a diminution of sovereignty, a world federation in control of trade and the air, a steady and gradual reduction of tariffs; if necessary, let the US and the UK begin it, as they were so near each other in view, language, and outlook. Above all else Wells called for an end to war-making ideas in schools, and the creation of a false patriotism through bad history. As he said, without this, 'Everywhere throughout the world, while the conferences meet and the politicians orate, war is being sown anew, steadily, day by day, in the schools.'[49] As Wells also said on several other occasions, what was needed was the creation of a 'competent receiver' to pick up after the bankrupt society in which his listeners lived. That was the work of the Open Conspiracy, and he then provided a list of seven parallel needs of the new world: this was the first effort at what would become the Declaration of Human Rights. Wells had thought the matter through clearly enough, but unfortunately the great slump had intervened, nations began to turn inward and to support nationalism in hundreds of new ways, and in its race with catastrophe, education began to seem the loser.[50]

The audience that Wells was reaching through these speeches and articles was one which had grown up with him, and one which looked forward to his new productions. It is remarkable how many of his books were sold. New editions proliferated — an Essex Edition of inexpensive hardbound books sold at 2s. 6d.; a larger edition was issued by Macmillans, and at least two ten- and twelve-volume collections were used to sell newspapers as they were given away as prizes, used in promotions, and to attract new subscribers. All these editions, now often found in bookshops, and some with brief new introductions by Wells as he strove to make his purposes clear to his readers, were dwarfed by the efforts from 1924 to 1927 to provide a de luxe collected edition, with new prefaces; and some revision of the texts by Wells himself. The Atlantic Edition volumes are beautiful books, each one numbered and signed by the author. Wells was at the height of his popularity, and these editions were an indication of the esteem in which he was held.[51]

As a result of all this work Wells did revise his opinion of agents. Watt had made him a wealthy man by his assiduous work on his behalf. As Wells said to him, 'And apart from that very material aspect I have to thank you for the most patient, sympathetic and ready understanding of the sometimes startling propositions we have discussed together, for your sedulous care of my literary good name.'[52]

Wells was under siege to reprint his short stories as well, and eventually Benn brought out an edition, still in print, although unfortunately it does not contain by any means all the stories. The other editions of his work, most of which included some short stories, used up the market, and when the slump came at the end of the decade, most publishers found themselves with excess stock. The Macmillan 6d. edition comprised 17 volumes, while the Collins version at 2s. 6d. had 22. The Essex Edition, envisaged by Wells as the inexpensive counterpart to the Atlantic Edition, eventually resulted in 26 volumes; 1,000 sets went to mail-order firms, but even so, it was remaindered in 1934. A table in the Notes lists Wells's sales in the year 1925, before any of the collected editions had appeared; based on Watt's records, it indicates that sales remained high long after publication.[53]

There was one more Wellsian fling in the educational activity of the late 1920s. He supported, with money and the use of his name, a short-lived magazine called the *Realist*, which carried the subtitle 'A Journal of Scientific Humanism'. Founded early in 1929, it lasted about six months, with Archibald Church as general editor and Gerald Heard as literary editor. Its reason for being was to offer a means for sophisticated writers and readers to ventilate their views on socialism and world government. The nearest analogue is the earlier *English Review*. The board of editors (some twenty-five names in all) included Bennett, A. M. Carr-Saunders, G. E. C. Catlin, Gregory, Haldane, Aldous and Julian Huxley, Laski, B. Malinowski, Naomi Mitchison, Eileen Power, Herbert Read, and Rebecca West, also Wells himself.

The journal began in arrears, in both production and funds, but although money was owed to the printers, enough was located (some of it from Wells) to produce the issues through June. No editorial salaries were paid; Sir Alfred Mond (the prototype of Clissold) lent his backing in general. Macmillans were interested, but were prepared to let this version go bankrupt, according to Gerald Heard, while hoping to pick up the pieces once that had occurred. The magazine had some problems with censorship, and Wells acted as a courier for some suspect material. He even used his good offices to approach Jung, but the magazine died before that article saw the light of day. When the slump came in the autumn of 1929, the magazine gave up, although some efforts were made throughout the winter and spring to locate another 'angel'. The New York Whitney family were asked to contribute funds, but far too late, as the stock market in America began to spiral down. Even Dorothy Straight Elmhirst (owner of the *New Republic*) was thought of. Although some funds were promised by her, by the Monds, and others, these were not enough, and even though the bills were met (some by Melchett, some by Mond), the brief effort at education came to an end, foundering on the shoals of capitalism, as did many such efforts of the time. The *Realist* produced a half-dozen issues, with several good contributions, but these were not enough.

Wells knew from this experience, as well as his other efforts in the 1929s, that once the slump had come, he and his friends had to redouble their efforts for peace and Cosmopolis. The pace was getting closer. It was time to take his message on the road. Writing was not sufficient. Speaking, sermonizing, arguing, all had to take their place in the arsenal of weapons to be brought to this grand enterprise.[54]

EDUCATING THE WORLD: WRITING AND TRAVELLING, 1929–1936

> The course of human affairs is little less chancy and unpredictable than the destiny of any other species of swarming animal. It is like the course of some great vessel without rudder, without charts, drifting and blundering down a swift, vast river. The unheeding multitude is carried along from reaches of sunlit steadiness, to rapids, to stern gorges, to places of infinite danger. Its mood changes the scene. It rejoices, it congratulates itself, it gives way to panic and anger. A few alerter individuals try to sketch charts, a few dispute about improvising a rudder and what sort of rudder, a few seek to impose some kind of helping discipline upon themselves and their fellows. And the drift goes on. . . . With local variations of accent and colours the mill of change grinds on and challenges us to solve a universal riddle.
>
> HGW, preface to Martha Gellhorn, *The Trouble I've Seen* (1936)

If, as Robert Graves suggested, the years between the wars were a long weekend, that expression really applies more to the earlier years than the later. For, from the failure of the Kreditanstalt and the great fall in the US Stock Exchange to the attack of the Japanese on Pearl Harbor, the world moved at an ever more rapid pace, and one in which larger and larger numbers of people began to concern themselves about what might be coming. It was as though in that long weekend the planning for Monday took up much of the time on Sunday. As the world whirled down into the vortex of the Second World War, H. G. Wells busied himself with the planning, organizing, and predicting of what that Monday would bring when it inevitably came.

He was extremely active, for a man who was in his seventieth year when the Spanish Civil War broke out. He produced a dozen novels during the period, as well as one of the famous autobiographies of this century. He also provided another half-dozen books from speeches, talks, and articles, and a major philosophical work. He travelled even more widely than before — visiting Germany, France, and Russia, as well as the Mediterranean, to do research and make speeches. He travelled to the United States four times, and made an arduous excursion to Australia. Throughout the period he also utilized the century's new methods of communication to increase his audience through film and wireless radio. He undertook to educate the world to the dangers of fascism, dictatorship, and the failure that would ensue if people did not work together to bring about Cosmopolis, world peace, and a promising future for mankind. As he reacted to his times, he treated the great themes of the period: the role of the individual in a mass society, the influence of dictators and strong men — understanding, however, that the world which produced Hitler and Mussolini also produced Franklin Roosevelt. His fiction of this period was caught up in these questions as he explored in a number of significant ways the impact of modern life on individual persons.

As time sped on, and the problems appeared to intensify, especially after the tariff battles of the early '30s, and the inward search for a way out of the declining days of capitalism in which Germany, Russia, the United States and Great Britain took the lead (each following a different escape route), Wells's messages seemed more apocalyptic to many in his day; although there is now a fusty air about them, as they were so clearly ignored by their audience. The acceptance by some and rejection by others of his theoretical proposals (both in Britain and in the world generally) makes an interesting counterpoint to his travels and writings.

How it was possible for him to maintain such a taxing schedule is still a mystery. He had good help, with Marjorie Craig Wells, his daughter-in-law, organizing his life, his appointments, and generally providing stability to his situation. Also, he had achieved so much fame that he could always travel first-class, being coddled and shepherded about. With Jane dead, and his tumultuous liaison with Odette Keun over early in this period, it is not too much to suggest that his supply of strength came partly from the diversion of emotional and physical energy from sex to the quest for peace. And, as the '30s wore on, this shift was probably intensified, at least on the evidence available — as we shall see in later chapters where his life and sexual activities are described against the backdrop of his fiction, from *Marriage* to *Apropos of Dolores*.

The failure of the peace of Versailles had led Wells to write, in the '20s, his trilogy of great textbooks. He began his project to educate the world with these books, and he moved the concept on with his writings, in two year-long stints of journalism, as well as in other articles and even in the fiction of the period, in which he attempted to understand moods and changes, especially in books like *The World of William Clissold*, *The Dream*, and *Men Like Gods*. Fascism triumphed in Italy, however, and this seemed to galvanize Wells again, as he produced, at the end of the '20s, his novel on the impact of fascism, *Meanwhile*, and his call to arms against such movements, *The Open Conspiracy*.

After the slump began, and it was obvious that isolationism was to prevail in major countries, Wells was forced to re-examine his premises. He continued to believe in the Open Conspiracy, but he now thought that it needed leaders to achieve its goals. He began to search for such leadership in the young of the older established parties in England, and also flirted with the possibility of following the lead of pacifism, if it were combined with better education. This last led him to a major effort at reforming teaching, and especially the teaching of history, as he returned to his old love, the classroom and its activities. The last years before the war in 1939, and before the US entered in 1941, were taken up with this educational crusade, as he attempted to warn the world of its danger, and to urge reform along international lines. His last great trips, to Australia, to Stockholm, and to the United States, are deliberate attempts to educate the world. But time ran out, for H. G. Wells, for the Allies in the face of Hitlerian demands, and perhaps for the species at Hiroshima and Nagasaki. In the race between education and catastrophe, the odds continued to lengthen perceptibly on education, despite Wells's efforts. No wonder that, when he was asked what his epitaph should be, he snapped at the questioner, "'Goddamn You All, I Told You So!'"

To a considerable extent the problem, for Wells as for most others who supported some form of collective action, was that the individual continued to obtrude. In the earlier part of this period Wells resorted to fiction, on three different occasions, to deal with the role of the individual; he produced *Mr Blettsworthy on Rampole Island* (1928), *The Autocracy of Mr Parham* (1930), and *The Bulpington of Blup* (1932), all in an effort to understand this problem. In a sense, *Christina Alberta's Father* (1925), although more important for its comments on women and men, was a precursor of these books.

Of the first three novels, probably *Blettsworthy* is the best written, and *Bulpington* the furthest from being realized, although both those judgements may stem from our expectations of a novel, and especially a Wells novel. Although each of the three sold fairly well in its time, none of them made much impact later, and must now be among the least read of Wells's books. One cannot dismiss them, however, as they do offer an attempt to understand the driving theme of the early '30s, the individual in society.

Parham is illustrated with ten cartoon sketches by David Low. It is the story of an Oxford don, captured by a modern leadership type and forcibly exposed to the world. This leads to an investigation into spiritualism, a seance, and the don's dreaming that he is a world leader, the Lord Paramount as Wells calls him. He is unfit for leadership, however, and a terrible war breaks out between England and America, fought in the midst of the North Atlantic. The work is a nice study of reaction under pressure, and the failure of contemporary education to prepare anyone for that pressure. Thinly disguised members of the British aristocracy inhabit the work, which ends with Parham rejected by his former patron as being out of touch, discarded once an early need has been fulfilled.

> All life has something dreamlike in it. No percipient creature has ever yet lived in stark reality. Nature has equipped us with such conceptions and delusions as survival necessitated, and our experiences are at best but working interpretations. Nevertheless, as they diverge more and more from practical truth and we begin to stumble against danger, our dearest dreams are at last invaded by remonstrances and warning shadows.

(Book IV, chapter 2)

Blettsworthy looks at these same problems through the eyes of a rejected person, tossed by the sea on to an unknown island. The life at sea, in South America, and the destructive storm are well described, as is the character of the beastly and violent captain who creates the disaster. Blettsworthy, a 'sacred lunatic', revered by the native population, is safe to observe the islands and their peculiar habits, which include a continuously practised cannibalism. A battle occurs, and Blettsworthy finds himself, awake, in a psychiatric clinic in New York, the entire episode having been the product of his deranged mind. The derangement had occurred as a result of his experiences in the World War, from which he emerged a victim of shell-shock and war neurosis. It becomes clear to the reader however that Rampole Island lurks in all our dreams, beneath (and not very far beneath) our sanity. We see life, only dimly lit, much as Plato described the Cave. On Rampole Island, down in the gorge where one crouches awaiting the attack of the enemy, dimly seen, reality takes on an intensity, but an external and terrible vagueness at the same time, which inhabits our lives always.

> "You and I, Blettsworthy, are very ordinary men. There is nothing in our brains that cannot be in the brains of thousands of other people. You haven't been alone in your visit to Rampole Island. Thousands, millions perhaps, have been there. You and I think rather figuratively, rather ineffectively, of getting out of the gorge. The movement hasn't really taken shape yet, and second-rate people like we are hang about afraid of the plain conclusions of our own brains."

(Chapter 4, sect. 14)

If Blettsworthy and Parham are examples of individuals under stress, in a world inhabited by unseen dangers from the great mass of ignorance, they at least come out into the world with some prospects. They understand their weaknesses, and look forward, although very tentatively, to joining with others to overcome them. It is true that the prospects for both are not strong. Parham and Blettsworthy may both fail, in fact probably will, but they do suggest that the effort is worth making.

Wells's other book of this period, *The Bulpington of Blup*, offers no such message, even of partial hope. Theodore Bulpington is an ordinary youth, representative of many trained by sloppy English methods in history and the allied arts. Throughout the book he is seen in conflict with science and modern thinking, often framed in terms of class, and he always comes out second-best. He turns out to be a liar, a cheat, a waste product of society, living from hand to mouth and on the gifts of those whom he can fool. He is not a pleasant character, as he treats all his companions in the same sort of shabby way, until they finally reject him as worthless and as a failure. Here the individual falls before the common and general good, cannot adjust, and we are led to think of ourselves with contempt as similar to Bulpington in all his tragedy. The book is filled with allusions to the Delphic oracle, and the endpapers of the original edition were even decorated with a visage of the Sibyl, which perhaps suggests that the oracle's pronouncements, here all bad, may not turn out that way — though in fact little hope or promise is held out. Bulpington, like many Wells heroes, is a dreamer and fantasizer, and some critics have described the book as highly autobiographical. It is the dreams and fantasies of Bulpington which represent the good in life, and the book illustrates clearly how he fails to achieve his dreams. The best-written parts deal with adolescent sexuality and the fears and hopes induced at that time. But, although we may sympathize with Bulpington, we cannot ever like him, as he flunks in every trial he is offered, whether personally, in sexual conflict, or in the greater conflict of the War and the front lines.

Wells is dealing in these books with individuality, and describing it without pity. Reading them in a simplistic way, with his other works of the period, one might come away with a view of this fiction as designed to demonstrate that individuality does not work very well in the modern world; but if that is the lesson, the reader begins to wonder why the emphasis on education and its ability to change lives and ideas. It is more likely that Wells is simply concerned with the growing significance of evil individuals, however — though of course he may also be haunted by the failure of education thus far to achieve his ideals, and his heroes may represent his concept of his own failures in the wake of Jane's death and his increasing age.

In fact, Wells left standard fiction for a time after publishing these three novels. He turned his attention to film and radio, and when he returned to fiction, it was with the four novellas of the middle part of the decade, dealing with the growing danger to world peace. At the end of the decade he returned finally to a discussion of the individual, especially in *The Holy Terror*, but also in his last novel, *You Can't Be Too Careful*. The novels discussed here mark a difficult period in Wells's life; in judging them one needs to look at his own specific efforts to provide a way to peace, even though in these he was perhaps no more effective in the long run than the Lord Paramount, Blettsworthy, or even Theodore Bulpington.

Whether it was the unusual topics (men under stress, at a time when Pollyanna books were wanted) or whether the public was surfeited with Wellsian books (the large numbers of cheap reprints must have hurt his sales), or whether the slump left people without as much money to purchase books, this trio of novels did not sell as well as his fiction had usually done. He had contracts with Ernest Benn for the books, but there was often difficulty now over the amount of the advance. Serial rights, always a big money-maker — especially in the States, where, for instance, *Collier's* had paid $20,000 for the serial rights to *Christina Alberta's Father* — were also now worth less than before, and this was especially true as the Depression went deeper. New magazines, such as *Liberty* and *Coronet*, were anxious to publish Wells's work, but wanted specially commissioned articles, and although the editors frequently discussed with his agents the serialization of his books, the talks rarely came to anything. When Wells was interviewed in the press about his new book, in the early days of the slump, Benns became anxious, as the headline had stressed a 'fantastic novel' by H. G. Wells, and they did not think that fantastic novels would sell. Wells told them he was hard at work on *Blettsworthy*, and that they should 'keep calm' until they had talked to him about it. Eventually the book was issued in a cheaper edition to enhance sales.[1]

His friends continued to like his books, of course. Sydney Olivier, in a very long letter, told him *Blettsworthy* was 'distinguishedly good stuff', and went on to discuss his own dreams, especially the set dreams he frequently dreamed. Eileen Power, who had read the book while on tour in Hungary, called it 'absolutely first class'.[2]

Parham gave even more trouble to Wells and Watt than *Blettsworthy*. Some people objected to the Low cartoons, which were thinly veiled caricatures of such persons as Beaverbrook and Churchill. Watt spent a tremendous amount of time with Ernest Benn, but the book was eventually rejected by Benns. He spent even more time on the serialization prospects, pushing the book with the *Pall Mall Gazette* (who accepted it), as well as with *Cosmopolitan, Pearson's, Collier's,* the *Saturday Evening Post, Liberty, Good Housekeeping,* and others. *Liberty*, described by Watt as having 'pots of money at their disposal, and in my experience they are willing to pay more than most people for what they want — or think they want', did not take this book, but were a useful outlet for Wells through the remainder of the decade.

Parham had a series of titles, 'The Master Spirit and the Spirit of the Times' being the most prominent, but the purchasers of the serial rights asked Wells to change it to the one it finally received. When Benns rejected the book finally, they told Wells it was because the press treated his work as 'sociology'. Wells balked at this, saying *Parham* was 'a comic novel', but

Benn finally let it go to Heinemann. Ernest Benn told Watt privately that he had just been on holiday to Sweden and found Wells's books everywhere unsold, and he was convinced that he could no longer move his stuff. Benn said, 'All this is not the sort of letter that a publisher should write to an author's agent, but we have surely got beyond that position with H.G.W.' He told of returns of 10,000 copies on the previous book. It had sold 12,000, but had not nearly reached its expected sale. In fact Wells took a lower royalty when shown the actual figures.

When Collins, a second publisher approached, refused *Parham*, Watt turned once more to Heinemann, and the book, when published, was one of Wells's better sellers in years. Wells as usual asked for a very high royalty and advance (in this case he wanted 20 per cent to 15,000, 25 per cent to 20,000 and 30 per cent thereafter, with an advertising budget of £2,000, and the rights to revert to him in seven years); some publishers felt they would not get their money back on such terms. Heinemann sold the US rights to Doran, and it was the US edition that went on sale first. The book sold well enough for second serial rights in England to be purchased by the Liverpool *Evening Express*.[3]

Bertrand Russell, who read *Parham* in serial form and later in its clothbound version, told Wells he liked the book, and especially his treatment of the ancient universities. In fact Russell told Wells that he thought the world was more sinister than Wells believed, as 'All the henpecked husbands are determined to prove they are he-men, and will soon try to prove it by bullying Europe.' Ivan Maisky, writing from Helsinki, told Wells he had met many persons such as those depicted in the book in his stay in England; 'military idiots of this kind are easily to be found in all countries', was his judgement. Maisky also told Wells that he was too optimistic about the international spirit of Russia, and he predicted to Wells that his character Bussy (Winston Churchill) would never remain neutral towards Russia. Maisky went on in this very long letter to discuss international affairs with his friend. He told Wells that the reason the French press had been hard on his book was that 'perhaps you are striking hard at the weak spot'.[4]

Much the same was true of the reception of *Bulpington*. Publishers were reluctant to meet Wells's terms, and he in this case went against his usual custom by sending out a descriptive synopsis of the book. Hutchinsons sought this book (after noting that Heinemann had lost £900 on *Parham*), but they offered much lower terms. Wells remarked that 'in view of current state of affairs', he found the offer 'quite satisfactory'. An early contract prepared by Watt was rejected by the publishers before another contract met approval.

Wells liked his own book very much, and remarked in a letter to Watt, sending on a précis, that the book was similar to *Kipps* in many ways, saying that Theodore Bulpington 'is an acutely differentiated character but there is something of all of us in his mental tangles and though he is an unfaithful lover, an outrageous liar, and narrowly escapes being shot for cowardice, he keeps more of our sympathy to the end than perhaps some of us will care to admit.' Perhaps so, but in any event, whether it was the time, the state of the economy, or the perception of H.G.'s work, the book did not sell, and it was to be some time before Wells returned to formal fiction of full length.[5]

Wells had much greater success in selling his shorter pieces, and giving talks for which he received payment when they were later published. Much of the rest of the decade would be taken up with this work. His message became clearer under the pressure of time and space, and his public round the world welcomed his comment. He found this success first in a series of talks he was invited to give near the end of the '20s and the beginning of the '30s. His speaking voice and platform manner had improved somewhat since the days of his talk at the Royal Institution in 1902. His voice remained high, but he spoke directly to his audience now, without smothering his comments in his moustache. His voice still tended to have a dying fall, and the high tone at first put people off, but continued practice aided even these defects. I have spoken to half a dozen persons who heard Wells speak on certain formal occasions, and all of them have remarked that although initially they were put off by his high-pitched voice, they soon forgot this in the physical presence of the man. Of course, the microphone, now in use in most places, and specified by Wells for his engagements wherever possible, enhanced his tone, and made him more intelligible. In any case, whatever the deficiencies of his voice, they remained minor as audiences crowded into lecture halls to hear him deliver his comments on the world and its future progress.

As the decade wore on and Wells perceived the increasing danger to the world, and as he became aware of the impact of his radio talks, he made more and more formal speeches. At the beginning of the period, however, he tended to save his remarks for specific occasions and important audiences. In 1927, for instance, after an invitation tendered first by J.D. Beresford, but then seconded by the French institution, Wells gave a major speech at the Sorbonne in Paris. He spoke here of the changes he perceived in democratic institutions, and urged his audience to follow them closely, to monitor their effects so that the French, in particular, leaders of the world's culture, would not be left at the post. He spoke of the tortuous road taken since the French Revolution, with the alluring byways of Marxism, controlled socialism, and a return to a benign aristocracy always beckoning. He urged his auditors to take the lead in the changes he noted, remarking, near the end of his speech, 'What is there to prevent a great politico-religious drive for social and world unity taking hold everywhere of the active and adventurous minority of mankind — that is to say, of the mankind who matters — even quite soon?'[6]

Wells also spoke at the Reichstag in Berlin, at a special meeting of a literary society in the spring of 1929. He returned to his topic of the need for world peace, and denounced patriotism as scamping the style of the peace-seeker. He discussed both the horror of modern war, and the promise implicit in cosmopolitan activities such as the Olympic Games, urging his German audience to participate in the Kellogg Peace Pact, to work as though peace were around the corner, to forget past wrongs and humiliations for the benefit of all the people of the world. He also urged the Germans to a new *Kulturkampf*, not in the sense of Bismarck's war on Catholicism but a new war against false history and patriotic teaching which poisoned the minds of children. Not just a new teaching was wanted, but the suppression of the old teaching, with its emphasis on military displays and outworn shibboleths; he ended his talk calling for a new 'War to end War', in which all could participate and benefit.[7]

Wells also spoke in Madrid to student audiences on medieval history, focusing on the significance of the silver and gold finds of the sixteenth century and their impact on modern capitalism. Eileen Power and her new graduate student, Michael Postan, provided detailed comments on this speech before he delivered it.[8]

Other important addresses in this period which established Wells's credentials not only as an orator, but as an orator on current events, were his remarkable talk to the Liberal Summer School in the summer of 1932; his speech to the National Peace Council in October 1934; and his later talks to the Oxford University Liberal Club in the spring of 1938. These are the papers which created the most controversy, and provided the widest response, so a brief look at them may be useful.[9]

The Liberal Summer School talk created a great storm, as Wells discussed the monarchy and the tired coalition government in control of Parliament, and suggested an alliance of left parties to replace the latter. This led to an invitation to provide a road map for these groups. He responded in the *Daily Herald*, and the New York *Daily American*, with 'I Demand a Creed to Save the World'. He called for a statement of general aims (this would become the 'Manifesto of Progressive Parties and Individuals'), and said that he made this call because

> There is, I believe, a great and growing stir in the minds of men to fight the sombre destiny that hangs over humanity. The gathering distresses of our race, deepening economic misery, the unrelieved threat of war and the lassitudes of governments are rousing a spirit which is in its essence revolutionary.

He urged replacement of private profits by collective production and collective enterprise, a new world system of finance and credit, scientific development of the world's resources, distribution of the resulting wealth to benefit all in the fullest amount possible for the entire species, organization of a world *pax* to end armaments, suppression of private manufacture of weaponry, and finally, the organization of education throughout the world 'to ensure to every human being the necessary knowledge and ideas and necessary habit of service, for conscious, willing and competent co-operation in the human commonwealth'. Free speech, free publication, and the right of free movement throughout the world were necessary adjuncts to this last.[10]

The Wells call for a new creed became the first chapter in the resulting Manifesto, published early in 1934, although Wells told Lord Allen of Hurtwood that he could only write and talk, and never was able to lead such groups. He told them he could not 'play Aaron to my own Moses'. The authors of the Manifesto remained as a ginger group outside the organized parties, and eventually spun off another organization, to which Wells was sympathetic, the Next Five Years Group. Dozens of prominent persons in England met and laid out a plan of action, submitting it to dozens more for signature. The group called for organized economic planning, especially for Britain, as well as a reorganization of industry, banking, finance, foreign trade, and agriculture along lines of social justice for all Britons. They urged joint action with the United States towards world peace. This group, active until after Munich, was the base force leading to much of the reconstruction of Britain after 1945, and deserves more mention that it usually receives. Wells, as was often the case, was the initial promoter. He saw that as his place in the world, and filled it very well.[11]

Wells also spoke more directly on the issues of peace to an audience at the Queen's Hall in November 1934, under the auspices of the National Peace Council. He told this group, 'We Peace Seekers are revolutionaries or we are absurdities. We stand for the World State or we stand convicted of either stupidity or imposture.' This speech, in a number of forms, was reprinted several times and in several different venues. It was widely used as well by persons who advocated the Oxford Peace Pledge.[12]

Writing on these subjects brought Wells back into the ambit of the League of Nations Union, and although he did not endorse the League, he did provide a number of interviews for League publications and others committed to putting an end to war. For instance, he had spoken with others in a series on the issues of world peace in 1920, and re-endorsed his views when the speeches were reprinted in 1933. He gave an interview to a League-supporting publication, the *New World*, in the autumn of 1930, calling for world education for peace, and also wrote for *No More War*, another journal with Quaker sponsors. This led to an interesting correspondence with Konni Zilliacus, active in Geneva for the League, and Wells eventually went to visit him and see the League in action. Wells sent him *The Open Conspiracy* and the two exchanged a number of letters concerning the peace movement, and what could be done about the growing fascist menace. Wells's talks and interviews came as a direct result of a significant first speech he made on the BBC.[13]

The BBC speeches, as was true of most of his public utterances in this period, were about the world and its quest for peace. He did turn once more to a local audience, calling for a revival of the classic Liberal creed, but even here he was only interested in the potential impact on the world. Wells had become a citizen of the world, based in England. His views were widely sought, and he spoke out constantly against the rising tide of terror, hate, and manipulation. He urged better education, wider understanding, and above all, the banding together of like-minded people to defeat these forces, and to create a new world, a *pax humana*. His essays written for the lucrative American market are all pieces of the greater dream. A brief description of some of these essays will indicate how far he had travelled, but also that his audience for this sort of thinking was growing — it was wider now in the US, perhaps, but growing nevertheless. In the final result, it did not grow quickly or widely enough, but a review of the period certainly leaves Wells free of guilt as to the final coming of the Second World War and its horror.[14]

Wells was under constant pressure to comment, and he utilized the pressure 'to extract as much' money in return as possible, as he told Ritchie Calder who solicited an article for the *Daily Herald*. He refused a great many offers, as when the *Sunday Referee* wanted a weekly column but did not offer enough. The *Reader's Digest* paid well but was so stuffy about editing and re-editing that after appearing there once or twice Wells was not interested. He told the *News Chronicle*, who asked for a statement on 'What is Happiness?', that the subject was dismal — 'All wet now', early in 1938; and although he was tempted to write an appreciation of Shaw, when he could not control the world rights he refused. He also refused to write on what he would do about Germany if he were Prime Minister, but this was largely due to the pressure of other work. His words were always valuable, though, as when the *Sunday Chronicle* editor, G. Drawbell, simply wrote asking for articles. Watt told Marjorie, when he relayed the offer, 'Mr Drawbell seems to be what the lawyers call a "willing buyer".' So he was, but so were many others, as Wells's ideas attracted attention, and sold newspapers and magazines, especially in the United States where he developed a great following, particularly among those who saw the German and Nazi menace for what it was. The United States was rapidly becoming politically split over whether it should interfere in European affairs, and Wells's comments provided strong support for those who wished American participation.[15]

He was constantly asked to prophesy what might be coming to the world. He used these occasions to discuss the failures of the past, as a way of avoiding them in the future, talking about possible disarmament and asking his audience a series of stiff questions as to their desires, making the point that what they wanted was what they would get, and if they were supine, they would only get more of the same. 'Are we at the dawn of another — a world-wide — Renaissance? Or is it indeed the ultimate bankruptcy of the human mind which is approaching?' were his queries to readers.[16]

In the earlier part of the decade Wells was a good deal more sanguine about future developments, holding out hope that a world *pax* could be achieved and possibly within the lifetime of his readers. All it would take would be tolerance, and he welcomed the Roosevelt New Deal as a possible, though ambiguous, start in these directions. Of course he knew full well, and constantly informed his readers, that it would take a massive effort, and the chances were no better than even, whatever the effort; but without the effort, there was no chance. One way to help was to provide truth in advertising, even in publishers' blurbs, as well as in other matters. The concept of honesty in all matters would achieve more than all the conferences one could imagine.[17]

Wells on occasion extended his view of the future to as much as a half-century away, but cautioned that the rate of change in life had recently become so great that any prediction was problematical. The overriding question to be solved was armament. Governments were also still a big problem because of their hidebound attitudes. His words, as he looked forward to the world of 1981, have a mordant and futile sting to them as we read them today:

> He [HGW] sees a world still firmly controlled by soldiers, patriots, usurers, and financial adventurers; a world surrendered to suspicion and hatred, losing what is left of its private liberties very rapidly, blundering towards bitter class conflicts and preparing for new wars.

To avoid this 'a renaissance of human courage and creativeness' was needed. If that occurred we could recondition the land, provide a world garden, 'a soundly educated world, aware of its origins, capable of measuring and realizing and controlling its destinies with an ever-growing sense of power'. But, without that concentrated effort he called for, 'when presently the rifles are put in our hands again, we shall kill. The whips will be behind us, and the "enemy" in front. The old history will go on with us, because we had not the vigour to accept the new.'[18] Readers of the present book will work out for themselves which of his possible worlds came to be.

Before mentioning very briefly Wells's work on the international situation, it might be well to remind ourselves of the world in which he was writing. It was a world which had suffered greatly in World War I, especially England, Germany, and France. The capitalist system seemed to be dying, and dictatorships had sprung up with many instant solutions to that decline, most of which found scapegoats for the failures of their governments in other people, other events. The expectations in life of ordinary people had been heightened by a freer press, cheaper newspapers, and wireless radio, but these had been in large measure unfulfilled because of the slump. The possibility of war, and future wars for unknown purposes, hung over the heads of the people, a large majority of whom took this as given, and lived out their lives without thought for tomorrow. Others worried, but were ineffective. The world seemed, to most of its citizens, to be a difficult, and worsening, place.

The *Sunday Chronicle* took a postal poll of readers on world affairs, in the wake of the re-occupation of the Rhineland and the invasion of Ethiopia, and just before a series of articles by Wells on world affairs. Sixty-five per cent of the response came from the north of England, with two-thirds of that figure from Yorkshire and Lancashire. The table indicates that response:

Question	Yes	No
Did you believe in League of Nations before Ethiopia?	72%	28%
Do you believe now?	61	39
Should members of League fight for League principles?	75	25
Should Britain retire from League?	71	29
Is there any cause for which you would fight?	95	5[19]

This poll preceded a long H.G. Wells article on 'The World Drifting to Future War'. The article had had even more frightening titles at other stages in its development: 'The World Shifting Towards a Universal Futile War — An Onlooker Speaks', was one such title; others were 'Staggering Towards World War', and 'The Drift to War'. In these articles Wells began to be much less sanguine about the immediate future. War seemed inevitable to him, as it did to many. Only a remarkably concentrated effort could prevent it. When Spain began to go under later in the decade, Wells was even less optimistic. 'Maybe a certain cringing immunity may be possible for a few years more if Eastern Europe and France are thrown to the wolves. Then, in a state of extreme disadvantage, the British Empire [and the USA] will come to its last accounting.' As he remarked in another place, Czechoslovakia had 'paid the moral price for us', but these events were not yet over. Everywhere one looked the horrors were mounting, and nothing seemed possible to prevent them.[20]

As can be seen by these recitals and summaries, Wells had become increasingly disconsolate as he viewed the world. This manifested itself in a number of ways. Perhaps the most important is the significant article which he wrote in 1935 for the very prestigious journal of the American Council on Foreign Relations, entitled 'Civilization on Trial', along with his effort to set out his own views, and those of others, in his book of the period, *The Anatomy of Frustration*. With these two pieces of work out of the way, he was able to concentrate on carrying his message of possible peace to the world. He then embarked on a series of novels reflecting on current events, undertook a major effort in the field of public education, and made a series of journeys in which he presented his views to large audiences, as well as a series of broadcasts and films. In a sense Wells adapted his attack on the affairs of his time to the new tools of the twentieth century as he fulfilled his destiny of prophet, gadfly, and Cassandra.

In his piece for *Foreign Affairs*, addressed, through the readership of the journal, to embassies and departments of state and external affairs, as well as to other top leadership positions in the world, Wells urged his audience to begin thinking of others than themselves when they set goals for the future. 'Is there not a possibility that in the future we can get away from the idea that human affairs are necessarily shaped and controlled in foreign offices and embodied in what are called foreign policies?' was his question. Following on his spring visit to the United States (the second in less than a year), he pointed out to his American readers that idle hands and idle brains could be put to good use throughout the world, rather than just at home:

> The surplus of energy which has accumulated in human affairs for several thousands of years has been partially expended in building up the standards of life. But the most natural method of relief has been war. War is a kind of excretion of the human social body. The energy accumulates — and human intelligence is not adequate to the problem of how to utilize it. So it has to get rid of it again. The chief corrective has been war.

Wells said that unless people understood this simple equation, war would come again. And although he knew that many Americans felt that they could remain out of that war, he warned them that this was very unlikely.

What was worse, in a world dominated by English-speakers, there was only a common language, but no common purpose to life. How tragic this misapplication of ideas seemed to him. Wells thought that a joint air patrol (similar to the one recently begun on the Maine—New Brunswick border) could be instituted in the world by Britain and the United States, to be followed by a joint fleet, joint police efforts, and so on, to lead the world into peace. For him, the answer was simple:

> The only thing to do is to invent a successful form of peace. That means a new sort of life for human beings. The choice before us is war or a new world — a rational liberal collectivist world with an ever rising standard of life and an ever bolder collective enterprise, in science, in art, in every department of living. Because so far we have not shown the intellectual power and vigour to take the higher, more difficult way, because we have not had sense enough to discover what to do with our accumulation of social energy, is why at the present time we are drifting and sliding back towards destruction. If humanity fails, it will fail for the lack of organized mental effort and for no other reason.[21]

Wells wrote this piece, or began it, on a ship returning to England. In the previous year he had made two trips to America, lunching and talking informally with Franklin D. Roosevelt on both occasions. He had also interviewed and talked with some of the major vocal forces in the United States, with Senator Huey Long of Louisiana, and with other important opposition senators such as Gerald P. Nye (North Dakota) and William Borah (Idaho). And he had listened to some of the private forces in opposition, Francis G. Townsend, leader of the old-age movement, and Father Francis X. Coughlin, the proto-fascist priest from Detroit, champion of social credit, who had an extremely popular radio programme. Wells also talked with most of the members of Roosevelt's Cabinet, and observed the New Deal methods in operation. The article in *Foreign Affairs* was a sober plea to Americans to harness their efforts even further; he was to make similar pleas after his 1934 visit to Russia, and his more formal interview with Joseph Stalin.[22]

His second trip to the US in the '30s was a formally planned one to produce articles for *Collier's*. They paid his expenses, his fares, for all of his necessary paraphernalia, and housed him in good clubs in Washington and New York, in return for three articles of 4,000 words each. Wells was interested in their overture, and when they increased their offer to $12,500 (from $10,000), he accepted the opportunity 'to comment on the New Deal'. *Collier's* wanted exclusive articles, and Wells agreed to give no speeches until after the book, on which he reserved the rights, should appear. The editors met him at quarantine; his baggage was not even inspected. He flew from New York to Washington, spent his time meeting the officials he wished to see, and left for London again on 30 March, on the *Berengaria*, after being in the US for twenty-three days. The articles appeared in *Collier's*, and in due course in a small book, *The New America — The New World* (1935). In it he summarized what he had seen, and the areas in which the New Deal was successful, although he was concerned about the right-wing opposition such as Long and Townsend, as well as Father Coughlin, of whom he heard more than he had expected. He used his metaphor of 'unexpended energy' in this work and called for a working New Deal in other places in the world.[23]

Wells's trip to the Soviet Union was very similar, although his interview with Stalin was much more formal. It was easy for him to go to Moscow when he wished, and apparently this trip occurred in part as he worked on his autobiography and wished to include a section on the changes since his visit at the end of the war. He and Maisky had kept up their friendship, supplying each other with comments and analysis, which led, for instance, to considerable discussion over the merits of the Five Year Plan instituted by Stalin in the late 1920s. The BBC broadcast a series of eight talks on Russia in 1931, and Wells summed up the series in the final broadcast. As he said in the last paragraph of that talk, the idea of longer-range planning in Russia might well come to be some salvation for Europe and America. Many in the world accepted this view with ease.[24]

Maisky was soon posted to London, and he and Wells met and discussed books, the future of the Soviet state, and many other matters on several occasions in the early years of the '30s. Maisky came to Wells's house to dine, and other more informal meetings also occurred. Wells introduced

Maisky to Brendan Bracken, at the former's request, and in return Maisky sent Wells a copy of an address he had given to the Anglo-Russian Parliamentary Committee, at Birmingham. Just before Wells left for the USSR he again had lunch with Maisky; they discussed which questions he should put to Stalin, and they met again when Wells returned, in order to compare notes.[25]

At this juncture it may not seem that a discussion/interview between Stalin and Wells can have been of much consequence. However, it needs to be thought of in context. Most western countries had not recognized the Bolshevik government after the Revolution. Distrust and fear greeted its ascendance to power, followed by intervention, spying, and consequent reservations and mistrust. The Russians on the other hand feared the capitalist nations as well, and although their ideology predicted their eventual victory, the timetable (especially by 1934) was very vague.

American financial pressures (from the steel and automobile industries and farm circles) had brought about US recognition in 1933. Each side still viewed the other with great suspicion, however. Wells, as an independent thinker of the left, with a reputation, was probably seen by Stalin and his advisers as a useful conduit for information of a more positive or benign nature. Wells, for his part, undoubtedly thought that he could break down Russian fears of the west, and that Russia and Stalin might join with F.D. Roosevelt to work together for world peace, in the face of rising fascism in Germany and a stagnant government in England.

These ideas were well understood at the time and account for the intense interest in the talks. The continued availability and reprinting of the book that came out of them also attests to their hoped-for significance in breaking down barriers of distrust between the two forces that have emerged as the chief powers since this century's German wars.

What appeared after Wells's visit was a transcript of his talk with Stalin, printed in the *New Statesman*, followed by detailed comments from Bernard Shaw, Ernst Toller, J. M. Keynes, Dora Russell, with still further responses and ripostes from Shaw and Wells. The text of all this was then published as a pamphlet, illustrated by David Low. In the talks Stalin and Wells sparred for a bit as to whether Wells could travel as an ordinary citizen, and then settled down to a discussion of the relative strengths and goals of the Soviet Five Year Plan as compared with the efforts of Roosevelt and the New Deal. Stalin, while paying a considerable compliment to the intellectual powers of Roosevelt, made the point that the two countries were pursuing different economic and social courses, so whether comparison was useful or not was a moot question.

Wells and Stalin then went on to discuss the role of the individual in a collective society; Wells tended to celebrate the individual more, at least in this talk, while Stalin dealt more in class groupings. They also disagreed on the role of the lower middle classes. Stalin said a more important group in the twentieth century were the technicians, who had to support the state and its efforts or all would be lost. There was then considerable discussion of the part played by strong leadership, and the violence that might be needed to achieve power, as the two men considered the means to what were very similar ends, at least in their separate views of historical necessity. More talk followed on revolutions, the succession of leaders in history, and, as had been the case when Wells spoke with Lenin, the discussion ended with an analysis of the British bourgeoisie. They concluded their meeting with comments about the mutual need for self-criticism, and Wells told Stalin that he and Roosevelt held the fate of the world in their hands.

Shaw, Toller, and others simply repeated, in their *New Statesman* comments, much of the dialogue; although typically, Shaw thought it basically a comedy of no utility. Keynes replied to Shaw, as did Wells, both pointing out that the playwright was simply proceeding as though he alone had the proper answers, and that he was ignoring what had gone before as well as the newer meaning of the dialogue. Wells hoped Shaw would actually listen and read what had been said, and called him to task for an unnecessary attack on PEN, which Shaw thought ineffectual. The correspondence then dwindled into a slanging match, and whether much was actually accomplished is difficult to say.

Stalin, for his part, was probably not much enlightened by Wells — he had a suspicious and difficult response to western intellectuals at the best of times. Wells was too close to the bone for him, at some points, as the writer felt able to criticize the Soviet Union, something which Stalin disliked. Wells, on the other hand, remained friendly to Russia, and to Russian ideals. He abhorred the violence, but at the same time, knew that Russia was different from Britain and America, and that violence there was perhaps more of a way of life. Some understanding of the two positions represented may have occurred in those who read the dialogue with relatively open minds, not always possible in Russian affairs, of course.[26]

Wells continued to remain sympathetic to the ideals of the Soviet Union, as did the Webbs and many other English intellectuals. He congratulated the Webbs on their mammoth book, *Soviet Communism*, sending them his 'unqualified respect', although he later told Sidney that they had under-represented the issue of 'personal autocracy' in the USSR. Beatrice told him, in return, that 'There is no one whose approval of our monstrous performance we so much relish as your own.' Wells continued his discussions on Russia with other visitors, and he and Maisky continued to exchange letters and visits. The Webbs and Wells later exchanged views on the 'show trials', although by this time both Wells and the Webbs were using Moura Budberg as a postbox for ideas, letters, and other comments from Russia. Wells even sent a letter (with others) to celebrate the twenty-first anniversary of the Revolution, and as it arrived after Munich, the reception of that letter was even more poignant. Russia had been isolated again, much as Stalin (and Wells) had feared. Solidarity was still important, but it seemed much less likely than in the late summer of 1934.[27]

If one thinks of these early visits to the US and the interview with Stalin as part of Wells's first efforts to study the world of the slump and the dictators, his response can best be seen perhaps in his unusual work, *The Anatomy of Frustration*, which appeared in early 1936. In this book, which is something of a milestone in Wells's efforts to understand human affairs, he used a prototype, the personal philosophic text by Robert Burton, *The Anatomy of Melancholy* (1621), as his model. Wells's book is a statement about his world in mid-decade between the slump and the coming of the war.

He thought that he was able to see the biological drives of our species becoming sublimated into a personal desire for immortality and for personal salvation, whether through religion, writing, or some other way of leaving part of one's being behind. 'That means in conduct that behaviour is shaped so that its main conception is the co-operative rendering and development of experience and the progressive development in the whole race of a co-ordinated will to continue and expand' (Chapter 4). For Wells this meant the development, although very slowly, of a new ethic. The failure to achieve this development as rapidly as was wanted had led to frustration, and in extreme cases, to suicide, thought Wells. This description might even apply to societies or groups, as well as individuals. Our desires for peace were those in most danger of this frustration and although the subconscious might overcome the lack of education, it would be much better if *Homo sapiens* could develop a moral code for everyone.

In this venture towards a moral code socialism had failed miserably, he said, because it had no idea of what constituted the transitional phases, a worthy enough goal on their own, leading up to socialism. This is where he describes his views of 'a competent receiver' at their fullest. Wells then provides for the consideration of his readers a plan to found a series of intermediate states, contracts, and directorates, to organize affairs on the way to the desired goal of the World State. As these new conglomerations did their work, a new religion and a new ethic would be hammered out to deal with the end results, or so he assumed.

It would be necessary to provide a peace as a substitute for war, and he called for the development of a new encyclopaedia of knowledge in the new phase of human life. He developed three theses which should govern the new world:

[1] whatever the origins of the ideas and practices of ownership may be, ownership is now made, protected and enforced by the laws of society, and there is no reason whatever except the collective welfare why any sort of ownership or any particular ownership should be enforced or permitted.

[2] whatever the distribution of sovereignties may have been in the past, all Mankind is now the ultimate owner of the natural resources of

the planet, earth, sky and sea, and that, failing for the present a complete general direction for the exploitation of these resources ... those who have them must be regarded as caretakers of treasure-trove and navigators of derelicts, all responsible to a final accounting.

[3] "money exists to pay wages." It is the mechanism of the producer's share-out. ... The expectation of security and satisfactions upholds the worker through the less interesting parts of his task and justifies the parts that are interesting.

Or, as he summarized the meanings of his theses for the future:

The Frustration of World Peace ... is due to the inadequate education of the human imagination and it can be defeated only by an immense poetic effort, by teaching, literature, suggestion and illumination. A vast Kultur-Kampf lies between mankind and peace. We must go through that battle; there is no way round.

(Chapter 13)

As one follows these ideas, it becomes apparent that education is for all life, not just the young. In this discussion Wells uses the concept of Jewishness as something which had had great value in sustaining the member group, but which must now be set aside to the greater good of all. Others, such as Catholics, Moslems, Communists, Nazis, all would have to give over their creeds as well, which were essentially selfish ways of maintaining life in the face of the growing need for change. Without doing this, frustration, already present in the world, would become unbearable.

He then goes off into a long discussion of the loneliness created by the need of humans to find a 'lover-shadow' who could aid in the great search. If man's full life is to be achieved, it will have to be in groups, not alone, and must accompany and be accompanied by love (an androgynous love, although he does not use that term). Without it, life is impossible, and although he remarks that his own life is possessed by a 'maleness' which he abhors and finds unnecessary, it has come from this world as it now is, not as he hopes it might become. If the human and sexual love he describes could be joined to the desires for world freedom and happiness, the frustrations which now prevent our species from full achievement would be completely overcome.

Most of us prefer to float half-hidden even from ourselves, in a rich, warm, buoyant, juicy mass of familiar make-believe. Until it overwhelms us. We were born in the morass and we are at home there. Our minds are still in the amphibian stage and cannot hold out in the dry clear air. ... A day will come when we shall cease to hide from each other. ... Candour, like everything else worth while, is a thing to be achieved with infinite difficulty. ... There are times when the whole spectacle of human life seems to me like a crowd of people without eyes for sight, tongues for speech or hands for gesture. . . . Our deeds are dreadful because our minds are dark. . . .

(Chapter 22)

This book is a profound cry from Wells's heart. Buried in it and driving the text are his own frustrations, ideals, and hopes. However, it still has a ray of hope for the human condition. Success for the species is all still possible, but . . . and it was with that 'but' that H.G. Wells faced the remainder of his life, in times which moved with great speed towards what seemed like Armageddon. However, as he was still optimistic, even in the face of all this knowledge and fear, he could not just let it come. He had to be busy in his work of educating the world. Now it was time to take his show on the road.[28]

REPUBLICAN RADICAL IN SEARCH OF HOT WATER

> The issue is a plain one. It involves us all; no part of the world of thought and creative imagination can escape it. It is a conflict between gangster adventurers or dull politicians on the one hand, trading on old national jealousies and resentments, stale and decaying and now poisonous dogmas and fear, who are blundering us down to destruction. That is one side of it. On the other hand, opposing this is the directive power of the fearless and unhampered human intelligence, expressing, educating and discovering. For this last, and for its supremacy, we of the PEN Club stand. This is the fundamental choice in life for every intelligent person, and by that choice mankind will triumph or end in complete disaster. We cannot avoid taking sides. No one can stand aloof. There is no neutral ground in this conflict; no middle way.... The whole intellectual life of man revolts against this intolerable, suffocating, murderous nuisance, the obsolescent national State. A world revolution to a higher social order, a world order, or utter downfall lies before us all.
>
> HGW, undelivered speech (to have been given at the Stockholm convention of PEN scheduled for September 1939, cancelled by events), reprinted as 'The Honour and Dignity of the Free Mind', *Travels of a Republican Radical in Search of Hot Water* (1939)

At first thought one might assume that H.G. Wells would have been among the earliest persons to use wireless radio and film for his messages. He was very tentative about both media, however, primarily because in the early days of these new forms of communication, censorship was usual, and he was adamant that others should not be allowed to tamper with his work. As with his writing, when he released a piece, it was ready for the press. He submitted to only minimal editing, and even protested at the practice of editorial cross-heads being supplied in his text. When he realized that the time allotted to a broadcast was often used as an excuse to shorten, cut, or otherwise alter his written words, he simply refused to participate.

The BBC, which began broadcasting on a regular basis in the Home Service in 1922, was very anxious to obtain Wells's participation. As early as 1925 they wrote to him asking him to take part in a programme on telepathy. He refused, as he also refused to read out his stories, although the producer assured him that this would consist 'simply of sitting at a table in a quiet room and reading aloud in your normal voice'. He did allow some bits of *Kipps* to be read aloud by others for use in a school programme on 'Heroes of Modern Fiction'. Another item in the series was Kipling's *Kim*. The BBC paid Wells, and Kipling, a guinea for every 1,000 words read in the programme. By 1930 that figure had risen to 2 gns. per 1,000 words of Wells's work. Wells continued to refuse invitations to talk, even when the BBC's director of programmes and talks, Lance Sieveking, a friend of Wells's from his club, came to Easton to implore him. Sieveking even asked Wells to come to the BBC and watch a broadcast, and offered to provide a radio in his flat so that he could hear the programming for himself.[1]

Wells finally succumbed to the BBC pleas, but only when they agreed that he was not to be censored. (Sir Henry Lauder and the Prince of Wales were the only others to be granted this exemption.) Shaw, as did many others, submitted his copy beforehand, and although Wells was willing enough to do this, he was not willing to have a single word changed. The person who finally persuaded Wells to accept the BBC offer was the assistant director for talks, Hilda Matheson. Now generally forgotten, this woman, along with Sieveking, shaped much of the BBC's programming policy through about 1935, and established, among other things, the freedom to treat any subject, along with a bias towards talks and appearances by significant persons in the world. Wells, in a memorial volume after her death, remarked that the BBC might have become a haven for vulgarity, and that Matheson had 'made a valiant and almost single-handed attempt to save us from this'. He called her 'courageous and indefatigable' on behalf of 'liberal thought and free expression'. Eventually she quarrelled with the BBC, and resigned, but she had made a major contribution by the time she left.[2]

As it happened, Wells met Hilda Matheson at Eileen Power's flat; Bertrand Russell was also present. In a comic contretemps, Wells left taking Matheson's handbag along with his hat and other items, leaving her without any money for transport. Russell provided the coins needed and the four exchanged amused letters. Matheson used the occasion to say to Wells, 'I have always found it to be pretty devastating that an internationalist like yourself — perhaps you are the only real internationalist? — shouldn't be making use of the most international means of communication there is. . . .' Wells accepted this comment, and with the censorship problem bypassed (apparently it was not an internal decision, but had had to do with the Postmaster General and control of the BBC), he said he would give a talk on 'World Peace'. She told him that something like his Reichstag address, which she had read, would be perfect. She also told him he should remember that the listeners could not respond, except by post, and that 'We are supposed to avoid the controversial handling of religious, industrial or political subjects except in discussion or debates.' She also asked him to refrain from any attacks on God or the King. Wells agreed to those provisions, said that he would speak primarily on the Kellogg Pact, and asked about copyright (which he reserved), especially after he learned that the talk would be reprinted in the *Listener*. They avoided seeming to take sides by putting Vernon Bartlett on the air the next night with a different view of the same topic. The BBC executives were concerned about the quality of Wells's voice and issued a statement that his talk was of 'outstanding importance'. They also engaged a symphony orchestra to stand by in case his timing was not accurate.[3]

Wells gave his talk on 10 July 1929. The BBC authorities were very concerned about his sensibilities, especially over how much to pay him (settling finally on 50 guineas). They gave him a dinner before the broadcast; he provided the guest list, which included Eileen Power, Rachel Crowdy, Count Bernstorff, Lady Whyte, Arthur Salter (who refused, as he was out of town), Desmond MacCarthy, Mrs Julian Huxley, Gerald Barry, Leonard and Virginia Woolf, and D. M. Matheson. The BBC also provided a bottle of whisky and a siphon of soda water if he needed it after the talk. His guests at the dinner sat in the studio while he spoke into the microphone.[4]

In the talk Wells asked his listeners what he termed the main question, 'How far is patriotism comparable with peace, now that weapons of war are so terrible?' He described the League as 'a debating society', and remarked that patriotism had 'defeated the new pacifism'. Answering his own query, he said that patriotism had been rendered defunct and counter-productive, but that governments, not people, had failed to adjust to the fact. He called for the abandonment of some sovereignty and 'ideas of national competition', asking his audience to relate to children and education to make the change. 'Let us set our face hard', he proposed, 'as learners, teachers, as parents and rulers, as people who talk and influence others, against the teaching of patriotic histories that sustain and carry on the poisonous war-making tradition of the past.'

Complaints flooded in to the BBC over the talk. One Bournemouth correspondent wrote to her MP, asking if nothing could be done 'to prevent broadcasting being used for dangerous teaching'. Others thought the BBC was 'entirely in Socialist hands now', and that the 'nationalization of the national life and character was next'. The BBC replied with a form letter assuring listeners of its impartiality, and citing the Vernon Bartlett talk the next night on the same topic.[5]

Comments in the press were much more positive about Wells and his views. The *Yorkshire Post* characterized his voice as 'light, high-pitched, and uncompelling', but said the listener soon overcame that, and they described the talk as 'brilliant speaking' and congratulated both Wells and the BBC. The *Observer* called his ideas 'wise and largely ignored', which they found appalling. They said, 'He may irritate some, but his lancet stabs only to heal,' and urged him to make many more speeches, to create a great public debate on the issues he raised. They thought that Vernon Bartlett's talk was good as well, and commended the BBC again. The *Listener* could barely contain themselves for self-congratulation over the talk, and allowed correspondence on it to fill the next several issues.

Wells was a huge success. His talk, somewhat modified and strengthened, was published by Ernest Benn to be used as Lenten reading in 1930. All in all the great experiment had been remarkably useful. Wells apparently enjoyed the experience; his friends and associates were happy with the quality of his voice, and those who supported his views could not have been happier with the wide airing they had received. The BBC knew that they too had made a coup, and pursued Wells to make other broadcasts immediately after the furore over the first talk died down.[6]

He and Hilda Matheson became quite friendly. When she returned from a holiday trip to Geneva, she wrote to him about several mutual friends 'you so illogically have in the Secretariat'. She asked him to do another talk, and Wells responded by describing her as a 'bully', but agreed to give the talk, one of a series, which was called 'Points of View'. The BBC raised the fee to 100 guineas for this talk, in the series which also featured J. B. S. Haldane, Shaw, Lowes Dickinson, Dean Inge, and Oliver Lodge. When Wells spoke they gave him another party, at which Lord and Lady Colefax were hosts, and Matheson told Wells that 'if there is anyone else you would like to hold your hand', they would invite them. (He asked J.M. Keynes; Lydia Keynes said she would come, but on the day mysteriously did not show up. She had told Matheson, 'I would like to try to help support the nerves of poor H.G.') At the end of the talk, before the microphones were completely shut down, Wells apparently remarked that he was 'whacked' — for which, on their next programme, the BBC felt constrained to apologize to listeners.

Others in the series had given their 'views' rather than points of view, according to Wells, so he went on to describe the versions of H. G. Wells that had already died, and how these versions related to the H. G. Wells of the broadcast, as well as how he related to his ancestors and to other citizens of the world in 1931. He closed his talk with this comment: 'Man, I take it, Man in us, is more important than the things in the individual life, and this I believe not as a mere sentimentality but as a vigorously true statement of biological and mental fact. . . . the best of today will become the commonplace of tomorrow.' He then told his audience that he wished he could turn the radio round so that he could listen to their points of view. That would make the day complete for him.[7]

This talk made HGW something of a radio star. Matheson told him of the great numbers of comments the BBC had had about his broadcast, and

Wells himself received over two hundred letters. He surveyed them generally, but, unfortunately for the BBC, threw the bulk of them away; the Corporation had hoped to study them closely for clues as to their listeners. Wells told the BBC he was surprised how many had agreed with his point of view, and urged them to have a follow-up programme of younger people on their Points of View.[8]

It was after this success that Wells became interested enough in radio to allow the dramatization of some of his work (see the list of works broadcast, in the Notes to Chapter 3 above). The BBC offered him 20 guineas for two performances of a short story, and 40 guineas for a novel. He agreed, but said that he would have to approve each script, and he continued to look these over up to the time of his death. Occasionally the BBC allowed other countries' radio services to broadcast their adaptations, and Wells received payment for these as well and at the same rate. Wells did not always allow them to do all they wished, especially if he hoped to sell the material elsewhere, and he was occasionally more liberal — as when a school friend of Gip's did an adaptation. By 1934 his rate, for a reading, had stabilized at 2s. 6d. for the first 800 words, and 2s. 6d. for each 400 thereafter. The words were to be counted exactly, according to the contracts.[9]

Wells's next real venture with the BBC was his participation in their Russian series of 1931, for which he summed up the talks of earlier speakers. Memoranda circulated internally showed that the top executives in the BBC remained concerned about his 'impartiality', but when this was dealt with, Matheson was instructed to 'get him *on any terms*'. She told Wells that she hoped he would speak as though he were writing a new *Outline of History* five hundred years later, and that this was his chapter on the Russian experiment. For this talk, the United States became part of the listening audience, although the Empire, later the World, Service did not make its formal début until 1932. Wells, Matheson, and Lionel Fielden had lunch to discuss the project and Wells agreed that his talk would simply be a summary. On the night the BBC again gave a dinner for him and Matheson appeared with 'a variety of lozenges'. This talk was later rebroadcast over Radio Ceylon, thus further extending his audience. Although the *Yorkshire Post* found his voice 'unimpressive', they did think that the talk was one of the best ever given, and they urged the BBC to bring him back soon.[10]

This success led very quickly to another series. It began as an idea called 'What Would I Do If I Were World Dictator?' Wells did not like that title and it was changed to 'What I Would Do With the World'. He gave the first talk and several others responded to his queries and comments. This idea originally came from Wells when he and Matheson were having luncheon and discussing what should go out over the wireless; it too was a great success. Wells told his audience that the reason for the rise in dictatorship was that the world was 'terribly out of gear', and the only persons who had any plans were the Russians. He predicted that twenty years of dictatorship were likely to ensue and said that the only way to avoid it was to insist on disarmament. He provided a twenty-year plan for the world, reducing tariffs, putting all transport under a world system, and called for the reorganization of all work, agriculture, and manufacturing over the next twenty years. He suggested a single standard world currency. He called for reorganizing all education, as 'every great change in political, social and economic life demands corresponding educational change.'

His listeners were in awe at his command of ideas. The *Evening Standard* described his performance as 'astonishing', and said that Wells had found a new medium. Right-wing listeners thought his opinions 'scandalous', and some said that his ideas cascaded forth with such speed that they could not be assimilated. The *Guardian* said that he had set an exam paper for others to answer and urged everyone to do so. Eventually, as critics came to discuss broadcasting as an art form, as was done in the *Observer* and the *Sunday Times* later in that year, it was Wells who was held up as an example of how the new toy, radio, could be used in education, in extending knowledge and providing a way for all citizens really to participate in modern life. Wells, for his part, contrasted the civilized way the BBC treated its speakers with America, where there were too many lights, too many reporters, and other things creating difficulties.[11]

Wells was enough of a celebrity on radio now to be able to decline to give talks which were proposed, such as one on his early life. Later he became unhappy with the BBC's 'disregarded ideals', and had to be 'wooed back', as they wanted to do more of his short stories. He turned down talks 'to average listeners', and refused to be on an early version of what sounds like Desert Island Discs, or to predict the future. He did not appear again until the BBC Tenth Anniversary broadcast, when he gave another of his talks, 'Wanted, Professors of Foresight'. Here he called for professors of futurology to be appointed to universities, citing the abolition of time and distance as reasons for a formal study of the future. Sir Alfred Zimmern replied to him, saying that the real issue was nationalism versus industrialization, but Wells pointed out in response that this comment had little to do with his ideas. Correspondence from others followed, lasting more than a month in the *Listener*.[12]

In 1933, as the slump deepened in Britain and the world, the BBC conducted a six-month survey programme entitled 'Taking Stock'. After this they asked Wells to give a talk, to be entitled 'Whither Britain?'. Wells urged that there be several other speakers besides himself; P. M. S. Blackett and R. A. Gregory were examples. When he did the talk it was from Bournemouth (where he was working on his film, *Things to Come*). This was one of the first remote broadcasts. It was recorded and rebroadcast in the United States. Recording was the method the BBC used to conduct the World Service at that time, preferring to control the quality of the sound directly. Wells told his audience that this was an uncensored talk, and he urged listeners to hear him out. He was not a patriot, and not a nationalist, he said, but still he had an intense pride in being English, even though he believed that Britain must become an integral part of the Commonwealth of Nations, or it would drift with the remainder of the world to catastrophe. As he said,

> But is it inevitable that the present poverty, underfeeding, under-education, and degeneration of great multitudes must continue indefinitely and that there must be an ultimate smash into another war storm? I think these are highly probable things. But they are not inevitable. Let us work to make British citizenship into world citizenship.[13]

Protests over Wells's talks continued to plague the BBC, but, to their credit, they went on using his services. He backed out, however, of a series on 'Freedom and Authority', after they cancelled a talk by J. B. S. Haldane on 'Causes of War'. Wells did provide a talk on T. H. Huxley for their series, 'I Knew a Man', in 1935, and they opened the series with it. They recorded this programme and rebroadcast it at a later hour for shift workers. There was more controversy over the issue of Wells's views, but the BBC said, 'After all, we can brave any storm with Wells, presumably. . . .' They did ask Wells to modify a phrase on Carlyle, whom Wells had termed an 'abusive ailing invalid'. As he told the BBC, 'I feel that editing by the BBC is a very undesirable practice. But I think "irritable dyspeptic" will be better than "ailing abusive invalid" and you shall have that instead.' After this talk, Wells was no longer as much in demand; not because his public did not like him, but because his old friends, Hilda Matheson and others, were no longer there to coddle him, and he did not like the editing, or censorship, of his material.[14]

The BBC continued to propose subjects for talks, but none was attractive enough to cause Wells to leave his other writing. They even proposed a special broadcast for the Coronation of George VI, but Wells told them that 'I shall flee London as a pestilence . . . during the Coronation and the only subjects I could possibly talk upon would be *The Advantages of A Republic*; or *The Deadly Influence of the Monarchy in British Intellectual Life*'. As he well knew, this was not acceptable.[15]

Wells's last major talk before the war came at the end of 1937. (He was sure after this that there was an unofficial blacklisting of his name for original talks.) The BBC asked him to provide a talk, to be used in both the domestic and foreign services, on 'As I See It'.[16] The talk focused on his ideas for a new encyclopaedia to be developed by the English-speaking nations, with the result to be a new international education.

After this time Wells's work was heard on both the domestic and the Empire Service of the BBC in the form of plays, or when portions were read to listeners. He watched out for and approved every item, but the

BBC was apparently interested only in dramatizations, adaptations, and readings from his earlier work. His script for *The Man Who Could Work Miracles*, an initially abortive film venture, was the only new material by him that was broadcast. A score for a fifteen-piece orchestra was composed specially for this work, and it was rebroadcast many times, from 1937 to 1943.[17]

The BBC did allow Lance Sieveking (with Wells's permission) to do a dramatized version of *Mr Polly*. Wells revised it, once written, and when the BBC did not take it, it was offered as a potential film script to Hollywood producers. When it appeared that the film might be produced, the BBC tried to claim it, but did not pursue the claim. *Polly*, in that version, went out as a BBC play in the autumn of 1941, and again to the European Service in 1942. Eventually the script was performed by a ship's company, and by the YMCA Dramatic Society in Gibraltar. These dramatizations were much easier matters for the BBC to deal with. The scripts, although Wells reviewed every one, were less expensive to put on, and the BBC did not need to worry about H.G.'s providing commentary which would bring in nasty and negative letters. There probably was no blacklist, but one imagines that the BBC simply took the line of least resistance.[18] The situation remained as it was until 1943, when his ideas came into vogue once more.

Wells had made very good use of the new media and told one of his friends that writing for the wireless and the cinema sharpened his prose. 'I find myself that when I do a radio talk I write and rewrite and weigh any words much more carefully than I do when I am writing for print.' He went on to say that film and radio gave him a better appreciation of music, as well as the spoken and written word. He had just finished his film masterpiece, *Things to Come* — the other new way in which the famous writer brought his message to the twentieth century.[19]

H. G. Wells had little interest in films originally, but his interest grew as he perceived the possibilities in the more sophisticated medium. In 1895, with a colleague, he had patented a special technique for possible film use with *The Time Machine*, but it came to nothing. Hollywood, French, and British producers continued to be interested in the film possibilities of his work, however, and in 1919 Samuel Goldwyn offered Wells a contract for five-year film options, at £1,000 per work, and with a guarantee of at least £2,000 a year. The offers were increased and Famous Players began to bid for his work as well. While in the United States at the Washington Conference, Wells had serious discussions with Goldwyn's representatives, and signed a contract with him for £2,000 a year for options on several books.

The rights to *The First Men in the Moon* and *The Invisible Man* had already been sold elsewhere, and eventually, between 1919 and 1922, silent films were made by the producer Stoll based on *The First Men in the*

Moon, The Wheels of Chance, The Passionate Friends, and *Kipps*. The only one of these to which Wells paid much attention was *Kipps*, which he watched being filmed. When he appeared at the Savoy Hotel at 2 a.m., filming ceased, in fact, while he held court for the actors and director. In 1932 Paramount paid him quite handsomely for the rights to *Dr Moreau*, which was filmed under the title of *The Island of Lost Souls*, starring Charles Laughton and Bela Lugosi. By 1933 Wells had earned £6,750 and $10,000 (or about $42,600) from his various film rights. He disliked the film medium at first, however, whether because of the tenor of the negotiations, which tended to be very mercenary, or because the actors he met, whom he described as 'cinema people', were 'utterly damned fools, beneath the level of a decent man's discussion'.[20]

But the money to be made in films, along with the growing potential of film as a message-bearer, especially after music, colour, and sound were added, were increasingly attractive to Wells. In 1927, apparently after a conversation in a Paris bistro, Wells sketched three one-reel shorts for Ivor Montagu. They, legend has it, were written on the table cloth, and were then transferred to the screen by Montagu and the stars Elsa Lanchester and Charles Laughton. Whether the legend is correct or not, in 1928 the three collaborated with Wells to produce *Bluebottles, The Tonic*, and *Daydreams*.

That same year Wells also began a new sort of novel, designed to be made into a film. It was originally called *The Peace of the World*, in its first draft in 1927, but early readers protested that peace came only after a war, so Wells changed the title to *The King Who Was a King*. In this film treatment he attempted to deal with a modern love interest, that is, one based on equality of emotion as well as purposive action, as well as using the film as propaganda urging an end to war. The idea (which was never made into a film) used a conflict over a miraculous metal compound to focus on the idea of the necessity of world control of resources for the betterment of all. Wells began this project as a film synopsis, first devised in 1926 for £1,000. The producer went bankrupt and the rights reverted to Wells, whereupon he turned his idea into written form. Wells told his agent that while he had been doing the new work, 'I have learned a lot or rather invented a lot of a new technique, and possibly I may follow this book up with another which will ostensibly be the book of a film.' Watt sent the film treatment on to Benn and to Doran (who had already read it and promised to buy it). Benn and Doran spent a fair amount of money advertising the book, using a special dust jacket showing a film projector screening the title. (Doran had got cold feet for a time, and the film treatment had been hawked about in America for several months, which led to some unnecessary publicity.) Although the film was not made, many film-makers were interested in Wells's ideas for the medium; this was especially true of his ideas on music, as up to that time the scores used in film had been of the music-hall variety, not very subtly performed. By the time his film treatment appeared, Wells was being widely sought after for new ideas, and his next effort eagerly awaited.[21]

That next venture proved to be Wells's most important use of film to make his didactic points. Beginning as a book, first called *An Outline of the Future*, and then *The Shape of Things to Come*, the work was a significant effort at prediction, which eventually led to the important predictive film, *Things to Come*. The book itself was widely distributed, and even more widely read. It predicts a world war of twenty-five years' duration, beginning in 1940, and ending with a world illness, the travelling sickness, all of which plunges the world into barbarism. The few remaining survivors are those with technical skills, mostly airmen, who gather at Basra and eventually take over the world, using a peaceful gas to subdue nationalism. Once those tendencies are suppressed, the citizens of the world begin to rebuild, and some centuries later have achieved an idyllic world of peace and universal harmony, with all humans reaching their fullest potential. In the book Wells forecasts a 'Puritan Tyranny' very similar to the idea of the dictatorship of the proletariat, which leads ultimately to the sublimation of personal interests in the interests of the state. Some of the more interesting passages in the book deal with the diminution and end of crime and aberrant behaviour of all kinds.

As Wells ended the book, he told Watt (through Marjorie) that it was in the form of a student's history of 2106, and 'It is not in any sense a fantasia or an extravaganza. It is not crowded with names or the thaumaturgic heroes.' Wells insisted on a cheap edition of the book, and within a year Hutchinson produced a two-volume paperback at 6*d*. As Wells said, 'I don't want this book kept out of the hands of the earnest young men and women, the labouring men, schoolmasters, journalists and all these low-price readers for an interminable time.' He did modify some of the descriptions in the original text, as they were felt (at least by Hutchinsons' solicitors) to be too close a caricature of Sir Basil Zaharoff, the arms manufacturer, and Montague Norman of the Bank of England. (This was the period of the revelations about the World War I arms trade and dozens of pamphlets and books were naming names and bringing charges.) Eventually Wells purchased libel insurance from Lloyds, but no suit or threat of a suit was ever offered on this book. The book sold well, and was serialized or excerpted in papers on both sides of the Atlantic.[22]

The book seemed a natural vehicle for film. Alexander Korda immediately sought out Wells, and the two, meeting at Bournemouth, decided on a film treatment of the latter parts of the book. Wells was given *carte blanche* by Korda to produce a treatment, rather than a regular screen play, for the director William Cameron Menzies. Korda rejected the first version, which was also seen by Menzies and by his assistant and cinematographer, Lajos Biros. Wells then wrote a second version, from which a scenario was derived; Wells used this as the basis for the published version, and essentially as the working script for the film. Changes were made on location as well — mostly, according to Raymond Massey, who played the male lead, to cut out socialism so the film could move more quickly.

Wells and Arthur Bliss, who composed the music for the film, worked very closely together on the production, which was overseen both by Wells, who spent a great deal of time on the set, and by his son Frank, who was the artistic limb of the Wells family and its chief film expert. The film is famous for its evocation of war, and especially of aerial bombing long before the numbing reality of the Blitz, and even before the Luftwaffe's attacks on Spanish villages in the Spanish Civil War. The film follows the book fairly closely, but is made more personal through moving scenes between the hero and his granddaughter, as they discuss past history and the new world to be. The sequence of the space gun (developed, again according to Massey, by German rocket experts soon to go to Peenemunde) and the promise of life to come are also vivid in the memory. The film ends with Wells's eternal question, 'Which shall it be?' — the choice of a future for all, or one of chaotic destruction.

Others besides Massey who made their mark in the film were Ralph Richardson and Ann Todd. The film was listed for a long time among the top twenty films of all time, and some would rate it higher. Critics of the time were very respectful, and the early portions of the film received high critical acclaim, as did the music. *Things to Come* is still often shown on television, and viewers of a later generation are generally impressed with it, although the prints available today are mostly heavily cut, and of poor quality. It was a milestone film, in its concept, execution, and in acting. Its prediction of war as being imminent was taken to heart by many, but not, unfortunately, by those who counted; and when war actually came, in another half-decade, many of the scenes from the film were re-enacted, especially in the earlier days of the war, by persons who had not been recruited as extras.[23]

Raymond Massey received outstanding reviews, and he and Wells were the focus of much attention at the London première on 22 February 1936. The film not only did well, the film treatment Wells had produced sold well, and was serialized in a number of places.[24]

Wells had one more good experience with films, although this time he did not take as active a part. However, he did have a good deal to say about the music, and even the staging, as well as writing a complete 'film story', as he always called his scripts or scenarios. This film treatment, called at first *The New Faust*, and printed under that title in magazines, became in its final form *The Man Who Could Work Miracles*, which was based on a short story of that same title. The basis for the story, and for the film, was that an unassuming man, a draper's assistant, is given the power to make the world in any form he likes. This works fairly well, although much conservative opposition is generated, until the hero, Fotheringay, stops the earth from rotating, and humankind is threatened. By mutual consent the power is withdrawn, and the world reverts to its previous state.

The film, also produced by Korda, starred Roland Young, Ralph Richardson, and Joan Gardner. It was a great comic hit, and Wells and his colleagues did well out of it, as well as out of the book on which it was based. Eventually both Wells's 'film stories' were republished in a single volume, and that also received much praise. Wells actually announced, while in the midst of this work, that he would not publish anything except film treatments in future, which frightened and disturbed many of his friends; but it was an idle threat, even though most of his later books have scenes and parts in which his film experience can be seen. His fling with the silver screen was really over with *The Man Who Could Work Miracles*.[25]

H.G. Wells sent Olaf Stapledon a copy of *Things to Come* soon after they first met. Stapledon liked the book, almost as much as he liked meeting Wells, whom he said he had 'always regarded . . . as one of those famous mythical beasts, like the lion and unicorn, that no one actually meets, no one at least except other mythical beasts like kings and great scientists and film stars'. Frank Swinnerton, who had listened to the BBC version of *The Man Who Could Work Miracles*, also enjoyed reading the film treatment, and told Wells that he would make as great a mark in that field as he had in fiction. George Orwell, reviewing the two 'film stories' when published together, thought them important, although by this time (1940), 'now that we are almost within earshot of Hitler's guns, the Wellsian Utopia, a super-Welwyn constructed by benevolent scientists, is somewhat unconvincing.' As Orwell said, by that time the machines were no longer in the hands of the progressives, but the fascists. Scientists had provided racial theories, poison gases and other horrors. Wells could have been right, but was not, as events overcame his hopes.[26]

Efforts continued to film Wells's work, as Charles Laughton and Famous Players tried to put together a company to do *Tono-Bungay*, for example. They failed, and the only other thing of Wells's that was done between the wars was the Orson Welles radio production of *War of the Worlds* on Hallowe'en of 1938. With this episode, covered elsewhere in this book, Wells's involvement with the new media essentially ended.[27] For the rest of the decade, as the Hitler menace came ever closer, H. G. Wells would attempt to use his old tools of fiction, oratory and journalism, but delivered now primarily to a world-wide audience, in America, in the Antipodes, and elsewhere.

Wellsian success, even if only relative, in cinema and wireless, did not diminish his interest in fiction. What it did do was to create an attitude towards fiction which produced work which was 'cinematic' in design, and this led to other work which was shorter, more rapidly paced, and with much of the message of the work carried in dialogue. In late 1936, and through 1937, Wells produced four such short works, *The Croquet Player*,

The Camford Visitation, The Brothers, and *Star-Begotten*. The four short novels (even novellas), although each stands on its own when read today, were part of his effort to warn of the danger of following out life to inevitable war and destruction, and are Cassandra-like works warning of the consequences of this behaviour.

To some extent they may reflect the failure of the publisher of his film books, Cresset Press, to gain enough currency for his work in that form, and their length and treatment may also be an indication of Wells's growing conviction that the novel, as known for many years, was undergoing a major change in the face of cinema techniques. More than likely, however, the novels are simply the product of Wells's recent writing experiences. Some of his publishers were concerned about his output, as these books followed one on another in rapid succession; they felt that the short novels would damage the sales of his more traditional fiction, especially *Brynhild, Apropos of Dolores*, and *The Holy Terror*. But Wells, through Marjorie, dismissed the idea, although when *The Brothers* was completed late in 1937, he assumed that this phase of his life was about over. As she wrote to Watt (using Wells's detailed notes as her guide to the letter),

> He likes writing these long–short stories and he wants to produce them when he is so disposed. These he has done have a more or less topical quality and should be published as they are thrown off. But practically if *The Brothers*, which is now nearing completion, cannot be published until spring, 1938, Mr Wells will be completely bunged up from writing any more of these long–short stories, unless he writes them to please himself and a few friends and then tears them up. . . . Meanwhile he has a really long novel in hand, *Happiness and the Evil Heart* [*Dolores*] to which he returns at intervals. It cannot be hurried and it is a much more considerable book than *Brynhild*. . . . These two are ships of the line. He wishes Scribners would not bother about these torpedo boats but just let Mr Wells end them up.[28]

The Croquet Player (1936) is told by an effete inhabitant of the inter-war years and involves a terrible ghostly presence rising from Cainsmarsh, a symbolic location, to overwhelm the world and the people in it. That the evil once interred with the biblical Cain is now abroad in the world is the symbolism of the little book. However, the narrator simply hears about it, shrugs, and after listening, returns to his croquet, as did nearly all others whom Wells saw or talked to in the mid-'30s.

The little book was serialized in the *Standard*, and was fairly widely read. Ada Galsworthy wrote to Wells after reading it, describing the mood on the Riviera as 'frightened'; and J. B. Priestley told him he enjoyed the symbolism, and said the book ought to be bound up with Thomas Mann's anti-fascist tract, 'Mario and the Magician', but true to the idea of the book most people simply shrugged and returned to their croquet.[29]

One who did not play croquet in the '30s was Winston Churchill, and Wells dedicated his next exercise in fiction to Churchill. This story involves an unusual character, very like Wells himself (or even like Churchill) and his much younger wife, described as 'fey' with a preternatural knowledge of music, art, and philosophy. This Joseph, and his wife, Mary (although her name is not revealed until the end of the book), are bombarded by (or, to be more precise, are more susceptible to) cosmic rays, especially Mary, and their offspring are 'unusual' — star-begotten.

The rays may emanate from residents of Mars, and are used, perhaps, to touch special isolated parents and children to produce a super race of Star-Begotten people, who have deeper and greater knowledge of the laws of the universe, and who, banded together, can bring about a good world for others less fortunate. Research into these ideas is conducted, and word of the possibilities of the rays is gradually circulated. Some regard the news as simply another manifestation of the communists in our midst, but most can accept it as a way out, a salvation of present problems. The book is heavily influenced by Stapledon's *Last and First Men*, and there is a good short discussion of genetic changes which occur as these 'sports' interbreed with 'normal' people. Power may accrue to the new citizens, '*Homo superbus*', as they are termed in one place. If it does a social revolution will occur. The Open Conspiracy will have triumphed in this scenario. The bankruptcy of civilization has produced its own competent receiver, if the people in the novel accept this view.

The book, *Star Begotten* (1937), serialized in three parts in the *London Mercury*, was well received. It was originally called (or had as alternative titles) *They Are Here, Arrows of Change, Here From Outside*, or *Sons of the Cosmic Rays* (along with eight other suggestions). Churchill was much moved by the dedication: 'It gives me real pleasure that my early admiration of thirty-five years ago for your wonderful books should have come to rest in our later times in a harbour of personal friendship.' J.B.S. Haldane reviewed the book in *Nature* (commenting mostly on the genetics); Swinnerton and Stapledon also wrote reviews. Stapledon told Wells that he appreciated the allusions to his own work, but that he didn't think he was really trying to find a formula for the entire universe, although he described himself as 'nearly a logical positivist'. Stapledon remarked that he thought about the universe as a whole, but let it come out in his work as a myth, which provided a greater 'emotional stability'.

Winifred Horrabin, writing in *Tribune*, described the book as 'one of the best, most characteristic and serious' of Wells's works, while Sydney Olivier, recovering from a stroke, wrote to say that although a bloody mess was sure to come, Wells's Star Begotten people could prevent it. Unfortunately, or so thought Olivier, they had waited too long to attempt their reform of education, and the battle was probably a losing one. As he ended this letter, 'What is it that underlies the illusion of reality, classical form and permanence in all foundations of logic, art, religion, love, etc.'

Of course for both Wells and Olivier, and perhaps for all others in the world in the mid-'30s, this was the overriding question to be answered, as Hitler moved and pacific responses seemed only to whet his appetite further.[30]

Wells's next short book was addressed to a specific audience, the students, faculty and graduates of Cambridge and Oxford. The book was even packaged in a plain cover of light and dark blues. Set in a college of Holy Innocents, the piece, titled *The Camford Visitation* (1937), opens in a common room, in a discussion of a possible modification of the curriculum, but one rejected and reviled by the Master. A penetrating Voice offers brief critical commentary on this and other academic scenes, culminating with a speech during the university Congregation Day. The voice ends this psychic Commencement Address with, 'There is no salvation for races that will not save themselves. Half the stars in the sky are the burning rubbish of worlds that might have been.' Of course, true to the symbolism of the story, all that actually occurs are a few 'learned' papers, for almost all who heard the Voice simply agreed to ignore it and carry on.

Wells's friends continued to be intrigued by his new work. Olaf Stapledon thought he was too hard on universities, from his position as a sort of peripheral don, but Ernest Barker, off to India, called the *Visitation* 'a wonderful *vade mecum* for the voyage'. The book was not widely noticed, with only Winifred Horrabin giving it a full review. She described it as 'seventy pages of concentrated common sense for two shillings' while remarking that if Wells's readers did not heed his quarter-century of warning, 'it will be our own fault'. The book sold surprisingly poorly. After its serialization, Methuen printed 10,000 copies, and on the very eve of the war still had 7,800 copies left, 5,000 of them unbound. Methuen wanted to remainder the book, but Wells said no; therefore, in the spring of 1940, the unbound sheets were destroyed, and the remaining copies sold off in dribbles until they were gone, sometime during the war.[31]

Wells now began speaking directly to his readers, with much less of the symbolism that had appeared in *The Croquet Player* and the other stories of the period. In *The Brothers* (1938), the last of these short didactic and fanciful stories, Wells used the old theme of two brothers, unknown to each other, who meet in battle. He refined the idea to make them mirror opposites to each other, one representing the fascist Right, and the other the hard and unyielding Left. The book was dedicated to J. F. Horrabin, and was originally to have been serialized in *Harpers* in the US, with much of the dialogue cut, subject to Wells's approval; but the magazine was too severe in its cuts and he withdrew the work. In Britain it appeared, relatively untouched, in the *Sunday Referee*.

The brothers meet (one is captured), and debate with each other over their differing views. The reader soon sees how similar they are. They are also vying to a considerable degree for the attention of Catherine, who listens, comments, mediates, and reflects on the discussion. The two men, under pressure of the battle, decide that they have been serving the same master, in fact, 'the Common Fool', but just as they decide to celebrate their common brotherhood — the brotherhood of man — both are destroyed by the forces they had actually created in their servitude to cant and passion.

As one brother says to Catherine, just before both are killed,

> 'Our minds are distorting mirrors and the wonderful worlds you see in them — ! Prisms and mirrors. That is all we are. Shatter the mirror and the story ends. . . .
>
> A day will come when we will have brought the hidden loveliness of a sunlit snow-crystal, drifting and melting on the other side of the moon a million years ago, into definite relation to the eternal human mind. Yes, and when the monstrous discrepancy between the scale of our lives and the starry intervals, will cease to be a disharmony. I don't know how such things can be achieved, but we shall achieve them.'

> (Chapter 6)

Olaf Stapledon thought Wells had gone too far in his characterization of the similarity between the two forces — communism and fascism, although he did accept some similarity and the streak of violence in communism. Winifred Horrabin, still loyal to Wells, but seeing deterioration or tiredness coming in the great mind, described the book as 'exciting, disturbing, exasperating, and disappointing', much as Wells himself was in this book. For her much more disturbing was the idea implicit in the book that there was no way out, no possibility of hope, and that the new world Wells had prophesied for so many was now to be put off to some far-distant time, and with no road map as to how to get there.[32]

Wells may have appeared overly pessimistic in this book, but he was simply reverting, in the face of reality, to his earlier stance that a new world was possible, but only just possible, and it would take a major joint effort to achieve it. On the evidence, in late 1937, that joint effort was not very likely to come for some time. Wells, however, was not giving up entirely. So, just as *The Brothers* was being set up in type, he began engaging the schoolmasters of the nation in a great dialogue, an effort at the modernization of knowledge, and the retrieval of its parts. He was also about ready to make his last great series of trips to spread his views. Hitler, Mussolini, fascism and terror were real. They would not go away. What Wells wanted was a method of analysing these phenomena to prevent their re-occurrence, and then to move on to the business of the species.

THE POISON OF HISTORY

The old history is by its very nature *useless* as the basis of a World Peace Ideology. It is antagonistic to that. It is a struggle to sustain the outworn story of personified Britannias, Germanias, Holy Russias, Israels, and so forth, meritorious races and chosen peoples. And that League of Nations, that little bit of paper hat on the top, not of a Colossus, but of a squirming heap of patriotisms, was only a last desperate attempt to carry on the old patchwork of nationalist ideas into a world that has no use for them at all. They have outlived their use, they decay, they become poisonous. Cosmopolis in its cradle was sick and crippled by their infection. We do not want Leagues of Nations, we want a ruling idea of a world in common. If the young Hercules of a new world is to live, its first feat must be to strangle the tangled coil of poisonous old histories in its cradle.

HGW, 'The Poison of History', from *Travels of a Republican Radical in Search of Hot Water* (1939)

By 1937, H. G. Wells had spent nearly twenty years in his efforts to educate the people of Britain, America, and the world to the dangers of nationalism, simple-minded patriotism, and the racism which often accompanied them. He had promoted a world peace — World Pax, in his terms — in which all members of the species, *Homo sapiens*, would have access to education, and a minimum life free from violence, attacks from others, and most of all, war, which stemmed directly from the claims of nationalism furthered by narrow-minded conservative diplomats. At the end of the twenty years he had converted many, interested even more, but had had almost no impact on those who remained in charge. And in many countries even worse horrors, still based nearly always on the false claims of nationalism, had begun to be routine. Italy, Germany, and China and Spain with their civil wars — all were scenes where a second world war might break out at any moment. And with the modifications in technology brought about, in great part, by the mismanaged advances of science, this war would probably be far worse than any other ever fought. As Wells surveyed the potential holocaust, he must have felt very disconsolate about the future of the species. However, H. G. Wells was not a natural pessimist. He believed that *Homo sapiens* could save itself — all that was needed was a continued campaign to educate a new leadership.

His educational strategy, although generally unplanned in detail, had taken two forms thus far. First, he had attempted to have curricula remodelled by bringing in much more science, and applied science, to replace outmoded Greek, Latin, and compulsory work in the classics. Secondly, he had written three massive textbooks by means of which any person could educate himself outside the hidebound and costly educational system provided either by the state or at public — i.e. private — schools. Now, with the threat of war and violence in the very air one breathed, Wells rethought his premisses. His two previous means of attack had been correct but insufficient. What was needed now was reform, a revolutionary reform, to root out the old nationalistic history and replace it with a history of the species, based on scientific investigation. That scientific investigation would also produce a new encyclopaedia (a new basis of knowledge, in fact) free from cant, error, and nationalistic bias. To ensure that these changes came about in time to achieve the overall goals he had in mind, H. G. Wells now began to carry his message personally to his listeners. Although he was an old and occasionally ill man, between 1937 and 1939 he made several extended trips with these purposes in mind, and even after the war had begun, made still one more major trip to the United States. That last time, after the US had proclaimed neutrality, Wells went with the message that although we live in two hemispheres, there is still only one world. Fascism and Nazism were the ultimate spawn of displaced and decadent nationalism, and the US must join in their destruction, and in the clean-up of the postwar world, or the species was still doomed. If the future was dark, H.G. Wells was willing to provide a miner's lamp and guide to the New World.

These ideas emerged, in their first form, in the Open Conspiracy. Certain aspects of these ideas, but within a British form of nationalism, matured in the 'Middle Way' ideas of Harold Macmillan, and in the views of Labour politicians such as Stafford Cripps and William Beveridge. After the war ended a general reform of British society actually took place, on the basis of such ideas. But England had suffered so greatly in the long war that these efforts, when they came, could be confined only to England and the British Isles, and even there were limited in focus. Wells could not wait for this, and, by that time, too, he was convinced that limited efforts were just that, limited: although admirable, they did not push the horizon very far forward. However, he was an Englishman, and it was from that base that he had to work.

In the spring of 1934, Wells was approached by a group led by Olaf Stapledon, Gerald Heard, Eden Paul, and Sylvia Pankhurst, to see if he would permit the use of his name for an organization that would work towards a Wellsian world. He agreed, and a meeting was held in Caxton Hall, 'to educate the world'. At the fifth such meeting, an annual general meeting, the name was changed from the H. G. Wells Society to the Open Conspiracy. About a hundred members were active at one time, but their number dwindled steadily, as little progress seemed possible, and their little newsletter even ceased publication in October 1935. Part of the reason for its limited success was that the group, exemplary as it might have been, still depended on H. G. Wells. He was honest enough about his problems of leadership; when Robert C. Galkins, of the University of California, wrote asking for his help, Wells referred him to Harold Laski, but then told his admirer: 'Because of all sorts of odd accidents and possibly something in my character, I have always had to do my thinking and expression alone and so I have no means of putting you in touch with any English planning groups. I have no aptitude for organization.'[1]

The Wells society also did not prosper because it had internal difficulties over the true role of pacifism, as well as territorial problems related to a parallel group, the 'X' Society, based in Edinburgh. Marjorie Wells attended one meeting of the Wells Society, but thought it not very inspiring, although some 200 to 300 people had attended the Caxton Hall foundation meeting. The group wrote out a 'Basis', attempted to increase its membership, and did offer a possible alternative to doing nothing. By 1936, with some of the early founders deposed, the group re-formed itself, this time under the name Cosmopolis. It was rejuvenated with a three-man advisory council, Olaf Stapledon, Gerald Heard, and Wells himself. This new group also began to publish a newsletter, called *Plan*. A new 'Basis' said its primary effort would be to end the sovereign independence of states; to eliminate that 'unmitigated evil', war; to abolish money credit; and to create the highest possible standard of education, available for all. The advisory group cautioned its members that 'integrity, service, and co-operation, based on a national and scientific attitude to life, are essential.'[2]

Many similar organizations emerged in the early 1930s. Wells and others attempted to organize them in a loose federation, with the Wells Society (Cosmopolis) more or less leading the group, although still submerged in it. The *Manifesto* of the group, for which Wells wrote the preamble, was published as a book. The *Manifesto* group also published a magazine, *News of Progress*, but by 1937 or so these organizations were overtaken by events, and the members began to turn their attention to Wells's hopes for a new encyclopaedia.[3]

Wells had never left the field of education, of course. He had helped write a proposal for a conference on unemployment, sponsored by the International Labour Organization, at the London School of Economics. This meeting in the spring of 1930, which Wells was unable to attend, dealt to some degree with the problems of outdated education. Wells also addressed the Liberal Summer School in 1932 on these matters, when he proposed the founding of the groups which led to Cosmopolis. He also went to Cambridge to speak and debate on education, and he maintained a slim but strong liaison with progressive 'alternative' schools such as Dora and Bertrand Russell's school near Petersfield, with Summerhill, and with Dartington Hall.[4]

Wells's views always commanded attention, so when he chose to write more formally on education it was well received, and although he did not think that committees on education sponsored by the League of Nations did much good, he did discuss some of their ideas. In 1936, after some pleading, he agreed to address an audience at the Royal Institution on his views on education.[5]

Wells's speech, delivered on 20 November, called for the establishment of a new world encyclopaedia. He proposed an organizing committee, to establish a basic bibliography, 'to provide a rehabilitation of thought and learning that ultimately may release a new form of power in the world', comparable to the religious revivals of earlier times. And he ended his talk to this learned audience with the warning,

> As mankind is, so it will remain, until it pulls its mind together. . . . Never was a living species more perilously poised than ours at the present time. If it does not take thought to end its present mental indecisiveness catastrophe lies ahead. Our species may yet end its strange eventful history as just the last, the cleverest of the great apes. The great ape that was clever — but not clever enough. It could escape from most things but not from its own mental confusion.

The speech was published as a pamphlet, and with a nine-page memorandum on a detailed organization for the encyclopaedia, it went out to a list of thirty-five significant people whom he thought might help. Several agreed to aid in some way, and Wells, encouraged by this response, enlisted A. P. Watt in the matter, and began to solicit help from his friends across the Atlantic, especially Nelson Doubleday. In addition his views on the potential of the encyclopaedia saw their way into *Nature, Harpers*, and *Survey Graphic*. He also spoke on his ideas of documentation to a Congress on Documentation in Paris, and contributed a special article to the new *Encyclopédie française*.[6]

Even with the interest that was shown in the project, it did not get very far. The world was in a financial Depression, and with possibly half a million dollars needed, a pious wish for an encyclopaedia was all that most people could raise. Wells, and his agents, felt that perhaps the United States was the best place to begin to find the necessary funds, so they began preparations for a lecture tour in the autumn of 1937.

While the preparations were going forward, Wells had yet another audience to address. A new section, Section 'L', had been formed in the British Association. R. A. Gregory, then very much a power in that body, had been instrumental in creating this section, whose mission was to provide discussion and papers on education and educational research. After the so-called Education Section was formed, its secretary, citing Wells's letters to *The Times* on the work of the Committee on Intellectual Co-operation (CIC), asked him to be the first president. An organizational meeting was held at Birkbeck College on 8 January 1937; Wells gave a dinner party for many of the participating members prior to the meeting.[7]

At the meeting the group roughed out a series of possible talks to follow Wells's presidential address. Wells then began to discuss with his friends what would go into that address, soliciting ideas especially from Gregory, Maisky, and Barker, as well as Eileen Power. As the conference news circulated, interest in Wells's speech caused the BA organizers to reserve the largest hall in Nottingham University, the site of the conference. Wells was assured of a bedroom near Gregory in their hotel, and his other needs were also met. There was slight apprehension when his neuritis began to trouble him, but on the day he was in good health, and delivered a strong address. A diagram, later printed with the speech (see illus. no. 21), was provided for his auditors.[8]

The speech, delivered on 2 September 1937, was a *tour de force*. Wells sketched an entire curriculum, complete with charts, for the whole of human life. It provided for 2,400 hours of teaching in specific areas of information in the actual school term. Wells asked questions, and himself provided the answers: What is the subject matter of a general education? What do we want known, and how do we want it known? What is the essential framework of knowledge, the irreducible minimum which a good citizen of the world needs to know? He put this all into a timetable which used the best knowledge of the period on how a human being learns and assimilates new ideas. As would be expected, his curriculum had a scientific basis, with history, geography, material on personal sociology, political training and analysis, and social organizational skills coming into it later in the pupil's career. Wells included no details on the teaching of languages, music, manual and physical training, as he felt he was not skilled enough in these subjects to provide the necessary detail, but he allowed time for this work. His education was entirely based on a developing set of data generated by his new encyclopaedia. His curriculum has some clear affiliations with earlier ideas of his, although this is clearly the most closely reasoned of all his attempts. As he lectured to a large audience, he related parts of his address to the chart, which graphically represented his views.[9]

The immediate response from his friends and associates was favourable, although Wells claimed that teachers were less enthusiastic: he had ruffled their feathers too much with his talk. Part of the problem was that the press had been supplied with an early draft of the speech, which was then modified to a considerable degree. Wells said, however, that the formal comments afterwards had only re-enforced his view that the chief objective

of education must be to analyse and prepare for the community that was
wanted by the educators.[10]

Wells now began to make plans for his American tour designed to carry
much of the same message, along with his ideas of a new encyclopaedia.
The Americans offered him $5,000 for ten speeches with all of his
expenses in the country paid as well; in the event he did five for the same
fees. In addition *Collier's* magazine, which had sponsored his 1933 visit,
wanted him to write an article or two, as he had done before. Wells's
neuritis and the need to have some teeth extracted threatened to postpone
this tour for a time. Eventually the details — the paraphernalia needed on
stage, an ear and throat specialist to be present on each occasion, the dress
he was expected to wear (a dinner jacket or tails), and the times of the talks
(8 p.m.–9:30 or 8:30–10 p.m.) were all fixed. An itinerary of Philadelphia,
Boston, Detroit, Chicago, Washington, and New York was arranged. The
talks went off without a hitch.[11]

His talk in America was called 'The Brain Organization of the Modern
World', and it was a summary of his feelings about education and the world
he was in. He reviewed his recent experiences at the BA, and with other
groups of intellectuals, including the centenary celebration at the University
of London. He remarked how much new knowledge there was, and called
for a reordering of knowledge, leading necessarily to a new encyclopaedism.
In his talk he also made mention of documentation problems and bibliography, as well as the new tool of microfilm, and urged his audience to
support his demands. The last time he gave the talk (the speech was the same
each time), at Town Hall in New York, it was broadcast over the radio.

After the talk he had discussions with possible backers in the United
States in an effort to raise money for his encyclopaedia project. He had
sent Nelson Doubleday another long memorandum (very similar to the one
of the previous year), and now asked him to set up some meetings. On 25
October, J. P. Morgan & Company gave a luncheon for Wells, at which
Frank Keppel of the Carnegie Corporation, R. C. Leffingwell of J. P.
Morgan, Henry Luce, Jackson E. Reynolds of the First National Bank,
Simeon Stansky, a prominent New York financier, and Wells's old friend
Thomas Lamont were present, and the idea of the encyclopaedia was given
a complete airing. The talk did not go very far, however, and although
Wells then approached Oxford University Press, while Doubleday also
remained interested, the pressure of events, the need for funds and for
organization, as well as the competition from the *Encyclopaedia Britannica*,
the recently published *Encyclopaedia of the Social Sciences*, and the French
Encyclopédie, simply did not allow the idea, good as it was, to go forward.[12]

While Wells was in Washington, he had a long and interesting talk with
Franklin D. Roosevelt over lunch, and this and his American experiences
led to several newspaper pieces, one commenting on the mood in America
in the autumn of 1937, along with an assessment of Roosevelt and the

Democratic Party. Later, after visiting the site of the impending New York World's Fair, going to Niagara Falls, and attending several plays, he returned to England. He continued to produce his musings on America, entitling one of them 'Transatlantic Misunderstandings' and urging his readers to make a greater effort to understand each other's feelings. By this time he had met FDR three times (in 1933, 1935, and 1937). He had been in America nearly every year in the decade, and in England had rapidly become an unofficial interpreter of intellectual opinion, at least, in the States.[13]

Although his presidential address to the BA had been published separately, apparently there was further demand for it. So it and his American talk, along with other recent addresses, his various pieces on encyclopaedias, and on his trip to America were brought together in 1938 in a slim volume, *World Brain*. For it he also wrote a long introduction. Wells sent copies of the book to 78 heads of colleges and universities in the States, in the hope of stirring up interest in his encyclopaedia, but little came of the gesture.[14]

Wells continued his interest in these topics, of course, although everything he did now risked being overtaken, as after Munich the events of the world seemed to speed up. He participated in an exhibit on new school buildings organized by the *News Chronicle* and wrote a piece about what schools could do. He continued to attend meetings of 'Section L', and endorsed the BA decision to increase the work of the group, giving it an injunction to report on ways of discussing social and political affairs. A 'Brains Trust' was created of Wells, Gregory, Julian Huxley, and Professor H. T. Tizard, with Gregory to report their views to the American counterpart society in December. When the Trust met it also co-opted Ritchie Calder, Lord Stampp, Boyd Orr, J. D. Bernal, John Russell, and P. M. S. Blackett. A questionnaire was prepared, and approved at the Cambridge meeting of the BA in 1938; the group agreed to report its findings the following year. That meeting, scheduled to be held at Dundee the first weekend of September 1939, never took place, and the findings of the group on the needs of education were never presented.[15]

The group so constituted did, however, accomplish another thing. They were the founders of a Fellowship of Scientific Workers, for whose charter Wells wrote much of the text. In 1940, when the BA did meet again, it was to hold a world-wide conference on the subject, in which Wells took a prominent part. The Charter was accepted, but again world events were in the way.[16] Wells continued to maintain his interest in these matters, but he was also interested in, and distracted by, his ideas on history, as well as his forthcoming trip to Australia.

As time ran out on him, and on the western world, through the late autumn of 1938 and the spring of 1939, Wells found it useful, but frustrating, to continue to write articles for the press and to hold meetings. So when the

Australian and New Zealand Associations for the Advancement of Science (ANZAAS) asked him, Boyd Orr, John Russell, and others from the BA 'Brains Trust' committee to come and discuss their ideas with them in Canberra, Wells turned his attention to their needs. A new audience, a chance to focus his desire for peace, for an end to war and militarism, called him, and like an old fire-horse hearing the bell and the siren, he responded.[17]

The Australians had a strong interest in Wells and his work. His books always sold well there, and there had been some interest, as early as 1933, in his making an Australian broadcast. Australia was a regular outlet for remaindered copies of his books when the other markets had been saturated. When he did agree to go there, the demand for his talks was immense. Although the Australian Broadcasting Commission explained that with only a million licence holders, they could not meet the BBC standard of payment, they did give him $220 Australian for each of his broadcast talks. In addition, he did rather well out of the articles written about the trip once he returned home. The trip out was leisurely, with the ship's band playing the 'Lambeth Walk' as the P. & O. liner, which Wells called the S.S. 'Pukka Sahib', made its usual calls, at Suez, Bombay, Colombo, and eventually at Fremantle.[18]

Wells left the ship at Fremantle and was guest of honour at a tea at the University of Western Australia, and later attended a dinner in his honour in Perth. The next day, 19 December 1938, he flew east to Adelaide, where he gave a speech over the Australian Broadcasting Company network. On New Year's Day, he and a companion began a motor trip to Melbourne where he arrived on 3 January. He gave a major radio address on the 8th from Melbourne, and another from Canberra on the 12th. He delivered the major address at the ANZAAS convention on the 16th. A further address was broadcast on the 18th, on 'Utopias'. A final nationwide radio address was read from Sydney on the 23rd. Wells left for home on the 26th.

On the surface this seems a routine journey for a distinguished, although elderly, author, but several incidents elevated the journey into a major event, once even bordering on a diplomatic crisis, stirring up world-wide comment, and causing especially widespread discussion in Australia itself.

Australia was isolated in 1939, as the bare account of Wells's journey suggests. Few authors of fame had been there before — Mark Twain, Kipling, and D. H. Lawrence, although Dickens had planned a trip that was not carried out, and Mr Micawber had settled there. Wells was well-known in Australia, however. Nearly every book in his bibliography was mentioned by analysts and reviewers during his stay, but it was apparent that for Australians the Wellsian novels best known were *Mr Polly*, *Kipps*, and *Mr Britling Sees it Through*, while the *Outline of History* was widely owned, if not necessarily widely read. The country he came to was a colonial outpost of Victorian England. Manners and morals were noticed and discussed. The adulation of the 'home country' was very great, and the wealthy often went 'home' on holiday, or at least on their version of the Grand Tour.

The Country Party, led by the Prime Minister, John A. Lyons of Tasmania, had been in power for many years, and Lyons himself was to break the longevity record for Australian Prime Ministers two months after Wells's departure. Lyons had supported Stanley Baldwin over the Abdication crisis and was an equally strong supporter of Neville Chamberlain, who had just returned from Munich. In the week before Wells's arrival, a Labour Party radio station, 2XY, had been suspended by the Postmaster-General for comment unfavourable to the Prime Minister. Its licence was renewed only after a reorganization of the affairs of the station, and an abject flight by the leaders of the rebellion to Kangaroo Island, where suitable apologies were extended to Lyons.

The weather during Wells's stay was as sultry as the politics. The day he arrived in Adelaide the temperature rose to 117° Fahrenheit, and it remained very high throughout his stay. In Canberra, Melbourne, and Sydney record temperatures, some of these still unsurpassed, greeted him. The heat, coupled with the worst drought of the century, caused huge and ferocious bush fires to race through the outback, destroying animals, farms, and even entire towns. More than sixty persons lost their lives in these fires. Wells toured the fire scene with the Governor-General, talking with and briefly addressing the fire-fighters. He, however, continued to dress in his typical British fashion, unbending only to the point of not wearing a coat or tie on one day in Canberra, when the mercury rose to 114°F.

Although the Australian heat was penetrating, oppressive, and exhausting, Wells was greeted with tremendous affection by the population. Even the sporting world made its contribution, when Don Bradman performed one of the great feats in cricket history by making six consecutive centuries in successive innings of first-class matches. And Don Tallon, the famous Queensland wicket-keeper, joined Bradman in welcoming Wells by dismissing twelve batsmen in two innings, against New South Wales. This equalled a record set in 1868 in a Surrey v. Sussex match at the Oval.[19]

The public sought Wells's autograph, which he would cheerfully give upon receipt of a cheque for 2s. 6d. payable to the Diabetic Foundation, of which he was then president. Only once did he give up his autograph without the donation, and this was to two young girls in Sydney who waylaid him in his hotel. For them he not only autographed a copy of *Men Like Gods*, but he also drew a 'picshua'. One of them told him, 'You really are brilliant, aren't you?', which must have pleased the old man.[20]

Those who could not get to speak to him, offer him a manuscript to read, or purchase an autograph, found that Wells's every moment was chronicled, almost as though he were royalty itself making a pilgrimage while showing the flag. Even when he went to visit a koala bear farm it was noted, as were his comments on Australian surfing, scenery, women, men, literature, and anything else the journalists could think of to ask him about. These statements were usually spread over the entire continent. Newspapers printed dozens of letters analysing H.G. and his remarks. Places such as Launceston, Tasmania, and Brisbane, Queensland, which were not favoured with visits, or which were fobbed off with airport stops, sent him telegrams hoping to inveigle a side journey. Clearly, when one considers the newspaper coverage, and the broadcast nationwide of six major addresses, it seems that Wells, at seventy-two, was still a major figure and one who could command a huge audience.

Prior to his departure Wells wrote a long article for the *News Chronicle* attempting to predict the course of events in the year 1939. He thought it was 'much pleasanter to prophesy at long range' as there was less chance to be caught out. However, in the world on the eve of war, the temptation to give short-range predictions was very great, and he had succumbed to the requests of the newspaper. For Wells, much of history consisted of mass movements of people, but sometimes just a few persons determined what really happened. The Germans and the Nazi Party were a case in point, as for Wells, 'The German people [were] an amiable, orderly, vain, deeply sentimental and rather insensitive people.' He thought they felt at their best when they were 'singing in chorus, saluting, or obeying orders'. Now they were led by a group of certifiable lunatics, who were weak until Neville Chamberlain reinstated their power at Munich.

Wells thought trouble was likely to follow. If the common people of the United Kingdom, the Commonwealth, and the United States could take charge of the situation the trouble might be thwarted, but sloth and inattention lay in the way. Parliament in the United Kingdom did not want the people in power, as it would mean the end of Hitler, and a social revolution, perhaps even an alliance with Russia. Still, said Wells, enforcing the Munich settlement was creating a great strain. Many Tories were in revolt, and H.G. predicted the demise of the Chamberlain Government by the end of 1939. He thought a radical, nationalist, or all-party government might replace it. He also predicted that the Commonwealth would come into line then, perhaps barring South Africa where the German tie was very strong. No peace was foreseen in the Far East, where economic exhaustion was more likely. Elsewhere the brink of war was at hand, and only a radical reform of government would forestall it.

Peace is not a foolish, faceless thing; it is not the retreating aspect of humanity. It is something more difficult than war, more exhausting of human energy. You have not only to arm and train for it; you have to educate for it.

Peace is the resolute, legal suppression of war by a world order. There can be no other peace than that, unless it is the temporary peace of the raped, robbed, exhausted, sleeping slave.[21]

Wells later remarked on what he expected to find in Australia, as he sat in London preparing for the trip, writing his predictions of the year to come. He said that his knowledge of Australia was based on reading Australian novels, and it was a world of kangaroos, koalas, eucalpytus, duck-billed platypus, and very primitive aborigines. When he arrived, he found that the blacks were less primitive, and the white population was supremely healthy. The island continent was very British, however, with its Labour Party a mirror image of the one he had left at home. Australians were slowly, wrenchingly, coming to understand that they were not alone, but were, in fact, part of the rest of the world. 'Crimes against humanity no longer know boundaries; they overflow them,' he informed his readers on both sides of the world.[22] With these strictures down on paper, Wells was able to enjoy his visit. However, his comments indicated that this was not to be just a trip of being lionized. The old man saw his journey as part of his effort to rouse the world to save itself.

Even on his way to Australia, Wells, try as he might, was unable to curb his rather abrupt comments. In Bombay, he asked his interviewers what India was planning for the future, and whether the tremendous amount of 'grey matter' in the country was to be used. He did not offer further comment, although he was pressed on independence, and his views on Gandhi were sought (he called himself an admirer). But at his next port of call, Colombo, his views on non-violence, given in Bombay, were quoted at length in the *Ceylon Observer* the day before he arrived:

Non-violence is the policy of the vegetable kingdom, and I cannot agree that that is the panacea for the world's present troubles. Animals tramp on vegetables and many eat them, and it is my opinion that in our present order of existence, there must be some reasonable use of force, even if only as a balancing factor.

In Colombo he toured the famous sites before dining with the Annesley de Silvas, local authors and London acquaintances. He was served arrack, which he liked, and told the press before embarking that the strength of the people was the 'manly vigour of their stimulating drink!'.[23]

When Wells arrived in Australia a few days later, his remarks to the waiting reporters were somewhat stronger. In response to queries he attacked the Munich settlement, said London would withstand bombing, if it came, and remarked that dictators such as Hitler, Mussolini, and Stalin were forced to make spectacular moves to retain their power. While talking about dictatorship and democracy he gave Australians an example of his credo when he told them: 'I am quite convinced that the most precious thing in life is to be able to express myself and I would rather be shot than stop expressing myself at the top of my voice to the best of my ability. I think that to not express oneself is suicide.'

The West Australian Federation of Writers tendered Wells a dinner in Perth, after which he held forth for an hour on a vast variety of subjects, and took questions from the audience. Walter Muirlock, professor at the local University, proposing Wells's health after this performance, likened the occasion to ones on which the admirers of Plato and Aristotle listened to those great men.[24]

In Adelaide he gave his first radio talk, entitled 'Fiction About the Future'. In the talk he reviewed futuristic fiction, concentrating on his own work. He said that fiction had a way of catching up with him, though, as he remarked, 'The more one goes ahead with this work the more he gets entangled with questions of his own time.' In *Things to Come* the director had reverted to contemporary modernism to make the film work. Wells also said fiction about the future was ephemeral, it was really written for one's own time and one's own problems. Future people would write 'fiction of their times and not read ours at all', thought H.G. As an example, he suggested that his audience write a story without male characters, dealing with the emotional status of women. How would they deal with life, with government? Wells said if the authors got past the comic giggles this might make a great story. Newspaper editors, columnists, and listeners were ecstatic with this speech. The Melbourne *Age* said Wells had 'delighted thousands' and he had.[25]

The pressure of the Australian crowds wherever Wells went tended to dampen his enthusiasm somewhat, however, as time went on. After two days in Melbourne, he was heard to remark to one interviewer, 'This really is a lot of nonsense, this publicity. I'm afraid I'm beginning to get very crotchety.' He accused his interviewers of not reading his latest work. The interviewers on their part asked him about *William Clissold* and whether, if war came again, *Mr Britling* would appear once more. Wells took this opportunity to complain of the scarcity of his latest work in Australian bookshops. He said that he had made enquiries about Australian libraries and their procedures. If a student were to ask for a specific work taking a radical view, he claimed that the librarians would also give standard and supplementary views to ensure that the radical view would not win out.[26]

Certain of Wells's comments to the press in Melbourne were not quite as generous as some others had been. 'You people here', he said, 'are under an illusion that you are quite different from the English and that you are a separate nation. Don't believe it. An Australian in England has to be pointed out as an Australian. You are part of the English-speaking world. The idea that Australians are something amazing and different has no reality at all.'[27]

Although most Australians had not noticed Wells's acerbic comments on Hitler upon his arrival, the Germans did. The day before Wells arrived in

Melbourne, the German semi-official newspaper *Angriff* issued a blast at Wells; they were duly reported, in London and in the Australian newspapers, as having said (in translation):

> The price that Wells is prepared to pay to maintain Britain's privileged position reveals his short-sightedness, also the egotistic way the British think, as this policy means that Germany and Europe can go to ruin so long as Britain is unharmed.
>
> Wells's declaration is criminal, coming from an Englishman who has a tremendous influence on the opinions of so-called intelligent people. It shows how great is the central significance of the Berlin-Tokyo-Rome fight against Bolshevism.[28]

When Wells arrived in Melbourne he was besieged by reporters. They were not just interested in his views on Australia now; they also scented a story related to the German response. Wells did not fail them. He gave a long, relaxed interview which he clearly enjoyed immensely. In it he described Hitler as 'a certified lunatic', and Mussolini as 'a fantastic renegade from social democracy'.

Later, speaking more slowly and with less regard for the newspapermen present, Wells ended his comments with a phrase that epitomized that last winter before the war. 'The trouble with us', he remarked,

> is that we haven't got a map of conditions under which we live. We have no way of telling what we are up against. So we are people wandering in a strange country — without a map. We may come upon terrible disaster. We may be lucky and get out of it. But our life is just chance. Until you organize knowledge, and have a better understanding between people, life like that has to go on.[29]

Prime Minister Lyons, apparently under pressure from the German Consul-General in Australia, Dr Aswin, decided that Wells's comments had gone far enough. From his home in Tasmania he issued a strong rebuke to Wells, reminding him that he was a visitor in a foreign place, and that courtesy called for moderation. The Germans and the Italians might well assume, said Lyons, that Wells was speaking for the Australian government and people. Lyons urged Wells to 'exercise his undoubted gifts for promotion of international understanding rather than international misunderstanding'. Wells did not respond at first; but at a dinner given in his honour on 9 January by the newly-formed PEN chapter in Australia, he was the guest speaker. The other major speaker was the Attorney-General, William Menzies. Leonard Mann, an Australian author, was toastmaster and he said that Lyons's comments ought to be 'treated with true Australian ribaldry' and called on Wells to respond. After a tremendous standing ovation, Wells gave a witty and courteous speech about PEN, in which John Galsworthy had been the major founding force. Wells described one meeting from which the Germans had walked out, and said that there was now a German branch in exile, located in Paris. From this gentle opening, Wells moved to a discussion of free speech, and with his audience laughing at every sally, he ended by remarking that Prime Minister Lyons had free speech to make his remarks 'in the worst possible taste'. Wells said he thought the only persons who did not have free speech in English-speaking countries were kings, 'who could not be allowed to choose their own wives'.

Menzies responded to the toast, 'Our guest', with a comment that Lyons was not really suppressing free speech, and that the audience should sympathize with the Prime Minister. This received a very tepid response, with some heckling, and the honours seemed universally on the side of Wells. Lyons, for his part, still in Tasmania, issued another rebuke to Wells. Wells refused to comment on this, and the controversy between the two died.[30]

It did not, however, die in the country, as the press, clergy, and others seized the opportunity to attack Wells or Lyons, depending on their political persuasion. There were many letters in the press, with a parson calling for 'restraint' and saying Wells had been 'swept away', while the Mayor of Newcastle, on the other hand, supported Wells and urged Lyons 'to mind his own business'. Most Australian newspapers offered commentary, occasionally very lengthy, on this contretemps between their Prime Minister and their distinguished visitor. The Brisbane *Courier-Mail* believed Wells's ripostes to Lyons precisely correct, as both 'enlightenment and entertainment', and the Sydney *Morning Herald*, in a long, balanced, and somewhat stately comment, although disturbed that Wells had resorted to calling names, did compare him to Tacitus.[31]

For home consumption, Wells was less forthcoming about Lyons and his role. In an article written in Australia and printed while he was still there in the *News Chronicle*, Wells said that Lyons by his activities revealed himself. He characterized him as an 'ultra-Chamberlainite' and said, 'He presents the complete, rounded-off, hand-made specimen of everything that is hampering the development of a valiant, generous and progressive policy common to the English-speaking and democratic communities throughout the world.' Wells went on to say that the Lyons attack was symptomatic of the Australian problem with censorship, citing the suppression of A.P. Herbert's *Holy Deadlock* (a hilarious farce about the difficulty of obtaining a divorce in England).[32]

In England the attacks on Chamberlain's foreign policy continued, this time by Lloyd George. The combination of the Welshman in England and the Kentish man in Australia was too much for Earl Winterton, the Father of the House of Commons. In a choleric speech to the Commons he called attention to 'these unamiable septuagenarians' who 'have recently been screaming defiance against dictators and against Mr Chamberlain'. Winterton called Wells, 'that absurd creature, an English Republican', and concluded that he and Lloyd George were 'scolding a world which has long ceased to take either seriously'. Australians hoped that Wells would respond with some of his vitriol to this attack, but in this case, again, he simply gave a soft answer. When pressed on the Winterton comment, Wells said, 'I have long been criticizing the education of the young men in England belonging to the so-called ruling classes. I note regretfully that Lord Winterton is an example that justifies all my criticisms.'[33]

The comments on Wells's foreign-policy remarks continued in the letter columns of the press through most of his Australian trip. One N. A. Vowles, of Spaulding, near Adelaide, wrote saying Wells ought to be silenced, as he was damaging the profitable German trade with Australia. And besides, no lives were lost by the persecution of Jews. The responses to this letter were very strong. Some called for more plain talk from Wells, and others wished a less supine government. Vowles was termed the 'peak of ignorance and impertinence'. The letters ventilated all sides of this argument for ten days, all over the subcontinent. Wells seemed to win in the heat of the exchange, and even in the numbers, but by the time the storm died down, a new one was in the making at Canberra.[34]

Before leaving for Canberra and the ANZAAS conference he had come to address, Wells gave an interview in which he was asked several questions about women. Having first referred the reporter to his novel *Brynhild*, Wells went on to say that women were as intelligent as men, they simply had a different will. For him, sexual equality or inequality was a male problem. As he said, 'Men are so ignorant, so uneducated, so lacking in judgement, so egotistical. Their attitude to women is all wrong. It is governed by jealousy — and what a dreadful thing is jealousy! and by the pride of possession. The sort of petty pride they feel over owning a gun, or a ten-acre field or a boat.'[35]

That same week, Wells's novel *Apropos of Dolores* was published in Australia. The novel, the story of a man who thinks it is possible to achieve peace and happiness for mankind, but whose wife, Dolores, nags him and prevents his reaching fulfilment, is widely seen today as a Wellsian view of his time and his relationship with the writer Odette Keun. Critics in Australia were ambivalent towards the book; they thought it was brilliant, but filled with half-truths, a work that was depressing, pessimistic, and at the same time 'entertaining and stimulating'. Those words could also be applied to the message Wells was now beginning to offer the Australian people in a rapid series of speeches.[36]

The weather was terribly hot. Weather records back to 1862 were broken, and the temperature in New South Wales and Queensland became unbearable, finally reaching 117°F. in Adelaide, 113° in Melbourne, and 114° in Canberra. Wells made the second of his public speeches while the nation gasped in the heat. Entitled 'The World As I See It', the speech was an uncompromising attack on the restriction and distortion of knowledge. 'In the modern world it is second only to murdering a child to starve and cripple its mind.' Wells reviewed his own boyhood in Bromley, and said that he was deprived of the knowledge of many great discoveries, as his parents simply did not know of these things. 'Even today,' he remarked, 'nobody is really bothering to give mankind an abundant supply of cheap new books. Our wonderful English-speaking democracies are still grossly ignorant and misinformed.'

He talked about the world of books he had encountered in the library at Up Park, but pointed out that he was still out of date when he came under the influence of T. H. Huxley. Many of the young were still out of date just as their education was out of date.[37]

The conference at Canberra was a major scientific event for the nations down under. The British Association had met in Australia in 1914, but this conference was an effort to provide an Australian–New Zealand scientific view for the entire world. The overall title of the conference was 'The Place of Science in World Affairs'. Great names from all over the world, and from all the scientific disciplines, met in the great heat at Canberra. Many appeared in linen suits, pith helmets, open-necked shirts; even Wells at the height of the heat (107.4°F.) appeared in white trousers, white shoes, and a blue open-necked shirt. The only relief came at an opening garden party when a terrible deluge caused these distinguished personages to run frantically for shelter. That torrential downpour, and a 'scientific cricket game' between visiting economists and Commonwealth statisticians, were the social highlights of the affair.[38]

Wells gave two addresses at the conference. The first, given on 12 January, was read to a huge audience both within and outside the hall, and it was transmitted over the country. He announced his title — 'The Future of Mankind' — and few newspapers missed the opportunity to headline their story 'Things to Come'. Wells told his listeners that the world was at a crossroads. Although it was the least probable way, he thought, we could 'abolish war through conscious co-operation and launch ourselves wilfully and intelligently upon a new and greater way of living'. However, when thinking about the possibility, he assumed that men would 'make the least possible concessions to the needs of war time. . . . The human mind will resist the humiliation and general disturbances involved in changing its ideas,' and eventually a single state would become dominant. He discussed 'those deep-seated delusions' of race and patriotic superiority. Again, as he had done for a lifetime, he proposed education as the panacea for the ills of the species.[39]

Although most newspaper editorial writers liked the speech — the Sydney *Morning Herald* headed its leader, 'All Wells with the World' — and urged Australians to follow Wells, many of the scientists at the convention were more tepid. The engineers felt that Wells had been too strong in his remarks, as they were more optimistic. J. R. Darling, however, the famous master of Geelong Grammar School, agreed with Wells completely. He described Wells's words as 'incontestable' and went on to remark, 'I believe that Mr Wells has given a great service to mankind. He has given people of my age an inspiration, for he is capable of criticizing existing institutions. He has a capacity for detaching himself from the environment.'[40]

The next day Wells attended a meeting on the relationship of science to society. Sir David Rivett gave the address, and when asked for comment after the speech, Wells remarked that Australians like Rivett would and should lead in this necessary work. 'Nationalism in Australia has gone far enough.' It was time to turn to broad issues, and he appealed for freedom of thought. The gathering, moved by Rivett's speech and Wells's comment, passed a motion affirming loyalty 'to the task of preserving truth, freedom of expression, and justice in the world'. The labour of the scientist must be utilized for the benefit and not the destruction of mankind.[41]

These addresses and appearances were the frosting on the cake for H.G. Wells's admirers down under, but he had been invited originally not to make public speeches but to give the major address to the convention of scientists. In various allusions to the address in his earlier interviews, he implied that it would make teachers squirm, and in the event it did. As he said in his first day in Australia, 'Teachers are a rather self-satisfied class, and some may be distressed that I do not think their work is perfection.'[42]

The address was a giant performance, dealing with the major theme of Wells's life — education — and his auditors were so stirred by it that at first almost nothing was heard, as if they had been stunned into silence. The newspapers, press, and politicians in Australia recovered quickly, however, and the honeymoon with H. G. Wells was over. He could attack Hitler and Mussolini with impunity, but when he attacked nationalistic history teaching, these patriots were not prepared to listen, or at least not to listen without responding. Wells entitled his speech, 'The Poison of History', a provocative beginning to a major confrontation in the great hall at Canberra.

He opened his remarks by describing his address as 'unmannerly' and 'aggressive'. He told his audience, many of them historians, that their profession blinded them to the present, because of their occupation with the past. He charged them 'with overstimulating patriotism in the young':

> Nationalism is the purest artificiality, and is made by the teaching of history and by nothing else, history taught by parents, friends, flags, ceremonies, as well as by the persistent pressure of the schools, but mainly in the schools. And by this school-made nationalism the very existence of civilization is threatened.

Wells said that there were two kinds of history, the old outdated type which relied on nationalism and a new sort based on human biology. A possible name for his new history was 'human ecology' or 'social biology'. He said that if we were to succeed in our great struggle for universal peace, 'If the young Hercules of the new world is to live, its first feat must be to strangle the tangled coil of poisonous histories in its cradle.'

He gave a number of examples of the poisonous past still being evoked. Caesar and Alexander were described as 'those two raiders' or 'those two wastrels'. He compared them unfavourably to Huey Long, the American demagogue, who had more political creativity, according to Wells. On another important matter, he felt the Jewish question was 'a particularly bad instance of the distortions of human life by the poison called history', which was useless as the basis for an ideology of peace. The most astounding story, he said, 'masked and hidden under the mis-representation of the old history', was the imposition of 'Judaeo-Christian mythology', first upon the Mediterranean world, and then, 'less effec-tively', upon the rest of Europe and America. 'I can imagine no more dreadful position in the world today than to be an intelligent Jew, with a clear sense of reality.'

The nationalist histories, he went on to say,

> have outlived their use, they decay, they become poisonous. . . . Without a proper teaching of the realities of the new history the outlook for World Peace is hopeless. . . . Let us make a burnt offering of our old history text-books to Cosmopolis, to the always natural and now necessary Fraternity of Mankind.[43]

The newspapers all hoped that the historians might respond to Wells at a session scheduled the next day. The session turned out to be quite dreary. Sir Francis Anderson opened by calling Wells's new history 'sawdust'. Anderson said he was speaking on behalf of a profession which was 'undertrained, underpaid, and a target for all'. Wells said that he could not understand why it was sawdust to discuss flying, building, and other great events, and why it was 'noble and invigorating to discuss Henry VIII and his six wives'. Dr A. N. Lewis (MLA, Tasmania) said that if he put Wells's teaching into practice he would be faced with political extinction. Others at the meeting said that Wells had some good points, and that great strides had been made in the schools in the previous thirty years. Wells responded to this by remarking that 'nationalism is like a stained-glass window which throws colours on a body on which a doctor is operating. The different colours make it impossible to see things in a true light.' The economics section offered, and then withdrew, a motion calling for optimism, saying that Wells was simply too pessimistic and this was having a bad impact on the world. The Tasmanian Minister of Education did say that he agreed with Wells and that changes should be forthcoming. However, on balance the response was tepid, and it was because the audience had been faced with an undigestible meal.[44]

Newspaper comment was not so restrained. The Melbourne *Age* called the address a 'shock', and the Melbourne *Leader* termed it 'aggressive'. The Brisbane *Courier Mail* headlined its editorial, 'Mr Wells Tilts Another Lance', and accused him of advocating book-burning. The *Argus* of Melbourne said that history was 'the crystal stream and nationalism the pollution', but they were more bemused with Wells than anything else, ending their remarks with 'There is no danger of boredom, however.'[45]

The Communist Party newspapers were the most pleased by the speech. The *Australian Worker* thought that 'only the organized workers can combat this fearful degradation of all our concepts of power', nationalism. But in the Brisbane *Worker* a writer in a column entitled 'Smoke Ho!' defended Julius Caesar against the attacks of Wells and described Caesar as essentially an early founder of the British Empire. A letter from the headmaster of Townsville Grammar School for thirty-four years might be taken as representative of most of the comments of the shocked population. As this man remarked, 'No, if the alternative is between scrapping history as we understand it, and scrapping Mr Wells there is not much doubt which alternative must be preferred.'[46] As the conference closed down with repercussions of the Wells talk still echoing, Australians had mixed feelings about the gathering which had been hailed originally with such enthusiasm.

Wells had two more radio addresses to give, neither of which was carried as widely, or reported as well as the earlier efforts. The first, on 18 January, was on 'Utopias of the Future'. In it he said all scientists were Utopians, and that as they gained perpetually in wisdom, they generally reflected the anxieties of their times. He discussed the various concepts of paradise, and dealt briefly with Plato's dilemma of freedom and justice. Recently, according to Wells, most Utopias had dealt with organization, and not conduct, with socialism the worst example of this error. Now we must return to the ideal of Sir Francis Bacon, of science working to achieve Utopia, and this was the reason that he was in Australia.[47]

Wells toured the fire scenes in South Australia with the Governor-General before returning to Sydney. He addressed the firefighters on their bravery and later was to write an article for the London newspapers, commenting on their strength and bravery, and calling for similar qualities to be used to fight totalitarianism.[48] In Sydney, he gave a final nationwide wireless address, 'The Way to World Unity'. The speech was another in his long series of prescriptions to end war. He again made his point about the young men of the world and their vigour and inventiveness being channelled into war by those who could not devise a method of using them. He called for the use of this surplus energy to raise the 'standard of life systematically' by replanning and rebuilding the countryside, 'and rebeautifying and reconditioning human life'. He closed his address with: 'Words and phrases are only manifestations of good intentions. The ideal to strive for is a world planned and disciplined to prevent outbreaks of the tragedy — war. World peace might be got by unity or world conquest. But the positive way is by creative exertion.'[49]

Wells remained 'down under' for a short time. He made a speech in Sydney to a luncheon of the Institute of Engineers, urging them to detach themselves more from English apron-strings, and concentrate on the United States. He told the engineers that Australia was about to be thrust into a central position in world events and she needed to be ready. Two days later, at a dinner of the Fellowship of Australian Writers, while seated close to the Australian poet 'Banjo' Patterson, Wells delivered himself of a massive attack on Australian and other censorship. He described the Aussie censorship as creating 'a half-Fascist nation'. He thought broadcast censorship the worst, as one could always turn the programmes off, or not listen. Referring again to the coming events for which Australia needed to be prepared, he discussed the Australian support of Munich which was given so slavishly without any regard to what Wells thought Australian interests really were. He also (in a later interview) mentioned Japan, when he urged the Australians to 'get right up and meet it now, as it will probably come down and meet you later with an overwhelming force'.[50]

Wells gave brief interviews in stops at Brisbane and Darwin when weather and petrol demands delayed his homeward flights for a time. Here he was full of praise for Australian men and women. When his plane took off for the north, it left behind a small continent somewhat bewildered by a month in the great writer's presence. R. B. Orchard, a member of the Australian Broadcasting Commission, waited only until the plane had left to say that Australia was pleased to say goodbye, not least to the liverish side of Wells's disposition. He described Wells as 'a rather quarrelsome bad-tempered old gentleman' who had abused his hosts' hospitality.[51]

Most Australians were probably as happy to have him leave. Too much of H. G. Wells for those who did not know him was a difficult cross to bear. Some Australian newspapers discussed his 'exaggeration', and the case for nationalistic history was made again and again after his departure, in the correspondence columns of the press. A few defended Wells, however, including one or two who had gone into teaching because of his influence. One said, 'Vale in pace'.[52]

Wells left for home on a Dutch airliner, stopping in Bali, Rangoon, Jodphur, Baghdad, Istanbul, and then Athens. Finally he arrived home in the second week of February. On the way home he wrote occasional despatches for the London papers. As the end of the Civil War came in Spain, he saw it as one more piece of evidence of the necessity to become aggressive. 'An Empire that awaits attack is a dying empire', he warned his readers. It was necessary to rally liberal forces everywhere. In Burma he saw the beginning of the new road to China, but he also saw antagonism to Britain. He said that he found the same short-sightedness of exclusion in Rangoon that he had found in Bombay and Colombo, although in his three-day stay there he made much more contact with the Burmese youth. They told him, 'We are the Irish of the East,' and Wells believed it. At the inevitable PEN meeting he spoke again of censorship, and his audience was receptive.[53]

He found London to be more jumbled and bad-tempered than ever, and he predicted that the war, especially from the air, would be horrible. The

Labour opposition simply bored him, they were so out of date. What was needed was massive education towards 'world radicalism'. Why not found a Radical Book Club? he asked. 'I wonder why the world has neglected that good strenuous word for so long,' he mused at the end of his piece.[54]

A week later Wells reviewed the past six months that had been so arduous for him. Democracy only occurred in patches, and it seemed to be breaking up everywhere. He called again for world-wide education, and mentioned his three textbooks. His Australian trip had been an effort to provide a focus, and now his United States agents wanted him to go there, but only if he would be less boisterous. And, said Wells, Japan reached down to Canberra, and the US, the Dutch, and the Australians appeared to be myopic about the danger. He seemed disconsolate and alone as he contemplated, in a public way, his recent journey: 'Until a great educational campaign gets to work, until a strenuous and explicit revival of world radicalism on world-wide lines occurs, democracy will be nothing more than a vague, unmeaning politicians' word.'[55]

The only thing he could do was to collect a few of his recent speeches and articles and try to lead the world through the medium he knew best, the printed page. Penguin welcomed the book, but events moved too quickly, and the book was still in the press when the Germans marched into Poland. *Travels of a Republican Radical* was published in November 1939, during the 'phoney' war which Wells and his followers knew well enough was only an interlude between the main events.

In evaluating Wells's Australian tour it is easy to say that he might have been too strong in his remarks. Certainly as the tour went on the Australians became more and more reserved in their comments, and most of them were happy to see him leave. When he died, only one Australian newspaper even mentioned the tour in its obituary. They hoped to bury it and its unpleasant message. To be this negative about the tour fails, however, to reckon with the force of Wells's personality. As he said in a letter to George Catlin, 'I had a good time blaspheming in Australia, but God has since got back at me with shingles and a spastic colon.'[56]

H. G. Wells had a major audience in Australia, probably larger and more attentive than any since the writing of the *Outline of History*, and certainly since *William Clissold*. He made the best of the situation. The Australians, prepared to do honour to the author of *Kipps*, *Mr Polly*, or even *Mr Britling*, found that Wells had changed and had become Mr Tewler, and the Wells of *The Fate of Homo Sapiens*; but this does not gainsay his effort, or diminish its impact. Unfortunately for Wells the events of the late '30s were speeding beyond his capacity to analyse them, and his words were overtaken by events. The poisonous nationalism called modern history had done its work. Wells was too good a prophet, even on this last trip, to win adulation. *Homo sapiens* was not prepared to take in his message; in fact, it was all the species could do even to listen to it. All that was left were the last motions possible before the horrors came down around his head.

By the time he returned home, very tired (he was, after all, about to turn seventy-three), and ill as he said with shingles, colitis, and neuritis, the weeks of peace were numbered. Within about six months, everything Wells had worked for was destroyed in the attack on Warsaw and the movement of German troops across the frontier into Danzig and along the Polish corridor. In that six months, as he recuperated from illness and debilitation, he was still able to write, and the work poured out of the typewriter, into the composing rooms, and to the booksellers. As at other times in his life when he had been under great strain, whether personal or in reaction to public affairs, he dealt with it through writing.

He had finished passing the proofs of *The Holy Terror* just before leaving for Australia. That book (1939) is the biography of Rud Whitlow, a weak snivelling bully who rises to be a world dictator. It was based on perceptions of both Hitler and Mussolini, and provided a Wellsian view of how personal power and authority could corrupt the soul. In this book an *eminence grise*, Chiffan, is almost a parody of Wells himself, and the book turns Wellsian ideas on their head, as he takes a sardonic look at his own life and his impact on world affairs. Other figures from the time, Mosley and Beaverbrook in particular, all appear briefly in sarcastic parody of themselves. Eventually the world revolution proclaimed by Rud deteriorates into a war of ideologies. Wells as always was able to describe war and other broad action, in this case giving his readers a strong foretaste of the aerial war soon to engulf Europe. Rud breaks with Chiffan, is gradually isolated from his friends and companions, becomes obsessed by antisemitic views, and is destroyed by a companion from college days. Wells summed up his views of the twentieth-century dictatorships he saw so clearly near the end of the book, when he remarked:

> Queer lot these twentieth-century Dictators. They broke out like wasps in a dry summer. Conditions favoured them. A peculiar species they were. A crescendo of scavengers because the unadapted world was rotten with shabby evasions and make-believes. It asked for blow-flies and wasps. Not a loyalty, not a religion left that was not dead and stinking. These Dictators were master stinks, stinks like burning rubber and creosote, in a world of cowardly skunks.
>
> (Book IV, Chapter 3)

This is Chiffan commenting on Rud, and his compadres, just after he has disposed of him. It, and other comments from Wells, earned him a place on Hitler's hate list, and very near the top. If Germany had invaded England, Wells would have been one of the first persons sought out for punishment — not a bad position to be in.

During the late spring and early summer of 1939, Wells continued to write steadily, producing *The Fate of Homo Sapiens*, eventually combined, in the early days of the war, with *The New World Order* (1940), as *The Outlook for Homo Sapiens* (1942). These books were re-statements of his views on religion, tyranny, dictatorship, the need to provide a goal for rootless young people without work, and the necessity to develop world goals of peace and justice, through better education. Those who read the books generally liked them. Gregory, about to retire from *Nature* and as president of the British Association, found the message in *The Holy Terror* alarming, but very true. He hoped that the 1939 meeting of the BA might use some of Wells's education ideas, but the meetings were cancelled, as the scientists found themselves mobilized for other work.[57]

Wells himself believed the novel might be dying: magazines and short topical books might replace fiction, he thought, as the affairs of the world speeded up. Hitler was moving so far and so rapidly that he went way beyond *The Holy Terror* while Wells was reading the proofs. Of his two books, *The Fate of Homo Sapiens* created the most interest, as he focused his attention more clearly on the causes of the forthcoming war. Published in August 1939, the book went through three impressions in the first fifteen days of its existence.[58] Beatrice Webb told her diary that 'It is the work of genius in its indictment of western civilization. . . .' although she thought Wells's alternatives were outworn panaceas. She wrote to him that she and Sidney (who had recently suffered a stroke, but could still read) had read it with 'unlimited admiration'. In fact, Sidney Webb had then gone back to *The Work, Wealth and Happiness of Mankind*, and became absorbed in it. Priestley, reviewing *The Fate of Homo Sapiens* in the *News Chronicle*, had had much the same reaction and he told his readers that they must read the book, 'For, he will do for you what he has just done for me. He sets us trying to think it out all over again.' Laski, writing in *Tribune*, felt the same way; he termed it 'one of the most invigorating books from Wells in years'.[59]

Whether Wells would write another novel or not, he did not know. Marjorie, writing to Curtis Brown who had become his New York agent for books, said, 'Mr Wells has not started another novel, but these things come very suddenly, and he may do so at any time. He will certainly continue with you if Michael Joseph and Simon and Schuster do as well with *The Holy Terror* as they seem to promise.' Wells did produce two more large novels, and one short one, but they did not emerge until after the war had begun. He, in the meantime, was concerned about Hitler's plans, and his own, now focussing on Stockholm and a world conference of PEN.[60]

In the last month before the war, as he was making his preparations for Stockholm, Wells took lunch with Hugh Walpole. Walpole described him as 'puckishly, gleefully pessimistic'. Wells himself said, in his last published words before the war, and knowing that it was close upon him and the world,

Is it an impossible dream that this time men — a considerable number of men — should not only fight for something called democracy, but also that they should have a sufficiently clear idea of what they intend by

Democracy, to insist that they get not merely the shadow, but the substance of it, when at long last the second world war that seems so unavoidable, blunders through blood and exhaustion to a more or less formal conclusion?[61]

When the war began, Wells was in Stockholm. The PEN conference, scheduled to focus on the problems of censorship, was cancelled, however. His speech, a great summary of the problems of censorship and a call to arms for writers all over the world to resist, as truth had become the only way to stop dictatorships, was never given. He printed it in the *Travels of a Republican Radical*, which appeared that November. In Stockholm, he and Thomas Mann, almost the only writers who actually appeared for the conference, could only talk, have a meal together, and commiserate with each other over the failure of their world.

The war, even though expected, came with such force that everyone seemed totally confused. Wells was stuck in Stockholm, but was finally able to fly, by Swedish civilian transport, to the Netherlands. His plane was buzzed by a Luftwaffe pilot, but no shots were fired. In the Netherlands he found himself caught up in the flotsam and jetsam of the war's beginning, but was eventually able to get a place on the ferry to Harwich, then travelled by train to London, where he arrived on 17 September. His experiences on the crossing led him to recommend a mine, to be dropped from the air by the RAF, and he mentioned the journey at other times as a comment on the world. But for Wells the war had come, and as he said in a book thrown off as the Declaration of Human Rights campaign began, the human race now was faced with the stark choice, 'Fight, Cheat or Yield' to the Nazi and Fascist terror. This time there were no alternatives.[62]

In the first year of the war, Wells finished two novels. The first, *Babes in the Darkling Wood* (1940), was a return to the themes of *Joan and Peter*. Two young people, caught up in a world they do not understand, try to determine what makes that world the way it is. It was cast as a dialogue novel, and is most famous today because of the long introduction in which Wells defended the dialogue technique as well suited to fiction with a specific didactic purpose. In the book, his characters, Stella and Gemini (the names are significant as representing heavenly, or, at least, non-earthly characters), meet, fall in love, and try but are unable to avoid the reality of the war which is threatening them. Gemini breaks down after actually viewing the terrible conflict, and part of the book deals with his recovery under psychoanalysis. There are good discussions of Russia, and why the Russian Revolution took the form it did. As Wells indicated, though, the world was too comfortable — reality too harsh — and no one wanted really to deal with the failure of the European system in the years between the wars. The Russian Revolution, the Nazi revolution, the Cliveden set, and isolationism in the United States were all, in their own way, evasions of reality. Using the metaphor of a block of alabaster ready for the sculptor, Wells and his characters imply that the block still exists, but if the sculptor is not allowed to work, the marble may be crushed. In the world of 1940 the sculptor had not yet thought about his statue. Wells ends the book by remarking that if the new world were to work, more had to be heard from both the mothers and the whores — all women must play a role. Men simply could not overcome their egocentric ideals.

As the two characters in the novel begin to think about remaking the world, they hear the guns across the Channel. But they are not afraid. As Gemini says,

> 'They will pass. . . . All that will pass. We fight by the way. To get rid of a dangerous nuisance. It is not our essential business. Incidentally our world may be blown to pieces and we with it. That cannot alter what we are while we are alive, nor what we have to do.'
>
> (Book IV, Chapter 3)

And as the Germans spill into the Low Countries, Gemini leaves for his minesweeper, and Stella for her nursing post, both with the firm belief that the war will be transitory, and a peace, a real peace, could still come. The thing that had forced the Germans twice within a quarter-century to erupt could be eliminated — it only wanted a will, and an attempt based on that will.

Wells's other book of the period was an allegory based on the story of Noah and the ark. He told his publisher, or Marjorie did for him, that 'He wrote it suddenly and he does not think he ought to release it except in co-operation with you for fear that it might detract attention from the *Babes*.'[63]

In the little allegory, *All Aboard for Ararat* (1940), the ark, symbolic of the world at war, is lumbered with a Jonah (the stupidity of man) who slows down the passage to the mountain. The Lord and Noah, as Captain, discuss the ark and its progress, both agreeing that it will attain Ararat eventually, but not without much struggle. Eventually those aspects that drag it down and keep it back must be shed, like barnacles from the vessel itself. After the Lord goes, Noah sits looking pensively at the sky, with its stars. '"No man is beaten [he says] until he knows and admits he is beaten, and that I will never know nor admit."' One might apply these words to Wells himself. He did not know he was beaten — he was not about to give up. At home he had launched the Sankey Declaration, and now he was off to America in one more attempt to lecture them, to educate them, as it were, to the Nazi horror, and to the need for joint action.

Marjorie had asked Alliance Press to time their publication of *Ararat* to take account of Wells's American lecture tour in October and November. Wells had signed a contract to give a half-dozen lectures, mostly in the West. He arrived, along with 250 refugee children, on the S.S. *Scythia* on 4 September. The United States was in the midst of a great debate over whether or not to enter the war, with Franklin D. Roosevelt attempting to lead the country into war against the fascist menace, but doing so in the face of a more or less hostile Congress, and in the midst of an unprecedented battle over his bid for a third term in the Presidency. Every word Wells uttered had an impact on that battle, and on Roosevelt's battle with the Congress. The press had already been following Wells's remarks in a regular way since the war began.[64]

In his first interview, while still on the ship, Wells called for a shake-up at home in the Foreign Office and in the Cabinet, saying Halifax, Gort, and the others in charge were representative only of upper-class views. (Wells got his wish, as Chamberlain resigned that very day from the chairmanship of the Conservative Party, while forming a new War Cabinet.) The interview repeated ideas in an article he had written before leaving; in both he issued a call for even more US aid, and, although he said he hoped that the US could remain out of the war, he doubted if it would be possible. In any case, American party politics would influence the peace settlement, much as it had done in 1919. Wells also delivered himself of an attack on Nicholas Murray Butler, who had recently called for an end to academic freedom during the present emergency.[65]

Wells rested for a couple of weeks at Thomas Lamont's, seeing Margaret Sanger for the last time. He went out once or twice, but mostly simply gathered strength for his tour. Back home in the Commons, as his splenetic remarks on the Government stirred comment, Lord Winterton asked if they could not keep people like Wells at home, or at least require that they keep their mouths shut while abroad. A debate ensued, in which Wells was called 'a great Englishman', and Emanuel Shinwell, speaking in rebuttal to Winterton, told him that his remarks would have gone down better in the Reichstag. Winterton said, in response, that Oswald Mosley should be sent after him to counteract Wells's observations. The free press, both in Britain and in the US, flew to Wells's defence, or more especially to the defence of free speech. The *New York Times* summed it up neatly enough: 'Earl Winterton leaves us cold.' After the squabble, Wells submitted to a long interview on his writing and his ideas, telling his audience that once his lecture tour was over, he was on his way back home: 'We're in the front line there, you see. I am only on furlough.' In the US Congress, however, Representative Delaney, an isolationist from New York, called for his deportation. No one else picked up the comment.[66]

Wells's talk, which he gave nearly a dozen times, was entitled, 'Two Hemispheres or One World'; it was published at least twice in pamphlet form under different titles. He told his audience, mostly located in the American West, that he had a propensity to view the world in broad terms. As time and distance had been virtually eliminated now, everything in the world was the concern of everyone else. He cited his old master, Winwood Reade, as saying that martyrdom might lead to a good end, and the world's martyrdom of the twentieth century could pay peaceful dividends if the species were willing. When the peace came, conservation of the world's resources, an economic control similar to that proposed so long ago by David Lubin, control of the air, and the elimination of Toryism would be the first priorities. 'We on this planet are caught', was his warning.[67]

Wells gave the same story to interviewers wherever he spoke. Appearing in Los Angeles on the eve of the election, for instance, he told newspapermen who met him at the hotel, 'We are fighting this war for human freedom, for ending the perpetual tension of war and a better way of living, or we are fighting for nothing worth fighting for.' He again urged the US to stay out of war if they could, but to continue to send supplies to Britain and her Allies. In the morning Willkie was defeated, and Wells could finish his tour, knowing full well that his old friend Franklin Roosevelt would not let Britain down.[68]

Wells completed his tour, and arrived back in New York to give his talk again, on a radio programme famous in those days, 'Town Meeting of the Air'. Introduced by Ray L. Wilbur, he modified his talk for the radio audience to call for 'cosmopolitan world socialism', and said, 'the true God, the God of Truth, has yet to be found, and in the world of my desires, the whole world will be seeking him.' A great many questions came from the audience after the talk, and Wells went on to urge control of the air, and to say that the Germans were losing. He reiterated his views on Lord Halifax, and described Joseph Kennedy, American ambassador to Britain and an isolationist, as 'a reckless talker in interviews'.

Later, before he left for home, the Town Hall Trustees gave him a luncheon where he reiterated his views on the need for federal control of air power, as well as a need for better history teaching. Flanked by Jacqueline Cochran, the famous aviatrix, Anne O'Hare McCormick of the *New York Times*, and Kingman Brewster, representing the *Yale News*, he was effusive in his praise for Americans, their press and their exploits. Two weeks later he left for home on the Yankee Clipper, asking in his last interviews for 'vigorous help' for Britain. Weather grounded the aircraft in Bermuda, where he was forced to stay in the same hotel as Otto Strasser. Once he arrived in Britain, from Lisbon, Wells was able to put his full efforts into the campaign for Human Rights, although he still had a few choice words for people like Strasser and Alfred Noyes, former Nazis who had changed sides, and who Wells felt were working for a soft peace which would only forestall his new world.[69]

Wells told Elizabeth Healey Bruce, soon after his arrival, that he had had a good time in America, 'successful and unregarding', as he had escaped the worst of the October bombing. Her house had been bombed, as had that of A. P. Watt, and damage had occurred at Hanover Terrace, but Wells was all right, as were they. He also told her, 'Now I have come back to be a thorn in the side of the Tories (D.V.).' He was always at home to lunch for his friends from the US and Great Britain, and much of the next few months was spent in entertaining them, along with carrying on his work;

and although he was asked to return once more to the US, it was now time to remain at home, on the front lines as it were.[70]

Wells had one more fictive shot in his bow as well. As he viewed his last few years' activities, while thinking about the progress of the war and the prospects of peace, he wrote one last novel, *You Can't Be Too Careful* (1941). He dedicated the book to Christopher Morley, 'who richly deserves it'. The work discusses the life of Edward Albert Tewler, representative of the genus *Tewler*, on his way, perhaps, to being *Homo sapiens*. Tewler (the name is evocative of a worker without brains or energy, the tool of anyone who wishes) lives a life of deeds, not words, the very rejection of books and ideas. He disdains any effort to better the world, in a comic arraignment of the lives of ordinary London people.

The book has a truly magnificent depiction of a North London lodging house and its inhabitants; one wonders how Wells could skewer that sub-group so well. Tewler marries, has a child, and his wife enforces a form of chastity upon him — leading to alarming outbreaks before she leaves him alone. Mrs Tewler the second, however, satisfies his physical wants occasionally, enough to keep him in line, and Tewler lives out his life, not happily but 'ever after'. He is completely surprised by World War II, but does his part as an air-raid warden and Home Guard, meeting as he does so representatives of Bolsheviks, Jews, and other groups important in England. But, as Wells puts it, just before Tewler ends his rather comic and yet pathetic existence, the real question is — can *Homo Tewler* become *Homo sapiens*, and what will it take? 'A Eutrophic world from which priest and pedagogue have been swept as unnecessary evils is quite within the range of human possibility', of course. But, in the meantime, Tewler is, as Everyman, 'what our civilization made of him'. Wells said that Tewler was not detestable, just pitiful, and asked his readers, 'How long are we unawakened Cosmopolitans to go on wasting one another and devastating the future?' As Daniel George said in *Tribune*, commenting on the book, *Kipps*, nearly a half-century earlier, had come to the conclusion that it was 'a Rum Go', and so probably did Tewler. But did he? As ever, even though this was the last novel, it was not the last of the old man, who still had some fire left, for his enemies, and for the enemies of his world.[71]

PART FOUR

PROPHET

WOMEN AND FICTION: II

She was a noble wife, a happy mother, and the maker of a free and kindly and hospitable home.... Some lives stand out upon headlands and are beacons for all mankind. But some, more lovely and precious, shine in narrower places and come only by chance gleams and reflections to the knowledge of the outer world.... All brave lives have been lived forever. The world of human achievement exists in them and through them; in them it has its being and its hope, and in it also they continue, deathless, a perpetual conquest over the grave and over the sting of death.... The city of the living world is a perennial city, founded deep in the immemorial past and towering up in the future to heights beyond our vision, its walls fashioned like a mosaic out of lives such as this one.

HGW, 'In Memory of Amy Catherine Wells' (Jane Wells), address — here slightly rearranged — read at the cremation service after her death, 7 October 1927

Most biographies of H. G. Wells skate fairly quickly over his personal and sexual life, often exhibiting distaste. To a considerable degree this must be because the biographer is uncomfortable with that aspect of his life. Wells was perhaps the best known socialist in the world for much of the twentieth century, an advocate of equality of education for all according to their talents, and a gifted author who provided his readers glimpses and vistas into a world set free — free of the dominance of upper-class rules, free of hidebound and narrow education, and above all, free from irrational nationalism with its pride in killing, in slaughter, bullying tactics, and oppression. How could a man with this reputation go through life bedding women other than his wife, sireing children out of wedlock, living in 'sin', and still justify that reputation?

If the question is put in this way, no useful answer is possible, except to skip over the unpleasant details, cover them in euphemistic language, and hope the reader will not put more probing and sticky queries. On the other hand, if the question is put from the point of view of the women involved with Wells, the answer may be different. This is especially true when one realizes, often with a sharp sense of recognition, that these women were not casual encounters, nor were they dull-witted slatterns looking for a moment's pleasure. One is left with the remarkable insight that these women, and H. G. Wells, enjoyed each other immensely, for shorter or longer periods of time — that both partners in these relationships came to them with the knowledge that its duration was not the significant aspect of the encounter, and that the ideas and comments of others were not of any great importance. What was important for the time involved was that these women and this man had a strong physical, mental, and psychological connection — on a give-and-take basis. In fact, with a single exception (Odette Keun), and for a short time in another case (Rebecca West), these women continued to see Wells, to meet him and discuss their ideas and the world's problems, and he, in his turn, regarded them as close personal friends, integral parts of his life, then and later.

For to cite the names of these women, before going on to discuss their life with H. G. Wells, and the meaning of that life for both individuals, provides an indication of the sort of persons we are dealing with. Not all his women friends were his sexual partners, although many were, and several of those who did not take that opportunity, according to their own testimony, did not because they chose not to. The opportunity was apparently there if one wished. In any case, so that the reader has some view of the external history of this side of H. G. Wells's life, a recapitulation and description of the more significant of these relationships is needed.

We have already dealt with Wells's life with Isabel Wells, his cousin and first wife, as well as his life with Amy Catherine Robbins (Jane), his second wife. In addition we have looked at his relationship with Amber Reeves, and a related friendship, with Violet Paget ('Vernon Lee'). His attitudes towards such persons as Beatrice Webb, and other Fabian women, have also been shown to be significant. In the later years of his life Wells had a remarkable relationship with Dorothy Richardson, the feminist stream-of-consciousness novelist, which went through a sexual phase, but continued afterwards as a friendship until Wells's death, and beyond. He had a passionate interlude with Elizabeth von Arnim ('Elizabeth of the German Garden') which lasted for over a year, led to an important novel by her, but continued as an analytical friendship for more than twenty years thereafter. He lived with Rebecca West, who needs no descriptive identification, for a decade. She gave him a son, Anthony West, a prominent novelist and critic. Although their relationship was clearly more stormy than most of the others, it never emerged into public acrimony, and West was a significant supporter of many of Wells's activities in later life. The two partners used their fiction to memorialize aspects of this life — Wells at the height of his

27 Dorothy Richardson, 1917

28 Elizabeth von Arnim, 1915

9 Amber Reeves (Mrs Blanco-White) with child, probably her
aughter

30 Rebecca West, aged 17

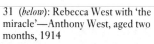

31 (*below*): Rebecca West with 'the miracle'—Anthony West, aged two months, 1914

relationship with Rebecca, and then later in a bitter-sweet memoir-novel. Richardson, for her part, focused on her relationship with Wells and his family in substantial portions of her long novel which has the overall title, *Pilgrimage*.

Wells's second wife died in 1927. During the dozen years after we last looked at the relationship, it remained strong. Amy Catherine Wells became an author of some little note, and when she died, Wells's grief and his efforts to deal with that grief provide a significant clue to their relationship. In this regard one must also look at the connection between Wells and such persons as the Countess of Warwick, his daughter-in-law, Marjorie Craig (Wells), Eileen Power, Cynthia Asquith, Christabel Aberconway, and, in his later life, the revival of his correspondence with Elizabeth Healey (Bruce). Partly as a result of Jane's death, Wells produced his remarkable *Experiment in Autobiography*, made even more remarkable by the recent publication of a suppressed portion of that work.

Coincidental with the ending of his relationship with Rebecca West, Wells was seduced by an extraordinary woman, Odette Keun. They had a stormy, passionate, and eventually bitter ten-year love affair. She wrote of it in several places, and he in turn wrote about her, in one of his most significant novels, *Apropos of Dolores*. While this was going on, he maintained a very long and quite passionate long-distance friendship with the famous advocate of birth-control, Margaret Sanger. Their correspondence is very interesting, in its implications for both their lives but also for our perception of male / female relations. Finally there was Wells's long-term liaison, as it must be called because of the freedom the relationship left to both parties, with Moura Benckendorff (Budberg); this was equally significant, not only for the role she played in his observable life, but also for her apparent role in his dream world.

It should be clear from this recital that we are dealing with remarkable individuals. These were not casual one-night stands. These women and this man loved and cared for each other. In most cases, they met on even ground, and each demanded from the other no more than it was possible to give. When a partner (in most cases, the woman) chose or wanted to change that ground, the relationship grew stormy, and eventually terminated. In the one case we know of in which it was Wells who wished to change the ground, and was denied, the relationship continued but was perceived differently, at least by Wells. Whatever one's feelings about these matters, it is crystal-clear that to know H. G. Wells, one must also at least attempt to know his life in the world of fiction and his life in love.

One other caveat ought to be stated. After Wells died, his daughter-in-law and secretary, Marjorie Craig Wells, bundled up much of the personal correspondence still in his files and posted letters back to their recipients / senders. Precisely what happened to that correspondence varied from person to person. There must be some letters surviving of the Amber Reeves relationship, but where they are one does not know. In the third volume of *Experiment in Autobiography*, entitled *H.G. Wells in Love*, there are some cryptic references to missing portions of the text, and one individual is identified only with an asterisk. This, taken together with Anthony West's recent biography of his father, in which he suggests that other items of correspondence were available to him, promises that much may still see daylight. Biographer of Dorothy Richardson have not seen much actual correspondence between her and H.G.; the only biography of Elizabeth von Arnim, by her daughter, is fairly coy about Elizabeth's relationship with Wells, as about an even more important one with the pseudonymous 'Mark Rainley', but as to correspondence, apparently little survives. The Rebecca West correspondence is at Yale University. It was made available to Gordon Ray for his book, *H. G. Wells and Rebecca West* (1974), but the correspondence was then closed to scholars for the lifetime of Rebecca's husband (now dead) and her son, as well as for her own lifetime (she died in 1983). The Margaret Sanger correspondence will be drawn on in the course of this chapter and the next. One more substantial batch of letters, offered for sale a decade ago but later withdrawn, may be Wells's correspondence with Odette Keun, or with Moura Budberg. In general one feels, however, that even if other letters were available, they would not change our understanding of Wells, his life, or his sexual and romantic relationships and entanglements.[1]

He fell in love easily, and with great passion. Succeeding encounters tended to be tempestuous, filled with secret nicknames for the partners, loving rendezvous, and other manifestations of strong physical love. Women adored H. G. Wells, accepted him readily, and found that his intellectual power dramatically opened new sexual avenues. Not all succumbed so easily, or even at all. For one such woman, Christabel Aberconway, probably the best-known of them, the relationship continued strongly until Wells's death — 'once', as she said, 'we had established that I was not going to go to bed with him.'[2]

For those women who did succumb (and apparently most did), Wells remained a firm friend and gracious lover. Whether the affair was a 'passade', to use his word for brief encounters, or lasted a decade, the woman in question knew that he was her friend, her supporter, that she was his equal (except perhaps mentally), and that she could rely on him for support, for aid if necessary, and for companionship once the relationship was over. Wells practised what he preached — sexual equality within the biological differences mandated by our genes. He was prepared to break down those inequalities created by social structures, and what is now described as 'male chauvinism'.

To return briefly to Amber Reeves and her daughter Anna Jane, one finds that she was 'paraded' at Chiltern Court for G.P. and H. G. Wells at about age twelve, and not only was she mentioned in Wells's will, but H.G. provided a trust for her when she became twenty-one. Amber remained close to Wells, of course; their mutual friends frequently carried messages, and eventually even Rivers Blanco-White found it possible to be entertained at Wells's table.[3]

Other women remained close to Wells after their early meetings. Rosamund Bland Sharpe, one of the Fabian kindergarten who chased, and caught, Wells in 1908, married Clifford Sharpe, another young Fabian, after that episode. Sharpe, an editor of the *New Statesman*, developed a severe alcohol problem. Eventually Rosamund wrote to Wells reminding him of their evening on the sands at Dymchurch, asking for help, moral support as well as work. Wells would not read a manuscript, apparently, but he did provide her with typing work, and introduced her to other potential employers, and perhaps lent her or gave her money once Sharpe died. This was the briefest of his early encounters, but he remained loyal to those who had helped him satisfy his physical wants.[4]

Wells was, as might be expected, a strong advocate of birth-control, and the dissemination of information and contraceptive devices to all who wanted them. Chief among the British organizations advocating this reform was the Neo-Malthusian League, founded in 1877 by Annie Besant and members of the Drysdale family. The League was founded when the first favourable court decision, freeing Besant and Charles Bradlaugh, found that information on birth-control could be made available, although not advertised. The League remained small, although Marie Stopes gave it a tremendous push forward when she began to provide information and contraceptive devices in birth-control clinics in the East End of London after World War One. Wells donated some funds to these efforts, and in 1915 he became a vice-president of the League, along with E.S.P. Haynes, Eden Philpotts, and very soon, Arnold Bennett. The League publication, the *Malthusian*, reviewed the second edition of *Anticipations* at about this time and highlighted Wells's stand on these subjects with, 'Thank goodness there are some who can see that the present trend of sentimental state help without the enforcement of parental responsibility is entirely against the real interests of the community.' The League leadership was thrilled with his acceptance of the vice-presidential honour.

Wells was not a token vice-president. He remained active until the group split over eugenics in the 1920s. He and Bennett could not accept the implications of the eugenics movement, but Wells did not resign with a fanfare; his name simply disappeared from the masthead of the journal. He remained active himself, however, in the movement. When Margaret Sanger was convicted in New York of giving out birth-control information in contravention of state law, Wells, along with eight others, wrote a letter to Woodrow Wilson, enclosing a petition urging her pardon, as her acts were legal in most areas in the US other than New York.

The editors of the *Malthusian* were not as favourably impressed with Wells's and other persons' socialism as with his views on birth-control. When Drysdale wrote an article attacking socialism, Wells responded, along with Bennett and others, threatening that he would withhold his support as long as such claptrap went out in the journal. Wells said that rather than issuing such 'silly' attacks, all should work together for their goals in an area of 'physiological enlightenment'. He wrote still another letter the next month, saying that he and Bennett had become vice-presidents of the League at some personal sacrifice, as the cause was so noble. As he noted that the editor had apologized, he, Bennett, and others (Philpotts?) would remain active in their support of the League and the cause of birth-control.[5]

In 1921 when Wells was in Washington for the Disarmament Conference, one of his articles mentioned birth-control as an issue, and the *Malthusian* quoted this and other newspaper comment favourable to him. When a major world conference on birth-control was called for July 1922 in London, Wells and Jane gave a reception at their home for the foreign delegates, and Wells took the chair at the great public meeting at Kingsway Hall on 12 July. The speakers at the meeting were Margaret Sanger, Baroness Ishimoto of Japan (the doyenne of the movement), and Sir Harold Cox.[6]

Wells sent his greetings to the next such conference in New York, saying, 'There is no subject of such importance as Birth Control. Knowledge of it makes a new and happier phase in the history of civilization.' In addition to contributing to the magazines within the movement, he introduced the subject and advocated wide adherence to these views in his other journalism, commenting on housing, the plight of the lower class, and specifically calling for birth-control measures to be understood and made widely available. As he said to one critic of his views, 'I think a married woman who knows nothing about birth-control is little better than a serf; a mere helpless breeding animal, and when I find an obscurantist Roman Catholic sitting in the light at the Ministry of Health, I think myself entitled to make a noise about it.' Later in that year of 1924 he told readers of his column in the *Westminster Gazette* that one of the most important questions of the world concerned, 'whether a woman has a right to clear and complete knowledge about her own body and the fundamental facts of her life'. He went on, after an attack on the Roman Catholic opposition, to take his bold stand: 'I hold that every man and woman should be the conscious and instrumental master of his or her own fate. . . . Sexual questions are coming into politics, and they are coming to stay.'[7]

In 1927 a Jubilee meeting was held to celebrate the founding of the Malthusian League by Annie Besant. J. M. Keynes was in the chair, and Wells was one of the featured speakers. He proposed 'The Malthusian League' as his toast and topic. After giving a short history of the League, and reminding the audience that it was only six years since the first major birth-control clinic had opened in Walworth, and much was left to do, he declared that the friends of birth-control were winning against their enemies.[8] In all ways H. G. Wells was a friend and advocate of this aspect of female emancipation. His stand of course attracted the attention of radical feminists of the time.

Although the Wells-Rebecca West relationship is very well known, through several recent books but also because they were more public with their love, and because their son, Anthony West, is also well known, the relationship which developed between H. G. Wells and Dorothy Richardson may be more important from the point of view of modern literature. All of Richardson's biographers agree on the main points of the relationship, but those books, well done as they are, have attracted only a limited audience.[9]

Richardson and Amy Catherine Robbins were schoolgirls together, at Miss Sandell's Southborough School, in Putney. In the year 1890, in particular, the two young women walked to school together most days along Upper Richmond Road. In their sixth-form year, they were fast friends (Amy was known as 'Perky'), and studied logic and psychology together. After Wells and Amy married, Amy invited Richardson to visit them at Worcester Park; Richardson was apparently, according to her own testimony in her fiction, fascinated by Wells: his eyes, his voice, and his mind. It was at the Wellses that she met Gissing, Grant Allen, Frank Harris. Wells began to prescribe reading for her. They read and discussed (arguing over) Kidd's *Social Evolution*, for instance. After Wells fell ill in 1898, they did not see each other much; Richardson was also working, and lived for a time in Germany.

Later she began to write brief pieces for the press. Amy/Jane Wells noticed these, and met her at a tea shop in London. Richardson was one of the earliest visitors to Spade House. According to her own testimony (and it is amply documented), Wells became, for the next decade, the 'vital centre' of her life. Richardson and Jane, both accomplished pianists, played duets for Wells when he was depressed. His and Richardson's conversations gradually moved on to a more physical plane. He pursued her. They exchanged many notes — over books and writing at first, but soon with more tender portions. She broke off the relationship for a time, but missed him, and they met again for a luncheon to renew their connection. Apparently they wrote long, open, 'totally uninhibited' and passionate letters to each other — letters probably destroyed either at the time of *Experiment in Autobiography*, or after Wells's death. They attended Fabian meetings together, often holding hands, and in May 1905, they became lovers. If we can accept Richardson's fictional account, this occurred at Spade House. The physical relationship lasted about two and a half years — it was less and less sexual, however, and more a struggle of wills, as their exchanges about fiction took a physical form. Richardson became pregnant in the spring of 1907, but miscarried in early summer. She moved to the country to recover, not only from the physiological ordeal, but also from the demanding nature of Wellsian love. He dedicated

The Future in America to her (to D.M.R.), and their relationship mirrored the events of the Fabian blow-up.

It seems clear that Richardson sustained him sexually during this period. By the time *Ann Veronica* appeared, however (and perhaps that book, as well as being about Amber and to some degree Jane, may also have some of Richardson in it), she and Wells had become the life-long friends they were to remain. It seems clear that Jane knew of their relationship, and the three remained close until Jane's death. Rosenberg quotes a letter, after that death, in which Richardson says, 'her disappearance mattered dreadfully to me, and still matters, and will always, though there was almost nothing we shared [except, of course, HGW]. Her life was "a work of art", and sheer poetry. And phrases. *Fabulous* shadows. I'll never forget. It is the uttermost about that sort of shadow in that-sort-of-environment-seen-as-secure. Whee.'[10]

Wells was extremely important to Richardson's fiction. He was a sharp critic, but at the same time constantly offered encouragement, and especially on her stream-of-consciousness style, so different from his own, but so remarkably expressive of life as she saw it and lived it. One of their mutual friends, J. D. Beresford, who lived in Cornwall, where Richardson and her husband, Alan Odle, settled, wrote an early critical biography of Wells, and his choice of subject as well as Wells's agreement to the proposed book probably owes a good deal to the Richardson connection. Wells is a significant figure in her fiction; in her long novel *Pilgrimage*, he appears as Hypo Wilson, from *Honeycomb* through to the end of the work. She, in turn, appears as Stella Satchel in *The Passionate Friends*. Wells likened Frank Swinnerton to her in his introduction to *Nocturne*, and gave her other public mentions, and support whenever he could.

He paid part of her debt to Duckworths in 1926, caused by the failure of *Pilgrimage* to sell, for instance, and a sketch by Alan Odle hung over his desk from 1918 on. She read proofs of the Atlantic Edition for him (paid for at £20 a volume), and Odle and Richardson paid lengthy visits to Easton in 1913, and in 1925. On the second visit Jane made sure that Odle had a studio room. Richardson was also given a locked study in which to write. Later Wells bought another drawing, and was instrumental in arranging Odle's remunerative sales to Theodore Roosevelt, Jr., to whom Wells introduced the artist. Later Wells helped obtain a Civil List pension for Richardson, while entrusting her and Marjorie with the job of shortening and tightening his *Experiment in Autobiography* while he was in America. Of course, she was always paid for such efforts, and in 1937 he settled on her for life an income of £4. 3s. 4d. a month — about $25 in pre-war money. That pension, and a similar one from her great friend, Bryher, made up the greater part of hers and Odle's income, as her books did not sell well. In 1938, Wells even helped Dent design a brochure promoting a new four-volume edition of her long novel. Wells, Hugh Walpole, Virginia Woolf, Swinnerton, and Rebecca West all provided quotations for the brochure.

Wells said of Richardson, at that time, that her books 'mark an epoch in the technical development of the novelist's art, a real and successful thrust towards a new reality and intensity of rendering that has exerted a powerful influence upon a multitude of contemporary authors'.[11]

She occasionally visited Wells in London, most notably at a party to meet Moura Budberg and Anthony West in the late summer of 1936, and they continued a correspondence. When Wells fell quite ill in 1944, Marjorie kept Richardson posted on his progress, and when he recovered, she was one of the first persons he wrote to, to thank her for her good wishes. He told her, 'thanks to disobeying my doctors and nurses in every possible way, I am now in rude health. Apart from gout (well-deserved, thank God!) and bores, I have no afflictions.' When he died, she said that it was 'an immense surprise', but she was unable to come to London for the cremation, as Alan Odle was very ill as well. Marjorie and others sent her all the obituaries, and other articles about him, so she was well apprised of how the world bade goodbye to him. Two and three years after his death, Marjorie and her children spent holidays in Cornwall visiting her. To Wells she had remained a constant friend and colleague, long after their months of passion earlier in the century.

She described him, in one of her novels, as having a not very pleasing-looking body, when it came time to make love, and he retaliated, to some degree, by leaving in his suppressed autobiographical piece, a description of her body as 'hairy'. These two comments aside, one can say that the relationship was important, and useful to both. She sustained him in a moment of great stress, and he became her mentor, her leader in writing fiction.[12]

Both Jane (as Alma) and Wells appear in Richardon's novel. *The Tunnel* describes their meetings, and Wells's 'disconcerting gaze', as well as their discussions of literature and a 'deadlock' which ensued, probably both physical and mental. In *Dawn's Left Hand* she presents scenes of returning from Europe to find his love letter, as well as a dinner and trip to the opera to discuss the affair. She remembered that it was Wagner they heard (perhaps *Götterdammerung*?!). In this book she described Wells and his views on people as, 'For so dismally, in everyone, he saw only what they were becoming, or might become, and of the essential individual one knew and wanted to know, nothing at all.' According to this novel, she and Wells embraced, but, although feeling great physical attraction for each other, did not have intercourse yet. She claimed to have a maternal instinct towards him, but that broke down when he entered her room at Sandgate and they made love. In *Clear Horizon* she discussed her pregnancy, and her miscarriage, as well as the meeting when she informed him of the latter. The note Wilson / Wells sends to her, as they agree to meet in future only as friends, says, 'the real difference between us is while you think in order to live, I live in order to think.' Wells appears again, in *Dimple Hill*, at meetings of the Lycurgus (Fabian) Society, a marvellous twist of names, as well as in scenes in *Revolving Lights*, and *The Trap*. It seems clear that Wells mattered terribly to her, and it might even be said that *Pilgrimage* is a sort of exorcism. *Dawn's Left Hand*, for instance, the most vivid depiction of him was written at the time of Jane's death.

Richardson's biographers have disagreed — not over her genius, which most critics will accept, but rather over whether she deliberately chose to be neglected, to be mastered, first by Wells, and later by the literary events which placed others ahead of her — others such as Virginia Woolf, who recognized Richardson's place in English literary history, as did May Sinclair and a host of others. It seems too much to believe that Richardson would toil on, through volume after volume of wrenched and passionate prose, only to court defeat. Rather, it is more probable that she was ahead, way ahead, of her time. H. G. Wells realized that, and he supported her claims to fame, and her rights to a more significant life. In another world it might have been different, but that was not to be. Their passionate but brief time remained for her the most significant event of her life, if one accepts her fiction as biographical evidence. It was not the most important event in Wells's life, but there is no evidence that she thought it should have been. She, like others, took what she was given.[13]

Another of Wells's women friends in this period, and one who played almost an interim part between Richardson, Reeves, and Rebecca, was Elizabeth von Arnim. She was exactly Wells's age, born in 1866, a cousin of Katherine Mansfield; after a conventional upper-middle-class girlhood she married, in 1891, Count H. A. von Arnim, who immediately took her away to Pomerania and East Prussia, where she became a subjected German *hausfrau*. That in itself is not terribly significant, perhaps, but Elizabeth Beauchamp, for that was her maiden name, felt oppressed by the German world, by her almost continuous pregnancies, or so they seemed to her, and she broke out with a famous novel, *Elizabeth and Her German Garden*, published in 1898, to immediate acclaim. From that time on she published a large number of novels, nearly all with autobiographical content, under the pseudonym of 'Elizabeth' or 'by the author of *Elizabeth and Her German Garden*'. Wells may have got some of his distrust of Germany from her, she having lived for a long time in a backward area of Prussia.[14]

Elizabeth von Arnim had difficulties with marriage, and with men in general. Her first marriage had fallen apart by the end of the '90s, and she found herself becoming increasingly attached to various of her children's tutors, who included Hugh Walpole, E.M. Forster, and C.S. Stuart (later a Cambridge don). She attracted and was attracted to younger men, and the results were occasionally quite comic, which became a focus of much of her fiction. She moved back to England in 1908 (having lived in England a good deal during the intervening years). By this time her books were the major source of the family income. Her husband was unsuccessful, was accused of fraudulent behaviour, and although he was cleared, life was very difficult. He died in 1910. Soon afterward Elizabeth met H. G. Wells, and for about three years they were seen together a good deal, much to the distress of her family, who felt that her association with this notorious socialist, and perhaps libertine, would damage her book sales as well as her reputation.

After her period of romantic entanglement with Wells was over, Elizabeth fell in love again, disastrously, with Francis, Earl Russell, older brother of Bertrand. She remarked to her diary at one point how much she admired Bertrand ('Bertie') Russell, who reminded her of H.G., whom she still missed very badly. She married Francis Russell in 1916, but the marriage failed almost immediately because of his drinking, and generally superior attitude. Not only was this marriage very unsuccessful, it seems not too much to say that most of her relations with men were unsuccessful. The marriage to Russell had disintegrated by 1919; he died in 1920. Later Elizabeth had a long relationship with a person, now known to us only as 'Mark Rainley', some twenty years her junior. Her novel about this affair, *Love*, published in 1928, is one of the most poignant comic novels of romantic attachment in our literature. Now undeservedly forgotten, it is useful to recall it here, as it too has some echoes of her relationship with H. G. Wells.

Eventually 'Rainley' broke off the affair, and Elizabeth, attended by servants and her family, moved from her home in Switzerland to Grasse (quite near Wells, in fact). Later she moved to the US with her sister, in 1939, dying in 1941.

Few writers of fiction, and especially fiction which is driven by feminist attitudes, have portrayed themselves and their lovers so dispassionately, and so ironically. Wells pursued her strongly throughout 1911–12, competing during this period with C. S. Stuart, who was some twenty years junior to both. Eventually (and it is difficult to say how much Elizabeth resisted, as her fiction usually gives her the better of the situations portrayed), the two older people planned a romantic interlude in Ireland; but she had become too 'emotionally involved' (the words are her daughter's) and she returned to her Swiss home. Wells, now very importunate, followed her to Switzerland, after 'reproachful' letters, and amid scenes 'of quite surprising violence'. In her autobiography (how does one separate these pages from her fiction?) Elizabeth remarked, apropos of H.G., 'Suitors are, after all, a strain. Even if they are the sort one turns a deaf ear to, one does, so long as they are about, give one's whiskers, as it were, an extra twist.' The use of the masculine metaphor to describe her reaction may be more revealing than she would have wished. In any case, Wells continued to pursue her throughout the year 1913, spending much time at her châlet, Le Soleil, while writing most of *The World Set Free*. At night, as he had done so many times with Jane, he read to her from his day's work.

The romantic interlude planned for Ireland finally took place in northern Italy, and although Elizabeth informed her daughter that 'his excessively trying behaviour' broke up the affair, it was an affair carried on, in the best of times, under difficulty. She liked younger and more adoring men, and did not especially care for the rough and tumble manner in which Wells usually conducted the early part of his romantic escapades. After this trip, they broke off the affair, but remained close friends. In the 1920s they shared the same address for their extensive London apartments, and in the autumn of 1923, for instance, Elizabeth rang up H.G. as soon as she arrived from the Continent. He came up to her flat, 'to tea and amused me as I was bored and depressed.' Later she purchased a house in Grasse, and spent a considerable amount of time there with Wells and Odette Keun, as well as his other guests.

Elizabeth's comments on Odette can await a description of that ménage, but they do occur frequently in her diary and journal, which form the basis for her daughter's rather reverential biography. While actively involved with 'Mark Rainley' who, she felt, was attempting to elude her much of the time, Elizabeth often discussed Wells, and his home, with Rainley, both in person and in their correspondence. She also discussed Wells from time to time with Hugh Walpole, who was always available as an escort when she was in London. At H. G.'s and Odette's she met Michael Arlen, the Aga Khan, Wilfred Grenfell, and other well-known persons. After she moved to the US, however, she apparently looked back with less warmth on Wells, and others; her letters are much more caustic. She continued to publish her accounts of love between persons of differing temperament (*Mr Skeffington*, of 1940, is an example). More significantly, she published her rather unrevealing memoirs, and died eventually a long way from home, bitter and resigned to a world dominated by primitive men, who were either too old, too young, or too distant. Since then her name has disappeared from most literature courses; but the best of her comic novels of love are delicious depictions of the folly and stupidity, the wan recognition of illusion, and the awkward efforts to retrieve a sense of reality which permeate most love affairs, and certainly those between individuals whose difference in age is as great as hers tended to be.[15]

Elizabeth memorialized her relationship with H. G. Wells in one of these novels, *The Pastor's Wife* (1914). In this novel her first husband also appears to no great advantage. The heroine, Ingeborg, marries a rather dull Germanic type, Herr Robert Dremmel. She is pictured as a free and open woman, wooed in a heavy and ponderous way by Dremmel. She is, in fact, swept away before she knows it, and is equally quickly pregnant. Her view is well stated, when she remarks, 'She greatly suspected, now that she came to a calm consideration of it, that that was the matter with marriage; it was a series of clutchings.' As she also remarks, she feels 'engulfed' by Dremmel, with her mind and body totally dominated by his presence. She ' . . . had no gift for honeymoons' is her comment. Love-making scenes are grotesque, 'without desire' apparently on the part of either, but she acquiesces, as she wishes only to make people happy, as she has done all her life. After the difficult birth, and increased isolation from Dremmel, she meets an English artist, Ingram (Wells). He tells her, almost at the first meeting, 'It really is *everybody's* duty to know at least something of what's being done in the world.' And, of course, he proposes to act as her tutor.

She has told Robert that she wants no more children, and she needs to be free of that aspect of marriage — a great insurrection, comparable to any that she has thought of ever before in her life. 'Fathers and husbands were not prepared for anything but continual acquiescence', but now she is done with that. She contemplates travel abroad, betrothal to a foreigner, refusal to her husband's desires — such are the thoughts which this casual encounter with Ingram places in her head and heart.

She experiences and accepts new sensations of freedom, youth, love, affection from Ingram, but she is torn between her 'duty' to her children, her need for rejection even, her desire for the old status as well as the cachet of the new. When Ingram calls her 'a perfect little seething vessel of independent happiness', she responds to her lover with, 'Teach me to seethe.' Even listening to him talk is provocative as it is 'mind-widening', greater than the greatest and strongest newspaper of the time. He kisses her, and entrances her with his use of words in his love-making, so far from Prussian stolidity.

Soon he becomes very importunate, however, and the platonic love of which she dreams is increasingly shown to be, as Ingram states it, 'in bad taste. Execrable bad taste . . . ' He tells her that in the mornings in which he does not see her, it is as though he were in the dark gloomy realistic world of Gissing, and he begs her to join him in love: 'I need you, my dear, I need you as a dark room needs a lamp, as a cold room needs a fire.' So, they go off to Italy, but their differing expectations doom the trip from the beginning. The hall porter who speaks of him as '*Monsieur votre père*', their ideas of clothing, Ingram's dissatisfaction with her naïveté — once they are away all these are bad omens; and, of course, there is the terrible fact that Ingram clearly wants his enjoyment, but he is not now prepared to pay with his mind for the pleasures of his body. He wishes to make love, but with no strong ties of emotion, just the romantic and physical ties which seem, on reflection, not to be enough. He wishes to love, and then to go to paint, which is clearly more important. His art always overcomes his ardour. He tells her to seek the 'freedom of spirit that disdains love'. 'Other lovers are engaged perpetually in sycophantic adaptations . . . ,' but there is no need for them to follow these ways and means. So, in the novel, but probably not in life, she decides to deny him her body, to remain true to her husband, no matter how dull he is, and how unforgiving and unfeeling.

There is one last comic scene in which Ingeborg appears in Ingram's room to claim her money. He thinks she is giving in, but she flees, taking only her toothbrush, returning home a prodigal. However, in the denouement of the novel, her husband does not even know she has gone. And the novel, extremely funny in many places, ends with Ingeborg looking back into her husband's study: 'In the middle of the room she hesitated, and looked back. "I — I'd *like* to kiss you," she faltered. But Herr Dremmel went on writing. He had forgotten Ingeborg.'[16]

I have paid a bit more attention to this novel than to some others because it is a novel in which Wells figures strongly, in this case as a sort of forlorn comic figure, chasing a sexual dream, but fleeing it once captured. That may well be an interpretation that can be placed on his affairs, but it seems to me to apply, if at all, only to the more casual affairs. Elizabeth von Arnim was a very complex woman. She too had strong feelings, usually directed towards unsuitable males. For that reason she probably exaggerates Wells's ardour, and certainly his reactions to her. Both chased — and both were caught. The result was a friendship, and an extremely amusing novel of the problems of love, and the impact of passion.

Wells himself would address many of these same problems from his own point of view. Before discussing them, however, it seems appropriate to discuss his life with his *grande passion* of this period, Rebecca West. Even here, there are many comic interludes, as she was much younger than he, and more ambivalent about their life together, at least in the later parts of their relationship. She first discovered him and his work, in a professional sense, while reviewing, appropriately enough, his significant novel, *Marriage*.

H. G. Wells had a hectic love life. And, although he managed it all quite well, at least as one looks back on the social, personal, and physical demands of that life, it still seems rather crisis-ridden. Things were always on the verge of falling apart. So, apparently, he alleviated some of the strain of this life by writing a rather remarkable group of novels which laid out the boundaries of normal male/female relations, while at the same time speculating on how his own life mirrored or reflected this other world. These novels, *Marriage* (published in 1912), *The Passionate Friends* (1913), *The Wife of Sir Isaac Harman* (1914), *The Research Magnificent* (1915), and later *The Secret Places of the Heart* (1922), are all related to his love life, but are also part of his educational effort. They are autobiographical in many passages, but as often they reflect Wells's ideas of a possible world. In fact, it is in the areas of frustration, and often even sputtering failure that they are closest to his own reactions. For they are often written, or so it seems to me, with the secondary purpose of exorcising unpleasant aspects of his life.

A decade after the last of these books, some years after the death of Jane Wells, and just after the break-up with Odette Keun, Wells collected three of these works in a volume along with *Love and Mr Lewisham*, and published them under the title, *Stories of Men and Women in Love* (1933). In a preface to this work, Wells remarked on how he had avoided, even in the

Atlantic Edition prefaces, saying much about his novels of love. After re-stating that he did not consider himself a novelist (again referring to comments of his and others about fiction), he reread these books, and delivered himself in this preface of a statement. He reminded his readers that it is in the dialogue in his novels (usually didactic in nature), that his work differed from more conventional fiction. But he felt that the books could be reprinted, because they did make some substantial points about love, not the act of falling into love, but the problems and situations which arose after 'the arrow has gone home'. For Wells, then, the chief interest in the novels (and in his life which he must have reviewed as he read) was the way in which various things repelled the lovers, or at least created centrifugal forces which allowed orbital activity within gravitational planes. 'Two words might be written over all these four stories, the words, "*And now?*"' However, as he went on in this preface, ' . . . now the love story is only the prelude to living. We remain *Men and Women in Love* and our problems unfold.'[17]

In *Marriage*, the first of the group of novels (although not included in *Men and Women in Love*), the opening part of the book recreates the life Wells lived with first Isabel, and later Jane, although mostly to tell the story of the man involved, not the women. But, in this treatment, a scientist leaves his science as love overcomes his need for research and intellectual life; he also experiences a growing disgust at the way in which science has been prostituted by the fortunes possible in a secret partnership with the financial and commercial worlds. All these relationships become prostitution, not only because of the payment tendered, but even more in the furtive, secretive way in which the transactions occur, just the reverse of the openness and sense of discovery in true science. This theme is carried on into Book the Second of the novel, with a growing sense of revulsion at the implications of the prostitution, not only for business, but at the ease with which the love and sexual interest in the marriage also creates a necessity for prostitution. Neither the male, Trafford, nor Marjorie, the controlling woman, are truly prepared to handle the demands of love, and modern life — their equality may be possible, but with all sorts of enticing by-ways in which to dally. They finally solve their problem by a long sojourn in Labrador — pondering such questions as, What is life to be?

This novel was monitored carefully, intensely by Jane Wells, who corrected the proofs of the book, and saw it through the press, as well as its serialization in the United States in the *American Magazine*. Wells was more concerned with persuading Macmillan to do more to advertise the book, especially when sales fell off six months or so after it appeared. He was, by this time, pressed for funds, as his various alliances and homes cost much money. By this time as well, however, he was also very concerned that his reputation, based on his books, and his 'infidelities', would prevent his sales from reaching possible heights.[18]

Ray Lankester realized that *Marriage*, as presented, might pose a problem for basic science, and he asked Wells to ensure that Trafford would return to science. Let him make a fortune and come through, if necessary, said Lankester, citing several scientists, notably Lord Kelvin, who had done so. Lankester later wrote Jane Wells that the book had 'a ripeness and breadth of view and sympathy — the best the dear man has yet done'. [19]

Wells's reviewers caught some of the ambivalence felt by Wells himself. Rebecca West, writing in the *Freewoman* (the review that led to their first meeting), thought that Trafford was the victim of a parasitic woman, but she went on to ask if Wells thought that Marjorie was a normal woman; she urged him to travel on the Underground and see 'how hopelessly unlovable' were most of the males travelling there. Rebecca said that the system had made Marjorie, but Wells was not sufficiently prepared to say so. Another woman reviewer, 'N.H.W.', in *T.P.'s Weekly*, was less critical, calling the book 'thrilling and inspiring' as well as saying that it could be placed by any Puritan family on their bookshelf. However, even this reviewer thanked Wells for his effort to understand the forces unloosed by 'the new woman' on the family. Another reviewer, who remarked that he had seen some of the book in proof, as well as hearing Wells read it, found the book the story of Everyman (intellectual life) and Everywoman (coquette and mother) working out their destiny in a new world, of which Labrador was only a symbol for the new world of every marriage if it were to succeed. [20]

Wells was not really discussing his marriage with Jane Wells in this book, of course. The boundaries of their relationship had been clearly defined long since, and its external aspects were quite well known. Wells, however, was fleeing the notoriety that had come from the Amber Reeves affair, which had been so widely discussed, while he fell in and out of love with Elizabeth. His life was in something of a turmoil. He wished to continue his sexual adventures, and had a substantial need for sexual release. Sometimes this was accompanied by real romantic love — as with both of these women, as well as with Isabel. Perhaps the evidence of sexual romance with Jane is slightly more tentative, as she so rapidly moved into the position of manager of his life. Still, *Mr Lewisham* suggests that the early period of his marriage to Jane was one of highly charged romance as well, and if my interpretation of *Ann Veronica* holds up, that too is evidence. But for Wells the question remained, how to have a love and keep it quiet?

His next novels also probed these questions. In *The Research Magnificent* he posed a love situation of a poor boy and a rich girl. The book is filled with the problems created by status and desire, as for instance, when Wells remarks, 'the servitude of sex and the servitude of labour are the twin conditions upon which human society rests today, the two limitations upon its progress towards a greater social order, to that greater community, those uplands of light and happy freedom.' The book strongly describes the lessons of possessive love, and the double standard which it has created for males, who Wells thought needed less love and more sex. The capitalist world is contrasted with the terror of jealousy, stemming from the same competitive instincts. In this book Wells is directly treating the early days of his life with Rebecca West, during which her possessive drive sometimes repelled him, but his sexual need brought him back. Gordon Ray, in his treatment of the two lovers, evokes those early days quite well, and at that stage, according to him, Wells was ambivalent while Rebecca was apparently besotted. We know, from Wells's few surviving letters to Jane, that sexual release was powerfully important to him, and even in Ray's account that must play some role. Wells and Rebecca were therefore both besotted, even though the initial drives were based on different needs.

In *The Research Magnificent* the pet names, the violent and passionate early encounters, and the words, gestures, and 'business' which Wells needed so badly in his romantic life, are clearly pictured, and not in a comic way as was so often his method for dealing with such matters. (As an aside, the paraphernalia of love worked much better with these upper-class and very young women, apparently, than with Elizabeth von Arnim, or others, such as Margaret Sanger, who were more realistic at this stage about Wells's needs, their role in his life, and their reasons for having the affair.)

We have Wells commenting, in this novel, about love as he sees it. 'Love is the most chastening of power.' And later, in a section entitled 'The Assize of Jealousy', he supports his point about the dominance of sex, and the roles in which fidelity, and infidelity crowd in on other thoughts. Of course, Rebecca, from the earliest days of their relationship, and certainly so after their child was born (4 August 1914), must have been hoping (and probably hinting to him) that as she had replaced Jane sexually, she should now do so at the altar, or in the Registry Office. Wells, in a letter quoted by Ray that is still among the West papers, made it quite clear that that would never happen — Jane was simply too important to him: as manager, as financial officer, as anchor (and, to a considerable degree, as personal sexual confidante). Jane Wells had become, as usually happens in the best and most stable marriages, his best friend.

Wells's friends, and especially those who knew Jane well, or Rebecca fairly well, thought *The Research Magnificent* quite remarkable. Violet Paget liked both the earlier books very much, though in her letters initially she praised their stress on internationalism. She and Wells had disagreed somewhat on world affairs, although they continued to meet and discuss various matters. Now she found she could still accept the Wells of these words, even though it was a different persona from the one in her head and heart. So she went on, in the letter discussing the books, to say: 'Of course the sex problem is one of the chief difficulties. Women are obstacles to progress, and women, as a result, would pay a very stiff price for their independence. It is by women working and competing with men that the hareem and the Paris fashion paper atmosphere . . . will be gradually got rid of.' She also remarked, agreeing with Wells, that women did not find these situations easy, and they were socialized to act in a way of which they often could not take advantage, even if they did find the chance. Paget ended this long letter by asking him to attempt some day, in his novels, 'to make amends to the poor "neuter", the woman who has left home and is typing or clerking, but always starving herself if not of food, then of other human rights often because of her blind, furious wish to independence.' She returned again to a brief discussion of these two novels in a later letter commending him for *The World Set Free*. She told him once more and finally (as the war would intervene in their discussions and meetings), that it was his ability to see things so vividly that was the key to his work, but also to much of the opposition to it.[21]

The Passionate Friends, another somewhat similar novel of sexual release, jealousy, and the configurations of love, was read with pleasure by Wells's friends Ford Madox Hueffer and Violet Hunt. Wells and Rebecca had been made welcome at South Lodge, Hunt's home, and there are a number of photographs of the four of them in various posed and artistic positions. Rebecca apparently considered living there with Hunt for a time. After the war, when C. F. G. Masterman and his wife Lucy, along with Violet Hunt (she was using the name Hueffer) and Hueffer himself travelled to Germany together, they sent Wells a postcard calling themselves 'The Passionate Friends'. Maurice Baring also liked the book, but thought that Wells should write about Catholicism, though whether he was likening the Church and its impact on women to that of capitalism is unclear (if he was, that is and was a brilliant suggestion). Most contemporary reviewers liked the novel, and there was even an effort to dramatize the work, but this fell through. The book was later translated to the screen without much difficulty; Wells himself had little to do with the script, however.[22]

In Wells's next novel of romantic love, *The Wife of Sir Isaac Harman*, he presents a picture of feminists of various kinds, especially suffragettes who were, according to him, defusing and re-focusing the battle for equality, by their attention to side engagements. 'Miss Alimony was one of that large and increasing number of dusky, grey-eyed ladies who go through life with an air of darkly incomprehensible significance', was his view. In our time such persons are best represented by those who engage in 'consciousness-raising', usually with new converts, but who, failing that, reiterate the same statements to their peers. Wells's novel focuses on naïveté, and the lack of realism among those who fail consistently to understand what others are thinking, hoping, dreaming. He again returns to his thesis that the emancipation of women can only come with the emancipation of jealousy — in other words, a removal of the blindfolds placed by naïveté.

In this book, however, the end seems to indicate that once the sexual and romantic part of love is finished, long, even intimate, friendships will and probably should ensue. This certainly reflected his own feelings about Dorothy Richardson, Elizabeth, and perhaps, by this time, even a hope for the end of his affair with Rebecca: that last had become increasingly burdensome, not least in the logistics of secrecy, which his own fears and life-style demanded, but also in her desire for open marriage, urged on by her mother and others. In *The Research Magnificent*, Wells remarked on the 'unquenchable demand, the wearisome insatiability of sex': that is, if one may paraphrase his feelings, if these women (and especially Rebecca) could only understand his need for release, and let life flow on, once the need was fulfilled, without the demands of jealousy and status intruding.

The first and early reviews of *The Wife of Sir Isaac Harman* were quite tentative, but when Holbrook Jackson treated the book with great respect in *T.P.'s Weekly*, Wells was much relieved. And eventually most reviewers liked the book, as it seemed to them that he was attempting to work out the significant questions of life in a period of growing independence.[23]

Wells had not quite finished with novels of this sort, although it was some time before he returned, except parenthetically, to the true themes involved. In 1921, he was beginning to break up with Rebecca (although the affair continued its stormy course for some months more), and was meanwhile spending a good deal of time with Margaret Sanger, who was living in England for a year while trying to adjust her life, and at the same time to dally with both Wells and Havelock Ellis. The novel Wells wrote at that time again discussed matters of marriage, love, sexual desire, jealousy, and their impact on the other work, especially of men, but on both partners to some degree. This book had a much better and more descriptive title, *The Secret Places of the Heart*.

The novel, set at the end of the war, begins with the leading character, Sir Richmond Hardy, taking a three-week trip with his alienist (the usual word of the period for psychiatrist) to work out his relationship with his wife (Rebecca), and his need for work. In this part of the book Hardy discusses his sexual life in some detail, and the relationship of sex to his marriage. Wells describes his dream of women, and the reality of women — his sexual anima which emerged from his study of Jung and which was to be so prominent not only in this novel, but in his other work, and especially in his treatment of women in *Experiment in Autobiography* (mostly in Volume III). The physician in the novel reacts in a more conventional way than Wells would have assumed, but eventually comes to the understanding that what Hardy is indicating is that women will need mental analysis and discipline as much as men if the world is to be better. Women are simply not 'biological machines', says Hardy/Wells. The trip continues to Avebury and Stonehenge, where they encounter an American traveller (Sanger) and from this time on the book turns on their growing relationship. Hardy (Wells as Rebecca's lover) dies at the end of the book, and the wife is apprised of the new relationship which had emerged on the trip. The question now beckons — should they treat these affairs conventionally, or as they really were? In the secret places of the heart, life is different, and should be recognized as such, but how? The book ends with the wife beating on the coffin of her dead husband, facing the reality of life — a life without him. Or, to put it into context, Rebecca, realizing that she cannot have Wells, is coming to grips with the fact, or at least so he hopes. From Wells's point of view, the last line of the book remains his testament on the affair: 'Always he had feared love for the cruel thing it was, but now it seemed to him for the first time that he realized its monstrous cruelty.'

These novels reflect H. G. Wells's efforts to deal with the complications of his life, and should be read and thought of in that vein. They can be complicated by the knowledge we have of his long liaison with Rebecca West. That relationship has been well treated by Gordon Ray. But, as one returns to that book, it seems increasingly clear that Ray's account owes too much to Rebecca West's efforts to control the past. West, christened Cicily Isabel Fairfield at her birth in 1892 (twenty-six years after Wells), grew up in upper-middle-class serenity, dominated by a mother who continued to play a strong role in her life. Much of her writing has an overly dramatic air about it, even her non-fiction, widely known and well-received, for which she is likely to be remembered. Among her early amateur dramatic roles was that of Rebecca West in *Rosmersholm*, Ibsen's play of sexual jealousy. Although Gordon Ray, undoubtedly following West's lead, says that she took the name without much regard for the role itself, she had played it on the stage. As everyone who has seen the play or read the text well knows, West, in that play, is a 'free woman' who has a very ambivalent and ambiguous relationship with her feminism, and at the end of the play in order to deal with it she sacrifices it and herself in a dramatic suicide. It seems much more likely that Fairfield was also ambiguous about her own feminism and her sexuality. Otherwise she would not have submitted to being moved from place to place at Wells's whim; she would not have hung on so long waiting for marriage, and would have been somewhat less dominated by him, not only in her writing, but in her treatment of their child. She never really discusses the Wells liaison in her fiction, although *The Judge* (1922) is about her coming of age and her break with her family. Much mist and veiling has been placed between her real life and her version of it, by West herself and by her son, who has adopted many different attitudes towards his mother (in his novel, *Heritage*, his articles in the press, and in his biography of his father). Anthony West has been on all sides of these questions, and remains remarkably adaptable in his attitudes towards his parents, although he was willing to attend the cremation of his father with his mother, and even to take a fairly important role in events surrounding the death.

Wells was clearly loved by Rebecca West. Whether he returned that love in the same depth remains somewhat unclear, although unlikely, even *with* the correspondence he left behind. He had a great physical need for her, but he was not really ready to sacrifice very much for it. She made the sacrifices, even to the obloquy she endured. As Mary Austin remembered in her memoir, *Earth's Horizon*, when Wells announced that Rebecca was pregnant, and he did so at table, with an audience, Jane Wells simply remarked how much help Rebecca would need to deal with the consequences of that pregnancy. Gordon Ray indicates that he thinks Wells instigated the pregnancy to claim West's allegiance, but it is just as likely that West importuned him to cement his role in her life. Some American women reviewers of Ray's book (Diana Trilling, and Lillian Hellman) were less forgiving of West than Ray was — one gathered that they had read the correspondence with interest, but with the general view that West had made her own bed. She, on the other hand, apparently did not think Ray went far enough towards her view, even though he dedicated the book to her; it was barely mentioned by her later, and the correspondence deposited at Yale was then closed. In later interviews she never attacked Wells, only remarking, but not with much antipathy, that if Wells had not entered her life, she might have written more.[24]

Some years after they separated Wells told Kay Boyle in Paris, when she mentioned the great impact *The Judge* had had on her fiction and her life, 'It was her [Rebecca's] way of beginning life again. It took courage but women have so much of that. It was her way of going on.'[25]

West did describe Wells as an 'uncle' in a much-quoted essay of 1927, while in 1929, in other essays, she discussed their life together very briefly in a description of his unwillingness to face reality. In the same collection, but much more politely, she urged the award of the Order of Merit to both him and Shaw, rather than to Galsworthy who had received it. As she said, 'If one took a census among young and middle-aged men who have reached positions of eminence in any department of life, and asked them what author had the largest part in inspiring them to their exceptional attainments, an overwhelming majority would give the name of H.G. Wells.' Later she ranked Wells and Shaw just behind George Moore as the pre-eminent writers of their time.

Wells, for his part, attempted to treat her fairly and honestly, but was clear as to just how far he was prepared to go. Therefore, one is ultimately faced with the knowledge that no matter how it appears today, she did accept his terms. He corresponded with Marie Stopes about her, and asked Gregory to ensure that Anthony West had proper schooling, as he was paying for it.[26] He provided Rebecca with an income, until she married, and settled a very large amount of money (£5,000) on her to meet her expenses once they had broken up. The demands of love and jealousy were great, on both parties. Wells gives his view, even with the evidence of the great abundance of letters, mainly in his fiction. Her view is hidden. The letters she wrote are no longer available — Wells may have destroyed them, or she may have done so upon their return. Some of them may survive in her still unopened archives. She lived longer, and had the satisfaction of being able largely to control how we view the long relationship. But perhaps we should also look at her remarks to Marjorie Wells (Jane's replacement in most ways, a fact which Rebecca well knew), after he died, for a clue to Rebecca's view of their life together:

> I loved him all my life and always will, and I bitterly reproach myself for not having stayed with him, because I think I was fairly good for him. But you know the reverse of the medal, the tyranny that was the incorrigible part of him. I could not have submitted to it all my life — nor do I think he could have loved me or that I could have loved him if I had been the kind of person that could. And indeed he got on pretty well without me.[27]

It is worth pointing out that the life of sham and prevarication that Rebecca talks about and which appears in the Ray treatment of the letters, was specifically laid at the feet and hands of Rebecca's mother and sisters in Wells's suppressed volume of his autobiography. He treats his relationship with Rebecca with a disarming innocence in that work, implying throughout that he was the pursued, for at least most of their time together. He describes their encounters over his failure to divorce Jane, and says that Rebecca hated Jane, as well as his work, *The Outline of History*. He describes *The Secret Places of the Heart* as being written 'at her'.

Wells also discusses their disagreements over fiction, and suggests that if Anthony had not appeared, they would have separated long before. In his chapter about her, however, he spends almost as much time on his affair with the young Austrian woman who, in a fit of rejection, attempted to commit suicide in Wells's flat, as he does on his relationship with Rebecca. In many ways this chapter is, of course, a self-serving document, now refuted in part by the correspondence; but it may reflect clearly Wells's actual feelings about her. Wells never really revealed his true feelings in most personal areas, and his letters are guides only, except perhaps when they are harsh and strident. He usually remained much more closely in control than has been realized by most biographers. Wells does go on in this revealing section of his book to invoke his ideal of the Lover-Shadow again, and makes it plain that Rebecca was not that woman.[28] They were close; they were physical lovers. For her this was not quite enough. The fantasy world in which she lived, and which he entered, dominated their life together. For him, though, the reality of life was his home with Jane, and hovering over all, the persona which was unavailable, the seeking spirit which would ultimately reveal itself, after Jane's death, to be Moura. However, the question remains as to whether that seeking spirit only really emerged when it was unattainable — much as Rebecca West was also unable to achieve her heart's desire.

A PRIVATE MAN IN A PUBLIC WORLD

> I think that in every human mind, possibly from an extremely early age, there exists a continually growing and continually more subtle complex of expectation and hope; an aggregation of lovely and exciting thoughts; conceptions of encounter and reaction picked up from observation, descriptions, drama; reveries of sensuous delights and ecstasies; reveries of understanding and reciprocity; which I will call the Lover-Shadow. It think it is primarily sexual and then social — I mean sexual in origin, because I do not see how a living creature could ever be anything but self-centred except through the development of sexual, family and group mental systems. I think it is almost as essential in our lives as our self consciousness. It is *other* consciousness. No human being faces the world in conscious complete solitude; no human being, I believe, lives or can live without this vague various protean but very real presence side by side with the *persona* ... That is what I mean by the Lover-Shadow. It is the inseparable correlative to the *persona*, in the direction of our lives.
>
> HGW, from 'Postscript to an Experiment in Autobiography', in G. P. Wells, ed., *H. G. Wells in Love* (1984)

These ideas of H.G. Wells's have been known about in very general detail for some time. Wells summarized his view in *The Anatomy of Frustration* (however, it was basically ignored in the comments on the book). This version was recently published by Wells's elder son, after the terms of his father's will were met, and the people involved either no longer cared or had passed away. It is from an addition to Wells's *Experiment in Autobiography*, a book originally published in 1934. The addition, a Postscript, contains Wellsian comment with regard to persons not mentioned in the original version, as well as philosophical remarks on his life as a sexual being. It cannot be and is not all that he might have said about his love life, for it bears the mark of selection even now. In addition it is filtered through Wells's own ideas of propriety (perhaps), libel (less likely), or self-delusion (most likely). In any case, it must now be added to our sources for the study of Wells's life: it offers some more luminescence on a private man in a public world.

Once H. G. Wells finished the *Outline of History*, he needed a long holiday in the warmth and humidity of the Mediterranean. He had been ill with influenza (as had Rebecca West), and the long intense hours of work left him a very tired, almost disconsolate human being. Jane, along with the boys, left for the Alps for skiing. Wells, unable now to face high altitudes as his breathing suffered, went off to Italy, Sicily, and then to Spain. Rebecca accompanied him on the Spanish portion of his journey, which took some two months. Although he was then able to return to work, his flu and bad chest returned, and he was forced to have another long sojourn in the South in 1922. After these visits, he turned increasingly to the idea of a southern home, for use in the winter months. Although he was not to build a house until later, when his liaison with Odette Keun appeared to be fairly long-lasting, he did, however, begin now to take lengthy winter holidays by the Mediterranean.[1]

With these regular vacations, better food, and proper rest, his health improved quite remarkably, and he was to be relatively free of health problems until much later in life. In 1935 he was involved in a trivial automobile accident, cutting his forehead. The cartilage in his knee acted up, and his success with an osteopath led him to endorse that branch of medicine. He became slightly diabetic early in the 1930s, had the flu again in 1937 (describing himself as 'emphysematous' while saying that he wished it 'was something that hurt more and deflated less'), but generally remained in good, if not robust health.[2]

He retained a strong interest in the education of his children, his home, and surroundings, and later in his grandchildren. The correspondence on G. P. Wells, his Russian studies, and his preparation for university science, is detailed, and by the time G. P. was seventeen, Wells urged Sanderson to involve his son in the discussions, especially as to whether he should remain at Oundle, or go on to Trinity somewhat early. In his last two terms at Oundle G. P. actually spent much of his time on classics, in order to catch up with more conventionally prepared youths. Of course he had had a superb scientific preparation, and he had the advantage of weekends, once he was older, with such people as G. D. H. Cole, J. F. Horrabin, and other political friends of his father's. S. S. Koteliansky, who had been G. P.'s Russian tutor, spent a week at Easton before Wells and his son went to Russia, carrying on conversations in Russian with his pupil. 'Kot' remained as part of Wells's following, doing some translation, often appearing at Easton for lunch, dinner, or the weekend. He was there the weekend Chaliapin came, for instance, as well as on a famous later occasion when Charlie Chaplin was the star attraction. In 1926 and 1927, he spent Christmas at the Wellses', along with Bennett, and later with Ernest Benn and Victor Gollancz, when they were Wells's principal publishers.[3]

With all his love affairs and needs, Easton Glebe still remained home base for H. G. Wells, until Jane died. She made it as comfortable for him as was possible, entertaining any and all, providing music, games, drama, while acting as his secretary, amanuensis, proofreader, and confidante. As he said to Sidney Low, after G. P. was born and she was convalescing, asking Low to delay his visit, the 'acting manager' was 'not very fit for social duties'.[4]

Jane did not just act as his manager. She protected H. G. Wells, probably overzealously, against rapacious publishers, agents, slurs in the press; when a good friend said something of which she disapproved, she wrote in protest. She even levied such a protest on someone as close as Frank Swinnerton, and although Swinny was able to demonstrate that it was American misquotation, he felt constrained to apologize very abjectly both to her and to H. G. As he said, whenever he spoke of the writer, he always spoke with the 'greatest enthusiasm', remarking that he had been smacked; but it was not until her death that further correspondence and meetings ensued. One assumes that H. G. did not even know of the incident.[5]

But eventually this great protector, friend, and the epitome of the Lover-Shadow in H. G.'s life, Amy Catherine (Jane) Wells, fell ill. She sustained a hysterectomy early in the 1920s, and was somewhat weakened by the rather invasive surgery of that period. Early in the spring of 1927, she began to feel increasingly weak, and tired, and when a physician examined her, he found that she had inoperable cancer. Their younger son, Frank, at Easton planning his marriage to his fiancée, broke the news to his father, who was in Grasse, still lingering in the southern warmth. George Doran, apparently visiting there, said later, in his autobiography, that this was the only time he ever saw Wells show emotion (Wells was later angry at this and tried to get the book suppressed, or the offending remark cut out). H. G. returned immediately to Easton, writing to Jane as he left to say, 'My dear, I love you much more than I have ever loved anyone else in the world and I am coming back to you to take care of you now and to do all I can to make you happy.'[6]

Once Wells arrived back in England, he realized quite quickly that Jane did not have long to live. The doctors assured him that there would be no pain to speak of, so he sat down to ease her life as much as possible, and to write to their friends to tell them the dread news. By July he was able somewhat to reassure some of these friends. He told R. D. Blumenfeld, their next-door neighbour, and the person who had introduced them to Essex, that 'We are really not unhappy here. I am able to watch over Jane quite effectively. There is no pain. We have roses, music, books, friendship and stoicism. If only we had more sun.' Just before she died he told his brother Frank that it was impossible 'to turn back the clock. We do all we can with flowers and music and books and visitors to make the days light for her.' She was able to get to her beloved garden till just before the end, on 6 October. Her only regret was that she could not attend Frank's wedding, scheduled for the day she was cremated. The planned-for nuptials were not delayed — in this family which had become inured to her impending death, and in a family whose only available solace was their own, there was no need. However, a year later, Wells wrote again to his brother: 'In a sort of way my life finished last year and I try to live a fresh sort of existence with the fag end of it.' Easton was still available for the grandchildren, 'But I can't live much in England. The heart has gone out of it.'[7]

As with much of Wells's personal life, the press intruded on his sorrow. This time it was a story associated with Jane's obituary, saying he had been in France and had had to rush home for the funeral. He, and Marjorie Wells, wrote to many newspapers attempting to put a stop to this story, but not without some sense of shock and disgust.[8]

The family did not want a religious service, so they sought a secular crematorium for the service. Wells told his agent in these matters, that he wanted a 'funeral service consistent with her life, which has been led always with a smiling disregard of all supernaturalism'. Dr C. Arnot Page conducted the brief service, although Wells had another speaker in reserve, as Page was quite old. Wells himself wrote the tribute to Jane which was read at the service, preceded by César Franck's 'Pièce héroique', and followed by Bach's Passacaglia. The words quoted at the head of the previous chapter will show clearly how H.G. Wells felt about his friend and lover, especially when one adds his statement that it is possible to learn from shortened, heroic days, 'that a precious use can be made of brief days and that the courage of a loving Stoicism is proof against despair'.[9]

As the coffin was about to enter the fire, G. B. Shaw urged Wells to go with the two boys and attend the burning. Ever after H. G. was grateful to his old friend, for he knew Jane had passed quickly into the void. Apparently Charlotte Shaw found the scene 'dreadful', but most who were there thought it was beautiful. Wells printed the brief address he had written and sent it to their friends who were away. Beatrice Webb thanked him for it, while recalling her last visit to Easton in 1924, and the 'development of a beautiful soul' to which she felt drawn. Ivan Maisky, writing from Tokyo, where the death was noticed in the *Japan Times*, told Wells, 'The men of your type are soldiers in the service of humanity. They have no right to give way before personal grief.' Eileen Power and Elizabeth Healey were equally mournful, and Elizabeth gave H. G. Isabel's address so she could have a copy of the funeral address. Isabel did not live much longer than Jane, but she responded to H. G. in this moment of trial. Four years later, when Wells dined alone with J. M. Barrie, they discussed Jane's funeral, and Barrie told Cynthia Asquith, his secretary, that Wells was still 'feeling very lonely'.[10]

H. G. began almost immediately to think about an appropriate memoir for Jane. She had always written, fey little pieces with much personality, in a light, buoyant, effort to capture moods, ideas, perceptions of reality, especially as the light changed or the view darkened. Some had been published in the 1890s; others had begun to appear in the three or four years before her death, as she refined her style in her secret study in Bloomsbury. H. G. collected these, in a book he entitled *The Book of Catherine Wells*, the name under which Jane wrote, with a personal memoir of their life as introduction.[11]

In it he remarked on the various Amy Catherines he had known, the girl in his laboratory, his lover, the mother of his children, the ardent skiier (with a marvellous photograph of her in the Alps), the prize-winning gardener, and the gracious hostess most persons knew. Throughout all these manifestations, however, she had remained the fairy queen — presiding over the extraordinary theatricals he recalled so vividly; then he went on to speak of the differences between them, which so many of their admirers must have wondered at. As he remarked, vivid and clear when one thinks of 1928:

> What is more difficult to tell is our slow discovery of the profoundest temperamental differences between us and of the problems these differences created for us. Fundamental to my wife's nature was a passion for happiness and lovely things. She was before everything else gentle and sweet. She worshipped beauty. For her, beauty was something very definite, a precious jewel to be discovered and treasured. For me beauty is incidental, so surely a part of things that one need not be directly concerned about it. I am a far less stable creature than she was, with a driving quality that holds my instabilities together. I have more drive than strength, and little patience; I am hasty and incompetent about much of the detailed business of life because I put too large a proportion of my available will and energy into issues that dominate me.

He then went on to pay her the ultimate tribute, in view of their marriage:

> We had to work out our common problems very largely by the light nature had given us. And I am appalled to reflect how much of the patience, courage and sacrifice of our compromises came from her. Never once do I remember her romancing a situation into false issues. We had two important things in our favour, first that we had a common detestation not only of falsehood but of falsity, and secondly, that we had the sincerest affection and respect for each other. There again the feat was hers. It was an easy thing for me to keep my faith in her sense of fair play and her perfect generosity. She never told a lie. To the end I would have taken her word against all other witnesses in the world. But she managed to sustain her belief that I was worth living for, and that was a harder task, while I made my way through a tangle of moods and impulses that were quite outside her instinctive sympathy. She stuck to me so sturdily that in the end I stuck to myself. I do not know what I should have been without her. She stabilized my life. She gave it a home and dignity. She preserved its continuity.

I have quoted so fully from Wells's writing on this occasion as his words seem to me to convey better than any others the extraordinary relationship of Bits and Bins — of Bertie and Jane — of H.G. and Amy Catherine. Wells. Their friends who received the book understood its message clearly. It was not an apology, for none was needed. What it was in a manly way is simply a farewell — *Vale*, to the dearest person he had ever known.[12]

Now it only remained to carry on. Wells did this in many ways. He spent much more time travelling in the next dozen years than he had ever done before. He worked harder than he had done for some time, and focused more on his goals of the World State and Cosmopolis. Eventually he wrote his *Experiment in Autobiography*, by way of partial exorcism, as such acts often are. He survived the blow, cruel as it was, but never forgot Jane's meaning to his life and his well-being. It was she who had helped make Bertie into H.G. No one else could make that claim.

In these years, he greeted and observed his grandchildren. Wells had always had an interest, although rather distant, in children. There is a remarkable vignette of his playing, in his bowler hat and lounge suit, with East End children on the occasion of the dedication of a playground at Bow. He told the adults present that although the East End had produced a Chaplin, humorous and funny, the life was still almost too poignant to watch. What children needed was a fair chance. The world owed them that much. His own children's nurse continued to receive gifts of money and books, often on the children's birthdays, well into the '30s. Two years after Jane's death, Wells told his biographer, Geoffrey Wells (West), that 'Easton is much given up to grandchildren nowadays but I am sometimes there ...' Marjorie reported to him from time to time on the grand-children, their progress, or their efforts at school. But, as he had said, it was lonely, and he usually went away. It was only a short time before the lease of Easton Glebe was sold, and he moved to town.[13]

After Jane's death, Wells's daughter-in-law simply replaced her as his 'manager', his guide, his *alter ego*. While in the South, he was incommunicado to all except Marjorie. All messages of any sort flowed through her: telephone contact war regular, but only by this method. At this point it may be well to mention again what Wells demanded of Jane and others. He left an excellent description of exactly what he needed from his secretaries in a letter to the mother of a prospective applicant:

My secretary has to live in London and she is quite free to live how and where she pleases provided she is in my flat in Whitehall Court from 10 to 1 and from 2 to 4. 30 on four days in the week and from 10 to 1 on two other days. She has a lot of typewriting to do. She has to answer the telephone and deal with callers and protect me from intrusion. She has to write a lot of letters and to be able e.g. to translate a pencilled 'No' into a polite refusal. She has to file letters, deal with accounts and so forth. She has to be loyal and silent. Every now and then she has to come down here [Easton Glebe] for some days to index books, put files in order and so forth. She will have to later (?run) gradually a tangle of human concerns with translations from Mrs Wells. She will be paid at first, £250 a year free of income tax, travel expenses and so forth and she will have to keep herself in London. She may have to travel with me.[14]

Marjorie increasingly became a force in Wells's life, as she took over his correspondence, his typing, and many of his relations with his agents, his publishers, and with the press. It may not be too much to say that his novel, *Brynhild*, the story of a young woman who dallies with dominating others in her search for personal success, is a tribute to Marjorie and the qualities Wells found so important to him. In the novel, a slight comic and ironic look at modern marriage and the literary life, the hero, Rowland Palace, after becoming a victim of modern publicity, finds he likes it, and tries to live that life. His wife, Brynhild, also observes it, and in her effort to control him, has some very slight adventures with a literary rival, Alfred Bunter. To a considerable extent this novel might be an ironic view of Wells himself, meeting modern publicity demands. All things appear to be 'show', and this is especially true in the reported conversations with agents, publishers, and a remarkable publicity man, Emmanuel Coote. Brynhild's meditations, at the same time, concern whether she will be able to adopt male attitudes towards sex, love, marriage, and life in general. The other novelist, with whom she dallies (too strong a word for a very mild flirtation), is done in by fate, as is she, for she finds herself to be pregnant by Palace. He goes off to his public life while she remains at home to have their child, and to maintain a home for him. Comic and ironic the book may be, but it is the character of Brynhild, steadfast, in control, above the battle, in whom we retain interest, just as Wells may have done as he contemplated his daughter-in-law becoming his manager, his Brynhild.

The copy for the book was in Watt's hands at the end of 1936, and was finally accepted by Methuen in England, and Scribners in the US. Wells was able to extract $5,000 as the American advance, and received royalties of 15 per cent on the first 10,000, with 17½ per cent thereafter. Methuen offered similar terms, to Marjorie who negotiated the entire matter while vacationing at Lou Pidou in France, with Wells and Odette.

Winifred Horrabin reviewed the book, calling it a 'kind of "raspberry", just a rude noise', although a most amusing one. The solemn world of book publishing was justly attacked, she thought. The first printing of the book, some 10,000 copies, sold out, as did an inexpensive edition at 3 *s*. 6*d*. which had disappeared by the end of 1941. It was a successful, even if modest, venture.[15]

One of the interesting things about H. G. Wells is how many casual friends, both men and women, he accumulated over time. One of the reasons for this was the free and open hospitality at his various homes, at least until Jane died; but it was also true that he was sought out for the strength of his personality, his willingness to meet nearly anyone to discuss matters, and, of course, the fact that he simply was attracted to and by young women. These young women in turn often found him delightful, as his voyeuristic eye provided a thrill at times, and his willingness to accept them as equals also worked as an alluring potion. There are very few memoirs or diaries of the rich and famous, especially those in literary or political circles, in the first half of the twentieth century, that do not have some entries concerning H. G. Wells.

Among those persons who found Wells interesting, attractive, and worth knowing, as he did them, was an American woman little known today, Mary Church Terrell. A very light-skinned black, born of slave parents, she was lucky enough to attend Oberlin College. She married a black, who rose to be a judge in Washington, D.C., while she served on the school board of the District of Columbia. She toured widely on behalf of the cause of feminist equality, better race relations, and peace. It was almost inevitable that she spend time with Jane and H.G. at Easton. After visiting Paris and Zurich with Jane Addams and Emily Balch (all three were delegates to an International Women's Peace Conference in 1907), she was invited to Easton by Jane Wells, who had been introduced to her by Florence Lamont. Mrs Terrell was in Paris in 1919 as well, lobbying Wilson, and paid a return visit to Easton. There she played tennis, the famous ball game, and talked with Wells at length. In 1930, she spent another weekend with Wells, and in 1937 returned again when the International Assembly of World Fellowship of Faith met in London. Each time they met she and Wells talked for long periods, and eventually, as he was intrigued by her story, he urged her to write an autobiography. In 1940, once the book was completed, he was persuaded to write a preface, in which he commended Mrs Terrell, and reiterated his own earlier comments on race relations in America, from his 1906 visit. Then he told the author's readers that 'The struggle for the assertive self is unending, and the greatest triumph of civilization and moral education, is to sublimate the self-respect of the individual so that he will put his pride into behaving like a gentleman and an equalitarian, in spirit and in truth.'[16]

Another interesting American female visitor was Mary Austin. Almost forgotten today, Austin wrote stories and books on the American West, many of which had Amerindian roots, even to including actual transcriptions of tribal folk-tales from the desert of the Southwest. She, a widow, was warned (by Herbert Hoover, later President of the United States, and his wife Lou) that it would be socially inexpedient for her to visit Wells, but Austin said that within an hour she was able to talk more openly with him than with any man she had ever met. She later said that that first acceptance of her as an equal could offset almost any disagreement she had with Wells's other views. Wells, for his part, read some of her work and commented on it, telling her how good her short story, 'The Walking Woman', was; it was about a woman who submitted to a passionate embrace, saying afterward that all that was necessary in life was equal work with men, love, and the act of giving birth.

It was while this story was being discussed that Wells, it is said, revealed that Rebecca was pregnant (although from other evidence it seems the revelation may have concerned Amber). Later, when the Hoovers became aware of her friendship with Wells, they tried to get Mary Austin to avoid him, but she went, instead, to a public dinner, with the Chestertons, the Wellses, and others. She and Wells did not enjoy the occasion, so went for a walk on Hampstead Heath to discuss his views on extramarital affairs. Wells introduced her to Conrad, Shaw (who she said had a witty way of missing the point), Belloc, James, Yeats, Mrs Humphry Ward, William Archer, and Edmund Gosse. Later, in her autobiography, she remarked that Wells had done much to enlighten her, open her eyes to the boundaries of literature, and without any thought of anything except advancing the cause of feminism, for which she gave him very high praise. She returned to England again after the war, but this time Wells asked Jane to see that either May Sinclair, Violet Hunt, or the Countess of Warwick was present to outflank Austin during the visit. In 1932, when she wrote her memoirs, Mary Austin submitted them to Wells, and he changed some remarks to suit his taste. This is another case of Wells going out of his way to do someone a favour — of course it helped that Austin was a bright comely female, but he was willing to do the same for other 'outsiders' such as Lewis Grassic Gibbon and 'Mark Benney'. Wells was interested in supporting the literary efforts of persons who were outside the norm, and that included both males and females.[17]

A remarkable number of letters survive from H. G. Wells to prospective authors, many of whom sent him manuscripts, or requests for advice. Although he did not respond promptly, and even if he liked the work usually refused to write a preface unless the author had some personal tie with him, he would often devote three or four pages to analysing a manuscript, suggesting publishers, or providing other advice. He usually suggested a writer begin by writing stories and then move on to longer work, as he had done.[18]

Better-known female friends were Eileen Power, Cynthia Asquith, Enid Bagnold, Christabel Aberconway; another, less of a friend, was Dora Russell. Power was a London University don, well-known for her brilliant new analysis of medieval society. She vetted parts of the *Outline of History*, and certainly knew H.G. fairly well by the time he stood for Parliament in 1922. By 1924, he was sending her copies of his books, and she usually settled in to read them immediately, even *William Clissold*, long as that was. She began, by the end of the '20s, to see Wells often, dining with him, at home or in restaurants, occasionally going to the theatre, and bringing people to meet him. Some of these were unusual, e.g., a Dr Maurice

Hindus, who wrote on the Russian peasant, and others from India, China, and elsewhere. She worked on H.G.'s Madrid speech, but could not come to a big dinner as it was in midweek and she had to lecture. After that Wells usually invited her for weekends. In 1932 she and Michael Postan were both seeing Wells, and when the two became engaged, Power brought Postan round for the old man's approval. When they came Wells gave them dinner, with Laski, Joad, and Amber Blanco-White as his other guests. After the Graham Wallas memorial, at which they could only wave to each other, Wells and Power had tea to discuss the dead colleague. She told Wells that she read *The Shape of Things to Come* on the night she was preparing a lecture for headmistresses in Brighton. 'I have been advocating world history with passion to the headmistresses', was her comment. Power was the feminine adornment (probably with Amber Blanco-White) at a dinner for scientists, and later when she suffered an attack of shingles, Wells sent violets and lilies, which overwhelmed her.

She and Postan did not marry until 1937, and even then she described their marriage as that of a 'semi-detached couple'. Wells continued to invite her, and with Postan in Cambridge, it was even easier to have dinner with an older man, who fêted her, thought her brilliant in conversation, and again, in every way, treated her as an intellectual equal. She and Moura Budberg became good friends, and she became very alert to the other woman's work, especially when Moura began to translate Gorky in 1939. At this time Wells himself contracted shingles, and Power was able to return the earlier favours. She remained, until her death, which occurred suddenly in 1941, a close friend and confidante, as well as a pretty, intelligent, witty, learned woman — and one who stood H.G.'s joking with pleasure, and looked forward to meeting him. The relationship was an epitome of what he wanted, especially in his later years. After she died he served on a committee to raise funds for a scholarship in her name; Wells contributed a small amount, but continued it on a yearly basis. Eileen Power was simply another of Wells's women friends, and a very good one indeed.[19]

Wells had met Cynthia Asquith, daughter of his early patron, Lady Elcho, at Stanway as a girl. She became J. M. Barrie's secretary, and so they knew each other casually. When Barrie died in 1937, and her mother followed soon thereafter, Wells renewed the acquaintanceship with letters of condolence. They became fast friends and saw each other frequently. She lived just across Regent's Park from him, and they were frequent guests at each other's houses for tea, up till the end of his life. He even did such an uncharacteristic thing for her, when asked, as to sponsor a fancy dress ball to raise money for guide dogs for the blind. He sent a fairly large donation, although probably did not attend the function itself. He was therefore willing to let his name be used even in such a cause, when a pretty young girl first flattered, and then charmed, him. Of course, in this case, the memory of her mother, who had sponsored and trained him would have overcome most prejudices.[20]

Ever since his first glimpse of the youthful and beautiful Enid Bagnold, Wells had had his eye on her. A good deal of correspondence and many meetings followed that first struggling attempt at seduction. Wells often drew pictures for her, and her papers include dinner invitations, 'picshuas', more of the special nicknames he often gave to favourites, as well as formal correspondence between her and her husband and Wells, when Wells came to visit at their country home. Although she married and became Lady Jones, *National Velvet*, and the other light novels and plays she produced, were published under her maiden name. She too asked Wells for help in her charities, and he sent her copies of books for auctions. And she continued to flirt with him, as when he suggested that she ask her husband for contributions to the charities, and she responded, 'And, anyway, damn it, dear H.G., you don't suppose a woman educated as I was, on *Ann Veronica*, goes in for "influence with her husband"! We are much too clumsy-fingered, "honest brave".' When Wells sent money for the Babies Fund, she thanked him in a provocative way, writing, 'Unlike you, I don't really care about the future of mankind. But unless I wrote you a very long letter which would bore you, I couldn't properly explain to you the imaginative and provocative side of the production of babies. (That is a perfect sentence, which allows you to read volumes into it.)' Wells, for his part, thought so much of her that he was willing to ask her, along with Eileen Power and Moura, to attend the dinner party at which he and Rivers Blanco-White gave up their estrangement. As he told Enid, '(They and I), we, have a common interest in their eldest daughter, Anna Jane, which you know all about. A cheerfully irrelevant guest will keep the little party extended. Come and be a cheerful irrelevant guest.'[21]

Another woman who enjoyed Wells's company, and with whom he was happy, was the 1920s author, Anita Loos. When she was in London they frequently dined together, often at a Russian restaurant, Kazbek, which they both enjoyed. She visited Wells in his Paris flat in the '30s, and it appears that he took her to dinner with Frank Wells and Ivor Montagu and their wives on that occasion.[22]

Wells always enjoyed being with 'bright young things', especially when he was in Hollywood, where the large British colony met regularly for tea, gossip, pink gins, and even occasional cricket. Wells was ever a welcome guest. Whenever he came to the West Coast he spent time with his compatriots, was usually entertained by Charlie Chaplin, who was a close friend, and occasionally by Charles Laughton and Elsa Lanchester, who had starred in one of his films. He also knew well Cedric Hardwicke, Basil Rathbone, Ronald and Bonita Colman, and others who were part of the British family-in-exile. The leader of the Hollywood colony was Sir C. Aubrey Smith, who as C. A. Smith played cricket for Cambridge and later captained Surrey and England. Wells was a very good companion for young women, and occasionally the Hollywood papers carried photographs of him with aspiring starlets. In 1937 or 1938 (the details are fuzzy)

Paulette Goddard gave a luncheon for him at the Vendôme at which the other guests were a dozen nubile young women. Wells was close to heaven, one supposes. Later Goddard and he went with Hugh Walpole to spend a famous week at William Randolph Hearst's castle, San Simeon. At one dinner that week, after a bit too much to drink, Wells gave an oration on US failures since becoming the most powerful nation in the world. On this visit Chaplin also gave him a dinner to which every Englishman in the area was invited. John Masefield was visiting as well, but it was H. G. Wells who was the guest of honour.[23]

Wells was very susceptible in such surroundings, although he did not always capitulate to temptation. When he was approached by the young correspondent, Martha Gellhorn, later to be Hemingway's wife, for some help, he wrote an introduction to her book, after first suggesting Sinclair Lewis. When he later told Lewis the story, he could not help adding, '(N.B. She hasn't seduced me and my interest is purely friendly, although she is 27 and quite attractive.)' It is no wonder then that when George Creel, who had met Wells when he worked with Woodrow Wilson during World War I, put Wells on a ship, he not only wished him 'Bon voyage', but told him that 'All your women friends ask about you tenderly and sigh guiltily. I've simply got to write a book on Sex. Nothing like it for an Open Sesame.'[24]

Wells also had some close women friends in his later years — women with whom he was frequently seen, and with whom the world assumed he had a close relationship. The most famous perhaps was Christabel Aberconway. She claimed (and Wells later sustained the claim) that they never slept together, by her choice, but they took great pleasure in making people think they were very intimate friends. Aberconway disliked Odette Keun very much, and Keun, sure that she was being traduced, did all in her power to drive her rival away. Christabel claimed in her memoirs that Wells had taught her much about the amenities of life. 'H.G. seemed to light glowing fires, fires by which we sat in happy intimacy both in and out of this world, but always within the universe.' Wells had helped her overcome a morbid fear of death. She also informs us of many lighter things: about Wells and his affection for his cats (the last one at Hanover Terrace was called Mr Peter Wells), or his views on how to judge an automobile.

Gordon Selfridge gave Wells a guided tour of the family's famous department store, after which Wells wrote his name with a diamond on a first-floor window reserved for this symbolic act; but he would not go through with the rigmarole unless Aberconway accompanied him. Wells used the opportunity to view again a modern drapery department, but was more interested later in employees' lavatories and recreation facilities. Aberconway occasionally helped H.G. with his proofs, and tells a story, perhaps apocryphal, of Wells writing a script for a Hollywood movie producer on the evolution of mankind, only to have it returned with a note that the story hadn't 'enough human interest' in it. Aberconway's daughter,

Anne, played the great-granddaughter in *Things to Come*, and Christabel herself was often part of the film crew, working occasionally as continuity girl. This friendship is another case of Wells at his most charming. He clearly desired Christabel, but, once rebuffed, accepted that as reality. They became close friends, and — to make the point once more — equal friends.[25]

Two women with whom Wells did not get on as well were Dora Russell, whom he apparently mistrusted from first sight, and Frances, Countess of Warwick, with whom he had trouble over some trivialities. His quarrel with the second of the two was assuaged, while Dora Russell always hovered on the same plane as Wells, but in an eccentric orbit, which finally terminated when she was apparently refused permission to attend his cremation. Dora Blake, as she was before marrying Bertrand Russell, had met and knew Jane Wells. She supported good causes, progressive schools and birth-control, so she was someone who was an ally. The difficulty occurred when she became a clinging, demanding ally. Jane began by making contributions to protests, demonstrations, and other causes of hers. Dora then asked H.G. to write an introduction to a book she was producing, and when he refused, she called him a 'liar', citing examples of his having done so for others. He sent her money, to help towards publication of a new version of Margaret Sanger's pamphlet, one which would meet British legal restrictions (i.e., on the use of photographs of contraceptive devices).

Later Dora and Bertrand Russell ran a school, and she always hoped Wells might visit, give money, talk to the pupils, and support her. He seldom did what she wished, other than give funds, but she kept on, and even ran a summer session at the school devoted to his ideas. The real problem arose when, because he and Russell were old friends, Wells did not wish to be in the middle of what became a sticky divorce situation. Dora, on the other hand, was only too willing to involve Wells as an ally. Bertrand Russell wrote to him, during this time, 'Thanks for a very pleasant afternoon and for understanding a fairly complex psychological problem.' Wells and Russell went on to discuss the values inherent in such schools as the Russells', Neill's Summerhill, and Dartington Hall.

Dora continued from time to time to ask Wells for contributions. He occasionally complied, mostly to keep her quiet, one supposes. One such appeal, in 1943, which elicited £10, was filed with 'N.A. We have not heard the last of her'. And they hadn't. Actually Wells was very forbearing, mostly because of her political stands, one supposes, but he also found it difficult to dislike a person once he had met them, and his affection for Bertie Russell also overcame his other dislikes.[26]

Although his landlady, the Countess of Warwick, was much less formidable than Dora Russell, Wells also had a somewhat mixed relationship with her. In his files is an immense correspondence with her over the minutiae of accommodation, clothing, electricity, and so on, but much of it is with Jane, and simply reflects the care of a home. Lady Warwick, a famous socialist, liked having Wells near by, as they could discuss matters of common interest, and each household could use the other to take in sudden extra guests. She and Wells worked together on *The Great State*, and it was at her table that the discussion with the Americans began which led, in part, to Wilson's Fourteen Points address. Lady Warwick was close to Jane, pitied her for Wells's apparent treatment of her, and thought that she was a gallant, courageous person. She also thought that Wells always prickled when Shaw was about, reacting to him, and each bringing out the worst in the other, which is a very perceptive comment. Wells always felt it necessary to debate with Shaw, and when Lady Warwick came to discuss the two, in her memoir, she asked if either really believed in the position he had taken up.[27]

The two families were quite close, but the first break came when a Warwick daughter developed a crush on G.P., and bragged of it in lurid terms. Lady Warwick brought the young people together for tennis, and a later talk on propriety. She told Wells that she was a 'turbulent neighbour'. A short while later they also had difficulty over a right of way, which she had granted H.G., but to no one else. As automobiles became a problem because of their numbers, as well as their noise, Wells's guests roared up and down the right of way (through the lodge gates), and from time to time frightened Lady Warwick's guests on their morning canters. She was concerned about the wear and tear on the driveway, and the question of the gates being locked at night to pen in the animals (deer). She proclaimed that the gate was to be locked after the last train had gone (5.45 p.m.). But such differences are the inevitable price of joint tenancy. When Jane died Lady Warwick was in the Isle of Wight, and may not have been at the cremation. From this time on her comments on Wells's novels, always sent to her, tend to be more personal.

She asked him if he was happy, after she read *Blettsworthy*, and she told him that *Rampole Island* was too close to home — however, the book had needed writing. They continued to have difficulty over the access to Wells's house. This became worse when Frank was refused entrance by the gatekeeper (who did not recognize a new car). Wells had a key to a special retreat on the estate used only by him, and by Lady Warwick's sister and herself, and he apparently gave the key to a guest, which also annoyed her. G.P. then hit and killed a cosset sheep while he was driving along the access road; he apologized, but while accepting his apology, she told him that she didn't like his speed, nor his control of the car. Wells then tried to purchase the property of Easton Glebe, but it was entailed in the estate, as it was part of the original church grant. He was unable to own it. She could not buy him out, as that was costly as well. In the end, he gave up the lease, after holding one more party, to which Lady Warwick came. She told him, in a thank-you note, that she understood the association the place had for him, his need for sun, and the fact that the boys were older — grown, in fact. 'Never shall I cease to mourn your departure—and forever cherish the memories of past years!'

They remained in touch, as when he saw her children, he wrote with news, and he sent her tickets to his seventieth birthday party. She was ill, unfortunately, and unable to attend, and although they had luncheon once more, she again fell ill, and soon died. Although her friends (including Wells) were able to provide a £500 scholarship fund, which she knew of before her death, she passed away, almost a relic of a different socialism and a country-house past. Those days had been pleasant, but by 1938, they had really ended, and she had lived on into a new and less pleasant time.[28]

Wells preferred friends, especially among women, of course, more compliant and supportive than the Countess of Warwick, but even though he and she had some difficulties these were of little consequence. In general she remained true to his ideals, and he was able to get on with her without trouble. She was, however, irrevocably associated with Easton, and after the autumn of 1927 that was an empty place. Once the children moved to houses of their own, it was time to leave.

At about the same time Wells renewed his correspondence with Elizabeth Healey Bruce. They had never remained far apart, of course, except in physical distance, but once Jane died, it was like a return to his earliest days to open Healey's letters, and reply, as he inevitably did, with reminiscences of their youth. He frequently sent her cards as he travelled, and he asked her to give Geoffrey West every help in writing his biography. When West reported on her great aid (she made abstracts for him of Wells's early letters to her, many of them quoted in this book from the originals), Wells told her, 'What a steadfast friend you have been always to my flickering self.' She thought Geoffrey West's book was good, but that it did not demonstrate enough 'delicacy and lightness', in describing her old friend, as she told Wells after an afternoon spent with him in London.

When her husband, ill much of his life, died in 1935, Wells learned that she had sold an early letter from him to raise money, as Bruce's illness had taken most of their savings. It was then that he settled a monthly pension on her. She was part of his youth. When Frank, his brother, died at seventy-seven in 1933, H.G. wrote to Healey an account of how Frank had acted to H.G., when 'the Buzzwhacker' had been young. He told her that Frank had helped him break out of the grasp of his parents, to do his writing. Healey helped H.G. with the autobiography, correcting early accounts, reading proofs, providing photographs, and sending him his early letters to use. He returned them to her later with the remark, 'I think the young man who wrote them was very young but if it is worth your while publishing them by all means do so.' She had begun contemplating a book, but never wrote it. She then offered him the letters once more, but he told her to keep them, and have them returned after her death.

When Wells received his honorary doctorate from the University of London, on the occasion of his seventieth birthday, he gave a tea party to his old friends. Gregory was there, and A.M. Davies; Healey came in from Cardiff. They talked all afternoon of the days at South Kensington. Wells continued to send her copies of his books, and wine in the winter, along with the pension. They went on exchanging letters until he died. When he sent her *The Fate of Homo Sapiens* in 1939, she wrote him a longish comment on the book, which may serve to end this account of Wells's first, oldest, and most loyal woman friend. She spoke of his 'clearing away of the perplexities of this horribly confused world', and said: 'You are the only great thinker of our time who can do anything to help in this problem.'[29]

Wells also had many male friends, of course, but they tended, with the exception of Arnold Bennett, Frank Swinnerton, and Richard Gregory, to be less close to him than the women in his life. Still, his correspondence is filled, as are the memoirs of others, with stories. He shed light and friendship to a remarkable degree and people were warmed by his presence. This accounts for the fresh nature of the correspondence and memoirs, and is what makes them difficult to abstract.

He knew Harold Nicolson well, meeting him occasionally for luncheon and talks. At early encounters they rejected social credit, and British fascism, for instance, as alternatives to the failing capitalism they saw everywhere. Accounts of dinners and luncheons abound in the memoirs and the correspondence, as Wells was a lion, and needed to celebrate victories by others, as well as changes in status. He and Churchill met occasionally, usually to discuss matters concerned with their views of the future. In fact Churchill nominated Wells again for the Other Club so they could meet even more regularly. In general, Wells knew more people on the left, of course, so there is a considerable correspondence with persons such as Vernon Bartlett (whom Wells supported in his successful effort to win a seat in the Commons), and Ritchie Calder, who organized the significant science column in the *Herald* as a forum for Wellsian views. Wells told Calder once that he was doing good work, but to beware the Labour politics he was so close to. 'Constructive politics and labour politics are absolutely divergent things — I realize that more and more, and so will they. And so will you.'[30]

Others drawn to Wellsian ideas were Konni Zilliacus, whom Wells met in Geneva, working for the League of Nations; Lord Beaverbrook, who took him to see *Porgy and Bess*; and George Creel, who, when Wells asked him to predict the outcome of the 1936 US election, thought Roosevelt would lose only six states. Another longtime friend was Gilbert Murray, who was happy to sign a letter urging that Eduard Beneš be admitted to England after Munich. Wells drafted the letter, and Murray, signing with pleasure, thanked Wells for his leadership 'in [a] time of dogmatic suppression, mass cowardice, violence and looting that devastates the world today'.[31]

Wells had very little trouble in getting people to sign the Beneš letter, which was published in *The Times*, and he was actively successful, along with many others, in aiding Albert Einstein to leave Nazi Germany. He also supported efforts to establish a home in Britain for Sigmund Freud, once the Nazi horror became clearly known. He supported the founding in 1934 of the National Council for Civil Liberties, acting as an observer at the foundation meeting, which he attended with Claude Cockburn. He refused to walk between the police and the platform, however, as he thought it might give fascist elements too good an opportunity. Wells sent funds, served as a vice-president, and in his work *The New World Order* (1940) urged membership in the group. And although he did not have much to do with the Communist Party, when the *Worker* came under attack and was suppressed, he joined in the battle to preserve free speech and civil liberties.[32]

Wells was more comfortable with his literary peers. He helped support James Joyce, as has been shown. Eventually he told Sylvia Beach he could no longer contribute, but this was not until 1927. And when he did withdraw, he was careful to inform Joyce that it had nothing to do with his work, which he accepted as being very important, although so different from his own. Wells remained close to Ford Madox Ford, sent him money, and was always courteous and friendly to Ford and Violet Hunt. Others whose work he admired were Katherine Mansfield, John Middleton Murry, and E. M. Forster. He and Forster served together on the Civil Liberties Council. With Sinclair Lewis also he exchanged letters and books, and he and Upton Sinclair had an association, meeting several times. Wells and Thornton Wilder became friends late in the 1930s, and occasionally had luncheon together, meeting originally through PEN, which was a source for many of Wells's friendships.[33]

Wells's older friends eventually began to leave him — J. M. Barrie, H. W. Massingham, and others. He began a new correspondence with his former colleague, A. M. Davies, after Davies read the *Outline of History*, and in the '30s, Davies was a frequent guest at Wells's, where they played bezique; Wells borrowed a microscope from him. Just before his death in 1943 Davies returned all his letters from H.G. Another friend from earlier days was Marie Belloc-Lowndes, who often came to Wells's parties, and to tea during the war, enjoying a dinner and a theatre party, as well as a trip to Bush House later to hear broadcasts to France. She and Wells also went to a famous cocktail party given by Hamish Hamilton for all the writers in London in the autumn of 1941. The most important of Wells's literary friends now, though, were Swinnerton, Olaf Stapledon, and J. B. Priestley.[34]

One of the more difficult matters to comprehend while writing a biography is how some persons meet others and immediately become fast friends, while other such encounters raise hackles, and the relationships remain prickly and uncomfortable. There appears to be little rhyme or reason in the outcome. A biological process, very similar to falling in love (as opposed to sexual chemistry), must play a role in such matters. H.G. Wells was not immune to these vagaries. For instance, one might have known that he would become friendly with Philip Guedalla, the biographer and essayist, but one could hardly have predicted that Guedalla would move to the Easton area, become close enough to Wells to help with proofreading, and eventually dedicate a book to him. And that Guedalla would be so miffed at the seating arrangements at the PEN dinner to honour Wells's seventieth birthday, that he would break off relations for nearly a decade, just does not seem possible. And yet, this is precisely what happened in their friendship.[35]

Ezra Pound, on the other hand, was often prickly, demanding, insulting, and in every way remote from Wells, philosophically, politically, and in their writing. Yet, in their correspondence, we find Wells and Pound being cordial to one another, even when Pound's letters become quite unanswerable. They agreed on James Joyce and his work, and conspired together to support him, and this apparently was enough to tie them together. Even so, Wells, writing about his rejection of social credit theories which Pound espoused, only remarked of Pound, with a sort of impatient camaraderie, 'He's like Belloc with his marvellous but untranslated European writers that no Englishman knows about. He's a poet dissolved in noise.' Later when Pound grew even more shrill in his letters, condemning Wells for his failure to attack the Semitic clutch on world affairs, Wells simply filed the correspondence, apparently without response or comment.[36]

Uncharacteristic as Wells's tolerance for Pound seems (especially with Pound's rather bizarre views), his relative irritation with Upton Sinclair seems even more peculiar. The two gurus of the left ought to have been close friends, and it seems clear that Sinclair regarded Wells as something of a mentor; but Wells tended to shrug him off, introducing him to the proper people, entertaining him when he was in London, but always on the outlook for a raid by Sinclair on what might be construed to be his own private intellectual property. Sinclair even went so far as to ask others to intercede for him when Wells did not respond, but Wells, although usually polite, did not take to Sinclair, and what might have been an unusually productive friendship scarcely progressed beyond an acquaintance.[37]

On the other hand, Wells apparently enjoyed the company and talk of A. P. Herbert, to the point of going to the University Boat Race with him, and even to Lord's Cricket Ground, places where he would never have been seen under normal circumstances. Herbert was remarkably, even savagely, ironic in much of his writing, and his book, *Holy Deadlock*, did much to improve modern marital relations in Britain; but other than that, and his standing as a University member of Parliament, he and Wells seem unlikely companions, except as casual dinner guests. But in 1930, we find Wells writing to Herbert to say,

You are the greatest of great men. You can raise delightful laughter and that is the only sort of writing that has real power over people like me. We secretly hate to be impressed by any other sort of work, even 'sheer loveliness' is highly irritating at times. But when we really have been got at and made to cackle, we want to follow the divinity about as a cat follows a cat's-meat man.[38]

As remarked earlier, Wells apparently never quarrelled with Frank Swinnerton or Arnold Bennett. One suspects that few people could have quarrelled with, or remained angry at, Swinnerton, who seems to epitomize the sophisticated and pleasant English man of letters. Of course, Swinny was really Jane's friend, but after she had passed on, Wells's and Swinny's affection for each other never diminished. Swinnerton had brought his new bride for Jane to inspect, later giving a private lunch to discuss their courtship and impending marriage, and his letters to Jane are often 'gossipy' accounts of mutual friends, and travel. But he was always on the lookout for a promising young author, or a way to aid the offspring of some unlucky literary figure — as when in 1925 he got Wells to help in obtaining a place at Christ's Hospital for a Barbellion child; Barrie, Galsworthy, and 'Arnold' were also asked, because, as Swinny said, 'They're so respectable.'[39]

After Jane and Swinnerton were mildly estranged over the badly reported remarks from America, and after her death, Swinnerton and his wife renewed the relationship with Wells, meeting him in Grasse when they were travelling in France. Swinnerton then returned the favour by offering lunch to Bennett and Wells, and later the old friends attended plays together in London, occasionally followed by supper at the Savoy. On a later occasion, Swinnerton hoped Wells could join him for another luncheon with Mrs Belloc-Lowndes and a New York acquaintance; Wells found he had a houseful of visitors, but the two met anyway, for coffee and dessert, with their respective guests. They continued, of course, to exchange comments, usually very flattering, on each other's work. When Swinnerton talked about Wells in his *Swinnerton: An Autobiography* his friend thanked him for the loving attention; Swinnerton found this almost too much to accept, telling Wells, 'You are a darling and no mistake. Thank you. It is splendid proof of your generosity to me that you should protest so gently against my roughly teasing, and even be doubtful of the turn your revenge will take.' Swinnerton promised even more of an appreciation of Wells in his next book, which turned out to be the famous *Georgian Literary Scene*, in which Wells is treated in some detail. Wells sent him *Brynhild*, on which Swinnerton lavished such praise as 'extraordinarily buoyant and full of knowledge . . . it makes the highbrows look the laboured prigs they are.' In return, Wells praised *William Harvest*, a good late Swinnerton novel. The two dear old friends simply went on through life with neither being able to give, or take, any offence to their friendship.[40]

Wells also began to make some new, strong friends. Olaf Stapledon, a Balliol D.Phil. who had driven an ambulance in World War I because of his pacifist ideals, and had devoted his working life to Workers' Educational Association lectures, adopted H. G. Wells as his mentor. Stapledon, who had money enough from an inheritance to indulge his WEA idealism, was a member of nearly every progressive club and association in inter-war Britain. He was a leading figure in the Federation of Progressive Societies and Individuals (the Manifesto group), as well as the League of Nations Union, Cosmopolis, the Common Wealth Party (for a time), the 1941 Committee, the British Interplanetary Society, and PEN. In his lifetime he acted as a one-person gadfly to others on the left, conducting a massive correspondence with Haldane, Huxley, Middleton Murry, Philip Toynbee, Laski, John Strachey, Aldous Huxley, Joad, Bertrand Russell, and Wells. From the list of organizations and correspondents, one can see that Stapledon was a 'man of the left', but without sectarian or 'received' views. He and Wells became stout friends, not least because the reviewers of Stapledon's science fiction continually compared him to the young Wells.[41]

When *Last and First Men* appeared in 1931, Stapledon wrote to Wells, saying that he had been influenced by Wellsian writing, especially by *The War of the Worlds* and *The Star*. 'They have helped very many of us to see things more clearly,' said the young writer, but 'My debt to you is too huge and I was not properly aware of it.' After all, he said, 'A man does not record his debt to the air he breathes in common with everyone else.'[42]

Stapledon sent copies of all his work to Wells, apologizing when he had differed from H.G., but using as an excuse, 'the times like these'. The day after his apology he sent Wells a drawing showing Wells free in a zoo full of people confined by bars. Wells, of course, was not disturbed by the minimal differences between the two, and gladly signed various petitions and ballots of one sort or another directed at the Tory leadership in England. When Wells told Stapledon that he was perilously close to supporting nationalism, the two men had lunch together and discussed the world they lived in. Stapledon spent a good deal of time urging Wells to work with groups of like-minded people, especially in the universities. Wells did not resist as much as Stapledon had anticipated, and, in fact, sent on one petition to Somerset Maugham and Hugh Walpole. Others involved in this particular venture were Aldous Huxley and J.B. Priestley. Wells would not visit Neville Chamberlain when the group handed in their long list of signatures, but he did give Stapledon lunch and sustenance before that visit.[43]

They continued with their close friendship as the '30s went on, still differing somewhat in style, and even in philosophical point of view, but, as Stapledon told Wells after Wells had offered fairly detailed comments on *Saints and Revolutionaries*, 'Basically I follow you, if not in the same tracks, on the other side of the valley,' pointing out that he simply paid greater attention to traditional culture patterns. After the war came, Stapledon went on active service, and the two continued their correspondence, with most of it now to do with the Universal Declaration of Human Rights. Wells had a strong influence on Stapledon and Stapledon was an ally against the fascist menace. The goals remained more important than the methods, for both.[44]

Another younger man, who grew up on Wells's writing, and was influenced by him, was the Yorkshire novelist and essayist, J. B. Priestley. When Priestley's novel, *Faraway*, received a highly critical appraisal from a representative of the more precious side of English literature, Wells wrote him a note of commiseration. Priestley was very grateful for the Wellsian support, telling him in return that what they needed was a broad-based middle-brow type of criticism, as he and Wells, and others like them, were 'being ground between the two mill-stones of silly high-browism, and equally silly low-browism'. Priestley said that the only significant test was good writing, and whether it furthered the cause of mankind, not 'disgruntled little devils in Bloomsbury and Greenwich Village'. Although the two had met previously at their clubs and at parties, this exchange led to a fond relationship at luncheon, dinner, the theatre, and in Wells's various Mediterranean hideways. They had dinner after Priestley's play *Eden End* opened and discussed Wells's *Experiment in Autobiography*, just released, which had been read by Priestley in his capacity as judge for the Book Society Selection Committee.[45]

They met in Hollywood in 1935 (Priestley was writing screen plays, and later his remarkable book, *Midnight on the Desert*). After renewing their friendship, Priestley dedicated his new novel, *They Walk in the City* (1936), to Wells, 'in ever renewed exasperation, admiration and affection'. Priestley told H.G. the exasperation was for his distrust of artists, and his support for scientists, who 'are busy making a hell on earth ready for us'.

Wells continued to go to openings of Priestley plays, offer good technical criticism, and Priestley, for his part, read and liked Wells's work, commenting especially on such novels as *The Holy Terror*, and on his *Fate of Homo Sapiens*. Wells liked *Midnight on the Desert* very much and urged Priestley to read *Flatland*, which had been a long-time favourite book of his. The two men continued to meet at dinner, read each others books, even to exchange chauffeurs when Priestley went abroad, and always, to admire each other's work. Eventually this friendship led to Wells's family asking Priestley to speak at his cremation service, an inspired choice as it happened.[46]

From the point of view of availability, the best-preserved correspondence of Wells with a female friend, especially in the later period of his life, is with the famous feminist and birth-control pioneer, Margaret Sanger. Although this may have seemed at first to be an odd liaison, it served the purposes of both individuals very well. Sanger was a very well-known person, who travelled unceasingly on behalf of her campaign. She and Wells met in 1920, although Wells had earlier signed the famous appeal to Wilson. They were both active in the same areas, and each felt free to fall at least a little bit in love with the other. Sanger spent one year in England, where she and H.G., and she and Havelock Ellis, could meet, make love, and discuss their mutual interests. To some degree, *Secret Places of the Heart* commemorates that summer.

Whenever Wells went to the States, he and Sanger were usually able to find some free time, either just before or just after a conference, in order to enjoy each other. Their mutual friends regarded this as their own time, not to be interrupted. Those friends often carried messages back and forth between them, as when Julian Huxley reported to Wells on her activities, and an attendance at a performance of *Lysistrata* that same evening. Edith How-Martyn and Gerda Guy of the British Birth-Control group also carried Sanger's love back to H.G. when they returned to England at various times.[47]

The two individuals were attracted to each other at their first meeting, and letters began to travel back and forth across the Atlantic after those early meetings. Sanger, for her part, remembered Wells as

> one of the most masculine men I have ever known. He has not only brains but a capacity for loving both individuals and humanity at the same time. He can be amusing, witty, sarcastic, brilliant, flirtatious, and yet profound at once. He is quick, sensitive, alert to the slightest meaning, or intonation, or feeling. To be with him means you must pull yourself up, keep alive every second or you miss Wells as he reveals himself to you in his writings.[48]

In addition to their personal and intimate friendship, Wells wrote a preface for her book, *The Pivot of Civilization*, in which he said that although birth control might not be the pivot, it certainly had the capacity to be the focus and test issue of the potential of civilization — that is, the life and conduct of everyday people. Science could provide a way out of the dilemma of the ages — improved conditions for all, but not if birth control were not introduced more widely. 'And we cannot go on, giving you health, freedom, enlargement, limitless wealth, if all our gifts to you are to be swamped by an indiscriminate torrent of progeny', was his message, and he went on to say of Sanger, and her work: 'She has lifted this question from out of the warm atmosphere of troubled domesticity in which it has hitherto been discussed, to its proper level of a predominantly important human affair.'[49]

Wells and Sanger had planned to meet on his American tour of 1920, which was cancelled after he fell ill. Disappointed at this, they were able to meet when he came to cover the Washington Conference in 1921. When Sanger told him she had something for his 'left ear' alone, he told her that they could meet in New York once he was finished in Washington, and that he was 'very much at your disposal'. He signed this letter, 'ever glowingly yrs, H.G.'. Later, when his plans were more firm, he told her that he planned to spend a week with her, and a week 'as much as possible without other people about'. He was willing to pay a good deal, he said, to get the freedom and privacy they wished, and to go anywhere, but 'not if it means just tantalizing glimpses'. He wanted 'a sure, sweet access to you'. As she knew the local scene, he urged her to book an apartment, which she did, so that they were able to enjoy each other, as he said, in the costume of 'the tropical island' he preferred.[50]

He congratulated her when she married J. N. H. Slee in 1922, saying that her friends would regard him with 'watchful and envious eyes'. That year, the Wellses gave a large reception for the international delegates to the birth-control conference, and Sanger spent at least one weekend with the Wells family at Easton. Her autobiographical writings include moving word-pictures of Jane Wells on those weekends. She and H.G. were also able to spend a half-hour alone together in his London flat prior to the great conference, but Sanger was in such great demand that he had to play second fiddle, until after the conference, when they had a short time together in London before she returned to America. As he said, in the letter making arrangements for the first rendezvous, 'Warmest desires to you.' When they did meet he invited her and her husband to visit him in Grasse, where, he confided, he was living with a 'very amusing and interesting Levantine writer, Odette Keun', whom he described as 'very observant and a little disposed to be jealous'.[51]

Wells hoped to get to the US in the autumn of 1924 for a brief visit, but Sanger came to London instead. The only relics of the visit are two or three postcards. He sat on her left at one luncheon, when they held hands and thought about the coming afternoon, which he remembered in a note as 'Wonderful! Unforgettable'. When she did get to London, he told her in a letter that he wanted her to reserve as much time as possible for him, 'because I want being taken care of just now.' He went on to say, 'Can't I carry you off somewhere for a day or so?' He told her, in another letter, to mark her correspondence 'Private' otherwise 'the little Craig opens them'. In this letter he urged an intimate dinner, the next week, and afterwards, 'we could see how we'll spend the evening. A music hall or so forth? or such like?'[52]

Wells wrote to Sanger when he learned of Jane's fatal illness, and she responded with a 'cancer cure' which Wells deflected with a note saying that these just raised desperate hopes, and he had been deluged with them. Wells told her that he was cancelling all engagements while Jane lay dying, although he would attend, and did, a general council meeting of the Birth Control Reform Society.[53]

When Wells came to New York in 1931, Sanger threw a magnificent dinner for him, with representatives of all the eastern state groups interested in birth control present, as well as all his friends such as the Lamonts. Wells spoke at the dinner, describing the need for further support for the continuation of Sanger's great work. They were able to meet again in 1937, although the passion of earlier days seemed to have lessened somewhat in their correspondence. Wells told her,

You are one of the loveliest and best people I have ever met and I'm deeply concerned that my secretary is not giving you a proper address ...Last spring I had neuritis very badly and had my doubts whether the fag end of life is worth living. But people like you and I have so many people getting a sort of courage to live out of us, weak as we may be in reality, that we cannot afford to [do] anything but live with the utmost apparent stoutness to the end. I can tell you now that I have loved you very deeply ever since I met you first and I always shall.[54]

This marks the end of the physical side of their relationship, which was warm and passionate, but also conducted with some difficulty as they were such prominent people. However, it was always conducted with due regard for each other's feelings. By this time Sanger was living much of the time in Tucson, Arizona. Wells and she exchanged a good many letters during the Second World War, always with the hope of better days, in each other's arms, while working for the cause of world betterment through birth control. She sent him a parcel of warm clothing to see him through the winter of 1942, for instance. He told her how sorry he was to hear of her husband's death, while sending her *Crux Ansata* and *The Rights of Man*. As he told her, 'There is still a lot of work you and I have to do before we go.' When she sent him an article which made a distinction between various Catholic groups, he cautioned her to be more careful; they were all the same, he said, 'tarred with the same brush'. He told her he might come to Arizona once the war was over, but 'so much is happening now about this little old London that I cannot tear myself away.' As Wells fell into longer and longer periods of illness, his letters grew shorter and shorter. He did meet her son while he was in London, and he gave her permission to reprint *Crux Ansata* in New York, asking only a nominal royalty of 1 per cent per 1,000 copies, but asking for a report of sales so he could keep track of the good work.[55]

There were few letters from H.G. after this time, and they dealt primarily with *Crux Ansata*. Sanger duly reported details of the publication: the cover, the inclusion of a Wells interview to fill out the book (it may have come from a Haldeman-Julius publication), and other matters, with further invitations to visit her in the warm air of Tucson. Marjorie responded to these letters, giving details of H.G.'s fight for life in 1944, and 1945. In the last week before his death, Margaret Sanger wrote to him again, but this time there would be no answer, for by the time the letters arrived, Wells had gone. She had hoped to see him once more, as she was going to London, after a trip to Stockholm, telling him that, 'My prayer is that you will be well enough to see me and I wish there was something I could bring you. . . .With fondest greetings and affections.' But she learned instead of his death. In her papers, there is a handwritten scrawl of goodbye, dated 14 August, the day she heard the news. As she told him, even though he was no longer there to listen,

So darling H.G. you have gone out to the Great Beyond. It is queer not to see your greatness, your mind, your vision, you dear most touched this aspect of our hearts now over there. You are such a darling and you know where you are . . . but I don't — that's interesting . . . I am flying overseas to Stockholm then to England. England means London and London means H. G. Wells, to me to many millions of Americans. Oh. darling H.G. you have been so dear to me, your great mind, or more human, perhaps your wit. . . . Remember the last, the meeting at your flat? How adorable when I got the wrong one? No you will not because you are too modest to recall. . . . So many many wonderful talks we had — about women, your women, your loves — my loves, our love — always we met and picked up all the threads of our last meeting and more again. A friendship which has endured for so long and now you are over there. Beyond my horizon. . . . I'll be in London a week and will see Frank and G.P. and your family if I can. It will be too awful not to see you there. My love wherever you are. Always,

MARGARET[56]

This letter is clearly not a letter written after a 'passade'. Wells and Sanger were lovers, and as was always true, the woman in the case was grateful to H.G. and to the world, which allowed them to love each other, even within the limits that had been set for them.

Although most of his relationships of a more casual nature, such as that with Margaret Sanger, were very successful, once H. G. Wells moved away from normally-behaved English or American women, his life became much more hectic. For instance, in the early 1920s he had a brief relationship with an Austrian woman who translated several of his books into German. She fell desperately in love with him, came to his flat in London, threatened suicide, and when he went for help, actually began to slash her wrists and throat. When he and the hall porter came back upstairs, she was walking about, streaming blood from her various cuts. She then collapsed. When the police and the ambulance arrived they found that she had in fact only inflicted some light wounds on herself; she was scantily clad in a nightdress under her coat. Prior to visiting Wells she had appeared at Rebecca West's threatening some sort of violent behaviour there as well. It is clear, or seems so today, that the woman was deranged, terribly jealous of Rebecca, and that she felt her suicide would cause Wells to regret his rejection of her. Wells called Lord Beaverbrook that night and he was able to silence most of the press coverage in London. The scene remained, however, a nine days' wonder among Wells's enemies, but of little importance to anyone except Frau Gatternigg.[57]

Whether it was because of this event, or his tumultuous love life in general, Wells returned in his writing of about this time to his themes of overweening love and possessive desire. He did so first in a novel, *Christina Alberta's Father* (1925), called in its serial version, *Sargon, King of Kings*. Its hero is convinced that he is a reincarnation of the ancient Near Eastern king, with a mission to reform the world. His daughter acts as his guide and protector in the modern world of the flapper, equality of the sexes, and the 'sophisticated' mores of the West End. Sargon may well be Wells — but who is Christina Alberta? She appears at this distance, perhaps, to be a mixture of Rebecca, Odette, Margaret Sanger, and perhaps even other women whom he knew well in the frantic world of the urban '20s. For us, though, the novel remains interesting for its snapshot view of boarding-house life (in Tunbridge Wells), the 'modern' scene, the ways of young men and women attempting to understand the message of equality, and, of course, the triumphant young woman of the title, who in the end is always in control, while the others simply observe, gossip, and are swept away by the running tides of the modern world.

A longish short story of the same period, 'The Pearl of Love', deals with the possessive nature of love, and its stranglehold on reality. An allegory, set in the East, it is the story of a remarkable building, built to house a pearl of love, so pure and lovely as to be almost legendary. As the building grows to house the pearl, however, the construction overshadows the pearl — just as the artifices and paraphernalia of love often come to overshadow the actual sentiment. This is a powerful story, back to Wells's older strengths, written to inform Rebecca perhaps, or Odette, that their constructions could never overcome the love he held for Jane — or so it seems to me. If one stripped away the building, the love might bloom again, but in the meantime, it was imprisoned and shunted aside by the external elements of passion.[58]

By the time Wells came to write this story, however, he was completely entangled with the most unusual of his mistresses, Odette Keun. She entered his life as an interviewer for a newspaper (she might be thought of as a predecessor of such modern female feature-writers and interviewers as Oriana Fallaci or Amabel Jacoby), but after the interview, when she was remaining overnight, she also entered his bed to fill out her impressions, or so she is supposed to have said. In any case, Wells obliged her, and found himself completely entangled in her life. She arrived from somewhere in the Levant, and had apparently had a rough childhood. She was extremely pretty in an exotic way (Elizabeth von Arnim remarked on her slender and beautiful legs), and Wells fell head over heels in love with her. It should be remarked, however, that Odette never achieved the status of being exhibited by him in London; he preferred her to remain in the more exotic and warmer climate of the Riviera, or in a Paris flat where they spent the spring and autumn. In the South, after a year or two of leasing fairly primitive lodgings, the two built a house, very remote from the world, in Grasse. They called it Lou Pidou, a local contraction, in Provençal, for *Le Petit Bijou* (Little Gift). Another interpretation is *Petit Dieu*, which Odette

32 Wells with Maxim Gorky and Moura Budberg, Petrograd, 1920

33 Odette Keun at Lou Pidou, the villa she and Wells built at Grasse

34 (*left*): Margaret Sanger in the 1920s

35 (*right*): Wells with Paulette Goddard at Palm Springs, California, 1938

adopted. Over the fireplace the lovers had a shield embossed with the worlds, 'Two Loves Built This House'. Here, for the next decade, until their final falling-out in 1933, Wells and Odette entertained a steady stream of visitors to the Riviera sun and warmth.

Wells introduced her to the world when he reviewed her translation of her own adventures in Russia, *Sous Lenine*, then appearing in England as *My Adventures in Bolshevik Russia* (1923). In his review he proclaimed that 'a heart so bold and a mind so fresh and vigorous as hers must have immense recuperative powers, and I refrain from any expressions of pity.' He went on to remark as well, in a prophetic sentence, that 'they do not realize how awfully she will tell about it [her experiences] when it is all over.'[59]

While their house was being built, Wells took Odette on an extended holiday tour of Spain and Portugal, where he first found out about her violent tempers, her consuming jealousy, and her vulgar and bitter tongue. For throughout the decade in which they continued as lovers, he found himself possessed by her jealousy, and the constant victim of her vulgarity, especially if his visitors were well known, or prestigious. She apparently delighted in using street and sewer words to describe their love life, which she was apt to do at table or at dull moments at tea. Wells realized that he had made his bed (or accepted her into it) and although he was apparently upset and shocked by her language, manners, and demeanour, he spent a good deal of time attempting to control her through education. She also importuned him to marry her: at first she wanted him to divorce Jane, and later, after Jane's death, she continued to insist on marriage, threatening to publish their correspondence, or bring suit for alienation of affections, or otherwise provide very adverse publicity. Fortunately for Wells, he was not moved by such manifestations, and told her to go ahead and do as she wished; it would not disturb him. Many of the visitors of the time mentioned her when they describe Grasse, but most were very circumspect, as they feared her tongue and her jealousy more than did Wells, who was bemused by her antics much of the time. Elizabeth, who purchased a house of her own near by, wrote fairly often of Wells and Odette in her letters and diary. She thought the house vulgar and oriental in style. She called Odette 'a foreign lady of much vitality'. . . . while going on to say, 'I was greatly amused.' Still later, as the house grew even more, she described it to her lover as 'an enormous sort of Kubla Khan dwelling, with maidens and dulcimers no doubt complete'. Others who offer similar descriptions are Lillah MacCarthy, who described how remote the house was from normal roadways. George Catlin tells of a dinner party with the Aga Khan, Sir Wilfred Grenfell, and their wives, at which Odette insisted on describing 'what Casanova did'. Catlin described her language as simple Anglo-Saxon learned in the port of Marseilles.[60]

We have a few other glimpses of this odd ménage in Grasse. Elizabeth remarked about a rather strange tea party, when Wells's other guests were the Aga Khan and his Begum. She also told of Wells's rudeness to Michael Arlen, but attributed some of that to Odette's temper. By February 1933, Wells confided to Elizabeth that he feared he was lumbered with Odette forever, 'a permanency he can never evade'. The last events of which we know at Lou Pidou were a play in 1933 about euthanasia, after which Wells, leaving soon for the PEN meeting at Dubrovnik, claimed he never returned except to pick up a few valuables. He left Odette in command — although he later tried to wall up the two halves of the house, and the matter went to court when she wanted to open them up again; but eventually he simply gave up the house as more of a problem than it was worth.[61]

Wells did not comment very much on Odette and her demands, although many times he was clearly at a loss to know how to deal with her and her behaviour. There is one revealing letter, however, which is worth analysis. It was written to a friend, Abel Chevalley, probably in mid-April 1927, begun at 3 a.m. when Wells found himself unable to sleep for indigestion. Odette had recently applied for French citizenship (her previous citizenship may have been Russian, Turkish, or Greek, it is difficult to tell). Upon the application, the French police revealed that they believed that she was a spy, and this disturbed Wells.

He told Chevalley that he hoped that she could become a French citizen, and went on to say, 'She has a very wild indiscreet nasty tongue and [is an] adventurous young woman, but I know her well enough to be assured that she has always been too honest, impulsive and headlong to be any sort of "agent" for any sort of political mischief-makers. That idea is pure nonsense and I am quite prepared to guarantee her future good behaviour, politically speaking, up to the hilt.'

As Wells continued in the letter, he revealed his real reason for desiring her to have French citizenship when he remarked:

> I want to do a few years of good work yet before I die. As it happens through odd compatibilities of taste and temperament, that she can give me a happiness and a serene friendly [?] contentment . . . there in Provence that no other person in the whole world will nor be able to do. She has devoted herself to me with extraordinary unselfishness and you can witness how completely she effaced herself during my little week of bright publicity. I want to make life safe for her and I can assure you that this faulty and defective dossier against her is as much an oppression on my mind as on hers.[62]

Whether this letter was sent or not, or sent in this form is not known. That is not even very important. What it does indicate is that the relationship was not entirely one-sided. Odette was extremely difficult to live with, from all accounts, but she did relieve Wells's emotional and sexual stress, and allowed him to do good work, at a difficult time in his life — Jane ill and dying, his children grown, and his reputation declining.

After Jane's death, Odette's demands apparently increased in intensity. And when he refused to marry her, her outbursts at table grew ever more dramatic. Finally he had had enough. She immediately began to attack him however, once he left for good. At first this was simply amusing, as when she published a small book in 1934 entitled *I Discover the English*. The book became a bit of a *cause célèbre*, with its dedication to Somerset Maugham, 'During a time of great bewilderment, you showed me a fearless, wise and steadfast friendship for which I do not cease to be grateful.' She, while describing herself as a 'Presbyterian schoolmarm and a spinster aunt rolled into one', remarked that she had lived among the English for a decade. All who knew the couple understood the reference very clearly. Then she went on to pay her debts to H. G. Wells.

She said the English were too prone to compromise, were too snobby, immature, and their insularity prevented them from living in a sophisticated society. So much for Wells and his friends. She went on, however, to be even blunter. In a chapter on 'The People of London', under the heading 'On Emotivity, Sex and Morals', she described Englishmen (that is, H. G. Wells) as 'undemonstrative', 'never profound', 'not amorous', and 'bad lovers', 'unawakened, clumsy, heavy, conventional; not disposed to caresses, . . . selfish . . . looking upon intercourse as a personal need to be satisfied as promptly as possible without paying any attention to the active participation or enjoyment of the woman'. She went on to use such other words as 'overbearing', 'primitive, morose, hasty, and reduced to the mere essentials. Nothing . . . charmingly capricious . . . about it', and further remarked that the Englishman 'will not give enough time, trouble or attention to the sexual act, and thereby makes it as flat, stale and deadly as a slab of one of his own cold suet puddings.' 'In brief: in bed, he's boring', was her judgement. But even with this frigid blast, she was not finished with H.G. Later in the book she said that the general attitude of the English 'towards sexual matters plunged me from first to last into an indescribable stupefaction and disgust. It gave me a perpetual wish to be sick, so as to spew it all out. I want to be very plain about this,' she said. 'I have little use for conventional morality, and a liaison in my own eyes is as justifiable, and may be as dignified and worthy of respect, as a marriage. I have acted upon this conviction as regards my own life. . .' She then went on to compare mistresses to wives among the British, whom she then described as 'promiscuous as dogs' or as 'a troop of monkeys mating in a cage', at least abroad, if not at home, and more usually among the upper classes.[63]

The book which this became apparently circulated in the form of letters, and *sub rosa*, in London for some time; the correspondence between Winifred Holtby and Vera Brittain clearly refers to these letters (sent to Holtby), and their salacious contents. In fact, the originals probably gave a chapter-and-verse description of Wells himself, at least if the Holtby-Brittain correspondence in to be believed. Vera Brittain told Holtby, 'Odette's letter is *delicious*. Can I send it on to G [George Catlin, her husband, and a friend of Wells]? What vitality! To think that the great Wells is so like the rest of human husbands!' Brittain was reading Odette's letters while she wrote *Testament of Youth*, her autobiography, and she thought Odette's comments on autobiography and objectivity useful in her writing.

While Odette's letters were being savoured, Wells came to visit Holtby, but she fortunately was not at home. Holtby was apparently intrigued by Wells, and his sexuality (although the context is unclear), but she seems also to have feared Odette and her jealousy, as at the time of the letters Odette and Wells still retained some contact, although the liaison was fast disintegrating. Keun, for her part, continued to give her views of Wells in her letters to Holtby, which were then shared with Brittain. Brittain commented, 'What a hell to go back to! She is wise to get rid of the place and some, at least, of her memories with it. What expressive and interesting letters she writes! Someday they should be published — though not, I fear, in the lifetime of anyone therein described.'[64]

All these women were contributors to *Time and Tide*, a quirky feminist magazine funded by Lady Rhondda, whose political beliefs varied widely. At first Lady Rhondda had the 'audacious notion' of having Odette review Wells's *Experiment in Autobiography* when it appeared, but this was felt to be too much; so Holtby reviewed it officially, while Odette wrote her views of Wells in three now famous articles for *Time and Tide*. Immediately afterwards Keun left for America, but she came once more to Holtby's house to read the final chapter of her Wellsian attack. As Holtby reported to Brittain,

> Odette came to lunch today and stayed till after tea, reading to me the unfinished chapters of her essay on Wells, her voice detached and steady, the tears pouring down her cheeks. It is a brilliant piece of work, incisive, penetrating, profound. It has cost her nearly a nervous breakdown to write it; but I think it is worth while. . . . She is a superbly courageous, indefatigable, tormented seeker after salvation.[65]

When Odette's articles appeared they created a great sensation. She described Wells's autobiography as the 'history of a gigantic personality', but she advised readers to take it with 'the salt of the oceans'. She said that he was activated by personal motives, none ignoble, but none abstract either, as he carried on his pugilism with the world. She said Wells was a 'pathological case' because he could not be cured from the early horrors and wrongs he had suffered. Now he suffered from an 'unconscious mental dishonesty' with 'no real self-knowledge'. She felt Wells had offered the youth of the world something, a release, but that the game had become more important than the result, and gave him the uttermost damnation of his generation by saying that he was the superb embodiment of *la trahison des clercs*. She said Wells was a destructive personality, citing his relations with the Fabians, the Labour Party, and with others as evidence, as by his 'brutality of method' he had 'wounded and injured beyond cure'; and finally, 'If he has failed to save us, the fault is in him. It is not we who left him.'[66]

These articles were a vicious attack, rivalled on the Left only by that levied by Christopher Caudwell. In a splenetic article published just before he went off to die in Spain, Caudwell said that the *Outline of History* simply pandered to the desires of the bourgeoisie, and had not pushed civilization or human history further along the dialectic. Writing in 1936, from a strict Marxist point of view, Caudwell may have been right, of course, although Wells had long since discarded that sectarian vantage point. Caudwell was flaying a horse of a different colour by the time he wrote. Odette's comments were more poignant, not only because of their personal nature, but also because there was just a germ of truth in them. Wells did not finish matters easily. He proposed, but left it to others to dispose. When they did not, chaos often resulted. He resented this attack, however, much more than the discussion of his sexual habits, and this time he struck back, but struck back at Odette and her possessiveness, not her politics.[67]

Wells's settlement of scores with Odette came in his novel *Apropos of Dolores* (1938), describing a two-month span in 1934. In this work, the narrator, Stephen Wilbeck, leaves his wife, Dolores, to muse over their relationship. She is described in the book as a 'superfluous dissatisfied woman', an essentially negative person. He goes on to remark of her, 'what is engaging my attention more and more and distracting it from all the larger aspects of life is the distressful immediate problem of close association with an unhappy, increasingly aggressive fellow creature and what I am to do about her. She will not let me be happy with her, although I have lengthened our phases of separation I am still with her altogether too much.' . . . And, 'What is the world to do with sad, insatiable, malignant, quarrelsome, grievance-cherishing people?' He then goes on to a bill of particulars, citing the woman's possessiveness, her jealousy, her seduction of him followed by a public announcement of the details, the continued vulgarity wherever she goes and no matter what they do, as well as her insatiable appetite for new and never digested ideas, simply for the experience. Wells gives an impression in the novel of what must have been Odette's almost pornographic taste in décor (see Elizabeth von Arnim's comments as well), using such terms as 'an exhibitionist bazaar'. He also describes her need to discuss in very frank terms, while at the table, such books (and their unwritten detail) as *The Well of Loneliness*; and he closes his attack with a bizarre and humorous incident of two dogs mating in the hotel dining room, cheered on, or not prevented, by Dolores. He claims that she has invented stories of his infidelity, even in one case implying incest. He goes on to compare her to Germany in the '30s with its desire for conquest and dominion over others. But Dolores dies in the book, perhaps by her own hand, perhaps from an overdose administered by Wilbeck himself — it is left unclear.

Wells then ends the novel by discussing his desire (or the narrator's) for a woman, only seen, never attainable. 'What I want to do is get this sex—beauty drive and this craving for close and peculiar individual intimacy that troubles me, into something like a rational relation to my life as a whole . . . ', says Wilbeck, as he looks back over the relationship and his life in general. Wilbeck also says that this relationship has shown him clearly how vulnerable he is to the demands of the sexual drive, but just as the world is going into decadence, so sex too is declining, leaving only the viler parts of the emotion. However, 'In spite of my experience with Dolores, I do not think that the average human is incurably perverse.' He does caution that as humans we need to ponder these malignant tendencies.

The manuscript of the novel arrived at Methuens early in April 1938. They accepted the book immediately, as did Scribners in the US. Soon, however, Methuens, and especially their editorial director and reader E.V. Lucas, who knew Odette, had second thoughts about the book. They began to fear libel suits. Wells sent them a note, signed by Marjorie, disclaiming anything in the book to be about Odette, but eventually he withdrew the book from them. Wells also withdrew it from serial publication, although *Esquire*, at that time a somewhat salacious magazine in the US, was very much interested in it. In the event Cape published the book, although by this time, with all the publicity, Methuens had changed their mind, but too late.[68]

Wells did his best to disavow the tie with his own life, as the novel was very close to reality for many readers. He had told Methuen, for example, that Dolores was in no way 'that vociferous lady at Grasse'. 'And *I repeat that in no particular except a community of temperament is Dolores like Odette Keun.* Thank God I got away with Kipps, and Mr Polly . . . before this sort of thing began,' he said, in a rather dissimulating letter. He also told Watt three weeks later that Methuens' fears of libel were groundless, and when he withdrew the book from them, he told Watt,

> I think that apprehensions in the matter are entirely baseless. I thought I made that plain to the meanest intelligence and I wish to reiterate it. But it is quite clear that some silly influence is at work in the firm of Methuen trying to suggest an identification of Dolores with Mme Odette Keun, but it is impossible for me to entrust my book to a publishing firm which is subject to such influences. . . . Simply I object to having the book published in an atmosphere of ill-informed gossip by a firm that has lost its directive intelligence. The only risk of trouble to the book lies in Methuen and Co. below stairs.[69]

His friends enjoyed the book immensely, knowing full well who was being skewered. Frank Swinnerton said that he had laughed all through the book, 'which is delicious, wicked, and beautifully *benevolent*'. Priestley also told Wells how funny the book was, and said, 'the lady is presented with devilish skill and the frame of general comment is equally grand'. The book came out while Wells was in Australia, and the support for the work there was unrestrained, as it was called 'brilliant', 'careful, swift clear writing'. One reviewer called attention to the likeness between Clissold and Wilbeck, a very penetrating comment, and went on, 'The Wellsian reader will find him such entertaining and stimulating company that the question whether he did or did not poison Dolores will trouble him as little as it did her husband.[70] Today that comment remains true, at least for this reader.

By the time H. G. Wells wrote *Dolores* he had become a very public man. He retained large amounts of his privacy, but he was a very well-known personage, not only because of his writing, but also because of his various public stands, the rumours about his love life and his sexual proclivities, as well as his highly publicized visits to the US and elsewhere. All of this attention had come about because he was rich, famous, and good newspaper copy. His books continued to sell very well, especially in a variety of reprint editions. As early as 1920, he had authorized reprint schemes, mostly through Sir Godfrey Collins of Collins & Sons. There was, as well, an Essex Edition, similar to the 6*d.* hardcover editions published by Nelson before the war, in which eventually some of his works appeared. Two separate schemes to sell newspapers, one through the Odhams syndicate and another through the *Daily Mail*, lasted off and on through at least 1933, and were several times revived; usually a set of Wells's books, in a uniform binding, was offered as an inducement to subscribers. When the publisher Ernest Benn began to court Wells, he found that the price was high. Benn told Wells that he hoped Wells's name would appear over their imprint; but, he said, 'I suppose that by and by, when you have finally perfected the human being, the best and the million [Benn's view of Wells's demands] will go together, but we haven't quite got there yet.' Eventually, of course, Benns published the *Short Stories* (1927), and were to have brought out two other collections, the *Stories of Men and Women in Love* and the *Scientific Romances*, which were in the end published by Victor Gollancz and Knopf. When a new magazine, *Argosy*, began in the States, they hoped to use Wells's name to sell the journal, asking for rights in a few hundred words in their January 1928 issue. Wells was able to get 10 guineas per 1,000 words (although he asked 20 guineas at first).

Even *Floor Games* and *Little Wars* were reprinted. As he became increasingly famous, excerpts from Wells's writing, especially passages from the great textbooks, found their way into school books. Finally, he and A. P. Watt set a standard price of $10 per 1,000 words for such use in the US. Of course, his various publishers hoped he would provide a new preface when they issued a collection of his work, and in the case of the love stories and the scientific romances, he obliged. On these books he was able to ask a high royalty, even though they were reprints: Gollancz and Knopf paid 10 per cent on the first 10,000 copies sold (at a price of 8*s.* 6*d.*) and 12 per cent thereafter. These collections are still in print. Even 'The Country of the Blind', so many times reprinted, could still bring in $30 when Somerset Maugham chose it for a travel book, along with stories from Beerbohm, Galsworthy, and others.

Eventually the short-story collection was offered as a premium by the Literary Guild in America, and Wells collected a further royalty of five cents a copy. Doubleday later offered a new edition of *The Outline of History* in a similar promotion.

It is interesting that fewer people remain interested in the *Short Stories*, which, even though they remain in print, are seldom cited or mentioned. Publishers in Wells's own time fell over themselves to use one, or a collection, of his stories. Single stories were reprinted, as when *Everybody's* paid $100 each for 'The Late Mr Elvesham', 'The Red Room', and 'The Magic Shop'. Wells insisted on reading proofs, 'as *Thirty Stories* [the edition to be used] is filled with various errors.' Hutchinsons also reprinted several stories in magazines they controlled, for £20 each. When the *Short Stories* were put together in 1927, Benn simply reprinted the various earlier collections (without seeking out other stories), and paid Macmillan a fee to release the rights. When Doran published the 1,000-page book in the US, they paid Wells $750 advance, and 25 cents a copy, sold mostly by mail order to their Book Club. Watt thought, as did Wells, that the US edition was a 'better turned out' book. Eventually Reuters bought the colonial serial rights for Africa and the Far East.

Wells told the *Sunday Express*, when the collection appeared, that his favourite stories were 'The Country of the Blind' and 'The Pearl of Love'. The paper reviewed the *Short Stories* with, 'What a magic carpet is here! . . . Where — or, when will Mr Wells give us more?' Hyman Levy, commenting in *Nature*, reminded his readers of Wells's scientific training and the use of it to strengthen the fiction, with the overall purpose 'to better and perfect mankind'. Levy said that English literature would have been the poorer if Wells's love novels had not been written, but that his real role in the twentieth century was as leader, charting a way to the future.[71]

He did very well indeed out of his writing, and some of this occurred because he was a public figure. Each of the two aspects of his life reinforced the other. But he drew the line at further exploitation of his name. When Horlicks asked him to lend his name, or his writing, to an advertising scheme for which they offered £300, Wells refused curtly, with the line, 'No. I prefer bankruptcy.' That never threatened, of course, which may have made the refusal somewhat easier, but it illustrates the dilemma he was in. He wanted to be a public man, and retain a private life. It was increasingly difficult to achieve that desire, and even more so after his *Experiment in Autobiography* appeared in 1934.[72]

The autobiography was bubbling up in Wells's mind for a long time before it appeared. To some degree the difficulty over Odette's demands and the anguish created by Jane's death probably combined to bring it out. Too many false or overwritten stories circulated in the press and in famous drawing rooms for Wells to delay much longer. By the time the book appeared he was sixty-eight, and although remarkably agile, both in mind and body, it was probably time to take stock — to ask himself, and report to his readers, from whence he came and for what he was seeking. One of the more remarkable things about him is that from about 1923, once he stabilized his diet and regimen, he seemed never to change physically until well into World War II. If one sees a photograph of him in the period from 1923 to 1943, without a caption, it is difficult to date it. This enabled him to live a public life much longer than many others, as he did not wither or deteriorate. But it also meant that interest in his life remained high, and especially from those who had some idea of his actual age.

William Clissold might be regarded as a trial run for the autobiography, although Wells specifically disavowed that in a long memorandum to his publishers. He described the book as 'the autobiography of a man of 60 [Wells's precise age] who reviews his world à la Montaigne and the story is discursive. . .'. Later he went on to say in a seven-page handwritten note, part of which found its way into the preface: *'The World of William Clissold* is not a *roman à clef*. No living person is introduced in it under another name. Many living persons are mentioned in it. Some are given thumbnail sketches; others portraits, not *always under their own names* . . .' It is not an autobiography of Wells, he went on. If he wanted to write one, he would. 'Mr Wells', he said,

> has taken an evangelistic and aggressive type in order to draw a particular view of the world consistently . . . Clissold moves about a London and world known to Mr Wells. It centres about a Villa Jasmin. This Villa Jasmin does not exist. The work is a work of fiction and the Villa Jasmin fictitious. It is described and with some particulars as being near Grasse and it is possible that many readers will believe it is a real villa . . . There is no original to Clementina. . . . The book includes therefore a *close-knit statement of modern behaviour* by an active man who believes in progress. He does his best to squeeze the activities of his life out of what he believes to be the general scheme of things. All these people are characters in a novel. Is it possible to have it discussed and treated as such?[73]

I have quoted at some length from this memorandum as it protests too much. *William Clissold* was a very autobiographical work; what it did not do was treat his views on writing, his fiction, or his relations with other women prior to Odette. To that extent he was correct; it was not autobiography. When the autobiography did come out, it treated these other matters, but also left out much, not least his relations with anyone other than his wives. So both books are incomplete, and both can be regarded as partially true, partially very selective versions of his life.

The autobiographical idea did not die easily, both because Wells's disclaimer about Clissold, in his 'Notes Before the Preface', was reprinted in several places, but also because the work seemed so close to Wells's observed life. He told his friend R.D. Blumenfeld, when discussing possible serialization of the book: 'Clissold is a big industrialist, metallurgical and chemical. He is a radical and a republican, but very acute in his criticism of Communism and rough on labour politicians. But he loathes the Duke of Northumberland more than he loathes Lenin (and the King bores him to death)'. That, with the exception of the first sentence, is a good, if superficial, description of H. G. Wells, of course. Benn wanted a different profile of Wells on the dust jacket each of the three volumes, but in the event Wells allowed them to use only one, by William Rothenstein. Frank Swinnerton passed the proofs of the novel, at least for the US edition. When the book was reviewed in *Nature*, the reviewer, Henry E. Armstrong, called it Wells's autobiography — 'a photograph taken with a wide lens, but not a very deep focus'. He revelled in the description of the Royal Society, terming it a 'True Bill', and ended his review: 'Society being composed of all sorts and conditions of men, to provide for all will always be very difficult, the less, however, the more we are alive to the differences and are not too immodest in our individual opinions.'[74]

Wells began work on the actual autobiography in 1932, and the publishing world soon heard rumours of the work, rumours which he and Marjorie were quick to deny. However, early in 1934 Marjorie notified Watt that the proposed book was nearly finished. Some chapters were at Chiltern Court, and the remainder in Bournemouth where Wells was spending the winter (free from Odette) while working on his film, and this book. Watt came by the London flat and read the chapters that were available. It was a very inchoate book at that time, and the final product was edited, fairly heavily in places apparently, by Marjorie Wells and Dorothy Richardson, who was, as we have seen, brought in to help. Wells, in fact, went off to America while the editing took place, although he passed the final product upon his return.

The publishing world remained anxious about this book, and the offers grew to be quite large for that Depression period. Wells was offered £3,300 by Hutchinsons, for instance, as an initial advance, and he eventually received £4,000 with a 20 per cent starting royalty, along with $1,000 for a three-part serial version in the US. Wells asked to supervise the cuts, and read proofs on the serial. When illustrations were used, the price rose accordingly. Even the Melbourne *Herald* paid £150 for excerpts, and Associated Newspapers of Ceylon £30 for a squib or two.[75]

Experiment in Autobiography, even with its partial view of its subject, is worthy of the claim made for it as one of the great autobiographies of this century. The frankness with which Wells treated his life with Isabel (and the love and affection which still suffused those sections), as well as the remarkable romantic way in which he depicted his life with Amy Catherine, caught the fancy of the pubic immediately. His descriptions of his early life, of learning to write, and the reception of his work, along with his involvement with the Fabians, and the great figures of the period before the First World War, were all done with affection, apparent frankness, and a willingness to adjudge himself guilty in many areas where another might have passed on the guilt. In addition, the book, subtitled 'The Story of a Very Ordinary Mind', used his own pictorial ability, along with excellent photographs (many of which were loaned to him by Elizabeth Healey Bruce), to lay out the first fifty years of his life in considerable detail. The last twenty years were treated very lightly, and the second section of the book is a restatement of his political and social philosophy.

As we read Wells's autobiography today, we are struck with the fidelity with which it depicts the life of the lower middle class, 'in the margin', to use one of his earliest subtitles. Since then we have had such books as C.P. Snow's *Strangers and Brothers*, with the bitter-sweet depiction of the Midlands, and Henry Williamson's *Chronicles of Ancient Sunlight*, but both are fiction. Wells's work is unsparing but true. It is always told with deep affection for his family, and for his education — with exasperation at the narrow horizons and displeasure at the waste of human potential in both, observed as fugitives in that unfair and creaky Victorian world. But Wells had escaped, and he knew by 1934 that escape was even more possible for his readers. By 1934 too he had reached a more dispassionate plateau as he viewed other humans. They were exasperating; he was irritated at their failure to use their potential. The world moved slowly, far too slowly, so *Experiment in Autobiography*, with its rich depiction of the steps he had taken, the roads fulfilled, as it were, was an effort to assist in the change of pace. The book remains one of the best testaments to the human condition and its possibility (but never to the necessity for change). Wells was never really a pessimist and he is still misread by those who project their own ideals and attitudes into his work. He tended to view the glass as half full, not half empty, and he only urged people to lift the wineskin, and turn it out.[76]

Wells originally offered *Experiment in Autobiography* through the *Daily Mail* as a further circulation-builder for the paper, and when he suspected a boycott on the part of booksellers as a result (it did not occur, although he was often sure his work was being boycotted when sales did not reach his somewhat lofty expectations), he suggested offering the book for sale in cinema lobbies.[77]

His friends found the book fascinating. Beatrice Webb congratulated him on the portrait of Jane in the book, and called it a 'marvellous gift for a disinterested analysis of your own opinions'. There was a sting in her letter, however, when she asked him again if he really believed that he could have a disciplined order and companionship 'without a definite metaphysic behind the projects which are advocated'. She also doubted whether FDR's controlled capitalism was really any better than the planned production for communal consumption as practised in the USSR. '... Time will show ...' was her last comment. (She and Sidney had just produced their famous book *Soviet Communism*, which accounted for that remark.)

Roosevelt himself, in a letter marked 'Personal', told Wells that 'Your experiment in autobiography was for me an experiment in staying awake instead of putting the light out. How do you manage to retain such vivid pictures of events and such extraordinarily clear impressions and judgements?' FDR went on in his letter to discuss the first two years of the New Deal, which he said had taught people to think, '— and your direction and mine are not so far apart; at least we both seek peaceable conveyances in our travels.'

All of Wells's closer friends were equally supportive. Gregory cited the parallels in their early lives; Eileen Power opened the book to a story about Einstein and Haldane, and immediately dissolved into laughter remembering Haldane at the time. She told Wells, 'I shall be deep in it tonight.' Frank Swinnerton, soon to write his own very moving and useful autobiography, commented on the interest sustained in the book and said that if Wells had done a bit more on the Fabians, and included a picture of Violet Hunt, it would have been nice. After telling Wells that Odette had sent him a copy of *I Discover the English*, Swinnerton remarked that he and his wife had found *Experiment in Autobiography* 'a living book. Splendid. We have both been engrossed by it. Thank you. I think it is a great book.' Jessie Conrad also thanked Wells for her signed copy, and reminisced about the wonderful days back at Spade House, ending the letter with, 'F. M. Hueffer will swell with pride and satisfaction when he reads your favourable comparison [of Ford to Conrad].' She went on to plead Conrad's case as a foreigner, unschooled in the English language or literature, to show that his triumph was all the greater. But, for her, 'your book has stirred early memories, brought into the foreground old friends and affections of many years ago. Stephen Crane, Henry James, and many others.'

Nearly all the reviews were good, but Wells must have been especially pleased by those which appeared in *Nature*. 'T.L.H.' (T.L. Humberstone) reviewed Volume I, saying that Wells had written to 'clear his mind', and urged readers to notice his maxims on the conduct of life. Hyman Levy, a sometime associate, but not really very close to Wells, reviewed the second volume, and in fact, the entire book. He was very gracious to one whose political views were not up to his own advanced standards. He remarked on how much the world owed to the creator of *Ann Veronica*, going on to cite the inspiration of Huxley, and to laud the great textbooks of the '20s. Levy said that Wells's great question, still unanswered, was and is, How do we get at the brains of those who are in charge? He thought a better social dynamic was needed, and that this autobiography with its standard of truthfulness, hitherto unmatched, would help. Even here, however, he said that although the book succeeded in the particular, because of its failure to heed the dialectic sufficiently, it had failed in general. This review is a very strong and analytical comment on what Wells had created, but from a special point of view. Taken all in all, though, it was conceded that Wells had created another masterpiece, even though today we also know that it is incomplete.[78]

Wells continued to work on fragmentary additions to the *Experiment*. Some of these, which dealt with his relations with Rebecca, Odette, Moura, and Jane again, have recently been republished as Volume III, under the title, *H. G. Wells in Love*. They continue Wells's unusual frankness, at least in the parts we now have, and recent reviewers have continued to be supportive. However, all three volumes have gaps and unfilled spaces, some of which may yet be filled — if the passages were ever written — while others await the biographer's interpretation. Wells was remarkably frank about his life, but even he was unwilling, or unable, to tell everything, not only about his active sexual life, but about his feelings for others. He apparently had much stronger feelings than he ever showed in public, or even in his personal writing. His seeming willingness to discuss personal affairs and the formative events of his youth, so far as he could remember them, led him to a private reticence about his deeper personal feelings — in fact to a public rejection of such feelings. Wells made a wonderful friend, and was willing to help his friends in any way he could. He was also uncommonly grateful for their aid. At the same time he was a harsh enemy, finding little good in those who aroused his hostility. True to his class and his upbringing, however, he tended to ignore such people where possible, and tried very hard not to slang them in print, or to attack them publicly. He preferred the distance of time to deal with these aspects of his life. He was a bundle of complex contradictions, stemming from his lower-middle-class Victorian background.

A good friend of mine, and a long-time reader of Wells, once dismissed him to me by saying that he 'remained a counter-jumper all his life'. At first I was indignant at the phrase, and still feel its uncaring sting, but there is, nevertheless, a thread of truth here. He did retain many of those values, but usually the better ones — truthfulness, candour, an effort to be absolutely democratic — and he attempted to bring these mores to all the world, and to cut away the excrescences he found: violence, nationalism, narrow statism, inequality, and an unwillingness to plan for the future. According to his lights, his autobiography was a remarkable effort to find the reality in his own life. When all the parts are taken together, it is clear that few since that time have come closer to the mark in surveying their own lives.

Wells continued to think about these matters, and occasionally he broke into print with his thoughts. He wrote a rather comic auto-obituary in 1937, at a time when a parlour game of some interest involved writing one's own obituary and tombstone epitaph. Of course, at about this same time he coined his own epitaph, 'God damn it, I told you so!' (to give one version of several attributed to him). In his auto-obituary he said that the crowning achievement of his life was not to accept his social inferiority and status, but that this had created a 'copious and repetitive essayist on public affairs'. He described his life as similar to a reef-building coral polyp, contributing to the greater good, but what that good would be was not yet revealed to him. 'Scarcely anything remains of him now, and yet, without him and his life, the reef of common ideas on which our civilization stands today could never have arisen.' Later, in 1938, he rewrote parts of his autobiography for serial publication in the *Sunday Chronicle*. These turned out to be very good pieces, and bear rereading in connection with the original work, for he modified his views somewhat. As he told his readers in the first of the new pieces, 'There are things I have to do to the best of my ability and things I will be damned if I do. To fail the former or to yield to the latter is a living death.' He described his creed as 'mystical stoicism': not a bad judgement after all.[79]

Wells thought further about these questions in his later life. He occasionally broached his views in letters to Gregory, as when he told him, 'the favourable difference between all religious creeds and science is that the former profess *finality*. The scientific must end in *Expectation*.' When Gregory responded with some very polite remarks about Wells's life, he was told, 'The fact of your long acquaintance has made my stuff very familiar to you, so that I become a symbol for what really is a very considerable body of thought in which we both have lived. Apart from that, I'm mostly to object to.' Wells refined these views in one of his last philosophical pieces for *Nature*, 'The Man of Science as Aristocrat', in early 1941. He had been prompted to write the piece, he said, after hearing Gregory give his Aldred lecture, entitled 'Discovery and Invention', as well as by an article by A.V. Hill called 'Science, National and International, and the Basis of Co-operation'. Wells said scientists came in two types, essentially. The first was interested in invention, and practical ideas. But the true scientist is responsive to the need to know, not need itself. This group celebrates 'free expression of thought'. The conclusion he drew from this (not lost on those who were further to the left than he had gone, at least in their adoration of Soviet science), was that 'the preservation, multiplication, and cultivation of the "pure" discovery is the primary solicitude for all progressives.' He recalled as an example of how this worked, that when he had been last in the US, on an avowedly political mission, he had spent time at the Lick Observatory in Pasadena, reflecting on the possible contributions of astronomy, and from there had gone to discuss the work of drosophila genetics with T. H. Morgan. 'The essential research worker must be a "stoical aristocrat" . . .' was his judgement.[80]

At the end of this section of the book, and before looking at how Wells spent his declining years, we might cast a retrospective eye back over his life. He took the lead in that venture at the remarkable birthday party given him in 1936 by his favourite group, the significant society, PEN. Wells often used PEN (Poets, Essayists, Novelists) to carry his message, and the concerns of that organization, as well as his last few years with Moura Budberg, sustained him after the blows life had dealt through death and through traduction (Odette) — blows not yet assuaged by the autobiographical effort recently attempted.

Several honours came to Wells as he grew older. He received the honorary freedom of the City of London and of Brissago, but refused that of

Bromley on the grounds that Bromley had not been very gracious to him, nor he to it. The University of London awarded him an honorary D. Litt. on his seventieth birthday, and his friends in PEN tendered him an immense birthday party to mark the occasion. All of his surviving old friends were there, including Cynthia Asquith who represented her mother for those ancient favours, and Moura who sat at his side. J. B. Priestley was in the chair. Wells gave them a speech, entitled 'Life Is Not Half Long Enough'. He told the audience that at seventy he felt like a little child, Master Bertie, told to put away his toys, and he said, 'I hate the thought of leaving.' He then went on to call for a new encyclopaedia, better use of films, and support, beyond all else, for 'the free activities of the human mind . . . above all political considerations'.

Among those who attended the dinner were Shaw, who paid Wells a handsome tribute for his authentic descriptions of English life, with only Dickens and Kipling his equal. G. B. Stern, Julian Huxley, André Maurois, and Arthur Bliss also spoke, and a message from J. M. Barrie, soon to be released from his deathbed, was read. Christabel Aberconway, Princess Bibesco, Vera Brittain, F. W. Crofts, Lovat Dickson, Gregory, Walter Greenwood, Guedalla, Hamish Hamilton, Laurence Housman, C. E. M. Joad, J. M. Keynes, Marie Belloc-Lowndes, E. V. Lucas, Rose Macaulay, Desmond MacCarthy, Somerset Maugham, Aylmer Maude, A. A. Milne, Leo Chiozza-Money, Mazo de la Roche, Stanley Unwin, and Alec Waugh were also in attendance. This was truly a gathering of literary lions to honour one of their leaders. Congratulatory messages also poured in, from correspondents whom he met and saw frequently, and even one from Stuart Blofield who reminded Wells of the time when he used to come to London to be tutored 'in the old booksellers' row off the Strand'.

Only Philip Guedalla was unhappy, mostly with where he was seated, as he felt he should have been at the head table. Wells told him, 'The cause of free speech is more important than an issue of personal dignity.' Later, in 1943, Wells wrote to Guedalla again, rehearsing the incident, telling him he was rereading his books, and reminding him, 'This is a time when all right — that is to say left-minded men should stand together.'[81]

That was an excellent sentiment, and one which Wells repeated many times to various gatherings of PEN. The society was initially brought together by John Galsworthy, with Wellsian help, and in Galsworthy's lifetime he was the only president and the group's chief spokesman. Wells was his successor as president, and took the society further into political controversy, especially on the issue of free speech. Ada Galsworthy worried that Wells would take the group too far, but in the '30s all had to stand up and be counted on this issue. Wells felt that Galsworthy would have been beside him, if he had lived, once the Nazis began their work of stifling free and open discussion of ideas. Wells attended every meeting of PEN he could, after its founding just after World War I, although at first he refused a vice-presidency, nominating Shaw instead. He acquiesced to the office, however, when Galsworthy noted that he himself was a Scot, while Shaw was Irish, and the English branch needed an English head. Galsworthy did not back Wells as strongly as he might have done at the time of the troubles with Thring, but otherwise the two men were in agreement. They saw the organization as one which could do good things, and always support the art of writing. After Galsworthy's death Wells often met with Ada Galsworthy to discuss PEN affairs. Both were concerned about who would follow Wells after he was elected international president in 1934, as the Nazi menace seemed to grow more terrifying every day, and especially as Wells had taken such a strong stand against them.[82]

By this time Wells was speaking out on this matter whenever he could, as when he wrote to G. Carson of the Anglo-German Club about his and PEN's views. He told his correspondent that he would be glad 'to learn what steps the Anglo-German Club is taking to assist in the defence and help of German science and culture against the present outbreak of violent black-guardism in Germany'. When he spoke at the PEN annual dinner on the same point, Gilbert Murray congratulated him on the speech, and said that they ought to go further and mobilize the cultural and literary world 'in defence of intellectual freedom and against certain extremes of cruelty'. At Barcelona in 1935, Wells reiterated his view, and although he was re-elected president, he told his listeners that younger persons were needed in these posts. Ada Galsworthy told him, when they discussed the matter further at tea, that he could not give up the presidency, as his voice in these matters was too significant. Eventually Priestley took over from Wells, as a worthy speaker on such questions, but not before Wells had made a speech at Dubrovnik (on which occasion the Germans left the meeting) and had sent an even stronger talk to be read at Buenos Aires. To some extent the Russians also constituted a problem, but the Germans and Italians who murdered and tortured writers were more important, for Wells and Ada Galsworthy as well as for others. Once the war began (and once Wells and Thomas Mann had made their unsuccessful pilgrimage to the PEN meeting in Stockholm), he and Priestley agreed to form a committee to ensure that authors would be made good use of in the work of preserving freedom. Wells served eagerly.[83]

By this time Wells was an elderly man. His interests, as with most elderly men, were with his creature comforts. Therefore it is remarkable to find that a man this old was able to bring enough energy to bear to conduct one more love affair.

If, as has been suggested, Isabel, Jane, and Amber were three true loves of his life, certainly Moura Budberg was a fourth. All four lurked in Wells's mind, as the Lover-Shadow — that mythical person who met and was met on even ground, supplying love, affection, support, psychic energy, each to the other, in equal amounts. The difference of Moura from the others was that she reciprocated that love, but not with the intensity or willingness of the first three. Wells, in fact, went to his deathbed unhappy that Moura had not reached in her own mind that peak, and that she had not been willing to marry him, once he was free.

She was born Moura Zabrewskaia in 1892, daughter of a Russian senator and landowner. She married H. von Benckendorff in 1911 when he was Russian ambassador to England. He was later shot, apparently by the Bolsheviks. She then married Baron Budberg, whose name she kept, although she later divorced him because of his addiction to gambling. She was briefly imprisoned in Moscow in 1918, but was released in the custody of Bruce Lockhart, a British agent with whom she lived for some time, and they remained friendly throughout his life. When he left for England, she transferred her affections to Maxim Gorky, and lived with him for some years. She was also friendly with Alexander Korda, the great filmmaker, and was Wells's mistress and companion from 1930 or so until his death. As Bruce Lockhart said of her, in his memoirs, 'Where she loved, there was her world, and her philosophy of life made her mistress of all the consequences. She was an aristocrat. She could have been a Communist. She could never have been a bourgeoise.'

She made her living as a translator, first of the works of Thomas Mann and Bruno Frank, and later of Georges Simenon. She spoke five languages well (Russian, English, Italian, German, and French) and was a true sophisticate, a marvellous companion for Wells in his last days, even though she would not marry him. Lovat Dickson said once, and he was close to them both, that the real reason for this was that she continued to be in love with Baron Budberg, and Wells himself indicated as much once or twice to intimate friends.[84]

Moura met Wells on his visit to Russia in 1914, but only at a brief social occasion. When he returned and stayed with Gorky in 1920, she and Wells seduced each other. On Gorky's letter of 3 December 1920, acknowledging receipt of several boxes of scientific books, she put a postscript to Wells: 'Just a few words, dear Mr Wells, from "The Trusty Girl Guide". We miss you very much here, in dear old Russia. Hope we shall meet again. Best luck to you and Gip.' Wells had earlier included a message for her in a letter to Gorky from Estonia, sending love to 'Dear Tovarisch Benckendorf'.

Moura made her way to Berlin, and when Gorky returned to Russia, she remained there, shuttling back and forth to Vienna and Florence, especially when Gorky came south for his health. Wells probably met her again in 1924, but it was 1930 before they renewed their acquaintance when she began to live part of each year in London. Wells certainly was smitten early on, for after the one physical embrace, he spoke often of Moura, telling Claire Sheridan, for instance, a good deal about her after they had met again. Sheridan called her 'beautiful and attractive', as she was, in a somewhat Eastern fashion. Bruce Lockhart is now one of the major sources on Moura, as he tended to see her, and to remark about her and H.G., when he wrote in his diary. At various dinners they attended together, many of them given by Lord Beaverbrook, Bruce Lockhart occasionally sat next to Wells, and across from Moura, where he was able to hear their backchat at the meal. Moura often went to lunch with her old admirer, and she told stories of Wells, Charlie Chaplin, William Gerhardie, Hilda Matheson (they were all in the audience at a Wells BBC talk), Arnold Bennett, Shaw, and others of Wells's friends. According to Bruce Lockhart, after one conversation, he and she agreed (although this sounds more like his invention) that 'Except for his women, he [Wells] has no real male friends. He takes little interest in young men and unlike Gorky does not put himself out to encourage them . . . Bennett was probably his only friend, and I doubt the two men ever comment very much to each other.' This sounds very like a gloss on Budberg's conversation, perhaps after Bruce Lockhart had expressed a wish for guidance of some sort.[85]

In the autumn of 1932 he and H.G. put Moura on the train to Paris after a long meeting over lunch and wine to discuss his memoir, *British Agent*, and the problem of how much one could say about the living in an autobiographical account. Moura was on her way to see Gorky. In 1934 they lunched again to report on Wells and Moura's visit to Up Park, for the first time since he was in his twenties, in order to describe it correctly for his autobiography. There were further discussions over lunch whenever the three were in town together, including several meetings to discuss education, and at least one occasion, at a lunch given by Emerald Cunard, when Mrs Wallis W. Simpson was also a guest. When Wells fell ill in 1936, he submitted to a medical examination, but Moura refused, and went to Estonia while he had five teeth removed on the doctor's advice.

Moura acted as agent for Wells with various women's groups, and she was a conduit for Soviet material from Gorky. Although she moved in some strange circles, one may doubt that she was a spy: a courier perhaps — but she was well known to Reilly, and others of the shadowy British intelligence underground of the inter-war period. As Wells dutifully reported to Elizabeth Healey Bruce, 'We live in open air and you must meet her some day. But for two grandparents with lives of their own there is next to [*word missing*] marrying nor giving in marriage.' Wells later told Guedalla that they would have been married (much as Mrs Belloc-Lowndes hoped when she remarked on the subject) 'except for the inconvenience of an inaccessible husband'. Whether that reflects reality or Wells's wishful thinking is immaterial at this stage. The two grandparents, for that is what they were, had a pleasant, but probably not too passionate, life together. Even here, though, one would not say it was too tame, from the latter-day publication of the secret portion of Wells's autobiography. Moura lived on nearly thirty years after his death, one of his heirs, but increasingly isolated as her old friends disappeared one by one. At her funeral, in the beautiful Russian Orthodox cathedral near Paddington Station, the service seemed very ornate, and out of place to some viewers. But there were very few of those by the time the priests had dealt with her remains.[86]

Wells found himself in constant demand to comment on his views on women, especially after his reputation grew and his autobiography was published. He never varied in public from what he said in private. He told an interviewer for the Melbourne *Age* when he was in Australia, that emancipation (the vote) had brought liberty to women, but no great achievements as yet. Women had not yet been able to see how much they could accomplish if they would only try. They showed courage, loyalty, and pertinacity, but no real pattern so far. And with modern birth-control methods available to all, together with the psychological ability to control the need to replenish the species, and to make an impact on evolution, a new set of goals was needed. He urged women to take up the new task of equality.

Men are so ignorant, so uneducated, so lacking in judgement, so egotistical. Their attitude towards women is all wrong. It is governed by jealousy — and what a dreadful thing is jealousy — and by the pride of possession. The sort of petty pride they feel over owning a gun, or a ten-acre field, or a boat . . . All history is plotted by the struggle for power that has its roots in the money tangle, and the continuation of human life depends ultimately on the outcome. And the women don't seem to care.

Once Wells returned to London he was approached by a publisher to write a book, under the tentative title *The Female of the Species*, based on these comments. Although he considered the proposal for a time, he eventually refused; he gave no reason, but it is my feeling that he refused because he thought what he wrote would be treated like a piece of old man's pornography. As he told a writer on *Tribune* later, who hoped for similar comments, Go ahead, write about the subject, but be careful of how you put it. For, he said, 'it is the old men who feel they haven't had their whack of fun who become nasty old boys at the end.' In the world to come, for which they both were working, 'sexual stress would go' and not get in the way of the other matters of concern to humankind. Still, in all, when one comes to these last comments on men and women in love, it is with the feeling that Wells could offer such remarks very easily, because no one could ever accuse him of not having had his 'whack of fun'.[87]

THE RIGHTS OF MAN

Within the space of little more than a hundred years there has been a complete revolution in the material conditions of human life. Invention and discovery have so changed the pace and nature of communications round and about the earth that the distances which formerly kept the states and nations of mankind apart have now been practically abolished. At the same time there has been so gigantic an increase of mechanical power, and such a release of human energy, that man's ability either to co-operate with or to injure and oppress one another, and to consume, develop or waste the bounty of Nature has been exaggerated beyond all comparison with former times. This process of change has mounted swiftly and steadily in the past third of a century, and is now approaching a climax. It becomes imperative to adjust man's life and institutions to the increasing dangers and opportunities of these new circumstances. . . . The history of the Western peoples has a lesson for all mankind. It has been the practice of what are called the democratic or Parliamentary countries to meet every enhancement and centralization of power in the past by a definite and vigorous reassertion of the individual rights of man. Never before has the demand to revive that precedent been as urgent as it is now . . .

HGW, Preamble to the 'Universal Rights of Man', from *The Rights of Man* (1943)

About a month before the German attack on Poland in 1939 Wells wrote an essay for the *Sunday Chronicle and Referee*. The essay actually appeared on the last weekend of peace, when he had gone to Stockholm to attend the aborted PEN meeting. In this piece Wells began to turn his attention to his major effort of the next several years. He said that the war was surely coming, that it was going to be very bad, and he remarked, 'if many of us are to die for democracy we better know what we mean by the word.' A real democracy should be the outcome of the forthcoming war, and he recalled the failure of the Allies during the First World War to lay out clear-cut war aims for discussion.[1]

Wells was no doubt remembering that he had spent the last weekend of peace in 1914 at Easton contemplating the defeat of German militarism and the world which might then result.[2] In 1939 others in Britain also thought of the necessity of clearly stated war aims as the peace was shattered on that last warm weekend of the old world. As the gas masks were readied for distribution, and the trenches dug again in Hyde Park, public discussion of war aims began in *The Times*. In H. G. Wells's contribution to the discussion, after his return, he stated the case for war aims very clearly. He called for a full-scale debate of the putative aims leading to a Federation of Man. He remarked, in fact, that, '. . . if we are to go on with this present regime of vague insecurities, mutual distrust and sabotage, I, for one, can see no hope for mankind, more of this sort of thing, and worse to the end'. The debate intensified steadily, as Wells and others began to call for an even fuller discussion.[3] The period of the 'phoney war' was a boon, as there was time for protracted analysis and discussion throughout the autumn and winter of 1939–40.

On the other side of the Atlantic, a discussion was also taking place. The Roosevelt–Willkie campaign of 1940, the ongoing debate between the America Firsters on the one hand, under their palatine leader, Henry Luce (see the *Life* editorial for 4 July 1940), and the Committee to Defend America by Aiding the Allies, led by William Allen White, need further analysis in terms of the actual war aims which were sought. In England, where the battle with Germany was already under way, the discussion was more direct, but the same issues were at stake: what to do with the European heartland, if the Allies won; and — an issue present as an unwanted guest since at least 1917 — what would be the postwar status of Russia? H.G. Wells was instinctively seeking the widest possible discussion and, he hoped, the best possible answers to these vexing problems of the twentieth century.[4]

Wells also fostered discussion in a number of other publications. Early in October he reappeared in the *Chronicle* in a piece analysing 'What We Fight For'. This article, published later in the US in *Liberty*, called for a broad-based democracy, and an organized collective control of modern life. Economic justice, the right to knowledge, and a unified police force to control economic robbery and gangster violence were musts in the new world, according to Wells. The next week Wells, and others, set out their views of war aims in *Picture Post*, and Wells's letter to *The Times* which had focused the discussion was reprinted. Later Wells and nineteen others signed a manifesto published in the *Manchester Guardian* which called for a federal government for the world in the final peace settlement. In the manifesto the signers also urged an international scientific effort to apply science to the common welfare, a demand which was part of the campaign in other places. The manifesto also suggested the surrender of arms to this federal government, and the establishment of a co-operative educational effort in backward areas. The education was to be offered without social discrimination, in preparation for self-government within the international federal union.[5]

By this time Wells and his associates, led by the *Daily Herald*'s science correspondent, Ritchie Calder (later Baron Ritchie-Calder), who became secretary of the drafting group, began looking towards initial publication of their first draft of aims, to further the discussion. Some courting of newspaper publishers took place, as a number of papers were unwilling to give sufficient space to what looked like being a long campaign. *The Times*, offered this first effort, kept the draft idea for nearly a month before they finally refused it. The editor who received it thought it would be good for the paper and for circulation, but his employers did not.[6] Eventually a combination of the National Peace Council and the *Daily Herald* agreed to serve as the forum for the discussion.

The Peace Council had first approached Wells at the end of October, but their discussion proposal was too limited for Wells and he refused comment. Francis Williams, Ritchie Calder's superior as editor of the *Herald*, however, saw the possibilities for the national Labour daily. By mid-November, probably urged on by Ritchie Calder, he had offered the newspaper's columns for a nationwide discussion, in which Wells was to act as general spokesman. Wells showed great interest, and sent Williams a draft outline which called for eight to ten articles. Williams, pleading the paper shortage, urged briefer and fewer articles, but did take the opportunity to offer prospective comments on free speech and free association to Wells when he returned the manuscript.[7]

Wells then sent a revised outline to Williams. In his response he mused about possible other outlets for publication, but Williams's desire to involve the Labour Party, and especially Herbert Morrison who had commented favourably on behalf of a declaration in a BBC broadcast, was so strong that he urged Wells to publish both with the *Herald* and with a wider-circulation illustrated weekly such as *Picture Post*. An offer of payment, as high as £350, was made, to sweeten the task of co-ordination and writing. In his plan Wells was to lead off the discussion with specimen articles for debate, and Ritchie Calder was to obtain reactions from prominent people. Others would respond in the natural way to the discussion, and this would create a great public forum and analysis. The idea of war aims had been completely set aside by this time in favour of the concept of human rights, and most discussions used this term thereafter. In Williams's plan the TUC was to be brought in to circularize their membership to alert them to the series, scheduled to begin early in the New Year. Discussion of publicity and the articles continued generally, and after some coaxing, Wells also agreed to participate in a public debate and forum sponsored by the National Peace Council, on the question, 'The New World Order — Its Fundamental Principles'.[8]

That meeting was held at Central Hall, Westminster, on 12 March 1940. C. E. M. Joad presided, and Wells, J. Middleton Murry, and Salvador de Madariaga addressed the audience. About 3,600 people attended, and when Wells spoke, he urged them not to applaud, as with so many people present, he felt the meeting was not a discussion, but had become a demonstration. In his talk Wells, refuting the case for imperialism as put in *The British Case*, published by the Government, asserted that a 'complete biological revolution' had occurred, and only a 'reorganization of the world into one political, social, economic, and educational community' would now do. A universal declaration of the Rights of Man, along with the development of a new education, and a new encyclopaedia of knowledge, was needed. In his peroration, Wells called for 'a worldwide coalescence of all the scattered forces of creativity present in the human heart into one consciously revolutionary movement based on the rights of man'.[9] The audience applauded the speech vigorously and went into the night buoyed by their attendance.

Even after this remarkable event, the *Daily Herald* remained the principal forum for the debate over the Declaration. A lead article, with five follow-up pieces by Wells, and several from other analysts, was originally planned. A redrafting committee, with Wells in the chair and Ritchie Calder as secretary, and made up of Lord Sankey, Sir John Orr, Lord Horder, Barbara Wootton, Norman Angell, and Francis Williams, was instituted. Among others who agreed to discuss the published draft were Harold Nicholson, William Holmes of the TUC, Richard Gregory, the Revd. Henry Carter (a prominent Methodist clergyman of Westminster), the Archbishop of York, Archibald Main of the Church of Scotland, General Carter of the Salvation Army, and many other private persons. Wells soon resigned his position as chairman in favour of Lord Sankey (thus accounting for the latter-day name of the Declaration), although he continued to chair the actual discussions at the meetings of the group. Sankey was never more than a convenient figurehead. Wells needed the freedom to comment which the chairmanship would deny him, or so he felt. After the discussions and the ensuing correspondence, Wells wrote three more analytical articles in which the debate was summarized, and a final draft of the Declaration was produced for further discussion and translation.[10]

The Declaration did not spring full-blown from the head of H. G. Wells or Ritchie Calder. Some ideas of this type had, of course, been abroad in the world at least since Wilson's Fourteen Points address in 1918, and certainly from the formation of the War Aims committee under the leadership of Lord Northcliffe in early 1918. (Wells's role in the Fourteen Points address is obscure, although as we have seen his views were apparently used in early drafts of that document). The Northcliffe committee produced, finally, and from Wells's hand, a memorandum to their masters, the Propaganda Ministry at Crewe House. It should be remembered, however, that Wells's further discussion of possible goals had also appeared in the week before the Armistice, but was lost in the furore over the end of the First World War. Wells reprinted the Crewe memorandum as part of his 1939–40 campaign to create discussion on the new Declaration, and as an example of what to avoid this time. In addition, he may also have used a statement he had prepared for Lord Esher in 1936 as a means of reviving the Liberal Party. The text is somewhat similar, although no mention of this document occurs in the 1939–40 discussions. Another somewhat similar document was produced in France in the mid–1930s and although Wells later acknowledged it, he claimed not to have known of it until after the Sankey Declaration was in its third or fourth revision.[11]

Whatever the original provenance, Wells was the primary and most essential author of the Declaration, and he, with Ritchie Calder, was the chief force in circulating it throughout the world. He did not hesitate to use his reputation and his position to foster publication and discussion of the various phases of the draft document. For instance, when the *Sheffield Tribune* hired a new editor, he wrote welcoming him as an ally in the fight for the Declaration. He produced articles for *Fortnightly Review*, *Picture Post*, and *Tribune*, which had offered some of the more trenchant comment on the drafts. His books on the subject also sold very well in the cheap paper-covered Penguin editions.[12]

Wells did not hesitate to distribute the draft to significant figures. Gandhi, Nehru, FDR, and others all commented on drafts. World syndication of the articles was made available at a nominal fee, and they were widely reprinted in neutral countries, in the Commonwealth, and in the US, especially in the black press. The *Daily Herald* made proofs available to the world press, and claimed to have 30,000 copies in circulation in the UK alone. Translation into ten different languages was provided immediately, along with a message from Francis Williams discussing possible press usage. A filing system was set up to handle the various comments which came in. When other papers were less appreciative Wells did not hesitate to remind them of their duty as he saw it. He sought further wide publication and discussion, as in a moving piece for the *Sunday Express* at the end of the year, 'The World of My Heart's Desire'. This brought a poignant letter in response from Eduard Beneš. He also wrote for *Horizon* (quite a different audience, of course), and finally sought publication of the more or less final document in an inexpensive form in 1943.

During the summer of 1941 Wells was host at a diplomatic dinner for John Winant, Ivan Maisky, and others. (This was after the German attack on the Soviet Union.) Wells's talk to his guests after the dinner focused on there being both an Eastern and a Western mind, and the role the Declaration of Rights could play in the postwar world by uniting the two intellectual strains. He continued his efforts with Maisky, as well as

Winant, through 1943, and by this time had enlisted another secretary, an Indian scholar, N. Gangulee (Rabindranath Tagore's nephew), to assist Ritchie Calder. He felt the need to go beyond Ritchie Calder's rather limited influence in these strata of society. This last recruiting led eventually to a book by Gangulee with a Wells preface, also in 1943.[13]

The Declaration was published in its final form in 1943 by Poynings Press, Brighton. Wells ostensibly contributed only a preface, but in fact wrote the entire text, and passed the proofs. In the preface, he disclaimed full authorship, although headquarters for the group was still 13 Hanover Terrace, and of course, he saw this copy through the press himself. He said, in his introduction, 'I am only in the most subordinate degree a contributor . . .' and only because he was 'a free man, too old for any sort of active service and too unorthodox for political affairs, with time, premises, resources, and competent assistance available, I have been convenient general secretary for the scientific examination and co-ordination of the vast welter of contemporary revolutionary and creative ideas.' In a further comment he also pointed to the problems of private property that had been raised, and said that the Declaration was far too western in orientation. He announced that he was about to ask Mass Observation, as well as scholars from the School of Oriental and African Studies at London University, to analyse the Declaration with special regard to such matters as the polling of opinion in lieu of elections. One idea he offered was that population groups of perhaps 20,000 each might be given a voice in a sort of world jury, the members to be chosen by lot. This jury would be the sovereign in the new world, according to Wells, and he went on to say, '[This law] is the fundamental law of a new free world that draws on all mankind.'[14]

Work on the Declaration revived and renewed H. G. Wells's interest in Basic English, one of the languages, like Esperanto, made up to act as a universal means of communication between different language groups. Basic English had a small but serviceable vocabulary and featured a greatly simplified grammar and syntax. Its inventor, C. K. Ogden, had come to Wells's attention at the time of the League of Nations committee in 1918. Ogden was a population expert and Wells consulted with him on such matters when the committee still hoped to produce a general textbook. Ogden came for a weekend to Easton where the two men talked of their various ideas in some detail.

In the '20s they exchanged books, and when Ogden's plans for his language matured sufficiently he, Fenner Brockway, and Wells met to consider the language over a luncheon at Wells's house. Later Wells submitted to Ogden a section of *The Shape of Things to Come* concerning a patron of Ogden's, Lady Welby, whom Wells had not liked when he met her earlier. Ogden wrote a good criticism for Wells, and later used the passage in a book of his own supporting the new language! Wells continued to be quoted by Ogden, occasionally anonymously, in support of the language-simplification effort.

Their correspondence languished, however, and it was not until Wells had turned to the Declaration that they renewed their acquaintance. As was so often with Wells, a change in his reader's ideas had not been anticipated, and at first he misread Ogden. Ogden then produced *The Time Machine* in Basic, as well as the Declaration in 1943. How many read the Declaration in this form (or, for that matter, in other translations) is not known, but the effort to give it a wide audience took in every facet of life.[15]

The Declaration appears in its final form as Appendix C in the present work, but its various articles deserve some comment. The first article, after a long introduction, was a statement of the free and equal right to 'all the resources, powers, inventions and possibilities accumulated by our fore-runners, without distinction', and including the right to medical care, good health, and mental development. Education and the right to knowledge was the second right, and the right of free choice of employment was third. The ability to buy and sell without restriction, except as affecting the general welfare, was granted to all, and freedom to hold personal property and from violence made up the next section. The right to move about freely, along with protection of one's own home, was the central point of number six, while number seven laid down the limitation on terms of imprisonment, for mental or other reasons, along with the right of habeas corpus and conscientious objection to military service. Freedom from lying, libel and slander, as well as secret dossiers, along with freedom from violation of person such as sterilization, mutilation, torture, and other punishments were outlined in the next two articles. A more detailed statement of rights was to be easily available to all persons. To ensure democratic control a majority of persons had to accept, not only this Declaration, but all changes in it thereafter. Secret treaties, unusual legislation acts, along with orders in council and the like, were also forbidden. The document closed with these words: 'There is no source of law but the whole people, and since life flows on constantly to new citizens, no generation of the people can in whole or in part surrender or delegate the legislative power inherent in mankind.'[16]

Although Wells was to devote much of his intellectual effort from 1939 to 1943 to the rights of man, at least twice he also became quite interested in other matters, both occurring as side-issues to the rights campaign. One of these, an effort in association with Sir Richard Gregory and *Nature*, was reasonably successful and forms a part of British science history. The other, a stormy interlude with Sir Richard Acland, was just that, stormy, but also only an ineffectual interlude.

Wells and many other men of science, as they always called themselves at that time, were concerned that science was constantly in danger of prostitution when government requests for scientific help were heeded without much discussion. For some scientists, of course, it was a case of my country right or wrong, and this led a few observers to assume that science could be either right science or left science. J. B. S. Haldane, J. D. Bernal, and others hoped that it would be a left science, that is, a science which would be devoted to solving the problems of ordinary people, and one which would also lead to some sort of world state. Wells wavered on this subject somewhat, as he had been taught that science was apolitical. In the event, he learned differently; for many scientists, their research was available to the highest bidder, inevitably the state, the military, and the causes of repression and crude nationalism. Wells had been part of the campaign to enable Einstein and Freud to leave Europe ahead of the Nazis, and this effort apparently helped convince him of the need to organize the potential of science, and drop the pose of neutrality. He was joined in this new cause by Sir Richard Gregory, his old friend from South Kensington, joint author of Wells's very first book, and since 1917 or so, editor of *Nature*, the leading journal of science in Britain.[17] Gregory used as a focus work in which he and Wells had been associated since 1917, through the British Science Guild.

Norman Lockyer, president of the British Association, had spoken at the Southport meeting of that group in 1903, calling for an effort under BA auspices to co-ordinate public opinion with regard to science. The Association felt that this was too political a gesture and did not act on his advice; therefore, Lockyer, Gregory, and R. B. Haldane formed another organization, called the British Science Guild, of which Lord Haldane served as president until 1913. The group met from time to time, and issued a yearly report of its views, and such progress as it found, but did not make much impact. In 1915, as a result of the wartime pressures on science, that publication was expanded to a journal, and the journal, although edited by others, came under the purview of R. A. Gregory, who essentially ran the organization. He saw the opportunity and accepted the responsibility, as it was possible that scientific ethics and standards, especially in teaching, could be reinforced. He knew that Wells would support him in the venture. From this time *Nature* also began to publish editorials on affairs of the day, the first significant scientific publication to do so.

Gregory also published a little book in 1916, *Discovery, or The Spirit and Service of Science*. It was a call to join the sciences and the humanities, to aid in the creation of a better world. Other scientists who held similar views now began to press for expanding the scientific content in the Civil Service examination, and in the school curriculum. A public meeting, which Wells attended, was held in May 1916, and a Neglect of Science Committee, subordinate to the British Science Guild, was founded as a result. A joint meeting was held that October with the humanistic societies to thrash out potential changes in the examination. The Neglect of Science group also began to hold regular meetings, with E. Ray Lankester in the chair, to investigate the claims of Greek and Latin, the teaching of history, and the further development of what would eventually become the 'modern side' in British public and state schools. A further public meeting was held in January 1917, which adopted a seven-point programme urging specific reforms in these matters. Wells advised Gregory, Lankester, and T.L. Humberstone (another scientist-educator active in this campaign) throughout the proceedings, and twice, at least, spoke to significant audiences on these ideas.

Ray Lankester, seeing this as an opportunity to gain further public attention and discussion, with funds from the British Science Guild and other interested groups, published two books which also provided ammunition for the change. The first, a reprinting of papers on similar topics first presented by Faraday and his colleagues, was simply offered as an indication of how long science had been waiting. The second book published speeches from a second formal meeting of the Guild and the Committee on the Neglect of Science, held in June 1917 at the Mansion House. Wells, a prominent speaker at that meeting, gave his standard nationalistic plea of the time: 'Education is the ring upon which all the keys of national greatness hang. If education is right all is right.' Wells also called for the introduction into the curriculum of French, German, Russian, a better mathematics, a history of mankind, and good experimental science, all of which he said were badly wanted. The greatest need, he said, was freedom from the backwardness of classical education as then presented. Education, he remarked, 'which begins with the beginnings of speech on the mother's knee, is first and primarily *a training in expression*, ... then *a training in understanding*.' Wells then turned the speech to his own life, as he ended his talk: 'I want my boy to be as highly educated, as well educated, as possible. He is, if I can manage it, to be an illuminated man ... I want as earnestly to see my country and my English-speaking race thinking more massively than it does at present, thinking more strongly and clearly.'

Further books were published and speeches given in that period, and some change occurred in the civil service examination, and in the curriculum, at least in the state schools, and to some degree in the public schools. Wells remained extremely concerned with the matter, and it is this well-spring that produced *Joan and Peter*, and later his work with F.W. Sanderson at Oundle School. During the 1920s, the British Science Guild focused much of its effort on the Labour Party, as that seemed the group most likely to support change, but also the one most likely to come to power in the near future.[18]

The Guild acted as a collection point for books for Soviet scientists, after Wells returned in 1921 from his visit to Gorky and Kamenev. Ernest Barker, Victor Gollancz, P. Chalmers Mitchell, Bernard Pares, and C. Hagberg Wright, along with Wells, Gregory, and others worked on this project intermittently. A joint committee on cultural relations with the

Soviet Union was created in 1924, with Gregory and Wells as vice-presidents. In fact, as Wells told Gregory after a meeting of the group in 1925, he could not have carried on without his support, and that of their old friend from Royal College days, A. T. 'Tommy' Simmons, before his death in August 1921.

One of the persons who replaced Simmons, in his editorial capacity, was A. G. Church. Church, after a brave wartime record, had become secretary to (and the chief force behind) the National Union of Scientific Workers, which had been founded in 1918 by a group of Cambridge physicists and chemists, predominantly young. The Union wished to have a social and political impact on the general public from its scientific perspective. These young and anxious scientists moved quickly to organize themselves but were less quick to proselytize, apparently because their mentor, Ernest Rutherford, urged caution. He suggested that scientists would be better employed in their laboratories, and that journalists who had scientific credentials could do the work of proselytizing with greater success.

It was partly because of this set-back, and the general change in the intellectual atmosphere, that Wells had agreed to stand in the 1920s for the London University seat. After his second defeat, Church stood, also as a Labour candidate, for a vacant seat at Leyton in a 1923 by-election, and was returned. He became Parliamentary Private Secretary to Sidney Webb, and he and Wells exchanged several letters in the next few years over the role of government in science and education, and over their efforts to move Sidney Webb further than he wished to go in these matters, from his position as president of the Board of Trade.[19]

The Guild was much less active in these years, although Gregory, and to some degree Wells, attempted to keep it alive. However, both were very busy on other matters. Both Wells and Sanderson spoke at the 1922 dinner meeting, discussing their topics of science in education, and the need for more scientific method in schools. In the main, though, the work of both the National Union of Scientific Workers and the British Science Guild was confined primarily to propaganda, a few editorials in *Nature*, and similar matters. The issue was not dead, but it was moribund. It was in this context that Wells discussed with Lloyd George in 1930 possible changes in attitude within the Liberal Party. Lloyd George, Wells, and several members of the Liberal executive met for two weekends at Lloyd George's country home. Among other matters, they discussed scientific development, and Lloyd George urged Wells to get Gregory to focus these efforts from his vantage point. It was time, according to the former Prime Minister, for scientists to band together in groups and join progressive and intelligent Liberals to push their ideas. Wells sought advice from Gregory, but neither man could do more than talk and hope.[20] Few people were interested in reviving the old World War I committees, no matter how much the effort appealed to the two old friends.

Wells instead became interested in his project for a world encyclopaedia and the earlier idea was allowed to drop. At his seventieth birthday party in 1936, Wells mentioned the subject again; in a series of orotund statements on a variety of subjects, he allowed himself to say, 'There is no left science. Science marches on and marches on, neither to the left nor to the right, but straight forward.' J. B. S. Haldane could not contain himself after this judgement, and responded to Wells calling attention to left science in the USSR, both in archaeology and palaeo-botany, and right science in Germany, where eugenics research was nothing but propaganda for the state. Haldane said this sort of perversion of science was being produced in Britain as well, and took the opportunity to call for subsidization of real science in Britain, and for the Labour Party to work towards that end.[21] So the general idea remained weakly alive.

After Wells's appearance at the 1937 BA convention, with all the fuss that it created, neither he nor his friends were content, and at the next meeting of the Association they debated a proposal to create a division of the group to deal with the social and international relations of science. The group was formed with Gregory as its first head. In fact it was meeting, at Dundee, when the war broke out. The group adjourned with the news and the failure of the speakers to appear. It did not meet again until 1941. Gregory, in the meantime, was elected president of the British Association itself.

The debate over the subjects in which that group was interested and over other world events led to a significant meeting of the British Association in 1941. Before that, however, discussion continued on the role of scientists and government, and when the war came and science was mobilized, the need to see that the end results of research would be broadly useful came increasingly to the fore. Gregory continued to make the columns of *Nature* available to the discussion, and himself contributed to the debate. Wells spoke at various student meetings, as did others, and eventually Gregory gave a talk over the BBC on British science in which he raised many of these issues again. Wells also spoke to a group of science teachers early in 1940, when he ventilated similar ideas.[22]

Early in 1941, the campaign to control the future of research grew more serious when Wells reviewed Gregory's new book, *Discovery and Invention*, for *Nature*. Wells described men of science as 'social aristocrats'. The ultimate reward to the researcher is not money, or so wrote Wells, but the 'innate conviction of the supreme value of his role'. The review called forth some critical response, and in his further remarks Wells challenged scientists to act like 'brains with a backbone'. Julian Huxley used the exchange, as well as the climate of opinion, to ask Wells to chair a session at the forthcoming BA meeting, and to be host at a dinner for foreign delegates. The general subject of the meeting was to be 'Science and the World Mind'. Wells seized his opportunity to bring attention to the Rights of Man Declaration, and he and Gregory in turn discussed a Charter of

Scientific Fellowship designed to establish the freedom of science from governmental pressures. Science, of course, was implicated in the present war by its failure to resist governmental misuse of its findings, and many scientists knew that. Such resistance could only come through joint efforts, or so thought Wells, Gregory and their supporters. A seven-point set of principles provided the focus for the debate in London. These had had their origin in the discussions held intermittently since the Cambridge group had been formed in 1910.[23]

When the meetings were held they seemed a bit incoherent, as too many speakers (ten) were scheduled in Wells's session alone. Wells, in the chair, was asked to cut back his remarks, and he was piqued by the request. He and Huxley had a brief exchange at the meeting, and later, although Wells could never long remain angry at Huxley. Some persons thought Wells's comments had been censored, and a tempest over this misunderstanding blew up in the press.[24] In fact the conference as a whole went off very well, and two major publications resulted, carrying the message of scientific freedom and, coincidentally, the idea of world fellowship and co-operation. The British Association published shorter versions of the talks in its *Transactions*, including an excerpt from Wells's speech, but discussion of the import of the whole meeting was so great that a separate book was eventually produced by the governing council of the Association and made available as a Penguin Special in 1942. The meetings had originally been set for Rothamsted, but interest in the conference, especially from the Nazis who monitored the BBC, was so great that London replaced Rothamsted as the venue. A month later Soviet scientists met in Moscow with a similar agenda.

In the three days of meetings in London, representatives of the USSR, China, the United States, and nineteen other nations discussed the postwar world, and the role that science could play in that world. Six major sessions were held. Gregory chaired the first, on 'Science and Government'. Ambassador John Winant of the US was in the chair for the second, 'Science and Human Needs'. Ivan Maisky, Soviet ambassador to Britain, chaired the third, 'Science and World Planning'. Wellington Koo, from China, presided over 'Science and Post-war Relief'. Eduard Beneš, exiled premier of Czechoslovakia, was in charge of the fifth session, 'Science and Technological Advance', while Wells presided over the final session, 'Science and the World Mind'. The Royal Institution was host to the event, and the proceedings were broadcast over the Empire Service (later the World Service) of the BBC. Featured in these events was a transatlantic radio round-table discussion by most of the major Nobel Prize winners of the time. Among the speakers at the meetings were several who had assisted Wells in drafting the Declaration of Human Rights. The air was charged with high purpose, and the ideal of world peace and freedom, led by the best scientific minds, must have seemed a real possibility once the war was over, and fascism defeated.[25]

The conference discussed the seven principles which Gregory (and probably Wells) had produced for the earlier discussions. Although a fellowship of science was not created, some progress towards that end was seen, and hopes for the results continued high. As Gregory said in his opening remarks to the conference, 'We stand as representatives of science for those very principles of order and fellowship within the human race by which alone we can hope to preserve what is best in civilization and to feel confidence in a higher destiny for humanity.[26]

Having been unable to give his entire speech to the session he chaired (his voice failed, and time was at a premium), Wells summarized his address, while introducing the other speakers. He felt, however, as did others, that the speech itself deserved a wider audience. Later in the year a small company was formed to publish the text, and copies appeared — not in large numbers, as paper was at a premium too, but nevertheless, appeared — along with appendices giving both the Declaration of Scientific Principles and the Declaration of the Rights of Man.[27]

The speech was a good statement of Wells's fairly well-known views on the shrinkage of time and space, the rapidity of change since the turn of the century, and the failure of education to note the change, especially in the area of history teaching. From these ideas he drew and reiterated the need for control of the air and international transport, control of world resources, and a declaration of fundamental human rights. He used, in his speech, as frequently before, his idea of a supernatural visitor who asks the difficult questions Wells himself was putting. He offered ideas on world language, as well as his views on the supposed lack of variety some felt was inevitable in the new world, and he called for science (or, as he termed it here, human ecology) to solve these problems, by developing a world encyclopaedia, a better language of communication, and the association of science with human rights which he was already supporting. The speech, as fitted the occasion, was somewhat optimistic. As Wells remarked,

> I do not know how it feels to belong to a species that is failing to adapt. I have lived my seventy-five years in an ascendant phase, but I should imagine our children and our children's children and all the young life about us will pay pretty bitterly, in ignominy, in privation, in straitened unwholesome lives and general brutalization, as Nature, without haste and without delay, after her manner, wipes them out.

And, although this was clearly the trend he saw, he still felt, as did most of his auditors and readers, that a mingling of hope with reality could avert these results. Wells said that this hope was the message of the conference.

When he came to publish his remarks Wells took the opportunity to discuss other speeches at the conference. He was specially moved by the talk by Sir John Orr, on human nutrition, as well as one by Sir John Russell, and by Philip Noel-Baker who spoke at the same session on feeding the world's population. All in all, Wells, as well as Gregory, Haldane, Huxley, and the others attending, must have been thrilled to contemplate the world which seemed to loom after the war. The cruel reality of modern science had not yet interfered with such feelings.[28]

Some people thought Wells's remarks reflected an anti-Bernal position, and he had to disabuse them of this. Young persons who heard him or read him had located Wells as a scientist again, however, and they began to put him forward as a candidate for fellowship in the Royal Society. Julian Huxley and Gregory were also active in this effort. The campaign forms a sort of leitmotif of Wells's last years, leading him eventually to seek a formal doctorate in science.[29]

A second, less useful, and much less significant result of the rights discussion was Wells's brief flirtation with the 1941 Committee, which later, in 1942, became the Common Wealth group. Wells was always a target for such potentially left-fascist type groups because of his isolation from party structures, as when he had been approached earlier both by Major Douglas on behalf of social credit, and by Oswald Mosley for his various ventures against the ruling forces. Wells rejected both of these earlier advances, and eventually he would do the same with Sir Richard Acland and his followers. Acland began his campaign to woo Wells very early. He wanted him to stand for Parliament at Ripon as an Independent Progressive in 1938. But Wells was about to leave the country on his trip to Australia, and not much interested anyway. Vernon Bartlett then became a candidate for another seat and was returned in a remarkable result. Both Liberals and Labour supported Bartlett's candidacy and Wells made a token two-guinea contribution to the effort.[30]

Acland was a member of the Liberal Party and Wells had known him in a vague way since the Fabian days. Acland called a meeting in February 1939 to ginger up the Government, as he put it. Wells agreed to speak at that meeting, but was ill when it was finally held. The meeting and the organization were rather ill-defined. Acland continued his efforts to win Wells, however, and early in 1940, while the debate on human rights was in full sway, he had a meeting with Wells and Ritchie Calder to discover whether there were joint interests to be pursued. Acland circulated to Wells and Calder a rather poorly constructed memorandum calling for the co-operation of progressive parties. Both Ritchie Calder and Wells were very suspicious of the possible tendencies of such a group towards fascism. Wells wrote to Acland and told him his views on the memorandum; in describing Acland's recent book, *Unser Kampf*, which had the same problems of structure, he apparently wounded Acland's sensibilities. Charges of personal Führerism went back and forth, and Wells broke off the correspondence early in 1941.

Still, when Acland revived his idea after the foundation of the 1941 Committee, also concerned about the direction of government, he invited

Wells to participate. Wells hoped the new group would adopt the Rights of Man as a working plan, and he apparently agreed to participate on this basis. One meeting was held which broke up in acrimony, ostensibly over the spelling and orthography to be used, but in fact, over Acland's methods and purposes which seemed to some of those who attended to be quasi-fascistic, whether Acland knew it or not. As Wells earlier said to Acland in one of his letters, 'They [Acland's objections to the Rights of Man document] bring out the peculiar confused quality of your mind. It slips to and fro between existing conditions and desirable conditions. . . . I think it is quite impossible to work with or lend countenance to you.' Wells later noted on this letter, 'There seems to have been a lull in our correspondence after this.' Both Violet Bonham Carter (representative of the real Liberals, of course) and Wells resigned from the committee after this April meeting. Wells continued to read their material for a time, but his flirtation with the group effectively ended soon after it began. Acland remained active, and his group did, in fact, go in the direction Wells and others predicted; after creating a stir in several wartime by-elections, however, it faded away.[31] The goals of the group were so inchoate that socialists as well as proto-fascists could be attracted to it. Eventually this was to be the reason it died out.

Wells was absolutely right in this particular situation, but false rumours of his interest in the group continued to appear in the press, and he found himself forced to correct the record several times. He finally asked Marjorie to prepare a chronology of events as he wished to protect himself against these smears. Eventually the press dropped the subject and Wells was now free to pursue his goal of getting the Declaration of Rights translated, discussed, and accepted by the world's population.[32]

Wells was indefatigable about the Declaration, promoting it, providing it in many forms for discussion, correcting errors in interpretation, and pushing it as a necessary aim of the world's population once the war was over. This activity on behalf of the Declaration took up much of his time through 1943, and into 1944. The Declaration continued to haunt him, but as he grew older, and more tired and ill, other things also claimed his attention. Ultimately, however, it is this activity for which he would wish to be remembered, one suspects, although the activity is much less well known than some of his wartime books. This campaign is the optimistic Wells at work — the Wells who believed, as he did all his life, that our species could prevent what seemed to be inevitable. Of course, the dark Wells — who knew in his heart that in human history there was little enough to suggest that the challenge would be met — was also present, as throughout his life. Both play a role in the last spurt of work, but the dark Wells is more subdued, repressed even, in the high excitement of the Declaration and its possibilities.

Olaf Stapledon, Wells's science-fiction writer friend, now serving in the forces, realized how important the Declaration might be, and he enlisted in the campaign to promote it. RAF Coastal Command Forces discussed world affairs at prescribed intervals in their units, and Stapledon saw to it that among the discussed items were the clauses of the draft Declaration. Wells was concerned that the discussions, without adequate leadership, would fall prey to propaganda, and he warned Stapledon especially of odious material emanating from the Polish government-in-exile. Stapledon reassured him, remarking that 'young men mean business and I want to strengthen their position . . .' However, he went on to suggest that giving them books such as *The Outlook for Homo Sapiens* and *Phoenix* would do the job better, as 'young people are roused not by appeals to rights but appeals to emotions.'[33] Wells needed more such supporters to circulate his message.

Wells was always on the lookout for misquotation and misinterpretation of his work, and his files contain many letters to the press, asking for, or demanding, retractions. The rights of man issue prompted fewer of these than some of his publications, although even here his watchful eye produced examples of the frailty of editors, or worse still, the stupidity of the breed. He subscribed from 1920 or so to a cuttings service which provided him with many comments he might not otherwise have seen. Three examples of his watchfulness show the range of his responses, especially on the Declaration. He was much more likely to be vehement or abusive when it was his personal life or work being discussed than on the Declaration, as here his sensibilities were less wounded if some discussion of the Rights ensued.

He always monitored *The Times* and the *Manchester Guardian*, and when one refused to print a comment, he usually sent it on to the other for publication. The *Listener* was also very important to him, as when they misinterpreted his thoughts, he felt their potential audience — the radio audience — was so great that the damage would be difficult to overcome. Consequently, in these cases he sent on documentary evidence of his thinking — in one case the Preamble to the Sankey Declaration itself. It was the organs of the Left which worried him most, however. The Progressive League published a cyclostyled journal called *Plan*. When they criticized the Declaration in *Plan*, he responded with a letter calling their remarks 'pretentious rubbish'. They published further criticism of the rights without printing his letter, and he resigned his vice-presidency of the group because of what he termed 'censorship'. However, this was a minor storm, and soon he again allowed *Plan* to publish his letters and continued his general support of the group.[34]

Much of the activity around the Declaration was good fun and exciting, of course. Most groups of the Left accepted the rights with little discussion, but they did on occasion discuss areas of disagreement. When *Plebs*, the organ of the National Council of Labour Colleges, commented on Wells's defence of the right not to work, he responded with thanks for the criticism, but he did note that 'The times are very late and unless we get our minds in unison and establish a clear world-wide common purpose, destruction will find us squabbling.' Wells, in fact, joined organizations in order to foster discussion, and in one case offered to adopt a position in opposition if it would stimulate constructive criticism.[35]

In the long run, his real concerns were not criticism but rather translation and circulation to other countries and areas. In the event, the Declaration was translated into Czech, Welsh, French, Danish, Spanish, German, Icelandic, Russian (Moura did this one), Italian, Polish, Gujerati, Hausa, Swahili, Arabic, Urdu (Gangulee did this one), Hindi, Bengali, Ganda, Yoruba, Basic English, Zulu, and Greek by 1944. Publication followed each translation, and Wells paid much of the translation and publication costs himself. Publication occurred in at least fifteen places, most of it through the foreign-language press based in England during the war. Wells was excited at the response, and as he said to Harold Keble when he was discussing translation into Asian languages, '. . . I am jubilant . . . We are letting something loose that will do *great* things for once.'[36]

By 1943, the *Daily Herald* and Ritchie Calder had become involved in other matters, and Wells (and of course Marjorie) now took over as the secretary of the group. It became their responsibility, self-assumed, to oversee the translation and distribution of the Declaration. Wells was roused by the new challenge and his correspondence in 1943 is filled with efforts to promote this crusade. In addition much of his formal writing, both for the press and of books, was concerned with the crusade. The old warrior, as we may call him in this regard, roused himself at the age of seventy-seven, tired, nearly alone, occasionally ill, to do remarkable work in his effort to preserve the species, or preserve the world for the species. As he said in a 1943 article on Russian prospects after the war, 'I am a full-time onlooker at the ever swifter world tornado through which we are all trying to steer.' After saying that his readers should hold back their comments on Russia until after the war, and calling for the Declaration as a guide to the future, he went on to remark, 'We have no alternative; we must come together. This is so manifest, so entirely inevitable, that it is only those who will not think or listen or whose minds have been perverted by dogmatic teaching who will resist its onset.'[37]

Wells circulated many copies of the Declaration himself, especially to persons whom he thought would be of use in further distribution; to Herbert Read, for instance, to whom he confided that he was 'greatly obsessed by the great revolutionary project'. He urged Read to join the campaign. Priestley, Wells, and Winant, along with some other Americans (Herbert Agar, probably) met for luncheon over the rights. Wells also attempted to enlist the *Daily Worker*, again being published, and favourable to Wells as he had supported them in the period of censorship. He called on Jan Masaryk as well, to whom he told his fears of 'the short-sighted advantages' which people would seek if nothing were done. He made up his old-time quarrel with Fenner Brockway, and Brockway, after meeting with Wells, printed the Declaration, along with another Wells letter calling for a 'fundamental equalitarian socialist law for the whole world'. Among others to whom Wells addressed special pleas for help were Chaim Weizmann, to whom he apologized for his general tactlessness on the matter of Jewish desire for a homeland, saying, 'In these urgent days there is a need for a fundamental solidarity in creative work that should rule out these minor resentments'; Alexandra Kollontai, whose aid was sought in getting the Declaration into the Soviet Union; Julian Huxley, as he wished the Brains Trust (a remarkably successful BBC programme) to discuss the matter; and finally, J. Christian Smuts, whom he invited to tea 'for a gossip' and to whom he said, 'The world is already committing suicide by misapplied, surplus energy, but there is no limit to what men can do to this largely unexplored planet if they really set about it.'

Among others to whom he appealed were Antoine Delfosse, Belgian Minister of Justice and Information, who complained about a translation. Wells sent on a better version. He wrote to Herbert Agar (of the US Embassy staff) to appeal for a release of paper for a new edition, and to S. Rostovsky (of *Soviet War News*) to ask for help in Russia, citing Stalin's popularity as a reason for possible world unification. Even in the summer of 1945, his spirit had not flagged, although his flesh was weaker, and he roused himself at the very end of the war to tell A. G. Watson, while supporting a project Watson had mentioned on world unification after the war, that he would 'co-operate to the extent of my limited and failing powers. Just let me know how precisely.'[38]

Wells was a remarkably prolific writer (there are about 3,000 separate items in his bibliography) and he had a knack of saying things pithily, and occasionally with venom. One of the problems his biographer faces is this ease of writing and the consequent desire to quote from his works. Even when the ideas are similar, as in the case of rights of man campaign, he is still eminently quotable. In addition, he had a knack of tuning the material to different audiences. Of course, he made a great amount of money out of his journalism, and always had since the *Pall Mall Gazette* and *Saturday Review* days. He was very comfortable while writing casual occasional pieces, and as such pieces sold newspapers, he was always in demand.

Soon after the war broke out, Francis Williams attempted to get Wells to agree to a regular column, and he did visit the *Herald* and discuss the matter with the editorial staff at their weekly luncheon. A published debate with Barbara Wootton ensued over world unity and federation. Wells did not like being under continuous pressure to write, however, and eventually his main outlet of publication during the war period became the *Sunday Dispatch*, still closely aligned with the Labour Party, of course. Just as when he wrote almost constantly for the *Daily Chronicle* during the First World War, he had an agreement that he would write when he wished for the *Dispatch*, and if he thought the material would be of greater use in another place, he was always free to place it elsewhere. He used *Reynolds' News* and the *Evening Standard* for substantial pieces of a more topical nature, but the *Dispatch* was the place for his analytical pieces.[39]

Wells did, of course, write for other papers for money, as when he reviewed Hamilton Fyfe's book, *The Illusion of National Character*, for *Reynolds' News*, but such work simply gave him another forum. He also occasionally tangled with old acquaintances such as C. E. M. Joad, who Wells always felt was a sloppy thinker, but even here the controversy was on behalf of the real cause, the Declaration. Joad nearly always brought forth a comment from Wells, whatever he wrote. People like Joad, and Clarence Streit, author of a famous wartime book, *Union Now*, were to some degree anathema to Wells, as he felt that their thought was too shallow and too protective of older nationalism; he did accept a vice-presidency of Streit's Commonwealth Institute, but again, this was primarily to get the Declaration of rights discussed by sympathetic, if (to him) narrow-minded supporters. Eventually these forums were too weak for him, and he devoted most of his efforts to new, young groups, and to his large numbers of famous friends and acquaintances.[40]

He was much happier writing his journalism and turning out his books on the subject of the rights Declaration, as this, he felt, meant that large numbers of readers would discuss what was written, rather than the petty controversies so dear to the press and his long-time antagonists, all with their own axes to grind (not that he was free from axes and grindstones). There are eight major articles in his *Dispatch* offerings, for instance, that deal with the rights campaign. Mostly, of course, he simply called for the Declaration, urged people to move on it, discuss the clauses, and especially so after Hitler turned on Russia. This provided the real opportunity, for, 'All over the world, once we have tackled this war problem, the inevitable necessity will be to build and rebuild and build again, to cultivate and innovate unceasingly. There is no way out but up.'[41]

Within a month of his welcome to Russian entrance into the war on the Allied side, Wells wrote perhaps his greatest piece, which had the Declaration of rights as its focus; it was entitled, strongly enough, 'The Greatest Opportunity the World Has Ever Had'. In this article he described himself clearly as an 'observer', trained by Huxley, 'to show the way, but not lead the way'. But this crisis, 'the crisis of destiny' in his phrase, called forth every ounce of strength, as there was a need to cast off old ideas and look for absolutely new ones:

> We have to rescue human affairs from the independent sovereign stage; we have to conserve human resources from the waste of national conflict and reckless exploitation for profit; and we have to substitute an equalitarian for a graded society. Then we can hope to go on. Otherwise there is no surcease to disaster. Can we map such a course? *WE* can.[42]

In this last quotation alone, the dark Wells and the more powerful and more significant Wells of light both appear, and the words still ring true, as one faces today many of the same problems he saw in 1941.

The next month he continued in his optimistic mode as he welcomed the Atlantic Charter as one way towards his goal, and he maintained his drum-fire beat through the year 1941. In the worst days of the war he was always able to find hope, and his voice was an important one for his readers in Britain, in the United States, where many of his articles were reprinted, and wherever copies found their way to the forces, even behind enemy lines. As he remarked in a later piece, ever since *The Time Machine* he had been predicting that science and the machine would destroy mankind unless humans adopted a social and political life to control them both. In this case he was attacking in particular the Left, which was dragging its feet, and he ended with the telling phrase, 'Red means stop . . . When this revolution comes, we shall still have Mr Harry Pollitt [the CP leader] at the harmonium in his Little Red Bethel, leading the dwindling congregation with the old *Internationale* — while the collection is made.'[43]

Usually Wells was not so sarcastic, and especially when his audience was less well tuned to his ideas and method of attack. When he wrote for the mass audience of *Picture Post*, for instance, he was almost coy, as when he remarked, 'Certain facts have to be realized by mankind . . . the world is now one . . . the common people are walking up everywhere, because they realize the house of human security is ablaze and its official guardians are inert . . .' He remarked, to a wide audience which had just played host to the American visitor, 'We have no Willkie — but that is the ideal. The Mills of God no longer grind slowly; they grind more and more swiftly. There is no time to waste.'[44]

Wells tended to write for this audience when he was in a mood to convert his readers. His *Dispatch* and *Reynolds' News* pieces conveyed his splenetic personality to a group made up essentially of those already converted. His books were directed to both audiences, but with the spleen tempered, and the coyness alleviated as well. They are more middle-of-the-road, if one can use that phrase, in putting the Wells position. He wrote prolifically during the war, but two works, in addition to his Penguin Specials, were written primarily to support the work of the Declaration. The first of these, *Guide to the New World* (1941), bore as its subtitle, *A Handbook of Constructive World Revolution*. It was a collection primarily of pieces written for syndication, although most of them were not published in England. In the work he dealt with the war itself, Catholic propaganda, world law, Poland, India, included a lovely piece entitled, 'The British Countryside in 1951', wrote on the future of cities, Spain, civil liberties, Comrade Stalin, and of course, education. The basis of the book, however, was a discussion of the three items he had cited elsewhere at the beginning of the war as absolute necessities: (1) immediate world and air transport control; (2) conservation of world resources; and (3) the Declaration of

Human Rights. This book was a more clearly thought-out version of *The Commonsense of War and Peace*, and *Science and the World Mind*. Gollancz published it, and the book did well through much of 1942.[45]

One reason for its success was that the book appealed to people suffering privation, bombing, and the rigours of war. As Wells ended the work, 'In the last year or so, since death became an everyday reality for everyone, I have come to realize as I never did before that there is an accumulating splendour latent in the hearts of men which justifies and makes reasonable the utmost endurance of which any of us is capable.' Victims of the blitz did not mind that sort of sentiment and it was well deserved.

Wells's other book of the period was written with the same verve and optimism. Its very title, *Phoenix: A Summary of the Inescapable Conditions of World Reorganization* (1942), indicates the optimism inherent in the book and in the author. It is a more retrospective book, dealing, among other matters, with a history of warfare, as well as analysing differing temperaments and their reaction to crisis. But it went on to provide necessary analyses of what Wells thought the rights of man Declaration would mean to ordinary people, and to deal, gently but analytically, with criticism of it. It is, in fact, a lovely book, with much hope for the future, and it went into two impressions within a week of publication. *Phoenix* deals with human sexual relations, the ending of disease, and the potential regeneration of the species, along with calls for a world art, world literature, and world crafts manufacture. To use a phrase well-known in our own time, it calls for a 'greening of the world' and challenged the wartime generation to do that work. As Wells said, 'The World Revolution is a transformation by release; it is not a clearance and a new start. The new human society we have sketched . . . , with its endless variety of types and occupations, its freedom of movement, its endless interestingness and its unending activities, is the logical realization of the latest accumulations of human experience. It is no more and it is no less.'[46]

Wells's only regret was that the book could not be published in the United States by a New York publishing house. He finally brought it out across the Atlantic with Haldeman-Julius, the famous producer of the Little Blue Books and other inexpensive democratic materials, in Girard, Kansas. In England, the book was published to very good reviews and comments. Many, if not most readers, found it a gleam of light, a return to the Wells who had heralded so many other good things throughout the lifetime of his readers. 'V.G.G.' was early off the mark in the *Standard*, where the book was welcomed for its 'eloquence, fire, vigour, and the cleansing, heartening mint of ideas . . .' The book was 'a brave one and clear with vision'. Barbara Cole, while disagreeing or arguing with much of it, said to her readers in *Tribune*, 'Get it quickly before it goes out of print.' Wells sent a copy to Beatrice Webb, and she liked it as well. In thanking Wells she told him that he and GBS had the satisfaction of knowing that they were read throughout the world, which was a generous comment. On the book itself, she remarked that he had said he was tired, and so was she, but, '. . . you and we have at least the satisfaction of having lived the life we liked, and done the work we intended to do. What more can a mortal want — except to die a sudden and painless death.' Lord Horder, who reviewed the book in *Nature*, said that '*Phoenix* lays bare for us our categorical imperative.'[47]

If the end had come at that time, one supposes that Wells would have been happy with his contribution to the debate over the postwar world. In retrospect, even though we know about that world, we have to salute him and his memory for this valiant crusade. No one could have done more. The failure to heed his message is ours, and our leaders', not his. Increasingly, as the war went on, Wells grew more tired, and the bleak dark Wells showed through his writing more and more. Still, until the very end, the shining and pure Wells of the Declaration was always present. The anomaly of his life and works in these last days on earth remains interesting, although perhaps not all of it can be approached with the same hope and vigour as the days of the Declaration and the meetings with Francis Williams, Ritchie Calder, and the others who pushed that cause forward.

SPINNING DOWN THE VORTEX

There is something more comprehensive than the individual, to which he belongs, out of which he arose, which existed before he appeared in the world, and which will outlast him. That in biological reality is the human species, but so far as a man's mental existence goes he may not think that. He may refer himself to a family, to a tribe, to a public school or a college, to a real or imaginary 'race', to a creed — indeed, to one or several of a vast variety of larger aggregations. In varying moods he may fluctuate considerably in his terms of reference. That is how he thinks and feels. The biological reality is that while he remains capable of communicating and inter-breeding with every variety of human being, his individuality goes on as a unit in the whole species, and, whatever the delusion of community to which he hitches his mind, it can have no narrower boundary than the species from the ecological point of view . . .

By education the harsh blows of natural selection were mitigated, and behind the screen of its protection a premium was put upon Educability. The history of the tertiary eutheria is a history of brain developing inevitably behind the screen of educability . . .

The integrality of the individual has been a necessary hallucination varying enormously with the gregariousness of the variety considered . . . In the face of the hallucinatory quality of personality . . . this [the emergence of some sort of super-individual], so far as it retains any validity, resolves itself into a demand for a new and broader education throughout the world in which a federated political and economic order and a common fundamental law of human rights may afford a protective screen . . . behind which the great impersonal society of the days to come, with its unprecedented range of variability, may develop to the best advantage.

HGW, *A Thesis on the Quality of Illusion in the Continuity of the Individual Life in the Higher Metazoa, with particular Reference to the Species Homo Sapiens*, submitted by H. G. Wells for the degree of D. Sci., granted 1943

When one considers the output of H.G. Wells during the Second World War, it is impossible not to be astonished at the amount, as well as the quality. When the war broke out he was just about to mark his seventy-third birthday, and over the next six years, in addition to carrying on the rights of man campaign, a full-time occupation for most persons, he wrote three novels, three other significant works of commentary, about fifty important articles for the press, and three other short works which reflect his views on life and the outcome of the war. In addition, he worked on his D. Sci. thesis, and lived the life of a man of affairs. Most of this, it is true, was accomplished by the summer of 1944, but even later he roused himself to make a few more comments as well as write his last three short books. In fact, as one scans his life, although it is true that he was always active as a writing thinker, or thinking writer, whichever one prefers, it was during the three periods of greatest stress that he produced the most work, almost compulsively commenting on events in the outside world. The first period, those days of learning to write in the early '90s, coincided with medical predictions of a possibly much shortened life, along with his marital difficulties and the adjustment to life, first with Isabel, then with Jane. The second occurs during the First World War period (also complicated by his relations with Rebecca), and the third, although he was now living comfortably with Moura, is the period of the Second World War. The German challenge, in some sense a secondary theme throughout his life, seemed to cause an outpouring of writing, and especially journalism.

Much of his comment reflected Wells's views on the conduct of the war. Just as he had during the First World War, he felt the need to keep up the pressure on the enemy — to fight a war to the finish, a goal which he always feared the Allied leadership would not pursue. In January 1940, as an example, he advocated the bombing of Berlin, and later when Churchill finally replaced Chamberlain, it was with Wells's full approval. He exulted that 'the lurking and demoralizing . . . irresolution in high places is lifted'. However, Wells also believed that Churchill would be dangerous in the long run — he was good as a war captain, but his vigour and loyalty also meant that he had an 'incapacity for understanding the limitations and meannesses of unimaginative people'. Wells was especially concerned that Lord Halifax and Selwyn Lloyd were still present in the Cabinet, although he welcomed the new Labour and Liberal members, who might have 'an influence upon the still open and active mind of Mr Churchill. . .'[1]

Wells was solicited for comment on the progress of the war effort in most years, on the anniversary date of the beginning of the war. These comments were occasionally quite trenchant. In 1940, for instance, he remarked that even though a year had passed, all of the country had not yet mobilized. However, the results thus far were a tribute to the extraordinary qualities demonstrated by the ordinary people of Britain (this is not far from a similar comment made in the summer of 1915 at the end of a year of that war). Wells also called for a refurbishing of the military leadership and for punishing the guilty who had created the year of disaster. He was not alone in placing blame for the disasters, of course. (Wells wrote this article after *The Times* had refused an article letter attacking Halifax and other Tory members of the Government.) Two weeks later he returned to his first theme, as the response had been strong and positive in support of his earlier work. In this article, Wells reviewed Hitler's career, commenting that he had risen to power on the strength of racial and sexual prejudice designed to keep one class and group in power. Wells also predicted that both Russia and the US were likely to enter the war, and if they did, it would be absolutely necessary to upgrade British knowledge of their leadership, especially that of Russia, as the Foreign Office was remarkably dull and ignorant of Soviet affairs and potentialities. Now was the time to rid the Foreign Office of Halifax and his sort, utilize the information available from anti-Nazi aliens, and 'reorganize the national imagination and the national resources for our supreme effort. We want a vigorous reconstruction of the War Office and the Foreign Office now.' Wells even went so far as to say that he believed, 'at the *core of this folly is deliberate fascist sabotage*'.[2]

He thought that the British ruling class deliberately did not prosecute the war strongly, and one indication of this was the unwillingness to bomb Rome. This evidence (at least in his view) of protection for Catholicism led Wells eventually to write one of the notable anti-Catholic books of this century. But, for now, he simply called for all-out attacks on Rome and other Axis cities regardless of the damage caused. Wells pointed out that both St. Paul's Cathedral and Lambeth Palace had been hit, and '. . . if Rome *will* make war, war is war'. This charge brought forth many responses in Britain and elsewhere in the world, as it struck close to home for many readers. Wells would later return to this theme, but in the meantime, he also called for stronger propaganda efforts on the part of the Allies. The Germans attacked him for his demand that Berlin and Rome be bombed, and he was furious that they classed him with the Tory leadership. As he sputtered, 'Let's have less about the Royal family, and more about ordinary people. It is time we got it plain and clear.'[3]

During the summer of 1941, Wells wrote to *The Times* urging aggressive action from the Government, and Stanley Unwin, one of his publishers, wrote directly to Wells thanking him for the call. Thus encouraged, Wells continued his onslaught and in a further letter called for paper to be released for propaganda purposes. In fact he urged the US to send paper, rather than 'Bundles for Britain'. Wells constantly urged the US to enter the war, as did many other Englishmen, and these propaganda items seemed a way to provide still more pressure. Wells had already welcomed the Russians, and he urged the British to forget their anti-Bolshevik stance of earlier days (he was thinking more of Churchill in this regard, but his remarks applied to the Foreign Office generally). Wells also called for hit-and-run attacks on the French coast, as a prelude to a full-scale invasion, and Churchill felt constrained to respond to this demand, welcoming the idea, but saying that the time was not yet quite ripe for raiding the coast. But, it would come, the Prime Minister assured his critic.[4]

Wells continued his attacks on the weak war effort as he saw it, both by urging the Government to locate the guilty parties, and by calling for stronger and more imaginative military action. He urged the Allies to drop such right-wing supporters as Otto Strasser, and ended that particular article with these prophetic words: 'But it may not be the Atlantic Powers who will get first to Berlin, and it may be that peoples who have learnt at first hand what the German considers suitable treatment for an invaded people will anticipate them.' Later he said that the strength of mind of the English common people was poorly mobilized, and he called for a complete cleansing of potential Quislings at home. He described the 'profound conceit and snobbishness' of the upper classes and called them not traitors, but 'frustraitors'. These men of the 'better-not brigade', as he termed them, were the same ones who had been in charge at Hong Kong and Singapore, and he proposed a new slogan, 'Go, Get On or Get Out'. On the third anniversary of the declaration of war he again called for a bombing of Rome. This famous article was reprinted in many places in the world as indicative of the class differences still apparent even in the 'democratic' war effort. Wells's last words in the article still bear quotation: 'Anti-bolshevism, big business, and that long-cherished isolationism that still subordinates affairs to party politics mutes the role of America in this horoscope of the Fourth Year, the cloudiest factor in all its cloudiness.'[5]

With both Russia and the US finally in the war, the tide turned, however, and Wells's comments diminished in shrillness, although there were many things with which he was still displeased. He could indulge himself from time to time now, though, as when he delivered himself, early in 1943, of the remarkable piece, 'A Patriotic Outburst: The True Greatness of the English'. In this article he said that although he was still committed to Cosmopolis, he was also profoundly proud to be English. He gave his readers a pocket history of his English heroes, beginning with John Ball, another man of Kent, and one to whom he would dedicate one of his last books. He then proceeded to list his other heroes: Roger Bacon, Sir Francis Bacon, Isaac Newton, Lyell, Darwin, Cavendish, Dalton, Joule, Faraday, Rutherford, Huxley (although he was a Scot, said Wells), Wycliffe, T. S. Raffles, Cromwell, George Washington, T. Payne, A. Lincoln, Blake, Godwin, Shelley, and the Tolpuddle Martyrs. He asked, '. . . can any other country or tongue produce a brighter constellation?' This piece is typically Wellsian; although he spent his entire life in working towards a world state — Cosmopolis, as he termed it — he remained an Englishman, even a cockney, at heart.[6]

Wells was very active during this period of the war in seeing to it that proper information was made available to the English people. Paper shortages cut down publication, and Wells and others were concerned that paper be made available for the Left. Books of information such as the Webbs' *Soviet Communism* and Philip Guedalla's *The Second Empire* were especially important, he thought. The Webbs' book caused a small furore, as *The Times* held a letter of Wells on the subject for some time then refused it. The letter was finally published elsewhere. Others also exerted pressure and as a result a new edition of the Webbs' book did appear.[7]

After this time most of Wells's comments were focused on the postwar era, and the need to provide a world better than the one which emerged from Versailles. For instance, he urged the war effort to go at full speed and force even though some art treasures might be damaged. The need to eliminate the Nazis would outweigh the loss of such treasures, which had been copied, stolen, transcribed, and studied for three hundred years, according to Wells. For him, education was essentially the struggle 'against those who won't, or can't'. It was more necessary to rid ourselves of unwanted kings and queens, and look for personal self-respect and education, than to worry over possible damage. In England, Norway and Sweden, kings and queens acted under law, and perhaps this might set them apart, but by and large, 'Their antics endanger the lives and happiness of hundreds of millions. Life grows grim and realistic everywhere and a certain ruthlessness is creeping into the behaviour of long-suffering common men.' At the end of 1944, he urged that Churchill now be replaced as well, 'He has served his purpose, and it is high time he retired upon his laurels before we forget the debt we owe him.'

Over and over again, in the last months of his life, Wells called for the creation of more republican forms of government everywhere and the end of royal families and privilege. As he said, in another such article, early in 1945, 'Mankind is now one universal brotherhood or a vast hopeless confusion of mean and petty motives and evasions. There is no self-respect now possible for a man unless he is prepared to treat every race and sort and colour and cult of human beings with an equal respect.' And, in one of his last published articles, he remarked that, 'Monarchy, as the word implies, is the antithesis of Democracy. It cannot be anything else. Where there is a court, there are necessary honours and titles; an artificial and insulting inferiority of the ordinary man is ensured.' Wells recalled that fifty years before he had been the only English republican, but 'now the whole world is going republican'. If necessary, he said, some district in America could be set aside for royalty, where they could live in exile, conferring titles and honours on each other, a royal reserve of all the courts in exile; the world would then be unencumbered by them, and 'World democracy would resume its age-long struggle against the indifference of nature, for the attainment of the Universal welfare of everyman, of Mankind.'[8]

Wells was forever convinced that aristocratic leadership was weak leadership. Nowhere was this better shown than in his campaign involving Lord Vansittart and 'Vansittartism'. He felt that the proper people should be blamed for the war, not only in Germany, but also those who, in Britain, had allowed the situation to deteriorate into the morass of the late 1930s. When Lord Vansittart, who had written fairly widely on the German menace (*Germany's Black Record* [London 1940]), wrote to *The Times* late in 1942 discussing German militarism and the need to re-educate the German people in more peaceful ways after the war, some of the left press in Britain attacked him. Wells came to his defence, and Shaw then attacked Wells. In response Wells said Shaw's views were worth relatively little, as Shaw came from those who conquered Ireland, while Wells came from those in Kent who had been conquered. The points of view were different. Harold Laski then attacked Vansittart, and Wells was simply unable to understand this, as Laski was usually more rational than Shaw. The issue was that of winning the war, and not of whether the German state, the Nazis, or only certain Germans were guilty. (Of course, this debate took place long before the truth of the German complicity in the Holocaust was known.) Others in Britain commented on the little battle, and Wells then felt constrained to defend himself.[9] The issue was a small one, perhaps, but it was symbolic of major problems relative to the rights of man Declaration, and the whole issue of what the postwar world might be like — a return to the old ways, or perhaps a new bright world with freedom and liberty for all.

Wells did not leave the issue alone, and when Vansittart published another book, his memoirs, Wells commented, saying that it was all true, but why not publish it ten years ago, when it would have really helped; why wait until now? He then called for a world teaching of history so that these nationalistic mistakes would be eradicated in the future. The real issue under discussion by this time was what to do about Germany, of course, and although it fizzled out in the actual event of occupation, it is instructive to remember the debate, a debate between Right and Left reflecting differing perspectives on the Soviet Union. Wells and his allies did not fear the Soviet Union and could focus on Germany. Others saw Germany as a bulwark against the Communists and could perhaps forgive more of their ways of behaving. It is worth mentioning again, however, that this debate took place before the horrors of the camps became fully known.[10]

Where a person stood on the issue of the Soviet Union was a key to understanding much else about his politics, of course. When Hitler and the Russians signed their non-aggression pact in 1939, most persons in the UK did not comment, as it came as such a surprise. A few, like Wells, who had had such a long and generally receptive relationship with Russia, did issue statements, but it was not until Hitler turned his attention to Russia in the summer of 1941 that most people were prepared to be heard in public. Even then Russian entrance into the war was viewed by many as a mixed blessing. True, it took Hitler's attention away from Britain, but at the same time the memories of that earlier alliance lingered, and for many, especially on the Right, the Russians remained the real enemy. Wells continued to meet and correspond with Ivan Maisky during the interim period, but as I have noted, their correspondence did not rise much above polite remarks on what people were reading.[11]

When the German attack did come, those in England who were well disposed towards Russia wasted little time in forming an Anglo-Soviet Public Relations Committee, and an Anglo-Soviet Friendship group. Wells joined as soon as he was asked. Rallies were held in England to build up the friendship, and although Wells did not attend many of them, because they were held in the winter when he rarely went out, his name appeared in the programmes as a supporter, and he wrote fairly continually urging others to support this cause. These articles appeared mostly in England and the US, but also in the Soviet Union itself.[12]

Wells and Maisky continued their correspondence during the wartime period, each apparently attempting to use the other for his own purpose. Maisky always responded in a friendly way to Wells, who sent him copies of all that he wrote. However, when Wells urged Maisky to call on Stalin to enter the war against Japan, the friendship cooled slightly, as Maisky felt he had to teach Wells some history. Maisky said that 'Hitlerite Germany was the main bastion of the world reactionary forces', and thus it was better for the USSR to concentrate its efforts there. Maisky later was instrumental in getting the Wells–Uspensky correspondence published in the USSR, but when Maisky supported de Gaulle at a slightly later time, Wells wrote in pencil on the letter, 'I don't think I'll answer. Later if only to take the opportunity of being amiable.'

Wells finally did write to Maisky, but only to urge his support for staging Gorky's play, *The Lower Depths*, in London. Maisky responded with the Russian aphorism, 'Every vegetable has its own season', and said that this was not a vegetable for this season. Wells continued his campaign in support of the play, pointing out that it was performed in Moscow, therefore why not London? Wells said to Maisky that the British people did not like the Communist Party because they had 'a strong aversion to being spoon-fed', and so let them see the play. The correspondence continued, and the two met to discuss the matter but the play was not performed. Essentially this marked the end of the correspondence. Wells continued to support the acts of the Soviet Union, and Maisky continued to see Wells from time to time, but these were the cordial meetings and salutations of old friends and without much content. Wells was a supporter of the Russian state, much as he had been throughout his life, but the support was distanced by events, especially in the very last years of his life, when the Russians moved more strongly on to the world (or at least the European) stage.[13]

Wells's relations with other Allied countries and groups were more sedate and less burdened with hidden meanings. He was a great supporter of France, but not of de Gaulle, and urged dropping a pamphlet addressed to the French people, of which he had written a draft, when the French surrendered in June 1940. Later he frequently took the occasion to write for French publications and to speak over the BBC to French listeners in their own language, which he spoke fairly well.[14] He was also quick off the mark to support the Czechs (and his old friend Beneš), Polish Jews, and the Spanish Republic. He spoke at meetings late in 1943 of the last two exile groups.[15] He sent fraternal greetings to the Chinese allies, which were duly translated and published in the press for the soldiers of China to read; he supported and spoke at meetings of Italians in exile, and supported Indian independence — not fast enough for Nehru, but certainly fast enough for Leo Amery, who was then in charge of the Indian Office.[16]

The one place where Wells stirred up a rather massive response to his comments was in the area of religion. His *Outline of History* had already been heavily attacked by Roman Catholics, of course, and these attacks had only served to solidify his views on Catholic irrationality. He extended that perception to most organized religion, but saved his strongest attacks for the Roman Catholic Church.[17] We have already seen how his calls for the bombing of Rome and attacks on Italian cities were received. This reaction simply reinforced his views and so he delivered himself in 1943 of a polemical diatribe against the Catholic Church, entitled *Crux Ansata*. This book, which appeared in hard cover in the United States, was published as a Penguin in England. Catholics were very unhappy with the book, and with Wells, not least because he called the Church 'the Black International', along with a number of other choice epithets. His earlier attack on Strasser had been part of a campaign of anti-Catholicism, and his views were inflamed more when the *Catholic World* supported Strasser. Wells then sought the aid of his friends Richard Gregory and Ernest Barker, for more bibliography supporting his position on Catholic ultra-montane influence in the war and before. Barker responded with a book list, and Gregory and Wells discussed the matter over lunch.[18]

Crux Ansata was a short book, which after asking again why Rome had been spared bomb attacks, responded with a short history of Catholicism. The history is quite straightforward, although the interpretation angered many, as when Wells described heresies as 'experiments in man's unsatisfied search for truth'.

As might be expected, Wells also gave considerable attention to the motivation for the Crusades — not religion but the need for capital and employment for rootless youth. Wells described again his 'typical Catholic' of the fifteenth century, Gilles de Rais, the rebellions against oppression, especially of Wat Tyler and John Ball, and the Reformation and Counter-Reformation with a strong account of the Jesuit order. In these sections Wells turned his knowledge of the life and work of John Milton to good account, and made use of contemporary British historical work. The book ends as Wells pays his respects to English and American Catholicism, along with the Church's then-recent manifestations of an increasingly aggressive proselytism under Pius XII.

Clearly the anti-Catholicism Wells had always entertained, and which had been inflamed by Belloc's attack on *The Outline of History*, had bubbled up again in the wartime atmosphere. *Crux Ansata* simply paid all his old debts.[19]

When *Crux Ansata* appeared it brought forth a storm of protest from the Catholic press, and a storm of support from persons on the other side. Wells was kept busy with letters, to the press and to his supporters, as well as with interviews, and meetings with Catholics who felt duty bound to try to cure him of his evil or at least misguided ways. Wells never recanted, and although his opponents carried on the fight even after his death, he had paid his tribute to Roman Catholicism as he saw it, and for him, that was the end of the matter.[20]

Wells, throughout his life, was engaged in what he described in one place as 'the race between education and catastrophe'. When he wrote or spoke with his acid tongue against a person or group it was always with the idea that they were contributing to the other side. It was his duty, and that of all right-thinking persons, to persuade them of their error, and to move them into the proper lane. As time went on and the science which he loved continued to produce more and more horrors, the future of the race seemed less and less sure. That was when the dark Wells, the Wells of *Mind at the End of its Tether*, emerged, although even here, surprising as it may be to those who have not read it, there was a residue of promise. For he always thought that this species, unlike the dinosaur or the trilobite, possessed a capacity for renewal and rejuvenation, through education, that would be in time to prevent the disaster. The other Wells, the optimistic force, although usually impatient, was the one which produced so much that is worth reading today, so much with its strong messages of the future, and so much that those who lived in his own time could cling to as a way to live their lives in the terrible wartime days, especially of the blitz and Dunkirk.

So, with all the other matters on which he wrote and spoke, there were these sanguine areas that deserve some attention, as he continues to speak to our time no less than to his own. Wells, for instance, was concerned that potential allies in the battle against Germany were interned and prevented from helping the cause, and he said so, loudly. Those who detained them were guilty of aiding the enemy, or so he thought.[21]

Wells thought that this sort of error would not have been made with a better education system. The two systems in England, one for technical knowledge and one for the upper class, had produced two thought patterns, and the crucial need was to bring them together. He called for the study of 'human ecology' and produced a new word, 'eutrophy', for what he had in mind. He closed his discussion with, 'A eutrophic world from which priest and pedagogue have been swept away as antiquated evils is now quite within the range of human possibility.'[22]

He called for 'Professors of Ecology and Professors of Foresight' to lead this educational revolution, as

> a rising tide of human common sense and consciousness threatens to swamp all the most cherished traditions of nationalist history by a realization of the common brotherhood of man . . . Man may fail in his last war. Many great and dominant species and classes of life have failed in the past. For a time they dominated and then they passed. Man may rise to this transformation of war. There is no guarantee whatever that he will. But he can. To that his whole past witnesses.[23]

He rejected premature efforts at drawing a new map of Europe, although he did attempt to enlist his friend, J.H. Horrabin, in a new atlas of substances for use in renovating the world. Eventually Horrabin produced, for Penguin, an atlas similar to Wells's ideas. For Wells, however, it *was* necessary to punish the war guilty in Germany, revamp German (and English) education, and work for the New World. 'A world education, a common science and philosophy for all men will not abolish the varieties of mankind. On the contrary, it will preserve them,' Wells remarked.[24]

Wells was often blunt, and when he was, those whom he attacked fairly danced with rage. One of his *causes célèbre* during the war was when he printed a letter from a Zulu Lance Corporal commenting on the lack of race prejudice among common soldiers, and asking why this was not true of South Africa. Wells, using comments from his relatives (brother and nephews) who had lived in the Union said that it was the only way the old guard there could preserve itself. His remarks on that country still ring true.

> What sort of black man do you want to have to face when the inevitable adjustment comes? If you let up these poor devils now, you will get a civilized deal. If not, race rebellion. They mutter of past glories and of toleration they enjoy no longer. The more you decivilize them the more savage and vindictive and merciless will the conflict be. I ask you, when all the rest of the world is made equal and free, how can the petty white tyranny of your system escape a convulsion?[25]

Other enemies danced their jig of frustration when he predicted the imminent decline of newspapers in this new world he was supporting. He said that newspapers were filled with bias and this had to be eradicated. Wells later backed away from this prediction somewhat, pointing out, in his defence, that he had followed a very boring speech, and had only five minutes to fill and was unprepared. He attempted to say that he was being facetious, but on the whole the comment rings true.[26]

The old man was on much stronger ground when he confined his judgements to education, speech, the role of religion in the proposed

Education Acts, and similar matters.[27] Here his listeners liked what they
heard and the promises held forth for them. In the cold bleak winters of
war, Wells's writings were a beacon of light pointing the way to a better
world. But, as with other promises of the future, the world could not be
that much different. Here his readers and listeners drew the line. Wells
knew this too, and usually did not allow himself to be caught out with the
sort of remarks he made at the newspaper meeting.

At the beginning of the war, Wells had published a book entitled *The
Fate of Homo Sapiens* (1939). Later he had offered a programme to deal
with the world he saw there and this appeared under the title *The New
World Order* (1940). At the height of the Axis triumphs, his publishers
asked him to rework the two books, as they felt that the promise possible in
them was needed by readers. He did redo them as one book, and entitled it
The Outlook for Homo Sapiens. It sold widely in late 1942 and throughout
1943, and was a selection of the book club, Readers' Union, so that its
message reached a fairly wide audience, at least among the middle class.
The subtitle describes it well: 'an unemotional Statement of the Things
that are happening to him [Homo sapiens] now, and of the immediate
Possibilities confronting him'. Lord Beaverbrook, the former Max Aitken,
to whom Wells sent a copy of the first version of the book, immediately
responded with what might have been the comment of most readers.
Aitken liked it all, disagreed with much of it, but said, 'It is a long time
since you set up in business as the governor of the world reformatory of
recalcitrant children. But now at least you look at the brats, not in hope but
in irritated dismay.'[28]

The new book marked the end of the sort of journalism and writing that
provided prescriptions for the world's ills, which Wells had been doing for
much of his life. From this time on his writing became more and more
personal (although not entirely so, of course). In the 1942 *Homo Sapiens*
book, with such chapter headings as 'What Man Has to Learn', 'Estimating
Hope', 'American Mentality', 'Resistance to Utopianism', 'Decadent
World', 'Disruptive Forces', 'Politics for the Sane Man', 'Declaration of
the Rights of Man', and 'Russia, the West and World Revolution', Wells
allowed both sides of his personality to have their say. As one reads it
today, both sides of the Wells message come across clearly. The race is still
on, and to the death. The winner is still not determined, although the odds
are lengthening on our species, and very rapidly. Those odds can be
closed, and the race can be won, but the effort of mind it will take, as well
as the necessary expenditure in the right plaes, is phenomenal. The
outcome is still unknown, but Wells put the challenge clearly. In the book's
last chapter, also published in translation in *Soviet News* and widely
circulated behind the Iron Curtain as well as to British and US readers, he
urged establishing the 'Final International', 'to guide us on this next great
step forward towards a liberated and unified Earth. . . . We world
revolutionaries of the West and the East need to get together now, to talk

plainly and exhaustively to each other now and to hammer out our common objective in the years ahead.'[29] This was his message at the mid-point of the war, and through the years, to today.

By 1942, Wells had also produced his last formal fiction. *You Can't Be Too Careful*, *The Holy Terror*, and *Babes in the Darkling Wood* were all written during the early days of the war, or before, and reflect the last educational campaign tours. The rights of man campaign, with its attendant journalism, took up most of his time and effort in the first years of the war. By his birthday in 1943, Wells was coming up to the last months of his life. He turned seventy-seven that autumn, and a lifetime of fighting enemies, in the guise of his various illnesses, and also those that beset him because of his personal life or his personal views, had taken its toll. He had a weak chest, but had fortunately been able since 1920 to spend nearly every winter outside London. Even as late as 1940–1 he had been on the road in the US, and had had a good month on the beaches and in the sun of Southern California. Now such travel was out of the question, and London (still the London of fog, wet, smoke, and bad air before the anti-pollution campaign of the 1950s) was where he must spend the rest of his time. The old ailments, some of them dating back to the last century, began to crowd in on his old age. His son, Anthony West, believes that Wells had grown senile as well. It is probably more to the point that old age had simply taken its toll, and while he could still rouse himself for a battle, for a meal, for a debate, even for a walk, in between such occasions he sat sunk in thought, and less responsive than in earlier days. Certainly his bodily activity slowed tremendously. By the autumn of 1944, most of the writing was finished. There were still two or three more projects, but they were the work of the good hours and the better days. The work habits of sixty years were perceptibly broken off. Even so, from time to time, even in the last year, flashes of the old Wells shone out. For the biographer, interestingly enough, more personal material from this essentially private man is available: since he could not travel, could not see his old friends, he wrote to them more frequently, and they to him, in these last few months of his life.

Wells was a highly private man in many ways, but it is clear that his neuroses about recognition also remained just below the surface. Perhaps his friendships among the upper middle classes and minor aristocracy were fostered by this need to be accepted. Certainly the thread of this need for acceptance runs through much of his writing and his personal journalism is filled with it. He 'knew' better than did those in charge, from experience, and others ought simply to accept his judgements. Only their inherited position, and their upper-class education, prevented these people from learning from him, or so ran the theme of much of his later work.

He began to receive even more recognition from some of his older comrades and friendly enemies. Shaw, reviewing *Outlook for Homo Sapiens*, said the book was good, that it must be read, and then, revealingly, described what he perceived to be the difference between himself and Wells. According to his own account, Shaw was a seventeenth-century Protestant Irishman using the tools of Swift and Voltaire, while Wells was a nineteenth-century English cockney always in revolt against unbearable facts and exasperating follies. To get what was needed, one must read them both, said Shaw — calling for a Wellshavian personality.

Although Shaw and Wells apparently did not meet many times after Wells's seventieth birthday party in 1936, they continued to exchange cheerful letters of abuse and friendship. Wells refused to sign a letter Shaw circulated, calling on the warring powers to respect art objects. 'I'd like to keep them but not if they lead to idolatry,' said H.G. Later Wells told Shaw that his education had been faulty, but that he was still citing him as an expert on phonetics in his British Association speech. Wells even asked his physician in to talk to Shaw about his and Charlotte's health. Apparently he gave them all tea and presided over the 'argy-bargy'.[30]

Beatrice Webb also strongly renewed her friendship with Wells, helped, no doubt, by Wells's gracious comments on her eightieth birthday. She wrote to him several times before her death in 1943. She also came and took lunch with him once or twice. Wells, after hearing that she had enjoyed *You Can't Be Too Careful*, was ready to renew their old connection. He remarked in his letter to the Webbs, that 'We wasted too much energy upon mere differences (of method and so on) in the Fabian movement that would have been better spent, perhaps, on aggressive attacks on the fundamental enemy. I and the Blands and G.B.S. were inexcusable coat-trailers.' In her reply, after a brief discussion of their differences over Soviet Communism, Beatrice accepted the overture with 'Meanwhile I greet you as one whose ideas do not substantially differ from my own — as well as an old friend of 40 years' standing'.[31]

One other from the old days was Sydney Olivier. Wells continued to send his books to Olivier and the very elderly man always read and remarked on what he found in them; however, *Boon* and *Tono-Bungay* remained his favourites. After receiving *The Outlook for Homo Sapiens*, Olivier told Wells that the species was 'played out', for 'Bladesover and the Wild Asses of the Devil are simply too much for us': 'You see I was bred among the hangers-on of county society, as a son of a clergyman, and know how deep its roots go. Hence I am not as sanguine as you, but do you go on writing books.' Later Olivier told Wells that he doubted that Homo Tewler could win out, and still later that year told his younger friend, 'Never say die until you are dead.'[32]

What Wells really wanted as much as anything, however, was to be elected a Fellow of the Royal Society. Many of his friends hoped for this as well. Although it is true that many of the 'no' votes were politically inspired, or so one assumes, it was also true that his career in science, except in the social sciences, had ended long before. So, in order to fill this gap, at the age of seventy-five, Wells began work on a doctorate in science. To receive an extra-mural degree from London University, he had no need to do any course work, as the degree reflected his lifetime of study; but he thought a piece of original research was called for. He presented his thesis to the faculty in 1942, and was granted the D. Sci. The subject, a logical choice, given his life work and training, dealt with the notion that members of the higher species, especially *Homo sapiens*, were somehow different from one another.

Wells maintained in the thesis that there were a few differences, but that the systems of behaviour which were the crucial factor and which appeared to be different, were really the same; the differences perceived were actually an illusion basic to this species. He described the growth of inhibition, the development of the concept of self, and other psychological matters, with an especially good section on dreams and other auto-sensitive behaviour, using to good effect the work of Jung, J. B. Watson, and Pavlov to help make his points.

The second part of the work dealt with the place that education had taken and might take in modifying natural selection and completely reflexive behaviour. In Wells's view, *Homo sapiens* was and is heterogeneous, and he brought in a good deal of evidence from palaeo-archaeology and anthropology to develop this point. In other parts of this rather remarkable work, he discussed the idea of an overall Creator, as an answer for those who refuse to think clearly, as well as the role of gregarious behaviour in aiding the illusion of difference and superiority. Wells felt that the only role of any real use this hallucinatory concept of personality might play was in demanding a newer, broader education and a fundamental law of human rights as a screen for adverse behaviour. There is, in addition, an interesting discussion of the role of sex and sexual drives, both in primitive peoples and in Wells's own time, given as an adjunct to the other aspects of the work. Wells ended the thesis with the statement that his view of individuality of personality as illusory need not inhibit individual behaviour, but would and could make that behaviour more group-oriented. He closed the work with, 'But the only way that will end these presumptuous idea-systems will be for them to die out, as those who are swayed by them die out, before that growing sense of reality which a younger, more completely revolutionary élite will create.'[33]

I have covered the thesis in this much detail because it is the scientific justification (with a heavy dose of psychological thinking) of Wells's life's work. It follows directly from what he learnt from T. H. Huxley, and could be transformed easily into *The Time Machine* or *Babes in the Darkling Wood*, to take two widely separated fictional treatments of somewhat similar material. Wells told Gregory in the spring of 1940, as he thanked him for his newest book, 'I have got very keen on what I might call psychosynthesis as a manual of the ideas of psychoanalysis.' This was happening because of his writing *Babes in the Darkling Wood*, which Wells described as about two young people who ask, 'what on earth *are* we — and why?'[34]

Scientists were quite impressed by the thesis. Julian Huxley made detailed comments on it for Wells, which were, in part, introduced into the final form of the work, and Huxley later borrowed some of the ideas of the thesis for his Romanes Lecture in 1943 (the fiftieth anniversary of T.H. Huxley's famous lecture under the same auspices). Still the FRS did not come. Gregory supported him, as did Haldane. Wells told Haldane in a letter addressed to 'Dear Jack' — 'I feel that if I am to pull my full weight in public affairs I must accumulate prestige of this sort.' Haldane told him in reply, 'If you can continue to outlive certain distinguished scientists I have very little doubt that you will be elected.' However, no matter what efforts were applied, the honour never came. Politics was simply too important, or inertia and the crust of custom too great.[35]

Wells spent much of his energy in these last years on more personal pursuits. He kept a sort of commonplace book during the period, and published the first half of it in an unusual work entitled, *'42 to '44*. This book is a sort of pendant to his autobiography and is almost entirely made up of his observations on how humans were behaving during the Second World War crisis. The thesis became an integral part of the work, and was properly published with it. Wells kept up the habit of making such notations and apparently had some idea of publishing a second part of the journal-like work, but in the event, abandoned that idea, and produced only a fragment, *The Happy Turning*, from the material. *'42 to '44*, published in a limited edition of only 2,000 copies, is quite personal in nature. It includes, in addition to the thesis, discussions of cruelty, personalities such as John Ball, Gilles de Rais, pieces on Irish neutrality and the U-boat war, interspersed with material on the Declaration of human rights, human rights in South Africa, and world education. From some writers this might seem bottom-drawer material, but from Wells it allows us to see somewhat more clearly how his mind functioned. Ideas came, were set down, refined, modified, and then made their way into more analytical work which was finally published. At this stage of his life, Wells was carrying out every stage of the process on paper. In earlier times, as we have seen, he usually wrote two drafts of each work — one after the first stage of synthesis, and that draft then interlined heavily with balloons, new sentences, crossings-out, and other attempts to refine the presentation. By that stage, however, the ideas were all clearly in place already. Now Wells was allowing his readers to see the earlier stages of the absorption of material.[36]

One issue on which Wells did not need to let the material soak up new concepts before he responded was that of press censorship. When, early in 1941, Churchill closed down the *Daily Worker* as being detrimental to the war effort, Wells reacted strongly. He had not supported the CP, and he thought the *Worker* an obscurantist journal, but closing one newspaper might herald the closing of others. It could not be countenanced. He wrote a powerful article, and later when the National Council for Civil Liberties took up the *Daily Worker*'s cause, he chipped in here as well. He was straightforward enough in his comment: 'Interference with free discussion in Great Britain in the interests of predominant political groups and persons has tainted British news with a flavour of untrustworthiness far more detrimental to our reputation abroad than the stark lying and falsification of the German propaganda.'[37]

Wells told the *Worker* Defence League that he had 'utter contempt' for the Communist Party, but he sent them a series of cheques to sustain their activities, especially so when paper became scarce, and the *Worker*, by then no longer banned, was being published only with difficulty. He continued to send his contributions and in 1942 also enclosed 450 copies of his correspondence with Lev Uspensky, a Russian aviator, on the Declaration of human rights, for their use. In December 1942, the *Labour Monthly*, Palme Dutt's publication, published a letter from Wells on Communism, which was a change of heart for them, but symbolic of how much his support had been worth. The *Worker* hoped to get him to make a personal appearance, and whenever a rally was held always sent him platform tickets, as well as invitations to dinners celebrating their right to publish. Wells never went, but he continued to send money from time to time, although he also took the opportunity to lecture them, especially on their support for de Gaulle.

At the end of 1943, the *Worker* was happy to publish an article of his on Oswald Mosley and his relation to the ruling class in Britain which Wells could not publish elsewhere. In fact, the *Worker* produced it as a leaflet in addition to its appearance in the paper. Wells thanked them, saying, 'Now it's socialism or hell. After all I backed you up when you were banned.' In 1945, while refusing one more invitation, Wells still had some good words for the *Worker* and its place in British journalism. After saying that he could not appear, he said his advice 'to every newspaper and every young man' was to 'bear hard to the left and keep to the left. Down with industrial ownership. To hell', he said, with 'Big Threes, Big Fours, Big Fives and any sort of Bigness' that was against the universal rights of man.[38] Wells and the CP were not quite done with each other, but this episode of press freedom had stirred up some ties which had lain dormant for years, and both sides benefited.

Before discussing the last days of Wells's social and personal life, the events surrounding his death, as well as the comments on his life by those who survived him, it may be useful in this summary of his last work to comment briefly on his later relationship with the BBC.[39]

Wells did write a five-minute talk in 1940 on the 500th anniversary of the invention of printing, but it was only part of a symposium and was never published. Once he had spoken, though, the letter of payment went on to say that 'Now that you have broken the spell of silence in broadcasting, I hope that you will be willing to keep in mind the possibility of giving further talks for us'. In fact several other talks were proposed, but did not come off — one on writing as more important than the sword of war (but Wells was in the US), and an abortive talk to the Near East (the Middle East today).[40] Eventually, at the end of 1942, Wells and several other scientists were asked to give talks in a series. Wells agreed, though he could not resist a gibe at the BBC for their delay in calling on him. He proposed a talk on science and the conservation of world resources, especially phosphates, once the war was over. Wells went on to say, 'I write slowly and polish carefully. How long can you give me for completion of my draft? I do not think I can get it into speakable shape until well in the New Year.'

The series of talks, eventually entitled 'Reshaping Man's Heritage' (the original title was 'Man's Place in Nature'), began with a memorandum early in August 1942. Wells was approached very gingerly by a student of Gip's, and through Marjorie. Originally he had been vetoed as a speaker, because of his membership in the Radio Freedom League, a group opposed to censorship. The plan for the series was kept alive, however, and when some months later it was revived, Wells was offered 40 guineas: 15 for the broadcast talk, and 25 for its publication in the *Listener*. His letter setting out his views, along with his comments on the Declaration of the rights of man, stirred more dovecotes at the BBC, and several internal memoranda circulated, worrying about whether he would attack classes or groups in his talk. As a result Julian Huxley was asked to monitor Wells's talk, and to urge him not to go too far on phosphorus; also to find out whether he could speak on either fisheries or whaling as well. Wells agreed to talk to Huxley, but said he would not comment on whaling. He then replied, within a month, that the talk was ready, but said he did not wish it to be touched, as it was timed to take exactly twenty minutes. As he had done on other occasions with the BBC, he asked if he could come on ahead, settle down, be comfortable, and if pressed, said he would not refuse a whisky and soda afterwards. In the event the BBC did ask him to modify one passage slightly, and to add a sentence. An orchestra stood by, prepared to fill a minute or so of the time, although it was not needed. Wells apparently got his whisky and soda as well, although the archives are vague on the subject.[41]

Wells's talk, broadcast in January 1943, was printed in the *Listener*, and later in a small volume along with other talks in the series by J. C. Drummond, W. F. Crick, W. G. Ogg, Haldane, Huxley, and others. In this talk, Wells put his case clearly on the need to catch the revolution now, or 'spin down the vortex to extinction'. He discussed the abolition of distance, the tremendous increase in mechanical power, and how these had made it possible and necessary for the new world order to be egalitarian.

This was the bright and cheerful Wells, saying that all were learning together, and final conclusions for the entire race must be reached as a group. Huxley thought the talk admirable and they exchanged references on phosphates and their location.[42]

Wells gave another talk on science on the BBC's Pacific and Australian Service at the end of April 1943. It was a summary of the Home Service talk, which by this time had appeared in the *Listener* and apparently attracted some attention down under. Wells also spoke on the French Service at least once, at the end of 1944. In that talk, after apologizing for what he called his atrocious French, he spent a half-hour on the work of F.D. Ommanney. He took no money for this talk, as it was a contribution to the war effort, or so he believed.

The BBC asked him several more times to talk, and even offered to record the talk at his home. He did give them a minute of comment, for someone else to read, on their hundredth programme on science, and there was a brief attempt to interview him after the atomic bomb was dropped on Japan. Wells declined, as he was too profoundly tired and unhappy; the young men now running the service were in any case not very happy with his voice, nor with his possible remarks, so the entire matter was dropped. After all, on the Bomb, Shaw spoke for most Britons when he remarked that Wells had made it all clear thirty years before, and there was nothing left to say.[43]

Wells had left the BBC well. The reviews of the science series and of his talks were favourable, and the *Perthshire Advertiser* topped them all with '. . . his intellectual activity is one of the wonders of the modern world.'[44] The old man and his friends must have been happy. With this bow to modern science and technology, he really left the public stage, however, and was now on the side-lines, active mainly with his friends and family, but without many more public appearances of any kind.

DESPERATELY MORTAL

So far as we can tell, death is not inherent in living matter.
Protoplasm may live forever, as a flame shielded from the wind and
fed from an endless store would burn forever. But the triumph is
barren as it is the individual life that appeals to the emotions.

HGW, unsigned article, 'Death',
Saturday Review, 23 March 1895

Space was extremely important to Wells — space and place. All one has to
do is think of Spade House, Lou Pidou, and Easton Glebe to know that
where he was had personal and psychological significance. Even an address
was significant. For nearly every residence Wells occupied in London, he
had stationery engraved with the address. The only places not so
distinguished were those he used to meet his women friends. Rebecca's
house, Amber's house, are not places we can easily identify today. Wells's
last home was 13 Hanover Terrace, on Regent's Park. As addresses go in
London, this was and is a very good one. Only a few locations, such as
Eaton Square or Cheyne Walk, could compete with it. Wells lived there
for the last decade of his life. It too mattered very much to him. With space
such as this, how one treated it was important.

In 1935, Wells had a formal garden planted at Hanover Terrace. An
expert gardener, Lady Allen of Hurtwood, wife of a radical companion of
Wells's in the birth-control battles, oversaw its care once she had planned
it. The plantings were special and a fig tree had pride of place. The flowers
were replaced regularly. This garden, of which Frank Wells's wife later
took over the management, was an important place in Wells's life; towards
the end of that life he mentioned it and described it in his short work, *The
Happy Turning*.[1]

Dogs were a problem at Hanover Terrace, however. Wells used the
garden as a place to work and dogs yapped and barked. Hammering,

singing, music lessons, children, parties, all these were all right, but dogs were difficult. 'Cats supply an ever present but inaccessible stimulus to canine self-expression, and also the little fellows bark to one another, gardens away, with the utmost gusto.'[2]

Hanover Terrace took a considerable pounding during the war. By the summer of 1944, Wells was apparently the only permanent resident left; all the others had gone to their country homes, or rented flats elsewhere. But his house escaped the worst of the bombing, save some broken windows and doors, and Wells would not leave, although he was under pressure to do so from some of his friends and family. One of the other sometime residents, Sir Thomas Moore, allowed his house to be used as a Salvation Army hostel, and a service club for military personnel on leave. He then erected a large sign calling attention to the hostel. The sight of this sign became intolerable to Wells. Signs were forbidden under the terms of the leases in Hanover Terrace, and so H.G. decided to invoke the lease.

Wells sent Moore a letter, signed by Marjorie, saying that the sign cheapened the site, and that he wanted it removed. Another part-time resident, John Harrison, at No. 1, apparently also protested against the sign. Moore was, in fact, fined 40 shillings, plus 5 guineas court costs, for going against the terms of his lease, and erecting the sign. Open warfare broke out with Moore.

The *Star* diary and gossip column reported the incident, and printed a picture of the offending sign. The story treated Wells with kindness, and agreed by implication that the sign was offensive. Moore then gave a reporter his version of the letters from Wells and Harrison, and The *Star* printed this aspect of the mini-battle as well. A day or two later, Lady Sinclair, who had paid for the hostel, chipped in with her comments about the sign, attacking Wells and Harrison, although not by name, while praising the sign. Her article was entitled 'Respectability'. Wells was incensed over the whole matter. He was convinced that Moore was a supporter of the worst elements in Britain, and his comments about him, and the sign, were not very restrained. He drafted a memorandum (whether or not it was sent is unknown) saying that Moore had learned his trade at the feet of the editor of the *Catholic Herald,* and he enclosed a copy of *Crux Ansata* for him to read. He went on to enquire if Sir Thomas was a member of the Catholic right wing, engaged in frustrating 'the efforts of the scientific intelligence to bring about a final rational phase in the world of mankind'. At the end of the letter Wells asked further if Sir Thomas was the MP who wished to restore flogging.[3]

The incident of the sign was too good to let pass. Other papers picked up the story, and sometimes Wells was not as well treated as by the *Star.* The leasehold of Moore's property (under which signs were illegal) was held by the Crown, and not everyone knew that. Wells told one newspaper that if he had painted his house red, and erected a sign, 'Long live Stalin and the Proletariat', it might have been more useful than a sign supporting the

Salvation Army. Moore and Wells exchanged comments in the press, with Wells getting rather the better of it, by calling attention to the heavy bomb damage in Hanover Terrace and asking why Moore chose to live elsewhere. It was not Wells who had prosecuted Moore, however, but the Crown, and as soon as this became widely known, Moore took down the more egregious of the signs; and although Wells had proposed to put up a Left Information board, he apparently did not follow through on his threat.

Eventually he wrote to the press again, pointing out that he had no objection to the hostel, and offering a contribution to the work of the Salvation Army. He complained of the sign, as it was a breach of contract, and demeaned the place. In this letter, he said the controversy over the sign had dragged on long enough, and suggested he and Moore meet for luncheon at some neutral spot, and negotiate peace. The luncheon apparently did not take place, but Wells had made his point, and in retrospect, although it was hardly a significant event, it did give Londoners, suffering under the rocket attacks of the end of the war, something to chuckle over. Wells had also, incidentally, shown again that place and location were important — that an Englishman's home, if not his castle, was certainly not to be demeaned or made shoddy by others.[4]

Wells did get out fairly frequently for lunch, at least during the early part of the war. He enjoyed such occasions, because he saw his friends, but also because he was increasingly lionized by others in the restaurant, by the waiters, by his companions. He had begun to be a celebrity, and to a considerable degree he enjoyed the experience. In 1940, at the height of the Nazi drive to the Channel, Wells dined with William Hickey, who reported their meeting in his column. Wells cautioned Hickey (and by implication, Hickey's readers) not to put so much emphasis on the threat of Nazi invasion. He said that Britain was much stronger than in 1916, the time of a similar shake-up in the First World War. The Labour men were better, more experienced, clearer-sighted. For all practical purposes, said Wells, a man like Herbert Morrison was better educated than an old Etonian Tory front-bencher. Wells also reported that he was in fine health, and planned to remain in London. He was simply making his preparations for the coming air raids. Later, when he travelled in the US on his autumn lecture trip, he also remarked to a reporter that he intended remaining in London and that he regarded his visit to the US as in the nature of a furlough from active duty. He reported that all Londoners felt the same, when away from the blitz.[5]

Vincent Sheean tells a marvellous story of September 1940, just before H.G. went to America for the last time. He describes a lunch at Sybil Colefax's flat with the other guests Diana Cooper, Somerset Maugham, and Moura. A heavy bombing attack ensued, but H.G. refused to go to the shelter, 'until I have my cheese. I'm enjoying a very good lunch. Why should I be disturbed by some wretched little barbarian in a machine? This thing has no surprises for me. I foresaw it long ago. Sybil, I want my cheese', was his view of that day.[6]

Wells had been proposed for the Athenaeum, once he was seventy-five, but the cost of membership was really too high (£45 a year was the annual fee at that time) and Wells felt that he wouldn't use the club enough to make it worthwhile, so he declined. He continued, of course, to belong to the Reform Club, as he had for many years. He declined a number of honours now as he began to curtail his activities, because of both the war and his age. For example, he was nominated once again as international president of PEN, but declined in favour of a five-person board during the war period. Wells also felt the organization was rapidly becoming a British province, and that this would not do, especially in the afterwar period.[7] When remarking on his own career, and the presidency, Wells said, 'I have not ever climbed up into an ivory tower nor proclaimed art for art's sake. I am always a journalist and proud of it.'

Throughout 1941, Wells continued to attend luncheons and other occasions. Some of these were very pleasurable, as when his friends gave him lunch on his seventy-fifth birthday. R. A. B. Butler came to discuss education with him over tea at Wells's house, as did Nye Bevan who wanted to talk about some of Wells's writings. Tea became the customary time for visits to Wells, as callers could come to the house, and if he were tired he could always retire upstairs. He did occasionally venture out to preside over an anti-fascist meeting of one sort or another, and he and Maisky often had lunch, usually at the Soviet Embassy. By 1944, though, Wells had begun to refuse invitations, as when the Churchill Club met and wanted him to sit at the head table. Originally he planned to go, but finally declined, with the following note to the organizer: 'As Mr H. G. Wells has to die in the next six months and the work he has in hand is far in excess of his energy, he is regretfully obliged to cancel his engagement with you.'[8]

Even when he could not get out there were letters to write, and interesting subjects to discuss. He and Ernest Barker exchanged notes on Aristotle, and the drive of man to set up the polis. H. Newman and Wells commented to each other on the martydom of Jews, although Wells said in the correspondence that he was not a Christian, and was certainly not responsible for the 'utterances of the Archbishop of Canterbury' (who may have quoted, or misquoted, Wells). In a discussion with E. N. Andrade, Wells said that physicists should read more biology, and develop a consciousness of time values. This exchange came about apparently as a result of Wells's research for his thesis. He told Andrade to look up his first published article, 'The Rediscovery of the Unique', in which Wells had commented on split personalities, selective memory, and the fact that members of this species are not identical. Wells said to Andrade, as a clinching point, 'We are social creatures and we have to keep up a story about ourselves to adjust ourselves to our social life and create and satisfy expectation about our selves.' They lunched at the Athenaeum to continue

Wells said he did not care what food was offered, if the drink were all right.[9]

To old friends he was more talkative than ever. We owe to Ernest Barker the sight of H.G. at Cambridge, sunk in thought, but making the sharp rejoinder about his epitaph, '"God damn you all, I told you so"', and to C. P. Snow, the delightful account of a dinner in Wells's honour at Cambridge with young scholars, at which Wells outstayed Snow in the talk, and rose before him for breakfast. The old man could screw himself up to put on quite a performance, especially if the young were around to observe. Like all old men he simply began to husband his time, and his talk.[10]

As mentioned earlier, he and Beatrice Webb had renewed their old acquaintance, and in the last year of her life she came to lunch with him from time to time at Hanover Terrace. At the end of the letter quoted earlier, about the Fabian days, he reminded her, 'It's hard to judge in the retrospect, because *what might have been* cannot be produced for comparison.' After she died, writing to Sidney Webb to express his sympathy, he said, 'My only consolation is that long ago all our ancient bickerings died out and that my relation with you both was one of warmest admiration.' Wells did, as we have seen, get some paper so 'that last fine book of yours', *Soviet Communism*, could be reprinted. Maisky congratulated Wells on his obituary note on Beatrice, which appeared in the *Guardian*, and Wells agreed to lunch with Maisky if it could be a real chance to discuss these and other matters. He told Maisky that the Webb note 'was difficult to write for many reasons'.

Of course, Wells always corresponded and exchanged books with Frank Swinnerton, although by now, their widely different styles of writing meant that the two men simply exchanged greetings, but did not generally comment on each other's books. Wells did remark on Swinny's 'knock-about' style in one book, but Swinnerton had already anticipated him by saying that the book was 'not spicy enough for sophisticated tastes'.[11]

Wells renewed many other old ties from the Fabian days, as when he wrote a long chatty letter to Alex Thompson ('Dangle'). In it he remarked on progress in the difficult days they were experiencing, 'But we always said it had to be worse before it gets better and we youngsters (I'm a mere child of 76) who were brought up on the *Clarion* more or less owe to your generation that anyhow we are seeing things with clear eyes . . .' Wells went on to discuss all the old gang, Olivier, Sidney, Beatrice, Shaw, Charlotte, and then his current work. He urged that memoirs be written by everyone from the old times: 'You ought to be working on some memoirs of the old cycling days. The bicycle has come back to the world. When I get up to look at the weather, the bicycles go streaming by. I never rode a pennyfarthing but I was blacking my shins before the day of the diamond frame and the free wheel.'[12]

Wells was somewhat given to looking back at the past at this time. For instance, he wrote the The *Freethinker* recalling the days of 1881, when he

36 Wells in his study in wartime London, 1940. The T'ang horse was a gift in recognition of his influential writing

37 Still defiant at the end of his life

used to buy the magazine at a little shop 'to strengthen my faith'. *Mistakes of Morris* was running as a serial then with, as Wells recalled, 'bright little illustrations'. In a response to the Readers' Union, which had asked him for a comment on book reviewing, he was very charitable, for a man who had suffered from reviewers, when he wrote, 'The city of literature has many mansions and it reflects on nobody that it harbours a multitude of mutually exclusive sets.' Wells did comment that reviews ought to be signed.

His oldest friends now returned in force in his correspondence. Elizabeth Healey, always close to Wells, but mostly as a recipient of his largesse in the 1930s, again became a regular correspondent. Wells was delighted to send her tidbits from his life. At the end of 1941, for instance, he told her, 'The war is going fairly well now — believe me. I am inclined to be grumpy and rather miserable these days but remain [?] clear-headed and cheerful. . . . And the older one grows the more one values the friends of one's youth.' She apparently wrote to him every time she spied his name in the paper: that he was ill, had gone out, or whatever. He was always telling her not to worry (she was in Cardiff), as when he wrote,

> The clamour or fuss made about these robot bombs is ridiculous. They do not humble the right and the grey sane people, but they have, thank God, led to a great exodus of panic stricken boors, who when they get to the country lie and exaggerate to justify their own disgraceful cowardice. Here I am in the middle of it and only one window cracked by the concussion of an A.A. gun on Primrose Hill. . . . We stood up so well to the Blitzkrieg in the beginning of the war and this silly behaviour is disgracing the country in the eyes of all the world.

Later he continued to show his good spirits, as he reassured her, 'I'm keeping remarkably fit, but public affairs irritate and disgust me. I mend clocks and fuss about the decorations of the house to keep my mind off the follies of mankind. Bombs come and go, they hit next door or down the street or out in the park, but they never hit me.'[13]

His correspondence with these old friends, now that travel was difficult and the demands of work, especially on his younger friends, were so great, became increasingly meaningful. Reading through it one gets the feeling that many people needed to touch base with the old man, and he with them. Frank Swinnerton, after receiving a favourable Wells comment on his book, *The Devil Breaks Through*, said it very well; thinking back (in a few words already quoted) to the days of the work on Gissing, and the first introduction to *Nocturne*, he wrote: 'But first of all believe how much your letter means to me, and how much you have always meant to me. Real affection and unalterable gratitude.' Wells quarrelled with his old friend David Low and then, realizing what he had done, said that he would enclose a 'Halo in an asbestos box by next delivery', by way of an apology.

Wells said that he had been irritated by platitudes about the war, and 'I'm dying for a change'. To Beatrice Webb in 1942, the year before her death, after reporting that he had lost half a stone, and commenting that she had been right years ago when she had said people ate too much, he also remarked that he had had insomnia, but solved the problem with a cup of tea, work for half an hour, after which he became moody and slept. But then he wrote the crucial words which heralded their reacquaintance: 'How this justification of our life's work drives us together.' He told her that if she came to London, he would break any engagement in order to have lunch with her. When Jack Haldane said he was coming to London and wondered if Wells was 'well enough to abuse me orally', his old friend replied that he was 'only too glad for a disputatious evening'. Eileen Power, with whom Wells had ordinarily had such evenings, had passed away, and he was lonely for academic voices.[14]

Wells went out to see a J. B. Priestley play in the spring of 1943, and Priestley was pleased with his comments. They had a meal or two together, and the two became closer than ever before. Wells was as conscious of his friends and their illnesses as they were of his; he wrote to W. E. Williams, commiserating with him on the loss of several teeth — but, said Wells, 'I have lost all mine and then you have peace. Teeth are one of the very worst bits of the mammalian design and that is saying a lot.'

He had a bout with gout, and diabetes flared up again in 1944 so he had to write and reassure many friends. One such was Florence Lamont, to whom he gave a lot of family news, including the fact that Anna Jane was in New Delhi. He assured Florence, however, that he was still working: 'I will die from the toes up, so shall go on writing to the end.' He was really quite ill this time, and doctors forbade any exercise or excitement, although he still continued to write a few letters. As he told Brendan Bracken, 'Apart from gout, influenza, a disagreeable infection of my feet, February with an extra day in it, lack of sunlight, Anno Domini, and an inability to stop the war for a few hours while I think a bit, I keep as well as can be expected.' He was too unwell to go out to lunch with Gregory, but told him, 'although I'm very seedy still and the doctors won't let me out of my bedroom, my household will be delighted to give you lunch downstairs and then come up and have a talk.'[15]

By July 1944, however, he and Swinnerton were exchanging their regular letters, as Wells had improved greatly. As Swinny said to him, 'Wells was not tired, just a little gouty', and later, '. . . I hope that it will be very long before you get tired of the human race, whatever you may think of human imbecility. Hooroo!'[16]

Bombs did do a fair amount of damage to Hanover Terrace, and this brought more letters, but Wells himself was all right. Even Fred, his elder brother, roused himself in Bournemouth to write to the 'Buzzwacker': 'I hope that it is nothing worse than the colds you always seem to catch to finish off the winter.' Fred offered a room for Bertie away from the war zone if the cold and raids were too difficult. Then Wells's old agent, A. P. Watt, dropped in to chat; 'no business', he assured Marjorie, who now handled these aspects entirely. Bertrand Russell, hearing that Wells was again ill, also renewed his old ties, but as Russell said, 'Your personal news is sad, and much distresses me. And the élite of the world is not such as to inspire me for a wish for prolongation of a painful life.' They met once more, in June of 1945, and had tea. Russell said later that it distressed him very much to see H.G. so clearly in a dying state.

However, Wells again roused himself, and reported to Elizabeth Healey in August, that he was downstairs again, 'louder and sharper and better than I have been for weeks'. 'Flags and reporters flying.' Wells remarked that his 'relapses into health' were short and uncertain nowadays, 'but this is the brightest for weeks'. He was now beginning to go into the garden and to walk about again. Fred, hearing the good news, welcomed the revival, and said, 'I hope that the Buzzwacker will not lose heart, but will beat my innings of 83 not out.' Again, early in 1946, he hoped that Wells could take a brief walk in the park, but that time had passed by the time the letter arrived.

The journalists were forever reporting Wells at death's door, but he delighted in informing Elizabeth Healey, in particular, that he had outfoxed them again. He told her, in one of the last of his personal letters, 'I'm stronger and more vigorous than I have been for a long time. I'm bored by the spectacle of humanity and get no sort of satisfaction from being able to say, "I told you so" fifty years ago.' However, he told her that he had been consistent, and careless observers were the ones who said that he despaired. He quoted Stevenson as a guide, 'Take who comes to you and help the weaker brethren to endure.'[17]

The minutiae of life continued. His friends supported him, with occasional gifts of a good malt Scotch, or when Priestley brought back a warm pair of socks from his Scandinavian publisher. Wells became concerned about small things too — the brewing of tea, the sycamore tree in his back garden, but these were really trivialities. Two letters will give a better view of his life in the war period. To H. G. Koppell, of Alliance Books, when writing about possible publications, he closed with 'Everything is hectic, and dangerous here but with a sort of gaiety.' To his oldest intellectual friend he simply said,

> Dear old RAGS,
>   . . . I spend two thirds of my waking existence getting myself fit to do some work in the remaining third. [After remarking that he never went out any more except in the very best weather] I haven't suffered much except by broken windows from the flying bombs. They are most exhilarating and one feels one is somehow *in* it . . . Take care of yourself oldest and dearest of my friends.

To others he was less forthcoming. To a newspaperman, visiting him on what was perhaps the last such occasion, he recommended stoicism: 'Do what you think is right, and if the heavens don't play their part — well, be damned to them.'[18]

Marie Belloc-Lowndes had dinner with H.G. and Moura in April 1945. She told her daughter the next day that she had 'a most interesting evening'. 'He is so *very* clear and shrewd and, of course, he and I have, roughly speaking, known all the same people. He is tolerant and broad-minded. I did think him much changed. He looked very thin (diabetes).'[19]

One of the last times Wells went out for a formal occasion was to go across the park to a party given by Cynthia Asquith; and probably the last time was an unexpected appearance at the Roadfarers Club in January 1944. He appeared at the annual dinner, and when recognized, delivered an impromptu speech on the place of cycling in his early life. He spoke of the early days in the streets of Bromley with his 'wheel', the grand days of weekend cycle trips in the 1890s, and predicted a return to bicycle usage after the war. His vision of a 'green and pleasant land' must have been nostalgic and enjoyable in the dark days of the wartime London winter.

He also continued a little political activity, and apparently got out to vote in 1945. He agreed to support Mary Stocks as MP for the University of London. (Stocks lost by only a few votes the seat that Wells himself had contested more than twenty years before.) He also told the *Daily Worker* that he would support a regenerate Communist Party if there were one in his Marylebone district. He said that the headquarters of the local Socialist Party was closed, with notices of whist drives 'rather than the vigorous campaign notices with which the constituency should be boiling at the present time'. He was also concerned about the concentrated whispering campaign that implied that the next war would be between the Anglo-American cousins and the USSR. He thought that it was too 'uniform not to be organized'.[20]

In his lucid and active moments Wells did work on his last three major publications. By January 1945, they were nearly finished, although he continued to work away at them. He told Curtis Brown that *Mind at the End of Its Tether* was ready to go, and although he was not certain of the proper publication date, 'I want to see it put into type and corrected for the press before I die.' He offered to hold it up, if it conflicted with *The Happy Turning*, which had already gone to press. In the event it came out in late 1945, and was reprinted in the US in early 1946. Another version of *Mind at the End of Its Tether* was also printed in the *Sunday Express*, at the end of the year.[21]

Mind was not a separate book at first, and a good deal of confusion has attached itself to the work. Wells had been asked to rework the last pages of, and to add a chapter to, his *Short History of the World*, first published in 1922, and used as a set book in most British sixth forms. These pages appear in one form in that earlier work, under the crosshead *Mind at the End of Its Tether*; in a different form (mostly of structure, although there are some eighty-odd other changes) in the book of the same title; and again under the same subtitle in the newspaper, which has a still different text in great part. The three versions are all overtaken by pessimism, but even so, an optimistic promise, or rather a remote possibility, still shines through. Man could adapt, but the harsh rule is, 'Adapt or Perish', and there is no real reason to assume from recent history that that will (or even can) occur. Wells was convinced that some new animal would replace our species. As he remarked,

> Deliberately planned legislation, food shortages, and such-like economic processes, waves of sentiment for or against maternity, patriotic feeling, or the want of it, the natural disposition of love coupled with a desire to fix a relationship by some permanent common interest, and a pride in physically and mentally well-begotten children, may play incalculable parts in the production of a new humanity, capable of an adaptation to the whirling imperatives about us, sufficient to see out the story of life on earth to its end.

As was often the case, he spoke about himself in the course of the writing. He said, 'The present writer is in his seventy-ninth year; he has lived cheerfully and abundantly. Like Landor he has warmed both hands at the fire of life and now, as it sinks towards a restrictive invalidism, he is ready to depart.'

> He awaits his end, watching mankind, still keen to find a helpful use for his accumulation of experience in this time of mental confusion, but without that headlong stress to come to conclusions with life, which is a necessary part of the make-up of any normal youngster, male or female.

But ordinary man was at the end of his tether, or so it seemed to Wells. Only a small, highly adaptable minority of the species could possibly survive. Our species, *Homo sapiens*, is 'at his best, curious, teachable, and experimental from the cradle to the grave'. But leadership is needed, and does not seem to be forthcoming. 'That is the darkest shadow upon the hopes of mankind.'[22]

Wells was not a pessimist, but instead a realist. He did not think that negative ends had to come, but there was little evidence that they would not. It was up to our species, the only one since the beginning of time with the capacity to change the future. From *The Time Machine* to *Mind at the End of Its Tether*, Wells had believed it possible, but thought it very unlikely. The pessimism which many see in his work reflects those readers' own incapacity to provide for change. The most recent publication of *Mind*, by an anarchist press on the US West Coast, shows how his work can be misread, if one comes to it with cultural baggage as to its inner meaning.

While Wells was producing this book, he was also writing *The Happy Turning*, which by using his old theme of dreams, the new road opening into the future, along with the biblical knowledge of his youth, provides a very optimistic version of what might come. To paraphrase the work, we simply need to eschew Paul, and follow Jesus — not the divinity created by Paul, but the historical Jesus, the human teacher of love and peace.[23]

At the same time Wells also produced a third version of his life's work, in an autobiographical piece, 'The Betterave Papers'. In this last work, Wells reviews his life, and to some degree, dismisses it as not significant enough; but let him have the last word on his fiction, much as he has had it earlier on his science and his education writing: 'Fantasies. Such stuff as dreams are made of. We make them up out of the drifting desires in our hearts and they vanish if we do not lay hold upon them. The heart is there always, beating with desire, the waking mind snatches at them as they fade . . .'[24]

When this appeared less than a year remained of Wells's life. He was tired, ill, and there were times when he was not terribly lucid. He was at the end of his bodily tether. However, it is remarkable how he could rouse himself to make another comment, another point, just as everyone assumed that he was finished. He wrote an extraordinary piece for the *New Leader*, 'That Mosley Money'. He petitioned the Nuremberg tribunal to find out whether there were any data on Leon Trotsky in the Nazi files. He reviled a manuscript which fell into his hands, saying, 'I can suggest nothing for her but a complete abstinence from any further literary efforts . . .' And he told a group to which he circulated a memorandum that he was working on a film scenario, 'The Way the World is Going', as a sequel to *The Shape of Things to Come*, following the explosion of the A-bomb. He said,

> it is urgently necessary to dispel many short-sighted, cruel, and dangerous misconceptions of the significance of these things. . . . Man should face his culminating destiny with dignity and mutual aid and charity, without hysteria, meanness, and idiotic misrepresentations of each other's motives . . . There is no copyright on the future; anyone may write anticipatory stories providing they are original and not patently *réchauffés* of stolen matter.[25]

He lived on, perhaps with dreams of his film, perhaps not, until the end finally came on 13 August 1946. He told his nurse that he wanted to go in and lie down for a bit. Ten minutes later when she looked in on him, he had gone. Nearly eighty, he did not go down easily, but in the end, 'desperately mortal' as he was, he too had to succumb.

Now all that remained was to bring together those who survived, to talk about their old friend and companion — before they, as Winifred Simmons said to Marjorie, gave him 'to the ages'.

Marjorie notified his old friends and the relatives, and on 16 August, many of them met at Golders Green crematorium for a brief service, an opportunity to meet and talk and think about this man who had had such a strong impact upon their lives and on most persons in the English-speaking world. Winifred Simmons, writing to console Marjorie, before coming to the service, recalled her early visits to Spade House when the children were small. She enclosed a letter she had written to H.G. when her son (in the RAF) had crashed. As she told him then, 'One could ill spare your wonderful capacity for friendship . . . only your friends know that, though the world knows all about your literary greatness.' Elizabeth Healey wrote immediately to Marjorie, also recalling their friendship, stretching back to 1885: 'Although I knew he was ill, I always felt he would rally after attacks — as he had done since I had known him. It is a last grief to know I shall never see or hear from him again.' Christabel Aberconway reminisced about a tea party just two months earlier. Wells had been frail, but had talked with 'zest, impudent zest and gaiety'. She recalled how much he had aided her, and that they had talked again of Amber's daughter, Anna.[26]

Most of his old friends attended the cremation. His family, including his older brother Fred, was there. Swinnerton, A.M. Davies, Winifred Simmons, Rebecca West, Cynthia Asquith, and of course Gregory, were present. J.B. Priestley spoke.

Those who could not attend were equally stunned. A.P. Watt, dictating to his wife from a sickbed in Swansea, regretted that he could not be present. G. D. H. Cole, writing under instruction from the Fabian summer school, remarked that, 'His Fabian connections were long ago; but he belonged to mankind and to Socialists in particular all his life and we all felt how much we owed him for his long stand for sanity and decency in human relations and in the ordering of the society of man.' Winifred Simmons, again writing in retrospect after the service: 'Now, of course, H.G. belongs to the ages as one of the greatest thinkers but on Friday he seemed just to belong to his children and grandchildren and friends and I do appreciate your letting me come as one of them.'

After the service, Anthony West and G. P. Wells scattered H.G.'s ashes from an aircraft flying over the Channel between the Isle of Wight and St. Alban's Head.

Plans were laid for a memorial service in the autumn, and for some permanent tribute to his memory. To date, however, only a Labour Party hall in Bromley, and a park bench on Primrose Hill, London, to mark where the last 'ululation of the Martian' invader was heard over London, serve as permanent reminders of him.

Wells's will provided generously for his children and grandchildren. His estate came to about £60,000, after some small bequests to Moura Budberg, Gregory, his nurse, and £1500 to Anna, then (as he had said) living and working in New Delhi. The rights to *The Science of Life* and *The Outline of History* were left to G.P. Wells, with all film, cinema, and dramatic rights going to Frank. Other literary rights remained with the estate. The residue of the estate was divided into eighteenths, with Marjorie receiving two shares, Anna two, Moura two, and the remainder divided among the three sons. Funds have continued to accrue to the estate ever since, of course: the *Outline* is still in print, as are many of the early science fiction works, and the demand for radio dramatizations, especially of the short stories in the decade just after the war, has brought in money from the BBC and other sources. H. G. Wells died a relatively wealthy man, which was a tribute to his ability, but also to the place his writing holds in the canon of educated persons.[27]

Reading the obituary notices, and the leading articles on Wells published after his death, one is struck by how differently people saw him, although nearly always in the context of optimism. J. B. Priestley, when speaking to his relatives and closest friends at Golders Green, simply said,

> For this man was a man whose word was light in a thousand dark places. Since the beginning of this century, whenever young men and women, from the Arctic to the Tropics, were determined to free themselves from mental squalor, from superstition, ignorance, cruelty, and fear, there was H. G. Wells at their side, . . . eager to instruct and inspire.
>
> He knew, far better than we did, that life need not be a sordid greedy scramble; and when he was impatient, it was because he knew there were glorious gifts of body, mind and spirit only just beyond our present reach . . . . At his worse he never diminished and hurt us. And at his best he made us feel, as he did, that we live on a star.

The *Manchester Guardian*, in a leading article, said that the world had lost a great Englishman. 'In him there was epitomized the whole of that period of hopeful progress against which our own age stands in such sad contrast.' The Sydney *Morning Herald* thought that with the death of Wells,

> we shall pass into a blackness we can only imagine. Without men like Wells, we should be much poorer. While they are alive to make themselves heard, men of good-will feel comparatively safe. When they are dead, the world is left to the mercy of the bookburners, the Communists, the Fascists, the Ku Klux Klan, the extremists of all kinds, the frightened little men with big whips. That is why, one says, with the death of Wells, that the lights are going out in Europe.[28]

On the Left, and in the weeklies, they were despondent at their loss. Swinnerton reviewed his life and his attachment to his friends, closing with, 'Wells's teaching has passed. Therefore we who knew him have a clear duty which is to keep alive the memory of the merry affectionate genius we knew so well.' Bertrand Russell, after recalling their long-ago meetings with the Co-efficients, simply said, 'For my part, his death leaves me with an increasing sense of mental isolation.' C.E.M. Joad remembered 'the sense of liberation Shaw and Wells brought to my generation', and ended by remembering Artie Kipps most vividly of all. Julian Huxley wrote in the *Spectator*, recalling as Wells's contribution, 'nothing less than having done more than any single man of the present century to alter the current of modern thought, and to alter it in a progressive direction'. George Orwell also remembered Wells's extraordinary influence on the writers of his time, and recalled *The Sleeper Awakes* as an 'astonishing feat of detailed imaginative construction', not a bad judgement for someone obviously heavily influenced by the book.

The *Daily Worker*, in the person of R. Page Arnot, entitled their piece, 'He Always Fought the Old Order'. In *Tribune*, there were articles from T. R. Fyvel, from Wells's old editor, Hamilton Fyfe, and best of all from Bruce Bain, recollecting a rumour of Wells's death that had reached him while his troopship was coming home through the Red Sea. The rumour, he said, had left them 'flat, bewildered, with a conviction of personal loss'. Bain, writing from Streatham, called for a continuation of the Open Conspiracy from the Trojan Horses Wells had left in Streatham, Balham, Lewisham, Battersea, Bangor, and elsewhere.[29]

As time went on the tributes diminished in number, but not in the savour of their comment. John McNair, writing in the *Socialist Leader*, recalled receiving a cheque from Wells two weeks before his death, for use in the Battersea by-election then being fought. They had met together with Jimmy Maxton, a well-known ILP figure, whose death preceded Wells's by twenty-two days. 'They are together now, in the Shades,' wrote McNair, 'and Life, for those of us who remain, moves on, more slowly and more painfully.' Richard Gregory, in an obituary that stressed the least known side of Wells, simply ended with, 'Wells was . . . the greatest international scientific educator of his time.' Desmond MacCarthy wrote and read the obituary for the BBC Home Service which he ended with:

> It was when he projected himself as Mr Polly, Mr Lewisham, Kipps, Mr Britling, or Mr Pribble, and let the comic spirit and the cross-lights of the grandeur and pettiness of human life play around those figures, that he showed himself most an artist; and, though I can hear H.G. protest as I utter the words, when perhaps he taught us most.[30]

As I look back on my own life, it is difficult to remember a time when Wells was not part of it, from the time I was given *The Time Machine* as a child, to later when a teacher introduced me to *The Outline Of History*, as a way of attracting my attention in otherwise boring history classes. It was Wells who sustained me as I read for my Ph.D. comprehensives, and, above all, it was that chapter, 'On the Novel of Ideas', which appears as an introduction to *Babes in the Darkling Wood*, that convinced me that the end does, did, and will always justify the means. If art must be sacrificed to truth, so be it.

Thinking of Wells always recalls a home movie of him made sometime in the 1930s, with the small, round, tiny-footed man coming towards you down a garden walk, gesticulating and talking to the camera. I have seen this only twice, and yet the power of the man, the sexual energy, the physical command, and the desire to communicate, simply suffuse this thirty-second piece of old film, and one no longer questions why he made the impact he did.

And now that I come to the end of this work on Wells, some words of his I have quoted above — words spoken on 24 January 1902 at the Royal Institution — come to mind, as he ended one of his greatest pieces with a vision of 'the day when beings, beings who are now latent in our thoughts and hidden in our loins, shall stand upon this earth as one stands on a footstool, and shall laugh and reach out their hands amid the stars.' Thus he remains — in Shakespeare's words, 'desperately mortal' then, but forever immortal now with that promise to us all.

EPILOGUE

As Wells lay dying in his Regent's Park home, Richard Gregory gave his last speech to the British Association. A passage in that speech could have served as an epitaph for Wells, to whom Gregory sent a copy: 'The earth is but a temporary home, not only for the short span of human life, but also for the whole human race. As tenants or trustees our duty is to make the best use of the resources of our heritage by the exercise of all our talents and with the belief and hope that by so doing we are contributing to make men Godlike — if not godly — in the sense of religious faith.' Wells, thinking about his last film project, and dreaming about the life he had lived, must have agreed with his old friend's view.

As the *News Chronicle* remarked in a front-page story on the day of Wells's cremation, 'He was a finger pointing the way to the salvation of man. It was not his fault that he could not put our feet upon the road.' In another piece Ritchie Calder reminisced on their last talk. Wells had said, as he often did in the last year or two of his life, that the males in his line simply tended to stop and die, giving as instances the way his father, his uncle, and his brother Frank had simply stopped in mid-stream, much as he did himself. In that last talk Wells also discussed the advent of British socialism, and said that he adhered to the Labour Party at the end. Ritchie Calder thought that the Royal Society warranted a strong reproach for their failure to give the old man the Fellowship he so much deserved. The paper agreed, in its leading article on his life:

> Whatever honours his countrymen may accord him on the path to the grave, whatever may be said or written about him in these next few days, no immediate tribute is likely to assess with full justice the scope and majesty of his contribution to human progress. . . . His career from obscurity to the forefront of the world's sages is one of the glories of British working-class history.[1]

But, as Wells's ashes were distributed by the wind, and his friends began to plan a memorial, the newspapers of the day told a different story. The headlines in the same papers were of the aftermath of the atomic bomb test conducted on Bikini Atoll on 1 July 1946; there were problems in Palestine (as it was then still called); and although Britain had just celebrated its first post-war Bank Holiday weekend, very sticky problems remained, about food, about bread.

Across the world in Los Angeles, members of an H. G. Wells Science Fantasy Society held a memorial meeting soon after receiving the news of his death. They gave it a simply title, 'Farewell to The Master'. Speakers reviewed, for newer members, his visit to California in 1941, and told how Wells had entertained members of the Society once his talk was over.

On 30 October 1946, in London, a formal memorial service was held at the Royal Institution, where he had given his talks, 'The Discovery of the Future' in 1902, and 'The Idea of A World Encyclopaedia' in 1936. William Beveridge was in the chair. Six hundred tickets were printed, and another two hundred of his old friends simply could not be accommodated in the space. Gregory was on the platform, and read a bit from *The Undying Fire*. David Low spoke about the famous 'ball game' and the wonderful charades so many remembered. G. D. H. Cole gave a short address on Wells as teacher and prophet. Desmond MacCarthy, who had been scheduled to speak, was very ill on the day, so Beveridge found himself called upon to speak in his stead. He read passages from *A Modern Utopia*, as the book which had influenced him most, describing Wells as 'a volcano in perpetual eruption of burning thoughts and luminous images'. For Beveridge, summarizing the other tributes, it was Wells's receptivity to ideas, his constructive and creative powers, his humanity, his honesty, and his sympathy which had made him the force he was. But now he was gone. A message was read from Clement Attlee, deep in a debate in the Commons on foreign affairs, and Stephen Potter closed the ceremonies by reading sections on love and death from *First and Last Things*. On the day of the service Penguin Books brought out paperback editions of ten volumes of Wells's most significant works, as their tribute to him.[2]

Gregory tried to set up a Wells Fellowship, without success. In November 1947 he gave a dinner for a half-dozen friends to try to revive the idea after a year, hoping that an annual H. G. Wells address could be given and published throughout the world. A fund was started, but in the follow-up planning, the lecture idea vanished. There was protest from the Left that this was not a fitting memorial, and scoffing from the Right that any memorial proposed tended to blunt the enthusiasm of the promoters. And Richard Gregory was a very old man. A committee continued to work, but without Gregory, who, as his biographer has shown, was depressed by the lack of support from such persons as J. B. S. Haldane and Rebecca West, both of whom thought the effort was too slim. The committee met only a few times, and by the summer of 1948 this idea of a Wells memorial was effectively defeated.[3]

Other short-lived attempts followed Gregory's death. The BBC broadcast a series of Wells programmes for the Forces network, the Home Service, and the European Service, and in 1947 three programmes for schools. The influence of H. G. Wells had been very great. When, in 1962, *New Society* ran a survey of Labour MPs, as to the significant events of their early life, 94 of the 110 responding mentioned specific authors as having an impact. Shaw was the author named by 32, and Wells by 26 (Marx by 19).[4]

A few books on Wells began to appear, a number from old friends or acquaintances, but the little serious discussion there was of his work came from Russia, France, Norway, and the United States. The world he wanted had been overtaken by the nuclear horror, the cold war, the need to supply food and sustenance to many of the world's hungry along with the problems of setting right the affairs of specific countries devastated by the Second World War and the increasingly narrow and limited views of those who felt that they had been denied their 'whack of fun'. It was not until 1966, at the centenary of his birth, that interest in Wells began to revive. A major exhibit was held at Bromley to mark the opening of that archive. (The bulk of his papers had gone to Illinois in 1947.) *Horizon* published interviews with G.P. and Frank Wells and with Ritchie Calder, which were also broadcast. C. P. Snow brought out a loving personal memoir in that year as well. The *New Statesman* noticed the centenary with an article on 'Wells and the Future'.[5]

Interest in Wells began to pick up. The H. G. Wells Society began to hold regular meetings, and a series of autumn conferences, each devoted to an aspect of his work, were held. Scholarly interest in aspects of his life resulted in a number of substantial books and articles. Books are being reissued, biographies written, and in 1986 — the 120th anniversary of his birth, and the 40th of his death — a major Wellsian conference is to be held in London. Wells shares are rising on the stock exchange: slowly, perhaps, but rising. He still speaks to us all — and a Wellsian world awaits, as it has always done, for those who are willing to use their brains and their will. The Trojan Horse that is the Open Conspiracy still stands in the courtyard.

APPENDIX A

THE AUTOCRACY OF MR PARHAM
Presentation List [1930]

This list must be returned without fail to Mr H. G. Wells, 614, St Ermins, Westminster, S.W.1.

1. Eliza — Mrs Aria, 8, Wimpole Street, W.1.
2. Max — the Lord Beaverbrook, Cherkley, Leatherhead, Surrey.
3. Arnold — E. A. Bennett Esq, 75, Cadogan Square, S.W.1.
4. Ruth — Mrs Walter Brooke, Shirley Hyrst, Kingsmead Road, Tadworth.
5. Elizabeth Bruce — Mrs Bruce, Gorphwysle, 57, Cardiff Road, Llandaff, Glam.
6. Abel Chevalley — M. Abel Chevalley, 19 Ave. d'Orleans, Paris.
7. Amabel — Mrs Williams Ellis, 14, Royal Ave, S.W.3.
8. Carmel — Mrs Haden Guest, 45, Gordon Square, W.C.
9. Dora — The Hon. Mrs Greville, 53, Springfield Road, St Johns Wood, N.W.
10. E.S.P.H. — E. S. P. Haynes Esq., 9, New Square, Lincoln's Inn, W.C.
11. Ettie Rout — Mrs Hornibrook, 4, Brendon House, Gt. Woodstock St. W.1.
12. Japhet — J. F. Horrabin Esq., 6, Mecklenburgh Square, W.C.
13. Julian Huxley — Professor J. S. Huxley, 31, Hillway, Highgate, N.W.
14. Pip — Philip Guedalla Esq., The Laundry, Little Easton, Essex.
15. Aldous Huxley Esq.,
16. Christabel — The Hon. Mrs McLaren, 38, South Street, Mayfair, W.
17. Odette — Mdme Odette Keun, 124, Quai d'Auteuil, Paris, XVIe.
18. Harold Laski — Professor Laski, 5, Addison Bridge Place, W.
19. Humpy — Lady Peacock, 3, Buckingham Gate, S.W.1.
20. Bertrand Russell — The Hon. Bertrand Russell, Telegraph Hse, Harting, Sussex.
21. R.A.G.S. — Sir Richard Gregory, 5, North Court, Wood St, SW.
22. Elizabeth — Mrs Lucas, 16, Davies Mews, Davies Street W.1.
23. Mrs Donald Craig, — Mrs Craig, Schoolhouse, Morebattle, Roxburghshire.
24. Little e — Lady Russell, White Gates, Wentworth, Virginia Water.
25. D.D. — Mrs Charles Petrie,
26. G.B.S. — G. B. Shaw Esq., Whitehall Court, S.W.1.
27. The best of Mothers in law — Mrs M. C. Robbins, Onslow Court Hotel, S.W.7.
28. Isabel — Mrs Fowler Smith, Cranford, Hillside Grove Mill Hill, N.W.7.

29. Miss Eileen Power, 22, Mecklenburgh Square, W.C.
30. President Masaryk, Pan President Masaryk c/o Miss Alice Masaryk, Czechoslavak Legation, London.
31. Walter Roch Esq., 24, Sloane Court, S.W.3.
32. Amber Pember — Mrs Blanco White, 44, Downshire Hill, N.W.3.
33. Rebecca — Miss Rebecca West, 80, Onslow Gardens, S.W.7.
34. Anthony — Mr Anthony West, School House, Stowe, BUCKS.
35. Mrs Florence Lamont, 107, E. 70th Street, New York City.
36. H.M.T. — H. M. Tomlinson Esq., 85, Waddon Road, Croydon.
37. Freddy — F. J. Wells Esq., 4, Leigham Vale Road, Southbourne, Dorset.
38. Brother Frank — F. C. Wells Esq., Roseneath, Liss.
39. Gip — G. P. Wells Esq., 19, Glenilla Road, N.W.3.
40. Little Frank — Frank Wells Esq., Bridge Cottage, Welwyn, Herts.
41. To Lady Warwick — Lady Warwick, Easton Lodge, Dunmow.
42. Gerald O'Donovan Esq., 8, Westbourne Gardens, W.2.
43. Moura — Die Baronin Budberg, 1, Koburgerstrasse 1, Berlin, Schoneberg.
44. Bokes — Mrs De Boer, 22, Park Mansions, Knightsbridge, S.W.1.
4   copies to 614, St Ermins, Westminster, S.W.1.
2   copies to 124, Quai d'Auteuil, Paris, XVIe.

APPENDIX B

A CHARTER OF SCIENTIFIC FELLOWSHIP [1941]

1. Man depends for his maintenance and growth upon knowledge of the properties of things in the world around him and the liberty to increase and use it.
2. People of all races and classes of society have contributed to the development of natural forces and resources and the understanding of the universe and mankind's relationships to it.
3. Every generation inherits the world's store of ascertained knowledge, and men of science are the trustees of this heritage with the duty of increasing it by faithful guardianship and devoted service.
4. The obligation to pursue scientific inquiry entails the right of intellectual freedom and international exchange of learning by unrestricted association in the common cause of the advancement of natural knowledge.
5. All natural or national groups of scientific workers are autonomous in their own domains but united in the fellowship of the Commonwealth of Science, with the whole world as its outlook and service to mankind its highest aim.
6. As freedom to teach, opportunity to learn, and desire to understand, are essential for the extension of knowledge, the democracy of science accepts these principles of progressive civilization and resolutely maintains them as basic elements in its constitution which cannot be abrogated without detriment to human development.

APPENDIX C

THE RIGHTS OF MAN [1942]

1. Right to Live.

By the word 'man' in this Declaration is meant every living human being without distinction of age or sex.

Every man is a joint inheritor of all the natural resources and of the powers, inventions and possibilities accumulated by our forerunners. He is entitled, within the measure of these resources and without distinction of race, colour or professed beliefs or opinions, to the nourishment, covering and medical care needed to realize his full possibilities of physical and mental development from birth to death. Notwithstanding the various and unequal qualities of individuals, all men shall be deemed absolutely equal in the eyes of the law, equally important in social life and equally entitled to the respect of their fellow man.

2. Protection of Minors.

The natural and rightful guardians of those who are not of an age to protect themselves are their parents. In default of such parental protection in whole or in part, the community, having due regard to the family traditions of the child, shall accept or provide alternative guardians.

3. Duty to the Community.

It is the duty of every man, not only to respect but to uphold and to advance the rights of all other men throughout the world. Furthermore it is his duty to contribute such service to the community as will ensure the performance of those necessary tasks for which the incentives which will operate in a free society do not provide. It is only by doing his quota of service that a man can justify his partnership in the community. No man shall be conscripted for military or other service to which he has a conscientious objection, but to perform no social duty whatsoever is to remain unenfranchised and under guardianship.

4. Right to Knowledge.

It is the duty of the community to equip every man with sufficient education to enable him to be as useful and interested a citizen as his capacity allows. Furthermore, it is the duty of the community to render all knowledge available to him and such special education as will give him equality of opportunity for the development of his distinctive gifts in the service of mankind. He shall have prompt and easy access to all information necessary for him to form a judgement upon current events and issues.

5. Freedom of Thought and Worship.

Every man has a right to the utmost freedom of expression, discussion, association and worship.

6. Right to Work.

Subject to the needs of the community, a man may engage in any lawful occupation, earning such pay as the contribution that his work makes to the welfare of the community may justify. He is entitled to paid employment and to make suggestions as to the kind of employment which he considers himself able to perform. Work for the sole object of profit-making shall not be a lawful occupation.

7. Right in Personal Property.

In the enjoyment of his personal property, lawfully possessed, a man is entitled to protection from public or private violence, deprivation, compulsion or intimidation.

8. Freedom of Movement.

A man may move freely about the world at his own expense. His private dwelling, however, and any reasonable limited enclosure of which he is the occupant, may be entered only with his consent or by a legally qualified person empowered with a warrant as the law may direct. So long as by his movement he does not intrude upon the private domain of any other citizen, harm, or disfigure or encumber what is not his, interfere with or endanger the happiness of others, he shall have the right to come and go wherever he chooses, by land, air or water, over any kind of country, mountain, moorland, river, lake, sea or ocean, and all the ample spaces of this, his world.

9. Personal Liberty.

Unless a man is declared by a competent authority to be a danger to himself or others through mental abnormality, a declaration which must be confirmed within seven days and thereafter reviewed at least annually, he shall not be restrained for more than twenty-four hours without being charged with a definite offence, nor shall he be remanded for a longer period than eight days without his consent, nor imprisoned for more than three months without a trial. At a reasonable time before his trial, he shall be furnished with a copy of the evidence which it is proposed to use against him. At the end of the three months' period, if he has not been tried and sentenced by due process of the law, he shall be acquitted and released. No man shall be charged more than once for the same offence. Although he is open to the free criticism of his fellows, a man shall have adequate protection against any misrepresentation that may distress or injure him. Secret evidence is not permissible. Statements recorded in administrative dossiers shall not be used to justify the slightest infringement of personal liberty. A dossier is merely a memorandum for administrative use; it shall not be used as evidence without proper confirmation in open court.

10. Freedom from Violence.

No man shall be subjected to any sort of mutilation except with his own deliberate consent, freely given, nor to forcible handling, except in restraint of his own violence, nor to torture, beating or any other physical ill-treatment. He shall not be subjected to mental distress, or to imprisonment in infected, verminous or otherwise insanitary quarters, or be put into the company of verminous or infectious people. But if he is himself infectious or a danger to the health of others, he may be cleansed, disinfected, put in quarantine or otherwise restrained so far as may be necessary to prevent harm to his fellows. No one shall be punished vicariously by the selection, arrest or ill-treatment of hostages.

11. Rights of Law-Making.

The rights embodied in this Declaration are fundamental and inalienable. In conventional and in administration matters, but in no others, it is an obvious practical necessity for men to limit the free play of certain of these fundamental rights. (In, for example, such conventional matters as the rule of the road or the protection of money from forgery, and in such administrative matters as town and country planning, or public hygiene.) No law, conventional or administrative, shall be binding on any man or any section of the community unless it has been made openly with the active or tacit acquiescence of every adult citizen concerned, given either by direct majority vote of the community affected or by a majority vote of his representatives publicly elected. These representatives shall be ultimately responsible for all by-laws and for detailed interpretations made in the execution of the law. In matters of convention and collective action, man must abide by the majority decisions ascertained by electoral methods which give effective expression to individual choice. All legislation must be subject to public discussion, revision or repeal. No treaties or contracts shall be made secretly in the name of the community.

'The fount of legislation in a free world is the whole people, and since life flows on constantly to new citizens, no generation can, in whole or in part, surrender or delegate this legislative power, inalienably inherent in mankind.'

A NOTE ON SOURCES

This book is based almost entirely on primary sources, either published material by H. G. Wells or letters and other unpublished documents written by him, about him, or to him. More than 3,000 items of published material by Wells, and perhaps as many as 35,000 letters and documents were consulted in various archives in the preparation of the work.

The principal archives of Wellsian material, published and unpublished, are:

Cited as

H. G. Wells Papers, in the Rare Books Room of the Library, University of Illinois, Champaign-Urbana. In addition to its immense Wells holdings, the largest single source of material by and on this author, the Library at Illinois has systematically acquired other related material, such as copies of the G.B. Shaw papers, the Macmillan Company papers dealing with Wells, and Wellsian and Fabian material in the Passfield Papers. Although I have not looked at every item in the collection, I have on several occasions scrutinized the excellent finding guide (published by G.K. Hall, Chicago) and called up every item which seemed to have any possible relevance; the only category of material of which I did not make extensive use are the MS versions of Wells's various books, although I did not altogether neglect this source. Unless otherwise indicated, this collection is the source of all the unpublished material cited in the Notes below, and of many of the published items referred to in text and Notes.   Illinois

H.G. Wells collection in the Bromley Central Library, Bromley, Kent. This second largest archive of Wells material includes many MSS and documents not in the Illinois collection, as well as an especially good selection of Wells's journalism and ephemera, and a very large collection of reviews of Wells's work, donated by Patrick Parrinder. In addition a number of unpublished theses and works of Wells scholarship are available here. I made use of all the items in the Bromley collection, but in the Notes have given it as the source for only those items which differ from the ones at Illinois.   Bromley

The MS archive in the Mugar Memorial Library, Boston University, Boston, Massachusetts, includes a third large collection of Wells material, especially rich in drafts of Wells's correspond-

ence, and contains some letters not found at Illinois. I have
looked at every item which does not duplicate material at Illinois
or at Bromley.   Boston

Wellsian MS material occurs in a great many other places, usually among the
papers of his friends or associates. Often, the other side of the correspondence,
with Wells's drafts of portions of his replies or occasionally carbons or copies of
those replies, may be seen at Illinois or Boston. The largest bodies of such
correspondence occur in:

Cited as

The Margaret Sanger papers, in the Sophia Smith Collection
(Women's History Archive), Smith College, Northampton,
Massachusetts, include both sides of the Wellsian correspondence, as Sanger's letters to Wells were returned to her after his
death. The collection has been augmented with much published
material from the Birth Control Pamphlet Collection at LSE
(cited here, however, in the original publications).   Smith

The MS collections in the British Library of Political and
Economic Science, London School of Economics and Political
Science, include the papers of Graham Wallas and William
Beveridge, both containing much Wellsian material. (Copyright
in the Graham Wallas papers is held by Newnham College,
Cambridge, whose Principal and Fellows have granted me
permission to quote from them.) I have also used material in
ancillary holdings of this Library.   LSE

The Violet Paget ('Vernon Lee') papers in the Special
Collections, Colby College, Waterville, Maine, include many
letters to Wells from Paget not at Illinois; I have had complete
access to material at Colby concerning their relationship, though
much of it is duplicated at Illinois.   Colby

The Walter Lippman papers in the Yale University Library.   Yale

The Upton Sinclair papers in the Lilly Library, University of
Indiana, Bloomington (with other Wellsian material at the same
location).   Indiana

Other collections containing Wellsian material are at:

The British Library, London   BL
Cornell University Library, Ithaca, N.Y.   Cornell
Hofstra University Library, Hempstead, L.I., N.Y.   Hofstra
Syracuse University Library, Syracuse, N.Y.   Syracuse

or in the hands of two private collectors:

the late Michael Katanka   Katanka
Eric Korn   Korn

In addition, large amounts of material concerning Wells are to be found in the archives of the Fabian Society at LSE, in the Shaw Papers, and in those of Sidney and Beatrice Webb (the Passfield Papers). Most of this material exists in xerox form in the Wells archives at Illinois or at Bromley, and although I have used the originals at LSE, for the other correspondence I have relied on the xeroxes. Much of the Shaw and Webb material has now been published, and I have cited the published editions where possible even though I am quoting from the original MSS.

Two other collections of material relevant to Wells have been made available to me:

Cited as

The T.H. Huxley papers at the Royal College of Science, London. These include some Wellsian papers, but are more valuable on the context of lectures and laboratory demonstrations in Wells's time; supplemented with the holdings of the Royal College itself — enrolment books, marking reports, précis of lectures, demonstrations, sample syllabi, and other related material — this is a good source for Wells's formal higher education.   Royal College

(Another source of some value was the archive perused at Oundle School, Peterborough; my visits there, and the resultant interviews, were of greater value, however.)

The BBC written archives at Caversham Park, Reading. These contain the correspondence concerning Wells's talks, or proposed talks, on various programmes of the BBC, together with internal memoranda about them, the texts of many of the talks (a few are also available on disc), and reviews of them in the contemporary press. The archives also contain correspondence on broadcast readings and dramatizations of Wells's work.   BBC

In addition, I have made extensive use of the newspaper files of the British Library at Colindale, North London. With two very small exceptions, all the published books and pamphlets by Wells cited or quoted in the text are from my own collection, although I have also consulted alternative editions or impressions, usually in the British Library, where possible.

In quoting from Wells's personal correspondence, I have silently expanded the ampersand to 'and'.

D.C.S.

LIST OF ABBREVIATIONS

In addition to the short forms indicated for the sources described above, the following abbreviations and short forms are used in the Notes:

Individuals:

HGW	H.G. Wells
ACRW	Amy Catherine Robbins, later Wells ('Jane')

GPW	G. P. Wells ('Gip')
MCW	Marjorie Craig, later Wells
EH	Elizabeth Healey, later Bruce
RAG	Richard A. Gregory
ERL	E. Ray Lankester
JBP	J. B. Pinker
APW	A. P. Watt
GBS	George Bernard Shaw
AB	Arnold Bennett
GG	George Gissing
GKC	G.K. Chesterton
FAS	Frank Swinnerton
ViP	Violet Paget ('Vernon Lee')
GrW	Graham Wallas

Published works frequently cited or quoted:

Atlantic	*The Works of H.G. Wells*: Atlantic Edition, 28 vols. (London and New York 1924–7)
ExA	H.G. Wells, *Experiment in Autobiography*, 2 vols. (London 1934; repr. 1984)
Armytage	W.H.G. Armytage, *Sir Richard Arman Gregory* (London 1957)
Hart-Davis	Rupert Hart-Davis, *Hugh Walpole* (London 1952)
MacKenzies	Norman and Jeanne MacKenzie, *The Time Traveller: The Life of H.G. Wells* (London 1973)
GBS *Collected Letters*	*Collected Letters of George Bernard Shaw*, vols. I and II, ed. Dan H. Laurence, (London 1965–72)
B. Webb, *Diary*	*The Diary of Beatrice Webb*, ed. N. and J. MacKenzie, 4 vols. (London 1982–5)
Webb *Letters*	*The Letters of Sidney and Beatrice Webb*, ed. N. MacKenzie, 3 vols. (London 1978)

Journals and newspapers frequently cited:

ET	*Educational Times*
PMG	*Pall Mall Gazette*
SR	*Saturday Review*
SSJ	*Science Schools Journal*
DTel	*Daily Telegraph*
NChron	*News Chronicle*
NYT	*New York Times*
WGaz	*Westminster Gazette*

D=Daily / E=Evening / M=Morning / S=Sunday

NOTES

Introduction

1 Beverley Nichols, *Are They the Same at Home?* (London 1927), ch. 56: 'H. G. Wells — or Multum in Parvo.' The chapter is also included in his *Oxford – London – Hollywood: An Omnibus* (London 1931), 556–60.
2 Vera Brittain and Geoffrey Handley-Taylor, eds., *Selected Letters of Winifred Holtby and Vera Brittain, 1920–1935* (London 1960): letter Brittain to Holtby, 9 Nov 1925.
3 'Shinwell's Century', *Sunday Times*, 14 Oct 1984.

PART ONE

Chapter 1

1 Geoffrey L. Eames, 'Joseph Wells: Father of H.G. and of the Bromley Cricket Club', a MS in Bromley. See any *Wisden* for the bowling record. The Bromley directories list Joseph Wells's shop at 47 High Street. The place is still marked with a small plaque as the first home of HGW. Wells apparently disliked cricket, although he used his father once or twice in his earliest essays in his persona as cricketer. Elizabeth Bond, 'Mr Wells and Joseph Wells', *Country Life*, vol. CLX (1976), pp. 1923–4.
2 *ExA*; HGW, 'Turning Points in My Life — My Mother Slaved for Me', *SChron*, 11 June 1939. Wells's most autobiographical novel is *The New Machiavelli* (1911). In that book we find some descriptions of what must have been the Wellses' kitchen and back garden. Even the gardening episode appears, although much twisted.
3 HGW, 'My Mother Slaved for Me'; *ExA*. HGW: 'My Lucky Moment', *View*, 29 Apr 1911; 'What Life Has Taught Me', *SChron*, 30 Oct 1938 (also in *Coronet*, Apr 1938). Wells recalled Wood's *Natural History*, as well as a trip to Crystal Palace to view the prehistoric plaster animals and a picture of a gorilla, in his introduction to E.G. Boulenger, *World Natural History* (London 1937), xv–xx.
4 Margaret Meade-Fetherstonhaugh and Oliver Warner, *Uppark* [sic] *and Its People* (London 1964). They quote HGW, *ExA*, 102–3. William Baxter, notes on an interview with Frank J. Wells, in Bromley. Baxter hoped to write a biography of HGW, and did produce several newspaper pieces. On Wells learning to write, HGW to 'Mark Benney' (Harry Degras), 15 Mar 1937. Wells's strip cartoons were exhibited at the Bromley centenary celebration in 1966; HGW, *The Desert Daisy*, ed. Gordon N. Ray (Urbana, Ill. 1957), reprints his earliest adventure story. The walks with his father also appear in *The New Machiavelli*.
5 W. Baxter's notes on his interview with Frank Wells, Bromley. Wells was influenced by the 'Punchinello' letters on simplified spelling; see *Punch*, Aug, Sept 1879. His comment on Thomas Morley is in the margin of a letter from Baxter to HGW, 12 Nov 1929 (but appears in almost identical words in HGW, 'The Academy for Young Gentlemen', *Journal of Education*, 1 Oct 1893, pp. 563–6). The description of Bromley

occurs in HGW, 'The Degeneration of the Ravensbourne — A Memory of Bromley, Kent', *PMG*, 12 July 1894. A boyhood friend at Morley's emerged, in poverty, in the mid-1930s. He was interviewed about their friendship, and Wells sent him a cheque for £5 'with my love'; *News of the World*, 11 Nov 1936. See M. Bowkett to HGW, 30 Sept 1935, in which he asks Wells from his hospital bed for help. This letter occasioned the gift. 'You have succeeded — I have failed. Think of us two together at Morleys, by God. But I am as pleased at your triumph as I am regretful of my own failure,' said Bowkett. They had retained some contact until the later '90s, as Wells exchanged visits with Bowkett and his brother Sidney at Surbiton; see S. Bowkett to HGW, 25 June 1898.

6   HGW to Mark Benney, 23 Aug 1940. The book in question was *The Big Wheel* (1940), although the book of Benney's which first attracted HGW was *Low Country*, published in 1936. Wells went on in this revealing letter to class Benney with James, Bennett, and Gissing as all of the curious persuasion 'that there is a real right thing to do on all occasions. James for all his expensive childhood moved in fear of all shibboleths.' F. Medhurst still owns the site of the Wells shop in Bromley. Joseph Wells could no longer pay the rent and a distress warrant for £13.3s.0d. was issued. See Medhurst's Advertising Supplement to *Southeast London and Kentish Mercury*, Oct 1979, for the history of the building. HGW's father was apparently over-fond of the bottle, which created part of the family problems. He eventually moved to Liss, Hampshire, to be near relatives.

7   *ExA*; HGW, 'I Escape from Drudgery', *SChron*, 18 June 1939; an undated letter (*c*. 1880) to Frank Wells describes HGW's Windsor hours of work. HGW, letter to editor of *Grocers' Assistant*, Feb 1900. The original letter, quoted here, was dated 3 Jan 1900; a longer and more poignant draft is at Boston. The second quotation is from HGW's review of T. Spencer Jones, *The Life of a Shop Girl: Pathetic Side of an Occupation Which Spells Drudgery and a Hopeless Outlook on Life for Many Thousands*, in *London Magazine*, vol. XIX (Sept 1907–Feb 1908), pp. 177–83. Also see his unsigned article, 'In a Little Shop', *PMG*, 11 Sept 1894, which describes setting up a new draper's shop with too little money and on credit. The desire to escape simply permeates this piece.

8   HGW to Frank Wells, 29 June 1881, reporting his holiday plans from 3 to 19 Sept 1881. He went on his wheel to the New Forest, Southampton, Stonehenge, and to Salisbury and Winchester to visit the cathedrals. He described this holiday life in one of his most remarkable early pieces, unsigned, 'The Holiday of the Draper's Assistant — Life in a Margin', *PMG*, 5 June 1894. The piece discusses the entire life he must have led. He was later to use his draper's experience and especially the holiday time in an article, 'A Perfect Gentleman on Wheels', *Woman at Home*, Apr 1897. This may have appeared in another form in *To-Day* in 1896, and he later extended the work to his comic novel, *The Wheels of Chance: A Cycling Holiday Adventure* (1896). Still later the idea was proposed as a play, although never performed. Michael Timko, ed., *Hoopdriver's Holiday* (Lafayette, Ind. 1964). The dramatization was done in 1903–4. The continued use of the material indicates the force of the experience and especially of the holiday periods. Even Wells's novels *The Wonderful Visit* (1895) and *Bealby* (1915) rely to some degree on what must have been his holiday experiences.

9   HGW to Frank Wells, 1 Sept 1880 (here he signs 'Busswuss'); 'I Escape from Drudgery'; *ExA*. See *Tono-Bungay* for a description of the walk to Up Park; HGW to Sarah Wells, July (two undated letters), 10, 22, 24, 28 July 1883.

10 Revd. Ernest Frederic Row, *A History of Midhurst Grammar School* (Brighton 1913), 126–7. Wells was noted there for 'his wonderful skill in pen and ink drawing'. Sarah Wells's comments are on an undated fragment of an 1883 letter from HGW; HGW to Sarah Wells, ?? July–Aug 1883. Wells on examinations, unsigned, 'The Subtle Examinee', *University Correspondent*, 15 Apr 1891. The quote is from a signed article in the same journal, 15 Mar 1893, 'What is Cram?' Two other comments which may be

expressive of life at Midhurst are 'On Capital Punishment', *SSJ*, Feb 1890, and 'Registration', his letter to *ET*, 1 June 1890, which comments on the quality of teaching in poor small schools. Wells received £40 in his second year at Midhurst. HGW to Sarah Wells, 17 July 1884. His poem, 'The Log of the Sausage Machine', appeared in *SSJ*, Nov 1890.

11   ERL to T. H. Huxley, 4 Apr 1892 (Huxley Papers). This is exactly what the Normal School of Science, with Huxley lecturing, meant to Wells, of course. Late in life he was to tell Gregory that he had never had an original idea or read a new book until he arrived at South Kensington, which expresses the matter well; HGW to RAG, 13 July 1943. For Huxley on the growth and change in science, see his 'Science, Past and Present', *Nature*, 1 Nov 1894, pp. 1–3, the lead article in the 25th anniversary issue of the journal. Huxley had also contributed the first article to vol. I, no. 1 of *Nature* (4 Nov 1869), calling in the latter for a full explication of the causes of evolution. Also see, on the impact of the new laws on science education in general during this period, RAG in *Nature*: 'The Progress of Technical Education', 21 Dec 1893; 'Some London Polytechnic Institutes', 24 May 1894; part ii of the same, 31 May 1894; 'The Advance of Technical Education', 14 Feb 1895. For a modern analysis, see R. MacLeod, 'Resources of Science for Victorian England: The Endowment of Science Movement', in P. Mathias, ed., *Science and Society, 1600–1900* (Cambridge 1972).

12   Wells's marks follow as well as the degree class of each:

Course	Class	Average	Date of Completion
Bio. Part I, Div. I	First	84	12/1884
Bio. Part I, Div. II	Second	76	2/1885
Maths — Class B	First	12.8 of 15	6/1885
Bio. Part II, Adv. Zoo	First	83	6/1885
Physics, Part I	Second	62	2/1886
Geom. Drawing	First	16.5 of 20	6/1886
Geol. I	Second	78	6/1886
Astro. Physics	Failed	53	6/1886
Geol. Parts I–II	Failed	54	6/1887
Astro. Physics	Second	71	6/1887

13   This paragraph is based on the standard syllabus at the Royal College (Normal School) in those days, now preserved in its archive, along with Huxley's correspondence. Huxley's illness was to force him from teaching within a year or two. Cyril Bibby, 'Thomas Henry Huxley and University Development', *Victorian Studies*, vol. II, no. 2 (1958–9), pp. 97–116. For Huxley's views, see, in particular, *Man's Place in Nature and Other Anthropological Essays* (New York 1898), which collects his statements. The foreword to the work explains his thought processes and their growth over time. Also useful is his *Evolution and Ethics and Other Essays* (New York 1898). This contains his Romaines Lecture of 1893, revised with other collected material. These were the substance of what Wells imbibed along with the factual material of the syllabus.

14   HGW, 'Huxley', *Royal College of Science Magazine*, Apr 1901, pp. 209–11. Wells also wrote of his old professor and gave a talk on the BBC in 1935, 'I Knew a Man (T.H. Huxley)', *Listener*, 9 Oct 1935, pp. 593–5. Incidentally, for the researcher into Wells's student life, a sharp shock of recognition comes when the marks books are produced and the names A. M. Davies, A. T. Simmons, Elizabeth Healey, and Richard A. Gregory are spotted near Wells's. Their friendship overcame the competition inherent in this intense atmosphere.

15   *ExA*, although he does not discuss his decisions much. HGW to Fred Wells, undated, sometime in 1884, and 31 Aug 1886. This last letter also discusses possible presents for Isabel Wells from Fred.

16   Unsigned HGW ('Z' and HGW are used for the author), 'At the Royal College of Science', *ET*, 1 Sept 1893, pp. 393–5, a long and very useful article for Wells's life at

the College. A. C. Robbins was hardly meek-looking, but very beautiful in a tender sort of way.

17   HGW, 'Preface — To the Average Man', *SSJ*, no. 1 (Dec 1886); By the First Editor, 'The Beginning of the Journal', *SSJ*, no. 48 (Oct 1893). Wells edited the first 38 numbers of *SSJ*.

18   EH to HGW, 6 Jan 1942. Two other *SSJ* pieces in which HGW comments on student life and its possibilities are 'Something Good from Birmingham', no. 19 (Aug 1889), and 'Specimen Day', no. 33 (Oct 1891). For another reminiscence of Wells by a friend, roommate of William Burton, and occasional illustrator of Wells's stories, see *St. Pancras Chronicle*, 6 Sept 1946, which prints and comments on a letter from Cosmo Rowe, describing the student life in the Euston Road. Rowe took in students as lodgers from 1884 to 1892 to supplement his income. He quotes a letter to him from HGW, *c.* Apr 1888, on a return visit to the College.

19   HGW, review article, 'The Well at the Worlds End', *SR*, 17 Oct 1896.

20   HGW to A. M. Davies, 13, 23 Aug and another undated, 1887; to EH, 10 Mar 1888. HGW, 'My Fight for Life,' *SChron*, 2 July 1939. Wells's best early comment on his education, which has sections on Morley's Academy, Holt Academy, and Henley House School, all thinly disguised, is 'The Academy for Young Gentlemen', *Journal of Education* (Supplement), 1 Oct 1893, pp. 563–6.

21   HGW to Sarah Wells, undated, 1887, on the injury; to EH at the end of 1887, undated; to A. M. Davies, undated, 1887 (Up Park): the literature quote is from here; to Davies, 3, 15, 31 Dec 1887.

22   HGW to A. M. Davies, 22 Feb, 29 Mar, and an undated letter of May–June 1888, probably early May, reported another spell of bad bleeding and coughing; to EH, 2, 19, 23 Mar, 1, 14, May, ?? June 1888, quote from the last letter. The poem is on the back of some bound handwritten Wells material from *c.* 1885. It is entitled 'An Aspiration'. The last two lines read, 'To dodge the chancel rails about / and carve my God and hand Him out'.

23   HGW to Fred Wells, 18 Jan, summer (undated), 7 Aug 1889; to Sarah Wells, 25 Feb 1890; to EH. Feb and late summer (undated) 1890. For Wells's rather jaundiced view of the examinations he was forced to take, see 'The College of Preceptors Science Examinations', *ET*, 1 Mar 1892.

24   *Henley House Magazine*: Mar 1889; Dec 1890; and HGW, 'Holiday Science', Aug 1889, p. 217. Wells also showed the depth of his knowledge in another piece, 'The North Sea', Aug 1889, which teaches more science. After he left the school, he continued to read the magazine and waken interest in the boys; he responded to a mathematical problem put by J.V. Milne, providing not only the solution, but also some implications to the problem not seen by Milne, who reciprocated by publishing Wells's solution in considerable detail. See 'That Problem', *Henley House Magazine*, Oct 1892. A.A. Milne, *Childhood Memories* (London 1937).

25   *ET*, 1 Feb 1890. His last examinations were held at Christmas, and the awards announced at a meeting held 22 Jan 1890. The certificate electing him an FZS is dated 20 Mar 1890. HGW, 'My Fight for Life'; *ExA*. See W. Briggs to HGW, 15 June 1891, which discusses a change in employment, as Wells is ill and will now be writing a book (*Honours Physiography*) while acting as correspondence tutor. Wells's brother Frank attended his wedding, along with his mother-in-law; whether others did is not known.

26   HGW, signed letter, 'School Zoology', *ET*, 1 Sept 1891; signed articles, *University Correspondent*: 'The Future of Private Teaching', 15 May 1892, and 'Biology for the Intermediate School and Preliminary Science Examinations: Hints for Practical Work', 25 Feb 1893. On Low see John Carswell, *The Exile: A Life of Ivy Litvinov* (London 1983), and her novel, *Growing Pains* (London 1912).

27   HGW, *University Correspondent*: 'The University for London', 15 Apr 1892, pp. 19–20; 'The Future of Private Teaching', 15 May 1892, pp. 12–13.

28 HGW, *Nature*: 'Popularizing Science', 26 July 1894, pp. 300–1; 'Science. In School, and After School', 27 Sept 1894, pp. 525–6; 'The Sequence of Studies', 27 Dec 1894, pp. 195–6.

29 RAG and HGW, *Honours Physiography* (London: Joseph Hughes & Co. 1893). The sections mentioned occur at pp. 65–8, 118–19, 174–81. HGW and RAG received £10 each for the book: HGW, 'Sir Richard Arman Gregory', Royal College of Science *Record*, ser. 2, no. 4 (Feb 1931), p. 35. For Gregory's memory of those days, see RAG to HGW, 9 Nov 1939, with its detailed account; the letter is reprinted in W. H. G. Armytage, *Sir Richard Arman Gregory* (London 1957).

30 HGW, *Textbook of Biology* (London: W. B. Clive & Co. 1892) [1893]; 3rd edn., rev. A.M. Davies, 1898; 6th edn., rev. J.T. Cunningham (London: University Tutorial Press 1913).

31 *Textbook of Biology* I: Preface, viii, 31, 35, 42–4, 56, 127–32, 'The Theory of Evolution'. *Textbook of Zoology* (1898) II: Preface, vii, viii, 143.

32 The review quoted appeared, unsigned, in *ET*, 1 Apr 1893, p. 188. Other substantial notices of the book appeared in the *Journal of Education*, 1 Apr 1893, and in *Nature*, 27 Apr 1893 (of vol. I), and 14 Dec 1893 (of vol. II), both these last signed 'W.N.P.' For the correspondence surrounding the change of illustrators for vol. II, see W. Briggs to HGW, 7 Nov 1893, where he hopes Miss Robbins will do the work as a labour of love, but is apparently prepared to pay her £5. Briggs also lists the journals to which he will send review copies.

33 HGW to EH, 23, 28 Feb 1888.

34 HGW to EH, 20 Mar 1888, 2 May 1892; the prayer is undated, from a letter to her in the early '90s. HGW, unsigned article, 'The Pains of an Imagination — An Experience', *PMG*, 20 Sept 1894; 'Books That Have Made Socialists', *New Leader*, 9 Sept 1944. Wells did apparently experiment with writing banal fiction. According to *ExA*, one such story was printed in *Family Herald*, but little resembling Wells's work is visible there to these eyes. One piece, 'A Romance on Wheels', using motifs of dreams, bicycles, contrast in class and struggle, appears under the house name Carl Swerdna (Andrews). To Davies Wells mentions other titles: 'The Death of Miss Peggy Pickersgill's Cat', 'The Professor', apparently offered to and rejected by *Family Herald*, *Household Words*, and *Home Chimes*. In *ExA* he mentions 'Lady Frankland's Companion'. By the time he wrote his autobiography, of course, Wells was not above disclaiming this sort of writing. HGW to A. M. Davies, 24 Dec 1887, 13 Jan 1888. At this time he told Davies that he was writing in a mood 'bordering on phrensy', and said that he would never criticize 'stuff *after it is printed* except to praise or because your enemy wrote it'. HGW to A. M. Davies, 30 Oct 1891, a letter written the day after his marriage.

35 HGW, 'The Chronic Argonauts', *SSJ*, Apr, May, June 1888, pp. 312–20, 336–71. Other versions of the work also appeared in *PMG*; see below, ch. 3. Bernard Bergonzi has dealt with this aspect of Wells's writing, and has reprinted parts of these works in *The Early H. G. Wells* (Manchester 1961). HGW to EH, 19 June 1888; to Editor, *Fortnightly*, 5 Sept 1891, in which he offers 'Chronic Argonauts' and another paper, which he later withdrew.

36 HGW, 'Socrates', *SSJ*, Dec 1886; 'Concerning Mr Welsted', *University Correspondent*, 7 Oct 1893; in *ET*: 'The Governess as Tutor: Charlotte Brontë's "Louis Moore"', 1 Dec 1893; 'Pestalozzi: How Gertrude Teaches Her Children', 1 Sept 1894; 'A Specimen of American Pedagogies' (a review of Parkes, *Talks on Pedagogics*), 1 Oct 1894.

37 HGW, 'The Scholastic Frame of Mind', *ET*, 1 Feb, 1 Mar, 1 Apr 1894. This three-part piece had as subtitles on parts ii and iii, 'Its Lack of Sympathy and Interest', and 'The Passion Pedagogic'. Earlier Wells had written a letter, 'Scholastic Isolation', to the same journal, 1 Sept 1893, which probably prompted the long and thoughtful follow-up.

38   HGW, *ET*: 'The Teaching of Geography', 1 Oct 1893; 'Geology in Relation to
     Geography', 1 July 1894; 'Science, in School and After School', 1 Nov 1894. This last
     piece had originally appeared in *Nature*, 27 Sept 1894, and was being reprinted
     because of the comment it aroused. The debate with R. H. Quirk appears in *ET*, 1 Jan
     1891, with HGW responding in a letter to the editor to Quirk's review, on 1 Dec 1890,
     of a book on Spencer. Quirk also responded to Wells, who had the last word on 1 Mar
     1891, when he dealt with the question of whether pure science was pure knowledge, or
     the application of knowledge.
39   HGW, *ET*, 'Professor Laurie on Herbert Spencer', 1 Dec 1892; a follow-up letter to
     Laurie's response, 1 Feb 1893; 'On Extinction', *Chambers's Journal*, 30 Sept 1893;
     Gentleman's Magazine: 'Zoological Retrogression', Sept 1891, pp. 246–53; 'Ancient
     Experiments in Co-operation', Oct 1892, pp. 418–22; 'Concerning Our Pedigree',
     June 1893, pp. 575–80 (the first of these was summarized in *Living Age*, 7 Nov 1891,
     and *Scientific American*, 10 Oct 1891). For other Wells comments on science and
     socialism which bear on this discussion, see *SSJ*: 'Are the Planets Inhabitable?', a
     speech to the debating society, Nov 1888; 'On Democratic Socialism', another speech,
     Dec 1886; Walter Glockenhammer, 'Mammon', Jan 1887; 'Mr H. G. Wells on
     Socialism', another talk to the debating society, Feb 1889. This last was followed by a
     debate with his friend, A. T. Simmons. Wells's best statement on the meaning of these
     matters was 'The Rediscovery of the Unique', *Fortnightly*, vol. L (July 1891), pp.
     106–11, where he put the point that unique qualities perceived by humans (that is,
     religious or other differences primarily) are illusory, although he did not use that word.
     The argument is similar to that in his thesis for the doctorate in science, completed in
     1943.
40   HGW to EH, 10 Mar 1888, and another dated 'Germinal', 1889. HGW, 'My First
     Romance', *SChron*, 25 June 1939; a photograph of Isabel printed there provides
     support for Wells's description. *ExA*.
41   HGW to EH, Mar 1888 (the first letter quoted; just below this is a section on 'My
     father' which is blacked out; apparently discussing alcoholism and tenseness in the
     parental marriage), May 1888, Sept ?1888; the second quotation, ??Dec 1890 (the
     letter reports inability to talk about college with Isabel, and says, 'Our social life is
     controlled by others and the autocrat will incite herself'). HGW to Fred Wells, just
     before Christmas 1891. RAG to HGW, 9 Nov 1939, remembers the end of the
     marriage and especially a walk with Wells towards Banstead discussing the marriage on
     the eve of H.G.'s leaving.
42   HGW, 'My Tragic Marriage', *SChron*, 9 July 1939: this article has another good
     photograph of Isabel. Wells's views on women after marriage may be seen in an early
     satirical story, 'The Lamias', *SSJ*, Feb 1889. HGW to A. C. Robbins, late May, 26
     May 1893. This last letter has a P.S. signed I. M. W. (Isabel), saying that HGW is still
     ill, and can't see her until Sunday next. That was apparently the date of the ultimatum.
     RAG was a witness to the second marriage and describes the Mornington Place flat
     originally inhabited by Wells, and the scenes of their first lovemaking, in his letter to
     HGW, 9 Nov 1939. Several other letters of HGW to A. C. Robbins appear in *ExA*.
43   HGW to A. M. Davies, 27 Dec 1893. *Ann Veronica* puts the same arguments in fic-
     tional form. See ch. 8.
44   HGW to EH, spring 1893, 22 Dec 1894.

Chapter 2

1   A good account of Wells's various residences from the time he moved to London is in
     Chrisopher Rolfe, 'From Camden Town to Crest Hill: H. G. Wells's Local
     Connections', *Camden History Review*, no. 1 (Autumn 1982), pp. 2–4. These houses are
     181 Euston Road (now demolished), Theobald's Road, 12 Fitzroy Road, Mortimer
     Road (now Mortimer Crescent, Nos. 6–7), 46 Fitzroy Road, 32 Red Lion Square, 7

Mornington Place, 12 Mornington Road (now Mornington Terrace), as well as the East Putney address mentioned in ch. 1.

2   This account comes from a dozen sources during Wells's life, including several photographs and from observation of the way in which he handled his correspondence. Time after time his draft reply on the incoming sheet ends with the injunction 'you sign', or 'I sign'. Usually these drafts were very complete. In the mid-1890s he wrote some of his correspondence on cards, occasionally as many as a dozen to a letter. He told Grant Richards that this saved time and made the letters more concise. He continued to write personal letters by hand until very late in his life, and quantities of these survive. How he discriminated between correspondence he would answer personally and that not, is not known, but it probably had a great deal to do with available time. HGW to Grant Richards, undated, *c.* Dec 1896, describing their move from Woking to Worcester Park, and discussed in Richards, *Memories of a Misspent Youth, 1872–1896* (London 1932), 329–30. In the letter Wells said they were always at home on Saturdays and welcomed visitors. Also see APW to HGW, 29 Aug 1894, after Wells and A. C. Robbins had moved to Mornington Road. See HGW, unsigned, 'In A Literary Household: Some Personal Confidences', *PMG*, 17 Oct 1894, p. 3.

3   APW to HGW, 3, 14 Sept, 21 Dec 1894, for details of short stories offered; 3, 29 Jan 1895, on terms offered to Wells by Dent. This is the correspondence about placing *The Time Machine*, both the magazine and book rights. The 29 Jan 1895 letter enclosed a book agreement from Methuen. On 24 Apr 1895 Watt and Wells discussed selling the latter's books in the US, and a letter from Watt to HGW, 25 Apr 1895, gives details of the discussion. Watt was educating Wells in the matter and closed his letter with 'Ours is by far the best way and we are the firm to do it'. Pinker, who had been an editor with *Pearson's Magazine*, began to act as an agent at this time; he offered his services to Wells, and indicated that *Black and White* was a source to which he had access. See JBP to HGW, 3 Jan 1896. When Wells for a time was using both Pinker and Watt, there was a good deal of jealousy between the two. See Pinker to HGW, 28 Apr 1897: 'Our friend A. P. Watt is up to some tricks again.' Pinker was very importunate with Wells; see JBP to HGW, 2 Jan, 5 Nov, 29 Dec 1898. Watt and HGW had an argument over sales and receipts from *The Stolen Bacillus*, and over Wells acting in part as his own agent. They broke off relations from 1902 until 1906. But by that time Pinker was also out of the running, and when HGW went back to Watt, the latter remained as his principal agent. See APW to HGW, 18 Oct 1901, 7, 10 Nov 1902; HGW to APW, 8 Nov 1902.

4   See the pseudonymous contributions to *SSJ*: Septimus Browne (HGW), 'A Talk with Gryllotalpa', no. 3 (Feb 1887), pp. 87–8; 'S.B.' (HGW), 'A Tale of the Twentieth Century: For Advanced Thinkers', no. 6 (May 1887), pp. 187–91 (a story set in July 1999, with a new electrically driven underground railway which runs from Victoria to Sloane Square); 'S.S.' (Sosthenes Smith: HGW), 'A Vision of the Past', no. 7 (June 1887), pp. 206–9. The last is a dream of his deep reptilian past which deals with scientific discovery and the pretensions of the powerful.

5   HGW to A. M. Davies, from Stoke, May–June 1888.

6   HGW to Fred Wells (who had gone to South Africa), summer '93. The letter has a drawing of the Wellses' new house in Sutton, and Wells says, 'Isabel is very well. I have been very busy with the floors, the blinds and all that kind of thing.'

7   HGW to A. M. Davies, (?) Mar 1894.

8   HGW to A. M. Davies, summer '94; to EH, 16 July 1894, *c.* May 1896. For his more advanced views see 'Popular Writers and Press Critics: An Informal Appreciation', *SR*, 8 Feb 1896.

9   See Grant Richards, *Author Hunting, by an old literary sportsman: Memories of years spent mainly in publishing, 1897–1925* (London and New York 1934), for Wells's letters to him dated 15 June, 7 July 1895; also p. 213 on his work.

10 JBP to HGW, 10, 14 Feb 1899, letters which summarize HGW's views of his work at that time; George Lynch, 'What I Believe: A Chat with Mr H. G. Wells', *Puritan*, Apr

1899, pp. 218–20. Also see 'Mr H. G. Wells', *Bromley Record*, Feb 1898, pp. 20–2, apparently also a report of an interview with Wells. The piece is more concerned with the role of Thomas Morley in HGW's early education, and refers to 'On Schooling and the Phases of Mr Sandsome' which Wells mentioned to the writer. A very busy cartoon dated Nov 1895 (see illus. no.7) shows the various stages of an article and story in the Wells home until it finally appears in print. By this time HGW was beginning to hear from earlier schoolmates, who thought he might be able to help them with their work. See S. Bowkett to HGW, undated letters (two) of 1895, 1896. HGW to W. Briggs, June 1898. Wells was vain enough of his name that he tried to get Davies to withdraw it from the 1898 revision of the *Textbook of Biology*. He had become a valuable 'property', to use the modern vernacular. Wells did not like the revisions at all; HGW to A. M. Davies, June 1898: Davies to HGW, 8, 16 June 1898. HGW's letter said, 'And so we go our separate ways. I shall call your name with considerable vehemence in private for some time for indeed you have been pitifully secretive, disloyal and shabby to me, but in the end I shall bear you no ill will.' He and Davies drifted apart for a time, but by 26 Mar 1902 they were discussing the Royal Society, and by 4 Apr 1909, reminiscing over the days at the old College. Wells simply could not remain angry at these earliest of his friends and supporters.

11   HGW, unsigned, 'The Dream Bureau — A New Entertainment', *PMG*, 25 Oct 1893; HGW to Rudolf Cyprian, 5 Apr 1902; and his autobiographical article, 'H. G. Wells, Esq., B.Sc.', in *Royal College of Science Magazine*, vol. XV, part vii (Apr 1903), pp. 221–4, where he again uses the dream motif to talk about the objects of his writing. A number of recent critics have offered comments on Wells's use of dreams, most especially John Reed, *The Natural History of H. G. Wells* (Athens, Ohio 1982).

12   HGW, 'My Dreams', *New Leader*, 21 Oct 1944. In this article he also remarked, 'More and more are my dreams what I believe the psychologists call compensatory; the imaginations I have suppressed revolt and take control.' This was in reference to his reaction to World War II, but it expresses quite clearly what went on in his mind from earliest childhood.

13   HGW, unsigned, *Lika Joko*: 'The Island of Opera', 24 Nov 1894; 'The Hygenic Country', 15 Dec 1894. HGW, 'Concerning the Nose', *Ludgate Monthly Magazine*, Apr 1896, pp. 678–81. HGW, *PMG*: unsigned, 'I Skate', 5 Jan 1894; Jane Crabtree (HGW), 'Hints on Visiting the Academy: Addressed to a Young Lady', 9 May 1894; unsigned, 'The Jilting of Jane', 5 July 1894 (this last later appeared over Wells's name).

14   HGW, 'Stray Thoughts in an Omnibus', *Black and White*, 4 Aug 1894; HGW, 'At a Window', *Black and White*, 25 Aug 1894; unsigned piece, 'The Very Fine Art of Microtomy: The Subtle Beauty of Next to Nothing', *PMG*, 24 Jan 1894, and its follow-up, also unsigned, 'In a Holborn Factory — Some More Microscopic Objects', *PMG*, 5 Mar 1894. For his short stories, signed, see HGW, 'Our Little Neighbour', *New Budget*, 4 Apr 1895; 'The Thumbmark', *Pall Mall Budget*, 28 June 1894; 'The Thing in No. 7', *Pall Mall Budget*, 25 Oct 1894. The last is a good suspense story with a twist.

15   HGW, *Select Conversations with an Uncle* (London and New York 1895). HGW to John Lane, 10 Sept, 14 Nov 1894, 20 Jan, another undated, 1895. Two short stories appear in the book, 'A Misunderstood Artist' and 'The Man with a Nose'. Uncollected 'Uncle' stories appearing in *PMG* were 'The Golden Gospel of Ugliness: A Jeremiad of Jewellers', 21 Dec 1893; 'The Ugliest Thing in London: An Inquiry', 3 Apr 1894; 'The Advancement of Humanity: A Serious Discussion', 11 June 1894. Others may yet emerge.

16   HGW, *Certain Personal Matters* (London 1897). See Sidney Brooks to HGW, 14 May 1895, asking him to revive Euphemia. Brooks, formerly an editor on the *Budget*, had moved to New York. He also told Wells that W. D. Howells was a supporter (letter of 17 Aug 1896). Brooks eventually published some HGW items in a pirated edition, for which he apologized in a letter of 8 Jan 1897. In one of the Euphemia papers already

cited, 'In a Literary Household — Some Personal Confidences', first published unsigned in *PMG*, 17 Oct 1894, HGW described his house and his writing, and ended with this remark directed to his family: 'However, there is a purely personal matter, though it illustrates very well the shameless way in which those who have the literary taint will make a market of their most intimate affairs.' HGW would carry this idea much further before he finished writing. For comments on *Certain Personal Matters* see J.M. Barrie to HGW, 13 Oct 1897, thanking him for a copy which he describes as 'long lost friends of mine'. The review quoted is from *SR*, 15 Jan 1898. On the reprinted edition, see JBP to HGW, 30 Sept, 10 Oct (the signed agreement) 1901. HGW received 100 gns. for the reprint rights over two years; the book sold for 6*d*. and 1*s*.6*d*. in the two editions. The publishers also had the right to reprint chapters in their journals for a fee of 5 gns. each. 'The Euphemia Papers', in the Atlantic Edition, is even more restricted, as 18 of the pieces from *Certain Personal Matters* are not reprinted.

17   Every serious writer on Wells in recent times has attempted to deal with his reviewing and his early work on science, usually separately. For that reason the literature on his contributions to periodicals, their location and number and context, is very large. The significant articles are Gordon Ray, 'H.G. Wells's Contributions to the *Saturday Review*', *Library*, 5th ser., vol. XVI, no. 1 (Mar 1961), pp. 29–36; Robert M. Philmus, 'H. G. Wells as a Literary Critic for the *Saturday Review*', *Science-Fiction Studies*, no. 4 (1977), pp. 166–93; Michael Timko, 'H. G. Wells's Dramatic Criticism for the *Pall Mall Gazette*', *Library*, 5th ser., vol XVII, no. 2 (June 1962), pp. 138–45. Significant recent books, which not only analyse the writing but also reprint some of it, are Patrick Parrinder and Robert M. Philmus, eds., *H. G. Wells's Literary Criticism* (Brighton, Sussex and Totowa, N.J. 1980), and Robert M. Philmus and David Y. Hughes, *H.G. Wells: Early Writings in Science and Science Fiction* (Berkeley and London 1975). I am indebted to these works, and especially to their annotation. However, any person wishing to write about Wells and his time must do a substantial amount of reading in the journals for which he wrote. To begin with, not every item has as yet been identified, and the content of the work which has not been reprinted often lends insight to other work. This is a highly prolific period for Wells, both in learning and production.

18   HGW, 'My Fight with G.B.S.', *SChron*, 23 July 1939. For an interesting contemporary view, probably not by Wells, see 'Ten Minutes with Mr Bernard Shaw', *To-day*, 28 Apr 1894, and for one which may well be by Wells, 'The Censorship of Plays: A Talk with Mr Bernard Shaw', *PMG*, 21 Mar 1895.

19   Unsigned reviews by HGW, *PMG*: '"Guy Domville" at the St James's', 15 Feb 1895; '"Delia Harding" at the Comedy', 18 Apr 1895; '"Vanity Fair" at the Court Theatre', 29 Apr 1895. Shaw's reviews of *An Ideal Husband* and *Guy Domville* are in *SR*, 12 Jan 1895.

20   Wells began with a spurt of 14 novels in his first three offerings, as Harris meant that he should earn his money. See HGW to Sarah Wells, 25 Mar 1895, when he remarked, ' . . . I am nearly off my head reading the silly things.' Wells later found himself having to review a book of Grant Allen's, and before he did so he thought he should reveal himself as the critic of Allen's earlier novel. Allen said that he had known it for some time, and he then remarked that he had reviewed *The Time Machine*. Eventually the two exchanged visits and views. Allen said to Wells, 'We may differ on our views of what constitutes good literature, and yet come together in a vast number of subjects, from argon to devilled kidneys. . . .' Wells and Allen continued to exchange notes and visits until 1899 at least, with the object of analysis almost always being 'the factor of determination in sexual freedom', to use Allen's words. HGW to Allen, Oct 1895; Allen to HGW, Oct 1895; HGW to Allen, 1896, on the occasion of his move to Worcester Park; Allen to HGW, late 1895, 4 Oct 1895 (on *Uncle*), 8 July 1899 (on *When the Sleeper Wakes*).

21   HGW, unsigned, 'The Disreputableness of Authorship', *National Observer*, 3 Nov 1894, pp. 637–8. The copy at Illinois bears Wells's emendations as if it were to be

reprinted somewhere, but as yet I have not located where. In addition to the writers cited who liked Wells's comments, one could add Arthur Conan Doyle, who visited Wells several times, and thanked him profusely for the comments in his review of one of Conan Doyle's books. A. Conan Doyle to HGW, prob. June or July 1898, although it may have been earlier.

22   Wells's review of *The Woman Who Did* is in *SR*, 9 Mar 1895. Others cited here from *SR* are 'The Method of Mr George Meredith', 21 Dec 1895; 'The Novel of Types', 4 Jan 1896; '"Jude the Obscure"', 8 Feb 1896; 'A Slum Novel', 28 Nov 1896; and 'The Lost Quest', 1 Aug 1896. This last piece was signed 'H.G.W.'.

23   HGW, 'Variorum: Of the Difficulties of Reviewing', *New Budget*, 9 May 1895. See *Academy*, 27 Mar 1897, which reports Wells's speech at a dinner in his honour at the New Vagabonds Club. HGW, 'Flickers of Imagination and a Flare' (review of R. Hichens, *Flames*, and Maures Jokai, *The Green Book*), *SR*, 3 Apr 1897. On a somewhat similar note see HGW's unsigned article 'The Sawdust Doll', *PMG*, 13 May 1895, which is not a review of a play, as some have had it, but an essay on the replacement of Victorian dolls with the doll figure of the 'new woman'. Why not either keep the old one, or give us a real one? Wells ended by remarking that the current mode was, '. . . if life is ugly we must take pains to alter it in fiction.'

24   See *Academy*, 16 Jan 1897, for the symposium and HGW's remarks.

25   HGW, 'The Examiner Examined', *University Correspondent*, 23 Sept 1893; A.T. Simmons and HGW, 'The Miscellaneous as an Educational Curriculum', *c.* 1893–4, cutting read at Illinois and as yet unlocated; perhaps *Science and Art?*

26   See for instance HGW's unsigned 'The Cultivation of the Faculty: A New Industry', *PMG*, 3 Nov 1894, and his running debate at about the same time in *Nature*: signed letter, 29 Nov 1894; a review, under the title 'The Sequence of Studies', of some textbooks, 27 Dec 1894; a response to his review in the issue of 10 Jan 1895; Wells's response to that letter, signed, 17 Jan 1895. Wells did not leave these matters entirely, for as late as 1911 in the *Eye-Witness*, 28 Sept 1911, he wrote a piece on an all-too-familiar subject, 'The Academic Committee'. He even continued to try to reform the Royal College by calling for a course in pedagogy for the students there. This issue was caught up in that of whether students should wear gowns in class, and the debate was finally terminated by Wells, who realized the futility of it. See *Royal College of Science Magazine*: HGW, 'The Value of the A.R.C.S.', Oct 1894; various responses in the Nov 1894 issue; further responses, and HGW's comments on these in 'The Scholar and the Gown', Jan 1895; further comments by Wells's readers in Feb 1895; HGW's final riposte, 'That Gown and Other Matters', Mar 1895.

27   HGW, unsigned three-part article, 'The Sins of the Secondary Schoolmaster,' *PMG*, 28 Nov, 8, 15 Dec 1894.

28   HGW, 'Science Teaching — An Ideal and Some Realities', address delivered on 12 Dec 1894, *ET*, 1 Jan 1895, pp. 23–9. See notice in *Nature*, 20 Dec 1894, urging scientists to read the piece.

29   Wells's articles in this period, with related material, include his comments on the London University question: HGW, 'The Threatened University', *SR*, 14 Dec 1895, a strong discussion of cramming and his education at the Royal. Wells was very forthcoming, and the *SR* editor took it upon himself to say HGW was using the letter as a puff for his own work. This brought an answer from another pen on 21 Dec 1895, defending Wells's facts. See also HGW's own signed letter, 'The London University Question', *SR*, 4 Jan 1896. The editor continued to respond rather heatedly to HGW. Also see Part iii of a debate among Wells, Sylvanus Thompson, and P. Chalmers Mitchell, on 'The Bill to establish a London University supervisory commission', *SR*, 31 July 1897. Other useful pieces for Wells's thought at this time are 'The South Kensington Revolution', 'The Science and Art of Education', *ET*, 1 Feb, 1 Mar, 1 May 1896.

30   Wells's finances at this period are discussed in his *ExA*. See A. Harmsworth to HGW, 18 Nov 1897, commending Wells's first article, and S.J. Penn, managing editor of the

Daily Mail, to HGW, 18 Nov 1897. Wells offered a series on his creed of what a proper school should be, in holograph on the back of the original letter. The cottage at Liss, 139 Station Road, was described in a recent real-estate brochure as having 4 bedrooms, 2 reception rooms, kitchen, breakfast room, garden, and an attached garage; the asking price was £42,000 freehold.

31 'The Root of the Matter — Some Reflections on the British Schoolmaster', *DMail*, 18 Nov 1897.

32 *DMail*: 'About the Principia — Dead Languages That Ought to Be Buried', 4 Dec 1897; 'A Parenthesis — Bookkeeping à la Maître d'École', 17 Dec 1897; letter to editor *in re* Sylvanus Thayer, 17 Dec 1897; another letter by HGW, 23 Dec 1897; 'Sums — The Fine Art of Not Teaching Mathematics', 24 Dec 1897; 'Stinks — The Cheerful Game of Teaching Science Without a Balance', 28 Dec 1897. For similar and related comments see the series by D. A. Williams, entitled 'Made in Germany', *DMail*, 6, 8, 9, 10, 11, 12 Nov 1897, with comments on 16 Nov 1897. HGW's articles began the day after this series closed with Williams's last article, on 17 Nov 1897.

33 See HGW, signed review, 'Peculiarities of Psychical Research', *Nature*, 6 Dec 1894, a description of a book on telepathy. Wells called for more scientific method in the research. Also see in *PMG*: HGW, unsigned, 'Angels and Animalculae', 9 Oct 1894, which demolishes a teleological attack on evolution; his 'Through a Microscope — Some Moral Reflections,' 21 Dec 1894 (in *Certain Personal Matters*); his article on the discovery of argon, 'The Strangeness of Argon — Some Very Remarkable Facts', 15 Mar 1895; and his response to a reader, 'The Writer of the Article', 18 Mar 1895, where he remarked that his science was written for general readers. The Wells-Gregory correspondence in this period, although slim (the two met fairly often, of course), is useful in this regard. See RAG to HGW, 2 Apr 1895, providing data for HGW, 'The Protean Gas' (on helium), *SR*, 4 May 1895. Wells sent Gregory *Jude the Obscure* to read, 16 Mar 1896. Also see, on the origin of volcanic craters on the moon, as well as gravity, RAG to HGW, 15, 22 June 1899. Other items from *PMG* in this period, mostly unsigned, include 'In a Holborn Factory: Some More Microscopic Objects', 5 Mar 1894; 'Jellygraphia: A New Vice', 28 Feb 1894 (in which Wells laments that copying only inhibits analysis, to which amen); 'The Polyphlorisballsanskittlograph: A Souvenir of the Royal Society Soirée', 8 May 1894, a very funny account of the incomprehensibility of a recent meeting; 'The Foundation Stone of Civilization: A Dissertation Upon a Flint', 22 May 1894, on the growth of tools from the first flints, some of which had punctured a bicycle tire and which led to the dissertation. For science-fiction writers in competition with Wells, see A. Kingsley Russell, ed., *Science Fiction by the Rivals of H. G. Wells* (London and Secaucus, N.J. 1979).

34 HGW, unsigned, *PMG*: 'The Advent of the Flying Man — An Inevitable Occurrence', 8 Dec 1893; 'The Extinction of Man — Some Speculative Suggestions', 25 Sept 1894. HGW, *SR*: 'The Cyclic Delusion', 10 Nov 1894; unsigned, 'Bye-Products in Evolution', 2 Feb 1895; unsigned, 'Intelligence on Mars', 4 Apr 1896.

35 HGW, 'Cheap Microscopes and a Moral', *SR*, 12 Sept 1896. The responses, mostly from British manufacturers, came in the issues of 19 Sept and 17 Oct 1896; in Wells's rejoinder on 26 Sept 1896, he challenged the British manufacturers to meet the German quality and price. See RAG to HGW, 28 Sept 1896, on the original article. Wells continued to press the matter in another *SR* letter, 24 Oct 1896, which prompted the manufacturers to say that they were in production with his requirements; see the issues of 14, 28 Nov 1896.

36 HGW, 'Morals and Civilization', *Fortnightly*, Feb 1897, pp. 263–8. Other pieces which deal with this argument are 'The Acquired Factor', his review of C. Lloyd Morgan's *Habit and Instinct, Academy*, 9 Jan 1897; his review of J. G. Nisbet's *The Human Machine, Academy*, 6 May 1899; and 'Physiography Rehabilitated', his unsigned review of his old friend and colleague A.T. Simmons's work, *Physiography for Beginners, ET*, 1 Feb 1897.

In addition one could cite HGW's review of Grant Allen's *The Evolution of the Idea of God*, *DMail*, 27 Nov 1897. Gregory kept up the drumfire by his comment on Wells's work in a letter to the *Academy*, and in *Nature*; in a letter to HGW, 1 Feb 1898, he described his review as having been written so people would take it as a scientist talking about the fiction, thus giving it strength. Also see HGW, 'The Limits of Individual Plasticity', *SR*, 19 Jan 1895.

37 This story is laid out in considerable detail in B. Bergonzi, *The Early H. G. Wells*. Also see 'The Man of the Year Million — A Scientific Forecast', *PMG*, 26 Nov 1893. W.E. Henley to HGW, 28 Sept, 24 Nov, 4, 6 Dec 1894; John Connell, *W. E. Henley* (London 1949), adds a bit to the story. Wells remained in debt to Henley for this help, and although the old man was to die fairly soon Wells followed his life until his death; see the letter from HGW to Henley, 30 Oct 1901, in Connell, on the occasion of William Nicholson's portrait of Henley being exhibited. The original letter, 5 pp. long, is at Boston; it is addressed to 'Dear "Man of Letters"'.

38 HGW, *The Time Machine* (New York: Random House 1931), special edn. illus. W.A. Dwiggins, with a new introduction by Wells, pp. vii–x.

39 APW to HGW, 7 Feb 1895; HGW to William Heinemann, 14 May 1895.

40 G. Richards, *Memories of a Misspent Youth*; *Review of Reviews*, vol. XI (June 1895), pp. 701–2; HGW to Sidney Low, 26 Oct 1895; HGW to T.H. Huxley, May 1895 (Huxley Papers, 'General', XXVIII. 233–4). Another who found *The Time Machine* and other works, especially *Anticipations* (1901), to be very important and who played a role in introducing Wells to the public was W.T. Stead, editor of the *Review of Reviews*. They became estranged over *Ann Veronica*, but before then, in correspondence, reviews, and generally, Stead aided Wells in his early career. J. D. Boylen, 'W. T. Stead and the Early Career of H. G. Wells, 1895–1911', *Huntington Library Quarterly*, vol. XXXIII, no. 1 (Nov 1974), pp. 53–79.

41 Quoted in G. Richards, *Misspent Youth*, 317–18. By this time Richards together with George Steevens had visited Wells at Worcester Park, and they had been visited in turn by Jane and HGW on their new tandem. Richards had also, when this letter was received, introduced Wells to Edward Clodd and Grant Allen; see Richards, 216–16.

42 W. E. Henley to HGW, 5 Sept 1895. APW to HGW, 3, 24 Sept, 21 Dec 1894, on the difficulty of placing his stories. Once Heinemann signed, Watt could remark, 'Should this book prove to be a success I would be able to do v.v. much better with a second volume. I trust that this may only be the first of many similar transactions between us ...' S. Bowkett to HGW, 8 Aug 1898; RAG to HGW, 18, 19 Aug 1898. G. Lynch, 'What I Believe', *Puritan*, Apr 1899.

Chapter 3

1 HGW, *Babes in the Darkling Wood* (London 1940). Introduction, Sir Thomas More, *Utopia* (London 1905), iii–viii, most readily located in *An Englishman Looks at the World* (London 1914), 184–7, and reprinted in an edition of *Utopia* by the Limited Editions Club (New York 1935). Preface, Atlantic I (1924).

2 HGW, *Seven Famous Novels* (New York 1934), preface, vii–x.

3 HGW, introduction to *The Sleeper Awakes* (London 1910). There is a third introduction (London 1921) with less in it about what was cut.

4 HGW, preface, Atlantic I (1924), xxii. The first foreign review was by Paul Valéry, 'H.G. Wells', *Mercure de France*, May 1899.

5 APW to HGW, 27 Apr, 6, 13 May, 12, 16, 25 July 1895. HGW to W. Heinemann, 7 Aug 1897, 22 Apr, 22 May, 22 July, Aug (undated) 1899. Wells asked the Society of Authors to vet his contracts. Society to HGW, 10 Feb, 11 June 1896. The correspondence with the Society fills three large file folders.

6 P. Chalmers Mitchell, 'Mr Wells's "Dr Moreau"', *SR*, 11 Apr 1896; HGW, signed letter on the review, *SR*, 7 Nov 1896, which also contains Mitchell's comment. Even

more horrified was the liberal anti-vivisectionist journal, the *London Echo*, whose reviewer, 'N.O.B.' (17 June 1896), liked Wells's work but was appalled at this book. Even though 'a narrative of consummate power', *Dr Moreau*, it was said, 'violates every canon of aesthetics'.

7   HGW to R. Cyprian, 28 Dec 1896. One wonders how Wells would have reacted to the various film versions (or perversions) of his moral tale. He certainly refused to license a dramatic version and in very strong terms. See APW to HGW, 7 Mar 1919, on a proposed Paris performance.

8   JBP to HGW, 14 Oct 1898; Pinker's accounts with HGW, 23 Jan 1935. APW to HGW, 10, 11 Nov 1926; HGW to APW, 15 Nov 1926 (there is an indication in this last that it was republication in the Essex Edition which aroused the new film interest). APW to MCW, 15, 26 Feb 1927. HGW gave another author the rights to his idea, and made his comment on transparency in a letter used as a preface to Keble Howard, *The Peculiar Major* (London ?1919), v–vi.

9   HGW, preface, Atlantic III (1924), ix, on Frank Wells's contribution, as well as his discussion in *Strand*, vol. LIV (Jan–June 1920), pp. 154–63, which is an introduction to HGW's own condensation of the novel. The *Strand* piece also discusses the illustrators of the work, but an analysis of the comments finds that one of these illustrators was a fraud, using work from a Dutch translation and passing it on to HGW as his own work. I am indebted to Eric Korn for this insight. 'Another Basis for Life', *SR*, 22 Dec 1894; *Honours Physiography*, 65–7; on canals, *Nature*, 27 Nov 1892; HGW, unsigned, 'Intelligence on Mars', *SR*, 4 Apr 1896. For other HGW comments see his letter, 'Is Earth the Only Peopled Planet?', *DMail*, 4 Nov 1903, one in a number of other comments, the result of remarks by Prof. A. Russell Wallace, who believed that only earth was inhabited. Also see HGW, 'The Things That Live on Mars', *Cosmopolitan*, vol. XLIV, no. 4 (Mar 1908), pp. 334–42, with marvellous illustrations. In this piece HGW proceeded from known science to his extrapolations, and his illustrator, William R. Leigh, followed his lead exactly. The illustrations remind one of the later cartoon version of HGW's story.

10 HGW was clearly thinking seriously about the idea in the *Saturday Review* piece, and it was under construction in this spring of 1896. W. (?) Marinslokes to HGW, 14 Mar 1896, commenting that Pearson had liked the first part of the MS. HGW adorned the letter with several 'picshuas' showing that he was still not sure what his ending would be, and that approval might be important to the outcome. HGW to Henry Hick, early 1897, although this letter may refer to another work. *Academy* (Supp.), 22 Jan 1898, calls attention to the rewriting in the book. HGW also offered the book (or a synopsis) for possible serialization to the agent W. Morris Colles; HGW to Colles, 26 Jan 1896.

11 JBP to HGW, 12 Jan 1896 (the success of HGW's work had enabled Pinker to place 'In the Abyss' in the US for 12 gns.), 25 Aug, (undated) Dec 1896. Unsigned review, almost a blurb, *SR*, 29 Jan 1898 J. M. Barrie to HGW, 22 Jan 1898, saying he had lain awake all night after reading the book thinking of the possibilities. Reality appears in his letter to HGW of 7 June 1898, however. On the first efforts to sell the film rights, see APW to HGW, 20, 22 Mar 1916. The discussion apparently did not lead to anything at that time. A letter from RAG, 'Mars in Fiction', *Academy*, 12 Feb 1899, discusses the scientific background to the book.

12 HGW, preface Atlantic VI (1925), ix. The book was serialized in the *Strand* in England in 1900, and in the *Cosmopolitan* in America soon after.

13 RAG to HGW, 15 June (on lunar craters and their origin: Gregory urges HGW to use Nasmyth and Carpenter, *The Moon*, as a source, and sends him some papers to read as well), 22 June 1899 (on gravity and its impact, and sending HGW specific mathematics done by F. Castle in response to HGW's request). These letters are quoted in detail in Armytage, *Sir Richard Arman Gregory*. But see *Nature*, 9 Jan 1902, which thought the gravity sequence good but challenged, incorrectly, some other scientific assumptions.

14 JBP to HGW, 10 Mar (first two chapters), 21 Mar (can you provide sequels?), 14 Apr (very good, will begin in *Strand* end of the year, just after a Grant Allen short story sequence), 18 Apr, 5 May, 24 July, 29 July 1899 (fragment setting out details of US sales from Elizabeth, Pinker's wife); JBP to ACRW, 29 Sept, 3, 10 Oct 1899; JBP to HGW, 8, 13, 14 Dec 1899. The last two also deal with *Tales of Space and Time*, and *Love and Mr Lewisham*, both of which were affected by the war as well. *Mr Lewisham* was delayed, in fact.

15 HGW, preface, Atlantic V, ix; the quoted sentence was underlined by HGW in the proof he corrected.

16 JBP to HGW, 8 Aug, 29 Sept 1902.

17 G. K. Chesterton, 'Mr Wells and the Giants', *Heretics* (London 1905), 76–88. This is one of Chesterton's more important books on the matters of his day, and the only one in which HGW figures. The two men remained good friends, and Chesterton understood Wells much better than did the other in the friendly triangle, Hilaire Belloc, of whom much more later.

18 RAG to HGW, 10 Oct 1904; Beatrice Webb to HGW, ? Sept 1904. The weekend was 12–14 Dec 1904: Sidney to Beatrice Webb, 15 Nov 1904; the evening party was early in Dec 1905: see B. Webb to GBS, 4 Dec 1905. All these are in N. MacKenzie, ed., *The Letters of Sidney and Beatrice Webb*, 3 vols. (Cambridge 1978), II. 204, 208, 215–17.

19 ViP to HGW, 31 Dec 1904; to ACRW, 7 Mar 1906.

20 *New Yorker*, 10 Nov 1980, p. 221.

21 JBP to HGW, 11 Feb 1902 (on Italian rights), 3 Jan 1908 (Spanish rights to *War in the Air*). On foreign rights, and on copyrights, see esp. Pinker to HGW, 24 Feb 1905, which summarizes the status and is a good guide to US publications as well. D. Pacey, ed., *The Letters of Frederick Philip Grove* (Toronto 1976), esp. F. P. Grove to R. von Poelhitz, Bonn, 14 June 1903. It is not too much to say that Greve, or Grove, brought HGW to the attention of Germans because of the quality of his translations. Grove also translated *Anticipations*. The Proust efforts are mentioned briefly in the biography of Proust by George D. Painter (London and New York 1959).

22 JBP to HGW, 22 Mar 1897, 14 Jan, 13 July, 9 Aug, 9 Dec 1898, 6 Jan, 20 Apr, 14 July 1899, 21, 28 June 1900, 9 July 1901, 12 Feb 1902. Filson Young (editor of the *Daily Mail*) to HGW, 6, 8 Jan, 6 Feb 1903. Young eventually turned to the idea of a regular column based on travel in a railway carriage, and urged HGW to think of a series like Oliver Wendell Holmes's *Autocrat of the Breakfast Table*.

23 JBP to HGW, 30 Dec 1908, 21, 25 Oct 1909; to ACRW, 7, 14 Nov 1910.

24 APW to MCW, 25 Oct 1926, 17 Feb, 6 Apr 1927 (to Miss Craig). *Argosy* paid 20 gns. for 'The Cone'. On a letter from APW of 12 Mar 1928, HGW writes at the top, 'Why did you bring Watt into this? He costs 10%.' Gernsback wrote occasionally to HGW about his proposed pulp magazine on 19 Mar 1928. The early pulp *Fantastic Stories* also reprinted HGW, and it is in these old volumes that a small boy in western Maine first found Wells. HGW to various Gernsback representatives, 20 Mar, 4 Apr, 30 May, 26 July, 7 Oct 1928, 8, 29 Jan 1929.

25 APW to HGW, 29 Mar 1933; to MCW, 31 Mar 1933, 26 Sept 1938.

26 APW to HGW, 15 Feb 1945; MCW to APW, 20 Sept 1945; APW to MCW, 19 Feb, 27 Aug 1945, 18 Apr, 17 Sept, 11 Oct, 2, 6, 26 Nov, 20 Dec 1945, 22, 28 Mar, 26 July 1946; MCW to APW, 9 Jan 1946. HGW continued to annotate some of this correspondence, setting out his wishes, well into 1946, although Marjorie Wells handled all routine details.

27

H.G. WELLS AND THE BBC 1927–1946

Title	Date of BBC broadcast
The Apple	11–19 Jan 1946
The Beautiful Suit	26–30 Sept 1927; 30 Sept 19 Oct 1944
The Blue Plaque (The Stolen Bacillus)	25 July–15 Oct 1934; 15–29 Apr 1944; 24 Aug–5 Sept 1945

The Country of the Blind	5–10 Apr 1934; 22–3 May 1935; June 1935; June 1936; 15 Feb–2 Mar 1938; 16–19 Mar 1945; 29 Oct–4 Dec 1945; 23 Jan–May 1946
The Door in the Wall	25 Nov 1933–July 1934; 14–17 Feb 1938
Experiment in Autobiography	26 Nov 1938–12 Feb 1939
The First Men in the Moon	14–20 Aug 1936; 23 Nov 1935–May 1936
The Invisible Man	24 July 1942; 7–16 Mar 1944; 6–10 Sept 1945; 7–29 July 1946; 8 Aug 1946
Kipps	25–31 Mar 1926; Aug 1944–Jan 1945
The Last Inheritance	21 May 1942–Mar 1943
The Late Mr Elvesham	29 Mar–3 Apr 1946; 20 July–2 Aug 1946
Mr Ledbetter's Vacation	4–5 Sept 1944
Love and Mr Lewisham	21 June 1943–Feb 1944
The Magic Shop	7–8 Sept 1934; 7–12 Dec 1939; 1–12 Mar 1943; 7–13 Oct 1943; 10–16 May 1945
The Man Who Could Work Miracles	16 Apr–22 June 1934; Dec 1934–June 1935; 29–31 Oct 1936; 23 Sept–6 Dec 1937; 19 Jan–25 Feb 1943; 25–8 Sept 1944; 16–31 Mar 1945; 22–30 Oct 1945; 1–18 Dec 1945; 3 Jan–6 Feb 1946
Mind at End of Its Tether	26 Nov 1944–Aug 1945; 18 Jan 1946; 4–11 Mar 1946
The New Accelerator	14–17 Mar 1938; 11–12 Sept 1945; 9–11 Apr 1946
The Outline of History	9–21 Jan 1945; Apr–23 May 1945
The Outlook for *Homo Sapiens*	5 May 1942
The Pearl of Love	29 July–21 Aug 1944; 14–19 Feb 1945; 4–6 Dec 1945
Mr Polly	18 Oct–11 Nov 1937; Oct 1940–Jan 1942; 16 Feb–1 Mar 1944; 14–19 Jan 1946; 17–29 July 1946
The Purple Pileus	25–7 Sept 1934; 19 June–27 July 1935; 10 Mar–18 June 1937; 23 Sept 1936–12 June 1937; 15 Sept–2 Oct 1939; 19–23 Sept 1944; 29 Apr–1 May 1946
The Red Room	29 May 1931; 17–18 Jan 1936
The Sea Lady	23 Feb–8 Mar 1946; 9 May 1946
The Sea Raiders	1–4 Jan 1932
The Shape of Things to Come	23 July–1 Aug 1945; 23 Feb–Sept 1946
A Slip Under the Microscope	30 Sept 1943
The Stolen Bacillus (Lord of the Dynamos)	20–1 July 1931
The Time Machine	Jan–Aug 1940; 31 May–26 June 1944
Tono-Bungay	26 Nov–11 Dec 1936; 21 June 1943–Feb 1944; 8–14 Feb 1946
The Treasure in the Forest	18–28 Feb 1930
The Truth About Pyecraft	20 Sept 1933–27 Feb 1934; 25–7 Sept 1934; 29 Oct–11 Dec 1936; 25 Feb–2 Mar 1938; 30 Jan–13 Feb 1941; 17 Mar–9 July 1943; 1 Mar–5 May 1944; 4 July–16 Aug 1944; 8 Nov 1944; 13–14 July 1945; 17 Dec 1945; 29 Apr 1945–5 Jan 1946; 24 Jan–5 Feb 1946

The Undying Fire	20 Dec 1934; 8–12 Feb 1946
The Valley of the Spiders	29 Apr–1 May 1932
The Vision of Judgement	18–26 June 1945; 23 Aug 1944–May 1945
The War in the Air	2–5 Nov 1936
The War of the Worlds	28 April–5 Mar 1945
The Wheels of Chance	21 June 1943–Feb 1944; 22–9 Aug 1944; 6–9 Apr 1945
When the Sleeper Awakes	22 June 1936–Apr 1937
The World Set Free	14 Aug 1945

Compiled from BBC written archives, Caversham Park, Reading: correspondence with HGW, files no. 2 (1936–8); no. 3 (1939–44); no. 4 (1944–6). There are about 500 pieces of correspondence about these broadcasts, nearly all concerning the detail of the performances. HGW's correspondence with the BBC about his own appearances on the air is treated in ch. 13.

28 W. Warren Wagar has discussed these books and others written in the western world in his *tour de force*, *Terminal Visions* (Bloomington, Ind. 1982); but by fitting them into a primarily eschatological analysis, he has diminished the impact of their message concerning capitalism; or so it seems to me. This is especially true of Wells's books, and it is interesting that Wagar does not discuss *When the Sleeper Awakes* at all in this work.

29 HGW, preface, Atlantic II, ix, as well as the prefaces to the 1910 and 1921 reissues of *Sleeper*. HGW to 'My Dear Connell', 28 Jan 1900, says he began work on the book at Worcester Park in 1896.

30 Orwell's comment appears in his obituary, 'H.G. Wells', *Manchester Evening News*, 14 Aug 1946; E. Zamyatin, in *Herbert Wells* (St. Petersburg 1922, 1924), most easily available in P. Parrinder, ed., *H.G. Wells: The Critical Heritage* (London 1972), 258–74.

31 JBP to HGW, 25 July, 15 Dec 1898. The quote is from the first of these.

32 J.M. Barrie to HGW, 16 July 1899. Unsigned review, *Academy*, 10 June 1899. The *Speaker*, 3 June 1899, urged Wells to leave fiction of the future as his gifts were too strong, although they gave quite a lot of space to the book.

33 HGW to P. Cazenove, 13 May 1908 (draft in HGW's hand).

34 RAG to HGW, 23 Sept 1906. *Outlook*, Sept 1906; *SR*, (?) Sept 1906 (only read cuttings).

35 HGW to Macmillans, 2, 11 Jan 1906. The second letter was written from Beatrice and Sidney Webb's home, where the title had received some discussion. Robert Blatchford, 'The Latest News From Utopia. H. G. Wells and the Comet', *Clarion*, 5 Oct 1906.

36 Joseph Conrad to 'My Dear Wells', 15 Sept 1906. The second letter, to 'Dear H.G.', 2 Nov 1908, is about *The War in the Air*, but Conrad is making the same point. Hueffer had come to visit Conrad, and they had apparently spent a substantial period of time discussing H.G. and his art.

37 HGW to A.T. Simmons, undated letters reprinted and discussed in Winifred Simmons, 'H. G. Wells as Atomic Seer', Sydney (Australia) *Morning Herald*, 23 Feb 1946. The *Herald* had printed an article the previous year commenting on the HGW novel, and Mrs Simmons had located these letters as a result of reading it. This was probably the last time Simmons was able to help HGW; he died very suddenly in 1921. RAG to HGW, 11, 19 Aug 1921, on Simmons, his death and the need to provide for his children. RAG, 'A. T. Simmons', *Nature*, 25 Aug 1921. Simmons, HGW, and Gregory had, of course, been inseparable at the old Royal College, and RAG's obituary was tinged with that old friendship.

38 RAG to HGW, 17 May 1914.

39 HGW, unsigned, 'The Literature of the Future: the Horoscope of Books', *PMG*, 11 Oct 1893.

40 HGW, 'Human Evolution: An Artificial Process', *Fortnightly*, Oct 1896, pp. 590–5; reprinted in *Review of Reviews*, Nov 1896, pp. 605–6, in excerpted form.

41 HGW interview with George Lynch, 'What I Believe', *Puritan*, Apr 1899.

42 HGW, *DMail*, 7 June 1906, a sort of pastiche of his views, along with those of nine other observers, on the future. He uses the phrase 'things to come' in this piece. Also see HGW, *NYT*, 30 Mar 1913, a special article on forecasting the future; 'The Tendency of Science', *T.P.'s Weekly*, Christmas 1909. See JBP to HGW, 27, 30 Aug 1909; to ACRW, 10 Jan 1910. Wells's mature views are in HGW, 'Fiction About the Future', *DTel*, 30 Dec 1938, and various Australian newspapers. Parrinder and Philmus reprint the version from the HGW archives in *H. G. Wells's Literary Criticism*, and I have reprinted the version actually spoken over Australian radio in George Hay, ed., *Pulsar One* (Harmondsworth 1978). HGW's introduction quoted here appears in Atlantic I, xvi–xvii. Another Wellsian comment on the same point appears in his preface to Gabriel Tarde's *Fragment d'histoire future*, transl. as *Underground Man* (London 1905). In this preface (pp. 1–19), discussing French and English views of these matters, HGW says that if you can't get the reader by serious study, you must use 'foolery' and both he and Tarde have done just that. Tarde is restrained and much more believable than some commentators, says HGW (is he thinking of Verne?). He goes on to say that society exists ultimately 'in the exchange of reflections', and urges readers to go beyond the froth in this work to the real meaning behind it.

PART TWO

Chapter 4

1 HGW, 'On Democratic Socialism', *SSJ*, no. 1 (Dec 1886), pp. 23–5: 'The Cornerstone of Socialism is the great principle of the merging of the individual in the State.' 'Mr H. G. Wells on Socialism', *SSJ*, no. 18 (Feb 1889), pp. 152–5: 'Scientific Socialism aims at equality of opportunity.' The description in the text comes from the opening of the debate.

2 HGW, unsigned, 'On the Use of Ideals: A Contribution to the Art of Living', *PMG*, 23 Feb 1894; 'The New Optimism', *PMG*, 21 May 1894, unsigned review of Benjamin Kidd, *Social Evolution*; HGW, 'The Acquired Factor', *Academy*, 9 Jan 1897, p. 39, a review of C. Lloyd Morgan, *Habit of Instinct*; HGW, 'Wanted: A Classification', *School World*, Jan 1899, pp. 4–5. The last was the lead article in a new journal, and it was reviewed in the *Academy*, 21 Jan 1899. Other pieces that show this side of HGW are his interview with George Lynch, 'What I Believe', *Puritan*, Apr 1899; HGW, 'Is Britain on the Down Grade?', *Young Man*, June 1899, pp. 222–3, one of a series on this query at the end of the century, to which A. Conan Doyle, the Dean of Canterbury, A.R. Wallace, Albert Spicer, H.W. Massingham, James Bryce, and Goldwin Smith also replied; HGW, 'The Causeries of the Week: The Philosophy of a Bacteriologist', *Speaker*, 31 Oct 1903, a review of Elie Metchnikoff, *The Nature of Man*; and the 1905 preface to Gabriel Tarde, *Underground Man*. Also see HGW's 1905 preface to More's *Utopia*, reprinted Limited Editions Club, 1935.

3 *Fortnightly*, Apr–Dec 1901; *North American Review*, June–Nov 1901. JBP to HGW, 26 Mar, receives 'The Great Prospectus', 7 May, mid-May (the quotation) 1900, early Apr, 19 Apr 1901. HGW received an advance of £100 for the US book rights, as well as a royalty of 10% on the first 5,000 copies sold and 15% thereafter.

4 JBP to HGW, 24 May, 21, 27, 29 Nov, another the same week, undated, 10, 19, 30 Dec 1901, 27 Feb, 18 Apr (from New York, where he reported early sales of 1,000 copies: 'I found the best men, ready and able to talk of your work, and have taken the line that you are only beginning; that now you have health and the time to give your

powers full scope they had better stand clear and look out'), 20 June 1902, 3 Nov 1903. HGW found himself with an increased correspondence as his ideas circulated. See HGW to Frederick A. Evans, 9 Nov 1902, on the intellectual prowess of first children and illegitimate children.

5   HGW, *Anticipations*, preface to 1914 edn., vii–xiii. He described a recent aeroplane trip, and implied, which was true, that he flew whenever he could.

6   ERL to HGW, 5 Nov 1901, 5 Jan 1902. RAG to HGW, 19 Nov, 28 Dec 1901, 8 Apr 1902. *Nature* noticed two of the articles when they appeared in serial form: 'Land Locomotion in the XXth Century', 4 Apr 1901, and 'Future Warfare Article', 5 Sept 1901.

7   E.R. Lankester, 'The Present Judged by the Future', *Nature*, 13 Mar 1902 (Supp.), pp. iii–v. Later another view, less roseate but at the same time extremely respectful, was provided by 'F.W.H.' (? Francis W. Hirst), 'The Future of the Human Race', *Nature*, 29 Dec 1904, pp. 193–4, which discussed *Mankind in the Making, The Food of the Gods*, and *Anticipations*. Other reviews liked the mechanical and scientific material, but balked at Wells's views on birth control; see *DChronicle*, 11 Nov 1901. One, in *Literature* (16 Nov 1901), asked him about the so-called 'inferior races', and whether he had rejected warfare as a method in this world. HGW responded to this letter saying ('Lions in the Path', *Literature*, 23 Nov 1901) that he had changed his mind since *Sleeper*, but, he remarked, the book was a judgement not a prediction.

8   *Academy*, 7 Dec 1901, for Sidney Webb's comment; HGW thought that the most important books were Shaw's *Three Plays for Puritans*, W.E. Henley, *Hawthorn and Lavender*, and G. Archibald Reid's *Alcoholism*. N. and J. MacKenzie, eds., *The Diary of Beatrice Webb*, 3 vols. (London 1982–5), II. 226 (undated comment Dec 1901). In this note is the seeds of the Co-Efficients. Webb *Letters* II. 143–5 prints S. Webb to HGW, 8 Dec 1901. They went to Sandgate soon thereafter. See B. Webb, *Diary* II, 28 Feb 1902. Sidney Webb thought he could remember meeting Wells at Kelmscott House in the 1880s, but this may have been simply a courtesy memory.

9   GBS to HGW, 12 Dec 1901, in Dan H. Laurence, ed., *Collected Letters of George Bernard Shaw*, vol. II: 1898–1910 (London 1972), 224–6; GBS to T. H. S. Escott, undated, *Collected Letters* II. 252–4. William James to 'My Dear Reid', 30 May 1902, from Edinburgh; Reid had apparently sent James the book. Another who was impressed by the articles, and wrote to Wells congratulating him before he had seen the book itself, was Rudyard Kipling; to HGW, 21 Jan 1902, from Cape Town: 'I am immensely blessed that you are in the game too! After the idiots have done roaring & swearing and prevaricating, they'll begin to take stock of the situation then they'll call you & me and a few others choice names and they'll do about 5% of the things they ought to have done years ago and pat themselves on the back for another three generations.'

10   Joseph Wells to 'Kate' (ACRW), 20 Jan 1902; ACRW to GrW, undated (writing in an interval 'snatched from the society of Mr and Mrs Webb'); HGW to RAG, 29 Dec 1901. These are all invitations to the lecture. HGW told Gregory that the new baby (his son G.P., born in 1901) was also taking some of his time from writing.

11   JBP to HGW, 28 Jan, 26 Feb 1902. GrW to HGW, 28 Feb 1902: 'I was at the back of the top gallery and heard all your lecture except perhaps some words — But I suppose you know that *secundum artem* you read quite 25% too fast.' ERL to HGW, 17 Feb 1902. *Nature*, 6 Feb 1902, pp. 326–31. HGW made a slight error in the lecture, misidentifying Procrustes; 'T.B.S.' wrote to *Nature*, 20 Feb 1902, pointing out the error, and HGW later apologized.

12   HGW, *The Discovery of the Future* (London 1902), 29–30, 39–40, 70, 94–5.

13   Joseph Conrad to HGW, undated (probably end of Feb) 1902.

14   HGW discusses Lady Elcho in *ExA*, 396, 541–2. He apparently met her at a dinner given by Beatrice Webb, whom Lady Elcho had introduced to A. J. Balfour at a country weekend. Others at the Webbs' dinner were John Burns, the Shaws, and H. H. Asquith. B. Webb said that HGW was not at his ease, and 'rather silent'. Shaw was

'egotistical and paradoxical'. Lady Elcho described the dinner as 'thrilling', however. B. Webb, *Diary* II. 263 (28 Nov 1902). HGW to 'My Dear Sir', 13 Dec 1901, accepting an invitation to a dinner, apparently in his honour, at the Whitefriars Club. Osbert Sitwell, *Laughter in the Next Room* (Boston 1947), 113–14, recalls Wells's great feeling for Lady Elcho.

15   B. Webb, *Diary* II. 320 (20 Apr 1904). G. W. Ramsay to HGW, 6 Dec 1905; HGW to A. J. Balfour, 1 May 1905. This last had to do with rewarding original contributions to thought by some sort of pension. Also see JBP to HGW, 17 Feb 1902, where after a party HGW toyed with writing an article on Rosebery's Chesterfield speech, although he abandoned the idea.

16   Gilbert Murray to HGW, 19 Sept 1906 (HGW stayed with the Murrays, and probably met Ben Keeling, a Fabian supporter, at this meeting). Ramsay MacDonald to HGW, 16 Mar (House of Commons lunch), 10 June (another), 10 Dec (lunch and dinner, as well as observing the debate) 1908, 26 Feb 1909, for a March dinner with J. M. Barrie, E. V. Lucas, Maurice Hewlett, as well as MacDonald. GrW to HGW, 10 Jan 1908, introducing H. Samuel; Eliza Hueffer to HGW, 2 Aug 1907, on suffrage; HGW to GrW, 15 Dec 1901, thanks for putting him up for National Liberal Club; later, in an undated letter (LSE), a 'picshua' showing HGW waiting for Wallas who missed an appointment at the Club.

17   James R. Thirsfield (*TLS*) to HGW, 30 Jan 1902; JBP to HGW, 14 Jan, 10, 19, 27 Feb, 5 Mar 1903. HGW did not take all offers, as he could not have fulfilled the requests. See R. MacDonald to HGW, 1, 14 Nov 1904, on his request that HGW write for a socialist monthly the Labour Party was proposing to found. They offered no pay. HGW said that he thought his name might hurt the review, and MacDonald accepted the refusal very graciously. HGW later told GrW, undated letter (LSE), with regard to a young friend of his, that he should avoid writing for the left-wing press if he wished to make a living at it. Instead he should write for the capitalist press — the audience needed the message more, and they paid; then, after achieving success, he could proceed to donate his time and money to the cause. HGW certainly did his share of free or poorly paid writing, but he also sold everything he could to the capitalist press, just as he advised this young aspirant to socialist journalism to do.

18   JBP to HGW, 22, 29 Apr 1902, 17 Aug 1903; HGW to GrW, undated (probably July) 1902; GrW to HGW, 17 Sept 1902 (an 11-pp. letter offering evidence and good commentary). HGW, *Mankind in the Making* (London 1914), preface to 2nd edn., ix–xiii.

19   L. S. Amery to HGW, 19 Oct 1903; A. T. Simmons to HGW, 10 Oct 1903; F.M. Hueffer to HGW, *c.* Oct 1903 (perhaps 1904, as there is evidence that Hueffer did not read this book until *A Modern Utopia* appeared). ERL to HGW, 23 Sept 1903: 'I don't believe we can change the faulty nature of the Anglo-Saxon, and I don't want him to over-run the globe and eat up all the other races.' M. Roberts to HGW, 11 Aug 1904, 15 Feb 1905 (a postcard). ViP to HGW, 15 Mar, 7 Apr 1904: these letters are part of an exchange about Gissing, as well as on HGW's books (Paget came to Sandgate for a long and analytical weekend to discuss ideas). C.F.G. Masterman to HGW, 29 (*sic*) Feb 1905: he dined with HGW, discussing the ideas.

20   *DChronicle*, mid-Sept 1903 (I have seen a press cutting only). JBP to HGW, 26 Sept 1903, saying that L. F. Austin had written the review, and did not mean to be offensive as he 'thought it the most interesting book he had read for years'. HGW, 'Fact in Sociology', *Nature*, 2 Feb 1905, a response to the portmanteau review by 'F.W.H.', 29 Dec 1904 (see note 7). HGW to Theodore Bartholomew, 2 Dec 1903, calling for inexpensive books so all can comment on ideas.

21   *A Modern Utopia* (1905) appeared first in the *Fortnightly* from Oct 1904 to Apr 1905. See preface to Atlantic IX, and 'Note to the Reader' in the original edn. Wells also reprinted in Atlantic IX a paper, 'The Scepticism of the Instrument', given to the Oxford Philosophical Society in 1903 and reprinted, somewhat reworked, in *Mind*, vol. XXII,

no. 51 (July 1904), as well as four other essays from the period. In the *Mind* essay he attempted to show how his scientific training in logic could be supplied to other matters, and how he was trying to do so. Unfortunately, as he said, '*The forceps of our minds are clumsy forceps, and crush the truth a little in taking hold of it.*' The essay was reprinted as an appendix to *A Modern Utopia*. See HGW to Sir Henry Newbolt, 9 Nov 1903 (Boston), offering the piece to *New Review*.

22   M. Roberts to HGW, 11 Aug 1904; RAG to HGW, undated letter, 1905, quoted in Armytage, 52–3; ERL to HGW, 10 Apr 1905 (he took the book to Paris to read on holiday). W. Churchill to HGW, 9 Oct, 17 Nov 1907. J. Conrad to HGW, 2 Nov 1903, another soon thereafter undated, another undated 'Monday to Friday', late 1904. Other correspondence on this book is C. F. G. Masterman to HGW, 11 May 1905. HGW to S. S. McClure, 25 Sept 1906, and to P. Cazenove, 18 Dec 1906 (Indiana), discusses US publication and his relations with his agents. Sydney Olivier to HGW, 20 May 1905; Wells spent the weekend with the Oliviers, 20 Aug 1905.

23   'F.C.S.S.', 'Sociological Speculations', *Nature*, 10 Aug 1905. ViP to HGW, 19 May 1906; Vernon Lee, 'On Modern Utopias: An Open Letter to H. G. Wells', *Fortnightly*, Dec 1906, pp. 1123–37.

24   Maurice Browne to HGW, 28 Dec 1906, 21 Jan, 21 Apr 1907. HGW to Browne, 3 Jan, 30 Apr 1907. *New Age*, 2 May 1907, pp. 9–11, for a full account of the meeting. Others continued to comment and HGW to respond. See HGW to 'My Dear Munro', 8 Feb 1908, on humanizing the Christian message and the slandering of a Samurai club, describing the end result as 'a hard artificial mostly barren group of ascetics'. On education see HGW to C. W. Adams, 2 Nov 1903, which refers the latter to *Mankind in the Making*, to appear later: 'The natural way is for knowledge to grow *step by step* between thirteen and eighteen in the case of western whites.'

25   HGW to S. S. McClure, 11 Nov 1906; to P. Cazenove, 22 Nov 1906; to W. Perrin, 8 Sept 1906; to Cazenove, 27 Sept 1906. ACRW to Perrin, 15 Jan 1907; to Cazenove, 12 Feb 1907. HGW to Cazenove, 15 Jan 1907 (Indiana). JBP to ACRW, 24 Sept 1906; HGW to JBP, 25 Sept 1906; JBP to HGW, 26 Sept 1906.

26   W. Archer to HGW, 18 Mar; RAG to HGW, 16 Mar; J. Galsworthy to HGW, 11 May; ERL to HGW, 28 Aug; R. Blatchford to HGW, 3 July (postcard); J. Conrad to HGW, 4 Mar, 25 Sept, all 1908.

27   Ben C. Apps to HGW, 2 Dec 1907; HGW to Apps, 5 Dec 1907. *New Age*, 14 Mar 1908; two articles entitled 'Mr Wells and His New Work', *Labour Leader*, 13, 20 Mar 1908.

28   For a good summary of other visits, as well as HGW's, see Richard L. Rapson, *Britons View America: Travel Commentary, 1860–1935* (Seattle 1971). HGW is treated in a dozen places in the book. Another book which deals with the subject is H. C. Allen, *Conflict and Concord, The Anglo-American Relationship Since 1783* (New York 1959), esp. 162. See HGW, *The Future in America: A Search After Realities* (New York: Harper & Bros. 1906), for the American edition. HGW always enjoyed a good reputation, and had occasional strong friendships with those on the American left such as Lincoln Steffens, Ella Winter, Upton Sinclair, and others. He was 'part of their world'.

29   The book was serialized in *Harper's Weekly*, July–Oct 1906, and in *Tribune* in London from 4 July to 6 Sept 1906. See *SR*, 6 Mar 1897, for HGW's review of G.W. Steevens, *The Land of the Dollar* (1897), perhaps the most perceptive journalistic account of the US before HGW, Bennett, and Chesterton wrote theirs in this century. HGW to W. Perrin, 20 May 1905; JBP to ACRW, 19 Mar 1906. B. Webb, *Diary* II; Webb *Letters* II (the latter on her own 1898 trip); B. Webb to Catherine Courtney, 29 Apr 1898. GrW to HGW, 25 Mar 1906; HGW to GrW, 23 Mar 1906; F. B. Miles to GrW, 16 Apr 1906; HGW to GrW, 30 May 1906 (LSE). L. Steffens to HGW, undated (Apr) 1906, on White House visit. Steffens met with HGW to discuss T.R. and prime him on what to say and when. HGW sent Steffens a copy of the book, which brought forth, 'You have helped us near-sighted American reporters'; also undated mid-1907. HGW to ACRW, 6 May 1906, on his Chicago visit. HGW was somewhat taken aback by Hinky-Dink's

saloon, an opium den, and what from his description must have been a brothel. He did not get to bed until 2 a.m., and faced the Hull House luncheon the next day. He spoke of Fabianism, and the coming need for socialism to that audience. For the two gentry controlling Chicago politics at the time, see Lloyd Wendt and Herman Kogan, *Lords of the Levee: The Story of Bathhouse John and Hinky Dink* (Indianapolis 1943).

30   HGW to GrW, 11, 22 June 1906 (LSE). Miles followed HGW to London, and apparently the three of them met for lunch at Sandgate. *The Future in America* (London 1906), 357. The standard source on Wellsian visits to America is Sylvia Strauss, 'H.G. Wells and America', unpub. Ph.D. thesis, Rutgers 1968, a useful if somewhat naïve look.

31   M. Roberts to HGW, 10 Dec 1906; EH to HGW, 28 Oct 1906; W. Churchill to HGW, 21 Nov 1906. M. Beerbohm to HGW, 7 Feb 1908: Beerbohm was reading Wells's book in the US, and at the injunction of Henry James. The three apparently had a luncheon once Beerbohm returned to England. R. S. Baker to HGW, 29 Mar 1907; HGW when he replied recalled their conversation on racialism. Baker was soon to publish a very influential set of articles, later a book, *Following the Color Line* (1908), which highlighted the evils of peonage and racialism HGW touched upon. B. Webb to HGW, mid-Nov 1906. The party was the 27th. B. Webb also announced her conversion to women's suffrage in this letter, saying that Jane would be happy. See *The Times*, 5 Nov 1906, and B. Webb to Millicent Fawcett, 2 Nov 1906, for more on the conversion. Review by 'J.A.H.', *Manchester Guardian*, 5 Nov 1906. HGW to Chapman & Hall, 24 Oct, 8 Dec 1906; to W. Perrin, 27 Feb 1906; to P. Cazenove, 18 Dec 1906. John Perry, 'Social Problems in America', *Nature*, 17 Jan 1907.

32   Among a host of possible sources on the Fabian movement, two stand out. N. and J. MacKenzie, *The First Fabians* (London 1977), is an excellent source on the early days, and Anne Fremantle, *This Little Band of Prophets* (London 1960), puts the entire history into easily accessible form. The *Fabian Essays* (especially the first dozen volumes in the series) are of major importance in understanding the significance of the group. HGW had a much earlier tie with the Webbs, although it does not appear to have been known when they first met. Among the friends of the Wellses when they lived in Worcester Park was Rosamund Dobbs, a sister of Beatrice Webb. She told Jane that she was very sorry they were moving as she would miss both HG and Jane, and Gissing, whom she had met at the Wells home. Two letters survive from 1898, and Dobbs later travelled to Rome with Gissing and the Wellses. R. Dobbs to ACRW, 23 Dec 1899. HGW wrote several times about his first meetings with the Webbs, but the most interesting account, because of the time it appeared, is in the 1914 introduction to *Anticipations*, 2nd edn., xi: 'This extraordinary couple, so able and energetic, so devoted, so perplexingly limited, exercised me enormously.' On the Co-Efficients, see Bertrand Russell, *Autobiography*, vol. I (London 1967). S. Webb to HGW, 12 Sept 1902. The first meeting was on 6 Nov 1902. HGW proposed Henry Newbolt as a member. See Margaret Newbolt, ed., *The Later Life and Letters of Sir Henry Newbolt* (London 1942), which quotes HGW to Newbolt, 21 Mar 1904 (original at Boston); Reeves and HGW to Newbolt, (?)9 Apr 1904 (they spent a weekend with the Wells family, along with Pember Reeves). The Co-Efficients published, for members only, a yearly summary of their papers and debates, often along with a list of members present. HGW's principal appearances were when he spoke on 'What is the Proper Scope of Municipal Enterprise?' on 14 Dec 1903; on 'What Part are the Coloured Races Destined to Play in the Future Development of Civilization?' on 16 Jan 1905; and on 'The Higher Stage of Education — Some Theorizing About It' on 19 Feb 1906; he also acted as rapporteur on Sidney Webb's paper, 'The Future Revolution in English Local Government', on 17 Apr 1903. For an example of a novel which used this idea of a club to solve problems, see John Buchan, *A Lodge in the Wilderness* (London 1904).

33   B. Webb to HGW, 21 Mar, 30 Apr 1903 (the first weekend, after the earlier visits, was 26 Apr), a second long undated letter in this period, 5 Apr 1903; HGW to GBS, 27 Jan

1902; B. Webb, *Diary* II. 239–41 (28 Feb 1902: a very detailed entry, with descriptions of the physical and mental attributes of the Wells family); 271–2 (2 Mar 1903); 342–4 (17 Apr, 11 May 1905). The intimate discussions are reported in her diary, II. 319–20 (19 Apr 1904), which recounts a long weekend at Sandgate. Beatrice specifically asked for comments on why Graham Wallas had become distant, and HGW gave her such personal answers that the conversation became quite 'heavy'. As a result of this conversation Beatrice said that she would withdraw for a time and let Sidney be in the forefront, although this remained a pious intention. For the dream, see HGW to B. Webb, 24 Apr 1904. The strain with Wallas had been a long time coming; the two differed greatly over the role of religious education in public schools, and eventually they broke over this issue. Wallas resigned from the Society over Fabian Tract 116, written by Shaw, *Fabianism and the Fiscal Question* (1904), which took a protectionist line, probably in support of the Chamberlain government which was in some difficulty. HGW also resigned at this meeting, but Edward Pease persuaded him to withdraw his resignation. B. Webb, *Diary* II. 225–6 (9 Dec 1901); 267–8 (16 Jan 1903, a meeting in the country of the Shaws, Wallases, and Webbs); 316 (27 Feb 1904). The resignation occurred 22 Jan 1904. On the continuing relationship and strain over schools, see S. Webb to GrW, 6 Sept 1910.

34   Although this matter has received a great deal of attention, much of the correspondence surrounding the case has not yet been printed, and no account uses all available correspondence. The following letters are important in an understanding of the event: HGW to L. Haden Guest, 12 Dec 1905 (describes HGW's hopes for the future society); GBS to HGW, 5 Apr 1904 (on *This Misery of Boots*, which Shaw wanted to rewrite); GBS to E. Pease, 4 July 1905 (says Wells will stir something up, and then the Old Gang can take over again); GBS to HGW, 24 Mar 1906 (a 'fatherly' lecture, and says he will rewrite *Faults of the Fabians* while HGW is in America); HGW to GBS, 26 Mar 1906 (keep your hands off my report); GBS to HGW, 14 Sept 1906 (dated by Dan H. Laurence: Wait awhile, the Old Gang really knows best); HGW to GBS, 18 Sept 1906, signed 'H. G. B. Shawells' (attempting to win GBS over); GBS to HGW, 22 Sept 1906 (an attempt at sweet reason); GBS to HGW, 17 Dec 1906 (gives a great deal of advice); GBS to H. Bland, about the same time (how to behave and how to control Wells at the meeting); GBS to HGW, 15 Feb 1907, on nominating him to the executive. The Wells speech, which was the final blow to Shaw, was on 7 Dec 1906, and he distributed proofs of his tract, placing copies on the seats before he spoke. Another meeting occurred on 14 Dec 1906 to discuss the matter further. This is the meeting at which Shaw spoke in debate. GBS to executive and members, an urgent whip postcard, 10 Dec 1906. Further meetings occurred on 11, 18 Jan, 1 Feb, 8 Mar 1907, on the issue of reform. GBS to HGW, 15 Feb 1907; GBS to S. Webb, 25 Nov 1906, 11 Oct 1907; B. Webb to HGW, ? Feb, 25 Feb 1907 (on the Poor Law work, but with a Fabian comment to keep HGW involved); B. Webb to Mary Playne, 10 Mar 1907 (how the Old Gang has triumphed and hopes it will continue). HGW to E. Pease, 16 Sept 1908 (what is needed in the Society, and why he can't do it; resignation letter). On the meetings also see S. Olivier to HGW, 7 Dec 1906; 7 Jan 1907, Wells spent another weekend with them.

35   The Wells special committee met on 7, 14 Dec 1906, 11, 18 Jan, 1 Feb, 8 Mar 1907 (usually just before the general meetings, or on the same or a close date). Charlotte Shaw reported the results of the meeting to her husband as a matter of course. G.R.S. Taylor to HGW, 22 June, 16 Sept, 19 Nov (talks witth Shaw, Pease, Keir Hardie reported), 6 Dec (talked to Mrs Reeves, Mrs Townshend), 13 Dec 1906 (talk with Pease, reports what GBS talk will be; Hardie not coming, will send statement backing HGW); Taylor to executive (an undated draft sent to HGW): no compromise possible, so wonders why they bother. Taylor told HGW, when enclosing this last, that Shaw had 'got his pound of flesh, not bad for a vegetarian'. Taylor to HGW, 20 Dec (encloses his letter of resignation from executive), 21 Dec 1906, 15 May: thanks for your vigorous defense of me at the meeting (apparently there was an attempt to censure Taylor for

discussing the executive meetings outside), 21 May 1907: all censure ideas withdrawn and Taylor awaits his pleasure. It is interesting to note that Jane Wells remained on the Fabian executive until Mar 1910, though whether she attended any meetings is unknown. For HGW's efforts to attract his friends, see M. Roberts to HGW, 29 Dec 1905 (postcard refusing); HGW to GrW, 15 Oct 1906 (LSE); GrW to HGW, 6 Dec 1906, thanks but I am out for good (this letter, in a copy made by Eric Hobsbawm in 1946, is now among the Wallas papers at LSE; where the original is, I do not know). Edward Carpenter to HGW, ? undated, if nearer, he might join; liked *Misery of Boots* very much. J. Galsworthy to HGW, 7 Mar 1907, not for him, they are divorced from English reality. Cecil Chesterton to HGW, 10 Mar 1906, reform is possible, so will help. Keir Hardie to HGW, 13 June 1906, a waste of time, join the ILP. HGW to Hardie, 17 Dec 1908, sending him 10 gns. to help that effort. A. E. Bishop to HGW, 11 Nov 1906, 'Dear Comrade Wells', join the ILP and the SDF. R. Blatchford to HGW, 15 Mar 1906, hopes Wells and Shaw will come around eventually. G.R.S. Taylor to HGW, 20 Feb, 22 June 1906, on bringing Hardie and Wells together. Joseph Fels to HGW, 20 May 1907, doubts efficacy of Fabian Society, but will try as long as HGW will. Gilbert Slater to ACRW, 4 Mar 1906, Fabian Society is an aristocratic Society, as we in the provinces who are members well know; urges HGW to form new group, rather than attempt to reform the unreformable. HGW to GrW, undated (LSE), on the Basis and his views. Shaw apparently made one attempt to go with HGW; see his letter to S. Webb, 29 Sept 1906, which is quite forthcoming.

36   Others who were part of HGW's reform group included Henry Newbolt. (See HGW to Newbolt, 30 June 1905, apologizing for his inattention at the Co-Efficients, as he was grieving for his mother.) More important were Victor Fisher and Richard Mudie-Smith. HGW to Fisher, 3 Dec 1906, discusses HGW's allies among the Fabian women, who included representatives from Croydon (illegible), West Central, and the Nursery groups; 29 Nov 1906, discusses possible formation of 'a *separate middle-class socialist party*'. This letter goes on to say, 'Webb is either mad or riding for a fall, Shaw is spring-heeled Jack, his favourite part, and the rest are — the Fabian Executive.' HGW to R. Mudie-Smith, 15 Oct 1906, late 1906, 20, 21 Feb 1907; telegram, 25 Feb 1907. HGW and Mudie-Smith had exchanged books in 1904: HGW to Mudie-Smith, 6 Feb (twice), 21 Feb 1904, as well as meeting to discuss sociology with a Dr Clifford; HGW to Mudie-Smith, 17, 23 Oct, 5, 14 Nov 1903 (Boston). Another good source on these matters in general is Samuel Hynes, *The Edwardian Turn of Mind* (Princeton 1968), and his *Edwardian Occasions* (London 1972).

37   GBS to S. Webb, 25 Nov 1906, 21 Oct 1907; to HGW, 22 Mar 1908. HGW to GBS, undated, and perhaps not even sent. In the letter HGW is referring to an attempt by Shaw to have HGW stop seeing Rosamund Bland, apparently, although some of the context is unclear. HGW did write a much more forbearing letter to Shaw, after the Fabian business, late in 1907 apparently, in which he says he had given up the friendship of the Webbs and Shaw 'for his gross of green spectacles'. He had said things that changed relationships, and although he didn't think they were wrong, still perhaps they should not have been said, but being HGW he had to say them. Both Shaw and HGW remained childlike especially to each other in their adult years, Shaw perhaps more than HGW, but as Dan Laurence has said, it was a sign of those years and perhaps of their class differences. See GBS to Erica Pottrell, early 1907.

38   Edward Garnett to HGW, 22 Mar 1907; R.C.K. Ensor to HGW, 21 May 1907, 23 May 1908; R. MacDonald to HGW, 29 Jan 1907; H.W. Massingham to HGW, undated 1908. HGW to editor, *New Age*, 2 May 1907. S. Olivier and HGW attended a Cambridge Fabian meeting, hosted by Ben Keeling. Francis Cornford and Rupert Brooke also spoke. See S. Olivier to HGW, ? Apr, 19 May, 20 Nov 1908.

39   GBS to HGW, 22 Mar 1908; HGW to S. Webb, 9 Mar 1908; HGW to GBS, undated, early 1908.

40 HGW, 'Liberalism and the Fabian Society', *DNews*, 13 Mar 1907; 'The Career of Fabianism', *Nation*, 30 Mar 1907; HGW, 'On the Alleged Diabolical Influences in the Fabian Society', *Nation*, 6 Apr 1907, p. 227, letter dated 'Sandgate, 30 Mar 1907'.

41 GBS, 'Mr H. G. Wells and the Rest of Us', *Christian Commonwealth*, 19 May 1909. HGW, 'The Minority Report as My Banner', *Christian Commonwealth*, 30 June 1909: here HGW said that he supported the work of the Webbs on the Poor Law without regard to the old Fabian entanglement. This was reprinted in a 1*d.* pamphlet, *The Charter of the Poor* (London 1909), although HGW's letter was dropped from the 1910 edition.

42 HGW to Sir F. Macmillan, 6, ? Oct 1910; Macmillan to HGW, 1 June 1910, ? (26?) Sept 1910.

43 HGW to Sir F. Macmillan, *c.* 26 Sept 1910; to W. Heinemann, 30 Sept, 1 Oct 1910; to Sir F. Macmillan, 1, 2 Oct 1910.

44 HGW to Sir F. Macmillan, Oct 1910. These letters are all either copies or drafts at Illinois.

45 B. Webb, *Diary* III. 146–8 (entry dated 5 Nov 1910).

46 GBS to HGW, *Collected Letters* II. 951 (18 Nov 1910).

47 C. F. G. Masterman to HGW, 10 Sept 1910 (this letter is 8 pp. long); Lord Northcliffe to HGW, 14, 20 Nov (from Paris) 1910: 'I very much agree with you, in regard to the people who control our Empire, and as to its future; and I realize my tremendous responsibility.' Northcliffe also urged HGW to read Lord William Cecil's *Changing China* (1910). Review of *The New Machiavelli* by 'A New Imperialist', *DMail*, 17 Jan 1911.

48 M. Roberts to HGW, 19 Jan 1911; ViP to ACRW, 24 May 1911. HGW apparently thought of taking a world cruise, and writing a column on it, in order to flee the critical heat. See HGW to P. Cazenove, 20 Mar 1911. Northcliffe liked the idea, but told him to wait. The trip never came about. Others liked the book for what it told them about the development of Wells's thought. See H. H. Reed, 'The Beginnings of H. G. Wells', *T.P.'s Weekly*, 10 May 1912.

49 Preface, *The New Machiavelli*, Atlantic XIV, x.

50 *Clarion*: HGW, 'Shaw vs Blatchford: Little Dunglas Interviewing', 3 July 1914; Shaw on Darwin and Huxley, 17 July 1914; letter by HGW, 'Little Dunglas', same issue; 'Little Dunglas', 24 July 1914; 'The Suckling Babe', 31 July 1914, this last possibly by HGW also. HGW, 'On Reading the First Number of *The New Statesman*', *New Witness*, 24 Apr 1913; HGW, 'Is Our World Collapsing?'. *DHerald*, 24 Jan 1923, review of S. and B. Webb, *The Decay of Capitalist Civilization*. HGW, 'Mrs Webb's Birthday', *New Statesman*, 22 Jan 1938: 'perhaps the greatest lady I have known', was his judgement here, after recapitulating their acquaintanceship.

51 HGW, 'Bernard Shaw', *DExpress*, 3 Nov 1950.

52 Introduction, *Anticipations*, 1914 edn., xiii. The Fabian Society for its part also recognized some of this, and attempted to make a liaison with the ILP. A meeting of R. MacDonald, K. Hardie, G. Wallas, and others was held to this end. C.M. Wilson to GrW, 5 July 1911 (LSE): 'Another thing is the intellectual dryness that has befallen the Fabians since the Wells tornado, and also the credo of the "minority" departers. There has been a general feeling of dissatisfaction lately and [we] resolve to take measures to revive.'

Chapter 5

1 A. Harmsworth to HGW, Nov 1897 (after HGW's article of 18 Nov 1897); HGW to Harmsworth (draft on back of AH's original); Harmsworth to HGW, 22 Nov 1897, for 'press or purse' comment. HGW said there were a number of things that needed discussion, the University of London, local government, and teaching skills. The original article had dealt primarily with education. HGW later wrote movingly of

Harmsworth/Northcliffe in 'What is Success', reprinted in Atlantic XXVII.

2   *DMail*, 1904: his subtitles were 'Religion is Not Altruism', 24 Mar; 'There is No People', 9 Apr; 'An Age of Specialization', 20 Apr; 'The Philosopher's Public Library', 28 Apr; 'The Drop in the Birth Rate: Does it Really Matter?', 19 May. See Arthur Mee to HGW, 8 Mar 1905, urging him to write even more articles. This letter did bring forth another series on Utopianisms; see below, ch. 8.

3   Among articles which might be noticed in this regard are HGW, 'Socialism', *Independent Review*, Oct 1906; 'Socialism and the Middle Classes', *Fortnightly*, Nov 1906; 'Socialism and the Family', *Independent Review*, 1 Nov 1906; *Grand Magazine*: 'Will Socialism Destroy the Home?', Dec 1907; 'Would Modern Socialism Abolish All Property?', Jan 1908; 'Socialism and the Middle Classes', *Eclectic Magazine*, Jan 1907 (a US version of the *Fortnightly* article listed above); 'The Middle Class Between the Millstones', *Independent Review*, 9 May 1907; 'My Socialism', *Contemporary Review*, Aug 1908; 'Ought Socialists to Live Poor?' *Labour Leader*, 14 Feb 1908, letter of HGW to the ILP paper. In this last response to criticism Wells said that his chief luxury was socialism, which cost him time, money, and energy, and damaged sales of his novels. He estimated the cost at £2,000 in the last four years, and 'it is quite well worth it. I want everyone to have at least as much ease, leisure, and freedom as I have myself and that is why I am a socialist. There is no reason to live badly to prove a point.' This was his considered judgement, and most persons probably accepted his view. He also signed, with many others, a manifesto which was published in mid-May 1907 as a broadside by the Secular Education League, calling for the end of religious education as part of regular school training, and reporting a meeting of a newly formed League, 4 Feb 1907. 'The Middle Classes Between the Millstones' also appeared, in a slightly different and cut form, in *Rapid Review*, Apr 1907. See proof sheets, and ACRW to P. Cazenove, 25 Mar, 30 Mar 1907.

4   *Nature*: 'F.W.H.', 'The Future of the Human Race', 29 Dec 1904; E. Ray Lankester, 'The Present Judged by the Future', 13 Mar 1902 (Suppl.)

5   HGW, 'Lions in the Path', *Literature*, 23 Nov 1901, p. 495; letter to 'My Dear Making', 20 Mar 1907; HGW, 'Mr Wells's Economics: A Reply to Sir R. K. Ensor', *Tribune*, 20 Aug 1906. John Beattie Crozier, 'Mr Wells as a Sociologist', *Fortnightly*, Sept 1905, pp. 417–26. HGW's article in the *Independent Review* which evoked Crozier's comment appeared, somewhat rewritten, as 'The So-Called Science of Sociology', in *Sociological Papers*, vol. III (London 1907), 357–77; it was originally given as a talk at a meeting of the Sociology Society at LSE, 26 Feb 1906.

6   *New Age*: HGW, 'The Socialist Movement and Socialist Parties', 13 June 1907, pp. 105–6; Chesterton letter, 20 June 1907; HGW, 'A Note on Methods of Controversy', 27 June 1907, p. 143; 4, 11, 18, 25 July 1907 for other items in the controversy.

7   William Archer, 'A Flag of Peace: A Plea for the United States of Europe', *Albany Review*, Aug 1907, pp. 491–7. G. Murray to HGW, 1 Mar 1909, and another undated letter (some letters in this period are missing). HGW, 'Race Prejudice', *Daily Chronicle*, 12 Feb 1907, a review of Jean Finot, *Race Prejudice*, and Sydney Olivier, *White Capital and Coloured Labour*; he liked the latter book very much. G. R. S. Taylor to HGW, 10 June 1909, informing HGW that he had resigned from the *New Age*. See HGW, 'The Schoolmaster and the Empire', *WGaz*, 21 Oct 1905, on what to teach in future. Vernon Lee, 'A Postscript to Mr Wells', *Albany Review*, Nov 1907, pp. 171–81.

8   R. MacDonald to HGW, 30 Sept, 17 Oct, 20 Dec 1907, 4 Jan, 28 Apr, 8 May 1908; HGW, 'An Answer', *New Age*, 28 Mar 1908; HGW, 'Conciliatory Socialism', *Socialist Review*, June 1908, pp. 200–6. *Christian Commonwealth*: HGW, 'The Position of the ILP', 12 May 1909, p. 554; GBS, 'Mr H. G. Wells and the Rest of Us', 19 May 1909, p. 570. The paper was filled with letters, commentary, and précis of arguments for the next several issues, and the controversy was even noted in other journals of the time such as *T.P.'s Weekly*, where it was summarized for their readership, 28 May 1909. The *Christian Commonwealth* carried a series of profiles of 'Leaders of Socialism' throughout

that spring. HGW was no. 19 in a series of 23, and his profile appeared on 14 Apr 1909. HGW, 'Why Socialists Should Vote for Mr Churchill', *Daily News*, 21 Apr 1908. The correspondence about this letter to the press, which did not spring full-blown from HGW's brow, includes A. G. Gardiner to HGW, 16 Apr 1908; W. Churchill to HGW, 16 Apr 1908, 'Thanks for the offer and I accept with pleasure.'

9   Surviving letters to Wells were sorted out very extensively by Jane Wells during the period just after World War I; Wells himself recovered many of his own letters when he was writing his *Experiment in Autobiography*, some of which were clearly destroyed at that time as well. More and more Wells letters turn up in the auction rooms as time goes on; and at least one large cache of his letters has been offered for sale, then withdrawn, within the decade since 1975.

10 The original version of *First and Last Things* (London: Constable 1908) — from which the quotations here are taken — appeared in two differently priced versions. The revision of 1917, with a new introduction, pp. v–ix, was published by Cassell; the introduction was dated 1 July 1917. Another introduction appears in Atlantic XI, with a bit more on the Fabian study group. The edition reprinted in 1929, without the introduction, in 1933 was circulated fairly widely, with other books, as a newspaper promotional stunt. The 1933 volume also contained *The Open Conspiracy*, and *Russia in the Shadows*.

11 L. S. Amery to HGW, 1 Jan 1909; J. Galsworthy to HGW, 9 Mar 1909. G. R. S. Taylor, 'H. G. Wells — Early Victorian Politician', *New Age*, 20 May 1909. The Galsworthy letter sounds like and may well be the germ of what was to become PEN, founded by Galsworthy with Wellsian help in the aftermath of World War I.

12 This was, of course, the period of Charles Booth's great series of investigations into *The Life and Labour of the People of London*, 17 vols. (1902–3); the studies of the Poor Laws which led to the Minority Report of Beatrice Webb; and one of the more famous of such books, C. F. G. Masterman, *The Condition of England*, first published in 1912, On HGW's contribution, see Northcliffe to HGW, 23 May 1910, 'To one of my prescience the position is very grave. To pathetic people, like the League of Frontiersmen and the Boy Scouts, everything, I have no doubt, is for the best.' HGW, *DMail*: 'The Case Against Socialism', 27 June 1910; 'Dull Work: The Real Source of the Labour Trouble', 10 Oct 1910. The latter was translated in the *Journal de Paris*, 14 July 1911. Northcliffe and HGW tried to time Wells's pieces so that the Government would not be affected at the wrong time, as this was the period of the difficult budgets, and the proposed increase in membership of the House of Lords. See ? G. Marlowe to HGW, 8 Feb 1911: 'As to the articles I am very anxious not to do anything which will make Mr Balfour's position more difficult than it is, and I think therefore that a little delay would be judicious.'

13 Lady Warwick, H. G. Wells, G. R. S. Taylor, eds., *The Great State: Essays in Construction* (London 1912); HGW's essay appears on pp. 1–46; the quotation is from p. 32. Although the others were credited with editorship on the title-page, the spine of the book carried only HGW's name, as it was clear that that would sell it. At the end of six months, the contributors had received an average of £42 apiece in royalties. The book is more important than it may appear, as it is an early form of how the 'Open Conspiracy' might work, and it follows logically from the Samurai phase. For correspondence about the book, see Lady Warwick to HGW, 28 May 1911, 28 Jan, 12, 16, 17 Feb 1912; G. R. S. Taylor to HGW, 29 July, 5 Aug, 7 Dec 1911, 28 May (receipt for £22), 17 Feb 1912 (proofs in circulation); Lady Warwick to HGW, 28 May 1912 (receipt for £16. 9s. 2d.). Not all receipts exist now.

14 HGW, 'Pot Shots at Criticism', *Nation*, 22 June 1912; *Labour Leader*: HGW, 'An Open Letter to Fenner Brockway', 23 Oct 1913; Brockway's first letter on HGW appeared on 2 Oct; see also letters defending HGW, from E. Pease and Agnes Hardie (although it was a damp defence in the first case), 30 Oct 1913. HGW was aware of how close he skated to apostasy: when he offered *The Great State* to Macmillan (Harpers actually

published it), he said that the essays would be 'socialistic rather than socialist'. HGW's essay from the book appeared, in slightly different form, in *Harper's Magazine*, Jan–Feb 1912, pp. 197–204, 403–9, under the title 'Socialism'.

15 *DMail*, 13 May 1912. The series of articles ran 13, 14, 15, 16, 17, 20 May 1912. Responses to it appeared on 24, 25, 27, 29, 30 May, 1, 2 June 1912. HGW returned with more comment on 5, 7 June 1912. Articles continued to appear, as late as 21 June 1912, with nearly every significant personage in the country offering comment. The *Daily Mail* then published the HGW articles in a pamphlet, *The Labour Unrest* (London 1912), 32 pp. The controversy continued, so the HGW pieces, plus all the comments, were reprinted in another pamphlet, *What the Worker Wants: The Daily Mail Enquiry*, by Hodder and Stoughton, for the *Mail*, 1912.

16 C. F. G. Masterman to HGW, ? June 1912 (undated, except for year). Galsworthy refused payment for his contributions as he thought the debate was so important: J. Galsworthy, *Glimpses and Reflections* (London 1937).

17 HGW, 'The Labour Revolt', *Everyman*, 7 Feb 1913, pp. 519–20.

18 HGW, 'What Are Liberals to Do?', *DMail*, 19 June 1913; also published as a pamphlet, *Liberalism and Its Party: What Are We Liberals to Do?* (London 1913). HGW, letter to editor, *Nation*, 3 Oct 1914, answering attacks on him on 26 Sept 1914, pp. 15–16.

19 HGW, *The Conquest of Time* (London: Watts & Co. 1942), The Thinker's Library, no. 92. The quotations are from pp. 65–6, and the last line is the last line of the work, p. 86. See Herbert Dingle, 'The Conquest of Time', *Nature*, 17 Oct 1942, a very long review which comes down on both sides in its comments.

Chapter 6

1 This period is discussed, in a limited way, in *ExA*. For an indication of the extent of Wells's earlier injury see HGW, 'My Lucky Moment', *View*, 29 Apr 1911, p. 212, which discusses a relapse, while walking down Villiers Street with a bagful of rock specimens. HGW spent the six weeks in bed in Hick's home, where he became very much attached to Hick's one-year-old daughter Marjorie. HGW, her godfather, wrote a book for her, illustrated with 'picshuas'. The copyright of the book, *The Adventures of Tommy* (London and New York 1929), was presented to Hick to help defray the costs of a younger daughter's medical education; copy of a letter from H. Hick, undated (Bromley). Marie Belloc-Lowndes, in her diary for 3 Dec 1911, describes talking to Jane at a party about the book and children's reactions to it; Susan Lowndes, ed., *Diaries and Letters of Marie Bellos Lowndes, 1911–1947* (London 1971), 25–6. *Tommy* was published in *Woman's Journal*, Dec 1928, with an introduction by G.B. Stein, 'Can You Find Something for Mr Wells to Play With?', about HGW and his love for children and their play. This discusses a production for toy theatre by HGW and G.K. Chesterton of the Minority Report on the Poor Law Commission! Chesterton also mentions the toy theatre in his *Autobiography* (London 1937).

2 G.W. Butler to HGW, 15 Oct 1896, recalls good cycling times that summer, but bemoans the bad roads; Marjorie Butler to ACRW, 31 Dec 1897, no longer trips as the baby interferes (the Butlers had been the Wellses' neighbours in Woking). HGW to Henry Hick, 2 May 1897, 16 July, Aug, Oct (2), Dec 1898. HGW, unsigned, 'Bleak March in Epping Forest', *PMG*, 16 Mar 1894. There are a half-dozen shorter pieces in which the bicycle is featured from the earlier days of Wells's writing, as well as a short humorous piece, 'A Perfect Gentleman on Wheels', *Woman at Home*, Spring 1897, repr. in Jerome K. Jerome, *The Humours of Cycling* (1897). The finest work, however, was the comic novel *The Wheels of Chance* (1896), serialized in *To-Day*, Apr–Aug 1896. It featured much discussion of trips, along with an abortive love affair, in which the differences in class and aspirations of the characters are significant. HGW to ??, offering American serial rights, 2 Jan 1896. I have discussed these works on

cycling in my 'Little Wars for Little People: Games, Sport and Leisure Time in the Life and Work of H. G. Wells', *Arete: A Journal of Sport Literature*, vol. II, no. 1 (Autumn 1985). On the play HGW attempted, based on the 1896 novel, see GBS to HGW, 29 Sept 1904, and see M. Timko, ed., *Hoopdriver's Holiday* (1964). For a description of the role of cycling at this period, see David Rubenstein, 'Cycling in the 1890s', *Victorian Studies*, XXI (1977), pp. 47–71.

3   With regard to Wells's illness, which disturbed many in England at the time, see W.M. Evans to HGW, 22 Aug, 26 Nov 1898 (Evans was a friend of both Gissing and HGW, and had spent part of a holiday in Italy with the two). A. Conan Doyle to HGW, two undated letters from late 1898, on Wells's health as well as commenting on the *Sleeper*; see HGW to A. Conan Doyle, undated 1898, on *A Duet, with Chorus* (1899), which HGW compares with his work in progress, *Mr Lewisham*; John Dickson Carr, *The Life of Sir Arthur Conan Doyle* (London 1949). *Academy*, 10 Dec 1898, reports that Wells is 'quite restored to health'. JBP to HGW, 18 Aug, 22, 28 Sept (sending £500), 4 Oct 1898, 17 Jan 1899, 17 Jan, 12, 22 Feb, 21 May 1900. Voysey did not build the Pinker house, as the cost was estimated at £4,000, which Pinker could not afford. RAG to HGW, 18, 23 Aug, on possible treatment by X-rays (Roentgen rays); HGW to RAG, late 1898, asking for information on the land slip: 'I'm getting efficient again, but still very easily fatigued and quite unable to travel or walk far because of the risk of reopening my abscess (damn it). But if this little house comes up trumps I may be settled again in a few months now'; RAG to HGW, also late 1898, in response. There are several good pages of HGW's 'picshuas' which deal with the recovery period, one dated 8 Oct 1898, as well as several undated which deal with cycling trips, learning to ride a bicycle, and other matters from this period (all at Illinois). A good description of building the house, and its situation, may be found in HGW to 'H.B.', undated; HGW to James Nicol Dunn, 16 Feb 1900. HGW also later had a bout with what he described as 'a rectal ulcer': HGW to Newbold Morris, 6 July 1904. He recuperated in Switzerland, 9 July 1904 (these last at Hofstra).

4   Roderick Gradidge, *Dream Houses: The Edwardian Ideal* (London 1980), describes Voysey houses, 177–83, although not discussing Spade House itself. HGW, 'The English Houses of the Future', *Strand*, vol. XXVI (1903), pp. 679–80, makes predictions, but what he describes is very similar to Spade House. For HGW's earlier ideas on houses, and studies, see Arthur H. Lawrence, 'The Romance of the Scientist: An Interview with Mr H.G. Wells', *Young Man*, Aug 1897, pp. 253–7, which has the best description of the house in Worcester Park. HGW described his real desires for a house (interior) in HGW to J. W. Robertson-Scott, postcard, p.m. 18 Mar 1911 (Hofstra).

5   For a good discussion of the England in which this life was lived, see W. H. Hudson, *Afoot in England* (1909), and Edward Thomas, *The Heart of England* (1906), both recently reissued in paperback. For an account of the Wells boys during their childhood, see M. M. Meyer, *H. G. Wells and His Family* (Edinburgh 1955). The games are described in HGW, *Floor Games* (London 1911) and *War Games* (London 1912). The books were widely reviewed: C. Chesterton, 'The Little Wars of H.G. Wells', *New Witness*, 28 Aug 1913, describes playing one of the games; Reginald R. Buckley reviewed *Floor Games* in 'A Work About Play — Mr Wells on Safe Ground', *T.P.'s Weekly*, 22 Dec 1911; another account of a game is in C. F. G. Masterman to HGW, 29 Dec 1914, in which he remembers the wars 'that break no hearts (only tempers)'. For an early account of his father, see an interview with Frank Wells, 'He's a Hell of a Good Fellow', *Star*, 23 Sept 1926, and Enid M. Nisbet, 'I Can See Again H. G. Wells in Those Country Tweeds', *Folkestone and Hythe Gazette*, 21 Sept 1966, with a very good account of life at Spade House, by an early secretary. Another HGW game, 'tishy-toshy', a form of table tennis, appeared later; see *DHerald*, 19 June 1924. Some amusing letters on the birth of the first Wells child are JBP to

HGW, 7 July; to 'My Dear Euphemia', 19 July; to HGW, 23 July, 1 Aug 1901; HGW to 'My Dear Rome', 27 Dec 1901, when G.P. was five months old.

6   It would be impossible to list all the sources which have commented on the Wells household, and only a few are noticed in the remainder of this chapter. Two, however, which show HGW and Jane at both their best and worst, are J.K. Jerome, *My Life and Times* (London 1926), and Alfred Noyes, *Two Worlds for Memory* (London 1943): especially good on the amateur theatricals. Others worth mentioning are Frank Swinnerton, *Swinnerton: An Autobiography* (1937) and *Background with Chorus* (1956); Julian Huxley, *Memoirs* (1956); William Rothenstein, *Men and Memories* (1922). For still more good but little-known accounts of HGW and his ménage, at different times, see Mrs L.T. Meade, 'Portraits of Celebrities at Different Times of Their Lives', *Strand*, Dec 1898, p. 675, which has five photographs of HGW; Constance Smedley, 'Some Storybook People, IX: H. G. Wells', *T.P.'s Weekly*, 11 Mar 1910, one of the better articles on the man in his own time. The house at Sandgate was rebuilt by Voysey after the children came, to provide nursery space. For Easton Glebe, see Lady Warwick to HGW, 21, 31 Aug; to ACRW, 6 Sept 1911; to HGW, 19 Nov 1913. The rent was lowered from £100 to £70 per year, as the Countess did not wish to lose the Wellses as tenants and neighbours. Lady Warwick to ACRW, mid-1918: the Warwicks lost some clothes in a fire, and Jane lent some for the maid, so they could travel to London acceptably. 'H. G. Wells and Bromley', *Bromley Chronicle*, 4 June 1914, an account of an interview with W. Baxter. On HGW, and a possible magistracy, which both he and Jane eventually held, Sir Henry C. Birm to HGW, ? Dec 1905, Jan, ? Feb, Mar 1906. On another weekend visit, C. F. G. Masterman to HGW, 7 Oct 1915. One of the more interesting weekends must have been at Christmas of 1899, when a two-act play, *The Ghost*, was presented; the authors included Henry James, Robert Barr, George Gissing, H. Rider Haggard, Joseph Conrad, H.B. Marriot-Watson, HGW, Edwin Pugh, A.E.W. Mason, and Stephen Crane. The *Academy*, 6 Jan 1900, prints a facsimile of the playbill. HGW, even in the salubrious surroundings of Sandgate, took a room outside Spade House in order to write with less interference; HGW to Enid Mary Nisbet, 5 Aug 1901. It was in Aldington, and he located it after a long bicycle trip exploring Kent. HGW also joined something called the Pope Joan Club; see G. J. Adams to HGW, spring 1911, 22 Sept 1915. A good description of the Church Row house is in Ivor Brown, *The Way of My World* (London 1954), where he describes 'the glorious bubble and squeak of H.G. Wells'.

7   HGW conducted an epistolary forum in the *Author* in which many of his views on agents were printed. See HGW, *Author*: 'Concerning Cat Athletics', 1 May 1913; 'Author and Agent', 1 June 1913; HGW comment on Arnold Bennett's letter, 'Author and Agent', 1 July 1913; also 'Beginning Agreements', in same issue; also Hall Caine, on 'Authors and Agents', 1 Oct 1913. HGW to James Warburg, 22 Nov 1939 (Eric Korn owns this letter). Some of this correspondence may be seen in Richard Findlater, ed., *Author! Author!* (London 1984), but not all of it, and the context is misunderstood as well. For the failure of publishing firms to do as much as they should, see HGW to Sir F. Macmillan, 3 Oct 1907. For HGW as he began his career and his work habits, Arthur H. Lawrence, 'The Romance of the Scientist', *Young Man*, Aug 1897.

8   On HGW and his agents, see JBP to HGW, 7 Oct 1901, arranging an interview with HGW; HGW to P. Cazenove, 2 Jan 1907, 'Don't let JBP know I showed the enclosed': the enclosed was an offer to publish his new novel. Place- and menu card, 18 Mar 1902, for a dinner at the Monaco Regent Saloon. Barry Pain was in the chair, and HGW responded to Pain's toast to J. B. Pinker. Pinker was a remarkable agent and the volume of his correspondence with Arnold Bennett, James Hepburn, ed., *Letters of Arnold Bennett*, I: *Letter to J. B. Pinker* (London and New York 1966), is a significant work in understanding this period of literary history.

9   Pinker's accounts with HGW, 1899–1933; Pinker's agency retained the right to sell some HGW items well into the 1930s, so money dribbled in from that source. HGW's

correspondence with Pinker ends essentially in 1904, although there are bits and pieces, usually handled by HGW's secretaries, throughout the period. HGW apparently introduced Bennett to Pinker. JBP to HGW, 6, 24 Jan 1899, 26 July, 17 Aug, 31 Oct 1900 (all on advertising), 12 Dec 1901: thanks for the introduction to Bennett, 10, 27 Feb (three) 1902 (on a prospective uniform edition which fell through), 13, 15 Jan, 6 Feb, 6, 9, 26 Mar, 8 July 1903 (all arguments over a contract with Methuen, and showing the disintegration of their relationship); also 26 Mar, 16 Apr, 19 May, 10 Oct 1903, 26, 27 Sept, 3 Oct 1904.

10   JBP to HGW, 3 Oct 1904 (quoted), 6, 20 Jan 1905; to ACRW, 12 July 1905; to HGW, 8 Jan, 8 July, 12 July 1904 (the diplomatic illnesses); to ACRW, 2 Aug 1904; to HGW, 12 Oct 1905, 2, 11 Aug, 19 Sept 1911, 11 Apr 1912; to ACRW, 29 Mar, 8 July 1913 (enclosing copies of agreements originally sent to HGW), 19 Jan 1909 (summarizing their arrangements); to HGW, 30 Mar, 2 Apr 1914. HGW to Eric Pinker, 5 Feb, 2 Apr 1920 (on possible sales of play version of *The Wonderful Visit*); Eric Pinker to HGW, 14 Mar 1926; series of memos MCW to HGW, 1929, on status of rights, especially translation rights.

11   *George Meek, Bathchairman, By Himself* (London 1910), preface by HGW, vii–xx, and a useful document on HGW's beliefs at this period. There is a memo in the Wells archive, dated 16 Sept 1908, in which HGW talks of publishing the book himself. HGW worked fairly extensively both on Johnson's novel and on Dunne's autobiographical piece. Maurice Baring, Hilaire Belloc, and HGW apparently supported Meek for a time until the book emerged. See Baring to HGW, 23, 29 Apr, 1 June 1910, 14 Apr 1916. Dunne's book was reprinted by John C. Winston, Philadelphia, in 1937. For Johnston and his visits to Easton Glebe, Sir H. Johnston to ACRW, 2, 14 June 1916; to HGW, 29 May 1916, 28 Sept, 23 Oct, 16 Dec 1918; to ACRW, 9 Jan 1919. Others to whom Wells gave support were B. F. Cummings (H. N. P. Barbellion), for whose *Journal of a Disappointed Man* (1919) he wrote an introduction. Cummings to HGW, 11 Mar, 12 Nov 1919. HGW was accused of collaborating on this book, as in *Boon*, and this led to a 'tempest in a teapot' in America where several of HGW's friends denied the charge, as did he. Also see H. Belloc to HGW, 23 May, 4 June 1911, on HGW's support for and contributing to the *New Witness*, their beginning publication. Another to whom HGW gave support was Nellie Shaw, author of *Whiteway: A Colony in the Cotswolds* (London 1935). She was a draper's daughter from Penge and that was her entrée. HGW read the manuscript, gave her an interview, 11 Nov 1933, and allowed her to use a copy of his letter as a frontispiece in the book.

12   *The Times*, 1, 28 Feb, 6 Oct (GBS letter; HGW letter also), 25 Oct 1906. HGW, Marie Corelli, Kipling, and Hall Caine, along with GBS, threatened to open their own bookshop unless *The Times* desisted. See *Glasgow Herald*, 26 Oct 1906. HGW began to subscribe to a cutting service after this issue arose. See also HGW letter to *Daily Mail*, reprinted in *Clarion*, 19 Oct 1906; 'Scrutator', 'Soap and Literature', *Truth*, 31 Oct 1906, thought *The Times* was wrong, and GBS 'muddle-headed'. HGW and Hall Caine came out better in this account. The controversy lasted in one form or another for two years. See GBS *Collected Letters* II. 677, for a speech by GBS, and a special edition of *John Bull's Other Island*, printed by *The Times*, which sold very well. Other letters are GBS to Otto Kyllman, 24 Mar 1906; to Constable & Co., 26 Mar 1907; to *The Times*, 17 Nov 1906. The issue of copyright also dogged this whole controversy. C. M. Moberly Bell to HGW, 14 Nov 1905, 28 Feb 1906. HGW wrote a long letter to GBS on *John Bull's Other Island*, undated 1907; Shaw's transcript is at Cornell.

13   On censorship, *The Times*: 29 Oct 1907, 70 signatures besides HGW's; 14 Feb 1912, many other signatures. A good statement of the problem is GBS, 'The Censorship of Plays', *Nation*, 16 Nov 1907. HGW joined the Society of Authors late in 1907. On an academy of letters, see long letter from HGW. *Academy*, 13 Nov 1897; H. Trench to HGW, 6 Jan 1903. Trench also contributed to *The Great State*; see Trench to HGW, 19 June 1912. They had several dinners together to discuss common literary problems

throughout this period. Academic Committee of the Royal Society to HGW, 20 Mar 1912, nominating him for election as a Fellow of the Society. He refused in letters to Henry James. HGW, 'The Academic Committee', *Eye-Witness*, late 1911.

14 Others who came, of course, included Barrie, Shaw, Galsworthy, Morley Roberts, Ford Madox Hueffer (Ford), as well as a few others to be mentioned later. Some of HGW's oldest friends also appeared, such as William Burton with whom he had stayed in the Potteries at the time of his first illness, and who had been with him at the Royal College. See Burton to HGW, 22 June, 17, 31 July 1900, about a weekend they spent together. A recent book has looked at some of these relationships, but is limited in that it chooses to study only one year: Nicholas Delbianco, *Group Portrait* (London 1982).

15 J. Galsworthy to HGW, 26 Oct 1907.

16 B. Webb to ACRW, Sept 1907 (Webb *Letters* II. 273).

17 GBS to William Archer, 9 July 1900 (on the possibilities of a play in *Mr Lewisham*); GBS to Charles Charrington, 20 May 1902; HGW to Mrs Charrington, 26 Feb 1904, describing the difficulties with the play. GBS to HGW, 29 Sept 1904 (GBS *Collected Letters* II). Later Shaw was to recount his adventures while bathing at Sandgate which led to his being drawn into an undertow. Shaw attributed his safe return to his vegetarian diet, and urged HGW to repent. HGW, for his side, remarked that it was too bad for the theatre that Shaw had not gone under. HGW could have put them all straight with a few obituaries which would reveal the truth, but, 'You will probably die about 1938 — obscurely.' GBS to HGW, 14 Aug; HGW to GBS, 23 Aug 1907.

18 There are several letters about this, along with the *dramatis personae*, in C. B. Purdom, ed., *Bernard Shaw's Letters to Granville Barker* (London 1956). The copyright performance was 24 Nov 1907.

19 The Shaws visited Sandgate in May 1905 and Shaw came alone in Nov and Dec 1905. This was the first visit with Coburn, to be mentioned later. Lillah MacCarthy, *Myself and My Friends* (London 1933), 124–7; GBS to HGW, 2 Mar 1908, of flying; to Granville-Barker, 31 Dec 1908, on his visit with L. MacCarthy.

20 Shaw's play opened on 1 Sept 1913 at the St. James's. See Shaw to Granville-Barker, Mar 1912 to 14 Oct 1913, in the Granville-Barker-Shaw correspondence. See the *Telegraph, Express, The Times*, as well as the *Church Times*, for one or another version of HGW's comment on the play.

21 C. F. G. Masterman to ACRW, 27 Nov 1902; to HGW, 31 Oct 1902, 2 Dec 1903, 19 Feb 1904; to ACRW, 19 Feb 1908: 'My visits to you at Folkestone are far the most stimulating and enjoyable of all my occasional excursions into the country and I will teach H.G. to golf — from the superior vantage of five months practice — when I come.' Ella Hepworth Dixon, 'As I Knew Them: H. G. Wells', *Queen*, 4 Sept 1929. She and HGW wrote a play for the toy theatre, enacted in 100°F. temperatures at the villa at Port de l'Arche, near Rouen, in 1911. Its title was *Dicky Touchwood*. ERL to HGW, 12 July 1900. Lankester gave HGW a guided tour of the Natural History Museum; also to HGW, 18 July, 29 Oct, 30 Nov 1900. HGW went at Lankester's request, representing Literature, to a dinner at which Stephen Phillips represented Poetry, with Sir James Frazer acting as their host. ERL to HGW, 10, 28 Aug (two) 1911; to ACRW, 15 Sept 1911; to HGW, 13 Sept 1911. On 28 Aug 1911, Lankester told Jane, 'I believe that talks with H.G. would restore my brain which is suffering from a bit of damp mould.' Also see his letter to Jane, 29 Nov 1910, about a Church Row dinner party at which the French visit was planned. There are a dozen letters from P. Guedalla to HGW, from 1911 to 1917. Guedalla met HGW when the former was president of the Oxford Union in 1911.

22 Martin J. Weiner, *Between Two Worlds: The Political Thought of Graham Wallas* (Oxford 1971); William F. Stone and David C. Smith, 'Human Nature in Politics: Graham Wallas and the Fabians', *Political Psychology*, vol. IV, no. 4 (Dec 1983), pp. 693–712.

23 HGW to GrW, 27 Nov 1900; Audrey Wallas to ACRW, 28 July, 12 Nov 1901; HGW

to GrW, 31 Oct 1902; ACRW to GrW, 25 Aug 1902; HGW to GrW, 20 Apr (postcard), 2 May (another postcard), 12, 16 Aug 1902.

24 HGW to GrW, 19 Sept 1902.

25 HGW to GrW, 6 Oct; ACRW to GrW, 23 Oct; HGW to GrW, 23 Oct 1902; GrW to HGW, 11 Aug, 8 Oct (signed 'Your Uncle, Graham Wallas'), 21 Oct (5 pp. of detailed criticisms of text; about educational practices primarily); HGW to GrW, end Oct (undated postcard, concerned that Wallas has the flu), all 1902.

26 HGW to GrW, 23, 28 Aug 1903; ACRW to GrW, undated (end of Aug) 1903. HGW introduced Wallas to A.T. Simmons, as a source for educational theory after the trip. HGW to GrW, 26 Sept, 14 Oct 1903.

27 ACRW to GrW, early 1905 (undated), on the occasion of Wallas bringing Herbert Samuel to Sandgate to meet HGW; GrW to HGW, 30 Oct 1905, on family illnesses; GrW to HGW, 4, 10 Nov (quoted) 1907. An exchange of letters, GrW to HGW, 6 Dec 1906, in response to HGW to GrW, 15 Oct 1906, on the process of thought in the Great Society, is cited by Weiner, p.141, although I have not seen it, and the topic suggests a misdate; perhaps 1913? HGW to GrW, 31 Oct 1907. The MS of Wallas's book was also read by Bertrand Russell: see letter to GrW of 21 May 1906, and by Logan Pearsall Smith, letter of 26 May 1906, as well as several others. On religious education see HGW to GrW, undated postcard, 'Personally, I don't like 2½ hours a week of religious instruction. It means that blasphemous rhymes and jokes will still be acceptable to our grandchildren.' The Wallas book, entitled 'Prolegomena', at one stage, and 'Men in Politics' at another, finally appeared as *Human Nature in Politics* (London and New York 1908), and interestingly enough, Wallas does not mention HGW in the acknowledgements, but this was probably because of the Fabian interest in the book, to say nothing of the LSE. On HGW and the proofs, two other undated letters survive from this period. (Many, but not all, letters to GrW are at LSE, the remainder, and those from GrW, are at Illinois.)

28 HGW to GrW, late 1908 (undated); one of the better reviews of Wallas's book was by Mildred Spencer, in *Christian Commonwealth*, 21 Apr 1909, and the only one really to deal with the religious implications of the book.

29 HGW, 'The Great Society: A Community Analysis', *Nation*, 4 July 1914, his review of Wallas's *The Great Society*, (London and New York 1914). The book is dedicated to Walter Lippman. See Thomas Burke to HGW, *c.* 1915; HGW to GrW, undated note at the Reform on American publishers; MCW to GrW, 26 July 1930, asking GrW to sign one of the two letters she was enclosing, one drafted by HGW and one by GBS, to the Home Secretary on the exclusion of Trotsky from England. GrW signed the HGW version. Others who signed were A. G. Gardiner, J. M. Keynes, Arnold Bennett, Sydney Olivier, Beatrice Webb, RAG, Martin Conway, Ramsay Muir, Lord Beauchamp, and Augustus Birrell. Also see MCW of 24 July 1930 to GrW on the same subject. HGW's obituary, entitled, 'Professor Graham Wallas: In Memoriam', appeared in *Literary Guide and Rationalist Review*, Sept 1932, pp. 165–6. HGW mentioned their early meeting at William Morris's and the two-week sojourn in the Alps as significant to his development, before writing the lines quoted.

30 HGW to ViP, 28 Mar, 11 Apr, 6 Aug 1904.

31 ViP to HGW, 6 Aug 1904.

32 HGW to ViP, 17 Oct 1906, late 1907 (undated).

33 Several undated letters, HGW to ViP, all 1908: one is from the Grand Hotel, Adelboden, late 1908; others are earlier. One, 17 Oct 1908, asks her who Mabel Dodge is, who wishes an introduction; ViP to HGW, 30 Oct 1908, explains about that lady's famous salon.

34 There are a great many letters, some of which will be cited again in a different context. The ones important for this discussion are: ViP to HGW, 16, 26 June, 4 July; to ACRW 9, 19 July, to HGW, 22 Aug, all 1909. ViP to HGW, 13 Feb 1909, on the *English Review*. HGW to ViP, end of Sept (Sister in Utopia); ?2 Sept, 3 or 4 Oct, end of Nov, 31 Dec 1909, 28 Jan 1910, two 1911 (undated), another 1912. ViP to ACRW, 3 July; to HGW,

11 July; to ACRW, 29 Aug, 11 Sept, all 1911. The long weekend near Rouen began 15 Sept 1911. HGW told another correspondent, unidentified, 2 Nov 1911 (Boston), that he had taken the Normandy house 'to escape the coronation' ViP's long letter on *The New Machiavelli* (quoted) is 19 Sept 1912, which would date HGW's as late Sept, or early Oct. The standard biography of her is Peter Gunn, *Vernon Lee: Violet Paget, 1856–1935* (London 1964), where the relationship is also described.

35 HGW's *Bealby* (London and New York 1915) was serialized in the US in *Collier's*, beginning with the issue of 20 June 1914 and in England in *Grand Magazine*, Aug 1914 – Mar 1915. HGW described the book to Frederick Macmillan, 26 Jan 1913, as 'a bye-blow, an illegitimate child; it came accidentally.'

Chapter 7

1 *SR*: HGW, unsigned, 'The Depressed School', 27 Apr 1895; 18 Apr 1896. Pierre Coustillas, ed., *London and the Life of Literature in Late Victorian England: the diary of George Gissing, novelist* (Brighton 1978); see entries for 20, 26 Oct, 16 Dec 1896, for Gissing's comments and their visits.

2 This short history can be followed in detail in Royal A. Gettmann, ed., *George Gissing and H. G. Wells, Their Friendship and Correspondence* (London 1961), and in Gissing's diary, where the relevant entries are 27 Jan, 9 Mar, 1 Apr, 5–12 Apr, 1–9 July, 16 Sept 1898, 1 May 1900, 8–10 Mar 1901, 7 Apr 1902. On the visit to Italy, see HGW to [Harry] Quilter, 20 Mar 1898, undated, same month, another in Apr 1898, 2 Jan 1899. HGW to James Welch, ? 1898 (Hofstra). Quilter was toying with a dramatization of *The Wonderful Visit*, at the time he was living in Florence. Also see P. Parrinder, 'The Roman Spring of George Gissing and H. G. Wells', *Gissing Newsletter*, vol. XXI, no. 3 (July 1985), pp. 1–12. A Gissing letter written from Wells's home, which has not been published as yet, is June 1901 to W. M. Colles, his agent, with regard to Gissing's prefaces for some Dickens reprints. See Pierre Coustillas, ed., *Henry Hick's Recollections of George Gissing* (London 1973). For an early Wells appreciation of Gissing's talent, see 'The Novels of Mr George Gissing', *Contemporary Review*, Aug 1897, repr. in a cut version, *Living Age*, 2 Oct 1897, and in full in Gettmann, ed., *GG and HGW*. The Pinker/Wells correspondence concerning Gissing: JBP to HGW, 5 Nov 1898 (Wells is a postbox), 24 June 1902 (the need of money and Gissing's novels simply do not do as well as they should), 24, 29 May ('How very ill he looks'), 13 Nov 1903 (rumour that Gissing's real wife is dead in an asylum: her death did not actually occur until 1917). Other items which bear on this friendship are: Brian Ború Dunne to HGW, 15 June 1912, recalling their 1898 meeting in Rome (this led to HGW's 1914 introduction to Dunne's *Cured*). Bernard Bergonzi, *The Turn of the Century* (London 1973), esp. 'The Correspondence of Gissing and Wells', 64–71 (repr. from *Essays in Criticism*, 1962), which discusses the two writers' common debt to Dickens. HGW's 'In Memoriam', in Edward Clodd, Clement Shorter, and Winifred Stephens, eds., *George Whale, 1849–1925* (London 1926), 39–46, discusses his meeting and relationship with Gissing. Whale and Wells were for a time joint trustees of the Gissing estate. Wells, commenting on Whale, said, 'for the most of us, perhaps dying is our private affair', which may in fact be taken for a comment on Gissing. A sketch of Gissing by Mrs Clarence Root, signed by both HGW and GG, is reproduced at the head of a long obituary notice by 'C.K.S.' (Clement K. Shorter), *Sphere*, 9 Jan 1904. HGW to E. Gosse, 4 Jan 1904, on Gissing's death. John H. Harrison, 'Gissing's Friendship with H.G. Wells', *Gissing Newsletter*, vol. XVIII, no. 1 (Jan 1982), pp. 9–39, which says Uncle Ponderevo's death scene was influenced by the last Gissing visit.

3 A description of Gissing's death, in a village in the Pyrenees, and of his funeral is given in Morley Roberts to HGW, 1 Jan 1904, along with an account of the interference of the local English chaplain who insisted on a religious burial. About 20 English residents attended the service. W. J. Ramsay (for A. J. Balfour) to HGW, ? 1904, granting a Civil

List pension to the Gissing children; also 29 July 1904, adding George Whale to the group of trustees. Clara Collet to HGW, 9 Apr, 21 May 1904, also 30 Dec 1903, 1 Jan, 5 Apr 1904, on Gissing and his estate. On the Civil List pension for the children, HGW to George Wyndham, 6 Feb 1904 (Boston), calling Gissing perhaps 'among the greatest as well as the most disinterested of contemporary writers'. To Wyndham he invoked Henley (they were old friends), as having liked *By the Ionian Sea* in particular.

4 JBP to HGW, 5 Jan; to ACRW, 6 Jan 1904. M. Roberts to ACRW, 7 May (postcard); to HGW, 12 Sept ('He should have been a scholar, a fellow of a college, a man of classics'), 14, 17, 29 Sept (they exchanged cuttings as well), 1 Dec 1904. On Roberts's book, see his to HGW, 2 Feb (long postcard which ends 'What shall any poor artist do when his most respected fellows can't see for wind? Aleiorum Salaam Effendi of the Shrine on the Hill of Pisgah'), 1, 6 Feb (postcard) 1905. See 'C.K.S.' (Clement K. Shorter), 'Literary Letter', *Sphere*, 6, 13, 20, 27 Aug 1904, for a running account of the Wells difficulties, and the proper proposed treatment of Gissing. HGW, 'George Gissing: An Impression', *Monthly Review*, Aug 1904, pp. 160–72, repr. in *Living Age*, Oct 1904, and in *Eclectic Magazine*, Nov 1904. This is a lovely piece which ends, 'Now at any rate he can bear to wait a little longer for the honour that will in the end be his in absolute security.' HGW to Henry Newbolt, 8 Mar 1904 (Hofstra), on the *Veranilda* difficulties (Newbolt was editor of the *Monthly Review*). P. Coustillas, 'The Stormy Publication of Gissing's *Veranilda*', *Bulletin of the New York Public Library*, vol. LXXII, no. 9 (Nov 1968), pp. 588–610.

5 M. Roberts to HGW, 20 June 1912. Morley Roberts, *The Private Life of Henry Maitland* (London 1912), reissued with revisions in 1923, and with a key to Gissing's life, edited by Morchard Bishop, in 1958. HGW figures in the book as G. H. Rivers, Roberts is J.H., or J.C.H., and Clara Collet is Miss Kingdon. Frank Swinnerton, *George Gissing: A Critical Study* (London 1912), remained the only significant study until Pierre Coustillas, Jacob Korg, and others created a new appreciation of the man. To my mind, however, the best modern life is by Gillian Tindall, *The Born Exile* (London 1974). All of Gissing's novels have now been reissued, along with most of his correspondence and his diary, in recent years. HGW, 'The Truth About Gissing', *Rhythm* (Literary Supplement), Dec 1912, pp. i–iv. Wells also discussed Gissing and his death in *ExA*, and again some readers were concerned with what was thought a cool treatment. Gissing partisans felt that Wells did not treat Gissing well enough after his death, but a careful reading of his comments suggests little amiss. Wells did not handle death well, and especially not at this period of his life. He did not, after all, have the cheap solace of religious belief. He had to face the reality of losing his comrades. Roberts became estranged from Wells soon after HGW's review appeared, when a servant failed to recognize Roberts and would not announce him to a working H. G. Wells. The Wellses' treatment of Gissing has re-emerged recently in the biography of his father by Anthony West, *H. G. Wells: Aspects of a Life* (London 1984). See the letters on West's book from Pierre Coustillas, *TLS*, 2 Nov 1984, as well as from Patrick Parrinder, 23 Nov 1984.

6 Swinnerton's most important books which bear on this subject are *The Georgian Literary Scene* (London 1935, and repr. in the Everyman series), a standard treatment of the subject; *A London Bookman* (London 1928), a collection of his columns for the *Bookman* (New York) from 1920 to 1927; *Swinnerton: An Autobiography* (London 1937), a remarkable and underrated book; *Background with Chorus* (London 1956). He also wrote a great many novels, most now out of print, but good books which give pleasure to readers still. His treatment of the Reform Club in his autobiography, pp. 291–314, is excellent.

7 Bennett treated the lecture in his guise as 'Jacob Tonson', in 'Lectures and the State', *New Age*, 25 May 1911. This piece and others of this period were collected under Bennett's real name, in *Books and Persons: Being Comments on a Past Epoch – 1908–1911* (London 1917); the *New Age* piece appears at pp. 315–16. Wells's lecture was published as 'The Contemporary Novel', in the *Fortnightly*, Nov 1911, and in the *Atlantic*, Jan

1912, pp. 1–11. It was an indirect cause of James's article on 'The Younger Generation', in the *TLS*, 19 Mar, 2 Apr 1913, and led eventually to Virginia Woolf's famous piece, 'The Wells and Bennett Novel', *TLS*, 23 Aug 1928.

8   HGW signed letter, dated 7 July 1917, 'About *Nocturne*', *Daily News and Leader*, 12 July 1917: 'a very vivid, entertaining and beautiful story'; it 'ought to be read and shouted about'. Swinnerton later revealed that the publisher at the same time gave him a larger advance, at Wells's behest: FAS to HGW, 12 July 1917; his preface to the 1954 reprint. HGW, 'Concerning Realists in General and Mr Swinnerton in Particular', *Bookman*, May 1918, pp. 252–5; Arnold Bennett, H. G. Wells, and G.M. Overton, *Frank Swinnerton* (New York 1920). In the book Bennett quotes Wells as saying, 'You know, Arnold, he achieves a perfection in *Nocturne* that you and I never get within streets of.' Wells's piece in the book, pp. 17–23, varies slightly from the magazine version. For *Nocturne* and its publication, see G. M. Overton, *If Winter Comes to Main Street* (New York 1922), which also reprints much of HGW's introduction, pp. 233–5, and is good on Bennett.

9   Swinnerton, *Georgian Literary Scene*, in general; *Background with Chorus*: on H. James and the meaning of literature, 123–5; on Bennett, Wells, and Galsworthy, as persons as well as novelists, 185–205; *A London Bookman*: 'The Letters of Henry James', 1–6; 'Chesterton – Belloc – Masterman', 76–81; 'Mrs Woolf on the Novel', 111–18; 'Mrs Woolf Again', 147–53. As Swinnerton pointed out, Virginia Woolf wrote beautifully but could not create characters, while that was precisely the strength of Wells, Bennett, and Galsworthy. FAS to HGW, 8 Aug 1934, lays out his intentions in *The Georgian Literary Scene*, and seeks HGW's permission, which was granted.

10 FAS to ACRW, 27 Mar 1912, 4 Mar 1914, 2 Dec 1915, 11 Apr, 16 Oct 1916, 29 June, 4 July, 15 Aug 1917, 9 July, 7 Oct 1918; to HGW, 3 Oct, 5 Dec 1918; to ACRW, 29 Oct 1918; to both, 22 Oct 1918, (from Thorpe-le-Soken) 21 Jan 1919; to ACRW, 5 June 1919; to HGW, 16 Aug 1920; on literary funds, to HGW, 16 Oct 1919; to ACRW, 16 Feb 1920 (on a trip to Portugal with Bennett).

11 FAS to ACRW, 11 Oct 1921 (the meal was 15 or 21 Oct).

12 FAS to ACRW, 14 Apr, 21 May 1923; FAS to HGW, 24 Oct 1939. One of the best accounts of HGW and his country life, as well as his views on Jane, occurs in *Swinnerton: An Autobiography*, ch. 9, 193–209. The first quote in this paragraph is from p. 194. Weekends are discussed, pp. 196–202; the ball game, pp. 199–200; and Jane Wells, pp. 200–5.

13 From a mass of source material, the most important are the biographies by Margaret Drabble (1977) and Reginald Pound (1952). An important work is F. Swinnerton, *Arnold Bennett: A Last Word* (New York 1978). AB's correspondence has been published in 3 vols., ed. James Hepburn (a 4th promised), and his letters to his nephew, ed. Richard Bennett (London 1935), are also important. His criticism is in *Books and Persons* (London 1917; the *New Age* material) and *Books and Persons* (London 1974, new edn. including the *Standard* articles). His journals were published in 1932, although fugitive material from them was published from 1929, and still more appears in F. Swinnerton, ed., *The Journals of Arnold Bennett* (Harmondsworth 1971). His correspondence with HGW is in Harris Wilson, ed., *Arnold Bennett and H.G. Wells* (London 1960). A few more HGW letters to Bennett have recently emerged, which buttress my interpretation generally: John R. Harrison, '"Yours, H.G.": Some Missing Letters to Arnold Bennett', *English Literature in Transition*, vol.XXV (1982), pp. 10–20. The most important are: concerning *Anticipations*, 20 Nov 1901; on Chesterton, 20 Dec 1901; on Bennett's work, 5 Nov 1905; offering his aid and comfort in the Marguerite affair, New Year's Eve 1921–2; on AB's and Dorothy's baby, 16 Nov 1925; on *Lord Raingo*, 26 Nov 1926; and six on Jane's illness and death, between 1 June and 7 Oct 1927.

14 Arnold Bennett, *Evening Standard*, 3 Mar 1927, discusses the matter, and the correspondence appears in Wilson, ed., *AB and HGW*. The Haymarket manager was

Frederick Harrison (d. 1926), not the same as the positivist Harrison (1821–1923) who wrote the introduction to Gissing's *Veranilda*.

15 E. A. Bennett (so signed), 'H.G. Wells and His Work', *Cosmopolitan*, vol. XXXIII (Aug 1902), pp. 465–71. JBP to HGW, 12 Feb 1902, in which he asks Wells to reconsider his decision not to help Bennett with the piece. Pinker wanted to 'advertise the benevolent tendencies of your teaching'.

16 'Jacob Tonson', 'H. G. Wells', *New Age*, 4 May 1909; AB also supported *Ann Veronica* against Yorkshire censorship, and noted that the banning of the book had increased sales: *New Age*, 13 Jan, 24 Feb, 3 Mar 1910.

17 'Jacob Tonson', '*The New Machiavelli*', *New Age*, 2 Feb 1911.

18 Bennett, *Evening Standard*, 10 Apr 1930, recounts the efforts to help Lawrence, although my impression is that Lawrence took some of the funds, which amounted to £10 a week, from Bennett, Galsworthy, and Wells. The Joyce story is told later in this chapter; cf. n. 49. George Beardmore, Bennett's nephew, and his wife Jean have edited some of Bennett's personal correspondence: *Arnold Bennett in Love: Arnold Bennett and His Wife Marguerite Soulié: A Correspondence* (London 1972).

19 HGW to AB, 7 Oct 1930. Wells wrote this from Paris, where he was speaking, otherwise we would not have it, as such comments were usually given in person.

20 Bennett was the last English figure of significance to have straw spread in the streets to deaden traffic noise as he lay dying. A memorial service for him was held 29 Mar 1931 at St. Clement Danes. Among those present as mourners were Hugh Walpole, Beaverbrook, J. M. Barrie, Wells, Pinero, St. John Ervine, John Drinkwater, and Virginia Woolf. Walpole unveiled a plaque to Arnold Bennett at Thorpe-le-Soken in July 1932. Walpole's journal, quoted in Rupert Hart-Davis, *Hugh Walpole* (London 1952), 321–2, 326. HGW was asked to unveil the plaque but could not: 'it is just because I knew A.B. so well that I dare not make off-hand comments on him.' HGW to Sir F. Joseph, 30 July 1931 (Boston).

21 HGW, unsigned, '*An Outcast of the Islands*', *SR*, 16 May 1896. The comment was applied both to this book and *Almayer's Folly*, which had come out the previous year.

22 J. Conrad to HGW, 18 May 1896 (pub. in Frederick R. Karl and L. Davies, eds., *The Collected Letters of Joseph Conrad*, vol. I [Cambridge 1983], 278–9); HGW to Conrad, May 1896 (pub. in G. Jean-Aubry, ed., *Twenty Letters to Joseph Conrad* [London: First Edition Club 1926]).

23 Conrad to HGW, 25 May 1896 (Conrad *Collected Letters* I. 282).

24 *Academy*, 8 Jan 1898, quoting HGW's letter to them. Henley's Burns volumes received second prize of 50 gns.

25 Conrad to HGW, 6 Sept, 11 Nov 1898. G. Jean-Aubry prints these and a number of later letters to HGW in his *Life and Letters of Joseph Conrad*, 2 vols. (London 1927).

26 Conrad to HGW, 17 Nov, another in Nov, 4, 23 Dec 1898. A comedy of errors occurs in this last letter, as Conrad and Jessie came to call on Wells and Jane, found them out, and returned to find that Wells and Jane had called on them in the meantime.

27 Instructive in this is an account by Arnold Bennett, *Evening Standard*, 3 Nov 1927, of his first meeting with Conrad at Wells's house. They discussed the difficulty of composition and Milton's work (especially *Lycidas* and *Comus*) which Wells defended against Conrad's imputation of their being second-rate. Conrad's life has been well treated by Frederick R. Karl in *Joseph Conrad: The Three Lives* (New York 1979). Karl discusses Wells and Conrad in 'Conrad, Wells and the Two Voices', *PMLA*, vol. LXXXVIII (Oct 1973), pp. 1049–66, which has influenced me, but with which I disagree in a few minor places. His biography supplants all earlier treatments, although those remain interesting to read, as the case of a reputation changing over time.

28 Conrad to HGW, p.m. 4 Jan 1899, 'Monday' (from the same period), 6 Jan 1900, and another undated in 1901 which complains that his work has prevented their meeting: 'Seriously I much rather talk with you than write. . . .'.

29 Conrad to HGW, 22 Dec 1902; to ACRW, 1 Mar 1902; to HGW, 30 Oct 1903.

30 These quotes are from the letter to HGW of 30 Nov 1903, and another undated, also from *c.* 1903.

31 Conrad to HGW, 13 Jan, 20 Oct 1905; the second of these is addressed to 'Dearest H.G.'.

32 Conrad to HGW, 'Dearest H.G.', 28 Nov 1905; two others from this period undated appear here as well. Dating is from internal evidence: a mention of Jessie Conrad having fallen and damaged her knee, and the similarity of the salutations of the letters.

33 Conrad to 'Dear Wells' (a New Year's letter), *c.* 1906, 2 Aug, 9 Aug 1906, 25 Apr 1907, another 'To My Dear Good H.G.', early 1907, to 'Dear Old H.G.' from Geneva, 30 Aug 1907.

34 Conrad to 'My Dear Wells', 27 Mar, 16 Apr, 25 Sept 1908, early 1909, 20 Jan 1911.

35 Hart-Davis, *Hugh Walpole*, 188, quoting Walpole's journal for 23 Jan 1918, is the source for the anecdote and the quotation, although Conrad seems to have repeated something like it in other places and at other times. Walpole had apparently asked for his version of the last meeting.

36 Wells sent a copy of *ExA* to Jessie Conrad, who had lent him a photograph of Conrad to use in the book. Jessie Conrad to 'My Dear Mr Wells', 3 Nov 1934. Mrs Conrad paid her respects to the Wellses in a page or two of her own memoirs, most of it concerned with the finicky neatness of Jane's house, and a somewhat heavy-handed portrait of Wells's mother. H.G. himself barely appears in her book, *Joseph Conrad and His Circle* (London 1935). Wells and EH exchanged comments on the Conrad friendship: EH to HGW, 7 Nov 1943, and his notes in the margin. This came after EH read Douglas Goldring's *South Lodge* (1943).

37 This story is a familiar one and was first and best told in Gordon N. Ray and Leon Edel, eds., *Henry James and H. G. Wells* (London and Champaign, Ill. 1958). Since then it has been illuminated in Leon Edel's remarkable five-part biography of James (1953–72). Some additional material is in G. K. Chesterton, *Autobiography* (1936), the source for HGW's notes to GKC over the wall as he talked to James. GKC is good, incidentally, on HGW in the controversy with James. Edith Wharton briefly discusses her meetings with Wells (most of which were in America, after the early encounter), in her *A Backward Glance* (New York 1934). On Howells, see HGW to W. D. Howells, 10, 12, 14 Apr, 14, 26 May, 23, 25 June 1904. Hamlin Garland discusses the James establishment in Rye in *Roadside Meetings* (New York 1930).

38 In addition to the earlier citations of this important essay, it has been reprinted in Edel and Ray, eds., *HG and HGW*, and was a centrepiece in Wells's collected journalism of the period, *An Englishman Looks at the World* (London 1914), along with pieces on flight, socialism, divorce, motherhood, and other matters. The book carried as its subtitle, 'Being a Series of Unrestrained Remarks Upon Contemporary Matters'.

39 'The Contemporary Novel', pp. 154–6 of the Edel–Ray volume cited above. The two papers alluded to had been prominent in the attacks on *Ann Veronica*, and caricatures of the editors of these papers were among Wells's unpublished drawings for *Boon*. It is interesting that Henry James does not appear in these drawings, at least not in his own person. The issues were widely discussed. See the correspondence cited and quoted between GBS and James, especially HJ to GBS, 20 Jan, GBS to HGW, 21 Jan, and HJ to GBS, 28 Jan 1909; Leon Edel, ed., *The Complete Plays of Henry James* (London 1949), and GBS *Collected Letters* II. 827–9.

40 Henry James, 'The Younger Generation', *TLS*, 19 Mar, 2 Apr 1913. Edel and Ray, eds., *HJ and HGW*, 178–215.

41 Reginald Bliss [H. G. Wells], *Boon, The Mind of the Race, The Wild Asses of the Devil, and The Last Trump, Being a First Selection from the Literary Remains of George Boon, Appropriate to the Times. Prepared for Publication by Reginald Bliss. . . with An Ambiguous Introduction by H. G. Wells* (London and New York 1915). Hilaire Belloc may have been responsible for one chapter title, as he urged Wells to write a book on the 'red devils from Hell' after he read *Tono-Bungay*: H. Belloc to HGW, 14 Feb 1909.

42 HGW, *Boon*, 341–2. Part of Wells's book appeared serially: HGW, 'Long, Last, Trump', *Century*, July 1915, pp. 369–78. Other parts were offered to magazines much earlier, but Wells withdrew them from his agents. See HGW to P. Cazenove, 2 Mar 1908, withdrawing 'Wild Asses of the Devil'. *Boon* is replete with 'picshuas', but a set of other drawings, not published at the time, were found in a copy of the book and they are even better. They include caricatures of Harold Bigbee, St. Loe Strachey (of the *Spectator*), J. L. Garvin, Richard Le Gallienne, the Archbishop of Canterbury, the editor of the *Westminister Gazette* (J. A. Spender), HGW himself, GKC, and GBS as 'Alice in Windy Land'. *Boon* has a closer relationship to the controversy over *Ann Veronica* than has been mentioned heretofore, in sources where the James connection is treated as paramount.

43 Maurice Baring to HGW, 11 May, 24 Sept 1915. Ray Lankester also liked the book, calling it a 'music-hall ragtime revue', but he was perplexed at the use of his name, and his villa by the sea. He thought it was a slip of the pen, Wells agreed, and he and Jane and Lankester had a long lunch the next week to discuss the book and its reception. ERL to HGW, 29 June 1915. G. R. S. Taylor also said *Boon* gave him 'joy of a most beautishly [?] sort': Taylor to HGW, 7 July 1915.

44 Hart-Davis, *Hugh Walpole*, 144, 165. It is a bit hard to tell exactly when these events took place, although the luncheon was in late Nov or early Dec 1917.

45 *Daily News and Leader:* Robert Lynd, 'Henry James', 1 Mar 1916; HGW, 'Mr H.G. Wells and Mr Henry James', 3 Mar 1916; Lynd responds, 4 Mar 1916, but with a soft answer and quotes HGW from *The Future in America*. James received the O.M. after his stroke on 5 Dec 1915. HGW supported the gesture; see letter to the Prime Minister, 18 Dec 1915, signed by GBS and others, in Edel, ed., *Complete Plays*, and cited in GBS *Collected Letters* II. 827–8.

46 Atlantic XIII, preface, ix–x.

47 HGW, *Babes in the Darkling Wood* (London 1940), introduction: 'The Novel of Ideas', 5–11.

48 HGW to Herbert Read, 30 July 1943. Also see HGW to *New Statesman and Nation*, 12 June 1943, after Logan Pearsall Smith brought the matter up again; HGW did not raise the AB issue in this letter.

49 William Rothenstein, *Men and Memories*, vol. II (London 1931); *Catalogue of Drawings Made in India by William Rothenstein* (Chelsea [London] *c.* 1911), HGW, preface, 3–5. HGW, review of Joyce's *Portrait of the Artist*, *Nation*, 24 Feb 1917: a 1917 handbill announcing the book includes Wells's review at the top of page 1 (copy in my collection). The review was reprinted in the *New Republic*, 10 Mar 1917, and again on 22 Nov 1954; W. Lippman to HGW, ? Mar 1917; to ACRW, ? Nov 1917 (Yale). Ezra Pound to HGW, five letters of late 1918, early 1919, most not dated except by year. Noel Riley Fitch, *Sylvia Beach and the Lost Generation* (Boston 1983), esp. p. 279, where Wells is said finally to have refused to support Joyce or publicize him any more, HGW to J. Joyce, 23 Nov 1928; Joyce to HGW, of the same period; both are printed in R. Ellmann and S. Gilbert, eds., *Letters of James Joyce*, vol. I (London 1959), 234–5. HGW, *Tono-Bungay: A Romance of Commerce*, *English Review*, Dec 1908 (vol. I, no. 1) to Mar 1909. Others appearing in these issues were James, Bennett, Belloc, Pound, Forster, Chesterton, Violet Hunt; the same numbers carry the first publication of Conrad's *Personal Record*, so are extremely significant. On Diaghilev and *Les Noces*, Nesta MacDonald, *Diaghilev Observed by Critics in England and the United States, 1911–1929* (London and New York 1929). Wells's letter of appreciation, distributed at the theatre in the entr'acte, spoke, among other things, of the ballet as expressing 'the present soul in its *gravitas*, in its deliberate and simple-minded intimacy, in its subtle voiced rhythms, with deep undercurrents of excitement'. It appeared in the *Graphic*, 25 June 1926, in response to a review by Hannen Swaffer in the *Express*, 16 June 1926. Also see Richard Buckle, *Diaghilev* (New York 1979). See Diaghilev to HGW, 18 June 1926 (letter appears in two forms at Illinois; one may have been

published in *Dancing Times* and another in W.A. Purogart, *The Russian Ballet, 1921–1929* [New York 1931]).

50 HGW to Mr Evans, probably about 1904; HGW to H. Newbolt, 3 May, 2 Oct 1904, undated, but after 1906 (all Hofstra).

51 F. M. Hueffer to HGW, 29 Sept 1908, 29 Jan, 1, 23 Feb, 9 Mar 1909, 2 Apr 1910; HGW to Hueffer, 7, 26 Sept 1908, memorandum of agreement, 29 Jan 1909; HGW to G. Duckworth, Jan 1909; E. O. Thomas to HGW, 14 Feb, 31 Mar, 2, 9 Apr 1909, on costs of production, proof sheets, etc., and Paget's payment. Hueffer to HGW, 20 Nov 1908, on reception of first issue by *Fortnightly*, *Glasgow Herald*, and generally. Other correspondence, especially on *English Review*, is HGW to Hueffer, undated 1909, 28 Jan, 5 Feb, 29 Mar, two others early Apr, 1 Apr 1909, two in 1910 (Indiana).

52 HGW to GKC, mid-1915, 10 Dec 1915. F. M. Ford on HGW and style, *English Review*, no. 141 (Sept, Oct 1920), pp. 107–17; responded to by HGW, 'A Footnote to Hueffer', pp. 178–9. The correspondence is F. M. Hueffer to HGW, 1 Aug 1920, 14 Oct 1923 (thanks for a letter congratulating him on his book), 28 July, 30 Sept 1930 (appealing for funds). Wells sent 2,000 francs. *Transatlantic Review*, vol. I, no. 1 (Jan 1924), p. 94; HGW, letter of 9 Oct 1923, wishing the new journal good luck; 17 Nov 1923, Wells could not contribute because of his journalism agreement with *Westminister Gazette* which forbade it. Also HGW to Ford, 'Dear Fordy', 26 Feb 1928, undated 1928–9, 5 Sept 1930 (Indiana), See F. Swinnerton, 'Vernon Lee', *A London Bookman*, 86–9: written in 1923. Ford's views of Wells are conveniently collected, along with much else, in his *Memories and Impressions*, ed. Michael Killigrew (Harmondsworth 1971). Wells especially liked Ford's *It Was the Nightingale* (London 1933). A marvellous view of the *English Review* circle, written as a personal memoir, is Douglas Goldring, *South Lodge* (1943). HGW and ACRW to Violet Hunt, 23 Oct 1904; HGW to V. Hunt, 23 Oct, 12 Dec 1904, 16 Jan, 12 Feb, 30 Mar 1907, 15 July 1908, and from others undated from same period. On her efforts to change her name (to Ford), see HGW to V. Hunt, 9 Mar 1923, where he advises against it (Cornell).

53 Alvin Langdon Coburn, *New York* (New York and London 1910), with a foreword by Wells, pp. 9–10, in which he extolls 'these records of atmosphere and effect', as 'welcome jewels, amidst the dustheap of accumulated fact with which the historian will struggle'. Coburn later illustrated Wells's *The Door in the Wall* (1911), with many photographs. A new edition of his book *New York* was issued in 1980. Herbert and Alison Gernsheim, eds., *Alvin Langdon Coburn, Photographer; An Autobiography* (London 1966), reprints several of the plates, along with much of Wells's foreword, and describes their meeting. They were introduced by GBS, and Wells invited them both to Sandgate. See GBS to Coburn, 1 Nov 1905. Wells provided trousers for Coburn to wear when he got his own damp while walking, and presented him with a copy of *First and Last Things*, inscribed, 'Our business is to see that we can render it'. Ella Hepworth Dixon, *As I Knew Them* (London 1930). Letters from HGW to her, May 1910, and several cards on a 1911 meeting, all addressed to 'Dear Zuleika'. See 'London Calling', *Daily News*, 5 Nov 1926, for a description of a very high-toned luncheon to say goodbye to Osbert Sitwell, who was on his way to the USA. Sitwell himself described the event in *Laughter in the Next Room* (1948), 267–8. Augustine Birrell was in the chair, and Sir Edmund Gosse, HGW, AB, and Siegfried Sassoon were guests.

54 *SR*: HGW, poss. unsigned, 'The New American Novelists', 5 Sept 1896; HGW, 'Another View of *Maggie*', 19 Dec 1896; two weeks earlier, 28 Nov 1896, he had reviewed Morrison, *Child of the Jago*, as well. HGW, 'On Stephen Crane', *North American Review*, vol. CLXXI (Aug 1900), pp. 233–42. Also see AB, 'Stephen Crane', *Academy*, 25 Aug 1900.

55 Cora Crane to HGW, 25 Apr 1900; undated to ACRW; to HGW, 1 Apr, 15 May 1900; JBP to HGW, 21 May, 12 June, 28 Aug 1900.

56 Paul Valéry, 'H. G. Wells', *Mercure de Paris*, May 1899, is a strong review of the translated *Time Machine*.

Chapter 8

1   The extended introduction to HGW in this matter owes much to Patricia Stubbs, *Women and Fiction: Feminism and the Novel 1880–1920* (Brighton 1979), a brilliant, although to my eyes somewhat flawed book. Stubbs leans too heavily on the novel *Ann Veronica* for her points and is not very well versed in Wells's other writings, especially those in the daily and weekly press. But she is good on Wells and Bennett and understands the relationship between these two, as well as the influence of Gissing and James on Wells. The introduction also owes much to *ExA* (2 vols., 1934), and to *H.G. Wells in Love*, ed. G. P. Wells (London 1984). Lance Sieveking, *The Eye of the Beholder* (London 1957), is a very good account not only of Wells and others in his world but also of how he was perceived in Sieveking's own family. HGW's correspondence with Jane, and with Isabel, is very sparse, and is non-existent for Amber Reeves, and for Moura Budberg, although one can find out much from other persons' perceptions. I am indebted to Patrick Parrinder, William J. Baker, Anne Bridges, Sylvia Smith, and some others for their willingness to listen to me, and to comment on these matters, which occupy such a significant place in Wells's thought but which many find too personal to discuss. I delivered a very early version of this chapter as a paper to a meeting of Phi Alpha Theta, the History honor society at the University of Maine, in 1978, and refined some of the comments in a seminar on H.G. Wells and his fiction that autumn and spring. One should read HGW's introduction to *Men and Women in Love*, a collection of four of his novels (London 1930), as well.

2   HGW to Fred Wells, two in 1893, both undated; Sarah Wells to HGW, 1 Feb, 21 May, 14 Aug 1898; Joseph Wells to HGW, several in 1899; Ruth Neal to 'Bertie', 31 Dec 1897, 18 Nov 1898: loan repaid, 23 Dec 1899, 21 Feb, 25 Mar ? (1901), to 'Bertie', 15 Apr 1934. ACRW to Fred Wells, 6 Dec 1916; HGW to Fred, 16 June 1914. G. P. Wells to Mother, *c.* 1916. Also see HGW, 'Master Anthony and the Zeppelin', in *Princess Marie-Jose's Children's Book* (London 1917), 12–16, a delightful little story for a child written to demystify the Zeppelin attacks and diminish fear. It was illustrated with Wellsian drawings, and probably written for Anthony West, who would have been the proper age.

3   A.T. Simmons to ACRW, 19 Nov 1896; to HGW, 16 Nov 1897, 27 Jan 1905; to ACRW, 6 Jan 1907; to HGW, 22 Oct 1909 (the Royal College dinner was 25 Oct). RAG to HGW, 11, 19 Aug 1921; Winifred Simmons to HGW, 17 Nov 1921, 20 July 1922 (and a later file of thank-you notes from the children). JBP to HGW, 19 Aug 1903, on HGW acting as an intermediary with Pinker and E. Nesbit (Mrs Hubert Bland). Lady Warwick to HGW, an undated fragment from World War I in which she tells him that she has reprimanded the vicar who had preached against Wellsian views from the Easton pulpit. She sent the vicar a proof to read. Also Lady Warwick to HGW, 13 Apr ?1918, perhaps on *Joan and Peter*; she thanks him for the wonderful book 'because you have raised what is lying at the back of the thoughts of the people who are living a hundred years too soon. Every word you write is re-echoed in something within me, and has made my heart – or soul – or whatever the thing is go out to you in sympathy.' It was not unusual for HGW to receive such letters from friends, and from female friends at that. The obvious thing here is that he did care, others knew it, responded to it, and were not afraid to put their inner thoughts down on paper to him with a sense of great trust and affection on their part.

4   HGW to EH, 29 Oct 1891; EH to HGW, 9 Apr 1892, 8 June 1893 (the quote on the party); EH to ACRW, 25 Jan 1907; EH to HGW, 13 Mar, 6 Apr 1910 (Bruce's visit with her to Wells); HGW to EH Bruce, 16 Oct 1912, reporting on seeing her father and other professors at opening of the RCS. See EH to HGW, 21 Sept, 25 Nov 1933; 11 Dec 1934, when HGW sent her £50 a year after Bruce became ill: it paid her rent. See HGW to EH, 1 May 1936, 17 May 1937. Her house in Cardiff was damaged in the wartime bombing; see EH to HGW, 8 Jan 1941, 'We never thought of such grim jests as

these in 1887.' Marjorie Craig Wells continued her income; see EH to MCW, 30 Nov 1946.

5 HGW to EH, 19 June 1888: an extract typed and in HGW file; the original was destroyed by HGW.

6 HGW to EH, 25 Dec 1894. (It is worth mentioning again that we have these significant letters because EH kept them, and posted them to the estate after HGW died; others, destroyed, may have been of equal importance.)

7 Isabel Wells to HGW ('Bertie'), Feb 1898, and thereafter in receipt of various cheques. HGW to EH, 18 Jan, as well as 21, 22 Jan 1904. In all these letters he vacillated on the burning of his correspondence. All are in his hand. Some letters may have been destroyed. EH to HGW, 6 Oct 1926, 30 July 1927, 14 July 1929.

8 Isabel Wells to HGW, 22, 27 Apr, 1 May, 19, 20 June, 4 July 1908, 1, 11 Feb 1912, 10 Dec 1913. 'It will help me very much if you grumble at any faults you find in the work.' EH Bruce to HGW, 17 Oct 1934. Isabel to HGW, 14 Oct 1921, 17 Jan (two, the second to ACRW), 1, 4 July, 22 Aug 1922, this last dealing with the laundry. He sent her £650 for this venture. She fell ill and recuperated at Easton, see Isabel to HGW, 3 Apr 1923. He sent her another £100 16 Jan 1923. Other letters are Isabel to HGW, 13 Feb, 15 Aug, 23 Dec 1923; HGW to Isabel, 2 Feb 1926. He sent her the funeral address for Jane, 7 Dec 1927. Also see Isabel to HGW, 8 Apr 1929, 27 Aug 1931, the latter in regard to Joy's visit to her mother's cousin.

9 HGW to P. Cazenove, 28 Nov 1906.

10 HGW, 'The Drop in the Birth Rate: Does It Really Matter?', *DMail*, 19 May 1904.

11 HGW, 'Utopianisms: I. The Garden Cities', *DMail*, 18 Mar 1905.

12 *DMail*: HGW, 'Utopianisms: II. A Cottage in a Garden', 30 Mar 1905; Keble Howard, 'The Dream Cottage: A Reply to H. G. Wells', 4 Apr 1905; Ebenezer Howard, 'Garden Cities: By Their Inventor', 22 Mar 1905.

13 HGW, 'State Babies – Utopianisms: III', *DMail*, 20 Apr 1905.

14 *DMail*: HGW, 'Joint Households – Daring Socialist Suggestion', 25 May 1905; HGW, 'A Woman's Day in Utopia', 7 June 1905. See Hamilton Fyfe to HGW, 29 Oct 1907 (Boston), asking him for a paper for the *DMail* to be entitled, 'Does Socialism Want to Change Human Nature?' HGW was 'not keen', but said he would for £30.

15 *Sociological Papers* (London 1905), HGW comment on Galton's paper, 58–60. For the conference, and HGW's role, see preface, xi. Letter from HGW, *DMail*, 18 Oct 1913, putting his position straight again. HGW was pursued, as were other socialists, by a person named Bolce who announced that he and his wife had become the parents of an eugenic baby, named Eugenetta. He visited HGW, Shaw, Jerome K. Jerome, Harry Lauder, and other celebrities, apparently seeking funds. Also see *Daily Chronicle*, 27 Dec 1915, for another effort by HGW to bring out his true position. Much the same thing was said with regard to his remarks on the endowment of motherhood, as his financial scheme began to be called. See, e.g., *DMail*, 13 June 1910; repeated in Fort Worth (Texas) *Star-Telegram*, 1 July 1910, HGW finally set forth his views in a signed article, 'The Endowment of Motherhood', *DMail*, 16, 22 June 1910. In this he said that if the falling birth rate was a problem, the state should pay mothers to produce children, but if they did so, they would need to provide better quality homes and schools. This was commented upon in *T.P.'s Weekly*, 15 June 1910, by E. A. M. Turner, who had proposed something similar in 1908, but said that HGW had done better and gone further. As HGW said elsewhere, 'whatever increases the personal and economic freedom of women concerns the welfare of the nation's children': *Christian Commonwealth*, 5 Jan 1910. His comment was part of a symposium eventually published in a pamphlet, *The Character of the Child* (London 1910). Wells was in considerable demand on these subjects. See L. P. Jacks, editor *Hibbert Journal*, to HGW, 11 June 1908 (Boston), accepting an HGW article.

16 HGW, 'Socialism and the Middle Classes', *Fortnightly*, vol. LXXX (1906), pp. 785–98. HGW was somewhat influenced in these matters by Benjamin Kidd, with whom he had

some correspondence. The issues, and others taken up by the two men, are described in D. P. Crook, *Benjamin Kidd: Portrait of a Social Democrat* (Cambridge 1984).

17 HGW, 'The Two Ways of Women: An Economic Revolution', *DMail*, 20 May 1916; HGW, 'The Church and the Illegitimate', *Nation*, 4 Aug 1917: letter to the editor in response to a letter attacking his views on women and children.

18 HGW, 'Mr Asquith Will Die', *Freewoman*, 7 Dec 1911.

19 'Mr Wells to the Attack: *Freewoman* and Endowment', *Freewoman*, 7 Mar 1912. The original article appeared on 24 Feb 1912.

20 *Freewoman*: HGW, 'Women Endowed', 21 Mar 1912. Also see his letter, this time from 'your sympathetic reader', 'The Policy of the Freewoman', 5 Sept 1912, urging them to focus their efforts better. The letter came about because of an editorial comment, 'The State and Freedom', 15 Aug 1912, on *The Great State*, which they did not review. The world outside the feminist movement heard and saw much of this debate by its being reprinted; see, e.g., *T.P.'s Weekly*, 22 Dec 1911, which quoted HGW extensively.

21 For various HGW comments, mostly on these same points, see 'Tyro' (HGW), 'A Devotee of Art', *SSJ*, no. 15 (Nov 1888), and Part II (Dec 1888), where he recounts a dream of his wife's death, and a promise to treat her more reasonably once he awoke. *Fortnightly:* HGW, 'The Artificial Factor in Man', Oct 1896, from which the quotations are taken; 'On Morals and Civilization', Feb 1897. The indigestion quote comes from Cyril Scott, *Bone of Contention: Life Story and Confessions* (New York 1969), 151, in which he recounts a walk along the beach during the period of the furore over the *Comet*. For the proposed article, see APW to HGW, 14 June 1918. The interview quoted is by W. R. Titterton, 'H.G. Wells Confesses I Don't Want to Be Immortal', *Daily Herald*, 7 Aug 1930.

22 HGW to Grant Allen, Aug 1896 (probable date); to Allen, 13 July 1899, a letter typed by HGW on his new machine (both at Yale). This was the period of his illness, and he closed the second letter with, 'I mustn't smoke, or drink the good alcohol God sends. I mustn't ride a bicycle or take any exercise. I am a mere sink into which Contrexville is poured. . . .' The review of Allen's book is in *SR*, 9 Mar 1895: 'It may not merit praise, but it merits reading.' Allen responded, *SR*, 16 Mar 1895.

23 HGW to GrW, 19 Sept 1902, a 9–pp. letter.

24 ViP to HGW, 16 May, 30 Oct 1908 (in which she enclosed detailed comments on the MS HGW had sent her).

25 ERL to ACRW, 10 Aug, 28 Aug (two letters, the second of which said, 'I believe that talks with H.G. would restore my brain which is suffering from a bit of damp mould'), 5 Sept 1911 (this last from Berne). The letter in question is from Lankester to HGW, 13 Sept 1911.

26 ERL to HGW, 1 Feb 1912.

27 HGW to Enid Bagnold, undated, sometime *c.* 1917. For Bagnold's view of life at this time see her *A Diary Without Dates* (London 1918); later in her *Autobiography* (London 1969, 1970), 131–4, she gives her version of the encounter.

28 For some other similar, but less pressing, relationships see HGW's letters to and from Mary Austin, an American novelist, with whom he exchanged letters in 1910–11; she interviewed HGW on sex, and his views of sex, and when she eventually wrote her memoirs, *Earth's Horizon* (1932), HGW changed the bits in the book about him to represent his views more precisely. See ch. 15. Another person of whom HGW saw a good deal was Claire Sheridan, a famous left-wing thinker, artist, and actress. She has left several accounts of their meetings, but the best for this subject is in her memoir, *Naked Truth* (New York 1928), in which she recounts coming to HGW for advice on education after her husband died. They had several lunches at his home, but he would not let her sculpt a bust of him. One of their meetings also included Arnold Bennett, when she claimed the two men talked to each other about love and marriage, 'but *at*' her. HGW gave his views in 'Sex Antagonisms: An Unavoidable and Increasing Factor in Modern Life', *WGaz*, 30 Aug 1924, in which while commenting on E. Rubins, *Ancilla's Slave* (1924), a novel of the time, Wells remarked that sexual antagonism was a

necessary result of the drive to freedom, but not as it was portrayed in the novel, as an innate matter. He claimed that women were not at war with men, but with sexual urges, and he counselled against 'foolish feminism'.

29 This section is based on *ExA*, esp. ch. 7, sections 2, 3, 4, as well as much discussion with a wide variety of people. Also see HGW, 'I am a Success at Last', *SChron*, 16 July 1939. *The Book of Catherine Wells* (London 1928), HGW introd., 3–44. The letter about his relationship with Jane is in E. Haldeman-Julius, *My Second Twenty-Five Years* (Girard, Kans. 1949), 100–1; there the author confirms that Jane Wells handled the business side of HGW's writing, and quotes several letters from HGW mostly written during World War II. (He also gives sales figures of HGW's work in the Little Blue Book series circulated so widely in the United States.)

30 ACRW to HGW, several in Aug, Sept 1903 (relatively few have firm dates). The ones quoted are dated by me from internal evidence as sometime in 1901; perhaps in 1902; 5 Aug 1903. HGW's letter to her is 16 Dec 1903.

31 For an early, humorous but prophetic HGW view, see 'On the Choice of a Wife', *PMG*, 16 Jan 1895. Jane's move to a flat in town occurred while HGW and Gip were in Russia. She discussed it briefly in a letter to their French agent, Marie Beets, 21 Oct 1920 (probably a draft). See HGW to 'Brightest and Dearest', sometime in late summer 1914 (Boston) as well.

32 HGW to ACRW, autumn 1914. This letter is written very rapidly, and in stress. The letters and words are small, crammed together, and yet filled with wide spaces, and words are missing. My reading is mildly conjectural in a few places. True, the letter was written as the war began, and Wells's mind was tremendously occupied with the journalism demanded of him, as well as with *Mr Britling*, beginning to emerge in his thoughts. But only a person whose relationship with his wife was absolutely secure could have written thus, one supposes. However the fact that it was written may indicate something of that security. HGW was, after all, always happier talking at someone through the printed or written word. He could always speak openly to Jane, however, as when he described visits to saloons and bordellos in Chicago (arranged, it seems, by Jane Addams, so he could see Chicago completely), as well as his talk and stay at Hull House. HGW to ACRW, 6 May 1906.

33 As an example of how such matters appeared to HGW in his days of journalism, one could look at an unsigned article, 'In The New Forest', *SR*, 27 Apr 1896, which ends with 'Here in the forest the problems of sex are as engrossing as the question of The New Woman in town'. Also see his remarks in a review, signed 'H.G.W.', of Richard Le Gallienne's novel, *The Quest of the Golden Girl*, in the same journal, 6 Mar 1897: 'Morality is only a selfishness, enlightened'; or his remarks in a review, also signed 'H.G.W.' and entitled 'The Democratic Culture', on G. W. Steevens, *The Land of the Dollar* (a book he later listed as one of the best of that year), *SR*, 13 Mar 1897: there he compared England to America with, 'Our country is an aristocracy in decay, an aristocracy with a leaky organization, a land of hyphenated names, bogus crests, and derived manners, where everyone is strenuously putting on a side – trying, imitating, presuming equality with some persons supposed to be "above" him, or imposing charity or patronage upon some other person supposed to be "below" him.' The impact of HGW's work on the aristocracy may be well seen in a letter from Alys Russell who was having problems in her marriage to Bertrand Russell. Beatrice Webb had offered to take her to the Continent for a rest cure, but Mrs Webb was too driven, and 'I do not feel I could discuss food and Wells's novels with her for three weeks': Alys Russell to Bertrand Russell, 1 June 1902. See B. Webb *Diary* II, for more on the trip, in which HGW was a topic of discussion.

34 The earliest version, *The Wealth of Mr Waddy*, has been published by Southern Illinois University Press (Carbondale, Ill. 1969), with an introduction by Harris Wilson. Kipps simply took over the book, and after chapter 7 when he first appears, the earlier book disintegrates.

35   JBP to HGW, 2, 17, 24 Jan 1898; to ACRW, 17, 19 Mar 1899; to HGW, 8, 20 June, 19 Dec (the quotation) 1904, 6 Jan 1905; HGW to F. Macmillan, 27 Sept 1905, an 8–pp. draft of a letter on the book, and on *The Food of the Gods*, which HGW also felt Macmillan did not understand. He told Macmillan that he would have been sceptical of Coleridge and Goldsmith as well, and that the publisher forced him to 'unbecoming lengths of self-assertion'. Macmillan to HGW, 9 Oct 1905; HGW to Macmillan, 9, 16, 23, 27, 29 Nov 1905.

36   C. F. G. Masterman, *Daily News*, 25 Oct 1905; Henry James to HGW, 19 Nov 1905; C. F. G. Masterman to HGW, 22 Oct 1905; Morley Roberts to HGW, 22 July (while reading the serial – a postcard), 9 Dec 1905. When EH Bruce gave a paper on HGW to the Wesley Guild in Cardiff in 1911, she reported that nearly everyone in the audience had read the book: EH to HGW, 31 May 1911.

37   Preface, *Tono-Bungay*, Atlantic XII, ix. HGW to P. Cazenove, 28 Oct 1906, 9 Jan 1909 (the quote is from the first letter). On the rearranging of sequence with the two novels, ACRW to Cazenove, 21 June 1907.

38   Hubert Bland, *Daily Chronicle*, 3 Feb 1909. B. Webb *Diary* III, entry for 24 Feb 1909; B. Webb to HGW, 10 Feb 1909, in Webb *Letters* II. 323. *DTel*, 10 Feb 1909. C.F.G. Masterman to HGW, Dec 1908. HGW to F. Macmillan, 11 Mar 1909, on the *British Weekly* attack, urging him to respond. In the event he did not need to, as Arnold Bennett took on the role of defender; in his piece, 'H. G. Wells', *New Age*, 4 Mar 1909, he praised HGW for 'stirring up the dregs', and called *Tono-Bungay* his 'most distinguished and powerful book'. Maurice Baring gave a dinner for HGW to celebrate the book, at which GKC was present: Baring to HGW, 2 Mar 1909.

39   Gilbert Murray to HGW, 9, 14 Feb, 1 Mar 1909. *T.P.'s Weekly*, 26 Feb 1909, 12 Mar 1909; the second is signed 'John o'London'. *Christian Commonwealth*, 14 Apr 1909; Fenner Brockway was a sub-editor and may have written the piece. The *Glasgow Herald*, 14 Nov 1908, ran a story while the book was appearing in the *English Review*, saying it was simply a piece of autobiography, although they did compare it to *David Copperfield*. HGW was angry at this remark, and on the margin of the cutting he wrote, 'Please track this *FOOL* who started this to his lair and cut his obscene throat.' Where HGW found the name for his patent elixir is not known, and he was somewhat coy on the subject when asked, but it does not tax belief too much to think that it is his tribute to Trollope. In the Palliser novels there is a character, the Duke of St. Bungay, who exercises great power, without ability and in a casual way, but is never in the forefront on the work, allowing others to carry out his suggestions. Especially one might instance *Phineas Finn*, or *The Prime Minister* as examples. By 1946 Wells's novel had been translated into eight languages, including Hungarian (1928), Portuguese (1943), Czech (1925), and Japanese (1934); MCW to APW, 11 Oct 1946.

40   Examples of good reviews of *Mr Polly* are those by H.L. Mencken, *Smart Set*, July 1910, who really liked the book. See Northcliffe to HGW, sometime in 1910, and an essay entitled, 'The Orientation of Mr Polly', *T.P.'s Weekly*, 27 May 1910. Wells tried to get Macmillan to react to a poisonous review in the *Field*, but the publishers would not file the libel suit he wished; see HGW to Macmillan, 25 May 1910. The *Field* had termed the work 'slime', and 'a poisonous stand of stagnant mud'. Wells refused the mantle of Polly when interviewed by Mrs. C. A. Dawson-Scott in 1923, saying that 'A man's novels tell you where he has been, but not what he has done', and that if he had set the fire, as Polly did, 'Oh, I would like a bigger conflagration – all the horribly ugly, inconvenient houses in the world – a holocaust of them.' 'As I Knew Them: Some Famous Authors of Today', *Strand*, vol. LXVI (July 1923), pp. 389–92. Wells discussed the provenance of the book in HGW, 'Drawn From Life? H. G. Wells and Mr Polly', *Strand*, vol. LXXVI (Aug 1928), pp. 595–6.

41   Unsigned review, *SR*, 26 Oct 1895. *The Wonderful Visit* remained a possibility for dramatization, at which at least three attempts were made. Two of these had copyright performances: Arthur Bourchier to HGW, 12 Apr, 25 May, 3 June 1896; HGW to

Charlotte Boucher, 11 July 1900 (was this one performed?): Wells asked her to change a name in her play. A performance of a play based on the book was given at the St. Albans Theatre in 1934; see Pinker's royalty accounts of 23 Jan 1935, crediting Wells with £2. 12s. 6d. for the work.

42 J. Galsworthy to HGW, 28 Jan 1906, discussing a long walk on the beach at Sandgate and a discussion of the inner meanings of *Kipps* and *The Sea Lady*. Galsworthy thought that the 'extreme precision' with which Wells dealt with 'an unimaginably difficult theme' set these novels apart from others of the time. On the business side, see JBP to HGW, 17, 18 Oct (the hussy comment) 1900, 20 June 1902. W. Archer to HGW, 22 Aug 1902, 24 Jan, 20 Mar 1903, for another play possibility. They produced a first act before abandoning the effort. HGW to D. Appleton, 17 Jan 1912, on US sales. JBP to HGW, 1, 24 Oct 1912, on a 6d. edition which sold some 25,000 copies within about 18 months. Wells got a 20% royalty.

43 Preface, Atlantic VII, ix. HGW to J.M. Dent, 12, 17 Sept, 10 Nov, 15, 17 Dec 1896; JBP to HGW, 20 Nov 1896.

44 JBP to HGW, 7, 9, 25, 28 Oct, 15 Dec 1898; to ACRW, 29 Nov 1898.

45 HGW to EH, Dec 1898. JBP to HGW, 19 Dec 1898, 5, 24 Jan, 14 Feb, 8 Mar, 14 Apr, 7 July 1899, 15, 21 June 1900. *DTel*, 6 June; *Daily Chronicle*, 14 June; *Morning Post*, 14 June (all 1900).

46 A.T. Simmons to HGW, 15 June; RAG to HGW, 10 July; EH to HGW, 12, 17 June; HGW to EH, 22 June (all 1900).

47 Doris Langley Moore, *E. Nesbit* (London 1932; rev. edn. 1966); John Carswell, *Ivy* (1984).

48 It is difficult to separate fact from fiction, or speculation here. Langley Moore did say in a footnote that the story of the relationship had not yet been told, and she retained that footnote in the 1966 version of her book.

49 HGW to [?] M. Perrin, 19, 28 June 1906.

50 HGW to *Standard*, 1 Nov 1907; to *Daily Express*, 19 Sept 1906; to Frederick Macmillan, 21 Nov 1906: Editor *TLS* to HGW, 19 Sept 1906. For a Wellsian view of the controversy, sent to a good friend, HGW to Henry Newbolt, *c*. Oct 1906 (Hofstra), a letter which also discusses male and female promiscuity.

51 ACRW to Jix (W. Joynson-Hicks), 11 Oct 1907; HGW to Jix, 12, 18, 23, 28 Oct 1907. The comments were summarized in the *Daily Telegraph* which is where Wells first spotted them as coming from Jix himself. His autobiography, *Jix* (London 1947), makes very little of the incident, although an earlier book by H. A. Taylor, *Jix: Viscount Brentford* (London 1933), discusses the election and HGW in ch. 10 as well as dealing with their Civil Air Transport Committee service. Wells wrote to Jix during World War I on aviation. In the event they became friends, even though remarkably different personages, and spent several holidays together on the Riviera. *Spectator*: 14 Oct; HGW, letter to the editor, 26 Oct; 2, 9 Nov 1907. HGW to *Standard*, 28 Oct 1907. *New Age*: HGW, 'Mr Wells and Free Love: A Personal Statement', 17 Oct; HGW, letter to editor, 31 Oct; another letter, 7 Nov 1907. The first letter to the press on this matter appeared in *Manchester Courier*, 24 Oct (written 22 Oct) 1907. *Lancashire Daily Post*, 23 Oct; *Manchester Dispatch*, 21 Oct; *North Devon Herald*, 7, 14 Nov; *Daily Chronicle*, 31 Oct; *Labour Leader*, 8 Nov; *Daily Express*, 8 Nov; *Bristol Mercury, Euston Morning News, York Daily Post*, 8 Nov; *Bristol Mercury, Euston Morning News, York Daily Post* (publication details not known: these letters were identical and were sent on 23 Nov); *Morning Post, Manchester Courier*, 22 Oct (all 1907). Horace Horsnell to *Advertiser*, 9 Nov 1907 (corrected by Wells before it went out). Also see HGW, 'Socialism and Free Love: The Relationship of the State to the Child', *Manchester Dispatch*, 10 Oct 1906. The *Clarion* letter, 'Mr H. G. Wells, Free Love and the Family', was published as a handout (London: A. C. Fifield 1907). Other items may have been printed as well.

52 ViP to HGW, 18 Dec 1906 (parts written as late as 29th). She goes on in a rambling bit to discuss platonic love, incest and so on before breaking off.

53   J. Galsworthy to HGW, 20 Sept 1906; HGW, 'Mr Wells and Free Love – A Personal Statement', *New Age*, 17 Oct 1907.

54   The relevant letters (of which many more might be included) are HGW to GBS, 24 Aug 1909: 'Matters are very much as you summarize. We should all be very happy and proud of ourselves if we hadn't the feeling of being harried and barked at by dogs.' Wells said that he liked Blanco-White, very much, went to the cottage often, and in fact, his two boys were there as he wrote, while Jane was in London. GBS to B. Webb, 30 Sept 1909, *Collected Letters* II. 869–71, a long letter warning her off the matter. Shaw said he thought one of the problems was that Amber was inclined to brag of her exploits. 'What will occur then is that W. will stand by Amber until "the ripping child" (who, alas, may not be a ripping child) is born.' (The Webbs had been close to the Reeveses; letters among the foursome go back to the Webbs' world tour of 1898. See S. Webb to Pember Reeves, 8 Aug 1898.) B. Webb, *Diary* entries, early Aug, 22 Aug, 27 Sept, 4 Oct (Beatrice visited Amber at the cottage), 27 Dec 1909. Beatrice vacillated considerably on the matter. Shaw's play *Misalliance* appeared at this time and that also gave her a good deal to think about. On the evidence of these diaries, Sidney was probably the more concerned of the two, and she simply aped him, or did not criticize him overmuch. In the diaries she assumes a more moral position on many matters, which suggests something of her character. HGW to P. Cazenove, 10 Aug 1908; to G. F. McCleary, 27 Feb 1907, on Amber's work and placing the article.

55   F. Macmillan to HGW, 7, 16, 19 Oct 1908 (the quotations are from the last letter). The official Macmillan version appears in Charles Morgan, *The House of Macmillan, 1843–1943* (London 1944), esp. 145–7.

56   W. Archer to HGW, 7 Oct, 1, 3 Nov 1909; RAG to HGW, 6 Oct 1909; C. H. Norman, 'Mr Wells's Polity of Babies: A Retrospect', *New Age*, 10 June 1909; in their review, 14 Oct 1909, the *New Age* called Ann Veronica 'a vulgar manhunter'. It is difficult to assume that any comment in this period is not directed towards the principals, rather than their fictional counterparts. Review by 'John o'London' (Winifred Whitten), *T.P.'s Weekly*, 22 Oct 1909. *Spectator*: 20 Nov 1909; Wells's response, 'An Open Question', appeared 4 Dec 1909. As has been pointed out by Wells and others (*ExA* [1934] II. 471), Wells had little to complain of in the review, which was not of his life but of his novel. During this same period *T.P.'s Weekly* was serializing Arnold Bennett's 'The Revolt of Youth', Oct-Nov 1909. In her memoirs, *The Tamarisk Tree* (London 1975), Dora Russell recalled the impact of this book and *The New Machiavelli* on her generation.

57   There are four letters from HGW to ViP in Sept-Oct 1909. From internal evidence (her responses in part), this last one is dated early Nov 1909. They all appear in Wells's hasty personal style, and I have corrected some punctuation.

58   ViP to HGW, 22 Dec 1909; HGW to Vip, 31 Dec 1909.

59   ViP to HGW, 5, 19 Jan 1910 (these are copies in her hand; the originals no longer survive in the Wells archive). HGW to ViP, 28 Jan (p.m.) 1910. Wells told EH at about the same time, 'I'm afraid I've behaved rather scandalous but no how mean in the past year. Believe enough [?] of scandalous and not mean about me and you will be fairly right': HGW to EH, very early 1910.

60   Wells sent a version of this to a Samurai conference in the late autumn of 1907; it had its genesis in a walking tour in the Alps with Jane in Sept 1907, although it was begun earlier, during the Bottomley/Jix business. See HGW to (?) Munro, 29 Sept, 28 Oct 1907 (Boston). Drafts of Credo: first one is dated from internal evidence from Jan 1907.

Chapter 9

1   I have treated this aspect of Wellsian thought, and the books and articles which followed from it, in my 'Little Wars for Little People', *Arete*, Autumn 1985. A.M.J. Balfour to HGW, 20 Dec 1911, says he looks forward to trying the games; C. F. G. Masterman to HGW, early in 1912, told HGW that he should have used a battle between the two of

them in which Masterman had won: they fought that battle from 12 to 2 p.m., then from 4 to 6, and finally again from 8 to sometime in the late evening. JBP to HGW, 12 Feb 1910, who could not understand the game prior to reading HGW's books and articles on it. Hilaire Belloc played the game, reviewed the book very well, and thought his days at Easton among the more pleasant he had spent. Cynthia Asquith, *Haply I May Remember* (London 1950), remembered a version of the game played up and down the stairs in their town house by her brother and his friends.

2 Possible unsigned HGW, 'The Locomotion of the Future – Leaders of Science Learning to Fly', *PMG*, 12 July 1894. JBP to HGW, 13, 14 Jan 1902, on placing 'Esau Common'. *The War in the Air* was included in Atlantic XX, along with 8 articles which bore on the subject, most of them to be found in HGW's 1914 collection, *An Englishman Looks at the World*. Some of the pieces in that volume had not previously appeared in England, as they were commissioned, mostly by the *New York World* – as was 'The Possible Collapse of Civilization', *World*, 1 Jan 1909. HGW to Viscount Esher, 25 Aug 1909 (on sources for his ideas on military matters). HGW to P. Cazenove, 16 Jan 1907, on his monetary needs for the novel: 'I've had my vision'; to F. Macmillan, 7 June 1907, asking to be freed from a contract in order to do his pot-boiler (his term) about flying machines. When the book was reprinted HGW wrote new forewords, in 1921 and 1941, the latter a source for his proposed epitaph, '"I told you so. You *Damned* Fools".' Another war novel (the sea story) also surfaced, although it was never written; see HGW to Cazenove, 5 Dec 1908, for a précis. Conrad liked *The War in the Air*, but perhaps not as much as did F.M. Hueffer; J. Conrad to HGW, 2 Nov 1908. HGW's work in this genre was important enough for him to be asked to comment on the death toll in early aeronautics; see *NYT*, 3 Jan 1911. He was a vivid advocate of flying, as was remembered by Jane Anderson who with several others listened to him in his flat: J. Anderson to HGW, *c.* 1932, 8, 11 Apr 1933.

3 HGW, 'Enquête sur l'influence allemande', *Mercure de France*, issue no. 1, 1903; 'Ce qu'on pense d'Allemagne', *Le Courrier Européen*, 10 Oct 1905. 'The War of the Mind', *Nation*, 29 Aug 1914, also appeared in *New York World*. HGW, 'The Perversion of Germany: A Study in Educational Organization', *Daily Chronicle*, 25 Mar 1915, a long review-article of F. M. Hueffer's *When Blood is Their Argument: An Analysis of Prussian Culture* (1915). Similar statements were put in a long letter from ViP to ACRW, 5 Aug 1914, saying how much she wished she could speak and listen to HGW on the subject of Germany and Prussianism.

4 HGW, 'The Common Sense of Conscription', 'Put Not Your Trust in Dreadnoughts', 'The Balance of Present and Future', *DMail*, 7, 8, 9 Apr 1913, collected as *War and Common Sense* (London 1913). See Twells Brex, comp., *'Scare-Mongerings' from The Daily Mail 1896–1914: The Paper That Foretold the War* (London 1915). From the quotations it will be apparent that HGW is still a Little-Englander, and has not made any transition to the idea of a world state.

5 The pieces appeared in *Daily Chronicle*, 7, 13, 20 Aug, 3 Sept 1914; *Daily News*, 14 Aug, 7 Sept (also HGW's letter in response to a critic, 21 Aug) 1914; *Nation*, 22 Aug 1914; *War Illustrated*, vol. I, no. 1 (22 Aug 1914). The piece for the *Nation* was his last for a time, as they were not belligerent enough for him; see his letter to them, 3 Oct 1914. Eleven pieces were conveniently collected in early October, and republished in a small book, HGW, *The War That Will End War* (London 1914). The book had a wide sale both in England and in the USA. It was published in paper and in boards and sold for a low price. Lillah MacCarthy happened to spend the first weekend of the war at home, with Gilbert Murray as her guest. The next weekend she was at Easton. She told, in her memoirs, of the seriousness of the two men. HGW said to her, when they met, 'The world is falling to pieces. I can do nothing but think, think. . . .' L. MacCarthy, *Myself and My Friends* (1933), 185. That last Bank Holiday weekend was the occasion of the annual flower show and fête at Easton; the Countess of Warwick presided but noticed that the men, John Robertson Scott, GBS, R. D. Blumenfeld, and

HGW, did not participate much. M. Blunden, *The Countess of Warwick* (London 1967), 245–7.

6   HGW, 'If England is Raided: The Civilian Force', *Daily Chronicle*, 12 Dec 1914. *The Times*, 5 Dec 1914, a letter supporting the organization of Home Defence, and urging people to participate in it; *NYT*, 25 Nov 1914, an earlier version of the same idea; 'Looking Ahead: The Organization of Foresight in Great Britain', *Daily Chronicle*, 19 Jan 1915; 'Why I Have Become a Protectionist: Free Confession', *Daily Express*, 20 Jan 1915. The *Express* newspaper had for years supported protectionism, and that is why HGW chose it for his recantation. See their leader, as well as letters on 22 Jan, from Walter Reynolds, and 26 Jan, from Sidney Bouverie. HGW also wrote a similar piece for the *Chronicle*, 31 Jan 1915, and this was answered by the *New Statesman*, 6 Feb 1915. They thought an indemnity to be paid after the war was sufficient for those who suffered war losses through protectionism. Also see HGW to *Nineteenth Century*, Apr 1915, on the same subject.

7   HGW, *Daily Chronicle*; 'Looking Ahead: After A Year of War', 3 Aug 1915; 'Looking Ahead: Braintree, Bocking and the Future of the World', 19 Feb 1916; 'The Liberal Aim in the War', 4 May 1915. HGW, *The Peace of the World* (London 1915); this was originally published in a slightly different form in the *New Review*, Mar 1915. HGW, 'The Kind of Peace That England Wants', *NYT*, 1 May 1915; HGW along with others endorsed meatless Thursdays, but had to be reminded of his pledge one night at the Reform. R.D. Blumenfeld, *All in One Lifetime* (London 1931), diary entry of 3 Oct 1915; *NYT*, 6 May 1916.

8   F. Macmillan to HGW, 21 Dec 1915 (they tried to cut his royalties); HGW to Macmillan, ?, 27 Jan 1916. HGW threatened to withdraw all his work from the firm, and they relented. Kurt Butow to HGW, 5, 15, 28 June, 18 July 1913, about the job; to 'Family Wells', July, Aug 1914, 14 Aug (sent via New York, 4 Sept 1914), 22 Nov 1914. For a brief comment on *Britling*, see Butow to HGW, 19 July 1918. He remained a significant foreign source for HGW after the war, and the letters continue until mid-1935. At the height of the German postwar inflation HGW lent Butow money, which was repaid on schedule. See, in particular, Butow to HGW, 16 Sept, 28 Nov 1919, 18 Apr 1920, 14 Dec 1921. On the actual writing of the novel, which was very similar to the scene sketched at its end, see memoirs of Newman Flower, *Just as It Happened* (London 1950); Flower was at Easton that weekend. And see R. D. Blumenfeld's diary entry of 14 Oct 1917, also as conversation in *Britling*. The book was serialized in the *Nation*, May–Oct 1916. The reviews of it were ecstatic; see, e.g., *Daily News*, 20 Sept, *Daily Chronicle*, 20 Sept 1916.

9   E[mily] T[ownshend], ed., Frederick Hillersdon Keeling, *Keeling Letters and Recollections* (London 1918), preface by HGW, ix–xiv. Keeling died 18 Aug 1916 in France.

10 *Daily Chronicle*, 19, 26, 31 Oct 1916; Rudyard Kipling, 'Our Destroyers at Jutland'. Also see John Buchan, *Francis and Riversdale Grenfell* (London 1920) and *These for Remembrance* (London 1919), for examples of another writer who found himself being hammered by the loss of friends. A. Conan Doyle to HGW, 9 May 1917, and Winston Churchill to HGW, 1 Oct 1916; both praise *Britling*.

11 HGW to Victor Fisher, undated, end 1916–beginning 1917. Also see his letter of the same time period to 'Dear M.', in which he says, 'This is a war of liberation. Beat Germany – German Inquisition that is – and you begin a new age in human history. I would rather see both my sons dead or mutilated in this war than have one of them a C.O. What is life for?' This letter was to someone in the Labour Party. (Both letters are now at Boston.) Socialists who had followed HGW blindly found this stage difficult, although most forgave him. *Britling* helped them understand his views. See the poignant essay by Douglas Goldring, who first met HGW at the *English Review* office, 'Mr Wells and the War', *Reputations* (London 1920), 79–98.

12 HGW to Marie Beets, 14 Feb, 19 Mar 1916 (trying to arrange translations into German); for the title change, see Martin Secker's remarks in Mervyn Horder,

'Conversations with Martin Secker', *TLS* 10 Dec 1976. The actual translations and transmittal to Europe are covered in C. F. G. Masterman to HGW, 12 Feb 1917; Northcliffe to HGW, 30 Mar 1917 (this led to HGW working on propaganda at Crewe House); Maxim Gorky to HGW, end Dec–beginning Jan 1917, 18–21 Mar 1917. John Galsworthy to HGW, 11 Sept 1919. F. W. Worsley, *Letters to Mr Britling* (London 1917), prints 8 letters, or sermons, addressed to Britling by the head of the chaplain force. Apparently hundreds of letters were addressed to Britling by soldiers, and they were read by the Corps of Chaplains as a guide to the state of morale. For the ups and downs of civilian feeling a good source is Marie Belloc-Lowndes's diary, Feb 1915, for dinner-table conversations with Henry James, Lord Haldane, Arnold Bennett; in the summer of 1916, conversations with Hilaire Belloc, and his letter to her of 9 June 1916. This last reflected a wave of optimism, but it would be the last such, as the Somme battles ended such feelings. Publishers wanted HGW to follow *Britling* with a sequel, but he could not; see HGW to 'My Dear Sir', early 1917: 'The War has dragged us all into journalism and I suppose I shall continue to author [?screeds] at intervals until after the peace.'

13 HGW, 'How People Think About the War', *Daily News*, 15, 18, 22 Dec 1916, 5 Jan 1917. HGW, 'A Reasonable Man's Peace', *Daily News and Leader*, 14 Aug 1917, reprinted as a pamphlet by the International Free Trade League (1917). Sir Harry Johnston to HGW, 6 Sept 1917, how right you are.

14 Northcliffe to HGW, 22 Apr, 8 May (these are summary responses to whole afternoons of talk), 18 June 1916, asking for the articles. *The Times* to HGW, 24 July 1916. The pieces, which appeared 17, 19, 24, 29 July, 1, 4 Aug 1916, were signed 'D.P.' (Dominating Personality), although HGW was named in the third article. They appeared signed in a pamphlet, *The Elements of Reconstruction* (London 1916), with an introduction by Viscount Milner.

15 The quotations are from the last chapter of the pamphlet version, pp. 112–13, 116, 120. For other Wellsian statements that bear on this problem see HGW to Marie Beets, 23 Nov 1917, urging her to work towards his ends; Northcliffe to HGW, 28 Oct 1916, on the reception of the articles. Also by HGW: *The End of the Armament Rings* (Boston 1914), a pamphlet; 'The War and the Workers', *W.E.A. Education Yearbook 1918* (London 1918), 66; 'Will the War Change England?' *War Illustrated*, 20, 27 Feb 1915; 'The Right Method in Elections', *Daily News and Leader*, 12 Apr 1917, and letters from him on 16, 23 Apr 1917. HGW to *The Times*, 29 Mar 1917, repr. by the Proportional Representation Society in *Letters to The Times by H.G. Wells. . . .* (London 1917). A good thesis is Bernard Carter, 'H. G. Wells as Critic of Society', unpub. diss. University of Wales, 1955.

16 W. Lippman to HGW, 29 Sept 1914, 25 May, 26 July, 13 Oct 1916. HGW to Lippman, end 1916 (which lays out an early version of specific points for a possible peace). Lippman's last letter in this series ends with 'As it is we rejoice in every Zeppelin you bag and every trench you take.' A. M. J. Balfour to HGW, 27 Jan 1917 (HGW apparently circulated some of his letters from America to Balfour, and this was the reason the Cabinet discussed his proposed visit to the US). Paul Hyacinthe Loyson, *The Gods in the Battle* (London 1917), HGW introd., xxii–xxiv; he urged readers of this translated work to look to Vernon Lee and Bertrand Russell for intelligent socialist and pacifist thought. Edouard Guyot, *L'Angleterre sa politique intèrieure* (Paris 1917), HGW preface, v–ix; he was complimentary of the French interest in English studies, but urged them to read the young as well as more established authors. Guyot went far beyond to create an England, 'vivantes et agissantes', but after calling for a joint system of trade and tariffs HGW went on to remark, 'ce que je sais, c'est qu'un tel projet est de ceux que l'imagination brittanique peut concevoir sans l'écouter en rien à ses tendances naturelles, et qu'il est entièrement acceptable pour la masse du peuple anglais.' Also see his 'The Lament of a Pacifist: An Open Letter to M. Romain Rolland', *Daily Chronicle*, 7 Mar 1916, which is a sort of review of *Above the Battle*. Winifred Stephens, ed., *The Book of France* (London

1915), contains a piece by Anatole France, 'Début pour la derniere guerre', which was translated by HGW under the title 'Let Us Arise and End War'. HGW would not write on Ireland, however: see Robert Donald to HGW, 25 Sept 1918.

17 HGW: 'Republicanism in Great Britain', letter to editor, *Daily Chronicle*, 27 Apr 1917; 'A Republican Society for Great Britain', *The Times*, 21 Apr 1917. He sent his *Daily Chronicle* letter to *Telegraph*, *Daily Mail* and *Manchester Guardian*, but I have not searched for other publications of it. ERL to ACRW, 21 Apr 1917. 'Mr Wells' Curse', *Independent*, 26 June 1915, on trade unions. HGW, 'The Imperfection of Democracy: A Reply to Arnold Bennett', *Daily News*, 5 Aug 1915; Shaw's letter appeared on 7 Aug, Bennett wrote again on 11 Aug, and William Archer on 12 Aug 1915: these are mostly on PR. HGW, 'The New Englishman: Mr Wells's Reply to His Critics', *Daily News*, 8 Feb 1916. See HGW to 'Capt. Charles' after his 1917 articles on royalty, saying they were prompted by 'the court playing the fool with the Greek princes and it has been necessary to start the warning discussions'.

18 HGW: 'Your Country Needs You: Body, Brains and Prosperity', *Illustrated Sunday Herald*, 21 Mar 1915; '"Can You Answer Yes?" Mr Wells's Blunt Questions', *Daily Chronicle*, 29 Mar 1917; letters to *The Times*: 'Playing the Enemy's Game', 14 May 1915; on Universal National Service, 3 Sept 1915; 'The Psychology of the Premium Bond', 3 Mar 1917; on the state of the monarchy after the war, 21, 23 Apr 1917. 'The Future of Monarchy', *Penny Pictorial*, 1 May 1917. *NYT*, 10 Jan 1915, 21 July 1916, 21, 23 Apr, 16 May 1917 (most of these last are reprints of his letters to *The Times*). *Daily Chronicle*: 'The Tariff as an Instrument of War', 4 Feb 1915; 'An Open Letter to Sir Hedley Le Bas', 1 May 1916. 'Ideals of Organization', *Nation*, 24 July 1915; *Daily News*: 'The New Englishman and the New Education', 1 Feb 1916; 'Property After the War', 12 Jan 1917.

19 HGW, *The War and Socialism* (London 1915). HGW, *Britain v. Germany, The Socialist Point of View* (London: National Socialist Defense League 1914), a letter to Victor Fisher released by Fisher as a leaflet to be handed out at Socialist meetings. Charles Reed to the Public, a letter calling for a meeting, 31 Dec 1917, of the Society for the Study of Republican Institutions; HGW was listed as a vice-president of the group.

20 HGW to *The Times*, 9 Jan 1915. Will Dyson, *Kultur Cartoons* (London 1915), foreword by HGW, repr. as 'The Goose Step – On the March of Civilization', *Daily Chronicle*, 22 Jan 1915. HGW, 'Looking Ahead: A Suggestion for Penalizing Germany's Commerce', *Daily Chronicle*, 1 Feb 1915; this stirred a controversy, and letters opposing, by J.A. Hobson and Leo Chiozza-Money, were printed 2, 3, 6 Feb, and some in favour on 3 Feb, along with a retort from HGW on 4 Feb in which he used the expression 'Hobson's really very bird-like mind'. HGW, 'Every Man's War', *Illustrated Sunday Herald*, 21 Mar 1915. Joseph Pennell, *Pictures of War Work in England* (London 1917), HGW introd., v-viii; J. Pennell, *The Adventures of An Illustrator Mostly in Following His Authors in America and Europe* (Boston 1925), discusses his relations with HGW in detail in ch. 37, esp. pp. 336–8. HGW to GKC, *c.* 1915; to *Daily Express*, end of 1914; to *The Times:* 'The Mobilization of Invention', 11 June 1915 (reprinted in *Evening News*); HGW, 'The Embodiment of Science: A Bureau for Inventors', 22 June 1915; *NYT* reprinted the 'Mobilization' piece, 11 June 1915. The quotations are from *Daily Chronicle*: letter to the editor, 1 Feb 1916: 'We Must Keep Pace With Essen Now – The War of Materiel', 15 Oct 1914. HGW to 'Mr Macker [?]', undated, on how to get his ideas to the inventions committee chaired by Lord Fisher.

21 HGW and G. S. Coleman, 'Descriptions of the "Leeming" Portable and Collapsible Aerial Ropeway', Ministry of Munitions, Trench Warfare Department, 26 Nov 1917: Min 5 198 y/K 6197; Northcliffe to HGW, 27 Nov 1916; ERL to ACRW, 8 Dec 1917 (on the plan and camouflage). HGW, letter to the editor, 'The Potential Officer', *Daily News*, 6 Nov 1916.

22 HGW, 'The Monster I Invented: Later Becomes a Tank', *SChron*, 30 July 1939; HGW discusses his inventions in the war in this piece. The word 'tank' came from an effort to

mislead the enemy as to the trials of the vehicle. C. F. G. Masterman to HGW, 25 Sept 1916, congratulations on the tank; W. Churchill to HGW, 1 Oct 1916, thanks for *Britling* and the tank idea. *Daily Chronicle*: article on leader page, 17 Sept 1916, giving long quotes from HGW's short story; HGW, 'Tanks: Land Ironclads and Their Function in War and a Permanent Peace', 18 Dec 1916. The uncensored version of his dispatch from the front appeared in Albert Stern, 'Tanks', *Strand*, vol. LVIII (July-Dec 1919), pp. 223–32; HGW cut material is at pp. 228–9. A special article by HGW, *NYT*, 7 Jan 1917, reprinted in part in *Current History*, Feb 1917, pp. 892–6. The trial as to who the inventor was is covered in *Daily Herald*, 26, 27 Nov 1925, which reprints Churchill's testimony. HGW's full article from the front was reprinted in 1949 in an anthology of important war reporting; C. Gabbertas to MCW, 20 Aug 1948, 9 Nov 1949.

23 HGW attended a banquet at the Ritz in May 1908 for the founding the Aero Club of the United Kingdom. His table companions were Sir Hiram Maxim, Moore Brabazon (an early pilot), and J. W. Dunne; see plan of seating and menu, 29 May 1908. Zeppelin raids were of great interest to HGW. One scene which has been described several times is of a Zeppelin raid when HGW, GBS, AB, and Thomas Hardy went on to the roof of the Reform Club to watch the ships in the floodlights. See several accounts, especially J.M. Barrie to Charles Scribner, 26 Oct 1917. Severe raids occurred on 2 Nov 1916; see Marie Belloc-Lowndes to Elizabeth Haldane, 2 Nov 1916 (*Diaries and Letters*). Baden Baden-Powell to HGW, 11, 28 June 1915, on inventions; A.D. Daily to HGW, 26 Jan 1912, on aeroplane inventions. Northcliffe to HGW, 19 Sept 1918. HGW to Walter Stamford, Mar 1915 (on bombing of Reims). HGW, 'The Quick Way to Essen: How to End the War', *Daily Express*, 23 June 1915: '. . .*it would be cheaper to launch two thousand aeroplanes at Essen than to risk one battleship. Two thousand aeroplanes could smash Essen to bits, and if we lost a thousand of them in the raid it would still be cheaper in money and lives than the victory of Neuve Chapelle*' (his emphasis); see follow-up stories 24, 25, 26, 28, 29, 30 July 1915. *NYT*, 23 June 1915; 'Looking Ahead: The Most Splendid Fighting in the World', *Daily Chronicle*, 9 Sept 1914; HGW, 'The First Class Air Fighter: Is He Going to be the Decisive Factor?', and leader, *Daily Mail*, 3 Oct 1917.

24 Claude Graham-White and Harry Harper, 'The Civil Aerial Transport Committee: A Milestone in the History of Flight', *Fortnightly*, vol. CII (1920), pp. 111–12. H.P. Harvey, Secretary to the Air Board, to HGW, 4 May 1917. *Reports of the Civil Aerial Transport Committee with Appendices* (London: HMSO 1918), Cd. 9218; HGW's report appears at pp. 68–70. He was unhappy the committee had no Labour representatives, did not discuss the future of the Empire, and showed a tenderness for private interests which was untoward; *Daily News*, 9, 10 Dec 1918, on the report, and HGW minority view. Jix (William Joynson-Hicks) shared his view. HGW was regarded as something of an authority on these subjects. He had written brilliantly of flying, and combat flying, in *Joan and Peter*, pieces of which were reprinted in *Daily News*, 22 Aug, 10 Sept 1918. *Catalogue of Paintings and Prints of the Earliest and Latest Types of Aircraft*, collected and arranged by the Countess of Drogheda (London: Grosvenor Gallery 1917). HGW wrote a preface to the catalogue, pp. 7–8, in which he said, 'Invention is always a flank attack upon the impossible.' Some 400 items were exhibited, and discussed in this 100-page catalogue.

25 Northcliffe to HGW, 12 Apr 1917, on tactics generally. HGW, 'Scientific War: The Lifeless Master That Kills the Souls and Bodies of Men', *Windsor Magazine*, Jan 1915, pp. 237–42; HGW, 'Looking Ahead: The Logic of the U39', *Daily Chronicle*, 22 May 1915. HGW, *War and the Future* (London 1917); in North America the book was called by its subtitle, *Italy, France and Britain at War* (New York 1917). The chapters all appeared as articles in the press, with the exception of an opening statement. On the trip see HGW to ? De Lima, 8 Sept 1916; to the Director of the Press Bureau, with regard to US publication, early 1917: HGW wanted as his title *The War of Ideas*, but the publishers did not. See Newman Flower to HGW, 31 Dec 1916; to ACRW, 4, 16 Jan 1917. HGW to ACRW, ? Aug 1916, on early days of his trip, in which he was briefly

under fire; he signed it 'Poor Bored Daddy'. Lady Warwick to HGW, 17 Feb 1917, 'a masterpiece of the war'. HGW used his first-hand knowledge to write a preface to a fictionalized account of the war by the son of an old schoolmate, A.D. Gristwood, *The Somme: Including Also The Coward* (London 1927). HGW's preface, pp. 9–12, was reprinted in Cape's Christmas Annual, *Now and Then* (London 1927), as 'Mr Gristwood's Somme', pp. 21–2. Also see letter to HGW from 'X', *Daily Mail*, 4 Jan 1918, on life in the trenches just before the last German offensive.

26 See *Daily News* to HGW, 13 Aug 1914; JBP to HGW, 18, 26 Jan 1915 (the quotation); to ACRW, 18, 31 May 1915; to HGW, 9 Mar 1915.

27 K.A. Wolff to HGW, 14 Apr 1913, for articles, 'Mr Wells and War'. The amounts of his fees occur in a series of receipts for articles in the *Daily News* (£331. 5s. 0d.) and the *Chronicle* (£1327. 15s. 0d.). J.A. Hammerston to HGW, 9, 13 Aug, 17 Dec 1914, 4 Jan, 2 Feb 1915, 15 Mar 1916, for pieces in *The War Illustrated*; these were reprinted in 1935 when the entire journal was reprinted. See J.A. Hammerston to HGW, 29 June, 2, 4 July, 5 Sept 1934. Robert Donald to HGW, 29 June 1916; Alfred (? Harmsworth) to HGW, 3 May, 15 June 1916 (the quoted line). APW to HGW, 28 Nov, 18, 21 Dec 1916, 9, 16 Jan 1917: this correspondence would lead eventually to the Atlantic Edition, first proposed by Watt and George Doran. Ivor Griffiths to ACRW, 15 Sept 1916; to HGW, 18, 25 Sept, 2 Oct 1916, on the appearance in translation of HGW articles in *La Victoire* (Paris). Mario Borsa to HGW, 24 May 1918, on translating *In the Fourth Year* into Italian. They kept up a correspondence and Borsa was a source of information to HGW on Mussolini and Fascism; see Borsa to HGW, 18, 26 Feb 1925, after which they met in France; 11 Jan, 19 Mar 1940, on the state of affairs in Milan; HGW to Borsa, 16 Apr 1946, cannot write for Borsa, but allows him to quote; HGW sent him several books, calling him 'a great man' for his resistance to fascism. On other pieces which HGW refused to change, ? Marlowe to HGW, 9, 26 Jan 1918. HGW told him not to say anything (apologize) 'until I squeak'. Marlowe to HGW, 15, 18 Mar 1918. J. Galsworthy to HGW, 11 May 1918. HGW allowed 'The Land Ironclads' to appear in what was called *The Blinded Soldiers and Sailors Book* (London 1918). Some work by him may also have appeared in their journal, *Reveille*, although I have never seen copies of the magazine.

28 Olivia Rossetti, *David Lubin: A Study in Practical Idealism* (Boston 1922; repr. Berkeley 1941), which quotes several of HGW's letters to Lubin, well-known for his views on international agriculture. In Oct 1916, for instance, HGW told Lubin, 'We are at one in looking to a world in which mankind is unified under God as King.' He defined God as 'the Divine in Man'. I. Zangwill to HGW, 3 Mar (enclosing an American Jewish review of *Britling*, and indicating that they had been discussing religion), 4 May (further to their discussions), 10 May 1917, when he tells HGW that the Chief Rabbi, as well as Claude Montefiore, are discussing the book and HGW's ideas. HGW and Zangwill had met and discussed Palestine as a 'Jewtopia' (Zangwill's word) as early as 1905. See Zangwill to HGW, 15 Apr, ? Nov 1905.

29 HGW, *God the Invisible King* (London 1917). S. Olivier to HGW, 27 Sept 1917; Alice Burgess to HGW, 30 July 1917 (his cousin); W. Temple (Archbishop of Canterbury) to HGW, 9 May 1917 (he called the book *Man the Invisible King*, in an interesting slip); Harry Johnston to HGW, 11 Apr, 23 May, 6 Sept 1917; ERL to ACRW, 23, 30 May, 12 Sept 1917; Northcliffe to HGW, 14 May 1917. Review by Robert Lynd, *Daily News*, 10 May 1917. The books spawned by HGW's effort included: William Archer, *God and Mr Wells* (London 1917); Leonard E. Binns, *Mr Wells's Invisible King* (London 1917); Aylmer D.T. Hunter, *That* Danse à Trois *and Mr Wells* (London 1917); J.M. Lloyd Thomas, *The Veiled Being: A Comment on Mr H. G. Wells's 'God the Invisible King'* (Birmingham 1917). HGW had been an object of religious study before; see Alexander H. Crawfurd, *The Religion of H. G. Wells and Other Essays* (London 1909), which dealt with Christians who liked Wells's message, but did not like his view of a world without religion. For HGW's American publication on this subject, see his 'Religious Revival', *New Republic*, 23–30 Dec 1916; 'Difficulties Inherent in the Belief

in a Struggling God' (an excerpt from the book), *Current Opinion*, Mar 1917; 'God and This New Age', *Ladies' Home Journal*, Sept 1917.

30 The literature on this subject is immense, but the version which best shows the impact on western observers of Russian acts is George F. Kennan, *Russia Leaves the War* (Princeton 1956). Several volumes of HGW's work had been translated into Russian, and he wrote a brief straightforward biography to be used as an introduction to the edition, of which an English version – HGW, 'Wells Reveals Himself' – appeared in *T.P.'s Weekly*, 11 Dec 1912.

31 HGW to ACRW, 24 Jan 1914; to F. Macmillan, ? June 1914; C. F. G. Masterman to HGW, 1 Mar 1914, a joky letter welcoming him home from Russia. HGW, 'Russia and England: A Study in Contrasts', *Daily News and Leader*, 21 Feb 1914.

32 HGW, 'The Liberal Fear of Russia', *Nation* (London), 22 Aug 1914; letter from HGW and C.H. Wright, 'Our Ally Russia: Some Misconceptions and a Protest', *Daily Chronicle*, 22 Sept 1914. G. Murray to HGW, 13, 18, 26 Oct 1914: the letter was sent to 33 Englishmen (Shaw wrote his own version, GBS to G. Murray, 5 Nov 1914; the original letter appeared in *Manchester Guardian*, 23 Dec 1914). HGW, 'Looking Ahead: The Future of the North of Europe', *Daily Chronicle*, 18 Dec 1914.

33 *Daily Chronicle*: GBS to HGW, a long letter dated 17 Dec, published 23 Dec 1914; Hueffer on Shaw, 24 Dec 1914; HGW, 'Muddleheadedness and Russia – With Some Mention of Mr Shaw', 31 Dec 1914. Robert Donald (*Daily Chronicle* editor) to HGW, 7 Jan 1915. *New Statesman*: J.M. Hare, 'The Man of Letters and the Junker', 16 Feb 1915; J. C. Squire, 'Men of Letters and Junkers', 23 Jan 1915; HGW, 'Mr H. G. Wells' Proposal', 13 Feb 1915. GBS to GrW, (postcard) 6, 13 Jan 1915 (LSE). (GBS and HGW met, and HGW went to lunch at Shaw's house.) Denis Garstin, *Friendly Russia* (London 1915), HGW preface, 9–12; he said Russia was not 'a mysteriously wicked tyranny'. A good account of Shaw at this time is Bernard Weintraub, *Bernard Shaw 1914–1918* (New York 1971, London 1973); the book has a subtitle, 'Journey to Heartbreak'.

34 HGW to GBS, 2 Sept 1913, 12 Mar 1914 (on *Androcles*, and the beginning of the *rapprochement*), 17 Nov 1915, 7 Dec, 18 Dec 1916, 12 Jan 1917 (BL). (Some of these now appear in GBS *Collected Letters* III. 439–42, 418–19, e.g., GBS to HGW, 11 Jan 1917.) HGW provided information for other authors as well, notably Northcliffe, and A. Conan Doyle. Shaw's material appeared in the *Chronicle*, 5, 7, 8 Mar 1917, Conan Doyle's 13, 15, 20, 22, 29 June 1916, Northcliffe's in his book, *At the War* (London 1917). A good short book could be written about the experiences by literary men at the front; one should begin with John Buchan, however.

35 HGW, *Daily Chronicle*: letter to editor, 17 May 1916; 'Tidying Up the Language Question: With Particular Reference to Russian', 6 June 1916; letter to editor, 25 July 1916.

36 HGW: 'Message to the Provisional Government of Russia', *NYT*, 1 Apr 1917: 'Free Russia', *Daily Chronicle*, 5 Apr 1917 (others mentioned in the text appear in these same pages). HGW, letter, *Manchester Guardian*, 22 June 1917, reprinted as a pamphlet, *The Labour Programme*, which also printed a communiqué from the Provisional Government, *The Times*, 17 May 1917; HGW, letter on Russia, *Bourse Gazette*, ? July 1917, reprinted in *Manchester Guardian*, 9 July 1918; HGW, 'Battleground of Freedom', *Daily News and Leader*, 21 Feb 1917, a reprint of this 'Study in Contrasts' piece. Robert Donald to HGW, 6 Feb 1917: 'The greatest drama of the war will take place in Russia now or a little later on.' HGW addressed a series of letters to 'Dear Sir', which were circulated privately by S. S. Koteliansky to English people who might be supportive of the Russian Revolution. Most are undated; one is postmarked 18 May 1917 (to Gorky); another, 19 May 1917 (to unnamed Americans), lists 11 items very similar to Wilson's Fourteen Points, but with emphasis on the east: statement dated 6 July 1917 (the item printed in the *Bourse Gazette*).

37 HGW, 'Mr Wells and the Bolsheviks: Some Disregarded Aspects', *Daily Mail*, 15 Jan 1918. Responses appeared on 17, 18, 19, 21 Jan 1918.

38 The best description of what European linguistic, climatic, and physical boundaries were like on the eve of the Great War is contained in Isaiah Bowman, ed., *Nationalities in Europe* (New York 1919), a book created by the American Geographical Society at the request of Woodrow Wilson and Colonel House. It is one of the few publications that resulted from 'The Inquiry', so-called, Wilson's think group preparing him for Versailles. HGW, 'Looking Ahead: The Need of a New Map of Europe Now', *Daily Chronicle*, 15 Aug 1914. On the same day in 'Opportunity', *Nation* (London), 15 Aug 1914, HGW called for much the same things, and in this case also for a world conference to undertake the work.

39 HGW, *Daily Chronicle*: 'An Appeal to the American People', 24 Aug 1914; 'Looking Ahead: Common Sense and the Balkan States', 28 Aug 1914; 'To: Mr Zangwill (Per Favour of the *Daily Chronicle*)', 4 Nov 1914 (Zangwill's reply is in 9 Nov 1914); 'Looking Ahead: World Languages', 13 May 1916. (*NYT* reprints much of the HGW–Zangwill correspondence, 28 Nov 1914.) HGW, 'Why the War Will Be Over by June: How to Offer Peace Before November', *Sunday Pictorial*, 17 Sept 1916. HGW, 'The Two Ways', *Nation* (London), 12 Sept 1914 (also in *New York World*). HGW, 'A Reply to Arnold Bennett', *Daily News*, 5 Aug 1915; Bennett's columns appear on 4, 11 Aug 1915. HGW, *NYT*: 'The Peace of The World', 21, 28 Feb 1915; 'The Kind of Peace That England Wants', 1 May 1915; 'Civilization at the Breaking Point', 27 May 1915; 23 June 1915 reprints most of his *Daily Express* piece of same date on bombing German factories; 23 Jan 1916, quotes his review (in *Saturday Evening Post*) on I. S. Bloch, *The Future of War* (London 1890); 4 Apr 1917, a message (with a dozen others) on US entrance, 'Fight. . . to make an end forever to all aggressive imperialisms'; 4 June 1917, quotes his *Chronicle* letter of same date on need for declaration of war aims. His most important piece in the *NYT*, 'Holland's Future', 7 Feb 1915, was censored in the UK. It also appeared as 'Avenir de la Hollande', in *La Revue* (Paris), May 1915, and in *Outlook*, 24 Feb 1915, pp. 411–12. Other important articles in the US were HGW, *Current History*: 'The Cause and Effect of the War', Nov 1916, pp. 203–6, with long quotes from *Britling*; 'Great Land Ironclads and Victory', Feb 1917, pp. 892–7; 'Death Knell of Empire', a four-part piece by Lord Grey, Lloyd George, AB, and HGW, Aug 1918, pp. 345–57 (HGW's piece is at pp. 353–4); 'Boycotting Germany: The Seriousness of the World Movement Against German Trade', Sept 1918, pp. 545–6. HGW to Holbrook Jackson, late 1916 (tipped into a copy of *War and the Future* in Bromley). His thought may also be followed in HGW, *What is Coming? A European Forecast* (London 1916), which reprints some of these articles, as well as others. HGW became very interested and was a supporter of the made-up language, Basic English.

40 HGW, 'The Incoherence of Liberalism', *Daily News*, ? June 1915. HGW, *Daily Chronicle*: 'The Allied Zollverein: Some Objections Considered', 13 Feb 1915; a letter correcting a proofreading error, 15 Feb 1915; 'The Liberal Aim in the War: Why Should We Not Discuss the Terms of Peace', 4 May 1915; letter to editor, 7 May 1915, replying to Holland Rose who had responded to HGW on 5 May; another HGW letter, 11 May 1915, saying he meant what he said, and does not wish interpretation of his words; 'Looking Ahead: The End of the War', 17, 18 Jan 1916. The later articles mentioned were commissioned in Robert Donald to HGW, 9 Aug 1916; they appeared in the *Chronicle* on 18, 25 Sept, 2 Oct 1916, under the general title, 'Some Liberal Ideas', with the subtitles 'Free Trade in Peace: Tariffs Are War', 'Nationalism and Nationality', 'The Ideal of Allied Combines'. Also see HGW's letter of 23 Sept 1916 saying, read the whole series.

41 Northcliffe to HGW, 26 Jan, 21, 23 May 1917; HGW was not formally appointed to the committee, which Northcliffe chaired, until 28 Feb 1917 (the date of the letter appointing him). He served until 30 July 1918, when he was replaced by Hamilton Fyfe; see Fyfe to HGW, 30 July 1918. C. F. G. Masterman to ACRW, 12 Oct 1915, on postal

censorship; to HGW, 29 Oct, 16 Nov 1915, on translation of *Britling* into German, and HGW's Italian articles: how shall they be got into Germany? HGW supervised some other translations (a book by G. Payot, e.g.); see Masterman to HGW, 6 Mar 1917; inability to send in materials by aeroplane drop, 4 May, 6 June, 12 July 1917. Payot also translated *Britling* and these later letters are to do with the publication of the translated work. Also Masterman to HGW, 20 Jan 1918, on a pamphlet by Lord Grey, and how will it get into the right hands? The two men had luncheon fairly frequently during the war to discuss the issues of war aims and propaganda. HGW's pamphlet, *A Reasonable Man's Peace* (1917), originated in these discussions and was a partial response to Lord Lansdowne's widely circulated article calling for a negotiated peace. See ? Marlowe to HGW, 25 Dec 1917; Marquis of Lansdowne to *Daily Telegraph*, 29 Nov 1917; Marie Belloc-Lowndes's diary, 30 Nov 1917, discusses its impact, and the fact that *The Times* refused to print the letter. Robert Lynd to HGW, 14 Aug 1917, for the first glimmering of the pamphlet, the text of which appeared in the *Daily News* that day. It too is a good statement of the war aims issue. The entire issue of propaganda is covered in Sir Campbell Stuart, *Secrets of Crewe House* (London 1920). HGW headed the German section at Crewe House for most of 1917–18. His memorandum on German and Allied war aims appears in Campbell Stuart's book, pp. 61–87.

42 HGW to *Glasgow Daily Record*, 3 Nov 1916: a draft on official Crewe House stationery headed, 'British War Medal Awarded to the Kaiser for Courage and Devotion to Duty'; whether it was actually used or not is not known.

43 HGW to Bainbridge Colby, Nov 1917, reprinted in *ExA* (1–vol. edn., 1936), 604–11. The minutes of the German propaganda committee show meetings on 14, 27, 31 May, 11, 25 June, 9 July, 14, 16 Aug 1918, but 1917 minutes are not available. HGW also received a number of letters and memoranda dealing with these subjects; see, e.g., H. K. Hudson to HGW, 22 May 1918; Hudson to HGW (with copy to Balfour and the memorandum), 4 July 1918; Balfour to Northcliffe, 11 June 1918, where the piece went to the Cabinet for discussion; Northcliffe to Balfour, 13 June 1918. Other letters which deal with some of these points are HGW to GrW, 11 June 1918, and the problem of getting the committee to appoint Jews and others who were not of the established orders in England; Northcliffe to HGW, 29 June 1918 (attacking the Prime Minister for not giving these ideas enough time, 'flying about Europe like a dragon fly, with one eye on the war, and one on Asquith'); Northcliffe to HGW, 25 July 1918, sorry you felt you had to resign; J. Headlam Morley to HGW, 23 July 1918, thanks for your effort. HGW to Philip Guedalla, sometime in 1918, 'Life is more crowded than ever since I have taken to advising Northcliffe on foreign policy.' Other Northcliffe letters which bear slightly on these discussions are Northcliffe to HGW, 15 Jan, 16 July, 24 Sept 1918. HGW to P. Guedalla, 27 Mar 1934. Countess of Warwick, *Afterthoughts* (London 1931), 122–3; Lansbury and Ben Tillett also attended the luncheon with Colonel House. Wilson's Fourteen Points address was delivered to Congress 8 Jan 1918, although he anticipated most of its ideas in a speech of 22 Jan 1917. The final statement on the Points came in a State Department document near the end of Oct 1918. Lippman, Frank I. Cobb (*New York World*), and perhaps Colonel House worked on it; all three were in London at the time. For others Lippman also introduced to HGW, see Lippman to HGW, 8 Aug (William Allen White), 20 Aug (S. H. Wolfe, an insurance actuary), 25 Oct 1917 (H. S. Canby). Canby, the well-nown American critic, was seconded to work with John Buchan.

44 HGW letter to unknown addressee, 19 May 1917, in which he listed his (or England's) war aims. They included:

1   liberation and *compensation* of Belgium by Germany
2   liberation of invaded areas of France, including those from 1871
3   reunion of Trentino and Trieste with Italy
4   liberation of Poles, including Posen and Galicia

     5   liberation of Servia and Servian peoples
     6   [none in the letter]
     7   evacuation and restoration of Romania
     8   liberation of Armenia, Arabia and Palestine from Turkish misrule
     9   abandonment of imperialist aggression by Germany
    10   a free access to Mediterranean for Russia
    11   home rule or autonomy of Czechoslovak peoples
   [12]   a permanent league of nations
   [13]   some control of international shipping

(The last two of these points were not given numbers, but I have done so in order that those who wish may compare this document with other listings of peace aims.) HGW to Chairman, National Conference on War Aims, 26 Dec 1917. See Walter Lippman to HGW, 24 Dec 1916; 27 Jan 1917, congratulates HGW on a *Saturday Evening Post* article on war aims ideas. 'You are regarded as authentic.' Lippman says that he is putting the ideas of 'our little group on the *New Republic*' before Wilson, as they are 'the only articulate force looking for a comprehensive peace'. Lippman felt that the Germans had to be defeated badly, however, before such a peace could come about, as they are 'too damned patriotic' for the health of the world. He said the Irish problem needed a solution, along with internal Russian reforms; as well as the territorial settlements over which HGW was so concerned. This letter, four long pages in Lippman's tiny handwriting, is significant, along with a few others to be cited below. See *New York Times*, 4 Apr 1917, for HGW's comment on American entrance into the war. HGW's work at Crewe House and his resignation are discussed in HGW to Edgar Jepson, summer 1918, in which he says he left over the anti-alien campaign in the Northcliffe press. The transition to the League committee can be seen in four letters, undated, to 'Dr Clark', all from the summer of 1918 (Boston).

45   HGW, *Daily News*: 'Ideas for a World Peace: I. How to End the War', 19 Jan 1917; 'II. The Last of the Conquests and After', 22 Jan 1917. HGW, 'Wanted: A Statement of Imperial Policy: Mr Wells and the Plain Lessons of the War', *Daily Chronicle*, 4 June 1917. HGW, 'Are We Sticking to the Point: My Views of Our War Aims', *DMail*, 26 Dec 1917; also see the discussion of 28 Dec 1917, with four letters from others, and the *Mail*'s leader on the same subject. Letter from HGW, *NYT*, 4 June 1917, urging British Government to define its aims. C. F. G. Masterman to HGW, 20 Apr 1918, a proposed series of pamphlets on the League of Nations and small nationalities, democratic idea, legal organizations, freedom of the seas, Christianity, biology, the future, conditions of labour, primitive peoples, and a no more war campaign. Masterman proposed either a book with these topics as the table of contents, or a series of pamphlets. This is the origin of the two League committee pamphlets of 1918 and 1919.

46   HGW, *DMail*: 'The African Riddle: My View of the Labour View', 30 Jan 1918; 'The League of Free Nations: Some Independent Opinions, I. Its Possible Constitution', 20 Feb 1918; 'II. Who is to Represent Us?', 28 Feb 1918; Part III, Continued, 1 Mar 1918. Also see his letter of 26 Feb 1918 to editor. Robert Donald to HGW, 28 Feb 1918, offers £100 for League of Nations series for *Lloyds News*; same to same, 19 Mar 1918, with HGW agreement to write the articles in margin of the letter; same to same, 2 Apr 1918, thanks for first two; 17 Apr 1918, series to appear in America as we delay for the great battle in west. *Lloyds News* in the spring of 1918 carried 10 articles by Arnold Bennett, but none by HGW. HGW, *New Republic* (New York): 'Question at Issue', 9 Feb 1918; 'African Riddle', 23 Feb 1918; 'League of Free Nations', 6, 13 Apr 1918; 'The Core of the Trouble', 23 Nov 1918. HGW, *In the Fourth Year* (London 1918); much of this book is reprinted in Atlantic XXI.

47   Reviews of *In the Fourth Year* appeared in the *Daily News*, 8 June 1918; *Daily Herald*, 15 June 1918; both urged wide readership for these chapters. W. Lippman to HGW, 6

Aug 1918. Robert Judd (*Morning Post*) to HGW, 11, 17, 24, 26 Sept 1918, setting articles up: HGW, 'The League of Free Nations', *Morning Post*, 30 Sept, 3, 9 Oct 1918.

48   The quotation conflates material from the ends of both the second and third articles. HGW may originally have prepared only one piece, but the response was so strong that he returned to refute the attacks, and the second and third articles are repetitive. For other items dealing with sovereignty and empires, see *Il Secolo* (Rome), 29 June 1918, for an HGW letter on Italian contributions to the League, and their leader of 7 July 1918 which translated some of the material from the *New Republic* and his book. HGW, 'British Nationalism and the League of Nations', *Daily Chronicle*, 5 Nov 1918, was reprinted as a pamphlet under the same title. In it he said, 'Failure [to get world peace and a commonweal of mankind] means a world unsettled and insecure as well as a world impoverished. It means a world therefore unable to recover from its strain and its impoverishment. It means a world staggering along through many generations to come, between phases of social disorder and phases of partial discipline, to great destruction.' British nationalism, as espoused by those attacking the League, 'has as much resemblance to that dear love of country that burns in the hearts of men as the mercenary leer of a painted harlot on the pavement has to the love of a mother for her child.'

49   HGW, *Daily News*: 7 Sept 1918, quoting his own piece in *Oeuvre* on the League in France; 'The League of Nations and the Foreign Office', 7 Nov 1918; 'No More Secret Treaties, Today's Great Opportunities', 8 Nov 1918.

50   A. Bennett, *Daily News*: 'Independence and Sovereignty', 2 July 1918; 'The Embargo *v.* the Gun', 16 July 1918; 'The Vindication of the Lord Grey', 7 Aug 1918; 'First Thoughts on Victory', 13 Nov 1918. These pieces support HGW's ideas precisely.

51   Jessie Brodie (L of N Society press secretary) to HGW, 19 Mar 1918; Aneurin Williams to HGW, 3 May 1918; David Davies to HGW, 3 Apr 1918; W. N. Dickinson to HGW, 9 May 1918. The committee – J. A. Spender, Wickham Steed, Aneurin Williams, W.N. Dickinson, and H. G. Wells – met first on 10 May, to plan a programme of action. Dickinson was in the chair at the meeting. Winifred Stephens (an expert on France) to HGW, 10 June 1918, what is happening in France where people are lukewarm; A. Williams to HGW, 15 June 1918, apologizes for outbreak at yesterday's meeting; W.N. Dickinson to HGW, 6 June 1918.

52   Minutes, L of N Society, 24, 26 June 1918. Memorandum to HGW, 18 July 1918, discussing who had responsibility for which nations; G. Lowes Dickinson to HGW, 10 June 1918; W. Archer to HGW, 27 July 1918, along with minutes of previous meeting when HGW was ill.

53   F. W. Dickinson to HGW, 27 July 1918; G. Murray to HGW, 15 Sept 1918; David Davies to HGW, 16 Sept 1918; W. Archer to G. Murray, ? Sept 1918 (copy to HGW); Archer to HGW, Sept (Monday morning) 1918; W. L. Williams to HGW, 20 Sept, 14 Oct 1918; Archer to HGW, 18 Sept, ? Sept (Wednesday) 1918; A.L. Zimmern to Archer, 26 Sept 1918; L. Curtis to HGW, 26 Sept 1918 (enclosed to HGW with comments); G. Lowes Dickinson to HGW, 25 Oct, 13 Nov 1918; David Davies to HGW, 20 Sept 1918 (thanks for funds); Archer to HGW, 13 Dec 1918, enclosing proofs of *The Idea of the League of Nations*.

54   The party is discussed in R. Meynell, ed., *The Letters of J.M. Barrie* (London 1951), 93; it occurred 17 Jan 1919. G. Murray to HGW, 14 Jan 1919, HGW to P. Guedalla, spring 1919; W. H. Dickinson to HGW, 15 Jan 1919, don't give up the ship yet. E. F. S. Lane to HGW, 23 Dec 1918, enclosing a draft of a pamphlet by J. C. Smuts supporting the League. J. C. Smuts to HGW, 28 Dec 1918, thanking him for his comments on the draft. 'The next stage is to move the big wigs forward, and that can only be done by the formation of a powerful and impudent [?] public opinion.' G. Murray to HGW, 19 Feb 1940, recalls the work of 1918, and says that HGW had been right as to their wrong direction (Murray had remained active in the L of N Society). He asks HGW to come back aboard for a new effort on war aims. HGW, of course, was already at work and he

joined Murray again. The standard accounts of Britain and the early days of the League, based on conventional sources, do not treat this period much, if at all. An article by Henry Winkler, 'The Development of the League of Nations Idea in Great Britain, 1914–1919', *Journal of Modern History*, vol. XX, no. 2 (June 1948), pp. 95–112, is better than a later book, George W. Egerton, *Great Britain and the Creation of the League of Nations: Strategy, Politics and International Organization, 1914–1919* (London 1979). Winkler's article has a good bibliography in its notes.

55   Drafts of these pamphlets in HGW's hand are among his papers, along with a number of drafts of possible constitutions, bases, etc. The pamphlets were published by Oxford University Press as from the research committee of the League of Nations Union, both in 1919. Other works of interest from this period (among thousands) are Robert Cecil, ed., *Fair Play for the League of Nations* (London 1921), from *Daily News* articles, 18–23 July 1921, and George Paish, *A Permanent League of Nations* (London 1918). HGW later attempted to obtain copyright in the pamphlets, as he had hopes of reprinting them, but eventually desisted. J. C. Maxwell Garrett to HGW, 3 Mar 1921, refers to a HGW postcard from Italy. Anon., 'Why Labour Left the Coalition', *Daily Herald* (London 1918), and in another form in the paper, 23 Nov 1918. The Government as constructed simply is not interested in the League, only the Empire, was this writer's view.

56   W. Lippman to HGW, 29 Jan, 14 May 1919. HGW to Lippman, end May 1919 (Yale).

PART THREE

Chapter 10

1   E. Ray Lankester, ed., *Natural Science and the Classical System in Education: Essays Old and New* (London 1918). HGW's two talks appear as chs. 6 and 7. Sanderson's talk is ch. 8, and Lankester's ch. 9. *Proceedings of The British Science Guild*, vol. XI (1917), HGW, speech, 75–80.

2   E. Ray Lankester, ed., *Science and Education* (London 1917), reprints seven lectures given at the Royal Institution in 1854, and first printed in 1855, all to the point of making natural science part of the education of all classes. [E. Ray Lankester, ed.], *The Neglect of Science* (London 1916), gives a summary of HGW's comments at pp. 23–4. 'Our Educational Future', *Fortnightly*, 2 Apr 1917: the first part is Lord Bryce's address to the Chemical Association in 1917, the second, pp. 567–74, a reworked version of HGW, 'The Case Against the Classical Languages', given before the British Science Guild, but in this instance reviewing R.W. Livingston, *A Defense of Classical Education*, as well. Lord Bryce and HGW also conducted a correspondence on the place of Greek, Latin, and science in the curriculum. See Bryce to HGW, 4, 15, 26 Apr, 7 May 1917. Bryce eventually agreed in good part with HGW but throught Greek still had a place. *Nature*: 12 Apr 1917, a review of HGW's review of Livingston; HGW, 'Education and Research', 19 Apr 1917, a review of *Science and the Nation*, a group of essays by Cambridge graduates, poorly edited: 'Against this strangle-hold of the Mandarins, the book is feeble ... '; 'The British Science Guild', 3 May 1917, reprinting Fisher's and HGW's speeches; letter from HGW, 10 May 1917, commenting on Livingstone's response to his review. HGW said the real issue was 'Who will get the better boys?' in a competitive curriculum. He had had to interfere with the education of his boys, he said, as the classics masters had 'muddled about' with them. *DNews*: HGW, 'The New Englishmen', 'Mr Wells replies to His Critics', 1, 8 Feb 1916, on the classics; Rebecca West, 'The Beginning of Wisdom', 27 Sept 1918, a review of *Natural Science and the Classical System in Education*. Background material for those who wish to go deeper into this subject is in Adam W. Kirkaldy, ed., *Industry*

and Finance: War Expedients and Reconstruction, the British Association reports on activities in the war, vols. for 1914, 1915, 1916–17, and a supplementary volume for 1920. Also see R. A. Gregory, *Discovery: or The Spirit and Service of Science* (London 1916), and reprinted many times. Armytage gives much of the background to the battle as well.

3 *TLS*, 19 Sept 1918, for V. Woolf review. T. Hardy to HGW, 23 Sept 1918, 29 May 1919; S. Webb to B. Webb, 2 Feb 1921 (Webb *Letters* III. 140).

4 ERL to HGW, 23 Sept 1918; Northcliffe to HGW, 29 Sept 1918, decrying the reviews that had appeared. He claimed that the average reviewer only mentioned the passages marked by his typist, and did not read or discuss the book. He urged HGW to suggest 'a Wellsian' to review the book in the *DMail*. Whether HGW did so or not is unknown. Atlantic XXIII and XXIV for *Joan and Peter*, with *Story of a Great Schoolmaster*. Caxton School in *Joan and Peter* is a thinly disguised Oundle, of course. For comments on *The Undying Fire* see FAS to HGW, 24 May 1919; Swinnerton also reviewed the book in the *DHerald*, where he spoke of its 'constructive quality'. In his letter he mentions the submarine episodes as being extremely vivid. Gilbert Murray to HGW, 9 June 1919: he read it twice and read parts of it aloud to his family. *Joan and Peter* was serialized in the US in the *New Republic*, 6 July–28 Sept 1918, as stating their view of what education should become.

5 On the surprising statement on the League, see HGW to Marie Beets, 16 Feb 1919, in a postscript: 'Don't you think that — all things considered — we are getting much more League of Nations than we had any right to hope for?' Later he wrote to her, 12 Apr 1919, about the *Outline*: 'I'm writing a vast *Outline of History* which aims at no less than the reconstruction of history teaching on a basis of the *history of mankind* rather than of national tendencies.' Often his letters to his French representative have such bits of philosophical remarks attached to their business portions. HGW had actually had the idea of the *Outline* in his head for some time, and had signed a contract in 1907 to contribute to a History of the World, which fell through. See P. Cazenove to HGW, 27 Mar 1907. HGW to Cazenove, undated, 'Could you get a thumping price from a paper?' He signed a contract with Amalgamated Press, 18 July 1907. Newman Flower recalled the idea of the *Outline* in conversations at Easton in 1918: Flower, *Just as It Happened* (1950), 175–7. HGW, *ExA*, esp. vol. III, *H.G. Wells in Love*, in which he describes his and Jane's decision to take the year to write the *Outline*. She played an important role in this book, more so perhaps than in any other, as can be seen in his remarks at the end of his introduction.

6 HGW and RAG, *Honours Physiography* (1891), preface.

7 Arthur Lynch, 'H. G. Wells as Historian: An Interview with the Famous Author', *Strand*, vol. LVIII (July–Dec 1919), pp. 464–8. HGW to Marie Beets, 19 Sept 1919; HGW to 'Dear Rev. Mitchell', undated (Eric Korn), *c.* spring 1920.

8 *DHerald*, 11 Apr 1923; H. A. L. Fisher chaired this meeting, at which HGW's address was entitled 'On the Teaching of History'. Most of HGW's address, 'The Teacher as Statesman', was reprinted in *WGaz*, 3 Jan 1924. In the chair on that occasion was A.H. Joslin, who had been one of HGW's students, probably at Henley House School. This second address was also reprinted as an article: HGW, 'The Teacher as Statesman', *Torchbearer*, July 1924, pp. 4, 6, 8. (The *Torchbearer* is a magazine for schoolmasters, and in the midst of HGW's speech appears a full-page advertisement for his biography of F.W. Sanderson.)

9 Copies of the various editions are in front of me as I write. The ones least likely to be found today are HGW and E.H. Carter, *A Short History of Mankind* (London and New York 1925); the German edition, *Die Welt Geschichte*, trans. by Otto Mendl (Hamburg 1928); and I. O. Evans, *Suggestions for Practice Work on World History. . . . based, by kind permission of Mr H. G. Wells, on The Outline of History* (London 1929). HGW's correspondence with Evans is interesting as to how he worked. See HGW to I.O. Evans, 9 Feb, 19 July, 25 Aug, 21 Oct, 25 Nov 1932 (recounting German protests, as

Evans's volume hurt their sales), 3, 10, 13 Mar 1933; W. A. Fuller to MCW, and telephone memorandum, MCW to HGW, 3 May 1933, on royalties to Evans, some of which had been withheld by overseas publishers as a protest. HGW gave the work his blessing, however, so they were released.

10 APW to HGW, 30 Oct, 19, 21, 27 Nov (HGW sent a response to this on the same date), 1, 3 Dec 1919. HGW to Watt, 30 Nov 1919. HGW began negotiations with publishers on the book, but eventually turned them over to Watt, who acted as HGW's main agent after this time. APW to HGW, 26 Nov 1930; HGW to Nelson Doubleday, 17 May 1931.

11 Harold F.B. Wheeler to HGW, 17 Mar 1915; ACRW to Wheeler, mid-spring 1925 (two letters): they eventually went to dinner and a play instead; HGW to Wheeler, 12, 20 Dec 1925: 'I'm a goad at times, I know, an impatient and rather heavy goad, but there's no bad feeling and you two have shed [?] it timely and played up well. . . . If I had my way there should be a little bit of royalty in every production for every man who took a responsible part in it.' HGW to Wheeler, 10, 16 June 1930; Wheeler to HGW, 3, 9 June 1930; HGW to Wheeler, postcard 26 Jan 1928 (all at Boston).

12 The material surrounding the collaboration is very rich, and one is tempted to discuss it in detail, as it shows us much about how Wells wrote and talked. However, that must wait for someone who is prepared to use this material and the various drafts of the book in the Wells archive, and to compare the final textual changes. ERL to HGW, late Oct, 9 Nov (two letters) 1919; to ACRW, 23 May 1920; to HGW, 8, 19, 22 Dec 1919, 12, 22 Jan, 13 Feb 1920.

13 G. Murray to HGW, 28 Mar, 29 Apr (with a note on how HGW rewrote the section on Aristophanes), 6 June, 15, 24 July (with detailed analysis of his friend's comments, and enclosing one letter), 9 Dec (on funds), end of 1919. The impact of the work can be seen in Murray's own work and can be followed in J. A. K. T[homson] and A. J. T[oynbee], eds., *Essays in Honour of Gilbert Murray* (London 1936), esp. in essays by Lord David Cecil, J. L. Hammond, and S. A. de Madariaga. A recent biography, Francis West, *Gilbert Murray* (London 1984), does not discuss this matter at all. A good example of the closeness of HGW's and Murray's views appears in Murray, *Faith, War and Policy* (Boston 1917). HGW to 'Dear Sir', undated, but *c.* 1920: '. . . I'm a mere compiler and Gilbert Murray who is my protector in things Greek is a novelist first' (Boston).

14 J. F. Horrabin to ACRW, 20 Feb 1919; H. S. Canby to HGW, 16 July 1918; RAG to HGW, end of 1919 (on meteors); Sir Harry Johnston, *The Story of My Life* (Indianapolis 1923), discusses his meeting with Wells (at a terribly warm session of the Committee on the Neglect of Science in 1915), and their collaboration (of sorts) on *The Gay-Dombeys*. Johnston to ACRW, Sept 1919; to HGW, 8 Dec 1919; to ACRW, ?, 28, 29 Jan, 6 Feb (on a new novel by Johnston), 29 May, 14 June 1920. Johnston contributed some illustrations as well. Ernest Barker to HGW, 17 Aug (4–pp. letter with further comments from his Oriental and Asian colleagues: HGW is 'a keen sympathetic imagination driving through history, the sweep of the panorama makes me almost breathless. . . . it is what I imagine an aeroplane is like in the material world'), 25 Aug, end Nov 1919; to ACRW, later Nov 1919 (he was to be in US but still would correct proofs); to HGW, end of 1919, 12 Jan 1923, on Amritsar. Ernest Barker, *Age and Youth. Memories of Three Universities and Father of the Man* (London 1953), 106–8. Anthony Powell, *To Keep the Ball Rolling*, vol. III: *Faces in My Time* (London 1980), 113–14. HGW to Barker, Oct 1942. ACRW to P. Guedalla, mid-Aug 1919. W.J.L. Abbott to HGW, 27 Sept, 3 Dec 1919 (on geology). A. M. Davies to HGW, 12 May 1925, further ideas from his work. This renewed the old friendship and a number of personal and friendly letters ensued until Davies's death in 1943. Revd. G. W. Bromfield to HGW, 16 Apr 1920. J. M. Keynes to HGW, 10 Jan 1920, with bibliographical suggestions. Sydney Olivier to HGW, 26 Feb 1920, urging HGW to do more with the Upanishads, and on the origins of religious rites throughout the world; and in later editions with material on blacks,

South Africa, and imperialism, 24 Sept 1926, 8 Apr 1929, 21 May 1931. Olivier wrote a famous book, *White Capital and Coloured Labour* (London 1906, rev. 1929). W. Sonnenberg to HGW, quoted and printed in *NYT*, 23 Apr 1921, on using the *Outline* in conjunction with the Bible.

15   HGW, *The Outline of History*; quotations are from the 'Definitive' edn. (London 1923), chapter locations as indicated.

16   J.H. Breasted to HGW, 11 Sept 1919; to ACRW, 24 Sept 1919; to HGW, 4 Oct 1921. Floyd Dell to HGW, late 1919, and two letters later, in 1920, all undated. W. Lippman to HGW, 10 Sept 1920. Others in this vein were Northcliffe to HGW, 11 Nov 1919; J. Galsworthy to HGW, 28 Aug 1920.

17   R. Blatchford to HGW, 15 Sept 1920; ERL to HGW, 26 Apr, 19 Aug 1920; F.W. Sanderson to HGW, 8 Sept 1920. B. Webb, diary, 29 Nov 1920; B. Webb to HGW, 8 Sept 1920 (Webb *Letters* III. 140–1). 'New World or Downfall: Mr H.G. Wells on the Next Step in History', *DNews*, 2 Sept 1920, was simply a reprinting of much of the last section of the *Outline*.

18   A.W. Gomme; *Mr Wells as Historian* (Glasgow 1921); 'Mr Wells as Controversialist', *Fortnightly*, July 1921, pp. 124–30. Richard Downey, *Some Errors of H. G. Wells, A Catholic's Criticism of the 'Outline of History'* (London 1921); Downey's criticism first appeared, in slightly different form, in the *Month*, Aug, Sept, Oct 1920. Fifteen years later, after the book had been widely used in schools, another attack occurred : W.A. Hirst, 'History as Taught in Our Schools', *Contemporary Review*, Apr 1938, pp. 452–7; but this is an American view, and isolated at that. For a contemporary English review of the *Short History*, see 'G', 'The Great Adventure of Living: H. G. Wells's New Record of the Past', *DHerald*, 11 Sept 1924. According to the paper the work sold 11,000 copies in the first week, at 2*s*. 6*d*., 1*s*. 6*d*. in paper. For HGW's answer to most of his critics, see his 'History for Everyone: A Postscript to *The Outline of History*', *Fortnightly*, June 1921, pp. 887–910. This is an important re-statement of HGW's view on history in general and its purpose in the curriculum.

19   *NYT*: 28 Nov 1920, 11 Sept 1921, 21 May 1922 (these are all editorials essentially in support of the Wellsian ideas). Letters opposing the work appeared on 13 Mar 1921; 13 Feb 1922 (an especially vicious one from the Revd. Dr Straton); 9 May 1922, which reported a pamphlet by college professors who disliked the book. But the *Times* reviewers liked the book (14 Nov 1920, 27 Nov 1921), and on 14 Feb 1922, Arthur Schlesinger Sr. refuted Straton; on 11 May 1922, another letter-writer (anonymous) praised the book, and when the Kansas State Normal School adopted the work, and the governor attempted to interfere, the *Times* was quick to report his retreat, 14 Oct 1922. HGW replied to his critics generally in *Current Opinion*, Aug 1921, pp. 207–9.

20   There is a huge bibliography on this controversy, most of it highly repetitive, and remarkably recondite. The major items are HGW, *Mr Belloc Objects* (London 1925), and Hilaire Belloc, *Mr Belloc Still Objects* (London 1926): nearly all of both these books also appeared in periodicals, in different form. H. Belloc, 'A Few Words with Mr Wells', *Dublin Review*, Apr, May, June 1920, pp. 182–202; HGW to *London Mercury*, Jan 1921, as 'Mr Wells and Mr Belloc'; HGW to *Tablet*, 22 Jan 1921; *WGaz*: HGW, 'The Fantasies of Mr Belloc and the Future of the World', 16 Feb 1924; G.K. Chesterton, 'Mr Wells and Mr Belloc', 21 Feb 1924; HGW, 'Mr Chesterton, Mr Wells, and Catholicism', 14 June 1924. 'Wells on Belloc', *DMail*, 15 Sept 1926. HGW to *Catholic World*, 11 Nov 1926. HGW to GKC, 2 Oct 1926, telling Chesterton that he is out of line with Belloc, even though the former had just converted to Catholicism. HGW to *G.K.'s Weekly*, 2 Apr 1927; HGW to *Truth*, 28 Apr, 19 May 1927 (five others as well). G. R. S. Taylor to HGW, 26 Sept 1926. APW to HGW, 28 June, 2 July 1926. HGW, *Crux Ansata* (London and New York 1943). A radio play on the subject, 'The Gallows in My Garden', featuring Belloc, HGW, and G. K. Chesterton, was given on BBC Radio 3 in July 1981. Chesterton, in the play and at other times, never defended Belloc's history, just his right to comment. For Belloc see J. B. Morton, ed., *Selected*

Essays of Hilaire Belloc (London 1948); Hilaire Belloc, *One Thing and Another* (London 1955); *The Essays of a Catholic* (New York 1931), esp. 'The Counter-Attack Through History', and 'Science as an Enemy of the Truth'. Recent biographies of Belloc by A. N. Wilson (London 1984), and by J. P. MacDonald, *Hilaire Belloc: Victorian Radical* (Indianapolis 1978), are disappointing on these matters.

21   *Nature*: 11 July 1925, 18 Dec 1926; Arthur Keith, 'Is Darwinism Dead?', 15 Jan 1927, pp. 75–7. RAG to HGW, 10 Dec 1926. Another defence occurred in Beverley Nichols, *Are They the Same at Home?* (1927), in his chapter on Belloc subtitled, 'Ignorance is Bliss'. Nichols intimates that this reproof had been administered in the Reform Club itself. For a brilliant summary of the *Outline* in terms of historical thought, see 'The Whole Story', *TLS*, 30 June 1972, pp. 750–1.

22   HGW, letter to I. Zangwill, *Strand*, Autumn 1922, on the omission of Shakespeare. R. Blatchford and V. Bonham Carter joined HGW in the controversy. It re-emerged in an *Anthology of Invective and Abuse* (London 1930), ed., Hugh Kingsmill, and yet again in 1939 in the *Star*: HGW, 'Mr Zangwill, Shakespeare, and *The Outline of History*', 7 Mar 1939, in which he points out the changes in the 1932 edn. esp. in these matters (drafts for the article at Boston), and HGW, 'H. G. Wells and Shakespeare', 31 Mar 1939. For HGW's views on Shakespeare, see *Shakespeare Day* (London 1917), which reprints a number of letters and speeches given in connection with the 300th anniversary of the Bard's death. HGW (pp. 26–30) refers to his 'varied sympathetic spirit', and spends most of the piece describing amateur efforts at his home in Shakespeare plays, esp. *A Midsummer Night's Dream*. The Odle drawing was offered for sale at Sotheby's on 20/21 Nov 1975; the catalogue of the sale carries a reproduction.

23   HGW, *The New Teaching of History. With a Reply to Some Recent Criticisms of 'The Outline of History'* (London 1921); the quotation is from pp. 32–3, 35. HGW, *History is One* (Boston 1919), originally in *Saturday Evening Post*, and in *John o'London's*, 12, 19 Apr 1919. C. David Stalling, ed., *Yea and Nay* (London 1923), which reprints the entire debate on 'Should History be Taught on a National or International Basis?': HGW's contribution, pp. 15–19. Other outlines which HGW liked were John Drinkwater and William Orpen, eds., *Outline of Literature and Art* (London 1923), also issued in 24 fortnightly parts from Newnes; and Lancelot Hogben, *Mathematics for the Millions* (London 1936, rev. 1940). HGW reprinted *History is One*, the *Short History*, and four other essays from the period in Atlantic XXVII. A useful work from this period, which began as proposed lectures in America, abandoned after HGW developed influenza, is HGW, *The Salvaging of Civilization* (London and New York 1921). The first chapter in this book appeared as four essays in the *Review of Reviews*. The remaining essays on teaching were the original lecture-tour talks, directed to an American audience, and are untouched from that form. Cassells inserted a bookmark advertising the *Outline* in each copy of this work, with quotations calling it, among other things, 'the Great Book of our Generation', and 'among the Most Exciting Books Ever Written'. HGW's later reaction to comments on the *Outline* appears in an interview, 'H. G. Wells on History', *New Era*, vol. II, no. 42, pp. 75–7. That journal, published in 15 countries as an organ of the League of Nations Union, was devoted to the teaching of history.

24   Examples, from among many, are R. L. Gwynne, *Estaines Parva: A Venture* (London 1923), HGW foreword, 5–6; this was a school in Essex. I.S. MacAdam, *Youth in the Universities* (London *c*. 1922), HGW preface, 3. T. L. Humberstone, *University Reform in London* (London 1926), HGW preface, 7–9; HGW to T. L. Humberstone, 22 May, 29 Sept, 10, 14, 18 Oct, 21 Nov 1922. M. Bentinck Smith, *Ad Vitam: Papers of a Head Mistress* (London 1927); ch. 1, 21–62, is entitled 'An Ideal in Education: H. G. Wells'. Oliver Holt, in 'H. G. Wells and I', *Newcastle M Herald and Miners Advocate* (Australia), 28 Jan 1939, tells of his school in Scotland which HGW aided, and their correspondence. Holt was Australian and eventually returned home, but met HGW again when Wells was on tour there in 1938–9. Another one of HGW's former students from Henley House School also met him on the tour, and is mentioned here as well. For

Wells's comments on these sorts of schools and what they need for books, see James Harvey Robinson, *The Mind in the Making* (London 1921, rev. edn. 1923), HGW intro. (also published as 'The Mind in the Making', *Now and Then*, Dec 1923), pp. 18–19. Also see HGW, 'Reconstruction in Higher Education', *Nation* (London), 2 June 1917, a review of John Burnet, *Higher Education and the War.*

25 Carl L. Becker, *American Historical Review*: 'Mr. Wells and the New History', vol. XXVI, no. 4 (July 1921), pp. 641–56; 'Everyman His Own Historian', vol. XXXVII, no. 1 (Jan 1932), pp. 221–36, and reprinted with other work dealing with the same points in *Everyman His Own Historian* (New York 1935). Harold Laski alerted Wells to Becker's views, and HGW sought out the articles to read: HGW to Laski, 1 Feb 1933. Albert Guerard, 'The "New History": H. G. Wells and Voltaire', *Scribners*, vol. LXXVI, no. 5 (Nov 1924).

26 E. Barker to HGW, undated, *c.* 1928; H. E. Barnes to HGW, 29 Mar 1928; G. Murray to HGW, 21 June, 13 July 1929, 21 Nov 1932. HGW to Gedge Fiske & Co., 26 Apr 1928: this memorandum is a good history of the League of Nations committee and reprints several letters of the time, discussing HGW's meetings at the Reform with Culbertson, 7, 9 Sept 1918, and with Canby, 15 July 1918. HGW obtained his own counsel on 14 Jan 1929, who also acted for him later in the Vowles – Thring case, and on a book pirated in Australia, in 1941. The judgement in the Deeks case was dated 27 Sept 1930. HGW to Canadian Authors' Association, 8 Nov, 5 Dec 1932; to Mr Kennedy, 8 Nov 1932, enclosing the Privy Council judgement. HGW, 'The Plagiarism Racket', *Author*, Spring 1933, pp. 83–4. APW to HGW, 16 June 1933. Florence Deeks's papers now lie in the University of New Brunswick archives, available to anyone who wishes to spend more time on the issue. HGW to Amalgamated Press, 12 Apr 1933, for the quotation. *The Times* was sympathetic to HGW: see J.J. Astor to HGW, 18 Oct 1932; HGW to *The Times*, 7 Dec 1932; J. Webb to HGW, 11, 12 Dec 1932.

27 William George Walker, *A History of the Oundle School* (London 1956). Richard Bennett, ed., *Arnold Bennett: Letters to His Nephew* (1935). *Report* of the University of London Joint Committee for the Promotion of the Higher Education of Working People (London 1914), which gives a history of efforts made since 1873, of the various conferences of 1907, 1909, and the development of a fourth-year curriculum, by dint of these efforts, just as the war began. Committee on the Neglect of Science (ERL) to HGW, 20 Mar 1916, 16 Feb 1917. *The Times*, 2 Feb 1916; Report of the Committee (Nov 1917). ERL to HGW, 27 July, 23 Sept, 11 Oct, 15, ?, 17 Oct 1917; to ACRW, 4 Nov 1917; to HGW, 11 Nov 1917; to ACRW, 15 Nov 1917. Northcliffe to HGW, 28 May 1918. F.W. Sanderson to HGW, 12 Aug 1917 (letter calling for 'Spaciousness' in schools, a new science block at Oundle, and the growth in literature and philosophy projected for after the war), 25 May 1919 (HGW had sent him *First and Last Things* and *The Undying Fire*, and Sanderson had used them in his chapel talks).

28 I spent an excellent day at Oundle School about a decade ago, as the guest of B.M.W. Trapnell, the then headmaster. Although it was clear that the school was no longer the revolutionary educational force it had once been, Sanderson's influence was still prominent. I was able to spend time with a student, Nicholas Martin, who showed me the various buildings and discussed his feelings about them, and with Malcolm Thyne, a master, as well as some time with L. Shaw, an old Oundelian who had been at school with HGW's children. Their insights were very valuable. On the Shaw play, see the *Laxtonian: The Oundle School Chronicle*, vol. IX (n.s.), no. 10 (Apr 1976), pp. 309–12; Shaw took a curtain call. F. W. Sanderson to HGW, 10 May 1917, 23 Jan 1918; to ACRW, 18 June 1918 (the Wells parents spent a weekend at Oundle). A 3–pp. fragment of a letter in 1918 lays out Sanderson's proposed new curriculum, using G.P.'s progress and attitudes as a guide for its analysis. V. Seymour Bryant to F.W. Sanderson, 16 Sept 1919; Bryant to HGW, 6 Oct 1919.

29 Mrs F. W. Sanderson to HGW, 30 June; to ACRW, 19 July, 16, 18 Oct, ? [3] Nov, 8, 9

Dec; to HGW, 12 Dec 1922. Apparently a very painful meeting of the three occurred early in Dec. L. Hickerson Barnes (head of the Grocers' Society, founders of the school) to HGW, 14 Aug 1922. K. Fisher to HGW, 13, 17 Dec 1922. ERL to HGW, 16 Aug 1922. Mrs Sanderson to HGW, 16, 20, 22 Dec (HGW to her, 19, 20 Dec) 1922. HGW to GrW, 27 Jan; GrW to HGW, 28 Jan; HGW to GrW, 29 Jan 1923. Mrs Sanderson to HGW, 29 Apr (thanks for *Men Like Gods*), 4 July (probable date) ? 1924, thanks for your biog; enjoyed *The Dream*; congratulations to you and Gip on his first in part II of the Tripos; 7 Apr 1936, asks HGW to meet and talk to her son-in-law, which he did. HGW was certainly not at fault in the matter of the biography. She simply wished the book to contain no personal matter at all. Sanderson and his wife had lost a son in France in 1918. HGW said the book was not worth much without this personal material. HGW, *The Story of a Great Schoolmaster* (London 1924), was translated into Swedish, and was reprinted in Atlantic XXIV, following *Joan and Peter* The other, official volume lists no author, although it is clear that HGW wrote much of it: *Sanderson of Oundle* (New York and London 1923).

30 HGW to G. Lowes Dickinson, 19 Jan 1925. I had an opportunity to read many reviews of HGW's Sanderson biography, kept in a folder at Oundle School and loaned to me. Representative reviews appeared in *EStandard*, 17 Jan (by R.K.L.); *DNews*, 17 Jan, by Wilson K. Midgeley; *MPost*, 18 Jan; *WGaz*, 19 Jan, by H. C. O'N, perhaps the most perceptive; *Birmingham Post*, 22 Jan; *Northampton DEcho*, 2 Feb; *Referee*, 20 Jan, all 1924. Reviews of the other volume appeared in *Sheffield Telegraph*, 16 May; *New Statesman*, 12 May; *Guardian*, 20 Apr 1923; all liked it, but urged a stronger book, and they nearly all mention HGW. Ada Galsworthy to HGW, 29 Feb 1925. B. Russell to HGW, 20 Jan 1924. Also see HGW, 'Education for Creative Science', *New Leader*, 6 Oct 1922 (a view of how to use Sanderson's ideas). HGW's biography appeared serially in the *New Leader* (London), 14 Sept to 26 Oct 1923, and in the *New Republic* (New York), 3 Oct to 21 Nov 1923.

31 Huxley was well known for his popular essays, collected in *Essays of a Biologist* (London 1923) and *Essays in Popular Science* (London 1926). Both these remained in print for years in Penguin editions. J. Huxley to HGW, 24 July 1925. Both men were elected Fellows of the Royal Society later in their careers. The basic agreement on the book is contained in a 'Memorandum of a Conversation', 18 Oct 1925, signed by both men. On G. P. Wells, see his obituary, *The Times*, 27 Sept 1985.

32 Julian Huxley, *Memories*, vol. I (London 1970), has a good and funny section on HGW's tyranny. There are dozens of letters among the three in 1927 and 1928. J. Huxley to HGW, 17 Jan, 5 Feb 1928, and HGW to GPW, 2 Dec 1928, are important. HGW to Huxley, 3 Oct 1928, is savagely analytical and critical of Huxley's rather sloppy habits: 'You can't work like a professional author at all' (2 single-spaced long pages, at Boston).

33 J. Huxley to HGW, 30 Aug 1929. There are about 30 letters between the two in this period, and Huxley spent several periods with HGW at Easton. Also see J.L. Hammerton to HGW, 24 Oct 1928, on an outside reader's criticism of some technical parts. GPW to HGW, 6 Jan (telling HGW to cut his stuff, as it was far too long and pedantic), 28 Jan, another late 1928, 31 Dec 1929, on rewriting, captions, and other illustrations. HGW to Cassell & Co. ('My Dear Flower'), 10 Jan 1927, urging him to discuss the proposed book with Watt, and its relationship to the *Outline of History*. HGW to Enid Bagnold (Lady Jones), 17 July 1929.

34 The number of letters on this subject in the Wells file is immense. The important ones are APW to HGW, 9, 26 Nov, 6, 12 Dec 1926, 4 Jan 1927; HGW to APW, 29 Dec 1926 (on the interview in Nice); APW to HGW, 2, 4 Feb; HGW to APW, 31 Jan, 9 Mar 1927; APW to ACRW, 5 May 1927; APW to HGW, 17 May 1927, 4, 7, 14, 15 Feb, 6, 18, 26 Mar, 20 June, 16, 26 Sept 1929. The book earned $50,000 over its advance through the mail-order version before it was actually published.

35 Again, a host of letters exist. The more important ones are HGW to Waverly Book Co., 4 Dec 1928 (memo), and 18 Mar 1934, on some publicity which focused on

reproduction which he and the collaborators detested. It was withdrawn. APW to HGW, 5 June, 16 Sept, 6, 17 Oct (a memo discussed at lunch), 3 Dec (the book club problems), 27 Oct, 18 Nov (thanks for new preface) 1930, 29 May, 22 June, 30 Aug, 29 Sept 1932. HGW to Nelson (Doubleday), 30 Aug 1932. J. Huxley to HGW, 6 Feb 1936. APW to MCW, 4, 8 Feb, 2 Mar 1937.

36 APW to MCW, 21 June, 11 Sept 1937, 12 Mar 1947. The book sold 3,000 copies that quarter in the Armed Forces edition. Reviews of the work may be found in *Nature*, 23 Mar 1929, 28 Mar 1931, 18 Sept 1937.

37 Closing words of the first edition, *The Science of Life* (London 1930). HGW followed the work carefully; when Lancelot Hogben did not mention it in his own book, *Science for the Citizen*, HGW wrote to Allen & Unwin, 10 May 1938, telling them that Hogben had put it in and their editors had cut out the reference.

38 From a 73-page prospectus with that title, 1928. HGW described the book as a 'spectacle of present-day activities', later in the prospectus, and also as following 'in the footsteps of Diderot and the Encyclopaedists'. The prospectus was sent to Watt. APW to Lucienne Southgate (HGW's secretary at the time), 20 Sept, 18, 19, 22, 26, 29 Oct, 5, 21 Dec 1928. APW to HGW, 15 Jan 1929, for an account of the Doran discussions. Flower (for Cassells), and Doran took the book eagerly, and on the same general terms as for *The Science of Life*. By 26 Feb 1929, it was being called 'The Science of Work and Wealth'. Terms were agreed and contracts signed on 5 Mar 1929.

39 The agreement with these men is laid out in APW to HGW, 19 Oct 1928.

40 The controversy can be followed in the *New Age*, 7, 14, 28 Aug, 11, 25 Sept, 9, 16 Oct 1930, which prints several letters from each of the combatants. HGW's view was published privately in *The Problem of the Troublesome Collaborator* (London 1930), but he was forced as part of the settlement to publish a second and clearer version: *Settlement of the Trouble Between Mr Thring and Mr Wells* (London 1930). HGW wanted Thring out, as he thought, and probably with some truth, that Thring and Vowles had manoeuvred him, to maximize Vowles's fee. Vowles should have been looked at more clearly before HGW agreed to use him, of course. An interesting set of letters, which led for a time to a slight estrangement between the friends, is J. Galsworthy to HGW, 13, 14, 29 Dec 1929, 18 Jan, 12 Feb, 4, 8, 10 Mar 1930 (these three to 'My Dear Madame'); to HGW, 8 Mar 1930. (Probably the Madame letters are to Odette Keun, who was able to hold her own in any contest of invective.) E. A. Bennett to Lord Gorrell (Chairman of the Society of Authors, of which Thring was Secretary), 10 Mar 1930. Ernest Benn to Society of Authors, 27 Mar 1930. HGW to Lord Gorrell, 9 Apr, 12 Apr 1930. He told Gorrell, 'You are scarcely an author. You are associated with a publishing firm, and your many and great engagements with public affairs, for which I am sure the Empire is grateful, give you an excellent excuse for disentangling yourself from these lowly dramas.' GPW to HGW, 3 Jan 1930; HGW to J. D. Beresford, 8 Jan 1930. There is another large sheaf of correspondence with Watt about the work. The second pamphlet came about because Thring threatened another suit. See G. Herbert Thring to GBS, 11 Apr 1930. Other correspondence is HGW to Edgar Jepson, *c.* 1930; HGW to Stanley Unwin, 18 May 1930 (Boston), which describes the second pamphlet and raises the possibility of Unwin's issuing them between covers for the public to read.

41 HGW to APW, 14 Nov 1929.

42 HGW to APW, 8 Jan 1930, 28 Jan, 19 Mar, 25 Aug 1931, 31 Nov 1933. By the summer of 1934, HGW had actually received $75,000 on account of royalties on the book, so the slump was more apparent than real for him.

43 In the preface to *The Work, Wealth and Happiness of Mankind* (London 1932), HGW says of Wallas, 'Another adviser has been Mr Graham Wallas. Years ago among the Swiss mountains we discussed Ostrogorski's fruitful studies of modern democracy, then newly published, and it has been very pleasant to link up this present work with those earlier trains of interest. Outside an all too limited circle of special workers on

both sides of the Atlantic, few people realize how much contemporary thought about political and administrative matters owes to the obstinately critical and enterprising mind of Graham Wallas.' HGW to GrW, 18 Feb, 9, 13 Apr, 25 Dec 1931. They had a long lunch on 28 Apr 1931. GrW to HGW, 11, 19, 20, 21 Apr, 19 Dec 1931. There is a sheaf of letters to and from Watt, as usual, throughout 1931, and a similar file of correspondence with Nelson Doubleday; some of HGW's letters are from New York. Odette Keun and Amber Blanco-White each received a one-eighth share of royalties on the book: APW to L. Southgate, 27 Nov 1931 (copies to Keun and Blanco-White).

44   APW to HGW, 22 Feb, 1 Mar 1932; HGW to APW, 14 Feb 1933 (a typed copy of only part of the letter, which is quite strong on Doubleday): 'Personally he's charming, but until he gives some evidence that his gang of mugs at Garden City has been replaced by men of some literary and general intelligence, I don't feel like burying any more books with his firm *at any price*. I write to be read'; 12, ?29 Jan 1934, on the publicity failures of the publishers. HGW to W. Baxter, 9 Nov 1929.

45   Last words of the book. It was published early in 1932, and was reprinted with some changes, enough to warrant calling it a new edition, in 1935.

46   HGW to Evans (of Heinemann), 9 July 1933, 21 Apr 1934 (the quote). A good review which urges using all three textbooks to frame a new ideology is in *Nature*, 16 Apr 1932.

47   RAG to HGW, 1 May 1932; Olaf Stapledon to HGW, 25 Nov 1931; GrW to HGW, 19 Dec 1931.

Chapter 11

1   R. D. Blumenfeld (for the *DExpress*) to HGW, 24 Feb 1926, 26 Sept 1927, 5 Dec 1929, 14 Apr 1931, proposing ideas for articles which were refused. Wells had been interested in Russia for a long time: see H. D. G. Addison to HGW, 15 Apr 1905, urging him to visit Smolensk. *NYT*, 1 Apr 1917, quotes the message he sent to the Provisional Government once the Revolution occurred.

2   HGW, 'The World in 1922: A Prediction by Our Greatest Prophet', *SExpress*, 25 Apr 1920. M. Gorky to HGW, end of Apr 1920; parts of this letter were published in the British press on 26 Apr 1920. Gorky's letters are at Illinois, but have also been published in Moscow, along with other letters which Gorky addressed to various well-known persons: Maxim Gorky, *Letters* (Moscow 1966). A photo of Wells and Gorky in Moscow in 1920 appears between pp. 96 and 97.

3   'RF', 'Mr Wells Seeing it Through', *SExpress*, 5 Sept 1920. 'A Londoner's Diary', *EStandard*, 20 Sept 1920, for details of the trip. R.D. Blumenfeld to HGW, 13, 15 Sept 1920, for details of payment. HGW's articles in the *SExpress*, 31 Oct, 7, 14, 21, 28 Nov 1920, were republished, somewhat revised and with more data, in HGW, *Russia in the Shadows* (London 1921). This edition has photographs of Wells and the trip which do not appear in later editions. He was welcomed in Petrograd by a delegation of Soviet authors: *NYT*, 4 Oct 1920. His speech to the Petrograd Soviet became a discussion point in the west: *DHerald*, 13 Oct 1920; *NYT*, 14, 16 Oct 1920; *Pravda* (Moscow), 12 Oct 1920.

4   Claire Sheridan, *Mayfair to Moscow: Claire Sheridan's Diary* (New York 1921), entries for 14 Sept, 4, 5, 6, 7, 24 Oct 1920. Her later memoirs use the diary for their treatment of this visit: *Naked Truth* (London 1929), 184–5, 188–9; *To the Four Winds* (London 1956), 120. Sheridan had an eventful time in Russia. She crossed paths with Ivy Litvinov in Oslo, and according to her diary they discussed their mutual friend H.G. Wells. (One would like to have a recording of that conversation.) Sheridan also met John Reed, soon to die of typhus; later on in her visit she attended his funeral. Sheridan and Wells spent much time in the evenings discussing and comparing their various views on Russia. They also discussed Madame Benckendorff, then acting as Gorky's secretary, who as Moura Budberg was to play a significant role in Wells's later

life. Wells was smitten with her, according to Sheridan's diary; in fact Wells had met her as early as his 1914 visit. Sheridan also describes Wells's visit to Lenin, another topic of their conversation. There are a few letters which substantiate this account: GPW to ACRW, 2, 3, 23, 25 Sept 1920. The interpretation in the last sentence comes from the last chapter of Wells's book on the subject — a chapter not published in the *Express*. Further Wellsian remarks appeared in the press: *MPost*, 25 Oct 1920; in the *NYT*, 27 Oct 1920, Wells denied saying them. L. Trotsky, 'H. G. Wells and Lenin: The Philistine Discourse on the Revolutionary', *Labour Monthly*, 1924, pp. 411–20 (from a cutting), discusses his view of the Wells–Lenin interview.

5 *SExpress*: Winston Churchill, 'This Frightful Catastrophe, Mr Wells and Bolshevism', 5 Dec 1920; HGW, 'Mr Wells Hits Back: Rejoinder to Mr Churchill's Criticism — The Anti-Bolshevik Mind', 12, 19 Dec 1920. ERL to ACRW, 20 Dec 1920, greatly enjoyed HGW's destruction of Churchill. For another view, favourable to Wells, see Hugh Brogan, *Arthur Ransome* (London 1985). Ransome was also in Russia at this time, and Wells's book simply eclipsed his *Six Weeks in Russia*; Ransome thought Wells's book was very good. Wells continued his comments. He blamed the Russian famine of 1921 in part on US intervention: *NYT*, 16 Aug 1921.

6 *EStandard*: H.A. Jones, 'An Open Letter to Mr H.G. Wells on His Approaching Visit to Russia', 16 Sept 1920; 'Mr H. A. Jones and Mr H. G. Wells on his Recent Trip to Russia', 17 Sept 1920; H. A. Jones, 'Mr Dear Wells', *MPost*, 4 Aug 1921, for his side of the correspondence. Some versions of these letters also appeared in the *Chicago Tribune* and the *NYT*. For Wells's responses, see *EStandard*, 16 Sept 1920 (HGW asked readers to see *DMail*, 15, 30 Jan 1918, for his views); *MPost*: 'H. G. Wells', 19 Aug 1921; HGW, 13 Aug 1921 (an interesting letter as it is a strong defence of Sidney and Beatrice Webb against the attacks of Jones). Also see *EStandard*: H. A. Jones, 'My Dear Wells', 3 Nov 1920; HGW, letter to Jones, 28 Dec 1920. Henry Arthur Jones, *My Dear Wells: A Manual for the Hater of England* (London 1921). HGW to R.D. Blumenfeld, 24 Nov 1925, no controversy with Jones as it takes two. Wells said Jones had had both the first and last words, as well as about 100,000 in between.

7 HGW to J. Middleton Murry, Oct 1920 (on Gorky's health and his visit). M. Gorky to HGW, 3 Dec 1920, Mar 1921, 16 Apr 1922, 21 Feb 1923, another sometime between Jan and Apr 1923, the last thanking Wells for what must have been *Men Like Gods*, and mentioning its forthcoming appearance in Russian in *Krasnaya Nova*. Bertrand Russell to HGW, 11 Apr 1923: what is Gorky's correct address? Russell also kept up a desultory correspondence with Gorky. Wells discussed his efforts to collect funds and books for the Russian intelligentsia in the *NYT*, 19 Oct 1920, and these were summarized in *Nature*, 11 Nov 1920.

8 HGW, 'Lenin and After: The Future of Communism in Europe', *WGaz*, 9 Feb 1924. Wells remained a Russophile, and there is a fair amount of correspondence with those who wanted information. Examples are: HGW to 'Dear Sir', early Nov 1920, reporting on British pensioners living in Moscow whom Wells had sought out. Wells said that his baggage was not checked at the frontier. HGW to A. C. Y. Bell, 9 Mar 1924, on Russian state religions. (Both at Boston.)

9 I. Maisky to HGW, 26 Jan, 23 May (9 pp. of info.), (?)26 May, 9 Nov 1927. Wells sponsored a new edition of Tolstoy to be published in 1928: HGW to editors, 21 Feb 1922.

10 See HGW, 'M. Briand, Mr H.G. Wells, and the *Daily Mail*', *DChronicle*, 28 Nov 1921, for his view of the contretemps, which was a nine days' wonder in England. Another letter, of which I have seen only a proof, went to the *EStandard* on same subject, and the *NY World's* backing of him in the attempt at censorship. Wells having had to cancel his 1920 lecture tour of the States, there was even greater interest in his visit: *NYT*, 29 July 1920, 4 Jan 1921.

11 Charles À Court Remington, *After the War* (Boston 1922). This is his diary, and the significant entries concerning HGW are 19, 25, 26, 27 Oct, 3, 9, 11, 12, 27, 28, 29

Nov, 2, 3 Dec 1921. Wells did not return to England immediately, taking a brief holiday at the home of Thomas Lamont in New York, and paying a visit to Margaret Sanger (see ch. 16). The problem with the French surfaced again in 1941: see *NYT*, 13 Nov 1941, for a gossipy version, inaccurate in many regards. When he left the US Wells was interviewed at least twice, *NYT*, 8, 18 Jan 1922. Wells had rejected disarmament or been sceptical of it earlier in his life. HGW to Ed. Bushey, 18 Mar 1903 (Boston): 'The quest for disarmament is one in which I am keenly interested but upon which I arrived at no conclusions of a definite sort . . . at the present time'. F. Chaliapin to Irina Chaliapin, 20 Oct 1921 (and added to for several days thereafter), briefly discusses the crossing with H. G. Wells; printed in Nina Froud and James Hanley, eds., *Chaliapin: An Autobiography as Told to Maxim Gorky* (New York 1967), 213–15. On the voyage Wells, Chaliapin, and Remington auctioned sketches they had made for the benefit of the Seaman's Fund and raised £70. A photograph of Wells, Gorky, Chaliapin, and others appears in F. Chaliapin, *Man and Mask: Forty Years in the Life of a Singer* (London 1932), opp. p. 376. A Wells shipboard interview appeared in *NYT*, 28 Oct 1921.

12 S. Webb to HGW, 28 Nov 1922 (Webb *Letters* III. 158), noting how well Wells had done as compared with himself in 1918. B. Webb, *Diary* III. 401–2, entry for 10 July 1922. *Labour Leader*, 20 July, 3, 10, 24 Aug 1922. A correspondence did continue on birth-control, with no mention of electoral politics. Wells was also nominated as Lord Rector of Aberdeen University but was defeated by Lord Birkenhead: *NYT*, 21, 22 Oct 1922.

13 HGW, *University of London Election* (London 1922).

14 HGW, *The World, Its Debts and the Rich Men* (London 1922). *DHerald*, 19 Nov 1922. S. Webb to HGW, 28 Nov 1922; RAG to HGW, 1 Dec 1922. Gregory remarked that the winner had done a great deal for the University, and especially its medical school. These election addresses were republished in Harry W. Laidler, ed., *Wells's Social Anticipations* (New York 1927). *Nature*, 29 July 1922, 24 Nov 1923, on HGW's election addresses and platform.

15 *DHerald*, 22 Oct 1923; 8 Nov 1923, Lady Warwick's election address, reprinting a letter from HGW to her. HGW, *Socialism and the Scientific Motive* (London 1923). RAG to HGW, 26 Mar 1923: Gregory told Wells that his address was 'on a level far above anything I have ever heard from a political candidate'. HGW, *To the Electors of London University, General Election, 1923* (London 1923). *WGaz*, 22 Nov 1923, reported his election address.

16 *DHerald*: 'Teachers for Freedom', 17 Nov 1923, with the text of HGW's speech to the teachers; a detailed report of his second Essex Hall address, 1 Dec 1923; HGW, letter, 5 Dec 1923, supporting Emil Davies, candidate for Romford; Webb and Shaw were also heavily engaged on Davies's behalf.

17 *WGaz*: letter from Wells's agent, M. Craig, 22 Nov 1923, on Pollard's candidacy; HGW, 'Politics as a Public Nuisance', 1 Dec 1923, and leader of the same date.

18 The list of supporters was carried as a fourth page to his 1923 election address in its second printing. *DHerald*, 7 Dec 1923, for election results. Lady Warwick polled 4,015 votes to Eden's 16,337, and the Liberal candidate's 11,135. *DHerald*, 11 Dec 1923, for Wells's statement on his retirement. The *NYT* covered both his campaigns quite fully, 3, 19 Nov 1922, 22 Nov, 1 Dec 1923.

19 HGW in *WGaz*: 'The Re-emergence of Lloyd George', 8 Dec 1923; 'The Parliamentary Tangle: Problems and Parties in the New House of Commons', 8 Jan 1924; 'Modern Government: Parliament and Real Electoral Reform: Labour's Hidden Hand', 12 Jan 1923; 'The Labour Party on Trial: The Folly of the Five Cruisers', 15 Mar 1924; 'Youth and the Vote: The Rejuvenance of the World', 29 Mar 1924; 'Labour Politicians Tarnished by Office: Evaporization of the Intelligentsia', 10 May 1924; 'Constructive Ideas in Politics: Where Labour is Deficient', 17 May 1924; 'P.R. and Party Extinction: Parliaments of a New Type', 31 May 1924. This last article was

reprinted as a pamphlet, somewhat modified, by the PR Society as HGW, *The P.R. Parliament* (London 1924). A bill for PR was actually put forward in the Commons in 1924, and defeated 238–144.

20 *DHerald*, 19, 20, 21, 22, 23 May 1924.

21 Thomas Lloyd Humberstone, *University Reform in London* (London 1926), HGW preface, 7–8. HGW to Humberstone, 22 May (2), 29 Sept, 10, 14, 18 Oct, 22 Nov 1922; RAG to HGW, 28 Nov 1927, on supporting him. Some funds dribbled out to Humberstone, who was never very successful, at least until 1939, when he disappears from the correspondence. Wells first met Humberstone in 1902 as a recent graduate of the Royal College. See HGW to T. L. S. Humberstone, 18 June 1902. Wells was good for occasional donations of 25 gns. over the intervening years. On the proposed Labour paper, see Philip Millward to HGW, 20 Apr 1923; H. Fyfe to HGW, 19 June 1923; Arnold Dawson to HGW, 10 Feb 1927. Wells donated the use of his short stories 'The Beautiful Suit' and later 'The Pearl of Love' to raise money for the paper and later for the Miners' Federation. A. Dawson to HGW, 18 Feb, 21 Apr, 2 May 1927. Stephen Koss, *The Rise and Fall of the Political Press in Great Britain*, vol. II (London 1984), 82, 394–5. H. W. Talbot to HGW, 12 Oct 1924, soliciting funds for his campaign. H.N. Brailsford to HGW, 21 Aug 1922. Wells was considered as a possible editor of the proposed paper. Webb *Letters* III. 168, describes as joint the efforts of Massingham, Wells, and Laski; eventually, in 1930, these led to the merger of the *Nation* with the *New Statesman*. HGW, 'Education for Creative Service: A Lead for the Labour Party in Education', *New Leader*, 6 Oct 1922, on F. W. Sanderson and Oundle School, and what these ideas meant. S. Webb thought this an excellent article, and told Wells so. Also see I. S. MacAdam, *Youth in the Universities* (1922), with a preface by Wells, for a further statement of these general views at the time HGW was a candidate.

22 HGW, 'The Six Greatest Men in History', *Strand*, vol. LXIV (1922), pp. 214–20, 361–7, 434–8. (I list only UK dates of publication; all of the following also appeared in the US.) When this series was reprinted in 1935 in the *Reader's Digest* only three names (Jesus, Buddha, and Aristotle) were featured. HGW, 'Christ Died — Do We Care?', *Pearson's*, Feb 1923. HGW, *John o'London's*: 'The Ten Most Important Books in the World', 31 Mar, 7, 11 Apr 1923; 'What Everyone Should Read — The Reading of History', 5 May 1923; 'The Pursuit of Wisdom', 19 May 1923; 'What Everyone Should Learn at School', 6, 13, 20, 23, 27 Oct 1923. HGW: 'H.G. Wells Prophesies — The Gifts of the New Sciences', *Strand*, 1924, pp. 152–8; 'What is Success?', *Cassells'*, 24 Nov, 1, 8 Dec 1923, and reprinted in Atlantic XXVI; 'The Teacher as Statesman', *Torchbearer*, July 1924, pp. 4–6; 'The Release of Man: The Ten Great Discoveries', *John o'London's*, 28 Feb, 7, 14 Mar 1925; 'The Greatest Dates in History', *Forum*, Nov 1930, pp. 269–72.

23 HGW, 'The Future of the British Empire', *Empire Review*, Oct 1923, pp. 1071–9. Brendan Bracken to HGW, 29 June, 23 July, 14 Aug 1923; Winston Churchill to HGW, 27 Sept 1923. Encyclopaedia Britannica, *These Eventful Years: The Twentieth Century in the Making*, 2 vols. (New York and London 1924): HGW, 'A Forecast of the World's Affairs', vol. II, pp. 1–17, and quoting p. 7. Also see Dan Griffiths, ed., *What is Socialism: A Symposium* (London 1924), HGW, p. 81; and *The Europa Yearbook*, ed. by M. Farbman, R. Muir, and H.F. Spender (London 1926), HGW, pp. 3–4.

24 S. Olivier to HGW, 25 Apr 1924. HGW to Marie Beets, 30 Sept 1919, sending on a letter from Jane asking for information. C. F. G. Masterman to HGW, 10, 21 Dec 1922 (Wells had objected to some phrases in Masterman's memoirs, and Masterman was hurt; the letters describe the friendship, and Wells's apologies). Léon Blum to HGW, ?1924, undated, sends tickets for the Chambre (des Deputés), and Wells then had dinner at Blum's home, to discuss world affairs. ERL to HGW, 26 Apr 1920, 22 May, 1, 28 Oct 1923, 18 Jan, 3 Nov 1924, 28 Oct 1925 (material exchanged on evolution and geology). By this time Lankester was basically confined to his home, and Wells made it a practice to have lunch there each year before leaving for the Mediterranean

and upon his return. ERL to HGW, 10 Jan, 1 Feb 1927. Bertrand Russell to HGW, 15 Dec 1924; to ACRW, 23 Feb 1925; to HGW, 4 Mar 1925, introducing Isaac Don Levine, an expert on Russia and Russian prisons, from which he had escaped. Fenner Brockway to HGW, 29 Jan, 12 Feb 1925, agreeing to sign a manifesto against conscription once Gilbert Murray had signed (Wells was at first mistrustful of Brockway). J.D. Beresford to HGW, 8 Oct 1926. HGW to RAG, 7 Nov 1925.

25   HGW, *WGaz*: 'Aviation of the Half-Civilized', 27 Oct 1923 (Wells made a tour of Europe by air in the summer of 1923, and was commenting on the need to set up an organized commercial/international network of airlines); 'Air Armament: The Supremacy of Quality', 3 May 1924. The *DHerald* had a long interview with Wells, 2 June 1923, on the future of air transport. HGW to *Airways*, published in the *Observer*, 20 Dec 1925. Wells was forced down in a windstorm while crossing the Channel: *NYT*, 30 Dec 1922. There are 7 articles on education in his series in the *WGaz*, later collected in *A Year of Prophesying* (London 1924); another is HGW, 'The Four Years of College are Wasted', in Roy Long, ed., *Literary Treasures of 1926* (New York 1927), 228–35 (the article probably appeared in *Cosmopolitan*, but I have not located it). There are 11 articles on the League in one form or another, and nearly every one of them stirred up comment, from 'Free Lance', from J. A. Spender, and hosts of others. The dates of the important appearances in the *WGaz* by HGW and/or his critics on this subject are 23 Sept, 6, 13, 20 Oct, 3, 7, 21 Nov, 27, 29, 31 Dec 1923; 2, 19, 23, 26 Jan, 8 Mar, 12 Apr 1924.

26   HGW, *WGaz*: 'The Other Side in France', 24 Nov 1923; 'Black and White France: The Spanish-Italian Challenge', 15 Dec 1924; 'On a New League: Latin America and the League', 22 Dec 1923; 'Cosmopolitan Citizens: World Control of Production, Trade, and Transport', 29 Dec 1923; 'The Spirit of Fascism: Is There Any Good in It at All?' (the quotation), 12 July 1924; 'Has Communism a Future? The Possibility of a Socialist Renascence', 9 Aug 1924. HGW's remarks on Fascism, coupled with the treatment of it in his novel *Meanwhile*, caused him to be barred from entering France by crossing from Italy. He normally took the train through the Simplon Tunnel and came back up the Riviera, but the Italian government forbade this, and he had to drive from Paris after that time.

27   HGW, *WGaz*: 'Olive Branches of Steel: Should the Angels of Peace Carry Bombs?', 5 Apr 1924; 'The European Kaleidoscope: The German Will in Default', 23 Apr 1924; 'Portugal and Prosperity: The Blessedness of Being a Little Nation', 1 Mar 1924; 'Dictators or Politicians: The Dilemma of Civilization', 22 Mar 1924; 'On China: The Land Out of the Limelight', 26 Apr 1924; 'Wembley: An Exhibition of Lost Opportunities', 24 May 1924; 'The Lawlessness of America and the Way to Order', 21 June 1924 (this reports his views of Rebecca West's trip to America); 'The Incompatibility of India: Divorce or Legal Separation?', 5 July 1924; 'The Race Conflict: Is It Inevitable?', 19 July 1924; 'The Impudence of Flags; Our Power Resources and My Elephants, Whales and Gorillas', 2 Aug 1924 (a remarkably prescient piece); 'After a Year of Journalism: An Outbreak of Autobiography', 20 Sept 1924, and see the *WGaz* leader in the same issue, on the year with Wells. FAS to HGW, 21 Dec 1924; Leo Amery to HGW, 26 Jan 1925. On similar ideas see Frank Swinnerton, 'Wembley', in *A London Bookman* (London 1928), his collection of journalism, 139–41, and Gilbert Murray, 'Our Debt to the League: The Lesson of the Recent Crisis', *DHerald*, 17 Sept 1923: both are reactions to Wells's articles. On the publication of *A Year of Prophesying*, see APW to HGW, 14, 24 Aug, 2, 4, 12 Sept 1924; ACRW to HGW, 13 Sept 1924 (in draft on the Watt letter).

28   Hamilton Fyfe to HGW, 16 Mar 1923. The first review in the *DHerald*, by W.J. Turner, 'A Milk White World', appeared on 4 Apr 1923. Wells responded on 5 Apr, with a letter to the reviewer; the *Herald* printed a letter from the reviewer defending himself on 7 Apr. Wells apparently asked how the *Herald* was owned during this period; letters went back and forth. Philip Millward to HGW, 9 Apr 1923; Fyfe to

HGW, 13 Apr 1923, saying he had rewritten the review, but the literary editor had total control of reviewers. *DHerald*: HGW, 'Men Like Gods: Mr H. G. Wells and the *D.H.* Critic', 9 Apr 1923, a discussion of Utopian thought; followed by letters on 7, 9, 19 Apr 1923. (The novel was serialized in the Liberal *WGaz*, which irritated some, but HGW said he had offered it to the *Herald*, which said it did not serialize books.) The Clydeside ILP, led by Jimmy Maxton, endorsed the book, 7 Apr 1923, and urged it be read, calling it the best book since Edward Bellamy's *Equality*. The prize-winning review, by Bernard Houghton of Hastings, was printed, *DHerald*, 2 May 1923; 14 other entries were also printed. Sydney Olivier liked the book very much and was impatient with the bad reviews; see Olivier to HGW, 26 Mar 1923.

29 C.V. Drysdale, 'Mr Wells's Interim Report on Utopia', *New Generation*, May 1923. H.M. Tomlinson, 'Mr Wells's "Men Like Gods"', *Adelphi*, June 1923. (The *Adelphi* remained influential, of course, and was to play a role in Orwell's life as well as in many of the intellectual summer schools of the 1930s.) *DHerald*, 29 May 1923. HGW, 'Winston', *WGaz*, 10 Nov 1923. W. Lippman to HGW, 11 Oct 1922. Wells wrote to Lippman thanking him for *Public Opinion*, and went on to discuss the serial in his letter of response. Richard Aldington to HGW, 9 June 1936. Aldington and Wells had met over the problem of James Joyce's pension: see Aldington to HGW, 2, 10 May 1919, 9 June 1929, 23 May 1931. 'J. S. H.' (Huxley), review, *Nature*, 5 May 1923. Edward Marsh was estranged from HGW for a time, until Lady Wemyss brought them together to, in Wells's phrase, 'bury the hatchet', in 1935. Christopher Hassall, *A Biography of Edward Marsh* (London 1959). They had met at Lady Elcho's in 1907. At a 1937 testimonial to Marsh Wells sat at the head table.

30 P. Tomlinson, 'Mr Wells's People', *Adelphi*, May 1924. Harry Johnston to Wells, 1, 11 Apr 1924, on the book. 'H.F.', review, *DHerald*, 4 Apr 1924.

31 *The World of William Clissold* was published by Benn in England in 3 vols. (1926), and by Doran in the United States in 2. The parody by A. A. M. Thomson, *The World of Billiam Wissold* (London 1927) is fairly laboured, although Book V, pp. 105–27, 'Wissold's the Open Expiry', is quite humorous. Ernest Benn had some interesting views, long after the fact, on Wells's relations with publishers: *Happier Days: Recollections and Reflections* (London 1949). On the interviews and so on, see *NYT*, 15 Apr 1925.

32 GBS to HGW, undated, and perhaps referring only to the first of the 3 vols. of *William Clissold*.

33 GrW to HGW, 8 Oct 1926 (only part of letter remains); Bertrand Russell to HGW, 7 Sept 1926; Thomas Hardy to HGW, 19 Nov 1926; ERL to HGW, 28 Aug, 3, 9 Sept 1926.

34 Patrick Parrinder's selection of reviews of the book (*Critical Heritage*, 275–307) illustrates very well the difference in reviewers. He includes comment from Conrad Aiken, H. L. Mencken, J. M. Keynes, and Geoffrey Wells, among others.

35 Correspondence is extensive on *William Clissold*. APW to HGW, 15 Dec 1925, 31 Dec 1925, 12, 20, 22 Jan, 5 Feb (agreement on terms of 21 Feb); to ACRW, 1 Mar 1926. HGW to V. Gollancz, Aug, Sept, 28 Oct, 3, 26 Nov 1926, 2 May 1927; Gollancz to HGW, 2 Aug 1927. APW to ACRW, 4, 23 May 1927 (this has a long comment by Wells on what was to be reprinted, and how). HGW to *Star*, 1, 4 Oct 1926; they objected to HGW's comments on the King and Ramsay MacDonald, but see *Star*, 1 Nov 1926, when they called the 3 vols. 'a splendid object. . . . and brilliantly accomplished'. APW to HGW, 26 May 1926. *William Clissold* excerpts, *Cosmopolitan*, July, Aug, Sept 1926. APW to HGW, 8, 10, 23 Feb; to ACRW, 18 Feb 1927, on inadvertent copying by *Liverpool Echo*. They apologized to Wells, and paid him a token £1. APW to HGW, 6 Mar 1929; to Lucienne Southgate, 15 Mar, 5 Apr 1929; Southgate to APW, 14 Mar 1929.

36 HGW, *SExpress*: 'Man Becomes a Different Animal: Delusions About Human Fixity', 2, 9 Jan 1927.

37 *SExpress*, 23 Jan, 6, 20 Feb 1927 for HGW articles. GBS to GrW, 7 Feb 1927 (on the article on fascism). HGW, 'Italy Under Mussolini', *Current History*, May 1927, pp. 175–9, a reprint of the *Express* article. HGW to Foreign Office, 11, 18 Apr 1929, calling for protection against the Italian ban. HGW to Meade Minnegerode (of *NYT*), 9 Nov 1926.

38 *DExpress*: 6, 20 Mar, 3, 17 Apr 1927.

39 *SExpress*: 1, 15 May, 5 June 1927. *Sacco-Vanzetti Dawn*, vol. I, no. 1 (June 1927): I have seen only this one issue, and that through the courtesy of my colleague, Charles Scontras.

40 *SExpress*: HGW, 12, 26 June, 10, 24 July 1927; GBS, 'The Scoundrels', 7 Aug 1927. The pamphlet, *Experiments on Animals: Voices for and Against*, appeared in 1927 from the British Union for the Abolition of Vivisection. E. Ray Lankester and Wells met several times in the month of July 1927 on the issue of spiritualism. See ERL to HGW, 31 July 1927 in particular. The Wells – Conan Doyle exchange which springs from these writings is in *SExpress*: HGW, 'What is Immortality?', 1 Jan 1929; A. Conan Doyle, 'Why H. G. Wells is Peeved', 8 Jan 1929. *The Science of Life*, Book IX. Wells and Shaw had been quoted before on spiritualism. See *Strand*, vol. LIX (1920), pp. 392–5 for interview.

41 *SExpress*: 7, 21 Aug, 4, 18 Sept, 2, 16, 30 Oct, 13, 27 Nov, 11 Dec 1927. The responses to the Birkenhead review appeared on 18 Dec 1927.

42 APW to MCW, 15 Sept 1927; to HGW, 12, 18 Oct (there was a meeting of the principals at the Reform Club this week as well); APW to MCW, 13 Jan 1928; APW to HGW, 2 Feb 1932; APW to L. Southgate, 8 Apr 1932. E. Ray Lankester received the book from Wells with pleasure, and Wells spent a day with him at his home, listening to the gramophone, and discussing the book, as well as the iniquities of editors. ERL to HGW, 24 Mar 1928. Lankester's obituary by Sidney F. Hamer, in *Proceedings, Linnean Society of London*, session 142 (1929–30), 206–11, discusses the Wells friendship.

43 HGW, *Playing at Peace* (London: National Council for the Prevention of War 1927). The original article appeared in the *SExpress*, 12 June 1927. Other statements at this time to the same point: HGW's introduction to J. M. Kenworthy, *Will Civilization Crash?* (London 1927), iii–xiii. HGW, 'Has the Money-Credit System a Mind?', *Banker*, vol. VI (1928), pp. 221–33, an article solicited after *William Clissold* appeared. HGW, 'The Next Phase in America', St. Louis *Post-Dispatch*, 9 Dec 1928, which also appeared in *The Drift of Civilization* (London 1930), 199–214, and in *Bermondsey Book*, June–Aug 1928, pp. 10–18. HGW, *The Way to World Peace* (London 1930), pamphlet in a series on Christianity; he published this only after a disclaimer on those views.

44 APW to HGW, 20 Jan 1926, 26 Jan, 10 Mar, 8 June 1927; to MCW, 23 June, 8, 13 July, 12, 14, 15, 28 Sept 1927; to Gertrude Press (Wells's secretary in late 1927 and early 1928), 13 Mar 1928; to MCW, 21 Mar 1928; to HGW, 26 June 1929. Bits of *Meanwhile*, characterizations of well-known persons, appeared in the *Observer* in July 1927; V. Gollancz to HGW, 28 June 1927. An interview with Gollancz appeared in the *Observer* and in the *Bookman* (US), July 1927. See *EStandard*, 25 Aug 1927, for A. Bennett's review.

45 APW to HGW, 16 Jan 1928, a long letter with extensive quotes from Gollancz's letters to APW. APW to MCW, 26 Jan 1928; to HGW, 3, 14 Feb, 2 Mar (Wells autograph on the side says, 'I want the book out as soon as possible': this is while the serial negotiations were going on), 13 Mar 1928; to MCW, 8, 12 Mar 1928. MCW to HGW, 8 Jan 1929. On the Book-of-the-Month Club see HGW to W. Lippman, 12 Sept, 4 Oct 1929; Lippman to HGW, 25 Sept, 15 Oct 1929 (both Yale).

46 Bertrand Russell to HGW, 24 May 1928. B. Russell, *The Autobiography of Bertrand Russell*, vol II, *1914–1928* (Boston and London 1968), 227–9. B. Webb to HGW, 25 May 1928 in Webb *Letters* III. 299; HGW to B. Webb, 9 June 1928.

47 Undated handbill, *c.* 1930 (Bromley); another very similar (Eric Korn). G. Henry to HGW, 9 Dec 1928, a 22-page report to the 'Hdqtrs' of the Open Conspiracy from Chicago. HGW to F. P. Crozier, 30 July 1929, urging members not to be so slavish in following his words. He describes himself as a writer and student, but also a 'sort of Prophet Patentee or Figure Head'. HGW to 'Mr Thompson', 13 Dec 1934, on an H. G. Wells Society and nationalisms; HGW to Ernest Bloch, 27 Sept 1935 (Boston) on his very negative views on nationalism of all kinds.

48 HGW to Victor Deznai, 24 Jan 1929; to Nelson Doubleday, 27 Oct 1930; George E. G. Catlin to HGW, 12 Oct 1929, urging him to read his wife Vera Brittain's book, which dealt with some similar ideas. HGW to Philip Guedalla, 17 Feb 1929. Wells returned to England to go to the Royal College of Science dinner on 22 Mar 1929, and the luncheon occurred then, apparently.

49 HGW, 'The ABC of World Peace: Disarmament is not Enough'; 'Let the "Big Two" Start a Peace Alliance'; 'Stop Warmaking in the Schools': a four-part article, *DHerald*, 17, 18, 19, 20 Mar 1930.

50 HGW, 'Project of a World Society', *New Statesman and Nation*, 20 Aug 1933, an address given at the Liberal Summer School in Oxford. 'Mr H. G. Wells Attacks', *Liberal Magazine*, Aug 1933, p. 393.

51 On the Atlantic Edition (1,600 copies of the sets) see HGW letter, *WGaz*, 2 Jan 1924, on tariffs, in which he describes rereading his books for the edition. APW to HGW, 22 Sept, 5 Oct, 16 Nov 1927, 15 May, 23 June, 5 July, 3 Aug, 4 Dec 1928 on the edition sales (several volumes were remaindered, in fact, as they were delayed by permissions problems). See APW to HGW, 7, 11, 27 Sept, 7, 13 Dec 1922, 16, 18 Jan, 1, 8 Feb, 9, 12 Mar, 11 Apr, 2 July 1923. This edition was actually thought of before World War I and begun in earnest in 1920; the correspondence is immense. Wells passed on the prospectuses for the travellers, all advertising and catalogue copy. One hundred and sixteen sets were sold in advance of publication: APW to HGW, 23 Oct 1924. My own set, No. 402 of the American version, is still uncut (except by me to verify changes). MCW to APW, 22 Feb 1928, a significant letter on Wells's view of the inexpensive editions. One of the best reviews of the Atlantic Edition is by J. C. Squire, 'Mr Wells', *Observer*, 29 Nov 1925: 'Mr Wells is a greater man than most sonnet writers, but he has scarcely grasped this truth.'

52 HGW to APW, 5 Oct 1925, republished in *The Writers' Handbook*, 1927; APW to HGW, 8 Nov 1926. The letter was reprinted later as well; see APW to MCW, 1 Aug 1939, and was also reprinted in an Indian book used to teach letter-writing.

53 Again the correspondence on this matter is prodigious. A few significant letters are APW to HGW, 17 Nov 1926, reporting an interview Watt had had with Macmillan; APW to MCW, 20 Sept 1927; APW to MCW, 21, 23 Sept 1933; APW to HGW, 15, 18 Oct 1928, on sales to mail-order houses; 27 Mar 1928, on recovering rights from other publishers. Occasionally Wells traded the reprint rights in a short story for these early rights to his work, although Dent gave Wells back his rights without charge. APW to MCW, 2 Feb 1928, on the film rights to *The Invisible Man* which were owned by Wells's son, Frank. The following table, from a memorandum in the Watt papers, is without date, but headed as below:

Sales of Wells Novels in 1925

Passionate Friends	1249
Tales of Unexpected	1049
Research Magnificent	943
First Men in Moon	2273
World Set Free	3329
War in the Air	3585
Modern Utopia	2239
Tales of Life	919

Marriage	1572	
In Days of Comet	744	
Tales of Wonder	1267	
Food of the Gods	1049	
Tono-Bungay	3508	
Mr Polly	4052	
Kipps	4067	[These editions sold for 2s. 6d. HGW received
Love and Mr Lewisham	1536	12½% royalty.]
Invisible Man	1534	[These two sold for 2s. HGW received 12½%
When Sleeper Wakes	3423	royalty.]
Wonderful Visit	409	[Dent sold this for 2d. HGW received a pittance.]
Bealby	5	[HGW received 25% of the 7s. 6d.]
Sea Lady	612	[HGW received 15% of the 2s 6d.]
Sea Lady	162	[HGW received 10% of the 2s.]
Tono-Bungay	21407	[These were 9d. paperbacks. HGW
Tales of Life	10072	received a small royalty.]
Wheels of Chance	442	[Dent published at 2s. HGW received 12½%.]
Dr Moreau	489	
Time Machine	2330	[Heinemann published these at 2s. HGW
War of the Worlds	1080	received 12½%.]
Total Sales	75,346	[at approximately 3s. 5d. each, these sales netted HGW around £1100.]

In 1927 *The Dream* and *Christina Alberta's Father* sold 47,488 in a 7s. 6d. edition. *William Clissold* sold 83,031, and *Meanwhile* sold 26,659 in the first three months of its existence, to give an indication of how Wells's newer books were selling.

54   A. G. Church to HGW, 25 Feb 1929; Gerald Heard to HGW, 25 July 1929. The paper lost £2,600 on the first three issues alone. Heard to HGW, 2 Aug (Wells courier duty), 2 Oct (money gone again), 9 Oct 1929; HGW to Heard, 4 Oct 1929, Melchett promised funds; Heard to HGW, 12, 15 Oct 1929. Church to HGW, 18 Oct 1929, on Elmhirsts. Wells gave a dinner to the board and their proposed donors, as well as a luncheon for others on the board in this week. Part of the problem was that Conway Davies, the first angel, did not live up to his written promises. Editorial board met on 9 Nov 1929 to discuss the future. Conway Davies to HGW, 24, 25 Oct 1929, claiming a misunderstanding. Another board meeting was called. Davies broke down and was hospitalized. Church to HGW, 3 Jan 1930; to Lord Melchett, 21 Dec 1929; to HGW, 25 Jan 1930, winding up the affair and meeting the bills. Some significant articles were published in the *Realist* even in its short career: Julian Huxley, 'What is Individuality?', vol. 1, no. 1 (Apr 1929), pp. 109–21; Vernon Clancey, 'Flicks Politics', vol. 1, no. 2 (May 1929), discussing Wells's ideas on cinema; HGW, 'Imperialism, The Open Conspiracy, Lord Melchett, and Lord Beaverbrook', vol. 1, no. 6 (Sept 1929), pp. 3–13, discussing international companies as a possible road for the Open Conspiracy, and relating the history of the Co-Efficients; Amber Blanco-White, 'Money and the Relief of Unemployment', vol. 1, no. 6 (Sept 1929), pp. 96–108. The correspondence on Wells's piece is G. Heard to HGW, 16 July 1929; APW to HGW, 13 Aug 1929, on getting it published to protect copyright. The *New Republic* printed it and paid Wells $50, and the *Realist* $50 for the privilege. See APW to HGW, 22, 23 Aug 1929.

Chapter 12

1   APW to HGW, 16 Apr, 17 Nov 1927, 30 Mar, 18 Apr, 7 May (on serial rights), 23 June 1928. 12 Mar 1928, on the interview, date-lined Paris, *EStandard*, 11 Mar 1928;

it was actually about Wells's earlier fantastic novels, and not about his new work. HGW's response to Watt was on the margin of the 12 Mar letter. 29 May, 6 June 1930.

2   S. Olivier to HGW, 20 Sept 1928; Eileen Power to HGW, 7 Oct 1928; ERL to HGW, 22 Sept 1928: 'It is rather alarming.' Olivier reread the book in 1934, on his 75th birthday, and found it one of Wells's best. His letter discussed racialism in detail and he reminisced of his own experience with racists; S. Olivier to HGW, 17 Apr 1934.

3   It seems worthwhile to follow some of these transactions, as they indicate a shift in Wells's popularity. *William Clissold* marks the shift, in fact, as that book sold, but acquired a reputation as a sermon or tract — a reputation which, when Wells reverted to less solemn books, damaged the sales of those books as well. APW to HGW, 1, 6 Mar (Wells's comment on back), and he agrees to remove some indelicate passages, 28 July (to L. Southgate); to HGW, 18 Apr, 14 July (to Southgate), 27 Aug, 16 Sept, 4 Nov, 6 Dec (this one quotes the Benn letter in the detail given here), 8, 19 Nov (Wells's note saying accept, but the Low pictures cannot be changed), to Southgate 28 Nov, 3 Dec (5-pp. letter on details of contract); telegram APW to HGW, 3 Dec; HGW to APW, accept, same date; 9, 12, 24 Dec, all 1929; 2 Jan 1930, to Southgate; APW to HGW, 9 Sept, 28 Oct 1930, on Liverpool *Express* sale. Ernest Benn, *Happier Days* (1949), is good on his relations with HGW. E. Benn to HGW, 13 Aug, 3, 29 Oct, 11 Nov 1929.

4   B. Russell to HGW, 24 July 1930; I. Maisky to HGW, 26 Aug 1930. The fiction of this later period is treated well in Robert Bloom, *Anatomies of Egotism, A Reading of the Last Novels of H.G. Wells* (Lincoln, Nebr. 1977).

5   APW to HGW, 2 Feb, 9, 26 Aug (Wells's comment here), 29 Sept to MCW reporting a telephone conversation with H.G., 10 Oct 1932 (the book was delayed for six months on account of the economy); 17 Jan, 3, 9 Feb 1933. On Wells and his book see HGW to APW, 9 Aug (on the contractual terms), 2 Sept (signed by L. Southgate, but in Wells's hand), 5, 12 Sept 1932 (on Delphic symbols, and the designs of the endpapers, which Wells insisted upon): his summary appeared in the draft of this letter, also signed by L. Southgate when it went to Watt.

6   The Sorbonne lecture, 'Democracy Under Revision', was printed separately by Leonard and Virginia Woolf, at the Hogarth Press (London 1927) as well as in HGW, *The Way the World Is Going* (London 1928). The invitation was tendered in J.D. Beresford to HGW, 28 Oct 1926. The intellectual élite of France attended. See *Nature*, 7 July 1928, for reviews: 'Men of Science owe a debt of gratitude to Mr H.G. Wells', review by 'A.M.C-S' (Carr-Saunders).

7   HGW, *The Common Sense of World Peace* (London 1929), and in *After Democracy* (London 1932).

8   The Madrid talk too is included in *After Democracy*, under the title 'Money and Mankind', and was given in May 1932. See Eileen Power to HGW, 8, 9 May 1932. On this topic Wells's pamphlet, *What Should Be Done — Now: A Memorandum on the World Situation* (New York 1932), calling for controlled inflation, an expansion of public employment and collective purchase, a readjustment of tariffs, and mutual disarmament, is a follow-up. Whether FDR read it or not is unknown, but there are similarities to New Deal measures in general. Wells's four-part series in the *DHerald*, 'The Road to World Peace', early in 1930, is important in his thinking. See below. The correspondence is A. Mellar to MCW, 9 Jan, 11, 20 Feb 1930.

9   Other talks worth mention at this time include Wells's introduction of Lancelot Hogben as the new Professor of Social Biology at the University of London in 1930, in which he heralded a new sense of responsibility in universities; HGW, introduction, *Economica*, Feb 1931, pp. 1–4. Hogben's talk was entitled 'The Foundation of Social Biology', and is also worth reading; *Nature*, 1 Nov 1930, pp. 694–5, 705–6, on the Wells talk and Hogben's speech. At the World Union of Freethinkers Conference in London, 9–13 Sept 1938, Wells spoke at the dinner on 12 Sept; see *Proceedings* (London 1939), 98–9. He discussed racial laws in South Africa, and said that once

Hitler was disposed of, it was up to his audience to create a truly free world: 'Why are we not getting a greater freedom ready for the world? Why are we always being anti-Nazi, anti-this, and anti-that and never exerting outselves to prepare for that wonderful community which must ensue?' See also his address introducing Eduard Beneš at Foyles' in Dec 1939, in E. Beneš, *Building a New Europe* (London 1939), 5–9. Wells reviewed the tragic history of Czechoslovakia since 1919, and his meetings with Beneš on these matters (Wells had sponsored his visits after Munich, and helped to arrange his exile in England). He said Beneš was not a foreigner, but a representative of world statesmanship to come, once the 'present stress and confusions are reorganized and unified'. Beneš ended his talk with 'Truth prevails'. On Beneš see HGW to *The Times*, 6 Oct 1938; to *Guardian, Telegraph, NChron*, 1 Nov 1938; J.M. Keynes to HGW, 12 Oct 1938; J. Huxley to HGW, Oct 1938, will sign. G. Murray to HGW, 22 Oct 1938, 'splendid letter' and will sign the letter of 'indignant sympathy' for Beneš.

10   HGW, 'H.G. Wells Attacks the Labour Party', *NChron*, 1 Aug 1932; G. E. C. Catlin to HGW, 22 Oct 1932, setting up a lunch to comment on H. N. Brailsford's Constitution for Socialist Leagues, which he enclosed. HGW, *DHerald*, 5 Dec 1932; G. D. H. Cole, 'Mr Wells's Creed', *DAmerican* (N.Y.), 4 Dec 1932: he endorsed it completely; *DAmerican*, 7, 8, 9 Dec, many letters endorsing it, but some also thought this was a call for Christianity; also 10, 13 Dec 1932. Wells received $250 from New York for the piece, which was entitled at various times, 'The Strategy of Progressive World Effort', 'The Common Objectives of Progressive World Effort'.

11   HGW to Lord Allen of Hurtwood (founder, with Bertrand Russell, of a No Conscription League), 17 Dec 1932, and another undated, ?9 Oct 1934. HGW, 'Keeping the Peace: A World Consortium', *The Times*, 28 Apr 1936, reprinted in a pamphlet by the Trustees for Freedom (London 1936), and in Swedish, as *Sla Vakt-om Freden*, by Oral Homstroms Farlag (Stockholm 1936). J. Chambrun to HGW, 25 Nov, 12 Dec 1932. C. E. M. Joad, ed., *Manifesto* (London 1934); on this book and its origin, J. Huxley to HGW, 6 Feb 1936. *The Next Five Years* (London 1936); earlier manifestos were dated Feb, July 1934. Wells endorsed the work. For a comment on the group and its impact see the marvellous book, Paul Addison, *The Road to 1945* (London 1975). The first conference of this group was 18 Oct 1930. Wells sent a supporting letter and they made him a vice-president. He signed the National Peace Petition in 1938.

12   HGW to Gerald Bailey (National Peace Council), 4 Oct 1934; their letter to a large group of addressees signed by Cust, Henry Chelmsford, G. P. Gooch, Walter Layton, Lords Lytton and Ponsonby, F. W. Norwood, HGW, 3 Dec 1934; MCW to Bailey, 22 Oct 1934, 19 June 1936. HGW, 'My Plan for World Peace', *DHerald*, 30 Nov 1934 (abridged version); see Ritchie Calder to HGW, 28 Nov 1934, on the difficulty of cutting it to 1,800 words. Wells actually helped in the abridgement then. See HGW, 'Stresa, Locarno, Versailles . . . they all, in the end, mean Disarmament', *SChron*, 14 Apr 1935; HGW, 'Arms and the World State', *Peace*, vol. II, no. 9 (Dec 1934), pp. 6, 8–9; HGW, 'Disarmament and How', *American*, May 1935.

13   F. S. Marvin, ed., *The Evolution of World Peace* (London 1920, 1933). On Geneva, APW to HGW, 24 Aug 1924 (Wells was in Geneva from 30 Aug to 12 Sept 1930); K. Zilliacus to HGW, 26 Sept 1928; HGW to Zilliacus, 3 Oct 1928. Maxwell Garrett to HGW, 11, 23 Nov 1930, and others throughout the 1930s on peace strategies. Advisory Committee for Wales (League of Nations Union), *The Teaching of Geography in Relation to the Community* (Cambridge 1933), 44–5; part of *The Way to World Peace* is reprinted with Wells's blessing. *No More War*: 'Mr H.G. Wells on the Enemy in Our Schools', vol. IX, no. 10 (Dec 1929); Leah Manning, 'History Text-Books and Peace', vol. IX, no. 11, urges people to read the *Outline of History*; C. A. Smith, 'History Teaching — Another View', vol. X, no. 1, says university syllabi are the problem; 'D', 'Way to Peace', vol. X, no. 2 (Apr 1930), reviews Wells's peace pamphlets: 'In them

[children] we must pin our faith. To their correct training we must bend all our energies'. HGW, 'H. G. Wells Throws Down the Gauntlet', *New World* (the follow-up journal to *No More War*), vol. I, no. 7 (Nov 1930), report of a speech to peace propagandists on 18 Oct 1930.

14 These pieces were read at the Oxford University Liberal Club on 4 Mar 1938, and were printed in *Liberty*, 5 Mar, 6, 30 Apr 1938, and in the *Star*, 11, 22 Apr, 3 May 1938, under the general title 'The Future of Liberalism'. Their subtitles were 'Signpost to Sanity', 'A Working Creed', and 'The Future of Liberalism'. Ritchie Calder to HGW, 28 Jan 1938, calling nationalism a form of constipation 'of a not yet properly digested mass of material'. The earliest form of this came from two weekends of discussion with Lord Esher. See HGW to Esher, 31 Oct, 2 Nov 1935, enc. 'A Memorandum on Liberal Principles and Policy', 7 pp. Wells specifically ties these matters together as I have done in his first letter to Esher.

15 HGW to Ritchie Calder, 20 Sept 1935, on margin of the letter. J. R. Steele (for Pinker) to HGW, 29, 31 Mar 1933; Steele (for *Reader's Digest*) to HGW, 31 Aug 1937 (the *Digest* published the *Star*);C.W. Ferguson to JBP, 11 Jan 1938, asking for 300 words ($200); F. Ralph Pinker to HGW, 21, 24 Jan, 14 Mar (HGW to Pinker, 11 Mar), 28 Apr, 11 May 1938 (Wells refused to rewrite the piece again and stopped the correspondence). His previous experience with the *Digest* over rewriting his squib on 'Six Greatest Men in History', which was used, also put him off this market. J. Chambrun to HGW, 26 Dec 1935, 23 Feb 1936; *Reader's Digest*, Mar, Apr 1936. Philip Jordan to HGW, 28 Jan 1938 (on happiness); to HGW, 30 June 1938 (in Wells's hand, response on the letter), 6 July 1938, 8, 25 July 1938 (on GBS offer); HGW to APW, 10 June 1938; Gerald Barry to HGW, 5 June 1938 (with Wells's response) on the Prime Minister piece; APW to MCW, 30 Oct 1936.

16 'The Man Who Let The World Down', *SChron*, 6 Sept 1936. HGW to V. Gollancz, 24 Dec 1930, and his preface, p. 13, to Victor LeFebure, *Scientific Disarmament* (London 1931). 'What Next?', *SChron*, 11 Oct 1936, also appeared in *MPost*, 11 June 1936, and in *Collier's*, as well as in South African newspapers. 'The Next War', *SChron*, 19, 26 July 1936, also in *Service in Life and Work*, vol. V, no. 19 (Autumn 1936), and *Collier's*, 4 July 1936. 'The Mobbing of Mrs Simpson', Hearst press in USA, 7 Dec 1936, and, much rewritten, in *SReferee*, 20 Dec 1936, as 'The Church Militant and Rampant'; 'The Map of Europe — 1949', *SChron*, 22 Jan 1939, also in *Liberty*, Jan 1939. HGW to *The Times*, 19 May 1936, on his opposition to League of Nations (a blind alley); 'The War Twenty Years After: How to Bring Peace on Earth', *Liberty*, 29 Dec 1934, also in *World War*, 8 Nov 1934. 'In Time of Peace, Prepare for War', *This Week*, 6 Nov 1938, and, in a different version, *Liberty*, 16 Sept 1938: a good deal of correspondence on this piece, as it was cut by *This Week*, and then partially restored.

17 'The New Phase of Human Affairs', *John o'London's*, 6 Oct 1934, also in *American*, Aug 1934 (they paid him $1,125 for the piece). J. Chambrun to HGW, 9 Apr, 7 Dec 1934. *Author*: 'Freedom of Expression', Summer 1934; 'Detrimental Wrappers and Blurbs and Advertisements', Christmas 1934 (read in proofs dated 25, 26 May 1934). 'Crystal Gazing: 1932 — What Does the Coming Year Hold for All of Us?', *Nash's Magazine*, Jan 1932. On 30 June 1934, George Catlin gave a dinner for HGW, Ernst Toller, Vernon Bartlett and Stephen Kinghall after the death of Röhm and other early Nazis. Wells held the audience spellbound with analogies of Rome, the fall of the Empire, and the current period. HGW thought the Romans at the time of Hannibal as complacent as the west in 1934. Sir George Catlin, *For God's Sake, Go!* (Gerrards Cross 1972), 221.

18 'The World Fifty Years Hence', *John o'London's*, 17 Oct 1931; *Liberty*, 17 Oct 1931. 'Ask for Your Schools and See that You Get them', *NChron*, 30 Dec 1937. 'Health in The Future', *DMail*, 12 Dec 1933, also in *Pictorial Review*, Jan 1934. 'The Sort of Man Your Grandson May Be', *DMail*, 13 Dec 1933: here he predicted that the children of

1983 would be brought up by 'professional educationists' to develop mind and body under doctors' supervision. Mothers would receive special training and specialists would be available for any problems or needs. 'Every-Day Life in 1988', *Star*, 17 Jan 1938: he foresaw a great war menace, but communities 'school-centred', with plastics as very important in life, but he doubted that contentment would be prevalent. 'The World Today — And Tomorrow?' *SChron*, 3 Apr 1938: 'The obstinacy of man is great, but the forces that grip him are greater, and in the end, after I know not what wars, struggles, and afflictions, this is the road along which he will go.'

19 *SChron*, 14, 28 June 1936. On the first day of the poll, five churchmen responded with written pieces to set up the questions.

20 MCW to APW, 5, 21 May 1936. *SChron*, 19, 26 July 1936. 'The Drift to War', and 'The World Drifting to Future War' (depending on where one reads it), *Collier's*, 4 July 1936, and *Science in Life and Work*, vol. V, no. 19 (Autumn 1936). This also appeared in another, slightly different, form in *Nineteenth Century*. 'After Spain — What?', *SChron*, 12 June 1938, also in *Liberty*, ? Apr 1938. 'The Dangerous Stratum', *SChron*, 5 Mar 1939, also in *Liberty*, 4 Mar 1939. 'The International Situation', *British Australian and New Zealander*, 5 Oct 1938 (on Czechoslovakia), signed by large numbers of people. On signing a letter on the bombing of civilians, published in *NChron*, W. T. Layton to HGW, 3 Feb 1938. His speech to China Society Dinner, mid-1935, was printed in several Chinese newspapers; and his message to China, sent by Shelley Wang, was printed in *China Times*, 16 Jan 1939. A clipping, in Chinese, is at Illinois. *DHerald*, 18 May 1939, a letter, also signed by Paul Robeson and D. N. Pritt, urging people not to forget the Scottsboro boys in all these other horrors; an address was given for funds.

21 *Foreign Affairs*, vol. XIII, no. 4 (July 1935), pp. 595-9.

22 The first US visit was private, although he did meet FDR. See 'The Place of Franklin Roosevelt in History', *Liberty*, ? Nov 1933, also in *John o'London's*, Nov 1934, and abstracted in *Reader's Digest*, Dec 1934. FDR wrote to HGW upon reading the piece, congratulating him and inviting him to come again: FDR to HGW, 4 Dec 1933. The visit had come about through an abortive US lecture tour, and Wells was looking out and planning for such a tour later. See J. Chambrun to MCW, 2 Dec 1932, with Wells's comments on letter. When he came back in 1933 he witnessed the sinking of the Nantucket lightship and wrote to the press about the event, but the letter was not published; Wells said that there had been several near-misses in recent years and called for an inquiry as a guide to joint efforts in the future: HGW to *The Times*, 25 May 1934. G. Dawson to HGW, 27 May 1934.

23 J. Chambrun to MCW, 7, 10 Mar 1935. For a review of the work, *The New America* (London 1935), see *Les Annales politiques at littéraires*, 10 Aug 1935, under the title 'L' Amérique de Roosevelt jugée par Wells'. Wells told one American that there was little prospect of socialism in the US of the mid-'30s and urged his reader to declare his movement a non-party one, which might work. HGW to Edward Kelly, undated draft, early '30s. 'Get Together With the USA', *SChron*, 19 Dec 1937, is a rehash of his views in *Foreign Affairs*. J. Chambrun to HGW, 19, 21 Feb 1935; telegram, HGW to J. Chambrun, 16 Feb 1935, specifies the details. *Nature*, 14 Sept 1935, reviewed the book which they called 'brilliant'.

24 I. Maisky to HGW, 27 Sept 1930 (from Helsinki). Maisky provided some material for *The Work, Wealth and Happiness of Mankind*, which Wells sent him with a very friendly inscription. Maisky to HGW, 29 Oct 1932. *The New Russia* (London 1931) reprints the BBC talks; HGW, 'Summing Up', pp. 110–26.

25 MCW to APW, 31 July 1934; I. Maisky to HGW, 28 Dec 1932, 13 Mar, 7, 14, 18, 21 Apr, 29 June (enclosing his speech, which is in the Wells papers), 7 July, 11 Aug 1934. Wells sent a message to the Committee of Russian Writers who had urged him to attend a meeting, although he could not: HGW to Committee, *c*. July 1934 (in draft). Gerald Barry to HGW, 30 May, 19 June 1934; Wells refused to write an article for the

Chronicle (note on the second letter, saying, 'No. I want to go to Moscow just as I went to Washington — to think about it afterward'). Beatrice Webb had urged Wells to go and observe, after they had recently returned, B. Webb to HGW, 21 Oct 1932 (Webb *Letters* III. 380–1).

26 *Stalin – Wells Talk* (London 1934) has remained as an interesting document of the between-the-wars period, and is still reprinted from time to time, although only the Stalin–Wells part usually now appears. (The most recent reprint I have seen, for instance, was published by the Bangladesh Communist Party, and appeared in English from Calcutta.) Those who wish to read the entire and highly repetitive correspondence should look at the *New Statesman*, beginning with the issue of 27 Sept 1934. Jan Masaryk (the Czech minister) gave a party when Wells returned at which Shaw, Wells, Bertrand Russell, and Frank Swinnerton discussed their various trips to the USSR, which may have led to the exchange in the press. See Hart-Davis, *Hugh Walpole*, 265–6, for an account.

27 HGW to the Webbs, mid-Jan 1936, 27 July 1937; B. Webb to HGW, 17 Jan 1936 (Webb *Letters* III. 410); Ralph Deakin to HGW, 10 Feb 1937, in response to his of 6 Feb; I. Maisky to HGW, 15 Mar 1938 (asking for copies of the Gorky letters for a volume to be printed. B. Webb to HGW, May 1937, on the Moscow trials (Webb *Letters* III. 419–20); Wells had asked for their opinion. Souvenir programme, 'Russia Today' meeting, 6 Nov 1938, at Earl's Court. Wells signed, with 26 others (and may have drafted), the letter which appears in this programme, 'A Common Front with the Soviet Union for Peace'. On the Shaw–Wells letters in the *New Statesman*, see HGW to GBS, 30 Oct 1934, after he had read Shaw's comments in proof. He told Shaw that he had a sister in Odette Keun, then slanging him in *Time and Tide*, and urged them to get together before it was too late. HGW to Charlotte Shaw, 28 Nov 1934, saying that the pamphlet had to come out, in order to square the accounts with GBS, although he did not like to hurt her feelings.

28 In addition to the book *The Anatomy of Frustration* (London: Cresset Press 1936), which was serialized in the *Spectator*, as well as *Harper's*, one is referred to 'An Article by H.G. Wells', *SChron*, 3 Oct 1937. Jewish groups were angry with him, which led to several exchanges; see HGW to G. Ellis, 25 June 1936; to *Jewish Chronicle*, 10 July 1938, with quotes from the book; the magazine ended the controversy with an apology of sorts: see 22 July 1938. Also see HGW, 'Palestine in Proportion', *Current History*, Jan 1938, which was the reason for the outburst against him. On the book and its serializations, see J. Chambrun to MCW, 10 Dec 1935. *Harper's* paid $1,000 for their bits and pieces: telegram, HGW to Chambrun, 22 Jan 1936. They appeared in Apr, May, June 1936. Wells sent presentation copies to B. Russell, Joad, RAG, Allen of Hurtford, Desmond MacCarthy, Wickham Steed, and others; see HGW to Cresset Press, 31 Aug 1936. F. Swinnerton told him it should be required reading for everyone, 20 Oct 1936. B. Webb was a bit more analytical, as she told her diary that the book was 'too bombastic'. However, see B. Webb to HGW, 20 Oct 1930, in which she took him to task, saying that it was too autobiographical and he should not have said it all. 'You have ranged throughout the world, living the life you liked, and doing the work you intended to do, amid multitudinous applause. You chose to fly in the air viewing the world, bombing what you did not like, and recording what you approve of.' She compared that to their own 'pedestrian life of toil, without frustration ... However, you are a genius, and on the whole on the side of the angels. Mind, I say "on the whole!" — in some ways you have combined the incompatibles', was her comment.

Chapter 13

1 Director of Education to HGW, 25 Mar 1926; MCW to J.L. Stobbart, 29 Mar 1926; Lance de Sieveking to HGW, 19 Oct 1925, 14 Dec 1926, 15, 31 Mar, 5, 14 May 1927. All these citations are from material in the BBC written archives at Caversham Park,

Reading, most of it in Box 910: file 1 (1925–33) and file 2 (1934–46). I am indebted to the BBC and to the persons who kindly guided me through the archive when I worked there in the summer of 1976. In subsequent citations from BBC material I give only the date, sender, and addressee, as with other correspondence, citing internal memoranda as well where relevant.

2 *Hilda Matheson* (Letchworth, Herts. 1941, a privately printed memorial volume): HGW's comment, 56–7. Matheson's book, *Broadcasting* (London 1933), in the Home University Library series, esp. chs. 3, 'Living Speech', 4, 'Public Opinion', and 9, 'Broadcasting and the State', gives her views very well. On Wells, the BBC, and censorship, also see a personal memoir by Lance Sieveking, *The Eye of the Beholder* (London 1957), 224–35.

3 H. Matheson to HGW, 14, 19 June 1929; HGW to Matheson, 25 June 1929 (he apparently telephoned her to respond initially). BBC internal memo, early June 1929, on his voice qualities, which they feared. *DTel*, 25 June 1929, which thought it terrible that he should be given air time. BBC memo, 28 June 1929, on preparations. Eileen Power to HGW, 15 June 1929. On censorship, *DNews*, 6 July 1929, which welcomed the breakthrough.

4 BBC memo, 10 June 1929. Eileen Power to BBC, 6 July 1929. HGW's talk, 'World Peace', appeared in the *Listener*, 17 July 1929, with a photograph of Wells at the microphone. The talk has since been reprinted at least once by the *Listener*, as it was an important breakthrough for them as well.

5 There were really very few complaints. The question, of course, is how many people had wireless sets in July 1929. See Harry Pye Croft to the Earl of Clarendon, 13 July 1929, in BBC files, and a few others. BBC memo, L. Sieveking, *c.* July 1929, saying that, although some wanted a disclaimer, he was opposed to it.

6 *Yorkshire Post*, 13 July 1929; *Observer*, 14 July 1929 (in BBC archives, Box 3A; Programmes: Collected Articles, 1929). *Listener*, 17 July 1929: leader, 'Mr Wells and Wireless'; V. Bartlett's talk, p. 85. The correspondence lasted until 2 Oct 1929. On the publication by Benn see APW to HGW, 14, 16 July, 1, 28 Aug 1929. Wells signed a contract on 6 Sept 1929. He had a talk with the Bishop of Liverpool, then nominal editor of Benn's Affirmations Series, in which the pamphlet appeared. He modified the text considerably, apparently on the galleys, after the BA meeting at which Sir T.H. Holland spoke on the same subject. Wells received 1¼*d.* a copy on the first 10,000 sold; and 1½*d.* a copy thereafter.

7 H. Matheson to HGW, 16, 18 Sept 1929; to Lady Colefax, 10 Oct 1929; to HGW, 21 Oct 1929 (the day of the broadcast). Lydia Keynes to H. Matheson, 15 Oct 1929. *DHerald* to HGW, 22 Oct 1929 (on the 'whacked' remark). HGW, 'Points of View – IV', *Listener*, 30 Oct 1929. The magazine version differs somewhat from the talk as given; the broadcast text appears (with others of his) on Film T638, in the BBC archives.

8 H. Matheson to HGW, 22 Oct; HGW to Matheson, 21 Nov; Matheson to HGW, 6, 7 Nov, all 1929. For some press comment, mostly summarizing HGW's talk, *DTel*, *Manchester Guardian*, both 22 Nov 1929; the letter termed his opinions 'provocative and interesting'. Wells broadcast a similar talk on the American CBS network on 2 Nov 1930, which must have been one of the earliest short-wave talks. CBS paid him $500 (£102. 17*s.* 7*d.*) for the talk.

9 R.J.C. Howgill to BBC Director of Programmes (D.P.), 20 Sept 1927; to HGW, 21 Sept 1927. BBC to MCW, 5 Apr 1934; MCW to H. Matheson, 21 June 1934, refusing 'Man Who Could Work Miracles'. BBC memos, 25 July, 3, 5 Sept 1934. MCW to H. Matheson, 26 Sept 1934.

10 BBC Director General (D.G.) memo, 24 June 1931; Mr Fielden to D.G., early July 1931; L. A. Fielden to D.P., 20 May 1931. H. Matheson to HGW, 27 May 1931; HGW to 'Hilda', postcard 1 June 1931 (from Grasse); H. Matheson to HGW, 22 June 1931. Their lunch was 3 July; H. Matheson to HGW, 10 July 1931 (Wells was on a diet

and concerned about what he should eat); the talk was 13 July 1931. Wells met the Director General on 5 Aug to discuss programming in general; HGW to H. Matheson, 6 Aug. The rebroadcast was later; HGW (secretary) to L. Fielden, 15 Sept 1931. *Yorkshire Post*, 18 July 1931; *Star*, 14 July 1931. HGW, 'Russia and the World', *Listener*, 22 July 1931.

11   H. Matheson to HGW, 17, 30 Sept 1931; HGW to Matheson, 25 Sept 1931. The talk appeared in the *Listener*, 30 Sept 1931. Arthur Salter to HGW, 31 July 1931; to H. Matheson, 31 July 1931. *EStandard, DDispatch, DTel*, all 29 Sept 1931 (the latter basically reprinted the talk). *Observer*, 4 Oct 1931; *S Times*, 22 Nov 1931: an interview, which sounds as though HGW had broadcast in the US, although he had done so only on short wave, as far as I can tell. Perhaps he was referring to that event, with US reporters present; the fact that it was one of the first times anyone had spoken on short-wave radio from a prepared script, would have accounted for the attention.

12   Sir John Reith to HGW, 18 Mar 1932; HGW to Reith, 22 Mar 1932, refusing 'Rungs of Ladder' idea. Wells said, 'I'm not very attracted to the "early struggle" business. I never wanted to get on. Mostly I wanted to get out of disagreeable things.' BBC internal memo, D.P. to D.T., 4 July 1932. C.J. Siepmann to HGW, 31 Oct 1932; L. Fielden to HGW, 14 Nov 1932, 3 May 1933. A Wells interview, on radio and how it can be abused, appears in *DTel*, 21 Nov 1932. HGW, 'Wanted – Professors of Foresight', *Listener*, 23 Nov 1932; some of this talk was rebroadcast early in Jan 1933, and reprinted in the *Listener*. HGW to *Listener*, 15 Jan 1933.

13   HGW, 'Whither Britain?', *Listener*, 10 Jan 1934. Reviews appeared in *The Times* and the *Star*, both 10 Jan 1934, the first a straightforward account, the second very favourable. I. Maisky to HGW, 12 Dec 1934, please send me a copy, and Wells did. BBC to HGW, 13 Oct 1933. HGW to BBC, 20 Dec 1933. MCW to HGW, 27 Jan 1934 (on receipt of the Victor recording). From this time on some of Wells's BBC talks are on disc, or tape, and may be listened to in the archives.

14   C. A. Siepmann to HGW, 30 Oct 1934; MCW to Siepmann, 2 Nov 1934, 28 Feb 1935. BBC to HGW, 12 June 1935; MCW to Siepmann, 14 June 1935; Siepmann to HGW, 19 June 1935; BBC to HGW, 20 Aug 1935; MCW to BBC, 29 Aug 1935; BBC to HGW, 4, 20 Sept 1935; MCW to M.D. Spicer, 21 Sept 1935. BBC internal memo to Mrs M. Adams and Mr Rose-Troup, 1 Oct 1935; Mary Adams to HGW, 3 Oct 1935; HGW to Mrs Adams, 3, 4 Oct 1935. HGW, 'I Know a Man: Thomas Henry Huxley', *Listener*, 9 Oct 1935.

15   M. Adams to HGW, 10 Jan 1936; MCW to Adams, 16 Jan 1936. Director of School Broadcasts to HGW, 21 Aug 1936 (he even used Hilda Matheson's name to Wells). Lucienne Southgate (secretary) to Mary Somerville, 24 Aug 1936: 'Too busy at present.' C.V. Salmon to HGW, 12, 15 Mar 1937; HGW to Salmon, 17 Mar 1937 (although he did suggest Frank Swinnerton as a possibility).

16   BBC D.G. to HGW, 27 July 1937; MCW to D.G., 29 July 1937. BBC internal memo, J. M. Rose-Troup (A.D.P.A.) to C(P.), 5 Aug 1937; C.A.S. to MCW, 6 Aug 1937. The broadcast was aired several times from 2 Nov 1937 to 25 Jan 1938. L. Southgate to C. G. Groves, 10 Aug 1937; HGW to C. G. Groves, 10 Aug 1937. John Pringle to HGW, 25 Nov 1937; MCW to Pringle, 26 Nov 1937. HGW, 'As I See It: The English Speaking World', *Listener*, 22 Dec 1937.

17   MCW to H. Mais, 24 Sept 1935. New Zealand Broadcasting Board to HGW, 31 Aug 1935; BBC to MCW, 26 Sept 1937; H. Mais to MCW, 26, 27 Sept 1937; MCW to H. Mais, 28 Sept 1937. M. T. Candler to MCW, 23 Sept 1937; MCW to M.T. Candler, 24 Sept 1937, 25 Jan 1943. R. Maconachie (?) to D.T., 14 Feb 1939. MCW to H. Marr, 18 Sept 1939 (his price went to 25 gns.), 1 Feb 1940. BBC memo, Miss Fields (schools) to Programme Controller, 5 Feb 1940; H. Marr to MCW, 7 Feb 1940.

18   MCW to M. T. Candler, 13 Feb 1941; to Lance Sieveking, 13 Sept 1941 (his story of the script is in his memoirs, *The Eye of the Beholder* [1957]). MCW to J. E. M. Waters, 10

Feb 1941; BBC to MCW, 10 Feb 1941. M. T. Candler to HGW, 1 Mar 1941; to MCW, 2 Sept 1941. HGW to BBC, 24 July 1942 ('no change' is a note from telephone conversation at bottom of letter). BBC to MCW, 4 July 1944; MCW to S. McGrath, 6 July 1944; BBC to MCW, 14 Aug 1944; MCW to McGrath, 16 Aug 1944.

19   HGW to B. Ifor Evans, 3 Feb 1936.

20   A Pathé version of *The Invisible Man* appeared in France in 1909. HGW, *The King Who Was a King* (London 1929), introductory chapter, 'The Development of the Film'. APW to ACRW, 30 July, 18 Nov 1919; to HGW, 7 (two), 12, 22, 28, 31 Jan, 3 Feb 1920. Interview and account of the Savoy visit, by 'H.V.M.', *EStandard*, 4 Nov 1920. Memo, MCW to APW, Motion Picture Rights to Wells's books, as of 9 Feb 1933. Symposium, 'The Novelist and the Film', *John o'London's*, 4 Aug 1923, HGW's contribution, p. 578 (quoted here). APW to HGW, 27, 31 Oct, 5 Dec (with HGW comments) 1930, on an infringement of rights. APW to MCW, 28 Sept 1933, can we film H.G. for a proposed cinemagazine? The early history of Wells's interest in film and his collaboration with Robert Paul, a pioneer cinematographer, is well told in Terry Ramsaye, *A Million and One Nights: A History of the Motion Picture* (New York 1926, repr. 1964), 152–62; their original patent for *The Time Machine*, 155–7.

21   HGW to APW, 11 Sept 1928; APW to HGW, 18, 27 Sept, 3 Oct, 23, 29 Nov, 28 Dec 1928; 4, 9, 11 (HGW comment on this letter), 21, 24 Jan 1929. HGW to APW, 28 Nov 1928 on the *DExpress* squib about the book. Vernon Clancey, 'Flicks Politics', *Realist*, vol. I, no 2 (May 1929). HGW, 'Predicts the Film of the Future', *Literary Digest*, 25 May 1929. Proofs of Benn's advertisements for the book: 'A Flash of Genius from H. G. Wells.' Frank Wells was important in HGW's developing interest in film; he talked of producing a film version of *Kipps*. HGW to APW, 10 Feb 1933.

22   MCW to Nelson Doubleday, 27 Sept 1932, announcing the possible book on which HGW was hard at work. APW to HGW, 10 Feb 1933; MCW (HGW) to APW, 4 Apr 1933; HGW to APW, 5 May 1933; MCW to APW, 21, 27 June 1933, enclosing some pamphlets on arms trade: Sgt. Maj. Franklin, 'A Suppressed Speech', and the Bishop of Hereford, 'The Secret International'. The second letter, dictated by HGW, indicates his proposed changes to meet legal complaints. HGW to L. Southgate, postcard, 12 May 1933, announcing new change in title, to final form. APW to MCW, 26 Apr, 2, 12, 18 May 1933. Benns paid 3,300 gns. as an advance. Twelve instalments of extracts, *SExpress*, 25 June–10 Sept 1933, which also appeared in *NY American* (repeated Dec 1933). Excerpts also appeared elsewhere. See *Education*, 25 Oct 1935, for an amusing correspondence.

23   HGW to APW, 29 Jan 1934, describes the early meetings with Korda at Bournemouth, where HGW was staying, having given up Lou Pidou after his split with Odette Keun. HGW wanted an inexpensive illustrated edition of the book, using stills from the film, published as a tie-in with the film, but this was later abandoned. Ritchie Calder to HGW, 25 Oct, 11, 19 Nov 1933, on a review of the book, which led to tea and a dinner. R. Calder was beginning to write weekly articles on science for the *DHerald*, on which HGW offered advice and much help: 24 June 1935, and HGW note on letter offering to take R. Calder on the set. Ritchie Calder, 'H.G. Wells's Amazing New World', *DHerald*, 8 July 1935, which is essentially a long interview with Wells about his ideas on film, and especially this one. Wells said in the interview, 'I must give people their money's worth – reach their sense through their senses, give them spectacles, give them action, give them the drama of human lives.' APW to HGW, 7 Mar, 12 Apr, 4 July 1935. Bliss and Wells spent three days together at the end of Sept 1934. The composer was not very tolerant either of actors or directors: Bliss to HGW, 24 Oct 1934; HGW to Bliss, 13 Apr, 29 June, 5 Sept, 17 Oct 1934, 5 Sept 1935. On music and films, also see HGW to Ernest Bloch, 27 Sept 1935; they later discussed a true film opera, but not one with Jewish or nationalistic overtones, as Bloch had originally wanted. See HGW to Bloch, 6 Nov 1935. Sir Cedric Hardwicke, also in the film, discussed his ideas of acting in such films (but not in this one), in *Let's*

Pretend (London 1938), while Raymond Massey told his version, not very complimentary to HGW, or Korda, in *A Hundred Different Lives* (Toronto 1979), 91–4. Massey thought the film powerful, but not thanks to HGW or Korda, which is an odd view, and different from the one expressed in Massey's letter to HGW, 28 Aug 1935, in which he agreed to redo a scene or two to meet HGW's needs, while thanking him for his help and comment. For a novel probably based in part on the film, see Nevil Shute, *What Became of the Corbetts?* (London 1938).

24 HGW, *SChron*, 23 Feb 1936, a long interview. Jacques Chambrun to HGW, 9 Aug 1935, on *Things to Come* in *This Week*, 27 Sept–29 Oct 1935. HGW received $3,000 for the pieces. MCW (HGW) to Drama Critic, *The Times*, 4 June 1936, which printed a college-magazine jape at the film, and later retracted its mistake. HGW to MCW, 6 Aug 1935, on veto of a photoplay edition. HGW to MCW, 31 Oct 1935, on *Architectural Review* reprinting an extract. The rights reverted to HGW and this is how *This Week* obtained them; see MCW to APW, 24 Jan 1936. *Nature*, 11 Jan 1936, reviewed the script, and covered the film début, 19 Feb 1936: 'Marvellous.' The best review of the work in its own time was by Graham Greene, *Spectator*, 28 Feb 1936, repr. *The Pleasure Dome* (1972). Wells was pleased with Greene's attention: HGW to G. Greene, 4 Sept 1936, although they quarrelled later over the virgin birth: HGW to Greene, 9 Mar 1940; MCW to Greene, 6 Mar 1940.

25 APW to HGW, 9 Aug 1932: *Man Who Could Work Miracles* sold to *Park Drive Magazine*, Oct 1932 (I have never seen this magazine). Jacques Chambrun to HGW, telegram, 3 Aug 1935, on *Nash's Magazine* publication of the film version (Dec 1935 or Jan 1936). MCW to APW, 27 May (on the film book of *The New Faust*, and *The Food of the Gods* – which last, if written, never appeared as far as I can determine), 23 June 1936. MCW to APW, 25 Jan 1936, Manchester papers also printed part of it; APW to MCW, 31 Jan 1936, also a Newcastle paper. Peter (Ritchie) Calder to HGW, 3 July 1935, on Wellsian plans. Review by Graham Greene, *Spectator*, 4 Sept 1936, also repr. in *The Pleasure Dome*. *Nature*, 6 June 1936. George Sanders also appeared in this film.

26 Olaf Stapledon to HGW, 24 Apr 1936; FAS to HGW, 14 May 1936; George Orwell, 'The Male Byronic', *Tribune*, 21 June 1940. For an example of HGW's influence in this film see Ritchie Calder, 'It Happened in 1963', *DHerald*, 15–29 Jan 1938: HGW had a considerable role in this predictive piece.

27 Memo, MCW to HGW, 19 Feb 1937, on telephone conversations on *Tono-Bungay*. On *War of the Worlds* and Wells's reaction, see above, ch. 3. Also see *DExpress*, 1 Nov 1938 (some English listeners heard the broadcast through a freak of skip distance); *Manchester Guardian*, *The Times*, *DTel*, 1, 2 Nov 1938. H.G. Wells and Orson Welles were in negotiation over the piece when the latter's broadcast went out, and eventually (within two weeks) Wells received his payment; Kathryn Chambrun to MCW, 11 Nov 1938; contract dated 20 Oct 1938. So much interest came from the panicked reaction to the Welles radio production that the *SChron* printed a serialized version of *War of the Worlds*, with a subhead, 'The Story That Scared America', 6, 13, 20, 27 Nov 1938. J. Chambrun to MCW, 30 Sept, telegram, 19 Oct 1938; telegram to HGW, 31 Oct 1938; to MCW, 1, 2, 3, 4 Nov 1938. The production was delayed in fact because of world affairs. HGW later congratulated Orson Welles on his remarkable film, *Citizen Kane*; see HGW to O. Welles, cablegram, *c.* 1941 (Indiana).

28 HGW to Jonathan Cape, 8 Oct 1938. In this letter HGW also proposes a new journal like the *English Review* to try out new techniques and ideas. HGW to D. Cohen (Cresset Press), 4 June 1936. MCW to APW, 22 July 1937: this is an excellent example, although nearly illegible now, of how HGW conducted his correspondence. He wrote out his ideas by hand, Marjorie then translated them into a letter, which he proofed before she sent it. Occasionally, if he were in the Mediterranean, she read the draft over the telephone, or simply signed it and sent it on. But normally, as I have said, he had an active part in all but the most mundane correspondence.

29 Ada Galsworthy to HGW, 3 Dec 1936. APW to HGW, 3 Dec 1936. J.B. Priestley's

encounters with Alexander Korda and potential film-making. They had lunch the following week to discuss literature in general. Wells sent a copy of *The Croquet Player* to Eleanor Roosevelt, and promised her *Star Begotten*; HGW to Eleanor Roosevelt, 2 Feb 1937.

30   APW to MCW, 26 Feb 1937 (although apparently HGW sold the serial rights to *Star Begotten* while Watt was still negotiating); MCW to APW, 6 Mar 1937; APW to MCW, 2, 9 Apr 1937; alternative titles are given in MCW to Chatto & Windus, 18 Feb 1937. (There was later some talk of re-issuing all four short novels in a single volume: Chatto & Windus to HGW, Apr 1944.) Winston Churchill to HGW, 4 July 1937. J.B.S. Haldane's review, *Nature*, 31 July 1937. FAS to HGW, 3 July 1937 (review in *Observer*). Olaf Stapledon to HGW, 23 June 1937 (review in *London Mercury*). *Tribune*, 11 July 1937. S. Olivier to HGW, 29 May 1937; Olivier was also rereading *Mr Polly*.

31   MCW to APW, 26 Aug 1937. HGW wanted the book published as a pamphlet with the cover in the two blues. It appeared only in boards, however. Olaf Stapledon to HGW, 12 Dec 1937; Ernest Barker to HGW, 29 Nov 1937. *Tribune*, 23 Dec 1937. APW to MCW, 1 Sept, 30 Oct 1939, 8 Mar 1940. *Nature*, 12 Feb 1937: 'stimulating, provocative and entertaining as ever'.

32   J. Chambrun to HGW, 2 Sept 1937: HGW's comments on letter; Chambrun to MCW, 4 Sept 1937, rejecting the *Harper's* offer ($5,000) on the grounds that the cuts were too severe. APW to MCW, 10 Feb 1938, on *SReferee* offer. Olaf Stapledon to HGW, 3 Apr 1938. W. Horrabin's review, *Tribune*, 4 Feb 1938, produced some letters in response, mostly on the nature of state socialism, as a possible transitional step.

Chapter 14

1   HGW to Robert C. Galkins, 3 Mar 1934.

2   H. G. Wells Society, *Newsletter*: June 1934, Nov 1934, Feb 1935 (Shaw became a member), Sept 1935 (Wells entertained them); Oct 1935, the last issue. HGW to William McCartney, 30 Sept 1932 (on the Edinburgh 'X' Society). Memo (?MCW) to HGW, 19 Apr 1934; another memo (in HGW's hand), 31 Jan 1934, about the character of some of the members. HGW to ? Hunot, ? Mar, 4 Apr 1936. Statement of Purpose, H. G. Wells Society (undated). Basis (typewritten, and also undated). Letter to prospective members, *c.* 1936. Cosmopolis handbill, 'For the World State', *c.* 1936.

3   *Manifesto*, ed. C. E. M. Joad (London 1934), preface by HGW. A folder at Illinois, marked 'Cosmopolis', but appearing to have been organized after HGW's death, contains among other material: 'Memorandum on the Co-operation of ALL Progressive Societies', 5-pp. TS, unsigned; *News of Progress*, July 1934, letter from HGW offering congratulations, and pledging support for at least a year; other letters, June 1937, and drafts of the Manifesto and Memorandum; a draft of a Wells letter on the World Encyclopaedia, enlisting the help of the members. In a bizarre development, the Wells Society led in another direction to the Common Wealth party of Sir Richard Acland (see ch. 17); see Acland to HGW, 4 Sept 1940, a call for the progressive societies to meet again. Wells was tentative in his response, but he did send Ritchie Calder, who was co-ordinating the efforts on the Declaration of Human Rights, to a meeting.

4   Programme, World Aspects of Unemployment, 25–7 Feb 1930: a proposal by Wells, Gilbert Murray, and A. Salter was apparently put forward, although I have not seen it. Fenner Brockway to HGW, 1 July 1930, asking for contributions to underwrite a campaign; Wells gave 2 gns. Brockway to HGW, 4 June 1931, asking him to speak to ILP summer school, but the dates were wrong. Ernest Barker to HGW, 6 May 1932, come to Cambridge. W. B. Curry (headmaster, Dartington Hall) to HGW, 7 Sept 1933, 28 Apr 1936; they met from time to time. A few letters also exist from A. S. Neill (mostly on rather bizarre topics). Dora Russell was after Wells almost constantly to

come to her school: D. Russell to HGW, 25, 27 June, 13, 27 Aug, 5 Sept 1935, 4, 10 Apr 1936. A conference on HGW's ideas was held at the Russell school 17–24 Aug 1935. Wells did not really like Dora Russell, and felt he was being used in her running battle with her husband during their widely publicized divorce. On the Liberal Summer School speech, 'Liberalism and the Revolutionary Spirit', and its aftermath, 'Project of a Liberal World Organization', see *New Statesmen*, 20 Aug 1932, which published the speech, and HGW, *After Democracy* (1932), where it and the essay also appear. James A. Hobson to HGW, 31 July, 29 Sept, 5 Oct 1932: Hobson covered the Summer School speech for the *NChron*, and interviewed Wells, to whom he submitted his copy for comment; T. Clark to HGW, 7 Oct 1932; *NChron*, 8 Oct 1932. HGW, 'Project of a World Society', *New Statesman*, 20 Aug 1932.

5   *Nash's Pall Mall Magazine*, Nov-Dec 1932 (I have only seen a press cutting); HGW, 'The Outlook for Education', *Cosmopolitan*, Dec 1932. Gilbert Murray to HGW, 3 Mar 1932; HGW to Murray, 18 Mar 1932, discussing world education. HGW to D. Lloyd George, 17 Dec 1934, soliciting his help. HGW to *Education*, 25 Oct 1935, on what he had actually said on the subject in *The Shape of Things to Come*; published with corrections, *Education*, Nov 1935; also HGW to *DIndependent*, 28 Oct 1935, same thing. HGW to *The Times*, 28 Sept 1936, on Committee on Intellectual Co-operation (CIC); G. Murray to *The Times*, 30 Sept 1936; HGW to *The Times*, 3 Oct 1936. On Gilbert Murray and the CIC, see Francis West, *Gilbert Murray: A Life* (1984), 193–208: Jean Smith and Arnold Toynbee, eds., *Gilbert Murray: An Unfinished Autobiography* (London 1960): articles by S. de Madariaga, 176–97, and Jean Smith, 198–204. Ritchie Calder to HGW, 28 Sept 1936. HGW to Sir William Bragg, 23, 26 June, 10 Aug 1936, setting up the Royal Institution speech.

6   'Project for a Modern Encyclopaedia', Memorandum for Private Circulation; copies were sent out in July 1936. *Nature*, 21 Nov 1936; Special Supplement, 28 Nov 1936; RAG to HGW, 22 Nov; HGW to RAG, 30 Nov 1936. HGW to APW, 18 May 1936. J. B. S. Haldane to HGW, 11 May 1936, doubts possibility; J. Huxley to HGW, 3 July 1936; Bertrand Russell to HGW, 3 July 1936. Russell, Wells, Gregory, and William Bragg of the RI met for lunch on 8 July 1936 to discuss the encyclopaedia. Bragg to HGW, 9, 20, 24 June; 8 Oct, 23 Nov 1936. HGW to Lancelot Hogben, 13 May 1938. J. C. Smuts to HGW, 29 Sept 1936. APW to HGW, 15 Sept 1936, on N. Doubleday's first reaction, quoting the letter from him. Doubleday thought it would take £100,000, and would need foundation backing. HGW's addresses appear in *World Brain* (London 1938), and were excerpted in *Science*, vol. XXXII (9 Oct 1937), on documentation; *Survey Graphic*, Jan 1938. *Harper's* paid $250 for their piece: J. Chambrun to MCW, 29 Jan 1937; *Harper's*, Apr 1937, pp. 472–82.

7   For material leading up to this, see also HGW to British Institute of Adult Education, undated (mid-'30s), which provided some queries for the group, based on a Barbara Wootton memorandum; HGW (MCW) to Ann Sitwell (British Youth Peace Assembly), 29 Oct 1936. A. Gray Jones to HGW, 28 Sept, announcing BA interest after the *Times* letters, 2 Dec 1936, HGW to be first president. RAG to HGW, 12 Dec 1936; HGW to RAG, 15 Dec 1936. Jones to HGW, 15 Dec 1936, 8 Jan 1937. Letter to Organizing Committee L, from A. Gray Jones, 18 Dec 1936. O. J. R. Haworth to HGW, 2 Dec 1936; HGW reply, in draft. Gregory suggested Wells discuss the role of teaching and research in education, as well as the role of history. A memo drafted by RAG, HGW, and O. J. R. Haworth was circulated, dated 21 Dec 1936, and early meetings of the Section used its points as their agenda. Ernest Barker to HGW, 26 Dec 1936. See HGW, 'Sociology and Economics', *Nature*, 23 Apr 1938; the entire issue is devoted to 'The Social Relations of Science'.

8   Draft Memorandum on Activities of Section L, undated; Suggestions for Papers at Nottingham Meeting, also undated; RAG to HGW, 15, 21 Dec 1936; A. Gray Jones to HGW, 8 Jan 1937, enclosing minutes of meeting. I. Maisky to HGW, 18 Feb 1937. A. Gray Jones to HGW, 18 Feb, 22 June 1937. RAG to HGW, 23 June 1937. HGW to

British Association, 24 May 1937. Jones to HGW, 21 Aug 1937.

9 For the BA speech, 'The Informative Content of Education', see *World Brain*, ch. 5; the text was published in the *Proceedings, British Association for the Advancement of Science* (London: British Association 1937). The chart HGW used is reproduced as illustration no. 26.

10 Olaf Stapledon to HGW, 15 Sept 1937; they dined together to discuss the ideas as well. HGW, 'Ruffled Teachers: The Breeze at the British Association', *SChron*, 12 Sept 1937; also in *World Brain*, App. I. The Manchester *DExpress*, 3 June 1938, printed the Wells memo on a proposed encyclopaedia, as did the *Scottish DExpress*.

11 J. Chambrun to MCW, 22 July 1936, first offer, news of sale of articles; to HGW, telegram, ? Jan 1937; memo, HGW to Chambrun, 30 Nov 1936, another 19 Mar 1937; Chambrun to MCW, 15 June, 22 July, 20 Aug (he sent on a report of FDR's Natural Resources Committee) 1936, 1 Apr 1937; also to MCW, 19 Feb, 3 Mar, 25 Oct 1936, about HGW's private trip to the US that year.

12 HGW to Nelson Doubleday, 12 Dec 1937, list of guests on a memorandum, 17 Mar 1938. 'Memorandum on the Project of a World Encyclopaedia', 9 pp. Draft letter to 'X', never sent, proposing a committee. HGW to APW, 22 Jan 1938; APW to MCW, 14 Apr 1938. HGW's talk in America appears in *World Brain*, as ch. 2. J. Chambrun to MCW, 10, 11, 30 Nov, 15 Dec 1937. *The Brothers* was delayed for Wells's topical pieces on America. The *Rotarian* paid $200 for 'More and Better Teachers', HGW's reaction to these talks, published at the end of 1937.

13 MCW to APW, 10 Nov 1937, alerting him to the articles HGW was writing in the States and on the ship coming back. HGW, *Collier's*: 'The Fall in America: 1937', 28 Jan 1938; 'The New Americans', 5 Feb 1938. *DTelegraph and MPost*: 'Why are America's Wheels Slowing Down? Handicaps of an "Olympian" President', 'Can Young America Escape Class Politics?', 1, 2 Feb 1938, which are slightly different versions of the *Collier's* pieces. For a minor controversy over a remark about the labour leadership, see the *Liberal Magazine*, Apr 1938, p. 174, which reprinted part of the second article with a comment. HGW's visit to the World's Fair site led to 'World of Tomorrow', *NYT*, 5 Mar 1939, an article in which he essayed a few predictions, nearly all of them based on better educational opportunities.

14 HGW received 15% on the first 10,000 copies sold, and 20% thereafter from Methuen's publication of *World Brain*. See APW to MCW, 30 June, 16, 28, 29 July, 15 Oct 1937. Doubleday published in the US, where HGW received a 15% royalty. MCW to APW, 16, 28 Sept, 9 June, 16 July, 27 Nov 1937, 9 Mar 1938; 6 Jan, list of recipients of complimentary copies, with a form letter, 17 Feb 1938. Alan Ferguson, review of *World Brain*, *Nature*, 23 Apr 1938.

15 Reginald A. Smith, *Towards a Living Encyclopaedia* (London ?1938). HGW's BA speech was widely reprinted in America, in *School and Society, Survey Graphic*, and excerpted in *Time*, which stimulated interest in the whole matter. Hubert E. Powell to HGW, 23 Apr, on the campaign for better schools: HGW served on an advisory committee, 27 Apr 1937. W. Layton to HGW, 29 Nov 1937. Gerald Barry to HGW, 29 Nov, 9, 13, 14 Dec 1937. HGW, 'Ask for Your Schools and See That You Get Them', *NChron*, 20 Dec 1937: leader-page article, for which he was paid 1,000 gns. Julian Huxley to HGW, 24 Aug 1938; Ritchie Calder to HGW, 20 Aug 1938. F. C. White to HGW, 27 Apr 1938, ensuring that he would come to Cambridge. *DHerald*, 24, 25 Aug 1938, reports the Cambridge meetings, the new committee, HGW participation, and so on; a later story is in 8 Nov 1938. *Journal of Education*, Sept 1938, pp. 573–4, an account of the preliminary report on HGW's ideas in the 1937 speech.

16 See ch. 17 for a discussion of this meeting. HGW, *Science and the World Mind* (London 1942). For another view see G. Werskey, *The Visible College* (London 1979).

17 Some little notice might be taken of HGW's later views on education, not much different from those of this period, except as the anxiety of the war, and the devastation, gave them greater poignancy. Gilbert Murray to HGW, 16 Mar 1939,

introducing C.D.L. Brereton who wanted to discuss these ideas. HGW: 'The New Educational Front in England', *Tomorrow*, vol. I, no. 3 (Nov 1941), pp. 7–8; 'An Article to Annoy Parsons and Professors', *SDispatch*, 23 Nov 1941: we need a eutrophic world, and only education can bring it; 'The Shape of Education to Come', *Educational Supplement* of County of London Red Cross *Bulletin*, Dec 1941; 'There's a Catch in the New School Plans', *SDispatch*, 21 June 1942.

18 ABC (Australian Broadcasting Corporation) (B.H. Molesworth) to HGW, 14 July, 17 Aug, 7 Oct 1938; HGW to ABC, 26 July, 17, 30 Aug; he refused an ABC shipboard interview: telegram to them 18 Nov 1938. ABC's earlier interest in Wells can be seen in APW to MCW, 12 May 1933, 5 Apr 1935, 18 Mar 1936; A. Hammerton to MCW, 16 Feb 1937; HGW to Hammerton, 17 Feb 1937; ABC to MCW, 9 Apr, 14 July 1938; Helen Dunbar to HGW, 10 Nov 1938, setting up the 'Poison of History' lecture. Other arrangements are seen in ANZAAS to HGW, 22 Aug, 9, 26 Sept, 10 Nov (on clothes, temperatures, etc.), and a whole sheaf of cablegrams on the ship, 10, 25, 28, 29 Nov 1938. On the articles, and their sales, see Gerald Barry to HGW, telegram, 4 Jan 1939, reporting the success of the forecast articles, and offering him more now; HGW cable to him of same date; Barry to HGW, cable, 6 Jan; to MCW, 10, 13 Jan; to Sydney *DNews*, 24 Jan; yours of 20 Jan a serious infringement. HGW to MCW, cable, 7 Jan 1939. Hugh Cumming to MCW, 1 Feb 1939. HGW, 'S. S. Pukka Sahib', *NChron*, 13 Feb 1939. For the views of another participant, much like HGW, Sir John Russell, *The Land Called Me* (London 1956). Russell was head of the Rothamstead Agricultural Experiment Station; he and HGW had known each other for years at the Reform.

19 Adelaide *Advertiser*, 1 Jan 1939. HGW's companion to Melbourne, and driver, was S.E. Gleeson of the latter city. For a description of such a motor tour, at about the time, see William Hatfield, *Australia Through the Windscreen* (Sydney 1939); chs. 17–18 cover this area. Melbourne *Argus*, 2, 4, 5 Jan 1939. Another account of the heat and English reactions to it is in Eric Newby, *The Last Grain Race* (London 1956). Newby was loading wheat near Adelaide while HGW was in Australia.

20 On diabetes, from which HGW suffered after 1933, *SChron*, 21 Mar 1937, for an interview. He helped found the Diabetes Association in 1935. *The Times*, 3 Apr 1933, and 3 Feb 1934, repr. as a flyer in an appeal for funds. Diabetic Association, Australia, to HGW, 14 Sept 1938; HGW to Nancy Parker, 27 Oct 1938: will meet the group, but no speech. Brisbane *Courier Mail*, 4 Jan 1939, on HGW, diabetes, and autographs.

21 HGW, '1939–What Does it Hold?', *NChron*, 2, 3 Jan 1939, and their very favourable leader on 2 Jan, 'Shape of Things to Come'. Philip Jordan to MCW, 6, 8, 13 Dec 1938; they paid 75 gns. for the article.

22 HGW, 'Crisis from Down Under', *NChron*, 16 Jan 1939.

23 Annesley de Silva to HGW, 1 Sept 1938; HGW to de Silva, 10 Oct, 17 Nov 1938; de Silva to HGW, 4 Mar 1939. *Ceylon Observer*, 27 Nov, 17, 18, 19 Dec 1938. *Times of India* (Bombay), 17 Dec 1938.

24 Melbourne *Argus*, 28, 29, 31 Dec 1938; Melbourne *Herald*, 28 Dec 1938. Nearly every Australian newspaper gave an account of HGW's arrival, and the first interviews, teas, dinners, and so on; the best appear in *West Australian* (Perth), 28 Dec; Adelaide *Advertiser*, 28, 29 Dec; leader, 'Mr Wells Arrives', Brisbane *Courier Mail*, 29 Dec; Melbourne *Herald*, 28, 29 Dec; Melbourne *Age*, 27, 28 Dec 1938, 3 Jan 1939. The extent of the reporting is indicated by the fact that the following newspapers all reported the arrival; many also provided editorial comment, and photographs: Sydney *MHerald*, 28 Dec; Maryborough (Queensland) *Colonist*, 31 Dec; Hobart (Tasmania) *Mercury*, 28, 30 Dec; Geelong *Advertiser*, 29 Dec; Newcastle *MHerald and Miners' Advocate*, 29, 30 Dec; and even the Christchurch (New Zealand) *Star-Sun*, 28 Dec 1938.

25 Melbourne *Age*, 30 Dec 1938. Other papers which treated the speech in some detail are Melbourne *Argus*, 30 Dec; Adelaide *Advertiser*, 30 Dec; Sydney *MHerald*, 30 Dec 1938; Melbourne *Leader*, 7 Jan 1939; North Queensland *Register* (Townsville), 31 Dec 1938.

For slightly different versions of this speech see P. Parrinder and R. Philmus, eds., *HGW's Literary Criticism* (1980) and my own version in George Hay, ed., *Pulsar One* (Harmonsworth 1978), 169–74.

26　Melbourne *Age*, 6 Jan 1939. Wells read a number of Australian books and MSS while in the island continent. One book that appealed to him was J. E. Hammond's *Winjan's People* which he found made the aborigines 'credible human people — instead of fantastic totem poles'. His letter to Hammond congratulating him on his work is repr. in the *West Australian* (Perth), 10 Jan 1939.

27　Melbourne *Leader*, 14 Jan 1939; Melbourne *Age*, 4, 7 Jan 1939; Brisbane *Worker*, 10 Jan 1939.

28　Most London newspapers carried the story on 3 and 4 Jan 1939; the best account in Australia, with the quoted translation, appeared in Brisbane *Courier Mail*, 5 Jan 1939. For others, see Melbourne *Age*, *West Australian*, Adelaide *Advertiser*, Sydney *MHerald*, all of 4 Jan 1939.

29　The interview is printed in considerable detail in several places. The best of the reports are Brisbane *Courier Mail*, Melbourne *Age*, Adelaide *Advertiser*, *West Australian*, Hobart *Mercury*, Launceston *Examiner*, all 5 Jan 1939. Later comments include the Newcastle *MHerald and Miners' Advocate*, 6, 7 Jan, and – the most detailed – the weekly Melbourne *Leader*, 14 Jan, and the *Australasian* (Melbourne), 7 Jan 1939.

30　Brisbane *Courier Mail*, 7, 9 Jan; Melbourne *Argus*, 6, 9, 10 Jan; Sydney *MHerald*, Adelaide *Advertiser*, both 9 Jan; Melbourne *Age*, 9 Jan (best account of the PEN dinner), 10 Jan; *West Australian*, 9, 10 Jan; *Worker* (Brisbane), 10 Jan; Newcastle *MHerald and Miners' Advocate*, 6, 7, 9, 10 Jan; Launceston *Examiner*, 7, 9 Jan; Hobart *Mercury*, 6, 7, 10 Jan; North Queensland *Register*, 7 Jan; Maryborough *Colonist*, 14 Jan; Geelong *Advertiser*, 10 Jan; Melbourne *Herald*, 6, 7, 9 Jan; *Australasian*, 14 Jan; Christchurch (New Zealand) *Star-Sun*, 6 Jan 1939.

31　Letters appeared in the Brisbane *Courier Mail*, Hobart *Mercury*, Melbourne *Herald*, Sydney *MHerald* and Newcastle *MHerald*. For the comments of the Mayor of Newcastle, see the last-named paper, 10 Jan 1939. The comments of the Prime Minister in Hobart were widely printed; in their most complete form, see Brisbane *Courier Mail*, 7 Jan 1939. The Germans did not let the issue die down either; in an editorial, the *Diplomatische Politische Korrespondenz* of Jan 1939 welcomed Lyons's 'pleasing adherence to the good traditions of civilized nations'. They contrasted this with FDR's 'wild west tones' heard in his State of the Union address, which was the other major news item in the world that week. Australian newspapers, with the exception of the Sydney *MHerald*, 9 Jan 1939, gave this editorial no space. Launceston *Examiner*, 6, 10 Jan; Adelaide *Advertiser* and *West Australian*, both 10 Jan; Sydney *Bulletin*, 11 Jan; Brisbane *Courier Mail* and Hobart *Mercury*, both 9 Jan; *Westralian Worker*, 13 Jan; *Australian Worker*, 11 Jan; Sydney *MHerald*: 'Free Speech and Mr Wells', 7 Jan 1939. The Newcastle *MHerald* supported HGW editorially, 6, 9 Jan 1939. Also see Hobart *Mercury*, 9 Jan 1939.

32　'H. G. Wells Makes an Attack on Mr Lyons Which is, in Effect, a Defense of the German People and Free Speech', *NChron*, 23 Jan 1939. Later, when HGW wrote about his Australian tour, he was quite dismissive of Lyons, preferring to remember other aspects of the trip. HGW, *Travels of a Republican Radical* (1939).

33　Geelong *Advertiser*, 21 Jan; Sydney *MHerald*, 23 Jan; Melbourne *Herald*, 21 Jan 1939.

34　Adelaide *Advertiser*, 6 Jan (the Vowles letter), 9, 10, 11, 12, 13, 14 Jan 1939; Hobart *Mercury*, 10 Jan 1939: these are perhaps the best examples of Australian letters to the press with regard to this topic.

35　Melbourne *Age*, 10 Jan 1939.

36　Melbourne *Herald*, 14 Jan; Sydney *Bulletin*, 25 Jan; *Australasian* (Melbourne), 14 Jan 1939, are all reviews of *Dolores*. HGW continued to pay for his remarks on women. At a luncheon in his honour in Sydney, after the conference, he claimed to be misunderstood and that those who quoted him on women had actually used his book, *Select Conversations with an Uncle*, published in 1895, representing his juvenile views. He went on to offer to his listeners such advice as 'never marry a beautiful woman', and said that half the Australian women were beautiful, and the other half knew they were as well. Later, at still another interview, he offered these comments: 'I think that women will always continue to be the female of the species *Homo sapiens* and never will be superseded'; and he described women of the press as 'attractive, insidious, and dangerous'. When asked why dangerous, he responded, 'Because they never get things wrong.' Sydney *MHerald* and Melbourne *Age*, both 21 Jan; Christchurch (New Zealand) *Star Sun*, 25 Jan 1939. See the *Australasian* (Melbourne), 28 Jan 1939, for his further remarks on women.

37   This important autobiographical fragment appears only in the Brisbane *Courier Mail*, 9, 10 Jan 1939.

38   Brisbane, *Courier Mail*, 4, 11, 12, 13, 16 Jan; Melbourne *Age*, 12, 14 Jan; Melbourne *Leader*, 21 Jan 1939. The last has good photos in the rotogravure section. The cricket match had one interesting local rule: 'Batsmen at either end could appeal for drinks.' Melbourne *Leader*, 14 Jan 1939, for the best and most thoughtful discussion of the purposes of the conference, although nearly all the newspapers devoted some space to this topic.

39   This speech received a tremendous press. It was reprinted in its entirety, or nearly so, throughout the country. See, for instance, the Brisbane *Courier Mail*, Christchurch (New Zealand) *Star-Sun*, Melbourne *Age*, Adelaide *Advertiser*, Hobart *Mercury*, Newcastle *MHerald and Miners' Advocate*, Launceston *Examiner*, Geelong *Advertiser*, all 13 Jan; North Queensland *Register*, 14 Jan; *Australian Worker*, 18 Jan; Melbourne *Leader*, 21 Jan; *Australasian*, 21 Jan 1939.

40   For an article on the impact of the speech, see Sydney *MHerald*, 16 Jan 1939; also Melbourne *Argus* and *West Australian*, 13, 14 Jan; *Launceston Examiner*, 17 Jan; Melbourne *Herald*, 13 Jan; Sydney *MHerald*, 14 Jan; Maryborough (Queensland) *Colonist*, 21 Jan 1939.

41   Brisbane *Courier Mail*, 14 Jan 1939.

42   Maryborough (Queensland) *Colonist*, 31 Dec 1938, although the comments and threats appeared in nearly every interview HGW gave.

43   There are a number of versions of this speech. It was first given in a slightly different form, in London, to an International Conference of Teachers of the League of Nations Union, and was reprinted, in a still slightly different form, in *Nineteenth Century*, May 1938. The text delivered in Canberra appears in many Australian newspapers: Brisbane *Courier Mail*, 17 Jan; Hobart *Mercury*, Melbourne *Herald*, 16 Jan; *West Australian*, 17 Jan; Adelaide *Advertiser*, Newcastle *MHerald and Miners' Advocate*, Launceston *Examiner*, Geelong *Advertiser*, all 17 Jan; and the *Australasian*, 21 Jan 1939. All reprinted most, if not all, of the address. The final text appears in *Travels of a Republican Radical*, 89–121. On the origins of this speech and its first delivery, see Gilbert Murray to HGW, 10 Feb 1938, asking him to make a speech to the education committee of the League of Nations Union; Murray reminded him of their visit to H.A.L. Fisher in 1922. Also Murray to HGW, 21–5 Apr 1938. Wells sent his greetings from Nice where he was avoiding the English winter, but agreed to speak if well. Murray to MCW, 18 Feb 1938; to HGW, 4 Apr 1938 (wrote response). L. W. Judd to HGW, 28 Mar, 24 Apr 1938; to MCW, 6, 30 Apr 1938 (the talk was on 24 Apr). Murray to HGW, 10 July 1938, asking for a copy to sell at a peace bazaar.

44   Melbourne *Argus*; Brisbane *Courier Mail*, Sydney *MHerald*, Melbourne *Age*, Hobart *Mercury*, all 18 Jan 1939.

45   Melbourne *Age*, 17 Jan; Melbourne *Leader*, 21 Jan; Adelaide *Advertiser*: 'Can We Abolish Nationalism?', 21 Jan; Sydney *MHerald*: 'The True History', 21 Jan; Brisbane *Courier Mail*, 18 Jan; Melbourne *Age*: 'Mr Wells and History', 18 Jan; Melbourne *Argus*: 'Poison in the Cup', 21 Jan 1939.

46   *West Australian*: 'The Value of History', 18 Jan; Sydney *Bulletin*: 'Mr Wells Improves', 18 Jan; *Australian Worker*, 18, 25 Jan; Brisbane *Worker*, 24 Jan; Brisbane *Courier Mail*,

18 Jan 1939 (for other letters, also see 19, 23 Jan 1939). Other supporters included Launceston *Examiner*, 'New Things and Prejudice', 19 Jan 1939; they called HGW one of 'the wonderful men of the age, steeped in deep thinking and daring in his conclusions'. Professor F. Alexander of the Univ. of Western Australian supported HGW quite strongly in the *West Australian*, 19, 21 Jan 1939. Others who simply covered the speech included the North Queensland *Register* 21 Jan 1939; the Newcastle *MHerald*, 21 Jan 1939, said HGW's pessimism was badly placed and his views were 'out of date and discarded'.

47   The best account of this speech is in the Adelaide *Advertiser*, 20 Jan 1939; others who covered it included the Hobart *Mercury*, Newcastle *MHerald and Miners' Advocate*, and the *West Australian*, all 20 Jan 1939.

48   HGW, 'I Saw the Bush Fires', *NChron* (London), 30 Jan 1939.

49   This speech was best covered in Brisbane *Courier Mail*, 23 Jan; Melbourne *Leader*, 28 Jan; Melbourne *Age*, Launceston *Examiner*, Melbourne *Herald*, 23 Jan; North Queensland *Register*, 28 Jan; *Australian Worker*, 1 Feb 1939.

50   For the engineers see Melbourne *Argus*, and Geelong *Advertiser*, both 24 Jan 1939. His censorship address appears in best form in Brisbane *Courier Mail*, 26 Jan; Adelaide *Advertiser*, Melbourne *Argus*, *West Australian*, all 26 Jan 1939. The Japanese menace remarks were reported in Adelaide *Advertiser*, 27 Jan 1939. Both the Australian *Worker* (1 Feb) and the *Westralian Worker* (20 Jan 1939) commended him for the censorship speech. On his visit generally see 'H. G. Wells – Project', *South Seas Review*, 16 Jan 1939. HGW to Roy F. Bennett (Millions Club), 9 Sept 1938; reprinted in Sydney *MHerald*, 18 Jan 1939. HGW to A.B. Walkow (ANZAAS), 26 Sept 1938.

51   Melbourne *Leader*, 4 Feb 1939; 'Darwin Notes', North Queensland *Register*, 4 Feb 1939; HGW was delayed a day in Darwin by bad head winds. The Geelong *Advertiser*, 27 Jan 1939, was the only paper to report some further attacks on the League of Nations in these last interviews. Wells called the League 'a spent force' and urged people 'to get a cross and erect it over the body to remind them of its status'. Also see Melbourne *Age* and Newcastle *MHerald and Miners' Advocate*, both 27 Jan 1939. Brisbane *Courier Mail*, 27 Jan 1939, gave his itinerary as tea in Sydney, breakfast in Brisbane, lunch in Cloncurry, and dinner in Darwin, travelling 2,528 miles. Sydney *MHerald*, 27 Jan 1939.

52   *Westralian Worker*, 3 Feb; Launceston *Examiner*, 28 Jan; Sydney *Bulletin*, 1 Feb; Melbourne *Age*, 28 Jan; Melbourne *Leader*, 28 Jan; Melbourne *Argus*, 23 Jan; Oliver Holt, 'H.G. Wells and I', Newcastle *MHerald and Miners' Advocate*, 28 Jan; 'Wells's generation brought on World War I Why Should I Listen to Him?', Melbourne *Age*, 28 Jan; Adelaide *Advertiser*, 27 Jan 1939. 'Burns on Fourth Estate', Sydney *Bulletin*, 1 Feb 1939: We are too serious.

53   *Rangoon Gazette*, 7 Feb 1939, reports his reception and a brief Wells speech. *NChron*, 6, 27 Feb 1939.

54   *NChron*, 6 Mar 1939; also see HGW, 'Britain Needs to be Told to Wake Up', *ETimes*, 18 Feb 1939. Gerald Barry to HGW, 17, 21, 24 (two) Feb; to MCW, 8 Mar 1939, on the details of publishing his pieces. Barry, Wells, and Philip Jordan also met for lunch on HGW'S return to London.

55   *NChron*, 13 Mar 1939.

56   HGW to George Catlin, 24 Apr 1939, quoted in Catlin's book, *For God's Sake, Go!* (London 1972).

57   RAG to HGW, *c.* Jan 1939, quoted in Armytage. RAG, 'Retrospect and Prospect', *Nature*, 7 Jan 1939, his farewell piece.

58   HGW to Jonathan Cape, 8 Oct 1938; he intimated in this letter that Cape should found a new review, as the lead time required for novels was too great. HGW, 'The Map of Europe – 1949', *SChron*, 22 Jan 1939; also in *Liberty*, 21 Jan 1939 (the world he predicted came by 1942). HGW, 'The Dangerous Stratum', *SChron*, 5 Mar 1939; also in *Liberty*, 4 Mar 1939. W. R. Inge, 'Victorian Socialism', *Nature*, 13 Jan 1940, a review

of *The New World Order* which brought an attack from Wells, 27 Jan 1940, especially for Inge's views on Spain. John Mann, 'Mr Britling Sees Through It', *Truth*, 12 Jan 1940, a more favourable review: 'No one should miss reading it.'

59 B. Webb, diary, 5 Aug 1939; B. Webb to HGW, 10 Aug 1939 (Webb *Letters* III. 429). *NChron*, 14 Aug 1939; J. B. Priestley, 'True, Mr Wells, But —', *Tribune*, 25 Aug 1939.

60 MCW to Curtis Brown, 25 Feb 1939. HGW wrote an article for *Look*, to be called 'The Amalgamation of Peace and War', which was accepted, paid for, but which they did not print. MCW to Vernon Pope, 16 Aug 1939, 25 Sept 1939. HGW, 'If Hitler Goes to War. . .He is a Catholic. Will he Appeal to the Pope?', *SChron*, 27 Aug 1939.

61 Walpole's diary, quoted in Hart-Davis. The lunch was at the beginning of Aug 1939. The quotation is from HGW's *SChron* article cited in note 60, which appeared the week before the invasion of Poland.

62 HGW, 'The Honour and Dignity of the Free Mind', in *Travels of a Republican Radical* (1939). HGW to Major H. J. Muir, 18 Sept 1939, 25 Feb 1942; HGW, 'If we do not Strike now, we Deserve Disaster', *DMail*, 3 Sept 1941, which recounts his trip home from Sweden. HGW to *Manchester ENews*, 17 Feb 1940: Their account of his life since the beginning of the war is libellous. He was in Stockholm, and since his return, he had remained in London. The *Saturday Review of Literature* (New York) negotiated with him for the Stockholm speech, but in the event did not print it. J. Chambrun to MCW, 1 Dec 1939. For HGW on nationalism, his changing views, and the coming of the war, see 'Nationalism – A Myth', *Reynolds's News*, 17 Mar 1940, which is a review of Hamilton Fyfe, *The Illusion of National Character*. The Penguin Special which emerged from all this was HGW, *The Common Sense of War and Peace: World Revolution or War Unending* (Harmondsworth 1940). In it he reprinted his war aims memorandum from the First World War as well.

63 The reviewer in *Tribune*, 8 Nov 1940, said that he had read Wells all his life and did not recoil from rereading him. He warned his readers that if you read *Babes in the Darkling Wood* you would run a risk with those who disliked him and his message. But it was 'the right book for the present moment. It is amusing, stimulating, encouraging. It is Wells.' On *Ararat*, MCW (in HGW's hand) to Alliance Press (draft), 8 Aug 1940. J. G. Crowther, reviewing *Babes* in *Nature*, 28 Dec 1940, called the work 'a major inspiration'. Fred T. Marsh, NY *Herald Tribune*, 6 Oct 1940, said, 'Anything Wells has to say is worth reading' in a very forthcoming review of *Babes* just after HGW arrived.

64 MCW to Alliance Press, 8 Aug 1940. HGW received $1,600 advance and standard royalties for *Ararat* in the US. For HGW and his earlier remarks on the Germans and the need to bomb Berlin, see *NYT*, 27 Jan, 12 Feb 1940: the Germans used this widely against HGW in their propaganda efforts in the US, and while the 'phony' war was still on; 28 Aug, 4, 5 Oct 1940, for his arrival and the dockside interview, when he said he slept through most air raids. *Herald Tribune*, 4 Oct 1940.

65 *NYT*: 'H. G. Wells Insists on British Shake-up', 8 Sept 1940; his press conference, as well as a signed article, 'Wells Says Nazis Would Embroil US', 4 Oct 1940: 'The human mind is no more guaranteed against extinction than was the Brontosaurus.' The Australians followed Wells's US progress with avid eyes. See Sydney *MHerald*, 4, 5 Oct 1940. A good article on Wells's life and work is in *NYT*, 27 Oct 1940.

66 *NYT*, 13 Oct 1940, for the Earl Winterton story; the Commons debate was on 23 and 24 Oct. 'Wells Upsets Blimps', *Reynolds's News*, 20 Oct; *NYT*, 25 Oct; Sydney *MHerald*, 25 Oct (a very complete story); *Tribune*, 25 Oct, an article by Raymond Postgate. *The Times* comment quoted was in their lead editorial, entitled, 'What We're Fighting For'. Rep. J.J. Delaney tried to get the US House to pass a resolution disapproving of Wells's visit. *NYT*, 9, 17, 24 Oct 1940; NY *Herald Tribune*, 8 Oct, also 24 Oct 1940.

67 *Two Hemispheres or One World* (n.d. [? 1940]). The speech was written after 29 June 1940, from the TS at Illinois. I have never seen the copy cited in the Wells Society bibliography. The talk given in San Francisco was published there as *The Immediate*

Future of Mankind, and I was able to use Eric Korn's copy.

68 Los Angeles *Times*, 2 Nov 1940; Los Angeles *Examiner*, 3 Nov 1940. The speech was 6 Nov, and the San Francisco one on 8 Nov. Wells had flown across the continent on American Airlines and this was of as much interest as his speech, or nearly so. For a first-hand memory of this talk, after HGW's death, see *Pluto*, the fan magazine of the Los Angeles Science-Fiction Society, issued 1946. For another interview in Phoenix, Arizona, on Russia (and Munich), NY *Herald Tribune*, 11 Nov 1940. *Arizona Republic* (Phoenix), 10, 13 Nov 1940.

69 *NYT*: Town Hall speech, 'What Kind of World Order Do We Want?', 29 Nov 1940; 4 Dec, summary of queries from his audience; 5 Dec, summary of his luncheon talk, which was also broadcast; 19 Dec 1940, his interview as he left. HGW, 'Future of the Finns and the Poles, and, if any, of the learned Dr Alfred Noyes', *Saturday Review of Literature*, 15 Dec 1940: Noyes had written an article about HGW in a Victoria, B.C., newspaper, and this was HGW's response (I have seen only the TS). *NY Herald Tribune*, 29 Nov, 4, 5, 19 Dec 1940. *Town Meeting*, vol. VI, no. 3 (2 Dec 1940): Wells's talk is at pp. 12–15; questions to him, Hu Shih and R. L. Wilbur (the other speakers), pp. 16–19. John T. Flynn offered a comment, pp. 20–2, and the panellists responded: HGW, pp. 23–4.

70 HGW to EH, 9 Jan 1941. Diana Bourdon to HGW, early in 1941, and his notes. He was attempting to get hold of Willkie. When the now emissary of FDR came to London he met HGW for luncheon as well. MCW to H. G. Koppell, 10 June 1941. *NYT*, 31 July 1941; HGW, 'The Strange Story of Otto Strasser: An Ally We Don't Want', *SDispatch*, 25 Jan 1942; also his reply to Strasser in *Dispatch*, 15 Mar 1942, and *Tribune*, 3 Apr 1942, for a mention of the *Catholic World's* support of Strasser. On HGW and America, also see HGW, 'Do We Want a Standing Anglo-US Alliance?', *Picture Post*, 29 Jan 1944. APW to MCW, 31 Oct 1940, recounts the bombing of his house, and asks for HGW's health. They met once again when HGW came home, just to chat.

71 *Tribune*, 2 Jan 1942. *You Can't Be Too Careful* has a marvellous picture of cricket as well, as HGW dipped deep into the well of his youthful experience.

PART FOUR

Chapter 15

1   The last substantial batch of Wells correspondence, offered as a package a decade ago to London dealers in H. G. Wells material but later withdrawn, was recently described over the telephone as 'juicy'; last said to be in Florence, it may one day surface again. The best speculation holds it to be the correspondence with Odette Keun; but the events of the last years of Moura Budberg's life indicate that these letters may be to and from her.

2   Christabel MacLaren, Baroness Aberconway, *A Wiser Woman?* (London 1966). I was fortunate enough to be able to see the corrected galley and page proofs for the book then called *My Memoir*; these have some emendations and comments not in the final version. The proofs were then in the possession of Michael Katanka who graciously loaned them to me. I do not know their present whereabouts.

3   GPW to HGW, 13, 19 Feb, ?1930 or 1931, on Anna Jane, her trust, and an earlier visit to Chiltern Court. HGW to GBS, 24 Oct 1928, on Amber, and (undated 1939) on a dinner party. Amber, for her part, carried news of others. See HGW to B. Webb, 29 Oct 1936. Apparently Wells saw her more often at Passfield Corner before his brother Frank, who remained at Liss, passed away. Wells told B. Webb, 'Let's all live to be 100.'

4   Rosamund Bland Sharpe to ACRW, 4 Mar 1908, discussing another friend's baby, and soliciting advice; 28 Jan 1908 or 1909, a bread-and-butter letter after a week at Sandgate. R. B. Sharpe to HGW, 19 Mar 192?, saying that she would work for him;

several letters, early 1920s, reminding him of their affair and discussing her husband's illness. HGW to Violet Hunt (postmark 9 Mar 1907): 'And I have a pure flame for Rosamund who is the *MOST* – quite!'.

5   *Malthusian*: 5 Dec 1914, 15 Jan, 15 Oct 1915; the first item coincided with Margaret Sanger's first London visit in Dec 1914. Letter to President Woodrow Wilson, 15 Nov 1915, pp. 85–6; others besides HGW who signed were William Archer, Bennett, Marie Stopes, Gilbert Murray, Alymer Maude, Edward Carpenter, Lever Ashwell, and Dr Percy Ames. (The letter was also published in the *New York Sun*.) HGW letter to editor, 'Malthusianism versus Socialism', 15 June 1917, pp. 43–4. (Drysdale and his wife resigned as editors, but came back when HGW accepted their apology.) Another HGW letter under the same title, 15 July 1917.

6   *Malthusian*, 15 Dec 1921. Programme, Fifth Annual International Neo-Malthusian and Birth Control Conference, London 1922. *New Generation*, vol. I, no. 5 (May 1922) and no. 6 (June 1922). *Report* of Conference, ed. Raymond Pierpoint, 1922. The conference took place on the centenary of Francis Place's first work in this field. *NYT*, 11 June 1922, 10 May 1924.

7   *New Generation*, June 1925, for HGW's greetings to the New York conference. HGW, 'Mr Wheatley's Little Houses: "As it was in the Beginning, etc."', *WGaz*, 16 Aug 1924. HGW letter, 'Mr H. G. Wells Replies', *DHerald*, 15 May 1924. HGW, 'The Serfdom of Ignorance: The Right of Women to Knowledge', *WGaz*, 7 June 1924.

8   Edith How-Martyn, *The Birth Control Movement in England* (London 1930), is good on this meeting. Programme, Fiftieth Anniversary of the Besant-Bradlaugh Trial, 26 July 1927. Wells's views can be seen in Betty Ross, *Heads and Tales* (London 1934), 36–52, which gives an account of an interview in 1931–2 which lasted for two hours. HGW was not publicly active in the movement after 1927 until, in the mid-'30s, Gerda Guy and others moved away from the eugenics issue to focus again on population control. Of course, his relationship with Margaret Sanger meant that he was seen to be involved when, on his trips to the US in the 1930s, he frequently sat at head tables with her.

9   Horace Gregory, *Dorothy Richardson: An Adventure in Self-Discovery* (New York 1967); John Rosenberg, *Dorothy Richardson* (New York 1973); Gloria G. Fromm, *Dorothy Richardson: A Biography* (Champaign-Urbana, Ill. 1977). The last is the standard life, although its citations are at times difficult to follow. The earlier books have more, and in Rosenberg's case stronger, analytical literary criticism.

10 J. Rosenberg, *Richardson*, 128.

11 For Richardson's writing in its early stages see D.M. Richardson, 'The Disabilities of Women', *Freewoman*, 5 Aug 1912, a review in which she claims that as feminism advances, the medical profession increases its opposition. APW to HGW, 26 May 1926; to ACRW, 2 June 1926. G. Fromm, *Richardson*, 111–13, on HGW's impact on her writing. HGW, letter to her on his autobiography, quoted in J. Rosenberg, *Richardson*, 128, and in Fromm, 272–3. Dent brochure, in 1938. An interesting undated (?1908 – 1912) letter, HGW to Thomas Seccombe, introduces Richardson to Constable as a possible author: 'She's got a real philosophical twist (which is rare in petticoats) . . . Will you give her an ear. I never do this sort of thing simply because I'm asked to, but I really believe in Miss Richardson' (Boston).

12 The letter from HGW in late 1944 is quoted in Rosenberg, and summarized in Fromm. I have not seen it. Marjorie typed one volume of Richardson's long novel in the summer of 1935, and HGW sent £50 when she and Odle were very short of funds. HGW mentioned her in the prefatory chapter in *Babes in the Darkling Wood*, a novel which she liked very much, apparently. Not all his female friends agreed, as Elizabeth von Arnim wrote to her daughter not to pay too much attention to HGW's talk in the book, and she also complained of its size and weight. Leslie De Charms (pseud.), *Elizabeth of the German Garden* (London 1958), 419: letter to Liebet, 9 Dec 1940. Von Arnim attacked Hugh Walpole's work at the same time.

13 'New Woman as Artist', a review of Gloria Fromm's biography of Richardson by

Elaine Showalter, *NYT Book Review*, 11 Dec 1977, is the best attempt to discuss the meanings in Richardson's life as seen by her major biographers.

14 The standard (and only) life of Elizabeth von Arnim is by her daughter, Liebet, writing under the pseudonym 'Leslie de Charms': *Elizabeth of the German Garden* (1958). In addition to von Arnim's *German Garden* novel, one is directed to her *Elizabeth in Rugen*, and her *Christine* (London 1927), published under the pseudonym 'Alice Cholmondeley'.

15 This material is based on Elizabeth's daughter's biography, and Elizabeth's own novels, as well as on some notions of her from reading the biographical treatments of, especially, Hugh Walpole. See De Charms, *Elizabeth*, 144–7. Also see Elizabeth's journal, 6 June 1915; diary, 17 Oct 1923; letter to 'Mark Rainley', 31 Jan 1927, which gives a physical description of HGW; diary entry of 7 Feb 1927; journal entries of 2 Jan, 18, 23 June 1932, 6 Feb 1933; letter to Liebet, 9 Dec 1940; journal entry of 8 Dec 1940; letter to Liebet, 29 Nov 1940 – all printed at least in part in the biography.

16 *The Pastor's Wife*, by the Author of "Elizabeth and Her German Garden" . . . (London 1914), 484 and *passim*.

17 HGW, Preface, *Stories of Men and Women in Love* (London 1933), v–viii.

18 The first part of the book was cut substantially in the serialization, which appeared in the *American* from Nov 1911 to Oct 1912. John S. Phillips to HGW, 12 Aug; to ACRW, 30 Aug 1911, 12 Jan 1912. John M. Siddall to HGW, 23 May 1919, seeking an opportunity to film the novel. This led to the sale of film rights to four novels, prior to those sold to Goldwyn. JBP to HGW, 15 Aug, 8 Sept, 11 Oct 1922, 24 Aug 1923; HGW to JBP, 11 Nov 1924; cannot help more as he is 'seriously ill'. HGW to F. Macmillan, *c.* early 1913.

19 ERL to HGW, 8 June 1911 (the date suggests that Lankester was reading proofs, or a typescript); Lankester had been for a weekend with Edward Clodd, J.B. Bury, and Flinders Petrie, and they may have discussed the problems posed, if not the book itself; Lankester to ACRW, 12 Sept 1912.

20 Rebecca West, 'Marriage', *Freewoman*, 19 Sept 1912, 'N.H.W.', *T.P.'s Weekly*, 13 Sept 1912, review of the novel. Thomas Secombe, 'Labrador', *New Witness*, 8 May 1913. A. C. Benson, writing in his diary, remarked of the book, 'But he's a poet, little Wells, and it's there he scores. . . .' (in Percy Lubbock, ed., *Diary of A.C. Benson* [London 1927], 273–4).

21 ViP to HGW, 7 Nov 1913, 8 June 1914. *The Passionate Friends* and *Marriage* took a great deal out of HGW physically and he was unable to meet some commitments for articles, even though they paid as well. HGW to P. Cazenove, 22 Dec 1911: 'Can't think of it just now. A novel absorbs me.' ACRW to Cazenove, end of 1911: 'HG is engaged in a very fatiguing struggle with the end of his *Passionate Friends* novel' (the word may be 'article'). HGW included *The Passionate Friends* in the Atlantic Edition along with articles on divorce, endowment of motherhood, and his prefatory first chapter to *The Great State*.

22 Violet Hunt, *The Flurried Years* (London 1926); for the German trip, where the novel was a leitmotif, at least for her, see esp. pp. 245–54. A number of Wells's letters to both her and Hueffer (Ford) survive. HGW had reintroduced them at the time of the *English Review*, and Hunt kept a pet owl for some years named Ann Veronica. W.H. Hudson freed it eventually. See postcard to HGW from the four, 13 Sept 1920. M. Baring to HGW, 4 Oct 1913. *Current Opinion*, Dec 1913, pp. 431–2, summarizes the reviews. JBP to HGW, 30 Sept, 2 Oct 1914. Later Vladimir Nabokov recalled *The Passionate Friends* as one of the most underrated novels of the past 75 years, *TLS*, 21 Jan 1971; he said it had a touch of high art denied Conrad and Lawrence. Arthur Mizener, *The Saddest Story: A Biography of Ford Madox Ford* (Cleveland and London 1971), is the standard life and treats the Wells relationship in detail.

23 HGW to Holbrook Jackson, *c.* Oct 1915.

24 Rebecca West, *Freewoman*, 25 July 1912, review of J.M. Kennedy, *English Literature*,

1880–1905, in which she refuted a claim that HGW was timid in his treatment of sexual life. Lillian Hellman, 'Love Letters, Some Not So Loving', *NYT Book Review*, 13 Oct 1974; Diana Trilling, 'The Jaguar and the Panther', *TLS*, 22 Nov 1974. Alec Hamilton, 'A Life of Interruptions', *Manchester Guardian Weekly*, 11 Mar 1979, an interview with West. R. West, 'The Confusion Which Is This Life', *Liberty*, 17 Sept 1927.

25   Robert McAlmon and Kay Boyle, *Being Geniuses Together* (London 1984), 145.

26   HGW to Marie Stopes, 12 Mar 1919, 15 Aug 1921 (after Rebecca's mother's death); RAG to HGW, 29 July 1926. Rebecca West, *Ending in Earnest* (New York 1931), a collection of her essays from the column, 'Letters from Europe', in the *Bookman*, 1929–30. The essays in question are 'O.M.', one on Evelyn Waugh later in the book, and 'Miss Gye'. For HGW on Rebecca's rather difficult American lecture tour, see 'The Lawlessness of America and the Way to Order', *WGaz*, 21 June 1924.

27   This letter appears in Gordon Ray, *HGW and Rebecca West* (New Haven 1974), 193: Rebecca West to MCW, 21 Aug 1946; the letter is owned by G. P. Wells.

28   G. P. Wells, ed., *H.G. Wells in Love* (London 1984), ch. 1, esp. 94–111.

Chapter 16

1   On 'flue' (as he called it), see HGW to Marie Stopes, 12 Mar 1919 (the first attack; whether it was Spanish influenza, or his usual susceptibility to upper-respiratory problems, is difficult to say). Sir Harry Johnston to HGW, 25, 30 May 1921, on how he seemed to look better than before the first trip. ACRW to Gertrude Stein, 25 Jan 1921, sorry he cannot see you, but after his pneumonia he has been sent to the South to recover. Series of postcards, HGW to ACRW, 1922, and esp. HGW to ACRW, 23 Mar ?1921: 'Rome is interesting, but – and the Vatican and the churches have narrowed all my Protestant feelings.' HGW to ACRW, 3 May 1923, on way to Paris, after attempting to fly from Prague; his plane ditched both times, cutting his forehead the second time. He spent four hours in the air in a heavy windstorm, which must have been quite a flight in the aircraft of that time. HGW, 'Portugal and Prosperity: The Blessedness of Being a Little Nation', *WGaz*, 1 Mar 1924, reports his most recent southern holiday.

2   Lord Beaverbrook to HGW, 2 Sept 1935; HGW to Beaverbrook, 4 Sept 1935, on the auto accident. It crept into the press, and Wells had a large number of solicitous calls and cards. HGW to Hugh Clegg, 1 Dec 1936, attacking medical doctors, and his preface to Charles Hill and H. A. Clegg, *What is Osteopathy?* (London 1937), v-vii (see his remarks to GBS, quoted in a later chapter, on medicine and Shaw). Diabetic Association to HGW, 14 Sept 1938, thanking him for his letter. In fact, he rewrote the Association's prospectus. Their brochure to raise money for diabetes research featured his photograph, as well as the letter. It was about this time that Wells began to charge 2*s*. 6*d*. for his autograph, with the funds going to the Association. Wells was an advocate of diet, rather than insulin, in the diabetic treatment. See, e.g., HGW to Henry Newbolt, 1 Aug 1933; to Vernon Bartlett, 26 Oct 1939. The letter quoted is to Tom Harrisson, 4 Jan 1937.

3   F. W. Sanderson to HGW, 24 Apr, 6 May 1916, 9 Sept 1918 (with HGW's comments on the letter), 6 Feb, 21, 25 Nov 1919. Sir Harry Johnston supervised some of G.P.'s dissections: ACRW to Johnston, undated; Johnston to ACRW, 30 Jan 1920. G.D.H. Cole to HGW, 3 May 1920. HGW to S. S. Koteliansky, 16 July 1920; ACRW to Kot, 21, 29 July, 17 Sept 1920; HGW to Kot, 4 June, 4 July 1921, 6 July 1922, 20 Apr 1923 (the Chaliapin visit), and many other letters through the decade. The only life of Kotel009iansky appears in the very useful book, John Carswell, *Lives and Letters: A.R. Orage, Katherine Mansfield, Beatrice Hastings, John Middleton Murry, S. S. Koteliansky, 1906–1957* (London and New York 1978). Kot lived on to Mar 1955. One of his friends in later life was Marjorie Craig Wells, who was with him when he died.

4   An excellent picture of the Easton and Essex weekends, with the attendant celebrities, is in R. D. Blumenfeld, *All in One Lifetime* (London 1931), esp. 173–6. HGW to Sidney

Low, 30 May 1901. *NYT*, 30 Apr 1922, reviewed Chaplin's *My Trip Abroad*, and discussed the Wells friendship.

5   FAS to ACRW, 17 Dec 1926.

6   George H. Doran, *Chronicles of Barabbas* (New York 1935). HGW to ACRW, ? May 1927. HGW to Methuen & Co., 19 June 1935.

7   Lady Oxford to HGW, end May 1927. HGW to R. D. Blumenfeld, 21 July 1927; to W. Baxter, 8 Oct 1927; to Frank Wells, 21 Sept, 7 Oct 1927, 16 Oct 1928. The letters to his brother are signed 'The Buzzwhacker'. Lord Beaverbrook to HGW, 16 May 1927. C. F. G. Masterman to HGW, 3 May 1927: 'Perhaps if she knows how much we [he and his wife, Lucy] care for her it may be a little gleam of happiness.' Lady Warwick to ACRW, 5 Oct 1927.

8   HGW to various newspapers, 7 Oct 1927. J. Webb to MCW, 10 Oct 1927, HGW's extended notes on the letter. HGW to MCW, 12 Oct 1927: please draft a statement of truth for the press, enclosing his notes and outline for her draft. With this act Marjorie Wells replaced Jane in his life. *DDispatch*, 18 Sept 1927. Eric J. Stovill to MCW, 17 Oct 1927, with apologies.

9   HGW to F. J. Gould, 26 Sept 1927; to F.H. Hayward, 3, 13 Oct 1927. HGW, *In Memory of Amy Catherine Wells (Jane Wells)* (n.p., n.d. [1927]), repr. *H.G. Wells in Love*, 42–6.

10 Charlotte Shaw to T. E. Lawrence, quoted in Webb *Letters* III. 294; B. Webb to HGW, 6 Dec 1927, *Letters* III. 295. I. Maisky to HGW, 12 Nov 1927, 3 Jan 1928. Eileen Power to HGW, 7 Oct 1927. J. M. Barrie to C. Asquith, 13 Apr 1931, printed in W. Meynell, ed., *Letters of J. M. Barrie* (London 1947), 223. Just before Barrie's death in June 1937, Wells wrote of his distress at the other man's illness, recalling Barrie's 'friendliness and generosity' over the forty years of their acquaintance. EH to HGW, 2, 7 Feb 1928. Kurt Butow to HGW, 19 Oct 1927.

11 APW to HGW, 19, 25 Oct, 3 Nov 1927 (which acknowledges receipt of the MS). HGW to EH, 24 Oct 1927. Pieces by Catherine Wells appeared in the *Transatlantic Review*: 'The Afternoon', May 1924; 'The Dragon Fly', Nov 1924; *Strand*, 'The Confusion of Mr Sackbut and Mr Densham', Aug 1925; *Windsor Magazine*: 'The Persistent Mr Bobbicombe', 'The Ghost', May 1928. APW to HGW, 3, 10 Feb 1928, for 'Ghost', and a *McCall's* reprinting. APW to MCW, 24 Feb, *McCall's* off now; 5 Mar 1928, Doran on way to London, and he has taken the book: $500 with a rising royalty, 15% to 5,000; 20% thereafter. APW to HGW, 15 Mar 1928. A few copies of the book were printed on special paper, 20 Jan 1928.

12 HGW [ed.], *The Book of Catherine Wells* (London 1928). The introduction also appears in its entirety in *H. G. Wells in Love*, by Wells's express wish, as a bridge to the 'Postscript' to his *Experiment in Autobiography*. FAS to HGW, 24 Apr 1928, as he renewed their friendship with his comment on this 'beautiful book'. EH to HGW, 7 May 1928.

13 HGW to Geoffrey West, 16 Sept 1929. *DHerald*, 26 Oct 1923, has a photo of Wells and the East End children with the caption, 'Mr Wells as a Good Fairy', *WGaz*, 25 Oct 1923, a series of photos, and a report of HGW's speech under the heading 'Children's House'. He may have given most of the money for the facility which had a roof garden, a nursery school, and offered evening classes for those over 14. The facility could house 170 children. MCW to HGW, 17 Dec 1931, reporting on a visit, with the Ivor Montagus, to A. S. Neill's Summerhill school.

14 HGW to APW, 8 Dec 1929, spells out the 'incommunicado' arrangement. HGW to Mrs Pedley (?Penley), undated 1924, 20, 21 July 1924 (Hofstra).

15 Sydney Olivier to HGW, 17 Apr 1934, on his daughter from whom Wells may have got the name Brynhild. APW to MCW, 5 Dec 1936, 13, 15 Jan, 12 Feb, 25 Mar 1937; to HGW, 18 Mar 1937. J. Chambrun to HGW, 22 Aug 1936, on serialization. APW to MCW, 26, 30 Aug, 15 Sept; to MCW, 20 July; HGW to APW, 23 July; APW to MCW, 25 Aug (on naval metaphors), all 1937. W. Horrabin's review, *Tribune*, 24 Sept

1937. APW to MCW, 18 Sept, 25 July; HGW to APW, 26 Apr 1941. The cheap edition of *Brynhild* was eventually sold at a cut price of 2*s*. 6*d*. and 2*s*., depending on the quality of the paper; Wells took a lower royalty of 7½% on the cheap edition.

16 Mary Church Terrell, *A Colored Woman in a White World* (Washington D.C. 1940); HGW's preface, i-v.. For the author's comments on the Wells family, see pp. 348–52, 358, 404.

17 Mary Austin, *Earth Horizon: Autobiography* (New York 1932); for her remarks on Jane and HGW, see esp. pp. 311–12. Her story 'The Walking Woman' appears in *Lost Borders* (New York 1919), but HGW read it in MS. See Austin to HGW, 25 Jan, 10 Apr 1910, 15 July 1911; HGW to Austin, 7 Aug 1911; Austin to HGW, 3 May 1921 (to which HGW appended a note to Jane), 4 Nov 1932.

18 Examples are HGW to Mr Clarke, 20 Oct 1906 (6 pp.), 28 Dec 1907; to Mr Oyler, 12 Sept 1909; to 'Dear Sir', 14 Aug 1926; to Mr Carling, 24 Dec 1919; to C. K. Ogden, 26 Nov 1922 (a significant friendship developed with the origination of Basic English); to Bluebell M. Hunter, 15 July, 29 Sept 1932 (Hunter to HGW, 14 July 1932: she dedicated a book to him, *Death Dams the Tide*, which he told her he stayed up past midnight reading), 9 Apr 1935, and another undated; to Mr Tilsby, 29 July 1933 (4 pp.); to Mr Burke, undated (sometime in '20s) (all Boston). Jane brought the last of these to his attention after he had rejected it. To Edgar Jepson, 30 Sept 1933, on *ExA*. Even well-known authors received long letters, as when HGW read Wyndham Lewis's *The Childermass* and wrote him 3 pp., 24 Sept 1928.

19 Eileen Power to HGW (most of his side of the correspondence is apparently lost), 30 Dec 1924, 22 Apr 1926, 27 Apr 1928, 19 June 1929, 8, 9 May (3½ pp. of comment on his speech draft), 22, 24 Oct 1932, 28 Oct 1933, two others undated: 2 Oct, 3 July (both early '30s), 5 Oct 1934, 8 Oct 1936, 22 Jan, 17 Dec 1937, 5, 17 Jan 1938, 20 Mar (with HGW note at foot of letter), 22 June 1939 (another HGW note at foot). Mrs E. A. Benians and M. G. Jones to HGW, Apr 1941; *The Times*, 15 Aug 1941; HGW to his bank, 18 Aug 1941; A. M. Carr-Saunders to HGW, 21 Aug 1941.

20 HGW to Cynthia Asquith, 1 May 1937, on her mother's death: 'It's like another light being turned out in a room that goes dark for me. . . .How life hustles us!' C. Asquith to HGW, 4 May 1937; on guide dogs, C. Asquith to HGW, 6, 14 Apr 1938.

21 There is a good deal of correspondence with Bagnold/Jones about dinners, weekends, and other social chatter. The letters I quote give a good flavour, and are important in themselves. See Herbert First to E. Bagnold, sent on to HGW, and adorned with many 'picshuas', 18 Sept 1918. A comic set of water-colour 'picshuas', from 1918, is in the papers as well, some of them quite revealing, but faded now, from hanging in frames in the sun. E. Bagnold to HGW, 21 Mar 1932; also 14 Feb 1927 (quoted), 7 Feb (quoted), 27 Feb 1929. The letter about the Blanco-Whites is quoted in MacKenzies, *The Time Traveller*, although I did not see it at Illinois. Bagnold was a guest (one of 30) at H.G.'s and Moura's 'wedding party'. E. Bagnold's *Autobiography* (1969, 1970).

22 HGW to Anita Loos, 4 Nov 1927, 4 Oct 1933; also two undated postcards and one letter from the same period.

23 The Hollywood cricket club and the British colony are well described in David Rayvern Allen, *Sir Aubrey: A Biography of C. Aubrey Smith. . . .* (London 1982), esp. 139–45. Hugh Walpole's diary, late autumn to Christmas 1935, quoted in Hart-Davis, 364–5, gives a good account of the English colony. Countess Lier De Maigret, 'On Hollywood', *SReferee*, 29 Nov 1936, with accounts of HGW and Goddard, and various lunches, dinners, and tennis. HGW and Goddard were an 'item' for a time.

24 Martha Gellhorn, *The Trouble I've Seen* (New York 1936), HGW's preface, vii–ix. HGW to Sinclair Lewis, 27 Nov 1935, written while he was at Chaplin's house. HGW was also thanking Lewis in this letter for *It Can't Happen Here*. The two were quite good friends; see HGW to S. Lewis, 4 Sept (?1929), 21 Sept 1931 (Syracuse). They met several times in Paris. George Creel to HGW, 24 Mar 1937.

25 Almost none of HGW's correspondence with Christabel Aberconway survives, apparently. But she devotes a substantial portion of her autobiography, *A Wiser Woman? A Book of Memoirs* (1966), to their relationship. The Selfridge window episode is also described in R. D. Blumenfeld, *All in One Lifetime* (1931).

26 Dora Blake (later Russell) to ACRW, 15 Jan 1919, 31 Jan, 2 Feb 1924; to HGW, 20 June 1924, 18 June 1930. Bertrand Russell to HGW, 26 Nov 1930. D. Russell to HGW, 1 Sept 1933. B. Russell to HGW, 12 Sept 1933 (quoted). HGW to W. B. Curry (postcard), June 1934; W. B. Curry (Dartington Hall master) to HGW, 5 June 1934: Don't get involved in the divorce. B. Russell to HGW, 30 Sept 1937 (telegram). D. Russell to HGW, 6 May, 9 July 1939; 12 Dec 1943, with his quote at the bottom of letter. In *The Tamarisk Tree: My Quest for Liberty and Love* (London 1975), 168–75, Dora Russell recalls her first meeting with HGW, when she went to Easton on a Sunday to protest a Wells letter; she walked through a snowstorm to get there. Wells was a very great help over a petition of May 1924 to the Minister of Health (a Catholic) on effects of birth on tubercular and syphilitic mothers.

27 All this, and a good account of HGW and Charlie Chaplin, is from Frances, Countess of Warwick, *Afterthoughts* (London 1931), a useful memoir.

28 A good deal of Warwick–Wells correspondence exists, on which these paragraphs are based, but specifically: Lady Warwick to HGW, Easter 1920, 17 Oct 1921, 10 Jan 1923, 21 Sept 1928, 13 July 1929 (with HGW's comment on the back). Lady Warwick to GPW, 27 Aug 1929; to HGW, 20 May, 20 July 1930, 12 July 1933, 13 Oct 1936. E. H. Pratt to HGW, 9 June 1938, with a note from G. R. S. Taylor, their colleague on *The Great State*. Margaret Blunden, *The Countess of Warwick* (London 1967), esp. 268–9 on her relations with HGW. Letter from Upton Sinclair to Lady Warwick, 30 July 1913, is an effort to arrange a meeting with HGW (in HGW files).

29 HGW to EH, 7 Sept, 16 Nov 1928, 8 Dec 1929; EH to HGW, 28 Apr 1930. *The Times*, 10 Sept 1935 (her husband's obituary). EH to HGW, 9 Oct 1936; HGW to EH, 7 May 1933, 13 Oct 1935, 30 Apr, 26 June, 25 July 1936, 5 Jan, 3 Aug 1939. The pension came after Healey was forced to sell letters from HGW after her husband died.

30 Harold Nicolson, *Diaries and Letters*; meetings at different times are mentioned in both the 3-vol. (1966–8) and 1-vol. (1980) edns. Nicolson went to a party at HGW's where the other guests were GBS and Brendan Bracken's wife, for instance; and they met as well on more political occasions. RAG to HGW, 22 July; HGW to RAG, 28 July 1936: a full-dress dinner for Mirza Ismail, Prime Minister of Mysore. Noel Brailsford to HGW, May 1933, 23 Dec 1941: two luncheons, one to discuss India, and the other H.W. Nevinson, who had recently died. George Doran gave a party at the Savoy, in late 1928, for HGW, Max Beerbohm, Philip Gibbs, A. P. Herbert, Bennett, Somerset Maugham, and Swinnerton. Asked by Ernest Benn for a MS, to be auctioned for a charity, HGW sent the MS of 'Aepyornis Island' and Benn bid it in for £950: E. Benn to HGW, 1 Mar 1934, 13 Apr 1937 (copy of a note from 'Peregrine' to Uncle Winston, 30 Mar 1937, enclosed). HGW to Michael Collis, 17 July 1935, rejection of social credit ideas, as well as Ezra Pound's poetry. Vernon Bartlett to HGW, 17 July 1929 or 1930, 27 July 1936, 29 Oct 1938; HGW to V. Bartlett, ? 1932 (aboard S.S. *Bremen*), 25 June 1935, 17 Jan 1936, 12 Oct 1937, 31 Oct 1938. HGW to Ritchie Calder, 31 Oct 1933 (quoted); R. Calder to HGW, 10 Oct 1935 (a long and important letter about the newspaper column and its direction), 17 Jan 1938.

31 Konni Zilliacus to HGW, 4 May 1935; Beaverbrook to HGW, 7 Apr 1929; George Creel to HGW, 19 June 1936, 29 Jan 1937; Gilbert Murray to MCW, 22 Oct 1938.

32 Sigmund Freud to HGW, 23 Sept 1936 (in German), in thanks: HGW sent a greeting on Freud's 80th birthday, along with Thomas Mann, Romain Rolland, Jules Romains, Virginia Woolf, Stefan Zweig, and many others; HGW gave 10 gns. towards a gift to Freud. HGW to Freud, 3 May 1936. Freud to HGW, 26 Nov 1938, after a meeting. HGW served on the Freud committee, giving them many ideas, addresses, and a list of

US names as possible subscribers. National Council on Civil Liberties, *1934–1984*, *Half a Century of Civil Liberties* (London 1984), their 50th anniversary pamphlet. See *Punch*, ?? 1955 (only read a cutting), for Claude Cockburn's account of the foundation meetings. Palme Dutt to HGW, 6 May; HGW to Dutt, 8 May; Dutt to HGW, 10 May 1937: this was the first olive branch from the CP. After the events of Munich that branch extended was not spurned. HGW and many others to *Manchester Guardian*, 24 Feb 1934, on hunger marchers and their treatment.

33 I have an article in preparation (1985) for *Paideuma*, on the Wells/Pound/Joyce relationship. See Sylvia Beach to HGW, 18 Dec 1926; HGW to James Joyce, 23 Nov 1928. For the reprinting in the *New Republic* of HGW's review of *A Portrait of the Artist*, see above, ch. 7. Walter Lippman to HGW, 1 Mar 1917; the piece carried an error, and Lippman apologized to ACRW who caught it, 13 Mar 1917. F. M. Ford, *It was the Nightingale* (1923), esp. 330–45, for the later days. The correspondence with Ford is relatively sparse, but interesting.

34 J.M. Barrie to HGW, 29 Mar 1931, on death of Bennett; HGW to Barrie, June 1937, five days before the latter's death. 'All through that time [the last forty years] I've had nothing but my affectionate admiration for you and nothing but friendliness and generosity from you' (in W. Meynell, ed., *Letters of J. M. Barrie* [1947]). A.M. Davies to HGW, 11 May 1925, 7 Apr 1927, 10, 22 Jan, 2 Feb (Davies received the Lyall Medal) 1929, 23 Sept, 29 Nov 1930, 31 Oct 1934, 10 Feb, 16 Apr 1935, 23, 27 July 1936, 2 Oct 1939, 8 Mar 1943. Alfred P. Havighurst, *Radical Journalist H. W. Massingham* (Cambridge 1984). H. W. Massingham to HGW, 19, 26 Feb, 14 Mar 1923. Marie Belloc-Lowndes, diary, 28 Sept, 1 Nov 1941, for the dinner party and theatre; the party was in honour of Alexander Woollcott. Their host at Bush House was Vyvyan Holland. At Grasse HGW also entertained certain literary figures, including, many times, Paul Valéry. A photo of the two in front of Wells's house (album in the Valéry papers, from 1930), has the legend, 'Avec Wells chez les Blanchenay à Grasse'. I owe this photo and the comment to my colleague M. J. McPartland, who found it when she was working on Valéry.

35 Letters between the two date from World War I, and the friendship as described here can be seen in HGW to P. Guedalla, 12 Apr 1926, several others that autumn, as well as 1 Oct 1931, 5 Jan 1932, 25 June 1936, 22 Nov 1943.

36 The letter quoted is HGW to Michael F. Collis, 17 July 1935. Letters between Pound and HGW date from 1917 to sometime in the late '30s. (The last letters from Pound bear no date. An extensive search in Pound correspondence files has turned up no response from Wells to these last outbursts.)

37 Upton Sinclair, *Autobiography* (New York 1962). Letters which demonstrate HGW's feelings are one to Sinclair, late 1920, thanking him for *The Brass Check*; HGW to Sinclair, 23 Sept 1921: 'I'm afraid of *you*. You always publish my letters to you and if I come across I shall want to be invisible and quiet.' The comment applies to one letter only, apparently, a perfectly innocuous facsimile of a Wellsian letter published in *Upton Sinclair's Magazine*, May 1918. Sinclair's letters to HGW, on the other hard, are quite effusive, especially several from 1911–13. Others from HGW are to 'Dear and Only Upton', 5 Aug 1921, signed 'Love'; a postcard of 27 Sept 1922; 5 Apr 1927, thanks for *Oil* which he promises to read by June: 'It looks a big thing. I've dipped in it. I send best wishes.' Sinclair's views did not change from those in *American Outpost* (Tarzana, Calif. 1935).

38 HGW to A. P. Herbert, 24 Oct 1930. The boat race letter is 28 Feb 1934; HGW took Moura as well. Also see 9 July 1935 (Boston).

39 FAS to ACRW, 9 May, 27 Sept 1924, 3 Sept, 21 Dec 1925, 31 Aug 1926. Jane and Swinnerton were frequent luncheon companions. Another good view of Swinnerton's later life is in his *Figures in the Foreground: Literary Reminiscences, 1917–1940* (repr. 1964), which uses letters to and from him to good effect, and provides another glimpse of Dorothy Richardson, Hugh Walpole, A. Bennett, and others of HGW's circle.

40 FAS to HGW, 10 Feb, 8 June 1929, 12, 14, 17, 21 Mar 1933. They went to the theatre

together on 30 Mar 1933, and the Swinnertons remained overnight at HGW's home in London. FAS to HGW, 23 Nov 1933 (with HGW's comments on the letter about the dessert and coffee), 24 Sept 1934, 26 Sept 1936, 30 Mar, 15 Sept 1937. These are the quoted letters.

41 The standard literary life of Stapledon, which, although short, is well constructed and very useful, Patrick A. McCarthy, *Olaf Stapledon* (Boston 1982). His correspondence with HGW has been published in *The Wellsian*, and the *Georgia Review*, edited by Robert Crossley, where he offers the text, although problems occurred in the printing, in 'The Correspondence of Olaf Stapledon and H. G. Wells, 1931–1942'; see also Gary Wolfe, ed., *Science-Fiction Dialogues* (Chicago 1982), 27–57.

42 Olaf Stapledon to HGW, 16 Oct 1931. Also see Humbert Wolfe's review of *Starmaker*, 'The Man With the Star-Duster', in the *Spectator*, 4 July 1937, which is expressly about HGW's influence on Stapledon's writing.

43 O. Stapledon to HGW, 15 Oct, 16 Oct (postcard) 1934, 27 Mar 1936, with draft of 'Open Letter to Peoples of the Earth', 6, 8 Apr 1936 (postcard: 'I shall be delighted to right the universe with you over lunch on the 20th'), 4 Feb 1937; letters and petitions, O. Stapledon to MCW, 7 Feb 1937. He and HGW had lunch again over this on 5 Aug 1937; see postcard of 4 Aug 1937. Letter to HGW, 25 June 1937, describes the 25 pages of signatures they had obtained, calling for a commission to investigate world social and economic problems. See O. Stapledon to HGW, 29 Oct 1937.

44 O. Stapledon to HGW, 16 Nov 1939; HGW to O. Stapledon, ?? Nov 1939. *Manchester Guardian*, 12 Feb 1940, reported a speech by Stapledon, 'Federate or Perish', which sounds almost like HGW, 'Unite or Perish', of the same period. O. Stapledon to HGW, 2 Sept 1940, commenting on his essay, 'I Believe'.

45 J.B. Priestley to HGW, 1 Sept 1932, 29 Sept 1934.

46 J.B. Priestley to HGW, 12 May 1936; HGW to J. B. Priestley, 1 Mar 1937; J.B. Priestley to HGW, 8 Mar 1937 (from Cairo). They spent time discussing the fourth dimension, and Priestley influenced HGW's thinking in *The Conquest of Time*; Priestley to HGW, 1 June 1937, 24 Feb 1939, 2 Jan 1940.

47 Julian Huxley to HGW, 29 Oct 1930; Edith How-Martyn to HGW, 23 Sept 1933; Gerda Guy to HGW, undated 1934. Sanger's own views are given in *My Fight for Birth Control* (New York 1931); *An Autobiography* (New York 1938). Most of the biographies of her pay little attention to her personal life. This is especially true of David Kennedy, *Birth Control in America* (New Haven 1970), but less so, in a disorganized way, in Madeline Grey, *Margaret Sanger: A Biography* (Marek, N.Y. 1978).

48 M. Sanger, *My Fight for Birth Control*, 274, but in almost the same words in her *Autobiography*, 269–71.

49 M. Sanger, *The Pivot of Civilization* (London 1923), HGW preface, 9–16. HGW to 'M.S.' *c.* 1922 from S.S. *Adriatic*, on the preface. HGW also had a long but much more prickly relationship with Marie Stopes, the English counterpart to Sanger. He wrote to her about his failure to perceive a male change of life, and was a frequent visitor at her home. HGW called Stopes 'bossy, self-opinionated'. But Jane and HGW, Stopes, the Shaws, and others devised strategy at HGW's house, and Stopes supported him very strongly at the time of H. Belloc's attacks on the *Outline*, so the two remained friendly. She termed HGW 'Brilliant. . .but how tiresome and didactic. . .rather a gross man'. Keith Briant, *Passionate Paradox: A Life of Marie Stopes* (New York 1962), esp. ch. 22, pp. 243–7; Ruth Hall, *Marie Stopes* (London 1976), is a good biography which also touches the subject. Ruth Hall, ed., *Dear Dr Stopes: Sex in the 1920s: Letters to Marie Stopes* (London 1978), prints a letter from HGW of 25 May 1936 on the change of life. (Hall dates this letter in the previous decade, but see the copy at Illinois.) HGW went on in the letter to say that there had been no observable periodicity in his sexual demands. He, good scientist that he was, had kept a 'very careful private diary for two or three years. I don't think there is any male equivalent to menstruation or to the menopause', was his judgement. I have not seen the diary.

50 HGW to M. Sanger, ? Aug, 21 Dec 1920, 26 Sept, 30 Nov, 7 Dec 1921. The last two were addressed to 'Dear Little Margaret Sanger'. These letters are now in the Sophia Smith collection at Smith College, Northampton, Mass.

51 HGW to M. Sanger, 22 Nov 1922, another undated at about the same time, to 'Dear and Much expected Margaret Sanger'; 12 Aug 1922, another undated at about that same time to 'Dear and Beloved Margaret Sanger', and still another, giving directions to his 'primitive *mas*' in Grasse, for about 5 Jan 1923.

52 There is a whole sheaf of letters and cards from HGW to M. Sanger in the period 1922–4, when they met in London and in Grasse several times. The useful ones (that is, with more than details of trains and so on) are HGW to Sanger (postcard) p.m. 8 Dec 1924; the quoted note, dated 8 Oct 1924; postcard of 21 Dec 1923; as well as six more letters and four postcards.

53 HGW to M. Sanger, postcard of 18 May, letter of 13 May 1927.

54 Draft letters to proposed guests at HGW dinner, and a draft thank you for a declination, 8 Oct 1931. HGW to M. Sanger, ? Aug 1930, 20 Aug 1931; 3 Nov 1931 (from Palisades, N.J., where he was on a sickbed); 28 July 1937 (this and another sheet are covered with details from a telephone conversation once he arrived in New York). M. Sanger to HGW, 12 Sept 1937, reporting from Honolulu on a recent visit to Japan, and a lost chance to visit Shanghai: she was delayed by having broken an arm on the ship, and was in hospital in Kobe at the precise time the Japanese invaded mainland China. HGW to Sanger, 4 Nov 1937, from Detroit, written after he heard about her arm, and the danger of her visit to the Far East.

55 HGW to M. Sanger, 26 June 1942; Sanger to HGW, 7 Nov 1942; an undated one from HGW at the time of *Babes in the Darkling Wood*; HGW to Sanger, 3 Jan, 7 July, 12 Oct 1943. Sanger to HGW, 31 May 1943; HGW to Sanger, 6 Apr 1944. MCW to Leo H. Lehmann, 6 Apr 1944; to Sanger, 6 Apr 1944. HGW to Sanger (copy to Lehmann), 17 July 1944. Sanger to HGW, 21 June 1944. HGW to Sanger, 19 Mar 1943 (thanking her for a gift of honey which went well at tea), 16 Apr 1944. Sanger to HGW, 8 June 1944. Wartime mail went slowly, and these repeat many things which had not been answered.

56 M. Sanger to HGW, 19 Sept 1942, 8, 23 May, 19 Sept 1944, 8 Aug 1945, 14 Aug 1946. (This last letter is extremely difficult to read, as she was clearly distraught at the time of writing. Some of the words are conjectural, therefore.) Sanger to Leo Lehmann, 4 Sept 1946.

57 The best account of the affair is Gordon Ray's, in *H.G. Wells and Rebecca West* (1977), in which he cites several letters in his possession from the woman in question. *DHerald*, 23 June 1923, 'Scene at Mr H. G. Wells' Flat', gives a version, as does *NYT*, 23 June 1923.

58 'The Pearl of Love', written at white heat in two to three days of Jan 1925, was published in a number of places: *Strand*, Dec 1925, pp. 594–7; *Forum* (New York), Dec 1925, pp. 889–93; and *Reynolds's News*, Jan 1931. In addition it was translated by Odette Keun into French, and appeared as *La Perle de l'amour* (Paris 1928). See APW to HGW, 23 July, 7 Aug 1925. *Forum* paid $300 and *Strand* the equivalent in pounds. *Strand* has a lovely colour illustration by Charles Robinson, at p. 593. On *Christina Alberta's Father*, APW to HGW, 29 July, 24 Aug, 22 Sept, 3, 8, 11 Oct 1924; telegram, *Collier's* to HGW, 6 Nov 1924. Wells's comments appear on margin of 29 July, 22 Sept (ACRW) 1924. Wells, Curtis Brown, and Watt were all involved. *Collier's* did the serial.

59 HGW's own account of Odette's life with him is in *H. G. Wells in Love*. The review is in *Adelphi*, vol. I, no. 1 (June 1923), pp. 62–3.

60 Leslie De Charms (pseud.), *Elizabeth of the German Garden* (1958), letter to 'Mark Rainley', 31 Jan, 3 Feb 1927. Lady Keeble (Lillah MacCarthy), *Myself and My Friends* (1933), 272. HGW to W. Baxter, sometime in 1922, 1924, 15 Apr 1925, which describes some of the life at Lou Pidou. Other letters are R.D. Blumenfeld to HGW, 7

Dec 1927; HGW to Daisy Blumenfeld, 14 Jan 1928, saying that Odette has had a painful sinus operation, and he has to attend to her in the clinic both afternoon and morning; Konni Zilliacus to HGW, 26 Nov 1930, describing a film of HGW and Odette, which he calls 'a bit libellous. . .'. MCW to HGW, 16 Dec 1931, saying that it would be a difficult journey (to visit Lou Pidou), but the children would like it. HGW took Odette to Spain again, and the innkeepers where he had lodged with Rebecca a decade earlier were circumspect, but always tipped him a wink; see HGW to Enid Bagnold, 20, 31 May 1932. They visited Valencia and Alicante. Sir George Catlin, *For God's Sake, Go!* (1972), 113.

61 Elizabeth von Arnim, diary entries of 2 Jan, 18, 23 June 1932, 6 Feb 1933, quoted in L. De Charms, *Elizabeth*. MCW to APW, 13 May 1933. HGW to Leon M. Lion, 8 July 1943 (Boston), a description of the last days at Lou Pidou for the couple. *Daily Herald*, 16 May 1938, describes the walling up, and the suit to prevent their being reopened. Odette returned from the USA for the trial. Also see Bernard Loing, 'H. G. Wells at Grasse (1924–1933)', trans. P. Parrinder, *Wellsian*, no. 7 (Summer 1984), pp. 32–7.

62 HGW to Abel Chevalley, ? 19 Apr, ? 1927, handwritten, at Illinois. Which week Wells refers to is unknown.

63 Odette Keun, *I Discover the English* (London 1934), 152–82, 186–7, 188, 193–7. She went on from this to write a book on the TVA (Tennessee Valley Authority) in America, but this work is her *pièce de résistance*. How widely it was read, I do not know; I have never seen much comment on the book among HGW's friends. But it is a remarkable work, clearly about HGW and their life together.

64 Vera Brittain and Geoffrey Handley-Taylor, eds., *Selected Letters of Winifred Holtby and Vera Brittain* (London 1960), V.B. to W. Holtby, 5 Mar 1932; W. Holtby to V.B., 7 Mar 1932; V.B. to W. Holtby, 8 May 1934. For other letters from Holtby see *Women and a Changing Civilization* (London 1935, repr. 1978). Holtby is, of course, famous for her novel, *South Riding*. If the Wells correspondence recently offered for sale (cf. n. 1, ch. 15) is that with Odette Keun, it may very well be 'juicy'.

65 Brittain and Handley-Taylor, eds., *Selected Letters*: W. Holtby to V. Brittain, 17, 27 Sept, 6 Oct 1934; an extremely good account of Holtby's views at this time is her *Women and a Changing Civilization* (1935).

66 Odette Keun, 'H. G. Wells the Player', *Time and Tide*, 13, 20, 27 Oct 1934. Wells apparently contemplated living in Malaya for a time after his breakup with Keun. HGW to 'Sir Herbert', 21 May 1936 (Boston).

67 Christopher Caudwell, *Studies in a Dying Culture* (London 1936). Caudwell, John Strachey, and others were unhappy that HGW did not join them in their adulation of Marxist ideology. HGW always remained immune to that lure; he did think that capitalism was dying, but disagreed on what would ensue, and certainly did not think it was inevitable, whatever it was. For him the only inevitable results were those of normal evolution and planetary physics.

68 APW to MCW, 9, 13, 20 June, 6, 14 July; HGW to APW, 14 July; HGW to Methuen, 23 June; Methuen to HGW, 22 July, quoting Lucas; APW to Scribner, 22 July; HGW to APW, 24 Aug; APW to HGW, 8 Sept, all 1938, cover these transactions.

69 HGW to Dakens (Methuen), 23 June; HGW to APW, 15 July 1938.

70 FAS to HGW, 13 Oct 1938; J.B. Priestley to HGW, 17 Oct 1938 (misdated 1937). Douglas Brass, 'Mr Wells Is as Young as He Likes', Melbourne *Herald*, 14 Jan 1939; Melbourne *Leader*, 21 Jan 1939; Sydney *Bulletin*, 25 Jan 1939.

71 APW to HGW, 22 Apr, 6 July 1925 (Wells comment on the first of these); to MCW, 7, 11 Jan, 23 Feb 1927; to HGW, 3 Aug 1927, 4 Oct 1928, 6 Mar, 20 Aug, 13 Nov 1929, 23 Nov, 21 Dec 1932. *SExpress*, 22 Aug 1927. H. Levy, 'Science in Literature', *Nature*, 8 Oct 1927.

72 This paragraph is based on a great many letters and contracts. Chief among them are HGW to Sir Godfrey Collins, 18 Dec 1920, as well as a half-dozen or so in 1933 when their agreement was extended for the last time; E. Benn to HGW, 20 Oct 1925; APW

to HGW, 4 Aug 1927; APW to MCW, 14, 16 Aug, 5, 7, 15 Dec 1927, 30 Oct 1930, 23 Feb, 20, 22 Apr, 26 June 1931; APW to HGW, 1, 11 Feb 1932; APW to MCW, 27 Oct 1932, 10 Feb, 3, 8 Mar, 5 Apr, 2, 9 June, 6 July 1933; APW to HGW, 16 June 1932 (many of these have HGW's answers written or typed on the original); APW to HGW, 24 May 1937; F. R. Steele (for Pinker) to HGW, 28 June 1938, with HGW's comment on the Horlicks offer in the margin.

73 APW to HGW, 10 Mar 1925, with a long HGW comment in the margin of the letter first describing *William Clissold*. HGW to MCW, 12 Feb ?1926, a 7-pp. handwritten memorandum on *Clissold* for Watt to use when he offers the book to publishers. On stories in the press, see HGW, 'The Mystery of the Perennial Paragraph', *English Review*, Oct 1922, pp. 288–94.

74 *Bookman* (New York), vol. LXIV (Sept 1926), remarks on the *Observer*'s printing of the *Clissold* 'Notes Before the Preface', and in Oct 1926, pp. 144–7, itself reprinted them as HGW, 'Notes on a Novel'. HGW to R. D. Blumenfeld, 3 Mar 1926; APW to HGW, 5 Aug, 9, 11, 15 Sept 1926; to MCW, 16 Mar 1926; to Lucienne Southgate, 8 Jan 1931. Henry E. Armstrong, 'Education, Science, and Mr H. G. Wells', *Nature*, 20 Oct 1926.

75 HGW to Miss Pearn of Curtis Brown, 5, 16 July 1932: no autobiography is contemplated. (These were signed by Lucienne Southgate although HGW wrote them.) MCW to Curtis Brown, 4 Aug 1932: this is a fantasy on your part, and you must stop hawking his name about. MCW to APW, 10 Jan 1934; APW to MCW, 27 Feb, 17 Apr, 23 May, 1, 20, 25, 27 June, 4, 20, 22 July, 1, 8 Aug, 24 Oct 1934. HGW to APW, 1, 24 July 1934. Vol. I of *ExA* was released on 15 Oct and vol. II on 12 Nov 1934.

76 Wells told Harold Laski, 8 Jan 1933, 'I have recently been writing an exhaustingly full and intimate account of my early life up to about the age of 35. There is a good mass of letters and sketches available, a sort of diary in pen and ink caricature that makes it rather specially entertaining. But I have not yet set myself to discuss how a large book of 200,000 words with two or three score pages of facsimile pictures and photographs can be published.'

77 Details of sales come from many letters in the files. HGW to V. Gollancz, 7 Nov 1934, for the cinema sales idea.

78 B. Webb to HGW, 1 Nov 1934 (Webb *Letters* III. 464–5). Franklin D. Roosevelt to HGW, 13 Feb 1935. RAG to HGW, 9 Nov 1934; Eileen Power to HGW, 29 Oct 1934; FAS to HGW, 30 Oct, 24 Nov 1934; Jessie Conrad to HGW, 19 Nov 1934. 'T.L.H.', 'Mr Wells Reveals Himself', *Nature*, 13 Nov 1934; H. Levy, 'The Autobiography of H. G. Wells', *Nature*, 8 Dec 1934, Supplement. The bit to which Levy was referring was repr. in *International Journal of Individual Psychology*, vol. II, no. 2 (1936), pp. 51–3, as 'Towards a Universal Social Life'. J. D. Beresford reviewed the book for *John o'London's*, 13 Oct 1934, saying that the ordinary mind idea had made him laugh. HGW to RAG, 23 Sept 1937; 'I'm vain but not so vain as to be blunt to the dominant share you have had in giving me a show in this B.A. affair.'

79 J. Chambrun to MCW, 24 Feb 1939, re an offer of $250 for a reprint in *Coronet* of 'What Life Has Taught Me' (it appeared in the May number). The original, first of a nine-part series, is in *SChron*, 30 Oct 1938. Also see HGW, 'My Obituary', *SChron*, 31 Jan 1935, repr. *Listener*, 15 July 1936, and also in *Coronet*; see Chambrun to MCW, 22 Dec 1936. HGW earned $500 on this reprinting. The piece was again repr., as 'My Auto-Obituary', *Strand*, mid-1943. The *DExpress* printed it the day after his death, 14 Aug 1946, and *Coronet* also reprinted it again at that time.

80 HGW to RAG, 14 Aug 1939, 11 Jan 1940. See HGW, *Nature*: 'Biology for the Million', 1 Mar 1941, on Julian Huxley, *The Uniqueness of Man*; 'The Man of Science As Aristocrat', 19 Apr 1941. Hills's piece appeared in *Nature*, 1 Mar 1941.

81 HGW to Thomas Heywood, 15 Oct 1934, on freedom of Bromley. The entire British press, 29 June 1936, on his honorary degree. *DTel*, 14 Oct 1936, for the best press account of the PEN dinner and guest list. Photographs appear in *Tatler* and the *Sketch*

as well; HGW's speech may be found in *PEN News*, Oct 1936. J. M. Barrie to J.B. Priestley, 10 Oct 1936: 'He is, of course, one of our chiefest glories, one of the two angels left to us, and I should have loved to be with you and have a go at him.' The programme for the dinner featured a Low cartoon as the cover, showing H.G. playing leap frog over a stile, or milestone, marked '70'. The menu featured oysters, smoked salmon, a soup, sole, lamb chops, green beans, potatoes, salad, an ice soufflé and petits-fours. Stuart Blofield to HGW, 21 Sept 1936; HGW to P. Guedalla, 16 Oct 1936; 22 Nov 1943. On HGW's 75th birthday, in Oct 1941, *Adam International Review* devoted an issue to Wells, with tributes from 30 of his colleagues, among them Beatrice Webb, Thomas Mann, Walter de la Mare, Eleanor Farjeon, C. Day Lewis, and others from all over the world.

82   J. Galsworthy to HGW, 1 Apr 1909 (they met at William Rothenstein's), 8 Apr 1923, 20 Apr 1928, 5 Dec 1929. Ada Galsworthy to ACRW, 29 Apr, 2 May 1926 (the two couples spent a weekend together at Easton); to HGW, 25 Feb, 30 Mar 1933, 13, 17 Jan 1934; HGW to Ada Galsworthy, 21 Feb, 28 Dec 1933. HGW, 'Freedom of Expression', *Author*, Christmas 1934, p. 36, summarizes a speech at the Jubilee Dinner of the Society of Authors. Count Albrecht von Bernstorff, counsellor at the German Embassy in London, detested Hitler, and when he was recalled to Germany late in 1933, Enid Bagnold gave a farewell luncheon for him, at which HGW and Harold Nicolson spoke. Bernstorff did not survive the attentions he received from the Nazis. Enid Bagnold, *Autobiography* (1969, 1970); Robert Bruce Lockhart, *Friends, Foes and Foreigners* (London 1957).

83   HGW (Marjorie signed it) to G. Carson, 6 Nov 1933; G. Murray to HGW, 18 Sept 1934. M. Wells (HGW) to Liverpool *Daily Post*, 28 May 1935, re an incorrect story filed from Barcelona. HGW to *New Era*, 28 Feb 1935, refuting an interpretation of Wellsian thought with regard to eugenics, also to Hertfordshire *Express*, 15 June 1935: another H.G. Wells, not he. Ada Galsworthy to HGW, 5, 7, 20 Sept 1935, 18 Oct 1936, 3 Mar 1937. J. B. Priestley to HGW, 30 July 1940, with Wells response in the margin. *Manchester Guardian*, 3 June 1933 and 5 Sept 1936, for HGW's addresses and letters to the PEN meeting at Dubrovnik and Buenos Aires; their leaders comment approvingly on his remarks.

84   Based on Moura Budberg's obituary, *NYT*, 2 Nov 1974; R. Bruce Lockhart, *British Agent* (London 1934). 'Moura: Citizen Baroness', a file produced by Lovat Dickson for the BBC, but shown only over CBC, apparently, on 14 Apr 1976. Moura Budberg, 'H. G. Wells–Maxim Gorky', *Adam International Review*, vol. XXX, no. 300 (1963–5), pp. 52–6, provides another look at the Wells-Gorky letters published in the USSR in *The Correspondence of M.M. Gorky with Foreign Writers* (Moscow 1960); Budberg produced a few more titbits in this piece. Also see an article on her, *Observer*, 5 May 1963.

85   Claire Sheridan, *From Mayfair to Moscow* (1921), her diary: the date when Moura is involved is 4 Oct 1920. Kenneth Young, ed., *The Diaries of Sir Robert Bruce Lockhart, 1915–1938* (London 1973): entries drawn on for this paragraph are 4 Oct 1930, 6 Mar 1931, 18, 19 Apr 1931. (At an all-male dinner, given by Beaverbrook to celebrate Bennett's sale of *Imperial Palace*, HGW told the story of his one night with a black prostitute in Washington after spending time with Teddy Roosevelt, whom he termed a 'poseur'.) 7, 26, 29 Sept, 3 Oct 1931, 27 Apr, 14, 16 Sept 1932.

86   R. Bruce Lockhart, diary entries of 8, 20 Oct, 17 Nov 1932, 16 Sept 1934, 14 Apr, 2 May 1935 (Mrs Simpson's attendance), 8 Feb, 25 July 1936. HGW to Lord Horder, 11 Jan 1945; Juliette Huxley to HGW, 13 Nov 193?; HGW to EH, 29 Oct 1934; HGW to Moura and others, 4 Nov 1932, on a tea to set up a women's progressive movement, attended by Amber, Moura, Lady Rhondda, Mrs Laski, and Miss Voysey. The tea took place on 3 Nov. HGW gave them £25 to set them going. HGW to P. Guedalla, 22 Nov 1943. Marie Belloc-Lowndes, diary, entry for ? Apr 1943. There are fewer mentions of Wells and Moura in vol. II of Bruce Lockhart's *Diaries* (London 1980). The useful

entries are those on a luncheon at Sybil Colefax's, 16 Sept 1940; on the Other Club, 24 July 1941; on Moura's reported views of Wells's latter days, 25 Aug 1944 and 18 May 1945.

87 'Mr Wells Talks of Women', Melbourne *Age*, 10 Jan 1939. APW to MCW, 21 Jan 1939, on the proposed book; HGW comment in the margin, asking for a more definite proposal, and APW to MCW, 8 Mar 1939. Wells's 1944 letters to W. F. Cooper deal with many of these personal judgements; see HGW to Cooper, 19 Jan, on Jesus and Paul; 20 Jan, on an article for *Tribune* in which HGW hoped to cite Cooper; 22 Jan, 4 Feb, all 1944. Both the last deal with the place of sexual activity in the human; I am quoting the second.

Chapter 17

1 HGW, 'If Hitler Goes to War. . .', *SChron and Referee*, 27 Aug 1939.
2 HGW, 'The Sword of Peace: Every Sword that is Drawn Against Germany is a Sword Drawn for Peace', *DChron*, 7 Aug 1914. Also see *The War That Will End War* (London 1914) and his article in *The Times*, 8 Aug 1914.
3 HGW, letter to *The Times*, 26 Sept 1939. The debate continued through the autumn. Other Wells letters appeared in *The Times* on 30 Sept and 25 Oct 1939. By the latter date he was referring to a trial statement already in circulation. The early days of the campaign are discussed well in Ritchie Calder, *On Human Rights*, a speech given on 7 Dec 1967, later published by the H. G. Wells Society (London 1968). An early meeting in Ritchie Calder's flat led to letters to various personalities who contributed to the first draft. The correspondence, published in 1939 by The Peace Book Company under the title *Peace and War Aims*, included letters from A. A. Milne, Maxwell Garnett, L. P. Jacks, Norman Angell, and others, as well as HGW. *The Times*, 4, 7, 14 Sept 1939. The discussion lasted in this form until early November.
4 MCW to Robert Randall, 13 Oct 1939; Randall to HGW, 15 Oct 1939, on pacifism, Anglo-Saxon expansion, and efforts to drive a wedge between Britain and the US: 'He is as much American as he is "British" and he is watching the campaign to estrange the English and Americans with great interest' (in Gerald Barry collection, LSE, file 9). The letter columns of the *Manchester Guardian*, in Jan, Feb 1940 on war/peace aims are relevant; see esp. 15, 16 Feb 1940 letters from F. N. Keen and D. Caradoc Jones. Christopher Hollis, ed., *Neutral War Aims* (London 1940), has useful articles by Herbert Agar, A. V. Baikalof, Merry DuVal, and many others. Dorothy Thompson to HGW, 20 Nov 1939: She wrote a column and gave a speech on Wellsian ideas. HGW to Vernon Bartlett, 24 Oct 1939: 'I have been hit by a great idea. Everybody wants to know what we are fighting for? . . . But what of Magna Carta over again? Why not a *Declaration of Rights* . . . Why not build the new world in that?' HGW to Bartlett, with a typed draft, July 1940. HGW, 'What the Allied War Aims Should Be', *Liberty*, 30 Dec 1939, pp. 5–7. HGW, 'The Transformation of War', *Tomorrow*, vol. I, no. 5 (Jan 1942), pp. 5–7: It will be possible to 'turn their whole surface of the earth into a smiling garden . . . Man may fail in his last war. Many great and dominant species and classes of life have failed in the past. For a time they dominated and then they passed. Man may rise to this ultimate transformation of war. There is no guarantee whatever that he will. But he can. To that his whole past witnesses.'
5 HGW: 'What We Fight For', *SChron*, 12 Oct 1939; *Liberty*, ? Oct 1939. 'What Are Our War Aims?', *Picture Post*, 21 Oct 1939; *Manchester Guardian*, 15 Nov 1939. Wells was apparently telling people at this time that he thought the war would be short; Marie Belloc-Lowndes to Susan, 1 Oct 1939, a letter discussing a recent lunch, pp.182–3 of her *Diaries and Letters* (1975). 'He is very shrewd' was her verdict. For other feminine writers and their views on England at this time, see F. Tennyson Jesse, *English Letters* (London 1943), and Vera Brittain, *England's Hour* (London 1941, repr. 1981), as well as Dorothy Sayers, *Begin Here* (London 1940). Also see George Beardmore (Arnold Bennett's nephew), *Civilians at War: Journals 1938–1946* (London 1984).

6 ? (signature illegible), for *The Times*, to HGW, 29 Nov 1939.

7 National Peace Council to HGW, 24 Oct 1939 (his draft answer appears on the letter). Francis Williams to HGW, 22 Nov 1939, a good summary of other meetings, and the state of the declaration.

8 Francis Williams to HGW, 9, 15 Dec 1939, 26 Jan 1940; undated HGW to F. Williams, early Dec 1939. National Peace Council to HGW, 26, 30 Jan 1940. Wells's responses appear in pencil on these letters. Carbons of many of his letters are lacking from this period on, because of the cost and scarcity of paper. Wells usually wrote his draft in pencil for Marjorie Wells to type and give to him for his signature.

9 H.G. Wells, et al., *The New World Order* (London: National Peace Council 1940); Wells quotes are from pp. 11, 21–2. The relevant correspondence is National Peace Council to HGW, 30 Jan (they sent out 1,000 invitations), 6 Feb (Wells's reply is 9 Feb), 18, 24 Mar (refers to publication proposals) 1940. A second meeting took place in Caxton Hall, 18 Mar 1941, and the discussion issued in stencilled form. N.P.C. to HGW, 4 Feb, 23 Mar, and the text of the discussion dated 22 Apr 1941. The Council continued its activities in 1943, although Wells was less active. By 1945 he was forced to refuse invitations to participate, citing his illnesses and that he was 'too preoccupied' to offer much. See N.P.C. to HGW, 9 Aug, and his answer, 31 Aug 1945. The preoccupation was over the Hiroshima and Nagasaki bombings.

10 A 5–pp. typed memorandum, unsigned, to the committee (*DHerald* file in HGW archive). Francis Williams to HGW, 2 Jan, 18 Feb 1940, which discuss payment, schedule for writing, proof correcting, along with the work of Calder, Williams, and others. The actual series appeared in *DHerald*, over HGW's name, and under the title, 'The Rights of Man', on 5, 6, 7, 12, 13, 16, 17, 22, 23, 24 Feb 1940. Comments were printed on 8, 9, 13 (J. B. Priestley), 15 (H. W. Nevinson), 16 (H. M. Tomlinson, Lancelot Hogben), 17 (Duchess of Athol), 19 (GBS), 20 (C. E. M. Joad, R. Acland), 21 (Earl of Lytton), 25 (A. A. Milne), 27 (Kingsley Martin, S. de Madariaga) Feb, 1 (C. R. Attlee) and 2 Mar (Ritchie Calder) 1940. See HGW to committee, 6, 10 Feb; Sankey to R. Calder, 7, 8 Feb 1940, for the internal discussion of chairing, and assessing the responses. HGW gives a view of these discussions, along with the texts of letters and various drafts in his Penguin Special, *The Rights of Man* (Harmondsworth 1940). A version of these events also appears in Armytage, 173–6.

11 HGW, *The Common Sense of War and Peace: World Revolution or War Unending* (Harmondsworth 1940), esp. ch. 14. Another source was a statement in his *The New World Order* (London 1940). Also see Sir Campbell Stuart, *Secrets of Crewe House* (1920), which discusses the First World War effort and prints the memo. The Liberal Party document occurs in HGW to Lord Esher, 31 Oct, 2 Nov 1935, which enclosed 'A Memorandum on Liberal Principles and Policy'. This 7–pp. document has an 11–point statement of principles very similar to the Declaration in its early forms. Also see the *Declaration des droits de l'homme*, passed at Dijon in 1936 at a meeting of the League for the Rights of Man, which HGW prints in his *Rights of Man* book. He also printed the Crewe memorandum in Atlantic XXI, *D News*, 8, 9 Nov 1918 for the early articles.

12 HGW to *Sheffield Tribune*, ? Feb 1940 (a MS read at Illinois). HGW, 'Interim Remarks', *Fortnightly*, May 1940, pp. 498–511; this was in response to a comment by H. A. L. Fisher in Feb 1940. HGW, 'Unite or Perish', *Picture Post*, 4, 11, 18 May 1940; the last of these reprints the Declaration. These articles in different form were also repr. in *The Common Sense of War and Peace*. Many of them were also repr. in the US and elsewhere. See *Tribune*, 15 Mar and 26 July 1940, for their comments; the second was by Raymond Postgate, in the form of an open letter to HGW, to which he responded on 2 Aug 1940. In this comment to *Tribune*, Wells said the Declaration called for a World Socialist state (Postgate had disagreed on the issue of private property) and went on to say, 'I, who am really in earnest about World Socialism and do not care a damn whether it strips me bare, kills me, and forgets me, repress a considerable anger at these mischievous, silly pseudo-extremists who

have done nothing but yap and hinder on the flank of every creative effort in this country over the last half-century.' This diatribe was directed at the British CP, not at Postgate, whom Wells congratulated on the new *Tribune* and its contributions to this debate. See Leland D. Case, ed., *A World to Like* (?1942), which prints the Declaration of Human Rights, pp. 6–8, and 'Essentials for Entering World Order', pp. 9–10; the latter appeared originally in the *Rotarian*, Sept 1941, as 'The Purpose of It All', pp. 6–10. The issue was entitled 'A World to *LIVE* In'.

13   FDR to HGW, 9 Nov 1939; Ritchie Calder to HGW, 20 Jan, 12 Feb, 23 Mar (this contains both Nehru's and Gandhi's comments) 1940; Eduard Beneš to HGW, 29 Dec 1941. HGW to *Guardian*, letter to editor, 23 Aug 1940. HGW, 'The World of My Heart's Desire', *SExpress*, 29 Dec 1940. He felt the idea that human nature was unalterable was now gone, and 'cosmopolitan socialism' would surely come. The *Documentary Newsletter*, Mar 1941, reprinted part of his Crewe House memo, under the title, 'Propaganda Plan 1918'. HGW, 'Fundamental Realities', *Horizon*, Mar-Apr 1941 (I read the TS at Illinois). On the diplomatic dinner see R. Calder to HGW, 11 Aug 1941, and HGW 'Very private memorandum' to himself, dated 14 July 1943, after a conference with Ritchie Calder and Gangulee on 13 July. Apparently this was circulated to Winston Churchill in some form as well (from internal evidence, as HGW offered to write to UN members, along with Winant and some neutrals). HGW to J. Winant, 12 June; to I. Maisky, 15 June; Maisky to HGW, 30 June 1943. N. Gangulee, *The Russian Horizon* (London 1943), with HGW preface. HGW to (?) A. Slonimski, 24 July, 7, 20 Aug, 15 Oct 1943, which led to the Polish version of the Declaration (after some minor changes were made over the issue of nationalism).

14   I am relying here on the copy of the 1943 *Rights of Man* at Bromley, which has a few interlineations in the text in HGW's hand. His preface is pp. 3–4; the other quotes are from pp. 9, 11, 12, 13, 15. HGW also thought sectional juries could solve regional problems as they emerged. I have found no evidence that Mass Observation did anything for HGW.

15   HGW to C.K. Ogden, undated (three) *c.* 1918, 13 Mar 1923, 29 June, 1, 10 July 1931. Lucienne Southgate to Ogden, 10 May 1933; HGW to Ogden, 4 Oct 1933. L. Southgate to Ogden, 4 June 1936. HGW to Ogden, 17 Sept 1943. Ogden to HGW, 16 May 1933, 3 June 1936, 17 Nov 1943.

16   Here I am relying on the text in HGW's *The Rights of Man* (1940), which came out before the Declaration was translated and widely circulated. It is, of course, a profoundly western document, and in its final form, as the Universal Declaration of Human Rights adopted by the United Nations in 1957, is substantially more even. Forms of the document appear in HGW's writings from 1939 to 1944, and vary somewhat in wording, but the provisions outlined here are his essential document. The article headings in *Science and the World-Mind* (London: New Europe Publishing Co. 1942), 55–63, are as follows:

           Introduction
    1.   Right to Live
    2.   Protection of Minors
    3.   Duty to the Community
    4.   Right to Knowledge
    5.   Freedom of Thought and Worship
    6.   Right to Work
    7.   Right in Personal Property
    8.   Freedom of Movement
    9.   Personal Liberty
    10. Freedom from Violence
    11. Right of Law-Making

The text also appears in HGW, *Guide to the New World* (London 1941); *Phoenix* (Girard, Kans. 1941, London 1942); *The New Rights of Man* (Girard, Kans. 1942); *The Outlook for Homo Sapiens* (London 1942); *'42 to '44* (London 1944). One area where the impact of the discussion can be noticed is in the so-called Atlantic Charter produced at the meeting of Churchill and Roosevelt in Newfoundland in 1941. FDR's widely quoted 'Four Freedoms' owe something to HGW's Declaration as well.

17   This argument, and its many side-effects, has been brilliantly treated in a recent book by Gary Werskey, *The Visible College* (London 1978). In addition, there is a good biography of J. B. S. Haldane, by Ronald Clark. I have also benefited from discussions with Patrick Parrinder, and from a paper which he delivered at the University of Maine some years ago, entitled 'H.G. Wells and "The Scientific Enlightenment"'. Gregory has been the subject of a good biography by W. H. G. Armytage (1956), cited frequently above, but one which concentrates on *Nature*, with less on politics. See RAG, 'Natural Aspects of Education', *Nature*, 17 Apr 1913, which cites Wells's roles.

18   The best account of these activities is in Armytage, esp. chs. 6–8. E. Ray Lankester, ed., *Natural Science and the Classical System in Education* (London 1918): HGW, 'The Case Against the Classical Languages', 183–95; and 'A Modern Education', 196–206; F. W. Sanderson, 'Science and Educational Reconstruction', 207–49. HGW, 'The Case Against the Classical Languages', *Fortnightly*, Apr 1917, pp. 567–74. Eleventh *Annual Report* of the Executive Committee of the British Science Guild (June 1917): HGW, 'Science and Curricula of our Schools and Universities', 75–80. HGW, 'Science and the Nation', *Nature*, 19 Apr 1917, pp. 141–2; *Nature*, 10 May 1917, for correspondence on one review. Also see E. Ray Lankester, ed., *Report, 1916–1918, on the League for the Promotion of Science in Education* (London 1919). See also G. Werskey, '*Nature* and Politics Between the Wars', *Nature*, 1 Nov 1969, pp. 462–72.

19   Armytage, chs. 8–9. *MPost*, 27 Sept 1922, on HGW's speech to B.S.G., apparently not reprinted anywhere. HGW to RAG, ?2 May 1921; RAG to HGW, 28 May 1921, quoted in Armytage; RAG to HGW, 11, 19 Aug 1921, on A.T. Simmons's death. Editorial, *Nature*, 25 Aug 1921. Statement of support for HGW's London Univ. candidacy written by Gregory. RAG to HGW, 1 Dec 1922, 28 Sept 1926. Also see the discussion earlier on the founding of the *Realist*, which partly stemmed from these matters; Church was the editor of that abortive journal. Also see HGW to RAG, 11 Mar 1930. (Most letters cited in these notes are not at Illinois, but were used and cited by Armytage, who quotes them fully.) *Nature*, 3 June 1922. J. Huxley to HGW, 9, 19 Oct 1926 (they had lunch on ?? Oct to work on the appeal to join the Union), 29 Aug 1928.

20   HGW to RAG, postcard 11 Apr 1930.

21   For HGW's speech on his 70th birthday, see *PEN News*, no. 82 (Oct 1936), and elsewhere. HGW was interviewed often on the birthday occasion, and quoted widely in the press. Whether he made the remarks to which Haldane responded, and if so where, is a bit obscure. J. B. S. Haldane, 'Of Course Science Can be "Left"', *University Forward*, Mar–Apr 1937, p. 3.

22   HGW, 'On the Social Relations in Science', *Nature*, 1938. *NYT*, 29 Mar 1940, reported a speech to a Leeds University conference of the British Students' Congress. There was less science here, and more of an attack on the government, at least according to the *Times*. See RAG to HGW, 2 Feb, 9 Aug 1940. HGW used Hilda Matheson as a go-between on Gregory's BBC talk. On a speech at Oxford arranged by Gilbert Murray, see L. W. Judd to HGW, 24 Feb, 15 Mar 1940. HGW, Judd, and Alan Ferguson of the BA had lunch to discuss the topic on 2 Apr. See Ferguson to HGW, 24 Mar 1940. The speech is discussed, with its aftermath, the formation of a Science Teachers group, in Judd to HGW, 22 Apr 1940. The acoustics were bad where HGW spoke.

23   HGW, 'The Man of Science as Aristocrat', *Nature*, 19 Apr 1941. HGW, letter to *Nature*, 17 Mar 1941. Julian Huxley to HGW, 6 Mar, 23 Aug, 22 Sept 1941. See memorandum to Division for Social and International Relations of Science, early in

Feb 1941 and follow-up 'Charter for Scientific Fellowship'. Both were discussed at an executive board meeting of 21 Feb 1941. The principles are printed as Appendix B of the present work. RAG to J. Huxley, Aug 1940, and other letters in which the place of the BA conference, its agenda, and the impact of the blitz are discussed.

24 *NYT*, 29 Sept 1941, covered the event in considerable detail, reprinting the 7-point principles and giving substantial quotations from HGW's speech, although they commented unfavourably on his voice and his age: 'Mr Wells', said the writer, Craig Thompson, 'was a strange and withered spectacle of a great spirit.' Julian Huxley to HGW, 23, 29 Sept 1941. RAG to *The Times*, 11 Oct 1941; RAG to HGW, actually reprints HGW's intended speech, 10 Oct, and HGW to RAG, 10 Oct 1941. RAG to *News Review*, 10 Oct; RAG to MCW, 13, 15 Oct, and *News Review's* apology to HGW, 16 Oct 1941. 'Wells the Censored', *News Review*, 9 Oct 1941, pp. 16–22; also 7 Feb, 20 May 1941.

25 I am following the description in ch. 1 of J. G. Crowther, O. J. R. Howarth, and D.P. Riley, *Science and World Order* (Harmondsworth 1942). The formal *Transactions* appear in *The Advancement of Science*, British Association, vol. II, no. 5 (Jan 1942), pp. 1–116. Those who wish to recall the remarkable hopes voiced at these meetings are urged to read ch. 5, on World Resources, 6, Health and Food, as well as 9, Science and World Planning. Another useful Penguin which may have had its origin in the committee is Raymond West, *Psychology and World Order* (Harmondsworth 1945), esp. ch. 9 (pp. 107–16), and the world chapter, pp. 124–5. Also see West's *Conscience and Society* (London 1942), for a Freudian analysis of these matters. See ch. 16 of Armytage, for another account.

26 Quoted as the culminating words in *Science and World Order*, 138. Readers may judge for themselves the results of this optimism.

27 HGW, *Science and the World-Mind* (London: New Europe Publishing Co. 1942); appendices, 51–63. It is difficult to determine how many copies were printed, but the pamphlet sold for a nominal 2s. 6d., and I have seen enough copies to suggest that several thousand must have been in circulation.

28 HGW, *Science and the World-Mind*, generally. The quote is from p. 40. The concept of science prevailing at this time permeates the fiction of C. P. Snow in his *Strangers and Brothers* series, in which many of the figures at this conference appear in other guises.

29 For the false efforts re the Royal Society, see HGW's correspondence with John R. Baker over Baker's book, *The Scientific Life*: Baker to HGW, 14, 17, 20 Aug, 3, 9 Sept 1942. HGW to RAG, 30 June 1942 on gingering the Royal Society to take in the new social scientists. HGW to C. Burrill and G. W. Denton, 22 May 1943, saying that scientific research did not need an FRS, but rather openness and willingness to work. HGW signed this letter, 'Your slightly elderly but still active Associate'. HGW also commented on these ideas in a roundtable discussion in 1943. The debate was printed first in 1943, and again in 1945 with an HGW article, 'Renvoi: How Are We to Get Out of This War?', in which these views were again raised. James Avery Joyce, ed., *World Organization – Federal or Functional?* (London 1945); I have not seen the 1943 version which appeared 24 Oct 1943, just after the roundtable. HGW's second paper appears at pp. 45–9. *The Advancement of Science*, vol. II, no. 8 (1943), reprints much of the dialogue held 20–1 Mar 1943 on 'Science and "The Citizen: The Public Understanding of Science"'; Wells's remarks appear at p. 337. Others who spoke were RAG, D. S. Evans, Ritchie Calder, and J. G. Crowther. Wells's remarks were a commentary on the other talks. *NYT*, 16 Jan 1943, reports similar remarks of his. Also see HGW's comparison with Soviet science organization in his note to Peter L. Kapitza, 'The Organization of Scientific Work in the Soviet Union', *Russian Review, 1945* (Harmondsworth 1945), 78–86; Wells's note is at p. 78.

30 Richard Acland to HGW, 3 Jan, 1, 3 Nov 1938. I am following a chronology of events typed out for HGW by Marjorie at the time of the 1941 Committee, when HGW thought he would need to have recourse to facts against his critics.

31 The correspondence on this matter is fairly extensive. See Paul Addison's remarkable book, *The Road to 1945* (1975), which places the group in context. Also see Sir Richard Acland's Penguin Special, *Unser Kampf* (Harmondsworth 1940). The significant letters are Acland to HGW, 26 Feb, 26 Mar 1939, 4 Jan, 29 Apr (the Wells–Acland–Ritchie Calder meeting took place at Hanover Terrace on 22 Apr 1940) 2, 7 May 1940, 24 Feb, 6 Mar, 17 Apr 1941 (two or three others undated in this period). HGW's responses, some in carbon, some in draft, are 21, 27 Mar 1939, 4, 11 May (the one quoted in the text) 1940, with HGW addenda on the carbon. 1941 Committee files, esp. memo of 13 Feb 1941; minutes of meeting 12 Mar, dated 9 Apr 1941 (HGW attended this one). HGW to Acland (to Committee, in fact), 7 May 1941. V. Bonham Carter to HGW, 17 Mar, 2, 8, 10 Apr 1941. Ritchie Calder to HGW, 12, 15, 16 Feb 1940, summarizing the three-way discussion, and later HGW and Ritchie Calder's extensive discussion of Acland, in memo in the files.

32 See HGW, letter to editor, *Manchester Guardian*, 9 Aug, and later 6 Sept 1940. In these letters he said the purpose of the meetings was to cut down Tory backbencher influence in the House of Commons. This may have been the beginning of the problems he later had with Earl Winterton, for which see an earlier chapter. Also see his letter, in draft, to *The Times*, written 24 May 1941, in which he disavowed membership in the 1941 Committee. HGW now said he had been only an adviser, had stopped attending, and was not responsible for their documents. Whether *The Times* published the letter or not has yet to be established, but in any case, HGW's association with the group was dead, and not before time.

33 Olaf Stapledon to HGW, 4 June, 3, 11 Aug 1942. HGW draft comments on the 3 Aug letter describe the Polish material sent to him via Moura. His views on bombing Berlin in the 'Sitzkrieg' period were the subject of press comment, and resulted in his letters on the correct view: *Freethinker*, 2, 19 Nov 1941; *Truth*, 2, 9, 23 Feb 1940.

34 HGW to *Manchester Guardian*, 23 Aug 1940; HGW to *Listener*, pub. 4 Mar 1943. HGW to Progressive League (Leslie Michen), 12 July 1943. Their comments appear in 12 Sept, 5 Oct 1943; HGW responded on 8 Oct, and they printed more comments on 15 Oct. He withdrew his support on 4 Feb 1944. However, also see his letters of 7 Jan, 26 Oct 1943, and their columns after 2 Nov 1943, when they print some of his familiar letters. He was scathing when the *Chicago Defender* published a garbled version of the Declaration, and took the occasion to attack their position on Gandhi and India as well. See their letter to him of 1 Oct 1942, and his notes on the margins. An interesting account of HGW and India is Mulk Raj Anand, 'In Conversation with H.G. Wells', *Journal of Commonwealth Literature*, vol. XVIII, no. 1 (1983), pp. 84–90, which reports a long and pleasant meeting in Jan 1932 of the 'Friends of India', called by Krishna Menon. They went on to discuss literature and general matters as well.

35 HGW to *Plebs* (J. M. P. Miller), 10 Sept 1943, and an undated letter of Nov 1943 in response to their two open letters to him. HGW to Charles A. Dana, of the British-American Council for World Government Organization, 1, 5 Nov 1943. HGW was more concerned about paper shortages than about opposition here, however.

36 I have listed only those translations I have actually seen. There were, in addition, translations into Chinese, Japanese, Dutch, Flemish, Finnish, and other languages. Publications containing the Declaration that I have actually seen include *Die Zeitung*, 24 Oct 1943; the *Czechoslovak*, 2 Oct 1943; *La Revue Danubienne*, 21 Mar 1940; *Esperanto Internacia Majo*, June 1942; the *New Leader*, 21 Aug 1943; *Public Opinion*, 3 Nov 1939 (one of the earliest versions); *Plan*, Aug 1943, *Forum* (journal of the Hull Youth Parliament), Jan–Mar 1944; *Plebs*, Oct 1943; *France*, early 1944; *Hellas*, 29 Oct, 5 Nov 1943 (HGW wrote a long introduction to this publication); *Nouveaux Cahiers*, 2 Jan 1940; *War Illustrated*, 20 Sept 1941 (with a comment comparing it to the Fourteen Points speech). The *DHerald* reprinted the text again on 20 Apr 1940, after the public debate. Edward Hulton printed it in *Thinking Aloud: What Price Peace Aims?* (London 1944–5). It was published in *Pririzaena Lidska Prava* (London: New Europe Publishing

Co. 1943), with an introduction by HGW. The Peace Pledge Union adopted it and printed it in July 1941, and a group calling itself the Research Co-ordinating Committee, in conjunction with the Engineers Study Group on Economics, published it in Feb 1942, with a postscript by J. B. Priestley. *Nova Polska* published it in Sept 1943. For some of the correspondence on costs and translations see MCW to E.R. Bushnell (the printers), several letters; on the Zulu translation, HGW to A. T. Bryant, 19 Oct 1943. Also see HGW, 'Buts de Guerre et carte du Monde', *La France Libre*, vol. XI, no. 7 (May 1941), pp. 26–9. HGW, 'The Outlook for the Small Nations', *Frit Denmark*, vol. I, no. 7 (Oct 1942), and reprinted in *Budou Cnost*, and *Mazych Narod*, where he attempted to bring out responses from the smaller powers. I am quoting from his letter to Harold Keble of Oct or Nov 1943, undated.

37   See his correspondence with G. E. C. Catlin on the early days of the Declaration: Catlin to HGW, 5, 15 Nov 1941, 1 Jan 1942, and HGW's note in which he says the rights must come from the bottom, not the top. Catlin and HGW had been associated over the *Realist*. HGW to J. Christian Moller, in which he lays out his new role on the committee, 24 July 1943 (Moller supervised the Scandinavian translations). HGW, 'Ourselves and Russia', *SPictorial*, 14 Feb 1943.

38   HGW to Herbert Read, 18 July, 18 Aug 1943; to J. B. Priestley, 21, 28 July 1943 (Priestley had some good comments on the Declaration); to Editor, *DWorker*, 26 July 1943; to Jan Masaryk, 26 July 1943; to Fenner Brockway, 29 July 1943; HGW, 'The Natural Rights of Man: An Essay in Collective Definition', *New Leader*, 21 Aug 1943. HGW to Chaim Weizmann, 3 Aug 1943; to Alexandra Kollontai, 6 Oct 1943; to Julian Huxley, 11 Oct 1943 (this one in his own hand; most of the others are typed copies); to Jan Christian Smuts, 22 Oct 1943; to Antoine Delfosse, 11 Nov 1943; to Herbert Agar, 8 Jan 1944; to S. Rostovsky, 7 Feb 1944; to A. G. Watson, 18 July 1945 (this in HGW's hand also). HGW also sent a new copy of the Declaration to Ivan Maisky, who had been in Russia, with a long covering letter, 15 June 1943, asking Maisky to circulate it, now called 'The Universal Rights of Man', widely. The letter is carefully written with the appropriate codewords.

39   Discussion of World War II journalism not directly associated with the human rights campaign appears in the next chapter. See Francis Williams to HGW, 13 Nov 1939. The letter offered 15 gns. for 600-word articles, and was the first contact which led to the rights of man publication in the spring. The debate with B. Wootton appeared on 22 Nov 1939, under the title 'Should the Nations Federate?' Her answer was, 'Yes, or perish'; HGW, on the other hand, headed his piece, 'But Dare You?'. This is a good place to see HGW's historical views on the League. See Ritchie Calder to HGW, 11, 14 Dec 1939 on the *Herald* luncheon which he described as an 'unqualified success'.

40   HGW, 'Nationalism: A Myth', *Reynolds's News*, 17 Mar 1940. C. E. M. Joad, 'An Open letter to H. G. Wells', *New Statesman*, 17 Aug 1940 (a review of *The Common Sense of War and Peace*); HGW, 'An Open Letter to C. E. M. Joad', *New Statesman*, 24 Aug 1940; Joad's rather weak answer appears on 31 Aug 1940; HGW, *New Statesman*, 18 Dec 1943, on Joad's review of *The Rights of Man*. On Streit and his organizations, see G. E. C. Catlin to HGW, 20 May, 17 July 1939; MCW to ? Kimber of the Federal Union, along with HGW's memorandum, 16 Nov 1939; HGW, 'Memorandum of the Federal Idea', *Union*, May 1940; HGW, 'The War and the U.D.C.', *New Statesman*, 31 Aug 1940, letter to editor with many others; HGW wrote and circulated this letter, although in the event he dissented from a half-dozen words in its final form. One group, the Abortion Law Reform Association, in which HGW had been active in the '30s, was revived and HGW urged more work. Gerda Guy to HGW, 28, 31 July 1936, Apr 1937; Janet Chance to HGW, 3 Dec 1943, and his marginal comments. HGW encouraged the publication of and wrote an introduction to L.W. Batten, *The Single-Handed Mother* (London 1939, rev. edns. 1943, 1945).

41   HGW, *SDispatch*: 'Hitler Has Lost the War, But Britain Has Yet to Win It', 5 Jan 1941; 'Russia and the Future', 29 June 1941. HGW did head this article with the

remark that it was difficult to write without saying, 'I Told You So', and he provided a sentence later which Hitler and Goebbels found maddening: 'This attack on Russia is the latest and perhaps the last of this poor blood-soaked world's convulsions.'

42 HGW, *SDispatch*, 27 July 1941.

43 HGW, *SExpress*, 24 Aug 1941; *SDispatch*: 'An Article to Annoy Professors and Parsons', 23 Nov 1941; 'Governments May Shut Their Eyes, But There IS a New World Coming', 28 Dec 1941. This article was answered by an acceptance of his principles, but with a cry from the heart about the large powers: Eduard Beneš to HGW, 29 Dec 1941. Beneš reminded HGW that their desires had been thwarted in Sept 1939 by only one nation. *SDispatch:* 'An Article – For Those Who Are Only Nagging for Victory', 3 May 1942, from which the quote comes; also see 'Genius in a New World', 21 Feb 1943; 'This Book is Massively Stupid;' ?? Apr 1943, where he analyses Leopold Schwarzschild's book as appealing only 'to the lumpen-intelligentsia, and the gentlemen saying, Hear!, Hear!, in the Senior Blimps Club'.

44 HGW, 'Do we Want a Standing Anglo-U.S. Alliance?', *Picture Post*, vol. XXII, no. 5 (29 Jan 1944).

45 There is a good deal of correspondence between HGW and W.L. Waddell about the syndicated articles which made up the book, some of which appeared in the US. See Waddell to HGW, 12 Dec 1940, and HGW to Waddell, 17 Mar 1941, along with a whole sheaf of cables. The idea for the pieces came after HGW's trip in the late autumn of 1940, and although many of them were never published, 31 altogether were written. Nearly all of them make up this book. HGW to V. Gollancz, 27 Mar 1941, sets out the financial terms for the work. HGW asked for 25% on the first 8,000, 10% on the second 8,000, and 5% thereafter with credit for book club editions. Gollancz agreed to put £500 into advertising on the day of publication. These were the final terms apparently. See HGW to *Tribune*, a mild rejoinder to their review, 13 Jan 1941, which referred to the book as Kippsian and the new world as a Kippsian one which HGW did not care for. A. C. Hardwick, 'Man's Present and Future', *Nature*, 21 Mar 1942, liked it very much.

46 *Phoenix* (London: Secker & Warburg 1942). The quote is from p. 163.

47 HGW to Curtis Brown, 20 June, 2 July 1942, on US publication, and the necessity to keep the UK title on the book. He urged Curtis Brown to consult with Corliss Lamont and Max Eastman as to potential publishers. HGW to Haldeman-Julius, 5, 28 Dec 1942. HGW also published *The New Rights of Man* with Haldeman-Julius in 1942, at the very end of the year, and in 1943 published his correspondence with Lev Upensky, of the Soviet Union, along with an article or two not published in the UK. See his letters to Haldeman-Julius, 24 Dec 1943 (text says 1944, but is probably wrong), and 10 Jan 1944. B. Webb to HGW, 17 Aug 1942 (Webb *Letters* III. 458–9). Lord Horder, 'World Deorganization'. *Nature*, 3 Apr 1943.

Chapter 18

1 HGW: 'Berlin Should be Bombed', *Liberty*, 3 Feb 1940 (also appeared in the UK, but as yet unlocated); 'The New Captain and His Crew', *Reynolds's News*, 19 May 1940; 'Churchill: Man of Destiny', *SGraphic*, 8 Dec 1940 (originally appeared in *Collier's*, 2 Nov 1940, as 'Winston Churchill: The Right Man at the Right Time'). The *Collier's* article was timed to appear when Wells was in the US, and may in fact have been written there.

2 HGW, *SDispatch*: 'What We Have Learned in the First Year', 1 Sept 1940; 'The Second Year of the War', 15 Sept 1940. These articles were widely distributed over the world as well as published in Britain. HGW pursued this tactic further in an article attacking Lord Swinton in particular: 'The Real Guilty Men', 20 Oct 1940, in which he said, 'War changes the British Fascist from ass to Murderer.'

3 HGW, 'Why Don't we Bomb Rome?', *SDispatch*, 19 Jan 1941. For a long comment

which reprinted much of HGW's original article see Sydney *MHerald*, 20 Jan 1941, on HGW's 'remarkable' article. HGW, 'War of Words', *SDispatch*, 23 Mar 1941. For a comment supporting HGW, at least on Winston Churchill, V. Bonham Carter to HGW, 18 Apr 1941. She described the other members of the Government as 'all pygmies and passengers'.

4   HGW, letters to *The Times*, 16 Aug 1941 (on fence-sitting), and 8 Dec 1941, on the need for paper. Stanley Unwin to HGW, postcard dated 16 Aug 1941: 'It crystallizes a point of view which badly needs expressing'. Philip Buck to HGW, 26 Sept 1941, HGW's notes on the letter, and his final letter to Buck of 10 Oct 1941. Buck wrote on 3 Nov 1941 asking permission to print the correspondence in Washington *EStar*. By that time events had overtaken the need to print it. *NYT*, 27 Sept 1941, which reprints a letter from HGW, Laski, and Priestley to John G. Winant expressing concern over the US–Japanese negotiations. HGW, 'Now Let Us Start Fighting', *SDispatch*, 12 Oct 1941. HGW, 'Raids *and* Raids', *DMail*, 6 Nov 1941. Winston Churchill to HGW, 8 Nov 1941. HGW then sent copies of the article to Churchill, Maisky, Strabolgi, Huxley, *Picture Post* and *Tribune*, 8 Nov 1941, urging the raids strategy even more widely. HGW also urged bombing the Black Forest. Churchill and his advisers discussed this idea in some detail. Martin Gilbert, *Winston S. Churchill*, vol. VI (London 1983).

5   HGW, 'The Strange Story of Otto Strasser: An Ally We Don't want', *SDispatch*, 25 Jan 1942. HGW had met Strasser in Bermuda on his way home from the States in early 1941, when bad weather grounded the Pan-American Yankee Clipper. HGW: 'The Frustraitors', *DMail*, 19 Mar 1942; 'Three Years of War and Still We Do Not Bomb Rome', *SDispatch*, 30 Aug 1942. The latter was reprinted in the *American Freeman*, Dec 1942, as, 'The Third Year of the War', and with a letter from Thomas Mann, and an article by A. de Seversky on air power, appeared as *The New Rights of Man* (Girard, Kans. 1943).

6   HGW, *E Standard*, 19 Jan 1943. HGW said the formation of the Royal Society was one of the greatest contributions of the English, as it had put forward the idea of scientific publication. He was not through with his criticism, however, as can be seen in HGW: 'Stir Up These Slackers', *SPictorial*, 27 June 1943, 'The Mediterranean Mess', *SDispatch*, 28 Nov 1943, and 'England the Unready', *Cavalcade*, 12 Feb 1944.

7   HGW to *Manchester Guardian*, 17 May 1943; to *The Times*, 24 July 1943. John Webb (*Times*) to HGW, 26 July; HGW to Webb, 27 July (notes on 26 July letter); MCW to *The Times*, 5 Aug 1943; Webb to HGW, 5 Aug, with HGW's comments (*The Times* set up the letter and sent a proof to HGW before declining to print it). HGW to *Tribune*, 20 Aug; *Bookseller*, 19 Aug 1943, reprinted this letter with comment. One of the problems was that Longmans' warehouse had suffered very heavily in the raids of 29 Dec 1940 and many copies of the Guedalla book were destroyed. HGW to P. Guedalla, 18 Dec 1943.

8   HGW, *SDispatch*: 'Hard Facts About Art Treasures', 4 Mar 1944; 'Unwanted Kings and Leaders', 9 Apr 1944. HGW, 'Churchill Must Go', *Tribune*, 15 Dec 1944, repr. in *Greek National Herald* (New York), 15 Dec 1944, and in a cut version in *Saturday Review of Literature*. HGW: 'A Republican's Faith', *New Statesman*, 23 Dec 1944; 'Orders is Orders. A Vanishing Excuse in the New World', *New Leader*, 19 May 1945; 'That Mosley Money', *Socialist Leader*, 6 July 1946. The last article was basically repr. in *NYT*, 7 July 1946, along with an editorial, and further discussed on 14 July 1946. The royal preserve Wells recommended was eventually established at Estoril in Spain.

9   HGW, 'Britain's Uncertain Voice', *NChron*, 20 July 1940, repr. in *Coronet*, March 1940, as 'My Advice to Churchill'. *Tribune*: HGW, 'German Militarism', 4 Sept 1942; Shaw and Laski letters, 11 Sept 1942; HGW, 'Why Lie About Vansittart?', 28 Sept 1942. HGW to *New Statesman*, 17 Oct 1942, 24 Oct 1942; HGW to *New Leader*, 21 Nov 1942. Brockway responded on this last with a comment saying, in essence, why bother with the invective – carry on with your good work.

10   HGW, 'Limitations of Lord Vansittart', *Tribune*, 14 May 1943 (Vansittart's response
      was printed 21 May 1943). HGW, 'Shall We Blame the Whole German People?',
      Picture Post, 31 July 1943. 'How they Would Deal with Germany', series in *DMail*:
      HGW's piece was entitled, 'The Price of Liberty is Eternal Vigilance', 6 Jan 1944.
      Others who commented were Shaw, Vansittart, and Emmanuel Shinwell. Vansittart's
      memoirs were *Lessons of My Life* (London 1943).
11   HGW to I. Maisky, 5 Aug 1940. Maisky was not in London during some of this time,
      of course. Of all the memoirs of the Second World War that are useful reading, I put
      Maisky's several volumes near the top. They give a picture rather different from that of
      some sources.
12   Hewlett Johnson (Dean of Canterbury) to HGW, 8 Aug 1941; 'The Constitution' and
      'Aims' of the Committee, headed by Lord Horder and Victor Gollancz. HGW, 'Russia
      and the Future', *SDispatch*, 29 June 1941. Letters from the Committee to HGW, 18
      May (rally held 20 June 1942); HGW to Director of National Academy, 7 Nov; letter
      to HGW, 9 Oct 1942, and his response. USSR Society for Cultural Relations with
      Foreign Countries (VOKS), *In Defense of Civilization Against Fascist Barbarians:
      Statements, Letters and Telegrams From Prominent People* (Moscow 1941): HGW's
      contribution, 'The Last of Hitler's Blood-Soaked Convulsions', 93–4; in which he
      defends the non-aggression pact of 1939 as giving Russia an easier way to attack Berlin
      when the war finally came. As he said, and thought, 'Not only alliance but friendship is
      possible with these people.' Wells was sometimes skittish about his associations, as
      when he attended an African Peoples Democracy and World Peace Conference in the
      summer of 1939, was interviewed, but did not allow publication of his remarks. Peter
      Blackhen to HGW, 14, 22, 30 June, 5 July 1939.
13   I. Maisky to HGW, 13 Nov 1941, 12 Jan, 2 July, 21 Sept 1942, 7 Jan, 25 Mar, 15 Apr
      1943; HGW to Maisky, late Mar–early Apr (seen in draft only), postcard 14 Apr 1943.
      HGW to *Manchester Guardian*, 17 May 1943. HGW to Registrar, Moscow Academy of
      Sciences, 26 Oct 1943, enclosing his thesis, and suggesting that he be nominated as a
      member, 'a distinction I greatly covet'. For his view of de Gaulle, see HGW, 'The
      Truth About de Gaulle', *World Review*, May 1943, pp. 57–8, a review of his memoirs.
14   HGW to several addressees, giving the draft text of his proposed pamphlet, 27 June
      1940 (whether it was used or not has not been determined). HGW, 'Marshall Smuts is
      Ignoring Facts', *Reynolds's News*, 19 Dec 1943, which also appeared in *La France Libre*,
      Dec 1943. Smuts had made a speech on 25 Nov denigrating the French and *The Times*
      printed it on 3 Dec, which called forth the HGW comment. HGW, 'Salut aux Trois
      Couleurs', in *Au Carrefour du Monde*, 28 Oct 1944; a version of this also appeared in *La
      France Libre* in Sept 1944.
15   HGW to E. Beneš, 17 June 1942. HGW was ill, and could not attend a meeting, but
      urged Beneš to determine the guilty parties after the Lidice massacre. Beneš and Wells
      kept up a correspondence until Beneš left for Prague. E. Beneš to HGW, 31 Oct 1941,
      24 Apr, 26 June, 17 July 1942, 27 Feb 1945; HGW to Beneš, 17 June 1942. HGW
      introduced an anti-fascist Polish Jew, Feffer Mikeels, at a meeting of PEN on 18 Oct
      1943, and his speech of introduction appeared in *Polish Jewish Observer*, 21 Oct 1943. I
      have seen it only in MS. HGW, 'Speech Made at the Opening of "Hagar Espanol"',
      Spanish News Letter, and *Español*, 17 Nov 1941. This event took place on 17 Oct 1941.
16   HGW to D. Camino, 2 July 1943, on what to read, and especially recommending S.I.
      Hsiung, *The Bridge of Heaven*, as 'a wholesome corrective to the missionary nonsense of
      Pearl Buck . . .' H. D. Lieu to HGW, 26 June 1942, 22 June 1943, asking for
      statements. The Chinese versions appeared in various Chinese newspapers, and copies
      survive in the HGW archive. Albert Baker to HGW, 6 Sept 1943, commenting on an
      anti-Italian Fascist meeting at which they both spoke on 26 Aug 1943. HGW, 'The
      Mediterranean Mess', *SDispatch*, 28 Nov 1943, in which he comments on the meeting
      over which he presided, and his introduction to T. L. Gardini, *Towards the New Italy*
      (London 1943). This is similar to his article and ends, 'the stars in their courses are

pointing mankind either to a unified socialist world or to disaster and misery and death
. . .' On India see Leo Amery to HGW, 29 Aug, 26 Sept 1941: 'I wonder what you
would do in my place?' HGW responded to a Nehru article, *NChron*, 17 Dec 1941,
with his 'On What Reasonable Men Want for India' in the same paper, 23 Dec 1941.
Wells felt the Congress Party was too limiting in its participation. Also see HGW to
NChron, 7 Jan 1942, on Nehru's response to him, in which he was disappointed.

17   HGW, 'Must We Believe in a Future Life?', *Strand*, Spring 1942. HGW to the *Friend*,
27 Mar 1942, commenting on Alfred Salter's speech to the Commons on 25 Nov 1941
on the role of violence in the Christian past. HGW to Archdeacon E. S. Daniel Litton
Cheney, 16 Oct 1943, on Uganda and missionaries.

18   HGW to *SDispatch*, 15 Mar 1942, on Strasser's response to his comment. *Tribune*, 3
Apr 1942. HGW to RAG, 15 July 1941; Ernest Barker to HGW, 19, 22, 24 Oct 1942.
HGW was very grateful for the booklist.

19   HGW, *Crux Ansata* (Harmondsworth 1943: New York 1944). The New York edition
reprinted (114–16) an interview Wells had given to John Rowland, *Literary Guide and
Guardian*, Mar 1944, pp. 14–16, on the reception of *Crux Ansata* in England. It was in
answer to attacks by M de la Bedoyère, editor of the *Catholic Herald*.

20   HGW to *Catholic Herald*, 15 Oct 1943, asking why they attack him, why not just review
the book. They apologized for the comment on his age in their next issue. See also his
letter to the *Universe* of the same date. (Did they print it?) W. Buckminster Taylor to
HGW, 10, 31 Nov 1943, sending each other anti-Catholic books. HGW to G.L.
Holliday, offering help in US distribution of *Crux Ansata*. HGW to G. J. Mayer, 25
Oct 1943, 12 Jan 1944 (out of print, for want of paper). *New Review*, 18 Nov 1943,
gives history of HGW's meetings with Catholic editors; eventually they were
postponed. Michel de la Bedoyère, *Was It Worth It, Wells* (London 1944) (also 1946?)
on their version of the aborted luncheon. John Rowland, 'A Talk with H. G. Wells',
Literary Guide and Guardian, Mar 1944, also published as a pamphlet, a rationalist view
of the matter. HGW was a member of the Society of Freethinkers and had been host to
a pre-war meeting in London; Society's *Report of Proceedings* (London 1939), 98–9,
reprints his speech.

21   HGW: 'J'Accuse: Doing Goebbels Work', *Reynolds's News*, 28 July 1940; 'The Real
Guilty Men', *SDispatch*, 20 Oct 1940. The first of these was published in the *New
Republic*, 26 Aug 1940, in a cut version, and the second was discussed widely as it
appeared during his US tour. He had some difficulty in publishing the article, and it
was subtitled, 'An Uncensored Article', He was assiduous in the cause of expatriates.
See HGW to 'Mr Omead(?)', 8 May 1939, on behalf of Dr Paul Eisner; to Ernst
Toller, 11 Nov 1938, on food for victims in Spain; telegram HGW and 15 others to
Toller, 19 Nov 1938 (Indiana). His criticisms stung, however; see a recent book, Nigel
West, *MI 5* (London 1981), which discusses Wells's letters to the press in ch. 4.

22   HGW, 'An Article to Annoy Parsons and Professors', *SDispatch*, 23 Nov 1941; also see
his 'The Shape of Education to Come', in County of London, *Red Cross Bulletin*,
Education Supplement, Dec 1941, as well as his article, 'The New Educational Front
in England', *Tomorrow*, vol. I, no. 3 (Nov 1941), where the same case is made and the
word 'eutrophic' is again suggested for what he wanted.

23   HGW, 'The Transformation of War', *Tomorrow*, vol. I, no. 5 (Jan 1942). HGW's two
articles in this little-known publication deserve wide circulation and much wider
readership than they received in their own time. Also see his piece, 'The New Society
is Here', *Star*, 4 Aug 1941 (the first in a series by several leaders of thought, after the
worst year of the war for Britain). The *Tomorrow* article cited in note 22 is a redaction
of this article.

24   HGW: 'Idiot's Delight: Drawing the New Map of Europe', *EStandard*, 6 Jan 1943 (this
also appeared in the Glasgow *ECitizen*, same date); 'How to Dispose of Hitler and Co:
A Problem in World Sanitation', *EStandard*, 29 Jan 1943 (he urged people to read
Vansittart's *Black Record*); 'Plan to Punish the War Guilty', *EExpress*, 14 Mar 1943; 'Are

the British an Educated People? A Dreadful Question to Ask', *EStandard*, 18 Feb 1943; 'Genius in a New World', *SDispatch*, 21 Feb 1943, from which the quotation comes. His letter to Horrabin was dated 5 Oct 1942. In it he said, 'If we would only instruct the common man he would take war by the throat.'

25   HGW, 'What a Zulu Thinks of the English', *EStandard*, 16 Mar 1943. HGW claimed that this letter had been censored by the BBC, to whom he had offered it, as Smuts was in the War Cabinet. Smuts responded with 'The Future of South Africa', *Standard*, 25 Mar 1943. Smuts apparently felt that racial harmony and co-operation were a very long way off, and he was right. HGW continued to enlarge on this theme in much of his other writing.

26   *Advertisers' Weekly*, 25 Mar 1943. Comment came from *Yorkshire EPost*, *Spectator*, *Church Times*, all 26 Mar 1943; *Densbury Reporter*, 3 Apr; *Horse and Hound*, 9 Apr; and *Newspaper World*, 3 Apr, which called it 'appalling nonsense'. This provoked HGW's apology, *Newspaper World*, 10 Apr 1943. Incidentally, for some of these periodicals it may mark the only time his name appeared there. Other comments worth mentioning are *Croydon Advertiser*, 9 Apr 1943; *Richmond Herald*, 10 Apr 1943 (which thought the ensuing discussion very useful), and *Advertisers' Weekly*, 15 Apr 1943, which called the remarks, 'Wells's farrago'.

27   HGW: 'We May Never Have a World Speech', *SDispatch*, 23 Sept 1943 (using his experiences in getting the rights of man translated); 'How Are We to Get Out of This War?', *SPictorial*, 24 Oct 1943, reprinted in slightly different form in *World Organization: Functional or Federal* (1945); 'The Pious Butler and the Religious Complex', *Tribune*, 28 Jan 1944, which brought down a storm of response on 5 Feb 1944; 'The Stupidity of Mankind in a World of Plenty', *SDispatch*, 19 May 1944, where his last words were, 'The hard clear facts of my hope in a glorious life for a rationally unified humanity remain'; 'Back to the Old Round? – No Fear', *New Leader*, 11 Mar 1944. HGW commented on the difficulty of being too far in advance of his audience in his Australian speech, 'Fiction About the Future', cited above, ch. 14, n.25.

28   Beaverbrook to HGW, 24 Oct 1939. This sort of comment on the first version of the book was one of the reasons why HGW wrote a sequel to it which is quite optimistic.

29   HGW, *The Outlook for Homo Sapiens* (London: Secker & Warburg, Readers' Union, 1942), 273.

30   HGW to GBS, 22 Apr, 28 Sept 1941 (BL); to Dr R.D. Lawrence, 7 Aug 1943 (draft); to GBS, 5 Jan, 21 Mar 1942: 'As we of the old gang grow older we grow more affectionate. I write nice love letters to Beatrice and wonder why it was we ever were antagonistic.'

31   HGW, 'Mrs Webb's Birthday', *New Statesman and Nation*, 22 Jan 1938. Shaw's review, *Tribune*, 27 Mar 1942. B. Webb to HGW, 4 Jan 1940, 5 Jan 1942; HGW to B. Webb, 5 Jan 1940, (postcard, quoted here) 6 Jan 1942 (Webb *Letters* III. 438–9, 453). Beatrice went on to ask about Frank and Gip.

32   S. Olivier to HGW, 13 Dec 1939, 16 Jan 1940 (long quote), 1 Jan, 28 Aug, 4 Sept, 10 Oct 1942. Olivier passed away in Feb 1943.

33   The thesis appears in its most complete form in HGW, *'42 to '44* (London: Secker & Warburg 1944), 169–96. It is accompanied there by two memoranda which bear on the same subject, 'On the Relation of Mathematics, Music, Moral and Aesthetic Values, Chess and Similar Intellectual Elaborations to the Reality Underlying Phenomena', 196–9, and a 'Memorandum on Survival', 200–12, in which he discussed the great climatic changes and other physical phenomena which have forced our species to modify its behaviour in order to survive. The point for HGW was that we were again in such a time: 'Knowledge of Extinction. There is no other choice for man' (p. 212). The thesis was privately printed as well (London: Watts & Co. n.d. [1942]); it appeared in abridged form in *Nature*, 1 Apr 1944, pp. 395–7, and was reprinted as a separate pamphlet, in its abridged form, as *The Illusion of Personality* (London 1944). The thesis has some minor changes, cf. p. 88, in later printings.

34 HGW to RAG, 24 May 1940.
35 HGW to RAG, (?) June 1942, quoted in Armytage; RAG to HGW, 29 June 1942.
HGW to J. B. S. Haldane, 3 July 1943; Haldane to HGW, 5 July 1943. HGW to RAG,
13 July 1943 (HGW was now attempting to get his thesis published in the *Philosophical Transactions* of the Royal Society; the abridgement in *Nature* and the attendant pamphlet were all that ensued). HGW in this letter to Gregory suggested burning old textbooks, as they tended to clutter libraries and 'put the self-educating man at a disadvantage. He starts behind the times. I never met new knowledge until I got to South Kensington'. For a favourable comment on the thesis from an unusual source, see Sydney *MHerald*, 30 Oct 1943, which quoted HGW as saying in an interview that he had undertaken the study necessary to write the thesis 'for pleasure'. Sydney Olivier to HGW, 28 Dec 1942, complimenting him on his understanding of 'human sexuality'.
36 HGW, *'42 to '44* (London: Secker & Warburg 1944). Some other unpublished work has been collected by W. Warren Wagar in *H.G. Wells: Journalism and Prophecy* (Boston 1964). HGW's obituary for Beatrice Webb appears in *'42 to '44*, 124–8; it was first published in *Manchester Guardian*, 4 May 1943. R. Brightman, 'The Supremacy of Reason', *Nature*, 29 July 1944, a review of *'42 to '44*, calling Wells 'indefatigable'. Brightman also said that if the illusion of personality is true, HGW nearly proved the exception to the rule.
37 HGW, 'Press Freedom in Wartime', *Labour Monthly*, Mar 1941. Press Freedom Committee of the National Council for Civil Liberties, *The Press and War* (n.p. [London] 1941).
38 HGW to *Daily Worker* Defence League, 14 July 1941; to editor, *DWorker*, 23 Oct 1942 (typed), and by hand, 26 Oct 1942 (a second £10 donation). William Rust to HGW, 27 Oct 1942, with HGW's handwritten comment on Dutt on the letter. See *Labour Monthly*, Dec 1942, a letter on the CP. A receipt for the donation dated Nov 1942; George Allison to HGW, 14 Oct 1942; Gertrude Morey to HGW, 21 Dec 1942 (the rally was held 3 Jan 1943). William Rust to HGW, 5 Apr 1943, with his handwritten comment on de Gaulle; 7 Dec 1943, accepting Mosley article, with the quoted HGW comment on the letter; 7 May 1945, the second quote also written on this letter. See HGW, 'That Mosley Outrage', *DWorker*, 7 Dec 1943, also published as a leaflet.
39 Lance Sieveking, *The Eye of the Beholder* (1957), for his views on HGW, both as personality and as a broadcaster. Wells and Sieveking also attempted several collaborations, and an interesting correspondence ensued: HGW to Sieveking, 7 Sept, 30 Oct 1942, 21 Feb 1943, 8, 14 Feb 1944 (Indiana).
40 ? Pringle to HGW, 23 Jan, 29 Jan 1940. For the talk, entitled 'The World Goes By', HGW was paid 20 gns. C.W. Salmon to HGW, 13 Sept 1940, and an internal memorandum, L.A. and N.E. Ex to P.C. Ex (Ivan E. Thomas to I.V.M.); the writer could not recall HGW's earlier talks and asked for information on his voice and diction for radio.
41 I am following the memorandum and files on this talk in the BBC archives. The internal memoranda begin 5 Aug 1942; HGW's first letter, to ? Barnes of the BBC, is 12 Dec 1942.
42 The talks are found in *Reshaping Man's Heritage* (London 1944): HGW, 7–14; Julian Huxley (whose talk uses HGW extensively), 89–96. HGW, 'Man's Heritage', *Listener*, 21 Jan 1943, pp. 67–8. J. Huxley to HGW, 22 Jan (with HGW's pencilled comments on back), 17 Mar (postcard) 1943. Also see HGW to *Listener*, 5 Feb 1943, on a listener mistaken about the talks; another on the same subject, 25 Feb 1943, was not printed. T.H. Hawkins, 'Science and Broadcasting', *Nature*, 8 July 1944, a review of the book by the original organizer of the talks, discussing their purpose.
43 ? Weymouth to HGW, 5 Apr 1943. The talk on the Pacific and Australian Service was broadcast from 26 Apr 1943, after being recorded on 15 Apr. *Northern Dispatch* (Priestgate, Darlington), 26 Apr 1943, printed the talk in 'Mr H. G. Wells and World

Peace', its only publication as far as I know. HGW's French Service talk is in the BBC file of 'French Scripts, 1944', 'La Demi-Heure du Soir', and was broadcast from 20 Dec 1944. Correspondence over the fee was BBC to HGW, 4 Jan, and MCW to BBC, 11 Jan 1945. Other talks are discussed in the files of the BBC: Z.A. Bokhari to HGW, 17 June 1943; Weymouth to HGW, 19 July 1943 (an appointment was made to discuss this one, before it was dropped), 9 Oct 1944: HGW sent his message on 14 Oct 1944 (although it does not appear in the BBC files); John Morris to Mr Wren, 2 Mar 1945; Peter Neeley to E. (O.N.B.), 26 Oct 1945; J. C. S. MacGregor to O.N.T.E., 30 Oct 1945, which says Wells really is not able (but at the bottom is the cryptic line, 'warned of our approach'). Last memo is Chalmers to Brown, 31 Jan 1946. See Shaw's comment in 'The Atom Bomb', *SExpress*, 12 Aug 1945. Also see A. M. Low, 'Can Our Scientists Produce the Little Bomb that would Destroy the Whole of Berlin?', *SDispatch*, 11 Jan 1942, which must have sent shivers down the spine of some readers. The *Saturday Review* did reprint a bit of *The World Set Free*, 1 Sept 1945, and a portion from the novel was read out on the BBC as well.

44   Reviews appeared in *British Medical Journal*, 9, 13 Jan 1943; *The Times Educational Supplement*, 23 Jan 1943; *Schoolmaster*, 21 Jan 1943. The *Perthshire Advertiser*, 23 Jan 1943, headed its comment, 'H.G.W.'

Chapter 19

1   Plans and correspondence on the garden appear in the Wells archive. See Lady Hurtwood to HGW, 17, 30 Oct 1935, 5 Mar, 18 May, 10 Oct 1936. She fell on hard times, and asked HGW for help near the end of the war; see her 6 July 1945 letter. HGW's comment on the bottom is simple, 'Can we ——?' leaving the decision up to Marjorie. On HGW and gardens see 'H. G. Wells, Back Gardener', *Countryman* (Summer 1945), pp. 221–1, a reprint of the *Happy Turning* material. HGW to *Countryman*, 20, 23 Feb 1945. Ronald Proctor to D. Robertson Scott, 15 Mar 1945 (Boston), which describes the occasion of the famous sycamore photo as well as H.G.'s appearance near the end.

2   HGW to Residents of Hanover Terrace, 24 Nov 1938. It is doubtful that this letter was ever sent; dogs and Englishmen are, to a considerable degree, inseparable, and HGW probably thought better of the letter once it was drafted.

3   *Star*, 10, 14 Aug 1944. HGW to Sir Thomas Moore, 12 Aug 1944. If this letter was actually sent, Moore was very forbearing. But I doubt that it was.

4   HGW to *DMail*, 12 Aug 1944; to *New Leader*, 26 Aug 1944 (also see *New Leader*, 19 Aug 1944). HGW to *The Times*, 28 Sept, 14 Nov 1944. HGW to *Star*, 28 Sept 1944; *Star*, 29 Sept 1944.

5   *DExpress*, 24 May 1940; *NYT*, Oct-Nov 1940. Later that autumn when he was given a luncheon at Foyles', air raids prevented RAG from attending, for which he was apologetic; he was at a memorial service for Sir Oliver Lodge, and could not get across town. RAG to HGW, undated, end of Sept 1940.

6   Vincent Sheean, *Between the Thunder and the Sun* (New York 1943).

7   RAG to HGW, 8 Oct 1941; HGW to RAG, 9 Oct 1941; *NYT*, 14 Sept 1941, which reported the PEN meeting in detail. The five-person governing board was Thornton Wilder, Thomas Mann, Jacques Maritain, H. G. Wells, and Hermon Ould (who was also the secretary). John Dos Passos, and Salvador de Madariaga also addressed the meeting.

8   Gilbert Murray to HGW, 27 Oct 1941, apologizing for not getting to the 75th birthday party: 'I am sorry that you are seventy-five.' R. A. Butler to HGW, 10 Sept 1941; HGW to RAB, 12, 16 Sept. The tea date was 3 Oct. Also see RAB to HGW, 2 July 1942, on the *SDispatch* piece on education. Aneurin Bevan to HGW, 20 Jan 1942, as well as 12 Nov 1941. The Italian anti-Fascist meeting was at the end of Aug 1943. Wells presided. They declared their 'solidarity with the Italian workers, soldiers, and

peasants in their struggle for freedom and a better life for mankind.' Ivan Maisky to HGW, 13 May 1943; Alan Pitt Robins to HGW, 20 April 1944 (*The Times* had said he was there and Marjorie dutifully wrote correcting their story; this letter is an apology). HGW to Churchill Club, Apr 1944, in his hand, perhaps as a telegram. At the top of the page in his hand is, 'Heil [or perhaps Hail] Churchill.'

9 Ernest Barker to HGW, 23 June 1941; HGW to H. Newman, 26 Nov 1943, 30 Apr 1943 (44); HGW to E. N. Andrade, 8 Jan 1943.

10 Ernest Barker, *Age and Youth* (1953), 107–8. C. P. Snow, *Variety of Men* (London 1967), where the story is part of a lovely essay on Wells by one of his earliest admirers. See the anonymous book by Snow, *New Worlds for Old* (1934), as well as HGW's rejoinder to a reviewer on both his and Snow's behalf: 'Power in Social Psychology', *Nature,* 22 Dec 1934.

11 HGW to B. Webb, 6 Jan 1942; to S. Webb, 30 Apr 1943. The obituary is in the *Manchester Guardian,* 4 May 1943. Ivan Maisky to HGW, 5 May 1943; HGW's comments appear in pencil on the original. They had their lunch on the 12th. F. Swinnerton to HGW, 28 Sept 1942, with HGW's comments on this letter as well.

12 HGW to 'Dangle' (Alex Thompson), 3 Sept 1942 (Bromley).

13 HGW to C. G. L. Du Cann; see the *Freethinker,* 6 June 1943. Proof and MS of a piece for Readers' Union, 15 May 1943 (the date of returning the proof). I do not know how or where they used it. HGW to EH, 14 Nov 1941, 4 July 1944 (signed 'A Buzz Buzz' under 'H.G.'), 26 Feb 1945. These are written by hand; they were willed to the Wells estate by Healey.

14 FAS to HGW, 24 Oct 1939; HGW to David Low, 20 June, 29 July 1941. The quotes are from a letter of 20 July 1942. HGW to B. Webb, 4 July 1942. J. B. S. Haldane to HGW, 18 Sept 1942 (HGW's comment on the MS in pencil).

15 J.B. Priestley to HGW, 26 May 1943; HGW to W. E. Williams, 24 Dec 1943; to Florence (Mrs T.) Lamont, 21 Jan 1944; to Andin Georges, 7 Feb 1944; to Brendan Bracken, 16 Feb 1944. RAG to HGW, 21 Mar 1944; HGW to RAG, in HGW's hand at the bottom of this letter.

16 FAS to HGW, 20, 24 July, 2 Aug 1944 (this is apparently the last letter, although they probably met again).

17 Ritchie Calder to HGW, 10 Sept 1944. Fred J. Wells to HGW, 1 Apr 1944. APW to MCW, 24 Jan 1945. Bertrand Russell to HGW, 15, 26 May 1945; HGW to B. Russell, May 1945. HGW to EH, 19 July 1945. Fred J. Wells to HGW, 25 Oct 1945, 5 Apr 1946. HGW to EH, 28 May 1946.

18 B. Bracken to HGW, 9 May, 2 June 1944 (for the Scotch); J. B. Priestley to HGW, 8 Nov 1945 (for the socks). John Webb to HGW, 12 Nov 1942, thanks for the tea recipe, and *The Times* will print it. (They were never able to find the space, so we still do not know how HGW liked his tea brewed.) For the sycamore, see *The Happy Turning,* ch. 8. HGW to H. G. Koppell, 22 Aug 1941. HGW to RAG, 25 Sept 1944, in HGW's hand. The interview, 'My Visit to Wells', by 'Colophon', appeared in *John o'London's,* 23 Mar 1946.

19 M. Belloc-Lowndes to Elizabeth, 8 Apr 1945, reprinted in her *Diaries and Letters.*

20 Cynthia Asquith to HGW, 27 May, and postcard, 31 May 1943. The party was 4 June 1943. For HGW's speech to the Roadfarers Club, see 'Back to the Old Round? No Fear', *New Leader,* 11 Mar 1944. It was remembered by F. J. Camm, in 'H. G. Wells's Last Day Out', *John o'London's,* Apr 1952. William Beveridge to HGW, 9 Jan 1945, soliciting support for Stocks. HGW, in his notes on the letter, said he would vote for her, but would not be on her committee; he was giving up all committees. HGW, letter to the *DWorker,* 24 May 1945. Michael Foot, 'H.G. Wells would vote if it killed him!', *DHerald,* 10 July 1945. Wells told Foot that the Tories 'would evade and cheat to the end . . . [But] in these matters the world is just beginning to realize that the appropriators are fighting against the stars in their courses.' Sir Ernest Graham-Little (Ind. Nat.) won the seat with 7,618 votes. Mary Stocks (Ind. Prog.) received 7,469,

after a recount. In 1935 G. Little had received 8,958 and Norman Angell, 3,918. *D Herald*, 27, 31 July 1945. Robert Bruce Lockhart (*Diaries* II, entry of 3 Aug 1945) reported that Moura took Wells to vote.

21   HGW to Curtis Brown, 23 Jan 1945; A. S. Frere to Curtis Brown, 31 Jan 1945; HGW to Heinemanns (My Dear Fred), 3 Feb 1945. *SExpress*: 'Life and Man's Future', 21 Oct 1945; 'The Nature of Life', 28 Oct 1945; 'How Man Began', 4 Nov 1945.

22   I am following, to some extent, G. P. Wells, ed., *The Last Books of H. G. Wells* (London 1968), an effort to place *Mind* and *The Happy Turning* in context. Most of the quotations here, however, do not appear in the versions he used, but are from the text of the newspaper publication, which seems to this writer, at least, to be a later, and a somewhat more positive, version.

23   HGW, *The Happy Turning: A Dream of Life* (London: Heinemann 1945). HGW to W. F. Cooper, 19, 20, 22 Jan, 4 Feb 1944: Jesus was 'a mere ventriloquist's dummy by that infernal creature Paul'.

24   HGW, 'The Betterave Papers', *Cornhill*, July 1945, pp. 349–63. The quotation is from p. 363.

25   HGW, 'That Mosley Money', *New Leader*, 6 July 1946. *NYT*, 27 Mar 1946, for the Nuremberg petition. Memo, HGW to MCW, dated (in another hand) 21 June 1946. Memorandum to 26 addressees, May 1946. 'Atom: Boon or Doom?', *DHerald*, 9 Aug 1945, subheaded 'H. G. Wells prophesied it in 1894'; a reprinting of sections of *The World Set Free*.

26   F. Swinnerton to MCW, 15 Aug 1946; HGW to Winifred Simmons, 8 May 1945; Winifred Simmons to MCW, 14 Aug 1946; EH to MCW, 15 Aug 1946; Christabel Aberconway to MCW, 14 Aug 1946.

27   A.M. Davies to MCW, 22 Aug 1946; to EH, 20 Aug 1946. APW to MCW, 15 Aug 1946; G. D. H. Cole to MCW, 15 Aug 1946; Winifred Simmons to MCW, 18 Aug 1946. Anthony West, *Principles and Persuasions* (London 1958), 4–20, and more recently his two journalistic accounts. *ENews*, 22 Nov 1946, for details of the will; MCW to D. L. Ross, 4 Nov 1947, for BBC film and drama information. *NYT*, 14, 15, 17, 18 Aug (reprinting the tribute in *Izvestia*), 25 Aug 1946.

28   Priestley's speech at the crematorium, 16 Aug 1946 (in HGW papers); J. B. Priestley, 'Good-bye to my Old Friend', *NChron*, 17 Aug 1946, reprints the oration and it apparently appeared as a pamphlet as well. Priestley also wrote on HGW in *DMail*, 14 Aug 1946. His later recollections of the day appear in his *Margin Released* (New York 1962), 169–70; on Wells and others of his circle, 163–71. Edward Shanks, 'One of the great formative spirits of our time', *DDispatch*, 14 Aug 1946. Michael Foot, 'We shall hear no more of that splendid scorn and soaring imagination', *DHerald*, 16 Aug 1946. *Manchester Guardian*, 14 Aug 1946. Sydney *MHerald*: a summary of HGW's life, 15 Aug 1946; a leader, 'The Novelist as Prophet', 17 Aug 1946, discussing his visit in 1938 and 1939; the quoted article by 'R. McC.', 'Wells and His Legend', in the book pages. H. N. Brailsford, 'H. G. Wells', *John o'London's*, 23 Aug 1946.

29   Frank Swinnerton, 'Genius'; Bertrand Russell, 'H. G. Wells: The Man I Knew', *Daily Sketch*, 14 Aug 1946. C. E. M. Joad, 'Salute to Wells', *EStandard*, 14 Aug 1946; J. Huxley, 'H.G.', *Spectator*, 16 Aug 1946. George Orwell, 'The True Pattern of H.G. Wells', *Manchester ENews*, 14 Aug 1946. *DWorker*, 15 Aug 1946. *Tribune*, 23 Aug 1946: Bain's paper was entitled 'Wells with the Red Cockade'.

30   *DHerald*, 24 July 1946, for several obituary articles on Jimmy Maxton, 'a man all M.P.s loved'. Labour kept the seat with Douglas Jay in Battersea, so Wells's last contribution was not in vain. GBS was 90 on 26 July 1946. *DHerald*, 26 July 1946. RAG 'H.G. Wells: a Summary and a Tribute', *Nature*, 21 Sept 1946.

Epilogue

1   *NChron*, 22 July 1946, for RAG's last speech; RAG to HGW, probably 22 or 23 July

1946, reprinted in Armytage, 201; RAG to EH, early Sept 1946; *Nature*, 31 Sept 1946, 19 Oct 1946. *NChron*: leader; Ritchie Calder, 'One World Will Be His Monument'; Robert Lynd, 'A Man of Genius Dies; He Taught a Generation to Think'; Hugh Pilcher, 'Wells – The Man Who Was Always Right', all 14 Aug 1946. Michael Foot, 'The Enemies of H. G. Wells', *DHerald*, 16 Aug 1946, a review of his obituaries.

2 Forest J. Ackerman and Arthur Lewis Joquel III, *In Memoriam, H. G. Wells, 1866–1946* (Los Angeles 1946). The booklet (Bromley) carried the *NYT* obituary of 14 Aug 1946; a talk given at the society's memorial service; and reprinted an account of HGW's 1941 Los Angeles visit, 'Wells of Wisdom', from *Pluto*, Jan 1941. *DHerald*, 30 Oct 1946; *NChron*, 31 Oct 1946. 'Homage to H. G. Wells', in Beveridge papers, LSE, file IXB 33, which gives a summary of the memorial, as well as Beveridge's notes on his own talk. 'H. G. Wells', *Penguin Progress*, Oct 1946, pp. 10–19, a good summary article which relies heavily on *Ex A*. The Penguin reissues, which sold for a shilling each, were *Kipps*, *Tono-Bungay*, *Invisible Man*, *New Machiavelli*, *Love and Mr Lewisham*, *War of the Worlds*, *Mr Polly*, *Dr Moreau*, *Short History of the World*, and a volume containing *The Time Machine* and some short stories. The last two have never been out of print with Penguin since.

3 Armytage, 201–12, covers this story, and reprints the significant letters to Gregory, and from him on the subject.

4 BBC to MCW, 21 Aug, 27 Sept 1946, 7 Aug 1947; MCW to BBC, 12 Aug 1947. R. J. W. Alexander and Alexander Hobbs, 'What Influences Labour M.P.s?', *New Society*, vol. I, no. 11 (13 Dec 1962).

5 *Horizon*, 31 July 1966. A recording of the broadcast interviews may still be heard at Bromley. *New Statesman*, 23 Sept 1946. C. P. Snow, *Variety of Men* (1966).

SELECT BIBLIOGRAPHY

As the Notes are so ample, I am not providing a formal bibliography, but give here a brief reading list, mostly of scholarly commentary particularly useful to me, arranged by date of publication. In addition to the items listed here, and those cited in the Notes, I have read every commentary on Wells and his work that I could locate in English or French, and a few in German. Most of the material in Russian exists in translation, but a few fugitive pieces were translated for me by members of the Foreign Language Department, University of Maine.

Academy, 29 Jan 1898, pp. 121–2.

R. A. Gregory, 'Science in Fiction', *Nature*, 19 Mar 1898.

Paul Valéry, 'H. G. Wells', *Mercure de Paris*, May 1899.

'A Novelist of the Unknown', *Academy*, 23 June 1900, pp. 535–60.

E. H. Lacon-Watson, 'Literature Portraits, XXIII: Mr H. G. Wells', *Literature*, 12 Oct 1901, pp. 33–5.

E. Ray Lankester, 'The Present Judged By the Future', *Nature*, 13 Mar 1902 (Supplement).

'F. W. H[irst]', 'The Future of the Human Race', *Nature*, 29 Dec 1904.

Jean Lionnet, *L'Évolution des idées chez quelques-uns de nos contemporaines*, ser. 2 (Paris 1905), 207–37.

'F.C.S.S.', 'Sociological Speculations', *Nature*, 10 Aug 1905.

'The Ideas of Mr H. G. Wells', *Quarterly Review*, Apr 1908, pp. 472–90.

G. K. Chesterton, *Heretics* (London 1909), ch. 5: 'Mr H. G. Wells and the Giants'.

Alexander H. Crawford, *The Religion of H. G. Wells* (London 1909).

'Jacob Tonson' (Arnold Bennett), 'H. G. Wells', *New Age*, 4 Mar 1909.

Firmin Roz, *Le Roman anglais contemporain* (Paris 1912), 227–71.

Sir Hume Gordon, Bart., 'The Popularity of H. G. Wells and Arnold Bennett', *Oxford and Cambridge Review*, no. 25 (Nov 1912), pp. 80–6.

J. D. Beresford, *H. G. Wells* (London 1915).

Van Wyck Brooks, *The World of H. G. Wells* (New York 1915).

H. L. Mencken, *Prejudices, First Series* (New York 1919), 22–35.

Edouard Guyot, *H. G. Wells* (Paris 1920).

'A Tour de Force', *Nature*, 30 Sept 1920.

Carl L. Becker, 'Mr Wells and the New History', *American Historical Review*, vol. XXVI, no. 4 (July 1921), pp. 641–56.

Sidney Dark, *The Outline of H. G. Wells* (London 1922).

R. Thurston Hopkins, *H. G. Wells: Personality, Character and Topography* (London 1922).

E. I. Zamyatin, *H. G. Wells* (Moscow 1922, later trans. into English).

James M. Gillis, *False Prophets* (New York 1923; 2nd edn. 1924): 'H. G. Wells', 20–44.

A. W. Tilby, 'Works of H. G. Wells', *Edinburgh Review*, vol. CCXXXVII (Jan 1923), pp. 113–32.

Ivor Brown, *H. G. Wells* (London 1924).

Albert Guerard, 'The "New History": H. G. Wells and Voltaire', *Scribners*, Nov 1924, pp. 476–84.

Georges A. Connes, *Etude sur la pensée de Wells* (Paris 1926).

F. H. Doughty, *H. G. Wells: Educationist* (London 1926).

Patrick Braybrooke, *Some Aspects of H. G. Wells* (London 1928).

Arnold Bennett, 'The Progress of the Novel', *Realist*, vol. I, no. 11 (Aug 1929), pp. 3–11.

Wilbur L. Cross, *Four Contemporary Novelists* (New York 1930).

'Geoffrey West' [Geoffrey H. Wells], *H. G. Wells: A Sketch for A Portrait* (London 1930).

H. G. Wells, Pages Choisis, avec une préface par Henri P. Davray (Paris 1931); the preface, 7–18, is by Wells's chief French translator.

Theodore Dreiser, Sandgate Edition, vol. I (London 1933), preface, v-xi.

Heinz Mattick, *H. G. Wells als Sozialreformer* (Leipzig 1935).

Frank Swinnerton, *The Georgian Literary Scene* (London 1936).

Percy Colson, *Georgian Portraits* (London 1938): 'Mr H. G. Wells', 37–63.

Norman Nicholson, *H. G. Wells* (London 1950).

A. Vallentin, *H. G. Wells: Prophet of Our Day* (New York 1950).

Vincent Brome, *H. G. Wells: A Biography* (London 1951).

Montgomery Belgion, *H. G. Wells* (London 1953).

Vincent Brome, *Six Studies in Quarrelling* (London 1958).

Bernard Bergonzi, *The Early H. G. Wells* (Manchester 1961).

W. Warren Wagar, *H. G. Wells and the World State* (New Haven 1961).

Ingvald Raknem, *H. G. Wells and His Critics* (Oslo 1962).

Colin Wilson, *The Strength to Dream; Literature and the Imagination* (London 1962; repr. 1979, 1982).

J. Kagarlitsky, *The Life and Thought of H. G. Wells* (Moscow 1965; English trans. London 1966).

I. M. Levidova and B. M. Parcheyskaya, *Herbert George Wells: A Bibliography of Russian Translations and Critical Literature in Russian 1898–1965* (Moscow 1966).

Kenneth B. Newell, *Structure in Four Novels by H. G. Wells* (The Hague and Paris 1968).

Sylvia Strauss, 'H. G. Wells and America', unpub. Ph.D. thesis, Rutgers 1968.

Lovat Dickson, *H. G. Wells* (London 1970).

Samuel Hynes, *Edwardian Occasions* (London 1972).

Patrick Parrinder, ed., *H. G. Wells: The Critical Heritage* (London 1972).

G. P. Vernier, *H. G. Wells et son temps* (Paris 1972).

Norman and Jeanne MacKenzie, *The Time Traveller* (London 1973).

Jack Williamson, *H. G. Wells: Critic of Progress* (Baltimore 1974).

Robert Philmus and David Y. Hughes, *H. G. Wells: Early Writings in Science and Science Fiction* (Berkeley 1975).

Robert Bloom, *Anatomies of Egotism: A Reading of the Last Four Novels of H. G. Wells* (Lincoln, Nebr. and London 1977).

J. R. Hammond, *Herbert George Wells: An Annotated Bibliography of His Works* (New York and London 1977).

Darko Suvin and Robert Philmus, eds., *H. G. Wells and Modern Science Fiction* (Lewisburg, Pa. and London 1977).

Brian Ash, *Who's Who in H. G. Wells* (London 1979).

Roslynn D. Haynes, *H. G. Wells: Discoverer of the Future* (New York and London 1980).

Patrick Parrinder and Robert Philmus. eds., *H. G. Wells's Literary Criticism* (Brighton and Totowa, N.J. 1980).

Frank McConnell, *The Science Fiction of H. G. Wells* (Oxford 1981).

John Batchelor, *The Edwardian Novelists* (New York and London 1982).

John R. Reed, *The Natural History of H. G. Wells* (Athens, O. 1982).

Peter Kemp, *H. G. Wells and the Culminating Ape* (London 1983).

William J. Scheick, *The Splintering Frame: The Later Fiction of H. G. Wells* (Victoria, B.C. 1984).

John Batchelor, *H. G. Wells* (Cambridge 1985).

In addition many important recent articles dealing with lesser aspects of Wells and his thought occur in

The Wellsian (Nottingham and London), 1966 to present.

Science-Fiction Studies, 1973 to present.

I have in preparation an annotated bibliography of the more than 3,000 H. G. Wells items I have located in print; when it appears I will ask readers to point out errors and omissions which I will then publish in *The Wellsian*.

D.C.S.

ACKNOWLEDGEMENTS

Over the past ten years I have been privileged to use a large number of libraries and archives in the writing and research for this book. The principal ones are listed in my Note on Sources, p. 493. Chief among them are the H. G. Wells Papers, in the Library of the University of Illinois at Champaign-Urbana. My work there, and the permission to use and copy huge amounts of material owes much to the remarkable custodians of the collection, Mary Ceibert and Fred Nash, archivists extraordinary. The second large H.G. Wells archive, in the Central Library at Bromley, in Kent, was put together by my good friend, A.W. Watkins. Bob and his wife Irmgard entertained me on several occasions and Bob provided a good and easy guide to the Bromley holdings. The archive was maintained for years by the redoubtable Miss H. Plinke who was of great help to me.

In addition, I have used, with permission, the BBC written archives at Caversham Park, Reading; the Huxley papers and the Royal College of Science archive in London; the papers of Graham Wallas (quoted by permission of the Principal and Fellows of Newnham College, Cambridge), as well as those of William Beveridge, and the Birth-Control pamphlet collection, all in the British Library of Political and Economic Science at LSE; the Walter Lippman papers at Yale; the Margaret Sanger papers (quoted by permission of Grant Sanger, Mt. Kisco, New York) at Smith College, Northampton, Massachusetts; the Upton Sinclair papers (by permission of David Sinclair, Martinsville, N.J.) at the Lilly Library, University of Indiana, Bloomington, as well as other Wells holdings in this library; collections at Hofstra University, Long Island, New York; Cornell University; Boston University, for which I wish to thank Howard Gotlieb for help 'above and beyond'; and various archives at Syracuse University. The papers of Violet Paget ('Vernon Lee') at Colby College, Waterville, Maine, were made available to me. The librarians and archivists at these libraries all put themselves out for me and hastened this work. In addition I have been privileged to use various papers and materials in the private collections of Eric Korn and the late Michael Katanka, both of London.

I have spent a great many days and hours in the British Library Newspaper Division at Colindale, North London, whose remarkable files enabled me to read just about everything of importance relating to H.G. Wells and his time; and in the British Library, Bloomsbury, and I wish to thank their staffs. Other libraries whose hard-working staffs have been of considerable help include those at the University of Reading; Fogler Library, University of Maine at Orono; and the public libraries of Boston, Massachusetts; Bangor, Maine; Los Angeles, California; and the New York Public Library. The library at Hobart and William Smith Colleges was of considerable assistance at an early stage of this work.

I wish also to acknowledge the financial support given me by the University of Maine at Orono – a major summer research fellowship, travel funds and a sabbatical year in which to write the book, as well as a lightened teaching load. In addition, a grant from the American Philosophical Society allowed me to make frequent journeys to Illinois.

A number of people have been of great aid and comfort to me while I was writing and researching this book. At the University of Maine at Orono, these include Edward O. Schriver, Howard Schonberger, J. J. Nadelhaft, R. H. Babcock, Arthur M. Johnson, Elaine Albright, Harold W. Borns, Jr., Anne Bridges, and my typists Carole Gardner, Jean Day, Sue Chambers, and most especially Kathy Moring and Carol Rickards. W.J. Baker and C. S. Doty have read, or allowed me to read to them large parts of this work. Richard Blanke has spent time in support of my work, and has interested himself in this project. Clark Reynolds, Charles Scontras, and my old and dear friend, Clyde Macdonald, have provided great help, as has Geddes Simpson. Louis Goodfriend has been a useful listener. My mentor, and dearest male friend, Robert Thomson, did not live long enough to read the book, but he knew more of it before the writing than any other. Tom Aceto provided me with an unpublished paper he had written, and students in an undergraduate Honors seminar in 1975 were of considerable assistance in focusing my thoughts.

Others who have been of help, mostly through their willingness to let me talk out my preoccupation when they were with me, include James L. Crouthamel, Wendell Tripp, and more than anyone else, for his intellectual sustenance over the last decade, W.R. Baron. Paul W. Gates, Edward Fox, and Gwilym Roberts have been of great help, as have William Stone, an invaluable friend, and Carroll Terrell. Judy Litoff has helped me to understand feminism.

In England my colleagues of the H.G. Wells Society have been wonderful to me, an invasive American. Parts of this book were read before various meetings of the Society, and elicited comments of major significance to my thinking. Dr Michael Draper scrutinized the final proofs. Michael Pattison, C. W. Rolfe, George and Molly Hay, Peter Hunot, John Hammond (with special thanks for the xeroxes), A. W. Watkins, Patrick Parrinder, and others make coming to England even nicer for me. Friends in England who have opened their homes, their hospitality, and their minds to me, are Mrs. O. Deutsch, Tom and Nancy Sharpe, Piers and Vivien Brendan, Michael Katanka, Eric Korn, B.M.W. Trapnel (of Oundle School), Ewe Parrinder, the owners of Spade House, and the present residents at Lynton, Woking. Another friend whom I met in England is David Hughes of the University of Michigan.

I am sustained in my work by my family. Sylvia W. Smith has lived with this book for over a decade, accepted my many absences, and my complete preoccupation at times, and remained throughout it all my lover and my best friend. Our children, Kit, Clayton, and their respective partners Jamie and Barbara, have been cheerfully tolerant. The book is dedicated to our first grandson, Joshua, who has made love into a new word. The confidence of my parents and my parents-in-law has helped support me in this and other work. All the errors, omissions, problems and shortcomings in this book are mine. What value it has should be shared by those above.

I must record a special thank you to Patrick Parrinder, who encouraged me from the beginning, has read and commented on every word in this book; and has provided an immense support to me. Catharine Carver has edited the text transatlantically, into a version of our shared but often divergent languages. Lastly, at a crucial point in the work I received encouragement from Robert Baldock; to a considerable degree, the finished product bears his imprint, as well as that of the press for which he works.

D.C.S.

INDEX